THE YALE EDITION

OF

HORACE WALPOLE'S

CORRESPONDENCE

EDITED BY W. S. LEWIS
(1895–1979)

VOLUME FORTY-EIGHT

HORACE WALPOLE'S CORRESPONDENCE

COMPLETE INDEX

COMPILED BY
WARREN HUNTING SMITH
WITH THE ASSISTANCE OF
EDWINE M. MARTZ, RUTH K. McCLURE,
AND WILLIAM T. LA MOY

V

SALLUST *TO* ZWEIBRÜCKEN

NEW HAVEN
YALE UNIVERSITY PRESS
OXFORD · OXFORD UNIVERSITY PRESS

1983

Library of Congress catalog card number: 65–11182

International standard book numbers:
0–300–02718–4 (*Complete Index*, vols. 44–48)
0–300–02717–6 (vol. 48)

10 9 8 7 6 5 4 3 2 1

Sallust (Caius Sallustrius Crispus) (86–34 B.C.), historian:
  Catiline by: quoted by HW, 39. 329; quoted by Hardinge, 35. 566
  'mystery of money would have barbarized,' 15. 49
  Wilkes compared with, 38. 188
Sally, Berrys' servant:
  Agnes Berry describes interview with, 12. 212
Sally, Mrs, Cts of Ailesbury's woman:
  HW thanks, for teapots, 38. 129
Sally, English merchant ship:
  capture of, 21. 16
Salm, Ps of. *See* Hornes, Marie-Thérèse-Josèphe de
Salm, Philipp Joseph (1709–79), P. of:
  Florence visited by, 24. 113n
  social relations of, in Paris, 7. 274, 290, 352
  son of, fights duel, 5. 175
  wife of, 6. 279n
Salm Kyrbourg, Friedrich Johann Otto (1745–94), P. of:
  Arpajon's duel with, 5. 175
  Lanjamet's duel with, 6. 278–9, 289
Salm Kyrbourg, Maria Maximiliane Luise von (b. 1744), m. (1763) Jean-Bretagne-Charles-Godefroy, Duc de la Trémoïlle:
  social relations of, in Paris, 7. 273, 300, 312, 318
Salmon, James (fl. 1772–81), carrier:
  book for Cole to be left with, 2. 259, 260
  Cambridge wagon of, 2. 259
  schedule of wagons of, 1. 263, 2. 260n
Salmon, Mrs Samuel. *See* Booth, Sarah
Salmon, William (1644–1713), apothecary; quack; writer:
  Pharmacopœia ('Bate's Dispensatory') translated by, 36. 140, 144–5
  Polygraphice by, 29. 6n
  treatises of Theophilus and Heraclius are in manner of, 29. 6
Salmon:
  pickled, served by monks, 13. 182
  sweet herbs with, as 'remove,' 19. 357n
Salm-Salm, Maria Franziska von (1731–1806), m. (1761) Georg Adam, Fürst von Starhemberg:
  Louis XV terrifies, though her French is good, 38. 220
  rouged too much to be bashful, 38. 220
  social relations of, in Paris, 7. 267, 301, 312, 352
Salo (Italy):
  Walpole, Bns, at, 17. 196, 217
Salom Mosse. *See* Solway Moss
Salomon, ——:
  subscription concerts of, 33. 471n
Salon (of paintings) in Paris:
  HW visits, 7. 317, 318
  See also Louvre
Salonica (Greece):
  La Pace bound for, 21. 274n

Salop, Cts of. *See* Beauchamp, Margaret (1404–67)
Salop, E. of. *See* Talbot, John (ca 1384–1433)
Salt:
  Genoese lease rents for, from Milan, 19. 337n
  HW's, envied by Hardinge, 35. 625
  Raynal discusses, 39. 168
  tax on, 25. 254n, 578n
Saltash, English ship:
  French vessels seized by, 19. 230n
Salt-baths. *See under* Bath; baths
Salt-box:
  played at *Old Woman's Oratory*, 9. 131
Salt cellar; salt cellars:
  at Dover inn, 18. 315
  at Trinity Hospital, Greenwich, 16. 91
  Du Deffand, Mme, orders, from Meunière, 7. 452
  Elizabeth (Q.)'s: 32. 324; at Burghley House, 10. 345; HW has, of Venetian glass, 17. 73n
  HW sends, to Mme du Deffand, 5. 156, 162, 172
  Mann's, acquired from Fane, 18. 472
  of Chelsea china, 22. 122
Salter, Rev. ——:
  Gloucester, 2d D. of, christened by, 24. 181n
Salter, Samuel (1713–78), D.D.:
  Hardwicke's chaplain (and tutor to his sons), and Master of Charterhouse, 31. 427n
Salter family:
  Rogers, Mrs, leases cottage from, 14. 25n
Salters' Company:
  Hinchliff of, 31. 86n
Salt fish. *See under* Fish
Salt Hill, Bucks:
  Gray's hearse to lie at, 1. 230
  Kingston, Ds of, at inn at, 32. 146–7
Saltire (heraldic device):
  on coin of Mary, Q. of Scots, 15. 166
Salt meat. *See under* Meat
Saltonstall, Capt.:
  print of, 40. 237
Saltonstall, Mrs, of Hillingdon, Middlesex:
  SH visited by, 12. 242
Saltonstall, Ricarda Posthuma (d. 1711), m. (1706) George Montagu, 2d Bn Halifax:
  genealogy of, 10. 352
Saltoun, Lord. *See* Fraser, Alexander
Salt provisions:
  Blakeney orders Dick to provide, for garrison, 20. 537
  English troops confined to, in America, 41. 313
  puppies may get mange from, 23. 40
Salts:
  bottle of, 30. 84
  HW gets, for Giovanardi, 17. 159, 416
Salt shaker:
  Du Deffand, Mme, receives, from Lady Mary Churchill, 20. 102
Salt water:
  baths of, 35. 247
  goldfish poisoned by, 35. 206

Saltykov, Cts. *See* Chernyshev, Daria Petrovna

Saltykov, Gen.:
captured at Zorndorf, **37.** 562n

Saltykov, Ekaterina Petrovna (1743–1817), m. Comte André Shuvalov:
Du Deffand, Mme, gives opinion of, **6.** 496, **7.** 26, 54, 73
——'s social relations with, **6.** 496, **7.** 431
England and Florence visited by, **22.** 460
Mann calls, 'pretty,' **22.** 460
Paris to be visited by, **8.** 205
Roissy to be visited by, **7.** 54
SH visited by, **12.** 226

Saltykov, Count Ivan Petrovich (1736–1805), Marshal; gov. of Moscow:
HW entertains, at breakfast at SH, **33.** 362
La Vallière, Duchesse de, recommends, to HW, **33.** 352
Ossory, Lady, hears news of, through Mr Vernon, **33.** 353

Salusbury, Hester Lynch (1741–1821), m. 1 (1763) Henry Thrale; m. 2 (1784) Gabriel Piozzi:
Anecdotes of the Late Samuel Johnson by: **43.** 139; first impression of, sold out on publication day, **25.** 640; HW criticizes, **25.** 638; Mann would rather see Wolcot's satire than, **25.** 643; published, **11.** 21n; to be published, **33.** 466, 512
Baretti, friend of, **28.** 97n
—— not alive to criticize, **42.** 245
books of, can readily be taken up and laid down, **42.** 273
Boswell mistreats, in *Life* of Johnson, **11.** 275
—— refutes, over opinion of Mrs Montagu's book, **25.** 640
British Synonymy by: **43.** 152, 153; HW refers to, **12.** 98; HW's unfavourable opinion of, **12.** 92–3, 174; to be published, **12.** 59
Calder's witticism on Dr Johnson and, **43.** 166
'Della Cruscan,' **25.** 612n
Du Deffand-HW correspondence owned by, **43.** 80
epigram by, on Reynolds's portrait, **10.** 158n
fête of, at Streatham, **11.** 106
Florence Miscellany has contributions by, **11.** 177n
Florence visited by, with second husband, **25.** 611n
HW calls: 'la Signora Piozzi,' **31.** 343; 'Mrs Frail Piozzi,' **33.** 512
HW imitates, **11.** 14n
HW likes preface by, to *Florence Miscellany*, **25.** 633–4
(?) HW nauseated by, **31.** 271
HW ridicules, **25.** 611–12
HW's letters to Montagu annotated by, **9.** 7, 9, 16, 18, 131, 142, 158, 207, 234, 236, 254, 256 (2), 259, 265, 269, 270, 271, 280 (2), 316, 320, 323 (2), 340, 342, 353, 389, 406, **10.** 14, 15, 16, 22, 40, 56, 69, 95, 101, 118, 148, 175, 177, 180, 228, 238, 254 (2), 265–6, 310, 348

HW's letter to Cole annotated by, **2.** 250n
HW's verses allude to, **12.** 258
Johnson, Dr Samuel, exposed by, **36.** 236, 241, 249
——'s letters to be published by, **31.** 255
——'s letter to, **12.** 22n
Lysons's letter from, mentions her letters to Pepys, Lort, Cadell, and Mrs Montagu about Boswell, **43.** 292
Mann's quarrel with, **25.** 633n
Meget's inn visited by, at Florence, **25.** 612n
Montagu, Mrs, gets letter from, disavowing Boswell, **25.** 634
More, Hannah, characterizes, **31.** 316
Observations and Reflections Made in the Course of a Journey through France, Italy and Germany by: Berrys read, **11.** 21; HW criticizes, **31.** 302, **42.** 244–5; HW dislikes style of, **11.** 14, 21, **42.** 244–5; More, Hannah, criticizes, **31.** 316; style of, vulgar, **31.** 202
St Giles's Pound evidently the scene of education of, **31.** 302
satiric prints of, **25.** 641
Seward a friend of, **16.** 189n
Siddons, Mrs, seen by, in *King Lear*, **34.** 2n
SH visited by, **12.** 242
style of, **11.** 14, 21, 21n
witticism by, on Sheridan, **31.** 343
Wolcot ridicules, **25.** 638, 640–1, 643

Salusbury, John (d. 1762), Mrs Piozzi's father:
daughter of, **11.** 21n
Halifax accompanied by, to Dublin, **9.** 340n

'Salutation,' tavern near Temple Bar, London:
Reynolds's painting resembles, **9.** 158n

'Salutation' (painting). *See under* Guido Reni

Salute; salutes:
cannon at Monaco fire, for D. of York as for French maréchal, **22.** 554
English ships fire, at Leghorn, **21.** 123
to English ships, disputes over, **22.** 156

Salvador, ——, m. (1760) Joshua Mendez da Costa:
(?) card sent by, to Q. Charlotte, **22.** 72–3

Salvador, (?) Esther (?d. 1788), m. (1751) Abraham Prado:
biographical information on, **43.** 78
HW mentions, **5.** 88
HW's enthusiasm for, **2.** 373
Raftor stays with, until Mrs Clive's burial, **31.** 238
SH visitors sent by, **12.** 228
Twickenham resident, **42.** 486

Salvador, Sarah, m. (1776) Francis Daniel Salvador:
(?) card sent by, to Q. Charlotte, **22.** 72–3
marriage date of, **43.** 278

'Salvator.' *See* Rosa, Salvator

Salver; salvers:
gilt, for gold pins, **33.** 163
Mann's, acquired from Fane, **18.** 472
Montagu wants, **10.** 98
Skrine serves drinks on, **20.** 145

Salvert. *See* Perier de Salvert

Salvetti, Lino, chancellor of Volterra:
Dumesnil avoided by, **19**. 493

Salvetti Antelminelli, Giovanni Battista (b. ca 1634), Tuscan Resident in England 1657–80:
hesitant to report Cromwell's death, **20**. 170, **32**. 210, **35**. 188

Salveyn, John (fl. 1440):
received into fraternity of Bury Abbey, **2**. 38

Salvi, Antonio, librettist:
Arminio (opera) by, **17**. 80

Salvi, Giovanni Battista (1609–85), called Sassoferrato; painter:
Abcedario pittorico does not include, **18**. 94
alleged Domenichino painting attributed to, **17**. 167n
Baldocci and Corsi have paintings by, **18**. 94
Madonna paintings by, famous in Florence, **18**. 94
Mann's Madonna by, sent to HW, **18**. 94, 182, 214, 291, 292
name of, on back of alleged Domenichino painting, **18**. 93, 162
painting finished by, **30**. 370

Salviati, Duchessa. *See* Buoncompagni, Anna Maria (1697–1752); Lante della Rovere, Maria Cristina; Rinaldi, Margherita (1712–90)

Salviati, Marchese:
HW civil to, in England, **18**. 459

Salviati, Antonio Maria (1683–1757), Duca di Giuliano-Salviati:
(?) Craon, Princesse de, entertains, **19**. 145
Dumesnil escapes from Florence with horses and servants of, **19**. 491
son of, **21**. *310*

Salviati, Averardo (1721–83), Duca di Giuliano-Salviati:
death date of, corrected, **43**. 275
(?) English visitors favoured by, **22**. 379
Gloucester, D. of, sends message to, **24**. *291*
Leopold accompanied by, to call on D. of Gloucester, **23**. 352n
—— sends, to D. and Ds of Gloucester, **23**. 405n
—— to be entertained by, **23**. 95
Tuscan Court makes, Grand Chambellan, against his will, **22**. 467
Villa Salviati may be rented by, to Cts of Orford, **21**. *310*

Salviati, Caterina Zephyrina, m. (1717) Fabrizio Colonna, constable:
Craon, Princesse de, tired of entertaining, **18**. 545

Salviati, Laura (1725–1802), m. (1742) Rodolfo Acquaviva, Duca d'Atri:
Orford, Cts of, talks with, **25**. 130

Salviati family:
banking house of, **14**. 67n
Tesi's banishment from Florence probably procured by, from Vienna, to protect Tempi and Corsi, **18**. 520

Salviati villa:
Orford, Cts of, may take, **21**. 310

Salvin, George (15th cent.) of North Duffield:
son of, **2**. 38n

Salvin, Mary (d. 1782), m. (ca 1760) Sir John Webb, 5th Bt:
(?) social relations of, in Paris, **7**. 270, 271

Salvini, Antonio Maria (1653–1729), poet and philologist:
(?) Gray's imitation of, **28**. 109

Salvini, Rev. Gregorio:
Theodore of Corsica calls, traitor, **18**. 156

Salvini, Salvino (1667–1751), canon; antiquarian:
(?) Mann attributes saying to, **22**. 511

Sal volatile:
HW's letter to act as, upon Mann, **18**. 117
Mann compares HW's letters to, **19**. 182
Townshend, Charles, has more of, than all France, **38**. 203

Salzburg (Austria):
Bavarian elector said to have entered, **17**. 108
treaty between Maria Theresa and Maximilian ratified at, **19**. 38n

'Samaritan woman':
Poussin's painting of, **35**. 149

Sambre (river in France):
Coburg's army crosses, **12**. 42n

Sambre Valley:
Saxe plans to reduce strongholds of, **19**. 261n

Sambrook, Mrs:
Isleworth house of, **33**. 524n

Sambrooke, Diana (ca 1731–78), m. (1754) Lord George Sackville (later Sackville Germain):
death of, **33**. 6
HW invited by, **43**. 301
HW, Vcts Milton, and, joke about Cts of Hertford's alleged death, **38**. 494
HW wishes to visit, **31**. 406
income of, **21**. 328
loo party wished by, **32**. 320
measles of, **33**. 3

Samminiati, Ascanio (b. 1678), senator:
annuity to be paid to, as Electress's executor, **18**. 168–9
Sansedoni replaces, as master of the woods and water, and councillor of finance, **17**. 181n

Samoggia (Italy):
Montemar encamps at, **17**. 427

Samoyed:
Catherine II's code of laws declined by, **28**. 476
reply of, to Orlov, **28**. 477

Sampieri, Valerio, Bolognese collector:
collection of, **21**. 231, 478
Strange applies to, for permission to engrave paintings, **21**. 231n

Sampson, James (d. 1768), D. of Richmond's servant:
Conway obtains place for, in Tower, **22**. 588n
——'s house robbed and set afire by, **14**, 183–4, **22**. 587–8, **23**. 9, **33**. 583–4
hanged, **4**. 40n, **33**. 583–4

Sampson, Mrs James (fl. ca 1760), Mrs Damer's maid:
husband of, 33. 584
Sampson, English packet boat:
Alderney chases, near Ostend, 24. 468n
Samson (Biblical):
pillars toppled by, 28. 479
Samson, ———:
Buyrette de Belloy's *Siège de Calais* to be translated by, 7. 262
Samson. See under Handel, George Frideric
Sanadon, Mlle, Mme du Deffand's companion; 'Mlle St-Chrysostome'; 'la Sanadona':
acts proverb well, 4. 277
apartment of, 8. 3
apartment of Marquise d'Aulan to be taken by, 4. 65
Auteuil visited by, 7. 347
Bagarotti, Mlle, and Contessa di Viry compared by, 5. 404–5
Caracciolo talks better than, 5. 108
Choiseul's opera box occupied by, 7. 331
Choiseul, Vicomtesse de, friend of, 5. 5, 130
Cholmondeley, Mrs, compared with, 6. 280
Cholmondeleys' stay in convent arranged by, 4. 220
Colmant disputes with, about letters, 5. 252
Comédie attended by, 4. 275, 277, 6. 75
Conway misspells name of, 39. 214
dines in town, 4. 45, 47
'donna Sanadona, la,' 4. 275
Du Deffand, Mme, accompanied by: at *Le Joueur*, 4. 75; to Mme de Mirepoix's, 6. 386; to Sceaux and Montrouge, 4. 443
—— asks HW to send message to, 6. 227
—— bored by, 5. 224–5, 282, 6. 179, 426
—— copied by, 5. 5–6
—— leaves diamond to, 8. 7
—— mentions, 5. 73
—— not displeased by Praslin's attentions to, 5. 333
—— reproached by, for going to Chanteloup, 5. 238
——'s arrangements made with, 3. 393, 406
——'s correspondence with, 5. 249, 251, 7. 460
——'s opinion of, 4. 484, 490, 5. 5, 44, 137, 6. 466
——'s relations with, 5. 248–50, 6. 40, 44, 66, 382, 466, 7. 349
—— takes refuge with, after fire, 6. 176
—— to depend on, for company, 3. 385, 4. 8, 65, 412, 5. 117, 152, 353, 6. 356, 367, 436, 476, 488, 7. 62, 198
—— tries to borrow piano for, 4. 452n
Foire Ste-Ovide visited by, 7. 329
grateful and happy, 4. 8
HW accompanies: to opera, 7. 339, 349; to theatre, 7. 326, 331, 332
HW inquired after by, 5. 139, 382
HW's correspondence with, 5. 244, 248–52, 254, 7. 395
HW sends compliments to, 3. *366*, 6. 234, 36. 55

HW's *Gramont* given to, 5. 305
Louvre shown to, by Abbé Lambert, 7. 339
Montigny secures income for, 4. 77n
Montrevel, Comtesse de, mourned by, 4. 151
name of, corrected, 43. 87
opera attended by, 5. 155, 325, 333, 7. 339, 349
Praslin, Duc de, favours, 5. 325, 333, 6. 66, 219
Praslin to be visited by, 5. 376, 380, 6. 78, 80, 356, 7. 64, 219
—— visited by, 5. 382, 6. 81, 84, 87, 358–60, 7. 64, 66, 68, 426, 461
—— visit forgone by, 5. 249–50
return of, 5. 388, 6. 361
Sceaux visited by, 7. 322
smallpox feared by, 7. 138
social relations of, in Paris, *see index entries ante* 8. 505
Sanadon, Père Noël (1676–1733), writer:
niece of, 3. 366n
San Antonio, Spanish ship:
artillery brought by, to Italian coast from Barcelona, 17. 286
Forrester, Sir Mark, takes command of, after its capture, 18. 344n
pieces of eight carried by, 18. 344n
San Antonio, Portuguese church at Rome:
edict posted at, 21. 423n
San Antonio Abbate, church of. *See under* Parma
San Antonio del Borgo, Naples:
'St Anthony Abbot' in, 42. 66n
San Barnaba, Venice:
Barnabotti of, 17. 75
San Bruno (Italy):
earthquake account mentions, 25. 376
San Carlo, ship:
Merlo defends, on the Danube, 19. 124
San Carlos, English ship:
French prisoners from Jersey on, 25. 115n
San Casciano (Italy):
Almada leaves, 21. 436
Corsini's villa at, occupied by Almada, 21. 426
San Casciano dei Bagni (Italy):
Lyttelton, Sir Richard, and Thomas Pitt at, 21. 524
Sancha (d. 1261) of Provence, m. (1243) Richard, E. of Cornwall:
Richard I not the husband of, 40. 298
Sánches, Tomás (1550–1610), Spanish Jesuit:
theories of, 28. 295
Sanchia; Sancia. *See* Sancha
'Sancho Panza.' *See under* Cervantes, Miguel de: *Don Quixote*
Sancourt, ———:
(?) made maréchal de camp, 7. 147n
Sancroft, William (1617–93), Abp of Canterbury:
James II's declaration not read by, 1. 319n
medal of seven bishops including, 1. 319, 321
nonjuror, 2. 345, 359, 360
transcript made by, 15. 74n

Sancta Sophia. *See under* Constantinople

Sand:

and rock constitute Minorca's terrain, **37**. 310

box for, in Q. Elizabeth's collection, **32**. 323

Conway's for blotting letters, thrown about by daughter, **37**. 435

HW furnishes, to Exchequer Office, **9**. 117n

Sandal Castle, Yorks:

York, D. of, lived at, **35**. 270

Sandal Magna, Yorks:

Zouch rector of, **16**. 1n, **37**. 560

Sandart. *See* Sandrart

Sandbeck Park, Yorks, Lord Scarbrough's seat:

near Tickhill, **1**. 275n

portrait at, **15**. 155

Scarbrough's seat, **15**. 139n

Sandby, Mr, of Teddington:

SH visited by, **12**. 230

Sandby, George (1717–1807), Master of Magdalene College, Cambridge:

Masters's retention of book belonging to Magdalene College is notified to, **2**. 351

notes by, on Charles II, **1**. 214, 223n

Sandby, Paul (1725–1809,) painter:

drawings by, for 'Des. of SH,' **33**. 576n, **43**. 72

engravings by, **2**. 245

Grafton asks Hertford for reversion to, of surveyorship of George III's pictures, **39**. 114n

——'s promise to, repudiated by George III, **28**. 342

HW permits, to trace rare Hogarth prints, **15**. 338

HW's correspondence with, **41**. 189

HW tells, to inform him when brother can sketch SH Gallery, **41**. 189

HW to consult, about, aquatints, **29**. 101

HW wishes, to engrave Lady Diana Beauclerk's drawings, **29**. 71

Harcourt's etching from drawing by, **43**. 364

has not come to SH, **29**. 77

Henshaw's engravings to be shown by, to Bartolozzi, **1**. 301

(?) Hertford consults HW about, **39**. 114

Hogarth prints traced by, **42**. 175n

King's College Chapel's description discussed by, **1**. 211

son of, **12**. 234

Stanton Harcourt view drawn by, **35**. 451n, 487n

SH visited by, (?) **12**. 221, **15**. 338, **42**. 175n

Windsor Park improved by, **10**. 44n

Sandby, Thomas (1721–98), architect:

designs by, disregarded, **2**. 177n

drawing by, of Gallery at SH, **2**. 274, **41**. 189, **43**. 383

Essex might be aided by, with George III, **1**. 211, 212

Harcourt's tomb should be designed by, **35**. 487

St Leonard's Hill built by, for Ds of Gloucester, **32**. 132n

—— improved by, **10**. 42n

sketches by, of King's College Chapel, **1**. 208, 211

Windsor Park improved by, **10**. 44n

Sandby, Thomas Paul (d. 1832), son of Paul Sandby:

(?) SH visited by, **12**. 234

Sandby, W.:

Lyttelton's *Dialogues* published by, **21**. 407n

Sanders family:

arms of, **2**. 220, 222

Sandershausen (Germany):

battle of: **21**. 227; Hanover exposed by, **37**. 554

Sanderson (*or* Saunderson), Nicholas (1683–1739), LL.D.: professor of mathematics at Cambridge:

HW hears mathematical lectures of, **12**. 208, **13**. 6

HW learns nothing from lectures of, **12**. 208

HW's lack of mathematical ability discerned by, **21**. 353, 359

visual images of, in his blindness, **41**. 292

Sanderson, Robert (1587–1663), Bp of Lincoln:

translation of lectures of, **15**. 109n

Sanderson, Sir William (?1586–1676), historian:

Aulicus Coquinariæ by, **2**. 34, 40

Sanderson. *See also* Saunderson

Sandford, Edward, army officer:

Bedford orders regiment of, assembled, **21**. 373n

Sandford, Francis (1630–94), Lancaster Herald:

Genealogical History of the Kings of England by: **33**. 249, **42**. 20, **43**. 70; cited, **2**. 49; Cole lacks, **1**. 222; genealogical tree of, now includes HW, **28**. 93; Montagu wishes to borrow, to get design for church window, **10**. 11; plate in, **2**. 365–6; SH hall copied from plate in, **35**. 150n

HW signs himself as, **21**. 532

History of the Coronation of King James the Second by, **21**. 532n

Sandford, Maj.-Gen. Robert (d. 1781):

Villinghausen battle includes, **21**. 516n

Sandiwell. *See* Sandywell

Sandleford Priory, Berks, Mrs Montagu's house:

Gothic windows at, **31**. 321

More, Hannah, at, **31**. 321, 327

—— to visit, **31**. 281

—— writes from, **31**. 319–22

oaks at, **31**. 321

parts of, finer than the whole, **31**. 321

San Domingo, West Indies. *See* Santo Domingo

Sandrart, Joachim von (1606–88), writer:

Academia nobilissimæ artis pictoriæ by: ascribes prints and painting to Holbein, **16**. 146; lacks Holbein drawing, **40**. 231

death date of, corrected, **43**. 219

Sandras, Marie-Anne-Jeanne (b. 1734), m. (1761) Bernard-Joseph Saurin:

social relations of, with Marquise de Monconseil, **7**. 297

Sandricourt, Marquis de. *See* St-Simon, Maximilien-Henri de

Sandridge, Herts:
Jennings of, **28.** 388n
Sandrini, Dr Baniere:
Lady Orford's attending physician, **43.** 288
——'s death certificate signed by, **43.** 288
Sands, Donaldson, Murray, and Cochran; printers:
English translation of *Candide* printed by, for Alexander Donaldson, **10.** 350
Sand walks:
HW sees, at Chantilly, **7.** 260
Sandwell, Douglas (ca 1724–1810), m. (1749)
Roger Mortlock Pettiward, D.D., of Putney:
SH visited by, **12.** 244
Sandwich, Cts of. *See* Fane, Hon. Dorothy (d. 1797); Montagu Dunk, Lady Elizabeth (1745–68); Wilmot, Elizabeth (1674–1757)
Sandwich, E. of. *See* Montagu, Edward (1625–72); Montagu, Edward (1648–88); Montagu, Edward (ca 1670–1729); Montagu, John (1718–92); Montagu, John (1742–1814)
Sandwich, family of earls of:
Hinchingbrooke wedding conducted in style of, **10.** 207
Sandwich, English ship:
Rodney detaches, **25.** 24n
Sandwich, packet boat:
Virginia news brought by, **25.** 167n
Sandwich, Kent:
Whaley and Dodd see, **40.** 4
Sandys, Bns. *See* Tipping, Laetitia
Sandys, Sir Edwin (d. 1607 *or* 1608), Kt, 1599:
lord of the manor of Latimers, **37.** 298n
Sandys, Hon. Edwin (1726–97), 2d Bn Sandys, 1770; M.P.:
Admiralty post for, **21.** 73
(?) HW thanks, for research on Butler, **40.** 272–3
succession of, to father's title vacates seat for Westminster, **23.** 206
Sandys, Samuel (1695–1770), cr. (1743) Bn Sandys; M.P.:
Argyll scolds, **17.** 335
Board of Trade may be headed by, **9.** 341
chancellor of the Exchequer, **17.** 249n, 332, 335, **18.** 51, 103, 118n, 350, 356, **40.** 39
cofferer, **17.** 249n, **18.** 350, 357, 365, 551
Conway's letter to Downing St may have gone to, **37.** 181, 185
Cuper's Gardens visited by, **9.** 35
Dashwood allied with, **17.** 249
death of, from fractured skull, **23.** 206
'dishclout,' **18.** 350
Downing St residence of, **30.** 74, **37.** 181, 185
dull, **18.** 142, **30.** 302
Earle's witticism on, **17.** 250
Essay on Woman debated by, **38.** 230n
Etonian proposed by, for King's College fellowship, **40.** 39
Exchequer acceptance defended by, **17.** 335
Exchequer resigned by, to Pelham, **18.** 350, 356
'Fountain' meeting attended by, **17.** 335

HW called on by, **19.** 25–6
HW ridicules, **13.** 14n, 249, **30.** 74
HW's verses on appointment of, to House of Lords, **18.** 357–8, 372
hackney coaches said to be hired to stand at the door of, **18.** 232
Halifax succeeded by, in Board of Trade, **21.** 489
Hardwicke succeeded by, as Speaker of the House of Lords, **21.** 25
House of Commons considered an unfair tribunal by, **19.** 26
Indemnity Bill opposed by, **17.** 437
Irish treasury post said to be assigned to, **9.** 181
justice in eyre, **20.** 25, 518, **21.** 489
Leeds to succeed, as chief justice in eyre, **9.** 341
levee (pretended) of, **18.** 232
Mann will be amused at reappearance of, **20.** 518
Mediterranean naval investigation discussed by, **19.** 25–6
neckcloth of, 'immeasurable,' **30.** 288, 302
New Ode, A, satirizes, **30.** 318
Ombersley the seat of, **40.** 13–14
Onslow said to be beckoned away by, **30.** 291
Ord secretary to, **18.** 320n
Parliamentary debate discusses, **18.** 118
Parliamentary motions by: for punishing sheriff, **17.** 294; to remove Sir Robert Walpole, **17.** 83n
peerage for, **17.** 249n, **18.** 142, 357, 365, **30.** 40
Place Bill to be prepared by, **17.** 295n
pocket of, picked, **9.** 35
'Prudence and Parts' satirizes, **30.** 318
Pulteney's protégé, **18.** 72n, 74, 91
Ranelagh frequented by, **37.** 164
reelection of, expected, **17.** 363
'republican,' **17.** 249n
Scrope defended by, **17.** 467
Secret Committee lists include, **17.** 385
Walpole, Sir Robert, enrages, by taking Orford title, **13.** 11n, **17.** 333
—— ordered by, to vacate Downing St house, **17.** 478, 495
wife of, **9.** 23n
Williams, Sir C. H., satirizes, **18.** 320, **30.** 315, 317, 318
Wilmington and Compton outvoted by, **18.** 50n
Wilmington offers Downing St house to, **17.** 478, 495
Worcester's instructions to, **18.** 103
Sandys, Mrs Samuel. *See* Tipping, Laetitia
Sandys, William (ca 1470–1540), cr. (1523) Bn Sandys:
Byng's fiasco would distress, **35.** 92
Henry VIII's lord chamberlain, who built chapel at the Vyne, **20.** 485n
Vyne, the, built, enlarged, and sold by, **35.** 641

——'s gallery fitted up by, **35**. 641
'Sandys and Jekyll.' *See under* Williams, Sir
  Charles Hanbury
Sandywell (*or* Sandiwell) Park, Glos:
  Conway at, **37**. 105
  Conway, Bn, expects HW at, **37**. 107
  Conway family's amusements at, **37**. 113
  Hertford inherits, from father, but sells it,
    37. 105n
  neighbours at, **37**. 106
  Whaley and Dodd visit, **40**. 11
San Eugenio, Spanish ship:
  lost on breakers, **25**. 16n
San Felice, church in Florence:
  Via Maggio leads to, **17**. 488n
San Felipe, Marqués de. *See* Bacallar y Saña,
  Vicente
San Fernando, Spanish ship:
  in Spanish fleet, **17**. 286
San Fernando de Omoa:
  English capture, **24**. 543
San Fiorenzo, Corsica:
  Corsican attack on, fails, **23**. 80
  France sends engineer to raise batteries at,
    20. 573n
  Genoa reserves, **20**. 273n
  Marbeuf wishes communication between
    Bastia and, **23**. 46
  rebels safe at, **19**. 258
  Rivarola may retire to, **19**. 437
  —— receives letter at, from Mann, **19**. 276n
San Gennaro; San Gennore. *See* Januarius, St
San Germano (Italy):
  Neapolitan troops at, **19**. 378
  Spaniards fortify, **18**. 438
Sanges. *See* Castello di Sanges
San Gillio, Contessa di. *See* Coardi di Carpa-
  netto, Caterina Maria Teresa
San Giorgio, Russian frigate:
  arrives at Leghorn from Paros, **23**. 326
San Giovacchino, Neapolitan ship:
  English prints in stateroom of, depict Lán-
    gara's and Grasse's defeats, **25**. 582n
  Ferdinand of Naples sails in, to Leghorn, **25**.
    581
San Giovanni (Italy):
  Spanish troops retire to, **18**. 154
San Giovanni, Augustinian church at Leghorn:
  falls in earthquake, **17**. 307
San Giovanni, Florentine church:
  procession to, **22**. 532n
San Giovanni (Lateran), church in Rome:
  possesso procession to, **24**. 136n
San Giovanni, convent of:
  Benedictine cloister for ladies, at Capua near
    Caserta, **20**. 429n
San Giovanni e San Paolo, convent at Rome:
  York, Cardinal, retires to, **20**. 332n
'Sangrenuntio.' *See* Stone, George
'Sanhedrin':
  HW's name for House of Commons, **23**. 555
Sani, Agata (*or* Prudenza Sani Grandi), singer:
  first singer in Leghorn opera, **18**. 160

'Ottajano de' Medici' accompanies, to Leghorn, **18**. 160
  sings in Florentine opera, **35**. 28
  ugly as Viscontina, **35**. 28
  (?) 'vile herd,' **17**. *463*
Sanisbury. *See* Sainsbury
San Isidoro (or *Isidro*), Spanish ship:
  Córdoba's fleet includes, **25**. 139n
  destruction of, **18**. 189
  in Spanish fleet, **17**. 286
Sanitary conveniences:
  at Westminster Abbey, for Q. Charlotte, **38**.
    122
  at Elizabeth Chudleigh's, **9**. 277
  French indelicacy about, shocks Lady Mary
    Churchill, **20**. 339
  Hervey's posture in, amuses ladies, **18**. 96
  on Ponte a Santa Trinità at Florence, **18**.
    286, **35**. 41
  See also Bath; Bedpan; Close stool; Jordan;
    Privy; Retiring-Chamber; Urinal, Water-
    closet
Sanitation:
  emptying of privies at Mme du Deffand's
    convent, **4**. 37–8
San Jenaro, Spanish ship:
  escapes, **25**. 16n
San Juan, Prior of. *See* Yecla
San Juan, Puerto Rico:
  English troops die of diseases at, **33**. 245n
San Julián, Spanish ship:
  runs ashore, **25**. 16n
San Justo, Spanish ship:
  escapes, **25**. 16n
Sankt Pölten (Bohemia):
  Bavarian-French army at, **17**. 194
San Lazaro (Italy):
  battle of, **19**. 266–7, 271
  HW hopes for Flemish victory similar to,
    19. 274
San Lazzaro e Sant'Antonio, Tuscan ship:
  seizure of, **21**. 269
San Lorenzo, Florentine church:
  chapel of: Electress to be buried in, **18**. 160;
    Electress to provide for completion of, **18**.
    113; left unfinished at Electress's death,
    18. 172; marble and timbers for completion
    of, sold, **18**. 172n
  Charles VI's obsequies in, **30**. 8n
  Craon, Princesse de, walks to, from SS. An-
    nunziata, **18**. 196
  Electress's funeral at, attended by Mann and
    Lady Walpole, **18**. 173
  Frenchman seeks Vandières at, **20**. 228
  Jadot designs catafalque for Charles VI in,
    17. 75n
  Mann attends Elizabeth Christina's requiem
    in, **20**. 227
  pompous tombs of Medici in, **25**. 202
San Lorenzo, convent of. *See under* Venice
San Lorenzo Library, Florence:
  Richard I's poems in Provencal MS in, **21**.
    156–7, 169, 186, **40**. 115

San Lucar, Duque de. *See* Guzman, Gaspar de
San Luigi Gonzaga, Tuscan ship:
　seizure of, **21**. 273–4
San Marcello, Cardinal. *See* Zacchia, Emilio
San Marco, procuratore di, at Venice. *See* Foscarini, Marco (1695–1763); Grimani, Pietro (ca 1677–1752); Morosini, Cavaliere Francesco (fl. 1744–85); Querini, Tommaso
San Marco, church of, at Florence:
　faithful to visit 15 times, in jubilee, **20**. 220n
　Sansedoni to visit, **20**. 228n
San Marco, convent of, at Florence:
　Bartolommeo's picture in, **23**. 276
　Branchi's essences equal those of, **18**. 177
　'odoriferous gardens' in cloisters of, **18**. 177n
San Marco, Place of, at Florence:
　HW's verses on, **37**. 96–7
San Marco, Venice. *See* St Mark's
San Marino:
　Austrian archduke would not be sent to defend, **21**. 96
　'Prudence and Parts' belittles, **30**. 318
San Martino, Duca di. *See* Pamfili, Benedetto
San Martino (Italy):
　Braitwitz to visit, **17**. 134
　garrison for, **19**. 11
　Leghorn troops sent to, **18**. 66, 76, 77
　mountain fortress of Francis I's, **18**. 66
　Traun orders Braitwitz to send troops to, **18**. 85
　villa of, **19**. 123
San Mignati. *See* Samminiati
San Miniato, near Florence:
　Grifoni, Mme, visits, **18**. 100
　Suares, Bp, brought from, **18**. 40
San Nicandro, Principe di:
　(?) Neapolitan orders relating to, **21**. 325
Sanosino. *See* Bernardi, Francesco
San Paolo, Russian frigate:
　arrives at Leghorn from Paros, **23**. 326
San Pasquale, Marchese di. *See* Würtz von Rudenz, Wolfgang Ignatz
San Pedro, Spanish ship:
　Córdoba's fleet includes, **25**. 139n
San Pieri. *See* Sampieri
San Pier Maggiore, Florentine church:
　faithful to visit 15 times during jubilee, **20**. 219n
　Sansedoni visits, **20**. 228n
Sanremaschi family:
　pro-Spanish, **19**. 123
San Remo (Italy):
　Francis I claims, as imperial fief, **20**. 429
　Genoese chastise, **20**. 429
　governor of, *see* Albero
　letter about bombardment of, **18**. 123–4
　Rowley destroys, **19**. 120–1, 123–4, 132
San Roque, near Gibraltar:
　Spanish camp at: expensive and pestiferous, **25**. 59; may be abandoned, **25**. 72
San Rosori (San Rossore), near Leghorn:
　camels bred at, **11**. 181n
　hunt in woods of, **22**. 220

'Sans culottes,' French regiment:
　Kalkreuth defeats, **39**. 505–6
Sans dépit, sans légèreté:
　Cambis, Mme de, sings, **5**. 137, 152, **6**. 338, **39**. 208, 218
San Sebastian. *See* St-Sébastien
San Secondo, Conte di. *See* Rossi, Federico
San Secondo, Contessa di. *See* Rangoni, Vittoria
Sansedoni, Signora. *See* Pannilini, Porzia; Venturi Gallerini, Ottavia
Sansedoni, Balì Giovanni (b. 1711):
　Bichi lives with, **20**. 228
　cats mistakenly forwarded by, **17**. 394
　cold caught by, in churches, in jubilee, **20**. 228
　Craon, Princesse de, favours, **20**. 228
　lottery ticket investigated by, **18**. 206
　Mann to ask, for cats from Malta, **17**. *181*, 212
　—— wishes sailor's report translated for, **17**. 471
　'master of the woods and water,' **17**. 181n
　(?) positions stripped from, **19**. 323n, 394n
　Samminiati replaced by, as councillor of finance, **17**. 181n
Sanseverino, Principessa di. *See* Carafa, ——
Sanseverino, Don Domenico (1707–60), Neapolitan physician:
　Neapolitan heir's incapacity certified by, **21**. 325
San Severino Albertini, Giovanni Battista, Principe di Cimitile; Neapolitan ambassador to England 1753–63:
　Albani recommends, to Mann, **20**. *369*
　Ammon to accompany, to England, **20**. 369
　courier of, **21**. 330, 453, 455, 461, 463, 465, 468n, 477
　expected in London, **20**. 372n
　George II to be thanked by, for promoting Sir James Gray, **21**. 159
　HW and Conway to welcome, in England, **20**. 370, 372
　Herculaneum book announced by, in England, **21**. 262, 272
　letter to wife of, forwarded by Mann, **21**. 331
　Mann entertains, in Florence, **20**. 369
　—— praises, **20**. 369
　Neapolitan envoy (ambassador) to England, **20**. 369, 372n
　new credentials of, in courier's pocket, **21**. 463
Sansidoni; Sansidonio. *See* Sansedoni
Sanskrit:
　inscription in, from Murphy's *Travels in Portugal*, **12**. 178
Sansom, Thomas (d. 1772), King's messenger:
　Hertford's letter to HW to be taken by, to England, **38**. 573
Sanson, Guillaume *and* Nicolas (1600–67):
　Atlas nouveau by, **35**. 435n
　geography of, **20**. 501
Sansovino, Jacopo Tatti (1486–1570), called; Florentine sculptor:
　Bacchus by, unhurt in Uffizi fire, **22**. 67

San Spirito. *See* Santo Spirito

'Sans Souci, philosopher of.' *See* Frederick II of Prussia

'Sans Souci,' Frederick II's villa:
Frederick II, 'philosophe' of, **34**. 34
Hobart, Mrs, borrows name and design of, **33**. 286

'Sans Souci,' Mrs Hobart's villa on Ham Common:
HW not invited to, **33**. 285
name and design of, borrowed, **33**. 286
rural breakfast at, **11**. 290, 294
See also under Ham Common

San Stefano, Order of, in Tuscany:
capitolo of, **19**. 238, 245, **20**. 473, **24**. 188n
Cerati, prior of, **21**. 147n
church of Pitti Palace to be built by, from prizes from Turks, **22**. 259
Cosimo I the founder of, **18**. 46n
Degli Azzi a knight of, **17**. 488n
Del Benino knight of, **17**. 122n
(?) knights of, in Florentine celebration, **35**. 27
Mozzi a knight of, **23**. 141
Ridolfi grand chancellor of, **17**. 104n
Viviani, Priore di Montalcino in, **17**. 116n

San Stephano on Mt Celio:
Beaton, Cardinal of, **2**. 20n

Santa Agueda, Minorcan mountain:
Moorish fortress and cavern on, **37**. 315

Santa Barbara, church of, in Castel Nuova, Naples:
'Adoration of the Magi' in, **42**. 66n

Santa Catarina, island of:
Spaniards capture, from Portuguese, **24**. 309, **32**. 357–8

Santa Cecilia, Spanish frigate:
escapes, **25**. 16n

Santa Croce, Principe di. *See* Publicola, Scipio

Santa Croce, Principessa di. *See* Falconieri, Juliana; Vecchiarelli, Isabella

Santa Croce, Florentine church:
English cocchiata ends at, **18**. 485
Pepi jokes about, to Abp of Florence, **18**. 41
Rinuccini's funeral at, **19**. 461

Santa Croce, convent of, at Florence:
Clement XIV was confrère of members of, **23**. 118

Santa Croce, Place of, at Florence:
alleged flirtation in, **17**. 150
flooded, **19**. 131

Santa Felicità, Florentine church:
Madonna dell'Impruneta remains at, for night, **30**. 4

Santa Lucia, in West Indies. *See* St Lucia

Santa Lucia, College of, at Bologna:
rector refuses to disband, without Clement XIV's order, **23**. 487

Santa Margherita, Florentine church:
Gavi flees to, **17**. 217, 223, 239

Santa Margherita, Via, at Florence:
church in, **17**. 217n

Santa Maria:
faction of, in Pisan Battle of the Bridge, **25**. 582

Santa Maria, convent of:
Benedictine cloister for ladies at Capua, **20**. 429n

Santa Maria, Forte:
reinforced by Genoa, **17**. 309

Santa Maria, Via, at Florence:
theatre in, *see* Teatro di Via Santa Maria

Santa Maria del Carmine, church at Florence:
Corsini's church, **23**. 287n
crucifix of, **21**. 510
fire damages Masaccio's paintings at, **23**. 276, 287

Santa Maria dell'Anima, church at Rome:
Albani has keys to, **23**. 36

Santa Maria in Cosmedin, church at Rome:
(?) Chute alludes to, **35**. 62

Santa Maria Novella, Florentine church:
(?) gens d'armes take refuge in, **17**. 79

Santa Maria Novella, Place (Piazza) of, at Florence:
celebrations in, **17**. 79, 100, **24**. 514
theatre in, *see* Teatro della Piazza di Santa Maria Novella

Santa Maria Nuova, bank at Florence:
Electress deposits money in, **18**. 169

Santa Maria Nuova, hospital of, at Florence:
Cocchi inspector of, **17**. 57n

Sant'Angelo, Duca di:
libretto for Cafaro's *Disfatta di Dario* written by, **21**. 127n

Sant'Antonio, convent at Parma. *See under* Parma

Santarelli, Giuseppe (1710–90), opera singer:
inaudible, **18**. 353, 361
opera performance of, **18**. (?) 302, 353

Santa Rosa, Spanish ship:
Grenville captures, **19**. 403

Santa Rosalia, Spanish frigate:
escapes, **25**. 16n

Santa Sophia. *See under* Constantinople

Sante. *See* Solis y Sante

San Teodoro, Duca di. *See* Caracciolo, Carlo Maria

Santerre, Antoine-Joseph (1752–1809), French Revolutionary army officer:
epigram on flight of, from Saumur, **34**. 183
HW denounces, **31**. 379

Santeul, Jean de (1630–97), poet:
verses by, at Chantilly, **7**. 260

Santiago, Cuba:
sea attack on, impracticable, **17**. 175
Vernon intended to attack, **17**. 96n

Santiago, Galicia:
road to, **12**. 40n

Santi Apostoli, church of, at Rome:
catafalque prepared in, for Old Pretender, **21**. 392
Jacobites congratulate Old Pretender at door of, **19**. 191, 196

[Santi Apostoli, church of, *continued*]
Old Pretender's funeral arranged for, **21**. 392n
prayers at, for Young Pretender, **19**. 171n
Santi Apostoli, palace of (Palazzo Muti), at Rome; Old Pretender's residence:
Clement XI puts, at disposal of Old Pretender, **19**. 85n
joy at, over Young Pretender's venture, **19**. 85
lease of, valued, **19**. 85n
Richecourt prefers, to St James's Palace, **19**. 441
rumours at, **19**. 362
Young Pretender called heir of, **22**. 383–4
Santi Apostoli, Via de', at Rome:
HW mistakes Mann's street in Florence for, **11**. 154, **23**. 107, 135, **43**. 145
Santi Barbieri, ——, opera soprano:
opera sung by, at Florence, **18**. 302
Santi Bargellini, ——, wine merchant:
Mazzei imports wine from, **23**. 204n
Santini, Marchesa. *See* Balbani, Lucrezia
Santini, Signora. *See* Minerbetti, Maria Teresa
Santini, Marchese Niccolò (1729–1812), Lucchese envoy to Tuscany 1758–1800:
becomes envoy to Tuscany, **22**. 319, 352
delivers credentials as envoy, **22**. 353
Dick asked by, for fans for fiancée, **23**. 295
HW's efforts to get a watch for Mann to send to, for sister-in-law, **21**. *293*, 295–6, 302, 303–4, 322, 330, 339, 340, 343, 355
honours at Lucca to be done by, to Joseph II and Leopold, **24**. 130
Leopold and Maria Louisa entertain, at dinner, **22**. 379n
Mann and Young Pretender invited by, to concert, **22**. 229
Mann asks HW to get fans for bride of, **23**. 295
ministerial dinner to be given by, **22**. 355
to wed Signorita Minerbetti, Mann's cicisbea's daughter, **23**. 295, 306
will give ball for D. of York, **22**. 171
York, D. of, entertained by, at Florence, **22**. 215
—— invited by, to Lucca, **22**. 221n
Santini, Marchese Paolino (1727–99):
brother of, **23**. 306
HW bought watch for, **23**. 306
heiress to wed, **21**. *293*
Santo Buono ('Santa Boni'), Principe di. *See* Caracciolo, Carmine Nicolò (1671–1726); Caracciolo, Marino (1696–1745)
Santo di Tito. *See* Tito, Santi di
Santo Domingo, West Indies:
Albemarle may now capture, **22**. 22
Choiseul serves in, **5**. 110n
Churchill has chief command in, **12**. 212n
earthquake of 1770 in, **4**. 440
English success in, against French, **12**. 85
France to have share in, with Spain, **25**. 180
French expect attack upon, **22**. 22n
French reverses at, **19**. 487–8
peace negotiations include, **21**. 526n

Prévost de Traversay second in command at, **6**. 403n
Spain presses France to send ships to, **24**. 300n
Spanish fleet of: captured by English, **19**. 424, 427, 487; said to be destroyed by storm, **24**. 531; unmolested by English, **24**. 501; *see also* Domingo-men
Santo Domingo, Spanish ship:
blows up, **25**. 16n, 26n
Santo Marco, Mme:
Maynard, Vcts, and Maria Carolina of Naples intimate with, **24**. 451n
'Santon Barsisa':
Hales called, **20**. 347
Santon Downham, Suffolk:
Cadogan's seat, **34**. 129n
Santo Spirito, Priore di (d. 1766):
church condemns, for giving plate to state, **22**. 475
Santo Spirito, Borgo di, at Florence:
Casa Manetti in, **43**. 179
HW's former residence, **18**. 561
Mann's house in, **11**. 154n, **13**. 237n, **18**. 561n, **19**. 317
Pecori's house in, on corner, **18**. 150n
Rinuccini palazzo in, **17**. 137n
Santo Spirito, convent at Florence:
bell installed in, **18**. 227
Franchini, Ugo, may take refuge in, **17**. 65
lodge of, overlooks Mann's garden, **20**. 446
nuncio lodges at, **20**. 446
Santo Spirito, Fondaccio di:
Sassi family operates bank at, **17**. 148n
Santuaré, Françoise-Augustine (ca 1754–94), m. Jean-Jacques Du Val d'Éprémesnil:
married name of, corrected, **43**. 140
Parisian cobbler's remark on, **11**. 32
Sanvitale, Contessa. *See* Scotti, Costanza
Sanvitale, (?) Marchese Giacomantonio (1699–1780), Gran Conestabile:
family reduce, to short allowance, **18**. 391
gendarme officer offers to fight, **18**. 368
libels against, **18**. 368, 391
Mann to be called on by, **18**. 281
Niccolini may sell jewels to, for Tesi, **17**. 135
Tesi breaks with, **18**. 391
—— receives gifts from, **17**. 70, **18**. 263
——'s dismissal leaves, almost penniless, **18**. 520
——'s dying lover, **17**. 70
——'s opera backed by, **18**. 281
theatre directors told by, to arrest Tesi's insulter, **18**. 368
San Vitali. *See* Sanvitale
Sanz, Frans:
captured at Velletri, **18**. 493
Sanzilla, Thomas:
captured at Velletri, **18**. 493
San Zirioco, Spanish ship:
Trial captures, **19**. 134, 138, 149
Saône, river in France:
Rhone's conflux with, **35**. 260

Saorgio (Italy):
French repulsed at, **18**. 461
Tenda guarded by castle at, **18**. 461n

Sap; saps:
for siege of Ft St Philip, **37**. 470

Sapieha, Maria Anna (b. 1728), m. (1750)
Prince Johann Cajetan Jablonowsky:
(?) Polish emissary to England, **23**. 319
(?) Young Pretender's negotiations with, **23**. 319

Saporiti, Giuseppe Maria (ca 1691–1767), Abp
of Genoa:
Clement XIII's letter received by, **21**. 411

Sapperton, Glos:
Atkyns of, **14**. 18n

Sapphire; sapphires:
Lorenzi's boast about, **20**. 107

Sappho (fl. 6th cent. B.C.), poetess:
'Castalian nymph' might be conceived by, **28**. 386
Craven, Bns, said to be HW's, **29**. 279
'methodism' of, **30**. 119
Miller, Mrs, is, **39**. 241
'mimic joys' of, **30**. 309
More, Hannah, compared with, **31**. 309
Ossory, Lady, compared with, **32**. 91
quoted in translation, **32**. 91
Rigby, Miss, compared with, **30**. 119
Westall's painting of, **12**. 193
Yearsley, Mrs, is, of parish, **33**. 538

Sappho. See under Mason, Rev. William

Saraband. *See under* Dance

Saracen; Saracens:
Gothic architecture not invented by, **42**. 305

Saracen architecture. *See under* Architecture

Saracen's head:
in Walpole crest, **9**. 36, **32**. 253

Saracin *or* Sarasin. *See* Sarrazin

'Sarag':
Mason (not HW) substitutes 'Cambridge' for,
43. 174

Saragossa, Abp of. *See* Garcia Mañero, Ludovico

Saragossa (Spain):
account of events at: **8**. 119–21; sent by Mme
du Deffand to HW, **3**. 19
from Segovia to, **31**. 21
parliament of, ordinance of, **8**. 119

Sarah (Biblical):
charms of, **34**. 21
Crewe, Lady, imitates, **35**. 74

'Sarah, Milady.' *See* Lennox, Lady Sarah

Saraka (Arabia):
Gray perhaps plays on name of, **13**. 69n

Sarao. *See* Serao

Saraswatee:
Murphy's *Travels in Portugal* mentions, **12**.
178

Sara Th . . . . See under St-Lambert, Jean-
François de

Saratoga, New York:
Acland, Lady Christian, attends wounded husband at, **32**. 402

battle of, Washington would like to repeat,
24. 408
Burgoyne at, **32**. 399
—— is questioned about, **28**. 401n
——'s surrender at, **6**. 486n, **7**. 185n, **24**. 340–
1, **28**. 395n, 411, **29**. 167n, 192n
capitulations at Yorktown and, erroneously
said to have been signed on same day, **25**.
212
convention at, about prisoners, **24**. 383n
Ft Edward near, **28**. 328n
Gates the hero of, **29**. 90n

Sarcenet:
drapery of, **32**. 115
white, sashes of, **32**. 102

Sarcophagus:
child's bones in, **24**. 462
for Ps Elizabeth, at Elizabeth Chudleigh's
ball, **38**. 205
in Pamfili palace, **42**. 268
Lucan, Bn or Bns, gets, at Rome, for HW,
24. 462
Wood's tomb might be copied from, **41**.
246–7, 308
See also under Tomb

'Sardaignais, le.' *See* Viry, Francesco Maria Giuseppe Giustino

Sardanapalus V (d. 625 B.C.), K. of Assyria:
bed at SH fit for, **28**. 42
reincarnation of, **21**. 7

Sardi, Giovanni Antonio:
San Remo deputy, **19**. 123

Sardini, Giovanni Battista Domenico (fl. 1722–
61), Lucchese emissary to Vienna:
Viennese mission of, **21**. 515

Sardinia, K. of. *See* Charles Emmanuel III
(1701–73); Charles Emmanuel IV (1751–
1819); Victor Amadeus II (1666–1732); Victor
Amadeus III (1726–96)

Sardinia, Q. of. *See* Élisabeth-Thérèse (1711–
41); Maria Antonia Ferdinanda (1729–85);
Marie-Adélaïde-Clotilde-Xavière (1759–1802)

Sardinia, Kingdom of:
Aix treaty acceded to by, **19**. 508n
—— not important to, **37**. 285
ambassadors from and to, *see under* Ambassador
Aranjuez treaty between Austria, Spain, and,
20. 294n
army of: Alessandria approached by, **19**. 259;
at Buon Porto, **18**. 151; Austrian army
meets, in Stura valley, **19**. 431–2; Austrians
to join, **19**. 323n; Gages attacks, **18**. 153;
Gages defeats, **19**. 119; Genoa thwarts, **19**.
75; Genoa to blockade, **19**. 344; Imola
approached by, **17**. 500n; Mann regrets having recommended Townshend to, **19**. 169–
70; Maria Theresa's troops to join, **17**.
424; Marseille threatened by, **19**. 323;
Mathews infuriated by failure of, to cooperate, **18**. 229; Mirandola to be besieged
by, **17**. 465; Montemar forced back by, **35**.
29; Nice should be taken by, **18**. 448;

[Sardinia, Kingdom of, *continued*]
Panaro the theatre of, **17**. 424, 432–3, 464, 489; Papal states may be traversed by, **17**. 342, 472, 482; Parma entered by, **17**. 342n, 392; Spaniards may be pursued by, **18**. 200; Spanish said to be defeated by, at Oneglia, **37**. 159–60; threatens Antibes, **19**. 323; Victor Amadeus III directs, **19**. 344; Villafranca abandoned by, **18**. 435–6
Austria guaranteed her possessions in Italy by, **20**. 294n
Austrian treaty with, **17**. 342, **18**. 311
British Empire may become as insignificant as, **39**. 354
Cavalchini, Cardinal, subject of, **21**. 215n
Charles of Naples alarmed by successes of, in Lombardy, **19**. 237
Choiseul settles boundary disputes with, **23**. 143
deserters from army of, **17**. 500–1
embassy chapel of, in Lincoln's Inn Fields, London: **21**. 46n; burnt, **29**. 51; Russian seized in, **29**. 60
England asked by, to finance Corsican campaign, **20**. 386
—— hoped by, to produce vigorous war measures, **19**. 441
——'s treaties with, **18**. 311
English minister to, instructs Mann to report on Spanish invasion, **17**. 265
envoys from and to, *see under* Envoy
France and Spain may be allied with, **17**. 85
France and Spain may divide Milan with, **23**. 469
France may order, to restore territory to Austria, **20**. 576
—— may pay, the equivalent of Placentia's revenue, **21**. 275n
——'s boundaries with, **23**. 143
—— signs armistice with, but delays its execution, **19**. 219n
——'s negotiations with, **12**. 148n, **19**. 230, 231
—— tries to influence, against Francis III and Maria Theresa, **20**. 400n
—— tries to prevent war between Naples and, over reversions, **21**. 275n
Francis I guarantees possessions of, **20**. 294n
French negotiations with, for treaty, **19**. 230n
galleys of, at Leghorn, **19**. 82
Gorsegno, secretary of state to, **20**. 386
grain not to be sent by, to Italy, till French and Spanish needs are filled, **23**. 430
Louis XIV tries to persuade Philip V to content himself with, **28**. 296
Maria Theresa not to meddle in claims of, under Aix treaty, to Placentia and Guastalla, **21**. 280n
Mathews gets diamond-studded sword from, **18**. 370
Oiseau escaped to a port in, **21**. 292
Osborne's squadron cruises off, **21**. 135n
preliminary Aranjuez treaty guarantees territorial integrity of, **20**. 294n

preparations in, to open spring campaign, **19**. 207n
reversionary rights of, to Placentia and Guastalla, **21**. 283n
Spain tries to bribe, **17**. 145
—— said to be making family compact with, **23**. 465
troops of: enter Modena, **17**. 464n; mobilized, **21**. 270n
viceroy of, *see* Ferrero di Biella, Filippo Francesco Maria, Conte della Marmora
Viry conspires to become prime minister of, **24**. 328n
See also Turin, Court of
'Sardinière, la belle.' *See* La Baume-le-Blanc, Françoise-Louise de; Scorailles de Roussilhe, Marie-Angélique
Sardonyx:
pocket-book of, **17**. 222, 414
Vicentino said to have cut, of Q. Elizabeth, **16**. 148–9
Sarendip. *See* Ceylon
Sargent, John:
petition of, for American lands, rejected, **23**. 424n
Sarjent, ——:
Hertford sends books to HW through, **38**. 476
Sark, island of (Channel Islands):
Conway might combine, with other Channel Islands, into United Provinces, **39**. 299
Sarlouis. *See* Saarlouis
Sarmiento de Acuña, Diego (1567–1626), Conde de Gondomar; Spanish ambassador to England 1613–22:
Buckingham's letter mentions, **14**. *107*
Chesterfield to repay Spain for, **33**. 430
portrait of, and print by Passe, **2**. 44
print of, **40**. 236
Wall resembles, **20**. 51–2
Sarpi, Paolo (1552–1623), historian; 'Father Paul':
authorities not cited by, **40**. 140–1
Bedell urged by, to have Wotton present James I's *Premonition* to Venetian senate, **20**. 198n
Histoire du Concile de Trente by, **32**. 273n
prayer of, 'Esto perpetua,' **32**. 273, **36**. 212
Venice anti-papal since time of, **23**. *56*
Sarrazin, Mme. *See* Vignolles, Maria Carlotta de
Sarrazin, Charles:
Leopold of Lorraine's Court councillor, **17**. *193*n
Sarrazin, Maria, m. Joseph-Claude de Juvrecourt:
husband of, **17**. *193*n
Mann may profit by Richecourt's friendship with, **19**. 452
(?) mother to be cared for by, **18**. 361
Orford, Cts of, may be supplanted by, in Richecourt's affections, **19**. 452, 457
Sarre, Marguerite, m. (ca 1740) Jacques de Chambon, Comte de Marcillat:
Ward, Mrs, femme-de-chambre of, **8**. 192

Sarria, Marqués de:
Spanish invasion of Portugal led by, **22**. 34n
Sarro, Domenico (1679–1744), composer:
Gray collects compositions of, **13**. 233n
Sarsfield, ——, Lady (d. 1724), m. (1718) Baron
Théodore Neuhoff:
father of, **18**. 207n
husband leaves, taking her jewels, **18**. 207n
Sarsfield, Guy-Claude (1718–89), Comte de, *or*
Jacques-Hyacinthe (1717–87), Chevalier (later
Vicomte) de:
biographical information on, corrected, **43**.
85
Du Deffand, Mme, gives parcel from, to Hon.
Thomas Walpole, **7**. 446
Hertford visited by, at Ragley, **39**. 85
London to be visited by, **42**. 141
Nivernais sends new copy of *Jardins modernes*
to HW by, **42**. 141
social relations of, at Livry and Paris, **7**. 270,
292, 307, 311, **10**. 211n
SH to be visited by, **30**. *179*
to go to England, **3**. 286
Sarti, Giuseppe (1729–1802), composer:
Idalide by, **11**. 248n
Sarti, Matteo, Florentine messenger:
Mann sends to England, with dispatches,
24. 443, 457, **25**. 42n
Sartine, Mme de. *See* Hardy du Plessis, Marie-
Anne
Sartine, Antoine-Raymond-Jean-Gualbert-Ga-
briel de (1729–1801), Comte d'Alby; lieuten-
ant of police at Paris:
Albert uncongenial to, **6**. 300
Brest visited by, to make Spanish admiral
give precedence to French, **24**. 528
Conti searched by, at the Temple, **23**. 453
Estaing entertained by, **7**. 439
HW consults, about theft, **7**. 267
HW jokes about consulting, in search for
Mme St-Jean, **30**. 217
letter from, about Brest fleet, **39**. 306n
letters and money sent to, after disaster at
fireworks, **4**. 419
lettre de cachet expected by, **5**. 48, 50
Louis XVI receives news of Senegal capture
from, **7**. 123
——'s letter to Penthièvre signed by, **8**. 210
——'s permission for Macartney to serve in
army declared in letter by, **7**. 445
Malesherbes may be succeeded by, **6**. 300
naval news brought by courier to, **7**. 52
Necker intercedes with, for Macartney, **7**. 211
Orvilliers ordered back to Brest by, **24**. 516n
police position regained by, **6**. 331
privateers ordered by, to sea, **33**. 28n
Prothée's loss subject of letter by, **7**. 446
Sade arrested by, **4**. 58
secretary of the marine, **6**. 87, **32**. 205
Tickell's pamphlet pretends to be Opposition's correspondence with, **39**. 326
war desired by, **7**. 40
war parley attended by, **7**. 459

Sarto, Andrea del. *See* Del Sarto, Andrea
Sartorogo. *See* Saratoga
Sarum. *See* Salisbury
Sarzana (Italy):
Spaniards threaten, **18**. 314
Sash; sashes:
black, Ferrers pinioned with, at execution,
21. 402
crape, worn by horse-guard officers at George
II's funeral, **9**. 322
Lippe-Bückeburg tears, from cowardly Portu-
guese general, **22**. 94
yellow, of Hanover, worn by George II at
Dettingen, **18**. 259n
Sassi, ——, Florentine banker:
Agdollo's creditor, **17**. 148–9
Sassoferrato (painter). *See* Salvi, Giovanni
Battista
Sassoferrato (Italy):
town of, **17**. 94
Sassuolo, Francis III's villa, near Modena:
Francis III reoccupies, **19**. 30
Hercules of Modena confined in, **22**. 171
Modena, P. and Ps of, visit, **17**. 489
Modenese Court moves to, **17**. 425
Sas van Ghent (Flanders):
French besiege, **19**. 389
Satan:
Devil's name as priest, **24**. 71
Milton's: **37**. 92; compared by HW to Apollo
Belvedere, **16**. 270
Orléans worse than, **31**. 379
'president of priests,' **33**. 230
Suares, Mme, 'bowed of,' **19**. 226
Satchell, Elizabeth (1763–1841), m. (1783)
Stephen Kemble; actress:
Count of Narbonne to be acted by, **41**. 453,
456
voice of, inadequate, **41**. 460
Satin:
black, worn by Keppels for mourning, **25**.
123n
blue: assembly-room hung with, **10**. 138; with
blonde lace, **32**. 110
blue embroidered robe of, worn by Duchesse
de Choiseul, **10**. 198
breeches of, **30**. 211
evening dress of, **9**. 240
hangings based on ground of, **21**. 468
uniforms of, for calcio players at Leghorn,
22. 423
waistcoats of: **30**. 211; jockeys wear, white,
31. 108
white: Chudleigh, Elizabeth, has wedding
gown of, **23**. 93; Craven, Bns, wears, **34**.
132; hangings of, **9**. 297; Kingston, Ds of,
has attendants wear, at her trial, **24**. 199;
masquerade costumes of, **10**. 80; running
footman wears, at races, **9**. 247–8; waistcoats of, **21**. 399n, **31**. 108
yellow, assembly-room hung with, **10**. 138
Satire:
HW's reflections on, **16**. 258

[Satire, *continued*]
Mann's reflections on, **22**. 272
modern, has no sting, **24**. 62
on Conclave, *see under* Conclave
on Sir Robert Walpole, *see* Miller, James: *Are These Things So?*
Satires and Epistles of Horace. See under Pope, Alexander
Satires of Dr Donne Versified. See under Pope, Alexander
Saturday:
House of Commons may have sessions on, **17**. 247
Saturday Club:
Richmond, Ds of, and, **43**. 185
Saturn:
More, Hannah, knows as little as if she lived on, **31**. 340
statue of, **32**. 169
'Saturnus':
HW's name for Henry Pelham, **35**. 263
Satyricon. See under Petronius Arbiter
Satyr Upon Plagiaries. See under Butler, Samuel
Sauce; sauces:
anchovy, **19**. 357n
'au bleu,' for large fish, **20**. 228
hot entremets of, **19**. 357n
sorrel, **19**. 357n
Sauceboat; sauceboats:
Mann to buy, **18**. 472
melted butter served in, **22**. 105
of Chelsea china, **22**. 122
Seymour, Lady Frances, orders, in vast numbers, **20**. 183
Saucepan:
silver, Lady Townshend carries supper in, to Brompton lodging, **30**. 70
Saucer; saucers:
for basins of Chelsea china, **22**. 180
HW buys, for Cts of Ailesbury, **39**. 146
Sèvres, given by HW to Mrs Gostling, **41**. 437, 438
Saucerotte, Françoise-Marie-Antoinette-Joseph (1756–1815), called Mlle Raucourt; actress:
acts at Choisy, **5**. 322
biographical information on, corrected, **43**. 94–5
Du Deffand, Mme, compares, with other actresses, **5**. 312
—— describes, **39**. 212
——'s opinion of, **6**. 213
no longer at Comédie, **6**. 213
Rhadamiste et Zénobie acted by, **7**. 349
Villette and, **6**. 157
Sauer, Gen., Austrian army officer:
Prussians checked by, **24**. 411n
Saufterre. *See* Sauveterre
Saul (Biblical):
Burney, Dr, to drive away evil spirit of, with music, **42**. 202
'has slain his thousands,' **12**. 12
Saul. See under Trapp, Joseph
Sault. *See* Saulx

Saulx, Marquis de. *See* Saulx-Tavannes, Charles-Henri de
Saulx, Charles-François-Casimir de (1739–92), Comte de Tavannes; Duc de Saulx-Tavannes, 1786:
(?) social relations of, in Paris, **7**. 311, 332
wife of, **7**. 67n
Saulx, Charles-Michel-Gaspard (1713–84), Comte de:
(?) social relations of, with Duchesse de Gramont, **7**. 451
Saulx-Tavannes, Duchesse de. *See* Lévis-Châteaumorand, Marie-Éléonore-Eugénie de
Saulx-Tavannes, Charles-Henri de (1697–1768), Marquis de Saulx:
death of, **4**. 118, 121
Du Deffand, Mme, likes March better than, **3**. 369
——'s acquaintance with, **3**. 197
——'s opinion of, **3**. 48, 55, **4**. 121
health of, **4**. 108, 118
Holdernesse compared to, **3**. 77
social relations of, in Paris, *see index entries ante* 8. 506
Saumarez, Lt Durell:
express from Jersey brought by, **39**. 357n
Saumur (France):
carabineers at, **3**. 230
Joseph II at, **8**. 201
Sade said to be imprisoned at, **4**. 57
Santerre's flight from, **34**. 183
Saunders, ——:
family deeds of, to be carried from Florence to England by courier, **25**. 204
Saunders, ——, Capt. of the *Thames*:
French privateer captures, **21**. 415n
Saunders, Sir Charles (ca 1713–75), K.B.; M.P.; naval officer:
Cadiz attack said to be planned by, **22**. 12
death of, **24**. 149
Dick told by, in letter, of possible visit, **22**. 507
Egmont succeeded by, in Admiralty, **22**. 449
England left by, for Gibraltar, **21**. 97n
French fleet to have been attacked by, **23**. 475
George II reassured by, about Byng, **35**. 95
Godheu's treaty with, inadmissible as basis for peace, **21**. 527n
HW thinks that Raynal refers to, **39**. 168
Hawke and, relieve Byng and West, **20**. 573n
Hawke followed by, in battle of Quiberon Bay, **21**. 351
—— leaves remainder of fleet under, **21**. 20n
—— succeeds, as first lord of Admiralty, **22**. 471–2
Leghorn governor expects to receive, **21**. 507
made admiral, **20**. 561–2
Mann must get, to defeat French and Spanish fleets, **22**. 48
—— receives letter from, promising English naval strength in Mediterranean, **21**. 97
mission of, to Gibraltar to punish Byng and West, **20**. 561–2

named commander of the fleet, 5. 348
near Cartagena, 21. 197
Pitt has report from, from the *Sterling Castle* off Point Levi, 21. 336n
resigns as first lord of the Admiralty, 22. 471
Richmond, D. of, names, to Admiralty, 41. 86
sails to America, 21. 306n
ships used by, against Quebec, 21. 306n
taciturn, 24. 149n
Toulon fleet pursued by, from Malta towards the Levant, 21. 431
Saunders, Thomas (fl. 1732–55), gov. of Madras:
Raynal discusses, 39. 168
Saunders, Mrs Thomas. *See* Pitt, Christian
Saunders family:
arms of, 2. 220, 222
Saunderson, Edward (d. ? 1755), high sheriff of Surrey, 1752:
Richmond Park ticket refused by, 20. 322
Saunderson, Sir William (1692–1754), 2d Bt:
Selwyn requests lord high steward's wand from, 9. 38–9
Saunderson. *See also* Sanderson
'Sauntering Jack.' *See* Prior, Matthew: *Epitaph*
Saurin, Bernard-Joseph (1706–81), dramatist:
À M. de Voltaire sur l'A, B, C, by, 4. 179–80
Beverlei (*Le Joueur*) by, 4. 44n, 75, 91–2, 94, 105, 107
brings play and verses to Mme du Deffand, 4. 92, 105
Helvétius's social relations with, 7. 299
Malesherbes's verses from, 39. 236
Mariage de Julie, Le, by, considered by Mme du Deffand inferior to *L'Indigent*, 6. 241
Orphéline léguée, L', by: 7. 271, 43. 106;
Anglomanie, L', intended title of, 31. 77;
HW criticizes, 31. 77; HW sends, to Bns Hervey, 31. 77; Hervey, Bns, criticizes, 31. 83; performances of, 31. 77; sent by HW to Cts of Ailesbury, 39. 32
Paul I's education not undertaken by, 32. 59n
Saurin, Mme Bernard-Joseph. *See* Sandras, Marie-Anne-Jeanne
Sauromatæ (Sarmatians):
Mason should do tragedy of, 28. 326
vague meaning of, 30. 73
Sausage, Bologna:
Bocchineri as small as, 35. 53
'favours' suggests bills for, 35. 31
HW not to receive, 18. 386
Saussure, Horace-Bénédict de (1740–99), Swiss naturalist:
HW invites, to call on him, 41. 165
HW meets, at Chatsworth, 41. 165
HW misses call by, in Arlington St, 41. 165
HW's correspondence with, 41. 165–6
HW to arrange for Ds of Portland's cabinet to be seen by, 41. 165–6
Pall Mall lodging-place of, 41. 165
Voyage dans les Alpes by, 41. 165n
Sauvage, Victoire-Françoise, m. (1771) Louis-Marie-Cécile, Comte de Ste-Maure:

(?) social relations of, with Mme du Deffand, 5. 138–40
Sauvé, Dame, chambermaid of D. of Burgundy:
poisoned and put in Bastille after plot, 20. 287n
Sauvé, Jean-Baptiste (1701–61), called La Noue; actor:
Œuvres of, owned by Mme du Deffand, 8. 33
Sauveterre, Mme. *See* Paganini, Rosa
Sauveterre ('Saufterre'; 'Sauvter'; (?) 'Soutter'; (?) 'Sovuter'), Francesco; dancer:
Bologna performances of, 17. *463*
choreographer at Florence and Venice, 17. 45n
dances in Florentine theatre, 18. 303, 322, 361, 19. 355–6, 439
may come to Florence, 17. 463
of French royal blood, 18. 303, 19. 355
Sauveur, ——:
attends session of parliament of Paris, 8. 171
Sauvigny, Mme Louis-Jean Berthier de. *See* Durey d'Harnoncourt, Louise-Bernarde
Sauzay, Marquis du. *See* Du Sauzay, Jean-Baptiste
Savage, Lady Elizabeth (fl. ca 1630), m. Sir John Thimbleby:
HW asks about portrait of, at Kimbolton, 10. 79
(?) Van Dyck's portrait of, at Hinchingbrooke, 40. 283
Savage, Henry (?1604–72), Master of Balliol College, Oxford:
Balliofergus by, 2. 231
Savage, John (fl. 1690–1700), engraver:
print by, of Armstrong, 1. 181
Savage, Richard, poet:
reputed mother of, 1. 181n
Savage; savages:
HW's reflections on, 33. 237, 34. 177
Savalette, ——:
attends session of parliament of Paris, 8. 173
Savannah, Georgia:
Estaing repulsed at, 24. 544, 25. 1
unsuccessful siege of, 28. 474n
Savannerola. *See* Savonarola
Savant; savants:
HW avoids, in Paris, 35. 116
Savary-Brèves de Jarzé, Marie-Renée-Bonne-Félicité de (ca 1743–68), m. (1755) Charles-René de Maillé de la Tour-Landry, Comte de Maillé:
Louis XV favours, 3. 373
ugly and disgusting, 3. 373
Savelli, Barbara (ca 1750–1826), m. (1765) Francesco Camillo Massimo, Marchese di Roccasecca:
Santini and Mann entertain, 23. 229
Savelli, castle of:
near Palazzo Albani at Gandolfo, 24. 214n
Saverin, château de:
burnt, 7. 428
Saverne, Battle of:
Hamilton, George, killed at, 42. 89n

Savile, Barbara (d. 1797), m. (1752) Richard Lumley Saunderson, 4th E. of Scarbrough:
Court presentation of Vcts Hinchingbrooke by Ds of Bedford displeases, 10. 210
(?) opera attended by, sitting back-stage, 38. 289
suggested as Bedchamber lady to Q. Charlotte, 38. 96

Savile, Lady Dorothy (1699–1758), m. (1721) Richard Boyle, 3d E. of Burlington:
Amelia, Ps, jokingly suggested as successor to, 9. 316
Bodens, Molly, companion to, 35. 165
death of, 9. 226
Devonshire, D. of, breaks promise to wife of not marrying son to daughter of, 20. 66n
Euston quarrels with, 17. 174, 18. 482
Garrick, Mrs, given mortgage by, 20. 74n
—— may have been spoiled by, 20. 180
—— may receive fortune from, 20. 74
HW's joke about St Peter, Lady Bath, and, 9. 226
Hartington, son-in-law of, 20. 74n
husband bequeaths all he can to, 35. 159
inscription by, on engravings of her portrait of her daughter, 18. 482
(?) masquerade attended by, 9. 79–80
picture designed by, 41. 452
Pope's conversation with, at Chiswick, 18. 449
profanity of, in illness, 37. 571–2
Pulteney's epigram mentions, 30. 24
Richmond's fireworks attended by, 9. 81
Thanet, Cts of, sister of, 35. 159n
'Violette' (Mrs Garrick) chaperoned by, 9. (?) 79, 81
—— protected by, 9. 28

Savile, Sir George (1633–95), 1st Vct, E., and M. of Halifax:
Character of a Trimmer, The, by, owned by HW, 16. 15n
HW's omission of maxims of, 16. 6, 15
HW's treatment of, in Royal and Noble Authors, 40. 139
Miscellaneous Thoughts by, satirizes 'mitred flattery,' 35. 569
Miscellanies Historical and Philological by, owned by HW, 16. 15n
Sunderland possibly confused with, 34. 255
'tawny Tuscan' of, 13. 64n

Savile, Sir George (1726–84), 8th Bt; M.P.:
Cavendish faction's retreat disapproved by, 29. 266
chariot of, demolished by Gordon rioters, 25. 54, 33. 177
Cust does not restrain speeches of, 23. 175n
delay on Wilkes's complaint proposed by, 38. 292
George III's pension list demanded by, to humour Yorkshire committee, 25. 18
Gordon rioters threaten, 2. 79n, 224–5, 29. 62
Grenville denounced by, 38. 499
—— opposed by, over Wilkes's complaint on privilege, 38. 292

House of Commons attacked by, 15. 130, 23. 169–70, 184, 289, 291
Militia Bill clause proposed by, 32. 279n
North accused by, of concealing Spanish belligerency, 24. 491n
——'s answer demanded by, 28. 359
Parliamentary bill moved by, for removal of Roman Catholic restrictions, 2. 66n, 197n, 25. 54n, 28. 395, 398, 29. 66n, 33. 177n
Parliamentary éclat of, over Newfoundland dispute, 38. 528
Parliamentary motions by: 36. 197–8; for inquiry into loan, 29. 123n, 36. 194n; for petition of county delegates for reform, 36. 198n
Parliamentary seat resigned by, 29. 321n
Parliamentary speech by, against Habeas Corpus Bill, 28. 283n
petition of, against Luttrell's election, 23. 114n
petition to be presented by, 29. 121n
reconciliation of, with rest of Opposition, 15. 128n
violent behaviour of, in House of Commons, alarms HW, 39. 121
witticism by, on Shelburne and Fox both being wounded in their groins, 25. 37
Yorkshire committee supported by, 28. 492, 29. 74

Savile, Sir Henry:
Rerum Anglicarum scriptores by, includes Hoveden's account of Richard I, 40. 117n

Savile, Sir John (1719–78), K.B., 1749; cr. (1753) Vct Pollington, (1766) E. of Mexborough; M.P.:
Bath ribbon awarded to, 20. 40, 71n
Parliamentary membership of, corrected, 43. 266

Savile, Lady Mary (1700–51), m. (1722) Sackville Tufton, 7th E. of Thanet:
Bathurst's conversation with, at Bath, 37. 87
Burlington, Cts of, sister of, 35. 159n
'Violette' (Mrs Garrick) protected by, 9. 28
Whitefield's preaching heard by, 9. 74

Savile House, Leicester Fields, London:
Court at, for George III's birthday, 35. 299n
Fox, Henry, confers with Pitt at, 21. 11n
plundered, 2. 224n
York, Edward, D. of, leaves, 35. 291n

Savile Row, London:
fire endangers, 9. 363
Gordon rioters in, 33. 185
Lort dies in, 16. 228n
—— lives in, 2. 335, 337, 16. 201, 228
—— returns to, 16. 282n
Prestage, auctioneer in, 21. 172n, 35. 220n
spelling of, corrected, 43. 221
Squibbs's in, sold by Carnivalli to Barrymore, 43. 143
Strawbridge, Mrs, lived near, 33. 556
Suffolk, Cts of, lives in, 9. 363
theatre in, 11. 101n, 216n

Saville. *See* Savile

Savoi, ——; singer:
in burletta company, 22. 474n

Savoie, Princesses de. *See* Marie-Joséphine- Louise (1753–1810) of Savoy; Marie-Thérèse (1756–1805) of Savoy

Savoie-Carignan, Marie-Thérèse-Louise de (1749–92), m. (1767) Louis-Alexandre-Joseph-Stanislas de Bourbon, Prince de Lamballe:
ball at Versailles attended by, 32. 255
dances at ball in honour of Dauphin's marriage, 4. 410
Dauphiness's heart to be carried by, 3. 263n
HW claims he never saw, 35. 389
HW may show SH to, unwillingly, 39. 456
head of, shown on pike to royal family, 34. 178
letter from Marie-Antoinette to, forged, 34. 179
London reached by, 39. 456
marriage of, 3. 225, 227, 229, 231, 245
murder of, 15. 219–20, 237, 35. 446
Orléans's death is atonement for, 12. 61
Queensberry gives dinner for, 35. 389

Savoir vivre, club in London:
goldfinch might belong to, 32. 205
house of, in St James's St, 32. 205n
Lyttelton the leader of, 24. 103
masquerades and gambling of, 24. 103

Savona (Italy):
Adorno, Agostino, commander of castle of, 19. 313n
bark from, reaches Leghorn, 19. 434
Brown to receive captured cannon from, 19. 353, 358
Charles Emmanuel III captures, 19. 313n, 352
—— to besiege, 19. 313
Cooper bombards, 19. 76n, 81, 35. 63
Della Rocca to attack, 19. 313n, 344–5
—— withdraws to, 19. 429n
English ships blockade, 19. 313n
French army drives from, 19. 54n
French fail to surprise, 19. 476
governor of, sinks powder-laden bark, 19. 81
Jesuits in disguise rejected by, 22. 546
Maillebois may be attacked from, 19. 237
Richelieu driven from, by counter-attack, 19. 476n
Young Pretender at, 18. 385

Savonarola, Girolamo Maria Francesco Matteo (1452–98), reformer:
medal struck in time of, 21. 201
party formed by, 15. 278n

Savonnerie, La. *See* La Savonnerie

Savorgio. *See* Saorgio

Savoy, Ds of. *See* Marguerite (1523–74) de Valois

Savoy, D. of. *See* Charles Emmanuel IV (1751–1819); Victor Amadeus II (1666–1732); Victor Amadeus III (1726–96)

Savoy, K. of. *See* Sardinia, K. of

Savoy:
ambassadors from and to, *see under* Ambassador
Charles Emmanuel III to expel Don Philip from, 18. 65
Corsicans hate people of, 19. 171
Cours de l'Europe satirizes, 17. 177
duke of, may be preceded by Richecourt, 20. 295
French emigrate to, 11. 140n
—— may join Don Philip in, 18. 295
HW writes from mountains of, 13. 181
ministers from and to, *see under* Minister
mountains of, surpassed by Rhine scenery, 37. 150
Neapolitan ambassador to, 4. 366n
Philip, Don, invades, enraging Charles Emmanuel III, 18. 58–9
—— may retire to, 18. 513
—— no longer rules, 18. 95
Piacenza ceded by Charles Emmanuel III in exchange for Nice and, 19. 508n
royalty of, visit England, 33. 567
Spain plunders, 19. 505
Spaniards from, awaited by D. of Modena, 18. 322
Spanish campaign in, will decide plans of Neapolitan Court, 18. 302

Savoy, the, palace in London:
guards at, 23. 12n

Savoyard girl:
Cumberland, D. of, rejected by, 9. 94
—— sends, to Windsor, 9. 94
HW sends print of, to Montagu, 9. 94

Savoyards, The, song:
Pont-de-Veyle sings, 7. 289

Sawbridge, Catharine (1731–91), m. 1 (1760) George Macaulay, M.D.; m. 2 (1778) William Graham; historian:
Anstey's indecent verses on, 33. 84–5
anti-monarchical views of, 2. 210, 32. 138
Boswell's complimentary letter from, about *Account of Corsica*, 41. 138–9n
Burke attacked by, in pamphlet, 11. 169–70
—— calls, a *poissarde*, 11. 169–70
——'s pamphlet attacked by, 23. 209
death of, 11. 301
Du Deffand, Mme, has social relations with, 6. 495, 497
—— wishes HW to recommend, to Mme Necker, 6. 488
—— would like, to bring tea, 6. 489
French cookery denounced by, 35. 485
(?) HW alludes to, 5. 199
HW and Duc de la Rochefoucauld to dine with, 23. 92
HW and Harcourt give recommendatory letters to, 28. 369, 371
HW asks for address of, 42. 62
HW calls: 'Dame Thucydides,' 33. 84; 'faction's brood-hen,' 23. 145; (?) 'virago,' 12. 258
HW finds, too much a Whig, 2. 90

[Sawbridge, Catharine, *continued*]
HW hopes for election of, as alderman, 32. 40
HW recommends, to Mme du Deffand, 6. 486
HW shocks, by views on Reformation, 29. 61
HW's relations with, 6. 495
HW talks with, about Luther and the Reformation, 29. 61, 34. 101–2, 160–1, 43. 307
HW to attend theatre with, in Mrs Cholmondeley's box, 39. 102
HW to tell, of Mason's remark about Barillon's letter, 28. 78
(?) Harcourt hears reports from, 35. 526
——'s letter from, returned to him by HW, 35. 485
health of, 6. 495, 497, 28. 142
History of England by: 6. 497, 15. 97n, 43. 66, 307; HW and Gray admire first volume of, 28. 3; HW expects England to be finished before, 29. 102; Mason to buy, 28. 4; published, 28. 3n
History of England . . . in a Series of Letters by: Mason asks about, 28. 369; 'wretched compilation,' 28. 371
husband of, 33. 84, 217
James I's letters not printed by, 15. 97
Junius papers attributed to, 36. 52
Modest Plea for the Property of Copyright, A, by, 28. 142
name of, corrected, 43. 93, 102, 366
Nice not to be visited by, 6. 497
Observations on a Pamphlet Entitled Thoughts on the Cause of the Present Discontents, by, 23. 209
Observations on the Reflections of . . . Edmund Burke, by, 11. 169n
Paoli lauded by, 23. 31n
——'s English visit not blighted by, 23. 150
——'s quarrel with, 36. 55–6
parentage of, Mason asks about, 28. 4–5
'Pride's Purge' approved by, 15. 129
Sidney to be defended by, 28. 78
suppers not liked by, 6. 488
Walpole, Sir Robert, abused by, 2. 127–8
wax figure of, by Mrs Wright, 32. 98
Sawbridge, Jacob (d. 1748), director of South Sea Co.:
grandfather of Mrs Macaulay, 28. 372
Sawbridge, John (1732–95), alderman; lord mayor of London; M.P.:
Barrington's speech provokes, in Parliament, 39. 125
Bastille Day celebrated by, at Crown and Anchor, 35. 399n
candidate for lord mayor, 23. 520n
dying, 23. 263–4
elected alderman of London, 39. 114
election defeat of, 36. 174
French Revolution praised by, 11. 89n
George III disrespectfully treated by, 23. 196
London remonstrance avowed by, 23. 198
Macaulay, Mrs, sister of, supports his political stand, 32. 40n
Maidstone meeting's chairman, 25. 290n
Opposition alderman, 35. 334n
Parliamentary motions by: for shortening Parliaments, 25. 290n; for Westminster election return, 25. 562n
weavers pacified by, 23. 163
Sawbridgeworth, Herts:
Cole's ancestor vicar of, 1. 50, 73
Sawdust:
execution scaffold sprinkled with, 19. 301
Saw mill; saw mills:
at Limehouse, 23. 21n, 30. 221n
Dingley's, 23. 21n
'Sawney.' *See* Wedderburn, Alexander
Sawyer, Edmund (ca 1687–1759), Master in Chancery:
fire in chambers of, 20. 321
Sawyer, Herbert (ca 1731–98), Capt., 1758; later Adm.:
Admiralty reached by, with Byron's dispatch, 24. 515n
Hermione captured by, 22. 44–5
Sawyer; sawyers:
mob of, rises in London, 23. 21
Saxe, P. of. *See* Franz Xaver
Saxe, Ps of. *See* Marie-Christine
Saxe, Hermann-Maurice (1696–1750), Comte de; Maréchal de France:
Aix treaty probably facilitated by fear of, of losing power, 19. 482–3
allied force defeated by, 9. 49n
Bellecourt, Mlle, mistress of, 7. 265
Belle-Isle's death does not distress, 19. 429
Bute quotes, 40. 189
Cumberland, D. of, blames, for prolongation of Maestricht's siege, 19. 480n
—— meets, at Laeffeld, 19. 409n
—— receives book from, for Chesterfield, 9. 52
—— sends Sackville to, about Maestricht siege, 19. 481
death of: expected, 19. 39; helps England's chances, 20. 506
Dieskau a pupil of, 35. 257
England supposedly visited by, 15. 134, 43. 197
—— to be invaded by, 9. 23
English army outnumbers that of, 18. 496
English army prevented, from preventing P. Charles's expulsion of Frederick II from Bohemia, 18. 526
English army to attack, 18. 481
English army to be intercepted by, 37. 152–3
English-French peace planned by, 19. 456n
Fontenoy command of, 36. 11
France needs, to resist English invasion, 21. 211
French invasion of England to be led by, 18. 402
generalship of, at Roucour, praised, 30. 108–9
Ligonier informed by, that his parole is ended, 37. 279–80

Louis XVI said to have ordered statue of, **7**. 23
MS of, about Königsmarck's murder, **7**. 278
Marigny orders statue of, **7**. 23
Paris house of, offered to Ligonier, **37**. 280
plans of, to reduce Sambre valley's strongholds, **19**. 261n
print of, **19**. 395–6
prudence of, **37**. 282
sieges started by, **19**. 395
tapped three times since Fontenoy, **19**. 91
Saxe, Marie-Josèphe de. *See* Marie-Josèphe
Saxe. *See also* Saxony
Saxe, Hôtel de, in Paris:
Wilkes stays at, **22**. 198n, **38**. 280n
Saxe-Coburg, P. of. *See* Friedrich Josias (1737–1815)
Saxe-Gotha, Ds of. *See* Charlotte (1751–1827) of Saxe-Meiningen
Saxe-Gotha, D. of. *See* Ernst (1745–1804); Friedrich III (1699–1772)
Saxe-Gotha, P. of. *See* August (1747–1806); Ernst (1745–1804)
Saxe-Gotha:
Wales, Augusta, Ps of, to visit, **4**. 420
Saxe-Gotha-Altenburg, Ds of. *See* Louise (1710–67) of Saxe-Meiningen
Saxe-Hildburghausen, Ds of. *See* Luise (1726–56) of Denmark
Saxe-Hildburghausen, Elizabeth Albertine (1713–61), m. (1735) Karl Ludwig of Mecklenburg-Strelitz:
marriage date of, corrected, **43**. 374
Saxe-Hildburghausen, Wilhelm (1702–87), D. of; Austrian field marshal:
Soubise joins Austrian army under, to recover Saxony, **21**. 137n
Tesi's affair with, **21**. 194
Saxe-Meiningen, Charlotte of. *See* Charlotte (1751–1827)
Saxe-Teschen, Ds of. *See* Maria Christine (1742–98)
Saxe-Teschen, D. of. *See* Albrecht Kasimir August (1738–1822)
Saxe-Weimar, Ds of. *See* Anna Amalie
Saxe-Weissenfels, D. of. *See* Johann Adolf II
Saxham, Little, Suffolk:
church of, described, **2**. 256
Saxlingham, Norfolk:
Gooch, rector of, **1**. 354n
Saxon; Saxons (Anglo-Saxons):
arches in style of, **42**. 103n
artistic skill of, **16**. 102
'bump in the ground' might be the work of, **28**. 37
Chatterton accuses Normans of destroying art of, **16**. 114, 115
contribution of, to England, **12**. 178
England fully exposed before its conquest by, **29**. 122
English, the, a mixture of, **35**. 392
Gothic architecture not invented by, **42**. 305
language corrupted by, **42**. 305

Normans' art compared to that of, **16**. 108
—— had corrupted liberty of, **42**. 78
Pownall thinks Whigs are heirs to, **42**. 78n
Wittenagemot held by, **10**. 274
Saxon; Saxons (inhabitants of Saxony):
Greenwich, Lady, discusses, with Lady Tweeddale, **34**. 17
Mann meets, in Florence, **20**. 327
Saxon architecture. *See under* Architecture
Saxon china. *See under* China
Saxon (Anglo-Saxon) history:
'Rowley' unlikely to be influenced by, **16**. 336
Saxon (Anglo-Saxon) kings:
mortuary chests of, at Winchester, **35**. 250
statue of, found under Westminster Hall, **16**. 198
Saxon (Anglo-Saxon) language:
Chatterton's imitators said to write poems in, **16**. 130
HW does not understand, **16**. 106
See also Anglo-Saxon
Saxon (Anglo-Saxon) MSS:
drawings in, **40**. 248, **42**. 67
Saxon (Anglo-Saxon) remains:
at Lincoln, **40**. 233
HW dislikes, **1**. 163, **2**. 116, 301
Saxony, Elector of. *See* Frederick Augustus II (1696–1763); Frederick Augustus III (1750–1827); Frederick Christian (1722–63)
Saxony, Electress of. *See* Maria Antonia (1724–80)
Saxony, P. of. *See* Frederick Christian (1722–63)
Saxony, Q. of. *See* Maria Theresa (1767–1827)
Saxony:
army of: Frederick II defeats, **19**. 189; Hessians oppose, **22**. 60; Leopold, P. of Anhalt, defeats, at Kesseldorf, **19**. 189n; may join English, **19**. 240, 255; Saxe-Weissenfels assembles, **18**. 495n; surrenders to Frederick II, **21**. 14–15
Bavarian relations with, **42**. 495
bishoprics may be obtained by, **22**. 119
Bohemian areas adjacent to, retained by Frederick II, **21**. 116
childbearing in, supposedly easy, **9**. 58
Du Deffand, Mme, has china from, **8**. 13, 24
Empire's 'vicar' and 'most material elector,' **42**. 496
England's treaty with, **20**. 299
France's treaty with, **20**. 510n
Frederick II discovers treachery of, by bribing Menzel to copy Brühl's dispatches, **21**. 5
—— disputes French and Austrian entry into, **21**. 137n
—— loses, **21**. 332
—— optimistic before invasion of, **21**. 90n
——'s alleged alliance with, **24**. 389
—— should not pause in, **21**. 2
Frederick Augustus II allows no French provisions to cross, **18**. 108
—— cuts off Maillebois's escape through, **18**. 89

[Saxony, *continued*]
French subsidy refused by, **42**. 496
Ginori imports workmen from, to make china, **18**. 184
HW imagines Frederick II bouncing into, **25**. 190
Maria Theresa's alliance with, **21**. 564
ministers from and to, *see under* Minister
paste of, excels all other, for porcelain, **25**. 635
prime minister of, *see* Brühl, Heinrich
Prussian-Russian battle expected in, **21**. 72
Prussian troops occupy, **21**. 271n
Russia refuses to join England in mediating between Austria, Prussia, and, **21**. 53n
Serbelloni, Cardinal, nuncio to, **20**. 428n
Soubise joins Austrian army under Hildburghausen to recover, **21**. 137n
subsidies for, **42**. 493, 496
troops of: contained in army of observation in Prussian service, **21**. 73n; defeated near Lutterberg, **22**. 60n
zaffre and smalt produced by, **18**. 184n
Saxthorpe, Norfolk:
Addison, Leonard, holds living of, **14**. 90n
Say, Charles Greene (ca 1721–75), printer of the *Gazetteer*:
French officers threaten, **23**. 231
(?) HW's correspondence with, **40**. 256
Say and Seal. *See* Saye and Sele
Sayde, ——, china merchant in Paris:
HW's bill from, **7**. 408, 413
Saye and Sele, Bn. *See* Twistleton, Thomas
Saye and Sele, Vct. *See* Fiennes, Richard (1716–81)
Saye and Sele, Vcts. *See* Tyrrell, Christobella
Saye and Sele, barony of:
descent of Clinton barony compared to that of, **25**. 165
Sayer, Frances Julia (1757–1850), m. (1805) Marie-Charles-Joseph de Pougens:
Boscawen, Mrs, gets letter from, from Paris, **11**. 45, **35**. 393
—— writes to, about Mrs Boyle Walsingham's ball, **42**. 222n
SH visitors sent by, **12**. 243
Sayer, Rev. George (ca 1696–1761), vicar of Witham:
HW praises parsonage of, **9**. 93
Sayer, Robert (ca 1725–94), printseller:
SH visited by, **12**. (?) 224, 225
Sayer, Mrs Robert. *See* Longfield, Alice
Sayer, William:
Henry VI's keeper, **14**. 180n
Sayer. *See also* Sayers; Sayre
Sayers, James (1748–1823), caricaturist:
satirical prints designed by, **33**. 401
Sayre ('Sayer'), Stephen (1736–1818), sheriff of London, 1773:
affair of, forgotten, **28**. 246
arrest and former career of, **24**. 138–9
biographical information about, corrected, **43**. 99

George III said to be object of plot of, **6**. 230, 231, **28**. 227, 229, **33**. 21
prosecution of, said to be expensive, **41**. 313
Sbirri (Italian police):
banditti murder, **13**. 221
Benedict XIV's, **18**. 56
Del Monte, Filippo, pursued by, in Castello, **20**. 442
Del Monte, Giambattista, arrested by, at Cortona, **20**. 422
Dumesnil (Alessandro)'s valet arrested by, **17**. 225
Dumesnil, Joseph, detained by, **19**. 493
Florentine children whipped by, for taunts against Richecourt, **21**. 85
foreign ministers in Italy do not allow, in streets near their embassies, **18**. 467n
Gavi's house searched by, **17**. 217, 223
Mann complains about, to Richecourt, **18**. 467
Mary's effects inventoried by, **17**. 102
Pepi arrested by, **17**. 136–7
prohibited weapons seized by, from suspected characters, at night, **17**. 136
Richecourt's, obey his orders on St John's Day, **19**. 8
satire on Conclave sought by, at printer's, **24**. 70
sentenced to the galleys after quarrel with grenadiers, **24**. 8–9
Serchio River to be diverted by, **20**. 514
See also 'Bargellos'
Scabby face:
occurrence of, **36**. 328
Scacciati, Andrea (1725–71):
medal by, engraved in Cocchi's *Discorsi Toscani*, **21**. 202n
Scadbury Park, Chislehurst, Kent:
HW compares, to Houghton Park House, **32**. 46–7
in print of Sir Francis Walsingham, **32**. 46–7
Selwyn, John, owned, **35**. 153n
Walsingham's seat, **32**. 46–7, **35**. 153
Scævola, Caius Mucius, legendary Roman:
chimney-piece adorned with history of, **1**. 3, 170–1
Scaffold; scaffolds:
at Coronation, **21**. 534, **38**. 126
collapse of, at Lovat's execution, **19**. 386
for Battle of the Bridge, at Pisa, **24**. 188
for execution of rebel lords, **19**. 299–302
for Ferrers's execution, **21**. 402
for fireworks celebration, **20**. 47
for fireworks in Hyde Park, **38**. 204
for seeing cocchiata at Florence, **22**. 158
French ladies might have, on French coasts to view English fleets, **37**. 537
hammering on, keeps HW awake on night before Coronation, **21**. 534
of St Paul's dome, **40**. 350
sheriff refuses to hold up Lovat's head on, **37**. 267

two, for Elizabeth Chudleigh's tradespeople, at party, **38.** 204

workmen fall off of, at Kew, **20.** 240

Scagliola:

Belloni makes table in, for Fetherstonhaugh, **20.** 194n

box of pictures in, sent to Strafford, **17.** 396, **18.** 13

chimney-piece at SH to have been made of, **35.** 407

HW orders tables of, for friend, **19.** 414, 423, 427, 430, 510, **20.** 23, 26–7, 37, 88, 93

HW's own table of: finished, **18.** 87, 106; HW receives, **18.** 291, 292; HW thanks Mann for his trouble in getting, **17.** (?) 24, **18.** 105; HW to have, **17.** 36, 41, 58, 123, 482, **18.** 214; HW wants two more of, **20.** 88, 93; Hugford begins, **17.** 58; Mann to send, **18.** 152; price of, **18.** 87, 106; spoiled, **17.** 199–200, 482

Hugford invents, **10.** 336

—— makes, **19.** 430n

—— no longer makes, **20.** 93

——'s pupils slow in making, **19.** 423, **20.** 93

Mann sends pictures made in, to E. of Strafford, **35.** 23

Richter and Bartoli make, in London, **35.** 407n

tables of: made for Leeson, **19.** 423; Mann orders, from Belloni for Fetherstonhaugh, **20.** 93n; Mann's, take four years, **20.** 93

Scaglivuola. *See* Scagliola

Scala, Via della, at Florence:

Mal Maritate in, **18.** 112n

Ridolfi, Palazzo, in, **17.** 59n

'Scala Santa':

HW's name for Lady Waldegrave's staircase, **31.** 394

Scala santa, La. See under Loredano, Giovanni Francesco

'Scaliger, Canis':

HW jokes about, **37.** 98

Scaliger. *See* Scaligero, Giulio Cesare (1484–1558); Scaligero, Giuseppe Giusto (1540–1609)

Scaligero, Giulio Cesare (1484–1558), scholar and controversialist:

Cardano's controversy with, **31.** 433n

Hume-Rousseau quarrel resembles those of, **41.** 51

Warburton resembles, **40.** 228

Scaligero, Giuseppe Giusto (1540–1609), classical scholar:

Brown, Dr John, compared with, **9.** 220–1

commentator on the classics, **13.** 132n

foul names thrown by, at adversaries, **43.** 291

Grattan and Flood imitate acrimony of, **25.** 438

Scaling-ladder; scaling-ladders:

British sailor boards Spanish ship with, **24.** 543

Carlisle assaulted with, **19.** 165

Scalken. *See* Schalcken

Scallop shells, purple:

Montagu may send, to HW from Ireland, **9.** 408

Scalp; scalps:

from Quebec, **31.** 22

Scalping:

HW jokes about Priestley and, **31.** 386

heroes would shrink from, **21.** 290

Scamozzi, Vincenzo (1552–1616), architect:

Cinq Ordres d'architecture by, Chute's copy of, **35.** 157n, **43.** 292

L'Idea dell'architettura by, perhaps bought by HW, **26.** 5, **43.** 292

Scandinavian; Scandinavians:

origins of, **16.** 378

Scandinavian antiquities:

Scottish historians should study, **16.** 379

Scandinavian poetry:

Jerningham's poem on, **29.** 331

Scapula, Johann (fl. 1572–9), lexicographer:

dictionary of, might be consulted, **13.** 240

Scaramouches:

at Ranelagh jubilee-masquerade, **20.** 47

Scarborough, Yorks:

Brompton near, **12.** 13n

Brown, Sir Robert, to visit, **9.** 16

Cayley has seat near, **12.** 13n

Grafton, D. of, to visit, **9.** 66–7

Hotham Thompson of, **9.** 132n

Mason to visit, **28.** 163, 165

Palliser's removal as governor of, asked, **24.** 446

Preston, Mrs, dies at, **2.** 23n

Seton, Mrs, to join Berrys at, **12.** 35

visitors to: Berrys, **12.** 22, 23, 26, 33, 34, 46; Bland, **30.** 84n; Hanmer, Lady Catharine, **30.** 84n; Pelham, Henry, **20.** 413; Shirley, **20.** 439; Townshend, Hon. Charles, **30.** 58n, **40.** 47

Waldegraves to visit, **34.** 53

Ward bookseller in, **29.** 294n

Scarborough, English frigate:

Boston to be reinforced by, **39.** 197n

galleon's capture reported by, **37.** 246

news from Boston brought by, **24.** 46n

Scarborough Castle:

Hill, governor of, **9.** 153n

Palliser resigns as governor of, **24.** 446n

Scarborough. *See also* Scarbrough

Scarbrough, Cts of. *See* Hamilton, Lady Frances (d. 1772); Savile, Barbara (d. 1797)

Scarbrough, E. of. *See* Lumley, Richard (ca 1650–1721); Lumley, Richard (ca 1688–1740); Lumley Saunderson, George Augusta (1753–1807); Lumley Saunderson, Richard (1725–82); Lumley Saunderson, Thomas (ca 1691–1752)

Scarf; scarves:

ecclesiastical, worn by Northumberland's chaplains at assembly, **38.** 401

of blue and gold tissue, apparently worn by Comtesse de Gramont in Lely's miniature, **10.** 12

[Scarf; scarves, *continued*]
  white, worn by Mann's mourners, **25.** 665n
Scarlatti, Alessandro (ca 1659–1725), composer:
  Arminio in Germania by, **17.** 80
Scarlatti, Domenico (1685–1757), composer:
  Alexander in Persia by, **17.** 184n
  contest between Handel and, **13.** 214n
Scarlatti, Filippo Maria:
  daughter of, becomes nun, **17.** 53n
Scarlatti, Giovanna Barbera (1723–46), nun:
  Craon attends *vestimento* of, **17.** 53
Scarlatti, Pompeo (fl. 1742–4), Imperial minister to Rome:
  Old Pretender often sees, **18.** 397
Scarlatti-Rondinelli, Elena Vittoria (ca 1728–82), m. (1740) Marchese Antonio Francesco Ximenes d'Aragona:
  Mann intimate with, **23.** 25
Scarlet fever:
  drinking and rioting occasion, **24.** 498
  occurrences of, **12.** 134, **18.** 430, 431, 444, **24.** 498, (?) **43.** 276
Scarlett ('Scarlet'), Edward, jr.; optician and dealer in pictures and curiosities:
  (?) HW buys spectacles from, **21.** 131
  HW to speak to, about picture for Selwyn, **30.** 150
  pictures and curiosities sold by, in Dean St near St Anne's, Soho, **21.** 131n
  reputed Van Dyck offered by, **30.** *149*
  Selwyn displeased by purchase at shop of, **30.** 149
Scarniccia, ——, son of Pascal Scarniccia:
  Leghorn reached by, after imprisonment in Spain, **25.** 430n
Scarniccia, James, of Gibraltar:
  Malborough Fort bought by Udny from, **25.** 199n
Scarniccia, Capt. Pascal:
  Leghorn reached by, after imprisonment in Spain, **25.** 430n
  Malborough Fort commanded by, **25.** 198
  Mann commissions, **25.** 249
  (?) —— receives news from, of Algiers, **25.** 416
Scarning, Norfolk:
  HW's will mentions, **30.** 369
Scarperia (Italy):
  Vitelli, Mme, and Mme and Balì Suares attend dinner at, in honour of Modenese princess, **17.** 56
Scarron, Mme. See Aubigné, Françoise d'
Scarron, Paul (1610–60), dramatist:
  Don Japhet d'Arménie by, **7.** 302
  Œuvres by, owned by Mme du Deffand, **8.** 33
  Roman comique by, **14.** 31
  Sévigné, Mme de, compared with, **5.** 390
  wife of, **4.** 44n, **14.** 62n, **33.** 497
Scarsdale, Bn. See Curzon, Sir Nathaniel
Scarsdale, Bns. See Colyear, Lady Caroline
Sçavoir Vivre Club. See *Savoir Vivre*, club
Scawby, Lincs:
  Preston, vicar of, **2.** 23n

Scawen, Miss:
  SH visited by, **12.** 224
Scawen, Tryphena (1730–1807), m. (1759) Hon. Henry Bathurst, cr. (1771) Bn Apsley; 2d E. Bathurst, 1775:
  agreeable, **32.** 236
  Dodd, Mrs, tries to bribe, to get Dodd a benefice, **32.** 185n
  Ossorys' neighbour, **32.** 236
  SH visited by, **12.** 221
Scawen, William (d. 1775):
  Butterfield, Jane, thought to have poisoned, **32.** 262n
Scawen's Park, Carshalton, Surrey:
  trees of, **33.** 111
Sceau (France):
  French wounded left at, **19.** 427
'Sceaux, M. de.' See Saulx-Tavannes, Charles-Henri de
Sceaux, château of the Duc and Duchesse du Maine, in France:
  ceiling of cabinet at: HW admires, **7.** 322; HW secures drawing of, **3.** 363n, 367, 373, 375, 378, 381, 384, 386, 389, 399, **4.** 1, 10
  curé of, entertains HW, Mme du Deffand, Selwyn, and Mlle Sanadon at dinner, **7.** 322
  Du Deffand, Mme, formerly lived at, **8.** 52, 56, 66
  Du Maine, Duchesse, assembles court at, **8.** 114
  guesses made at, **3.** 78n
  HW's happiness at, **30.** 258
  Pavillon d'Hanovre at, **7.** 322
  visitors to: Bauffremont, **4.** 442–3; Beauvau, Chevalier de, **4.** 443; Boufflers, Marquise de, **4.** 442; Cholmondeley, Mrs, **4.** 243, 442; Cholmondeley, Henrietta Maria, **4.** 442; Du Deffand, Mme, **4.** 243, 442–3, 496n, **6.** 145, **7.** 322; Elliot, Gilbert, **4.** 442; Elliot, Hugh, **4.** 443; HW, **6.** 145, **7.** 322; Sanadon, Mlle, **4.** 443, **7.** 322; Selwyn, **7.** 322; Sickingen, **4.** 442; Sigorgne, **4.** 443
Scellières, Abbey of:
  prior of, *see* Potherat de Corbière, Dom Gaspard-Edmé-Germain
  Voltaire buried in, temporarily, **7.** 46n, 48
Scelta di xxiv vedute delle principali contrade, piazze, chiese e palazzi della città di Firenze. See under Zocchi, Giuseppe
Scenery:
  More, Hannah, learns cant for discussing, from Gilpin's book, **31.** 320
Sceptre; sceptres:
  Harcourt despises, **35.** 462
  kings and emperors must abandon, to others, as actors abandon their stage properties, **25.** 552
  on monument in Trinity Hospital, Greenwich, **16.** 88
Scey-sur-Saône, Prince de Bauffremont's château in France:
  Bauffremont occupies, **5.** 97, **6.** 281, **7.** 246

visitors to: Boisgelin, Comtesse de, **6.** 281; Boufflers, Marquise de, **6.** 281; Mirepoix, Mme de, **6.** 281

Schaffgotsch, Philipp Gotthard (1716–95), Graf von; Bp of Breslau, 1748–95:
Frederick II appoints, coadjutor of Breslau, without Benedict XIV's consent, **20.** 269n
——'s letter to, about Hungarian Protestants, **20.** 269

Schairner, Col. (d. 1743):
killed at Campo Santo, **18.** 164

Schalcken, Godfried (1643–1706), painter:
Bentley draws light effects as well as, **35.** 243
portrait by, of woman with torch, **10.** 335

Schalken. *See* Schalcken

Schall, Comte de:
SH visited by, **12.** 237

Schärdingen (Germany):
restitution of, to Bavaria, **19.** 37n

Schaub, Lady. *See* Ligonier du Buisson, Marguerite de (d. 1793)

Schaub, Frederica Augusta (1750–1832), m. (1767) William Lock:
(?) HW sends parcel to, **7.** 378
SH visited by, **12.** 232, **43.** 161

Schaub, Sir Luke (1690–1758), Kt, 1720; diplomatist:
Ædes Walpolianæ owned by, **9.** 88
auction of, **21.** 199–200
Frederick, P. of Wales, makes offer to, for pictures, **21.** 200
—— sends, to HW, to get *Ædes Walpolianæ*, **9.** 88–9
Houghton collection should bring three times the price of that of, **21.** 208
remark by, on wife, **17.** *181*
Spanish pictures cheaply bought by, **21.** 199–200

Schauenberg, Alexis-Balthazar-Henri-Antoine (1748–1832), Gen.:
reinstated, **12.** 28n

Schauensee, Franz Joseph Leon Meyer von (1720–89), organist of St Leodegar:
Trionfo della Gloria, Il, composed by, **19.** 354n

Schedula diversarum artium. See under Theophilus

Scheemakers, Peter (1691–1770), sculptor:
biographical information about, **43.** 360, 361
Shakespeare's monument by, **35.** 151n
Stowe busts attributed to, **35.** 75n

Scheffer, Carl Fredrik (1715–86), Greve; ambassador from Sweden to France:
Aiguillon, Duc and Duchesses d', entertain, **5.** 40
Du Deffand, Mme, hears from, that Gustav III wants to receive her, **5.** 36–7
French interference blamed by, in election of K. of the Romans, **20.** 394n
Gustav III's supper with, **5.** 39–40
Louis XV receives: **5.** 36; after going to bed, **5.** 36

Swedish princes brought to Mme du Deffand by, **5.** 26
to return to Sweden, **5.** 37, 40

'Scheherezade,' character in *Arabian Nights*:
Du Deffand, Mme, a new, **6.** 398
HW criticizes narratives of, **11.** 21
HW's stories shorter than those of, **29.** 101
Ossory, Lady, describes Macartney with eloquence of, **33.** 317
See also under *Arabian Nights*

Schelda; Schelde. *See* Scheldt

Scheldt ('Schelda'; 'Schelde'), river:
Austrian-Dutch clash over navigation on, **25.** 530n, 543–4, 554, **39.** 428n
Dutch-English reinforcement goes up, **37.** 205
English army crosses, **18.** 481, **37.** 174
English make bridges across, **18.** 448
Joseph II's quarrel with Holland over navigation of, **25.** 530n, 543–4, 554
Pisa's Battle of the Bridge preferable to invasion of, **25.** 583
Tuscany must be interested in, through Austrian connections, **25.** 544

Schelestadt (Alsace):
Beauvau to command at, **6.** 322
—— to visit, **6.** 325, 331
military division of Alsace, **6.** 322

'Scheme for a Tax on Message Cards and Notes':
HW contributes, to *The Museum*, **13.** 16

Schemnitz, Hungary:
mines in, visited by Conway, **39.** 181, 182, 538

Schenck, G. F., engraver:
Law's portrait engraved by, **42.** 387n

Schencker *or* Scheneker, Nicolas (1760–1848), engraver:
Hardinge's drawings engraved by, for Lysons's *Environs*, **34.** 131n
(?) print by, of Ds of Cleveland, **16.** 323

Scherbenin, Mme. *See* Dashkova, Anastasia Mikhailovna

Schetland. *See* Shetland Islands

Scheuchzer, Johann Jakob (1672–1733), Swiss naturalist:
engraving of, **16.** 67

Schiller, Johann Christoph Friedrich von (1759–1805), German poet:
Parsons eulogizes, **11.** 177n

Schimmelmann, Heinrich Carl (1724–82), Greve:
HW can tell more about, **35.** 329

Schindel, Vice-Adm. Conrad von (1715–94):
Danish squadron under, **25.** 60n, 61n

Schio, near Valdagno, Italy:
Mann, Horace II and Lady Lucy, at, **24.** 122

Schleswig:
Peter III of Russia claims, **22.** 54n

Schleswig-Holstein-Augustenburg, Ds of. *See* Louisa Augusta (1771–1843) of Denmark

Schlüsselburg (Russia):
Ivan VI assassinated at, **17.** 256n

Schmeling, Gertrud Elisabeth (1749–1833), m. Johann Mara; singer:

[Schmeling, Gertrud Elisabeth, *continued*]
HW hears, at Westminster Abbey in Handel jubilee rehearsal, 25. 648
not so much in fashion, 25. 648
Rubinelli and, in Mortellari's *Armida*, 25. 646n
sings at Pantheon, 11. 202n
Schmelwitz (Germany):
Conway sees Frederick II's encampment at, 39. 538
Schmettau, Karl Christoph (1696–1775); Graf von; Prussian Lt-Gen.:
Dresden suburbs burnt by, 21. 257–8
Schmidt, Georg Friedrich (1712–75), engraver:
Law's portrait engraved by, 42. 387n
print by, 15. 180n
Schnebbelie, Jacob (1760–92), engraver:
cross engraved by, 1. 241n
drawings by, for Gough's *Sepulchral Monuments*, 42. 217n
(?) HW called on by, in Berkeley Sq., 42. 217n
SH visited by, 43. 161
Schola Italica picturæ sive selectæ. See under Hamilton, Gavin
Scholasticism:
More, Hannah, disparages, 31. 290
Scholemaster, The. See under Ascham, Roger
Schomberg, D. of. *See* Schönberg, Frédéric-Armand de
Schomberg, Maréchal de:
Forth, aide-de-camp to, 41. 6n
Schomberg, Ferdinand, cook to E. and Cts of Hertford:
attacked in Gordon riots, 33. 188–9
Schomberg, Lady Frederica (ca 1688–1751), m. 1 (1715) Robert Darcy, 3rd E. of Holdernesse; m. 2 Benjamin Mildmay, 19th Bn Fitzwalter; cr. (1730) E. Fitzwalter:
'at home' in London, 9. 15
brag played by, 9. 90
Schomberg, Gottlob-Louis (d. ca 1792), Comte de:
(?) Chanteloup visited by, 5. *245*
Choiseul, Duchesse de, has social relations with, 7. 328
HW disliked by, when at Choiseul's, 39. 292
Necker, Mme, recommends, to HW, 39. 292
Schomberg, Isaac (1714–80), physician:
testimony by, at House of Lords, about Ds of Kingston, 24. 151, 28. 234
Schomberg, Jeanne-Armande (ca 1632–1704), m. Charles de Rohan, Prince de Guéménée:
tomb of, 7. 282
Schomberg House, Pall Mall, London:
Cosways live in, 11. 285n
Cumberland, D. of, takes, 9. 316
fracas near, 33. 335
Graham's 'Temple of Health' in, 33. 335n
Schönberg, Frédéric-Armand de (1615–90), cr. (1689) D. of Schomberg:
Swift's epitaph for, 10. 11
Schönborn-Heussenstamm, Maria Theresia Josepha (b. 1758), m. (1781) Johann Rudolf,

Count Czernin von Chudenitz:
SH visited by, 12. 230
Schönbornlust (Germany):
Calonne at, 11. 310n
Schönbrunn, Austrian imperial palace:
Maria Josefa dies at, 22. 561n
School; schools:
English, should teach English constitution, 42. 403
English public, House of Lords appoints committee on, 16. 151
Schoolboy; schoolboys:
executed for joining Gordon riots, 33. 214
pastimes of, 9. 3
School Dialogues. See under Frere, Eleanor, Lady Fenn
School for Greybeards, A. See under Parkhouse, Hannah
School for Scandal, The. See under Sheridan, Richard Brinsley
School for Wives, The. See under Kelly, Hugh
Schoolmaster; schoolmasters:
erroneous ideas derived from, 30. 221
foreign, wrote Jacob Colomb's will, 42. 299
ignorant of the world, 30. 221
Schoolmistress, The. See under Shenstone, William
'School of Athens, The.' *See under* Raffaello Sanzio
Schooner; schooners:
American, on Lake Champlain, 24. 261n
news of Pigot's having taken, should not have been put in the *Gazette*, 25. 318
sent by Gage, burnt by the Americans, 28. 211
Schöpflin, J. D.:
Valtravers a pupil of, 20. 393n
Schoppe, Kaspar (1576–1649), called Scioppius; scholar and controversialist:
Brown, Dr John, compared with, 9. 220–1
Grattan and Flood imitate acrimony of, 25. 438
Hume-Rousseau quarrel resembles those of, 41. 51
Schouallow; Schoualoff; Schoualow; Schouvaloff; Schouvalow. *See* Shuvalov
Schröder, ——, George II's valet-de-chambre:
George II's death discovered by, 9. 311, 21. 443
Schroeder, William, Hanoverian soldier:
affair of, makes counties and cities send instructions to Parliament, 35. 291n
arrest of, 21. 12, 34
Schualoff; Schualow. *See* Shuvalov
Schulembourg. *See* Schulenburg
Schulenburg, Count Adolph Friedrich von (1685–1741):
George II resembled by, 2. 124
Schulenburg, Ermengarde Melusina (1667–1743), Bns von der, cr. (1716) Ds of Munster, (1719) Ds of Kendal; George I's mistress:
arms of, 41. 451
Bolingbroke favoured by, 20. 455
Chesterfield inherits nothing from, 18. 231

death of, **18**. 231

George I said to be younger than, **18**. 231

——'s drinking to be prevented by, **20**. 455

——'s mistress, **2**. 123n, **25**. 248n

——'s reputed daughter by, **43**. 286

HW sees George I going to supper with, **25**. 248

name of, corrected, **43**. 250

nephew of, **19**. 64

'niece' of, **18**. 231, **24**. 283n, 412n, **25**. 248n

St John buys Custom House place from, **20**. 18

Walpole, Sir Robert, hated by, **20**. 455

wealth of, **18**. 231

Yarmouth, Cts of, the counterpart of, **19**. 419

Schulenburg, Georg Ludwig (d. 1759), Graf von Oynhausen; army officer:

brother sends, on embassy, **19**. 64

Schulenburg, Ludwig Ferdinand (1700–54), Graf von Schulenburg und Oynhausen; Gen.:

army command assumed by, **19**. 47

army command refused by, from dislike of Pallavicini, **19**. 50–1

Bartolommei to aid, at Turin, **17**. 196n

Botta succeeded by, in command of Austrian forces against Genoa, **19**. 363n

brother of, sent on embassy, **19**. 64

Brown succeeds, in army command, **19**. 393

Charles Emmanuel III grants requests of, **19**. 367

——'s troops to join, **19**. 393n

(?) Estevenon accompanied by, to Florence, **17**. 200

(?) Faiola reconnoitred by, **18**. 530–1

fall of, from horse, **19**. 393

Gages deludes, into defending Milan, **19**. 119

Genoa approached by army of, **19**. 384

—— to be reduced by, **19**. 367

Genoese message to, **19**. 65

Genoese must be intimidated by, **19**. 363

Lobkowitz replaced by, **19**. 41, 50, 55, 58

Lomellini's letter denying entrance to, **19**. 67

Medley to assist, against Genoa, **19**. 384

Novi the station of, **19**. 58

Spanish invalids will embarrass, **19**. 55

Venice and Vienna visited by, **19**. 50

Schulenburg, Petronille Melusine de (1693–1778), m. (1733) Philip Dormer Stanhope, 4th E. of Chesterfield; she was cr. (1722) Cts of Walsingham, s. j.:

(?) at Chesterfield's assembly, **37**. 326

'aunt' of, **18**. 231n, **24**. 283n, 412n, **25**. 248n

death of, **2**. 123–4, **24**. 412

George I came over with, when she was not young, **24**. 412

—— creates, Cts of Walsingham, **24**. 412n

—— reputed father of, **18**. 231n, **43**. 286

——'s legacy to, **2**. 123–4

HW's relations with, **31**. 173

HW taken by, to kiss George I's hand, **25**. 248

health of, stroke of palsy, **24**. 283

mother of, dies, **18**. 231

name of, corrected, **43**. 250

St-Germain intimate with, **26**. 21

Schulenburg-Oynhausen, Margarete Gertrud von (1698–1726), m. (1721) Albert Wolfgang, Graf von Lippe-Bückeburg:

son of, **22**. 43n

Schuma. *See* Shulma

Schutz, Mr:

Mme du Deffand sends parcel by, **4**. 77

Schutz, Mr:

SH visited by, **12**. 234

Schutz, Armand Johann (d. 1773), army officer:

HW's servant told by, of D. of Cumberland's alleged death, **38**. 445

Vanneck's legacy to, **9**. 112

Schutz, Augustus (1690–1757), Baron of the Holy Roman Empire; Master of the Robes to George II:

Carteret said to leave, with George II to play cards with Cts of Delorain, **18**. 82

death of, **9**. 207

Frederick II might seize, **35**. 221

HW's letter to Morrison might have been dictated by, **9**. 306

legacies often left to, **9**. 207

(?) Lorenzi mistakes, for Chute, **20**. 89

Vanneck's legacy to, **9**. 112

Schutz, George Augustus (1722–49), page:

(?) HW's letters conveyed by, to England, **20**. *15*, 23, 54, **26**. 36

(?) puny, **20**. 15, 23

(?) St John, Vcts, escorted by, **20**. 15, 23

Schutz, George Frederick (1724–1802):

groom of the Bedchamber, **20**. 247, **21**. 460n

(?) HW's letters conveyed by, to England, **20**. *15*, 23, 54, **26**. 36

(?) puny, **20**. 15, 23

(?) St John, Vcts, escorted by, **20**. 15, 23

(?) Vergy's affidavit attested by, **22**. 262n

Schuwalof. *See* Shuvalov

Schuyler, Philip John (1733–1804), American Gen.:

army of, to invade Canada, **24**. 133n

Schwalm River, Germany:

Broglie opposes P. Ferdinand on, **40**. 181n

Schwartzenberg, Lt-Gen. ——:

Waldeck leaves his command to, **19**. 428n, 429n

Schwartzenberg, Johann Nepomuk (1742–89), Prinz von; chamberlain:

Clement XIII thanked by, **23**. 23

Schwarz ('Schwartz'), Frederik (1753–1838), Danish actor:

SH visited by, **12**. 243

Schweidnitz (Silesia):

Conway and Scott visit, **39**. 538

Frederick II captures, **21**. 198, **22**. 87

—— gets between Daun and, **22**. 60

—— loses, **22**. 544

—— said to have captured, **21**. 166

garrison of, defends itself with honour, **22**. 87

Schwellenberg (*or* Schwellenbergen), Elizabeth Juliana (ca 1728–97), Keeper of the Robes to Q. Charlotte:

[Schwellenberg, Elizabeth Juliana, *continued*]
Burney, Frances, second keeper of robes under, 31. 247n
Charlotte, Q., accompanied by, 21. 530
Clarence, D. of (William IV), scolds, for not curtseying in passage at Kew, 39. 464
Garter not to go to, 32. 168
George III's 'seraglio' includes, 35. 323
HW imagines conversation of, 33. 319
HW imagines Windsor Park ploughed up by, 34. 215
Hurd dines with, 29. 35n
Moss, William, former servant to, 42. 296n
Selwyn might get a hint favourable to Kennedy conveyed by, to Q. Charlotte, 30. 254
Wales, P. of (George IV), might be put under tutelage of, 29. 181
Schwerin, Kurd Christoph (1684–1757), Graf von; Prussian Gen.:
death of, 9. 206, 21. 92, 95
Frederick II orders, to march to Brünn, 17. 316n
Prague's capitulation accepted by, 18. 511n
Schwerin (Poland):
Wobersmow and Hårdt fail to capture, 21. 247n
Schwichelt, August Wilhelm von:
Hanoverian privy councillor, 20. 212n
Schwichelt, Ernst Otto (d. 1750), Baron von:
Frechapelle kills, in duel, 20. 184
——'s accompanying George II resented by, 20. 184n
Sciarelli, Bernardino:
Lady Orford's will probated by, 43. 288, 289
Sciatica:
Laurenti diagnoses Old Pretender's illness as rheumatism or, 20. 442n
occurrences of, 6. 408, 31. 205
Science; sciences:
Conway an amateur in, 37. 59
Du Deffand, Mme, has poor opinion of, 4. 247
HW and Robertson discuss the East as 'cradle' of, 34. 132
HW implies that greed is real motive for, 25. 545
HW's animus against, opposed by Hume, 41. 63
HW's ignorance of, 21. 368
HW thought, never haggled about blood when considering experiments, 39. 419
HW to write treatise or panegyric on, 37. 292–3
Orford, Cts of, 'flings herself into the arms of,' 25. 121
Pineda believed Adam understood all, but politics, 37. 293
Pinkerton's defence of works of, 16. 306
tediousness of, HW's reflections on, 20. 555
westward course of, 28. 166, 217
Scientific discoveries:
HW's reflections on, 20. 292

Scientific experiments:
with diamonds and other jewels, 31. 158
Scilla città (Italy):
earthquake account mentions, 25. 376
Scilly Islands:
combined French-Spanish fleet appears off, 25. 182, 28. 457n, 29. 156n
Scimitar; scimitars:
HW buys, at Mrs Kennon's sale, 37. 439
Mogul, through Clive, gives, to George III, 22. 540
Scio. *See* Chios
Scione:
harbour of, scene of Russo-Turkish naval battle, 23. 233
Scioppius. *See* Schoppe, Kaspar
Scipio Æmilianus Africanus Numantinus, Publius Cornelius (ca 185–129 B.C.), statesman and general:
Carthage demolished by, 33. 49
(?) toothpicks introduced by, from Spain, 33. 246
Scipio Africanus Major, Publius Cornelius (?237–183 B.C.), Gen.:
Anson imitator of continence of, 9. 55, 90, 37. 535
breeches of, continent, 24. 426
Carthaginian author would be proud to be translated by, 42. 129
Clodius must be discussed for want of, 23. 499
continence of: 9. 55, 24. 426, 29. 71, 32. 265, 327, 33. 113, 41. 238; depicted at Wanstead, 35. 238
HW recommends good breeding of, 18. 518
HW's name for Christian VII, 35. 327
HW would rather see, playing leapfrog, 33. 49, 552
military career of, unhampered by financial intrigues, 21. 559
noble mind of, 31. 439
Roman enamellers might eclipse, 21. 313
'romantic delicacy' of, 30. 270
statues of, in Pomfret collection, 20. 390
'Scipio,' race-horse:
the only Scipio that Clermont should be aware of, 33. 246
Scipione in Cartagine. See under Galuppi, Baldassare
Scipioni, ——, Corsican murderer:
escape of, 20. 206
Scipioni, Signora, of Bastia (Corsica):
suspected by husband, 20. 206n
Scissors:
cases for, Parisian best, 31. 85
Du Deffand, Mme, loses, 7. 119
gold: Mann tells Lincoln to buy, at La Frenaye's, 17. 99; ordered by Lincoln through HW and Mann in care of Charles Selwin, 17. 93
HW furnishes, 9. 117n
HW seeks, 6. 359, 367
HW superstitious about, 11. 67

Hervey, Bns, obtains, for HW, 31. 76, 84–5, 95, 113, 114
ladies', of English steel, 31. 76
manufactured at Sheffield, 9. 295
mercer pretends not to have, 24. 153–4
Salisbury famous for, 40. 8
Selwyn procures, for Mme du Deffand, 7. 131
street-criers advertise, 21. 154
Sclater (later Bacon), Thomas (?1664–1736):
  biographical information about, corrected, 43. 43
  collection of: bought by Cole, 1. 19; HW's Kneller from, 1. 19n
Sclavonians. See Slavonians
Sconce; sconces:
  Electress leaves, to Rinuccini, 18. 169
  in Westminster Hall, 38. 126
  ormolu, at Paris, 32. 261
Scone, Scotland:
  Charles II at, before Restoration, 33. 163
  regal chair of, 33. 349
  Scottish history's source at, 37. 217
Scorailles de Roussilhe, Marie-Angélique (1661–81), Duchesse de Fontanges:
  (?) Ennery has medallion of, 7. 325
  HW's verses mention, 31. 12
Scorel, Jan:
  portraits attributed to, 43. 123
Scornful Lady, The. See under Beaumont, Francis, and John Fletcher
Scorpion; scorpions:
  HW does not find, in bed, 39. 498
  Italian feature, 37. 73
  oil of, 30. 197
Scot (surname). See Scott
Scot; Scots ('the Scotch'):
  Americans are driving out, 28. 270
  at Ds of Gordon's dinner, speaks only Erse, 35. 82
  avarice of, HW hints at, 21. 87
  baneful influence of, 28. 430–1, 39. 372
  banknotes circulated by, 23. 418–19
  believed in 'second sight,' 29. 373
  British Coffee-House much frequented by, 20. 124n
  bullets deserved by, 33. 147
  Bute does not dare to promote, 22. 295
  Charles II coerced by, at Scone, 33. 163
  cling together, 35. 568
  Coke, Lady Mary, does not love, 31. 8
  Danish and Russian fleets to be commanded by, 25. 60
  defence of country by, 33. 133
  delicacy of thought might be inspired by women of, 37. 260, 263
  dissect each other, skilfully, 32. 90
  Dutch Jews said to trade with, in gold, 23. 418n
  Earle satirizes, 17. 243
  Edward I promised victory over, 1. 323
  England inundated by, bringing cold weather and war, 35. 473
  ——'s disgrace often occasioned by, 33. 122

English enslavement planned by, 24. 448–9
English heroes and authors traduced by, 29. 105
English newspapers attack, 23. 419
envoys often are, 33. 232
favouritism shown to, by Court, 28. 91
Foote's witticism on, 12. 254
Fox, Henry, hated by, 20. 412
Gibbon flatters, 29. 98–9
(?) —— not liked by, 32. 297
Gordon, Lord George, would have been martyrized by, 25. 131
government positions rumoured for, 9. 320–1
HW abused in Public Ledger for praising, 38. 208
HW accused by Wilkes of flattering, 13. 37–8
HW blames, for England's plight, 28. 374, 403–4, 411, 416, 29. 84, 105
HW calls, 'Ossianites,' 28. 324
HW compares himself to, runner for ministry, 33. 138
HW compliments, in Royal and Noble Authors, 1. 139, 2. 264, 29. 358
HW expects, to call English 'lousy,' 29. 105
HW loves, 31. 8
HW prefers Americans to, 33. 302
HW's low opinion of, 30. 96–7
HW's 'Patapan' denounces, 30. 287
HW's praise of, ridiculed by North Briton, 38. 175n
HW's second assembly to be attended by, 10. 107
HW stipulates that his gardener should not be, 35. 473, 479
HW urges Mason to satirize, 29. 105
Hamilton's marriage enrages, 20. 303
historians of: lie, 33. 319; will not decry present English commanders, 33. 215
Hume's life, supplement to, shows morality and taste of, 28. 308–9
incapable of delicacy of thought, 37. 260
India and America are escaping from, 29. 123
in India, bring about Pigot's arrest, 28. 293
Ireland exposed to, 35. 478
Irish origin of, 28. 71, 192, 233
itch for command in army, 37. 32
Junius papers attack, 23. 247–8
letters against, 42. 505
Luttrell's election pushed by, 23. 104n
Mary, Q. of Scots, overpraised by, 15. 27
Mason resolves not to offend, 28. 157
metaphysics of: HW 'elbowed' by, 33. 319; HW has read little of, 32. 374
migrate to London and America, 23. 569
ministers, HW expects inundation of, 33. 340
national pride of, 1. 139, 152, 2. 264
North infuriates, 29. 206
'odious nation,' 35. 479
Opposition's triumph must surmount attacks from, 35. 617
portraits of, see under Portrait
Regency Bill opposed by, 38. 553
second sight of, 24. 356, 33. 13, 269

[Scot; Scots, *continued*]
Stormont will be disliked for being, **24.** 526
Stuart is, **35.** 486
threaten to break union with England, **29.** 271
Townshend, Vcts, entertains, **30.** 58
unfashionable, **31.** 8
villainy of, **28.** 441
Walpole, Sir Robert, to be defended by, **17.** 338
Wilkes forgets, **38.** 362

Scotch Adventure. See under Goldwin, William

Scotch Greys (regiment):
Hamilton, Charles, former capt. in, **33.** 218

Scotchman; Scotchmen; Scotchwoman; Scotchwomen. *See under* Scot; Scots

Scotch reel:
HW proposes that Bathurst dance, **33.** 256-7

Scotch Tast in Vista's. See under Bramston, Rev. James

Scotland, K. of. *See* David II (1323-70) (Bruce); Duncan I (d. 1040); James I (1394-1437); James II (1430-60); James III (1451-88); James IV (1473-1513); James V (1512-42); James VI (*see* James I of England); Robert I (d. 1329) (Bruce); Robert II (1316-90); Robert III (ca 1340-1406)

Scotland, lord clerk register of. *See* Campbell, Lord Frederick (1729-1816)

Scotland, primate (titular) of. *See* Macdonald, Hugh (1701-73)

Scotland, Queen of. *See* Jane (d. 1445) Beaufort; Margaret (1489-1541) Tudor; Mary (1515-60) of Guise; Mary (1542-87) Stuart; Matilda (d. 1130-1)

Scotland, solicitor-general of. *See* Murray, Alexander

Scotland:
accounts of rebels' success in: printed at Rome, **19.** 158; vary, **19.** 108
Aiguillon to embark troops for, **21.** 296n, 328n, 346n, 350n, 351n
ambassadors from and to, *see under* Ambassador
American independence caused by people of, **24.** 378
American news from, **32.** 380
American privateers infest coast of, **24.** 315, 377-8
Anne, Q., strikes medal for repulse of invasion of, **21.** 357n
Anstruther unpopular in, **20.** 230
appeal by, to House of Lords, **35.** 622
Archangel, Father, from, **16.** 203
Argyll, D. of, insists on control of patronage in, **20.** 5n
—— managed Sir Robert Walpole's elections in, **20.** 5n
——'s death leaves Bute the chief power in, **21.** 527n
——'s patronage in, to be inherited by Bute, **9.** 358

——'s plan for colonizing forfeited estates in, **20.** 310
artists in, discussed in Dalrymple's missing letter, **15.** 99
authors of, countenance HW, **40.** 135
ballad tunes of, used for hymns, **35.** 118
bankers of, remit bills and draw cash from England, **23.** 418-19
banks of, fail, **23.** 418-19, 498
Belle-Île no better than islands off the coast of, **21.** 505
Belle-Isle, Maréchal de, plans invasion of, **20.** 535n
bishop of, would not use same dialect as Somersetshire monk, **16.** 351-2
books of, engravings from, sent to HW by Colquhoun, **42.** 431-3, 436
boroughs of, supposedly betrayed by Ilay, **15.** 153
Buccleuchs visit, **10.** 284
Buchan and HW correspond about portraits of kings of, **29.** 107
Buchan informed by HW about kings and queens of, **33.** 368
—— plans biographies of illustrious men of, **15.** 179-80
Bute shows no favouritism to people of, **21.** 465
Byres from, **42.** 101
Cameron arrested in, **20.** 373
—— collects subscriptions in, for Young Pretender, **20.** 373n
Carlisle boasts of its superiority to, **19.** 165
Charles I in, **40.** 264
charters from, **42.** 280
church of, *see* Church of Scotland; Episcopal Church of Scotland; Presbyterian, Presbyterians
clan, clans of: attack in columns, **37.** 240; do not support George II, **19.** 102; urged to revolt, **18.** 402-3; Young Pretender waits for, at Inverness, **37.** 238-9
(?) Common Council to summon members from, **17.** 329
contractors in, **41.** 312
Conway jokes about HW tracing revolutions in, **37.** 217
—— may visit, **39.** 147
—— not prevented from going to, with D. of Cumberland, **19.** 204
——'s aversion to, **37.** 217, 225, 231-2, 253, 255, 256
——'s campaign in, **37.** 261
—— stationed in, **38.** 59
Cordiner's letters on, **29.** 37
Corsican rebels swifter than those of, **19.** 162
counties in, send petitions, **23.** 151
Court of Session of, Haddington's collection of cases in, **15.** 29
Craufurd does not care for, **3.** 230
—— in, **3.** 23, 156, **6.** 3, 4, 76, 82, 93, 457, 462, **32.** 139
Crawford was premier earl of, **20.** 109n

Cumberland, D. of, denounces Jacobites in official posts in, to George II, **20**. 311n
—— hated by, **19**. 288
—— may go to, **19**. 193
——'s baggage returned from, **19**. 242
——'s conduct in, investigated by Lyttelton, **20**. 240
——'s return from, awaited, **19**. 271
——'s stay in, prolonged, **19**. 228
—— takes Fawkener to, as secretary, **19**. 382n
—— to pacify, **19**. 205, 257
—— unpopular in, **37**. 352
Dalrymple is HW's 'sensible friend' in, **38**. 205
De Wet's work in, **42**. 346–7
dinner hour in, by 3 P.M., **38**. 530
Douglas visits, **31**. 287
Drummond, Lord John, reaches, **19**. 187
—— said to escape from, **19**. 270
dukes from, said to become English peers, **36**. 222, 223
Dutch troops to land in, **19**. 103, 109
Earl Marischal of, see Keith, George
elections in, **17**. 294, **26**. 32–3, **39**. 186
Elliot in, **4**. 435
emigration from, to London and America, **23**. 569
emissaries from, at Rome, **17**. 145
England, if armed, might have speedily crushed rebellion in, **19**. 130
—— must share lunacy with, **33**. 165
—— never governed by, **32**. 296
—— once harassed by, **35**. 497
—— said to be betrayed by Cornwall and, **17**. 346
English civil wars caused by, **24**. 124
English prisoners in, released, **19**. 204
English settlement in, proposed, **26**. 31–3
English severity said to have enraged, **19**. 399–400
English union with: HW's 'Patapan' denounces, **30**. 287; may be broken, **17**. 159, 160, 202, **25**. 280, 310
English victory in, pleases Hobart, **40**. 56
English weather might make, more Arcadian, **21**. 267
episcopal church of, see Episcopal Church of Scotland
Findlater in, **15**. 151
Fitzjames captured on ship bound for, **19**. 222
—— in, **3**. 259, 264
——'s regiment to go to, **19**. 208–9
Forbes from, **22**. 162
Fordyce from, **23**. 418
forfeited estates in: mortgaged, **26**. 31–3; restored, **25**. 520; to be purchased, **20**. 310
'45 has different meaning for, than for Wilkes, **23**. 30
Fragments of Ancient Poetry defended in Highlands of, **14**. 115–16
France might recruit secret agents from, **20**. 491

—— said to have sent Irish regiment to, **19**. 170
French expedition may be sailing to, **21**. 315
French fleet may attack, **18**. 404, **19**. 261
French invasion of, indicated by Don Giuseppe, **19**. 85
French invasion said to be encouraged by, **18**. 415
French will use troops from, **20**. 508
gentlemen from, at Vienna, **19**. 290
George II might give up, to keep Hanover, **17**. 202
—— would be joined by clans of, if his army were strong, **19**. 130
Gordon, Ds of, goes to, **11**. 274
Gordon, Lord George, might have started revolt in, **25**. 64
—— reported to have gone to, **33**. 193, **35**. 506
Grant, Maj. John, from, **21**. 153n
Grattan's 'character' of Chatham too good to be from, **32**. 179
Gray returns from his tour in, **14**. 140, 141
——'s *Catalogue* should be extended to include antiquities of, **41**. 251
——'s poetry not valued in, **28**. 217
Grenville ministry demands dismissal of Stuart Mackenzie from 'direction' of, **38**. 564
Grosett from, **25**. 410
HW as untruthful as a runner for the ministry from, **33**. 138
HW buys golden heart from, **42**. 12
HW denounces, as hotbed of traitors, **25**. 62
HW does not expect poetry from, **37**. 260
HW expects addresses from, on D. of Gloucester's return, **28**. 340
HW hopes, will be disheartened by Association for Preserving Liberty and Property, **15**. 235
HW's attitude to, **32**. 179n
HW says, 'never produced one original writer in verse or prose,' **29**. 105
HW's partiality for, **15**. 32, 41, 47, 54, 55, 85
Hamilton, Ds of, arrives from, **38**. 458
—— in, **32**. 19
Hamiltons descended from kings of, **32**. 364
Hawley condemned by jury of, **19**. 241
—— sent to, with Wade's army, as military magistrate, **19**. 193
heart of, unsafe for English messenger, **19**. 247
Henry VIII releases captured nobles of, **16**. 80
heritable jurisdictions in, debated, **37**. 268
Hertfords visit, **38**. 91, 92–3
Hesse, Landgrave of, should be unpopular in, **9**. 27
Hessians to be kept longer in, **37**. 226
—— to be sent to, **19**. 188, 205
Highland chiefs of: Lovat's execution an example to, **19**. 386, 399; Scotch bills to humble, **19**. 388–9

[Scotland, *continued*]

Highlander; Highlanders of: acknowledge Irish origins, **16**. 378, 379; *Caledonian Mercury's* term for rebels, **19**. 107; Carleton's, said to be cut to pieces by Montgomery, **24**. 156; Charles II not accompanied by, to Worcester, **19**. 107; Conway must combat demons in the form of, **37**. 231; Corsicans differ from, **19**. 157; Edinburgh Castle's garrison captures, **19**. 133; English repulse, at Culloden, **37**. 239; Fontenoy distinction of, **36**. 13; HW's 'Patapan' denounces, **30**. 287; highwaymen compared with, **33**. 267; King's Road taken by, to mountains, **37**. 216; must not suspect that Young Pretender is not in Scotland, **19**. 198; not likely again to invade England, **19**. 188; not to be defeated by unbuilt navy, **19**. 168; rebels dislodged by, from the Spey, **37**. 238n; regiment of, due in Boston, **24**. 197n; regiment of, sails to America, **37**. 434; regiment of, to be raised, **24**. 175n; said to be the ancient Caledonians, **16**. 378; Seaforth's, repel Jersey attack, **24**. 472n; Seymour-Conway dressed as, **23**. 194n; tend English gardens, **32**. 359; well-trained by system of rotation, **19**. 116; will rebel as long as France pays, **37**. 226; Young Pretender joined by, **35**. 61; Young Pretender might not be followed by, to England, **19**. 107, 137; Young Pretender's speeches to, **19**. 170

Highlands of: **14**. 115–16; air of, sharpens Conway's appetite for London, **37**. 255; army recruiting in, discouraged by England, **41**. 313n; colonization attempts in, **26**. 31–3; Conway finds poem in, **37**. 260; Conway jokes about HW visiting, **37**. 217; Cumberland, D. of, severe in, **9**. 34; English army to march to, **37**. 247; fogs of, **33**. 144; HW imagines Ds of Hamilton and John Campbell in, **38**. 7; HW should visit scenes and historic sites of, **37**. 217; Macphersons the first authors produced by, **16**. 379; Montagu said to inherit prophetic ability from, **9**. 137; 'nasty and barren,' **35**. 480; Norwegian lords, not Scottish crown, in control of, **16**. 379, 380; penury of, **33**. 218; rebels may retreat to, **19**. 137; regiment from, mutinies, **18**. 236–7; seat of superstition and oppression, **16**. 375; wilds of, **30**. 38

history of: Pinkerton asks HW about, **12**. 9; *see also* Robertson, William: *Histoire d'Écosse*; *History of Scotland*

Hume settles in, **3**. 137, 207, 208, 230, **4**. 269

inn at, 'the worst,' **38**. 92

invasion of: possible, **9**. 246; would please HW, **28**. 370, 454

Irish merchant at Nantes formerly in, **38**. 405n

itch, the, said to be fatal in, **32**. 97n

Jacobite estates in: might be forfeited, **19**. 247; mortgaged, **26**. 31–3; restored, **25**. 520; to be purchased, **20**. 310

Jacobites call, 'the Pretender's own dominion,' **17**. 145n

Jacobites from: always provoke civil wars in England, **24**. 124; betrayed, **23**. 338; persuade Old Pretender that English union with, may be broken, **17**. 145, 159; restored to forfeited estates, **25**. 520; said to have encouraged Louis XV, **18**. 426

James II shipwrecked near, **32**. 390

Jamesone's portraits of kings and queens of, **40**. 264–5

Johnson's coarse comments on, **11**. 275

——'s tour of, interests Mason, **28**. 172

jubilee in, celebrating 1688 revolution, **16**. 296

Keith may invade, **19**. 261

Keppel, Laura, and Hon. George Fitzroy elope to, **25**. 508

kings of: drawn by Jamesone for Charles I, **40**. 264; Scots College has charters of, **7**. 359

kirk of, Charles II lectured by, **23**. 386; *see also* Church of Scotland

laws of: more favourable to perpetuities, **42**. 13n; will replace those of England, **28**. 67

lord advocate of: sketched by Boswell, **33**. 462n; *see also under* Lord advocate

lord privy seal for, *see under* Lord privy seal

Lorn in, **23**. 7

Loudoun defeats rebels in north of, **19**. 153

Lovat's body not sent to, **19**. 386

——'s body to be sent to, **37**. 267

Lowlanders of: Conway must combat demons in the form of, **37**. 231; descended from ancient Caledonians, **16**. 379; Macphersons enemies of, **16**. 379

Lowlands of, the source of liberty, **16**. 375

Macpherson promotes study of Celtic in, **16**. 377

'maiden' used in, **12**. 260

Mansfield's origins in, a disadvantage, **20**. 412

marches of, London as lawless as, **25**. 619–20

Marchmont, first commissioner of police in, **20**. 5

men of power in, come to London when needed at home, **30**. 96

'merchants' of, ridiculed, **41**. 401

monotonous landscape of, **37**. 250

Montagu, D. of, sets out for, **29**. 68

mountains of, to be patrolled, **20**. 35

Nairne from, **25**. 536

nobility of: flock to Lombard St, **38**. 476; form theatre, **19**. 468; to be humbled by Hawley, **19**. 201

Nova Scotia order of 80 knights of, **32**. 279

Old Pretender receives emissaries from, **17**. 145, 149

orators from, in Parliament, unbearable, **35**. 620

painters of: discussed in Dalrymple's missing letter, **15.** 99; listed by Dacre, **42.** 72

paintings in, *see under* Painting

Parliamentary bills for control of, endangered, **19.** 388–9, 396, **20.** 310–11

Parliamentary members from: **37.** 416; criticize Lestock and Mathews, **19.** 25; laugh at Grenville, **38.** 500; take refuge at Sir Robert Walpole's, **17.** 496

Parliament of, **15.** 121

partiality to, had no merit in reign of George II, **13.** 38

pedant of, defines vanity, **35.** 561

peerage of, Elibank's pamphlet on, **16.** 292

peers of: elected, **9.** 42; HW considers, 'household troops' in House of Lords, **25.** 368; in danger of bankruptcy, **23.** 426; involved in plot, **35.** 229; oppose Turnpike Bill, **20.** 124; outvote Camden, **35.** 588; to raise regiments in London, **19.** 167–8

Pennant's books on, **1.** 328–9, 332, 334, 336, **2.** 20

—— sees Tollemache's portrait in, **16.** 285

petitions not signed by counties of, **33.** 167

Pinkerton is writing ancient history of, **16.** 286

——'s 'Hymn to Liberty' praises, **16.** 373–4

poetry of, James I's rules for, **40.** 297

poor rate not the custom in, **15.** 91

Porteous affair in, **20.** 230

Presbyterians of: forswear the Pope, **24.** 475; Gordon leads, against Roman Catholics, **25.** 11

Pretenders may be joined by, **17.** 160

privateers captured on way to, **19.** 173

Privy Council of, letter to, **40.** 131

Privy Seal of: Campbell, Lord John, indecently accepts, after Stuart Mackenzie's removal, **32.** 11n; Stuart Mackenzie restored as keeper of, **22.** 444, 453; to appoint commissioners for colonization, **26.** 33

proxies sent to, for Paddington Road Bill, **37.** 458

rebel clans in, unite to capture Inverness, **19.** 221

rebellion in: crushed, **32.** 347; may be prolonged, **19.** 188, 228; may divert troops from Flanders, **19.** 222; possible, **18.** 237; precautions against, **26.** 31–3

rebels in: Bland to attack, at Strathbogie, **19.** 233n; expected to invade Cambridgeshire, **14.** 2; no more remote than Charles Emmanuel III's camp, **19.** 190; retreat to Carlisle, **19.** 185n

rebels may retreat to, **19.** 179

rebels may wait in, for French support, **19.** 117

rebels on defensive in, **19.** 201

rebels said to be about to recapture, **19.** 235

regiment from, mutinies, **18.** 236–7, **25.** 362, **33.** 384

regiment goes to, from Flanders, **37.** 209

representative peer from: **35.** 622; Marchmont to succeed Crawford as, **20.** 110–11

roads in: bad, **38.** 92; Crosne asks about, **35.** 335–6

Robertson's *History* of, **28.** 243; *see also under* Robertson, William

Roman Catholicism not to be tolerated in, **24.** 439, **26.** 33

Roman Catholics in, said to encourage French invasion, **18.** 415

royal and noble authors of, included by HW in his *Catalogue of the Royal and Noble Authors,* **15.** 26, 28

Rutherfurd of old family in, **24.** 453

secretary from, may not be liked in Ireland, **22.** 549

(?) Selwyn visits, **30.** 137

Sinclair from, **19.** 456

soldier from, finds glove and meets Selwyn, **18.** 524

Spanish ships leave for, **19.** 134, 137–8

Stair to visit, **18.** 494

statute law of, **15.** 122

Stone deals with place-seekers from, **20.** 366

Stormont becomes lord justice general in, **24.** 179n

—— in, **6.** 203

——'s character will be forgotten since he is from, **24.** 526

—— will go to, by way of Greenland, **38.** 36

Stuart-Mackenzie succeeds Argyll in post in, **21.** 511n

taxes not paid by, **20.** 311

thirst for knowledge in, **15.** 181

Thurot hovers over coast of, **21.** 352

—— ordered to invade, **21.** 315n

——'s fleet destined for, **21.** 328, 346n

torture used in, **16.** 376

Townshend may raise regiment in, **18.** 566

troops in, to be cantoned near sea-coast, **21.** 300n

Tweeddale resigns as secretary of state for, **19.** 195

—— secretary of state for, **20.** 209

upholders of, to be defeated in national points, **20.** 100

Vertue probably did not visit, **16.** 51

'volunteers' forcibly enlisted in, **28.** 360

Wade to advance on, from Doncaster, **19.** 137

Walpole, Sir Robert, overthrown partly by votes from, **17.** 346n

Whigs in, plundered by Highlanders, **16.** 375

Wilkes hated by people of, **22.** 189, **23.** 6, 99, 317n

William III and Hamilton discuss, **19.** 103

wisest heads said to grow in, **32.** 296–7

writers of, Mackenzie's lives of, **15.** 34

Young Pretender and Frenchmen to embark from coast of, **37.** 218

Young Pretender calls a Parliament in, **19.** 118

—— invades, **35.** 61

—— joined by few people in, **19.** 104

[Scotland, continued]
—— may go to, 18. 373, 375, 378–9, 20. 35
—— may wait in, for French support, 19. 117
—— said not really to be in, 19. 140–1, 172, 174, 198–9, 205, 227
—— said to be still in, 19. 270, 311
—— said to have escaped from, 19. 269–70
—— said to invade, 19. 85–90, 93, 95, 96, 98, 99, 112
—— sails from Belle-Île to, 19. 85n
——'s flight from, reported, 19. 213–14
——'s projects with, not laid aside, 17. 202
—— threatens to confiscate estates in, of loyal M.P.s, 19. 138
—— unlikely to invade, again, 20. 35
—— will conquer, 19. 103
See also Antiquaries of Scotland, Society of the, and under Dalrymple, Sir David: Annals of Scotland; Robertson, William: History of Scotland
Scotland's Skaith. See under MacNeill, Hector
Scotland Yard, Whitehall, London:
Éon lodges in Eddowes's house in, 38. 467
fire strews, with burnt grain, 11. 213n
land revenue office in, 42. 417n
Lort lodges in, 16. 164
Scots College, Paris:
charters of Scottish kings preserved at, 15. 182
Cole describes, 15. 107n
confiscation of, 42. 286n
Gordon, principal of, 7. 307
—— shows HW the library of, 29. 294
HW describes, 7. 358
HW seeks information at, for Dalrymple's pursuits, 15. 107
HW sees papers at, of Atterbury, James II, and Mary, Q. of Scots, 42. 286–7
HW sees treasures of, 15. 107n
HW visits, 7. 307, 308, 15. 107n, 29. 294
James II, and entrails of his wife and daughter, buried at, 7. 308
James II's memoirs or journals at, 15. 103n, 107n, 38. 443n, 478, 479
portrait at, of Mary, Q. of Scots, 15. 158–9
Scottish papers may have been sent to, at Reformation, 15. 187
Smith, Adam, visits, 7. 307
Scots dialect:
Montagu would not speak, 10. 142
Scots Magazine:
Donaldson's publication of English translation of Candide announced in, 10. 350
Scott, ——, Irish attorney-general:
mob pulls down house of, 24. 535n
Scott, Mr and Mrs:
SH visited by, 12. 231
Scott, Mrs (?):
SH visited by, 12. 241
Scott, Ann Dorothea, m. William Richard Stokes:
Herbert's MS inherited by, 43. 67

Scott, Arthur (1718–56), naval capt.:
Mann not readily obeyed by, 18. 507
——'s permission awaited by, 18. 453
Rome visited by, 18. 461
Scott, Benjamin (? d. before 1761), Customs official:
HW's correspondence with, about Cts of Ailesbury's contraband imports, 38. 124, 130
Scott, Hon. Campbell (1747–66):
death of, 3. 157n, 31. 132
(?) Foire St-Germain attended by, 7. 309
HW praises, 31. 109
Hôtel du Parc-Royal to be lodging of, in Paris, 31. 109
Sèvres visited by, 7. 309
Scott, Caroline (fl. ca 1750):
Cumberland, D. of, has, as mistress, 20. 203n
Scott, Lady Caroline (1774–1854), m. (1803) Charles Douglas, 5th Bt, 1783; 6th M. of Queensberry, 1810:
Reynolds's portrait of, 32. 337–8
Scott, Caroline Frederick (d. 1755), army officer:
Young Pretender almost caught by, 37. 251
Scott, Lord Charles (1727–47):
death of, 20. 138
matriculation of, at Christ Church, Oxford, 19. 387n
Oxford servant's death attributed to, 19. 387
Scott, Charles (ca 1739–1813), American army officer; gov. of Kentucky:
American news reported by, 33. 199
taken prisoner, 33. 199
Scott, Capt. David (d. 1792), army officer:
Conway's continental tour with, 39. 175, 536–9
Scott, Folliott (1758–before 1829), mercer:
dates of, 43. 68
HW asked to aid, 2. 112
Scott, Lady Frances (1750–1817), m. (1783) Archibald James Edward Douglas, cr. (1790) Bn Douglas:
Berrys entertained by, 12. 135
birth of, 20. 138
birth of daughter of, 11. 165
Buccleuchs visited by, 10. 302
Bulstrode visited by, 31. 287
HW admires, 11. 172
HW's correspondence with, 42. 407–8
HW's informant about Ds of Portland, 33. 489
HW's social relations with, 11. 152, 12. 117, 135, 31. 275, 33. 404
HW told by, to have his portrait painted, 42. 408
HW wishes to be in a bracelet on the arm of, 42. 408
health of: better, 42. 407; eyes affected, 34. 103; illness, 11. 165, 172, 176, 34. 105
heiress of Lady Jane Scott, 33. 145, 146
house of, at Petersham, 33. 146
loo played by, 10. 302

marriage of, **33**. 399
Onslows entertained by, **12**. 117
presented at Court, **33**. 404
Richmond visited by, **11**. 148
SH visited by, **12**. 226, 248
Stuart Mackenzies entertained by, **12**. 117
Scott, Francis (1695–1751), 2d D. of Buccleuch:
rebels camp at park of, **19**. 152
son of, **19**. 468n, **20**. 137n
Scott, Francis (1721–50), styled E. of Dalkeith:
Argyll refuses to sign marriage articles of, **17**. 479–80n
death of, **20**. 137
HW's opinion of, **9**. 171
marriage of, **7**. 360
smallpox fatal to family and, **20**. 137–8
wife of, **11**. 63n, **19**. 468n, **28**. 447n
Scott, George (1721–80) of Wolston Hall:
collection of, **2**. 324n
Scott, George Lewis (1708–80):
Bolingbroke recommends, as George III's underpreceptor, **20**. 203, 344
—— recommends, through Bathurst, **20**. 203n
——'s disciple, **20**. 323n
George III's subpreceptor, **20**. 246, 344
Harcourt objects to ascendancy of, over princes, **20**. 343n
—— refuses to act with, **20**. 343
Hayter and Harcourt oppose, over George III's tutorship, **20**. 323
name of, corrected, **43**. 269
wife of, **28**. 35n
Scott, Mrs George Lewis. *See* Robinson, Sarah
Scott, Henrietta (1774–1844), m. (1795) William Henry Cavendish Bentinck, styled M. of Titchfield; 4th D. of Portland, 1809:
fortune of, smaller than Lady Sarah Fane's, **12**. 68, 72
husband of, **11**. 205n
Scott, Henry (1746–1812), 3d D. of Buccleuch, 1751:
Adderbury may be left by, temporarily, **10**. 262
Banbury visited by, to see play, **10**. 266
Bath to be visited by, **10**. 266
brother of, dies, **3**. 157
cards to be played by, with Montagu, **10**. 268
Christmas to be spent by, at Adderbury, **10**. 284
daughter of, in picture, **32**. 337–8
dowry of daughter of, **11**. 121
Eton training of, approved by Montagu, **10**. 268
expected in Paris, **31**. 79
Fitzwilliam visits, **10**. 302
Foire St-Germain visited by, **7**. 309
French clergy's relief fund subscribed to by, **31**. 383n
genealogy of, **10**. 351
goods of, detained at Calais, **3**. 92
Guines's ball attended by, **32**. 96n
HW accompanies, to theatre in Paris, **7**. 305

HW mentions, **31**. 132
HW praises, **31**. 109
HW's opinion of, **10**. 259, 262
Hallam visits, **10**. 268
heir of Lady Jane Scott, **33**. 146
Hertford entertains, at dinner at Paris, on way to Toulouse, **38**. 337
Holland visited by, **33**. 562
house of: at Grosvenor Sq., **33**. 399n; HW wishes to see, in owner's absence, **10**. 262
lodges with Lennoxes, **3**. 157
loo played by, **10**. 302
Montagu accompanies, to Banbury, **10**. 266
——'s neighbour at Adderbury, **10**. 259
——'s relations with, **10**. 261, 266, 268, 302
Paris residence of, to be Hôtel du Parc-Royal, **31**. 109
Queensberry, D. of, leaves nothing to, **31**. 189, **33**. 67
Scotland visited by, **10**. 284
Scott, Lady Frances and Lady Jane, visit, **10**. 302
servant, servants of: SH visited by, **12**. 246; to convey Mme du Deffand's parcel, **3**. 160
Sèvres visited by, **7**. 309
sister of, **11**. 148n
Smith, Adam, travels with, **40**. 321
social relations of, in Paris, **7**. 306, 308, 309
Toulouse visited by, with Adam Smith, his tutor, **31**. 79n
unmarried, **10**. 29
Scott, Henry (b. 1762, d. ca 1845), commissioner of police:
dates of, **43**. 68
goes to India, **2**. 112n
Scott, Lady Isabella (d. 1748):
HW jokes with, about Rigby's mistake, **30**. 54
Orford, Cts of, writes to, **19**. 61
painting from collection of, **15**. 191n
parentage of, corrected, **43**. 257
Townshend, Vcts, visited by, **30**. 54
whist played by, **30**. 54
Scott, James (1649–85), cr. (1663) D. of Monmouth:
beheaded, **11**. 347
daughter of wife of, **43**. 257
descendants of, attend Ds of Buckingham's funeral, **18**. 203
mother of, **9**. 16n
not an author, **16**. 11
Ossory, Lady, 'dancing a dream' with, **32**. 263, 264
Scrope involved in rebellion of, **17**. 458n
suggested as 'Man in the Iron Mask,' **4**. 114
Scott, Rev. James (1733–1814), D.D.; 'anti-Sejanus':
'anti-Sejanus' letters of, **31**. 57, **32**. 20
hooted off the stage, with Sandwich, **22**. 410
'Repeal, The,' caricatures, **22**. 400
Sandwich inspires diatribes of, in *Public Advertiser*, **22**. 323n
takes refuge at York, **28**. 465–6

Scott, Lady Jane (1723–79):
Amelia, Ps, offends, **31.** 147
(?) at Chesterfield's assembly, **37.** 326
Bedford and Grafton, Duchesses of, and HW entertained by, **9.** 232
Blandford, Lady, has social relations with, **31.** 181
Browne, Lady, has social relations with, **31.** 142
Buccleuchs visited by, **10.** 302
buys mourning for Ds of Queensberry, **32.** 366
death of, **33.** 144
Dutch friends of, **32.** 92
Dysart fines, for inheritance at Petersham, **31.** 191
Grafton, Ds of, attended by, at accouchement, **38.** 421
Greenwich, Bns, inherits miniature from, **33.** 110n, 146n
HW gives Lady Ossory's compliments to, **33.** 110
HW jokes about reported marriage of, to Newcastle, **31.** 142
HW knows nothing of, **32.** 92
HW to invite, to SH, **31.** 406
Lincoln, Cts of, visits nobody but, **37.** 454
loo played by, **10.** 302, **32.** 28
low spirits of, **33.** 144
Petersham inherited by, from D. of Queensberry, **33.** 67
SH visited by, **31.** 147
unable to dine with HW, **32.** 366
will of, **33.** 144–5, 146
York, D. of, dances with, at Kew ball, **35.** 229n
Zincke miniature found by, at Ham, **33.** 110
Scott, Jane Elizabeth (ca 1773–1824), m. (1794) Edward Harley, 5th E. of Oxford, 1790:
HW receives letter addressed to, **12.** 80–1, 84
Scott, John:
Foundation of the Universities of Oxford and Cambridge, The, by, given by HW to Cambridge, **28.** 27n
Scott, John, bookseller:
Rider's translation of *Candide* to be published by, **10.** 349
shop of, in Paternoster Row, **10.** 349
Scott, John (1725–75), army officer and gambler; M.P.:
daughter of, **11.** 205n
Selwyn's epitaph on, **12.** 258
successful gambler, **12.** 68n
wealth of, **32.** 289
Scott, John (1730–83) of Amwell, Herts; Quaker; poet:
Amwell by, quoted and praised by HW, **28.** 257–8
Scott, John (1739–98), cr. (1784) Bn Earlsfort, (1789) Vct Clonmell, (1793) E. of Clonmell:
English government defended by, **33.** 141
house of, in Dublin, attacked, **33.** 141

Scott, John (1745–9), styled Lord Whitchester or Bn Scott of Whitchester:
death of, **20.** 137
Scott, John (1747–1819), Maj. in East India Co.; M.P.:
in India, **2.** 112
Letter to the Right Hon. Edmund Burke by, **12.** 169n
one of HW's favourite authors, **33.** 466
Parliamentary memberships of, corrected, **43.** 356
'probationary ode' attributed to, **33.** 465
Scott, Sir John (1751–1838), Kt, 1788; cr. (1799) Bn Eldon, and (1821) E. of Eldon; M.P.:
MacDonald succeeded by, as solicitor-gen., **34.** 9n
Scott, Mrs John. *See* Young, Isabella
Scott, Jonathan (ca 1722–78):
Cole's correspondence with, **43.** 67
HW asked by, to place his son, **2.** 112
MS of, of Lord Herbert's account of French court, **2.** 111–12, 113
Scott, Jonathan (1753–1829), orientalist:
Herbert's account of Court of France inherited by, **43.** 67
in India, **2.** 112
Scott, Marjory (d. 1746), m. (1688) David Murray, 5th Vct Stormont:
Jacobites aided by, at Perth, **19.** 283
Scott *or* Scot, Martha, m. (1748) Charles Churchill:
Churchill parts with, **7.** 374, **38.** 234
Tatton's mistress, **7.** 374
Scott, Lady Mary (1769–1823), m. (1791) James Stopford, styled Vct Stopford; 3d E. of Courtown, 1810:
at Mrs Boyle Walsingham's ball, **42.** 222n
marriage of, **11.** 121
mother of, **10.** 281
SH visited by, **12.** 239
Scott, Richard (b. 1750, d. before 1829), Lt-Col.:
in India, **2.** 112
Scott, Robert (1771–1841):
Allan's frontispiece engraved by, **42.** 432
Scott, Samuel (ca 1702–72), painter:
birth date of, corrected, **43.** 121, 266, 362
celebrated Twickenham resident, **35.** 234
disposition of, **10.** 329, 330
HW's opinion of, **10.** 330
health of: **10.** 329, 330; gout, **10.** 330
house of, in Covent Garden, **10.** 331
Marlow a pupil of, **23.** 299
Martyn lodges with, **10.** 330, 331
Müntz inspired by, to be landscape painter, **9.** 261
sea-pieces by: **20.** 38; at Hinchingbrooke, **40.** 283, 284
Twickenham resident, **42.** 481, 482
visited by Deacon, (?) Platel, Sir Edward Walpole, and Yeo, **10.** 330, 331

Walpole, Sir Edward, hopes for death of, **10.** 329, 330
—— writes to, **10.** 329–31, **43.** 138
wife of: prevents visitors from seeing him, **10.** 329; takes care of Laura Walpole, **9.** 61
Scott, Mrs Samuel:
HW's opinion of, **10.** 330
husband protected by, from visitors, **10.** 329
Walpole, Sir Edward, writes humorous letter to, given by her to HW, **10.** 329–31
Walpole, Laura, lodges with, **9.** 61
Scott, Mrs Sarah. *See* Robinson, Sarah
Scott, Sir Walter (1771–1832), author:
Berry, Mary, mentions, **11.** 67n
Scott, Sir William (1745–1836), Kt, 1788; cr. (1821) Bn Stowell; judge:
candidate for Parliament, **29.** 36n
disbelieves in Ireland's MSS, **15.** 321
Scotti, Costanza (ca 1736–94), m. (1756) Alessandro Sanvitale:
Mann to entertain, in garden, **22.** 45
Strathmore's affair with, **22.** 45, 69, 88, 145
Scottish books:
Montagu's opinion of, **10.** 182
Roland, Mme, reads, **10.** 182
Scottish soldier:
HW intercedes for, **31.** 8
Scott Montagu, Mrs. *See* Douglas, Jane Margaret
Scottow, Norfolk:
HW's will mentions, **30.** 344
Scott Waring. *See* Scott, John (1747–1819)
Scrafton, Mr, of Moulsey:
SH visited by, **12.** 251
Scrafton, Luke (1732–?70), East India Co. official:
ship of, lost, **23.** 282
Screen; screens:
at Crewe Hall, carved, **10.** 96
at Navestock, **9.** 244
at SH: **40.** 150; given by Lady Ossory, **33.** 273
Chinese, **20.** 191, 193
Indian, of tiger-killing, lacks perspective, **35.** 445
in Gloucester Cathedral, **35.** 154
in HW's exchequer chest, **23.** 285
in La Borde's dining-room, **7.** 280
in St George's Chapel, Windsor, **11.** 362
linen, taken by Princesse de Craon to opera, **19.** 357
lovers correspond by flinging letters over, **32.** 263
See also Fire-screen
Screveton, Notts:
Sutton of, **29.** 146n
'Scribonia':
HW's or West's error for Vipsania Agrippina, **13.** 117
Scrine. *See* Skrine
Scrip (financial):
price of, rises, **30.** 166

Scriptural Confutation of the Arguments Against the One Godhead, A. See under Burgh, William
Scripture. *See* Bible
Scrivelsby, Lincs:
Dymoke, lord of the manor of, **9.** 161n
Scrivener:
Conway would rather be, than a mere soldier, **37.** 129
Scrofula; or 'King's Evil':
Fitzgeralds said to have, **19.** 241–2
Gloucester, D. of, might have, **36.** 138
HW says that kings are the evil that they pretend to cure, **25.** 423
Romans believe Old Pretender to be last English king capable of curing, **21.** 392
royal bastards may claim ability to heal, **19.** 242
royal touch said to cure, **28.** 94, **32.** 334
Scrope, Bn. *See* Le Scrope, Henry (ca 1373–1415)
Scrope (Le Scrope), John (1435–98), 5th Bn Scrope of Bolton:
house of, in Holborn, **1.** 148
Scrope, John (ca 1662–1752), judge; M.P.:
death of, **17.** 458n
George II and Sir Robert Walpole not to be betrayed by, **17.** 459
Holland visited by, in disguise, **17.** 457n
Monmouth's rebellion participated in by, **17.** 457n
nephew's Treasury clerkship said by *London Evening Post* to be reward for silence of, before Secret Committee, **18.** 33
Perry and Pitt almost fought by, **17.** 458
Pulteney examines, **17.** 458
Rushout and Sandys defend, **17.** 467
secretary to the Treasury, **17.** 457n, 467
Secret Committee drops investigation of, **17.** 467
—— examines, **17.** 457–9
Tower not dreaded by, **17.** 458–9
Scrope, Richard:
Clarendon's *State Papers* edited by, **33.** 549n
Scrope, Mrs William. *See* Long, Emma
Scrots ('Scroets'), Guillim (d. ca 1544), painter:
Knole portraits perhaps done by, **35.** 134n
'Scrutator':
letter by, on Chatterton and HW in *European Magazine*, and *Cambridge Chronicle*, **34.** 148–51
Scrutiny; scrutinies:
of papal conclave, **17.** 16n
of Westminster election, **20.** 108, 112–13, 122–3, 223–4, **25.** 565, **36.** 177, 231
Scrutoire *or* scrutore:
gentleman's, robbed while owner was with maid in garret, **20.** 215
Mann's, HW's letter lies unanswered in, **25.** 429
Volterra vases to adorn, **17.** 394–5

[Scrutoire *or* scrutore, *continued*]
Walpole, Sir Robert, receives accounts at, **9.** 349

Scudamore, Miss:
Pope's elegy not about, **42.** 123

'Scudamore, Sir.' *See under* Spenser, Edmund: *Faerie Queene*

Scudamore, Charles. *See* Fitzroy, Charles (ca 1707–82)

Scudamore, Hon. Frances (1711–50), m. 1 (1729) Henry Somerset, 3d D. of Beaufort (divorced, 1744); m. 2 Charles Fitzroy:
divorce of, **17.** 452–3, **18.** 185, 199
Fitzroy weds, **17.** 452n
silver lace on gown of, **17.** 453
Talbot's adultery with, **17.** 452n, 453, 486, **18.** 199

Scudamore, James (ca 1678–1716), 3d Vct Scudamore:
daughter of, **17.** 452n

Scudder, Rev. Henry (d. ca 1659), Presbyterian divine:
Christian's Daily Walke, The, by, **16.** 66n
engraving of, **16.** 66

Scudéry, Georges de (1601–67):
Bachaumont mentions, **5.** 187–8
Observations of, on the *Cid*, **5.** 188
sister of, **5.** 188
wife of, **3.** 387n, **5.** 187

Scudéry, Mme Georges de. *See* Du Montcel de Martinvast, Marie-Madeleine

Scudéry, Madeleine de (1607–1701), novelist:
Anson's sea-piece worthy of, **20.** 38
Artamène ou le grand Cyrus by: **3.** 272, **5.** 188; HW knew, by heart, **37.** 189; HW reminded of, **10.** 22, **18.** 69
Cassandre by, superseded by Crébillon, Mme de la Fayette, and Marivaux, in HW's esteem, **37.** 203
Clélie by: **3.** 272, **4.** 71, **5.** 188, **9.** 3; Conway longs to read, **37.** 151; old gentlewomen study no map but that of *tendre* in, **25.** 530
Du Deffand, Mme, admits resemblance to, **3.** 142
—— annoyed by charge that she resembles, **3.** 55, 142, 248, 272, 273, 276, 279, 294, 312, 346, 363, **4.** 51, 304, 305, 374, 391, 441, **5.** 43, **6.** 428
—— dislikes, **5.** 392
—— has never read, **3.** 248, **4.** 304
goldfish splendid enough for, **35.** 221
HW jokes about, **9.** 378
Ibrahim, ou l'illustre Bassa by, HW reminded of, **18.** 69
Miller, Mrs, as romantic as, **39.** 241
Scudéry, brother of, **5.** 188

Scudo; scude, coins:
Florentine currency, **18.** 348
Florentine value of, **17.** 82n
Roman value of, **25.** 588n

Scullery:
window of, in Gothic farm, **37.** 579

Scully, ——, Irish tailor at Florence 1741–3:
English naval captain lodges with Bosvilles to avoid expense of renting another room from, **18.** 251
English people lodge with, in Florence, **17.** 450n
house of, near Mann's, may receive overflow of guests, **18.** 212
(?) Karl Friedrich lodges with, **20.** 149
Mann said to have persuaded, to take large house to receive Walpole family, **17.** 426, 450, **18.** 14
Mary's lawsuit with, to be decided by Mann, **17.** 101–2
Pomfret, Cts of, says that Mann splits the fees of, **17.** 130
—— scolds, **17.** 102–3

Sculptor; sculptors:
'drunken' English, at Florence, *see* Harwood, Francis
England has one or two, **24.** 93
English, Bowle has data on, **40.** 306
Florentine, would not understand English heraldry, **25.** 227
'little English,' to be employed by Chute, to buy eagle, **19.** 101
See also under names of sculptors

Sculptura. See under Evelyn, John

Sculpture:
Agincourt's project on monuments of, **42.** 102
alabaster, **42.** 68
ancient, seldom expresses passion, **35.** 444
antique marble, **15.** 16–17
at low ebb in England, **20.** 86
Boyle, Charlotte, does, **31.** 251n
—— imitates Mrs Damer in, **35.** 385
Damer, Mrs, has taste and judgment in, **25.** 203
—— has talent in, **25.** 184
——'s works in, listed, **12.** 271–4
declining taste in, **20.** 398
Greeks' grace in, **16.** 270
Greeks set standards for, **33.** 479
HW may get aid in treating history of, when he has finished that of painting, **16.** 37
in wood, **2.** 175, **42.** 68
Mann gives Mrs Damer an antique foot, **25.** 287
monumental, by Fishers, **28.** 97
Proctor's prize in, **25.** 577
statues, HW discusses expression in, **11.** 338
Venus Callipygus, casts of, **12.** 268
See also Antiquities; Bas-relief; Cast; Eagle; York Minster: choir-screen of; *see also under* Wax

Scurvy; scurvies:
ancestors of gouts, **2.** 292, 294, 303
French may wait for English ships to be eaten up by, **38.** 37
occurrences of, **10.** 61, 142, **13.** 48, **15.** 332, **18.** 86–7, 289, **20.** 413, **22.** 154, 413, **23.** 240, **24.** 39, **37.** 218

Orford's eruption might be caused by, **23.** 460

poverty and fasting cure, **29.** 95

remedies for, **37.** 314

treatment for, mercurial unctions, **18.** 87

Scutcheon. *See* Escutcheon

Scuvaloff. *See* Shuvalov

Scylla:

and Charybdis, **12.** 145

Scythe; scythes:

garden-swords to be used as, **39.** 499–500

Gothic ancestors said to have armed themselves with, **10.** 273

(?) HW mentions, **20.** 441

man almost cut in two by, at election, **39.** 183

rebels armed with, **19.** 116n

Scythes, Les. See under Voltaire

Scythia:

Greek arts not influenced by, **15.** 211

Scythians:

HW has no regard for, **33.** 479

Hancarville ascribes universal knowledge and invention to, **33.** 478

Ovid exiled among, **31.** 289

Scythian Diana. *See under* Diana

Sea; seas:

consumption thought to be cured by voyage on, **24.** 220

English princesses and P. Alfred bathed in, **25.** 413

excursions into, at low tide, at Holkham, **30.** 37

HW avoids, in bad weather, **35.** 342

HW compares effect of, on claret to that of distance on news, **10.** 113

Joseph II anxious to see, **22.** 548

Montagu unable to see, **10.** 321

See also Ocean; Sea air; Seasickness; Sea voyages; Sea water

Sea air:

Gloucester, D. of, may go to Bordeaux for, **24.** 360

——'s health improved by, **33.** 233

HW considers, beneficial, **11.** 60, 68, 77, 113, **12.** 22, 35, 208, **33.** 438, 481, 485

HW helped by, **24.** 227, 272, 311, 318, **25.** 49

HW recommends, to Mann, **24.** 311, **25.** 49

HW to seek, for health, **32.** 192, 200, 304

Sea-bathing:

at Southampton, **35.** 251

Berry, Mary, practises, at Bognor Rocks, **31.** 402

Fox probably to benefit from, **30.** 235

HW now neglects, **25.** 49

HW prescribes, for Mrs Damer, **12.** 145

horse-racing more fashionable than, **35.** 247

Lort to visit Boulogne for, **16.** 211

Seabright. *See* Sebright

Sea captain. *See* Captain; captains

Seafield, Cts of. *See* Seaforth, Cts of

Seaford, English war ship:

Caroline Matilda escorted by, **23.** 409n

involved in war, **19.** 207

name of, corrected, **43.** 260

sent to Adriatic, **19.** 220, 231, 235

Seaforth *or* Seafield, Cts of:

print of, **40.** 236

Seaforth, E. of. *See* Mackenzie, Kenneth (1744–81); Mackenzie, William (d. 1740)

Seaforth, English merchant ship:

French squadron carries, into Brest, **18.** 463n

Seaforth, Lancs:

election at, **19.** 449

Potter's speech on election at, **19.** 449n

Sea Horse, English vessel:

Braddock's defeat made known by, **20.** 494n

release of, **17.** 8

Spaniards capture, **37.** 56–7

Sea horse; sea horses:

teeth of, made into artificial teeth, **18.** 289n

Seal; seals (for documents and letters):

Anderson's, shows he is of Whig family, **16.** 376

antique, of a woman's head, **1.** 223

bloodstone, belonging to Gray, given to HW, **28.** 43

by Costanzi, **26.** 7

charter of Robert Bruce without, **15.** 159

conventual, **1.** 31

cornelian, for Robert Child, **32.** 361

Edmund, K. of Sicily's, **42.** 266

engraver of, *see* Major, Thomas

Fitz-Othes, William, makes, **42.** 87

'flying,' **25.** 176

from deeds at Earls Colne, **2.** 175

HW changes on his letters, **17.** 421

HW obliges ministers to open, if they would read his letters, **37.** 568

HW recovers, after robbery, **20.** 99n

HW's: **1.** 11, 6. (?) 355; Maclaine offers to return, **40.** 64; 'vulgar,' **35.** 586

HW's 'antique sacrifice,' made by Wedgwood, **28.** 236

letter sealed with five, sure to be read, **37.** 573

Mann opens, on Craon's letter to daughter, **20.** 55–6

—— replaces Rowley's, which was lost, **19.** 9

—— tells HW to put, on inside of cover, **17.** 98

Mann, Galfridus, to have, cut for Mann, **20.** 480

medal for Francis I's election under Mann's, **19.** 185

Natter's, of Sir Robert Walpole's head, **16.** 299

of Henrietta Maria, **2.** 128–9, 130

of St Leonard's Hospital, Leicester, **2.** 295

on cabinets and coffers at Welbeck, **35.** 271

on HW's letter, **24.** 72

on HW's watch, **40.** 64n

on monk of Glastonbury's chair, **35.** 106

on Nell Gwyn's letter, **1.** 349

Prieto cuts, well, **16.** 170

prints of reginal, **2.** 163

[Seal; seals (for documents and letters), *cont.*]
17th-century letters preserve, with ribbons, **9.** 224
sharp impression of Mason's, convinces HW that letters are opened, **28.** 440
Stosch's, **30.** 11
Townshend's witticism on, **35.** 392
Waldegrave, Cts, gives her late husband's, to his brother, **22.** 164
wax, on warrant, **10.** 116
with figures of justice, **1.** 233
Seal; seals (of public offices):
lord chancellor's (Great Seal): De Grey cannot accept, **23.** 175; Irish attorney-general thinks, should be set to Irish regency act, **25.** 682; Mansfield refuses, **23.** 174; must be put into commission, **23.** 179; Pitt prefers Pratt to Charles Yorke for, **38.** 285; Pulteney refuses, **18.** 72; Ryder may be promoted to, **20.** 202; to be put into commission if not given to a lord keeper, **21.** 18; Willes, Wilmot, and Smythe succeed Hardwicke as commissioners of, **20.** 25; Wilmot may receive, **23.** 175, 179; Yorke's rejection and acceptance of, **23.** 175, 178
of Exchequer chancellorship, **37.** 481
of secretaries of state: Egremont may receive, **21.** 72, 76, 98; Fox, Henry, accepts, **20.** 502; George II wants Newcastle to resume, **21.** 76; Granville resigns, **18.** 537; Hardwicke refuses, **21.** 92; Harrington receives, **18.** 537; North declines and then accepts them, **22.** 552; Pitt (Chatham) kisses hands for, **21.** 103; Pitt (Chatham) threatens to reject, **21.** 30; Pitt (Chatham) to take, **21.** 22; Weymouth resigns, **23.** 255; *see also under* Secretary of state
patent has to pass, **16.** 84
privy, *see* Privy seal
Tuscany's official, awaited by Leopold, **22.** 356
Seal-cutter:
Deuchar is, **42.** 432
Seaman; seamen. *See* Sailor; sailors
Sea monster; sea monsters:
Berrys see, at Scarborough, **12.** 27
Seamstress:
Charles II's, *see* Wall, Ellen
Sea-piece; sea-pieces:
at Hinchingbrooke, **40.** 283, 284
Seaports:
air travel may make, into deserted villages, **39.** 425
English, guarded against smuggling, **10.** 288–9
Search, right of. *See* Right of search
Seascape:
Anson's, **20.** 38
Seashore:
HW may go to, **24.** 272, **32.** 192, 200, 304
Seasickness:
HW escapes, **39.** 70
HW's first experience of, **1.** 124
Hertfords but not their entourage escape, **38.** 212

occurrences of, **10.** 250, **11.** 120, **30.** 250, **37.** 405, **38.** 119, **39.** 255, 260
Seaside. *See* Seashore
Seasons. See under Thomson, James
Seaton. *See* Seton
Seats of the Nobility and Gentry, The, published by Watts:
Devonshire, D. of, criticized in, **2.** 274
Sea voyages:
HW has previously taken, six times without seasickness, **10.** 250
Montagu dislikes, **9.** 385, **10.** 214, 299
'Sea-war':
Selwyn's witticism on, **35.** 261
Sea water:
bathing in, **36.** 324
See also Sea-bathing
Sebastian (1554–78), K. of Portugal 1557–78:
uncle and successor of, **25.** 482n
Sebert (d. ?616), K. of the East Saxons:
pictures of, **2.** 183, 184–5
Sebright, Lady. *See* Knight, Sarah
Sebright, Henrietta (1770–1840), m. (1794) Henry Lascelles, 2d E. of Harewood, 1820:
breakfasts with HW, **11.** 286
drawing given by, to HW, **11.** 286, **43.** 149
HW invites, to SH, **42.** 326
SH visited by, **12.** 238
Sebright, Sir John (1725–94), 6th Bt, 1761; M.P.; army officer:
(?) at Chesterfield's assembly, **37.** 326
Bedford, D. of, orders regiment of, assembled, **21.** 373n
burglars pursued by, **9.** 133
HW calls on, to invite him to SH, **42.** 326
HW entertains, at SH breakfast, **11.** 286, **35.** 225
HW's correspondence with, **42.** 326
Knight, Sarah, infatuates, **10.** 210
name of, corrected, **43.** 373
SH visited by, **12.** 238
Whiteboys pursued by regiment of, from Cork, **22.** 24n
Sebright, Mary Anne (ca 1779–1854), m. (1811) Nicholas Lewis Fenwick:
breakfasts with HW. **11.** 286
SH visited by, **12.** 238
Sebright, Sir Thomas Saunders (1723–61), 5th Bt:
Furini's 'Sigismunda' bought by, **21.** 200n
Secchia, river in Italy:
Berrys cross, **11.** 149n
'Se cerca, se dice':
Mann's favourite song in *Olimpiade*, sung by Monticelli, **17.** 401
Séchelles. *See* Herault de Séchelles; Moreau de Séchelles
Sechenov, Daniil Andreievich (1709–67), known as Dimitri; Bp of Nizhni Novgorod and Alatyr, 1742, of Riazan and Murom, 1752; Abp (1757) and Metropolitan (1762) of Novgorod and Velikie Luki:
Catherine II aided by, **22.** 64

crimes of, **22**. 66

Peter III said to be murdered by, for building Lutheran churches, **38**. 164

Samoyed and, **28**. 476

Sechford Common, Norfolk:

foxes flee to, **37**. 181

Seckendorf, Friedrich Heinrich (1673–1763), Graf von; Marshal:

Austrians fail to capture, **18**. 230

—— formerly injured, **18**. 230

Frederick II arrests, sending him to Magdeburg for disclosing plan for seizure of Dresden and Leipzig, **21**. 266

Seckendorff, Baron von:

SH visited by, **12**. 225

Secker, Thomas (1693–1768), Bp of Bristol 1734–7, of Oxford 1737–58; Abp of Canterbury 1758–68:

American war fomented by ecclesiastical policy of, **29**. 23, 28

Augusta, Ps, married by, to Karl Wilhelm Ferdinand, **22**. 197

Bedford, Ds of, calls, *sage-femme*, **38**. 264

Bute's first levee attended by, with lame excuse, **10**. 35

Canterbury archbishopric no longer expected by, **20**. 187

career of, **30**. 304n

Cock Lane ghost séances not forbidden by, **10**. 6

confinements enjoyed by, **9**. 58

Court visited by, on Ps of Wales's rumoured confinement, **9**. 58

Cumberland, D. of, jokes with, after being trod upon, **9**. 318

death of, **23**. 40

Ducarel continued in employment by, **40**. 128

Ferrers's trial attended by, **9**. 281

Foote's joke on censorship of his *Minor* by, **9**. 326–7, **10**. 6

former midwife, **39**. 104

Frederick, P. of Wales, may be advised by, **17**. 451

——'s representative in dealing with George II, **17**. 296n, 320n

—— talks with, **17**. 328–9

George II's message to P. of Wales jotted down by, **17**. 296

George III's Court frequented by, **9**. 318, 325

——'s favour sought by, **9**. 318, 324

George IV baptized by, **38**. 174n, 180–1

Gregory's marriage arranged by, **30**. 304n

HW satirizes, in verse, **20**. 134

HW's 'character' of, **30**. 304n

Hardwicke gives service of silver plate to, for arranging son's marriage, **30**. 304n

—— recommends, as Abp of Canterbury, **21**. 185n

Henry VIII's statue in Tower made decent by, **9**. 70n, **38**. 379

hypocrisy of, **23**. 43

jesuitical and popish, **20**. 133

Kent's daughter's marriage arranged by, **30**. 304n

Lambeth Palace mentioned by, **10**. 35

Newcastle, D. of, aided by, in Oxford clergy appointments, **22**. 324n

—— plied by, with smelling-bottle, **9**. 323

——'s last levee not attended by, **10**. 35

Oxford bishopric given to, **17**. 451n

Pearce's resignation from Rochester bishopric opposed by, **38**. 364

prebend of Portpool held by, **20**. 187n

rectorship of St James's, Westminster retained by, until he became dean of St Paul's, **20**. 133n

St Paul's deanery wanted by, **20**. 187

sermon on earthquake preached by, at St James's, Westminster, **20**. 133n, 155

started as a Presbyterian, **20**. 188

witticism on, by Sir C. H. Williams, **30**. 304n

women told by, not to flee from London earthquake, **20**. 133

Secker, Mrs Thomas. *See* Benson, Catharine

Seclusion:

HW's reflections on superiority of, to politics, **10**. 177, 254, 263

See also Politics: HW's aversion to

Second Anticipation. See Exhibition, The

Secondat, Charles de (1689–1755), Baron de Montesquieu; writer:

Christian VII praises, **4**. 165–6

comment by, on Niccolini's banishment, **20**. 4n

Esprit des lois, L', by: **3**. 334n; critics of, answered, **15**. 239; Du Deffand, Mme, owned, **8**. 33; Florentine opinion of, **21**. 17; Gray is anticipated in, **15**. 53n; HW praises, **20**. 126; Jansenists accuse, of atheism, **20**. 107n

Gibbon as sly as, **28**. 243

Gray agrees with, **29**. 335

Guasco proof-reader to, **22**. 530n

—— publisher of letters of, **22**. 575

HW praises, **5**. 397

Helvétius tries to imitate, **16**. 23

letters of; printed, **3**. 373n; should not have been printed, **42**. 121

Lettres de Monsieur de Montesquieu by, (London edn), **43**. 86

Lettres familières by: **43**. 86; authenticity of, doubted, **22**. 529, 530; Duclos takes, to France in rage, **22**. 531; Du Deffand, Mme, sends, to HW, **3**. 334; Galiani said to be editor of, **22**. 524n; Guasco said to be editor of, **22**. 529; HW receives, from Florence, **3**. 335; HW's opinion of, **3**. 335; HW thanks Mann for, **22**. 523–4

'portrait' of Mme de Mirepoix by, **8**. 78

satiric print or drawing of, **22**. 531

Saurin defends, against Voltaire, **4**. 180

vanity in, would offend, **33**. 537

Voltaire's discussion of, **4**. 171, 180

Secondat, Jean-Baptiste (1716–96), Baron de:

Borde, friend of, **3**. 110

Second courses:

misers should save money by not having, since they are never eaten, **25**. 609

Second Dialogue between G-s E-l and B-b D-n, A: poor imitation of Sir C. H. Williams's 'Giles Earle . . . and Geo. Bubb Dodington, Esqrs: A Dialogue,' **30**. 314

Second Epistle of the Second Book of Horace Imitated. See under Pope, Alexander

Second Epistle to the Reverend Mr Brooke: title of, corrected, **43**. 212

Second in command:

never remembered, in warfare, **38**. 181

Second Letter to a Late Noble Commander: Sackville attacked in, **38**. 31–2, 35

Second Letter to the Reverend Mr Brooke: Middleton's attack on Sherlock provokes, **15**. 300

Second Part of the Full and Impartial Account. See under Middleton, Conyers

Second sight:

HW will consult Craufurd about, **33**. 13

Johnson, Dr Samuel, believes in, **32**. 225

See also under Scot; Scots

Second temple of Jerusalem:

'Sarahs' of Twickenham still talk about, **28**. 447

Secousse, Jean-François-Robert (ca 1696–1771), curé of St-Eustache:

Choiseul's social relations with, **4**. 373

Secretary; secretaries:

Almada's, **21**. 430, 476

Barbantane's, **24**. 369

French, at Florence, informs Mann about Duc de Chartres, **24**. 408–9

HW's, *see* Kirgate, Thomas

HW tells Mann to dictate a few lines to, instead of writing, **25**. 602

HW uses, to spare his eyes, **24**. 501

HW when ill usually employs, for letter-writing, **25**. 354

Lorenzi's, replaced, **17**. 157

Mann dictates common letters to, **25**. 585

—— grieved that HW is compelled to use, **24**. 513

—— seeks, **17**. 156–8, 172, 189, 190, 207, 216, 246, 255, 257

——'s, *see* Giberne, Gabriel George; Gregori, Antonio; Palombo, Domenico

—— tells HW to have notes written by, about health, when HW is unable to write, **25**. 359

Newcastle's, **17**. 24n

Richecourt's, *see* Niccoli

salary of, **19**. 93n

Secretary at war, English:

Barrington becomes, **35**. 253–4

—— remains as, instead of Sackville, **21**. 109

—— to be, **20**. 502

Clare or Ellis may succeed Barrington as, **39**. 93

Conway proposed as, **38**. 563

Fitzpatrick becomes, **33**. 397

Fox, Henry, appointed as, **19**. 256

—— remains as, **20**. 417

—— transformed office of, from sinecure to laborious employment, **30**. 334

—— urged to remain as, **20**. 39

—— wishes to remain as, **35**. 169

Frederick, P. of Wales, prefers Elizabeth Chudleigh to Pitt as, **19**. 175

George II and D. of Cumberland persuade Fox to remain as, **30**. 319

George II rejects Pitt (Chatham) as, **19**. 209, 211

—— rejects Sackville as, **21**. 109

Granby should be consulted on choice of, **39**. 94

HW proposes Sackville as, **21**. 48n, **37**. 487n

Pitt (Chatham) covets post of, **18**. 552, **19**. 168, **37**. 200–1

—— may become, **19**. 155, 175

—— said to be, **37**. 219

Sackville said to succeed Barrington as, **21**. 104

Townshend, Charles, replaces Barrington as, **21**. 490

—— to be, **21**. 486

Townshend, T., becomes, **25**. 264n

Walpole, Sir Robert, was, **22**. 26

Secretary at war, French. *See under* Secretary of state, French

Secretary at war, Irish:

Conway 'civi-military' as, **37**. 456

Secretary at war, Portuguese:

'Migas Frias' applies to, **23**. 166

Secretary at war, Tuscan:

Antinori was, **22**. 124

Rinuccini, Carlo, was, **17**. 40n

Secretary of state, English:

American appointments shifted to, from Board of Trade, **21**. 488n

aspirants to office of, **20**. 202n, 461, **22**. 159, 161, **41**. 86

Barré praises present incumbents in office of, **22**. 283

Bedford, D. of, is, **19**. 463

—— to be succeeded by Holdernesse as, **20**. 258–9

Bute succeeds Holdernesse as, **21**. 487

Carlisle wishes to be, **33**. 104n

Carmarthen is, **25**. 583

changes in office of, **20**. 259, 265, and *passim*

Chesterfield resigns as, **19**. 463

circular letters by: about D. and Ds of Cumberland, **23**. 543; on Grafton's resignation, **23**. 190; usually sent to correspondents upon retirement, **25**. 299

Conway changes departments in, **22**. 427

—— proposed as, **38**. 563

—— refuses salary of, **22**. 559, **36**. 47

—— succeeds Halifax as, **22**. 309

—— to resign as, **22**. 571

—— was, **25**. 129, 526

dancing by, **35**. 213

Dartmouth, 1st E. of, served as, under Q.

Anne, **20.** 208n

Dartmouth, 2d E. of, almost becomes, for America, which might have been separated from southern province, **22.** 444

departments of, defined, **22.** 429n

dissension in office of, **20.** 38–9

Egmont may become, **22.** 159

Egremont may be, **21.** 72, 75–6, 540, 541

—— might be succeeded as, by Bubb Dodington, **22.** 17

—— succeeds Pitt as, **38.** 132, 134

—— too sensible to become, **21.** 76n

fashionable to leave one's name with, when newly appointed, **22.** 17

for American department: Ellis succeeds Germain (Sackville) as, **25.** 237n, 241; Germain (Sackville) succeeds Dartmouth as, **24.** 142; Hillsborough becomes, **22.** 569, 571; Shelburne may resign as, **22.** 569

foreign: Grenville succeeds Leeds as, **34.** 109n; see also Grenville, William Wyndham (1759–1834); Osborne, Francis Godolphin (1751–99)

for home affairs: Shelburne may succeed Sydney as, **25.** 487; see also Dundas, Henry (1742–1811); Grenville, William Wyndham (1759–1834)

Fox, C. J., is, **25.** 262, 391, 460

—— resigns as, **25.** 293

Fox, Henry, becomes, **35.** 87–8

—— may become, **20.** 502, **21.** 6, 11

—— refuses to be, since he cannot control House of Commons, **20.** 417, **35.** 168–9

—— replaces Robinson as, **35.** 253

——'s health prevents his becoming, **38.** 184

Gage predicts that Chesterfield and Carteret will be, **17.** 296

George II usually sees both, at once, **20.** 346

—— wishes D. of Newcastle to resume seals as, **21.** 76

Germain (Sackville)'s declaration as, **24.** 282n

——'s place as, for the colonies, not to be filled, **25.** 237

——'s resignation as, for the colonies, expected, **25.** 236, 240–1

Grafton, D. of, or Pitt expected as, by Hertford, **39.** 1

Grafton, D. of, succeeded by D. of Richmond as, **22.** 419–20

—— succeeds Sandwich as, **22.** 310

Grantham, 1st and 2d Bns, are, **25.** 296n

Granville (Carteret) does not notify Italy of his becoming, **19.** 213

—— is to be, **17.** 296, 333

green velvet bags used by, **18.** 225, **20.** 346

Grenville, George, becomes, **22.** 37

—— recommends Egremont for, **31.** 24n

—— refuses to replace Pitt as, **21.** 541n

HW advises Henry Fox against becoming, **30.** 122–3

HW implores, not to peek into his mail, **22.** 373

HW jokes about becoming, **9.** 311

HW's letters harmless enough not to be intercepted by, **35.** 212

Halifax prevents Holdernesse from becoming, **20.** 249

—— succeeds Grenville as, **22.** 91, **38.** 184

—— succeeds Sandwich, **23.** 268

—— to replace Holdernesse as, **20.** 346

Hanoverian soldier delivered from English prison by warrant of, **20.** 12

Harrington resigns as, **19.** 326

Hillsborough becomes, **22.** 569, 571

—— may be, **39.** 93

—— succeeds Weymouth as, **24.** 534

—— to resign as, **23.** 423

Holdernesse, Pitt, and Robinson nominated for, **20.** 202

Holdernesse becomes, **21.** 103

—— reappointed as, **35.** 282

—— remains as, for northern province, **21.** 17

Jenkinson rumoured to be, **35.** 528n

'Junius' acquainted with office of, **36.** 52

Lyttelton angered by failure to become, **24.** 465

Mann hopes for instructions from a new, **25.** 299

—— may be affected by changes in department of, **19.** 338

——'s ignorance of identity of, results in delaying letters, **25.** 306

Minorcan papers from, presented to House of Commons, **21.** 76n

Newcastle, D. of, and Harrington resign as, **19.** 211

Newcastle, D. of, changes provinces as, **19.** 463

—— offers to shift from, to President of the Council, **20.** 201n

—— reportedly recommends Grantham and Hardwicke as, **30.** 185

——'s candidates for, **21.** 86n

North and C. J. Fox become, **25.** 391

North and C. J. Fox requested by George III to turn in their seals as, **25.** 460

North succeeds Charles Townshend as, **22.** 552

office of: Deyverdun employed in, **13.** 44; for southern department, moved from Whitehall to St James's, **22.** 176n; Gloucester, D. of, to receive packets from, at Genoa, **23.** 328; HW brings letter to, **22.** 176; HW had barely time to send letter to, at 7 P.M., **25.** 467; HW inquires about Mann's courier at, **25.** 228; HW sends letter for Mann to, **17.** 359, **20.** 165, **25.** 326; HW sends to, for Mann's servant, **25.** 215; HW's letter intercepted on way to, **25.** 564; HW's letter to Mann must have stayed a week at, **25.** 395; HW's letter to Mann sent through, delayed, **25.** 179–80; HW's new footman puts letter in post instead of carrying it to, **25.** 118; HW to write to Conway by Stair's packet from, **37.** 135; Hertford receives no letters from, **39.** 1;

[Secretary of state, English, *continued*]

Hertford's letters perhaps delayed by, **38.** 513; Hertford's letters to, **38.** 219; Larpent first clerk in, **39.** 21; Larpent to have successor in, **23.** 443–4; Mann asks about punctuality of people at, in forwarding letters, **23.** 542; Mann sends weekly gazette under blank cover to, **24.** 396; Mann still dictates and signs letters to, **25.** 660; Mann, Horace II, quarrels with, over salary, **25.** 671–6, 678; Murray's letter to Mann produced by, as evidence against Murray, **25.** 349; Polish nuncio's expulsion fully told by, in letter to Mann, **22.** 192; procedure at, for incoming and outgoing letters, **22.** 319n; royal happenings announced through, **33.** 379; Sneyd's continuance in, unknown to Mann, **25.** 272; to discover nothing in HW's letter, **39.** 316; travellers get letters of recommendation from, to diplomatists abroad, **35.** 440; under Holdernesse, might eclipse those of France and Italy, **35.** 166

opera singer obtained by, **35.** 257

Pitt (E. of Chatham) asks D. of Newcastle not to meddle in department of, **21.** 91

—— becomes, **21.** 103

—— becomes, for southern province, **21.** 17

—— does not permit department of, for West Indies, **21.** 104, **30.** 135n

—— may become, **20.** 461

—— may succeed Henry Fox as, **20.** 12

—— names himself and C. Townshend for, **22.** 161

——'s designs on, **20.** 223, 235

Pitt, William II, may become, **25.** 295, **35.** 518

Robinson becomes, **17.** 497n, **20.** 417

—— may become, **20.** 202, **35.** 169

—— to be, **21.** 92

Rochford, E. of, acting as, commits Sayre to Tower, **24.** 138n

—— becomes, **23.** 62

—— becomes, for southern province, **23.** 255

—— was, **25.** 191n

Sandwich becomes, **22.** 159, 167

—— dismissed as, **20.** 258

—— may replace Suffolk as, **24.** 445n, 450

—— may succeed D. of Bedford as, **20.** 217, 235

—— succeeds Weymouth as, but in northern province, **23.** 255

—— to resign as, **23.** 263

Shelburne and C. J. Fox become, **25.** 262

Shelburne becomes, **22.** 439, 443, 447, **25.** 262

—— may resign as, for America, **22.** 569

—— may succeed Sydney as, for Home Affairs, **25.** 487

—— remains as, **22.** 571, 581

—— wishes to be, **22.** 159

Stormont succeeds Suffolk as, **24.** 525, **39.** 342

Suffolk, E. of, may become, **23.** 263

—— may succeed Halifax as, **23.** 304, 310

——'s death leaves vacancy in, **24.** 450

Sydney and Carmarthen are, **25.** 583

Temple, 1st (2d) E., attributes political breach to Pitt's refusal to appoint Gower as, **30.** 228

Temple, 2d (3d) E., briefly becomes, **25.** 465, **36.** 215n

Temple, 2d (3d) E., Carmarthen, and Sydney appointed as, **25.** 460n

Temple, 2d (3d) E., rumoured to become, **25.** 295

Townshend, 2d Vct, was, **25.** 423

Townshend, Thomas, is, **25.** 355n

Tweeddale resigns as, for Scotland, **19.** 195

—— was, for Scotland, **25.** 209

vacancy in, unfilled, **24.** 455

warrant from, for St-Germain's arrest, **26.** 21

Weymouth may become, **22.** 570

—— succeeds Rochford as, for southern province, **24.** 142

—— succeeds Shelburne as, **23.** 62

—— to succeed Conway as, **22.** 571, 578

Wilkes writes to, accusing them of robbing him, **22.** 138

Yarmouth, Cts of, advises George II to make D. of Bedford Master of the Horse if he would resign as, **20.** 183n

See also Conway, Edward (ca 1569–1631); Conway, Edward (ca 1623–83); Dundas, Henry (1742–1811); Grenville, William Wyndham (1759–1834); Williamson, Sir Joseph (1633–1701); *and under* Seal; seals, of public offices

Secretary of state, French:

Choiseul ousted as, **41.** 192–200

Du Châtelet rumoured to be, **22.** 586n

for war: Du Muy becomes, **23.** 258, **24.** 17; Du Muy to be, **39.** 134; Du Muy's death leaves place of, vacant, **24.** 133

Pecquigny fears lettre de cachet from, **38.** 295

St-Contest succeeds Puisieux as, for foreign affairs, to Nivernais's disappointment, **20.** 286

St-Florentin is, **22.** 342

Turgot replaces Boynes as, for the marine, **24.** 26

Secretary of state, Irish. *See* Carter, Thomas

Secretary of state, Neapolitan. *See* Guzmann, José Joaquin, Duca di Montallegre

Secretary of state, Papal. *See* Archinto, Alberigo; Pallavicini, Lazzaro Opizio; Torreggiani, Luigi Maria; Valenti, Silvio

Secretary of state, Sardinian. *See* Del Carretto, Leopoldo, Marchese di Gorsegno

Secretary of state, Spanish:

Wall to succeed Carvajal as, for foreign affairs, **20.** 426

Secretary of state, Tuscan:

HW hopes that letters are not opened by, **24.** 38

See also Degli Alberti, Giovan Vincenzo; Piccolomini, Tommaso; Tornaquinci, Giovanni Antonio

Secretary of the Latin Briefs. *See* Giacomelli, Michelangelo

Secret Committee, English, on East India Co.: appointed, 39. 168

Secret Committee, English, on Sir Robert Walpole:
Bristow, Burrell, and Hanbury Williams to be examined by, 17. 411
defeat of, 17. 363–4, 379, 388
dissolution of: pleases Mann, 18. 14, 29; predicted, 17. 438
Edgcumbe created a baron to prevent examination by, about Cornish boroughs, 17. 399n
forgotten, 17. 502, 18. 29
Labour in Vain satirizes, 18. 19
lists for, voted on, 17. 383–6, 403
Lyttelton proposes, 18. 117
may consist of Sir Robert Walpole's friends, 17. 375, 429
members absent from, 17. 401
Paxton and Wendover borough exposed by, 17. 425
Paxton examined by, 17. 397, 502
Pitt discusses, in speech, 19. 370
proposed in Parliament, 17. 297–300, 355, 375
Rawdon reveals Wallingford expenses to, 17. 400
report expected from, 17. 450, 467
report of, on Bristow, Burrell, Weymouth election, and secret service money, 17. 475
Scrope examined by, 17. 457–8
——'s investigation dropped by, 17. 467
——'s silence before, said by *London Evening Post* to be rewarded by giving Treasury clerkship to Fane, 18. 33
second attempt to form, expected, 18. 89
secret service money investigated by, 17. 399, 475
Tilson's persecution from, causes his death, 18. 33
voting for, attended by P. of Wales's friends, but not by Lytteltons and Pitts, 17. 366
Walpole, Sir Robert, investigated by, 13. 248, 22. 27
—— not impeached by, 42. 79
—— not mentioned in report of, 17. 425
——'s supporters in, support Indemnity Bill, 17. 429
—— unharmed by, 17. 419, 421
Weymouth customs officials examined by, 17. 420

Secret committee, English, to investigate Q. Anne's last administration:
Prior examined by, 13. 186
Walpole, Sir Robert, chairman of, 22. 26

Secret committee, Swedish:
power of King and Senate vested in, 23. 436n

Secret expedition. *See under* Expedition

Secret History of the Rye-House Plot. See under Grey, Ford, E. of Tankerville

Secret Memoirs . . . from the New Atlantis. See under Manley, Mary de la Rivière

Secret service, English:
Mann's allowance for, 21. 149
money for: 35. 168; Newcastle refuses to reveal disposal of, 30. 123n
Secret Committee investigates money for, 17. 399, 475
Stosch manages, at Rome, 21. 149–50
Stuart Mackenzie's pension from, 30. 184n

Sectarianism, religious:
More, Hannah, deplores, 31. 335

Sects, religious:
HW's reflections on, 31. 333
jarring chaos of, deplored by Conway, 37. 193–4

Sedaine, Michel-Jean (1719–97), dramatist:
Déserteur, Le, by: 4. 274, 276, 278, 5. 376, 378, 379; parodied, 4. 301n; played at Versailles, 6. 127; seen by HW, Louis XVI, and Marie-Antoinette, 5. 378; verses to air from, 5. 226
Gageure imprévue, La, by, 4. 84
Maillard, ou Paris sauvé, Le, by, heard by Mme du Deffand, 4. 376, 384–5, 5. 379
Philosophe sans le savoir, Le, by: 4. 274, 275, 384, 5. 379, 7. 280, 283, 285; censorship of, 31. 104n; HW criticizes, 31. 105; HW sees, on second night, 33. 180–1; HW sends, to Bns Hervey, 31. 104; O'Brien's *Duel* adapted from, 28. 58–9; performances of, 31. 104–5
Richard Cœur-de-Lion by: Burgoyne's version of, 33. 546; HW criticizes, 31. 255; HW sees, at Drury Lane, 11. 8; suggested to D. of York, 34. 186
Roi et le fermier, Le, by, 7. 314, 320
Rose et Colas by: Caraman family acts, 5. 269; HW sees, 7. 316
Tom Jones libretto revised by, 38. 519n

Sedan chair. *See* Chair, sedan

Sedan chair, carriers of. *See* Chairman; chairmen

Seddon, John:
print of, 40. 237

Sedgwick, Mr and Mrs:
SH visited by, 12. 222

Seditious meetings bill. *See under* Parliament: acts of

Sedley, Catherine (1657–1717), m. (1696) Sir David Colyear, 2d Bt; cr. (1699) Bn Portmore, and (1703) E. of Portmore; she was cr. (1686) Cts of Dorchester; James II's mistress:
daughter of, 9. 244n, 28. 389n
equal of Nell Gwyn, 33. 564
Radcliffe's conversation with, about pox, 39. 54–5
Selwyn, Mrs, told by, that Graham was Ds of Buckingham's father, 18. 193
witticism by, on meeting other royal mistresses at Windsor, 33. 528–9, 34. 260

Sedley, Sir Charles (ca 1721–78), 2d Bt; M.P.:
  Cornish's situation resembles that of, **10.** 190
  Kingston, Ds of, tells, of intention to live in France, **24.** 59n
Sedley, Henry. *See* Venables Vernon, Henry
Seduction. See under Holcroft, Thomas
Sedworth, Hants:
  Smith of, **12.** 154n
Seed; seeds:
  Cotton, Mrs, spreads, in Gloucester Cathedral for dead daughter reincarnated as a bird, **34.** 16, **35.** 154
  Egmont, Comtesse d', sends, to Bns Hervey, **31.** 103
  from SH and the Vyne, sent to Bentley, **35.** 185, 198
  grass, *see* Grass seeds
  HW orders, through Mme du Deffand, **6.** 305, 306, 308
  HW procures, for Montagu, **9.** 155
  HW receives, from Mann for Galfridus Mann, **18.** 560
  HW sends, to Conway, **37.** 370
  ivy, **21.** 457, 466
  Mann sends, to Galfridus Mann, **18.** 330, 560
  —— wishes to send, to HW, **20.** 25
  Mann, Galfridus, gets, for Duncannon, Whithed, and others, **20.** 25
  melon, *see under* Melon seeds
  of cypresses, **35.** 161
  pimpernel, sent to Marquise de Broglie, **30.** 251
  tea, *see under* Tea
'Seeds of Poetry and Rhyme,' by HW:
  sent in letter to West, **13.** 121–3
Seeley, B.:
  Stowe by, verses in, ascribed to Cts Temple, **35.** 75n
Seeman, Mrs Frances:
  HW's bequest to, **30.** 372
  HW's 'poor old pensioner,' **30.** 372
'See the Conquering Hero Comes':
  band plays, to compliment M. of Granby, **38.** 401n
Sefton, Cts of. *See* Craven, Hon. Maria Margaretta (1769–1851); Stanhope, Isabella (1748–1819)
Sefton, E. of. *See* Molyneux, Charles William (1748–95); Molyneux, William Philip (1772–1838)
Segar, Sir William:
  Honour, Military and Civill by, extracts from, **13.** 48n, **28.** 39n
Seghezzi, A. F.:
  Crescimbeni's *Dell' Istoria* annotated by, **40.** 299n
Segni, Bp of. *See* Angelis, Cesare Crescenzi de
Segni, Duchessa di. *See* Orsini, Eleonora (d. 1634)
Segovia (Spain):
  to Saragossa from, **31.** 21
Segrais. *See* Regnauld de Segrais

Segretario dell'ambasciate:
  York, Cardinal, to have, **19.** 416
Séguier, Antoine-Louis (1726–92), advocate-general of parliament of Paris:
  HW scandalized by speeches of, **41.** 346
  indictment by, of condemned books: Du Deffand, Mme, sends, to HW, **4.** 470, 472, 483; essence of condemned books in, **8.** 177; parliament declines to publish, **4.** 450n, 470
  La Galaisière answered by, for cour des aides, **5.** 59
  La Harpe censured by, **7.** 375
  Maupeou's address elicits reply from, **5.** 66n
  (?) mentioned by Mme du Deffand, **6.** 168
  parliament at odds with, **4.** 450, 470, 491
  requisition of, registered, **4.** 491n
  speaks at lit de justice, **5.** 61, **8.** 166
Séguier, Nicolas-Maximilien, Comte de St-Brisson:
  social relations of, in Paris, **5.** 191, **7.** 310, 349–50
  wife of, **5.** 192n
Séguier, Sidoine-Charles-François (1738–73), Marquis de St-Brisson:
  D. of Richmond's social relations with, **7.** 301
Ségur, Comtesse de. *See* Froissy, Philippe-Angélique de
Ségur, Joseph-Alexandre-Pierre (1756–1805), Vicomte de:
  Auteuil visited by, **7.** 348
  Luxembourg, Mme de, fond of, **7.** 200
  social relations of, in Paris, **7.** 348, 351, 352
  verses by, **7.** 200
Ségur, Philippe-Henri (1724–1801), Marquis de:
  La Tuilerie visited by, **7.** 345
  model for letter to Orléans sent to, **8.** 183
  social relations of, in Paris, **7.** 296, 345
Seignelay, Marquis de. *See* Colbert, Jean-Baptiste (1619–83); Colbert, Louis-Jean-Baptiste-Antonin (1731–living 1780)
Seignelay, Marquise de. *See* Béthune, Catherine-Pauline de (b. 1752); Montigny, Marie-Anne de (1748–67)
Seigneur, Le. *See* Le Seigneur
Seilern, Gräfin von. *See* Solms-Sonnewalde, Charlotte von
Seilern, Christian August (1717–1801), Graf von; Austrian ambassador to England 1763–9:
  assemblies and dinners given by, **10.** 138
  biographical information on, corrected, **43.** 132
  Council considers complaint by, on mob stopping his coach, **23.** 7
  dances at Court, **38.** 402
  Du Châtelet thrusts himself between Chernyshev and, at George III's birthday ball, **23.** 125–6
  fierce and stiff, **23.** 125
  Guerchy and foreign ministers meet with, **38.** 369–70
  HW at dinner given by, **38.** 365
  HW calls, 'his Uprightness,' **32.** 19

HW jokes about formality of, **31**. 150, 152, **38**. 250

HW prefers Belgioioso to, **31**. 152

Hertfords entertain, at card party, **32**. 19n

irresistible in mourning cloak, **32**. 20

Leopold's notification of accession delivered by, in London, **22**. 345n, 361n

receives company after Francis I's death, **32**. 19

wife told by, to continue dinner and assembly despite daughter's death, **38**. 510

Seilern, Maria Anna von (1743–63), m. (1761) Raimund, Graf von Vilana Perlas:

death of, a widow, **38**. 510

Seillern. *See* Seilern

Seilly, Mme de:

Conti has son by, **32**. 329n

Seine, River:

Avon paltry enough to be, **39**. 76

Boulogne on, **7**. 326n

Burgoyne's defeat reported from, **32**. 392

Choiseul-Beaupré, Comtesse de, embarks on, **5**. 352

'dirtier ditch,' **35**. 342

'filthy,' **1**. 113n

floods, **4**. 331

Hertford's new Paris house on, **38**. 351

island in, **6**. 459n

Marly machine turned by, **21**. 354n

Paris linen washed in, **10**. 232

Paris mob drowned in, **23**. 218

Pascal nearly thrown into, **7**. 117n

Place de Grève on, **5**. 190n

Plaine de Grenelle near, **3**. 118n

Port-à-l'Anglois on bank of, **5**. 79n

St-Port on, **5**. 386n

Watelet's Moulin Joli in middle of, **28**. 215n, 220

water of, injurious, **3**. 234

Seine, Rue de, in Paris:

La Rochefoucauld, Hôtel de, in, **6**. 26n, **7**. 226n

Seinsheim, Adam Friedrich von (d. 1779), Bp of Würzburg 1755–79, of Bamberg 1757–79:

Nuremberg to be punished by, **21**. 29

Seise. *See* Sezi

Selby, Henry Collingwood (ca 1748–1839), D. of Northumberland's steward:

avarice of, **11**. 16–*17*, 50, 56

Berrys' landlord, **11**. 1n, 17n, 50, 54

Cathcart, Lord, rents Twickenham house of, **11**. 60

Davenport, John, quarrels with, **12**. 169

SH visited by, **12**. 241

SH visitor sent by, **12**. 242

Twickenham resident, **42**. 486

Selby, William (fl. 1483), porter of Warwick Castle:

grant to, **15**. 221

Selden, John (1584–1654), jurist and scholar:

engraving of, **16**. 65

Kent, Lady, said to have married, **1**. 39n

Mason uses notes of, for *Caractacus*, **29**. 64

portrait of, **2**. 327–8, 329

Whitelocke persuaded by, to safeguard Inigo Jones's things, **40**. 208n

Select Collection of Poems, A, ed. John Nichols:

Cato's speech in, **42**. 18

Select Fables of Æsop. See under Æsop

Select Society:

Townshend becomes member of, **15**. 42n

Seleucia, Abp of. *See* Doria Pamfili, Giuseppe

Seleucidæ:

Russian crimes reminiscent of, **22**. 54

Seleucus:

Demetrius, son of, **18**. 421

Self:

deaths are felt most, when they relate to, **35**. 127

Self-criticism:

HW's reflections on, **18**. 518

Self-denial:

HW's reflections on, **31**. 268

Self-denying Ordinance. *See under* Parliament: acts of

Self-interest:

HW's reflections on, **16**. 283, **30**. 273

Selfishness:

HW's reflections on, **11**. 56

Self-knowledge:

HW's reflections on prevalence of, despite maxim to the contrary, **25**. 539–40

Self-love:

HW's and La Rochefoucauld's reflections on, **24**. 373

hopes never to want compassion, **7**. 361

inclusiveness of, **34**. 5–6

love of virtue founded on, **28**. 122

Self-murder. *See* Suicide

Selibury family:

Horton formerly the seat of, **10**. 333

Selim III (1761–1808), Sultan of Turkey 1789–1807; 'Grand Signor':

at war with Russia, **11**. 161

'Selima,' HW's cat:

Gray laments death of, **13**. 22, 23–4

St-Simon knows Gray's ode on, **35**. 238–9

(?) Selincart, Henriette (ca 1644–80), m. (1662) Israel Silvestre:

tablet to, **7**. 277

Selkirk, E. of. *See* Douglas, Charles (1663–1739); Douglas, Dunbar (1722–99)

Selle, Charles de (1730–86):

(?) attends session of parliament of Paris, **8**. 173

Selle, Marie-Françoise de (b. 1746), m. (1763) Anne-Joseph-Marie de Verdusan, Marquis de Miran:

social relations of, with Comtesse de la Marche, **7**. 301

Sellières. *See* Scellières

Sellwood, Thomas:

transcribes letters of Lady Rachel Russell, **28**. 85n

Selsey, Bn. *See* Peachey, James

Selsey, Sussex:
bishop of, **16.** 109
Seltzer, Christopher:
letter by, about Chatterton, **34.** 149n
Selva Florida, Conde de. *See* Ponce de Guerrero,
Don Manuel
Selwin, Charles (ca 1716–94), banker at Paris:
Conway addressed in care of, **37.** 309, 315
—— to receive packet from, **20.** 285
HW addressed in care of, at Rue Ste-Apol-
line, **37.** 99, 105
HW asks Hertford to notice, **38.** 266
HW asks West to address letters to, **13.** 239
HW jokes about 'drawing on' for compli-
ments, **30.** 20–1
HW receives letters through, **30.** 19
HW sends presents through, **17.** 181, 183
HW's esteem for, **31.** 31–2
HW thanks Hertford for attentions to, **38.**
277–8, 281
Hertford entertains, at dinner, **38.** 269
—— neglects, **31.** 31–2
Hervey, Augustus, addressed in care of bank
of, **26.** 29
Lincoln orders gold scissors sent to, from
Siries at Florence, **17.** 93
Mann sends letter to HW through, **17.** 115
Maynard receives letter through, **18.** 371
Pitt, Anne, sends letter from, to HW, **31.**
31–2
Veers forges signature of, **19.** 507
Wilkes asks, about Webb's indictment for
perjury, **38.** 297
Selwin, Richard:
Selwin, Charles, partner of, **13.** 239n
Selwyn, Albinia (ca 1715–39), m. Thomas Town-
shend:
marriage of, **13.** 3n
Selwyn, Charles (1689–1749), Maj.; M.P.:
biographical information on, corrected, **43.**
256
'dirty pensioner,' **19.** 25
naval investigation proposed by, **19.** 25
Selwyn, George Augustus (1717–91), M.P.; wit;
HW's correspondent:
Ampthill visited by, **32.** 395, 398
anecdote by, about Paris president's family
arguing about names of dinner courses,
22. 163
Bath visited by, **3.** 265, **30.** 145, 242, **32.** 341
Bedford, Ds of, accompanied by, to Paris, **22.**
105, **38.** 178
Bedfords entertain, **9.** 233
Bentheim, Gräfin von, has business relations
with, **4.** 11
—— sent compliments by, **30.** 213
Bentley recommended by HW as deputy to,
30. 154
Bibliothèque du Roi visited by, **7.** 323
Blake's confession of murder elicited by, **38.**
193–4
Board of Trade engrosses, **33.** 136

Board of Works position of, attacked by
Burke, **33.** 169
Bolingbroke 'advised' by, to seek rehabilita-
tion by HW, **30.** 252
brother of: **37.** 56n; asked to recommend
Maynard to Mann, **20.** 451
Bunbury, Lady Sarah, accompanied by, **3.**
201, 208
Bute's levee attended by, **10.** 35
Byron's trial will bring, from Paris, **38.** 503
Calais to be visited by, **7.** 85, 86, 88, 151
—— visited by, **7.** 89
Campbell asked by, if George III knows where
expedition goes, **37.** 531
Caraman's correspondence with, **7.** 217
Carlisle, Cts of, corresponds with, **7.** 63
—— visited by, **33.** 236
Carlisle, E. of, friend of, **3,** 152n, **5.** 361, **6.**
74, **7.** 185
—— in Paris with, **3.** 152, 154, 170
——'s correspondence with, **7.** 63, **30.** 266
——'s election as K. T. unsuccessfully pressed
by, **30.** 246
—— to receive *Historic Doubts* from, **30.**
251–2
Carlisles may be accompanied by, to Cheltenham, **34.** 13
—— to meet, en route to London, **32.** 103, 108
Cassiobury Park visited by, **32.** 77
Chanteloup to be visited by, **7.** 124
Chantilly to be visited by, **7.** 151, 152
characteristics of: does not go out until late
evening, **30.** 278, 281; does not pretend to
be supernatural, **30.** 274; drowsy, **30.** 207;
equally uninterested in condition of France
and England, **30.** 264; forgets engagements,
30. 259, 280; witty, **30.** 210, 283
Charles I's bust erected by, **1.** 341, **30.** 121n
Cheltenham may be visited by, **34.** 13
—— visited by, **31.** 287
Choiseul's reprimand of Fréron known to, **3.**
228
chokes and falls, with injured head, at Coventry's, **38.** 348
Coke's death may prevent Thomas Hervey
from publishing letter of, **30.** 120–1
Compiègne visited by, **38.** 413
Conti visited by, at Paris, before going to
Fontainebleau, **38.** 452
Conway's refusal of salary told to, **3.** 371,
372
Cornbury visited by, with Abergavenny and
Mrs Frere, **20.** 182
Coventry, Cts of, shows costume for King's
birthday to, **9.** 253–4
Coventry, E. of, butt of joke by, **30.** 210, **31.** 85
Craufurd attended by, **3.** 363
—— says HW finds, witty, **3.** 374
——'s death rumoured by, **3.** 156, 160, 162,
171, 193
Craufurd, Mrs, pitied by, **33.** 221
'Crawford, Mrs,' lamented by, **30.** 137

criminals interesting to, **9.** 133
cup used by Q. Charlotte labelled by, **33.** 28
dead people preferred by, **41.** 111
death of, **11.** 182, 183, **30.** 283, **34.** 106–7
designing of coat-of-arms aided by, **9.** 186
did not 'mimize,' **33.** 6
difficulties of, in Paris, **7.** 110, 112, 114, 189
dolls suggested as joke between Mme du Deffand and, **3.** 377
Dorcas, Mrs, entertained by, **9.** 47
Du Deffand, Mme, aided by: in purchases, **4.** 27, 28, 39; in sending parcels and letters, **3.** 160, 183, 184, 191, 199, 200, 201, 203, 210, 213, 219, 221, 364, 367, 371, 373, 374
—— believes, to be at Newmarket, **3.** 291
—— buys porcelains for, **4.** 69
—— confided in by, **7.** 146–7, 150, 189
—— contrasts Bièvre and, **6.** 241
—— does not know plans of, **4.** 131
—— doubts promised Paris visit of, **30.** 262
—— gives commissions to, **3.** 292, 295, 297, **4.** 28, 67–8, 189, **7.** 120, 123, 124–5
—— gives fan of, to Duchesse de Choiseul, **3.** 89, 111
—— 'good old friend' of, **30.** 267
—— hears nothing of, **3.** 291, 389, **4.** 32, 116, 119, 124, 224, 229, 233, 428, **7.** 88, 167
—— hopes, will write about HW, **3.** 220
—— hopes to see, **5.** 406, 413
—— inquires about, **4.** 69, **5.** 184, 228, 351, **6.** 187, 214, 381, **7.** 6, 168, 174, 187, 235
—— introduced to HW by, **30.** 203–4
—— mentions, **3.** 46, **4.** 163, 180, **7.** 132
—— permitted to speak of HW to, **3.** 157
—— pleased by probable Paris visit of, **30.** 218
—— receives compliments of, **6.** 74
—— receives fan from, **3.** 87, 89
—— receives gifts from, **7.** 131
—— receives regrets from, about delayed Paris visit, **7.** 34
—— receives tea from, **3.** 87, **7.** 423
——'s correspondence with, **3.** 41, 49, 57, 59, 87, 213, 221, 222, 227, 231–2, 237, 238, 252, 258, 265, 268, 291, 292, 295, 297, 317, 324, 329, 380, 381, 384, 387, 395, 401, 407, **4.** 17, 19, 21, 35–7, 62, 67–8, 73, 83, 84, 108, 124, 125, 189, 191, 229, 236, 332, **5.** 8, 127, 309, **6.** 116, 296, 302, **7.** 36, 37, 65, 72, 89–91, 93–5, 99, 101, 102, 105, 106–8, 112–14, 117, 119–20, 124, 126, 127, 156, 190–4, 196, 198, 206, 207, 213, 217, 226–8, 233, 422, 438, 440–2, 444, 446–8, 458, 460, **30.** 261, **43.** 81
——'s debts to: **3.** 308; to be paid by HW, **3.** 224
—— seldom talks of HW with, **3.** 186
—— sends letter through, **7.** 82
—— sends parcels by, **7.** 96–7, 101
——'s French criticized by, **5.** 316, 319
——'s opinion of, **3.** 162, 168, 170, 181–2, 191, 199, 204, 205, 210–11, 252, 355, 360, 374, 376–7, 381, **4.** 125–6, 249, **5.** 189, 193, 421, **6.** 390, **7.** 67, 78, 105–6, 130, 146, 150, 154–5, 155, 195
——'s portrait copied for, **8.** 216
——'s portrait desired by, **4.** 32, 35
——'s relations with, **3.** 355, 360, 391, **4.** 33, 156, 267, 435, **6.** 390, **7.** 199
——'s verses applied to, **3.** 204
—— talks with, **3.** 162, 184, 353
—— to inform, of Pulteney's death, **3.** 365
—— to receive news of HW from, **3.** 182, **7.** 84, 87
—— to receive *Pièces fugitives* through, **3.** 152
—— to send letter by, **7.** 40, 87
—— to send parcels by, **7.** 75–6, 82, 86, 141, 143, 151
ebony cabinet of Mme de Sévigné given to, **7.** 80
Edgcumbe's dropsy will sadden, **30.** 165
election contest prevents, from coming to London, **30.** 162
election defeat of, **33.** 227
election problems of, **33.** 221, 227–8
election progress of, pleases HW, **30.** 165
England to be revisited by, **33.** 64
English great men ridiculed by, **30.** 217
English princes overly tenderly treated by, **30.** 217
epigram by, on Elizabeth Chudleigh lamenting her mother, **37.** 447
executions and corpses delight, **9.** 133, 362, **20.** 181, **29.** 206, **30.** 120, 121
eyes of, 'demure,' **35.** 170
Fagnani, Marchesa, vexes, **7.** 143, 148
Fagnani, Marchese, corresponds with, **7.** (?) 133, (?) 135, 137, (?) 145, 146, 152
Fagnani, Maria, adored by, **7.** 43, 50, 77, 130, 131, 133, 139, 145–8, 150, 154, 174, 178, 181, 198, 217, **36.** 205
—— and, compared with Abishag and David, **33.** 142
Fagnani, Maria, arrives with, **33.** 134
—— entrusted to, **7.** 152, **33.** 107
—— given money by, **7.** 145, 154
—— probably not to be redemanded from, **30.** 268–9
—— suspected of being daughter of, **7.** 145
—— to be fetched by, from Paris, **33.** 67
—— to be obtained by, **33.** 27, 36–7
—— to be taken by, to England, **7.** 133, 137, 145, 146, 150
—— to receive gift from, **6.** 482
Fagnanis' claim on Maria Fagnani feared by, **33.** 197
——'s correspondence with, **7.** 133
Fagnanis make agreement with, **7.** 77–8
—— might poison, **30.** 266
falls asleep at gaming-table after heavy losses, **35.** 192–3, **38.** 481–2
Fanshawe invites, to dinner, **30.** 252

[Selwyn, George Augustus, *continued*]
—— recommended by, to Mme du Deffand, 4. 238

Fanshawes introduced by, 6. 402n

Fitzpatrick's parody of advertisement by, 29. 30, 375–6

Fitzroy's letter to Mme du Deffand forwarded by, 3. 227

Foire Ste-Ovide visited by, 7. 322

fondnesses of, for: anything fashionable in Paris, 30. 210; Carlisle's children, 30. 265; executions, 9. 133, 362, 20. 181, 29. 206, 30. 120, 121; Fagnani, Maria, 7. 43, 50, 77, 130, 131, 133, 139, 145–8, 150, 154, 174, 178, 181, 198, 217, 30. 263, 265, 268–9; 'foreign ecstasy,' 30. 239; 'Raton,' 30. 265

Fox, C. J., under tutelage of, 4. 287n

Fox, Henry, considers his letter of dismissal a trick by, 6. 24

—— jokes about occupations of, 30. 191

——'s correspondence with, 30. 171, 176, 201, 202

—— to give pictures to HW through, 30. 171

franks letter for HW, 1. 292

French of, 3. 161, 170, 7. 150

French people misjudge, 31. 43

gambles, 3. 208, 308, 4. 75, 282, 289

gambles no more, 4. 191

Gem, Dr, to accompany, 7. 43

—— to be repaid by, for book for HW, 37. 242

Geoffrin, Mme, consents to, having a copy of her portrait, 30. 213

George III and Gower concerned about absence of, from Parliament, 38. 492n

George III and Q. Charlotte to visit, at Matson, 34. 7

George III not willingly offended by, 38. 506

Gloucester borough canvassed by, 39. 180

Gloucestershire left by, for Richmond, 33. 533

Gordon, Lord George, answered by, 33. 181

—— brought by, to White's, 33. 169

Gray and HW expect visit from, 13. 177, 180

Greville criticized by, 9. 354

Grignan visited by, 7. 80, 33. 85

HW abuses, for sending him to Ashridge, 30. 120

HW accompanies, to shops in Paris, 7. 323

HW advises, on Q. Charlotte and Kennedy, 30. 254

HW aided by, in search for burglars, 9. 133

HW and, may dine with T. Townshend, 30. 261

HW and, may live to be the least mad in England, 30. 137, 210

HW and, might visit G. J. Williams at Bath, 35. 89n

HW angry at, for expressions used in dictated letter, 7. 93

HW applies quotation from Pope's *Satires* to, 30. 271

HW asks: for Sourches's address, 30. 277; to carry subscriptions and letter to England,

15. 8; to deliver message to Marquise de Broglie, 30. 251; to execute commissions punctually, 30. 214; to forgive him for cancelling Matson and Bath visits, 30. 144; to make inquiries to the Guerchys for him, 30. 213–14; to obtain proof of 7-shilling piece from the Mint, 30. 276; to pay his debt to Guibert, 30. 251; to provide Mme du Deffand's correct address, 30. 266–7; to tell Fox that publications have been sent, 30. 206; to thank Carlisle, 30. 258; to write his verses to Carlisle under paintings at Castle Howard, 30. 257–8

HW calls, 'foolish boy,' 30. 85

HW cannot attract, 34. 13

HW compares, with Cleitus, 30. 216

HW dines in party with, 30. 252

HW disagrees with, over Norfolk dukedom, 30. 259

HW discusses America with, 6. 151

HW discusses Swift's *Letters* with, 10. 219

HW entertains: at dinner, 11. 13; at dinner at SH, 6. 64n; at SH, 10. 127, 38. 276

HW executes commissions for: in Paris, 30. 211; punctually, 30. 214; to get prints, 30. 217, 264; to Mme St Jean, 30. 210, 213, 217, 219; to purchase lottery tickets, 30. 251

HW expects, at SH, 32. 197, 35. 200

HW frequently visited by, during illness, 30. 201

HW 'friendly' to, about change in administration, 30. 201

HW from age of 8 had known, 34. 106

HW gives arms in painted glass to, 1. 341

HW has not seen, 33. 307

HW hears calamities from, 33. 348

HW hears dismal stories from, 32. 77

HW hears from, about Mme de Bentheim, 39. 4

HW hopes to see, in London, 40. 113

HW informed by, of Henry Fox's decline, 30. 218

HW inquires about travel plans of, 30. 149

HW intends to visit, 38. 16

HW jokes about: (?) March and, 30. 149; political indifference of, 30. 271; Vice-Chancellor of Oxford and, 30. 149

HW jokingly forbids, to visit SH, 30. 282

HW leaves subscriptions for Middleton's *History of . . . Cicero* with, 37. 98

HW loves to please, 30. 256, 268

HW may receive letter from Henry Fox by, 30. 179

HW meets, during Gordon riots, 33. 184

HW mentions, 5. 75

HW misunderstands Mme du Deffand concerning, 3. 397

HW not sorry for discontent of, 33. 27

HW offers copy of Mme du Deffand's picture to, 30. 252

HW pleased at decision of, to live in Richmond, 30. 279

HW preferred company of, to that of wiser men, **32.** 191

HW receives money from, **7.** 411

HW's affection for, **11.** 182, **33.** 348

HW scolds, **4.** 84

HW's correspondence with: **7.** 378–81, 396, **17.** 2n, **30.** (?) 117–18, 120–1, 124, 133, 136–51, 154–8, 160–6, 171–2, 179, 203–21, 239, 250–2, 254–83, **38.** 167, 469, **40.** 113, 151, 163; MSS of, **36.** 310

HW's *Counter Address to the Public* criticized by, and sent to Guerchy, **30.** 176

HW's distresses would gladly be exchanged by, **30.** 266

HW sees, **33.** 107, 136

HW sends ballad to, **30.** 124

HW sends 'grubs' to, **30.** 144

HW sends letter by, **7.** 43

HW sends money to Mme du Deffand through, **7.** 131, 133, 135

HW sends parcel by, **7.** 131

HW sends wine to Lady Diana Beauclerk by, **42.** 451

HW sent by, to Ashridge, **30.** 120n

HW's enthusiasm for, **32.** 327

HW serves tea to, at SH, after Hampton Court visit, **39.** 104

HW's *Historic Doubts* criticized by, **30.** 252

HW's *Historic Doubts* joked about by, **2.** 31, **31.** 138

HW's host, **1.** 340n

HW shown Queensberry House by, as 'concierge,' **33.** 541–2

HW's inclusion in public prayers hoped for by, **5.** 247

HW's intentions to exchange meetings and visits with, **30.** (?) 118, 120, 139–43, 150, 151, 155, 161, 166, 171, 179, 244, 258, 259, 277, 280, 281

HW's letter explained by, **7.** 145

HW's letters to, shared by G. J. Williams, **30.** 218

HW's letter to be explained by, **7.** 146

HW's letter translated by, **7.** 84

HW's long friendship with, **30.** 150, 268, 279, 281, 283, **34.** 106

HW's opinion of, **5.** 201, **31.** 214

HW's pendant in his letters, **4.** 31

HW's praise of Castle Howard will please, **30.** 256

HW's publications given to, **30.** 238, 251, 278

HW's query from, **32.** 395

HW subscribes to Middleton's book through, **37.** 98

HW surpassed by, in wit, **32.** 42n

HW thanks: for introduction to Mme du Deffand, **30.** 203–4; for kindnesses, **30.** 281; for present, **30.** 136; for promising Bentley a position, **40.** 163

HW to be visited by, at SH, **33.** 427, **34.** 49

HW to desert, for Ds of Grafton, **38.** 176

HW to dictate letters to, **7.** 192, 197

HW to have news of Mme du Deffand from, **7.** 83, 154

HW to send parcels by, **5.** 205, 207, **7.** 40

HW to talk with, **3.** 374, 375, 400

HW to visit, **9.** 243, 293, **40.** 113

HW uncertain of address of, **30.** 136–7

HW urges return of, to England, **30.** 251

HW versifies epigrams of, **14.** 88

HW visited by: **25.** 274–5, **30.** 266, **32.** 139, 398, **33.** 6; at SH, **9.** 186, 417, **12.** 229, 237, **33.** 468; with Maria Fagnani, **33.** 347

HW visits: **6.** 83n, 86; at Matson, **35.** 152–3, **39.** 179, 183; in Cleveland Court, St James's, **33.** 236; in evenings, after he has walked, **34.** 62

HW wishes, not to concern himself with Fitzpatrick genealogy, **33.** 414

HW wishes to dine with G. J. Williams and, **40.** 151

HW would have liked company of, at Castle Howard, **30.** 258

hanged in effigy by political opponents, with 'Mimie' pinned to breast, **34.** 227–8

has *malapropos* almost as much as *apropos*, **33.** 307

health of: **5.** 227, **7.** 138, 140, 147; fever, **32.** 108, **33.** 533, **34.** 7; tooth pulled, **9.** 52

Hénault sent message by, 4 125

Heralds Office searched by, for precedents of K. T. elections of under-age men, **30.** 246

Hertford, Cts of, charms, **38.** 527

—— entertains 'Mimie' and, **33.** 314n

—— talks to, **38.** 481

Hertford, E. of, discusses HW's itinerary with, **38.** 16

—— entertains, at Fontainebleau, **38.** 465

—— hears news of HW from, **38.** 176

—— sees, in Paris, **38.** 409

Hervey, Thomas, might publish letter to, **30.** 121

—— presses, for debt to Coke, **30.** 120n

Holland, Lady, visited by, **32.** 398

Hollands attract, **3.** 375

house of, at Matson, **12.** 154–5

Howe, Hon. Charlotte, provided with humorous letter-ending by, **9.** 140

inquires about soldier, **4.** 5

in the country, **3.** 394

Isle-Adam visited by, **3.** 345, 349

Italy to be visited by, **7.** 6, 37, 43, 44

Jamaica or Barbados losses reported by, **33.** 266

Keene, Col., on Hampton Court Green visited by, **33.** 347

leaves Paris, **3.** 204, 205, 210, 213, 371–4, 376, **7.** 44, 46

Le Neve, Isabella, 'particular friend' of, **30.** 133

letter from, about Princesse de Talmond, **38.** 469

letters of: **11.** 88n; described by Mme du Deffand to HW, **33.** 55–6

[Selwyn, George Augustus, *continued*]

Llanthony gateway begged by, **35.** 154–5

London addresses of: Chesterfield St, **30.** 216, 261; Cleveland Court, **30.** 277; Curzon St, **30.** 138; Stanhope St, Berkeley Sq., **30.** 262

London reached by, **38.** 527

—— to be visited by, **3.** 384, **7.** 151, 155

Louis XIV would have called, 'votre partialité,' **30.** 257

Lucan, Lady, entertains, at musicale, **33.** 139

Luckyn the village counterpart of, in wit, **33.** 206, **34.** 22–3

Lyon to be visited by, **7.** 80, 133

Lyttelton, Charles, calls, 'good creature,' and defends him until profanation incident, **30.** 89

Mackreth's speech partly written by, **32.** 215

Maillé spoken of to HW by, **3.** 373

Mann has heard much of, without seeing him, **22.** 105

March, E. of (D. of Queensberry), accompanies, in Paris, **3.** 349, 350, 360, **38.** 506

—— does not visit 'Mie Mie' and, **39.** 262

—— keeps, in France till Parliament meets, **38.** 465

—— left by, at Richmond, **32.** 139

—— liked by, **3.** 374, **6.** 74, 186

Marchais, Mme de, would delight, **30.** 265

Marie Leszczyńska admired by, **30.** 204, 218–19

——'s Court frequented by, but Princesse de Talmond cheats him there, **38.** 465, 469

Matson and Danson Hill punned upon, as homes of, **33.** 55

Matson might have been stripped by, of Charles I's relics before George III's visit, **34.** 16

—— occupied by, **7.** 162, 168, 169

may fear that Mme du Deffand shows his letters around, **4.** 229, 231

may have mentioned HW's 'Modern Gardening' to Mme du Deffand, **5.** 195n

Maynard, friend of, **43.** 254

Maynard visited by, in Essex, **30.** 88n

Mézières, Marquise de, described by, **37.** 353

Midleton, nephew of, **30.** 144

'Mie Mie' or 'Mimie' of, see Fagnani, Maria

Milan to be visited by, **7.** 44, 50

—— visited by: **7.** 65; to fetch Maria Fagnani, **33.** 27n, 33n, 36n

'Mimie' or 'Mie Mie' of, see Fagnani, Maria

Mistley visited by, **30.** 51

Monson intimate with, **9.** 369n

Montagu inquires about, **9.** 267n

Morfontaine known to, **3.** 219

mother of, **9.** 104n, **14.** 120n

mother's witticism worthy of, **23.** 94

never reads, **29.** 271

Newcastle's appearance derided by, in stage whisper, **9.** 233

Newmarket may be visited by, **30.** 244

—— to be visited by, **38.** 440

Newton the principal of, at Oxford, **30.** 88

Nivernais's *Jardins modernes* given to, **12.** 260

not expected soon, at Richmond, **34.** 13

Onslow succeeded by, as paymaster of Board of Works, **20.** 518

Opéra-Comique attended by, **3.** 345

Ossory, Lady, to be visited by, **32.** 103

—— told by, that HW is out of spirits, **33.** 251

owner of Grignan identified by, **34.** 85, 86

Oxford criticizes, for recommending La Rochefoucauld's maxims, **30.** 88

Oxford misconduct of, **30.** 85, 88–9

Paris cannot be left by, without E. of March, **38.** 506, 516

—— left by, for Newmarket, **38.** 440

—— may be visited by, **4.** 173, **6.** 204

—— pleases, **3.** 374, 376–7, **4.** 199

—— to be left by, **7.** 83–6, **38.** 516

—— to be visited by, **3.** 83, 119, 137, 317, 324, 338, 376, **4.** 170, 343, **5.** 55, **7.** 36–9, 42, 63, 70–3, 75, 124, 126, 127, 130, **31.** 126

—— visited by, **7.** 76, 131, 321, **30.** 171, 218, 240, 250, **31.** 136, **33.** 64, **38.** 409, 448, 485

Parliamentary voting by, on land tax, **30.** 243n

passport wanted by, **7.** 36–8, 40, 65, 66, 123, 152

paymaster of Board of Works, **9.** 181

Pelham, Frances, quarrels with, at Ranelagh, for giving rose to the Rena, **32.** 6n

Piozzi, Mrs, fails to understand joke by, **9.** 254n, 256n

—— quotes joke by, **10.** 238n

Pitt (E. of Chatham) might brain, with crutch, **30.** 217

—— ridiculed by, **30.** 216

plans of, **3.** 268

political interests of, **4.** 189

portrait of, by Reynolds, **9.** 417

pretends to be shocked by Henry VIII's statue, **9.** 70n

purchase at Scarlett's displeases, **30.** 149

Queensberry, Ds of, routs, from warm room at her ball, **38.** 343

rebel lords' executions witnessed by, **19.** 298n

reputed Van Dyck may interest, **30.** 149

return from Paris postponed by, **38.** 492, 516

returns to London, **33.** 106

returns to Richmond, **34.** 28

Richmond preferred by, to Gloucestershire, **30.** 279

—— residence of, **11.** 148, **31.** 287, **42.** 451n

—— visited by, with 'Mie Mie' instead of going to Castle Howard, **39.** 262, 266

riddle by, **28.** 102–3, 107, 108, **43.** 295, 296

Rigby and C. H. Williams visit, at Oxford, **30.** 330n

Rigby reports probable expulsion of, from Oxford, **30.** 85

—— to dine with, **30.** 280

Rochechouart attracts, 4. 71
Rochers ground plan owned by, 41. 258
Roubiliac's bust of Charles I placed by, at Matson, 30. 121n
sacrament profaned by, 30. 89
St Giles's vault visited by, 20. 181
St John, Hon. Henry, friend of, 4. 73n
Saunderson, Sir William, asked by, for lord high steward's wand, 9. 38–9
Sceaux visited by, 7. 322
Scottish officer meets, on Bexley Heath, 18. 524
secure during ministerial change, 30. 201
Sévigné, Mme de, admired by, 3. 405
—— interests, 30. 206–7
——'s cabinet given to, 33. 150–1
——'s letters collected by, 3. 405n
silver of, stopped at customs, 7. 77
sister of, 13. 3n
sleeps when bored, 5. 205, 7. 86
social relations of, in Paris, see index entries ante 8. 511
source of story about Atterbury and Wynne, 13. 33
Storer visits, 33. 236
story told by, 33. 314
suggests that Mme du Deffand send him Wiart, 3. 393
takes house for Lord Carlisle, 1. 326n
Thistle order sought by, for Lord Carlisle, 39. 97
Thomas, Lady Sophia, might have medicine brought from Paris by, 38. 511, 514
'Tonton' commented on by, 11. 13
Townshend brother-in-law of, 19. 444n
Townshend, Vcts, abuses, behind his back, 30. 51
—— discovered by, in Roman Catholic chapel, 10. 216
—— has bag of counters thrown in her face by, 30. 50
—— infuriated by, 9. 47
—— tells HW of probable departure of, from London, 30. 139
Townshend family annoyed with, for revealing their faro-playing, 30. 69
Turgot's reforms would not interest, 30. 264
(?) Usson, Comtesse d', disparages friend of, 7. 94
Vauxhall visited by, 10. 127
war may prevent Paris visit of, 7. 27, 32
Westminster Abbey visited by, with Abergavenny, 20. 181–2
Weymouth's pun on marriage answered by, 9. 236
White's frequented by, 9. 133, 145, 202, 10. 259
Wiart's correspondence with, 6. 225
—— sends wine to, 5. 370–1
—— to get lodging and carriage for, 7. 127
(?) Williams, Sir C. H., expects to meet, at SH, 30. 118

—— friend of, 11. 93n
Williams, G. J., corresponds with, 30. 120, 125, 171, 176–7, 203, 238–9
—— scolds, for reading HW in translation, 30. 238
—— urges, to persuade HW to join in Bath visit, 30. 125
will swear child to Lord March, 32. 178
windbound at Calais, 38. 527
Winnington's wit equals that of, 15. 331
wit can be struck by, out of politics, 32. 38
wit of, 3. 161, 162, 168, 204, 374
witticisms by: 4. 23, 6. 64, 12. 258, 263, 271, 13. (?) 200, 14. 171, 28. 173, 204–5, 250, 383–4, 29. 185, 190, 193, 195, 206, 271; about French ladies making scaffolds to watch English sail by, 37. 537; about Lyttelton's being called, 'nuncio,' 35. 195; about Ponsonby 'passing the money bills' at Newmarket, 20. 7; HW does not expect to receive, from him, 30. 208; HW fond of, 30. 208; on Amelia, Ps, 9. 318; on Anson getting Rochester title, 35. 170; on Ashburnham, 9. 153; on Bedford as 'mamamouchi,' 39. 107; on Bethell, Mrs, 9. 41; on Boone's marriage, 10. 32–3; on Bute's levees, 10. 35; on Cabinet's including D. of Richmond, 36. 222; on Calcraft and butlers, 32. 38; on Chartres's display of indecent buttons, 25. 409; on collar-day and May-day, 25. 275; on Cooke's sermon, 20. 186; on Coventry, Cts of, 9. 254; on Deering, Mrs, 9. 188; on Duncan, Dr, and Lady Mary, 9. 360, 24. 49; on Falmouth, Cts of, not walking at Coronation, 38. 122; on Fawkener, 9. 145; on Fox, Charles, and Mrs Robinson, 35. 523; on Fox, Henry, and Pitt, 33. 393, 36. 209; on George III, 10. 219; on going from Gloucester to Ludgershall, 33. 228; on Gordon, Lord George, as candidate for Ludgershall, 34. 181; on Gordon, Lord George, as sole Opposition voter, 33. 169; on Guilford, Cts of, 9. 188; on HW's Historic Doubts, 31. 138; on Hardwicke's getting title for Anson, 35. 170; on Harrington, Cts of, 9. 387; on Haszlang, 9. 185; on Hesse, Landgrave of, 9. 30; on Hillsborough, 9. 265; on Irish union, 9. 265; on Jacobites at St James's Palace, 9. 321; on Jeffreys, 9. 145; on Jersey, E. of, 9. 339; on Leake, 20. 391; on Leicester House, 9. 202; on Louis XVIII, 39. 477; on Lovat's head being cut off and sewn on again, 37. 267–8; on Lyttelton and Miss (?) Ashe, 35. 195; on Newcastle making Darlington a paymaster, 30. 125, 35. 263; on Newcastle's levees, 10. 35; on Oxford chancellors and the Pretender, 32. 3; on Oxford vice-chancellor mistaking Lady Sarah Lennox for Q. Charlotte, 21. 531n; on Pelham's plate being used by toad-eaters, 35. 220–1; on Pelham, Lady Cath-

[Selwyn, George Augustus, *continued*]
erine, **35**. 170; on Pembroke's bridge, **9**. 52; on Pitt's gout, **21**. 43; on Pomfret, E. of, **9**. 153; on Pomfret, E. of, and the Parks, **30**. 120; on Rockingham, Cts of, **9**. 116; on St John, Mrs, and her 'breastwork,' **32**. 251; on Sandwich, E. of, **20**. 155; on sea-war and 'continent' admiral, **35**. 261; on Sulkowsky's diamonds, **33**. 280; on Townley's *High Life Below Stairs*, **31**. 14; on Townshend, Vcts, and her fear of fires, **33**. 195; on Vane (perhaps made into epigram by HW), **30**. 125; on waiter at club, convicted of robbery, **9**. 256; on Winchilsea, Cts of, **9**. 185; outmoded at White's, **10**. 259; thrown away at Newmarket, **30**. 224; to D. of Richmond, when presented to Louis XV, **22**. 163; to Wilkes, quoting Pope on ear-cropping, **38**. 223

Selwyn, Col. John (1688–1751), M.P.:
biographical information on, corrected, **43**. 113, 243
Caroline, Q., had, as treasurer, **20**. 114n, **23**. 94n
Danson Hill rented by, **33**. 55n
daughter of, **13**. 3n
Gloucester city controlled by, through water supply, **35**. 153
HW satirizes, **13**. 14
House of Commons calls no re-election for, despite appointment to Household by George II, **20**. 247n
Scadbury Park owned by, **35**. 153n
son of, **9**. 47n
son's character discussed by, **9**. 47
son's death will distress, **37**. 310
son's recovery pleases, **37**. 94
Walpole, Sir Robert, advised by, to decline pension, **17**. *329*, **18**. 465
wife of, **4**. 73n, **9**. 104n, **14**. 120n, **20**. 114n, **23**. 94n

Selwyn, John (ca 1709–51), the younger, George Selwyn's brother; M.P.:
appearance of, sleek, well, and rubicund, **37**. 80
balls attended by, make him ill, **37**. 50
brother of, **18**. *451*, **37**. 56n, **43**. 254
business prevents, from writing to HW, **37**. 28
Conway, Bn, met by, in Park and at Sir Robert Walpole's, **40**. 27–9
Conway, H. S., awaited by, in hackney coach, **37**. 13
—— congratulated by, on HW's approach, **37**. 13
—— hears from, of Townshend-Winnington duel, **37**. 112
—— mentions, **37**. 16
——'s correspondence with, **37**. 45, 111, 114
—— sees, at Bns Hervey's, **37**. 88
death of, **37**. 310
enlistment of, amuses Conway, **37**. 125
Good gives supper to, **37**. 14

HW asked by, to recommend Maynard at Florence, **18**. 367, 451
HW's correspondence with, **37**. 56, 71, 85, 95, **40**. 27–9
HW's love for, **37**. 56, 88, 89, 95
HW to receive compliments of, **37**. 6, 15, 26
health of: bark alleviates, **37**. 89; better, **43**. 180; blisters applied, to ease fever, **37**. 94; doctors hopeful about, **37**. 93; ill, **37**. 77; illness approaches crisis, **37**. 88; pleuritic fever, **37**. 50; recovered, **37**. 56; recovery of, pleases HW, **37**. 95–6; Tunbridge visit revives, **37**. 80–1
Hervey, Bns, entertains, **37**. 88
—— receives HW's compliments through, **40**. 28
(?) Houghton to be visited by, **30**. 64
Maynard a friend of brother of, **43**. 252, 254
Parliamentary vote by, on privately-raised regiments, **26**. 19
Robinson's ball may be described by, to Conway, **37**. 114
starving in coach at Conway's door, **37**. 13
(?) Walpole, Sir Robert, advised by, to decline pension, **18**. 465
(?) —— met by, on his journey to London, **18**. 536n
Williams replaced by, as paymaster of the marines, **19**. 341n

Selwyn, Mrs John. *See* Farrington, Mary

Selwyn, William (d. 1702), Brig.-Gen.:
royal occupation of Matson described by, **1**. 341

Selwyn. *See also* Selwin

Selwyn family:
'gentleness' of, **30**. 133
HW and Sir C. H. Williams would dislike presence of, at Houghton, **30**. 64
HW dines with, **36**. 1
Houghton probably not to be visited by, **30**. 65
Le Neve, Isabella, may have been 'jolted' by, **30**. 133

Semele:
Stormont, Cts of, compared with, **38**. 60
Williams, Sir C. H., compared with, **30**. 159

Semele. See under Handel, George Frideric

Semenovsky Guards, in Russia:
Catherine II proclaimed by, **22**. 61n

Seminara città (Italy):
earthquake account mentions, **25**. 376

Semiramis, legendary Q. of Assyria:
HW compares Catherine II to, **22**. 71, 253
See also under Catherine II

Semiramis. See under Ayscough, George Edward (d. 1779); Voltaire

Sémonville, Comte and Marquis de. *See* Huguet de Sémonville, Charles-Louis

Sempill, Francis (d. 1748), styled Lord Sempill (Jacobite peerage):
agent of English Jacobites in Paris, **18**. 426

Sempill, Hew (1688–1746), 12th Bn Sempill, 1727; army officer:
  regiment of: at Perth, **37**. 249n; called the Black Watch, **18**. 236n
Sempill, Hon. Sarah (d. 1751), m. (1750) Patrick Craufurd:
  (?) Selwyn grieved for death of, though he had never seen her, **30**. 137, **33**. 221
Semplice spiritosa, La:
  Vanni, impresario of, takes refuge in church, **19**. 356n
Semplicetta pastorella:
  Mann sends, to HW, **17**. 181, 212
  Rich, Elizabeth, desires, **17**. 166
Sempy, P. A. (living, 1720), glass-painter:
  Elias's designs executed by, **7**. 282
Sénac de Meilhan, Gabriel de (1736–1803):
  intendent of war, **6**. 311
  La Tuilerie visited by, **7**. 345
  social relations of, with La Reynières and Mme du Deffand, **7**. 345
Senapisms:
  applied to Mann's feet, **25**. 560
Senart, forest of, in France:
  Louis XV loses way in, **3**. 291n
Senate:
  Florentine, escorts Madonna dell'Impruneta, **30**. 4
  Genoese, *see under* Genoa
  of Bologna, **22**. 236, **25**. 85
  of Sweden, **18**. 305
  Roman: *conservatori* represent, **19**. 428; duels not prevalent in, **25**. 31; House of Commons compared to, **9**. 3; York, Cardinal, receives visit of, **19**. 428
  Venetian, *see under* Venice
Senate House, Cambridge:
  examinations in, described by Gray, **13**. 78–9
  juniors at Cambridge elect a fictitious Hardwicke in, **38**. 363
Senator; senators:
  at Florence and Rome, keep Adonis wigs with robes of ceremony, **24**. 32
  Florentine: **22**. 363n; Englishmen may become, **35**. 52n; St John celebration avoided by, **18**. 251
'Senator of Rome, while Rome survives.' *See under* Addison, Joseph: *Cato*
'Senatus, St':
  Cincinnati interpreted as, in Paris, **33**. 431
Senauki, Q., m. Tomo Chachi; Indian chieftainess:
  costume and missing eye of, **42**. 236
  HW sees, at Eton, **42**. 236
  Oglethorpe brings, from Georgia, **42**. 236
  swims from Chelsea to Fulham, **42**. 236
Seneca, Lucius Annæus (ca 3 B.C.–A.D. 65); philosopher; dramatist:
  Apocolocyntosis by, **28**. 280
  Du Deffand, Mme, mentions, **3**. 328
  HW mentions, **3**. 151
  HW quotes, **12**. 265, **28**. 280

  paintings of: (?) by Giordano, **10**. 346, **15**. 205; by Guercino, **35**. 38; (?) by Meulen, **10**. 346
Senegal:
  England to demand, from France, **21**. 526
  —— to keep, by peace terms, **22**. 76n
  Lauzun captures, **7**. 123
  war extends from, to Russia, **21**. 290
Senegal River:
  French surrender Ft Louis on, **21**. 212n
'Sénèque.' *See* Barthélemy, Jean-Jacques
Senesino. *See* Bernardi, Francesco
Sénezergues de la Rode, Étienne-Guillaume (1709–59), brigadier:
  wounded at Quebec, **21**. 338
Senhouse, Grace (ca 1695–1755), m. (1721) Richard Boyle, 2d Vct Shannon, 1699:
  ball given by, attended by royal children, **19**. 398n
  daughter of, **18**. 481
Seni. *See* Sani
Senile consumption. *See under* Consumption
Senlis (France):
  Du Deffand, Mme, receives letter sent from, **6**. 235
  Grand Cerf, Le, inn at, **7**. 342
  visitors to: Craufurd, **5**. 290; HW, **5**. 90, **7**. 316, 342
Sennert, Daniel (1572–1637), physician:
  Institutiones medicinæ by, Gray's note on, **14**. 127
Senneterre, Comtesse de. *See* Crussol, Marie-Louise-Victoire de
Senneterre, Charles-Emmanuel (1752–83), Marquis de:
  social relations of, with Duchesse de la Vallière, **5**. 233
Senneterre, Marie-Charlotte de (1750–94), m. (1770) Louis de Conflans, Maréchal d'Armentières:
  social relations of, in Paris, **5**. 233, **6**. 221, **7**. 345, 349, 352
Senonches (France):
  Louis XV purchases, **4**. 419
Sénozan, Comte de. *See* Olivier, Jean-Antoine
Sens, Abp of. *See* Albert de Luynes, Paul d' (1703–88); Loménie de Brienne, Étienne-Charles de (1727–94)
Sens, Mlle de. *See* Bourbon, Élisabeth-Alexandrine de
Sens (France):
  Marie-Josèphe buried at, **3**. 263
Sense:
  HW's reflections on, **33**. 12
Sense of St Peter, The. See under Cooke, William
Senses, the:
  possible improvement of, **15**. 168
  variations in, in individuals, HW's reflections on, **41**. 394–5
Sensibility:
  HW's reflections on, **32**. 344–5

Sensible, French ship:
  Adams sails in, to France, **39**. 345n
Sensidoni. *See* Sansedoni
Sensitive plant:
  HW's nerves as tender as, **24**. 272
Sentença que em 12 de Janeiro de 1759 se proferio:
  Almada gives, to Mann, **21**. 275n
  being printed at Rome, **21**. 275
Sentiment; sentiments:
  Du Deffand, Mme, defends, **4**. 289
  —— on, **3**. 381
  HW annoyed by the word, **4**. 303
  HW's reflections on absurdity of, when reduced to human infirmities, **9**. 83
Sentimental Journey through France and Italy, A ('*Sentimental Travels*'). *See under* Sterne, Rev. Laurence
Sentinel; sentinels:
  in Boboli Gardens, Florence, **24**. 204
  in Germany, may be frozen, **21**. 369
  in London park, accosted by mad parson, **17**. 197
Separation; separations:
  Paris does not have, **31**. 92
Septchênes. *See* Le Clerc de Septchênes
September:
  a dry month, **1**. 271
  a quiet month, **1**. 256
  'betweenity' of, **32**. 282
  Greenwich, Bns, enlivens, with speaking trumpet, **39**. 251
  HW usually dislikes, **35**. 397
  partridge shooting in, **1**. 256, 263
Septennial Act (Bill). *See under* Parliament: acts of; Parliament, Irish: acts of
Sept-et-le-va; Septleva. *See under* Faro
Septizonium:
  Severus's, **14**. 240
Sepulchral Monuments of Great Britain. *See under* Gough, Richard
Sepulchre; sepulchres. *See* Tomb; tombs
Sepulchre, St, church of. *See* St Sepulchre
Sépulcre, Rue du, in Paris:
  Aulan lives in, **8**. 11
'Sequel to Gulliver's Travels,' by HW:
  HW sends, to Lady Ossory, **32**. 71–3
Sequin; sequins. *See* Ruspi; Zecchins
Serafini, ——, opera singer:
  HW's opinion of, **9**. 157
Seraglio:
  HW jokes about, **31**. 162, 279, **32**. 5
  inside accounts of, valuable, **42**. 183
Séran, Comtesse de. *See* Bullioud, Marie-Marguerite-Adélaïde de
Serani, Elisabetta:
  paintings by, in Colebrooke's sale, **23**. 569n
Serao, Francesco (1702–83), physician:
  Philip Anton's incapacity considered by, **21**. 325, 329, 337
Serapis, English ship:
  defeated by John Paul Jones, **28**. 467n

Seravalle. *See* Serravalle
Seravezza (Italy):
  iron worker goes to, from Pistoia, **18**. 242
  Mann orders gun barrels from, **18**. 243
Serbelloni, Gen.:
  Austrians to join, in Saxony, **21**. 229n
  Daun relieves, at Prasek, **21**. 95n
  Puebla ordered by, to join P. Charles near Prague, **21**. 96n
Serbelloni, Fabrizio (1695–1775), cardinal, 1753:
  Benedict XIV tells, to negotiate with Francis I about Monte Santa Maria, **20**. 428
  nuncio to Cologne, Saxony-Poland and the Empire, **20**. 428n
Serchio, river in Tuscany:
  Brunelleschi advises diversion of, in wartime, **20**. 514
  Regency orders, to be diverted into Lucca, **20**. 514–16, 521–2
Serenade; serenades:
  at Naples, **19**. 439
  Mann avoids, **17**. 105
  on Lung'arno at Florence, **17**. 95, 105
  See also Cocchiata
Serenata:
  at Haymarket Theatre, for Frederick II's birthday, **38**. 1
  for George III's birthday, **38**. 87
  performed at London opera, **20**. 49
'Serendip, Isle of':
  Ceylon called, in *Arabian Nights*, **25**. 277
  See also Ceylon
Serendipity:
  HW alludes to, **31**. 325
  HW explains, **20**. 407–8
  history of, **26**. 34–5
  Mann's explanation of, **20**. 415
Sérent-Kerfily, Marquise (later Duchesse) de. *See* Montmorency-Luxembourg, Bonne-Marie-Félicité de
Sérent-Kerfily, Armand-Louis (1736–1822), Marquis (later Duc) de:
  Mme Geoffrin's social relations with, **7**. 327
  wife of, **6**. 105n
Sergaux, Alice (d. 1452), m. 1 Guy de St Aubyn; m. 2 (1406 *or* 7) Richard de Vere, 11th E. of Oxford; m. 3 (before 1421) Nicholas Thorley:
  burial of, at Colne Priory, **43**. 114
Sergeant; sergeants:
  Cope's, *see* Molloy, ——
  HW mentions call of, **10**. 259
  pen brought to HW under conduct of, **37**. 67
  recruiting, Townshend, George, says lords are all, **37**. 446
  Walpole, Edward, restrained by, **21**. 240
Sergeant-at-arms. *See* Serjeant-at-arms
Sergères. *See* Surgères
Sergison (formerly Warden), Thomas (1701–66), of Cuckfield, Sussex; M.P.:
  Middlesex opposed by, in Sussex by-election, **30**. 20

Séricourt, Marie-Michelle de (1713–78), m. (1737) Augustin-Joseph, Comte de Mailly, Marquis d'Haucourt:
marriage of, **7**. 216
Series of Adventures in the Course of a Voyage, A. See under Irwin, Eyles
Series of English Medals, A. See under Perry, Francis
Sérieux, Le, French ship:
captured off Cape Finisterre, **19**. 410
La Jonquière on board, **20**. 38n
Namur defeats, **20**. 38n
Sérigny. *See* Le Moine de Sérigny
Seringapatam (India):
Cornwallis promises capture of, **11**. 350
——'s victory at, **11**. 186n
Serious Call. See under Law, William
Serious matters:
HW's aversion to, **10**. 171–2, 184
Serjeant-at-arms, of House of Commons. *See* Bonfoy, Nicholas (d. 1775); Odiarne, Wentworth (d. 1762)
Serjeant's Inn, London:
Pratt writes from, **40**. 79
Serjeantson, Elizabeth (d. 1744), m. Thomas Norton:
son bargains for better house for, at Preston, **38**. 454
Serle, Elizabeth, m. Thomas Trevor, 1st Bn Trevor:
genealogy of, **10**. 352
Serle St, Lincoln's Inn Fields, London:
White, bookseller in, **36**. 216n, **42**. 93n
Serlio, Sebastiano:
ceiling designed by, in inner library of St Mark's, Venice, copied for ceiling of gallery at Houghton, **18**. 63n, **32**. 141n
Serlupi-Crescenzi, Teresa (d. 1779), m. (1723) Antonfrancesco Acciaioli:
Bolognetti, Contessa, to meet, **18**. 65
Loreto visited by, for daughter's wedding, **18**. 65
Mann takes Marchesa Bichi to call on, **19**. 407–8
Rome left by, for Florence, **19**. 408
Sermon; sermons:
at Mayfair Chapel, on Frederick, P. of Wales, **20**. 241, 243–4
charity, by Bp Porteus at Twickenham, attended by HW, **31**. 359
Churchill's, **22**. 261–2
city, in London, attended by Wilkes, **23**. 208
Cooke's, against Middleton, **20**. 185–6
Coyer's *De la prédication* ridicules, **31**. 113–14
futility of, for reforming morals, **31**. 114
HW calls, 'dullest of all things,' **34**. 115
HW disgusted by, in bad English, **30**. 25
HW's mock, for Lady Mary Coke, **31**. 25, 423–6, **43**. 330
HW wishes Hannah More to write, vindicating Providence for permitting French Revolution, **36**. 285–6
Henley's, on Pelham and Lady Catherine, **35**. 170–1
in French style, **9**. 274
Methodist, **39**. 493
Nowell's, deplored by HW, **28**. 40
on earthquakes as judgments, **20**. 133–4, 154–5, 158
Wesley's, **35**. 119
See also under Ashton, Thomas; Atterbury, Francis; Mason, William; Wesley, John; Whitefield, George
Sermoneta, Duca di. *See* Gaetani, Michelangelo (ca 1689–1760)
Sermoneta-Gaetani, Duchessa di. *See* Corsini, Maria Teresa (b. 1732)
'Sermon on Abstaining from Birthdays,' by HW:
MS of, **43**. 172
'Sermon on Painting, A,' by HW:
HW writes, for father's amusement, **13**. 13
Sermon Preached at the Visitation at Basingstoke, A. See under Toll, Frederick
Sermon Preached Before the University of Cambridge, A. See under Lort, Michael
Sermon Preached by Order of her Imperial Majesty. See under Hinchliffe, John
Sermon prêché . . . sur la tombe de Pierre. See under Vorontsova, Ekaterina Romanovna
Sermons. See under Whitefield, George
Serocold, Walter (1758–94), naval officer:
returns from East Indies, **2**. 303n
Serocold, Mrs Walter. *See* Richardson, Mary
Seroux d'Agincourt, Jean-Baptiste-Louis-Georges (1730–1814), Chevalier d'Agincourt:
HW given comments by, on *Anecdotes of Painting*, **42**. 65–9
HW's correspondence with, **42**. 63–9, 101–4
HW visited by, at SH, **42**. 102
Hamilton, Lady, recommends, to HW, **39**. 291, **42**. 102
Histoire de l'art par des monuments by: **42**. 64, 102; engravings for, **42**. 64, 103
prints by, of Duc de Chartres, valet, and ornaments, **42**. 64
Serpent, English ship:
French ships pursued by, **37**. 246
Serpent; serpents:
Conway and Lady Ailesbury left to converse with, **38**. 14
flying, **37**. 117
ministry to strangle, **35**. 559
on monument in Trinity Hospital, Greenwich, **16**. 89
Serpent (musical instrument):
accompanying chanters at Mass, **4**. 210–11
Serpentine River, Hyde Park, London:
construction of bridge over, **37**. 560
Moone's cottage on, **32**. 135n
Serra, Angelina, m. —— Durazzo:
daughter of, **22**. 236

[Serra, Angelina, *continued*]
York, D. of, attentive to, at Genoa, **22.** 201, 236, 251, 260, 267, 553
Serragli, Via de', in Florence:
Casa Feroni in, **17.** 33n
Rinuccini, Palazzo, on corner of, **17.** 137n
spelling of, corrected, **43.** 234
Serrant, Comte de. *See* Walsh, François-Jacques de
Serrao. *See* Serao
Serrati, Santi, of Florence:
Lady Orford's Declaration signed by, **43.** 288
Serravalle (Italy):
Austrians capture, **19.** 297
Rossi, governor of fortress of, **19.** 78n
Spaniards capture, **19.** 84
—— to retire through, **19.** 292
Serre, Del. *See* Del Serre
Serre, Étienne de (b. 1698):
(?) attends session of parliament of Paris, **8.** 173
Serres de la Tour, Alphonse:
Courier de l'Europe edited by, **25.** 71n
(?) Lamotte, Mme, aided in her *Mémoires* by, **11.** 5n
Serristori, Signora. *See* Del Monte Santa Maria, Giovanna (b. 1684); Guadagni, Maria Maddalena Teresa (1719–97)
Serristori, Andrea (1716–95):
Gabburri, Mme, dismisses, **17.** 136, 157
(?) Hervey's memorial to, **12.** 63n
Modenese princess gives cane and snuff-box to, **17.** *64*, 70
Regency appoints, to attend Modenese princess, **17.** 64
(?) Ricasolis entertain, **17.** 136
Serristori, Anna Maria Luisa (1722–98), m. (1741) Cavaliere Anton Vincenzo Bartolini Baldelli:
Bartolini to wed, **17.** 40, 53
Serristori, Anton Maria (1712–96), senator:
Albizzi challenges, **17.** 381
—— has, as cicisbeo, **19.** 322
—— regains, after his marriage, **20.** 95
Guadagni, Maddalena, to wed, **19.** 322
(?) Hervey's memorial to, **12.** 63n
(?) Mann asked by, to get from HW a design for machine for raising water, **21.** 348
Pistoia and Leghorn visited by, for affairs of his farm, **20.** 442
sister of, to wed Bartolini, **17.** *40*, 53
Suares, 'Cecco,' rebuked by, **17.** 149
travel used by, to dissipate grief, **20.** 442
wedding festivities for, expected, **19.** 461
Serristori, Averardo (1675–1744), cavaliere:
(?) dies a year after Electress, **19.** 23
(?) Electress leaves money and silver to, **18.** 169
(?) —— leaves pension to, **19.** 23
Rinuccini's adherent, **17.** *473*
Sersale, Antonio (1702–75), cardinal, 1754:
archbishopric of Naples to go to, **20.** 429

Benedict XIV told by, that the March moon caused Livizzani's death, **20.** 429
Jesuits' suppression not demanded from, at Conclave, **23.** 527n
Maria Amalia will enjoy, **20.** 429
Sertor, Gaetano (fl. 1774–ca 1792), abbé:
Conclave dell'anno 1774, Il, by, **24.** 64–5, 69–70, 73
Sertorius. See under Corneille, Pierre
Servan, Gen.:
dismissed from Pyrenees command, **34.** 186n
Servandoni, Chevalier Jean-Jérôme (1695–1766), architect; scene-painter:
death of, **7.** 397
Ranelagh fireworks supervised by, **20.** 47n
spectacles staged by, **4.** 211, **20.** 47n
Servant; servants:
acting by, at Sluys, without knowing languages, **38.** 10
agent; agents: Beaulieu's, to consult Cts of Cardigan, **10.** 189; HW's, discusses business with him, **31.** 366; HW's, in Devonshire, **42.** 377; HW's, to go to Orford's executors, at Houghton, **42.** 356
Ailesbury, Cts of, to send, for copper plate, **37.** 525
Albany, Cts of, maintained with, by Cardinal York, **25.** 150
Amelia, Ps, leaves legacies to, **33.** 535
—— refuses to dictate voting by, **25.** 489n
——'s: visit SH, **42.** 96; warn her of fire, **38.** 527
Americans said to be carried on shoulders of, **23.** 420–1
Amyand's, **9.** 138
Angelelli's, sent to Young Pretender for message, **22.** 374
appears in picture of Mme du Deffand, **12.** 14
arrows meant for their sovereigns intercepted by, **36.** 245
at: Adderbury, **10.** 312; Chatsworth, **9.** 295; Cowdray, **12.** 16; Drayton, **10.** 90; Hall Place, **9.** 92; Ham Common play, armed like conspirators, **33.** 370; Houghton, bad, **32.** 142, 143; Kimbolton Castle, **10.** 77; Petworth, **9.** 98; Windsor Castle, **10.** 137; Wrest, **9.** 4
attachment of, **32.** 53
Aylesford's, attentive to Waldegrave in illness, **36.** 270
bailiff: Granville's, on Jersey, **35.** 161; Wakering's, at Essington, *see* Wilkinson, James
ball given by, **9.** 295
Bath's, do not dare tell of daughter's breaking window, **30.** 89
Bathurst's, attempts assassination, **9.** 84
Beauchamp to be accompanied by, to SH, **39.** 154
Beauclerk's, inherits his clothes, **36.** 192
Bedford's, *see* Butler, Robert
Bedfords': **11.** 201, 284; brings message to HW, **40.** 65

bedmakers, at Oxford, 35. 368

Berrys': 12. 163, 211; see also Croft, William; James; Sally

Berwicks', do not speak English, 10. 131

Bessborough's, die of fever and sore throat, 21. 362

Bichi, Marchesa's, breaks leg, 19. 408

Biron, Duchesse de, not allowed to have, in prison, 12. 61

—— to have been betrayed by, 39. 492n

Boscawen's, 9. 141

Braitwitz to give, to Mme Vitelli, 18. 334

Bristol collects, for Spanish embassy, 21. 202

——'s, carry him, 33. 148

Browne, Lady, may be affected in health by loss of, 31. 286

——'s, tells HW of Lady Blandford's illness, 31. 195

Buccleuch's, visit SH, 12. 246

Bull sends note by, 42. 184

Burlington's, delivers letter and china to Mrs Bracegirdle, 25. 74

Burney, Fanny, employs Moss as, 42. 296n

—— loses Jacob Colomb as, 42. 290

butler; butlers: at Trinity Hospital, Greenwich, 16. 85; Braber or Draper was, to Vcts Townshend, 30. 224n; Clement XIV's, dies of chocolate that poisoned his master, 24. 49; Conway's, see Lantun; Dacre's, see Murcott, John; Gerrard is, to Cts of Albemarle, 41. 333; Gower, Cts, rolled in carpet by, to put out fire, 33. 460n; HW's, see Jones, Henry; Hapsburgs originated in, 20. 409; Mann's, sends ices every day to D. and Ds of Cumberland, 25. 644; Mann's, see also Beaushini or Brianchini, Giuseppe; Montagu, Charles's, to pay for muff, 10. 151; (?) Somerset, D. of, and, 37. 307; Wilkes's, see Brown, Matthew

Catherine of Aragon attended only by, 18. 537

chairman; chairmen: boar and sow run away from, 37. 347; burglars pursued by, 9. 133; costume of, 10. 204; Lodomie sends insults to Lady Caroline Petersham by, 37. 355

chambermaid; chambermaids: Braber or Draper, Molly, succeeds Dorcas as Vcts Townshend's, 30. 224n; Coventry wishes to take, in vehicle, 20. 324; Duncannon, Lady Caroline's, 30. 90n; Eleonora, Ps, desires HW's room for, in Venice, 17. 74; lying, 38. 471; of Cts of Orford, 19. 238; recommended to Lord Talbot, 11. 278; shares Ds of Northumberland's bed, 32. 128–9; terrible to be, of Lady Mary Coke, 37. 572; ticks at chandler's shop, 33. 201; Walpole, Lady, has, 10. 22–3

Chichester, Bp of, has, 12. 109, 110

Chute's, see Martelli, Francesco

Clarence, D. of, locks up, at night, 34. 72

coachman; coachmen: at Rome, resents being treated as valet, 22. 286, 300n; Azzi mis-

treated by, at Florence, 17. 488; Du Deffand, Mme, has, 32. 260; Du Deffand (Mme)'s, has accident, 3. 55, 56; Du Deffand (Mme)'s, see also Decla; Electress's, separated from postilion, 19. 370; Eleonora's, see Bacci, Lorenzo; Ferrers's, cries all the way to scaffold, 21. 399; Florentine, crack whips, 17. 488; Frederick, P. of Wales's, see Biddel, Thomas; Bradshaw, Robert; HW mentions, 32. 384; HW's, 11. 153, 370, 12. 185, 193; HW's, admires pig, 37. 347–8; HW's, seduces cook, 32. 291; HW's, tells him of Lady Blandford's illness, 31. 195; HW's, to bring bootikins from London, 10. 320; HW's, see also Jenkins, John; Peter; in bas-relief of Margaret Nicholson, 11. 363; in chaise, 35. 306; Lauraguais's, English, goes to England to buy horses, 39. 22; Leopold's, is Clement XIV's near relation, 23. 118; Masserano's, in livery, 38. 399n; ministers', tumbles off box, 17. 503, 18. 21–2; Modenese princess gives money to, 17. 65; Northumberland, D. of, said to be descended from, 20. 124–5; old English, brought to Florence by eccentric English-woman, 24. 260; Orford, Cts of, robbed by, 19. 88; Orford's, 17. 503, 18. 21–2; Rice, Lucy, has, 9. 49; stolen watch of, to be returned by Maclaine, 40. 64; Townshend, Vcts's, see Osborne, John

Coke, Lady Mary, dismisses, at Genoa, 23. 553

—— has difficulties with, 31. 175–6

—— learns news from Cts of Suffolk's, 31. 129

—— might have had to appear before public tribunal because of, 23. 535

Cole's: 2. 136, 166; copies inscription at Burghley House, 10. 347; see also Wood, James; Wood, Thomas

companion, Lady Mary Coke has, 39. 7

concierge, at Chantilly, 31. 46

confectioner: Clement XIV's, poisoned, 24. 43; HW must borrow, for dinner, 39. 404

conversation about religion should be restrained in the presence of, 10. 176

Conway's: at Park Place, retained by Lord Malmesbury, 15. 334; Conway sends, to get desserte from Custom House, 37. 328; HW to answer by return of, 37. 391; return to England with him, 37. 461; wear favours, 32. 125; see also Genet or Gennet; Mathews; Tom

cook; cooks: Berwick resembles, 38. 406; Conway's, sets out from Dover to Sluys, 38. 4; Craon's, asks guests if they stay for supper, 18. 122; Derby's, resents serving supper at 3 A.M., 24. 310; Du Deffand, Mme, in a passion with, 39. 269; French, in Florence, 19. 356–7; French, may be replaced by Negro butchers, 24. 21; French, waste English money, 37. 172; French antechambers full of, 31. 55; Gaubert said to have

[Servant; servants, *continued*]
been, **33**. 499; German Protestant, of Cts of Hertford, attacked by Gordon rioters, **33**. 188–9; Gloucester, Ds of, has, good at black cock pies, **36**. 324; HW mentions, **38**. 157; HW must borrow Ellis's, **39**. 404; HW's, from town, incompetent, **31**. 147; HW's, has dropsy after miscarriage, **33**. 291–2; HW's, in Reggio, **17**. 57; HW's, seduced by coachman, **32**. 291; Lovat's, poisons enemies, **19**. 380; Mann's, **17**. 57; Mann's, *see also* Bambi, Michele; Mann's, prepares dinners for D. and Ds of Cumberland, **25**. 644; Montfort's, *see* Joras; Newcastle's, **17**. 485n, **20**. 17, *see also* Chloé; St John offers to preside over, at Mann's house, **21**. 533; to join Young Pretender in France, **18**. 434; Walpole, Bns, has, **18**. 4; (?) Walpole, Horatio (1678–1757) has, **35**. 65

cook-maid, has affair with D. of St Albans, **21**. 172

Corsini's body rescued by, **23**. 276

costumes of, magnificent in mourning period, **10**. 204

courier: Barrymore, Lady, steals, from Lady Mary Coke, **31**. 184–5; Coke, Lady Mary, believes her life saved by, from Maria Theresa's plots, **31**. 183

Cowper's: Mann might have to tip, at christening, **24**. 219; takes Mann's letter to Conway, **22**. 345n

Craon, Princesse de, attended by, **18**. 196

Craons': **17**. 9; wait badly on dinner guests, **21**. 248

Craven, Bns, said to have amour with, **36**. 210

Crawford's, *see* Kopp

Crewe, Mrs, sends lights by, to coach accident, **39**. 454

Cumberland's, placed by George III, **32**. 65

dairy maid: Boadicea's, **31**. 326; HW asks Lady Sophia Fermor not to dress like, **30**. 29

doorkeeper: Electress's, **17**. 236; Mann's, *see* Bianchi, Antonio

Douglas, Ds of, carries body of, tied to her chaise, **39**. 9

drawer; drawers, *see* Waiter; waiters

dresser, Anne Kemp is, to Princesses Amelia and Caroline, **19**. 427n

Duchess of Newcastle's, *see* John

Du Deffand, Mme, has 10 or 12, **4**. 386
—— resents Craufurd's gratuities to, **41**. 4
——'s annuities for, **4**. 365–6, 387

Electress's livery, taxed on Electress's pensions to them, **19**. 23–4
——'s provision for, **18**. 169

Ellis's, visit SH, **12**. 241

English: employed by Chartres in London, **33**. 399n; of Ds of Richmond, uses slang French to get from Paris to Aubigny, **40**. 28; of Q. of Denmark, **23**. 386n; Orford, Cts of, does not take, to England, **19**. 61

English gentlemen should never be unattended by, **18**. 344

English liberality to, imitated by Duc and Duchesse de Mirepoix, **20**. 89

English officers', ignorant of languages, **37**. 134

'factotum,' Conway's, *see* Stokes

'fanciulla,' Marchesa Gerini's, **17**. 41–2, 62

farmer, HW's, sent to Hampton Court for portraits, **10**. 103

female servitors represented in statues at Herculaneum, **16**. 89

femme-de-chambre, friend of, has amour with Comtesse d'Artois, **36**. 220, 223; *see also* Chambermaid

firearms learnt by, **24**. 512

Fitzpatrick's hair curled by, **32**. 200

Fitzroy Scudamore leaves nothing to, **33**. 554

Fitzwilliam's, received legacies, **34**. 59–60

floorsweepers at Versailles, **35**. 112

Florentine, must be searched for brand-marks, **20**. 144

footboy, HW's: **11**. 51; always drunk, **21**. 300

footman; footmen: actor worse than, as son-in-law, **38**. 367; Aiguillon, Duchesse d', has, open her coach door, **22**. 163; Almodóvar's, left by him at brothel door with flambeaux, **24**. 413; at Kimbolton Castle, **10**. 77; Beauclerk, Lady Diana, has, **12**. 170; Bettina's, from Naples, absconds after her illness, **17**. 421; Biblical misreading by, **32**. 268; Brown, Sir Robert, tells, to carry map of London by-lanes in pocket, **25**. 609n; carry effigy in chair, **17**. 391; coach flanked by, bare-headed, **42**. 380; Conway's, reports on Gordon riots, **33**. 188; Craggs and Moore start as, **20**. 181; Dacre's, *see* Blake, Daniel; dismissed by Mrs Craster and hired by Cts of Harrington, **38**. 421; Dysart, Cts of, takes, in boat, **39**. 311; eccentric Englishwoman does not have, for her carriage, **24**. 260; Eleonora's, running, **17**. 39; Fox's, fires at highwayman, **33**. 267n; Fox's father was, **18**. 450; Fox Strangways, Lady Susan, eludes, when eloping, **38**. 367; Frederick, P. of Wales's, ordered to give letter to Harrington, in Yonge's presence, **19**. 175; French, always powdered, but may wear handkerchiefs at necks, **35**. 112; French, carries his lady's goblet to every dinner she attends, **20**. 340; French, enters Lady Mary Churchill's bedroom, **20**. 339–40; French, shows Lady Mary Churchill all sanitary conveniences, **20**. 339; French, to join Young Pretender, **18**. 434; French, wear dirty nightcaps, **31**. 55; French, wins fortune, but forgetfully climbs in back of coach, **20**. 195; French antechambers full of, **31**. 54; French running, father of Ps Eleonora's son, **17**. 39; gallery for, in Drury Lane Theatre, **20**. 231; George III's, may have written verses,

33. 299 (see also Toplin); Giovanni Gastone de' Medici's, see Giuliano; HW accompanied by, while coursing, 30. 81; HW and nieces with, in little boat, 39. 311; HW expects, only to execute errand, 25. 337; HW's, 11. 276, 12. 140, 141; see also Colomb, James; Fitzwater, John; John ——; John —— (ca 1773–91); Monnerat, David; Sibley, James; HW's, carry him in and out, 31. 402n; HW's, robbed by Maclaine, 40. 64, 65; HW's, to accompany him to Houghton, 18. 498; HW's new, cannot read, 25. 118; HW's new, puts letter in post by mistake, 25. 118; HW scolds, unfairly, 32. 326; HW talks French only to, 37. 110; Hertford, Cts of, has, wearing orange-tawney, 32. 191n; James II's, becomes father of Sir James Gray, 20. 409; Kingston, Lady, has lover fetched by, 34. 258; lace stripped from livery by, 23. 535n; laugh at HW and Mary Rich, 35. 276; Lobkowitz's, in new liveries, bearing torches, 37. 288; Mann's, running, 17. 81; Marlborough sends, to show observatory to Archduke, 33. 531n; Masserano's, in livery, 38. 399n; Mirepoix followed by, 9. 154; Molesworth's, tries to save family, 22. 140; Morelli was, to Cowper, 33. 587n; Murray, Lady, had Arthur Grey as (see under Grey, Arthur); Neapolitan nobleman demands that dukedom be conferred on his, 22. 32; Northampton's, running, at races, 9. 247–9; Northumberland, Ds of, adds, 38. 473; Northumberland, Ds of, has more, than Q. Charlotte, 34. 23; Northumberland, Ds of, has 7, preceding her chair, 38. 469; Orford's, committed to prison by Bn Walpole, for fathering a bastard, 25. 355; Petersham, Lady Caroline's, see Richard; Prescott's, see Sith, John; prude's amours may begin (and gallant woman's end) with, 36. 210; ride in back of coach, 20. 181, 195; running, considered by HW as good as a learned man, 35. 226; sex of newly-born child confused in mind of, 7. 375, 32. 268; throng Twickenham churchyard, 34. 115; Townshend, Vcts's, 10. 216; tries to be actor but ends as candle-snuffer, 37. 141; Walpole, Sir Edward, promises, to Mrs Scott, 10. 329; Wasner's, delivers letter, 19. 29; watch ladies urinate, 34. 257; Watson Wentworth, Lady Henrietta, elopes with, 38. 456–7; Whitehall thronged with, 9. 325; Yarmouth, Lady's, waits with HW in Kensington Lodge, 9. 315; Zoffany's, 33. 358

foreign ministers at mercy of, if abuse can be printed, 38. 357

Francis I's, in his livery, 18. 196

Frankland's, 33. 335

French: amazed by HW's costume, 10. 278; differ from English ones, 35. 112; female,

dying of cancer at Rome and tended by Anne Pitt, 24. 344, 353; French antechambers full of, 31. 55, 80; untrustworthy, 39. 204

friseur of Q. Charlotte waits on table, 38. 434

gamekeeper; gamekeepers: at Laughton Place, killed by Dacre, 35. 139; D. of Cumberland's, treats Montagu's family brutally, 9. 93; HW meets, at Houghton, 9. 349

gardener; gardeners: attend Hardwicke, to Montagu's neglect, at Blenheim, 10. 309; Berrys', 12. 163, 166; Conway's, to be his 'first minister,' 37. 472; French, at Fulham, 31. 94n; HW's, see Cowie, John; Farr, Thomas; Vickers, Christopher; HW wishes, at SH, but not if Scottish, 35. 473, 479; Northington's, disobeys orders to cut trees, 23. 368; Orford's at Houghton, 36. 97; Ossory's, see Gibbs, Robert; Trinity Hospital's inmates have often been, 16. 85

gatekeeper at convent of St Joseph in Paris, 3. 55

gentleman; gentlemen: Chute's, attends his death-bed, 24. 211; Kilmorey's, 20. 298; of D. of Grafton, 21. 78

gentleman-usher, see Griffith

George III's, hear him ridicule Mansfield, 32. 235

George III's and Q. Charlotte's, ordered to keep new clothes for Queen's birthday, 38. 286

George III's page of the Bedchamber, 33. 225–6

German, sent by Ds of York to strollers' theatre and Methodist sermon, 39. 493

Giberne resents being, 17. 454, 480

girls hanged for participating in Gordon riots, 33. 214

Gloucester, Ds of, sends message by, 36. 262

——'s, 12. 24

Gloucester, D. of, leaves Gloucester House in charge of, 42. 463

godparent might give money to, at christening, 24. 199, 219

Gordon, Ds of, has, 11. 187

governess; governesses: Dee, Leonora, to be, to Ps Sophia Matilda, 36. 247; Molesworths', see Morelle, Mrs

gratuities to, see Vails below; see also under Tip; tips

groom; grooms: Conway's, refuses to go with him because wife not adequately insured in case of accident, 21. 155; English, suspected of poisoning race-horse, 31. 107, 41. 6; Ferrers's, see Williams, Peter; Gunning's, see Pearce, William; Harcourt not expected to drench, 35. 507; Ligonier's, see Harding, John; Orford's, expensive, 36. 96; Orford's, gives him medical advice, 23. 460, 36. 332; Orford's, help wreck his estate, 23. 511

[Servant; servants, *continued*]

groom (grooms) of the chambers: at Kimbolton Castle, **10.** 77; at Petworth, has list of paintings, **40.** 318; Giberne may become, through Lady Yarmouth, **20.** 91; HW asks Bns Hervey's, to buy scissors, **31.** 76; Harris and wife wheeled by, **33.** 525; of Ds of Montrose, **33.** 296

groom-porter's annals, Lord William Manners famous in, **20.** 418

Guerchy's, delivers HW's letters to Hertford, **38.** 571

HW able to have, in old age, **39.** 318

HW carried by, **31.** 204, 402

HW delivers Mann's letter to Horace Mann II's, **24.** 512

HW detains Fanny Burney's, **42.** 296

HW rings bell for, at SH, **35.** 373

HW rings up, at night, **15.** 327

HW's: **1.** 33, **9.** 191, **10.** 40, 103, 296, 320, 322, **11.** 33, 112, 129, 145, 173, 174, **12.** 41, 68, 194, **28.** 128–9, **66.** 337; Ailesbury, Cts of, receives message through, **37.** 511; at Arlington St, *see* Favre; at Berkeley Sq., gets letter too late, **25.** 57; at SH, listed, **21.** 300; bring account of Hannah More's health, **31.** 259; brings letter from Mann, **25.** 185; carry blunderbusses after dark, **35.** 367; carry him around house, **42.** 446; carry him to bed, **22.** 316, **25.** 347, **34.** 211, **35.** 303, **38.** 65, 68; defend SH against housebreakers, **31.** 298; delivers Ds of Gloucester's letter, **36.** 88; delivers *Historic Doubts* to Lady Mary Coke, **31.** 137; dies, **19.** 132; fit for an infirmary, **32.** 292; forced to display lights for Rodney, **25.** 280, 343; frightened by earthquake, **20.** 130; HW fortunate to have, in old age, **39.** 318; HW lays up a little money for, **39.** 408; HW's correspondence with, **7.** 389, 393; HW sends, to bookseller, **42.** 277; HW sends, to Richmond, **42.** 277; HW sends, to Thames Ditton for news, **30.** 272; HW sends, to Twickenham from London, **31.** 37; HW sends, to Tyburn to ransom watch, **41.** 64; HW sends S. Lysons a message by, **15.** 195; hear gossip about Martha Ray, **33.** 98; help him to climb stairs, **16.** 320; hold him up when he walks, **34.** 217; ill, **3.** 325, **31.** 235; in Italy, neglect his chaise, **37.** 66; invitations delivered by, **31.** 406; Johnston, Lady Cecilia, gives drams to, **35.** 474; Jones, Henry, quarrels with, **38.** 175; lop trees at SH, **24.** 48; mistakes chimney-back for armour, **20.** 396; move him from bed to couch, **36.** 90; Müntz's affair with one of, **40.** 169n; must not carry contraband goods in chaise, **37.** 39; named, **41.** 433; 'new,' **42.** 83; not allowed to identify donor of Q. Elizabeth's portrait, **37.** 531; noticed in HW's will, **15.** 338; not to be called on by their friends, **40.** 259; reminds him of forgotten invitation, **35.**

455; rest at Ware, **40.** 197; run to light candles for mob, **25.** 563; tax for, to be paid by Bedford, **41.** 433; tell about mob's activities, **24.** 442; tell him of Colman's gift, **41.** 351; tell him that Ps Amelia is coming to SH, **31.** 147; to be under charge of his steward-butler, **40.** 258; wakes him with false news of Cts of Hertford's death, **38.** 494; wife of, treated by Dr Hunter, **41.** 422

HW's and Fox's, bungle transport of pigs, **37.** 347

HW's 'French boy,' **35.** 11

HW's Swiss, *see* Favre

HW's Swiss boy, *see* Louis (d. 1767)

HW's upper, HW sends to Arlington St from SH, **23.** 284; *see also* Favre

handbell calls, to dinner, **9.** 405

handmaid, brutally treated by D. of Cumberland, **9.** 93

Hardinge's, *see* Moody, John

Harrington's, questioned about robbery, **38.** 259

Harrington, Cts of, dies in passion at, **39.** 418

Henrietta Maria's dwarves employ, **41.** 160–1

Hertford's: at Paris, *see* Demange; drowned in boat at Liverpool, **38.** 108; have suitable table, **38.** 253; ill and cannot go to ask about HW, **38.** 156; unavailable to convey letter, **37.** 384; *see also* Brian

Hertford, Cts of, has, well-dressed to attend her to Court, **38.** 237

—— protected by, from robbers, **32.** 207

Hewet's, interrupt his wife-beating, **24.** 204

Holdernesse's, unfairly treated in his will, **33.** 13

Holland's, tells HW of D. of Gloucester's reported death, **23.** 343

horrors of French Revolution must be impressed on, **15.** 221, 232

housekeeper; housekeepers: annuity suitable for, **32.** 384n; at Althorp, **35.** 305; at Berkeley Castle, **39.** 183; at Castle Howard, gives 'Rosette' a basin of water, **30.** 258; at Castle Howard, shows and tells HW everything, **30.** 258; at Hampton Court, SH, or Windsor, must exhibit Bentley's paintings, **35.** 243; at Houghton, **32.** 158; at Kimbolton Castle, **10.** 77; at Knole, poisons HW's enthusiasm, **33.** 224; at Knole, puts HW out of humour, **29.** 78; at Letheringham, **35** 248; at Petworth, visits London, **9.** 98; at Raynham, new and does not know portraits, **30.** 81; at SH, **11.** 25 (*see also* Bransom, Ann; Catherine; Young, Margaret); at Wrest, HW converses with, **9.** 4; Burnet gives Wolsey's hat to, **41.** 333; Collier, Susan, is, to Sir Edward Walpole, **36.** 317n; Granville's, on Jersey, **35.** 161; HW prefers to be shown castles by, rather than by owners, **39.** 434–5; HW's, garrulous, **15.** 271; HW's, to attend Fanny Burney, **42.** 150; HW's, to receive Cowley portrait, **42.** 203; Mason's, **28.** 166; Molière's, trusted by him to judge plays, **41.** 372; Montagu's, at Adderbury, **10.** 312; Montfort's, at his suicide, **35.** 202; Orford's, **15.** 333; Ossory's, congratulates him on death of heir, **32.** 61n; pictures baptized by, **42.** 75; typical legacy for, **20.** 11; Walpole, Sir Robert's, deciphers chambermaid's letter, **10.** 23

housemaid; housemaids: at Drayton, **10.** 343; converted to Methodism are the usual converts, **35.** 192; HW interviews, **28.** 391; HW's in Arlington St frightened by explosion, **32.** 75 (*see also* Fare, Martha; Mary); HW's in Arlington St, sends him word by waterman, **35.** 229; mint kept by, for sake of greenery, **30.** 218; obituary of, who drowned herself for love, **37.** 189; Townshend's, bears him three children and inherits money, **22.** 211; Townshend's, is his mistress, **38.** 346n; wounded by negro, **37.** 8–9

Hungarian, Polish, French, and Swiss, at Lady Mary Wortley Montagu's, **22.** 3n

huntsman, Beckford's, *see* James

in France, to be sent to prepare horses, **37.** 41

inquiries made by, seldom elicit truth, **41.** 392

Jewesses', sent with card to Q. Charlotte, **22.** 73

Joseph II attended by only one, **23.** 112

kitchen boy, Mann's, wears tricolour cockade, **18.** 544

La Borde's antechambers full of, dirty, **31.** 80

lackey; lackeys (laquais): Du Deffand, Mme, has, **3.** 55, 330, 338, **6.** 408; HW's, returns from Mme du Deffand's, **39.** 271; Praslin's, **3.** 56; *see also* Footman; Laquais de louage; Laquais de voyage

laquais de louage, HW's, in Paris, 31 78

laquais de voyage, **17.** 59n

La Trémoïlle, Duchesse de, has, **12.** 3

laundress, Anne Kemp is, to D. of Cumberland, **19.** 427n

laundry-maid, reveals alleged plot, **35.** 230

Leicester's, at Holkham, get paltry gratuity from E. of Bath, **19.** 443

Leopold and Maria Louisa take only two, to Poggio Imperiale, **23.** 449

Leopold's and Maria Louisa's, when travelling, **23.** 220

letters sent by, **31.** 236

livery, at Burghley House, **10.** 347

Lorraine officers', **17.** 162

Louis XV's, starving, **39.** 143

Lovat's, imprisoned for marrying each other, **19.** 380

Lucchese, attend D. of York in livery, **22.** 222

Lyttelton's *Henry II* too valuable to be entrusted to, **40.** 133

maid; maids: Albemarle, Ds of, pretends, are ladies of the Bedchamber, **25.** 564; at brothel, gets niggardly fee, **24.** 413; at Standon, **40.** 198; Bath's, go to bed in uncurtained room, **30.** 89–90; Burlington, Cts of, scares away, by profanity, **37.** 572; Burney, Fanny, asked to bring, to SH, **42.** 150; captain of ship leaves, in pirates' clutches, **25.** 480; Clement, Anne, sends message by, to HW, **36.** 157; Conway, Hon. Henrietta Seymour's, *see* Pelham, ——; Cornelys, Theresa, left by, because of excessive bed-making, **23.** 272; counterfeiter's, tried at Old Bailey, **19.** 242–3; Craon, Princesse de, makes room odorous with, **18.** 78; Damer, Mrs, has Mrs James Sampson as, **33.** 584; dances performed by, at Blenheim, **38.** 462; Dothwaite is, to Sir Edward Walpole, **36.** 325; for Henrietta Maria's dwarfs, **41.** 160–1; French, employed by Cts of Hertford, **39.** 20–1; French, steals pearls, **23.** 535n; French officer's wife does not have, **10.** 283; from Richmond, wishes to stay in town to see Ds of Montrose, **21.** 535; Goldsworthy, Mrs, brings, to Mann's house, **17.** 306, 313, 395; HW jokes about Sunday occupations of, in Berkeley Sq., **31.** 235; HW's, **11.** 94, 316; HW's at Arlington St, **9.** 191, **10.** 40, 296, **23.** 286 (*see also* Fare, Martha; Mary; Sibley, Maria); HW's at Arlington St belittles his gout, **39.** 162; HW's, in Berkeley Sq., **42.** 176; HW's, posts his Paris correspondence, **30.** 267; Hamilton's, escape storm, **33.** 82; killed in fire, **35.** 210; ladies', HW compares watering-places to, **10.** 229; Mann, Lady Lucy, reveals extent of illness to, **24.** 346; Maule's, reveals coats-of-arms, **19.** 107; Molesworths', *see* Patterson, Mrs; Niccoli brings, from England, **19.** 290; of Cts of Orford, seduced by abbé-secretary, **19.** 224, 238; patriarchs accompanied by, **37.** 290; sleeps in garret when not in employer's bed, **20.** 215; Strathmore, Lady's, *see* Morgan, Mary; Parkes, Ann; Suffolk, Lady's, shown ring by Miss Hotham, **10.** 114; Walpole, Sir Edward, promises five, to Mrs Scott, **10.** 329; Windham's assignation with, **31.** 421; *see also* Chambermaid; Dairy-maid; Handmaid; Housemaid; Laundry-maid; Milkmaid; Nursemaid; Nursery-maid; Waiting-maid; Wright, Mary

maître d'hôtel: Blandford, Lady, has, **32.** 208; Conway's, suspected of arson, **33.** 583–4; of Cts of Orford, *see* Waters, Charles; Tencin's, *see* Goudine; Tylney's, made executor and residuary legatee, **25.** 534; Windham's assignation with, **31.** 421

major-domo: Beauclerk, Lady Diana, has, at Little Marble Hill, **35.** 625; Clement XIII's, gives presents to D. of York, **22.** 229

male, not allowed in Maria Louisa's chamber, **22.** 529

Mann furnishes, to Lady Mary Coke, **23.** 544–5, **31.** 177

[Servant; servants, *continued*]

—— praises Conway and Lady Ailesbury for refusing to suspect, of robbery, **23**. 9

——'s: delivers letter to Horace Mann II, in London, **24**. 446; Florentine furniture to be sold for benefit of, **25**. 669–70; frightened of thunder-storm, **17**. 117; Gloucester, D. of, dismisses, **23**. 394; HW sends to secretary of state's office for, **25**. 215; honoured by carrying message to Mann from Leopold's son, **25**. 282; Leopold exempts, from 8% tax on legacies, **25**. 666; Mann may have to take to Leghorn, for clothes, **20**. 205; Mann's funeral attended by, **25**. 665n; Mann's legacies and annuities to, **25**. 677; Mann, Horace II, forms fund for, for employees' benefit, **25**. 669–70; Mann, Horace II, retains, while still in Tuscany, **25**. 667; Mann, Horace II, to sell furniture for benefit of, **25**. 678; may wear mourning for Maria Theresa, **25**. 102n; mourning clothes for Electress too expensive for, **18**. 206; not told where Lady William Campbell is going, **25**. 272; return of, to Florence from London, delayed, **24**. 450; sent on horseback to Castello, **25**. 329; sent with message, **17**. 51; serve dinners out of town for D. of York, **22**. 220, 222; suffer from influenza, **25**. 304; to attend Ds of Gloucester at theatre with ice refreshments, **24**. 291; tricolour cockades worn by, **18**. 544; writes letter to Horace Mann II, **25**. 570

—— sends, to Horace Mann II, **24**. 94

——'s nephew's, may be lodged at neighbour's, **24**. 72–3

Mann, Galfridus, has, cut his bread and butter, **20**. 554

Mann, Horace II, tells, to tell Mann's servant of wife's death, **24**. 356

manservant; menservants: Chute's, **10**. 261; Clive, Mrs, has, **10**. 238; Goldsworthy, Mrs, brings, to Mann's house, **17**. 313

Mary, Q. of Scots's, **9**. 297

may be put into mourning on Electress's death, **18**. 175

Middleton's, assist him, **15**. 313

Mill's, **19**. 407

ministers', made drunk at Claremont, **17**. 503

Modenese princess brings, on journey, **22**. 201

Molesworth, Hon. Charlotte, probably learns of mother's death from, **22**. 146

Molesworths': burns house to conceal theft of plate, **22**. 140n; perish in fire, **38**. 201

Montagu, D. of, leaves legacies to, **9**. 94

Montagu's: armed against thieves, **10**. 120; false rumour of Halifax's death to be repeated to Montagu by, **10**. 296; former, awaits HW in Paris, **37**. 41; HW to be escorted by, to Greatworth, **10**. 82; Montagu does not dare to scold, **10**. 275; *see also* Ann, Mrs; Glass; Nicolò

Montagu, Lady Mary Wortley, has only men as, **22**. 3

Mount Stuart dismisses, **25**. 345

necessary woman at Trinity Hospital, Greenwich, **16**. 85

negro: of Ds of Manchester, **37**. 8–9; of Irish merchant at Nantes, **38**. 405n; of Lady Philipps, **34**. 29; of Porto Bello governor, **37**. 54; Usher's, **22**. 141

Newcastle's: die of sore throat, **21**. 312; HW to be notified by, **40**. 362; keep Mann waiting for credentials, **17**. 24; ransack house for source of cryptic card, **37**. 437

Newcastle, Ds of, has, **16**. 367–8

Norfolk's and Northumberland's, want to be stylish by wearing mourning for Ps Caroline, **21**. 165

nurse; nurses: **11**. 72, 73; Anne Seymour Conway's, *see* Jones, Mrs Elizabeth; at Paris, gives child a farthing for beggar, **10**. 209; Charlton's, repulsed by him, **33**. 414; Englishwoman brings, to Florence for her child, 24 260; 'Isabel' in HW's 'Patapan,' **30**. 296–8; Lorenzi's, causes child's death, **20**. 306; Stadtholder's children tended by, **37**. 287; to P. William of Gloucester, **36**. 142

nurse-maid, trains children by hand, **30**. 84

nursery-maid: Abergavenny's mistress, **38**. 510n; ill of fever, **36**. 288

officer's, at Ghent, *see* Doyne, Mrs Mary

old: HW lays up money for, **39**. 408; status of, **11**. 336

'old man,' Hillier's, calls at HW's for painting, **16**. 97

Old Pretender dismisses, **19**. 96

Orford's: at Eriswell, **36**. 118, 121, 122; conceal his illness and hurry him off, **34**. 130; dismissed for dishonesty, **16**. 19; Gordon, Lord William, to be obeyed by, **36**. 157–8; HW and Moone discharge, **36**. 97; HW writes to, enjoining deference to Lord William Gordon, **41**. 379; persist in pilfering, **23**. 521; *see also* Herbert, Thomas

Orford, Cts of, neglects, in will, **25**. 122

Ossory's, *see* Farr, Thomas; Gordon, William; Hawkins, ——

ostler, at Worcester inn, **35**. 150

Oxford college's, said to have been killed by Abergavenny and others, **19**. 387

page; pages: Botta's, to wear new liveries, **22**. 330; Bristol's to have, for embassy, **21**. 202; carries Princesse de Craon's train, **18**. 196; Charles III's, puts hooks in wigs, **23**. 238; Craon, Princesse de, has, **17**. 414; for Cts of Hertford's presentation, **38**. 237; Frederick, P. of Wales's, **20**. 232; George III's, **33**. 225–6, 497–8; Karl Alexander does not bring, **20**. 376; Mirepoix followed by, **9**. 154; Northumberland's, **38**. 401; of the backstairs, Louis aspires to be, **9**. 305; Penthièvre's, **20**. 466n; Pucci, Mme, has, **17**. 39, 42; to D. of Gloucester, *see* Bryant,

Robert; Stiell, Alexander; York, D. of, leaves, at Florence, **22.** 225; Young Pretender sends, to France, for French songs, **30.** 92

Page's, spoil paintings by not shutting sun out, **33.** 137

page-in-waiting, George III's, **22.** 96

peeresses', exhibit their mistresses' costumes for Coronation, **21.** 535

Pelham's, **9.** 417

Pembroke's: **10.** 17; call in dog-doctor, **31.** 126

Pembroke, Cts of, lends, to protect French visitors, **33.** 404
—— sends, to HW, **39.** 447

Philip, Don, quarters, on chief families, **20.** 45

Philipps's, **17.** 67

picture to be delivered by Hon. Anne Seymour Conway's, **37.** 385

pipers, employed by Ds of Northumberland, **20.** 341

Pitt's, precede his chair to Buckingham House, **22.** 159

Pomfret, Cts of, employs Mary as, **17.** 101

porter; porters: Ailesbury, Cts of, asks that eggs be sent to, **37.** 484; at Burghley House, **10.** 347; Charles I's, *see* Evans, William; Conway's, reports on Gordon riots, **33.** 188; creditors have C. J. Fox's goods carried off by, **39.** 376; drunken, Parliament members compared to, **38.** 325; Exchequer, **40.** 308; HW gets information from Ds of Richmond's, **37.** 288; HW may send letter to Lady Ailesbury by, **37.** 511; HW's, knows nothing of Belle-île, **40.** 199; Hardinge's legs like those of, **35.** 588; Harrington's, *see* Wesket, John; Hertford's, tells HW about courier, **38.** 494; Hertford's, to deliver things to HW, **38.** 170; Lincoln, Cts of, sends, with invitations to assembly, **37.** 453–4; Mann's, repels visitors on post days, **19.** 59; Mann's, to open door at any hour of night for express from Leghorn, **25.** 9; Montagu, Mrs Elizabeth, has, **9.** 255; of Q. Elizabeth, **20.** 49, **35.** 206; Ossorys', HW sends packet by, **32.** 171; Parisians murder, because called *Le Suisse*, **31.** 373; Perceval's, **17.** 301; Pitt's, **35.** 195; Swiss, kept by Northumberlands, **20.** 341; two, brings HW's purchases from Mrs Kennon's sale, **37.** 439; Walpole, Sir Robert's, 'customers' of, now go to Carteret, **18.** 96; Walpole, Sir Robert's, told by HW to shoo away the mob, **18.** 96; *see also* Shields

postilion; postilions: **32.** 154; drunk at Mereworth, **35.** 144; Hertford's, responsible for accident, **38.** 387; Ligonier's, *see* Harding, John; Montagu's, may be sent to meet HW, **10.** 83; Montagu, Mrs Elizabeth, has, **9.** 255; North's, wounded by highwaymen, **24.** 47; Werpup's, overturns chaise, **22.** 306; wheel runs over, **9.** 195

Richecourt brings, for Tesi, **18.** 263
—— gives, to Cts of Orford, **19.** 49

Richmond, D. of, pensions his wife's, **34.** 222
——'s, *see* Sampson, James

Rinuccini's generosity to, in will, **19.** 462

royal family have few, at Richmond, **38.** 418

running footman, *see under* Footman

Salviati's, Dumesnil escapes with, **19.** 491

Sandwich's, reports Martha Ray's death, **33.** 100–1

Scarbrough's, fetches sedan chair, **37.** 47

scolding of, an old-age occupation, **39.** 209

'scrub,' given by Florentine Regency to Modenese princess, **17.** 60

secretary; secretaries: at Richmond House, *see* Sampson, James; Dumesnil's, assists him at Mass, **19.** 493; HW's, *see* Kirgate, Thomas; Mann's, *see* Giberne, Gabriel George; Gregori, Antonio; Palombo, Domenico; Tylney's, made executor and residuary legatee, **25.** 534

Shorter's Swiss, suspected of killing him, **35.** 159n

Shrewsbury's, **17.** 14

Simco is, **41.** 388

Somerset, D. of, survives old ones and distrusts their successors, **40.** 318

stable boy; stable boys: at Tower of London, taken by Vcts Townshend as Kilmarnock's bastard, **37.** 268; Orford's, at Newmarket, **36.** 97

steward; stewards: Ailesbury, Cts of, pleased with extravagance of, **37.** 509; at Welbeck, cuts passage through oak, **35.** 271; Carlisle's, at Castle Howard, **41.** 250; Cullum's accounts kept by, **41.** 103–4; Devonshire's, **16.** 369; Devonshire's, falls off horse from drinking to victory, **37.** 567; Ferrers's, murdered by master, **9.** 272 (*see also* Johnson, John); Fox's, *see* Ayliffe, John (d. 1759); Grandison, Lady, has, **33.** 334; HW confers with, in London, **35.** 464; HW's, at Crostwick, **36.** 291; HW's, *see* Jones, Henry; HW's life invaded by, **23.** 497; Harcourt's, uses house in Rockingham Forest, **10.** 214; Hertford's, **16.** 17; Hertford's, uses MSS for household paper, **35.** 104; Lincoln's, *see* Reade, Henry; Marlborough (Ds of)'s, **9,** 245; Montagu's, visits Gloucestershire, **9.** 242; Montagu's landladies', to order alterations at Adderbury, **10.** 266; Newcastle's, *see* Turner, Richard; Northampton's, **16.** 88–9; Northampton's, to forward box of medals to HW, **21.** 272; Northumberland's, *see* Selby, Henry Collingwood; of Cts of Orford, **25.** 440; Orford's, **32.** 141–2, 143, **41.** 266 (*see also* Cony, Carlos; Moore, William; Withers, William); Oxford's, **12.** 80; Talbot's, **19.** 176; Walpole, Sir Robert, has Jenkins as, **36.** 2

steward-butler, HW's, *see* Jones, Henry

[Servant; servants, *continued*]

Strafford's, Townshend's indelicate witticism in front of, **37.** 430

strange, make HW afraid of Goodwood, **39.** 295

Strozzi's, **18.** 146

suspicion of, when houses burn, **33.** 583–4

sweepers entitled to loose silver on floor, **38.** 295; *see also* Firmin

Swiss (*suisse; suisses*): from London, to form regiment, **18.** 409; of Duchesse de Choiseul, **4.** 423–4; of Mme de Guerchy, **3.** 349, 362

tableau decorations painted by, at Elizabeth Chudleigh's, **38.** 204

tax on, **25.** 578n, **41.** 432, 433

Townshend accompanied by, when raising mob, **21.** 138

Townshend, Vcts, accuses, of robbing her, **30.** 224

Tripolitan minister's, die of plague, **23.** 24

tutor; tutors ('governors'): Buccleuch's, **10.** 268; Castlecomer's *see* Roberts, Rev. Thomas; Chewton's, seen by HW in Paris, **7.** 288–9; Christian IV's nephew's, **17.** 339; Christian VII does not have, **23.** 40; English, HW's opinion of, **20.** 170, 454; English, have Jacobite sympathies, **19.** 112; HW to avoid, in Paris, **10.** 173; Hérault's, **35.** 222–3; Jamaïque's, **10.** 129; Osborn's, **10.** 170; pupils should be taught by, to have no ideas, **38.** 181; Tylney's, *see* Hold, Richard; *see also* Daniel, Samuel

Tylney's: have new laced clothes, **23.** 60; to get proceeds of sale of his Neapolitan possessions, **25.** 534

umbrella carried by, **31.** 215

unable to carry messages because of epidemic disorders, **25.** 284

under-cooks, Young Pretender to be joined by, in France, **18.** 434

upper, have garret rooms, **35.** 301

vails for, **20.** 89n; *see also under* Tip; tips

valet-de-chambre; valets-de-chambre: Acciaioli's, returns Clement XIII's letter, **21.** 340–1; Barbantane's, conveys threat to Leopold, **24.** 405; Beauvron (Marquise de)'s, **3.** 62; Borghese's, drowns in Tiber, **19.** 444; Chesterfield's, *see* Walsh, Thomas; Choiseul (Duchesse de)'s, **4.** 309; Cowper's, hurries back to Florence with Conway's letter to Mann, **22.** 374, 380; Cowper's, takes Mann's letter to HW, **22.** 361, 366; discarded clothes the perquisite of, **17.** 158, 172; Du Deffand (Mme)'s, *see* Wiart, Jean-François; Dumesnil (Alexandre)'s, arrested, **17.** 225; Dumesnil (Giuseppe)'s, proclaims him bishop, **19.** 493; footman might be promoted to, **37.** 41; French, **30.** 211; George II's, **9.** 311, **35.** 307 (*see also* Schröder); Guerchy (Comtesse de)'s, **3.** 349, 362; HW's announces Chute's death, **24.** 211 (*see also* Colomb, Philip); Hertford's, at Naples for

health brings HW a black spaniel, **23.** 56; livery not worn by, **17.** 207; Lorenzi to have, as secretary, **17.** 157; Louis XIII's, *see* Dubois; Louis XVI's, *see* Binet, Gérard, Bn de Marchais; Mann's, *see* Galletti, Giuseppe; Giarlii, Giuseppe; Mann thinks St-Aignan's surgeon is, **17.** 81; Mann wants, out of livery, **17.** 207; Marlborough's, receives Marlborough's father's robes, **9.** 280–1; Medici (Ottaviano de')'s, **17.** 238; Mordaunt accompanied by, **30.** 144; no man a hero to his, **32.** 223; Pomfret, Cts of, has Stephan as, **19.** 46; Rushout's, **18.** 299; Stormont's, **21.** 2; Tencin's, aids Pretender's sons to escape from Rome, **19.** 98–9; Tornaquinci's, issues passports, **21.** 482; Voisins's, **41.** 174; wages of, **17.** 157; Walpole, Sir Robert's, *see* Jones, John; Werpup's, killed by overturned chaise, **22.** 306; Whithed's, *see* Ferreri; Young Pretender's, *see* Stewart, John (d. after 1788)

valet-de-place; valets-de-place: Agincourt's, **42.** 64–5; coachman at Rome refuses to serve as, **22.** 286; Rena well known to, **21.** 162

Veers's, stripped of lace liveries, **19.** 507

Verelst's, **28.** 128

Vertue's sister's, **16.** 74–5, 81

Villettes's, takes news to England, **19.** 431

Virrettes's, **38.** 313

Vitelli, Mme, solicitous about Braitwitz's health in presence of, **18.** 353

wagoner, Montagu's, to transport Montagu portraits, **10.** 67, 104

waiter; waiters: at Arthur's, talk publicly of Sackville's story, **37.** 20; at St James's Coffee-House, says he could thrash Nivernais, **22.** 84; at Star and Garter, **38.** 502 (*see also* Edwards, John); at White's, **18.** 174; Cumberland, D. of, ousted by, from reserved seat, **38.** 296; Mackreth was, at White's, **24.** 53n; makes pedantic remark about violinist, **34.** 173; Rumbold and Sykes formerly were, at tavern, **25.** 141; Rumbold was, at White's, **25.** 400; watch Frances Pelham expose herself, **32.** 169–70; wear brown frocks and blue aprons, **20.** 209

waiting-maid, *see* Patience

Waldegrave's, wear Queen's livery, **33.** 541

Waldegrave, Cts, puts, into mourning for Louis XVI, **36.** 285n

Wallmoden's, summoned from Rome, **22.** 357

Walpole, Bns, dismisses, for being Mann's spy, **18.** 14

Walpole, Sir Edward, and Jane Clement involved with, **36.** 318, 319 (*see also* Collier, ——)

Walpole, Hon. Thomas to send message by, **36.** 192

washerwoman: at Rome, **17.** 461; Bootle's, told to tell him of George II's death, **20.** 245, 254; English, at Florence, refuses Mrs Richmond's proposals, **19.** 46

waterman; watermen, taken in boat by Cts of Dysart, **39.** 311

weeding-girl, Orford's, bears him a daughter, **25.** 355

Wilkes's: inserts books in Stanley's trunk, **38.** 484; to give evidence, **38.** 292

Williams's, writes letters for him to Winnington, **30.** 68

Wilson, Ann, acquitted as accomplice in coining, **19.** 242n

woman; women: Ailesbury (Cts of)'s, *see* Sally, Mrs; does not have book for Hillier, **16.** 93; Du Deffand, Mme, has, **3.** 115; follows mistress in second coach, **42.** 380; Walpole (Lady)'s, intimate with Mrs Gates, **25.** 92n

women of fashion never give tips to, **20.** 89

Woodford's, saves house from rioters, **33.** 185n

Worsley's, *see* Cardini, ——

Wright's, **17.** 449

York, Ds of, takes, to hear Methodist preacher, **39.** 493

Yorke's, dies of sore throat, **21.** 312

Young Pretender's: aid him when he goes to theatre corridor to be sick, **24.** 244; bring his effects, **18.** 434; support him as he walks, **25.** 442; *see also* Stewart, John

Young Pretender said to have left Rome with, **17.** 113

Servants' hall:

at Burghley House, **10.** 347

Serva padrona. See under Pergolesi

Servetus, Michael (Miguel Serveto) (1511–53), Spanish physician and theologian:

Calvin burns, **20.** 555, **34.** 111

Servi, Costantino de':

Henry, P., instructed by, in art, **25.** 224n

Servi, Via dei:

Florentines frequent, **18.** 445

Servites, Order of:

France suppresses, **39.** 147n

Servius Tullius (fl. 578–534 B.C.), K. of Rome:

Fortune said to be in love with, **14.** 20–1

Sesac. *See* Sesostris

Sesostris (legendary K. of Egypt):

Bruce finds harp painted by order of, **28.** 249–50

HW's letter might have been written in time of, **25.** 15

Vesuvius would have felled, **24.** 515

Sésostris. See under Voltaire

Sessaracoa, William Ansah (b. ca 1721, living 1752) African chief's son:

Oroonoko resembles story of, **20.** 40

sea-captain sells, as slave in Barbados, **20.** 40n

Session, Lords of. *See under* Edinburgh, Court of Session

Sesster, Levina Benjamina, m. (1764) Henry Goodricke:

'Dutchwoman,' **28.** 375

Sestorio, Giuseppe Maria, Genoese secretary of state:

Austrian-Genoese agreement signed by, **19.** 316

Sestri (Italy):

Philip, Don, flees to, **19.** 304

Spaniards at, **19.** 40

Setauket, Long Island, N.Y.:

American attack on, **24.** 331n

Setbury (? Sedbury):

food riots at, **22.** 460n

Seth, John:

HW settles with, for furniture at Little Strawberry Hill, **42.** 306–7

Pope, Jane, to settle with, for pictures, **42.** 307

Seton, Lady. *See* Gordon, Lady Henrietta (d. 1651)

Seton, Sir Alexander (fl. 1311–40), keeper of Berwick:

Jerningham's *Siege of Berwick* concerns family of, **12.** 62, 63n

Seton, Sir Alexander (ca 1555–1622), 1st E. of Dunfermline:

Birch calls, a good poet, **16.** 140

Seton, Barbara Cecilia (d. after 1838), m. (1807) Rev. James Bannister:

Berry, Agnes, visited by, at Little Strawberry Hill, **12.** 198, 210

Berrys' correspondence with, **11.** *116*–17, 159, 162, 165, 167

HW mentions, **12.** 62

HW's correspondence with, **11.** 129, 141, 165, 167, **12.** 213

HW tells, of Berrys' landing, **11.** 117

HW visited by, **11.** 120, 121, 129

HW visits, **11.** 120, 124

mother and, at Caversham, later at Chepstow and in Wiltshire, **43.** 144

Seton, Elizabeth (1719–97), m. John Seton; grandmother of Berry sisters:

Berrys' affection for, **12.** 74

—— leave Scarborough at request of, **12.** 46

—— loved by, **12.** 27

—— visit, **11.** *19*, 51, 60n, 69, **12.** 27, 46, 64, 68, 74

HW calls, 'Grandmama,' **11.** 19, 69, **12.** 8, 10, 100

lives with daughter in Yorkshire, **12.** 8n

Lovedays visited by, **11.** 137

mentioned, **11.** 156, 157, 165, 166, **12.** 16, 21, 22, 30, 33, 35, 50, 83, (?) 101, 106

not alarmed about Berrys, **11.** 159, 162, 164

Seton, Elizabeth (ca 1744–67), m. (1762) Robert Berry; mother of Mary and Agnes Berry:

marriage and death of, **34.** 24

Seton, George (1531–86), 5th Lord Seton, 1549:

painting of, at Pinkie House, **16.** 51

Seton, Mrs George:
  daughter and, at Caversham, later at Chepstow and in Wiltshire, **43**. 144
Seton, Isabella (d. 1828), m. (1763) Thomas Cayley, 5th Bt, 1791; aunt of Berry sisters:
  Berrys visit, **11**. *18*. 51, 60n, **12**. 8n, 64
  (?) HW sends love to, **12**. 101
  mother lives with, **12**. 8n
Seton, Jane (ca 1745–1803), m. (1770) Sir Walter Synnot, Kt, 1783; aunt of Berry sisters:
  Berrys to be visited by, **12**. *124*
  daughter of, **12**. 88n
  HW thinks, disagreeable, **12**. 124
  illness of, **12**. 124
  SH visited by, **12**. 243
Seton, Mrs John. *See* Seton, Elizabeth
Seton, John Thomas (fl. ca 1760–1806), painter:
  Hailes's portrait by, **42**. 432n
Seton, Mary, m. Dr William Robertson; great-aunt of Berry sisters:
  (?) HW franks letter from Mrs Seton to, **12**. 106
Seton family:
  Siege of Berwick concerns, **12**. 65, 69, 82, 83
  of Dunfermline, **16**. 51n
Settee, The. See under Crébillon, Claude-Prosper Jolyot de (1707–77)
Settee; settees:
  at SH: **11**. 51; HW lies on, **39**. 475; linen-covered, **20**. 382, 387
  in Vyne parlour, **35**. 639
Settignano. *See* Masoni da Settignano
Settimia. *See* Guadagni, Settimia
Settlement, Act of. *See under* Parliament: acts of
Sève. *See* Sèvres
Sevenoaks, Kent:
  Chevening Park near, **11**. 97n
  Chute and HW visit, **35**. 132
  Grove, The, at, is Hardinge's address, **35**. 595, 597
  Knole Park near, **29**. 77n
Seven-shilling pieces:
  proofs of: HW asks Selwyn for, **30**. 276; struck but not uttered, **30**. 276
1739:
  Mann's happiest year because it brought him HW's friendship, **25**. 9
1741. See under Williams, Sir Charles Hanbury
1745:
  rebellion of, Voltaire exaggerates executions in, **35**. 284
  See also 'Forty-five'
1762:
  Wesley celebrates conversions to Methodism in, **22**. 17n
1770:
  treads in footsteps of 1641, **23**. 170
Seventeenth century:
  gravity of, tires HW, **33**. 550
Seven Towers, prison at Constantinople:
  Mann unlikely to be confined in, **23**. 88, 92
  Russian minister released from, **23**. 308–9
  Sultan may confine Murray in, **23**. 479

Seven Years' War:
  America makes, but peace will be made for Germany, **21**. 369
  causes of, **7**. 285–6
  commissaries in, compared with Beast of the Gévaudan, **31**. 53
  conclusion of, **15**. 54n
  extends from Muscovy to Alsace, and from Madras to California, **35**. 290
  Pitt (Chatham) wants to continue, **38**. 75
  progress of, *see under* War
Severambians:
  HW's letters discuss people as unknown as, **21**. 552
Severn, English war ship:
  scagliola tables to be sent by, **20**. 27
Severn, river:
  at Worcester, **40**. 13
  Bewdley on, **40**. 42
  Bridgnorth on, **40**. 14
  Matson overlooks, **35**. 152
  Rhine's banks no more inspiring to Conway than those of, **37**. 143
  Shrewsbury almost surrounded by, **40**. 14
  source of, a great discovery, **34**. 93
  views of, near Worcester, **35**. 152
Severn End, Lechmere's seat:
  HW visits, **35**. 152
Severus, Alexander. *See* Alexander (208–35) Severus
Severus, Lucius Septimus (146–211), Roman emperor:
  arch of, **16**. 61
  'septizonium' of, **14**. 240
Sévery, Monsieur:
  SH visited by, **12**. 229
Sévigné, Marquise de. *See* Bréhan de Mauron, Jeanne-Marguerite; Rabutin-Chantal, Marie de (1626–96)
Sévigné, Charles de (1648–1713), Marquis de:
  letters of, better than his mother's, **35**. 602
  Ninon de Lenclos's remark about, **37**. 531n
  wife converts, from pleasure to devotion, **41**. 257
Sévigné, Françoise-Marguerite de (1646–1705), m. (1669) François de Castellane-Adhémar de Monteil, Comte de Grignan:
  biographical information about, corrected, **43**. 82, 361
  descendants of, **41**. 257
  Du Deffand, Mme, mentions, **5**. 330
  'great-granddaughter' of, **3**. 405n
  HW admires letter of, **4**. 141, 144
  HW likes only one letter of, **35**. 601
  HW's verses mention, **31**. 12
  (?) La Harpe ignores mother's affection for, **5**. 420
  Lely's miniature of Comtesse de Gramont resembles, **10**. 12
  letter of, after her mother's death, **32**. 171–2
  letters from, awaited by her mother, **10**. 212
  letters from, printed, **6**. 275

medallions of: at Ennery's, **7.** 325; at Livry, **10.** 212
miniature of, by Müntz, at SH, **10.** 12
mother admires letters of, **20.** 84
mother gives pearl necklace to, **18.** 291
mother leaves, at Paris, to economize in Brittany, **35.** 198
mother neglected by, in last illness, **41.** 257
mother's affectionate remarks to, **3.** 127, 196, **4.** 24, **5.** 420
mother's laments to, on parting, **4.** 1n
mother's letter to, **41.** 109
mother's letter to, of 13 Sept. 1679, sent to HW, **3.** 402, 405, **4.** 1–3, 6, 24
mother's letter written on departure of, **34.** 82
mother sorrows too much for, **16.** 273
mother's replies from, lost, **28.** 297
mother visits convent on evenings of departure of, for Provence, **30.** 207
portrait of: **3.** 70; at Grignan, **7.** 80; *see also* medallion of; miniature of
Sévigné, Rue de. *See* Culture Ste-Catherine, Rue de la
Sévigné family:
HW describes, **41.** 257–9
Sévigniana. See under Barral, Pierre
Seville (Spain):
Charles III may settle at, **22.** 415
climate of, **11.** 244n
English ship at, **20.** 572n
Torrigiani starves at, **1.** 82n
Seville, Treaty of:
Aix treaty does not renew Separate Article I of, **20.** 198n
Assiento and Madrid treaties renewed by, **20.** 198n
Sèvres (France):
china made at: Cupid's statue in, **2.** 373; Du Deffand, Mme has, **8.** 12–13, 24–6; given by HW to Mrs Gostling, **41.** 437–8; HW's, **7.** 402, 404–7; Hertfords will use, for HW if he visits Dublin, **39.** 40; imitating lapis lazuli, wanted by HW, **36.** 207; in Colebrooke's sale, **23.** 569n; landscape in, **43.** 89; mustard pots of, **38.** 278; Spencer, Cts, gives piece of, to Mann, **25.** 645
china manufactory at: **4.** 348, 356; HW jokes about, **31.** 125; HW visits, **4.** 348; Holdernesse attends Hertfords to, **38.** 237; Necker to retain charge of, for a few months, **7.** 453
customs duty makes china from, a rarity in England, **41.** 437
Dumont, Mme, has brother living at, **4.** 492
horses changed at, **4.** 399
visitors to: Dumont and son, **4.** 492; HW, **4.** 348, **7.** 271, 309, 331; Irwin, **7.** 331; Richmond, D. of, **6.** 441, **7.** 271n; Richmond, Ds of, **7.** 271n
Seward, Mr:
HW denies having written to, **35.** 181

HW might have to write to, if Bentley died, **35.** 188
HW's correspondence with, **35.** 182
(?) HW sees, at Southampton and discusses postal service to Jersey, **35.** 249
(?) HW writes to, about Bentley's trees, **35.** 205
Seward, Mrs:
Bentley told by, that HW wrote to her husband, **35.** 181
Seward, Anna (?1742–1809), poetess:
father of, **14.** 37n, **33.** 422
HW dislikes 'piping' of, to Hayley, **31.** 271
HW sick of poetry of, **33.** 463
Hayley and, discuss Mason, **29.** 259
lacks imagination and novelty, **33.** 533
'Muse of Lichfield,' **33.** 422
Williams, Helen Maria, gets subscription from, to *Poems*, **33.** 533n
writes no better than Ann Yearsley, **33.** 475
Seward, Rev. Thomas (1708–90), canon of Lichfield and of Salisbury; poet:
Gray dismisses poems of, **14.** 37
HW astonishes, at Ragley, **9.** 225
HW at Lyon bored by epic poem read by, **39.** 233
HW probably met, at Lyon, **43.** 182
Hertfords visited by, at Ragley, **9.** 225
poem by, on Lord Charles Fitzroy's supposed cure at Genoa, **33.** 422–3
Seward, William (1747–99), writer:
Burney writes to, **42.** 330n
HW's correspondence with, **42.** 388, 399
HW sends pieces to, and thanks him for sight of 'picture,' **42.** 399
HW thanks, for Taylor's *Contemplatio*, **42.** 388
HW wishes print of Brook Taylor from, **42.** 388
Houghton collection missed by, **16.** 189
'Memoirs' of Lady Fanshawe contributed by, to *European Magazine*, **34.** 147n
(?) Nivernais's *Jardins modernes* given to, **12.** 260
oddities of, **15.** 332
SH to be visited by, with friends, **16.** 189
(?) SH visitors sent by, **12.** 228, 232, 235 *ter*, 238
Sewell, George (d. 1726):
prefaces by, to Shakespeare, **24.** 267n
Sewell, John (ca 1734–1802):
publisher of *European Magazine*, **15.** 196n
Sewell, Sir Thomas (ca 1710–84), Kt, 1764; Master of the Rolls; M.P.:
birth date of, corrected, **43.** 281
De Grey persuaded by, not to sign Wilkes's writ of error, **23.** 12
HW receives favourable decree from, on purchase of house, **33.** 115–16, **36.** 166n
insulted, by mistake for Mansfield, **22.** 464
Master of the Rolls, **22.** 263n, **38.** 472
Townshend's ridicule of, **35.** 360

Sexton; sextons:
  at Gloucester, sells tiles to HW, 35. 151–2
  at King's College, Cambridge, 34. 62
  at Westminster Abbey, 37. 107
  Edward (1453–71)'s coffin discovered by, 30. 274
Sexual perversions:
  Edwards's theory about, 9. 270
Seychelles. See Moreau de Séchelles
Seyer. See Sayer
Seyffert, C. G., printer in Pall Mall (formerly of Dean St, Soho):
  pirated work printed by, 21. 403n
Seymour, Lady:
  Caulfeild said to have married, 38. 124
Seymour, Algernon (1684–1750), styled E. of Hertford 1684–1748; 7th D. of Somerset, 1748:
  agents of, carry off Percy papers, 40. 318
  daughter and mother of, 23. 365n
  daughter of, 9. 265n
  death of, 20. 124
  dukedom of, corrected, 43. 270
  earldom wanted by, for son-in-law instead of daughter, 20. 81
  estate settled on, 20. 10
  father blames son's death on, 18. 522
  father reconciled with, 17. 364
  father renounces, 40. 318
  father's bequest to, 20. 10
  George II discusses earldom with, 20. 12n
  —— gets letter of resignation from, through Beauchamp, 17. 346
  Newcastle, D. of, writes on behalf of, to George II, 20. 12n
  Northumberland peerage for Wyndham opposed by, 20. 12
  Northumberland title to go to daughter after death of, 20. 81
  regiment not to be resigned by, 17. 345–6
  Sturrock's correspondence with, 18. 544
  wife of, 9. 126n
  Wyndham's relations with, strained, 20. 81n
Seymour, Lady Anna Horatia. See Waldegrave, Lady Anna Horatia
Seymour, Berkeley (d. 1777):
  Somerset dukedom claimed by, 20. 139n, 167
Seymour, Lady Caroline. See Cowper, Lady Caroline
Seymour, Caroline (b. 1755), m. (1775) William Danby:
  Danby to wed, 7. 43n, 24. 94
  father's fiancée lives with sister and, 39. 266
  (?) HW sees, dishevelled, 39. 391
Seymour, Lady Catherine (d. 1731), m. (1708) Sir William Wyndham, 3d Bt:
  marriage of, 29. 69n
  Percy estate settled on children of, 20. 11n
  portrait of, 10. 338
  son of, 21. 24n
Seymour, Charles (1662–1748), 6th D. of Somerset, 1678:
  Ancaster, D. of, sells house to, 20. 11
  assets of, discovered, 20. 18

butler and, 37. 307
country fellow thrusts pig in face of, 20. 10n
daughter of: 20. 183, 21. 24n, 429n; punished for letting him fall off a couch, 20. 18
death of, 14. 21n, 20. 9
Egremont descended from, 29. 69
Gray may allude to, 13. 83n
HW imagines presents that would be given by, according to Italian custom, 18. 141
health of, 9. 71
Henley's address for, 32. 322
Mann shocked by inhumanity of, 18. 544
marriage of, to Percy heiress, 9. 97n
marriages of, 40. 318
Newcastle, D. of, succeeds, as chancellor of Cambridge, 20. 9–10
Palace, the, in Newmarket leased to, 20. 373n
pride and tyranny of, 20. 18, 28. 455n
pride of, from wife's family, 42. 380
servants survived and lists locked up by, 40. 318
settlements not divulged by, 20. 12
Seymour, Sir Edward, retorts to William III about, 18. 523
son blamed by, for grandson's death, 18. 522
son reconciled with, 17. 364
son renounced by, 40. 318
statue of, 2 330
wife of, 9. 126n
will of, 20. 10–12, 18
Seymour, Lady Charlotte (1730–1805), m. (1750) Heneage Finch, styled Bn Gernsey; 3d E. of Aylesford, 1757:
  daughter of, to be married, 32. 369
  father punishes, for letting him fall off a couch, 20. 18
  father's bequest to, 20. 10, 18
  HW and Waldegraves attend ball given by, 33. 283
  (?) Hervey woos, 9. 98
  money squandered by, 20. 183
  uncle marries, to his relative, 20. 183
Seymour, Edward (ca 1500–52), cr. (1536) Vct Beauchamp, (1537) E. of Hertford, (1547) D. of Somerset; Protector:
  Beauchamp title recreated for, to deprive son, 20. 138
  birth date of, 43. 56
  brother of, 12. 165n
  Calais visited by, with D. of Suffolk's expedition, 20. 139n
  execution of, 1. 221
  France visited by, when 'son' was begotten, 20. 139
  letter from, 16. 5n
  letter of, possibly mentioned in Royal and Noble Authors, 16. 4–5
  letters of, at Corpus Christi, Cambridge, 41. 159
  note on, 1. 220
  St Paul's chapels pulled down by, to build Somerset House, 16. 47

Seymour, Edward, and E. of Hertford contest estate of, **20**. 139n

son by first wife disinherited by, in favour of son by second wife, **18**. 523, **20**. 138–9

Surrey's prestige undermined by, **1**. 186

Thynne, Sir John, steward to, **28**. 303

wife of, **9**. 98

wife repudiated by, **20**. 139

Wolsey, Cardinal, accompanies, on embassy to France, **20**. 139n

Seymour, Sir Edward (1529–93), of Berry Pomeroy; Kt, 1547:

father disinherits, **18**. 523, **20**. 138

Hertford's alleged trial with, **20**. 139

Seymour, Sir Edward (1537–1621), styled E. of Hertford 1547–52; cr. (1559) E. of Hertford:

father disinherits elder brother in favour of, **18**. 523

Seymour, Sir Edward, has legal contest with, **20**. 139

Seymour, Edward (1561–1612), styled Lord Beauchamp:

(?) portrait of, **32**. 353, **35**. 411

Seymour, Sir Edward (ca 1563–1613), cr. (1611) Bt, of Berry Pomeroy:

Hertford's contest with, **20**. 139

Seymour, Sir Edward (1633–1708), 4th Bt; Speaker:

William III receives retort from, about D. of Somerset, **18**. 523

Seymour, Sir Edward (1695–1757), 6th Bt; 8th D. of Somerset, 1750:

Bruce's estate may be claimed by, **20**. 331

Hertford title granted to Francis, Bn Conway, with consent of, **20**. 167

Lord Chancellor refuses writ to, **20**. 139

Seymour, Berkeley, disputes Somerset title with, **20**. 139n, 167

Somerset title goes to, **18**. 522, **20**. 124, 139

Seymour, Edward (1718–92), 9th D. of Somerset:

brother of, **10**. 337

complaint about newspaper attack on Hertford bashfully seconded by, in House of Lords, **38**. 347

unmarried, **10**. 29

Seymour, Mrs Edward. See Fillol, Catherine

Seymour, Lady Elizabeth (1685–1734), m. (1707) Henry O'Brien, 7th E. of Thomond: nephew of, **21**. 24n

Seymour, Lady Elizabeth (1716–76), m. (1740) Sir Hugh Smithson, 4th Bt, 2d E. of Northumberland, 1750; cr. (1776) D. of Northumberland:

Amelia, Ps, thanks, after entertainment, **9**. 334

another footman added by, **38**. 473

Armagh, Abp of, wears stone of, in ring, **10**. 132

assemblies of: **32**. 27; given up on Ps of Orange's death, **38**. 8

(?) at Chesterfield's assembly, **37**. 326

Batheaston's verse contributions from, **32**. 225

Bath visited by, **38**. 143

Bedchamber lady to Q. Charlotte, **21**. 518, **38**. 96

Bedford House receives, with insults, **38**. 562–3

Bentham's *Ely* might have, as subscriber to a plate, **1**. 161n, 162, 164–5, 177

bouts-rimés by, on a buttered muffin, **39**. 241

Christian VII to attend York races with, **35**. 329

Cock Lane séance attended by, **10**. 6

Conway does not envy Lothario qualities of, **37**. 358

crowds entertained by, **9**. 337

Cumberland, D. and Ds of, to be called on by, **23**. 433n

début of, before HW's time, **38**. 470

dinner delayed by, at Northumberland House, **38**. 529–30

Dublin visited by, **10**. 132

dying, **24**. 99, 102

epitaph for, HW consulted by Percy about, **41**. 411–12

Ernst, P., entertained by, **10**. 34–5

extravagant construction by, **20**. 341

father wants title to go to husband instead of, **20**. 81

footmen of, more numerous than Q. Charlotte's, **34**. 23

Fuentes family entertained by, in lighted garden, **35**. 301

Gloucester, D. and Ds of, excluded by, from Alnwick Castle, **36**. 323

Grafton, Ds of, talks with, about alleged kick, **9**. 264

Guines's ball attended by, **32**. 96n

HW calls: 'Duchess of Charing Cross,' **32**. 211; 'Irish Queen,' **38**. 469; 'Vice-Majesty of Ireland,' **10**. 108; vulgar, **9**. 264

HW does not know, well enough to recommend Muzell to her, **21**. 514

HW entertained by, **9**. 334

HW gives *Fugitive Pieces* to, **38**. 78

HW informs, of heralds belonging to Percy family, **40**. 178–9

HW invited by: to meet Ps Dashkov, **39**. 132; to play cards, **40**. 153, 237, 246

HW jokes about characteristics of, **31**. 125

HW mentions, **37**. 467

HW's correspondence with, **38**. (?)555, **40**. 153, 162, 178–9, 237, 246

HW thanked by, for *Royal and Noble Authors* and (?) *Fugitive Pieces*, **40**. 162

HW told by, of Queen's message for Cts of Hertford, **38**. 473–4

Hamilton disliked by, **38**. 251n

health of: injured leg, **9**. 264; stone, **10**. 132

house and garden of, decorated for festino, **10**. 34–5

husband of, **9**. 265n

Irish post granted to husband of, **10**. 65

[Seymour, Lady Elizabeth (1716–76), *continued*]
Jewesses' servant rebuked by, for improper delivery of card to Q. Charlotte, **22**. 73
junkets of, imitated by Conway, **38**. 59
levee of, for Irish, **10**. 75
Magdalen House visited by, **9**. 273–4
March visits, **9**. 265
marriage of, **23**. 365n
mob forces, to drink Wilkes's health, **23**. 7
mourning by Queen's household, discarded at request of, **38**. 204
Newmarket visited by, **10**. 108
Northumberland title to go to, **20**. 81
opera attended by, **10**. 6, **38**. 470
opera opened by, for Guadagni, **23**. 271
Paris to be visited by, **31**. 125
—— visited by, **3**. 191
pays 40 guineas for bed at Portsmouth, **32**. 128
'pearls and diamonds' scattered by, in Irish post, **38**. 235
Percy estate does not go to, **20**. 11n
Percy papers unobtainable from, **40**. 318
pipers and Swiss porters kept by, **20**. 341
portrait of Lady Catherine Grey given to, **35**. 411
post-chaise ridden by, in deluge, with legs out the window, **34**. 207
Poulett, Lady Rebecca, pushes, **9**. 264
'private mobs' entertained by, **10**. 139
returns from Ireland, **38**. 393
servility of, to royalty, **34**. 23
seven footmen precede chair of, **38**. 469
sits on hustings, **32**. 209
subscription masquerade attended by, in fantastic headdress, **20**. 49–50
supper given by, for Cts of Yarmouth, **21**. 191
Westminster electioneering by, in Covent Garden, **24**. 51–2, **32**. 209, **39**. 196
witticisms by: on Ds of Hamilton, **9**. 264; to Cts Talbot's remark on Thermopylæ, **38**. 526
York, D. of, entertained by, **9**. 334
Seymour, Lady Elizabeth (1754–1825). *See* Seymour Conway, Lady Elizabeth
Seymour, Lady Frances (1728–60), m. (1750) John Manners, styled M. of Granby:
death of, **9**. 271, **21**. 429
father leaves house to, hoping mother can live with her, **20**. 10–11
father's bequest to, **20**. 10, 18
fortune of, £150,000, **20**. 183n
Granby to wed, **20**. 91, 183
(?) Hervey woos, **9**. 98
husband of, **9**. 108n
lease to Palace, in Newmarket, inherited by, **20**. 373n
money squandered by, **20**. 183
Piozzi, Mrs, comments upon, **9**. 271n
son sells estate inherited from, **32**. 287
Seymour, Francis (1697–1761), M.P.:
Sandwich's widowed mother married by, **20**. 216n

son at Florence told by, of Sandwich's prospects, **20**. 216–17
son quarrels with, over estate, **37**. 340, 343
son's fiancée's beauty displeases, **37**. 343
wife of, **9**. 94n
Seymour, Lady Francis. *See* Payne, Catherine
Seymour, Lord Francis (1726–99), Canon of Windsor; Dean of Wells:
Bath and Wells diocese may go to, **32**. 168n
wife of, **10**. 337
Seymour, Lady George. *See* Hamilton, Isabella
Seymour, Lord George. *See* Seymour Conway, Hon. (later Lord) George
Seymour, George (1725–44), styled Vct Beauchamp:
death of, **18**. 510, **20**. 11n
father sends, with letter to George II, **17**. 346
Mann never saw, **18**. 510
Somerset blames death of, on Hertford, **18**. 522
Sturrock tutor to, **18**. 544
Seymour, Sir George Francis (1787–1870), Kt, 1831; Adm.:
Bathursts visited by, in Sussex, **36**. 288
HW visited by, at SH, **12**. 158, 160
(?) illness of, **36**. 288
Seymour, Georgiana (b. 1756), m. (1794) Comte Louis de Durfort:
birth date of, corrected, **43**. 104
father's fiancée lives with sister and, **39**. 266
(?) Gem attends, **7**. 43
(?) HW sees, dishevelled, **39**. 391
Seymour, Hon. Georgina Augusta Frederica. *See* Elliott, Hon. Georgina Augusta Frederica Seymour
Seymour, Lord Henry. *See* Seymour-Conway, Hon. (later Lord) Henry
Seymour, Henry (ca 1626–54), styled Lord Beauchamp, 1646:
Ailesbury, E. of, grandson of, **20**. 331n
Seymour, Henry (1729–1807), M.P.; groom of the Bedchamber:
Albany, Cts of, attached to, with husband's consent, **24**. 94
Egerton, Lady Diana, breaks match with, **37**. 338, 339–40, 343
father of, objects to fiancée's beauty, **37**. 343
father tells, of Sandwich's prospects, **20**. 216–17
fiancée brought from France by, **39**. 266
fiancée lives with daughters and, **39**. 266
Florence to have been summer resort of, but for daughter's engagement, **24**. 94
—— visited by, **20**. 216–17
goes abroad, **37**. 340
HW sees, with daughter, **39**. 390–1
lover of Mme du Barry, **20**. 216n
Paris the home of, **7**. 43n
resignation of, expected, **30**. 196
Sandwich's half-brother, **20**. 217
Somerset's relative, **32**. 119
will try for a son, **32**. 119

Young Pretender and wife must be followed by, to Paris, **24.** 102

Seymour, Mrs Henry. *See* La Martillière de Chançay, Anne-Louise-Thérèse

Seymour, Horace Beauchamp (1791–1851):
Bathursts visited by, in Sussex, **36.** 288
(?) illness of, **36.** 288
mother of, **12.** 158n

Seymour, Lady Hugh. *See* Waldegrave, Lady Anna Horatia

Seymour, Lord Hugh. *See* Seymour Conway, Hon. (later Lord) Hugh

Seymour, Hugh Henry (1790–1821), army officer:
Bathursts visited by, in Sussex, **36.** 288
birth of, **31.** 352
HW visited by, at SH, **12.** *158*, 160
(?) illness of, **36.** 288
mother's beauty inherited by, **12.** 158
SH entail mentions, **30.** 351

Seymour, James (1702–52), animal painter:
HW thinks Bentley may succeed, **35.** 243

Seymour, Jane (?1509–37), m. (1536) Henry VIII of England:
arms of, **1.** 342
brother of, **28.** 303n
costume for play copied from portrait of, **9.** 335
Henry VIII's wife, **12.** 165n
print of, by Vertue, **2.** 323
Richmond, Ds of, dresses as, **17.** 338
said to have lain at Prinknash, **1.** 342

Seymour, Sir John (d. 1536), Kt:
daughter-in-law's alleged relations with, **20.** 139

Seymour, John (d. 1552):
begotten while 'father' was in France, **20.** 139
father deprives, of title because of illegitimacy, **20.** 139
father disinherits, **18.** *523*, **20.** 138–9

Seymour, Dr John (d. ca 1749):
Somerset dukedom said to be claimed by, **20.** 167

Seymour, Lady Mary (d. before 1673), m. (before 1653) Heneage Finch, 2d E. of Winchilsea:
Sultan flings handkerchief to, in his harem, **9.** 91n

Seymour, Lord Robert. *See* Seymour-Conway, Hon. (later Lord) Robert

Seymour, Sir Thomas (ca 1508–49), cr. (1547) Bn Seymour of Sudeley; lord high admiral:
birth date of, corrected, **43.** 137, 155
Catherine Parr wife of, **42.** 113, 116
Sudeley Castle owned by, **10.** 285, **12.** 165
wife jealous of, on account of Elizabeth, **16.** 207

Seymour, Hon. Thomas (1563–1600):
(?) portrait of, **32.** 353, **35.** 411

Seymour, Lord William. *See* Seymour-Conway, Hon. (later Lord) William

Seymour, William (1588–1660), 2d D. of Somerset, 1660:
Russell, Lord, praised by, **29.** 224n

Seymour, William John Richard (1793–1801):
Bathursts visited by, in Sussex, **36.** 288
(?) illness of, **36.** 288
mother of, **12.** 158n

Seymour. *See also* Seymour-Conway

Seymour-Conway, Lady Anna Horatia. *See* Waldegrave, Lady Anna Horatia

Seymour-Conway, Lady Anne (1744–84), m. (1766) Charles Moore, 6th E. of Drogheda:
aunt rejoices at marriage of, **39.** 69
character of, **33.** 448–9
death of, **33.** 448–9, **39.** 426
drawing by, awaits HW's approval, **38.** 482
Drogheda to wed, **39.** 50, *51*–2, 54
fashionable at Dublin, **39.** 45
father accompanied by, at Dublin, **39.** 19, 25
father and sister entertained by, **39.** 278
father expects, at Paris, **38.** 427–8
father may leave, in Ireland, **39.** 39
father's letter from, from Spa, about Brest fleet, **39.** 315
Forbes proposes to marry, **38.** 575–7
Fox, Hon. Stephen, said to be marrying, **38.** 489, 492
HW does not see, at Hôtel de Brancas, **39.** 9
HW supposes, grows talkative at Paris, **38.** 343
health of, fever, **39.** 287
husband accompanied by, to visit his sisters, **39.** 59
Keene, Col., arranges match for, **39.** 51
March said to be marrying, **38.** 453, 489, 492
Montagu deplores rumoured engagement of, **10.** 107
Paris left by, **38.** 427–8
settled and pregnant after marriage, **39.** 59

Seymour-Conway, Hon. Rev. Edward (1757–85):
death of, at Lyon, **33.** 500, **39.** 433–4
height of, **39.** 379

Seymour-Conway (later, Seymour), Lady Elizabeth (1754–1825):
brother's generosity to, **34.** 200
father accompanied by, at Sudbourne, **39.** 423
HW entertains, at dinner, **11.** *323*
Lincoln, Lady, visited by, **11.** 323
marriage of, rumoured, **32.** 358, 360
more beautiful than elder sister, **23.** 323
mother of, gives party, **33.** 283

Seymour-Conway, Lady Frances (1751–1820), m. (1775) Henry Fiennes Pelham Clinton, styled Lord Clinton 1752–68, and E. of Lincoln 1768–78:
brother and sister-in-law to visit, **36.** 245–6
brother's generosity to, **34.** 200
daughter of, to inherit Clinton barony, HW thinks, **25.** 165
father dies at house of, at Putney, **39.** 509n
HW praises, **24.** 71
HW's guests come from, **11.** 323

[Seymour-Conway, Lady Frances, *continued*]
HW to have been called on by, 39. 162
HW to meet Hugh Seymour-Conway at house of, 39. 453–4
house at Putney Common taken by, 12. 158, 36. 245 (*see also* Copt Hall)
husband's body brought back to England, 24. 420
Lincoln, E. of, to marry, 24. 71
marriage of, 6. 132, 134, 28. 303n
more beautiful than elder sister, 23. 323
son of, dead, 33. 123
Seymour-Conway (after 1807, Ingram-Seymour-Conway), Francis (1743–1822), styled Vct Beauchamp 1750–93 and E. of Yarmouth 1793–4; 2d M. of Hertford, 1794; M.P.:
admired in Paris, and speaks French well, 38. 219
apartment of, in Hôtel de Brancas, available for HW, 38. 477, 481, 485
appearance of: 10. 237; tall, 38. 215
(?) brothers accompany, at Warwick, 10. 300
brothers and servants to accompany, to SH, 39. 154
brothers and sisters generously treated by, 34. 200
brothers' and sisters' legacies from father augmented by, 34. 200n
brother's letters shown by, to HW, 38. 180
Christ Church, Oxon, attended by, 9. 287, 38. 43–6, 50–1, 52–3, 62
Combe marries mistress of, 28. 303–4
Compiègne to be visited by, 5. 388
—— visited by, 38. 408
convention signed by, 12. 34n
Coronation to be attended by, 38. 114
Cowslade a play-fellow of, 9. 251n
deposition of, against Lord Mayor, 33. 199
Dublin Castle constable's post declined by, 39. 77
Du Deffand, Mme, cannot procure society for, 5. 385
—— pities, for death of wife, 5. 189, 219
——'s opinion of, 5. 387–8
Edgcumbe brings, into Parliament, 22. 471n
enclosure sent by, to HW, 38. 314, 323
Eton re-entered by, 38. 26
—— speech by, 38. 15
father accompanied by, to Dublin, 39. 19, 25
father expects, at Paris, 38. 427–8
father's instructions awaited by, 22. 319, 327
father visits 'all the town' with, 38. 238
Florence visited by: 38. 514, 531; from Milan, 22. 319
Fontainebleau to be left by, for Turin, 38. 448
franks letter for HW, 2. 123
French of, will pass, 38. 219, 237–8, 277
Frenchwomen's freedom defended by, against mother's criticism, 38. 268
George III's train-bearer at Coronation, 38. 122
Grafton wrests Coventry from, 23. 186n

Gulston intimate with, 1. 313n
HW and Conway to visit, at Oxford, 38. 54, 59–60, 61, 62
HW asked by, for (?) *Essay on Modern Gardening*, 39. 461–2
HW called on by, with news of K. of Spain's death, 34. 33
HW calls, 'great news-merchant,' 33. 214
HW consulted by, about Jesuit possibly fleeing to London, 38. 349
HW hears Mann's praises from, in Paris, 22. 344
HW not again to exhaust, at Oxford, 38. 68
HW offers to lend SH to, after wife's death, 39. 153–4
HW praises good heart of, 38. 152–3
HW probably not to make, his heir, 15. 335
HW rebukes, as 'stock-jobber' for East India Co.'s stock, 39. 81–2
HW receives china from, 39. 177
HW's advice to, 38. 152–3
HW's advice to father to be repeated only to mother and, 38. 391
HW's correspondence with, 9. 285, 303, 38. 42–3, 45, 50, 52, 61, 62, 150, 152, 157, 251, 349, 39. 81, 155, 177, 249, 461
HW sends box by, 7. 404
HW sends epitaph on wife to, 39. 155–6
HW sends letter by, 5. 384, 387, 7. 376
HW sends tooth-powder by, 5. 387
HW sends verses to, on destruction of French navy, 13. 35, 38. 50–1, 52–3
HW shown Mann's letter by, 22. 495
HW's letter carried by, 10. 183n
HW's letter to, better for postal inspection than letter to Hertford is, 38. 354
HW's letter to Hertford on Conway's downfall can be communicated only to, 38. 391
HW's Oxford explorations exhaust, 9. 288
HW's rumoured settlement of SH on, 12. 143, 146
HW thanked by, for *Anecdotes of Painting*, 38. 150–1, 152–3
HW to entertain, at dinner at SH, 38. 74
HW to hear about Mme du Deffand from, 5. 401
HW to receive compliments of, 38. 337
HW to tell, of Mann's readiness to oblige him, 23. 213
HW to visit, at Oxford, 9. 282, 285
health of, mumps, 39. 52
Holdernesse, Cts of, entertains, 43. 304
horses obtained by, 22. 338
Horsham borough might be inherited by, 39. 300
House of Lords ejects, 23. 256n
Irish liberalism of, may be a thrust at Shelburne ministry in England, 39. 396n
Irish success of, pleases father, 39. 39, 45
Irish Volunteers' addresses to, 33. 382n
Irvine visited by, in Yorkshire, 39. 265
Italian itinerary of, from Florence, 22. 336, 344, 38. 531

Italy to be visited by, **38**. 441, 451
Letter to the First Belfast Company, A, returned to, with criticism, by HW, **39**. 394–7
liberty preferred by, to prerogative, **39**. 395
London probably reached by, **5**. 395
—— reached by, just in time to go to Dublin, **39**. 25
Macdonald a friend of, **22**. 344
Magdalen House visited by, **9**. 273–4
Mann conceals false news of mother's death from, **22**. 468
—— congratulated by, on HW's recovery, **22**. 466
—— encloses letter to, **22**. 470, 476, 486, 495
—— praises, **22**. 282
—— procures Italian wine for, **23**. 200, 204, 213, 215, 279, 302
——'s civilities to, at Florence, **38**. 514
——'s correspondence with, about Bath knighthood, **22**. 480, 486, 502
—— tells, of father's Irish post, **22**. 327
—— to entertain, at dinner, **22**. 327
Mannheim, foreign minister at, writes military news to, **12**. 89
marriages of, **10**. 237, **39**. 265, 268
Montagu hopes HW will visit, **9**. 361
—— hopes to see, **9**. 286
—— invites, to Greatworth, **9**. 288, 290, 303
—— sees, at Warwick, **10**. 300
Montagu, Lord Charles Greville, to accompany, to Greatworth, **9**. 303
mother accompanied by, to Dublin, **32**. 14
mother regrets trip of, to Italy, **38**. 451
mother's fondness for, **33**. 448
mother's letter from, mentions Turin visit on way to Genoa, **38**. 482
mother vainly awaits, at Paris, **39**. 25
Mount Stuart to be visited by, **39**. 154
mules sought by, to facilitate departure from Florence, **22**. 336
Nivernais's *Jardins modernes* given to, **12**. 260
Oxford residence to be resumed by, **38**. 99
paper copied by, for HW, **38**. 314
parents' interest centred in, **4**. 410
parents send compliments to Mme du Deffand by, **5**. 386
Parisians consider, extremely knowledgeable, **38**. 268
Paris left by, **5**. 219, **38**. 427–8
—— visited by, **7**. 265
Parliamentary membership expected for, **25**. 488
Parliamentary motion by, for modifying Clandestine Marriages Act, **39**. 375n
Parliamentary speech by, opposing London's remonstrance, **39**. 126n
Patch's painting owned by, **26**. 45
popularity of, in Ireland, **10**. 204
Ragley to be visited by, **38**. 80
Reims visited by, **5**. 388, 394, 395, 401
rumoured to be war secretary, **7**. 49
secretaryship to father in Ireland rumoured for, **22**. 320n

secretary's post in Ireland given up by, without reward, **39**. 77
social relations of, in Paris, **5**. 384, 388
son of: taken by him on tour, **39**. 463; well, **33**. 97
Stanhope St the address of, **39**. 249
SH visited by, **12**. 223 *bis*
Thames Ditton visited by, **33**. 214
threatened by rioters, **11**. 317
Times mentions, as HW's possible heir, **12**. 139n
Turin to be visited by, **38**. 448
—— visited by, on way to Geneva, **38**. 482
tutors of, **1**. 345, **9**. 288
uncle to receive letter from, through Mann, **22**. 320
unpopular at Eton, **38**. 219n
unpopular literary pretensions of, at Oxford, **38**. 44n
Warwick to be visited by, **39**. 78
—— visited by, **10**. 300
wife's death distracts, **23**. 381
Wilkes asks, to deliver message to Mann, **22**. 281–2
Windsor, Hon. Alice, to wed, **22**. 480
Windsor left by, for Suffolk, **38**. 179
Seymour-Conway, Francis Charles (1777–1842), styled E. of Yarmouth 1794–1822; 3d M. of Hertford, 1822:
Conway papers left by, to Croker, **9**. 121n
father takes, on tour, **39**. 463
health of, well again, **33**. 97
wife of, **5**. 387n, **11**. 184n
Seymour-Conway (after 1794, Seymour), Hon. (after 1793, Lord) George (1763–1848), army officer; M.P.:
Austrian-Dutch clash reported by, **39**. 428
baptism of, **38**. 209
biographical information about, corrected, **43**. 152
brother's generosity to, **34**. 200
Conway mistakes P. of Wales for, **12**. 44
dances at mother's party, **33**. 283
Foote says Hertford would not license play when, was not boxkeeper, **39**. 252
Gibraltar army service of, might be followed by one in America, **39**. 379
HW called on by, **39**. 379
(?) HW encourages Conway to be impartial towards, **29**. 305
HW to be visited by, at SH, **39**. 284, 285, 286
'handsomest giant in the world,' **39**. 379
height of, compared to brothers', **39**. 379
marriage of, **12**. 169
Parliamentary membership expected for, **25**. 488
Saarlouis, news of surrender of, brought by, **12**. 73
Wurmser, Gen., dispatch about, brought to London by, **12**. 40
Seymour-Conway, Sir George Francis (1787–1870), naval officer; Kt, 1831:
birth of, **39**. 457

[Seymour-Conway, Sir George F., *continued*]
HW visited by, at SH, **12**. 158, 160
Hertford visited by, at Sudbourne, **39**. 463–4
SH entail mentions, **30**. 351
Seymour-Conway, Lady Gertrude (1750–93), m.
(1772) George Mason Villiers, styled Vct
Villiers; 1st (2d) E. Grandison, 1782:
fashionable at Dublin, **39**. 45
father accompanied by, to Dublin, **39**. 19, 25
father hears of Conway's illness from, **39**. 278
father may leave, in Ireland, **39**. 39
Frankfurt and Vienna to be visited by, **39**.
261
Hatton known to Hertford's daughters who
accompanied, **39**. 433
health of: fears for, **39**. 261; low and uncomfortable at start of journey, **39**. 265
Henley revisited by, fat, **39**. 209
husband should not drag, to Germany's vile
inns, **39**. 252, 261, 265
marriage of, **1**. 236, 237n, 238, 240, 243, **5**.
139, **23**. 323, 381, **36**. 76, **39**. 151
mother-in-law consults parents of, **36**. 76
mother-in-law forces, to travel with husband,
39. 261
mother-in-law to live with, **32**. 369
sister visited by, on return from Henley, giving father news of Germany, **39**. 278
Vienna to be visited by, **32**. 251
Seymour Conway (after 1794, Seymour), Hon.
(after 1793, Lord) Henry (1746–1830), M.P.:
abbreviated address by, on letter to T. Tighe,
25. 608
at Sudbourne, choosing Orford mayor, **39**.
265
(?) Beauchamp accompanied by, to SH, **39**.
154
brother's generosity to, **34**. 200
brother shows to HW letters by, **38**. 180
Compiègne to be visited by, **5**. 388
Conway gets courier from, on mother's alleged death, **38**. 494
Du Deffand, Mme, cannot procure society
for, **5**. 385
—— inquires about, **7**. 229–30
——'s opinion of, **5**. 387–8
Eton re-entered by, **38**. 26
father accompanied by, at Sudbourne, **39**.
423, (?) 431
father hopes E. of Orford will find borough
for, **39**. 192
father sends, to fetch pens, **39**. 540
father writes to, at Park Place to tell Conway
and wife of Damer's suicide, **39**. 281
Fox, Hon. Stephen and Lady Mary, accompanied by, in dressing-room, **23**. 392
grief of, at mother's death, **33**. 371
Guines's ball attended by, **32**. 117
HW asked by, for leave to bring breakfast
party to SH, **39**. 74–5
HW gives 'character' of Lady Hertford to,
33. 373
HW invites, to SH, **32**. 42

(?) HW plays with, at Ragley, **9**. **225**
HW's 'character' of, **39**. 544
HW's correspondence with, **39**. 74–5
HW sends letter by, **5**. 387
Hampton Court to be visited by, **39**. 75
height of, **38**. 538
Hobart, Mrs, surprises, by her agility, **32**. 117
indolent and humorous, **25**. 608
Lincoln's Inn the address of, **39**. 74
London probably reached by, **5**. 395
Montagu sees, at Warwick, **10**. 300
——'s landlady admires, **10**. 300
Orford not left by, for Garter pageants, **38**.
179–80
Oxford to be entered by, **38**. 99
parents send compliments to Mme du Def-
fand by, **5**. 386
Parliamentary membership expected for, **25**.
488
Ragley to be visited by, **38**. 80
Reims visited by, **5**. 388, 394, 395
reports on Gordon riots, **33**. 188
social relations of, in Paris, **5**. 384, 388
watch bought by, from Griegson in Paris, **39**.
117–18
Seymour-Conway, Lady Hugh. *See* Waldegrave,
Lady Anna Horatia
Seymour-Conway (after 1794, Seymour), Hon.
(after 1793, Lord) Hugh (1759–1801), M.P.;
naval officer:
absent, **36**. 288
Agincourt to be recalled by, to HW's remembrance, **42**. 104
Berry, Mary, identifies, **11**. 261n
brother's generosity to, **34**. 200
dances at mother's party, **33**. 283
death of, **43**. 370–1
father entertains P. of Wales with, **39**. 439n
father, on his marriage, presents, to George
III, **39**. 438n
fever in family of, **36**. 288
HW appoints, trustee under his will, **30**. 353
HW called on by, at SH, **39**. 502
HW entertains, at dinner, **11**. 323
(?) HW hopes, has recovered, **38**. 260
HW praises, **25**. 632
HW to talk to, at Cts of Lincoln's, **39**. 453–4
HW visited by, **34**. 199
Hambledon the address of, **39**. 489
health of: (?) ill at Tours, **38**. 246; (?) re-
covered, **38**. 268, 277; suffers from blow
on head, **11**. 261–2
Lennox, Lady George, tends, after accident,
31. 352–7
Lennox, Lord and Lady George, to be repaid
by, with dog, for kindness, **39**. 490
Lincoln, Lady, visited by, **11**. 323
marriage date of, corrected, **43**. 378
marriage of: HW congratulated on, by
Thomas Walpole, jr, **36**. 235–6; results in
HW's dining with P. of Wales at Hertford's
and at Leicester House, **25**. 647
marriage settlement of, **42**. 173–4, **43**. 369

Parliamentary membership expected for, **25.** 488

Portsmouth visited by, **12.** 179n

(?) 'pretty,' **38.** 246

promotion of, **43.** 379

Richmond, D. of, accompanies, to France, **42.** 104n

Seymour-Conway, Hon. George, almost as handsome as, **39.** 379

sister to be visited by, at Putney Common, **36.** 245–6

to return to Lord Hood's fleet, **39.** 502

unable to come to London, **11.** 262

Waldegrave to receive from, Box A of HW's MSS, **36.** 313n

Waldegrave, Lady Anna Horatia, to marry, **25.** 632

wife expects, to return from sea, **12.** 158

wife of, **2.** 55n, **10.** 63n, **28.** 445n

wife's relationship to, **25** 632n, 647

wife still the passion of, **39.** 443

Seymour-Conway, Hugh Henry (1790–1821), army officer. *See* Seymour, Hugh Henry

Seymour-Conway, Lady Isabella Rachel (1755–1825), m. (1785) George Hatton:

baptism of, **37.** 428, 430

birth of, **37.** 430

brother's generosity to, **34.** 200

father accompanied by, to Sudbourne, **39.** 423

HW dances with, **33.** 284

HW to be visited by, at SH, **39.** 284, 285, 286

Hatton engaged to, **39.** 432–3

marriage of, **33.** 500

mother of, gives party, **33.** 283

Seymour-Conway (after 1794, Seymour), Hon. (after 1793, Lord) Robert (1748–1831), 'Colonel Conway'; M.P.; army officer:

American news reported by, **33.** 305–6

arrives with bad news from America, **29.** 161

(?) Beauchamp accompanied by, to SH, **39.** 155

brother's generosity to, **34.** 200

Clinton's aide-de-camp, **33.** 305n

Conway accompanied by, to Jersey, **39.** 358, 361–2

——'s calmness admired by, **25.** 115

(?) Cumberland, Ds of, resembles, **32.** 65n, **36.** 88n

(?) HW plays with, at Ragley, **9.** 225

height of, **39.** 379

marriage of, **32.** 125

masquerade attended by, as highlander, **23.** 194n

Montagu sees, at Warwick, **10.** 300

Parliamentary membership expected for, **25.** 488

storm described by, **33.** 269–70

wife of, miscarries, **33.** 270

wife's uncle's paltry bequest to, **39.** 274–5

Seymour-Conway, Hon. Mrs Robert. *See* Delmé, Anne (d. 1804)

Seymour-Conway, Lady Sarah Francis (1747–70), m. (1766) Robert Stewart, cr. (1789)

Bn Londonderry:

death of, from fever, in pregnancy, **39.** 129

Du Deffand, Mme, thinks parents of, will scarcely regret her, **4.** 440

fashionable at Dublin, **39.** 45

father accompanied by, to Dublin, **39.** 19, 25

father may leave, in Ireland, **39.** 39

Moore plans to wed, **39.** 50, 51–2, 54

son of, **39.** 444, 445

Stewart to wed, **39.** 71, 72

Seymour-Conway (after 1794, Seymour), Hon. (after 1793, Lord) William (1760–1837), army officer; M.P.:

brother's generosity to, **34.** 200

HW's correspondence with, **31.** 352–3

HW's esteem for, **31.** 356

HW to be visited by, at SH, **39.** 284, 285, 286

Parliamentary membership expected for, **25.** 488

reports on Gordon riots, **33.** 188

Seymour-Conway. *See also* Conway; Seymour

Seymour-Conway family:

daughters of, accompanied by HW to Soho masquerade ball, **23.** 194

Seymour family:

Caulfeilds and Stauntons not related to, **38.** 133

Chute discovers scandal in, **20.** 138–9

descent of titles of, **18.** 523, **20.** 138–9, 167

HW would decorate Ragley salon with portraits of, **9.** 223

Osterley Park must be envied by, **32.** 125

Seymour Place, London:

Cole at, **1.** 308, 311n

Grafton, Ds of, has house in, **32.** 28n, 29, 30n

(?) HW's error for Grosvenor Place, **32.** 272

Sézanne (France):

French losses admitted at, by officers, **19.** 427

Sèze, Raymond (1748–1828), Comte de:

Défense de Louis by, good sense of, **31.** 375

Sezi *or* Seise (Italy):

Spaniards arrive at, **19.** 225–6

Sforza, Duca:

Rosenberg keeps, waiting, **23.** 104n

Sforza, Duchessa. *See* Orsini, Eleonora (d. 1634)

Sforza, Giovanni Galeazzo Maria (1468–94), D. of Milan 1476–94 *or* Ludovico Maria (1451–1508), D. of Milan 1494–1500; 'il Moro':

(?) portrait of, at Wimbledon, **9.** 120

Sforza Cesarini ('Cetarini'), Marchese [? Francesco (1773–1816)]:

Lepri heiress engaged to, **25.** 385

Pius VI will be opposed by, over Lepri donation, **25.** 385

Sganarelle. See under Molière

SH. *See* Strawberry Hill

Shackerly, Mr:

Twickenham resident, **42.** 487

Shackerly. *See also* Shakerley

Shackleton, ——, painter:

George II's portrait by, **40.** 284

Shackleton, Abraham (1697–1771), Quaker:

Burke's teacher, **29.** 63

Shaddocks:
climate of India suitable for ripening oranges to, **25.** 153
Shade; shades:
green, for candle, **18.** 228
Shadrach, Meshach, and Abednego:
jewels, put in furnace, resemble, **31.** 158
Shadwell, Lady. *See* Binns, Ann
Shadwell, Miss (elder):
Conway calls, 'Miss T'other,' **37.** 46, **43.** 372
—— meets, **37.** 46
costumed as Mary, Q. of Scots, at Ds of Norfolk's ball, **17.** 338
HW meets, at Court, **17.** 185
Shadwell, Catherine, m. (1737) Edward Allen, English consul at Naples:
biographical information on, corrected, **43.** 239, 257
Charles of Naples may seize, as hostage, **19.** 57–8
Florence to be visited by, from Naples on way to England, **19.** 477
(?) HW meets, at Court, **17.** 185
Shadwell, Charles (fl. 1710–20), dramatist:
Fair Quaker of Deal, The, revision of, **28.** 110
Shadwell, Sir John (1671–1747), Kt, 1715; physician:
Conway meets, **37.** 46
(?) Cope to be cured by daughter of, **14.** 87
HW meets, at Court, **17.** 185
Seward's ode to, for supposed cure of Lord Charles Fitzroy, **33.** 422–3
'sudden death' the nickname of, **37.** 46
widow of, **24.** 282–3n
Shadwell, Molly:
called 'Mademoiselle Misse Molli' in Italy, **17.** 185n
Conway meets, **37.** 46
(?) Cope should drink Bath waters from hand of, **14.** 87
HW meets, at Court, **17.** 185
Pulteney, E. of Bath's verses on, **43.** 184
Shadwell, Richard (d. 1785), clerk in secretary of state's office:
Larpent recommends, to handle Mann's affairs, **23.** 443–4
Mann advances money to, **25.** 87n
Shadwell, Thomas (? 1642–92), dramatist:
Libertine, The, by, **9.** 256
Virtuoso, The, by, **13.** 232
Shadwell, Thomas (d. 1786), undersecretary to Bn Grantham:
goes to Madrid, **5.** 87n
Shadwell (near London):
Ford, police magistrate at, **11.** 368n
New Gravel Lane in, **23.** 39n
Shaftesbury, E. of. *See* Cooper, Anthony Ashley (1621–83), Cooper, Anthony Ashley (1671–1713); Cooper, Anthony Ashley (1711–71)
Shaftesbury, Dorset:
Beckford and Delaval meet at, as election opponents, **35.** 171

Shafto, Jenison (ca 1728–71), M.P.:
betting prowess of, **40.** 197
Castle Rising allotted to, **36.** 47
Huntingdon races visited by, **43.** 130
Meynell's wager with, over ride by Woodcock, **38.** 272n, **40.** 197n
Newmarket winnings of, predictable, **38.** 272
Shag, scarlet:
underpetticoat lined with, **18.** 333
Shagreen:
watch-case of, **40.** 64n
Shah Alam (1728–1806), Mogul emperor, 1759:
East India Co. awarded revenue rights by, **22.** 479n
George III and Q. Charlotte get 'presents' from, through Clive, **22.** 540, 547
(?) grandmother of, **21.** 378
Spencer's letter to, **23.** 381n
Shah Goest, Indian animal:
Pitt gives, to George III, **21.** 378
Shakerley, Mrs Peter. *See* Morris, Margaret
Shakerley. *See also* Shackerly
Shakespear. See under Pignotti, Lorenzo
Shakespear, George (d. 1797), architect; carpenter:
Darnley's mausoleum said to be entrusted to, **16.** 197
Shakespeare, William (1564–1616), dramatist:
Addison excelled only by, in humour, **16.** 269
'allicholy' used by, **43.** 110
Antony and Cleopatra by: Du Deffand, Mme, cites, **7.** 162; monument in, **32.** 147
application of quotations from, **33.** 52
'argosie' a word used by, **18.** 202
As You Like It by: George III sees, **32.** 235; quoted by HW, **11.** 126
Barrett writes worse than, **31.** 331
Beauclerk, Lady Diana, does illustrations worthy of plays of, **24.** 524
Bentley ridicules formal commentators on, **35.** 262
'bodkin' used in, **41.** 295, 373
Boufflers, Comtesse de, dislikes, **6.** 304
Boydell's illustrated edition of, **33.** 546–7, 549
bust of, repaired, **9.** 120
Caliban's style formed by, **41.** 292
Capell's notes on, **35.** 599
contradiction to Milles's definition of forgery, **16.** 340
Coriolanus by: to be translated, **6.** 298; translated, **7.** 69
counterfeiting of, impossible, **31.** 260
Cymbeline by, **7.** 70, **9.** 408
deed signed by: Garrick, Mrs, owns, **31.** 259–60, **42.** 211, 426; Malone wants to borrow, for facsimile, **31.** 260, **42.** 211, 426
'divine plays' by, **1.** 248
Droeshout's print of, **1.** 132
Du Deffand, Mme, compares Sedaine's plays to those of, **4.** 384
—— does not appreciate, **5.** 390
—— influenced by, **4.** 174

—— mentions, **4.** 168

—— praises, **4.** 167, 174

—— reads, **5.** 347

——'s acquaintance with, **3.** 270, **4.** 167, 171, 174

editors' prefaces to, **24.** 267n

Elfrida shows influence of, **14.** 46

England gets pre-eminence in genius from, **31.** 256

English commentators on, inadequate, **33.** 547

English still prefer, to Pope and Addison, **40.** 379

Farmer's *Essay on the Learning of*, **1.** 257, **2.** 269, 293

Felton's *Imperfect Hints towards a New Edition* of, **34.** 10

——'s portrait of, **34.** 10n

festival for, at Stratford, **10.** 287, 298

first folio of, Heming's and Condell's dedication to Pembroke in, **35.** 629

forgeries of, prevalent, **42.** 426

French cannot approach, **31.** 256

French critics ignorantly disparage, **41.** 289, 297

French stage etiquette fortunately unknown to, **42.** 213–14

French translation of, in progress, **28.** 258–9, 276

Garrick builds temple to, **9.** 198–9, **35.** 242

—— contrasted with, **33.** 86, 88

—— should not be admired as much as, **38.** 524

genius: **32.** 289; but wanting in taste, **40.** 352

Goldsmith envies, **28.** 277

Gray adores, **28.** 277

——'s lines written in name of, to Mason's housekeeper, **28.** 166

——'s odes mention, **40.** 101

—— to join, **28.** 20, **29.** 295

HW alludes to, **28.** 86

HW calls, 'first of men,' **41.** 373

HW compares, with Correggio, **23.** 350

HW compares Mason to, **28.** 161, **29.** 295

HW consigns to the Americans, **35.** 597

HW defends, against Voltaire, **35.** 558, **41.** 149, 152–3, 158

HW discusses, **31.** 331

HW grieved that English admire, but write worse than he, **39.** 120

HW guides Mme du Deffand's reading of, **4.** 174

HW on commentators of, **2.** 293

HW praises, **4.** 98, 119, **5.** 389–90

HW prefers, to French dramatists, **6.** 44

HW prefers, to Voltaire, **3.** 256, 261, 270, **4.** 96, 98, 129

HW's correspondence with Voltaire on, **4.** 90, 95–6, 98–9, 101–4, 106, 113, 116–20, 122–3, 126, 127, 129, 146, 237, 286, **6.** 361, **7.** 387, **8.** 144–6

HW's defence of, in *Castle of Otranto*, **8.** 141–3; Barthélemy inquires about, **6.** 268

HW's letter resembles historic plays of, **25.** 68

HW's model in depicting domestics, **1.** 92n

HW's *Mysterious Mother* shows influence of, **36.** 53

HW's notes on characters of, kept at SH, **42.** 137, 138–9

HW's opinion of, **6.** 303

HW's veneration for, **33.** 543

HW's works deserve no edition like that of, **42.** 372

had several souls, **14.** 188

Hamilton and guests discuss, at Bushey Park, **9.** 380

Hamlet by: **4.** 281, 282, **8.** 141; Bentley's criticism on Queen in, **35.** 262; Berrys and Greatheeds to see, **12.** 129; Bromfield quotes, **40.** 326; Chute quotes, **35.** 60; close mourning of Hamlet in, **32.** 316; costumes of King and Hamlet in Macklin's production of, **30.** 55; Ducis's adaptation of, **7.** 332, **35.** 121, **42.** 213–14; Garrick alters, **28.** 58, **29.** 368–70; Genlis, Mme de, makes witticism on, **12.** 257; 'Gertrude' in, should be counterpart of Catherine II, **22.** 426; ghost in, **39.** 197, **41.** 297; ghost in, wears scanty costume, **20.** 209; (?) grave-digger in, **35.** 565; grave-diggers in, have no chance against French tragedies, **35.** 122; grave-diggers' scene in, **29.** 368–9, **41.** 289; grave of, **20.** 240; Gray alludes to, **13.** 79, **14.** 69; HW alludes to, **28.** 120; HW compares himself with 'Polonius' in, **33.** 582; HW compares politicians with actors exchanging parts in, **38.** 511; HW echoes grave-digger's speech in, **30.** 137, 210; HW paraphrases, **9.** 136–7, **30.** 57; HW quotes, **23.** 345, **24.** 366, **25.** 48, **32.** 214, 281, 316, **33.** 106, 338, 522, **35.** 177; Hardinge paraphrases, **35.** 600; Hardinge quotes, **35.** 568; keeper reads, to Ferrers, **21.** 408; Mason alludes to, **29.** 80, 303, 342; More, Hannah, alludes to, **31.** 274; More, Hannah, paraphrases, **31.** 320; parts in, exchanged, **35.** 263; Polonius in, **39.** 127; Pulteney alludes to, **17.** 298; Russian translation of, performed in St Petersburg, **22.** 426; soliloquy in, on Yorick's skull, **25.** 7; source of character, **28.** 244; Voltaire condemns phrase in third soliloquy, **29.** 370; Waldegrave, Cts, quotes, **36.** 290

Hanmer's edition of, **18.** 566–7, **30.** 302n, **43.** 256

Hardinge's sonnet refers to, **35.** 557–8

Hénault imitates, **4.** 166–7n

Henry IV, parts i and ii: cabin-boy in, **41.** 373; Falstaff and Mrs Quickly in, **32.** 154; Falstaff in, **15.** 206, **38.** 127; Falstaff in, acted by Quin, **33.** 87, 547, **38.** 524; Falstaff in, greater than *Iliad* or *Æneid*, **32.** 334; Falstaff in, resembles HW, **33.** 284; Garrick as Hotspur in, **33.** 87, **38.** 525;

[Shakespeare, William, *continued*]
Glendower in, **28**. 350; Gray alludes to, **13**. 56, 82, 148; Gray quotes, **13**. 82n; HW alludes to, **43**. 151; HW and Dr Johnson admire, **33**. 574; HW paraphrases, **35**. 286; HW parodies lines from, **19**. 443n; HW quotes, **10**. 298, **29**. 108; Hardinge quotes, **35**. 571, 573; 'hostess' in, **11**. 68n; Hotspur's mockeries of Glendower in, **41**. 373; Lady Percy's speech in, better than Voltaire, **41**. 294, 294–5; lines from, repeated at Drury Lane, **17**. 336; Montagu refers to, **10**. 239; More, Hannah, paraphrases, **31**. 341

Henry V: error in dramatis personæ of, **42**. 138; HW paraphrases, **20**. 402; Hardinge quotes, **35**. 571; Kemble produces, **11**. 64n; Mason alludes to, **29**. 60; 'Shrewsbury clock' in, **40**. 14

Henry VI: **4**. 167, 174; Gray mentions, **14**. 75; HW quotes, **2**. 221; Kemble adapts, **11**. 64

Henry VIII: **18**. 537; Catherine of Aragon speaks English in, **16**. 207; etiquette in, **9**. 100; Henry VIII perfectly drawn in, **41**. 290; performed at Covent Garden, **43**. 257; Wolsey's dying speech in, **32**. 338

historic scenes in, mere versifications of Holinshed and Stow, **41**. 294

Homer compared to, **7**. 181

Hurd praises Warburton's notes on, **16**. 37

imitators of, seldom produce a *François II*, **41**. 29

Ireland's forgeries of, complete triumvirate with Macpherson and Chatterton, **34**. 213–14

Johnson's strictures on, **29**. 370, **41**. 294, 372–3

—— thinks bombast essential to sublimity of, **41**. 294, 373

Johnson-Steevens edition of, **28**. 116, **29**. 179, **43**. 299

jubilee of, described by Le Tourneur, **6**. 287

Julius Cæsar: Cinna the poet in, **34**. 162–3; Du Deffand, Mme, cites, **6**. 298; Du Deffand, Mme, gives opinion of, **6**. 298, 304; Gray alludes to, **13**. 61, 126; HW quotes, **16**. 158, **22**. 367, **33**. 428; More, Hannah, discusses Brutus in, **31**. 249; West alludes to, **13**. 91

Kent's design for monument to, in Westminster Abbey, **35**. 151

King John: **4**. 174; Arthur and Constance praised in, **41**. 294, 373; HW describes scene in, **29**. 370; HW quotes, **10**. 168; Montagu alludes to, **9**. 356; Northcote's painting from, **15**. 206; reveals nature in some parts, **41**. 294

King Lear: Beauclerk, Lady Diana, does picture to illustrate, **33**. 573; Dover cliff in, **40**. 5; Du Deffand, Mme, gives opinion of, **7**. 162, 165, 167; Garrick as Lear in, **33**. 87, **38**. 524; HW alludes to, **29**. 368; HW quotes, **11**. 69, **12**. 174, **32**. 66, **39**. 480; HW sees Garrick's last performance in, **28**. 277;

Hardinge quotes, **35**. 588; Mason quotes, **28**. 172; Montagu alludes to, **9**. 309; Siddons, Mrs, is seen in, by HW, Reynolds, Mrs Piozzi, and Hothams, **34**. 2n; to be translated, **6**. 298

King Lear and *Othello* show uses of misery and pity, **35**. 588–9

King wants Latin translation of, **32**. 311n

La Place makes poor translation of, **6**. 290

life of, in Le Tourneur's *Shakespeare traduit de l'anglois*, **6**. 287

Love's Labour's Lost and *Titus Andronicus* the only plays by, now imitated, **39**. 120

Macbeth: **7**. 69; account in, of two grooms, **41**. 373; art in, by chance, **41**. 294; Bartolozzi could not illustrate, **33**. 547; Beauclerk, Lady Diana, does illustration for, **33**. 573; Duncan's castle in, **33**. 547; English act, at Geneva, **37**. 44; Garrick inferior to Quin as Macbeth in, **38**. 525; Gray alludes to, **13**. 105; HW alludes to, **15**. 206, **29**. 85; HW paraphrases, **31**. 294; HW quotes, **33**. 157, 385, 464, **35**. 531; Harcourt, Lady, alludes to, **29**. 235; Leveridge acted Hecate in, **28**. 271; 'Lord George Macbeth,' **33**. 190; Mason alludes to, **28**. 484, **29**. 212; More, Hannah, paraphrases, **31**. 375; murder in, **35**. 446; Selwyn quotes, **9**. 360, **24**. 49; Siddons, Mrs, refuses rôle of Lady Macbeth in, **33**. 377; Stanislas I's situation reminiscent of scene in, **22**. 253; terrible incantations in, **41**. 297; train of kings in, **38**. 7

Malone's edition of, **11**. 291–2, **43**. 149

Marshall's print of, with laurel, **42**. 140

Merchant of Venice: HW mistakenly puts 'Sandy' in, **15**. 198; Portia in, preferred by Mrs Siddons, **34**. 2; Shylock the only good part in, **34**. 2

Merry Wives of Windsor: Gray alludes to, **14**. 7, 152; Mason quotes, **28**. 317; Old Slender in, **33**. 450, **41**. 404

metaphoric diction of, should not be imitated, **41**. 374

Methodists ban, **35**. 578

Midsummer Night's Dream: Fairies, The, based on, **35**. 209–10; Gray alludes to, **14**. 7n

Milbourn's print to, **11**. 114

Milles compares Rowley to, **2**. 314

mirth can be rendered pathetic only by, **41**. 289

'modern' characters from, **28**. 489

Montagu, Mrs Elizabeth, defends, **8**. 204

Much Ado about Nothing: 'Beatrice' in, **11**. 64, **33**. 88; 'Benedick' in, as acted by Garrick and Kemble, **11**. 64, **33**. 88; 'Dogberry' in, a favourite of Hannah More's, **31**. 358; Mallet cites, **40**. 152; More, Hannah, paraphrases, **31**. 358

nature dictated words to, **41**. 382

Œuvres of, owned by Mme du Deffand, **8**. 34

Othello: afterpiece to, **43**. 245; art in, is by chance, **41**. 294; Barry's performance in,

14. 6–7; Barthélemy likes, **6.** 287–8, 288; Delaval family act, in Drury Lane, **20.** 230–1; Du Deffand, Mme, likes, **4.** 167, **6.** 288, 291, 298, 304; French translation of, **28.** 258; Garrick ridiculous as Othello in, **38.** 525; Gray alludes to, **13.** 126; Gray sees, at Drury Lane, **13.** 114; HW praises Desdemona in, **41.** 373; HW quotes, **29.** 136, **33.** 92, **38.** 131; Hanmer's alteration of, **18.** 567, **30.** 302n; Kemble and Mrs Siddons act, **11.** 237; King Stephen's breeches in, **34.** 224; Mason alludes to, **29.** 342; Mason quotes, **29.** 286, 320; Parliament adjourns to see, **20.** 231; Quane, Mrs, as Desdemona in, **9.** 189n; Stephens acts in, **13.** 63n; West alludes to, **13.** 127

Otway next to, in boldness, but not in strokes of nature, **41.** 290

'our Raphael poet,' **2.** 221

Palladius and Irene imitates, **28.** 118

Percy's observations on, **40.** 373

Pignotti's *Shakespear*, poem on, to Mrs Montagu, **24.** 536

pity often praised in, **35.** 588–9

plays of, include half a century and half Europe, **33.** 553

poor actor but good author, **32.** 177

portrait of, owned by Felton, **15.** 197n

prints for, HW asks about author of plan of, **15.** 197

prologues necessary to, **33.** 553

prologues of, 'endurable,' **41.** 291

Racine inferior to best scenes and speeches in, **41.** 294

Richard II: **42.** 138–9; Garrick as Richard in, **33.** 87; horse in, used by Bolingbroke, **41.** 373; Kemble did not stage, **11.** 64n; quoted by Felton in application to HW, **34.** 10

Richard III: Conway quotes, **37.** 278; Du Deffand, Mme, reads, **4.** 171; Garrick as Richard in, **33.** 87; George III goes to, **9.** 325; HW cites, **32.** 160; (?) HW echoes, **31.** 246n; HW quotes, **18.** 248, **23.** 195, **28.** 458; 'Jocky of Norfolk' in, **33.** 505; More, Hannah, paraphrases, **31.** 341; Northcote's painting from, **15.** 206; Smith resembles Garrick in, **28.** 177

Romeo and Juliet: Gray alludes to, **13.** 62; HW praises Juliet in, **41.** 373; Satchell, Miss, acts in, **41.** 456

Rowe's edition of: corrected by later editors, **42.** 138; HW's notes to, **42.** 137n, 138–9

Royal Academy unable to do justice to, in illustrations, **33.** 547, 549

Sherlock's enthusiasm for, **2.** 302

Southampton friend of, **10.** 104n

Steevens's edition of, **2.** 293, 294, **11.** 357

Stratford's tragedy compared to those of, **29.** 223, 225

Taming of the Shrew: Kemble and Mrs Siddons in, **11.** 236

Tempest, The: 'Ariel' in, **34.** 105; Du Deffand, Mme, gives opinion of, **6.** 298; Gray's *Odes* has passage resembling, **40.** 103; HW alludes to, **18.** 117; HW alludes to characters in, **31.** 291–2; HW cites Trinculo in, **39.** 56; Hardinge quotes, **35.** 562; Mason quotes, **28.** 55; More, Hannah, alludes to, **31.** 339; 'Trinculo' name of, applied to Prescott, **33.** 424

Theobald's edition of, **13.** 131n, **20.** 215n

Thompson's poem mentions, **39.** 120

Timon of Athens: altered by Cumberland, **32.** 69; to be translated, **6.** 298

tomb of, **9.** 120

Twelfth Night, HW quotes, **35.** 534, **39.** 104

Two Gentlemen of Verona, acted at Drury Lane, **22.** 120n

Voltaire attacked by Pignotti for pillaging and reviling, **24.** 536

—— attacks, **6.** 345, 348, 354, 373n, **8.** 141, **13.** 43n, **28.** 275–7, 278–9, **32.** 340, **40.** 373, **41.** 465

—— calls, 'buffon,' **13.** 45

—— condemns, for dignifying vulgar or trivial expressions, **41.** 295

—— criticizes, without adequate knowledge of English, **42.** 121

—— first praised and then disparaged in France, **24.** 267, **28.** 279, **41.** 152

—— thinks, suffered from his unrefined age, **41.** 153

Warburton's edition of, **9.** 117n

Winter's Tale: 'improprieties' in, **41.** 291; is said to be wrong in referring to Delphos, **29.** 12; Robinson, Mrs, acts in, **28.** 44n

works of, to be taken by HW to Mme Roland at Montagu's request, **10.** 170, 174, 180, 182

worst plays of, on level with those of modern playwrights, but best ones far above theirs, **24.** 415

Yearsley, Mrs, has read a few plays by, **31.** 218

——'s *Earl Goodwin* expected to excel, **31.** 331

York and Gloucester, Dukes of, remind HW of, **38.** 475

See also under Felton, Samuel: *Imperfect Hints*; Ireland, William Henry; Malone, Edmond, *and under names of actors and actresses*

Shakespeare Gallery, The, a Poem. See under Jerningham, Edward

Shakespeare Gallery, Pall Mall:
  Boydell's and Nicol's civilities to HW at, **11.** 81
  Damer, Mrs, does bas-reliefs for, **12.** 274, **43.** 167
  Farington visits, **15.** 321
  HW dissatisfied with, **15.** 206
  Nicol addressed at, **42.** 283
  pictures in, **11.** 247

Shakespeare Press:
  Nicol establishes, with Bulmer, **42.** 283n

Shakespeare Tavern, London:
  Boswell, Macklin, and Davies at, **29.** 145n
  (?) Paine dines at, **11.** 319

Shakespeare traduit de l'anglois. See under Le Tourneur, Pierre-Prime-Félicien

Shamela. See under Fielding, Henry: *Apology*

'Shane.' *See* Conway, Hon. Jane

Shannon, Cts of. *See* Ponsonby, Catharine (1746–1827)

Shannon, E. of. *See* Boyle, Henry (ca 1682–1764); Boyle, Richard (1728–1807)

Shannon, Vct. *See* Boyle, Francis (1623–99); Boyle, Richard (1675–1740)

Shannon, Vcts. *See* Senhouse, Grace

Sharawadgi *or* Sharawaggi:
  Bateman founder of taste for, in England, **35.** 359
  HW admires, **20.** 127

Shark; sharks:
  Sloane's museum contains, **20.** 358
  Spaniards, submerged at Gibraltar, must please, **35.** 367

Sharkskin case:
  Du Deffand, Mme, sends, to Cts of Ailesbury, **6.** 325

Sharman, William:
  Irish Committee of Correspondence headed by, **39.** 405n

Sharp, Capt.:
  Mercury packet ship commanded by, **23.** 561n

Sharp, Mrs:
  SH visited by, **12.** 247

Sharp, Granville:
  Sierra Leone founded by, **31.** 371n

Sharp, John (ca 1729–72), D.D.; fellow of Corpus Christi College, Cambridge 1753–72:
  Edward VI's letter copied by, for HW, **40.** 158–60
  HW receives remarks of acquaintance of, for *Anecdotes of Painting*, **40.** 253
  HW's correspondence with, **14.** 104, **38.** 167, **40.** 158–60, 253

Sharp, Samuel (ca 1700–78), surgeon; writer:
  Hawkwood's picture in Florentine Duomo claimed by, as ancestral portrait, **23.** 428

Sharp, William (1749–1824), engraver:
  print by, of Wynn, **2.** 167n

Sharpe, Christopher (1722–97), engraver:
  gives print to Cole, **1.** 365
  prints by: **1.** 207, 210, 212, 213, 216; of Cromwell, **1.** 360, 362; of Gray, **1.** 296

Sharpe, Fane William (? 1729–71), M.P.:
  (?) HW mentions, **37.** 478

Sharpe, Gregory (1713–71), LL.D.:
  death of, **1.** 290n

Sharpe, Horatio (1718–90), gov. of Maryland:
  (?) borough for, **24.** 52

Sharpe, John (? 1700–56), M.P.; lawyer; solicitor to the Treasury:
  (?) HW mentions, **37.** 478
  (?) Orford, Cts of, may have left documents with, **25.** 160
  (?) —— receives documents from, **20.** 547
  papers saved by, from fire, **20.** 321n

Sharpe, Joshua (d. 1788), lawyer:
  biographical information about, corrected, **43.** 348, 364
  conduct of, shameful in disloyalty to clients, **25.** 172
  (?) Conway writes to, **39.** 343
  counter-demands against Orford should be produced by, **25.** 333
  courier may have reported Cts of Orford's death to, **25.** 121
  denies having objected to Duane, **25.** 320
  division of money held by Hoare may have been suggested by, **25.** 426
  Duane feared by, because of honesty and intelligence, **25.** 217
  —— finally approved by, **25.** 315, 324
  —— probably would not be approved by, **25.** 304
  ——'s nomination disapproved by, **25.** 217, 235
  —— told, that he would accept no reward, **25.** 519
  —— will tell, of Orford's indecent letter to Mozzi, **25.** 330
  duplicity and dishonesty of, surprising to Mozzi, **25.** 335
  fire in Lincoln's Inn nearly destroys papers of, **25.** 350–1
  former opinion of, that Cts of Orford's jointure should be made good, will surprise him, **25.** 172
  HW advised by, to sell Orford's horses, **32.** 134
  HW asks consent of, in Cts of Orford's name, to manage Orford's affairs, **36.** 93
  HW asks, to tell Cts of Orford of her son's latest insanity, **24.** 292
  HW calls, rogue and fool, **25.** 315
  HW complains of delays of, **25.** 433
  HW condemns, for forcing Mozzi to come to England, **25.** 315
  HW consults, about E. of Orford, **23.** 496, 503, 545
  HW does not wish treachery of, shifted to himself, **25.** 289
  HW, Duane, and Lucas confer with, about Mozzi's affairs, **25.** 391, 419, 421, 439, 444, 448
  HW glad to sow division between Lucas and, **25.** 315
  HW hears from, of Duane's apoplexy, **25.** 495
  HW hopes, will be afraid of Duane, **25.** 331
  HW impeded by difficulties from, **24.** 308
  (?) HW mentions, **37.** 478
  HW not aided by, in keeping E. of Orford from renting farm to jockey, **24.** 52
  HW not allowed by, to raise Cts of Orford's jointure, **25.** 140
  HW not to be influenced by, **25.** 172
  HW praises, in Mozzi affair, **25.** 410
  HW receives copy of paper sent by, to Morice, **25.** 186

HW reproached by, at same time that he asks for aid, **25.** 308

HW returns to, a draft of the Hugh Conways' marriage settlement, **42.** 173–4

HW scolds, in letter, for asking him to take Mozzi's affair upon himself, **25.** 315

HW's correspondence with, **35.** 417, **42.** 173–4

HW's letter from: about Hoare's payment, **25.** 509; laments E. of Orford's conduct, **24.** 53; telling of reception of Mozzi's letter, **25.** 500

HW's note of resentment to, **25.** 509

HW's relations with, **25.** 154–5, 172, 439–40, 444–7, 471–2, 477, 496

HW suspects collusion between Lucas and, **25.** 286

HW told by, of Cts of Orford's habits, **23.** 545

HW to tell, of Mozzi's resolution, **25.** 466

HW urged by, to resume care of E. of Orford's affairs, **23.** 308

HW writes to, complaining of delay, **25.** 500

Hertford told by, about Orford's horses and dogs, **39.** 171

less zealous for Mozzi than Lucas appears to be for Orford, **25.** 200

Lucas acts in concert with, **25.** 328

—— and, had settled on £6000 for E. of Orford, HW thinks, **25.** 335

Lucas's agreement over Cts of Orford's estate desired by, **25.** 150

Lucas scolded by, for his delay, **25.** 286

——'s demands against Mozzi are sent to him by, **25.** 333

——'s possible collusion with, **25.** 150, 328, 492

——'s summary delivered to Duane by, **25.** 335

—— told by, that Cts of Orford's money in England should be divided between Orford and Mozzi, **25.** 160

Mann and secretary to receive legal instrument from, **25.** 167

Mann censures, for treatment of Mozzi, **25.** 161–2

—— does not trust, to convey Mozzi's letter to Duane, **25.** 304

Morice advised by, to call for papers, **25.** 289

—— receives papers from, **25.** 184

Mozzi advised by, to divide sum with E. of Orford, **25.** 419

—— asks HW to conceal doubts about, **25.** 341

—— assured by, that Orford will act honourably, **25.** 144

—— awaits letter from, **25.** 479

—— claims he always answers letters of, **25.** 465

—— desired by: to list Cts of Orford's things, **25.** 151; to return release from E. of Orford to HW, **25.** 527; to send him copy of paper signed by Yorke, **25.** 169

—— employs, because of having been Cts of Orford's lawyer, **25.** 320

—— fears, might secrete papers in his favour, **25.** 333, 341

—— glad to escape from, **25.** 161

—— has bad opinion of, but must retain him, **25.** 181

—— may go to England unless prevented by, **25.** 431

—— mistakenly employs, **25.** 160, 182, 320

—— neglected by, **25.** 390

—— receives adverse opinion from, before considering justice of Orford's claims, **25.** 217

—— safer in HW's hands than in those of, **25.** 158

——'s claims against Cts of Orford's estate requested by, **25.** 168

——'s correspondence with, **25.** 144, 156, 166, 216, 300–1, 315, 324, 412, 459, 471, 478, 492, 500, 504, 511, 514, 524, 540

——'s employment of, surprises him, **25.** 320

—— sends power of attorney to, **25.** 137, 144

——'s relations with, **25.** 181

——'s release as Cts of Orford's executor to be drawn up by, **25.** 498

—— suspects Lucas and, of wishing him to go to law, **25.** 322

—— to pay, through Hoare, **25.** 492

—— urged by, to come to England, **25.** 144, 435

Orford and Mozzi advised by, to divide money in Hoare's hands, **25.** 154–5, 157, 160, 217, 335, 419, 426

Orford does not answer expresses from, about elections and boroughs, **24.** 46

—— persuaded by, to reject Duane, **25.** 265

—— represented by, against Mozzi, **33.** 281, (?)372, (?)404

—— to receive from, a letter from Mozzi, **25.** 300–1

—— would probably be favoured by, **25.** 421–2

Orford, Cts of, allowed salary to, as agent, **25.** 492

—— can convey hint to HW through, **23.** 514

—— corresponds with, about her son, **23.** 464, 472, 476, 477, 486, 491–3, 496, 500–1, 503, 509, 514, 516, 525, 537, 548, **24.** 46–7, 57, 304, 305, 317, 318, **35.** 417

—— disappoints, by not leaving him a legacy, **25.** 162, 320, 328

—— had, as her lawyer, **25.** 160, 320

—— has confidence in, **23.** 477

—— may consult, **23.** 537, **24.** 91

—— mistakenly trusted, **25.** 172

—— offers borough to, for his nephew, **24.** 52

—— preferred by, to have left less to Mozzi, **25.** 162

—— probably does not open letters of, **24.** 318

—— refused to send order for money to, **25.** 129

[Sharpe, Joshua, *continued*]

—— represented by, against Mozzi, **33.** 281, (?) 372, (?) 404

—— should have given fuller powers to, **24.** 67

—— will be made by, to regret her want of confidence in HW, **24.** 317

—— will be told by, of her son's neglect of boroughs, **24.** 47

probable author of Cts of Orford's 'case,' **25.** 162

proposed marriage settlement drawn up by, for Lady Anna Horatia Waldegrave and Hon. Hugh Seymour-Conway, **43.** 369

rent arrears to be collected by, **25.** 511–12

rents not neglected by, to earn salary, **25.** 496

sale of E. of Orford's boroughs advised by, **24.** 52

(?) Shirley has, send deed to Cts of Orford, **20.** 547

Zincke's portrait of Cts of Orford sent by, to HW, **25.** 501

Sharpe, Mary (ca 1753–1807), m. 1 (1782) Osmund Beauvoir, D.D.; m. 2 (1791) Andrew Douglas, M.D.:

HW jokes about marriages of, **31.** 360

Shaving:

Cavaliers postpone, till the Restoration, **35.** 256

Italians practise, on their bodies, **19.** 437

Townshend's witticism on Ds of Newcastle's, **35.** 256

Walpole, Sir Robert, has John Jones as barber for, **38.** 55

Shavings, wood:

SH full of, **37.** 352, **38.** 175

Shaw, Charles:

Customs place of, **26.** 52

Shaw, Elizabeth (d. 1788), m. (1747) William Byron, 5th Bn Byron:

Byron later marries, **19.** 19n

Coke breaks with, on her flirtation at ridotto with Stuart Mackenzie, **19.** 27

—— rumoured to be marrying, **19.** 19

fortune of, **19.** 19

Shaw, James, deputy ranger of Richmond Park ca 1751–ca 1761:

Bird consulted by, in Ps Amelia's behalf, **20.** 323

Shaw, Sir John (d. 1702), cr. (1679) Bt:

son of, **26.** 52

Shaw, Sir John (d. 1721), 2d Bt; M.P.:

Customs place of, **17.** 27n, **26.** 52

Shaw, Peter (1694–1763), M.D.; physician and writer:

Bacon praised by, **37.** 294

biographical information about, corrected, **43.** 274

Bute's dosing from, would make Newcastle jealous, **38.** 83

George II's physician in ordinary, **21.** 79n

Grafton attended by, **37.** 482

Keck, Lady Susan, harangues, about her palsy, **30.** 54

mushrooms poison, **31.** 10

Newcastle's physician, **31.** 10n

Newcastle, Ds of, attended by, **21.** 79

Townshend, Vcts, visited by, **30.** 54

Shaw *or* Shaa, Rev. Dr Ralph (d. 1484):

Edward IV's pre-contract mentioned by, **35.** 609

Richard III's mother charged by, with adultery, **14.** 179

sermon by, says Richard III resembles his father, **40.** 110

Shaw, T. W.:

The Crisis printed by, **28.** 180n

Shaw, William (1749–1831):

Inquiry into the Authenticity of the Poems Ascribed to Ossian, by, **29.** 239n

Shawfield House. *See under* Glasgow

Shawl:

Indian, worn by Emma Hart, **11.** 337–8

Shawnee Indians:

Dunmore's war against, **24.** 88n, **41.** 312n

Sheba, Q. of:

Arundel Castle, painted glass window at, represents, **12.** 205n

Coke, Lady Mary, compared with, **23.** 539, **31.** 177

HW jokes about Solomon and, **31.** 160

HW's 'The Dice Box' mentions, **31.** 156

Solomon given dish by, **37.** 320

——'s polygamy admired by, **33.** 555

Shebbeare, Dr John (1709–88), political writer:

broken Jacobite physician, **21.** 87

Camden prosecutes, for libel, **35.** 551n

career and writings of, **21.** 39n

Conway may meet fate of, **37.** 569

Guthrie's *Address to the Public* attributed to, **38.** 422

HW calls, ungrateful, **28.** 41

HW's epigram on Hume Campbell's attack from, **21.** 87

Hardwicke attacked by, **21.** 39

—— attributes attack from, to Fox, **21.** 39n

Letter to his Grace the D—— of N——, by, **21.** 87

Mason couples, with Johnson, **28.** 438

Monitor, The, written by, **21.** 39

pilloried and pensioned, **28.** 182n

revises 'Memoirs of a Lady of Quality' for the press, **14.** 48n

See also *Epistle to Dr Shebbeare*

Shee, Sir Martin Archer (1769–1850), painter:

HW unacquainted with name of, **42.** 395

Sheen, Surrey:

Blandford, Lady, dies at, **15.** 152, **33.** 121n

Sheen. *See also* East Sheen

Sheene, Mrs Mary, (?) weeding-girl:

Coutts & Co. invest legacy of, **42.** 377n

(?) Orford, E. of, begets daughter on, **25.** 355

Sheep:

Arcadian, not to be tended by Mrs Yearsley, **31.** 221

Blake might order, for supper at Almack's, **24.** 21

Clinton captures, **24**. 419

eaten at Cambridge banquet, **20**. 83

England will tend, **23**. 116

floods endanger, **35**. 365

French obtains hyenas clad in clothing of, **42**. 375

HW busy with, at SH, **37**. 287

HW imagines, replaced by camels and dromedaries, **33**. 212

HW jokes about tending, with Lady Mary Coke, **31**. 156

HW rescues, from SH flood, **35**. 228

HW's, at SH: **4**. 394; Turkish, **10**. 94, **19**. 414; Turkish, with four horns, to be folded on lawn, **30**. 116

HW's ignorance of, **36**. 96

HW vends: **23**. 497; at Houghton, **32**. 142

in portrait, **30**. 37

Mann obtains, for English fleet, **21**. 114

market of, at Tunbridge, **35**. 135

on medals of Charles I and of Leicester, **16**. 50

Orford's militia consume, **25**. 12n

Powis, E. of, has roasted, in every village, **32**. 302n

price of, falls, **42**. 393

visible from SH, **20**. 380, **25**. 532

Sheep paddock:

at the Vyne, **35**. 640

Sheep-shearing:

HW's, at SH, **9**. 134

Sheep's pluck:

sold in St James's Market, **9**. 365

Sheerness:

George II delayed at, **18**. 224

—— out of sight of, **36**. 13

storm at, **12**. 175n

Sheerness, English ship:

Bully, Capt., commands, **19**. 173n

Hazard captured by, **37**. 235–6

Soleil taken by, **19**. 173n

Sheet; sheets:

Benedict XIV's attendants carry off, before his death, **21**. 81

clean, in Paris, **35**. 124

Gévaudan beast covered with, **39**. 14

HW has changed only once a week during gout, **33**. 73

HW puns about making Hannah More stand in a white, **31**. 323

HW tears, for his cows, **40**. 252

of holland: **42**. 182; Anne of Denmark has, **32**. 325; William IV and wife under, **37**. 287

penitent might wear, of Brussels lace, **38**. 87

Pope and Lady Mary Wortley Montagu quarrel over, **34**. 255

'reindeer,' **32**. 194

Strozzi's servants borrow for him, **18**. 146

white: Kingston, Ds of, may have to stand in, if condemned, **24**. 162; Shore, Jane, does penance in, **24**. 163n

Sheffield, Bn and E. of. *See* Baker Holroyd, John (1735–1821); Holroyd, George Augustus Frederick Charles (1802–76)

Sheffield, Bns. *See* Howard, Douglas (ca 1545–1608); North, Hon. (after 1790 Lady) Anne (1764–1832); Way, Abigail (d. 1793)

Sheffield, Cts of. *See* North, Hon. (after 1790 Lady) Anne

Sheffield, Sir Charles (ca 1706–74), cr. (1755) Bt; D. of Buckingham's natural son:

Buckingham, Ds of, has law suit against, **17**. 254n

Cori accused of being in league with, **17**. 254

George III buys Buckingham House from, **22**. 130n

Sheffield, Lady Douglas. *See* Howard, Douglas

Sheffield, Edmund (1564–1646), 3d Bn Sheffield of Butterwicke; E. of Mulgrave:

arms of, **1**. 149

patron of Ferne, **1**. 149

Sheffield, Edmund (1716–35), 2d D. of Buckingham, 1721:

burial of, **18**. 193n

wax figure of, dressed by mother for Westminster Abbey, **18**. 193n

Sheffield, John (ca 1538–68), 2d Bn Sheffield, 1549:

HW has Mor's portrait of, **41**. 352

Sheffield, John (1647–1721), 3d E. of Mulgrave; cr. M. of Normanby, and D. of Buckingham:

Character of King Charles by, **1**. 223n

Ferrers imitates epitaph of, **21**. 408

HW acknowledges mistake about, **16**. 15

HW attributes allusion to, in Pope's poem, **21**. 140

Sheffield, Sir Charles, natural son of, **17**. 254n

wife of, **9**. 244n

will of, **17**. 254n

Sheffield, Yorks:

Aston near, **28**. 21, 23

Byron raises recruits at, **28**. 472

HW visits, **9**. 295

iron prices might be raised by, **38**. 101

manufactures of, **9**. 295

Mason visits, **28**. 316

parcel for Mason is left at, by mistake, **28**. 317

'Repeal, The,' indicates American trade of, **22**. 400

scissors from, **11**. 67, **17**. 302n

steel industry of, competes with Woodstock, **17**. 302n

Walker dies at, **1**. 9n

Sheffield:

earldom of, rumoured for Horatio Walpole (1678–1757), **17**. 430, 469n

Sheffield Place, Sussex:

Gibbon visits, **32**. 341

Sheffield silver:

box of, **7**. 416

See also Silver: plated

Sheinton, Salop:

Stephens rector of, **11**. 195n

Shelburn. *See* Shelburne

Shelburne, Cts of. *See* Carteret, Lady Sophia (1745–71); Fitzmaurice, Mary (d. 1780); Fitzpatrick, Lady Louisa (1755–89)

Shelburne, E. of. *See* Petty, Henry (ca 1675–1750); Petty, William (1737–1805)

Shelburne House, London. *See under* Petty, William, E. of Shelburne

'Shelburne Square.' *See* Berkeley Square

Sheldon, Frances (1714–90), m. 1 (1736) Henry Fermor; m. 2 Sir George Browne, 3d Bt, 1751; HW's neighbour and correspondent:
Barnewall known by, 7. 358
Berry, Mary, preceded by, as HW's 'wife,' 12. 205–6
Blandford, Lady, entertains, 32. 48n, 41. 278
——'s social relations with, 31. 180–1
—— tended by, in last illness, 31. 196–7
characteristics of: good-humoured and cheerful, 31. 72; loves laughing, 31. 65
Coke, Lady Mary, corresponds with, about HW, 31. 93
—— friend of, 31. 72
——'s social relations with, 31. 142, 43. 102
Fifes friends of, 31. 72
French country visit of, 31. 64
(?) grandson of, dies, 31. 198–9
HW accompanies, to Twickenham Park, 35. 365
HW and, are robbed, 29. *160*, 33. 295–6
HW and, in ferry-boat accident coming from Lady Blandford's, 38. 187, 41. 278–9
HW buys cup and saucer for, 7. 414
HW calls: 'Catholic neighbour,' 33. 37; 'the Catholic,' 7. 358
HW condoles with son of, on her death, 42. 276–7
HW escorts, to fireworks, 33. 183
HW impatient for return of, to Paris, 31. 65
HW invites, to SH, 31. 406, 407
HW jokes about marriage to, 31. 180, 209, 409
HW jokes with, about Lady Blandford, 31. 49
HW, Lady Anne Conolly, and, return from Twickenham Park with guard, 35. 355
HW laments absence of, from Twickenham, 31. 199
HW may summon, to SH for whist, 39. 285
HW may visit, 31. 407
HW plays tredille with Ds of Newcastle and, 39. 187
HW receives partridges from, 31. 170
HW's correspondence with: 31. 170, 188–99, 201–5, 209–10, 217–18, 235–9, (?) 263, 286–9, 405–11; MSS of, 36. 310
HW's 'nominal wife,' 33. 359
HW's relations with, 31. 406–11
HW's social relations with, 31. 142
HW's verses about, 31. 440
HW to accompany: to Lady Blandford's, 31. 406; to Twickenham Park, 31. 203, 204, 205, 218
HW to be landed from boat at house of, 39. 311

HW unable to accompany, to Twickenham Park, 31. 205
HW unable to visit, 31. 201, 408
health of: cold, 31. 239; illness, 33. 334; improved, 31. 192; recovered, 35. 373
house of, at Twickenham, 31. 287
leaves Twickenham, 33. 472
liveries and temper lost by, 39. 420
loo played at house of, 31. 142
maid of, dies, 31. 286
marriages of, 31. 180
Montagu desired by, to live at Twickenham, 10. 252
Montrose, Ds of, misses, 31. 199
Newcastle, Ds of, often visited by, at Twickenham Park, 35. 349–50
not at Lady Blandford's, 31. 180
Paris visited by, 31. *49*
picture of, at Arundel Castle, 12. 205
Roman Catholicism of, 7. 358, 10. 252, 33. 37, 39. 187
Scott, Lady Jane, entertained by, 31. 142
screams to saints, 39. 187
social relations of, in Paris, 7. 260, 269, 271, 274, 277, 285, 292, 294, 300, 311, 312
SH visited by, 12. 224, 31. 147, 297
Tusmore visited by, 31. 192–3, 198–9, 288
Twickenham residence of, 31. 147, 188, 190, 209, 42. 482
visits by, to: Fermor, 31. 192–3, 198–9, 288; Fitzwilliam, Vcts, 31. 236; Langdale, Bns, 31. 235; Throckmorton, 31. 237
visits planned by, to: Conolly, Lady Anne, 31. 205; Hertford, Cts of, 31. 410; Langdale, Bns, 31. 411; Pococks, 31. 203

Sheldon, Gilbert (1598–1677), Bp of London 1660–3; Abp of Canterbury 1663–77:
portrait of, 10. 338
print of, 1. 180

Sheldon, Father Henry (1686–1756), Jesuit:
Bower's alleged letters to, 20. 532, 580

Sheldon, John (1752–1808), surgeon; anatomist; aeronaut:
balloon ascent by, 39. 424n
HW imagines, as balloon commander, 39. 425
visible in balloon, 35. 631

Sheldon, William (d. 1570):
tapestry works established by, 16. 195n

Sheldon, William (d. 1780), of Weston, Long Compton, Warwickshire:
HW's purchases at sale of, 2. 327–8, 12. 101n, 16. 195, 198, 33. 292
portraits of kings and queens of England owned by, 42. 443

Sheldonian Theatre, Oxford:
(?) box built in, for Cts of Pomfret, 20. 579
concert in, 12. 258n

Sheldon maps:
HW visits Nuneham to see, 29. 360
Harcourt receives, from HW, 16. 195n
See also under Map; Tapestry

Shelford, Cambs:
Wale of, 2. 97n, 29. 41n

Shelford, Little, Cambs:
Palavicini and Finch houses at, **1**. 3, 3n
Shelford Field, Cambs:
ring found in, **2**. 152
Shell; shells:
Bentley sends, to HW, **35**. 207
book of, HW will be glad to receive, from Mann, **18**. 105; *see also* Regenfuss, Franz Michael: *Choix de coquillages*
clam, with mahogany stands, **37**. 439
'flowers' made of, **42**. 307
HW's cabinet of, **23**. 285
HWs collection of, **43**. 126
HW's verses on, **32**. 87–8, 95
in Ds of Portland's collection, **36**. 237
See also Ormer shells
Shell; shells (projectiles):
magazine of, belonging to French, destroyed by Murray, **25**. 207
Voyer and Paulin take, past Lyon, **20**. 536
Shelley, Lady. See Pelham, Margaret (ca 1700–58); Woodcock, Elizabeth (d. 1808)
Shelley, Miss (?) Catherine:
Constantinople to be visited by, with Cts of Pomfret, **20**. 53
Florence to be visited by, **20**. 70, 116
Mann advises a convent for, **20**. 70
Pomfret, Cts of, tries to introduce, at rebels' trials, **19**. 294
Uguccioni expects to be in love with, **20**. 70
Winnington calls 'filial piety,' **20**. 53
Shelley, Henrietta (1731–1809), m. (1753) George Onslow, 4th Bn Onslow, 1776; cr. (1801) E. of Onslow:
Chichester, Bp of, anecdote about, told by, **12**. 109, 110
Coke, Lady Mary, has social relations with, **31**. 347
Conway sees, at Chatham, **38**. 33
Darell, Edward, visits, **12**. 103
Douglas, Lady, visited by, **12**. 117
goes home in chair from Mrs Crewe's at Richmond, **39**. 454
HW entertains, at dinner, **12**. 5
HW goes to, at Richmond, **39**. 418
HW hears anecdote of, about Major and prudish lady, **34**. 18
HW's social relations with, **31**. 347, **32**. 156
HW visits, **12**. 103
HW with, at Mrs Crewe's, **39**. 454
Malden, Vct, visited by, in Herefordshire, **31**. 288
Newcastle entertains, at Oatlands, **32**. 250
Richmond residence of, **11**. 148, **31**. 288
SH portrait of Lady Ossory astonishes, **32**. 156
Shelley, J., printer:
prosecution of, threatened, **18**. 33
Shelley, Sir John (1692–1771), 4th Bt, 1703; M.P.:
daughter of, **19**. 294n, **20**. 53
(?) nose of, **21**. 4
'shabby man' seen with, at Hampstead, **9**. 19

wife of, **34**. 258
Shelley, Sir John (? 1730–83), 5th Bt, 1771; M.P.:
Arundel to be succeeded by, as Clerk of the Pipe, **21**. 26
Chatham aped by, **22**. 470n
customs place lost by, **22**. 109n
Edgcumbe replaced by, as treasurer of the Household, **22**. 470
(?) Lyttelton hears indiscreet remark from, at Covent Garden about Beard's marriage, **9**. 265, **43**. 122
(?) Pelham, Frances, entertains, at Esher, **10**. 72–3
Pelham, Mary, rejects, **43**. 122
wife of, **12**. 132n
Shell-work:
by Mrs Delany, **9**. 391
grotto of, **34**. 8
Shelly. *See* Shelley
Shelvock. *See* Sherlock
Shelvocke, George (d. 1760), secretary to post office:
HW's correspondence with, **20**. 436, **37**. 379
secretary to General Post Office, **20**. 436n
tutor to Vct Coke, **20**. 436n
Shene:
Henry VII's exchequer and hoard at, **42**. 223
Shengay. *See* Shingay
Shenstone, William (1714–63), poet:
appetite of, for fame, **1**. 166, 169
'Arcadia' of, **32**. 244
HW characterized by, **1**. 165n
Leasowes the seat of, **29**. 268n
letters of: **1**. 165–6, 309, **32**. 244; belittled by HW, **28**. 233, 347
Luxborough, Lady, idolizes, **28**. 233
——, neighbour of, **28**. 233n
——'s correspondence with, **11**. 65n, **17**. 127n, **32**. 244
Mason to see house of, **29**. 259
never wrote a perfect song, **16**. 257
Percy introduced by, to Lyttelton, **40**. 373n
quill of, mentioned by Lady Luxborough, **32**. 283n
Schoolmistress, The, by: Gray admires, **14**. 35; his only good poem, **28**. 384
Tickell eulogizes, absurdly, **28**. 384
Works of, **43**. 54
Shepheard, Francis:
Dodd and Whaley travel with, **40**. 3n
Reste, 'governor' of, **40**. 3n
Shepheard. *See also* Gibson, Frances; Ingram Shepherd; Shepherd; Sheppard
Shepherd, Anne. *See* Sheppard, Anne
Shepherd, Rev. Antony (1721–96):
calls on Cole, **2**. 226
dines with Dean of Ely, **2**. 226
Shepherd, Elizabeth (ca 1700–88), m. (1725) Sir John Philipps, 6th Bt, 1743, of Picton Castle, Pembrokeshire:
daughters of, **34**. 29
death of, **34**. 29

Shepherd, Frances. *See* Gibson, Frances
Shepherd, Samuel (d. 1748), M.P.:
  illegitimate daughter of, **2**. 181n
Shepherd. *See also* Ingram Shepherd; Sheppard
Shepherd; shepherds:
  HW jokes about times when kings were, **39**. 127
Shepherdess; shepherdesses:
  at Ranelagh masquerade, **17**. 495
  Conway jokes about being cared for by, **37**. 189
  HW jokes about times when queens were, **39**. 127
  Walpole, Catherine, portrayed as, **30**. 371
Shepherd's Bush, Middlesex:
  Nicoll, Miss, visits, **14**. 230
Sheppard, Mr, near Uxbridge:
  SH visited by, **12**. 231
Sheppard, Anne (d. 1707), m. (1641) Richard Gibson:
  dates of, corrected, **43**. 291
  print of, by Walker, **15**. 97n, **42**. 39n
Shepperton, Middlesex; Hawke's seat:
  near SH, **32**. 381n
Sheppey, Isle of:
  Hogarth and friends tour, **41**. 435n
Shepreth, Cambs:
  Wortham of, **2**. 88n
Sherard, Lady. *See* Sidney, Mary
Sherard, Hon. Lucy (ca 1685–1751), m. (1713) John Manners, 2d D. of Rutland:
  anecdotes about, **12**. 25–6, **31**. 120
  Brooke takes house of, **9**. 135
  daughter ordered by, to put down gossip to fill country letters, **18**. 129–30
  (?) mother-in-law confused with, **34**. 259
Sherard, Lady Lucy (d. 1781):
  (?) Bath visited by, **10**. 229
  (?) HW calls on, **10**. 230–1, 234
  (?) HW fears he may not recognize, **10**. 229
  (?) HW's opinion of, **10**. 231
  (?) HW to call on, **10**. 229
  (?) house of, at Bath, **10**. 231
  (?) Montagu sends compliments to, **10**. 230
Sherard St, near Golden Sq., London:
  Montagu at, **9**. 2, 6
Sherbatow, Prince:
  Richecourt takes house of, in St James's St, **20**. 90n
Sherbet; sherbets:
  Florentine nobility scramble for, at conversazioni, **20**. 75
  Mann serves, to visitors before theatres open, **25**. 585, 592
  —— to serve jar of, to Mrs Damer, **25**. 650
  snow from Vallombrosa imported for, when ice fails, **20**. 25
Sherborne, Bp of. *See* Aldhelm (? 640–709)
Sherborne, Dorset, Digby's seat:
  HW visits, **40**. 251
Sherborne St John, Hants:
  Vyne, the, at, **35**. 640

Sherfield, Henry (d. 1634), recorder:
  breaks painted glass, **1**. 8
Sheridan, Michael:
  arrival of, in Scotland, **19**. 138
  Young Pretender accompanied by, to Pont-de-Beauvoisin, **20**. 9
  ——'s effects guarded by, at Avignon, **20**. 9n
Sheridan, Richard Brinsley (1751–1816), dramatist; M.P.:
  at Richmond, **34**. 62
  ball given by, **11**. 321
  borrows Lady Craven's play, **29**. 43n
  borrows money from William Taylor, **11**. 191n
  buys share of Drury Lane patent, **28**. 245n
  Combe receives book from, **33**. 465n
  Cornwall's dinner attended by, **33**. 588n
  Count of Narbonne unlikely to be opposed by, **42**. 437–8
  Courtenay demolished by, **29**. 116
  Critic, The, by: **43**. 305; acting of, said to be admirable, **28**. 487; allusions in, escape HW, **33**. 159; HW reads, and finds it flat, **28**. 487; prologue to, by Fitzpatrick, **33**. 141–2, 145; Sir Fretful Plagiary in, **29**. 12n
  Crown and Anchor attended by, during Bastille Day celebration, **35**. 399n
  Drury Lane visited by, **16**. 227n
  evicted from house in Bruton St, **11**. 321
  Familiar Epistle attributed to, advertised, **28**. 150, 155, **43**. 296
  Fitzpatrick, Richard, friend of, **33**. 577
  French Revolution admired by, **11**. 89n, **31**. 343
  grandfather of, **20**. 334n
  HW never spoke to, **41**. 459
  HW tells Lady Ossory to admire, **33**. 566
  HW wishes that Catherine II and Joseph II were worried by, **35**. 392
  Haymarket theatre taken by Harris and, **28**. 632, **33**. 301n
  house of, at Isleworth, **11**. 341n
  Jephson unharmed by emissaries of, **41**. 459
  ——'s *Count of Narbonne* refused by, **33**. 301
  Keppel, Mrs, lets house at Isleworth to, **11**. 320
  Knight places, above Gray, **29**. 338
  More, Hannah, returns ticket for speech of, at Hastings's impeachment, **31**. 265
  oratory of, extempore, **33**. 543
  Parliamentary speeches by: on resuming committee on state of nation, **33**. 432n; opposing Burke on French Revolution, **31**. 343n
  people pay 50 guineas to hear, in Westminster Hall, against Hastings, **42**. 221–2
  Pizarro, prologue to, **29**. 44n
  'Portrait; Addressed to Mrs Crewe, A,' **32**. 388
  prologue by, for Lady Craven's comedy, **29**. 44, **33**. 182
  protectors of, push new comedy, not his, **33**. 243–4

remark of, on Humberston, **28.** 482

Revolution Society's jubilee not attended by, **11.** 314

Rigby's clause on Thurlow in Exchequer reform bill opposed by, **33.** 406n

Rivals, The, by, Miss Farren appears in, **12.** 107n

Robinson Crusoe; or, Harlequin Friday by: HW sees, **33.** 361–2; said to be contrived by him, **33.** 361n

Rubinelli and Pacchierotti not paid by, **31.** 343

School for Scandal by: HW disappointed in reading, **28.** 487, **29.** 35; HW likes, with reservations, **28.** 309; HW praises, **41.** 363; HW thanks Henderson for, **42.** 5; 'Lady Teazle' in, **33.** 87, 564; 'Mrs Candour' in, **31.** 191; satirical imitation of, dealing with American war, **42.** 5n

Short Review attributed to, **33.** 557n

slavery may be opposed by, **31.** 269

speech by, in Westminster Hall at Hastings's trial, **33.** 560, **35.** 391–2

takes part in debate on loan to Francis II, **12.** 214

Vestris's 'Grand Entertainment' at theatre of, a failure, **39.** 381–2

witticisms by: on Mrs Piozzi, **31.** 343–4; on Tarleton, **29.** 189, 195

Wraxall's *Short Review* shows fear of, **33.** 558n

Sheridan, Mrs Richard Brinsley. *See* Linley, Elizabeth Ann

Sheridan, Sir Thomas (ca 1672–1746), cr. (1726) Bt (Jacobite); Young Pretender's sub-tutor:

death of, **19.** 312n

Excerpta said to be written by, **18.** 419

grandson of, **20.** 334n

nephew of, **19.** 270n

Swift wishes piles for, as sign of health, **20.** 334n

Young Pretender's companion on return to France, **19.** 270n

——'s tutor, **19.** 312n

—— to be joined by, **18.** 433

Sheridan, Thomas (1719–88):

HW procures *Count of Narbonne* from, **41.** 406, 409

Sheridan, Mrs Thomas. *See* Chamberlaine, Frances

Sheriff; sheriffs:

at trial of rebel lords, **19.** 301

county, murderer's property goes to, **21.** 398

Dublin's, *see* Smith, ——

eat and drink on execution scaffold, **21.** 402–3

election of, London populace may win, from Court party, **23.** 419

Ferrers attended by, **21.** 399–402, 408

high, of Denbighshire, **17.** 44

insolence of, to George III, **6.** 31

London's remonstrance presented by, to George III, **23.** 196

Macaronies might be fined for not serving as, **35.** 334

Mann, Edward Louisa, gets exemption from being, **24.** 146–7

of Berwickshire, *see* Home, David

of London: House of Lords calls, for report on Wilkes mob, **38.** 257; London Common Council's defeated motion to thank, for behaviour at Wilkes riot, **38.** 262; proposes to marry Jane Shore, **16.** 171; warn House of Lords of new riot, **38.** 562; *see also* Alsop, Robert (d. 1785); Blachford, John (d. 1759); Blunt, Richard (d. 1763); Cokayne, Francis (d. 1767); Errington, George (d. 1769); Harley, Thomas (1730–1804); Sawbridge, John (1732–95); Townsend, James (1737–87); Vaillant, Paul (ca 1715–1802); Wilkes, John (1727–97); Winterbottom, Thomas (d. 1752)

of London and Middlesex, Wilkes and Bull elected as, **32.** 52n

of Middlesex, summon Wilkes, **24.** 475

Parliament may punish, for remonstrance, **23.** 197

picked by 'committees of council,' **26.** 26

robes of, worn by Vaillant, **21.** 400

Sayre was, under Wilkes, **24.** 138

Wilkes becomes, **23.** 317, 360

—— canvasses for, **23.** 314

Sheriff Hutton, Yorks:

castle of, Q. Elizabeth conducted from, **14.** 79

Sheriffmuir:

Balmerinoch, captain under D. of Argyll at, **19.** 283n

battle of, **37.** 217

Sheriff's Account, The. See under Vaillant, Paul

Sheriff's officers:

Harley turns out, for not arresting Wilkes, **23.** 13

Sherrington, Bucks:

Barton rector of, **1.** 117n

'Sherley, Lady Elizabeth':

print of, **1.** 182

Sherley. *See also* Shirley

Sherlock, Rev. Martin (ca 1750–97), writer:

bluestocking meeting at Lady Lucan's attended by, **29.** 104

Consiglio ad un giovane poeta by, **29.** 228n

dedicates book to Bp Hervey, **2.** 301

does not write in English, **34.** 240

HW's opinion of, **2.** 301

Italian and French of, poor, **34.** 240

Letters on Several Subjects by, **29.** 228n

Lettres d'un voyageur anglois by, **29.** 228n, **43.** 75

Mason mistakenly assumes, wrote *Lord Russell,* **29.** 228–9, 233

miscalled Shelvock, **2.** 307

Nouvelles lettres by, **43.** 75

sketch of Yorke by, **29.** 114n

Sherlock, Thomas (1678–1761), Bp of Bangor, 1728, of Salisbury, 1734, of London, 1748:
argument of, upon prophecy, **15**. 307
Canterbury see refused by, **19**. 511
Chute and HW do not believe, **20**. 137
Cole collated by, to rectory of Hornsey, **2**. 378
futility of answering bigotry of, **20**. 555
HW hopes Lyttelton may succeed, **40**. 125
HW not to tell, about Voltaire's *Pucelle*, **20**. 548
Letter to the Clergy and People of London by, on earthquake, **20**. 133–4; 548
London bishopric accepted by, **18**. 203n, **19**. 511
Master of the Temple, **20**. 133n
Middleton's controversy with, **14**. 43n, 236, **15**. 298, **20**. 134
——'s death will please, **20**. 167
——'s interview with, **15**. 307
——'s preferment obstructed by, **15**. 306
Paddington Road Bill upheld by, **37**. 464n
Pilkington, Mrs, draws picture of, in bawdy book, **20**. 134
Regency bill obstructed by, **20**. 248
Shirley, Rev. Hon. Walter, said to have been suspended by, **9**. 279
Use and Intent of Prophecy by, **15**. 298
York archbishopric refused by, **18**. 203
Sherman, Mary (d. 1767), m. (1765) William Mason:
fortune of, retained by father, **29**. 227
Sherman, Thomas (ca 1741–1803), Mason's brother-in-law:
HW sends letter of, to D. of Richmond, **29**. 230, 233
HW too ill to see, **29**. 249
Mason asks HW to recommend, to D. of Richmond for place at Hull, **29**. 227–8, 229–31, 236–8, 240, 242, 249, 260, 352, 362–3
transferred to Isle of Man, **29**. 362–3
Sherman, William (d. 1786), Mason's father-in-law:
memory of, gone, **29**. 227
Sherriff, Mr, in Ash's nursery, Twickenham:
SH visited by, **12**. 252
Sherriff. *See also* Shirreff
Sherrington, Mary (1663–1749), m. (1681) Sir William Luckyn, 3d Bt:
Hall Place the home of, **9**. 92
Sherry:
priest offers, to HW, **40**. 199
Sherwin, Capt. John:
Peggy commanded by, **25**. 579n
Sherwin, John Keyse (ca 1751–90), engraver:
drawings by: of attack on Portsmouth, **2**. 8; of 'Finding of Moses,' exhibited, **29**. 185
engraves heads for Johnson's *Poets*, **28**. 413n
print by, of Pennant, **2**. 191, 203
Sherwin, William (ca 1645–ca 1711), engraver:
engravings by, **16**. 66

Sherwood, Mrs. *See* Jones, Elizabeth
Sherwood, (?) James (d. 1757), surgeon:
actors attended by, **13**. 113n
Sherwood Forest, Notts:
'a trist region,' **32**. 375
HW refers to Rockingham Forest as, **10**. 191
needs outlaws to enliven it, **32**. 375
Thoresby in, **20**. 321n
She Stoops to Conquer. See under **Goldsmith, Oliver**
Shetland horses:
HW selling, at Houghton, **32**. 142–3
Shetland Islands:
Christian I pledges, **37**. 298
She Would if She Could. See under **Etherege, Sir George**
Shield *or* Shields, ——, porter:
Bryant writes to, **36**. 126
Waldegrave, Cts, gets letter from, **36**. 247
Walpole, Sir Edward, gets news from, of D. of Gloucester, **36**. 138
Shield; shields:
arms of Sidney family on, **33**. 350–1
at SH: **20**. 375, 341; depicting Medusa, **33**. 518; Gothic painted, given to HW by Hamilton, **35**. 419, 420; oriental, **20**. 375n; Persian, **31**. 26
Herbert of Chirbury's, **42**. 43
lady carries, in *Réduction de Paris*, **32**. 268
Surrey's, **35**. 420
Shields (place):
Dutch troops sail from, to Willemstadt, **19**. 221n
Shift; shifts:
Gramont, Comtesse de, wears, in Lely's miniature, **10**. 12
French princesses might be reduced to, **37**. 535
Hervey, Mrs Thomas, had holes in sleeves of, before marriage, **16**. 116
ladies escape in, from fire, **35**. 210
Montagu, Lady Mary Wortley, wears, of coarse cloth, **18**. 306
Senauki, Q., does not wear, **42**. 236
Shilling; shillings:
Bath waters turn, yellow, **31**. 364
counterfeit, **19**. 242–3, **31**. 277
French equivalent of, **37**. 39
Henry VII's, **40**. 219
Shillinglee Park, Sussex ('Shillingley'):
Winterton's summer home, visited by Bromfield, **40**. 317
Shimay. *See* Chimay
Shin; shins:
Flobert breaks, at Carrickfergus, **21**. 386
Shineker. *See* Schencker
Shingay, Cambs:
Cole's notes on, **1**. 253
Shingles (disease):
Saturn's belt resembles, **28**. 160
Ship; ships:
African, *see* Slave-ship

American: destroyed by Collier, **28.** 467, in Jacobite service, **37.** 237; not yet taken, **28.** 282; received at French ports, **28.** 277
American news brought by, **39.** 210
anecdote concerning, **12.** 261
at Hurstmonceaux, **35.** 139
at Rotterdam, **37.** 134
at Southampton, **35.** 251
balloons might replace, **39.** 425
'beastly,' crossing Channel, **39.** 251
Blake sinks, to see if man can live under water, **24.** 20
Caracca, **37.** 166
cartel, Minkette's boat to be, **38.** 12n
Danish and Dutch, news of Lord Howe brought by, **12.** 76
Dutch: Brest fleet being supplied by, **29.** 2; lost in storm, **31.** 136
England recalls, from Mediterranean and borrows from Dutch, **37.** 163
England's 'bastions, ravelins, and hornworks,' **37.** 71, 72
England sends, to West Indies or to intercept Spanish ones from there, **37.** 164
England to send, to Gen. Gage, with presents for Indians, **41.** 312n
English: attack Cherbourg fort, **37.** 558; cannot prevent French aid to rebellion, **37.** 226; captured at Nootka by Spanish, **39.** 479n; captured by Conyngham, **28.** 324; destroyed at New York, **28.** 206; France lays embargo on, **28.** 376; go to West Indies, **37.** 164; hunt Spanish, from West Indies, **37.** 164; not to be admitted to Leghorn, **28.** 461; reported to have taken Spanish galleons, **37.** 246; rout French, **15.** 71; sent to intercept French men-of-war, **37.** 246; *see also* England: ships of
English capture, **35.** 294
English embargo on, **37.** 446
English merchant, French capture, **39.** 308
for Coromandel, bought in England, and turned into Tuscan navy, **20.** 102, **22.** 548
France has, built in Boston, **24.** 386
French: English aim at, at St Malo, **37.** 533; English capture, **35.** 251, 254; *see also* France: ships of
French may wait for English to be eaten up by scurvy, **38.** 37
from Canada, at Bordeaux, **21.** 344
from Liverpool to Ireland, **38.** 107
from West Indies brings news to D. of Newcastle, **37.** 246
frozen in the Thames, **22.** 579n
George IV's emblem, in tableau, **38.** 204
Greek brigands seize, but are captured, **42.** 102
guard, filled up, **20.** 468n
HW does not understand ratings of, **33.** 171
HW offers to get, for the Vyne, **35.** 90
Holland augments, **38.** 6
hospital, in Russian fleet, **23.** 187n

hulks used as prisons, **25.** 316
Joseph II anxious to see, **22.** 548
Kingston, Ds of, has, **24.** 7
—— has, in Thoresby Lake, **31.** 289n
launching of, at Greenwich, **10.** 70
Lowther donates, to nation, **33.** 433n
Mann orders, to be purchased, for relief of Minorcan garrison, **25.** 199
——'s, for Minorca, see *Dolphin*; *Fly*; *General Murray*; *Indian King*; *Malborough Fort*; *St Philip's Castle*; *Tartar*
merchant: Holland must not send, under convoy, **25.** 8–9; plundered by English fleet, **35.** 63
mermaids painted on, **32.** 264
Mexicans' reactions to, **41.** 292
model of, on artificial river, **35.** 521
Naples cannot send, direct to England, **35.** 432
Neapolitan, *see under* Naples
news will soon be confined to topic of, **33.** 147
New Yorkers seize, with provisions for Boston, **41.** 303
ordnance, captured, **29.** 77
Richelieu's, reported to have sailed, **37.** 462
Roman, prow of, at Genoa, **37.** 320
shot from, hits Greenwich Palace, **16.** 80
slave-girl forced on board, at Bristol, **31.** 340
South Sea Company sends, to Spanish West Indies annually, **20.** 198n
Southwark fire destroys, **25.** 577
Spanish: captured, **38.** 169–70; *see also* Spain: ships of
Spanish sink, to block Havana harbour, **38.** 170
Swedish, Lady Shelley captured on, **12.** 132
Turkish, Christian slaves abduct, to Malta, **21.** 493n
victualling, England gets news by, **24.** 327
See also *Achilles*; *Actæon*; *Active*; *Æolus*; *Agamemnon*; *Aigrette*; *Ajax*; *Alarm*; *Alcide*; *Alcmena*; *Aldborough*; *Alderney*; *À Leon Franco*; *Alert*; *Alfred*; *Alliance*; *Amazon*; *Ambuscade*; *America*; *Américaine, L'*; *Andrea Doria*; *Andromache*; *Andromeda*; *Ann*; *Anne*; *Anson*; *Antelope*; *Apollo*; *Appollon*; *Aquila*; *Aquilon*; *Ardent*; *Arethusa*; *Argo*; *Arnoux*; *Asia*; *Augusta*; *Augustus Cæsar*; *Aurora*; *Baltimore*; *Barfleur*; *Beaumont*; *Bedford*; *Belle Perle*; *Belle Poule, La*; *Bellona*; *Bellone*; *Berwick*; *Bethia*; *Biddeford*; *Bienfaisant*; *Blandford*; *Blenheim*; *Blonde*; *Bonefoy*; *Bonetta*; *Boreas*; *Bottetourt*; *Bouffon*; *Brederode*; *Bretagne*; *Brilliant*; *Brilliante*; *Bristol*; *Britannia*; *Bruna*; *Buckingham*; *Buffalo*; *Cabot*; *Cæsar*; *Cambridge*; *Capitana Hali Bey*; *Captain*; *Carysfort*; Catalan ships; *Caton*; *Centaur*; *Centurion*; *Cerberus*; *César*; *Champion*; *Charité, La*; *Charlotte*; *Charmante*; *Charming Kitty*; *Charming Molly*; *Charming Nancy*; *Charon*; *Chatham*; *Chester*; *Chi-*

[Ship; ships, *continued*]
chester; Childers; Chimère; Colchester; Columbus; Comandante; Committé; Commodore; Comtesse de Bentheim; Conqueror; Conserva; Constante; Constantine; Constant of Teneriff; Conte d'Urbeck; Cornwall; Crawford; Cruiser; Culloden; Cumberland; Cygnette; Dankbaerheid; Daris; Dartmouth; Dauphin Royal; Defiance; Deptford; Devonshire; Diadème; Diamant; Diamond; Diana; Diligente; Discovery; Dolphin; Dorset; Dorsetshire; Doutelle; Dragon; Dreadnought; Duke; Duke of Cumberland; Dunkirk; Dursley; Eagle; Earl of Besborough; Edgar; Elena Fortunata; Elisabeth; Elizabeth; Ely; Emerald; Endeavour; Espérance; Esperance; Essex; Europe; Éveillé; Evstafiĭ; Experiment; Falcon; Falkland; Fame; Familia Real; Fantasque; Favourite; Fénix; Ferrytoat; Feversham; Fier; Fire Drake; Florissant; Fly; Folkstone; Formidable; Fortune; Foudroyant; Fowey; Fox; Friendship; Fubbs; Furnace; Galatea; General Barker; General Lally; General Murray; Gentille; George; Gibraltar; Glasgow; Gloire; Glorieux; Gloucester; Goodwill; Gracieux; Grafton; Grand Duchess of Tuscany; Gran Duca di Toscana; Great Duchess of Tuscany; Greenwich; Greyhound; Guadaloupe; Guarland; Guernsey; Halifax; Hampton Court; Hannah; Hannanel; Hanover; Happy Jennet; Hardwick; Hartwell; Harwich; Hastings; Hawke; Hazard; Hebe; Hector; Helena; Hermione; Héros; Heureux, L'; Hibernia; Hippopotame; Hunter; Hyæna; Illarim; Il Postiglione; Inconstante, L'; Indian King; Infernal; Inflexible; Invincible; Ipswich; Iris; Isabel; Isis; Jason; Jersey; Joseph; Juno; Junon; Jupiter; Kennington; Kent; King George; Kingston; Kite; Kouli Kan; Kuty and Reggi; Lady Juliana; La Flore; La Fortuna; Lancaster; Languedoc; La Pace; Lapwing; Lark; La Santa Fortuna; Lemon; Lenox; Leopard; Leviathan; L'Heureuse; Liberty; Licorne; Lightning; Lion; Litchfield; Lively; Liverpool; Lizard; L'Océan; London; Lord Howe; Lord Hyde; Louis; Lowestoft; Ludlow Castle; Lyme; Lynn; Lyon; Lys; Magnanime; Majesteux; Majestieux, Le; Malborough Fort; Maréchal de Belle-Isle; Maria Theresa; Marie-Louise; Marlborough; Mars; Marseillais, Le; Martin; Mary; Medway; Mercury; Merlin; Mermaid; Middleburg; Mignonne, La; Milford; Minerva; Modeste; Monarca; Monarch; Monmouth; Montagu; Montgomery; Montreal; Namur; Nassau; Natalia; Neptune; Newcastle; Nonsuch; Nostra Signora della Misericordia; Nostra Signora del Rosario; Nottingham; Novum Aratrum; Nuestra Señora; Numero Due;

Oiseau; Olive Branch; Orford; Oriflamme; Orphée; Otter; Oxford; Paerl; Pallas; Paloma; Panther; Patrique; Peacock; Pegasus; Peggy; Pembroke; Peter Peloquin; Phaeton; Philibert; Philip; Pitt; Pléiade; Pluto; Plymouth; Poder; Portland; Postilion; Postillion; Prince; Prince Charles; Prince de Conty, Le; Prince Ferdinand; Prince Frederick; Prince George; Prince of Orange; Prince of Piedmont; Prince of Wales; Princesa; Princes Royaal; Princess Louisa; Princess Royal; Prince William; Proserpine; Prothée; Providence; Provvidenza; Prudente; Prudente, La; Quebec; Queen, The; Quero; Raisonable; Raisonnable, La; Ramillies; Ranger; Raven; Real Filipe; Rennommée; Reprisal; Repulin Bacha; Repulse; Resolution; Revenge; Reynolds; Richmond; Rippon; Robuste; Rochester; Roebuck; Romney; Rosario; Royal Anne; Royal Charlotte; Royal Constantinople; Royal George; Royal Louis; Royal Oak; Royal Philip; Royal Sovereign; Ruby; Rumney; Rupert; Rye; St Caroline; St Domingo; Ste Anne; St Esprit; St Estevan; St George; St Joseph; St Laurance; St Paul; St Philip's Castle; St Quintin; Salisbury; Sally; Saltash; Sampson; San Antonio; San Carlos; Sandwich; San Eugenio; San Fernando; San Giorgio; San Giovacchino; San Isidoro; San Isidro; San Jenaro; San Julián; San Justo; San Lazzaro e Sant'Antonio; San Luigi Gonzaga; San Pablo; San Pedro; Santa Cecilia; Santa Rosa; Santa Rosalia; Santo Domingo; San Zirioco; Scarborough; Seaford; Seaforth; Sea Horse; Sensible; Sérieux; Serpent; Severn; Sheerness; Shrewsbury; Singe, Le; Sobervia; Solebay; Soleil Royal; Solitaire, Le; Somerset; Sophia; Sophia Wilhelmina; Southampton; Speedwell; Spence; Speronara; Sphinx; Sprightly; Spy; Sterling Castle; Success; Sukey; Sultan; Superb; Superbe; Surprise; Surprize; Surveillante; Sutherland; Swallow; Swan; Swiftsure; Syren; Syrène; Tamer; Tartan; Tartar; Teresa; Terpsichore; Terrible; Terror; Thamas Kouli Kan; Thames; Thésée; Thétis; Theÿlinger; Thomas; Thompson; Three Sisters; Thunder-Bomb; Thunderer; Tilbury; Tocha; Tonnant, Le; Torbay; Trepid; Tre-Primati; Trial; Trident; Triton; Trolle; Trusty; Tryal; Unicorn; Union; Vainqueur, Le; Valiant; Valk; Vanguard; Vengeance; Venus; Vespa; Vestal; Vestale; Victory; Vigilant; Ville de Paris; Vine; Viper; Volunteer; Vulcan; Vulture; Warren; Warwick; Weazle; Weymouth; William; William and Mary; Willingmi; Winchelsea; Windsor; Worcester; Wyville; Xavier; Yarmouth; Zebra; Zélé, Le
See also under Bark; Bilander; Boat; Bomb-ketch; Bomb-ship; Brig; Carvel; Cockboat;

Cod smack; Collier; Cutter; Dogger; Domingo-men; Felucca; Ferry-boat; Fire-ship; First-rates; Fishing-boats; Fleet; Frigate; Galleon; Galley; Gondola; Gunboat; Gunship; Hoy; Jamaica-men; Lighter; Longboat; Mackerel-boat; Man of war; Merchant-man; Merchant ship; Messenger sloop; Packet-boat; Polacre; Privateer; Register ship; Schooner; Ship of the line; Ship of war; Sloop; Smack; Smuggling vessel; Snow; Store-ship; Tartan; Tender; Transport; Trekshuit; Wherry; Xebec; Yacht

Shipbrook, E. of. See Vernon, Francis

Ship-carpenters:
at Portsmouth, 35. 178

Shiplake, Oxon:
Granger, vicar of, 1. 56n, 151, 177, 28. 47n
—— writes from, 40. 322, 41. 133, 187, 217
Gray dislikes visit to, 9. 285n

Shipley, Mrs. See Mordaunt, Anna Maria

Shipley, ——, drawing master:
Romney, friend of, lives near him in Kent, 26. 48
Society of Arts and Sciences 'invented' by, 26. 48

Shipley, Anna Maria (ca 1749–1829), m. (1783) Sir William Jones:
Lucan entertains, 33. 254

Shipley, Georgiana (ca 1756–1806), m. (1783) Francis Hare Naylor:
Franklin and sister of, 43. 147–8
HW describes, 11. 268–9
marriage of, indiscreet, 11. 269

Shipley, Jonathan (1714–88), D.D.; Bp of Llandaff, 1769, of St Asaph, 1769:
Blair's letters seen by, 29. 239
daughter of, 11. 269
HW expects, to become Bp of Salisbury, 33. 338
Nivernais's Jardins modernes given to, 12. 260
pro-American, 33. 338n
Rockingham's levee attended by, 29. 231
shows HW a letter from son, 29. 32
social relations of, 31. 210–11, 213
Stratford's Greek verse admired by, 29. 234

Shipley, Rev. William Davies (1745–1826), Dean of St Asaph 1774–1826:
political activity of, in Cheshire, 29. 32

Ship of the line; ships of the line:
England prepares, 35. 208
English: Hawke brings, towards Minorca, 20. 581; in English invasion of France, 21. 204; put in commission, 24. 252; ready to sail to Mediterranean, 23. 474; York, D. of, to take, to Italy, 22. 260, 267; see also England: ship, ships of
French: at Gibraltar, 24. 541; Estaing's squadron to be reinforced by, 24. 397; from Brest, 25. 345; Guichen returns to Europe with, 25. 94; in French fleet at Minorca, 20. 558; in Toulon squadron, 21. 431, 23. 474; see also France: ship, ships of

French and Spanish, threaten Minorca, 25. 173–4
Spanish: captured at Havana, 38. 181; Rodney defeats, 25. 16; said to be bombarding Algiers, 25. 416; see also Spain: ship, ships of
Turkish: defeated by Russians, 23. 234; see also Russia: ship, ships of

Ship of war; ships of war:
English: at Leghorn, 17. 455; to have access to Genoese and Corsican ports, 20. 588; see also England: ship, ships of
French: at Toulon, 20. 545; see also France: ship, ships of
Russian: leave Leghorn for Calais without waiting for Ds of Kingston's treasure, 24. 404, 409–10; must sail direct from Leghorn to England, 24. 114; see also Russia: ship, ships of
Tuscan: at Leghorn, to be visited by Joseph II, 23. 108; rescue Tuscan prize from Prussian privateer, 21. 349; see also Tuscany: ship, ships of

Shippen, Elizabeth, m. Benedict Arnold:
pension for, 25. 242n

Shippen, William (1673–1743), M.P.:
army proposals opposed by, 17. 370
army voting opposed by, 17. 343
English subsidies and troops for Maria Theresa opposed by, 17. 231n
Jacobite, 17. 231n, 343n
Jacobites led by, in Parliament, 17. 231, 410n
Murray's apostasy enrages, 18. 123
Walpole, Sir Robert, does not know price of, 17. 343n
—— saved by, from impeachment, 17. 232n

Ship Tavern, Gate St, Holborn:
priest hiding at, 33. 178n

Shirewood. See Sherwood

Shirley, ——:
Vane, Vcts, elopes with, 37. 1n

'Shirley, Mrs.' See under Richardson, Samuel: Sir Charles Grandison

Shirley, Lady Anne (1708–79), m. (1729) Sir Robert Furnese, 2d Bt:
HW attends ball given by, 35. 80

Shirley, Sir Anthony (1565–?1635), Kt; traveller:
an adventurer, 1. 62
Dalrymple's mistake about, 15. 79, 82
England might send, to hire troops in Persia, 37. 498, 500
extracts from letters of, 15. 79–82
HW's interest in, 15. 84
Sir Anthony Shirley: His Relation of his Travels into Persia by, read by HW, 16. 173, 37. 498n

Shirley, Lady Barbara:
madness of, 21. 388n

Shirley, Elizabeth (1694–1741), m. (1716) James Compton, styled Bn Compton, 5th E. of Northampton, 1727; Bns Ferrers, s.j.:
(?) family piece of, 10. 336

Shirley, Lady Frances (ca 1706–78):
Chesterfield requests pension for, 19. 463n
(?) ——'s song about beauty of, 24. 401n, 42. 489, 490
death of, 24. 401, 28. 412–13
'Fanny, blooming fair,' 28. 412–13, 42. 489, 490
Ferrers's salvation ignored by, 9. *284*
HW calls, 'Saint Frances,' 35. 309
HW does not hear Methodist scandal from, 35. 309
HW hints at hypocrisy of, 9. 284
HW jokes about: Methodism of, 10. 7; possible elopement of, 35. 303
HW mentions, 37. 337
HW to be reported by, as nuisance, 10. 2
Huntingdon, Cts of, heir to, 24. 401
Methodism of, 20. 52, 24. 401, 42. 490
senses lost by, 24. 401
sister receives unintelligible letter from, 35. 346
turns Methodist when no longer admired, 20. 52, 24. 401
Twickenham resident, 42. 485, 489, 490
Whitefield preaches at house of, 20. 52n
Williams, Sir C. H., writes 'The Evening' as soliloquy of, 30. 317
Shirley, Hon. George (1705–87):
HW mentions, 5. 88
Heath Lane Lodge the Twickenham house of, 43. 363
new house of, at Twickenham, called 'Spite Hall,' 35. 358
Townshend puts up, for Tamworth election, 30. 194n
Twickenham field of, scene of goldsmiths' dinner, 39. 310–11
Twickenham resident, 42. 481, 485
wife of, 14. 120n
Shirley, Mrs George. See Sturt, Mary
Shirley, Henry, 3d E. Ferrers:
madness of, 21. 388n
Shirley, Laurence (1720–60), 4th E. Ferrers:
children of, 21. 396, 397, 398
Cornwallis's correspondence with, 21. 399
date of trial of, fixed, 21. 385
excommunicated, and therefore unable to give evidence, 21. 184
execution of, 9. 283–4, 11. 265n, 21. 394–403, 410–11
family said to have forced, to plead insanity, 21. 396
foreigners cannot understand ignominious treatment of, 21. 410–11
George II consents that India bonds of, go to mistress and Johnson family, 21. 397–8
groom supposedly killed by, 21. 395
HW sends *Trial* of, to Mann, 21. 388, 407
hanging of, announced by cousin in circular letter, 21. 406, 25. 658
Hertford assizes attended by, 21. 184
House of Lords ties, to the peace, 21. 184, 396
Huntingdon, Cts of, visits, in prison, 21. 398

imprisoned, 9. 272, 21. 374
insanity may preserve, from execution, 9. 272–3, 279
keeper of, reads *Hamlet* to him, 21. 408
mistress of, see Clifford, Mrs
Monro affirms lunacy of, 21. 397
mother of, seeks his pardon, 21. 388, 397
piquet played by, with warders, 21. 397
robber fought by, 21. 184
steward murdered by, 9. 272, 21. 367, 396
trial of: 9. 279–81, 13. 35, 21. 388, 406; decorations for, 19. 280n; ticket for, 30. 160; to take place, 9. 276
wedding clothes worn by, at execution, 9. 283
wife and mistress ill-treated by, 21. 395–6
wife's bill in Parliament for separation from, 21. 367, 396, 37. 529
wife's murder attempted by, 21. 183, 396
Shirley, Mrs Laurence. See Clarges, Anne
Shirley, Lady Mary (1712–84), m. (1730) Thomas Needham, 9th Vct Kilmorey:
almost a Methodist, 20. 271
Cheroffini, Contessa, at Rome called by, *più meretrice di me*, 21. 406
cousin's hanging announced by, in circular letter, 21. 406, 25. 658
Dick, Lady, called 'Dyke' by, to avoid indelicate word, 25. 108
Florence visited by, 20. 271
malapropisms of, to Niccolini and Salins, 20. 298
mother lived with, in France, 20. 298
Nightingale family to separate from, 20. 278
Nightingales' relationship to, 20. 271, 278
scandal whispered by, about George II's amours, 20. 278
Shirley's aunt, 20. 271
Taylor recommended by, to Albani, 20. 458
Shirley, Sir Robert (ca 1581–1628), adventurer:
Dalrymple's mistake about, 15. 79, 82
great traveller, 37. 498n
wife of, 1. 183n
Shirley, Robert (1650–1717), 1st E. Ferrers:
daughter of, 28. 412n
son of, 1. 342n, 9. 113n, 20. 481n
Shirley, Robert (1723–87), 6th E. Ferrers, 1778:
family insanity described by, at trial, 9. 279, 21. 388
HW mentions, 9. 278
'Ragged and Dangerous,' 9. 279
Shirley, Lady Selina (ca 1701–77), m. (1720) Peter Bathurst:
sister's letter to, 35. 346
Shirley, Selina (1707–91), m. (1728) Theophilus Hastings, 9th E. of Huntingdon:
Bowles's print of, trampling on a crown, 35. 346
chapel built by, at Bath, 10. 179
chapel of, in Harlequin Row, 35. 118n
Chelsea home of, 9. 74
Cornwallis told by, to exclude Ferrers's mistress, 21. 398

daughter not allowed by, to accept Bed-chamber post, **20.** 33–4
daughter of, **12.** 72n
death of, **11.** 296–7
Ferrers not converted by, **9.** 283–4
——'s courage expected by, to fail, **21.** 399
——'s cousin, **9.** 279n
——'s insanity pleaded in petition signed by, **21.** 397n
—— visited by, in prison, **21.** 398
HW calls: 'Lady St Huntingdon,' **28.** 93; 'Pa-triarchess of the Methodists,' **11.** 296; 'Pope Joan of Methodism,' **35.** 323; 'Queen of the Methodists,' **20.** 33; 'St Theresa of the Methodists,' **21.** 398
HW jokes about Methodist sympathies of, **31.** 69, 431
house of, in Park St, **20.** 52n
Madan the friend of, **11.** 12n
Methodist seminary in Welsh mountains at-tended by, **24.** 90
Methodists' patroness, **24.** 401n
Ossory, Lady, to pray with the appetite of, **32.** 22
religious activities of, **1.** 124
Rockingham, Lady, may depose, as Methodist leader, **35.** 323
Shirley, Lady Fanny, makes, her heir, **24.** 401
sister less Methodist than, **20.** 271
tickets with mottos distributed by, for Bath chapel, **10.** 179
title of, corrected, **43.** 360
Whitefield begs for watch and trinkets of, but gives them to his wife, **35.** 309
—— one of the chaplains of, **20.** 52n
—— preaches at home of, **9.** 73–4
—— sent by, to convert Ferrers, **21.** 398
Shirley, Hon. Sewallis (1709–65), M.P.:
Bedford's play could not be memorized by, **19.** 309, **20.** 395
death of, **7.** 397, **22.** 366
document in duplicate sent by, through Sharpe, to Cts of Orford, **20.** 547–8
Ferrers's uncle, **9.** 279n
HW calls: 'Hercules,' **20.** 439; 'Hornadatus,' **20.** 248
Kilmorey, Vcts, aunt of, **20.** 271
Mann pities, **20.** 443–4
marriage of, **9.** 113
name of, might be placed on Cts of Orford's monument, **25.** 227
Orford, Cts of, cohabits lovingly with, for several years, **20.** 239n
—— discards, **20.** 438–9, 443–4, 476
—— disparages, **20.** 476, 479, 481, 487
—— gives separate maintenance to, **20.** 439, 547–8, 568–9
—— keeps, as slave of her jealousy, **20.** 433
—— may forsake Richecourt for, **19.** 385
—— might be made pregnant by, **20.** 254
—— picks up, **19.** 309
—— probably does not write when accom-panied by, **20.** 143

—— receives dunning letters from, **20.** 479
—— to wed, **20.** 239, 250
picture of, perhaps being claimed by E. of Orford, **25.** 227
Scarborough visited by, **20.** 439
Vane, Vcts, describes her affair with, **20.** 439
wife of, **1.** 342n, **5.** 360n, **9.** 78n, **13.** 227n, **29.** 106n
Shirley, Teresia (d. 1668), Lady:
print of, **1.** 182
Shirley, Sir Thomas (1564–ca 1630), adventurer:
Dalrymple and HW refer to, **15.** 79, 82
great traveller, **37.** 498n
Shirley, Hon. Thomas (1733–1814), naval of-ficer:
deputy rangership of St James's and Hyde Parks resigned by, **41.** 378–80
HW acquainted by, with change in park rangership, **41.** 380
North may have been misinformed by, about HW's consent regarding Parks post, **36.** 157–8
Orford, E. of, allows, to treat regarding Parks rangership, **36.** 158
Parks deputy rangership of, corrected, **43.** 368
Shirley, Hon. Rev. Walter (1725–86):
biographical information about, corrected, **43.** 122
bishop said to have suspended, for Method-ism, **9.** 279
brother makes, trustee of fund for family of man he murdered, **21.** 398n
brother prefers services of, **21.** 398
brother procures porter from, **21.** 397
family insanity attested by, **9.** 279, **21.** *388*
HW mentions, **9.** 278
Shirley, Washington (1677–1729), 2d E. Ferrers:
daughter of, **11.** 296n, **20.** 33n, **21.** 398n
Shirley, William (1694–1771), army officer:
discredited in England, and succeeded by Loudoun, **21.** 13n
Massachusetts governor, **21.** 13n
regiment of, arrives at Plymouth, **21.** 18n
Shirley, William (fl. 1739–80), dramatist:
dates of, corrected, **43.** 302
Roman Sacrifice, The, by, disliked by HW, **28.** 343, **32.** 409–10
Shirley brothers:
HW intended to clear confusion about, **37.** 498n
Shirley family:
arms of, worn by Cts of Orford, but not to be used on monument, **25.** 240
Ferrers said to have been forced by, to plead insanity, **9.** 279, **21.** 396
——'s scaffold decorated at expense of, **21.** 402
insanity of, **9.** 279, **21.** 388, 397
undertaker for, prepares Ferrers's scaffold, **9.** 283
Shirreff (*or* Sherriff), Alexander, father of Charles Shirreff:
carries print to Dalrymple from HW, **15.** 117
HW advises, **15.** 116

Shirreff (*or* Sherriff), Charles (ca 1750–ca 1831), miniature painter:
 deafness of, **15**. 116
 HW advises father of, not to send him to Italy, **15**. 116
Shirt; shirts:
 dirty: fashionable for young men, **11**. 273; worn by Norborne Berkeley, **35**. 102
 Falkland wants, clean, in case of death, **40**. 137–8
 Franceschi's, sold, **17**. 122
 HW jokes about Harvey's sending for, to HW's room, **30**. 86
 HW sees Louis XV put on, **35**. 113
 regulation of, in ecclesiastical costume, **41**. 222–3
 Strozzi's servants borrow, for him, **18**. 146
 Young Pretender said to want, at Albano, **18**. 378
Shivering fit; shivering fits:
 occurrences of, **18**. 268, **24**. 76, **39**. 248
Shock-dog; shock-dogs:
 wax bas-relief of, by Mrs Damer, **38**. 198n
Shoe; shoes:
 black or white, ladies to wear, for Court mourning, **32**. 101n
 Carlisle's, red-heeled, **33**. 268n
 chamois, HW to wear, **39**. 44
 cloth, HW wears, when recovering from gout, **31**. 59, **39**. 23, 235
 Coventry, Cts of, has, made at Worcester, **20**. 324
 Devonshire, Ds of, complains of room dirtied by, **37**. 341
 embroidered: Hertford, Cts of, wants HW to get, from Paris, **39**. 264; raffled at Bath, **10**. 187
 England sends, to Portugal, **20**. 512n
 for jackass, prize for jackass race, **37**. 311
 for winner of foot race, **37**. 311
 gold, French procure, for mourning for Dauphin, **31**. 89
 gouty, Churchill practises dancing in, **33**. 283
 HW's, split, **35**. 596
 HW unable to wear, **30**. 200, 202
 Harris's, big, **39**. 235
 high-heeled, Chute should design, **35**. 110
 Kilmarnock, Cts of, requests, **37**. 218
 large, HW uses, for gout, **10**. 180
 Mann wears galoches over, **24**. 79
 Montagu, Lady Mary Wortley, does not wear, **10**. 5
 Percy, Bp, can identify on tombs, **34**. 225
 red-heeled: Carlisle wears, **33**. 267; 'exploded,' **18**. 148; Richelieu wears, **31**. 79
 regulation of, in ecclesiastical costume, **41**. 223
 slave-girl loses, **31**. 350
 'split gouty,' to be worn by Chute, **35**. 86
 wadded with flannel for gout-sufferers, **33**. 534
 white, running footman wears, at races, **9**. 248

wooden, gone from France, **39**. 8
Young Pretender's forces repair, at Perth, **19**. 105
Shoe-buckle; shoe-buckles:
 Barnard's tongue droops to, **35**. 166
 Carlisle, E. of, might ask about fashion in, **35**. 359
 diamond, broken in dancing minuets, **35**. 577
 English ladies' bosoms do not hang to, **25**. 641
 silver, not to be contributed by HW to Polish relief, **34**. 156
 Wortley Montagu wears, of diamonds, with a frock, **20**. 226
Shoe Lane, Fleet St:
 Cox in, **28**. 325n
 Gordon rioters set fires in, **29**. 56
Shoemaker; shoemakers:
 at Worcester, exhibits Cts of Coventry's shoe, **20**. 324
 riot of, predicted, **30**. 181n
Shoestring; shoestrings:
 on Charles II's statue at Lichfield, **9**. 294
Shonen, ——:
 Marmet replaces, as cashier of Sèvres workshop, **4**. 348n
Shooter's Hill, Kent:
 Christian VII ambushed at, by Cts of Harrington, **35**. 327
 resort of highwaymen, **12**. 134
 Walpole, Sir Edward, writes from, **36**. 319
Shooting:
 at Newmarket, **38**. 29
 Conway and Freeman join at, **37**. 476
 Conways' pastime at Sandywell, **37**. 105
 Ferdinand of Naples enjoys, in Florentine cascines and woods, **25**. 600
 —— includes Hamilton in parties for, **35**. 439
 HW refuses to join party for, **37**. 127
 Hertford and Orford may be at, in Norfolk, **36**. 87
 Hertford's diversion at Dublin, **39**. 39, 45
 ——'s pastime at Ragley, **38**. 80, 81
 Neapolitan Court interested only in, **35**. 433
 Richmond, D. of, wants to rent Ennery for, **41**. 11
 season for: **11**. 349, **25**. 433; begins, **15**. 164; London deserted during, **25**. 433
 Wickes to go to Norfolk for, **11**. 72
 See also Game; Hunting; Shooting-party
Shooting-party; shooting-parties:
 Hertford's, from Paris, **38**. 409
Shop; shops:
 Ailesbury, Cts of, may now afford any, of old china or Dresden, **38**. 145
 at Genoa, plundered, **19**. 338
 at Leghorn Fair, **22**. 423
 at Ranelagh jubilee-masquerade, **20**. 47
 Ghent people live at doors of, **37**. 124
 in London: full of favours, **17**. 196; looking-glass sought in, from Pall Mall to Cheapside, **20**. 141

lights in all, near London, **39.** 498

Parisian: HW unable to visit, **31.** 64; HW visits, daily, with Ds of Richmond, **31.** 93; have nothing new, **39.** 145–6

retail, tax on, **25.** 578n

See also Apothecary's shop; Laceman; Pastry shop; Ponte Vecchio; Snuff shop; Upholsterer's shop

Shopkeeper; shopkeepers:

in future, will be descended from aristocracy, **38.** 367–8

Methodism attracts, **20.** 82

Shop Tax Bill. *See under* Parliament: acts of

Shore, Jane, née (?) Wainstead (d. ?1527), m. (before 1483) William Shore; mistress of Edward IV:

'Blagrave,' Mrs, friend of, **24.** 162

HW compares Cts of Hertford and Frances Pelham with, **9.** 274

HW's print of, by Faber, **1.** 144, 150n

HW wrote account of, after impetus was chilled, **14.** 167–8

More knew, in her old age, **41.** 112

picture of, at Eton, **1.** 144

print of, by Tyson, **1.** 142, 144n, 149, 150

Richard III's letter about, **1.** 156, **2.** 108, 115, **14.** 160

——'s order relating to marriage proposal for, **16.** 171

——'s withered arm attributed to spell cast by, **41.** 112

supposed picture of, at Cambridge, **1.** 142, 144, 150

Waldegrave, Cts, said to be costumed as, **23.** 193n

See also Rowe, Nicholas: *Jane Shore*

Shore, Samuel (1738–1828), of Norton Hall, Yorks:

probable delegate from Yorks, **29.** 140n

Shore, William (d. ca 1480):

husband of Jane Shore, **1.** 156

Short, James (1710–68), optician:

glasses should be approved by, **4.** 31

'Short Account of Osney Abbey.' *See under* Huddesford, Rev. William

Short Address . . . to the Public. See under Sackville, Lord George

Shorter, Arthur (d. between 1746 and 1753), HW's uncle:

biographical information about, corrected, **43.** 45, 167, 171

Conway asks about Jacobitism of, **37.** 256

HW may get dirges from, on brother's death, **37.** 224

HW tries to reconcile, to Erasmus Shorter, **37.** 255, 256

left no children, **1.** 52

stone, gravel, gout, rheumatism, and ruptures of, **37.** 256

youngest brother survives, **13.** 25n

Young Pretender's coronation would be hailed by, **37.** 255

Shorter, Catherine (ca 1682–1737), m. (1700) Sir Robert Walpole, K.B., 1725; K.G., 1726; HW's mother:

ancestry of, **1.** 52, **33.** 454

apartment rented by, for George II's coronation, **21.** 536

at Godolphin's death-bed, **28.** 390

believes in return of departed spirits, **15.** 5

birth date of, corrected, **43.** 146

Boothby Skrymsher's mother a cousin of, **21.** 497

brother of, **20.** 403

bugles purchased by, **11.** 212

Burton, Mrs, milliner to, **9.** 385

Caroline, Q., dines with, **15.** 333, **33.** 248

chambermaid of, **10.** 22

Cholmondeley's sisters entertain, at his Windsor Castle apartment, when tending HW in his illness at Eton, **43.** 169

courage of, when dying, **40.** 24

daughter of, **30.** 371

death of: **13.** 7, 140, 144, **40.** 23–4; HW mourns, **37.** 36, 37; Middleton condoles with HW on, **15.** 4–6; one of HW''s heaviest blows, **22.** 226

Eccardt's and Wootton's picture of, **19.** 511, **35.** 173–4, **42.** 249

enemies of, **17.** 403

engraving of, in *Ædes Walpolianæ,* **19.** 511

father of, **28.** 24

finds relics, **2.** 24

gout not experienced by, **9.** 291

grotto of, **13.** 117, 118, **43.** 175

HW addresses envelope to, **9.** 4

HW alludes to, **13.** 221

HW compares Mme du Deffand to, **10.** 290

HW embarrassed by affection of, **4.** 59

HW looks on Conway as his nearest relation by, **37.** 170

HW said to foment anger of, against Sir Edward Walpole, **36.** 18

HW's correspondence with, **36.** 1–4

HW seeks statue for memorial to, **17.** 212n

HW's letters to, shown to Sir Edward Walpole after her death, **36.** 18–19

HW's love for, **37.** 170

HW's medicine mixed by, **36.** 3, 4

HW's monument to, in Westminster Abbey: **13.** 25, **22.** 98n, **35.** 178, **40.** 80; payment for, **38.** 111; *see also* Livia: statue of

HW taken by, to see George I, **25.** 248

HW to receive things from, at Cambridge, **37.** 15

Hertford receives playthings from, **39.** 517

——'s boyhood letter to, **39.** 517

husband of, **9.** 348n

husband's defeat cannot injure, **17.** 246

husband's portrait by Richardson kept by, **41.** 234

India ink obtained by, from China after Sloane would not give her any, **17.** 436

marriage of, **22.** 27

nephew of, **20.** 468n, **24.** 71n

[Shorter, Catherine, *continued*]
Philipps cousins of, **17.** 67n, 384n, **19.** 310n
'rump-days' a term used by, **35.** 86
son of, **25.** 462n
statue for monument of, in Westminster Abbey, *see* Livia, statue of
tomb of, at Houghton, **9.** 348
Voltaire dines with, **41.** 149
woman of, intimate with Mrs Gates, **25.** 92n
Shorter, Charlotte (d. 1734), m. (1716) Francis Seymour Conway, cr. (1703) Bn Conway:
brother of, **20.** 403n
children of, **9.** 156n
Hertford's correspondence with, **39.** 517
son of, **20.** 468n
Shorter, Erasmus (d. 1753):
Chancery Lane lodgings of, **20.** 403n
death date of, **43.** 45
death of, intestate, **9.** 156, 161, **20.** 403, 436, **37.** 372
estate of: **4.** 359n; Camden advises HW about, **40.** 79
HW receipts promissory note from Anthony Wright to, **20.** 403n
HW receives share of fortune of, **13.** 25, **36.** 161, **40.** 79
HW rejoices in inheritance from, **35.** 84
HW's interview with, **37.** 224
HW tries to reconcile, with Arthur Shorter, **37.** 255, 256
heirs of, **9.** 156, **20.** 403
left no children, **1.** 52
Mann disapproves of, for not making a will, **20.** 404–5
Park Place, St James's, the address of, **37.** 372n
Swiss servant of, suspected of hastening his death, **35.** 158–9
Shorter, John, of Staines, Middlesex, HW's great-great-great-grandfather:
genealogy of, **12.** 266
Shorter, John, of Staines, Middlesex, HW's great-great-grandfather:
genealogy of, **12.** 266
Shorter, Sir John (1624–88), Kt, 1675; HW's great-grandfather:
descendants of, **1.** 52
HW's great-grandfather, **28.** 24n
James II gives coat of arms to, **12.** 266
parentage of, **12.** 266
Shorter, John (b. ca 1660), of Bybrook, Kent; timber-merchant; HW's grandfather:
daughter of, **1.** 52n
family of, **1.** 52
HW does not think himself better than, **28.** 24, **29.** 232
Shorter, Sir John (*or* Sir Joseph) (d. 1733):
obituary notice of, **12.** 267
Shorter, John (d. 1746), HW's uncle:
biographical information about, corrected, **43.** 45, 167, 171
death of, **37.** 224
left no children, **1.** 52

youngest brother survives, **13.** 25n
Shorter, Mrs John. *See* Philipps, Elizabeth
Shorter, Sir Joseph. *See* Shorter, Sir John (d. 1733)
Shorter, Robert. *See* Shorton, Robert
Shorter family:
arms of, **12.** 266
note on, **28.** 24n
Shortgrove, Essex; Thomond's seat:
HW visits, **10.** 30
landscape effects at, **10.** 30
Shorthand. See under Macaulay, Aulay
Shorthand:
Hodgson, reporter in, **34.** 99n
Shortness of breath:
occurrences of, **20.** 523, **21.** 1, **25.** 394
'Short Notes' by HW:
dating of, **43.** 169
provenance of, **43.** 168–9
text of, **13.** 3–51
Short Observations on the Remarks of the Rev. Mr Masters, by HW:
published in 1798, **28.** 247n
Short Observations on the Right Honourable Edmund Burke's Reflections:
Burke's *Reflections* answered by, **11.** 169n
Shorton, Robert (d. 1535):
Cole asks about, **1.** 42–3
Short Review of the Political State of Great Britain, A. See under Wraxall, Sir Nathaniel William
Short Treatise on the Game of Whist. See under Hoyle, Edmond
Short View of the Dispute . . . Concerning the Regulation of the African Trade, A:
HW owns, **20.** 126n
Shorwell, Isle of Wight:
North Court at, **42.** 127n
Shotesham, Norfolk:
poor men from, eligible for Trinity Hospital, **16.** 90
Shotley, Suffolk:
Aston, rector of, **14.** 38n
Shotover, Oxon:
Schutz inherits manor of, **9.** 207n
Shottesbrook, Berks:
Dodwell, rector of, **15.** 302
Shoulder; shoulders:
Salimbeni breaks, **17.** 116, 132
Shovel (surname). *See* Shovell
Shovel; shovels, fire:
Newcastle colliers said to feed their children with, **20.** 450
Shovell, Sir Clowdisley (1650–1707), Adm.; Kt; M.P.:
daughter of, **34.** 257
naval operations in winter criticized by, **9.** 268
Shovell, Elizabeth (1692–1750), m. 1 (1708) Robert Marsham, cr. (1708) Bn Romney; m. 2 (1732) John Carmichael, 3d E. of Hyndford:
marriages of, **34.** 257

Shove to a Heavy-Arsed Christian, A:
  Presbyterian tract, **29.** 271
Show; shows:
  London full of, **25.** 502
  See also Opera; Play; Theatre
Shower, Sir Bartholomew:
  print of, **40.** 237
Shreeve, Edmund (d. 1779), Capt. of *Earl of Besborough* packet-boat:
  Tuscans want satisfaction from, **24.** 417
Shrewsbury, Cts of:
  figure misidentified as, **42.** 247
  See also Beauchamp, Margaret (1404–67); Brudenell, Lady Anna Maria (d. 1702); Cavendish, Mary (d. 1632); Hardwick, Elizabeth (ca 1521–1608)
Shrewsbury, Ds of. *See* Paleotti, Adelaide (d. 1726)
Shrewsbury, D. of. *See* Talbot, Charles (1660–1718)
Shrewsbury, E. of. *See* Talbot, Charles (1660–1718); Talbot, George (ca 1528–90); Talbot, George (1719–87); Talbot, Gilbert (1552–1616); Talbot, John (ca 1384–1453)
Shrewsbury, English ship:
  Keppel awaits, **39.** 307
  —— mentions, **28.** 415n
  Palliser pursues La Rochemaure in, **21.** 431n
Shrewsbury, Salop:
  Dodd and Whaley visit, **40.** 12, 13, 14–15
  election in, **19.** 447n
  mayor of, *see* Corbett, Sir Richard
  post-house at, **40.** 12
  Scottses and Stokeses of, **43.** 67
  Severn almost surrounds, **40.** 14
'Shrewsbury clock':
  Pitt talks by, **37.** 444
Shrine, mosaic (of St Simplicius and St Faustina):
  from church of Santa Maria Maggiore, Rome, **43.** 284
  given to HW by Hamilton, **35.** 406–7, 409, 429
  Hamilton's, put in SH chapel, **35.** 421
  Hamiltons to see, at SH, **35.** 429
Shropshire, Walter (d. 1785), bookseller in New Bond St:
  HW imposed upon by, **41.** 271
Shropshire:
  Clun in, **16.** 87
  Mason to pay visit in, **28.** 429
  Mawley Hall in, **40.** 42
  Stafford, E. of, to exile wife to, **9.** 95
  Walpole, Sir Robert, has lands in, **36.** 25n
Shroud; shrouds:
  Balmerinoch wears, **19.** 299
  Elgin, Cts of, depicted in, on tomb, **39.** 139
  Sandys must shudder in, **35.** 92
Shrove-tide:
  carnival at, in England, since Reformation, **13.** 201
Shrove-tide cock. *See under* Chicken
Shrove-Tuesday:
  solemn jousts on, **16.** 80

Shrub; shrubs:
  at St John's, Oxford, **33.** 57
  Conway's: growing, **37.** 486; improve, **37.** 528
  English, are often in full leaf by end of April, **25.** 497
  flowering, at the Vyne, **35.** 640
  HW jokes about planting, at Notting Hill, **31.** 163
  HW to send, to Bentley, **35.** 196
  in bloom in February, **21.** 268
  laurustinus, **1.** 133
  lettuce mistaken by HW for West Indian flowering, **37.** 292
  Radnor's, **35.** 174
  walks edged with, **21.** 417
  See also under Flower; Plant; Tree; *and under names of varieties*
Shrubberies:
  HW ridicules, **21.** 418
Shrub's Hill, Windsor Park:
  Sandbys build summer-house on, **10.** 44n
Shuckburgh, Sir Richard (1596–1656), Kt:
  hunts during Edgehill battle, **2.** 75n, **29.** 147, **38.** 543
  name of, corrected, **43.** 66
Shuckburgh, Richard (1728–72), Col.:
  Mann called on by, at Florence, **20.** 160
  Orford, E. of, said to have recommended, to Mann, **20.** 160
  whist addict, **20.** 160
Shuckburgh, Mrs Richard. *See* Hayward, Sarah
Shugborough, Staffs:
  Anson of, **9.** 294n
Shuja-ud-daulah (d. 1757):
  defeat and decapitation of, **21.** 181n
Shuja-ud-daulah ('Sujah Dowla') (ca 1731–75), Nawab-Vizir of Oudh 1754–75:
  East India Co.'s dealings with, **21.** 181n
  Oudh belongs to, **25.** 13
Shuldham, Molyneux (ca 1717–98), cr. (1776) Bn Shuldham; naval officer:
  Barré's and Manchester's motions for dispatches of, **24.** 205n
  Edgcumbe persuaded by, to cut trees down, **33.** 212n
  Esquimos brought by, to England, **32.** 357n
  George III's remonstrance from, for Keppel trial, **24.** 432n
  Keppel hears from, **39.** 307
  Mercury sees, near Block Island, **24.** 229n
  naval news from, **24.** 506n
Shulma ('Schuma'):
  Danville's maps do not include, **24.** 29
  Rumiantsev to attack Grand Vizir at, **24.** 29
Shute, ——, Mrs:
  Pomfrets entertain, and her two daughters, **17.** 169n
Shute, John. *See* Barrington, John
Shuter, Edward (ca 1728–76), comedian:
  Luxborough, Lady, compared with, **32.** 244
Shutter; shutters:
  altar, from Bury St Edmunds, **43.** 65
  at Matson, hacked by James II, **35.** 152

[Shutter; shutters, *continued*]
Bath, E. and Cts of, will not permit, in maids' room, **30.** 89–90
Le Brun designs, for Louvre gallery, **35.** 344
of Pall Mall taverns, have Townshend's caricatures, **37.** 444
Shuttle; shuttles:
used in knotting verses, **33.** 263
Shuttlecock; shuttlecocks:
Middleton, Mrs, plays at, **15.** 310
Pembroke, Cts of, calls, 'shuttlesomething,' **17.** 496
Shuttleworth, Anne *or* Elizabeth (d. 1788), m. (1737) John Crewe:
son and Montagu to be entertained by, **10.** 96
Shuttleworth, (?) James (1714–73), M.P.:
biographical information about, corrected, **43.** 241
Nourse angers Windsor by accusing, of pretended illness, **17.** 248
Shuttleworth, Richard (1683–1749), M.P.:
birth date of, **43.** 241
Shuttleworth, Thomas (b. ? 1674) *or* Richard (1708–before 1748), absconding bank clerk:
clerk of South Sea Co., **19.** 76n
death of, at Naples, **19.** 76n
Mann almost catches, before his escape to Naples, **19.** 76–7
Shutz. *See* Schutz
Shuvalov, Comtesse. *See* Saltykov, Ekaterina Petrovna
Shuvalov, Lt-Gen., Russian army officer:
Florence visited by, with Orlov, **23.** 191n
Shuvalov, André (1744–89), Comte; Gen.:
Du Deffand, Mme, gives opinion of, **6.** 496, **7.** 26, 54, 73
——'s social relations with, **6.** 496, **7.** 429, 431
England visited by, **22.** 460
Épître à Ninon de l'Enclos by: Du Deffand, Mme, attributes, to Voltaire, **6.** 28; Du Deffand, Mme, sends, to HW, **6.** 28, 42
Épître à Voltaire by, **21.** 175, 426, 428
Mann entertains, at Florence, **22.** *460*
Paris to be visited by, **8.** 205
Roissy to be visited by, **7.** 54
uncle of, **7.** 55, 175
wife of, **6.** 496n
Shuvalov, Ivan Ivanovich (1727–97), called Comte:
absent from Paris, **7.** 176
Auteuil visited by, **7.** 347
blameless career of, when given absolute power, **22.** 289n
Britannicus applauded by, **7.** 277
Catherine II makes, grand chambellan, **7.** 72
—— receives, **6.** 492, **8.** 205–6
—— said to be cicisbea of, **23.** 149
—— said to have made, a chief minister, **22.** 59
——'s fall may be desired by, **10.** 157
Choiseul, Duchesse de, pleasantly surprised by, **3.** 365, 381
—— talks with, **3.** 111

Du Barry, Comtesse, called 'Mme Barbari' by, **6.** 51
Du Deffand, Mme, receives blue-fox mantle from, **7.** 72, 80–1
——'s correspondence with, **3.** 248, 290, 365, **5.** 144, **6.** 492, 496, **7.** 72, 80, **8.** 205
——'s friendship with, **3.** 9
—— to be accompanied by, **3.** 13, 16
Elizabeth of Russia's favourite: **3.** 129n, **10.** 156, **12.** 254; in disfavour with Catherine II, **38.** 516n
——'s minion, **22.** 59, 455, **23.** 149
——'s supposed husband, **22.** 289n
England charms, **10.** 157
—— to be visited by, **3.** 111, 112, **38.** 516, 524
—— visited by, **22.** 289, 455–6
Florence visited by, **23.** 149
Frederick II visited by, **6.** 492, **8.** 205
Genoa visited by, **3.** 365
HW and Mme du Deffand discuss, **6.** 335
HW disappointed in, **22.** 289
HW entertains, at SH, **10.** 156–7
HW given Dorat's *Fables* by, **6.** 182
HW knew, in Paris, **22.** 455
HW's correspondence with, **6.** 307, 308, 310, **41.** 348–9
HW sends parcels to, **6.** 335
HW sends regards to, **39.** 214
HW sent messages by, **3.** 290
HW's esteem for, **22.** 289n, 455–6
HW's remarks on Marmontel to be repeated to, **6.** 424
HW to consult, about medal, **6.** 400
HW to receive compliments of, **22.** 565
Italy may be visited by, **22.** 456
Jesuits' sufferings pain, **3.** 365, 381
Jonzac, Marquise de, gives commission to, **3.** 129
London visited by, **3.** 129
Luxembourg, Mme de, exchanges presents with, **6.** 415, **12.** 254
(?) —— writes verses to, **6.** 415
Mann entertains, **22.** 564
—— will expect, **22.** 460
(?) Marmontel's verses to, **6.** 424
nephew and niece of, **7.** 55
nephew of, **6.** 28n
Paul I and wife receive, **6.** 492
Razumovskiĭ accompanies, **22.** 456, 564–5
Roissy visited by, **6.** 72
St Petersburg visited by, **6.** 492, **7.** 72
social relations of, in Paris, *see index entries ante* **8.** 508
verses for, **12.** 254
Vienna visited by, **3.** 248
Shveidnitz. *See* Schweidnitz
'Shylock':
HW calls Hardwicke, **30.** 141
See also under Shakespeare, William: *Merchant of Venice*
Siam:
ambassadors from and to, *see under* Ambassador

Sibbald, Sir Robert (1641–1722):
MSS left by, **15**. 104n
transcribed Jonson's conversations with Drummond, **15**. 166n
Siberia:
Apraxin exiled to, **21**. 159
Catherine II would rather plunder Constantinople than develop, **25**. 545
death preferable to exile in, **22**. 68
England in May worthy of, **38**. 196
—— may resemble, **35**. 171
forces of, oppose Frederick II, **21**. 327
HW compares Norfolk to, **17**. 495, **18**. 68, 467, 481, **30**. 63, 73
HW imagines Russian ex-favourites passing each other on way to and from, **10**. 39
HW jokes about the Walpoles going to, when Sir Robert falls from power, **28**. 48
HW might as well be in, **32**. 259, **33**. 420
Menshikov's death in, **6**. 167
next door to the Russian Court's drawing-room, **22**. 55
O'Hara unlikely to be sent to, **11**. 236
Paris as cold as, **31**. 90
Peter III may banish Vorontsov to, **22**. 11
Pomerania worth more than, **22**. 11
Russian leaders recalled from, **22**. 11, 59–60
travels in, *see* Chappe d'Auteroche, Jean: *Voyage en Sibérie*
'viceroy' of, **5**. 357
Sibilia *or* Sibilla (d. 1406) de Forciá, m. 1 Artal de Foces; m. 2 (1377) Pedro IV, K. of Aragon:
Calveley said to have married, **41**. 445
husband said to have been given potion by, **41**. 445
Sibilla, giuoco della. *See* Giuoco
Sibley, Anne, of Teddington, wife of James Sibley:
HW's bequest to, **15**. 338n, **30**. 362
Sibley, James (d. in or before 1793), HW's footman:
(?) donor's name forgotten by, **35**. 431
(?) HW scolds, **32**. 326
(?) HW sends, for blunderbuss after robbery, **33**. 296–7, 298
(?) illiterate, **25**. 118
(?) letter mistakenly posted by, **25**. 118
(?) messages sent by, **31**. 205
(?) reports on Gordon riots, **33**. 189
'seized by Bird,' **12**. 261
widow of, **30**. 362
(?) with HW during attempted robbery, **32**. 308
Sibley, Maria, (?) maid:
Waldegrave, Cts, praises, **36**. 288
Sibly. *See* Sibley
Sibton, Suffolk:
Derehaughs held lands in, **1**. 377
Sibyl; sibyls:
Domenichino's: **17**. 267–8, 313, 325, **35**. 19; *see also under* Domenichino
gold tapestry of, after Guercino, **22**. 233n

Jamesone's paintings of, **40**. 267
old women guides in Derbyshire resemble, **40**. 16
pictures of, at Dulwich, **11**. 289
portraits of, at Standon, **40**. 198, 199
Sibylla. *See* Sibilla
Sibylline Leaves. See under Poulett, John
Sibylline Leaves:
HW will not dispose, over Europe, **25**. 105
Sicard, —— (d. 1752), French traitor:
Ciotat in Provence home of, before going to Tripoli to turn Mohammedan, **20**. 319n
France demands, from Tripoli, **20**. 319
Sicilies, Two:
Montemar conqueror of, **17**. 427
See also under Naples; Sicily; Two Sicilies
Sicily, K. of. *See* Alfonso V (1416–58); Edmund (1245–96); René I (1409–80)
Sicily, Q. of. *See* Isabelle (1410–53)
Sicily:
arms of, **1**. 242
art objects from, brought by Hamilton, **32**. 70
Bute would have written to HW from Otranto, had he visited, **23**. 103
Caracciolo to be viceroy of, **7**. 452, **10**. 216n
Charles of Naples may take refuge in, **18**. 453
Cicero in, compared to Conway, **24**. 526
earthquake and fire in, **35**. 373
earthquake damage in, less than was represented, **25**. 391
earthquakes in, **11**. 298, **33**. 396, 444
Fogliani viceroy of, **18**. 183n
France and Austria give up, to Charles III, **21**. 280n
frequent upheavals in, **32**. 159
Gothic paintings in, **35**. 409
grain not to be sent by, to Italy, till French and Spanish wants are filled, **23**. 430
honours of, may be conferred on Mann, **18**. 484
Inquisition suppressed in, **25**. 383
Leghorn bans ships of, because of plague, **18**. 252
Louis XVI treated like a tyrant of, **34**. 87
Malta imports all supplies from, **20**. 405
medal from, **35**. 432
Naples isolated from, because of plague, **18**. 252
Otranto not in, **23**. 107
Phelps's secret expedition into, **21**. 124
plague in, *see under* Messina
Pomfret, Cts of, describes tour in, **21**. 579
rebellion in, **24**. 39
ships from, do quarantine before Gravesend, **18**. 276n
Squillace from, **21**. 330n
travels in, *see* Brydone, Patrick: *Tour through Sicily*
Van Dyck sails from, **7**. 371
Verres plunders, **37**. 432
viceroy of: **10**. 216n; *see also* Caracciolo, Domenico

[Sicily, *continued*]
Wortley Montagu may embark from, for Egypt, **22.** 77
Sickingen, Karl Heinrich Joseph (1737–91), Reichsgraf von; minister from Elector Palatine to France:
Du Deffand, Mme, accompanied by, to Sceaux and Montrouge, **4.** 442
—— entertains, at supper, **41.** 195
——'s social relations with, **5.** 5
Sickness:
HW's reflections on, **35.** 331
Sida, Abp of. *See* Onorati, Bernardino
Sida Tunez Bey, son of Bey of Tunis. *See* Yūnus Bey
Siddons, William (d. 1808), actor:
SH visited by, **12.** 229
wife of, **29.** 282n
Siddons, Mrs William. *See* Kemble, Sarah
Sideboard; sideboards:
Ailesbury, Cts of, wants, for Park Place, **37.** 465–6
at Burghley House, **10.** 346
Brown, Sir Robert, saves money by not having orange or lemon on, **25.** 609
fruit on, at ball, **35.** 301
HW seeks granite for, **35.** 178n
Pesters's, **37.** 465n
Selwyn tries to get water at, **38.** 348
Side-saddle:
for Pegasus, **32.** 88
Sidi Mahmūd Aga, envoy from Tripoli to Holland:
Elizabeth brings, to Leghorn, **23.** 24
Sidi Yannes. *See* Yūnus Bey
Sidmouth, Vct. *See* Addington, Henry
'Sidney, Lady.' *See* Sidney, Elizabeth
Sidney, Lady. *See* Dudley, Lady Mary (d. 1586); Walsingham, Frances (ca 1567–1632)
Sidney, Algernon (1622–83), republican; M.P.:
Barillon's letter to, perhaps forged, **28.** 75–6
Beckford compared with, **35.** 339
born at Penshurst, **2.** 240n, **28.** 464n
brothers of, **41.** 470
Dalrymple accuses, of accepting bribes, **28.** 66–8, 85–6, 95
epigraph from, in pamphlet, **28.** 337n
'freedom's martyr,' **10.** 164
genealogy of, **10.** 352
HW compares himself to, **9.** 137, **10.** 164
HW condones French intrigue of, **32.** 105
HW will not be traduced like, **39.** 277
'half-divinity,' **29.** 262
Heroic Postscript does not include defence of, **28.** 127
Hume's *History* attacks, in note, **29.** 104
Macaulay, Mrs, defends, in her *History*, **28.** 78, **29.** 102
Macpherson and Dalrymple unsympathetic to, **2.** 66n
Mason to be inspired by shade of, **28.** 78
Montagu includes, in his roster of heroes, **10.** 124

—— related to, **9.** 304, **10.** 139, 164, 352
one of HW's heroes, **2.** 60, 66–7
Park Place would be approved by, **10.** 126
picture of, jokingly worshipped by Montagu, **10.** 141
print of, in Hollis's *Memoirs*, **29.** 19
quotation from, **32.** 383n
Scots traduce, **29.** 105, 135
Stratford's tragedy includes, **29.** 223
successors to, inferior to him, **28.** 411
Sidney, Ambrozia (ca 1565–75), sister of Sir Philip:
HW 'utter stranger' to, **34.** 94
Sidney, 'Beau':
HW speculates about, **41.** 470
Sidney, Lady Dorothy (1617–84), m. 1 (1639) Henry Spencer, 1st E. of Sunderland; m. 2 (1652) Robert Smythe; 'Sacharissa':
cipher of, not carved on beeches, **35.** 141
Montagu confused about relationship of, **10.** 128
—— hopes he has portrait of, **10.** 125, 128
portrait of, at Penshurst, **35.** 141
'Sacharissa,' **28.** 203n
Smythe descended from, **23.** 248
Waller's reply to, **34.** 226
Sidney, Lady Dorothy, m. Col. Thomas Cheke:
Lely's portrait of: Bonus not to be allowed to clean, **10.** 256; HW buys, at Lady Yonge's auction, **10.** *123*, 256; Montagu consults HW about mildew on, **10.** 256; Montagu finds mezzotint of, in Guilford's library, **10.** 128; Montagu removes mildew from, with lemon, **10.** 261
Sidney, Elizabeth (d. 1783), m. William Perry; 'Lady Sidney':
children of, **10.** 122
HW thinks Romney portrait kept by, **10.** 123
HW to direct Montagu's letter to, **10.** 125
marriage of, **20.** 389n
Montagu does not need information from, about portraits, **10.** 128
——'s correspondence with, **10.** 125
sister's property left away from, to Lady Yonge, **10.** *122*
Sidney, Frances (ca 1531–89), m. (1555) Thomas Radclyffe, 3d E. of Sussex, 1557:
foundress of Sidney Sussex College, **33.** 350
shield perhaps belonged to, **33.** 350
Sidney, Sir Henry (1529–86), Kt, 1550; lord deputy of Ireland:
daughter of, **34.** 94
portrait of, too expensive for HW at Yonge auction, **10.** 124
seeks dispensation, **1.** 194
widow of, **33.** 350
See also *Letters and Memorials of State*
Sidney, Hon. Henry (1641–1704), cr. (1689) Vct Sidney, (1694) E. of Romney; M.P.:
birth date of, corrected, **43.** 131
earldom of, cost £5,000, **9.** 51n
Irish parliament prorogued by, as lord lieutenant, **23.** 156n

portrait of: HW thinks, kept by Lady Sidney, **10.** 123; Montagu fond of, **10.** 123; Montagu hopes he has, **10.** 125; not in Lady Yonge's auction, **10.** 123

probably not the 'Beau Sidney,' **41.** 470

removal of monument from Dover Castle permitted by, **16.** 86

Sidney, Jocelyn (ca 1692–1743), 7th E. of Leicester, 1737:

coheirs of, **10.** 122n

Sidney, Lady Lucy (d. 1685), m. (1647) Sir John Pelham, 3d Bt:

genealogy of, **10.** 352

Montagu hopes he has portrait of, **10.** 125

——'s great-grandmother, **9.** 304n

Sidney, Lady Mary. *See* Dudley, Lady Mary

Sidney, Mary (1561–1621), m. (1577) Henry Herbert, 2d E. of Pembroke, 1570:

bust of, at Houghton Park House, **33.** 351, **34.** 184

'Countess of Arcadia,' **34.** 184

HW has billiard sticks used by brother and, **39.** 294

Sidney, Mary (fl. 1604–21), m. (1604) Sir Robert Wroth:

Countess of Montgomery's Urania by, HW glad to hear of, **16.** 28

Sidney, Mary (d. 1758), m. (1738) Sir Brownlow Sherard, 4th Bt:

co-heiress to Earls of Leicester, **20.** 389n

drunken, **10.** 122

Yonge, Lady, attends, and inherits property from her, **10.** 122

Sidney, Sir Philip (1554–86), Kt:

arms of, **32.** 47

born at Penshurst, **2.** 240n, **28.** 464n

Brooke's friendship with, commemorated on tomb, **37.** 524

(?) bust of, **33.** 351

Countess of Pembroke's Arcadia by, disparaged by HW, **9.** 26

Defence of Poesie by, **40.** 137

Discourse in Defence of the Earl of Leicester by, read by HW, **9.** 25–6

Dyer a friend of, **1.** 5n

Erskine, Sir Harry, compared with, **37.** 524

European acclaim for, **40.** 136

HW as antiquary venerates, **32.** 47

HW has billiard sticks used by sister and, **39.** 294

HW includes, in *Royal and Noble Authors*, **21.** 196

HW's attack on: approved by Lort, **16.** 367; criticized by Lady Mary Coke, **31.** 200–1

HW's *Royal and Noble Authors* improves at, **37.** 524

—— makes comments on, **40.** 136–7

HW unfair to, **32.** 47n

Herbert, Edward, rivals, as hero, **10.** 140

Houghton, Beds, perhaps built by, **32.** 46–7

Languet, friend of, **35.** 141

Poland said to have considered, as possible king, **9.** 26, **40.** 136

portrait of: **1.** 170, 180n; at Woburn Abbey, **9.** 123

portraits of, at Penshurst, **35.** 141

sister proud of, **33.** 351

wife of, **32.** 15, 47

See also *Letters and Memorials of State*

'Sidney, Sir Robert.' *See* Sidney, Sir Henry

Sidney, Robert (1563–1626), cr. (1603) Bn Sydney, (1605) Vct Lisle, (1618) E. of Leicester:

Arundel refers case to, **1.** 5

steward of Anne of Denmark, **33.** 350

Sidney, Robert (1595–1677), 2d E. of Leicester, 1626; M.P.:

anecdotes of, **41.** 270

(?) apology by, **16.** 11

daughter of, **10.** 125n

Desmond, Cts of, said by, to have died in fall from nut-tree, **40.** 113n

genealogy of, **10.** 352

Montagu confused about kinship of, to 'Sacharissa,' **10.** 128

—— mistakenly thinks he has portrait of, **10.** 128

——'s relationship to, **10.** 128

reports death of Cts of Desmond, **7.** 370n, **40.** 108

Temple cites, on Cts of Desmond's age, **40.** 108

wife of, **10.** 123n

See also *Letters and Memorials of State*

Sidney, Robert (1649–1702), 4th E. of Leicester:

portrait of: Bonus not to be allowed to clean, **10.** 256; HW buys, for Montagu, at Lady Yonge's auction, **10.** 123, 256; Montagu consults HW about mildew on, **10.** 256; Montagu finds mezzotint of, in Guilford's library, **10.** 128; Montagu removes mildew from, with lemon, **10.** 261

son of, **10.** 122n

Sidney, Col. Thomas:

daughters of, **10.** 122n

Sidney, Sir William (ca 1481–1553):

Edward VI gives Penshurst to, **35.** 141

Sidney. *See also* Sydney

Sidney family:

Ampthill formerly owned by, **33.** 350–1

arms of, **33.** 350

co-heiress of, marries Perry, **20.** 389n

Penshurst the seat of, **28.** 464n

Townshend, George (1753–1811), descended from, **43.** 68

Sidney papers. See *Letters and Memorials of State*

Sidney Sussex College, Cambridge:

foundress of, **33.** 350

new chapel of, **2.** 27

portrait of Cromwell at, **1.** 360, 362

Whigs at, **13.** 58

Sidon:

Arlington St's resemblance to, **20.** 469

Sidy Jones. *See* Yūnus Bey

Siècle de Louis XIV, Le . . . [and] *un précis du siècle de Louis XV. See under* Voltaire

Siege; sieges:
  HW jokes about uselessness of, **30**. 34–5
  may be popular in London, **30**. 35
Siège de Calais, Le. See under Buirette de
  Belloy, Pierre-Laurent; Ferriol, Antoine;
  Guérin, Claudine Alexandrine
Siège d'Orléans, Le:
  given at Nicolet theatre, **7**. 66
Siege of Aquileia. See under Home, John (1722–
  1808)
Siege of Berwick. See under Jerningham, Ed-
  ward
Siege of Damascus. See under Hughes, John
Siena (Italy):
  Bichi, Mme, of, **18**. 206
  cantata and ball given for D. of York in
    theatre at, **22**. 232
  Carmelite friar from, **22**. 438
  coaches not to be hired at, **19**. 232
  cold very severe at, in winter, **24**. 130
  commissary of, welcomes D. of York, **22**. 224
  countess of, will not sit at table with actor,
    22. 170
  Duomo at: HW copies inscription from, **13**.
    205; overpraised by Addison, **13**. 204
  epidemic at, **22**. 511
  fen country makes air at, unwholesome, **24**.
    130
  figure of, dressed in red velvet, at St John's
    Day celebration, **18**. 251
  Fortini-Oxenden feud divides, **19**. 374
  Franchini, governor of, **19**. 492n
  Guercino painting at, **20**. 263, 313
  HW describes, **13**. 203–4
  HW proposes, to D. and Ds of Gloucester as
    winter residence, **24**. 125, 130
  Hervey to visit, **22**. 430
  inn at, **22**. 223
  lady from, calls on Princesse de Craon, **17**.
    481
  legend of founding of, by Romulus and
    Remus, **13**. 204
  Leopold to visit, **24**. 343
  Mann gets marble from, for Chesterfield, **19**.
    423
  —— hopes not to accompany Tuscan Court
    to, **22**. 511
  —— plans Sir Robert Walpole's visit to, **18**.
    212–13
  marble of, **19**. 423, **35**. 144, 184; *see also*
    under Marble
  nobles of, to be enrolled in two classes, **20**.
    192n
  Oxenden may visit, to learn Italian, **19**. 232
  Palazzo Pubblico at, houses Accademia degli
    Intronati, **20**. 391n
  passeggio out of gates of, **22**. 232
  republic of, suppressed by Cosimo I, **37**. 97n
  Spanish army blocks approach from, to Tus-
    cany, **17**. 289
  Strozzi fails to visit, **17**. 111
  Taviani auditor-general of, **17**. 63n
  Te Deum sung at, **21**. 112

  theatre at, burnt, **18**. 46
  theatre, new, at, **20**. 391
  Tuscan Court pleased by shows at, **22**. 515
  Tuscan Court to go to, **22**. 511
  visitors to: Almada, **23**. 26; Bruce, **20**. 391;
    Damer, Hon. George, **22**. 286; Gascoigne,
    22. 286; Leopold, **22**. 515; Mann, **20**. 391,
    22. 223, 228; Montemar, **18**. 46; Orford, Cts
    of, **24**. 70; Oxenden, **19**. 232, 374; Rocking-
    ham, **20**. 263; York, Cardinal, **25**. 394;
    York, D. of, **22**. 223–4, 228, 231–2
  Young Pretender leaves, for Florence, **23**. 318
  —— lives at, **5**. 218n, **43**. 94
Sierra Leone:
  inhabitants of, superior to the French, **31**. 371
  More, Hannah, interested in, **31**. 371
Siestrzencewicz, Stanislaus, Abp of Mohilew:
  Jesuits under control of, **16**. 192n
Siette. *See* La Siette
Sieyès, Emmanuel-Joseph (1748–1836), Comte;
  abbé; politician:
  Paine engaged in controversy with, **11**. 319
  speaker's post declined by, because he writes
    Constitution, **34**. 61
'Sigismonda':
  character in E. of Carlisle's tragedy, **33**. 410
  Furoni's painting of, attributed to Correggio,
    21. 200
  Hogarth's painting of, **9**. 365
  See also Tancred and Sigismonda
  See also under Hogarth, William
Sign; signs:
  Anson's head may replace D. of Cumberland's
    on, **37**. 272–3
  Kildare's face blackened on, **37**. 410
  notice written under, **30**. 24
  of removed tradesman, 'Burnt out from over
    the way,' **33**. 195
  Ormond's and Vernon's heads, replaced by
    D. of Cumberland's on, **37**. 266, 272
  with Vernon's head, pulled down by rioting
    sailors at Rochester, **30**. 29
Signature; signatures:
  to letters in newspapers, **42**. 500
Signet, the, at Edinburgh:
  joint keeper of, *see* Dundas, Henry
  writer to, *see* Tait, John (d. 1800)
Sign manual, royal:
  witticism about, **10**. 116
Sigonio (Sigonius), Carlo (1524–84), scholar:
  Scotland lacks, **16**. 379
Sigorgne, Pierre (1719–1809), abbé; philosopher; 'un grand vicaire de Mâcon'; Mme du
  Deffand's 'professeur':
  Bastille imprisonment of, **4**. 407
  Du Deffand, Mme, accompanied by, to Sceaux
    and Montrouge, **4**. 443
  ——'s correspondence with, **7**. 440, 456
  ——'s efforts in behalf of, **4**. 407, 421, 453,
    484
  ——'s opinion of, **4**. 411–12, 421, 435, 453,
    484, 490, **7**. 56
  ——'s social relations with, **6**. 182

—— takes, to Hénault's, **4.** 416
HW hopes Mme du Deffand may keep, in Paris, **4.** 453
Paris left by, **7.** 62
—— to be left by, **7.** 51
—— to be visited by, yearly, **4.** 453
—— visited by, **4.** *407,* 439, **7.** 46
professor at Collège du Plessis, **4.** 421
Si le Roi m'avait donné Paris:
verses to air of, **5.** 353, **7.** 104
See also *J'aime mieux ma mie*
Silesia:
arms of, on Hyndford's plate, **18.** 89
Austria hopes to regain, **20.** 528, 576, **21.** 360
Bohemian areas adjacent to, retained by Frederick II, **21.** 116
borders of, in dispute, **20.** 187
Charles VI mortgages, **20.** 348n
Conway and Scott visit, **39.** 538
Frederick II agrees in Breslau treaty to take over mortgage of, **20.** 348n
—— demands, **17.** 144
—— may be given Holland or Flanders in lieu of, **19.** 223
——'s demands in, presented through Hyndford and Robinson, **17.** 76n
——'s victory in, discussed at Rome, **35.** 58–9
guarantee of, **42.** 496
HW imagines Frederick II galloping to, **25.** 190
Hohenfriedburg defeat in, **19.** 58, 65
Hungarians invade, **18.** 543, 547
Hyndford secures, to Frederick II instead of to Maria Theresa, **18.** 89
Lobkowitz transferred to, **19.** 58
Maria Theresa demands, **19.** 38n
—— loses, **18.** 521
—— may obtain, at expense of English and Dutch alliance, **19.** 238
—— persuaded by Robinson to give up all of, to Frederick II, **18.** 108
—— refuses to give up, **17.** 87n
——'s attempt to recover, disastrous, **20.** 588, **21.** 15, 502, 519, **22.** 51–2
negotiations for peace settlement in, **17.** 121n
Prussian-Russian battle expected in, **21.** 72
Prussian troops occupy, **21.** 271n
Schweidnitz the only fort in, in Austrian hands after the fall of Liegnitz, **21.** 166n
Tilenus a native of, **14.** 130
Silesian loan:
Frederick II may demand, **20.** 360
—— stops payments on, **30.** 321
Prussian manifesto stops payment of interest on, **20.** 348
Silhouette, Étienne de (1709–67), controller-general:
Berthier de Sauvigny succeeds, **21.** 349n
French trade and credit ruined by financial device of, to raise money, **21.** 349
Silhouette; silhouettes:
Hamilton, Lady, does, **43.** 96
Huber's, **5.** 285–6, **43.** 96; of Ds of Grafton,

21. 548, 554; of Voltaire, **43.** 94
Silistria:
Russians threaten, **23.** 479, **24.** 29
Silius, C. (d. A.D. 48):
Messalina marries, in her husband's life-time, **24.** 333
Silk:
artificial flowers of, **34.** 237, 238
at 55 shillings a yard, **33.** 218
Augustus Cæsar has cargo of, **19.** 13n
bag of, for Great Seal, **25.** 481n
black: breeches of, **21.** 399n; for Court mourning, **32.** 101n; mask of, **37.** 5; sacque of, **24.** 192n
blue, warrants strung together with, **10.** 116
brocaded, Mrs Rudd pays mercer for, **24.** 153
cargo of, captured, **21.** 415n
cherry-coloured, Mann should not be paid with, **22.** 226
coat of, **21.** 410
crimson, Ps Amelia's body wrapped in, **33.** 535n
damask of, **21.** 447
dresses of: **32.** 256; blotched, **37.** 116
dyer of, **37.** 104
evening dress of, **9.** 240
figured, hangings of, **42.** 314n
flambé, curtains of, **32.** 261
Florence to send, to Constantinople, **19.** 437
flowered, canonici and abbés forbidden to wear, **21.** 224
for filet, **5.** 20, 23, 27, 32, 65, **7.** 392
French, seized by Customs, **38.** 415n
French, the, shiver in, **35.** 343
gowns of, **37.** 17
green, 'woods' of, for Dublin ballroom, **37.** 412
Guido Reni's painting copied on, **17.** 41n
HW buys, in Paris, for Lady Ossory, **32.** 53
HW procures, for Mme Pucci, **17.** 159, 222, 416, **18.** 112
handkerchiefs of, contraband, **9.** 105
hangings of, **21.** 468, 471, 481, **32.** 106
importation of, from France opposed, **30.** 181n
in nutshell, **35.** 49
Irish, worn by Cts of Hertford and daughters, **39.** 20n
Montagu prefers watered tabby, **9.** 355
Persian, HW's 'Persian letter' to Lincoln wrapped in, **30.** 35
Probyn dealer in, **31.** 199n
'run,' **10.** 133
stockings worn as sleeves are tipped with, **18.** 109
tapestry of gold and, **35.** 143
tinsel from, **38.** 198n
umbrella of, **39.** 267
velvet worked in, **35.** 132
waistcoats of, **9.** 355, **20.** 396
warriors' eyes sealed with, **32.** 251
white: shoes to be worked with, **39.** 264; stockings of, **21.** 399n

Silk merchants, Tuscan. *See* Dreier; Nutini
Sill, John:
 Glasgow's second pilot, **21**. 268n
Sillery, Marquis de. *See* Brulart, Charles-Alexis
Sillery, Marquise de. *See* Ducrest de St-Aubin, Stephanie-Félicité (1746–1830); Le Tellier de Louvois de Rebenac, Charlotte-Félicité (1707–82)
Sillery:
 battle of, **21**. 416, **38**. 56
Silva, Mr:
 acts as agent in loan, **2**. 35n
Silva, Jean-Baptiste (1684–1742), physician:
 Du Deffand, Mme, quotes, **6**. 79
Silva, Maria Teresa de (1716–90), m. (1738) James Francis Edward Stuart Fitzjames, 3d D. of Berwick:
 Alva, brother of, **10**. 129
 ——'s sister, not handsome but easy and genteel, **38**. 406
 bad French spoken by, **10**. 129
 clergyman directs, to inn, **10**. 131–2
 England visited by: **38**. 404, 406; 'to see relatives,' **10**. 129
 HW entertains, at SH, **10**. 129
 HW's opinion of, **10**. 129
 Hertford entertains, in Paris, **38**. 337
 Hertford, Cts of, related to, **10**. 129
 Marlboroughs entertain, at Blenheim, **10**. 129
 Paris visited by, **38**. 298–9, 337
 servants of, **10**. 131
 social relations of, in Paris, **7**. 261, 269, 272, 292, 311
 Spanish, but speaks a little French, **38**. 298–9
 Stowe visited by, **10**. 131–2
Silva Álvarez de Toledo, Fernando de (1714–76), 12th Duque d'Alba (*or* Alva):
 Berwick, Ds of, sister of, **10**. 129, **38**. 406
 tapestry of, at Madrid, **16**. *169*
Silva Gruenemberg, Odoardo de (ca 1693–1771), Marchese della Banditella; Spanish consul at Leghorn 1718–62:
 biographical information on, corrected, **43**. 238
 Braitwitz hears from, **17**. *180*
 Charles of Naples sends, to Mann with expostulations, **19**. 57
 Mann might have been compared by, to Telesephorus, **19**. 383
 —— negotiates with, **19**. 65
 ——'s correspondence with, **19**. 57
 ——'s negotiations with, approved by George II, **19**. 86
 —— thanked by, **19**. 383
 protest by, about passage of artillery, **18**. 542
 Richecourt belittles complaints of, **18**. 542
 Salas, D. of, sends complaints of Court of Naples to, **19**. 65n
Silver:
 andirons of, at Ham House, **10**. 306
 at Burghley House, **10**. 346
 bell of, for inkstand, **23**. 383
 bells of, tinkling, **30**. 308

 Bolivian, discovery of, **23**. 562n
 buckles of, **21**. 399n
 candlestick inlaid in gold and, **40**. 259
 candlesticks of, **23**. 285, **34**. 98–9
 Cellini's chest of, **23**. 427
 coffee-pot of, *see under* Coffee-pot
 coinage of, **16**. 77
 coins of, scarce in late 18th century, **30**. 276n
 copper superior to, for medals, **11**. 271
 customs rate and regulations for, **10**. 289
 double-plated, Mann wants dish-covers of, **24**. 27, 32
 Du Deffand, Mme, has (inventory), **8**. 27–9
 dutiable, **7**. 77
 ecclesiastical, basins and ewers of, sacred according to Dr Johnson, **35**. 497
 écus of, given by Lady Mary Wortley Montagu to son, **18**. 567
 Electress leaves, to courtiers, **18**. 169
 embossed, at Knole, **35**. 132
 engravers' plates of, **41**. 219
 Ferrers's wedding clothes embroidered with, **21**. 399n
 Florentine coin of, **42**. 439
 flowers of, on riding-coat, **22**. 3
 flutes of, **35**. 419
 gilt, plate of Charles V meeting François I, **35**. 423n
 glasses framed in, **18**. 169
 HW cannot bring, to Montagu because of Customs, **10**. 288–9, 296
 HW's waistcoat, for wedding, worked with, **34**. 110
 Hilliard's portraits of Q. Elizabeth and James I usually painted on, **42**. 462
 hoard of, in Mme Gavi's small coal, **17**. 223
 incense pot of, **38**. 362
 ink-standish of, **23**. 383, **38**. 259n
 Invincible carries, **19**. 411
 Jesuits', weighed, **23**. 512–13
 knives of, **30**. 207
 lamps of, **25**. 55
 leaf, wanted by HW, **37**. 15–16, 24
 Mann to buy, **18**. 472
 medals of, **16**. 49, **18**. 406, 424, 447, 478, **21**. 189, 201, 203, **24**. 469n
 medals sold for their content of, **18**. 478
 Montagu asks HW to buy, in Paris, **10**. 286
 —— disappointed that HW cannot bring, from Paris, **10**. 295, 300
 objects of, in Q. Elizabeth's collection, **32**. 323–5
 opera ticket of, **10**. 139n, **43**. 391
 Parliamentary bill to ban imported fabrics woven from, **35**. 36n
 pencil of, **17**. 194
 pennies of, **12**. 45, **25**. 15, **33**. 339, **35**. 535
 picture-frame of, **18**. 171
 plated: Bolsover invents process for, **9**. 295; manufactured at Sheffield, **9**. 295; wears badly, **24**. 27; *see also under* Sheffield
 saucepan of, **30**. 70
 scarcity of, in Rome, **17**. 4
 service of plate of, **30**. 304n

Sheffield, **7.** 416
snuff-box of, **18.** 553
standish of, **18.** 126, **35.** 315
strainer and spoon, pawned by HW's foot-man, **11.** 368
suit laced with, **17.** 183
table and stands of, **18.** 169
teaspoons of, **21.** 221
tortoise-shell case studded with, **35.** 429–30
trunk of, for perfumes, **26.** 56
tubes of, **20.** 203
Walpole, Sir Edward, promises, to Mrs Scott, **10.** 329
William I gives, to Westminster Abbey, **40.** 223
See also Silver plate
Silver dust:
Nuestra Señora del Cabadonga has, in cargo, **18.** 463n
Silver faro. *See under* Faro
Silver hazard. *See under* Hazard
Silver Hill, Sussex:
HW and Chute visit, **9.** 141, **35.** 137, 141
HW imagines D. of Newcastle showing Sus-sex from, to smugglers, **35.** 141
Silver lace. *See under* Lace
Silver Lion (inn). *See* Lion d'Argent
Silver loo. *See under* Loo
Silver mines:
Conway goes in search of, **39.** 181
Silver pharaoh. *See under* Faro
Silver plate:
considered essential for a diplomatist, **17.** 135n
cost of Fane's, **17.** 135n, **18.** 472
Mann to buy, **18.** 472
Silversmith; silversmiths:
Munro to consult, about double-plated dish covers, **24.** 32
See also Demetrius; Siries, Cosimo; Siries, Louis
Silver St, Whitefriars, London:
Woodfall bookseller in, **42.** 455n
Silver stuff:
HW's suit of, for George III's wedding, **23.** 285
Silver Tankard, The. See under Berkeley, Lady Elizabeth (1750–1828), Bns Craven
Silvester. *See* Sylvester
Silvestre, Israel (1621–91), engraver:
tablet for wife of, **7.** 277
Silvestre, Mme Israel. *See* Selincart, Henriette
Silvio, Enea (1631–1701), Conte Caprara; Gen.:
trophies taken from Turks by, **13.** 194
Simbach:
battle of, **18.** 230, 234, 249, **37.** 137n
Simco, John (ca 1750–1824):
HW's correspondence with, **41.** 388–9, **42.** 258
HW to give ticket to, for SH, **42.** 258
SH visited by, **12.** 234, 241
Simeon, Simon (fl. 1322), Franciscan:
Itineraria Simonis Simeonis et Willelmi de

Worcestre by: Nasmith's edn of, **2.** 54, 57, 73–4, 76, 79, 82; quoted, **1.** 175
'Simeon and the Child.' *See under* Guido Reni
Simiane, Marquise de. *See* Adhémar de Monteil de Grignan, Françoise-Pauline d'
Simiane, Anne de:
nun with the Filles du Calvaire, **41.** 257n
Simiane, Julie-Françoise de (1704–28), m. (1725) Jean-Baptiste de Castellane, Marquis d'Esparron and de la Garde:
husband of, **41.** 109, 257–8
marriage of, **3.** 255n, **34.** 81, 85
name of, corrected, **43.** 359
relative of Mme de Sévigné, **4.** 72n, **34.** 81
Simiane, Marquise de, mother of, **7.** 320
Simiane, Madeleine-Sophie de, m. (1723) Alex-andre-Gaspard de Villeneuve, Marquis de Vence:
'daughter' of, **3.** 405n
family of, **41.** 257
lives at Aix, **3.** 405n
'Simile, Printed in Geoffrey Broadbottom's Journal, A.' *See under* Williams, Sir Charles Hanbury
Simiramis. *See* Semiramis
Simmonds. *See* Symons
Simnel, Lambert (ca 1477– living 1525), pre-tender to English throne:
Burgundy, Ds of, unlikely to have set up, just 'to try the temper of the nation,' **14.** 163–4
supported by E. of Lincoln, **15.** 172
Warbeck, Perkin, thought to be identical with, **42.** 255
Simnel, Thomas, of Oxford, joiner:
son of, **14.** 163n
Simolachri, histoire, e figure de la morte. See *Imagines mortis*; see also *Simulachres et his-toriées* below
Simolin, Ivan Matveevich (1720–ca 1800), Rus-sian minister to England 1779–85:
brother of Ps Dashkov rescued by, **29.** 60
Copie d'une note by, asks Montmorin for passports for French royal family, **34.** 229n
(?) Courland asked by, to reinstate Biron, **22.** 60n
Fox's letter to, about Dutch-English treaty, **25.** 266n, 267n
George III told by, about Russo-Turkish peace, **25.** 486
Paul I of Russia sends message by, **34.** 229
Stormont receives Russian dispatches through, **25.** 118n
Vorontsov rescued by, **33.** 179n
Simon, St:
HW refers to Savile as, **23.** 170
Simon, the Pharisee:
Dodd's sin not that of, **32.** 185
Simon, Abraham (1617–92), medallist:
Anecdotes of Painting omits, **40.** 238
Vertue mentions, in *Medals, Coins, Great Seals,* **16.** 159
Simon, M. and Mme Antoine:
Louis XVII under care of, **34.** 185n

Simon, John (? 1675–1751), engraver:
plate by, of Baker, **2**. 354
Simon, P. G.:
printer to parliament of Paris, **8**. 169
Simon, Thomas (1618–65), medallist:
Anecdotes of Painting omits, **40**. 238
medal by, of Cromwell, **1**. 319, 321
Vertue mentions, in *Medals, Coins, Great Seals*, **16**. 159
Simon. *See also* Simon Magus
Simonburn, Northumberland:
Scott, James, is forced to leave rectory of, **28**. 465
Simonet, ——, maître de ballet at Paris and London ca 1772–ca 1792:
dances at Pantheon fête, **39**. 331n
(?) daughter of, **25**. 585
Simonet, Mme, dancer:
daughter of, **25**. 585
Simonet, Mlle, dancer, aeronaut:
balloon ascent by, with Blanchard, **25**. 585
Simonetta, Contessa. *See* Castelbarco, Teresa di
Simonetti, Mme, hotel-keeper in Paris:
Du Deffand, Mme, asks, to notify her of HW's arrival, **3**. 342
HW to lodge with, **4**. 258, 270
proprietress of Hôtel du Parc-Royal, **6**. 81n
Simonetti, Francesco:
government post given to, **23**. 294
Simonetti. *See also* Simonetta
Simonin. *See* Simolin
Simon Magus, founder of simony:
Dodd's sin that of, **32**. 185
Simple; simples:
Gray educated in, at Eton, by uncle, **43**. 190
Simons. *See* Symmonds; Symonds; Symons
Simpson, ——:
witness at Mrs Cornelys's trial, **23**. 272n
Simpson, Lady Anne. *See* Lyon, Lady Anne
Simpson, Rev. Peter (ca 1710–80), (?) assistant at Mayfair Chapel:
(?) sermon by, **20**. 241, 243
Simpson, Bucks:
Leicester, curate at, **1**. 84n
Sims, William (fl. 1778–1814), Customs official:
Mann, John, to be succeeded by, **24**. 368
Simulachres et historiées faces de la Mort. See under Trechsel, Kaspar and Melchior; see also *Imagines mortis*
Sinai Peninsula:
Wortley Montagu visits, **22**. 113n
'Since Now the World's Turned Upside Down':
song in D'Urfey's *Wonders in the Sea*, **12**. 33, **43**. 152
Sinclair, Capt.:
ship of, from Boston, in Jacobite service, **37**. 237
Sinclair, Lady Dorothea (1739–1818), m. (1759) James Duff, 2d E. Fife:
Browne, Lady, friend of, **31**. 72
social relations of, in Paris, **7**. 271, 277, 292, 294, **30**. 211
travels of, **31**. 65, 72, 109

Sinclair, Hon. James (1688–1762), army officer; M.P.:
birth date of, **43**. 263
English regiments and engineers under, land at Pouldu Bay, **19**. 319n
Port l'Orient attempt bungled by, **19**. 456
Quiberon Bay expedition of, **19**. 456n
Wentworth to be succeeded by, **19**. 456
Sinclair, Sir John (1754–1835), cr. (1786) Bt; M.P.:
Statistical Account by, may mention De Wet, **42**. 347
'Sindbad the Sailor' in *Arabian Nights*:
voyages of, superior to Æneas's, **11**. 20
Sinecure; sinecures:
HW jokes about Burke's attempted reform of, **31**. 241
HW jokes about his, **31**. 14–15
Singe, Le, French ship:
Lauzun embarks in, **4**. 135n
Singer, Elizabeth (1674–1737), m. (1710) Thomas Rowe:
Jeffreys's epigram attributed to, **2**. 202n
Singer; singers:
amateur, might walk at Coronation, **24**. 86
bankers recruit, abroad, for English opera, **17**. 191
English, articulate badly, **28**. 347
French: crack eardrums, **31**. 46; distressed at not squalling, **7**. 338
from Canterbury, Oxford, and the farces, to sing *Miserere,* **17**. 211
Gallini collects, in Italy, **25**. 431
in *King Arthur,* worse than actors, **39**. 133
Italian: Conway, Bns, has, at assembly, **17**. 334; English poetesses imitate flourishes of, **16**. 257; Pembroke, E. of, pursues, to Florence, **25**. 497n; pronounce English more distinctly than natives do, **28**. 354; *William and Mary* visited by, **17**. 141
Mann may have to hire, for Holdernesse, **20**. 259
poor, in Handel's oratorios, **18**. 180, 186
See also under Opera
Singing:
French, HW comments on, **32**. 18, 22
modern, ruins Purcell's music for Dryden's *King Arthur,* **31**. 152
popularity of, in England, **24**. 89
Singleton, J., engraver:
Jephson's portrait engraved by, **42**. 409n
Sinigaglia (Italy):
Spaniards march to, **18**. 16
Spanish invalids to sail to, **18**. 76
Young Pretender at, **23**. 225
Sinistri, ——:
Mulinari nearly as big as, **18**. 138
Sinking fund:
Pitt attacks Lyttelton over, **37**. 432
Sinopoli (Italy):
earthquake account mentions, **25**. 376
Sinsheim, Count:
at Aix-la-Chapelle, **18**. 304n

Sinzani, Gen.:
   reinforcements under, to be sent to Lobkowitz,
      19. 22n
Sinzendorff, Nikolaus Ludwig (1700–60), Count
   Zinzendorff and Pottendorff; Moravian
   leader:
   (?) Austrians cut down trees in garden of,
      at Dresden, 21. 361n
   biographical information about, corrected,
      43. 271
   Lindsey House, Chelsea, bought by, for Mo-
      ravians, 20. 359n
   Reuss assistant to, at Herrnhut, 20. 359n
Sinzendorff, Philipp Ludwig (1699–1747), Graf
   von; Bp of Breslau; cardinal:
   anecdotes of, at Conclave, 13. 212–3
   Conclave entered by, 37. 57
   Corsini's party supported by, 17. 21n
   mother of, prescribes pig's blood for gout,
      13. 213
   Old Pretender may receive, 17. 11
Sion Hill, Middlesex, Holdernesse's seat. See
   Syon Hill
Sion House, Middlesex, Northumberland's seat.
   See Syon House
Siracusa (Sicily). See Syracuse
Sir Anthony Shirley: His Relation of His Trav-
   els into Persia. See under Shirley, Sir Anthony
'Sir Cauline,' ballad:
   'Tancred and Sigismonda' resembles, 40. 374
Sir Charles Grandison. See under Richardson,
   Samuel
Sir Courtly Nice. See under Crowne, John
Sirens:
   England imports, from Italy, when superan-
      nuated, 24. 149
Siries, Cosimo (d. 1789), Florentine jeweller:
   (?) medal by, 24. 469–70, 478, 500
Siries, Louis (d. ?1759), French silversmith at
   Florence:
   Astley's copy mistaken by, for Guercino orig-
      inal, 20. 313–14
   at Palazzo Vecchio, 17. 213, 20. 475n, 24. 500
   biographical information on, corrected, 43.
      236
   Correggio painting shown by, to Mann, 20.
      314
   edict will be resented by customers of, 20. 475
   French goldsmith, buying and selling curiosi-
      ties at the Palazzo Vecchio in Florence,
      20. 475n
   French silversmith settled at Florence, 24.
      500n
   HW's old acquaintance of Palazzo Vecchio,
      20. 313, 24. 500
   HW's patch box praised by, 17. 414
   Mann to order scissors from, 17. 93, 99
   medallist probably grandson of, 24. 500
   razors to be made by, for Sultan of Turkey,
      19. 437
   spectacles blamed by, for mistake, 20. 313–14
   stairs to rooms of, 25. 169
Siries, Luigi (1743–1811), Florentine jeweller:
   (?) medal by, 24. 469, 478, 500

Siris. See under Berkeley, George
Siristori. See Serristori
Sirius, the dog star:
   agrees with HW, 34. 182
Sirloin:
   Albrecht, Maréchale d', ordered, 30. 220
   country gentlemen exude as much gravy as,
      35. 42, 46
Sirtema, Anton, Baron van Grovestins, grand
   écuyer to Stadtholder:
   William IV sends, to pacify Haarlem, 37. 286
Sirtema van Grovestins, Mme. See Bouwers, Ja-
   coba Johanna
Sirtema van Grovestins, Anna Wilhelmina (ca
   1738–1820), Baroness:
   friend of Lady Jane Scott, 32. 92
Sirven, father and daughter:
   Élie de Beaumont's mémoire on, 3. 251
Sisera, Capt. of Jabin's army:
   Jabin mistaken for, 33. 25
Siskovics, Gen.:
   Frederick II's supply train under Von Zieten
      destroyed by, 21. 224n
Sismani, Principe di. See Corsini, Bartolom-
   meo (1683–1752)
Sissinghurst, Kent:
   Chute and HW visit, 35. 144–5
   Mann family owned, 35. 144n
Sisson or Sissons, Jeremiah, of Beaufort Bldgs,
   Strand, scientific instrument-maker:
   biographical information about, corrected,
      43. 275–6
   design of, for water-raising machine, 21. 390
   HW and James Mann hurry, to finish draw-
      ing, 21. 384
   HW delivers Perelli's letter to, 21. 354, 359–
      60
   HW's correspondence with, 21. 407
   'low indigent mechanic,' 21. 407
   Mann, James, to treat with, 21. 414
   model of machine of, to be sent by sea, 21.
      375–6
   payments to, 21. 384, 407, 414
   Perelli praises performance of, 21. 430, 432–3
   ——'s correspondence with, 21. 348, 354, 359–
      60, 375, 414, 432–3
Sisson, Jonathan, scientific instrument maker:
   successor to, 43. 275
Sistrum (musical instrument):
   HW's, very rare, 15. 13
'Sisygambis':
   HW's name: for Augusta, Ps of Wales, 38.
      315; for Vcts Townshend, 37. 196
Sith, John (b. ca 1761), footman:
   Clive, Mrs, employs, 33. 424–5
   testifies at Isaac Prescott's trial, 33. 424–5
Sittingbourne ('Sittinbourne'), Kent:
   HW visits, 17. 142
   HW writes from, 30. 19–21
Situbaldi, Abbé; Jesuit:
   Cicognani college to be directed by, 23. 513n
Sivrac, Jean:
   HW's Castle of Otranto translated by, 35.
      436n

Six Clerks Office, London:
Woodcock, attorney at, **42**. 297n
Six Letters from A——d B——r to Father Sheldon. See under Douglas, John
Six-livre piece, French:
English equivalent of, **37**. 39
Six Overtures for Violins. See under Handel, George Frideric
Sixpence; sixpences:
French equivalent of, **37**. 39
HW wins, at faro, **19**. 494
1641:
1770 treads in steps of, **23**. 170
1683:
Austrian-Turkish war of, represented in ballet, **25**. 361n
1688:
anniversary of, **34**. 31
centennial of, **34**. 31n
'great-grandchild' of, **33**. 388
revolution of: anecdotes forged against supporters of, **29**. 192; compared to Irish revolution, **39**. 395; HW's principles go back to, **29**. 351; Hardinge reveres, **35**. 561n
Six Town Eclogues. See Pierrepont, Lady Mary: eclogues of
Sixtus V (Felice Peretti) (1521–90), pope 1585–90:
casino of, at Villa Negroni, **24**. 7
Clement XIV imitates, **23**. 157
edict by, against bandits, **17**. 29n
Elizabeth, Q., supposedly excommunicated by, **22**. 177
Italy unused to severity of, **21**. 395
print of, **1**. 257
treasure deposited by, in Castel St Angelo, **22**. 446, 448
Villa Negroni, villa of, may be used by Ds of Kingston, **23**. 567, **24**. 14, 24–5, 31
—— built by, when cardinal, **20**. 69n
Six Voyages. See under Tavernier, Jean-Baptiste
Skating:
George III's, **33**. 163
in Hyde Park, **33**. 507
Omai learns, **24**. 175
on Florentine ponds, **24**. 434
on the Arno, **33**. 95
Skavronska, Anna Karlovna (1723–75), m. (1742) Count Mikhail Ilarionovich Vorontsov:
appearance and costume of, masculine, **22**. 193
Catherine II rejects proposal of, to surrender Order of St Catherine, **22**. 65
Craon, Princesse de, quarrels with, **21**. 248–9, 259
Elizabeth, Czarina, is related to, **21**. 248, **22**. 173
—— jealous of nephew's attentions to, **22**. 173
Italy to be revisited by, **22**. 173
Mann knew, at Florence, **23**. 245
name of, corrected, **43**. 275
Skeffington, Hon. Clotworthy (d. 1739), 4th Vct Massereene:

match with, arranged by Lady Mary Wortley Montagu's father, **14**. 244n
Skeffington, Clotworthy (1743–1805), 2d E. of Massereene:
ball given by, at Paris, **30**. 211
HW calls, 'Adonis,' **30**. 211
HW had never visited, before ball, **30**. 211
Hertford supports, in Irish election, **38**. 343
imprisoned in Paris for debt, **30**. 211n
social relations of, in Paris, **7**. 271, 274, 294
Skeleton:
HW compares himself to, **32**. 12
nobody in France excels in portraying, **39**. 32
soldier in Conway's company looks like, **37**. 136
'Skelton,' Young Pretender's officer. *See* Sheridan, Sir Thomas
Skelton, Jonathan:
Stephens criticizes paintings by, at Rome, **23**. 423n
Skene, Sir John:
De verborum significatione by, **43**. 57
Skerrett, Maria (ca 1702–38), m. (ca 1738) Sir Robert Walpole, K.B. 1725; K.G., 1726; HW's stepmother:
arms of, **1**. 342, 343
biographical information about, corrected, **43**. 182, 193, 243, 258
daughter of, **1**. 165n, **4**. 173n, **11**. 97n, **13**. 15n, **17**. 320n, **22**. 262n, **25**. 418n, 464n, **28**. 389n
death of, **13**. 8
Exchequer funds advanced by, before marriage, **36**. 24n, 25n
HW's opinion of, **30**. 74
HW's stepmother, **9**. 68n
husband makes, burn papers, **34**. 256
husband of, **10**. 348n
Leneve, Isabella, cares for daughter after death of, **25**. 609n
Lincolns to sleep in room where, died, **30**. 74
marriage of: **13**. 151n, **14**. 42n, **22**. 27; Etough performs, **40**. 69n
Montagu, Lady Mary Wortley, relative and correspondent of, **34**. 256
——'s relation and *élève*, **14**. 242n, 245
Pleydell, nephew of, gets legacy from Sir Robert Walpole, **19**. 32n
tomb of, at Houghton, **9**. 348
Walpole, Sir Robert, has liaison with, **15**. 5n
—— makes financial agreement with, on their marriage, **43**. 176–7
Sketch; sketches:
by Anne Seymour Damer, of foreign officers, on cards, **38**. 156
HW and Chute make, on trip to Kent and Sussex, **35**. 140
HW copies, from Vertue's MSS, **42**. 217
of Charles VI's head, **42**. 217
Sketches and Characters of the Most Eminent and Most Singular Persons Now Living. See under Thicknesse, Philip
Sketches of the History of Man. See under Home, Henry, Lord Kames

Sketch of the Life of John Barclay. See under Dalrymple, Sir David

Sketch of the Life . . . of . . . Richard Trevor. See under Allan, George

Skie. *See* Skye

Skiff; skiffs:
HW 'sails' in, to Lady Cecilia Johnston, 35. 474

Skin:
HW jokes about shedding, after gout, 10. 277
HW's 'humorous' recipe for beautifying, 9. 138
stag's, worn at party for Louis XV, 37. 340
Strange's paintings on, in water-colour, 22. 108n

Skin diseases:
Pisa baths thought to cure, 24. 83

Skin eruption:
occurrence of, 1. 298

Skinner, ——, auctioneer:
Hindley's Twickenham house sold by, 33. 105n, 180n, 183
Lovibond's sale at Hampton by, 32. 295n

Skinner, ——, Walker's nephew:
Walker's estate left to, 19. 511n

Skinner, Brinley (d. 1764), consul at Leghorn 1724–34:
Charles III snatches wig of, 23. 238

Skinner, Matthew (1689–1749), serjeant-at-law; M.P.; chief justice of Chester 1738–49:
(?) insanity confines, 30. 22
MS memorandum by, defending Barrington, 15. 148
rebel lords tried by, 19. 282
speech by, disparaged, 9. 38
treason defined by, 19. 282n

Skinner, Stephen (1623–67), physician:
Etymologicon linguæ Anglicanæ by, could not be read by Chatterton, 16. 178–9

Skipper; skippers:
Dutch, share Conway's cabin, 37. 208–9
HW jokes about hat style of, becoming fashionable, 38. 2

Skipton Castle:
child born at, 2. 324n

Skipwith, Sir Thomas:
Copt Hall occupied by, 35. 346n

Skittles:
Chatsworth guests play, 9. 295, 21. 433
Conway overheats himself playing, 32. 309n
—— plays, 39. 278n

Skottowe, Ann (1732–1803), m. Robert Wood:
biographical information about, corrected, 43. 99
HW mentions, 6. 202
HW's correspondence with, 41. *245–9*, *254–5*, *307–8*, *317–18*
husband's *Essay* presented by, to HW, 41. 306, 307–8
husband's *Essay* published by, 28. 212
South Audley St the address of, 41. 245, 249
South St the address of, 41. 307, 317

tombstone of husband and son of, designed by HW, 41. *245, 246–9, 254–5, 307–8, 317–18*

Skreen (Ireland):
Sherlock rector of, 29. 104n

Skreene. *See* Skrine

Skrine, Louisa (1760–1809), m. (1777) Sir Thomas Clarges, 3d Bt, 1759:
SH visited by, 12. 243, 252

Skrine, William (ca 1672–1725), apothecary:
son of, 20. 145

Skrine, William (? 1721–83), M.P.:
birth date of, corrected, 43. 267
Callington election declined by, for fear of expense, 35. 416
circumstances of, said to be distressed, 25. 386
elected M.P., 32. 212
extravagance of, in entertaining at Florence, 20. 145
marriage of, 38. 394
Nugent, Lady Louisa, thought to be daughter of, 24. 417n
obligated to E. of Orford, 25. 158, 166
Orford, E. of, sends, to Callington borough, 24. 46
—— wishes, to assist in settlement with Mozzi, 25. 158, 162, 164, 166, 33. 274
referee in Orford-Mozzi negotiations, 33. 274
Roman's letter to, enclosed by Mann to HW, 22. 447, 450
son of Bath apothecary, 20. 145
suicide of, 25. 385–6, 36. 210, 43. 369
wife's death will be a relief to, 22. 402

Skrine, Mrs William. *See* Sumner, Jane

Skrymsher. *See* Boothby Skrymsher

Skull; skulls:
sacred, listed at Genoa, 37. 320
savages drink ale from, 10. 255

Skye, Island of:
Gibraltar might be sent to, for safe-keeping, 29. 110
HW's letter might as well have been written on, 28. 292
Loudoun marches towards, 37. 237
Young Pretender escapes from Macdonald's house on, 30. 103
—— lands on, 37. 251
—— with Flora Macdonald on, 37. 252

Skylight; skylights:
at Kedleston, 10. 230
at SH, 35. 228
HW's, in town, demolished by storm, 33. 81–2

Skyrocket; skyrockets:
(?) at Marybone, 10. 156
(?) at Ranelagh, 10. 156
at Ranelagh, for George III's birthday, 38. 88
Beauvau, Princesse de, has no more effect than, 39. 143
English impoverish themselves on, 38. 105
for Culloden anniversary, 37. 266
HW would like to drink, 19. 249
seen from SH, 10. 156
See also Fireworks

'Slamerkin, Miss,' E. of Orford's horse:
foal of, **32.** 131n
Slammerkin. *See* Andrienne
Slapton, Bucks:
Higgate, rector of, **1.** 288n
Slate; slates:
HW may write on, **33.** 310
Slater, Thomas, carpenter:
Barnwell church repaired by, **16.** 193n
Slaughter, Stephen (d. 1765), keeper of the King's pictures:
Bedford to ask, about portrait, **40.** 142
drawings bought for HW by, **15.** 95n
Slaughter:
Mann's reflections on, **25.** 282
Slave; slaves:
African, observe destruction of men-of-war by hurricane, **25.** 109
American Indian, in Brazil, **23.** 452n
'black boys,' given to Mann and Dick by Russians, **23.** 228
Christian, seize Turkish ship, **21.** 493n
Circassian, might be freed by Lady Craven, **42.** 184
Codrington's will provides that 300 be always employed on his estates, **35.** 178
Du Deffand, Mme, accused by HW of seeking, **43.** 94
English shipping of, preyed upon by French, **21.** 101n
Eskimos', **35.** 187n
galley: at Leghorn, eat venison, **20.** 83; escape from galleys, **20.** 206; sent to work at Messina, **18.** 262
girl, escapes at Bristol, **31.** 340, 350–1
HW expects alleviation of lot of, rather than immediate emancipation, **31.** 324
hurricane kills, at Barbados, **25.** 109n
Las Casas suggests supplying Spanish settlements with, **28.** 315
mechanical sugar cultivation might relieve, **31.** 324–5, 328
Moroccan, accompany ambassador at Leghorn, **24.** 469
of Society for Propagation of Gospel, have 'Society' branded on their chests, **35.** 178n
Parliamentary regulation of trade in, **31.** 269n
popular attitude towards, **31.** 328
Roman, painting of, **40.** 4
Somerset freed by King's Bench against Stewart, **35.** 565–6
statue of, in chains, **40.** 11
Turkish: girls given to Lady Dick and Maria Louisa by Russians, **23.** 228; Petersham, Lady Caroline, costumed as, **35.** 206
See also Negro; negroes
Slavery:
abolition of: delayed, **31.** 268; supported by English admirers of French Revolution as measure of faction, **31.** 362; Wilberforce advocates, in Parliament, **31.** 296n
Acton and sailors might be carried into, **20.** 473

Darwin criticizes, in *The Botanic Garden*, **31.** 293
defenders of: call humanity romantic, **31.** 331; use custom house records to defend it, **31.** 331
French situation favourable to abolition of, **31.** 331
HW attacks, **20.** 126
HW opposed to, **31.** 268, **35.** 178
House of Lords defends, **31.** 280
in British West Indies, **31.** 274
in England and France, not abolished, **11.** 252
instance of, at Bristol, **31.** 340, 350–1
kings and sugar-planters will preserve, **31.** 284
Montesquieu attacks, **20.** 126
More, Hannah, opposes, **31.** 260, 296, 297, 319, 340, 342, 350, 362
—— writes against, **31.** 269
pamphlets vindicate, **31.** 280
Parliament to decide on, **31.** 296
Sheridan may speak against, **31.** 269
Tarleton to defend, as Liverpool delegate, **31.** 297
Turkish pirates put captive seamen into, **17.** 16
Slavery. See under More, Hannah
Slave ship; slave ships:
Burgess applies Dante's inscription over Inferno to, **31.** 296
More, Hannah, shows section of, **31.** 297
Tarleton interrupts Hannah More's discourse on, **31.** 297
Slave trade:
African Company's, debated in Parliament, **20.** 126
Barbauld, Mrs, verses of, on rejection of bill to abolish, **31.** 357–8
Bishop Bonner's Ghost discusses abolition of, **31.** 314
defence of, published, **28.** 77
England to assist France in, **21.** 526
French Revolution may lead to abolition of, **31.** 324
HW calls, 'horrible traffic,' **31.** 324
Mason's sermon on, **29.** 361
Roscoe protests against, **15.** 282
souls of American merchants should be troubled by, **28.** 135–6
Slavonians:
Mann grants commissions to, for their protection against French, **25.** 249
sailors who capture *Great Duchess of Tuscany* are, **25.** 479
'Slay-Czar, Catherine.' *See* Catherine II of Russia
Sleaford, Lincs:
HW sups at, **28.** 36n
Sleech, Dr Stephen (1705–65), provost of Eton:
death of, **1.** 106n, **7.** 397
Sleep:
Du Deffand, Mme, would give 22 hours to, and 2 to eating, **4.** 496
HW has lost little of, despite gout, **25.** 620

HW's, 'marvellous,' **25**. 558

Sleepwalker, The. See under Berkeley, Lady Elizabeth, Bns Craven; Ferriol, Antoine, Comte de Pont-de-Veyle

Sleeve; sleeves:
close, in Fenn's unidentified portrait, **16**. 232
Conway, F. S., wants *galon de mousquetaire* for two laces on, **37**. 106
lawn: Bp Hervey wears, **25**. 455; bishop wears, in play, **9**. 336; bishop wears, in portrait, **10**. 336; HW mentions, **10**. 305; legal robe opposed to, **35**. 603; of bishops, **35**. 587, 603; put on Hume's bones, **35**. 587
long, to be worn by Venetian doge's nephew or grandson, **17**. 75
Mann wears, at baptism, **17**. 473
slashed, worn by Richard III, **41**. 132
stockings worn as, **18**. 109

Sleidan, Johann (1506–56), historian:
print of, **1**. 179

'Slender, old,' comrade of P. of Wales. *See under* Fortescue, William Henry (1722–1806), E. of Clermont; Shakespeare, William: *Merry Wives of Windsor*

Sleter, Francesco:
paintings by, at Mereworth, **35**. 143

Slew, Joseph (d. 1771):
murder of, **32**. 68n

Sligo, Ireland:
chapel at, inherits from Cts of Desmond, **40**. 109
Conway and Cts of Ailesbury at, **37**. 336–8, 364
Conway's regiment quartered at, **37**. 353n
—— writes from, **37**. 355–60
monument at, **40**. 107–10

Sling; slings:
Conway busy with, **37**. 358

Slinger, the:
statue of, destroyed in Uffizi fire, **22**. 68n

Slingsby, ——:
dances at Guines's ball directed by, **32**. 109n

Slingsby, Barbara (ca 1669–1721), m. 1 (1688) Sir Richard Mauleverer, 4th Bt; m. 2 (1693) John Arundell, 2n Bn Arundell; m. 3 (1708) Thomas Herbert, 8th E. of Pembroke:
relationships of, **20**. 108n, **25**. 178n

Slippers:
Charles of Naples escapes in, **35**. 52
HW gives, to Princesse de Craon, **17**. 415
HW prefers celebrities to be wearing, in their memoirs, **38**. 444
HW saunters in, till dinner-time, **39**. 127
HW unable to put on, **39**. 475
HW wears, in snow, to see fire, **35**. 210
of gold brocade, Bootle wears, at breakfast, **20**. 184
worn: by HW before dressing, **9**. 304; by HW outdoors, **9**. 225; by Lady Mary Wortley Montagu, **10**. 5, **22**. 3

Sloane, Mr:
HW's social relations with, in Paris, **7**. 266

Sloane, Elizabeth (after 1695–1768), m. (1717) Charles Cadogan, 2d Bn Cadogan, 1726:
Richmonds to be reconciled to Foxes by, **30**. 112n

Sloane, Sir Hans (1660–1753), cr. (1716) Bt; physician:
estate from, at Chelsea, **33**. 161
HW named in will of, **43**. 171
Histoire de la Jamaïque by, owned by Mme du Deffand, **8**. 34
house of, at Chelsea near Physic Garden, **20**. 358n
India ink. coloured, imported by, **17**. 436
museum of: HW a trustee of, **13**. 24, **20**. 358–9; House of Commons votes purchase of, **20**. 358n; Macclesfield trustee of, **20**. 557n; offered for sale after Sloane's death, **20**. 358
Pulteney's epigram mentions, **30**. 24
Walpole, Lady, refused India ink by, **17**. 436

Sloane, Hans (1739–1827). *See* Sloane Stanley, Hans

Sloane, Mrs Hans. *See* Fuller, Sarah

Sloane, Sarah (d. 1764), m. (1719) George Stanley:
husband of, commits suicide, **29**. 5

Sloane Stanley (formerly Sloane), Hans (1739–1827), M.P.:
Stanley, Hans, leaves bequest to, **33**. 161–2
SH visited by, **12**. 223
wife of, **12**. 146n

Sloane Stanley, Mrs Hans. *See* Fuller, Sarah

Sloley, Norfolk:
advowson of, mentioned in HW's will, **30**. 344
HW's will mentions, **30**. 344

Sloop; sloops:
American, burnt on the Delaware, **24**. 386
American Congress's news to be brought by, **39**. 210–11
at Horton, **10**. 334
Conway has order for, to enable him to return from Jersey, **39**. 341
Dodd and Whaley sail in, to Isle of Wight, **40**. 8
English, puts in at Antibes, **18**. 385
English captain of, reports bad bread at St-Malo, **12**. 77
French ships off Scotland pursued by, **37**. 246
Gage dispatches, with news of Lexington battle, **24**. 110
in English invasion of France, **21**. 204
See also *Bonetta; St Paul; Viper; Weazle*

Sloper, Margaret (ca 1707–53), m. (1726) Smart Lethieullier:
(?) Paris visited by, **37**. 47

Sloper, Lt-Col. Robert (d. 1802), K.B.:
testimony of, at Sackville trial, **9**. 276
Walpole, Sir Edward, friend of parents of, **43**. 122

Sloper, William (1709–89):
Walpole, Sir Edward, friend of, **43**. 122
—— thanks, for Mrs Sloper's being godmother to Edward Walpole, **43**. 365

Sloper, Mrs William. *See* Hunter, Catherine

Sloper, Col. William Charles (after 1728–after 1813), M.P.:
Spencer's candidate for St Albans's, **33.** 225n

Slough, Bucks:
Herschels move to, **33.** 569n

Slow, William, of Millman Place, Bedford Row:
HW's codicil witnessed by, **30.** 369

Sluys:
cartel arranged at, for French-English prisoner exchange, **37.** 584, **38.** 1, 5, 7, 10, 11
Conway to visit, **21.** 261
—— visits, **9.** 230
—— writes from, **38.** 3–6, 9–11
French besiege, **19.** 389
governor of, reprimanded for not admitting English troops, **19.** 91
landlord at, overcharges, **38.** 10–11
London compared with, **38.** 9
ramparts of, **38.** 10
See also Hellevoetsluis

Smack; smacks (ships):
Dutch, **38.** 2
See also Cod smack

Smalbroke, Richard (1672–1749), Bp of St David's, 1723, of Lichfield, 1730:
sleepy, **40.** 43

Smallpox:
age of victims said to be important in, **10.** 56
children's complaint, **42.** 412
Chute discusses, with Mme Sarrazin, **17.** 498
——'s joke on Primate of Lorraine's death from, **17.** 480, 498
epidemic of, in London, **19.** 224, **20.** 434
French and Spanish fleets ravaged by, **24.** 519, 527, 530
Guilford, Cts of, fears, **10.** 189, 197
HW inoculated for, **13.** 3
inoculation for, *see under* Inoculation
Italian peasants want, to reduce number of children, **22.** 150
little chance of, after two inoculations, **33.** 89
Lorenzi's daughter has, after inoculation, **22.** 153
Louis XV's, **6.** 46–8, **24.** 1, 2, 8
Mesdames have, **6.** 55, 57
occurrences of: **3.** 112, 114, 306, **4.** 281, 321, **5.** 121, 123, **7.** 41, 138, 443, **9.** 372, **10.** 55–6, 58–9, 189, **17.** 148, 150, 255, 416, 432n, 468, 480, 498, **18.** 65, 341, 510, **19.** 224, 334, 454n, 467, **20.** 137–8, 175, **21.** 42–3, **22.** 126–7, 153, 525–6, 558, 561, **23.** 238, 527, **24.** 1–2, 5, 8, 13, 19, 330, **25.** 413, 414, **31.** 92, **32.** 26, **33.** 140n, **35.** 28, 236, **37.** 27–8
occurrences of, despite inoculation, **4.** 321, **6.** 336
Octavius may have had, on the brain, **25.** 414
Piozzi, Mrs, comments on treatment for, **10.** 56n
precautions against, **6.** 50
prevalent in Florence, **22.** 559
quarantine against, **6.** 50
treatment for, **6.** 47, **33.** 12

'Smallwares, Mr' (HW's name for haberdasher at Twickenham):
proves alibi for highway robbery, **33.** 298

Smallridge, Mrs George. *See* Capper, Mary

Smalridge, George (1663–1719), Bp of Bristol, 1714:
preface to Clarendon's history attributed to, **16.** 8

Smalt:
Saxony produces, **18.** 184n

Smart, Mr:
SH visited by, **12.** 246

Smart, Christopher (1722–71), poet:
copyist for, **14.** 54n
Old Woman's Oratory by: HW sees, performed, **9.** 131; Piozzi, Mrs, comments on, **9.** 131n
The Midwife published by Newbery and, **9.** 131n

Smart, John (1741–1811), miniature-painter:
Pars lives with estranged wife of, **35.** 425n

Smart, Mrs John:
Pars accompanied by, at Rome, **35.** 425n

Smell; smells:
Chute and HW enjoy, **18.** 230

Smellie, William (1740–95), printer; naturalist:
Account of . . . the Society of the Antiquaries of Scotland by: **15.** 164, 165–6; error in, **33.** 368

Smelling-bottle:
Secker plies D. of Newcastle with, at George II's funeral, **9.** 323
goldfish too fat to carry in, **39.** 404

Smelt, Anne Jessie, m. (1774) Nathaniel Cholmley:
Leonard Smelt's daughter, **28.** 491

Smelt, Leonard (ca 1719–1800), of Langton, Yorks; deputy-gov. to royal princes 1771–6:
Account of Some Particulars by, **28.** 493n
HW jokes about Mason being put under, **29.** 85
Hunter outdoes, in absurdity, **29.** 86
Mason satirizes, **29.** 287, 351
resigns as George IV's sub-governor, **24.** 217, **28.** 273n, **35.** 497
royal favour intoxicates, **29.** 5
social relations of, with Mrs Garrick and Hannah More, **31.** 228
speech of, resigning pension: described by Mason, **28.** 491–2; George III hurt by, **29.** 1: to be published, **28.** 492

Smelt, Mrs Leonard (d. 1790):
social relations of, with Mrs Garrick and Hannah More, **31.** 228

Smerna; Smirnia. *See* Smyrna

Smilowitz:
French defeated at, **17.** 452n

Smissaert, Joan Carel (1684–1747), Lt-Gen.:
Dutch troops under, ordered from England, **18.** 449n
witticism by, on being sent from England without orders, **18.** 458

'Smith, Capt.' *See under* Hawke, Hon. Chaloner

'Smith, Capt.' *See* Callis, Smith

'Smith, Vice-Chamberlain.' *See* Howe, John Grubham

Smith, Lady. *See* Brydges, Frances

Smith, ——, Conway's landlord:
Conway leaves books and plays with, **37.** 189
——'s landlord in London, **37.** 184

Smith, ——, gilder:
(?) coronet forgotten by, **9.** 282
(?) delays of, **9.** 276
(?) Montagu's picture frames to be finished by, **9.** 276, 282

Smith, ——, sheriff of Dublin:
riot quelled by, **39.** 421n

Smith, Mr, Irish M.P.:
Speaker threatens to name, **30.** 299n

Smith, Mr (fl. 1749):
'puny spark,' **20.** 23
St John, Vcts, accompanied by, **20.** 23

Smith, Mr:
SH visited by, **12.** 225, 251

Smith, Mr, of Twickenham:
SH visited by, **12.** 228

Smith, Adam (1723–90), political economist:
Argyll's last years described by, **7.** 360
Buccleuch's tutor, **3.** 92n
—— travels with, **40.** 321
constitutional knowledge of, good, but his French is poor, **40.** 321
Fragments of Ancient Poetry considered authentic by, **14.** 115
Gibbon praises, **29.** 99
HW accompanies, to theatre in Paris, **7.** 305
HW called on by, **15.** 107n
HW scoffs at, **29.** 105
HW's social relations with, in Paris, **7.** 302, 306–8, 310, 312
Hôtel du Parc-Royal to be Paris residence of, **31.** 109
Preston discussed by, at Beauclerk's, **32.** 286–7
Reid may replace, at Glasgow, **40.** 321
Scots College visited by, **7.** 307
Theory of Moral Sentiments by, recommended by Robertson to HW, **15.** 52
Toulouse visited by, with Buccleuch, **31.** 79n
Wealth of Nations by, **16.** 31n, **29.** 99n

Smith, Andrew:
HW to address letter to Bowle to, **40.** 299

Smith, Anker, engraver:
Fuseli's title-page to Erasmus Darwin engraved by, **42.** 269n

Smith, Charles:
Ancient and Present State of the County and City of Cork by, mentions Cts of Desmond, **40.** 112

Smith, Charles Loraine (1751–1835), M.P.:
Tyrconnel, Cts of, said to have eloped with, **39.** 279

Smith, Mrs Charlotte. *See* Turner, Charlotte

Smith, Edmund (1672–1710), poet:
Phædra and Hippolitus by: admired by Dr Johnson, **29.** 111; 'fine poetry,' but wants nature, **41.** 296–7

poems of John Philips and, published together, **14.** 27

Smith, Lt-Col. Francis:
Gage sends, to Concord, **24.** 110n

Smith, Francis ('Frank'), mason; architect:
Ombersley Court designed by, **40.** 13
Warwick church mostly rebuilt by, **40.** 348

Smith, George (1693–1756):
father's works published by, **2.** 354n

Smith, Hannah Catherine Maria (ca 1707–86), m. 1 Richard Russel; m. 2 (1736) Hugh Boscawen, 2d Vct Falmouth:
Lincoln, Cts of, entertains, because Ds of Bedford had snubbed her, **37.** 454
Selwyn's witticism on failure of, to walk in Coronation procession, **38.** 122
Townshend's witticism on diamonds and stomach of, **37.** 429, 442

Smith, J. R.:
Reynolds's 'Lady Anne Fitzpatrick' engraved by, **33.** 201n

Smith, J. T., of British Museum:
Deere, J., gives lock of HW's hair to, **43.** 326

Smith, Rev. James (1605–67), D.D., 1661:
Musarum deliciæ by Mennes and, **15.** 266n, **42.** 234–6, 238–9

Smith, James:
(?) stocking-weaver at Nottingham, **25.** 104n

Smith, Capt. John (1580–1631), soldier; colonist:
Generall Historie of Virginia by, De la Warr's *Relation* printed in, **16.** 140

Smith, John (ca 1652–1742), engraver:
catalogue of works of, not found by Dalrymple, **15.** 102–3
print by, **1.** 175
print by, of E. of Warwick, **1.** 183

Smith, Rev. John (1659–1715), editor:
epitaph on, **2.** 354

Smith, John (1705–75), fellow of King's College, Cambridge:
corrections by, for HW's *Anecdotes*, **1.** 167, 177
HW's tutor, **13.** 5
services of, to King's College, **1.** 166–7

Smith, John, sergeant in St George's Dragoons:
Murray, Sir John, seized by, **19.** 274n

Smith, John (d. ? 1772), pugilist; called 'Buckhorse' or 'Lord Buckhorse':
Anstey's *Epistle* addressed to, **1.** 310
(?) Boehm fears, **10.** 273
death date of, **43.** 59

Smith, Capt. John (d. 1804), gentleman usher to Q. Charlotte; Sackville's aide-de-camp:
boastful letters of, from army in France, **21.** 211
declaration by, about Sackville, **38.** 32
Fitzroy repeats P. Ferdinand's orders to, **38.** 21–2
Pitt said by, to have spoken to George II on Sackville's behalf, **21.** 320n
wife's sister to marry, **32.** 52

Smith, John, under-sheriff of Middlesex:
Wilkes cannot again be returned by, as M.P., **23**. 110
Smith, John, pamphleteer and print-seller:
implicated in plot to assassinate George III, **12**. *115*, 118, 123
revolutionary clubs suspected of instigating plot of, **12**. 119
Townsend pursues, **12**. 116
Smith, Mrs John. *See* Fair, Mary (d. 1810); Wilkinson, Mary (d. 1800)
Smith, John Christopher (1712–95):
Fairies, The, by: (?) put on by Arne at Dublin, **37**. 412n; produced by Garrick, **35**. 209–10
Smith, John Silvester (1734–89):
(?) Berkeley's supper attended by, **37**. 530
Smith, Rev. Jonathan (fl. 1673–93):
incorporated at Oxford, **2**. 354
Smith, Joseph (ca 1675–1770), English consul at Venice 1744–60:
appointment of, **18**. 244n
Canaletto employed by, for English trade, **35**. 185
Chute and HW amused by ignorance of, **18**. 465
Chute and Whithed informed by, of Mann's operation, **35**. *4*
English newspapers probably shown by, to HW, **17**. 84
George III buys art collection and library of, **22**. 107, 115, **25**. 93, **35**. 186n
Goethe's appreciation of, **18**. 465n
Gray draws money from, **17**. 82
HW's lack of influence with opera directors to be repeated to, **18**. 211
library of, **18**. 465n
Mann's correspondence with, **17**. 82, 88, 101, 195
—— sends letter through, to HW, **17**. *58*, 86
paintings of, shown to Chute and HW, **18**. 465
Pertici and 'tinca nera' sought by, for English performances, **18**. 198
title-pages alone known to, **18**. 465
Smith, Joseph (ca 1733–90), Gen.:
booty of, at Tanjore, **23**. 561
(?) gambling success of, **7**. 6
Smith, Lucy Assheton (d. 1815), m. (1790) Thomas Sutton, cr. (1806) Bt:
Broadie, Miss, visits, **12**. 157
HW visits, **12**. 154, 157
Hampton Court house of, admired by HW, **12**. 157
Hotham, Miss, visited by, **12**. 154
landscapes by, **12**. 157
SH visited by, **12**. 249
Smith, Margaret (d. 1814), m. (1760) Sir Charles Bingham, 7th Bt; cr. (1776) Bn and (1795) E. of Lucan:
artistic activities of, **24**. 462, 475
aunt of Lady Camden, **12**. 152
baroness's title expected for, **32**. 293

Beauclerk, Lady Diana, admired by, for artistic skill, **6**. 340
Beauclerk, Topham, gives book commissions to, **6**. 373
Choiseul, Duchesse de, portrayed by, **6**. 371
Coigny, Comte de, visits, **12**. 79
Craufurd to deliver Mme du Deffand's gift to, **6**. 500, **7**. 6
daughter of, to wed, **25**. 104, 108
daughters taught by, **24**. 417
Du Deffand, Mme, given presents by, **6**. 395, 400
——'s correspondence with, **6**. 375, 395, 400
—— sends letter by, **7**. 159
—— sends regards to, **7**. 51
——'s opinion of, **6**. 330, 340, 350, 356, 358, 363, 366
—— to receive parcels by, **6**. 328
—— to send letter by, **7**. 157
Florence visited by, **24**. 417, 462
French Court said to favour, **32**. 312
Gordon, Ds of, attends assembly of, **11**. 273
Greuze surprised by artistic talent of, **6**. 333
HW called on by, **32**. 341, **33**. 373
HW calls, 'my new friend,' **32**. 124
HW diverted at home of, **33**. 313
HW entertains, at breakfast at SH, **39**. 390
HW gives 4th vol. of *Anecdotes* to, **41**. 418
HW has not seen, **32**. 124
HW informed by, of Sir Joshua Reynolds's illness, **33**. 373
HW invited by, to dinner, **32**. 122
HW invited to meet, at Lady Shelburne's, **32**. 152–4
HW persuaded by, to write epilogue for *Braganza,* **32**. 233
HW prints *Muse Recalled* to please, **35**. 362
HW's correspondence with, **7**. 396, **41**. 418–19
HW's cuffs to be chosen by, **6**. 358
HW's neighbourhood visited by, **24**. 517
HW's nuptial ode for, **33**. 260–1
HW's preface to 4th vol. of *Anecdotes* praises miniatures of, **41**. 418
HW's relations with, **24**. 417, 462, 475
HW's translation verified by, **6**. 359
HW the 'master' of, **32**. 312
HW to hear La Bastardella at house of, **39**. 223–4
HW to visit, **31**. 410
HW visited by, **12**. 92
HW visits: **12**. 76, 79; to hear singing, **33**. 138–9
Hamilton's pastel portrait of, **41**. 418n
Hampton Court visited by, **43**. 345
Harenc de Presle's miniatures seen by, **6**. 333
Henri IV's portraits copied by, **6**. 340
Hobart, Mrs, entertains, at Ham Common play, **33**. 370
husband follows volatile leadership of, **24**. 475
husband of, **12**. 152n
Italy may be visited by, **6**. 373

Johnson, Dr, at bluestocking gathering of, **29.** 104, 116

Mann loves, **25.** 108

—— praised by, **24.** 517

—— saw, with her daughter and niece, **25.** 620

—— to entertain, at dinner, **24.** 462–3

—— to take, to opera, **24.** 418

Marie-Antoinette befriends, at horse race, **6.** 366

—— given miniatures by, **6.** 349

miniatures of, praised in Paris, **32.** 298

Moulin-Joli visited by, **6.** 333

musicale given at Mme du Deffand's by family of, **6.** 356–7, 363, 366

Nivernais's *Jardins modernes* given to, **12.** 260

painting executed by, for Mann, **24.** 462

paintings copied by, **15.** 192nn

painting the pursuit of, at Rome, **24.** 462

paints in miniature, **32.** 155

Paris left by, **7.** 423

—— may be revisited by, **6.** 373, **7.** 13, 71

—— to be left by, **6.** 372

—— visited by, **7.** 157, **32.** 293, 298, 312

—— visit of, may be prevented by war, **7.** 27, 32

poetic turn of, **24.** 475

(?) sarcophagus from Rome to be presented by, to HW, **24.** 462, 475

social relations of, in England, with: Bedford, Ds of, **33.** 139; Brudenells, the, **33.** 139; Bute, Cts of, **33.** 139, 313; Clermont, Lord, **33.** 246; Cornwallis, Mrs Frederick, **33.** 313; Gibbon, **33.** 313; HW, **33.** 139, 246, 313; Jerningham, **33.** 139; Keenes, the, **33.** 139; Macartney, **33.** 139; Selwyn, **33.** 139; Walsingham, Mrs, **33.** 139

social relations of, in Paris, **6.** 330, 335, 356–8, 371, **7.** 157, 423

story of Irish couples told by, **11.** 37

studio at Palais-Royal given to, **6.** 333

verses by, **34.** 131

Voltaire's *Mémoires* brought to HW by, from Paris, **39.** 414

Woburn portrait copied by, **9.** 124n

Smith, Richard (1734–1803), Brig.-Gen. in East India Co.'s service; M.P.:

candidate for director of East India Co., **38.** 371n

chooses numbers in lottery betting, **33.** 255

withdrawals at East India Co. election, **38.** 378n

Smith, Robert (ca 1690–1768), LL.D.; D.D.; Master of Trinity College, Cambs:

has promise of mastership of Trinity, **15.** 292n

Pratt's letter to, **14.** 135

Smith, Mrs Robert Percy. *See* Vernon, Caroline Maria

Smith, Rev. Sydney (1771–1845):

Berry sisters discussed by, **43.** 138

Smith, Sylvester. *See* Smith, John Silvester

Smith, Sir Thomas (d. 1609):

wife of, **1.** 149n, **9.** 7n

Smith, Thomas (ca 1707–62), naval officer:

commodore, and commander-in-chief at Leith, gets news of galleon, **37.** 246

death of, **38.** 167

Lyttelton's relative, **35.** 149

Miller builds Rockingham Hall for, **35.** *149*

orders of, to watch for invasion, **20.** 506n

Smith ('Smyth'), Rev. Thomas Jenyns (ca 1759–1830):

HW and Lysons received by, at Dulwich College, **11.** 288

Smith, W. M. (fl. ca 1842):

Mme du Deffand's picture bought by, **8.** 215

Smith, William:

condemned at Old Bailey for forgery, **20.** 199n

Smith, William (ca 1739–1819), actor:

Braganza acted by, **28.** 177, **41.** 287, 362

Elfrida acted by, **28.** 110

HW thinks, would expect to play 'Theodore' in Jephson's *Count of Narbonne*, **41.** 408

Smith, William, Chatterton's friend:

Chatterton advised by, to learn French not Latin, **16.** 332

——'s genius said by, to be universal, **16.** 361

unlikely that MSS would have been relinquished by, **16.** 360

Smith, William (1747–1836), of Bristol:

dialogue between Glynn and, **2.** 288n

Smith. *See also* Smyth; Smythe

Smith; smiths:

Queensberry, Ds of, orders, to remove door from warm room, **38.** 343

Smith, name of:

Young Pretender assumes, **23.** 318

Smith Barry, Miss (b. 1747):

dancing of, **32.** 116

Stanley and, in quadrille, **32.** 115n

Smithfield, London:

burning of books at, **2.** 61

burnings in, **31.** 361, **37.** 445

earthquake effects expected in, **20.** 130

fires of, would be rekindled by Bp Butler, **35.** 497, 507

Hog Island is Boston's equivalent of, **28.** 211

Warburton measures ground in, for Wilkes's execution, **22.** 185

Smithson, Lady Elizabeth. *See* Seymour, Lady Elizabeth (1716–76)

Smithson, Sir Hugh (d. 1733), 3d Bt:

said to have been a coachman, **20.** 124–5

Smithson (afterwards Percy), Sir Hugh (1715–86), 4th Bt; 2d E. of Northumberland, n.c.; cr. (1766) D. of Northumberland; M.P.:

Adam's gateway and screen for, **28.** 102

administration may be headed by, **22.** 521

Alnwick inhabited by, **9.** 265n

Amelia, Ps, entertained by, **9.** 334

arrives late at his dinner party, **38.** 530

Bedford, D. of, dislikes rumoured marquisate for, **38.** 392–3

[Smithson, Sir Hugh (1715–86), *continued*]
Bedford House receives, with insults, **38**. 562–3

Bentham's *Ely* may have plate contributed by, **1**. 161n, 162, 164–5, 177

biographical information about, corrected, **43**. 263

Bute may make, prime minister, **38**. 497

—— wants Grenville to be replaced by, **38**. 429

cabinet councillor, and chamberlain to Q. Charlotte, **22**. 103, **43**. 127

chamberlain's post sought by, **10**. 29

chaplains of, **22**. 239

(?) Chesterfield's assembly attended by, **37**. 326

Cumberland, D. of, discusses Regency Bill with, **22**. 296n

—— urged by, to make overtures to Pitt and Temple, **22**. 300n

Dashkov, Ps, received by order of, **33**. 172n

Delineator, The, charms, **39**. 293

dukedom conferred upon, **21**. 191n, **22**. 462

Dutens, chaplain to, **11**. 35n

election of, **19**. 425

Erskine aide-de-camp to, in Ireland, **30**. 198, **31**. 41n

etiquette of, **20**. 341

extravagant construction by, **20**. 341

father-in-law wants title to revert to, **20**. 81

Fielding's *Fathers* dedicated to, **33**. 77n

gallery of: Brettingham brings measurements of, to Albani, **20**. 329n; HW condemns, **20**. 340–1, 507, **21**. 88, 90, 96–7; HW sees, by candlelight, **21**. 88; Mann defends, to Galfridus Mann, **20**. 340–1; Mann procures copies of Italian paintings for, **20**. 328–9, 340–1, 352–3, 490, 507n, **21**. 88, 90, 96–7; Mann receives drawing of, **21**. 209; will be opened with masquerade, **20**. 507

gambling loss of, at Almack's, **33**. 6

gate of, at Syon, endangered, **32**. 213

George II confers Garter on, **37**. 480

George III picks, as prime minister, and sends him to get D. of Cumberland to bring Pitt and Temple in, **38**. 557n

George III will not entail dukedom of, on children by another wife, **24**. 99n

Gloucester, D. and Ds of, may be excluded by, from Alnwick Castle, **36**. 323

Gordon rioters pick pockets of, **25**. 54, **33**. 175

grandfather of, a coachman, **20**. 124–5

Grenville ministry demands exclusion of, **38**. 562–5

Guines's ball attended by, **32**. 96n

HW calls: 'antiquated Duke,' **33**. 259; 'His Royal Highness of Sion,' **33**. 109

HW declines dinner by, as being political manœuvre for Middlesex, **39**. 101

HW does not know, well enough to recommend Muzell to him, **21**. 514

HW entertained by, **9**. 334

HW invited by, to meet Ps Dashkov, **39**. 132

HW mentions, **5**. 88, **37**. 337

HW proposes idea of Syon House gallery to, **38**. 429

HW thanks, for Northumberland 'Household Book,' and sends him a book, **41**. 181–2

Halifax's anti-Stone Irish policy reversed by, **38**. 251n

health of, gout and stone, **34**. 210

Hertford persuades Conway to let, be ambassador to France, **22**. 431n

—— told by, of Carlisle's political change, **39**. 96–7

Irish Parliament discussed by, with Halifax, **43**. 131

Irish post granted to, **10**. 65

Irish post not to be resumed by, **38**. 533–4

Irish post to be quitted by, **38**. 492, 497

Italian connoisseurs pleased by plan of, to have decaying masterpieces copied, **20**. 328n

K.G., **21**. 27

lease of Syon Hill to be settled with, **28**. 399

levee of, for Irish, **10**. 75

light horse troop to be raised by, **37**. 446n

Lockhart, Mrs, intends to marry, **35**. 489n

lord chamberlain's post suggested for, **22**. 308n

lord chamberlain to Q. Charlotte, **32**. 78

lord lieutenant of Ireland, **11**. 3n

Malpas recalled from Ireland by, at Grenville's request, **43**. 279

Mann receives snuff-box from, **21**. 209, 222

——'s correspondence with, **21**. 209

March, E. of, visits, **9**. 265

marquessate may go to, **38**. 392

marriage and peerages of, **23**. 365n

Master of the Horse to George III, **24**. 407n, **34**. 210

Mastership of Horse accepted by, **33**. 93

may be prosecuted for hiring mob at Brentford, **23**. 79

Middlesex Parliamentary seat of, vacated, **20**. 125

mob forces, to drink Wilkes's health, **23**. 7

mob pelts, **23**. 99

Morton contends with, for presidency of Royal Society, **38**. 463

Newcastle, D. of, sends, with letter to George II on Hertford's behalf, **20**. 12n

newspapers name 'vice-admiral of all America,' **38**. 492, 497

Northumberland title goes to, **20**. 124

Ogiński resembles, **33**. 511

Parliamentary act procured by, to boost his rent by erection of powder mills, **23**. 365–6

'pearls and diamonds' scattered by, in Irish post, **38**. 235

peerages suggested for, but not granted, **38**. 377

Percy, Rev. Thomas, employed by, as domestic chaplain and as tutor to younger son, **43**. 309–10

Pitt (Chatham) allegedly to aid, **30.** 226
—— and Temple differ over, **41.** 23n
—— hints at, to Richmond, for prime minister, **41.** 304n
plate might be inscribed to, **1.** 161n
political failure of, **23.** 216
Poor Bill upheld by, **38.** 529
pretensions of, to Percy blood, **9.** 265
prime ministry proposed for, **22.** 302n
quinze losses of, at Duc de Guines's ball, **32.** 100
remarriage of, unlikely, **24.** 99
resignation of, for age, declined, **33.** 245
returns from Ireland, **38.** 393
Revely, William, maternal grandfather of, **20.** 125n
Robinson gets Armagh archbishopric through influence of, **22.** 276
Rockingham ministry shows civilities to, **22.** 431
slow to illuminate his house, **33.** 93
son of, **11.** 127n, **21.** 512, **24.** 315n, **25.** 422n
son of, marries Bute's daughter, **22.** 302n
supper given by, for Cts of Yarmouth, **21.** 191
Swiss porters kept by, **20.** 341
Syon House shows magnificence of, **38.** 429
—— villa of, **35.** 330n
Temple asks Pitt's intentions towards, **30.** 226
upper servants of, want to be stylish by wearing mourning for Ps Caroline, **21.** 165
volunteer companies of, to protect London, **28.** 455
Wagstaff, Elizabeth, misses seeing, **31.** 431
Westminster electors promised subscription by, for militia, **33.** 109
Weymouth to succeed, as lord lieutenant of Ireland, **22.** 302
wife of, **3.** 191n
wife of, does not inherit Percy estate, **20.** 11n
York, D. of, entertained by, **9.** 334
Smithson, Hugh (1742–1817), 2d D. of Northumberland. *See* Percy, Hugh (1742–1817)
Smithson, Robert:
assisted in building Longleat, **14.** 111n
Smithson family:
Stanwick Park, Yorkshire, ancestral estate of, **20.** 341n
Smith Stanley, Edward (1752–1834), styled Lord Strange *or* Lord Stanley, 12th E. of Derby, 1776; M.P.:
appearance of, round face, **12.** 90
ball given by, **32.** 115–16
Bath order offered to, for Burgoyne, **32.** 380n
brother of, **1.** 362
Burgoyne's *Heiress* dedicated to, **33.** 514n
Conway's play acted by, **31.** 268n
cook of, protesting against 3 A.M. suppers, is asked how much he valued his life, **24.** 310
Damer, Mrs, entertains, at supper, **11.** 369, **12.** 76
daughter of, **12.** 159n
Farren, Miss, object of anxiety of, **12.** 107

—— 's constancy from, **11.** 291, **12.** 17–18, 161
—— visited by, **11.** 141, **12.** 17–18
fête-champêtre of, **35.** 421
(?) fêtes, for, **6.** 64
fiancée to be entertained by, at fête champêtre at the Oaks, **24.** 14
gout of, **11.** 337
HW reports military successes to, **12.** 90
HW told by, of Drury Lane Theatre as seen from Westminster Bridge, **12.** 56
HW visited by, **12.** 90
Hamilton, Lady Elizabeth, to marry, **35.** 422
house of, filigreed, **32.** 371
maiden speech of, in Parliament, **32.** 231, **39.** 248
marriage of, **6.** 68
Murphy's *Way to Keep Him* acted by, at Richmond House, **33.** 563n
prologue to Conway's play delivered by, **35.** 391
quadrille danced by, **32.** 115–16
speaks in House of Lords, **29.** 266
wife of, **11.** 64n
wife of, to wed Dorset after her divorce, **24.** 436
Smith Stanley, Hon. Henrietta (Harriet) (1756–1830), m. (1778) Sir Watts Horton, 2d Bt, of Chaderton, Lancs:
quadrille danced by, at Lord Stanley's ball, **32.** 116
Smith Stanley, James (1717–71), styled Bn Strange; M.P.:
army appropriation vote opposed by, **43.** 256
Augusta's dowry may be opposed by, **38.** 249
biographical information about, corrected, **43.** 265–6
death of, leaves chancellorship of Duchy of Lancaster vacant, **23.** 313
Egmont clashes with, **20.** 32
England's subsidy to Hesse-Cassel opposed by, **38.** 8
face of, 'black,' **38.** 499
Grenville supported by, in Parliamentary debate, **38.** 499
militia bill to be presented by, **21.** 552
Onslow's exemption from place tax sought by, **21.** 199
Parliamentary Address may be opposed by, **20.** 510n
Parliamentary speech by, on Dresden treaty, **42.** 496
Pitt's speech distresses, **38.** 320
retracts stand on Wilkes and warrants, **38.** 309
son of, **1.** 362n
Tories usually joined by, **20.** 32
ugliness and busy disposition of, **30.** 302
Smith Stanley, Hon. Thomas (?1753–79). *See* Stanley, Hon. Thomas
Smitsart. *See* Smissaert
Smock Alley Theatre:
at Dublin, **39.** 39n
Brooke's *Earl of Essex* performed at, **41.** 293n
Gustavus Vasa acted at, **13.** 171n

[Smock Alley Theatre, *continued*]
Jephson's *Hotel* performed at, **42.** 124n
Mossop acts at, **37.** 412n
Smoke:
Conway's experiments on, **35.** 437, 438–9
of London, beneficial to HW, **33.** 544, **42.** 200
'Smoke-kilns,' Conway's. *See* Coke-ovens
Smoking:
Howe pursues, in chimney-niche, **35.** 71
Stanislas I's, **20.** 26
Smollett, Tobias George (1721–71), novelist:
Adventures of Peregrine Pickle by: Gray calls, poor, **14.** 48; Lady Vane's memoirs in, **17.** 209n, 459n, **20.** 439n, 459n; Lyttelton is attacked in, **14.** 48
Adventures of Roderick Random by: Powlett the 'Capt. Whiffle' of, **18.** 301n; Wentworth's West Indian failures mentioned in, **18.** 143n
capable of dealing with parties, not with factions, **22.** 306
Complete History of England by: **22.** 306; **23.** 198n; Stuarts 'whitened' by, **16.** 30
False Alarm attributed by, to Dr Johnson, **23.** 189
HW attributes review of *Royal and Noble Authors* to, **35.** 107
HW calls, indolent, **28.** 41
HW warns Mann against, **23.** 198
Humphrey Clinker by, a 'party novel,' **28.** 41n, **43.** 294
Mason quotes, **28.** 113n
settled at Pisa for health, **23.** 189
'Tears of Scotland, The,' by, perhaps referred to by Mason, **28.** 73
translates *Gil Blas*, **14.** 47n
Smuggler; smugglers:
articles smuggled by, **9.** 105
balloon travel will be improved by, **33.** 458
body of, hangs in chains, **35.** 141
called 'mountebanks' in Sussex, **35.** 137
East India Co. buys tea at Ostend to cheat, **25.** 577–8
English ports guarded against, **10.** 288–9
excise officers shoot, **35.** 137
HW's Calais trip worthy of, **32.** 252
Hawkhurst infested by, **9.** 105–6
Holdernesse, Lady, 'queen' of, **33.** 64
Monte Santa Maria inhabited by, **20.** 424, 428
names of, in old newspaper, **9.** 105–6
Newcastle, D. of, might show Sussex to, from Silver Hill, **35.** 141
Orford's militia clashes with, at Southwold, **39.** 304
wine importation a trade imperilled by, **35.** 191
Smuggling:
at Dartford, **1.** 101
Blakiston twice convicted of, **20.** 261n
Haszlang conducts, **25.** 55
of Burgundy wine, **20.** 289
of Chamier's parcels, **4.** 439, 453

of vest for HW, **4.** 143
Smuggling vessel:
American privateer might pretend to be, **33.** 24
Smyrna:
Chishull, chaplain at, **1.** 20
Craven, Bns, at, **25.** 654n, **42.** 176n
Pars shut up in consul's house at, during plague, **26.** 48
Santa Fortunata, La, bound for, when captured, **21.** 274n
Turkish cruelties to Christians at, **23.** 232, 235
Smyrna (London coffee-house):
Cogan hears at, of D. of Newcastle's pension, **21.** 26n
politician at, **29.** 159
Smyth, Mrs:
Van Dyck's portrait of, at Horton: **10.** 335; HW has copy of, **10.** 335
Smyth, Arthur (1706–71), Bp of Clonfert, 1752, of Down, 1753, of Meath, 1765; Abp of Dublin, 1766:
HW's financial dealings with, **17.** *10*
Mann to receive compliments of, **17.** 25
Naples visited by, **17.** 16, 23
Rome visited by, **17.** 10, 15, 16, 23, 25
Shrewsbury's servant discusses Young Pretender's departure with, **17.** 14
translated to Dublin see, **10.** 187n
Venice the destination of, **17.** 23
Wiseman to be instructed by, **17.** 15
Smyth, Corbetta:
Manners, illegitimate son of, **32.** 121n
name of, corrected, **43.** 347
Smyth, Sir Edward Skeffington (1745–97), cr. (1776) Bt:
Beauvau asks about family and wealth of, **41.** 331–2
(?) lodges at Hôtel du Parc-Royal, **4.** 258
Smyth, Elizabeth (d. 1843), m. (1776) Marie-Charles-Rosalie de Rohan-Chabot, Vicomte de Chabot, later Comte de Jarnac:
Beauvau asks about family of, **41.** 331–2
HW's attentions to, **6.** *452*
migraine keeps from SH dinner, **32.** 357
Paris visited by, **4.** 258n, **41.** 331
Smyth, Ellis *or* Elisha (ca 1743–81), m. (1764) Francis Mathew, cr. (1783) Bn, (1793) Vct, and (1797) E. of Landaff:
Beauvau asks about family of, **41.** 331–2
costume of, at Duc de Guines's ball, **32.** 111
HW meets, **4.** 258n
'most perfect beauty' at Q. Charlotte's wedding, **38.** 117
Paris visited by, **41.** 331
sister of, **6.** 452n
(?) social relations of, in Paris, **7.** 271, 294
Smyth, Lady Georgiana. *See* Fitzroy, Lady Georgiana
Smyth, James (d. 1771):
(?) lodges at Hôtel du Parc-Royal, **4.** 258

Smyth, Mrs James. *See* Agar, Mary

Smyth, John (1748–1811), of Heath, Yorks; M.P.:
good qualities of, **32**. 352
marriage of, to Lady Georgiana Fitzroy, forbidden, **32**. 351–2, 356, 360, **34**. 15–16

Smyth, Rev. Richard (? b. ca 1726):
elopement of, **15**. 154

Smyth, Mrs Richard. *See* Powlett, Annabella

Smyth. *See also* Smith; Smythe

Smythe, Lady. *See* Clifford, Hon. Mary

Smythe, Miss, —— (d. 1796), m. (1768) Charles Dodgson, Bp of Elphin 1775–95:
SH ticket not used by, **12**. 226n

Smythe, Constantia (d. ca 1792), m. Marmaduke Langdale, 5th Bn Langdale of Holme:
Browne, Lady, addressed at house of, **31**. 235
—— to visit, **31**. 411
HW unable to visit, **31**. 411
relatives of, at Lady Clifford's, **33**. 528

Smythe, John, brother of Mrs Fitzherbert:
George, P. of Wales (George IV), accompanied by, **25**. 625n

Smythe, Maria Anne (1756–1837), m. 1 (1775) Edward Weld; m. 2 (1778) Thomas Fitzherbert; m. 3 (1785) George, P. of Wales:
Albany, Cts of, introduced to, **11**. 284–5
assertiveness of, **34**. 41n
Bentinck sups with, **34**. 41n
brother of, **11**. 195n
Cosway paints eye of, **33**. 503n
George, P. of Wales's connection with: **11**. 50, 71, **12**. 113, 120, 138, 149, **25**. 625n, 637; Mann tries to discredit rumour of, **25**. 627; reported in Berlin gazette, **25**. 628; reported in *Gazette de Leyde*, **25**. 628–9
——'s marriage to, **11**. 53n, **33**. 514, **39**. 453n
HW calls, 'Inés de Castro,' **33**. 528
Marble Hill occupied by, **12**. 138
Margate visited by, **12**. 113, 120
mother of, **12**. 231n
Queensberry, D. of, entertains, at dinner, **11**. 152
satisfaction and ostrich feathers wanted by, **34**. 201
SH visited by, **12**. 248
Treves said to push P. of Wales towards, **33**. 565n
Twickenham resident, **42**. 482, 483

Smythe, Robert (d. before 1684):
Smythe, Bn, descended from, **23**. 248
wife of, **10**. 125n, **28**. 464n

Smythe, Sir Sidney Stafford (1705–78), Kt; Bn of the Exchequer; M.P.:
becomes commissioner of the Great Seal, **21**. 25
birth date of, corrected, **43**. 273
Great Seal to be delivered by, to Bathurst, **23**. 269n
lord chancellor's seals in commission to, **23**. 179n
Methodist, and Sacharissa's descendant, **23**. 248

to be lord keeper, **23**. 248

Smythe, Walter (d. 1788), Mrs Fitzherbert's father; of Brambridge, Hants:
at Lady Clifford's, **33**. 528
wife of, **11**. 195n

Smythe, Mrs Walter. *See* Boycott, Louisa Victoria Maria Sobieski Foxhunter Moll (1778–1849); Errington, Mary

Smythe. *See also* Smith; Smyth

Snail; snails:
HW compares himself with, **31**. 368

Snake; snakes:
Ailesbury, Cts of, thanks HW for, **37**. 466
Grifoni, Signora, appears as, in HW's 'Patapan,' **30**. 294, 296
in portrait of Lady Digby, **10**. 332
taming of, **20**. 454
See also Asp

Snelling, Miss:
Mme du Deffand's social relations with, **4**. 241

Snelling, Althea (d. 1805), m. (1753) Simon Fanshawe:
(?) Du Deffand, Mme, gives opinion of, **4**. 242, 247
(?) ——'s social relations with, **4**. 241, 242
Karl Wilhelm Ferdinand accompanied by, **38**. 312
SH visited by, **12**. 223

Snelling, Thomas (1712–73):
Thirty-Three Plates of English Medals by, edited by Pinkerton, **16**. 299

Sneyd, Jeremiah (fl. 1770–91), 1st clerk in secretary of state's office:
bills drawn on, **25**. 303n
continuance of, in secretary's office, unknown to Mann, **25**. 272
HW hopes, will be more regular in forwarding letters, **23**. 454
Mann offered services of, as Larpent's successor, **23**. *443*

Snow:
England has: in late March, **25**. 483; in March for 10 days, **35**. 171; in October, **25**. 613, **36**. 231
Fiesole cut off by, **24**. 347
Florence cut off by, from Rome, **25**. 470
—— imports, from Vallombrosa, **20**. 25
French post impeded by, **17**. 207
HW confined by, at Ampthill, **6**. 262
HW kept in town by, **25**. 258
in Florence: in April, **17**. 369; in March, **25**. 628; plentiful, **19**. 466; prevents use of coaches, **22**. 385, 574, 575; streets covered, **22**. 479
in Paris, **7**. 6, **22**. 396
in Rome, **17**. 21n
near Florence: falls daily, **19**. 471; in October, **20**. 336
on Bologna mountains, **21**. 435, **25**. 22
on Bologna road, **25**. 2
on Florentine hills, in April, **19**. 391

[Snow, *continued*]
on Tuscan mountains: in April, **25.** 397; in January, **22.** 575, **25.** 2; in late October, **25.** 334, 441; in March, **19.** 472; in May, **17.** 34
Orford, Cts of, turned back by, at Siena, **24.** 70
Pisa covered by, in late March, **23.** 294
third in winter, in London, **28.** 284
Snow; snows (vessel), French:
English brig captured by, **21.** 334
Snowdon, mountain:
may be reproduced in one's garden, **29.** 283
Snowdrops:
Cole's, blooming, **2.** 210
Snuff:
Ailesbury, Cts of, gives, to HW, **38.** 87
café au lait taken for, **38.** 215
Du Deffand, Mme, arranges for, **5.** 231
—— sends, to Mrs Greville, **4.** 37
Florentines sacrifice, for lottery tickets, **20.** 389
HW does not take, **20.** 377
HW does not throw out, before presenting snuff-box to Ps Amelia, **31.** 141
HW urges Bentley to draw in, **35.** 243
Mann lists advantages of, **20.** 392
——'s headache may be caused by, **20.** 376, 377
—— tries to stop taking, **20.** 376, 377, 389, 392
—— uses, to appear nonchalant, **20.** 392
Montagu, Lady Mary Wortley, is suspected of smuggling, **14.** 245
Spanish, given by Huntingdon to HW, **42.** 464
'tabac vert,' from Portugal, **4.** 55, 62, 64
writing under sign recommends, **30.** 24
See also Herb-snuff; Rappee
Snuff-box; snuff-boxes:
agate, Ottoboni presents, to Carlisle, **13.** 214
Ailesbury, Cts of, gives, to HW, **38.** 87
Barbantane supposed to have sent, to Mann, **25.** 206
Barnewall, Vcts, has, with Comtesse de Gramont's picture, **10.** 12
Capponi receives, from Modenese princess, **17.** 70
Catherine II gives, to Chesterfield, **23.** 376
Choiseul's portrait frequently found on, in France, **23.** 303
Cibber's, given by Raftor to HW, **42.** 158
Clermont, Cts of, passes, to D. of Portland, **35.** 533
Coke, Lady Mary, brings, to HW, **22.** 94, **31.** 146
crystal, jewelled, given by Maria Theresa to Forrester, **18.** 107
diamond: Catherine II said to have promised, to Mann, **25.** 84; Maria Theresa gives, to Giustiniani, **22.** 465
Du Deffand, Mme, collection of, inventoried, **8.** 26, 27
Electress gives, to Kaunitz, **17.** 48
Farinelli collects, in England, **38.** 476
Florence to send, to Constantinople, **19.** 437

French, affected by Palladian architecture, **31.** 99
French excel in designing, **25.** 635
Gibbon orders, from Paris through Mme du Deffand, **6.** 296, 297, 302–6, 308–9, 316, 319, 325, 329, 331, 333, 341, **43.** 100
Gordon rioters snatch, from members of Parliament, **25.** 54
HW asks for miniature the size of, **15.** 279
HW does not want, from Ireland, **9.** 398
HW knows faces of, in all Paris shops, **39.** 145
HW orders, for Montagu, **9.** 239, 247
HW owns, **20.** 377n
HW presents, to Ps Amelia, **31.** 141
HW's: balloon looks no bigger than, **25.** 579; jubilee causes restitution of, **6.** 319; Richmond to take, to HW, **6.** 325, 331; Wiart, Mme, finds, **6.** 312; with Mme de Sévigné's portrait, **3.** 51, 70, 73, **31.** 119
HW sends, to Mann, **17.** 436
HW's price limit on, from Paris, **39.** 234
HW to buy, in Rome, **17.** 29
HW to procure, for Mann in Naples, **17.** 26, 29
HW to show, to Rucellai, **17.** 30
Harrington's, stolen, **38.** 259
horn, Frederick II gives, to Giustiniani, **22.** 465
Huntingdon gives, to HW, **42.** 464
in Paris, HW tired of, **32.** 23
Kilmarnock's, **9.** 47
Lucan, Bns, gives, to Mme du Deffand, **6.** 400
Mann procures, from Naples for Stone, **17.** 26, 29, **18.** 115, 330, 445, 496n
Modenese princess gives, to Capponi and Mme Grifoni, **17.** 70
Montagu, John, carries, for Montagu, **9.** 204n
Müntz does not work on, for Montagu, **9.** 250
musical, from Paris, brought by George (IV), P. of Wales, **11.** 214
Neapolitan: HW and Galfridus Mann receive, **18.** 496; sent by Mann to HW, **18.** 330
new ones, not available in Paris, **32.** 54
Nicoll, Miss, receives, from Chute, **14.** 230
Nivernais's, has portrait of Merlou, **31.** 54
Northumberland, D. of, gives, to Mann, **21.** 209
of Battersea enamel, sent by HW to Bentley, **35.** 252
of cannel coal: **31.** 105; HW sends, to Comtesse de Guerchy, **30.** 214
of goat's horn, **42.** 322n
of gold: lined with wood, **31.** 113; with cameo, **22.** 234n; with false bottom, **33.** 539n; with Tonton's portrait, **8.** 26, **33.** 235, **36.** 182
of tortoise-shell: for Cts of Hertford, **6.** 173, 175, 181, 183, 185, 186, 188, 190, 196; hearts not to be compared with, **30.** 219
Orlov's, stolen at Covent Garden, **24.** 143n
pillow no bigger than, **17.** 481
Portland, Ds of, inherits, from mother, **36.** 237

—— leaves, to Mrs Delany, **33.** 484n

price of, **4.** 50

Richmond, Ds of, brings, from Paris for Hon. Henrietta Seymour Conway, **38.** 384

Serristori, Andrea, receives, from Modenese princess, **17.** 64, 70

Shuvalov gives, to Mme de Luxembourg, **6.** 415

silver, Uguccioni gives, to Granvilles, **19.** 553

stone, given by Bp of Apamea to Kaunitz, **17.** 48

Stuart Mackenzie loses, in Gordon riots, **33.** 175

Suares, Mme, receives, from Modenese princess, **17.** 64

Wade's, stolen at gaming-house, **20.** 110, **43.** 267

with miniature of Mme de Sévigné, **3.** 51, 70, 73, **31.** 119, **43.** 82

with Tonton's portrait: **43.** 105; Du Deffand, Mme de, leaves, to HW, **8.** 26, **36.** 182; given to Mme du Deffand, **7.** 2; HW receives, **36.** 190

with views of Spa, sent to HW by Mary Churchill, **36.** 112–13

with Zincke's portrait of Cts of Orford, received by HW from Sharpe, to be sent to Mozzi, **25.** 501

Wortley Montagu collects, **20.** 226

Snuff-box-wrights:
  HW's, in Paris, **31.** 44

Snuffer; snuffers:
  Du Deffand, Mme, has, **3.** 345
  in Q. Elizabeth's collection, **32.** 324

Snuff shop; snuff shops:
  Mann's abstinence from snuff will distress, **20.** 389

Snyders, François (1579–1657), painter:
  paintings by: **10.** 78n; at Blackheath, **33.** 137; at Burghley House, **10.** 345; at Chantilly, **7.** 260; at P. of Monaco's, **7.** 335; of eagle, at Kimbolton, **10.** 78; to be sold at Brussels, **33.** 487

Soame, Mrs:
  SH visited by, **12.** 230

Soame, Mrs Henry. *See* Bunbury, Susan; Wynn, Frances

Soame, Stephen (ca 1709–64), of Little Thurlow, Suffolk:
  birth date of, **43.** 63
  Cole borrows MS from, **1.** 377
  —— visits, **15.** 309
  death and marriage of, **38.** 463

Soame, Mrs Stephen. *See* Alston, Anne

Soap:
  HW's economy in, at Houghton, **32.** 143
  remedy beneficial to Horatio Walpole (1678–1757), **19.** 510n, **20.** 3
  symbolic of Christ, **35.** 156
  tax on, **25.** 254n

Soap pills:
  Beauvau takes, **7.** 3, 8

Soberton, Hants:
  Lewis of, **13.** 176n

Sobervia, galleon:
  in Spanish fleet, **17.** 286

Sobieska, Maria Carlotta (1697–1740), m. (1724) Charles-Godefroy de la Tour d'Auvergne, Duc de Bouillon:
  Beauvau's wife related to Young Pretender through, **43.** 260

Sobieska, Maria Clementina (1702–35), m. (1719) James Francis Edward Stuart, the 'Old Pretender':
  bare-bone knees of, **25.** 106
  Barigioni designs mausoleum of, with Bracci's sculptures, **21.** 391n
  Benedict XIII gives furniture to, **25.** 525n
  cost of funeral of, exclusive of mausoleum in St Peter's, **21.** 391
  husband of, **11.** 271n
  Mann calls, 'Santa Sobieski,' **19.** 362
  medal of, owned by HW. **11.** 271
  miracles of, will cause her to be declared a saint, **21.** 424
  Orsolene convent the refuge of, from husband's tyranny, **19.** 362n, **25.** 106

Sobieski, Prince James Lewis (1667–1734):
  daughter of, **11.** 271n
  grandsons sell rights to Polish property of, **22.** 387n
  mother's bequest to, **22.** 385n

Sobieski, Johan. *See* John III

'Sobieski, Santa.' *See* Sobieska, Maria Clementina

Sobieski family:
  Jablonowska, Ps, related to, **23.** 319n
  Princesse de Talmond's bed hung with saints and, **14.** 157

Sobieskists, Polish:
  HW pities, **23.** 338

Sobiize. *See* Soubise

Sobriety:
  HW defines, **11.** 14

Soccage:
  Hurstmonceaux recalls days of, **35.** 138

Sochet, Charles-René-Dominique (1727–94), called Chevalier Destouches; French naval officer:
  Arbuthnot balks, **25.** 146n
  ——'s clash with, **25.** 150
  name of, corrected, **43.** 290

Social customs. *See* Customs, social

Social rank:
  HW's reflections on corruptions resulting from, **31.** 282–3

Società Botanico Fiorentino:
  Fossi writes *Elogio istorico di Antonio Cocchi* for, **21.** 170n

Society, high:
  solitude of, **5.** 13

Society for Arts and Sciences. *See* Society . . . for the Encouragement of Arts, Manufactures, and Commerce

Society . . . for the Encouragement of Arts, Manufactures, and Commerce:
  Barry's paintings in, **29.** 296n

[Society . . . Arts, *continued*]
Élie de Beaumont visits, **38.** 461
establishment of, **21.** 173
HW a 'contributory member' of, **43.** 172
HW elected a member of, **13.** 37
HW leaves, **15.** 155
HW neglects, **24.** 284
Ossory awarded medal by, **33.** 480
Transactions of, **33.** 480
Society for the Propagation of the Gospel in
Foreign Parts:
Codrington leaves estates to, subject to em-
ployment of negro slaves, **35.** 178
Markham's sermon to, **28.** 314–15
missionaries of, should be recalled from
America, **28.** 255
Society for the Reformation of Manners:
HW proposes project for, **21.** 418
Society of Antiquaries. *See* Antiquaries, Society
of
Society of Apothecaries:
garden of, at Chelsea, **18.** 250
Society of Artists Associated for the Relief of
their Distressed Brethren:
exhibit of, **23.** 210–11
(?) Müntz's paintings exhibited by, **13.** 34n
Society of Arts and Sciences. *See* Royal Society
of Arts
Society of Friends of the Constitution. *See*
Jacobins
Society of the Antiquaries of Scotland. *See* An-
tiquaries of Scotland, Society of the
Society of the Cincinnati. *See* Cincinnati,
Society of the
Society of the Dilettanti. *See under* Dilettanti
Society of the Supporters of the Bill of Rights:
organization of, at the London tavern, **23.**
114n
Wilkes aided by, **23.** 92n
Socinian:
Bagot calls Hoadly, **29.** 125
Socinianism:
Church of England deserted by adherents of,
31. 328
More, Hannah, accused of, **31.** 329
—— and Priestley would quarrel over, **31.** 333
—— thinks adherents of, sincere, **31.** 329
Socinios, K. of Abyssinia:
Páez converts, **39.** 476n
Socorro, Marqués del. *See* Solano y Bote, José
Socrate. See under Voltaire
Socrates (469–399 B.C.), philosopher:
Aristophanes ridicules, **41.** 55
Du Deffand, Mme, cites, **3.** 214
—— mentions, **4.** 41, 42, **7.** 176
house of, compared to that of Ds of Queens-
berry, **20.** 226, 235–6
Louis XVI compared with, **34.** 179
Macaulay, Mrs, thinks she resembles, **39.** 102
Paar's mistake in speaking of, **3.** 214
West alludes to dancing of, at four-score, **13.**
123

Soderini, Signora. *See* Cenci, Porcia (ca 1700–
72); Mignanelli, Prudenza (ca 1691–1775)
Soderini, (?) Giulio Maria, Venetian Resident
in London 1786–9:
attends Archduke and Archduchess to SH, **33.**
530
Södermanland, D. of. *See* Karl (1748–1818)
Sodi, Pietro, dancer:
(?) handsome but ineffective, **38.** 250
opera performance of, pleases, **18.** 104
Sodor and Man, Bp of. *See* Pepys, Henry (1783–
1860); Wilson, Thomas (1683–1755)
Sofa, The. See *Sopha*
Sofa; sofas:
Du Deffand, Mme, orders, for HW, **4.** 435
Fane likes to recline upon, **19.** 100
Middleton rests on, **15.** 313
Montagu's, of ribbed velvet with black frame,
9. 247, 248
Patapan's, **35.** 45
Sofa-bed; sofa-beds:
HW sits on, **15.** 322, 325
Soffi, Abbé, Jesuit:
Cicognani college to be directed by, **23.** 513n
Sofie Karoline (1737–1817) of Brunswick-Wolf-
enbüttel, m. (1759) Friedrich Wilhelm, Mar-
grave of Brandenburg-Bayreuth:
George III does not want to marry, **35.** 255
Söhlenthal, Baron Henrik Frederik (ca 1672–
1752), Danish ambassador to England:
order of the Elephant given to, **30.** 55
Soho, London:
ball at, **23.** 193
Carlisle House in, **38.** 289
Dean St in, **21.** 131n
St Anne's in, **13.** 28, **21.** 32n, 140, 148
subscription masquerade in, **4.** 371, 375
tailor in, known to Theodore of Corsica, **21.**
45
Soho Factory, Birmingham:
Boulton establishes, **24.** 32n
Soho Square, London:
Banks lives in, **16.** 202n, **42.** 320
Beckford's house in, **23.** 205
Bolingbroke, Vcts, dies in, **20.** 136n
Carlisle House in, **10.** 138n, **29.** 31n
Cornelys, Theresa, takes Carlisle House in,
23. 193n, 271
Dalrymple, Alexander, lives in, **15.** 127n
Duberly in, **11.** 365n
English Court would not exile people to, **23.**
298
Guerchy's house in, **3.** 151n, 317n
Harvey, William, lives in, **21.** 47n
Masserano's house in, **24.** 111n
Ramsay writes from, **40.** 150, 370
Soirée; soirées:
Tylney gives, at Naples, **24.** 280n
Soissons, Bp of. *See* Fitzjames, François de
Soissons, Anne-Victoire de, P. Eugene's heiress:
Zanetti acquires cameo from, **21.** 562n

Soissons (France):
  Bernis exiled to, **21.** 262n
  Morfontaine intendant of, **3.** 205
  visitors to: Gloucester, D. of, **3.** 117; Marie-Antoinette, **4.** 406
  Young Pretender said to be at, **18.** 433n
Soisy, Marquis de (d. 1789):
  (?) social relations of, with Mme du Deffand, **4.** 415
Soisy (France):
  Le Droit, Mme, lives at, **3.** 359n
Sol, French coin:
  value of, **37.** 39
Solander, Daniel Charles (1736–82), F.R.S.; D.C.L.; botanist:
  Beriea 'discovered' by, **31.** 162
  Berry, Mary, learns botany from, **11.** 12
  HW dines with, **32.** 122
  HW has satiric print of, **43.** 337
  HW jokes about geographical discoveries of, **31.** 157
  Omai met by, in Tahiti, **24.** 21n
  voyages of, **2.** 225
Solano, Joseph:
  captured at Velletri, **18.** 493
Solano y Bote, José (1726–1806), cr. (1784) Marqués del Socorro; Spanish naval officer:
  fleet of, joined by Guichen's fleet, **25.** 73n
  said to return to Europe with Guichen, **25.** 94
Solar, Comte de. *See* La Fontaine-Solar, Vincent-Joseph de
'Solar, Comte de.' *See* Joseph (ca 1762–ca 1792)
Solar, Comtesse de. *See* Clignet, Jeanne-Paule-Antoinette
Solar, Guillaume-Jean-Joseph de (1762–74):
  Joseph the deaf-mute claims to be, **7.** 134
Solar microscope. *See under* Microscope
Solaro di Breglio, Roberto Ignazio (ca 1715–65), Sardinian minister to France 1758–65:
  Choiseul, Duc and Duchesse de, aided by, **3.** 373
  Choiseul, Duc de, proposes to, that France pay Sardinia the equivalent of revenue of Placentia, **21.** 275n
  Choiseul, Duchesse de, liked, **3.** 359, **4.** 302
  employed in Paris peace treaty, **22.** 105
Soldier; soldiers:
  borough towns vacated by, during elections, **25.** 489n
  Botta's solicitude for, **22.** 124
  Braddock's, sacrifice him from objection to being drafted, **35.** 245
  Conway considers, men and not beasts of burden, **37.** 183
  —— describes defects of a mere, **37.** 129
  disbanded, Nova Scotia lands granted to, **20.** 40n
  elections invalid if supervised by, **17.** 252
  England and America can enlist, **24.** 81
  English: cuts ring from old woman's finger, **21.** 221; in good health and spirits, **37.** 214; remark by, to French, **21.** 191; spirit of,

37. 135–6; take to robbery when disbanded, **20.** 111
equinoctial rain sends, to hospital, **37.** 204
foot, Mann receives letter through, **17.** 52
found drunk on post, **39.** 240
Frederick II forbids, to receive any more presents from a Madonna, **25.** 499–500
French, fight fatal duel, **38.** 506
HW thanks Conway for kindness about, who will get substitute, **39.** 510
hard lot of, when retired, **15.** 90
hat retained and musket shouldered by, when delivering message, **19.** 439–40
Henri IV among, sketching, **35.** 243–4
human weaknesses inappropriate for machine-like efficiency of, **37.** 223–4
hussars and court martials of, terrify the civilians, **38.** 82
Joseph II encourages copulation to get more, **25.** 280
old women see that hats of, are cocked right, **37.** 292
Palliser's house protected by, **24.** 442
physicians induce more deaths than, **25.** 342
risings and riots not rebellions made by, **42.** 252
sbirri quarrel with, **24.** 8–9
Sundon's election invalidated by presence of, **17.** 251–2
wife of, is Cts of Ailesbury's only attendant, **37.** 295
will not, like priests, be suppressed, **25.** 237
'Soldiers at Cards.' *See under* Van Dyck, Sir Anthony
Soldini, —— (d. 1775), Abbé; Dauphin's confessor:
  Dauphin guided by, in marital relations, **5.** 50
Sole, J. C.:
  letters by, from Florence, **23.** 225n, 348n, 352n, 355n
Solebay, English ship:
  news brought by, **25.** 257n
Soleil, French privateer:
  arrival in London of prisoners from, **19.** 180
  English ship captures, on way from Dunkirk to Montrose, **19.** 173
  Henry Benedict (Stuart)'s capture on, believed certain, **19.** 173, 177
Soleil Royal, French ship:
  Conflans forced to burn, **21.** 351
  runs aground, **21.** 357
Solemeni. *See* Solimena
Soleure (Switzerland):
  Breteuil goes to, **11.** 36n
Soley, Mrs. *See* Dixon, ——
Soley, John (d. ? 1780):
  HW's correspondence with, **41.** 96–8
Solferino, Duque de. *See* Pignatelli, Luís
Solferino, Duquesa de. *See* Gonzaga, María Luisa (1726–73); Pignatelli d'Egmont, Alphonsine-Louise-Julie-Félicie (1751–86)

Solicitor-general; solicitors-general:
Dunning resigns as, **23**. 175, 180
Hardinge contends with, in law case at Norwich, **35**. 633–4
Murray is, **17**. 250n, 344n, 494, **18**. 118, **19**. 283, 379
—— succeeds Strange as, **18**. 118
—— to succeed Strange as, **17**. 494
Scott succeeds MacDonald as, **34**. 9n
Wallace becomes, **39**. 136n
Wedderburne becomes, **23**. 269
Wilkes not proved by, to be author of *North Briton*, **22**. 189
Yorke, Charles, may become, **20**. 202
See also Arden, Richard Pepper (1744–1804); De Grey, Sir William (1719–81); Dunning, John (1731–83); Lee, John (? 1733–93); Mansfield, James (1734–1821); Mitford, Sir John (1748–1830); Murray, William (1705–93); Norton, Sir Fletcher (1716–89); Ryder, Sir Dudley (1691–1756); Strange, Sir John (1692–1754)
Soliman II. See under Marmontel, Jean-François
Solimena, Francesco (1657–1747), painter:
Furnese has pictures by, **21**. 172n
Mariette has drawings by, **7**. 273
Montagu wishes paintings by, **10**. 97
painting not by, left by Electress to Benedict XIV, **18**. 171, 207
Solis de Folck de Cordona, Francesco (1713–75), cardinal, 1756:
Conclave entered by, **23**. 113
—— expects, **23**. 95n
'dried blackish parchment only covers his little bones,' **24**. 69
Jesuits' suppression agreement demanded by, at Conclave, **23**. 527n
reaches Conclave in dying condition, **24**. 68–9
Solis y Rivadeneyra, Antonio de:
Historia de . . . Mexico by, basis for *Motezuma*, **24**. 90n
Solis y Sante (d. 1744), Don; Duque d'Atrisco; field marshal:
detachment of, **18**. 443
Solitaire, Le, French ship:
Chartres reaches Cadiz on, **32**. 301n
Solitaire; solitaires (jewels):
San Vitale gives, to Tesi, **17**. 70
Solitaire (neckcloth):
Cholmondeley affects youth by wearing, **38**. 470
Solitaire (game):
Montagu, Henrietta, plays, **9**. 49
Solitary people:
peevishness of, **33**. 576
Solly *or* Soly, Arthur (fl. 1683), engraver:
Boehme's portrait engraved by, **16**. 66
Crisp's portrait engraved by, **16**. 67
Solms-Sonnewalde, Charlotte von (1725–83), m. (1741) Christian August, Graf von Seilern:
at home but twice a week, **31**. 57
circle of, **32**. 29
HW calls on, **38**. 494

Hertfords entertain, at card party, **32**. 19n
husband insists on dinner and assembly by, despite daughter's death, **38**. 510
receives company after death of Emperor, **32**. 19
'Solomon.' *See* Pitt, William, E. of Chatham
Solomon (fl. ca 970 B.C.), K. of Israel:
Arundel Castle window portrays, **12**. 205n
botanist, **34**. 123
Churchill asks question about, **20**. 367
dish given by, to Q. of Sheba, **37**. 320
Du Deffand, Mme, cites, **3**. 158, **4**. 48
Frederick II compared to, **21**. 94, **23**. 539
HW attributes saying to, **35**. 253
HW calls D. of Norfolk, **12**. 205, 206, 209
HW compares himself to, **11**. 72, **12**. 4
HW has not sagacity of, **23**. 555
HW jokes about Q. of Sheba and, **31**. 160
HW's 'Dice Box' mentions, **31**. 156
HW's mock sermon mentions, **31**. 426
HW's name for: D. of Norfolk, **12**. 205, 206, 209; James I, **35**. 329; Louis XV, **23**. 157; Pitt, William, E. of Chatham, **9**. 164
HW's 'Persian Letter' mentions, **30**. 36
lilies of the field and, **35**. 461
'old Carr's cousin' contrasted with, **35**. 107
proverbs of, **32**. 191
saying attributed to, **23**. 198
seal of, wielded by Burke, **34**. 102
Song of, version of, **33**. 261
temple of, **39**. 182
wisdom of, as polygamist, attracts Q. of Sheba, **33**. 555
Solomon I (d. 1784), K. of Western Georgia 1752–65, 1768–84:
Turkish warfare of, **22**. 420
Solomon on the Vanity of the World. See under Prior, Matthew
'Solon, Lord.' *See* Darcy, Robert, E. of Holdernesse
Solon:
HW at Paris compared with, **35**. 337
Lyttelton's gravity like that of, **32**. 387
travelled to Egypt, **33**. 399
Solre, Prince de. *See* Croÿ, Emmanuel de
Soltau, Mr:
SH visited by, **12**. 226, 227 *bis*
Soltikoff. *See* Saltykov; Soltykov
Sołtyk, Kajetan (d. 1788), Bp of Kiev 1749–59, of Cracow 1759–88:
Russians remove, **22**. 574
Soltykov, Count Petr Semenovich (ca 1700–72), Russian field marshal:
Berlin menaced by, **21**. 441n
Fermor replaced by, **21**. 312n
Frederick II defeated by, **21**. 317n, 331n, 332n
name of, corrected, **43**. 276
Prussian oath of allegiance taken back by, **22**. 75
Turkish sortie repulsed by, **24**. 29n
Vistula left by, to cross Poland, **21**. 419n
See also Saltykov

Solway Moss:
  battle of, **16**. 80
Sombreuil, Vicomte de. *See* Virot, Charles
Some Account of . . . Legge. See under Butler, John
'Somebody':
  prints of, **34**. 194
Some Considerations upon Clandestine Marriages. See under Gally, Henry
Some Cursory Reflections on the Dispute . . . at Antioch. See under Middleton, Conyers
Some Farther Remarks on a Reply to the Defence. See under Middleton, Conyers
Some Farther Remarks . . . upon Proposals, etc. *See under* Middleton, Conyers
Some Observations on a Book Entitled an Essay. See under Ashton, Thomas
Somer, Paul van (1576–1621), painter:
  portrait by, **1**. 88n
  (?) portrait by, of Henry, P. of Wales, **10**. 102, 103n
  portrait probably by, of Northampton, **16**. 92
Somerby Hall, Lincs:
  Markham, Mrs, at, **1**. 6, 20n
Somercote, John de:
  patent to, for custody of the Mint, **40**. 223
Some Reflections on the Present State of the Nation. See under St John, Henry, Vct Bolingbroke
Some Reflections upon a Late Pamphlet Entitled an Examination:
  Middleton's attack on Sherlock provokes, **15**. 299
Some Reflections Upon the 7, 8, and 9th Verses of the 2d Chapter of Genesis. See under 'Philalethes.'
Some Remarks on a Book Entitled a View, etc. *See under* Heathcote, Ralph
Some Remarks on Mr Walpole's Historic Doubts. See under Masters, Robert
Some Remarks Upon a Pamphlet Entitled, The Case of Dr Bentley. See under Middleton, Conyers
Some Remarks Upon Mr Church's Vindication. See under Toll, Frederick
Somerfield. *See* Somerveldt
Somerford Park, Cheshire:
  Shakerley of, **11**. 47n
Somerleyton, Suffolk:
  Fitzosbern family's seat, **1**. 387
Somers, Bns. *See* Pole, Anne
Somers, John (1651–1716), cr. (1697) Bn Somers; lord chancellor:
  Addison's character of, **2**. 95, 98
  Demosthenes' orations said to be translated under direction of, **16**. 370
  Dunning's *Inquiry* the best work since, **38**. 474
  HW mistakes Hardinge's reference to, **35**. 552, 557
  Jacobites offered services of, **20**. 322n
  Miscellaneous State Papers does injustice to, **35**. 603

Sophia's letter among papers of, **7**. 362
  subject of, 'chaste and sacred,' **35**. 561
  Swift disparages, in history, **21**. 185
  Tories humoured by, in 1688, **35**. 613
  wrote for liberty, **14**. 137n
  Yorke's papers of, lost in fire, **20**. 322, 331–2
Somersby, Thomas, jr, mayor of King's Lynn, 1773:
  HW's correspondence with, **41**. 262
Somerset, Cts of. *See* Howard, Lady Frances (1589–1632)
Somerset, Ds of. *See* Alston, Sarah (d. 1692); Fillol, Catherine; Finch, Lady Charlotte (1693–1773); Percy, Lady Elizabeth (ca 1667–1722); Stanhope, Anne (ca 1497–1587); Thynne, Frances (ca 1699–1754); Webb, Mary (1697–1768)
Somerset, D. of. *See* Beaufort, Edmund (ca 1439–71); Seymour, Algernon (1684–1750); Seymour, Charles (1662–1748); Seymour, Edward (ca 1500–52); Seymour, Sir Edward (1695–1757); Seymour, Edward (1718–92)
Somerset, E. of. *See* Beaufort, John (ca 1371–1410); Carr, Robert (ca 1587–1645)
Somerset, M. of. *See* Beaufort, John (ca 1371–1410)
Somerset, Ladies (? sisters of Henry, 5th D. of Beaufort):
  SH visited by, **12**. 247
Somerset, Anne (1673–1763), m. Thomas, 2d E. of Coventry:
  (?) Hertford, Cts of, visits, **38**. 134
Somerset, Lady Anne (1741–63), m. (1759) Charles Compton, 7th E. of Northampton, 1758:
  appearance of, **10**. 337
  Bagot and physician accompany, to Rome, **22**. 142
  death of, **10**. 337, **22**. 150
  Florence visited by, **22**. 132
  handsome, **21**. 294
  HW admires appearance of, at Coronation, **9**. 387, **38**. 127
  health of, consumption, **10**. 337, **22**. 132, 142, 145
  Mann tries to comfort, **22**. 132
  marriage of, **35**. 295
  Naples to be visited by, **22**. 132, 142
  Northampton, E. of, to wed, **21**. 294, 313
Somerset, Lady Arthur. *See* Boscawen, Hon. Elizabeth
Somerset, Sir Charles (ca 1460–1526), K.G., 1496; cr. (1514) E. of Worcester:
  ancestor of Dukes of Beaufort, **16**. 233
Somerset, Lord Charles Henry (1767–1831):
  declines invitation to ball at Windsor, **11**. 329
Somerset, Lady Charles Noel. *See* Berkeley, Elizabeth
Somerset, Lord Charles Noel (1709–56), 4th D. of Beaufort, 1745:
  brother succeeded by, **19**. 26n, **20**. 50n
  daughter of, **2**. 167n, **11**. 187n, **24**. 54n, **29**. 185n

[Somerset, Lord Charles Noel, *continued*]
Jacobites led by, **17.** 231, **19.** 26
Opposition meeting addressed by, at St Alban's Tavern, **20.** 50
political capacity of, questioned, **17.** 231n
widow of, **11.** 86n, **24.** 46n, 120, **25.** 564n
Somerset, Edward (ca 1550–1628), 4th E. of Worcester, 1589:
commissioner for Greenwich Hospital, **16.** 83n
Somerset, Edward (ca 1603–67), styled Lord Herbert of Chepstow 1628–45, E. of Glamorgan 1645–6; 2d M. of Worcester, 1646:
Century of Names . . . of Such Inventions: machines described in, **37.** 294; resembled by HW's 'Inventionary,' **35.** 252
Charles I countenances, **34.** 103
—— empowers, to raise force of Irish and foreign Roman Catholics, **40.** 138
'Papist,' **40.** 130
Parliamentary membership unlikely for, **40.** 130–1
Somerset, Elizabeth (d. 1691), m. (1654) William Herbert, 3d Bn Powis, cr. (1674) E. and (1687) M. of Powis:
marriage of, **7.** 265
Somerset, Lady Elizabeth (d. 1760):
mother loses, by consumption, **23.** 372
Somerset, Lady Henrietta (1748–69), m. (1769) Sir Watkin Williams Wynn, 4th Bt:
mother loses, by consumption, **23.** 372
Somerset, Henry (? 1495–1549), E. of Worcester:
daughter of, **1.** 6
Somerset, Henry (ca 1576–1646), 5th E. of Worcester, cr. (1643) M. of Worcester:
'Papist,' **40.** 130
Somerset, Henry (1629–1700), 7th E. and 3d M. of Worcester, cr. (1682) D. of Beaufort:
creation of, **16.** 233n
Somerset, Henry (1684–1714), 2d D. of Beaufort, 1700:
Bubb Dodington's ballad mentions, **33.** 557, **34.** 262
Somerset, Henry (1707–45), 3d D. of Beaufort:
brother succeeds, **19.** 26n, **20.** 50n
divorce of, **17.** 452–3, **18.** 185, 199
HW well acquainted with Badminton and, **40.** 11
Raphael painting may be bought by, **18.** 239, 273, **35.** 37
Talbot pitied by, **17.** 486
wife's accusation of impotence disproved by, before witnesses, **18.** 185, 199
Somerset, Henry (1744–1803), 5th D. of Beaufort, 1756:
ball given by, at Paris, **7.** 271, **22.** 365, **32.** 24
Deerhurst's accident while hunting with, **33.** 242n
first of his family to forsake Jacobitism, **23.** 174
George III to visit, **34.** 47n
HW and Chute afraid of, **10.** 228
lieutenancy of Welsh counties contested by, with Morgan of Tredegar, **23.** 174

Mastership of the Horse to Q. Charlotte resigned by, **23.** 174
Paris visited by, **31.** 71–2
sister of, **10.** 337, **21.** 294
social relations of, in Paris, *see index entries ante* **8.** 516
travels improve, **31.** 71–2
unmarried, **10.** 29
Somerset, Henry Charles (1766–1835), styled M. of Worcester, 6th D. of Beaufort, 1803:
marriage of, **11.** 244
SH visited by, **12.** 238
Somerset, James (slave):
King's Bench court frees, **35.** 565–6
Somerset, John (d. ? 1455), physician:
Baker's materials on, **2.** 355
Somerset, Lady Lucy (? 1524–83), Bns Latimer:
daughter of, **1.** 6
Somerset, Lady Maria Isabella (1756–1831), m. (1775) Charles Manners, styled M. of Granby 1770–9, 4th D. of Rutland, 1779:
Barry includes, in allegorical painting, **29.** 296, 297, 300
beauty of, **25.** 282
beauty of, not so striking to HW, **24.** 54
Burlton's gaming-house said to be sponsored by, **32.** 131n
feathers and hat of, **32.** 216–17
Florence to be visited by, **23.** 397
George, P. of Wales, envies husband of, **33.** 411
Granby to wed, **24.** 54, 120–1, 148
health of, indifferent, **39.** 266
Hertford, Cts of, sees, **39.** 265–6
husband of, **6.** 190n
marriage of, **32.** 287
mother accompanied by, to Pisa, **23.** 372, 397
Paget leaves pursuit of, to De Visme, **12.** 120
——'s rumoured marriage to, **11.** 187, 244
Ramsgate, admirer at, pursues, **12.** 113–14
'reigning toast,' **25.** 411n
Sherwin includes, among beauties, **29.** 185
turns Hon. John Townshend out of her coach, **2.** 167n
Tuscan Court favours, at Florence, **23.** 406
Somerset, county of. *See* Somersetshire
Somerset, English ship:
American destination of, **39.** 197n
at Port Mahon, **17.** 285
Somerset, dukedom of:
descent of title of, **18.** 522–3, **20.** 124–5, 138–9
Seymour will try to perpetuate, **32.** 119
Somerset, dukes of:
Buckingham, D. of, descended from, **16.** 234
Somerset family:
Beaufort, D. of, the first member of, to forsake Jacobites, **23.** 174
George II to perpetuate, with earldoms, **20.** 81
Somerset House (old), in the Strand, London:
Anne of Denmark's furniture at, **32.** 324–5
Ashton seeks news of HW at, **13.** 246
Bedford, Grosvenor, familiar with, **40.** 142
Boden, Mrs, at, **41.** 241

Brietzcke, Catherine, housekeeper of, **40**. 142

chapel of, Ashton preaches in, **13**. 249–50

Chernyshev to give masquerade at, **35**. 199

Chute, Mrs, of, **14**. 195n

Frederick II may have to live at, **22**. 38, 320

Grosvenor, Anne, under-housekeeper and housekeeper of, **10**. 276n, **13**. 220n, **17**. 230n, **42**. 491

HW mentions, **37**. 186

HW writes from, **17**. 230, 263

Harris, Mrs, housekeeper at, **9**. 167n

John of Padua supposedly built, **14**. 110–11

Karl Wilhelm Ferdinand gives levees and dinners at, **22**. 197

lodgings for poor gentry in, **17**. 230n

Miremont and sister at, **34**. 257

old gallery at, ruinous, **35**. 344

Portuguese royal family may flee to, **22**. 38, 95

Somerset builds, **16**. 47

Wimbledon's portrait said to be at, **40**. 142

woman at, tries to split hairs, **37**. 576

Somerset House (new):

Bindley lives at, **16**. 301

Chambers builds, **29**. 37, 42

——'s masterpiece, **28**. 28n

exhibition at, full of Brobdingnag ghosts, **31**. 221–2

from Southwark, **12**. 258n

Hunter, Dr William, lectures at, **43**. 307

praise of, in newspapers, on removal of scaffolds, **16**. 187

Royal Academy at, **2**. 246, **29**. 33, 138, 296, **35**. 344n, **43**. 307

Society of Antiquaries moves to, **2**. 242n, **28**. 40n

Zoffany's 'Tribuna' exhibited at, **24**. 540n

Somerset House Coffee-house, in the Strand:

HW tells Bedford to investigate needy case at, **41**. 384, 385n

Somersetshire:

Damer sells lands in, **10**. 233n

dialect of, **31**. 265

HW to visit, **10**. 34

HW visits, **1**. 14

man from, meets Pitt at Bath, **22**. 425–6

monk of, would not use same dialect as Scottish bishop, **16**. 351–2

North, Lord, lets house in, to woman, **33**. 232

Pynsent subject of scandal in, **38**. 493

—— supposed to be from, **22**. 276

Walpole, Sir Robert, has lands in, **36**. 25n

Somerset St, London:

Berrys' house in, **11**. 3n, 107, 145, **34**. 68n, **43**. 143

Somers Town:

Gunning at, **11**. 366n

Somerton, Bns and Vcts. *See* Benson, Jane

Somerveldt, Georg Friedrich (1711–60), Hanoverian general:

Maidstone mayor refuses to deliver up Schroeder to, **21**. 12n

Somerville, William (1675–1742), poet:

Chase, The, by, **37**. 16

'Elbow Chair' of, may be 'Wicker Chair' published as *Hobbinol*, **37**. 16n

Luxborough, Lady, erects monument to, **11**. 65n

Somery family:

arms of, **33**. 350

Some Seasonable Advice. See under Vernon, Edward

Some Short Remarks on a Story. See under Middleton, Conyers

Sommerfield. *See* Somerville

Somméry, Comtesse de. *See* Riquet de Caraman, Cécile-Agathe-Adélaïde de

Somméry, Mlle de, m. Jean-Baptiste-Nicolas-Louis de Villicy, Chevalier de Tourville: marriage of, **3**. 393n

Somnambule, Le. See under Ferriol, Antoine, Comte de Pont-de-Veyle

Somodevilla y Bengoechea, Zenón de (1702–81), Marqués de la Ensenada:

Campillo to be succeeded by, as secretary at Madrid, **18**. 253

Ferdinand VI retains, **19**. 278n

Keene brings about downfall of, **21**. 166n

Mann asked by, for passport to take furniture to Spain, **18**. 253

recall of, rumoured, **39**. 64

Sonata; sonatas:

Veracini's, includes 'Tweedside,' **20**. 148

Sonde. *See* Tort de la Sonde

Sondes, Bn. *See* Watson, Hon. Lewis (1728–95); Watson, Lewis Thomas (1754–1806)

Sondes, Bns. *See* Pelham, Grace (ca 1731–77)

Sondes, Vcts. *See* Tufton, Lady Margaret

Sone. *See* Poutier de Sone

Sonetto; sonetti:

affair in Mann's garden satirized in, **19**. 498–9, 502

Song; songs:

English language now too worn-out to produce, **16**. 257

French: with double entendres, **30**. 45; sung by Lady Cecilia West, **38**. 100; Young Pretender sends page to France for, **30**. 92

HW has, made, **37**. 126

HW has no talent for writing, **16**. 257

HW sends, to Lord Lincoln, **30**. 46

Handel's, **35**. 350

parliament of Paris's return hailed by, **39**. 207

Russell, Lady Caroline, signs risqué stanza of, **37**. 565

Shenstone never wrote, perfectly, **16**. 257

sung at election at King's Lynn, **9**. 350

See also Ballad; 'Black Joke'; 'Phœbe is Gone'; Madrigal

Song of Solomon:

Du Deffand, Mme, mentions, **3**. 158

'Song on Miss Harriet Hanbury, A.' *See under* Williams, Sir Charles Hanbury

Songs and Sonnettes. See under Howard, Henry (ca 1517–47), styled E. of Surrey

Sonnet; sonnets:
  buried on Laura's bosom, **40**. 377–8
  Craon's on Lady Sophia Fermor, **30**. 12–13
  Frederick II writes, to Voltaire, **21**. 168, 171
  HW finds, intolerable except in Italian, **15**. 260–1
  HW receives, from Lincoln, **30**. 30
  HW's verses on, **12**. 271
  Hardinge's, to 9-year-old girl, **35**. 557–8
  ——'s, 'writ in . . . Chancery Lane,' **35**. 557
  political, Mann sends, to HW, **17**. 302
  Prussian, by Frederick II, **37**. 65
  Surrey's, **18**. 497
Sonning, Mme Louis-Auguste. *See* Puchot des Alleurs, Marie-Sophie
Sontete, Mme de:
  Monaco, Ps of, accompanied to Bellechasse by, **4**. 438
Soor, in Bohemia:
  Frederick II defeats P. Charles at, **19**. 127
Soothsayer; soothsayers:
  visions of, not revealed until fulfilled, **22**. 562
Sootwater:
  Beauclerk, Lady Diana, does drawings in, **24**. 524, **28**. 244
  HW urges Bentley to draw in, **35**. 243
Sopha, Le. See under Crébillon, Claude-Prosper-Jolyot de
Sophi, of Persia:
  etiquette for, **23**. 550
Sophia (1630–1714), m. (1658) Ernst August I of Hanover:
  Old Pretender recommended by, for K. of England, **7**. 362
  (?) print of, **40**. 237
  William III plays loo with, **7**. 362
Sophia (1777–1848) of England, Ps:
  Eastbourne visited by, **33**. 232n
  father asks provision for, **24**. 372
  (?) HW visited by, at SH, **39**. 510–12
  inoculation of, **25**. 405n, 406
  miniature of, **11**. 145n
Sophia, Dutch ship:
  Waldegrave captures, **33**. 272n
Sophia Dorothea (1666–1726) of Celle (Zell), m. (1682) George of Hanover, later George I of England:
  George I ill-treats, **2**. 125
  HW wants copy of Ps Amelia's portrait of, **42**. 180–1
  Königsmarck's affair with, **7**. 278
Sophia Dorothea (1687–1757), m. Frederick William I of Prussia:
  death of, rumoured, **35**. 189, 192
  legacy to, **2**. 125
Sophia Matilda (1773–1844) of Gloucester, Ps:
  annual sum granted to, **7**. 40n
  baptism of, **32**. 129–30
  birthday and ball for, attended by HW, **33**. 171
  birth of, **1**. 321n, **5**. 346, 370n, **23**. 483, **28**. 89, 94, **32**. 118

brother will probably not be preferred to, **24**. 302
Cressen barons liked by, at Trent, **36**. 129
Dee, Leonora, made governess to, by George III, **36**. 245n
—— to be governess to, **36**. 247
descendant of both HW and George I, **25**. 248
Du Deffand, Mme, inquires about, **6**. 328, **7**. 130, 177
father dotes on, **24**. 86
father essential to welfare and happiness of, **24**. 329
father may be amused by, **24**. 306
father may take, to southern France, **24**. 76
father pleased with, **36**. 326
father's anxiety for, **34**. 246
father seeks provision for, **36**. 306, 307
father's plight may arouse sympathy for, **24**. 321
father to arouse pity for, to get more income, **36**. 102–3
father to supplicate George III for aid to, **36**. 110–11
George III demands provision for, **24**. 372, 376
godmother to Chatham Horace Churchill, **11**. 264
HW calls, 'a dear soul,' **24**. 302
HW dances minuet with, **33**. 46
HW discusses, with Cts of Albemarle, **31**. 172
HW kisses, **32**. 403
HW sees, at Gloucester House, **25**. 68
HW solicitous about, **36**. 107–8, 111–12
HW would be thanked by, were she not a 'fallen angel,' **36**. 116
Humphry's portrait of, at SH, **42**. 71n
Kingsgate not to be visited by, **33**. 24
lands at Dover to go to Gloucester House, **36**. 155
Leopold sees, **24**. 297
legitimacy of, might be questioned if her father applied to Parliament, **36**. 108
less pretty than she was, **24**. 332
Mann called on by, **24**. 297
—— to be called on by, **24**. 291
mother angers, by snatching off cap to show her hair, **24**. 297
mother consoled by, **36**. 330
mother's concern for, **33**. 36
mother's 'evil representations' to, **36**. 244n
mother would have trouble travelling with, if father died, **24**. 326
Princesses to be visited by, at Kew, **36**. 329
Ranelagh visited by, **25**. 68
recovers from inoculation, **24**. 86
regards herself as grown up, **36**. 155
royalty of, acknowledged, **32**. 118
'sauciness' of, **36**. 324
seventh birthday of, **29**. 47
to be inoculated, **24**. 82
'Tonton' invited by, to Pavilions, **33**. 276
Wales, Ps of, will enliven, **36**. 330

Σοφια Θεηλατος Σολομων. *See under* Cooke, William

Sophia Theresa (1751–1835), m. (1772) Joachim Egon, Landgrave of Fürstenberg:
husband's fondness for, **11**. 133

Sophia Wilhelmina, Dutch ship:
Feilding captures, **25**. 3n

Sophie Karoline (1737–1817) of Brunswick-Wolfenbüttel, m. (1759) Friedrich Wilhelm, Margrave of Brandenburg-Bayreuth:
(?) George III may wed, **20**. 494

Sophie-Philippine-Élisabeth-Justine (1734–82), dau. of Louis XV; 'Madame Sophie':
announcement to, of coming presentation of Comtesse du Barry, **4**. 191, 192
ball at Versailles attended by, **32**. 255
Beauvilliers scratched by, from party list, **23**. 115–16
Boisgelin, Comtesse de, tells anecdote about, **7**. 121
Choisy visited by, **6**. 50, 55
Du Barry, Comtesse, to be presented to, **4**. 191–2, **23**. 78
English might reduce, to shift and no rouge, **37**. 535
expense of coffee and rouge for, **20**. 500
father nursed by, though she had never had smallpox, **6**. 50, **24**. 1–2
HW describes, **35**. 113
HW not spoken to by, at Versailles, **39**. 14
HW presented to, **7**. 266
HW sees, dine, at Versailles, **7**. 330, **10**. 292
health of: smallpox, **6**. 55, 57, **24**. 13; smallpox cured, **6**. 60, **24**. 13, 19
Hertford, Cts of, well received by, **38**. 261
household of, **4**. 442
Louis XVI to see, at Compiègne, **6**. 60
Marie-Antoinette governed by, **23**. 321
(?) Marie-Josèphe's funeral oration attended by, **7**. 318
meals of, public spectacles, **10**. 292
mother not addressed by, across father at dinner, **20**. 340
stiff, **38**. 221
well-behaved, **38**. 218

Sophocles (ca 496–ca 406 B.C.):
Addison's prologues mention, **33**. 553
Chatterton's poems imply a knowledge of, **16**. 362
Electra and *Œdipus* by, lack Shakespeare's buffoons, **41**. 153
Elfrida singers as unintelligible as choruses of, **28**. 109
Glover compares Van der Does to, **13**. 197
Homer's 'bantling,' **29**. 169
Philoctète, La Harpe's translation of, **7**. 236

'Sophy,' HW's cat:
'Luna's' gifts envied by, **35**. 86

Soprapporta; soprapporte:
Mann offers HW views of Florence for, **23**. 275, 287–8

'Soquxkin soqubut':
Japanese term for 'heart,' **19**. 308

Sora, Duca di. *See* Boncompagni, Gaetano (1707–77)

Sora, Duchessa di. *See* Boncompagni, Maria (1686–1745)

Sora (Italy):
Francis III occupies, **18**. 438

Sorans, Comtesse de. *See* Cléron, Marie-Anne-Victoire de

Soranus (fl. 2d century) of Ephesus; physician:
Cocchi publishes Greek and Latin versions of, **20**. 34n

Sorba, Mlle:
brother of, dies, **5**. 159
Louis XV gives pension to, **5**. 170

Sorba, Agostino Paolo Domenico (1715–71), Marchese; Genoese minister to France:
born at Paris, **23**. 363
Choiseul instigated by, to invade Corsica, **23**. 363
death of, **5**. 159, **23**. 363
Genoa proposes sending, to England to congratulate George III, **21**. 509
—— told by, of French withdrawal from Corsican ports, **22**. 536
social relations of, in Paris, *see under entries ante* 8. 516

Sorba, Giambattista (d. 1738), Genoese diplomatist; chargé d'affaires at Paris:
son of, **23**. 363

Sorba, Julie-Thérèse-Mélanie (d. 1784):
(?) brother of, dies, **5**. 159
(?) Louis XV gives pension to, **5**. 170

Sorbe. *See* Sorba

Sorbonne, la, at Paris:
HW visits, **7**. 264
Marmontel persecuted by, **8**. 132, 150
——'s *Bélisaire* condemned by, **8**. 132
Richelieu's tomb at, **13**. 165, **39**. 201
Syndic of, invoked by Voltaire, **8**. 152
'Trajan' flays, **8**. 151
verses satirize, **4**. 454
Voltaire ignored by, **7**. 36

Sore foot:
occurrence of, **9**. 83

Sorel, Agnès (1422–50), Charles VII's favourite:
Doumenil has portrait of, **7**. 313
Hôtel de Bouillon has portrait of, **7**. 317

Sore leg:
occurrences of, **18**. 139, **24**. 118, 480, **37**. 428, 429

Sore mouth:
occurrence of, **18**. 148, **21**. 543

Sore throat:
epidemic of, in England, **9**. 244, 271–2, 275, 287, **17**. 398n, **21**. 312, 362, 369, 416
HW jokes about, **10**. 262
HW on, **1**. 271
occurrences of, **9**. 198, 244, 271–2, 275, 287, **10**. 26, 80, **13**. 197, **32**. 27, 139, **33**. 95, **37**. 474, **38**. 58n, 462, **39**. 289

[Sore throat, *continued*]
Wilmot cures, by lancing, **21.** 369
Sorgental. *See* Görgenthal
Sorhouet, ——: *Correspondance secrète de. See* Pidansat de Mairobert, Mathieu-François: *Suite de correspondance . . .*
Soria, Giovanni Battista (1581–1651):
church of S. Carlo ai Catinari built by, **14** 20n
Soriano (Italy):
earthquake account mentions, **25.** 376
Sorrel:
sauces of, **19.** 357n
Sortes Virgilianæ:
Dashwood mentioned in, **17.** 247n
HW and others draw, at Florence, **10.** 5
HW quotes, **37.** 79
Mann's opinion of, **17.** 108
Sortes Walpolianæ:
Chute designates HW's discoveries by serendipity as, **20.** 407, 415
HW gives instance of, **35.** 163
Sotelte:
Cole asks meaning of, **1.** 137
HW on, **1.** 144
See also Sotilties *below*
Sotheby, William (d. 1766), Col.:
death of, **7.** 397
Sotheby's (auctioneers):
sales at, **36.** 315
Sotilties:
for Robert de Winchelsea's enthronement, **16.** 47
See also *Sotelte* above
Sotomayor, Marqués de. *See* Masones de Lima y Sotomayor, Don Jaime
Soubise, Maréchal de. *See* Rohan, Charles de (1715–87)
Soubise ('Soubize'), Prince de. *See* Rohan, Charles de (1715–87); Rohan, François de (1631–1712)
Soubise, Princesse de. *See* Rohan-Chabot, Anne-Julie de (1648–1709); Hesse-Rheinfels, Anna Viktoria Maria Christina von (1728–92)
Soubise, Hôtel de, at Paris:
fête at, **7.** 457
HW visits, **7.** 283, **31.** 87
Soufflot, ——:
social relations of, with Mme Geoffrin, **7.** 291, 304
'Souillard,' Louis XI's dog:
bons mots by, **33.** 385–6
Soul, the:
Gray's reflections on, **14.** 188
immortality of, **32.** 79–83
Mawhood disputes about, **39.** 250
Stosch's witticisms on, **17.** 404
transmigration of, **32.** 79–83
Soup; soups:
and biscuits, for breakfast, **39.** 447
at Florentine dinner, **19.** 357
beef, for royal family, **38.** 434

Du Deffand, Mme, takes, **4.** 393, **6.** 219, 343, **7.** 129, 243, 245
—— to take, **3.** 281
four, at Bns Athenry's supper, **37.** 442
HW takes, scalding hot, **31.** 93
Mann takes, at dinner, **17.** 104
Marie-Antoinette takes basin of, **31.** 372n
radish, ordered by abbé for HW and Gray, **13.** 181
scraps of paper, with holy words, made into, **20.** 430
Soup plates:
from Chelsea china set, **43.** 278
Sourches, Comte de. *See* Du Bouchet, Jean-Louis (1750–ca 1782); Du Bouchet, Louis–Hilaire (1716–88)
Sourches, Comtesse de. *See* Le Voyer, Louise-Françoise; Riquet de Caraman, Marie-Anne-Antoinette de (1757–1846)
Sourches, Marquis de. *See* Du Bouchet, Louis
Sourches, Vicomte de. *See* Du Bouchet, Jean-Louis
Sourches, Vicomtesse de. *See* Riquet de Caraman, Marie-Anne-Antoinette de
Sourdière. *See* Meulan de la Sourdière
Sourdine:
Brown marches to, **18.** 488
Sousfermiers:
France abolishes, **20.** 500
South, Mrs. *See* Mann, Margaret
Southacre, Norfolk:
Harsick of, **1.** 33n
South America:
Charles III suspects England of designs on, **25.** 339n
revolts in: rumoured, **36.** 277; would distract Spain from Gibraltar, **25.** 292
Spain and Portugal fight over colonies in, **6.** 339n, **24.** 262n
Southampton, Bn. *See* Fitzroy, Charles (1737–97); Fitzroy, Hon. George Ferdinand (1761–1810)
Southampton, Bns. *See* Keppel, Laura (1765–98); Warren, Anne (d. 1807)
Southampton, Cts of. *See* Leigh, Elizabeth (living, 1654); Pulteney, Anne (1663–1746); Vernon, Elizabeth (living, 1655)
Southampton, D. of. *See* Fitzroy, Charles (1662–1730)
Southampton, E. of:
Grafton, D. of, may inherit title of, **24.** 5
See also Fitzroy, William (1698–1774); Fitzwilliam, Sir William (ca 1490–1542); Wriothesley, Henry (1573–1624); Wriothesley, Thomas (1607–67)
Southampton, Hants:
Bentley's books to go to, **35.** 217
Berkeley sails from, to conquer France, **35.** 102
Campbell dies at, **7.** 63n
Chamier, Mrs, dies at, **4.** 439n
coach to, from London, **35.** 161

Conway writes from, 37. 519–20
Cumberland, D. and Ds of, go to country seat near, 33. 56n
Gray and Chute visit, 14. 83
HW might confuse, with Durham, 37. 271
Hessian troops land at, 20. 526n
Isenburg astonished by tide at, 20. 563
mob at, murders Bp Molyneux, 14. 76
Ossory, Cts of, at, 33. 47, 68
—— sees Stuart at, 33. 79n
—— suggests air of, for HW, 33. 124
sea-baths at, 35. 251
visitors to: Chute, 14. 83, 35. 249, 250–1; Gray, 14. 83; HW, 35. 249, 250–1, 37. 407; Ossorys, 33. 38n, 47, 68, 79n; Stuart, 33. 79n
wagon to, from London, 35. 204, 205
Whithed's re-election in, 19. 420n
Southampton, English ship:
Caroline Matilda sails on, to Stade, 23. 409n
French and Spanish fleets chase, 28. 457
(?) French and Spanish fleets chase, into Plymouth, 24. 506
Southampton family:
portraits of, brought from Place House, Titchfield, to Bulstrode Park, 10. 102
Southampton Row, London:
Gray occasionally lodges in, 14. 184n
—— writes from, 14. 117
Southampton St, London:
Abingdon, Mrs, lives in, 41. 215
South Audley St, London:
Boscawen, Mrs, lives in, 32. 335n
Bradshaw dies in, 32. 214n
Bute's house in, 12. 42–3n, 21. 531n, 23. 312n
Chesterfield's house in, 20. 302n, 23. 471n
Johnston, Lady Cecilia, in, 11. 214n, 34. 142n
Luttrell's house in, 23. 105n
Portuguese king buys house in, for embassy, 20. 164n
Pye, Mrs, dies in, 43. 63
Wood, Mrs, writes from, 41. 245, 249
South Barrow, Kent:
Reynolds's house at, 23. 205n
South Carolina, Governor of. *See* Campbell, Lord William (ca 1732–78); Lyttelton, William Henry (1724–1808); Montagu, Lord Charles Greville (1741–84); Pownall, Thomas (1722–1805)
South Carolina:
Campbells of, 6. 158n
Cherokee chiefs sail in, 10. 36n
English forces in, 19. 69n
Hoyland unable to take living in, 29. 267
Leigh, chief justice of, 20. 108n
See also under Carolina, North and South
'Southcoat.' *See* Southcote
Southcote, Sir Edward (d. ca 1751–8):
house of, near Witham, Essex, 9. 93
Roman Catholic, 9. 93
Southcote, Philip (d. 1758):
Brown, Lancelot, borrows landscaping ideas from, 9. 121

Conway and wife to visit, at Woburn Farm, 37. 374
forced to close garden to visitors, 2. 275
house of: 9. 71; compared with SH, 9. 169
marriage of, 34. 258
Sayer's parsonage improved by, 9. 93
Townshend, Vcts, jokes about wife's arrangements with, 30. 11
Woburn Farm of, 1. 44, 35. 71, 237
Southcote, Mrs Philip. *See* Andrews, Bridget
Southcote, Thomas, O.S.B.:
Fleury procures abbey for, at request of Horatio Walpole (1678–1757), 9. 116
Pope, Alexander, friend of, 9. 116
South Downs:
Park Place's view of, 39. 550
Southern continent:
necessity of, postulated, 35. 383
Southerne, Thomas (1660–1746), dramatist:
agreeable, despite failing memory, 13. *107*
Fatal Marriage, The, by: 13. 107; Garrick alters, 33. 359n; Porter, Mrs, plays 'Isabella' in, 33. 360n; worthy, in some parts, of a Shakespeare disciple, 41. 374
Gray a neighbour of, 13. *107*
HW prefers tragic scenes in *The Fatal Marriage* and *Oroonoko* by, to Otway's plays, 41. 290
Isabella by, acted by Mrs Siddons, 11. 163n, 176n
Oroonoko by: 13. 107; HW paraphrases, 31. 7; 'Imoinda' in, 19. 18; Sessaracoa overcome with emotion on seeing, 20. 40n; worthy, in parts, of a Shakespeare disciple, 41. 374
Southesk, Cts of. *See* Hamilton, Lady Anna *or* Anne
Southey, Robert (1774–1843):
Bedford, Grosvenor Charles, friend of, 42. 492
Southgate, Rev. Richard (1729–95), numismatist; official at British Museum:
death of, 16. 325
(?) Pinkerton hopes to succeed, 42. 212n
Southgate, Middlesex:
Heckstetter of, 14. 200n
Nicoll, Miss, to go to, 14. 228
Minchenden House at, 14. 193n
South Lynn:
orders of friars in, 15. 2n
South Pole:
horrible metropolis may rise near, 24. 154
South Scotland Yard, Whitehall, London:
Great Wardrobe in, 15. 117n
South Sea Bubble:
East India Co. speculation comparable to, 22. 498, 23. 467
South Sea Co.:
Burrell, Peter, sub-governor of, 19. 17n
Conway's stock in, 37. 166n
English-Spanish negotiations over, 20. 197–8
Goosetree, solicitor to, 17. 272n
governor of, *see* Bristow, John; Burrell, Peter

[South Sea Co., *continued*]
Knight, cashier of, **19**. 419n, **24**. 174n
Montagu, Ds of, has bonds of, **9**. 95
Sawbridge involved in collapse of, **28**. 372
Shuttleworth, clerk of, **19**. 76n
stock of, **21**. 497n, 504n, **22**. 38n, 74n, 81n
Walpole, Sir Robert, profits by, **42**. 81
South Sea House:
Chute's fortune may bring him to, **35**. 86
hours for payment at, altered, **35**. 156
South Stoneham, Hants:
Sloane of, **12**. 146n
South St, Grosvenor Sq., London:
Wood, Mrs, writes from, **41**. 307, 317
South Uist, Scotland:
Coradale in, **37**. 252
Southwark, London:
Astley establishes amphitheatre at, for riding and rope-dancing, **25**. 451n
banks and brothels in, **1**. 137–8
East India Co. stores tea in, **25**. 577–8
election in, won by Polhill, **39**. 197n
fair at, Goldsmith's comic muse from, **32**. 108
fire in, **25**. 577–8, **33**. 190
Forth, Samuel, brewer in, **20**. 556n
Gordon rioters start fires in, **25**. 57, **33**. 190
HW not in, before 1740, **11**. 212
HW will not pack up until the French are in, **20**. 469
Horseshoe Inn in, **23**. 20n
Hume, M.P. for, dies, **7**. 396
Parliamentary members instructed by electors of, **23**. 98n
rioting in, **39**. 197
slaughter in, during Gordon riots, **33**. 192
southward expansion of, **24**. 228
Southwell, Betty:
Bristol, Cts of, teased by, about Col. Cotton, **34**. 260
wit of, **34**. 260
Southwell, Edward (1705–55), M.P.:
motion against Sir Robert Walpole opposed by, **37**. 90
wife of, **14**. 119n
Southwell, Edward (1738–77), 20th Bn Clifford, 1776:
King's Weston, seat of, **1**. 172
(?) SH to be visited by, **14**. 119
Southwell, Mrs Edward. *See* Watson, Hon. Catherine (d. 1765)
Southwell, Hon. Frances (b. 1708), and Hon. Lucia (b. 1710):
flee to London from Lumley's dinner at Hampstead, **9**. 367
Southwell, Thomas (1698–1766), 2d Bn Southwell, 1720:
Payba claims, extorted notes from him, **20**. 288n
Southwell, Notts:
Kaye, prebendary of, **29**. 40n
Southwick, Hants:
Henry VI married at, **14**. 70

Margaret of Anjou at, **14**. 72, 74
priory of, **14**. 76
Southwick Park, Hants, Whithed's seat:
burns down, **20**. 185
HW was to have gothicized, **20**. 185
Thistlethwayte of, **14**. 49n
Whithed of, **14**. 18n
Southwold, Suffolk:
militia at, clash with smugglers, **39**. 304n
Soutter. *See* Sauveterre
'Souvenir':
Luxembourg, Mme de, gives, to Shuvalov, **6**. 415
Souvré ('Souvray'), Marquis de. *See* Le Tellier, François-Louis (1704–67)
Souvré, Marquise de. *See* Sailly, Félicité de
Souza Coutinho, Mme de. *See* Montboissier-Beaufort-Canillac, Louise-Agnès-Élisabeth de
Souza Coutinho, Dom Vicente de (ca 1726–92), Portuguese minister (1763–74) and ambassador (1774–92) to France:
birds imported by, **5**. 129
Choiseul, Duchesse de, fond of, **3**. 392
Du Deffand, Mme, gets account from, of attack on José I, **4**. 328–9
—— receives snuff from, **4**. 55, 64
Gennevilliers visited by, **7**. 328
marriage of, **5**. 342
Mirepoix, Mme de, yields house to, **5**. 105
Œiras writes to, of attack on José I, **4**. 328–9
social relations of, in Paris, *see* index entries *ante* **8**. 517
Sovrano, Emanuel, Capt.:
captured at Velletri, **18**. 493
Sovuter. *See* Sauveterre
Sow:
Conway's, given to HW, pregnant, **37**. 344, 347, 349
'Sow and puggis':
HW's reference to, **35**. 41
Sowden, Rev. Benjamin (d. ca 1779), Presbyterian clergyman 1748–ca 1779 at Rotterdam:
Montagu, Lady Mary Wortley, entrusts MSS to, **22**. 84
Sowle, Marmaduke (d. 1766), army officer:
wounded and captured at Roucour, **30**. 108
Soyecourt, Hôtel de, at Paris:
Fuentes and Aranda occupy, **5**. 405–6
Fuentes at, **4**. 367n
Soyres, François de (d. 1807):
Bauffremont recommended, to HW and D. of Richmond, **25**. 518
Edgcumbe travels with, **25**. 518, 551n
English well spoken and written by, **25**. 519
HW mentions, **12**. 270n
HW recommends, **25**. *518*–19, 551n
HW told by, from Florence, that Mann is better, **25**. 551
Nivernais's *Jardins modernes* given to, **12**. 259
youngish French Protestant, of good family, who left the army, **25**. 518

Sozomen (Hermias Sozomenus Salamenes) (fl. 400–50), historian:
Gibbon cites, 29. 114–15

Spa (Germany):
accounts from, of D. of Devonshire's illness, 40. 364, 43. 380n
Bath, Cts of, to visit, 20. 116n
Beauvau not to visit, 7. 453
Carteret (Granville) ordered by physicians to go to, 19. 26
Cholmondeley and wife to go to, 11. 255
Cholmondeley to visit, 23. 316
Cumberland, D. and Ds of, to go to, 25. 645
Devonshire, D. of, may go to, 38. 422
Grandison, Lady, dies at, 33. 334
HW mentions, 10. 282
HW recommends, for Cts of Hertford, 38. 169
Hertford, Cts of, refuses to visit, 31. 27
Holland, Bn and Bns, to visit, 22. 129n
Mirepoix, Duc and Duchesse de, leave London for, 20. 116n
Orlov to visit, 24. 113
Pitt, Anne, to visit, 20. 116n
Poyntz, Mrs, to visit, 22. 164
views of, on snuff-box, 36. 113
visitors to: Ancaster, Ds of, 11. 255; Bath, E. of, 20. 80; Boufflers, Comtesse Amélie de, 7. 235, 239; Boufflers, Comtesse de, 7. 230, 235, 239, 459, 461, 11. 76n; Bucquoy, Gräfin, 4. 460; Bunbury, Lady Sarah, 3. 314; Cardigan, Cts of, 17. 141; Carlisle, 30. 258; Churchills, 6. 207, 36. 113; Coke, Lady Mary, 33. 293n; Craufurd, 3. 311, 338, 5. 267, 268, 32. 250–1; Cumberland, D. and Ds of, 32. 386n; Damer, Mrs, 7. 160, 33. 71n; Devonshire, D. of, 10. 133, 38. 429, 444–5, 447, 40. 364, 43. 380; Drogheda, Cts of, 39. 315; Du Barrys, 33. 71n; Fifes, 31. 65; Fox, Henry, 30. 171; Gloucester, D. and Ds of, 33. 336; Greville, 5. 351, 362; Greville, Mrs, 5. 362; Guéménée, Princesse de, 39. 315; Gustav III, 7. 230, 235, 239; Harrington, 39. 269n; Holland, Bn and Bns, 22. 129n; La Marck, Comtesse de, 7. 239; Lloyd, Rachel, 4. 116; Lyttelton, Charles, 40. 82; Montagu, Lady Mary Wortley, 17. 141n; Montesson, Marquise de, 5. 356; Pitt, Anne, 24. 405; Rice, 33. 71n; Rodney, 33. 495; Spencer, Lady, 5. 351, 362, 6. 488, 22. 173; Spencers, 6. 488, 7. 177n; Stanhope, Lady Harriet, 39. 269n; (?) Usson, Comtesse d', 7. 239
York, D. of, to visit sister at, 22. 524

'Spaccatavola' (dancer):
Pantolomina compared with, 19. 356

Spada, ——:
York, D. of, greeted by, at Bologna, 22. 232n

Spada, 'Conte' or 'Marquis':
Young Pretender accompanied by, at Florence, 23. 225n, 229
—— sends, to Leopold, 25. 102

Spada, Leonello (1576–1622):
paintings by, 19. 314n

Spade; spades:
England sends, to Portugal, 20. 512n

Spa Fields:
Huntingdon, Cts of, dies at, 11. 297n

Spagna, Piazza di, at Rome:
Acquaviva considers, under his jurisdiction, 19. 113–14
capitano della, see Capitano
miquelets on guard in, 19. 114n

Spagnolet; Spagnoletto. See Ribera, José de

Spaight, ——, merchant of Carrickfergus:
Thurot captures, 21. 376

Spaight, Mary, m. (1764) Francis Morice:
husband of, 13. 33n

Spain, Infant of. See Philip, Don

Spain, K. of. See Charles II (1661–1700); Charles III (1716–88); Charles IV (1748–1819); Charles V (1500–58); Ferdinand V (1452–1516) of Aragon; Ferdinand VI (1713–59); Philip II (1527–98); Philip III (1578–1621); Philip IV (1605–65); Philip V (1683–1746)

Spain, Q. of. See Bourbon d'Orléans, Louise-Élisabeth de (1709–42); Elizabeth (1545–68) of Valois; Elizabeth (Farnese) (1692–1766); Louisa Maria Theresa (1751–1819); Maria Amalia (1724–60); Maria Anna (1635–96); Maria Barbara (1711–58); Marie-Louise-Gabrielle (1688–1714)

Spain:
Acquaviva is 'protector' of, at Rome, 19. 339n
admiral of, Du Chaffault refuses precedence to, 24. 528
Admiralty, English, gets islands missed by, 28. 94
Aix treaty awaits accession of, 19. 485
Aix treaty benefits, 37. 284–5
Aix treaty not yet signed by, 19. 511
Aix treaty preliminaries do not mention, 19. 480
Algerian hostilities of, 24. 121–2, 179, 25. 26, 415–16, 32. 239n
Alhambra in, 42. 53
allodials claimed by, 18. 176
ambassadors from and to, see under Ambassador
ambassador's wife from, 9. 10
ambassador to, not yet appointed, 22. 444
America may get underhand aid from, 24. 139, 271, 366, 459
American conquests of, less cruel than slave trade, 20. 126
America now a hindrance instead of a help to England in fighting, 24. 485
American policy of, announced by Almodóvar, 33. 60
Americans helped by gold from, 33. 199
Aranjuez treaty between Austria, Sardinia, and, 20. 294n

[Spain, *continued*]

armada of: 'call of sergeants' of the time of, **10.** 259; Elizabeth's medal on defeat of, **21.** 357; Gibraltar defeat of, **35.** 367; tapestry in House of Lords depicts, **23.** 242

armaments said to be prepared by, **24.** 98

army camp of, at San Roque, pestiferous, **25.** 59

army of: Abruzzo approached by, **18.** 438; Acquaviva sends Roman recruits to, **18.** 542; advance of, reported from Rome, **19.** 15; Alessandria the theatre of, **19.** 36, 75, 120, 137, 226; Ambrose harasses, **19.** 37; ammunition and artillery received by, despite English fleet, **18.** 296; Apremont and other officers captured by, **18.** 153–4; Aqui approached by, **19.** 225; Aquila reached by, **17.** 265; Arezzo approached by, **17.** 289, 341, 350; Asti captured from, **19.** 226; at Cartagena may threaten Gibraltar, **23.** 261; at Presidii, lack horses, **17.** 262; at Rome, **18.** 531–4; Austrians defeat, at Campo Santo, **18.** 161, 163–5, 312; Austrians may resist, in Lombardy, **23.** 474; Austrians try to cut off, **18.** 66; Barcelona the embarkation point of, **17.** 182, 192, 290, 312, 361, **18.** 106; Birtles tells Haddock of approach of, **17.** 305–6; Bologna the theatre of, **17.** 289, 341, 350, 432, **18.** 45, 55, 58, 76, 99, 154, 175, 199; Bomporto the theatre of, **18.** 151, 189; Botta attacks, **19.** 291; Braitwitz prepares order of battle of, **18.** 127n; Burgoyne checks, **38.** 178; called 'Ligur-Napolispani,' **19.** 82; campaign of, compared to country dances, **18.** 55; cannon captured by, **19.** 119–20; Castro and Ronciglione may be winter station of, **17.** 204; Charles III to send, to son, **21.** 335; Charles Emmanuel III attacks, near river Lambro, **19.** 278–9; Charles Emmanuel III deters, from invading Tuscany, **18.** 58; Charles Emmanuel III dislodged by, from Monte Castello and the Tanaro, **19.** 120; Charles Emmanuel III may resist, in Lombardy, **17.** 266; Charles Emmanuel III not alarmed by junction of, **19.** 47; Charles Emmanuel III said to have defeated, on the Var, **18.** 466; Charles Emmanuel III's news intercepted by, **19.** 190; Charles Emmanuel III to pursue, **19.** 292; Colligara reached by, **18.** 151; convoys of, to Italy, **17.** 323, 350; courier robbed by, **18.** 515–16; couriers may be intercepted by, **19.** 156, 163–4; Cuneo the theatre of, **18.** 519; deserters from, **17.** 349, 379, 427, 432, 455, 464, **18.** 216, 412, 454, **19.** 36, 231; Eliott defeats, at Gibraltar, **35.** 367; Elizabeth Farnese's appointments to, insane, **18.** 135; Empoli the theatre of, **17.** 341; encamped near Prati della Masone, **17.** 424; English at Leghorn to be respected by, **17.** 215; English fleet does not keep, from Italy, **19.** 9; Europe Point said to be occupied by,

25. 324; expects reinforcements from Majorca and Barcelona, **18.** 106; Faenza the theatre of, **18.** 175; Fano the theatre of, **18.** 7, 45, 55, 335, 339, 412; Farlo to be entered by, **18.** 45; Ferrara the theatre of, **17.** 464, 500: Fleury may permit, to invade Tuscany, **17.** 205, **18.** 42; Florence's gates to be passed by, **17.** 342; Florence threatened by, **17.** 342, 349, 365, **35.** 10, 11, 13–14, 15, 22, 25; Foligno the theatre of, **17.** 265, 289, **18.** 18, 27, 42, 76, 174, 200, 331, 529, 542, **19.** 15; Forlimpopoli the theatre of, **18.** 257; fortifies itself at Codogno and Lodi, **19.** 276n; Fossombrone the theatre of, **18.** 18; France forbids, to enter Tuscany, **17.** 197–8, 214, **19.** 7; France to give orders to, **17.** 265; Francis I orders Braitwitz to keep, out of Tuscany, **18.** 66, 127, 134; Francis III of Modena commands, **18.** 222, 228, 235; French troops withdrawn from, **19.** 8; Garfagnano may be invaded by, **19.** 65; Genoa abandoned and plundered by, **19.** 305–6; Genoa aids, **19.** 64–5; Genoa approached by, **18.** 454, 554, 559, **19.** 35, 36, 47, 292, **23.** 469; Genoa invaded by, **19.** 40, 51, 58; Genoese and Neapolitan barks thought to supply, **19.** 56–7; Genoese provisions for, **19.** 266; German cavalry to cut off, from Ferrara, **19.** 197; German deserters bribed by, **18.** 243; German troops oppose, **18.** 200, 267; Gibraltar besieged by, *see under* Gibraltar; Gibraltar threatened by, **21.** 20, **23.** 261; Imola the theatre of, **17.** 289, **18.** 175; infantry of, outnumbers Lobkowitz's, **18.** 312; invalids of, *see under* Invalid; Irish deserters give news of, **18.** 432; Italy to be invaded by, **40.** 36; kettle drums captured by, **18.** 161, 189; La Cattolica the theatre of, **18.** 58, 200, 331; large cannon lacked by, **18.** 151; Leghorn might be menaced by, **17.** 196, 212, **18.** 77; Licanians captured by, **18.** 459–60; lives on biscuits, **19.** 35; Loano reached by, **19.** 559; Lobkowitz has insufficiently crushed, **18.** 359; Lobkowitz may be pursued by, **18.** 508; Lobkowitz pursued by, near Rome, **18.** 530–4; Lobkowitz pursues, **18.** 412–13; Lobkowitz's advance awaited by, **18.** 335; Lobkowitz said to defeat, **37.** 160; Lobkowitz to drive, to Naples or Pesaro, **18.** 405; Lodi pillaged by, **19.** 267, 268–9; Lombardy may be invaded by, **17.** 180, 192, 198, 204, 208, 213, 214, 219, 229, 261, 266, 311, 323, 341, 349, **18.** 45, 76, 547, **19.** 22, 278, 367; Lucca approached by, **19.** 35; Madrid to send orders to, **17.** 265–6; Maillebois joins, at Piacenza, **19.** 263n, 266; Majorca said to be base of, against Minorca, **23.** 261; Mann discusses, with Braitwitz, **17.** 182; Maria Theresa's hussars pursue, **18.** 199; Martin demands that Charles of Naples withdraw troops from, **18.** 15, **21.** 564; Massa the theatre of, **17.**

314, 323; Mathews awaits, **18**. 106; Mathews to protect Nice against, **18**. 312; Mathews wants Charles Emmanuel III to coop up, in Tuscany, **18**. 108; may be cut off from Naples, **17**. 500; may be transported from Antibes to Genoa, **23**. 469; may embark at Naples, **19**. 410; may retire to Naples, **18**. 325, 397–8; Milan attempt abandoned by, **19**. 225; Milan may be captured by, **17**. 198, **19**. 119; miquelets in, **17**. 432, **18**. 101; Miranda besieged by, **22**. 38; Mirandola besieged by, **17**. 489; Modena besieged by, **17**. 455, 464, 465; Modena threatened by, **17**. 226, 379, 424, **19**. 22, 30, 65, 156; money shortage prevents Traun from marching against, **18**. 257; Montale the theatre of, **19**. 30; Nádasdy pursues, **19**. 244; Naples may not receive, **18**. 412–13; Naples receives troops from, **19**. 367; Neapolitans may join, **17**. 198, 265, 350, **18**. 10; Neapolitans separated from, **18**. 15, 66; near Rome, **18**. 530–4, 546; Nice may be traversed by, **18**. 395, 461; Nice reached by, **19**. 9; Novi the theatre of, **19**. 58; officers of, devout, **17**. 427; Oneglia the theatre of, **18**. 454, 459, 461; Orbetello the theatre of, **17**. 178, 192, 198, 204, 214, 226, 239, 262, 265, 289, 350, 389, **18**. 7, 16, 27, 243, 253, **19**. 55; Pallavicini escaped by, **19**. 244; Pallavicini exposes Milan to, **19**. 120; Panaro valley the theatre of, **17**. 432, 455, 464, 472, 489, **18**. 45, 55, 76, 151, 154, 164–5, 196, 197, **19**. 30, 35; Papal states threatened by, **18**. 444; Papal states traversed by, **17**. 261, 323; Parma captured from, **19**. 244, 245; Parma threatened by, **17**. 198, 204, 214, **18**. 454, **19**. 22; 'patrimoine de St-Pierre' reached by, **18**. 546; Pavia may be invaded by, **19**. 41; Perugia the theatre of, **18**. 42, 76, 542, **19**. 11, 15; Pesaro the theatre of, **17**. 379, **18**. 76, 174, 335, 339, 412, 419; Philip, Don, to command, at Nice, **18**. 547; Philip, Don, to join, in, **19**. 47; Piacenza casualties of, **40**. 56–7; Piacenza occupied by, **19**. 156, 258, 262, 266, 268, 275, 276; Piacenza threatened by, **17**. 198, 204, 214; Pironi confined by, **18**. 253, 257; Po controlled by, **19**. 276; Pontremoli and the Lunigiana threatened by, **17**. 289, **18**. 76, **19**. 35, 245; Presidii the theatre of, **17**. 192, 262, **18**. 27, 325, 547, **19**. 410; provisions stored by, in the Lunigiana and Tuscany, **19**. 10; Rimini the theatre of, **17**. 379, **18**. 13, 16, 199, 216, 243, 253, 331, **19**. 36; Ripalta captured from, **19**. 262; Riviera di Ponente plundered by, **19**. 306; Ronciglione occupied by, **18**. 527; St Philip's on Minorca to be attacked by, **25**. 229; St Philip's to be stormed by prisoners released for, **25**. 180; San Giovanni the theatre of, **18**. 154; San Lazaro (Piacenza) defeat of, **19**. 265–7, 274; San Roque encampment of, **25**. 59,

72; San Stefano the theatre of, **17**. 197; Sardinians may pursue, **18**. 199–200; Sardinians said to defeat, at Oneglia, **37**. 159–60; Sarzana threatened by, **17**. 314; Savoy campaign of, to decide Neapolitan plans, **18**. 302; Seravalle the theatre of, **19**. 84, 292; Sestri the theatre of, **19**. 40; Sezi reached by, **19**. 226; sickly, at Minorca, **25**. 197; Sienese approach to Tuscany blocked by, **17**. 289; Sinigaglia the theatre of, **18**. 16, 76; Spanish and Neapolitan letters to, captured, **18**. 85–6; Spezia the theatre of, **17**. 182, 198, 206, 262, 289, 314, 323, 350, **18**. 405, 413; standards captured by, **18**. 189, **19**. 119; supplies stored for, at Leghorn, **19**. 10; taxes levied by, in Italy, **18**. 344; tied up at Gibraltar, **25**. 345; to receive artillery by way of Adriatic, **19**. 30; Tortona the theatre of, **19**. 36, 41, 75, 82, 267, 291–2; transports hired by, at Genoa and Leghorn, **19**. 304; Traun may dislodge, **18**. 253, 271; Traun's nephews captured by, **18**. 154; Traun's troops too weak to attack, **18**. 127; Traun tells Braitwitz not to fight, **18**. 295; Turin threatened by, **19**. 120; Tuscan area may be passed by, **17**. 226, 341, **19**. 35, 58, 65; Tuscan negotiations with, **17**. 228; Tuscans may aid, **19**. 10–11, 31; Tuscany said by Fleury to be safe from, **17**. 197–8, 205; Valenza may be captured by, **19**. 120, 137; Velletri fortified by, **18**. 454; Velluti to protest against route of, **17**. 341; victories of, in Lombardy, **19**. 119–20; 'victory' claimed by, **18**. 161; Villafranca captured by, **18**. 437; Villettes asks Mann to report progress of, **17**. 265; vineyards and olive trees destroyed by, **18**. 344n; Viterbo may be left by, to cross Tuscany to join Gages, **19**. 58; Viterbo the theatre of, **18**. 243, **19**. 55, 58; Viviani deserts to, **20**. 350

artillery of: at Algiers, **24**. 121–2; at Genoa, **18**. 244, 257; in Italy, **18**. 27, 296, **19**. 35–6, 147

Ascanio supports faction of, at Florence, **17**. 86–7

Assiento treaty with England to be renewed by, **19**. 480

Asturian mines in, **7**. 288, **35**. 349n

Austria guaranteed her European possessions by, **20**. 294n

Austrians may resist, in Lombardy, **23**. 474

Austria's war with, *see* War: Austrian-Spanish

bad taste discarded by, along with the Inquisition, **41**. 154

Banks tries to find islands not discovered by, **23**. 436

barks of, **17**. 262, 350, 433, **18**. 288

batteries of, *see under* Battery

Bavarian treaty with, reported, **17**. 183

Beauvau a grandee of, **19**. 1

Bedford, D. of, tells Fane that he cannot go to, **20**. 203

[Spain, *continued*]

bee-keeping in, **40.** 256–7

Benedict XIV acknowledges Francis I despite cabals of, **19.** 183

—— fears cabals of, **19.** 157–8

—— receives indemnity from, for right to appoint to its own benefices, **21.** 437

——'s advisers said to favour, **18.** 56

—— said to be betrayed to, by Valenti, **18.** 56, **19.** 492

—— threatens, with excommunication, **18.** 56, 344

'bombastly unsuccessful' in war, **25.** 338

Bourbons and Austria fought over, **21.** 199–200

bravado of, below par, **25.** 351

Brest fleet said to be off coast of, **19.** 274

Bristol, E. of, ambassador to, **21.** 166, 175, 190, 194–5

—— assembles servants for post at, **21.** 202

—— recalled from, **38.** 120

—— returns from, **21.** 548–9, 558

——'s demands upon, **21.** 563–4

—— treated by, with derision, **22.** 5

—— writes from, **10.** 224

cardinals fear exclusion by, at next papal Conclave, **22.** 387

cardinals from: awaited at Conclave, **23.** 95; reach Rome, **23.** 113

Cartagena should not have been left in hands of, **17.** 96

Castellar recalled to, **18.** 44

Castro and Ronciglione may be taken by, from papacy, **23.** 36, 45, 413

Catherine II's manifestos illiterate enough to be from, **22.** 71

cavalry of: captured on way to Havana, **38.** 169; convoy to bring, **17.** 323, 350; inferior to Lobkowitz's, **18.** 312; ruined, **35.** 51; to pass through Loreto to Fano, **18.** 45; to repass the Var, **19.** 51

Charles I's pictures in, Waddilove writes to Lort about, **16.** 179

Charles III behaved better at Naples than at, **21.** 560

—— displeases, **25.** 32

—— does not send couriers to, **18.** 486

——'s departure to, **21.** 318, 335, 363

—— to be king of, **21.** 264, 270, 275, 335

—— to observe neutrality when called to throne of, **21.** 271

Charles Emmanuel III may be lured by, from Maria Theresa, **17.** 312

—— urged by, to permit troops to pass, **17.** 145n

chess games formal in, **9.** 2

Chesterfield expects England and Ireland to be attacked by, **38.** 154–5

Choiseul's fall may displease, **23.** 259

Clement XIII 'carted' by, **23.** 32

—— relaxes Lenten rules for, **22.** 5

——'s disputes with, over Jesuit expulsion, **22.** 517–19, and *passim*

Clement XIV detaches Portugal from negotiations with, **23.** 221

—— may disappoint, **23.** 157

——'s negotiations with, over Jesuits, *see under* Jesuit

clergy of, in America, were compassionate, **28.** 315

conquests of, in New World, **28.** 175

consuls from and to, *see under* Consul

conundrum concerning, **12.** 266

corn shortages in, **22.** 206

Corsica may be ceded by, to Tuscany, **23.** 469n

Corsican relations with, **18.** 156

cortes's struggle in, **15.** 46

couriers from and to, *see under* Courier

Cours de l'Europe satirizes, **17.** 177

Court of: conceals fleet's destination, **25.** 173–4; Mann considers publication by, about Minorca, scurrilous, **25.** 188–9; memoirs of, **15.** 137; Montemar expected by, to relieve Modena, **17.** 501; neutrality said to be the policy of, **20.** 498, **24.** 463; tells Roman minister to disavow Young Pretender, **22.** 399; *see also under* Charles III; Ferdinand VI; Philip V

Craon accuses England of alliance with, **17.** 180

Cumberland's book on painters in, **29.** 225, 232

——'s mission to, a failure, **29.** 146

defeat of, at Gibraltar, attributed to faithless allies, **25.** 149

Del Campo sent gift plate by, to serve Q. Charlotte, **39.** 465n

'desolate abode of nobles and priests,' **28.** 412n

disarms, **5.** 66n, **23.** 297

dress of, **17.** 399

Du Châtelet draws, into attack on Falkland Islands, **23.** 258

Du Deffand, Mme, has no news of, **3.** 16

Dutch ships may be searched by, **18.** 116

Eliott's success against furious attack by, **25.** 325

Elizabeth Farnese fonder of Naples than of, **17.** 291

—— must be infuriated by defeats of, **18.** 331

Elizabeth of Russia's death should help England to defeat, **22.** 1

England again permitted by, to use Channel, **25.** 191

—— assured by, of pacific intentions, **21.** 541

—— captures quicksilver from, **24.** 543

—— denies right of search to, **19.** 255

—— disputes with: over Falkland Islands, **4.** 479, 482, 488, **5.** 16, **10.** 321n, **23.** 239–42, 245–6, 250–2, 255, 258, 359, **31.** 150, **35.** 340–1; over Honduras logwood and Manila ransom, **38.** 432

—— does not frighten, **21.** 78

—— does not know decision of, **24.** 467

—— excels, in avarice and cruelty, **23.** 400

—— feels that armada of, is bound for Lisbon, **24.** 111

—— makes head against, only by sufferance of Eastern powers, **25.** 201

—— may be baffled by underhand aid by, for America, **24.** 139

—— may be forced by, to give up America, **39.** 330, 333

—— may be preferred by, to France, **19.** 278

—— menaced by fleet of France and, **16.** 189

—— resembles, in lust for gold, **23.** 381

——'s agreement with, **5.** 16n

—— said to have accepted mediation by, **24.** 440

—— saved by slowness of, in joining France, **24.** 448

——'s commercial relations with, **19.** 480, 504, **20.** 170–1, 197–8

——'s feeble enemy, **25.** 149

—— should send Moors to invade, **22.** 100

——'s manifesto from, **33.** 102–3

——'s negotiations with, questioned, **39.** 324

——'s peace with, **31.** 150, 356

England's relations with: Assiento Treaty, **19.** 480; English rejection of Spanish ultimatum, **24.** 486; Ferdinand VI may improve, **19.** 278; may yet be neutral, **24.** 463; Portugal a factor in, **22.** 99–100; predicted to be harmonious, **21.** 544; punned upon by West, **43.** 178; quarrel over Falkland Islands, *see* England disputes with; rescript from Spain, **35.** 615; rupture, **33.** 202; Spanish bullying for France strains, **21.** 536; wanted by Pitt for discussion in House of Commons, **21.** 553; war possible, **20.** 487, 491, **21.** 171–2, 260, 553–4, 555, **24.** 17; Young Pretender may inflame, **17.** 14

——'s sea-power compared with that of, **33.** 116

——'s wars and peace treaties with, *see under* War: English-Spanish

——'s wars with, in poem, **40.** 25, 26

——'s war with, hopeless, **39.** 330, 356

—— takes no advantage from slowness of, to make war, **39.** 355

—— thought herself trampled on by, **19.** 69

—— told by, that France humbled, should not be ruined, **38.** 120

—— too disunited for war with, to unify her, **22.** 540

—— to prevent invasion of Italy by, **17.** 192n

—— will love to humble, now that Pitt rules, **22.** 441

English army in, under Peterborough, **18.** 180, **24.** 482

English capture Central American fort of, **24.** 543

English consuls in, reassured about English-Spanish relations, **21.** 544

English convention with, *see under* Convention

English defeat, at Gibraltar, **33.** 358

English fleet's ambush by fleet of, unlikely, **39.** 313

English fleet unable to interrupt Genoese commerce with, **19.** 207

English-French naval disarmament pact rejected by, **24.** 299–300

English-French rift over America might be mediated by, **39.** 303

English-French war might be joined by, **20.** 487, 491

English manufacturers solicited by, **20.** 170–1

English messenger from Hanover to, **20.** 498

English negotiations with, over Nootka controversy, **39.** 478–9

English out-quixote, **39.** 368

English sailors must precede Sir James Gray at, **21.** 560

English war not wanted by, when France can fight it, **38.** 121

envoys from and to, *see under* Envoy

expedition against settlements of, perished, **33.** 263–4

expedition by, from Cadiz to Minorca, would have little chance of success, **25.** 59

expedition of, threatening Tuscany, *see* Tuscany: Spanish expedition in

family compact of France and, *see* Bourbon family: family compact of

Farinelli said to have escaped from, **18.** 119

Ferdinand VI makes changes in ministry of, **19.** 278n

—— orders unlimited export to Portugal from, after Lisbon earthquake, **20.** 512n

——'s will appoints Elizabeth Farnese regent of, **21.** 327n

Ferdinand of Naples ordered by, to admit no guests to his table, **23.** 191

finances of, inadequate, **23.** 244

fleet armed by, **21.** 494, **24.** 412

fleet of: Algiers and Tunis preoccupy, **24.** 120; Algiers to be attacked by, **25.** 416; arrives in Gulf of Spezia, **17.** 290n; at Cadiz, not to join Brest fleet, **25.** 72; at Spezia, may go to Barcelona and Toulon, **17.** 323; at Toulon, **18.** 93, 360, 370; Brest fleet may be joined by, **25.** 16; Cadiz fleet of, probably to join Gibraltar siege rather than French fleet, **30.** 271; Cadiz said to be retreat of, **25.** 145, 344; Cadiz the station of, **39.** 368; cautious conduct of, **25.** 147; Charles III orders, home to escape disease, **24.** 530, 538; Charles III to be escorted by, from Naples, **21.** 324, 333; crippled, **25.** 344; Darby braves, at Cadiz, **25.** 147; Darby not opposed by, **25.** 145, 147, 149; decisive battle avoided by, **25.** 156; defeated at Algiers, **28.** 217; destroyed in Seven Years' War, **28.** 411; does not alarm English ministry, **24.** 101; English East and West Indian fleets captured by, **29.** 75; English merchant fleets gobbled up by, **25.** 78; English merchant ship seized by, near Majorca, **18.** 354; English ships cap-

[Spain, *continued*]

tured by, **33**. 216; Estaing said to be taking, against Jamaica, **25**. 345; estimated size of, **28**. 396; expected in English Channel, **33**. 338; fire-ships and bomb-ships in, **17**. 286; Florentine Jacobites expect victory from, **18**. 415; France may borrow, to besiege Minorca, **24**. 437, 443, 467; French fleet does not aid, against Darby, **25**. 149; French fleet joined by, **7**. 425, **17**. 269n, **24**. 502, **25**. 73; French fleet may join, against Gibraltar, **24**. 484; French fleet quarrels with, **24**. 528; French fleet separates from, **18**. 415, **24**. 541; George II orders Haddock to intercept, **17**. 259, 260, 267, 269, 281, 306, 380, 405; Gibraltar left unblocked by, **25**. 145; Gulf of Lyon alleged location of, **17**. 179; Haddock alarms, **17**. 322; Haddock keeps, at Cadiz, **17**. 219; Haddock to keep, at Barcelona, **17**. 259, 266–7, 290–1; Haddock too weak for, **17**. 269, 281; Keppel's fleet menaced by, **33**. 48; leaves Cadiz, **17**. 23; Lisbon said to be target of, **24**. 111; list of ships in, **17**. 286; Mann must get Saunders to defeat, **22**. 48; Mathews eluded by, at Majorca, **18**. 244; may be sent to America, **24**. 224; Minorca expects surprise from, **24**. 114; off Gibraltar, and detains Dutch vessel, **24**. 541; plays hide and seek, **33**. 347; preparation of, rumoured, **5**. 348n; Rodney defeats, **25**. 16, 17, 21, 24; runs away, **29**. 138; Russian fleet to be intercepted by, **25**. 415; said to have sailed, **39**. 250; sails, **29**. 72; should not intimidate England, **33**. 222; size of, **17**. 286; Spezia gulf patrolled by, **17**. 317; storm said to have damaged, **33**. 289; to accompany French and Dutch to India, **25**. 485–6; Toulon squadron joins, **17**. 269; very sickly, **25**. 145; West Indies menaced by, **17**. 17, 20

fleet of France and ('combined fleet'): about to come out, **33**. 126; at Brest, **24**. 525; at mouth of Channel, **25**. 297; attempts invasion of England, **41**. 402; avoids Hardy's in Channel, **24**. 506; Cadiz left by, **25**. 82, 173, 181; Cape St Vincent said to be approached by, **25**. 173, 181; contradictory reports on, **33**. 133; Conway prevented by, from leaving Jersey, **39**. 341; Darby did not attempt to beat, **33**. 304; disappears from Plymouth, **24**. 511; dispersed by storm, **25**. 336; does not engage Howe, **25**. 337; Dutch fleet may have joined, **25**. 188; engagement by, rumoured, **39**. 338; England expects reappearance of, **33**. 126; English fleet outnumbered by, **39**. 332, 336; English fleet plays hide-and-seek with, **25**. 306; English fleet said to have defeated, **17**. 35; expected to sail from Brest, **33**. 131–2; French fleet's separation from, **25**. 197; French ships join, **24**. 502; Gibraltar bay to have been closed by, **25**. 16; Gibraltar to be captured by,

before Howe's arrival, **25**. 323; HW fears appearance of, **33**. 129; Howe criticized for not fighting, **25**. 439n; Howe may be engaged by, **35**. 367; Howe to be attacked by, **33**. 358; in Channel, **25**. 182, 185, 186, 188; Mann hopes that English fleet will drive, from Minorca, **25**. 205; Minorca attacked by, **25**. 178–9, 180–1, 182; Minorca instead of Gibraltar the objective of, **25**. 173–4; near Cartagena, **25**. 174; now separated but could reassemble, **25**. 201; Penobscot news will frighten, **33**. 123; Plymouth approached by, **24**. 506, 511; reported to have departed from English coast, **25**. 302; reported to have returned to Brest, **25**. 186; rumoured about to sail, **30**. 274; thought to have gone home, **25**. 191, 192; to engage Howe, **25**. 326

fleets prepared by, **23**. 474

Florentine adherents of, avoid Mann's parties and want Ferdinand VI to send Don Philip, **19**. 498

Florentine agent of, *see* Vernaccini, Ranieri

Florentine jewels claimed by, **17**. 238

France advised by, to refuse English peace terms, **22**. 66, 76

France and, seek defensive alliance because of Modenese treaty, **20**. 400n

France at odds with, **18**. 416, **23**. 322, **25**. 32

—— coining gold from, **38**. 120

—— grudgingly aids, against Gibraltar, **25**. 292

—— invokes family compact to get aid from, **21**. 563–5, **22**. 5, 95, **24**. 478, 495

—— is unlikely to aid, under family compact, **23**. 244

—— lures, by family compact, **21**. 563

—— manages, in family party, **21**. 4–5

—— may act with, in Mediterranean to aid Turkey, **23**. 470n

—— may aid, against Algiers, **24**. 179

—— may alienate England from, **19**. 378, 393

—— may be compelled by family compact to aid, **23**. 244

—— may be joined by, in spring of 1757, **21**. 20

—— may borrow fleet from, to besiege Minorca, **24**. 437, 443, 467

—— may cede Minorca to, in return for alliance, **20**. 545, 572, 575

—— may induce, not to suppress Jesuits, **23**. 372

—— may sacrifice England to, at Aix treaty, **19**. 511

—— might bribe, with offer of Minorca and Gibraltar, **20**. 571n

—— not aided by, against England, **20**. 490n

—— not to join, in Portuguese war, **24**. 262n

—— opposed by, **11**. 54, **12**. 40, 53, 89

—— said to be ready to negotiate with England through, **21**. 360n

—— said to permit, to invade Tuscany, **19**. 30–1, 38

——'s alliance with: **21.** 536, 539, **24.** 486; England asks terms of, **21.** 559; England ignorant of terms of, **21.** 548; must be to England's disadvantage, **21.** 544; not countenanced at Naples, **21.** 551, 555; not yet announced, **24.** 486–7; would align Europe towards France, **20.** 528; would defeat England, **24.** 448

—— sends Dunn to urge, to make peace, **22.** 65n, 66n

——'s peace negotiations with Charles Emmanuel III broken by, **19.** 223

——'s treaty with: England demands sight of, **21.** 557; England does not know terms of, **21.** 548; must be to England's disadvantage, **21.** 544

——'s war with, rumoured, **7.** 127–9

—— to answer for, at Aix treaty, **19.** 480

—— to share Santo Domingo with, **25.** 180

—— will not be aided by, **20.** 498

—— will permit lawful pretensions of, to dominions in Italy, **17.** 230n

Francis I's election forbidden by, to be celebrated, **19.** 183–4

Francis III will easily be reinstated by, **19.** 156

Frederick II refuses plea of, to continue war, **17.** 315n

French and Italian ministers in, dismissed to England's advantage, **22.** 420

French-Bavarian alliance may be affected by, **17.** 119

French-Bavarian treaty with, rumoured, **17.** 183

French guarantee may not save Tuscany from, **18.** 502

French junction with, would defeat England, **24.** 448

French negotiations under Choiseul with, **41.** 196

French presumption may be checked by, **24.** 396

French rifts with, **18.** 416

French rift with England said to be disapproved by, **24.** 375

French ships wanted by, at Santo Domingo, **24.** 300n

French vessels mistaken for those of, **17.** 46

French victory may deflect, from peace, **25.** 83

French war preparations instigated by, **32.** 301

frequent upheavals in, **32.** 159

frigates of, *see under* Frigate

Fuentes delivers declaration of, to England, **21.** 559

Gabburri, Mme, returns to, **18.** 46

Gage and Lady Mary Herbert meet in, **7.** 288, **35.** 349

Gages, Comte de, ordered by, to attack Lobkowitz, **19.** 15

gallantry in, **31.** 21

galleys of, *see under* Galley

Genoa and France agree with, for Jesuits' landing in Corsica, **22.** 535n

Genoese alliance and negotiations with, **18.** 455, 509, 546–7, 554–5, **19.** 65, 237, 304, 343–5, 363–4

George II's orders may deter, from attacking Francis I's possessions in Tuscany, **17.** 288

Gibraltar allowed by, to cool, **25.** 345

—— and Jamaica objectives of, **39.** 332

Gibraltar and Minorca unlikely to be taken by inefficient fleet of, **24.** 119

Gibraltar attacked by, **29.** 65, 145

—— blockade abandoned by, **25.** 59

—— may be besieged by, **24.** 501

—— regarded by, as a point of national honour, **20.** 575

——'s capture no longer hoped by, **25.** 48, 331

——'s exchange for Port Mahon suggested to, by Henry Fox, **20.** 574n

——'s prisoners from, may infect garrison with the itch, **25.** 59

——'s siege exaggerated by accounts from, **25.** 334

governor from, in West Indies, **17.** 7

grandee of, less dangerous than Irish papist, **20.** 171

grandees of, despise painters, **16.** 170

Grantham made ambassador to, **5.** 87n

—— stays in, despite war declaration, **24.** 487

Gray, Sir James, expected to be ambassador to, **21.** 150, 159, 165–6, 174, 556, **22.** 107, 112

—— goes to, **22.** 463

greatest losers by war, and last to make peace, **37.** 284–5

Grenville, George, defends pretensions of, **38.** 487

Grimaldi minister of foreign affairs in, **6.** 376n

HW anticipates war with, **32.** 303

HW expected France to instigate, to fight England, **39.** 288

HW fears France's alliance with, **39.** 330, 332

HW hears nothing about, in Paris, **39.** 17

HW hopes for war with, **4.** 479, 483

HW sees minister to, **33.** 140

HW's fears of, **28.** 396, 425, **29.** 82

HW's joke about king's fool and king of, **9.** 389

HW's letters may be intercepted by, in revenge for interception of galleons, **35.** 15

HW wants Mann to be minister to, **21.** 166

HW would give Gibraltar to, **33.** 14

Harcourt is offered embassy to, **29.** 348, 350

Havana may not be restored to, **22.** 99–100

havocked world for gold, **25.** 142

hostility disclaimed by, **24.** 384

Huntingdon seeks embassy to, **21.** 166, 175

Inquisition but not changes in costume tolerated by, **39.** 61

Inquisitors of, will not be able to oppress newly-discovered stars, **25.** 614

invulnerability of, **33.** 132

[Spain, *continued*]

Ireland may be invaded by, 9. 418, 21. 539, 28. 196

Irish unrest said to be aroused by gold from, 22. 24

Italy develops tragedy ahead of, 41. 153

—— devastated and taxed by, 18. 344

—— will not be upset by succession of, 21. 280

Jamaica said to have been captured by, 24. 196–7

James I's letters to Charles I and D. of Buckingham in, 15. 339–42

Jesuits expelled from, 3. 365, 22. 509–10, 513, 515–19, 535–6, 23. 136, 376, 26. 49; *see also under* Charles III

Joseph II forbids Leopold to negotiate with, 25. 46

Keene asks for recall from, 21. 159

—— must continue as ambassador to, 20. 203

Keppel, Capt., escapes to, 9. 307

king of, mentioned in 'The Peach in Brandy,' 32. 60

King's messenger expected from, 11. 119–20

kings of, ungrateful to their 'assassins' in America, 32. 359

Labour in Vain mentions, 18. 18

'lamb' symbolizes, 30. 126

La Vauguyon ambassador to, 6. 87n

Leghorn houses no subjects of, 22. 351

'Leghorn' is Mann's code name for, 25. 43

Leopold forbidden to negotiate directly with, 25. 43

—— receives complaints from, about supplies sent to St Philip's, 25. 250

——'s accession announced to, 22. 345

——'s possible loss of grand ducal title enrages, 22. 330

——'s remonstrances to, 24. 509

letters from, to army, captured with courier, 18. 85

letters to Maria Louisa from, must be delivered by Spanish minister, 25. 334

Llano goes to Parma from, 23. 445

Lombardy may be exchanged by, for Tuscany, 17. 206

—— threatened by, 18. 295

—— to be invaded by, through Nice, 18. 395

losses of, through family compact, 22. 95

Madrid's grievances less than those of other cities in, 39. 65

Maillebois to attack Gibraltar if aided by, 20. 538n

Majorca filled by, with troops, 23. 261

manifesto of, tries to justify rupture with England, 21. 563

Mann has Leopold and Maria Louisa urge Charles III to release, from war with England, 25. 43–4

—— hopes for English fleet to drive away, from Minorca, 25. 205

—— speculates on reactions of, to Young Pretender's separation from wife, 25. 100

man *or* men of war of, *see under* Man-of-war

Maria Amalia of Naples refuses to flee to, 18. 3

Maria Amalia of Parma's extravagance subject of complaints by, 23. 412

Maria Louisa brings dogs from, to Florence, 22. 330

——'s jewels from, 22. 481

——'s letters from father in, must be delivered by Spanish minister, 25. 334

Maria Theresa's designs on Naples known to, 18. 390

Massa claims of Cybo relinquished to, 17. 35

Masserano dies on reaching, 24. 328n

mediation of, rejected, 33. 116, 119

Medici allodials in Tuscany claimed by, 17. 238, 18. 176

Mexican revolts against, would guarantee peaceful policy in Europe, 24. 384

ministers from and to, *see under* Minister

ministry of, pro-French, 38. 233

Minorca cannot receive Russian warships for fear of attack by, 24. 114

—— formerly under, 37. 311, 314

——, if France cedes it to Spain, might be exchanged by, for Gibraltar, 20. 575

—— may be attacked by, 24. 114, 25. 48

Minorcan news comes only from, 25. 205

Minorca's garrison prisoners in, 25. 430

——'s siege by, *see under* Minorca

miquelets of, 18. 100

Miranda siege indicates belligerency of, 22. 38

missionaries of, in Mexico, 35. 505

Modena may be allied with, 17. 216

Moniño will oppose Court intrigues of, if detrimental to country's welfare, 24. 478

Montemar awaits advice from, before daring to return there, 18. 54

—— awaits orders from, 18. 27

—— recalled to, 18. 46

—— sends courier to, 18. 42

Mount Stuart does not go to, 25. 398n

—— promised ambassadorship to, 25. 345–6

munitions of, to be deposited in Corsica according to Genoese treaty with Villettes, 18. 271

Muzell to sail to, 21. 527

Naples advises Gages to await orders from, after Charles Albert's death, 19. 8, 10, 11

—— and Portugal not invaded by, 22. 1

Naples exchanges couriers with, weekly, 22. 349

—— hopes that Sardinia can be bribed by, 17. 145, 291

—— ordered by, to send food to Tuscany, 22. 448

navy prepared by, at Cadiz, 24. 496

Neapolitan cardinals and nobles forbidden by, to celebrate Francis I's election, 19. 183–4

Neapolitan Court assures Gray that letters from, promise rapprochement with England, 21. 551, 555 neutrality of: an excuse to invade Ireland, **21.** 539; expected, **24.** 467; Frederick II must be encouraged by, **21.** 271

Newfoundland fishing rights demanded by, **38.** 120

Noailles's *Mémoires* contain secret history of, **28.** 296

North administration powerless to confront, **39.** 326

O'Brien, Mrs, discloses Tencin's secrets to, but loses pension, **20.** 28

officers of, shipped to Scotland, **37.** 236

Old Pretender acknowledges help of, by not celebrating Francis I's election, **19.** 184

——'s pension from, **22.** 387

Onslow teaches George II to plunder, **30.** 302

Orsi expect defeat of, **17.** 427

Ossory, Lord, might go to, as ambassador, **32.** 209

Pallavicini former nuncio in, **23.** 118

Papal states and Sicilies may export grain to, **23.** 430

papers sent to, during Reformation, **15.** 187

Parma to be supported by, in quarrel with Clement XIII, **23.** 10

party of, at Florence: avoids Mann's parties, **19.** 498; wants Don Philip, **19.** 498

peace may leave, to mercy of Maria Theresa and Charles Emmanuel III, **19.** 219

peace preliminaries to be ratified by, **25.** 365

peace with: declared in House of Commons, **23.** 268; in doubt, **29.** 118

Pensacola captured by, **25.** 172

Peru and Mexico a burden to, **33.** 328

Peruvian cruelties of, outdone by English in India, **23.** 387, 396–7

Peterborough hunts for army in, **18.** 180, **24.** 482

Phelps to be given post in, **22.** 112

Pitt (Chatham) falls from conquest of, to a pension, **38.** 135

—— insists on war with, **38.** 131

—— lures London with hope of plunder from, **21.** 549

—— should not want war with, **21.** 544, 549

——'s resignation will make, bolder, **21.** 538, 539

Pitt, George, may be transferred to, from Turin, **22.** 500

Pius VI may fear, more than poison, **24.** 86

pleased by unrest between England and Ireland, **33.** 129

Polish partition may inspire, to divide Milan with France and Sardinia, **23.** 469

Porto Longone belongs to, **23.** 131

ports of France and, surround those of Italy, **25.** 352

Portugal about to be conquered by, to replace Havana, **38.** 186

—— at odds with, **6.** 339

—— can be taken by, from the Portuguese but not from the English, **38.** 178–9

—— may be attacked by, **21.** 559–60, **22.** 1, 23–4, 31, **24.** 253

——'s conquest means more to, than Havana's loss, **22.** 48, 51, 92

——'s independence disappoints, **22.** 95, 99

——'s invasion by, violates law of nations, **39.** 302

——'s war with, *see* War: Portuguese-Spanish

—— to be freed from, **22.** 76n

—— to exchange territories with, in Paraguay, **21.** 341

Portuguese campaign of: fails to live up to boastful manifestos, **22.** 66; minimized by HW, **22.** 23–4; pleases HW, **22.** 31

Portuguese conquest by: may be pushed to exchange, for Havana, **22.** 99–100; would make France more insolent, **22.** 76

Portuguese island seized by, **24.** 309–10

Potosi's wealth can be procured by, only by digging, **23.** 561–2

prints of castles in, **2.** 151–2

prisoners from and to, *see under* Prisoner

privateer from, captures English, **17.** 153

Protestant manufacturers exempted by, from Inquisition, **20.** 170n

recognition by, of American independence expected, **28.** 376

register ships of, **17.** 175, 208, 377, **24.** 543

religion used by, as an excuse for plunder, **25.** 400

reluctance of, for peace, gives enemies a chance to make gains, **19.** 488

Rigaut de Barbezieux retires to, after sweetheart's death, **21.** 169

Rio Grande settlement of, attacked by Portuguese, **24.** 223

Rochford wants post in, **21.** 166

Rome's revenue lowered by act of, in buying nomination to benefices, **21.** 349

Rosenberg's debts in, paid by Maria Theresa, **23.** 294

royal family of, addicted to playing with tapestry, **23.** 242

royal progeny of, **15.** 188

Rubens's pictures in, **11.** 266

Russian shift enrages, **22.** 12

Russian ship captured by privateers of, **25.** 39n

St Bona walks across rivers in, **13.** 88n

Sandwich rumoured to be ambassador to, **22.** 103, 112, **38.** 534

Santa Catarina captured by, **32.** 357–8

Sardinia may be allied to, **17.** 85, **23.** 465

—— not bribed by, **17.** 145

Savoy plundered by, **19.** 505

Schaub buys pictures cheaply during wars in, **21.** 199–200

secretary of state of, *see* Secretary of state, Spanish

secret expedition of, will be abandoned if Sultana produces an heir, **21.** 494

1715 a frightful era for, **4.** 46

ship of: brings arms to Young Pretender, **19.**

[Spain, *continued*]

138; British sailor boards, **24**. 543; English attack on, **24**. 306–7; English captain throws cannon from, **18**. 406; lacks *corpo santo*, **25**. 26; lost on Irish coast, **19**. 138; Scotland to have received arms and money from, **19**. 134

ships of: at Genoa, **17**. 262, **18**. 244, 257; captured, **17**. 175, **38**. 169–70, 181; cruise near the Gorgona, **17**. 182; Dutch ship detained by, **24**. 541; English merchant ships watched by, **18**. 354; from West Indies, **37**. 164; join French near Greece, **36**. 220; may intercept English corn shipments to Italy, **22**. 206; near Port Mahon, listed, **17**. 286

ships sunk by, to block Havana harbour, **38**. 170

siege of Minorca not yet begun by, **25**. 196

South American revolt might distract, from Gibraltar, **25**. 292

Spanish ministry of, pleased by disgrace of Italian colleagues, **39**. 65

Squillace's difficulties in, **22**. 414–15

stocks rise and fall on news from, **23**. 250

subjugation of, to Carthaginians, **29**. 232

Swinburne's account of, shows Moorish buildings, **16**. 180

——'s *Travels through*, **2**. 149, 151

Tabuernigas flee from, **17**. 277–8

Talbot advises strong diplomatic treatment of, **9**. 389

Te Deums not to be sung by, for victories in Naples, **18**. 486

Te Deum sung by, for supposed victory, **18**. 161, 163

threats of, **22**. 12

tilting in, Charles I's horses caparisoned for, **32**. 325

toothpicks introduced from, **33**. 246

Townshend, Charles, employed in, **25**. 392n

travel books on, superficial, **15**. 137

treasure expected by, may make policy anti-war, **24**. 375–6

treasure's arrival at, rumoured in Florence, **17**. 83

treasury of, Musquiz, first *commis* of, succeeds Squillace, **39**. 64

troop movements of, near Gibraltar, **21**. 20

troop shipments of, to Italy, not impeded by English fleet, **19**. 9–10

troops of: 14,000 tied up at Gibraltar, **25**. 345; on Majorca, may threaten Minorca, **23**. 261; plunder Lodi, **19**. 269n

troops of France and, landed in Minorca, reported sickly, **25**. 197

troops sent by, to Naples, **19**. 367

tumult in, over suppression of slouched hats, **7**. 311

Turkey's treaty with, **25**. 415n

Tuscan envoy's witticism on, **32**. 210

Tuscan independence of, would please England, **18**. 2

Tuscan neutrality with, preserved by Francis I, **18**. 92

Tuscan regency does not welcome English protection for fear of antagonizing, **18**. 37–8

Tuscans told by, that goods bound for England will be confiscated, **24**. 508–9

Tuscany hopes for aid from, **17**. 144

—— may be invaded by, when P. Charles invades France, **18**. 285, 295

—— said to be resigned to, by England, **17**. 180

—— threatened by invasion from, *see under* Tuscany: Spanish invasion threatens

Twiss describes as dull, depopulated, and despotic, **28**. 190–1

Tyrawley may get embassy in, **21**. 166

undependable, **20**. 571, **24**. 424

verses refer to projected alliance of France, Austria, and, to restore Pretender, **30**. 126–7

visitors to: Damer, Mrs, **11**. 181, 190, **12**. 273; Herbert, Lady Mary, **7**. 288; Mengs, **16**. 170n; Pitt, Thomas, **21**. 501; Strathmore, Lord, **21**. 501; Young Pretender, **7**. 288, **19**. 377, 390, 392

Viviani gets envoy's credentials from, **22**. 349

—— language-master at Court of, **20**. 350

Wall probably tries to lure English manufacturers into service of, **20**. 170–1

—— recalled by, to succeed Carvajal as secretary of state, **20**. 426

—— secretary of state in, **20**. 426n

——'s recall to, **35**. 78–9

Walpole, Sir Robert, advised England to cultivate, **21**. 121

—— arouses opposition by project for settling England's disputes with, **17**. 187n

war expenses of, futile, **19**. 432

war waged by, differently from Frederick II, **25**. 190

William III and succession to throne of, **42**. 496

xebecs of, *see under* Xebec

Young Pretender disregarded by, **22**. 399

—— ill-treated in, **19**. 392n

—— may be aided by, **17**. 14, **19**. 97, 105, 130, 137–8, 330, 335

—— may be set up by, in Ireland, **23**. 328

—— receives money and promise of pension from, **19**. 392

—— said to be going to, **17**. 6n, 13, **19**. 140, 198, 377–8

——'s departure may embroil, **17**. 119

——'s invasion not helped much by, **19**. 105, 137–8, 139

——'s negotiation with, **17**. 15, **19**. 97

——'s Polish attempt probably does not involve, **23**. 338

—— urged by Farinelli and Carvalho to leave, **19**. 390n

—— will probably urge, to make Clement XIII give him royal honours, **22**. 369

See also Spaniard; War: English-Spanish

Spalato, Abp of. *See* Dominis, Marcantonio de

Spalato:
Diocletian's palace at, **10**. 230n
spelling of, corrected, **43**. 135

Spalding, Lincs:
Heighington gives concerts at, **13**. 84n
in 'Marshland,' **1**. 378
Priory of: benefactor of, **1**. 378; Cole transcribes register of, **1**. 278
Rousseau writes from, **3**. 300n

Spangle, ——:
Conway sees, at Court, **37**. 62

Spangle; spangles:
French fond of, as ornament, **25**. 635
gown embroidered with, **10**. 198

Spanheim, Mary Anne von (ca 1683–1772), m. (1710) François de la Rochefoucauld, Marquis de Montandre:
arrogance of, **11**. 306
dull parties of, **9**. 163
refugee in England, **11**. *305*
Spectator, The, mentions, **11**. 305
tea-party precedence maintained by, **11**. 305–6

Spaniard; Spaniards:
American throats cut by, for gold, **32**. 358
Cartagena victory causes consternation among, **17**. 68
cocchiata given by, in Florence to lady, **22**. 158
Conclave gets appeal from, over ship's capture, **17**. 8
Conway, Henrietta Seymour, considers, boastful and harmless, **38**. 160
dogs employed by, against Indians, **28**. 332
English captains damn, **18**. 38
English fleets captured by, **33**. 216
French hated by, **7**. 360
in East and West Indies, discussed by Raynal, **39**. 168
in Peru and Mexico, savages and barbarians, **34**. 177
said to be good friends of English, **33**. 382
tyranny of, over Peru, **32**. 272

Spaniel; spaniels:
Dorset's, **9**. 368
King Charles: Charles II's favourites, **18**. 351n; Dacre promises, to HW, **22**. 479; Dacre's bitch miscarries, **22**. 534, 546; HW alone has true small breed of, **19**. 59; HW gets puppies, for Maria Louisa, **23**. 40; HW has, **10**. 283, 312, **19**. 71; HW jokes about Charles I's descendants as, **19**. 71; HW promised, to Mari, **18**. 293; HW promised, to the Tesi, **18**. 280, 293, 351; HW's gift of, rejected by Mme de Mirepoix, **22**. 534; HW's tanned black, **23**. 200; HW tries to get, for Maria Louisa, **22**. 479, 534, 546; Hertford's valet-de-chambre brings, to Mann, **23**. 56; Mann asks HW to get, for Maria Louisa, **22**. 438, 470; Mann has two, **19**. 59; Mann's 'Pompey' is, **18**. 530n; Maria Louisa asks Mann about, **22**. 438, 519, 546; Maria Louisa receives, from Mann, **23**. 56;

puppies about to have offspring, **23**. 97; puppies on way to Mann for Maria Louisa, **23**. 45, 48, 50, 54, 57, 66, 72, 79; puppies to be housebroken by Mann before being given to Maria Louisa, **23**. 72; seized by wolf, **13**. 189–90; true breed of, lost, **35**. 191; unprocurable after Halifax's death, **18**. 293; Voelcker has smallest breed of, **23**. 56; *see also* 'Rosette'; 'Tory'

Spanish Armada. *See* Spain: armada of

Spanish brooms:
HW to send, to Montagu, **9**. 177

Spanish Friar, The. See under Dryden, John

Spanish Gazette:
Mann sends HW an abstract of, **25**. 325–6
news of destruction of floating batteries confirmed by, **25**. 329

Spanish Guards:
casualties of, at San Lazaro, **19**. 267
MacDonel commands, at Campo Santo, **18**. 336n

Spanish language:
Boyle, Charlotte, studies, **31**. 251n
Bubb Dodington speaks, **35**. 301
Carteret and his daughter speak, **17**. 278
Craon does not understand, **17**. 280
Gray comments on passages of, in Herbert's *Life,* **14**. 128
HW's ignorance of, **15**. 67
Pomfret, Cts of, does not speak, **17**. 277
(?) St-Germain's native tongue, **26**. 20

Spanish Town, Jamaica:
Knowles moves capital from, **37**. 432n

Spanish West Indies. *See under* West Indies

Spanocchi, Gen.:
Karl Ludwig tutored by, **25**. 569n

Sparke, Bowyer Edward (1760–1836), Bp of Ely:
Ely Cathedral window finished by, **1**. 204n

Sparre, Baroness. *See* Deritt, Elizabeth

Sparre, Alexandre-Séraphin-Joseph-Magnus (b. 1736), Comte de, *or* Ernest-Louis-Joseph (b. 1738), Comte de:
(?) social relations of, with Comtesse de la Marche, **7**. 298

Sparre, Amelia Wilhelmina Melusina (1733–78):
Granby, M. of, flirts with, **9**. 108
Lloyd, Mrs Gresham, deplores bad company of, **9**. 108
March, E. of, incited by, to resent Mrs Lloyd's remarks, **9**. 108
Petersham, Lady Caroline, includes, in Vauxhall party, **9**. *107–10*

Sparrow, ——:
engraving by, **2**. 148n

Sparrow, John, convict:
highwayman, **29**. 6on
released by Gordon rioters, **33**. 194
said to have been shot while encouraging Gordon rioters, **33**. 191
trial of, **25**. 67

Sparrow; sparrows:
Catullus's, **35**. 45

[Sparrow; sparrows, *continued*]
  cock, resembled by Christian VII, **10**. 265, **35**. 327
  Du Deffand, Mme, has, **3**. 76
  HW has bones of, **33**. 304
  hedge, sits on cuckoo's nest, **36**. 85
  sooty, in London back gardens, **34**. 196
'Sparta, Q. of':
  character in *Ballet de la Paix*, **18**. 496
Sparta:
  authorized thievery and communal property in, **15**. 227
  Bedford, Ds of, compared to 'dame' of, **33**. 115
  Hervey, Bns, and Cts of Albemarle unlike mothers of, **31**. 28
  occupations of ladies of, **31**. 21
  Parliamentary opposition compared to defenders of, **38**. 315
  Windham imbibes notions of, **25**. 50
'Spartan'; 'Spartans':
  in England, **5**. 199
'Spartan delicacy':
  of Behn and Cowley plays, **33**. 544
'Spartan mother':
  Townshend, Vcts, to be represented as, **40**. 167
Spasm; spasms:
  of stomach and bowels, **34**. 6n
Spatterdash; spatterdashes:
  Cumberland, D. of, regulates number of buttons on, **19**. 464n
Spay. *See* Spey
Speaker of the (English) House of Commons. *See* Cornwall, Charles Wolfran (1735–89); Crewe, Sir Thomas (1565–1634); Cust, Sir John (1718–70); Hanmer, Sir Thomas (1677–1746); Lenthall, William (1591–1662); Norton, Sir Fletcher (1716–89); Onslow, Arthur (1691–1768)
Speaker of the (Irish) House of Commons. *See* Boyle, Henry (ca 1686–1764); Pery, Edmund Sexten (1719–1806); Ponsonby, John (1713–89)
Speaker's Coach:
  slowness of, **37**. 378
Speaking trumpet:
  Craon, Princesse de, would need, to talk to Vorontsovs at dinner, **21**. 248
  Greenwich, Bns, enlivens August and September with, **39**. 251
Spear; spears:
  at SH, **20**. 381
  HW's wooden, with 50 points, **31**. 26
  lady carries, in *Réduction de Paris*, **32**. 268
  tiger killed with, **35**. 445
Spearing, ——, attorney:
  Kingston, Ds of, brings, to Amis at Winchester, **24**. 195n
Specimen of Naked Truth, A. See under Vernon, Edward (1684–1757)
Specimens of Arabian Poetry. See under Carlyle, Joseph Dacre
'Speckle-belly':
  Montagu's name for fish, **35**. 205

Spectacle; spectacles (public entertainments):
  cease at Marie-Josèphe's death, **3**. 263
  Christian VII attends all, **4**. 154
  forbidden at Eastertide, **3**. 264
Spectacles (eye-glasses):
  Balmerinoch uses, to read speech, **19**. 301
  Finch wears, **30**. 300n
  green, bought by HW from Scarlett, **21**. 131
  HW reads without, **21**. 139, 157
  HW should use, in reading invitations, **35**. 455
  Hillier wears, **16**. 95
  La Condamine wears, in street, **22**. 146
  Leneve, Mrs, uses, **37**. 181
  Neapolitan ambassador sees his legs enlarged by, **41**. 101
  Siries blames his mistake upon, **20**. 314
  Stuart Mackenzie loses, in Gordon riots, **33**. 175
  Zouch wears, **16**. 51
Spectateur français, Le. See under Marivaux, Pierre-Carlet de Chamblain de
Spectator, The, by Addison, Steele, etc.:
  character in, **9**. 16n
  Byrom contributes pastoral to, **12**. 35n
  Du Deffand, Mme, reads, **4**. 261
  epitaph given in, **1**. 40
  HW cites, **33**. 158, **35**. 396
  HW expected Pulteney's writings to resemble those in, **20**. 374
  HW's bulletins no longer can be called, **33**. 388
  HW takes title from, **13**. 14n
  hacked phrases from, **35**. 262
  journal of retired tradesman in, **33**. 464, **41**. 278
  Montandre, Marquise de, mentioned in, as Mlle Spanheim, **11**. 305
  Pinkerton 'translates,' into gibberish, **33**. 490
  Pinkethman's petition in, **18**. 565
  quoted during Cambridge 'guzzling affair,' **13**. 63
  'Sir Roger de Coverley' in, **35**. 562–3
  Walpole, Sir Edward, imitates, **36**. 188
  West alludes to, **13**. 117
  See also under Addison, Joseph; Cocchi, Raimondo
'Spectator No. None,' by HW:
  sent to Lady Ossory, **32**. 78–83
Speculation:
  HW dislikes, and is unequal to it, **33**. 571
Speculations on the Perceptive Power of Vegetables. See under Percival, Thomas
Speculum:
  Dr Dee's, **33**. 323–4
  on monument in Trinity Hospital, Greenwich, **16**. 89
Speculum Britanniæ. See under Norden, John
Spedale degli Innocenti (Florentine foundling hospital):
  Eleonora's bastards put in, **18**. 40
  Lucchi, Sophia, rescued by Chute from, **18**. 406n, **22**. 265

Speech; speeches:
(?) at opening of new parliament of Paris, sent by Conway to HW, 39. 230
See also under Parliament; Parliament (Irish); Parliament of Paris, etc.
Speech of Edmund Burke, Esq., on American Taxation. See under Burke, Edmund
Speech of Richard White-Liver, The, by HW: copies of, 43. 171
HW replies to Campbell in, 13. 21
Speed, Henrietta Jane (1728–83), m. (1761) Francesco Maria Giuseppe Giustino, Barone de la Perrière, Conte di Viry, 1766:
Aigueblanche enemy of, 6. 477
Ailesbury, Cts of, to visit, 6. 106
Bagarotti, Mlle, resembles, 5. 404
Boufflers's witticism on seeing, at Mme du Deffand's, 39. 219
Chute's house bought by, 9. 330
Conway to visit, 6. 106
Creutz brings regrets of, to Mme du Deffand, 5. 426
Damer, Mrs, to visit, 6. 106
death of: on eve of visit to England, 33. 384; sudden, 33. 384n
disgrace of, 41. 343n, 43. 102
Du Deffand, Mme, scolded by HW for writing name of, 5. 416–17, 424
——'s opinion of, 6. 15
——'s relations with, 6. 106, 294–5
French conquered by fêtes of, for Ps of Piedmont's wedding, 39. 259
friends of, 41. 343n
Gloucester, Ds of, to visit, 35. 522
Gray inquires about, 14. 123
—— makes, heroine of 'Long Story,' 24. 328n, 41. 342n
——'s intimacy with, 14. 61n, 43. 191
——'s verses prompted by, 38. 144
HW accompanies, to theatre, 7. 347
HW's account of, 41. 342n, 343n
HW saw social triumphs of, at Paris, 41. 343
HW's correspondence with, 6. 308, 310, 41. 203–4, 342–4
HW's opinion of, 5. 360
HW's social relations with, 7. 345, 347–50, 352, 414, 31. 182–3, 39. 259
HW warns Mme du Deffand against, 5. 360, 364, 409
husband of: arrested, 6. 474, 24. 328; disgraced, 6. 470, 483
husband's fall caused by intrigues of, to have him made prime minister, 24. 328n
large cheeks of, 32. 254
marriage of, expected, 9. 406
presented at French Court, 5. 401
Shelburne friend of, 24. 328n, 35. 522n
social relations of, in Paris: 31. 182–3, 39. 259; *see also index entries ante* 8. 517–18
Stanhope, Lady Harriet, to visit, 6. 106
Stormont, Cts of, may be presented by, 6. 306
success of, in Paris, 5. 410

Voltaire's verses to Aranda presented to HW by, 41. 203–4
wit of, 41. 342n
Speed, Mrs Henry. *See* Montagu, Augusta (d. 1849)
Speed, John (ca 1552–1629), chronicler and cartographer:
Fabyan copied by, 14. 71
HW refers Gray to, 14. 171, 173–4
Historie of Great Britaine, The, by: Gray derives passage from, 40. 103; HW refers Dalrymple to, 15. 118–19, 120
parliamentary roll printed by, 14. 181
print of Chaucer by, 14. 108–9
Theatre of . . . Great Britaine by, has Nonsuch painting, 40. 254
Warbeck's proclamation extracted and discussed by, 14. 168, 180
Speedwell, English sloop:
Berrys cross Channel in, 11. 116n
Lyn, captain of, 11. 116n
news from Cancalle brought by, 35. 289n
Speenhamland, Berks:
Donnington Castle near, 35. 642
Speiss, Mr (fl. 1770), dancing-master:
print of, 1. 363
Speke, Anne (ca 1740–97), m. (1756) Frederick North, styled Lord North 1752–90; 2d E. of Guilford, 1790:
at Bushey Park, 32. 193
Bushey House home of, as ranger of Bushey Park, 32. 156n
children of, prevented by fever epidemic from visiting Wroxton, 10. 287
cribbage liked by, 12. 167
Eden entertained by, 33. 214
fecundity of, 10. 287
genealogy of, 10. 352
HW dines with: at Bushey House, 11. 114; at George Onslow's, 32. 156
HW entertained by, 33. 284
HW entertains, at SH, 12. 164, 32. 156
HW makes annual visit to, 33. 214
HW mentions, 12. 120
HW visits, 11. 82, 12. 167, 33. 235
Hertford, Cts of, entertains, 33. 283
Hobart, Mrs, entertains, at play at Ham Common, 33. 370
Hotham, Miss, visited by, 12. 154
humility and civility of, 33. 214
husband tended by, in his blindness, 33. 580
Keene, Mrs, entertains, 33. 232
Keppel, Mrs, entertains, at Isleworth, 33. 481
Montagu to receive compliments of, 10. 250n
mother of, 10. 197n
Payne entertained by, 33. 284
Pynsent, Lady, related to, 38. 493
slighted after husband's fall from power, 33. 338
Somerton, Lady, visited by, 12. 164
SH visitors sent by, 12. 236, 244
uncomeliness of, 38. 493
Waldegrave ladies entertained by, 33. 284

[Speke, Anne, *continued*]
  Williams, G. J., visits, 9. 203
Speke, Mrs George. *See* Williams, Anne (d. 1782)
Speke, Philippa, m. Edward Bridges; Mann's great-great-grandmother:
  (?) Chute investigates, in Heralds' Office, **20.** 13
Spelling:
  HW unsure of, **32.** 158
Spelling-book:
  (?) answer to charade, **33.** 533, **39.** 445
Spelman, Mrs, Conyers Middleton's housekeeper:
  equivocal character of, **15.** 310
Spelman, Sir Henry (? 1564–1641), historian; philologist:
  Concilia by, describes Glastonbury Church, **16.** 46
  Garnett quotes Bourchier from, **41.** 222
Spence, Miss:
  SH visited by, **12.** 248
Spence, Elizabeth (ca 1694–1764), Ds of Newcastle's companion:
  death of, **38.** 459
  Newcastle promises, to be lord treasurer, **35.** 165
  Pelham, Thomas, to inherit sister's bequest from, **38.** 459
Spence, Rev. Joseph (1699–1768), writer; professor of poetry at Oxford 1728–38; regius professor of modern history, 1742:
  Apology for the Late Mr Pope by, **20.** 61n, 65n
  blindness of, to Pope's mortality, **35.** 262
  Blythe and Chetwynd met by, at Turin, **43.** 178
  Byfleet, Surrey, home of, **20.** 188n
  Cocchi gives book to, **20.** 438
  Dodsley travels to Scotland with, **15.** 37n
  Duck, Stephen, described by, **13.** 124n
  dullness of, **30.** 17–18
  Genoa visited by, **17.** 91
  HW attributes verses on Rollin's death to, **30.** 24
  HW calls on, **20.** 188
  HW compares, with Bp Hume, **30.** 1
  HW found ill at Reggio by Lincoln and, **30.** 17
  HW hopes, busy about gods and goddesses, **30.** 9
  HW hopes to be friendly with, in England, **30.** 11
  HW jokes about 'quarrel' with, **30.** 178
  HW mentions, **14.** 52, **17.** 475
  HW often told, of desire to visit Lincoln, **30.** 174
  HW puns on name of, **30.** 178
  HW rides in chaise with, **30.** 17
  HW's admiration for countryside around Swallowfield would please, **30.** 26
  HW's correspondence with, **30.** 3, **40.** 34–6, 62, 68–9, 115–17

HW sends compliments to, **30.** 1, 15, 17, 21, 28, 31
HW sends messages to, **30.** 11
HW sends Pope's epigram to, **30.** 4–5
HW's inquiries about Lincoln's love affair not to be mentioned to, **30.** 24
HW's mock epitaph on Lincoln to be shown to, **30.** 2
HW's opinion of, **2.** 216–17
HW told of engraved gem of Virgil by, **30.** 11
HW to travel with, **17.** 86
HW travels to Paris with, **13.** 10–11, **17.** 61n, **30.** 17
Impostor Detected and Convicted by, **20.** 65n
letter of, about Cooke, **2.** 214
Lincoln, E. of, esteemed by, **30.** 11
—— gives house at Byfleet to, **40.** 62
——'s grant to, witnessed by HW and Ashton, **30.** 32
Mann bored by pedantry of, **17.** 107
——'s correspondence with, **17.** 51, **30.** 4, **40.** 34
—— sends thanks to, **17.** 96
marriage duties explained by, to Lincoln, **30.** 73
mother cherished by, **20.** 188–9
mules counted by, with HW in chaise, **17.** 91
Oxford University appointment of, **17.** 475n
Parallel in the Manner of Plutarch, A, by: Cole comments on, **1.** 40; Cole's copy of, **43.** 45; HW lists number of copies printed of, at SH Press, **43.** 79; HW prints, at SH Press, **13.** 29, **28.** 23–4, **35.** 107, **37.** 552n; HW sends, to Bibliothèque du Roi, **41.** 58n; Mann receives, from HW. **21.** 289
Parker, Mark, known to, at Rome, **17.** 82n
Polymetis by: **2.** 214–15, **17.** 51n, **43.** 71; Gray read, in MS, **14.** 14, 18; Gray's criticism of, **14.** 18–21; Gray scoffs at, as 'a pretty book,' **14.** 14; Gray's letter on, **28.** 124; HW sends Middleton a print from, **15.** 20; Spence's portrait in, **14.** 14
Pope defended by, in pamphlet by, **20.** 62n
——'s imitation of Horace copied by, **37.** 8n
Ramsay's anecdote to, about Reims and Lord Peterborough, **24.** 112n
Rosalba's portrait of, **18.** 243n
Rubens's 'Prometheus' attributed by, to Titian, **10.** 78
'Sir Harry Beaumont,' nom-de-plume of, **42.** 131
Smyth friend of, at Oxford, **17.** 10n
travel diary of, **17.** 58n
Turin visited by, **13.** 191
Venice visited by, **17.** 86
works of, **20.** 188n
Spence, Mrs Joseph. *See* Collier, Mirabella
Spence, Ruth (d. 1767):
  sister's bequest to, **38.** 459
Spence, Thomas (d. 1737), serjeant-at-arms to House of Commons:
  sister of, **35.** 165n

Spence, English sloop:
   Forbes and Capt. Laurence reach Leghorn on, from Port Mahon, 19. 192n
   Laws commander of, 17. 71n
   Mogg, commander of, 18. 404n
   Spanish galleys attacked by, 17. 471
Spencer, Bns. *See* Poyntz, Margaret Georgiana (1737–1814)
Spencer, Cts. *See* Bingham, Hon. Lavinia (1762–1831); Poyntz, Margaret Georgiana (1737–1814)
Spencer, Mr:
   SH visited by, 12. 246
   SH visitor sent by, 12. 248
Spencer, Mrs:
   SH visited by, 12. 246
Spencer, Anne (d. 1618), m. 1 William Stanley, Lord Monteagle; m. 2 Henry Compton, Lord Compton; m. 3 Robert Sackville, 2d E. of Dorset:
   Dalrymple prints letters of, 15. 82–3
   imprisonment of, 15. 83–4
Spencer, Lady Anne (d. 1769), m. (1720) William Bateman, cr. (1725) Vct Bateman:
   brother forces separation of, from husband, 30. 309n
   house of, in Green Park, 31. 22n
Spencer, Lady Caroline (1763–1813), m. (1792) Hon. Henry Welbore Agar, 2d Vct Clifden, 1789; 2d Bn Mendip, 1802:
   HW calls, 'the silent woman,' 12. 156
   Ramsgate visited by, 12. 156
Spencer, Charles (ca 1674–1722), 3d E. of Sunderland, 1702; prime minister:
   Barrington, Lord, attached to, 15. 148, 33. 470
   Halifax possibly confused with, 34. 255
   Newcastle served under, 10. 192n
   son of, 9. 34n
   wife of, 34. 258
Spencer, Charles (1706–58), 5th E. of Sunderland, 1729; 2d (3d) D. of Marlborough, 1733:
   address of loyalty to George II moved by, in Parliament, 18. 399
   Aiguillon returns teaspoons of, 37. 544, 547
   alleged appointment of, 18. 556
   at battle of Dettingen, 17. 353n
   Blenheim, seat of, 9. 6
   brother disinherits, 9. 34
   brother of, 19. 272n, 25. 78n
   brother's bond to be repaid by, 9. 34
   Cherbourg attempt reported by, 35. 102n
   command in Flanders may be given to, 17. 353
   Cornbury bought by, 11. 152n, 33. 541n, 35. 155
   daughter of, 5. 392n, 22. 148n, 24. 524n
   death of, 21. 259
   Devonshire, D. of, succeeded by, as lord steward of the Household, 20. 67
   English invasion of France led by, 21. 204, 211

English troops in Germany commanded by, 37. 555n
estate and will of, 21. 259
Ferdinand, P., joins, at Coesfeldt, 21. 228n
Fox, Henry, wants Bedford to replace, as lord privy seal, 35. 89n
France not conquered by, 37. 535
Frederick, P. of Wales, does not speak to, at Carlton House, 17. 337
French may be frightened by presence of, in Flanders, 30. 34
genealogy of, 10. 352
George II wants, to replace Gower, 20. 418n
—— offered services by, 18. 400n
—— told by, that 'old women' were the only French he saw, 37. 544
Gower succeeded by, as lord privy seal, 35. 203
—— succeeds, as lord privy seal, 20. 517
grandmother conciliated by resignations of, 18. 350
health of: camp fever and bloody flux, 40. 144; in great danger, 21. 251
Hyde sells Cornbury to, 33. 541n
in cavalcade at Henley, 37. 371n
land poor, 21. 527
Lennox, Lady Georgiana Caroline, given away by, 18. 451
letters by, dated from Cancale, 21. 210n, 212n
Lincoln receives officer's apology before, 17. 412, 30. 32
Lowther rich enough to hire, 37. 459
Master of the Ordnance, 20. 517
Mastership of the Horse may go to, 20. 182–3
military procession to be watched by, 9. 192
Moore favoured by, 16. 280n
parents of, 34. 258
Piozzi, Mrs, comments upon, 10. 15n
regiment of, 17. 411n
Richmonds friendly with, 18. 451
Rochefort inquiry conducted by, 21. 155
St-Malo attempt by: 37. 533n; satirized by HW, 35. 287
secret expedition planned by, for George II, 21. 205n
sister of, 21. 156n
sister's separation from husband forced by, 30. 309n
Somers's papers preferred by, to be burnt, 20. 331–2
son gives robes of, to valet, 9. 280–1
son of, 9. 357n
teaspoons abandoned by, in retreat from St-Malo, 21. 221
troops commanded by, under Lord George Sackville, 21. 198
Walpole, Sir Edward, told by, of son's bravery, 21. 240
(?) wife inseparable from, 39. 3
wife of, 9. 392n
Spencer, Lord Charles (1740–1820), M.P.:
   Admiralty place offered to, 22. 569n

[Spencer, Lord Charles (1740–1820), *continued*]
biographical information on, corrected, **43.** 319
(?) Bologna visited by, **21.** 512n
Germain, Lady Elizabeth, gives Arundelian gems to, **42.** 204n
Harcourt may be succeeded by, as chamberlain to the Queen, **23.** 66
Marlborough, at Bedford's request, summons, to Blenheim to prevent anti-Court voting, **38.** 327
Moore tutor to, **16.** 280n
Opposition joined by, **38.** 320
Oxfordshire election falsely predicted for, **9.** 320
Parliamentary activity of, on Regency Bill, **38.** 551
Parliamentary motion by, for removal of ministers, **33.** 432n
resignation of, **30.** 192
royal ball for Christian VII attended by, **23.** 57n
(?) Spencer, Lord Robert, represents, at Oxfordshire election, **9.** 357
weepers for mother retained by, at private Court ball, **38.** 144
white staff held by, as comptroller of the Household, **38.** 320
Spencer, Lady Charles. *See* Beauclerk, Mary (b. 1743)
Spencer, Charlotte. *See* Spenser, Charlotte
Spencer, Lady Diana (1734–1808), m. 1 (1757) Frederick St John, 2d Vct Bolingbroke (divorced, 1768); m. 2 (1768) Topham Beauclerk:
adultery reportedly will be acknowledged by, **30.** 250
approaching marriage of, **30.** 137
bas-reliefs modelled by, in wax, **35.** 425
Bateman's auction attended by, **32.** 241
Bath visited by, **6.** 460, **15.** 270
Beauclerk makes, miserable, **15.** 320
—— persecutes, **30.** 269
——'s relations with: 'patched up' for moment, **30.** 269; reported smooth at Brighton, **30.** 272
—— the husband of, **28.** 237n
—— to wed, **22.** 567
Bedchamber position to Q. Charlotte given to, **9.** 377, **21.** 518, **22.** 104n, **38.** 96
Bedford, Ds of, gives watch to, for Q. Charlotte, **22.** 104–5
Bedford House scene of disgrace of, **31.** 71
Blenheim visited by, **32.** 77
Bolingbroke rouges, for Coronation, **9.** 388
——'s separation from, rumoured, **14.** 141
—— to wed, disappointing Hamilton and West, **37.** 499–500
Bouveries and Selwyn visit, **42.** 451n
Brighton visited by, **7.** 73, **28.** 421, **30.** 272
brother and sister given paintings by, **42.** 490
children drawn by, in bistre, **35.** 426
Clarence, D. of, at suppers of, **11.** 163

comes to tea during HW's absence, **32.** 293–4
Damer, Mrs, excelled by, **35.** 438
daughter and son of, elope, **34.** 56
daughter-in-law of, dies, **11.** 190
daughters of, **30.** 275, **33.** 334
Devonshire, Ds of, painted by, **28.** 385–6, 419, **43.** 303
Devonshire Cottage home of, at Richmond, **35.** 506n
divorce of, **22.** 567
drawings by: described by Harcourt, **29.** 353–4; for *Mysterious Mother*, housed by HW in Beauclerk Tower at SH, **15.** 317–18, **24.** 524, **28.** 244, 259, 275, 315, 317–19, **29.** 71, 142, 144, **31.** 206, 216, 297, **32.** 289, 294–5, **35.** 385, **39.** 443, **43.** 147
Du Deffand, Mme, hears of, **5.** 392, **6.** 460
—— inquires about, **6.** 384, 390, 471, **7.** 6, 42, 173
Dysart visits, **36.** 328
ebony cabinet decorated by, **43.** 378
Felton quotes HW on, **34.** 10n
Foote-Ds of Kingston letters sent by, to HW, **41.** 309–10
genius of, **31.** 297
George III's coronation attended by, **9.** 388, **38.** 127
gipsies by, copied by Agnes Berry, **34.** 25
gown desired by, **6.** 480, 483
Gunning match not credited by, **11.** 120
HW and Hardinges to be entertained by, **35.** 632
HW and Lady Jersey meet at house of, at Richmond, **35.** 506
HW asked by, to consult Harcourt about making green paint, **35.** 530
HW asks, to get copy of Hampden's poems, **42.** 397–8
HW breakfasts with, **11.** 341
HW called on by, at SH, **6.** 334n
HW calls on, **35.** 636
HW calls on, as 'most unfortunate of all mothers,' **34.** 56
HW compares, to Michelangelo, **29.** 272
HW concerned for, in Bolingbroke's illness, **30.** 267
HW dines with, at Muswell Hill, **32.** 122, 241
HW does 'portrait' of, **6.** 79, 80
HW entertains, at dinner, **32.** 365
HW gives *Mysterious Mother* to, **41.** 428n
HW hints about morals of, **10.** 53
HW hopes, will return in week from Bath, **32.** 341
HW jokes about suitors of, **30.** 137
HW may have sipped coffee with, **35.** 624
HW meets Miss Lloyd at house of, **33.** 290
HW mentions, **9.** 402, 403
HW procures wine for, **42.** 450–1
HW receives drawings from, for *Mysterious Mother*, **41.** 321–2
HW's accident at house of, **33.** 225
HW's correspondence with, **7.** 395, 396, **41.** 321–2, **42.** 397–8, 450–1

HW's painting of gipsies by, **29**. 272, **34**. 25
HW tells Hardinge not to drop into Little Marble Hill in absence of, **35**. 625–6
HW to be visited by, at SH, **6**. 460
HW to console, for husband's loss, **7**. 214, 215, (?) 239
HW told news of Catherine II by, **11**. 323
HW to transmit Mason's method of combining oil and water-colours to, **29**. 311
HW visited by, **32**. 242, **39**. 276
HW visits, **11**. 81–2, 247, **12**. 99, 142, 169, 170
HW wants Hardinge to help console, **35**. 636
Hamilton's 'old passion,' **35**. 425
Hamilton, Lady, 'attitudes' of, admired by, **11**. 350
Hardinge's 'passion' for, **35**. 630
—— spies HW sipping coffee with, **35**. 624
—— to deliver HW's note to, when Charles Beauclerk is not there, **35**. 632
—— wants to see garden in absence of, **35**. 624–5
Hardinge, Mrs, emulates, **35**. 627
Hardinges called on by, at Ragman's Castle, **35**. 631
Hare's story about Craufurd told to HW by, **33**. 415
health of: black vomit, **32**. 77; gallstone colic, cured at Bath, **15**. 270
Houghton not to be visited by, **32**. 319
—— to be visited by, **32**. 313
house of, **12**. 36n
house taken by, at Richmond, **43**. 307, 364
husbands of, **30**. 267
in black gloves, and pregnant, at private Court ball, **38**. 143
Little Marble Hill and Devonshire Cottage (at Richmond) inhabited by, **42**. 451n
Little Marble Hill decorated with lilac festoons painted by, **29**. 272, 354, **33**. 473, **35**. 624, **36**. 238
Little Marble Hill, Twickenham, occupied by, **42**. 484, 490
Lloyd, Rachel, lived with, **38**. 457
Lucan, Bns, admires artistic talent of, **6**. 340
major-domo of, demands Hardinge's name when he trespasses on her garden, **35**. 625
marital infelicity of, **6**. 286
Moore, Abp, consulted by, about Pinkerton, **16**. 280, 281–2, 286, 291, 311–12, 327
Muswell Hill house of, **43**. 299
Nivernais's *Jardins modernes* given to, **12**. 259
'not the worst' figure at Coronation, **38**. 127
O'Brien, Nelly, to be imitated in portrait of, **10**. 53
paintings by: **42**. 489, 490; illustrations for Dryden's *Fables*, **11**. 247; Spencer Grove, room at, **12**. 252n; water-colour of gipsies, **11**. 248
pictures by, for *Macbeth* and *Lear*, **33**. 573
pictures, drawings, and busts by, at SH, **31**. 206
Reynolds paints, **10**. 52

Richmond House masquerade and fireworks attended by, **22**. 148
Richmond house occupied by, until she moved to Little Marble Hill, **43**. 364
Richmond visited by, **11**. 148
room painted by, with lilacs, at Little Marble Hill, **29**. 272, 354, **33**. 473, **35**. 624, **36**. 238
sister distressed at miseries of, **30**. 269n
social relations of: with Brudenell, Georgina Herbert, HW, and Lady Pembroke, **33**. 195; with HW, Mrs Dixon, and Lady Payne, **32**. 407
son of, **11**. 118n, 190n
SH Closet dedicated to, *see under* drawings by, for *Mysterious Mother*, housed by HW in Beauclerk Tower at SH
Twickenham residence of, **34**. 56
watches boat-race from Richmond Castle, **11**. 341
Spencer, Elizabeth (d. 1632), m. (1599) William Compton, 2d Lord Compton, 1589; cr. (1618), E. of Northampton:
letter of, printed, **34**. 194
Spencer, Elizabeth (1618–72), m. 1 John Craven, Bn Craven of Ryton; m. 2 Henry Howard; m. 3 William Crofts, Bn Crofts of Saxham:
monument for, **2**. 256n
Spencer, Lady Elizabeth (1737–1831), m. (1756) Henry Herbert, 10th E. of Pembroke, 1750:
appearance of, ghostly, **9**. 264
balls attended by, **4**. 26
Beauclerk, Lady Diana, visited by, **33**. 195
beauty of: **3**. 406, **4**. 26, **22**. 9, 19, **43**. 122; at Coronation, **38**. 122, 126; at Russian masquerade, **35**. 206; HW admires, **9**. 376, 387; 'not glutinous,' **10**. 52
brings French guests to SH, **33**. 403
Carlisle, E. of, attentive to, **4**. 190, 199, 200, 205
Chantilly visited by, **4**. 159
club at Almack's founded by, **10**. 305
comment by, on staging of Jephson's *Braganza*, **41**. 295
daughter taken by, to Nice for health, **25**. 497n
Du Deffand, Mme, misses, slightly, **4**. 93, 205
—— 's correspondence with, **4**. 223–4
—— sends messages to, **4**. 207
—— 's opinion of, **4**. 16, 26, 37, 59, 86, 93, 116, 201, 205, 223–4
George III's Coronation attended by, **9**. 387
HW notified by, of Ps Lubomirska's visit to SH, **39**. 447
HW visited by, **4**. (?) 249, **32**. 345, **39**. 276
Historic Doubts sent to, **4**. 31–2
husband deserts, **22**. 9–10
husband leaves, at Nice, **25**. 493
husband may be charmed by, into forsaking La Rena, **21**. 156
husband's relations with, **5**. 309, **10**. 14–17, 52, **22**. 16

[Spencer, Lady Elizabeth (1737–1831), cont.]
husbands called 'powerful animals' by, 30. 269n
husband wishes to take leave of, before joining army, but is repulsed, 22. 33
husband writes begging letters to, while eloping with mistress, 22. 25
Isle-Adam visited by, 4. 54, 69, 159
Italy to be visited by, 4. 116
Langley Park visited by, 31. 126
lends servant to Duc de Guines for protection, 33. 404
Lloyd, Rachel, accompanies, 3. 406, 4. 7, 37, 59, 66, 86
—— fond of, 4. 78
lodge of, 11. 98n
Lubomirska, Ps, to be brought by, to SH, 33. 565–6
Mann hoped that husband would make amends to, 22. 22
—— pities, 22. 19
marriage of, imminent, 9. 181
Midleton entertains, 10. 14
Montagu pities, 10. 20
Nivernais's Jardins modernes given to, 12. 259
Palais-Royal visited by, 4. 159
Paris to be left by, 4. 86, 159, 199, 200
—— to be visited by, 4. 116, 139
—— visited by, 3. 396
(?) Parliament attended by, after opera, 38. 318
Pelham, Frances, entertains, at Esher, 10. 72–3
Piozzi, Mrs, comments on, 10. 15n
Richmond's masquerade attended by, as a pilgrim, 22. 149
sister gives paintings to, 42. 490
sister's misery distresses, 30. 269n
social relations of, in Paris, 3. 396, 406, 4. 7, 30, 31–2, 37, 59, 66, 86, 159, 169, 200, 201
son of, bitten by mad dog, 31. 126
(?) SH visited by Carlisle and, 4. 249
to winter in Paris, 4. 139
Spencer, George (1739–1817), 3d (4th) D. of Marlborough, 1758:
appearance of, at Ferrers's trial, 9. 278, 280–1
Archduke and Archduchess of Austria not courteously treated by, at Blenheim, 33. 531
at Mrs Boyle Walsingham's ball, 42. 222n
Beauclerk, Lady Diana, visited by, 11. 81–2
Bedford, D. of, seeks place for, 22. 463n
Bologna visited by, 21. 512n
brother summoned by, to Blenheim at D. of Bedford's request, 38. 327
Brown's 'flippancy' to, 32. 148, 152
chamberlain's office vacated by, for D. of Devonshire, 22. 130–1
colour-blind, 12. 253
conduct of, regarding children, 11. 198
costume almost conceals beauty of, at George III's coronation, 9. 388

daughter of, 10. 15n
Doge's espousal of sea attended by, at Venice, 21. 512n
Ealing Grove sold by, 11. 8n, 31. 239
expense of, at Venice, 22. 6
father's death benefits estate of, 21. 259
footman sent by, to show observatory to Archduke Ferdinand, 33. 531n
Garter suggested for, 30. 236n
—— to be conferred upon, 22. 572
gems of: copied by Miss Boyle, 42. 204; mostly from Arundelian collection, 42. 204n
Gulston's house bought by, 1. 357
Gunning affair involves, 11. 123–4, 197–8, 199, 217, 279
HW entertains, at breakfast at SH, 39. 418
health of, camp fever and bloody flux, 40. 144
house of, in Pall Mall, 21. 512n
London not visited by, 11. 120
loo played by, 38. 341n
lord chamberlain, 15. 160n, 22. 103
lord privy seal, 10. 6on
marriage of, 38. 170
Masserano entertains, at supper, 38. 399n
Master of the Horse, 22. 130
not at Blenheim but at Syon Hill, 11. 201
old privy seal, perquisite of, 30. 177
Paduan house taken by, 21. 512
Pembroke's letter to wife opened and read by, 10. 17
Poor Bill supported by, 38. 529
'Prince of Mindleheim,' 33. 531
quinze winnings of, at Duc de Guines's ball, 32. 100
Russell, Lady Caroline, to wed, despite his dislike of her mother, 22. 73
Sandwich opposed by, 24. 435
shyness of, when winning at quinze, 32. 100n
sister of, 22. 9n
SH visited by, 12. 221
Syon Hill occupied by, 33. 13n
Temple offered his place by, 30. 187
unmarried, 10. 29
weepers for Ds of Marlborough retained by, at private Court ball, 38. 144
will be eclipsed by Margrave and Margravine of Ansbach, 34. 133
Zanetti's gems said to have been bought by, at Venice, 21. 561
Spencer (after 1817 Spencer-Churchill), George (1766–1840), styled M. of Blandford to 1817; 4th (5th) D. of Marlborough, 1817:
Dashwood, Sir Henry, visited by, 11. 201
Gunning, Elizabeth, said to be marrying, 11. 120, 39. 479
Gunnings' matrimonial plot against, 11. 104, 123, 128n, 136n, 142, 185n, 196, 201, 204, 229, 279
London to be visited by, for match, 11. 120
Lorn has not seen, 11. 108
marriage of, forbidden by Ds of Marlborough, 11. 108n

marriage of, impending, **34.** 125
marriage of, to Lady Susan Stewart, **11.** 348–
9, 352, 366
peerage of, corrected, **43.** 143
sister of, **11.** 82n
son of, **11.** 198n
Sturts visited by, **11.** 141–2
wife of, **9.** 406n
Spencer, George John (1758–1834), styled Vct
Althorp 1765–83; 2d E. Spencer, 1783; M.P.:
arrives in England, with wife, **25.** 632
Du Deffand, Mme, mentions, **7.** 111
——'s social relations with, **6.** 219, 483, 488
engagement of, **25.** 104, 108, **33.** 249–50,
253–4
Fontainebleau to be visited by, **6.** 484
—— visited by, **6.** 488, 490
French navy opposed by, **34.** 230
HW calls, 'our Neptune,' **34.** 230
HW entertains, at breakfast at SH, **39.** 390
HW's nuptial ode for, **33.** 260–1
Italy visited by, with wife, **25.** 613n, 618n
Jones, Sir William, makes nuptial ode for,
33. 287, **35.** 362n
—— tutor to, **29.** 36
mother offered houses by, **33.** 428n
Paris visited by, **6.** 482
Portsmouth visited by, **12.** 179n
Spa visited by, **6.** 488
Vesuvius ascended by, **33.** 509
wife of, **6.** 349n, **12.** 202n
Spencer, Lady Georgiana (1757–1806), m.
(1774) William Cavendish, 5th D. of Devonshire, 1764:
balls attended by, but does not dance when
pregnant, **36.** 233n
Barry includes, in allegorical painting, **29.**
296, 297, 300
Beauclerk, Lady Diana, paints, **28.** 385–6,
419, 421, **43.** 303
beauty of: **5.** 280, 292, 358, 362, **32.** 232; dis-
paraged by HW, **25.** 411
Blagden, Sir Charles, visits, **12.** 214
captured by French, **7.** 177
Combe's satires on, **28.** 313
courier to England sent by, before leaving
Paris, **39.** 467
Craven, Lady, persuaded by, to attend her
play, **29.** 43n
Crewe, Mrs, compared with, **5.** 362, 367
Damer, Mrs, makes bust for, **12.** 272
Derby, Cts of, not visited by, **31.** 194n
Du Deffand, Mme, has social relations with,
5. 358, 403
Egremont's engagement to Lady Charlotte
Maria Waldegrave broken by, **29.** 72n, **35.**
506n, 532n
'empress of fashion,' **35.** 357
eyesight of, threatened, **12.** 202, 214
faro punter, **39.** 377n
Fox, C. J., supported by, in Westminster

election despite indecent abuse by Court
party, **25.** 489
George, P. of Wales (George IV), advised by,
34. 40n
—— envies husband of, **33.** 411
Gordon's scandal about, in *Morning Post*,
33. 117n
Guines, Duc de, gives supper for, **32.** 277
HW jokes about John Paul Jones abducting,
33. 135
HW jokes about wedding presents for, **32.**
194
HW requests copy of 'Ode to Hope' by, **29.**
173, 175, 183, 189
HW to receive, at breakfast, **33.** 21
Hare Naylors receive annuity from, **11.** 268n
Isle-Adam to be visited by, **5.** 403
Keppel, Mrs, tried to entertain, **33.** 481
Ladies' Club's ball attended by, **32.** 232
late hours of, **33.** 21
London reached by, from Basel, **39.** 502
long reign of, in world of fashion, **34.** 534
losses of, in Exchange Alley, **11.** 213
lottery winnings of, **33.** 255
low spirits of, **32.** 392
marriage of, **23.** 562, **24.** 14
Montpellier visited by, **5.** 280
moves from Chatsworth to London, **32.** 392
'Ode to Hope' by, may be printed by HW,
29. 175n
Palmerston's verses written to, **28.** 203
Paris left by, **11.** 27, 36
—— to be left by, **39.** 467
—— visited by, **5.** 280
play planned by, for Richmond House, **33.**
580n
Polignac, Duchesse de, exchanges presents
with, **25.** 427
pregnancy of, influences fashion, **33.** 379–80
pregnant, **36.** 233
probably not a good nurse, **33.** 408
regimental uniform worn by, **33.** 20n
'reigning toast,' **25.** 411n
Roissy to be visited by, **5.** 367
Rutland, Ds of, rival of, **11.** 187n
Sherwin includes, among beauties, **29.** 185
(?) sister-in-law will eclipse, **33.** 250
sister of, **29.** 185n
Uranus may have a counterpart of, **33.** 365
verses to her father written by, sought by
HW, **28.** 203
Spencer, Lady Georgiana Caroline. *See* Carteret, Lady Georgiana Caroline
Spencer, Henrietta Frances (1761–1821), m.
(1780) Frederick Ponsonby, styled Vct Duncannon to 1793; 3d E. of Bessborough, 1793:
Chartres, Duc de, displays indecent buttons
to, at dinner, **25.** 409, 417, **29.** 302
Du Deffand, Mme, has social relations with,
6. 483, 488
Fontainebleau to be visited by, **6.** 484
—— visited by, **6.** 488, 490

[Spencer, Henrietta Frances, *continued*]
Fox, C. J., liked by, **25**. 489n
HW thinks, may not be gentle enough for future husband, **35**. 357
Hobart, Mrs, entertains, at play at Ham Common, **33**. 370
Keppel, Mrs, entertains, at Isleworth, **33**. 481
losses of, in Exchange Alley, **11**. 213
Paris visited by, **6**. 482
'reigning toast,' **25**. 411n
Sherwin includes, among beauties, **29**. 185
Spa visited by, **6**. 488
Spencer, Lord Henry John (1770–95), English ambassador to Holland 1790–3:
Gunning forgery detected by, **11**. 198
London visited by, **11**. 198
Spencer, Hon. John (1708–46), M.P.:
arrested in Covent Garden bagnio, **17**. 505
brother gives bond to, **9**. 34
death of, due to brandy, beer, and tobacco, **19**. 272
house left to, **9**. 119n
Marlborough, Ds of, makes her heir, **19**. 272, **22**. 277n
Pitt gets reversion of estate from, **22**. 277
Vernon's bust at Wimbledon supposedly erected by, **9**. 120
wife of, **9**. 301n, **25**. 78n
will of, **9**. 34
Spencer, John (d. 1767), East India official:
letter from, **23**. 381
Spencer, John (1734–83), cr. (1761) Bn and Vct Spencer, (1765) Vct Althorp and E. Spencer:
Althorp seat of, **9**. 5n, **16**. 324n
Amelia, Ps, entertains, **32**. 307
Barré's pension signed by, **29**. 264
Bath visited by, **31**. 130–1, **35**. 319
becomes Vct, **21**. 490
Bisshopp, Miss, to marry, **37**. 359
Bologna visited by, **22**. 173
Calais visited by, **6**. 231
Cambridge committee member, **2**. 208n
captured by French, **7**. 177
children of, act in Lady Craven's play, **29**. 235n
Cowper, step-brother to, **43**. 280
Craufurd addressed in care of, at Althorp, **41**. 281
——'s social relations with, **6**. 221, **7**. 353
daughter of, **25**. 409n
Devonshire's death reported by, **38**. 450
——'s decline reported by, **38**. 447
Dick to be proxy for, at baptism of Cowper's child, **24**. 233, 239
Ds of Devonshire's verses to, sought by HW, **28**. 203
Du Deffand, Mme, mentions, **7**. 111
——'s social relations with, **5**. 404, **6**. 219, 483, 488
entail of Sunderland estate broken by, **22**. 277n

(?) extravagance of, **21**. 200
financially embarrassed by election expenses, **10**. 256n
Fontainebleau to be visited by, **6**. 484
—— visited by, **6**. 488, 490, **38**. 448, 450
HW jokes about, **33**. 250
HW mentions, **10**. 7
HW sees, in chariot, **31**. 204
health of, **5**. 351, **25**. 78, **31**. 204
Isle-Adam to be visited by, **5**. 403
Jones, Sir William, quarrels with, **29**. 36
Mann encloses letter to, **22**. 336
Montpellier visited by, **5**. 280
mother's bequests to, **33**. 217
mother's house bought for her by, **32**. 318n
mother's jointure inherited by, **25**. 78
Naples and Rome visited by, **22**. 180n
Northamptonshire's moderate petition disappoints, **25**. 10
Paris visited by, **5**. 280, **6**. 482
peerage granted to, **9**. 344
portrait of, **33**. 265
Queensberry House given by, to mother, **33**. 541n
Roissy to be visited by, **5**. 367
Sacchi painting bought by, **21**. 172
Sloper candidate of, for St Albans, **33**. 225n
(?) son's match disapproved by, **25**. 104
Spa visited by, **6**. 488
Stanley at house of, **29**. 5n
——'s social relations with, **7**. 442
——'s suicide in park of, **33**. 161n
stepbrother will entertain, at Florence, **22**. 173
Van Dyck paintings owned by, **15**. 95n
Warton might be aided by, **41**. 164
wife of, **9**. 387n
will of, HW does not know about, **33**. 428
Spencer, Mrs John. *See* Poyntz, Margaret Georgiana
Spencer, Lady Louisa (d. 1769):
death of, **31**. 141
Spencer, Robert (1641–1702), 2d E. of Sunderland, 1643:
birth date of, corrected, **43**. 254
James II dethroned by, **18**. 458, **34**. 101
Maratti paints, at Rome, **42**. 159
Spencer, Robert (1701–29), 4th E. of Sunderland, 1722:
etchings by, **41**. 145
Spencer, Lady Robert. *See* Fawkener, Henrietta (ca 1751–1825)
Spencer, Lord Robert (1747–1831), M.P.:
Beauclerk, Lady Diana, entertains, at breakfast, **11**. 341
Beauclerk, Topham, visited by, **32**. 292
Berkeley Sq. room of, painted by sister, **42**. 490
Berry, Mary, identifies, **11**. 341n
Boufflers, Marquise de, tries to fleece, **5**. 150
collar-bone of, broken, **5**. 170
colour-blind, **12**. 253
Cowdray fountain moved by, to Woolbeding, **43**. 115

defeated in Parliamentary election for Oxford, **11**. 82

Du Deffand, Mme, has said little about HW to, **5**. 21

—— sends parcels by, **4**. 22, 37, **5**. 136, 142, 150

—— to send letter by, **5**. 8

Fox, Hon. Stephen and Lady Mary, accompanied by, in dressing-room, **23**. 392

gambles, **5**. 140

letter to, tells of house-breaking at HW's Arlington St house, **23**. 295

Mann entertains, at dinner, **23**. 295

Marlboroughs entertain, at dinner, **11**. 82

marriage of, **5**. 75n

Moore tutor to, **16**. 280n

Norton moved by, for Speaker, **24**. 60n

Paris left by, **5**. 142

—— to be left by, **5**. 8, 11, 128, 130, 135–6

quadrille danced by, at Duc de Guines's ball, **32**. 110

quietness of, **32**. 292

Richmond boat-race cup given by, **11**. 337, **43**. 150

Richmond Castle visited by, to watch boat race, **11**. 341

social relations of, in Paris, **3**. 396, 406, **4**. 16, 31, **5**. 10, 120, 135, 139, 140, 144

(?) Spencer, Lord Charles, represented by, at Oxfordshire election, **9**. 357

SH visited by, **33**. 403

wife of, **5**. 75n, **11**. 163n

Spencer, William *and* Mary (servants): in Mrs French's will, **11**. 184n

Spencer. *See also* Spenser

Spencer family:

Beauclerk's marriage to Vcts Bolingbroke approved by, **22**. 567

'countenance' of, **35**. 206

Lucan entertains, **33**. 253–4

Pembroke entertains and deserts, **10**. 16

——'s elopement resented by, **22**. 10

Spencer Grove, Twickenham:

Giles lives at, **24**. 243n

see also Little Marble Hill

Spencer Stanhope (Stanhope before 1776), Walter (1749–1822), M.P.:

biographical information about, corrected, **43**. 305

Fitzroy, Lady Georgiana, given away as bride by, **33**. 15n

Smelt's speech ridiculed by, **28**. 492

Spenser, ——:

extravagance of, **21**. 200

Spenser *or* Spencer, Charlotte (d. 1789):

Devonshire, D. of, has daughter by, **25**. 455n, **32**. 139n

Spenser, Edmund (? 1552–99), poet:

Chatterton's imitations unconvincing to readers of, **35**. 584

——'s poems resemble those of, **16** .117

Damer, Mrs, inspired by, to make knight in wax, **12**. 273, **38**. 198n

Faerie Queen by: 'Archimage' in, **35**. 522; Birch's edition of, with Kent's illustrations, **9**. 116; HW compares himself to 'Sir Scudamore' in, **31**. 26; Warton's *Observations* on, **1**. 170, **16**. 146, **40**. 253–4, 368

frontispiece to *Life of Edward Lord Herbert of Cherbury* reminds Montagu of, **10**. 134

Gray's *Odes* mention, **40**. 103

HW calls, 'John Bunyan in rhyme,' **29**. 256

HW censures, **1**. 91

HW mis-attributes Chaucerian lines to, **11**. 62

HW mistakenly attributes poem about strawberries to, **10**. 84–5

HW not fond of, **11**. 68

Mother Hubbard's Tale by, dedicated to Cts of Dorset, **15**. 84n

posterior to 'Rowley,' **16**. 338

sonnet form injured, **15**. 261

stanza said to be in use before the time of, **16**. 114, 115

SH resembles castles described by, **40**. 255

verses not by, **10**. 84–5

Warton's *History* does not extend to, **29**. 118

Yearsley, Mrs, unfamiliar with, **31**. 218

Spenser. *See also* Le Despencer; Spencer

Speranze della terra, Le, opera:

Charlotte, Q., sees, **38**. 123, 126

Sperelli. *See* Manciforte Sperelli

Speronara, Tuscan vessel:

(?) launching of, **22**. 548

Spey, river:

English vanguard approaches, **37**. 229

rebels may defend, **37**. 224

rebels run away at, **37**. 238

Speyer (Germany):

English army approaches, **37**. 148

Spezia (Italy):

English squadron guards, **19**. 55

fleets said to leave, for Toulon, **17**. 323

France said to have demanded, of Genoa, **20**. 277

French ships between Genoa and, **17**. 322

governor of, warns Genoa of arrival of Spanish fleet, **17**. 308–10

limit set to English ships which can stay at, **20**. 588

Lowestoft and *Terrible* cruise off, taking prizes, **19**. 277n

Mann receives letter from, about attack on San Remo, **19**. 121

Montemar said to have reached, **17**. 195

pope's ship carried to, **17**. 16

Spanish army's landings at, **17**. 179, 182, 198, 314, 323, 350, **18**. 405, 413

Spanish army leaves garrison at, **17**. 289

Spanish barks at, **17**. 262

Spezia, gulf of:

importance of, **17**. 309

Spaniards patrol, **17**. 317

Spanish expedition may aim for, **17**. 206

two fleets in, **17**. 311

Sphinx, French ship:

in Vilaine river, **21**. 351

Sphinx; sphinxes:
'a harmless dicky-bird' compared with Lady
Anne Fitzpatrick, **33**. 258
at the Vyne, **35**. 640
'coquet, with straw hats and French cloaks,'
7. 357
HW describes modern versions of, on gate-
posts near Livry, **10**. 212
Spice; spices:
caravan of, from India, **24**. 510n
French, inferior, **35**. 485n
Raynal discusses, **39**. 168
'spicy gale,' **30**. 308
Spice-plate:
Harcourt serves, to Charles VI, **35**. 486
Spider; spiders:
Argyll's interest in, **37**. 150
scarlet, procured by HW from Adm. Bos-
cawen for Ds of Portland, **9**. 114
Sloane's museum contains, **20**. 358–9
Spierincx, Frans (1551–1630):
tapestries by, **23**. 242n
Spina, Jean, Cadet:
captured at Velletri, **18**. 493
Spinach:
tarts of, **17**. 218
Spinage, John, London magistrate:
(?) house of, in West Drayton, interests
Montagu, **10**. 255–6
(?) Montagu's correspondence with, **10**.
255–6
(?) Wilkes applies to, **22**. 138
Spindler, ——, Maj. (d. 1743):
killed at Campo Santo, **18**. 164
Spindle tree:
HW has, **33**. 304
Spinelli, Marchese:
Mann to procure flute for, through Croft,
23. 377
passport in name of, **18**. 388
Spinelli, Ferdinando Maria (1728–95), cardi-
nal, 1785; gov. of Rome, 1778:
Clement XIII summons, to advisory congre-
gation, **21**. 308n
Pius VI urged by, to suppress Carnival, **25**.
383
Spinelli, Gaetano (1688–1766), senator:
Lady Walpole's cases opened by, **17**. 224
Spinelli, Giuseppe (1694–1763), cardinal, 1735:
Louis XV wants French candidate elected by,
17. 20–1
Old Pretender visited by, at Albano, after
Benedict XIV's audience, **20**. 590
—— writes to, of grudge against Benedict
XIV, **20**. 590
Spinelli, Scipione or Carlantonio, Principe di
Cariati:
earthquake destroys manors of, **33**. 197
Spinhamlands. See Speenhamland
Spinnage. See Spinage
Spinola, Marchesa. See Durazzo, Pauline (ca
1755–73); Lévis, Gabrielle-Augustine-Fran-
çoise de (b. 1762)

Spinola, ——:
Ferdinand VI admits, to his Court and min-
istry, **19**. 278n
Spinola, Cristoforo Vincenzo, Marchese; Geno-
ese minister to France:
marriage of, arranged, **7**. 453
social relations of, in Paris, **7**. 344, 347, 348,
351, 460
Spinola, Giorgio (1667–1739), cardinal:
HW and Gray ask about nephew of, **13**. 193
Spinola, Giovanni Battista (1681–1752), car-
dinal, 1733:
votes for, at Papal election, **17**. 16–17
Spinola, Girolamo (1713–84), vice-legate to
Bologna:
HW and Gray see, **13**. 193
Molinari succeeds, as vice-legate, **18**. 138n
Spinola, Palazzo, at Genoa:
plunder of, by mob, **19**. 352n
Spinola de la Cerda. See Cordova Spinola de la
Cerda
Spinola family:
Los Balbases of, **17**. 13n
Spinoza, Baruch (1632–77):
Voltaire defends Bayle against, **3**. 113n
Spinster; spinsters:
college for, proposed, **42**. 305
'Spintria' (pornography):
HW's, **15**. 22
Spintrian medals. See under Medal
Spire; spires:
Gothic, HW suggests, at Mistley, **30**. 87
of Salisbury Cathedral, **40**. 8
on 'Priory of St Hubert,' **35**. 644
to be added to Vyne barn, **35**. 640
Spires. See Speyer
Spiridov, Alexei Grigor'evich (fl. 1770–90),
Russian naval officer:
escape of, at Tchesmé battle, **23**. 227, 233
(?) on board *Winchelsea* at Leghorn, **23**. 233
Spiridov, Grigorii Andreevich (1713–90), Rus-
sian naval officer; Kt:
fleet of: **23**. 146n, 148n, 226n; Orlov to join,
23. 326n
Orlov notified by officer from, **23**. *162*
Port Mahon left by, for the Levant, **23**. 172n
Russian ship arrives with, at Port Mahon,
23. 162
ship of, blown up, **23**. 227, 233, 234
ships of, at Port Mahon, **23**. 185
Turkish fleet, said to be burnt by, at Lemnos,
23. 319
Spirit of lavendar. See under Lavendar
Spirit of Patriotism. See St John, Henry (1678–
1751), Vct Bolingbroke: *Letters*
Spirits (distilled liquors):
casks of, staved in Gordon riots, **35**. 505
duties on, removed, **24**. 542n
fœtuses preserved in, in Sloane's museum,
20. 359
Middlesex, Cts of, preserves miscarriage in,
19. 447

Spirits of camphor:
 gout remedy, 35. 259
Spiritual Quixote. See under Graves, Rev. Richard (1715–1804)
Spitalfields, London:
 damask hangings made in, 32. 107
 mob from, supports Crosby, 23. 290n
 weavers in, 36. 55, 38. 461
Spital Sq., London:
 Giles and Mesman live in, 24. 243n, 244n
 Rice lives in, 20. 397
'Spite Hall':
 Shirley builds, 35. 358
Spithead, near Portsmouth, Hants:
 Boscawen's fleet arrives at, 20. 511n
 Brederode reaches, 19. 556
 Conway, Hugh, goes to, 11. 262n
 Cornwallis, Effingham, and Hervey arrive at, 21. 23n
 English fleet at, 39. 338, 40. 8
 George III and Q. Charlotte at, 24. 377n
 Hardy anchors at, 28. 462n
 Heroic Postscript mentions, 28. 113
 Norris's squadron returns to, 13. 230n
 West, Adm., arrives at, in *Antelope* with Byng, 20. 583n
 witnesses for Byng's trial sail from Gibraltar to, 20. 590n
Spithead Expeditions:
 of Sir Robert Walpole, 34. 201
Spithead Squadron:
 Roquefeuil to destroy, to clear English Channel for invasion, 18. 383n
Spitting of blood:
 occurrence of, 33. 370
'Spittlefields':
 HW's name for Lady Powis's great room, 32. 107
 quarrel in, 32. 107, 112
 See also Spitalfields
Spittle *or* Spittal Sq. *See* Spital Sq.
Spitzer, 'hussar-dog':
 Fitzroy, Lady Caroline, romps with, 30. 84
Spleen, The. See under Green, Matthew
'Spleen, English':
 English weakness, 20. 1
 Mann claims to have, 20. 404
Spon, Jacob (1647–85), antiquary:
 Middleton writes against, 15. 295
Sponge; sponges:
 eyes to be helped by, 18. 386
 hot: Mann applies, to breast, 19. 8; Mann uses, for pain in stomach, 22. 469
Sponging-house:
 Poniatowski, Prince, carried to, 11. 243
Spoon; spoons:
 at Trinity Hospital, Greenwich, 16. 91
 Croat carries, 37. 142
 for frankincense, 32. 324
 gold, for Leopold's household, made from furnishings in Palazzo Pitti, 25. 231
 Mann's, acquired from Fane, 18. 472
 See also Teaspoon

Spooner, Charles (1720–67):
 mezzotint by, of George III, 21. 554n
Spoon-meat:
 Parliament should limit eating to, 33. 526
Spörcken, August Friedrich (1698–1776), Freiherr von; army officer:
 Conway meets, 39. 537
 (?) Cumberland, D. of, sends, to surprise French troops, 21. 117n
Spork, Johann Joseph (1695–1749):
 (?) at Aix-la-Chapelle, 18. 304n
Spours, battle of:
 near Morguesson, 35. 641
Sprain:
 HW tries to pretend that his gout is, 35. 259
Sprat, Thomas (1635–1713), Bp of Rochester, 1684; historian:
 flower-pot that held evidence against: formerly at Bromley, 35. 132; seen by HW at Matson, 35. 153
 Hurd's dialogues the 'offspring' of, 16. 34
 not educated at Westminster, 29. 259
Sprengporten, J. M.:
 Swedish revolution planned by, 23. 436n
Sprig:
 Walpole, Sir Edward, promises, to Mrs Scott, 10. 329
Sprightly, cutter:
 Portsmouth left by, for Guernsey, 39. 362n
Sprimont, Nicholas (1716–71):
 Chelsea china made by, 22. 121–2
Spring; springs (mechanical):
 bent in coach accident, 39. 454
 HW's servants allow chaise to come away without, 37. 66
 to cables of Turkish fleet, 23. 234
Spring Garden Gate:
 cane shop in, 35. 365n
Spring Gardens (between St James's Park, Charing Cross, and Whitehall, London):
 Berkeley's house in, 17. 210n
 Cox's museum in, 28. 325n
 exhibition at, of Jervais's works, 2. 170
 HW escorts two ladies to Cts of Albemarle's in, 24. 442
 Pelham lives in, 30. 22
 Royal Incorporated Society of Artists in, 23. 210n
'Spring Gardens, new.' *See* Vauxhall
Sproken. *See* Spörcken
Sprotborough, Yorks:
 Copley of, 11. 352n
Sproule *or* Sprowle, Mrs John Rowland. *See* Masters, Anne
Spruce firs:
 HW to send, to Montagu, 9. 177
 placing of, as accents, 9. 177
Spry, Sir Richard (1715–75), Kt, 1773; naval officer:
 Orford, Cts of, to be taken by, in ship from Naples to Marseille, 23. 2
Spry, Mrs William. *See* Pitt, Amelia

Spur; spurs:
Conway busy with, **37**. 358
Danvers wears, **35**. 70
Elizabeth's, not bought by HW, **15**. 19
lack of, in portrait shows that subject has not been knighted, **41**. 431
man wears, to London theatre, **17**. 172
Vorontsov wears, to dinner table, **21**. 248
William III's: given to HW by Harcourt, **35**. 477–8, 488; HW owns, **28**. 339; Hardinge wants evidence about, **35**. 598
Spurs, Battle of:
erroneous name for Spours, **35**. 641
Spy, English sloop:
news brought by, from Guadeloupe, **21**. 289n
Spy; spies:
English, seized by French at Brest, **19**. 182n
French: hanged in Isle of Wight, **37**. 496; Hawley hangs, **19**. 201, 241; surgeon asks Hawley for corpse of, to dissect, **19**. 201
French ministers employ, on foreigners in Paris, **39**. 17
Gordon at Brest as, **23**. 183n
Mann's, at Rome: abbé is, **17**. 113, 114, 140; gets information from valet, **17**. 202n
St-Germain arrested as, **19**. 181–2, **26**. 20, 21
Virrette arrested as, **19**. 182n
Spyers, John (d. 1798), draughtsman:
SH visited by, **12**. 221
SH visitors sent by, **12**. 241, 246
Spy-glass; spy-glasses:
(?) Amherst's, **9**. 248
Du Deffand, Mme, buys, **3**. 393, 404, **4**. 5, 7, 10, 19, 27, 28, 30–1, 36
(?) Montagu uses, at Waldershare, **10**. 321
to see thoughts, **33**. 365
Spying-glass; spying-glasses:
Macaronis use, **38**. 306
on cane, **35**. 86
pocket, for viewing China, **37**. 293
Square; squares:
London's, new, **24**. 228
Squawking:
HW mentions, **37**. 465
Squib; squibs:
for Rodney, disturb HW's sleep, **25**. 281
Frederick makes, from papillotes, **37**. 297
in London, for Amherst's capture of Montreal, **21**. 437
in London bonfires, after battle of Minden, **21**. 314
Jupiter lights, in English opera, **19**. 370
mob throws, in London, **24**. 442
Squibb, George (ca 1764–1831), auctioneer:
in Savile Row, **11**. 101n
Squibb, James, auctioneer:
(?) room of, converted into theatre, **11**. 101
Squillace, Marqués de. *See* Gregorio, Leopoldo de
Squillace (Italy):
earthquake account mentions, **25**. 376
Squinancy. *See* Quinsy

Squire, —— (d. 1763), m. John Newcome:
print of, **1**. 280, 281, 282, 284, 284n, 285
Squire, Rev. Samuel (1713–66), rector of St Anne's, Soho; Bp of St David's, 1761:
Bute believed by, to be Ps of Wales's lover, **21**. 6n
dubious about HW's inscription to K. Theodore, **21**. 140
Squire; squires:
country, in uniform, **21**. 311–12
Montagu's companionship with, **10**. 140, 142, 144
stammering, described by Swift, **35**. 30
'Squire of Low Degree':
HW quotes, **32**. 193–4
Squires, Mary, gypsy:
Canning, Elizabeth, accuses, **35**. 175
Squirrel; squirrels:
HW needs activity of, **39**. 258
HW's, **31**. 36
jerboa resembles, **9**. 142
Strafford, Cts of, has, **35**. 275n
See also 'Hunt the Squirrel'
Sreemunth Mhade Row Narrain, Pundit Purdhan:
English make Convention of Wurgaon with, **24**. 509n
Staal, Baronne de. *See* Cordier de Launay, Marguerite-Jeanne
Staal. *See also* Staël
Stabat mater:
Brown and Mingotti sing, in Passion Week, **9**. 219
Stable; stables:
arch in, at Sissinghurst, **35**. 144
at Newmarket, **41**. 6
Ghent people live in, **37**. 124
HW refuses to accommodate Goodere with, **42**. 317
Leopold's, visited by Maria Amalia, **25**. 301
Welbeck riding-stable converted into, **35**. 271
Stable-boy. *See under* Servant
Stable Yard, St James's St, London:
Harrington's house in, **33**. 97n, **38**. 259
York, D. of, builds house in, **20**. 48n
Stackelberg, Comte de:
Craven, Bns, presented by, to Stanislas II, **25**. 633n
Stade (Germany):
convention at, *see* Klosterzeven: convention of
Cumberland, D. of, should not have marched towards, **21**. 146
—— takes route of, to Hanover, **21**. 28
Rochefort expedition might be diverted to, to aid D. of Cumberland, **37**. 501n
suspension of arms at, *see* Klosterzeven: convention of
Stadler, Joseph Constantine (fl. 1780–1812):
engravings by, **15**. 218n
Stadt (Germany):
Hanover ministry flee to, **37**. 554

Stadtholder. *See under* Holland

Staël-Holstein, Baronne de. *See* Necker, Anne-Louise-Germaine

Staël-Holstein, Eric Magnus (d. 1802), Baron de; Swedish ambassador to France:
arrives in Paris, **11.** *45*
Gustav III's instructions to, **11.** 336, 346
social relations of, with Mme du Deffand, **7.** 430

Staff; staves:
chamberlain's, **21.** 91, **22.** 96
Devonshire, D. of, leaves, with Egremont, **22.** 96
lord steward's, **41.** 73
lord treasurer's, **35.** 148
pilgrim's, **17.** 339
white: Bateman and Edgcumbe receive, as comptroller and treasurer of the Household, **37.** 481; carried by Magdalen-House governors, **9.** 273, 274; comptroller of the Household's, held by Lord Charles Spencer, **38.** 320; comptroller of the Household's, Hillsborough fond of, **9.** 181; Hertford does not imitate Devonshire in breaking, **38.** 424; of lord chamberlain, **22.** 103n; of treasurer and comptroller, **37.** 481; of treasurer of the Household, **33.** 104n; used by state officers but not coveted by HW, **35.** 340

Staffa, Isle of:
Banks's account of, **1.** 329n, 336

Stafford, Bn. *See* Jerningham, Sir George William Stafford (1771–1851); Stafford, Edward (1573–1625); Stafford, Henry (ca 1534–66)

Stafford, Cts of. *See* Cantillon, Henrietta (d. 1761); Gramont, Claude-Charlotte de (ca 1659–1739)

Stafford, E. of. *See* Leveson Gower, Granville (1721–1803); Stafford Howard, John Paul (1700–62); Stafford Howard, William (ca 1690–1734); Stafford Howard, William Matthias (1719–51)

Stafford, Lady. *See* Howard, Douglas (ca 1545–1608)

Stafford, Marchioness of. *See* Stewart, Lady Susanna (ca 1743–1805); Sutherland, Elizabeth (1765–1839)

Stafford, M. of. *See* Leveson Gower, George Granville (1758–1833); Leveson Gower, George Granville (1786–1861); Leveson Gower, Granville (1721–1803)

Stafford, Anne (d. 1472), m. Aubrey de Vere:
received into fraternity of Bury Abbey, **2.** 38

Stafford, Anthony:
Honour and Virtue by, commemorates 5th Bn Stafford, **42.** 44n

Stafford, Edward (1469–99), 4th E. of Wiltshire:
at Henry VII's Court, **2.** 365

Stafford, Edward (1478–1521), 3d D. of Buckingham, 1485:
claim of, to throne, **33.** 454

Fenn's unidentified portrait may be of, **16.** 234

'Plotting Closet' of, at Thornbury Castle, **32.** 322

print of, **1.** 207n

put to death by Henry VIII, **15.** 172, **42.** 208n

Stafford, Edward (1573–1625), Bn Stafford:
arms of, **1.** 149

Stafford, Francis, Young Pretender's tutor:
Young Pretender sends, to brother, **18.** 377–8
—— to receive effects of, in France from Rome, **18.** 433–4

Stafford, Henry (1455–83), 2d D. of Buckingham:
Clarence, D. of, executed under supervision of, **41.** 324
extent of power of, **15.** 172
mentioned in 'Coronation roll,' **14.** 182
rebellion of, mysterious, **15.** 175
spurious portrait of, **1.** 207
takes up arms against Richard III, **14.** 165
widow of, **2.** 363

Stafford, Henry (d. 1481), 2d son of 1st D. of Buckingham:
received into fraternity of Bury Abbey, **2.** 38

Stafford, Henry (ca 1534–66), 2d Bn Stafford, 1563:
Mirrour for Magistrates licensed by interest of, **16.** 367n

Stafford, Henry (1621–37), 5th Bn Stafford:
Honour and Virtue eulogizes, **42.** 44n

Stafford, Henry (fl. 1744–64), Young Pretender's companion:
Bath's former 'creature,' **20.** 9
Young Pretender accompanied by, at Avignon, **20.** 9n
—— said to be banished with, to Pont Beauvoisin, **20.** 9

Stafford, Humphrey (1402–60), 1st D. of Buckingham:
children of, **2.** 38n
daughter of, **3.** 38n
Meir or Mere Manor granted by, to Macclesfield, **42.** 145
Penshurst owned by, **35.** 142
portrait of, at Penshurst, **35.** 141–2
received into fraternity of Bury Abbey, **2.** 38
son of, **16.** 234n
wife of, **14.** 75n

Stafford, Humphrey (d. 1455), styled E. of Stafford:
received into fraternity of Bury Abbey, **2.** 38
wife of, **16.** 234n

Stafford, John (d. 1452) Abp of Canterbury 1443–52:
Henry VI gives jewel to, **14.** 75
opens Parliament at Bury, **2.** 37
perhaps shown in HW's picture, **14.** 75

Stafford, Staffs:
races at, **21.** 421, **22.** 174n

Stafford family:
Arundel collection sold by, **15.** 114

Stafford House:
  Arundel collection in, 1. 192n
Stafford Howard, Lady Henrietta Maria (d.
  1756), m. (1748) Claude-Prosper Jolyot de
  Crébillon:
  E. of Stafford's aunt, 7. 281
  husband takes, to provinces, 20. 325
Stafford Howard, John Paul (1700–62), 4th E.
  of Stafford:
  picture owned by 'Popish family' of, 1. 281
Stafford Howard, Lady Mary Apolonia Scolas-
  tica (1721–69), m. (1744) Guy-Auguste de
  Rohan-Chabot, Comte de Chabot:
  affairs of, 7. 285
  England to be visited by, 3. 301
  father of, 31. 29n
  French country visits of, 31. 45, 64
  good nature of, 31. 69
  HW fails to find, at home, 31. 50
  HW's attentions from, 31. 69
  HW's card from, says she will take letter to
    Hertford, 38. 430
  HW's correspondence with, 31. 29
  HW to see, in Paris, 10. 172
  Hervey, Bns, admired by, 31. 64
  —— inquired for by, 31. 75, 81
  —— receives compliments of, 31. 60
  Historic Doubts received by, 4. 33
  Jonzac, Mme de, receives allegory on Rous-
    seau from, 3. 37
  —— receives news of HW from, 3. 314, 324
  marriage of, 18. 430
  narrow escape of, in Channel crossing, 31. 136
  Rohan-Chabot, Duchesse de, mourns, 4. 265
  social relations of, in Paris, 31. 60, 62, 64;
    see also index entries ante 8. 519
Stafford Howard, William (ca 1690–1734), 2d E.
  of Stafford:
  daughter of, 31. 29n
Stafford Howard, William Matthias (?1719–51),
  3d E. of Stafford, 1734:
  Crébillon marries aunt of, 7. 281
  England revisited by, before invasion threat,
    18. 429
  France preferred by, 17. 135
  —— revisited by, for sister's wedding, 18.
    429–30
  HW on round of dinners with, 17. 131
  Histoire de Dom B—— bound by, like prayer-
    book, 17. 273–4
  (?) Knight, Mrs, has affair with, 17. 126
  London and Paris to be residences of, 18. 277
  marriage of, 18. 219, 277
  peerage of, corrected, 43. 249
  returns to England, with stories of Primate of
    Lorraine, 17. 273
  St Gregory's College, Paris, attended by, 17.
    135n
  wife left by, in France, 18. 430
  wife to be exiled by, to Shropshire, 9. 95
  Winnington entertains, with HW, 18. 283
  —— jokes with, about Catholicism and fast-
    ing, 18. 283

Stafford Row, Buckingham Gate, London:
  Bedford, Charles, lives at, 42. 492
Staffordshire:
  Allen collects materials for history of, 1. 4n
  Child family wrongly said to have seat in,
    12. 72
  Conolly, Lady Anne, to meet daughter in, 31.
    199
  Etruscan vases made in, 23. 211; see also under
    Wedgwood, Josiah
  Garrick visits, for nephew's wedding, 41. 367
  Jacobites in, 9. 115
  Leake and Stone in, 19. 178
  Meir or Mere Manor in, 42. 145
  visitors to: Mason, 28. 224; North, Lord, 33.
    347
  Wyatt's great-grandfather a farmer in, 41. 232
Staffordshire ware. See under Wedgwood,
  Josiah
Staffort. See Stafford
Stag; stags:
  French princes hunt, 40. 387
  Henry, P. of Wales, depicted when killing,
    35. 73
  Wortley builds lodge to hear belling of, 35.
    269
Stage:
  elephant breaks, 17. 358
  England, like Athens, as fond of, as of the
    state, 24. 435
  enlarged, for Venetian scene in opera, 17.
    302
  HW thinks royalty are like actors on, 25. 552,
    624
  See also Opera; Theatre
Stage box. See under Theatre
Stage-coach; stage-coaches:
  at Hatfield, 9. 349
  Damer, Mrs, sends plants to SH by, 12. 36
  evening, to Twickenham, 11. 162
  forward place in, 32. 374
  HW leads the life of a, 33. 11
  HW likes landscape views to include, 24. 196
  HW receives message by, of E. of Orford's
    insanity, 24. 293
  jumbling of passengers in, 9. 200
  leave from Whitehorse Cellar, 21. 313
  letters to be forwarded by, 12. 16, 37. 511
  regularity of, 11. 260
  Richardson, Mrs, goes by, to London, 12. 134
  Russian fleet as slow as, 23. 224
  Salisbury, E. of, imitates manners of driver
    of, 10. 348
  state: 'a gold glass-case,' 34. 210; slow, 33. 156
  string of, on road, 39. 498
  See also Coach
Stage scenery:
  in Nature Will Prevail, 41. 243
  See also under Opera; Theatre
Stag-hunting:
  humans as stag and hounds enact, for Louis
    XV, 37. 339, 340

INDEX

Stagione:
Mann's slow convalescence attributed to, **24.** 479

Stahremberg. *See* Starhemberg

Stainberg, Bn, secretary of state for Hanover: Arenberg entertained by, **18.** 97n

Stainbrook. *See* Stainforth

Stained (and painted) glass:
account of, by Thomas Wilson, **1.** 21
at: Abbot's Hospital, Guilford, **16.** 197; Balliol College, **9.** 289n; Battle, **35.** 140; Beckley, **9.** 326, 336; Bristol Cathedral, **10.** 232; Bromley, stolen from Westminster Abbey, **35.** 132; Castle Ashby, **10.** 336; Chenies, **9.** 102; Copt Hall, **9.** 92; Coughton, **9.** 224–5; Crewe Hall, **10.** 966; Dublin, **10.** 11; Fotheringhay, **10.** 91; Fulham Palace, **31.** 313; Gothurst, **10.** 332; Hall Place, **9.** 92; Hartlebury Castle, **35.** 149; Hinchingbrooke, **40.** 283, 284; Hurstmonceaux, **35.** 138; Letheringham, **35.** 248; Malvern Priory, **35.** 151; Mereworth, **35.** 144; Messing church, Essex, **9.** 91, **33.** 206, **34.** 22; New College chapel, **39.** 435; New Hall, **9.** 92; Outwell, **40.** 225; Oxford, **9.** 288–90, **10.** 42, **35.** 155, **39.** 435; Prinknash, **1.** 342, **43.** 60; Ragley, **9.** 224; St Margaret's, Westminster, **41.** 142; SH (*see below under* HW's, at SH); Trinity Hospital, Greenwich, **16.** 86; Vyne, the, **20.** 485n, **35.** 641; Walpole St Peter, **40.** 224–5; Warkworth, armorial, **35.** 77; Wroxton, by Van Linge, **35.** 73
Brown, Lady, gives pane of, to HW for SH, **40.** 89
Carter to draw, at Fairford, **16.** 198
Chatterton's remarks on, **16.** 103, 113, 221, **31.** 326, **34.** 150
church windows in, for stage scenery, **39.** 133
Cole begs, **1.** 143
—— given, by HW, **2.** 47, 48, 321
—— quotes Chishull on, **1.** 20
Du Deffand, Mme, wishes to send, to HW, **5.** 172
Ewin's apparatus for, **1.** 161n
for Gothic castle at Nuneham, **29.** 263, 270
French, **1.** 194
HW continues buying, despite invasion threats, **37.** 444
HW does not remember seeing, in Italy, **20.** 111, 119
HW gets, from Flanders, **20.** 199–200
HW grateful for Zouch's present of, **16.** 43
HW lacks, **1.** 145
HW mentions, **10.** 61
HW's, at SH: **4.** 439, **5.** 172, 224, 235, **9.** 102, 146–7, 150–1, 385, **10.** 61, 64, 72, 120, 274, 307, **20.** 371, 382, 391, 396, **23.** 365, **31.** 216, **35.** 494; broken by Lord Holland, **34.** 88; explosion breaks, **23.** 365; HW amasses, **20.** 111, 119, 371–2; HW describes, **20.** 382; in Beauclerk Tower, **28.** 318; in every window, **31.** 216; Palmer glazier for, **20.** 396; red ivy would look well through, **21.** 457–8;

sunshine illuminates, **25.** 532; transfigured by 'Delineator,' **28.** 329; West asks who was maker of, **40.** 312
HW's memory of rose window in, **9.** 224
HW still buys panes of, **37.** 444
HW to give, to Mason for Nuneham, **35.** 521
HW vainly asks Mann to get, for SH, **20.** 111, 119
HW wants, **16.** 40
in Stowe temple, from Warwick priory, **35.** 77
Liotard's, **33.** 417n
modern: armorial, at Knole, **35.** 134; in Bulstrode chapel, **35.** 233
Montagu inquires about, for HW, **9.** 328
—— seeks design for rose window in, for church, **10.** 11
——'s remarks on, **16.** 146–7
——'s rose window in, finished, **10.** 18
origins of, discussed in Chatterton's letters to HW, **31.** 326, **34.** 150
painters of, should study false jewels, **28.** 253–4
Peckitt's: at Hinchingbrooke, **40.** 283, 284; for Exeter Cathedral, **41.** 102
Price's, in bishop's house at Gloucester, **35.** 153
—— to paint, for the Vyne, **35.** 639
prices of, **1.** 21, 145n, 147
sale of, **38.** 340n
Selwyn given, by HW, **1.** 341
—— gives, to HW for SH, **30.** 136n
Sherfield breaks, **1.** 8
window painted by Jervais from Reynolds's 'Nativity' for New College Chapel, **29.** 301
Wolsey satirized in, at Oxford, **16.** 47
York minster's, **16.** 47
Zouch procures, for HW, **16.** 41
See also under Elias, Matthew; Michu, Benoît; Sempy, P.A.

Staines, Middlesex:
ground floors uninhabitable at, in flood, **35.** 265
Thames, above, **11.** 124n

Stainforth, Mr, of Weybridge:
SH visited by, **12.** 233 *bis*, 246

Stainforth, Mrs:
SH visited by, **12.** 238

Stainmore (*or* Stanemore, *or* Stanmore):
'wintry wild' of, **10.** 307, **33.** 540

Stainsted, Norfolk:
Orford, 3d E. of, carried to, **41.** 260n

Stainville, Comte de. *See* Choiseul, Jacques-Philippe de (d. 1789); Choiseul-Stainville, Étienne-François de (1719–85)

Stainville, Comtesse de. *See* Clermont d'Amboise, Thomassine-Thérèse de

Stainville, Marquis de. *See* Choiseul, François-Joseph de (1695–1769); Choiseul, Jacques-Philippe de (d. 1789)

Stair, E. of. *See* Dalrymple, John (1673–1747); Dalrymple, John (1749–1821); Dalrymple Crichton, William (1699–1768)

Staircase; staircases:
  at Cowdray, **41**. 105
  at Knole, not good, **35**. 132
  at SH, *see under* SH
  at the Vyne, **35**. 642
  Du Deffand, Mme, inquires about, in HW's Berkeley Sq. house, **30**. 272
  HW has difficulty in walking down, **10**. 269
  handing of ladies at, **10**. 269
  Templars try to kiss Ps of Wales and Lady Middlesex on, **30**. 95
  to Cts Waldegrave's lodgings, very bad, **31**. 394
  to Uffizi gallery, **22**. 123
  window on, **30**. 89
  wooden, peculiar to England, **22**. 143
Stairs. *See* Staircase
Stake and crossroads:
  old custom for burial of suicides, **31**. 267
Stalbridge, Dorset:
  Colman rector of, **2**. 72n
Staley, Andrew (ca 1733–1813), King's Messenger:
  HW sends letter and parcel by, **7**. 378
  Stormont sends news of Louis XV by, **24**. 1
Stalham, Norfolk:
  HW's will mentions, **30**. 344
  HW's will mentions Stalham Hall with Brunstead in, **30**. 368
Stamford, Cts of. *See* Bentinck, Lady Henrietta (1737–1827); Booth, Lady Mary (ca 1703–72)
Stamford, E. of. *See* Grey, George Harry (1737–1819); Grey, George Harry (1765–1845); Grey, Harry (1715–68)
Stamford, Lincs:
  Burghley House near, **10**. 91n
  Cole and HW to visit, **10**. 344
  Cottesmore near, **25**. 222, 461, 546, 678
  Cust of, **9**. 398n
  distance to, from Drayton, **10**. 343
  Dodd and Whaley to visit, **40**. 17
  George Inn at, **11**. 33n
  Great Road superb as far as, **35**. 266
  HW writes from, **10**. 88–91, **43**. 130
  Harrod bookseller at, **16**. 194
  Langton's glass at, **1**. 176
  Peck's *Annals* of, **1**. 176
  print of St Leonard's Priory at, **1**. 176
  rebels reported at, **14**. 2
  St George's Church in, **1**. 176
Stamford Baron, Lincs:
  Plumptre dies at, **2**. 154n
Stammer. *See* Stanmer
Stampa, Marquis de:
  SH visited by, **12**. 231
Stampa, Carlo Francesco (1685–1751), Gen.:
  Botta to succeed, **20**. 320
  death of, **20**. 295
  Francis I's commissary for Italy, **20**. *24*, 295
  Grand Duke of Tuscany's villa occupied by, **20**. 116
  'paragino' at Pisa, **20**. *24*

Richecourt disputes with, over chairs and stools, **20**. 320
  —— fears that Craon will be succeeded by, **20**. 24
Stamp Act. *See under* Parliament: acts of
Stamperia Bonducciana:
  Arno Miscellany printed at, **25**. 507, **26**. 46
Stand; stands:
  at Elizabeth Chudleigh's, **9**. 277
  silver, left by Electress to Rinuccini, **18**. 169
Standard; standards:
  captured at Piacenza, **19**. 267, 270
  English and French lose, at Laeffeld, **37**. 274
  French: captured at Louisbourg and carried to St Paul's, **21**. 238; HW might wrap, in postscript, **21**. 518
  of Blenheim, in Westminster Hall, **25**. 337
  recaptured from Spaniards, **18**. 189
  Spaniards capture, **19**. 119
  —— send, to Madrid, **18**. 161, 189
Standgate Creek:
  Mediterranean vessels perform quarantine at, **18**. 276n
Standish; standishes:
  HW keeps letter in, **19**. 372
  HW might have thrown, at Wolfe, **38**. 69
  metal, HW's, at Arlington St, **23**. 285
  owned by Q. Elizabeth, **32**. 323
  silver: Pomfret, Cts of, gives, to Uguccioni, **18**. 126; Vere robbed of, **35**. 315
Standon, Herts:
  HW visits ruins of, **40**. 198–9
Standon School:
  Kendal master of, **40**. 198
Standstead. *See* Stanstead Park
'Standup, Phil':
  HW's name for Lord Chesterfield, **40**. 88
'Standup, Will':
  HW's name for Harrington, **40**. 88
Stanford. *See* Stamford
Stanford Court, Worcs:
  Winnington of, **10**. 49n
Stanford Hall, Leics:
  Cave of, **41**. 236n
Stanhoe, Norfolk:
  Robert, Bn Walpole, has house at, **13**. 13, **18**. 249
Stanhope, Cts. *See* Grenville, Louisa (1758–1829); Hamilton, Grisel (ca 1719–1811)
Stanhope, Lady. *See* Delaval, Anne Hussey (1731–1811)
Stanhope, Maj.:
  Conway behaves kindly in affair of, **42**. 74
Stanhope, Hon. Alexander (d. 1707), envoy to Spain and Holland:
  d'Ayrolles, clerk to, at The Hague, **19**. 404
  d'Ayrolles, Mme, mistress to, **19**. 404
  witticism by, on relations with clerk's wife, **30**. 308n
Stanhope, Lady Amelia ('Emily') (1749–80), m. (1767) Richard Barry, 6th E. of Barrymore:
  admired when in Paris, **30**. 264, **31**. 183

affairs of, with Ancaster and Deerhurst, **32.** 144n

ball given by, **6.** 265

Barrymore to marry, **31.** 125

coiffures from Paris preoccupy, **35.** 477

Coke, Lady Mary, discusses servant's health with, **7.** 350

—— quarrels with, **31.** 183–5

Compiègne visited by, **32.** 55, **35.** 344

Damer, Mrs, friend of, **35.** 414–15

death of, falsely reported, **33.** 212

Egremont might marry, **39.** 176

French sojourn contemplated by, **6.** 317

HW's verses on, **32.** 144

health of, better, **33.** 212

house taken by, in Paris, **39.** 258

husband may soon be replaced by, **35.** 415

income of, **32.** 144

lies in, after death of husband, **32.** 139

Liotard to depict, **37.** 355

social relations of, in Paris, **6.** 229, 232, 273, 282, **7.** 345, 347–51, **31.** 183

Stormont attentive to, **6.** 282

—— lends house to, **6.** 265

'Tonton' bites, **30.** 265, **39.** 258

Stanhope, Lady Anna Maria (1760–1834), m. 1 (1782) Thomas Pelham Clinton, styled E. of Lincoln 1779–94, 3d D. of Newcastle-under-Lyne, 1794; m. 2 (1800) Lt-Gen. Sir Charles Gregan Crawfurd, G.C.B.:

bequest to, from father, **33.** 97

St John, Mrs, invites, to ball, **28.** 403

Stanhope, Anne (d. 1587), m. 1 (by 1535) Edward Seymour, E. of Hertford, cr. (1547) D. of Somerset; m. 2 Francis Newdigate:

husband disinherits stepsons of, in favour of her own son, **19.** 523, **20.** 139

picture of, at Petworth, **9.** 98

print of, **9.** 98n, (?) **40.** 236

Stanhope, Lady Caroline (1747–67), m. (1765) Kenneth Mackenzie, cr. (1766) Vct Fortrose, (1771) E. of Seaforth:

death of, from white lead, **10.** 237, **22.** 484, **30.** 240

Hertford congratulates mother on engagement of, **38.** 575

Liotard to depict, **37.** 355

mother forbids, to speak to debauched Pecquigny, **38.** 234

Stanhope, Charles (1673–1760), M.P.:

birth date of, corrected, **43.** 267

Crawford's servant rewarded by, **2.** 110, 118–19

fits discussed by, at Lady Townshend's, **35.** 80

HW answers questions of, with news of fictitious appointments, **35.** 281

HW mentions, **36.** 8

HW's correspondence with, **40.** 100

Pembroke taken home by, in chariot, **20.** 108

reputation of, as a bore, **9.** 158

Townshend, Vcts, to be escorted by, to SH, **40.** 100

Williams, Sir C. H., describes love of, for Ds of Manchester, in 'Isabella or the Morning,' **30.** 317

Stanhope, Charles (1708–36), M.P.:

(?) Suares, Mme, afflicted by death of, **17.** 39n

vanity of, **17.** 39n

Stanhope, Charles (1753–1816), styled Vct Mahon 1763–86; 3d E. Stanhope, 1786; M.P.:

ancestry of, **24.** 67

Bastille Day jubilee to be attended by, **11.** 88–9

Calonne attacked by, in Parliament, **11.** 150–1

Chatham father-in-law of, **28.** 207

—— is attended by, **24.** 371

Considerations on the Means of Preventing Fraudulent Practices on the Gold Coin, by, **28.** 207

Court opposed by, in Westminster election, **39.** 186

defeated as Wilkes's candidate for Westminster, **24.** 52

English countryside belies, **11.** 98

father will not permit, to powder hair, **39.** 183–4

French Revolution approved by, **31.** 343

'furious republican citizen of Geneva,' **25.** 32

Geneva, scene of education of, **6.** 29

Gordon, Lord George, counteracted by, **29.** 53

Gordon rioters harangued by, **33.** 177

Gordon rioters prevailed upon by, to disperse, **25.** 54

HW jokes about *poissardes* taking rank away from, **11.** 97

HW's letter from, about Devonshire property, **34.** 184

Lee's acquaintance with, **6.** 68n

Letter . . . to . . . Edmund Burke, A, by, is lunatic's raving, **34.** 98

Mann, Horace II, opposes, at Maidstone meeting, **25.** 32

marriage of, **11.** 128n, **24.** 67

Marsham to have been opposed by, in Kent election, **25.** 490, 494

'mischievous lunatic,' **11.** 88

Paris visited by, **6.** 29

'Presbyterian conflagrations' would be raised by, in England, **34.** 80

republican sympathies of, **34.** 184

resigns from Revolution Society, **11.** 131, 135, 313n, 314

Voltaire not seen by, **6.** 29

vulgar, though he cannot be M.P., **35.** 399

wife of, **6.** 225n, **11.** 128n, 260n

witticism on Court presentation of, with black hair and white feather, **39.** 184

Stanhope, Charles (1753–1829), styled Vct Petersham 1756–79; 3d E. of Harrington, 1779; army officer:

brother of, **12.** 33n, 136n

Burgoyne defended by, in Parliamentary inquiry, **39.** 325

candidacy of, supported by Gen. Burgoyne, **32.** 336

[Stanhope, Charles (1753–1829), *continued*]
father displeased with, **39**. 141
father's house at St James's to be bought by,
33. 97
Pitt, Anne, entertains, **32**. 48n
Stanhope, Lady Elizabeth, m. Hon. Edward
Darcy:
ancestry of, **1**. 375
HW's ancestress, **1**. 375n
Stanhope, Elizabeth (d. 1761) m. (1747) Welbore Ellis, cr. (1794) Bn Mendip:
father of, **12**. 158n
husband of, **21**. 417n
marriage of, alienates her father, **19**. 485
Pope's villa inherited through, from father,
11. 41n
taciturnity of, **35**. 298n
witticism by, to father on his remarriage, **35**.
298
Stanhope, Lady Emily. *See* Stanhope, Lady
Amelia
Stanhope, Hon. George (1717–54), army officer:
Argyll's aide-de-camp, **17**. 356
Chesterfield requests colonelcy for, **19**. 463n
Stanhope, Lady Gertrude (ca 1696–1775), m.
(1724) Sir Charles Hotham, 5th Bt:
Chesterfield's witticism to, when she invites
him to Methodist retreat in Welsh mountains, **24**. 90–1
death of, from fire, **24**. 90
house of, in New Norfolk St, **24**. 90n
witty, but a Methodist, **24**. 90
Stanhope, Lady Harriet (*or* Henrietta) (1750–
81), m. (1776) Hon. Thomas Foley, 2d Bn
Foley, 1777:
Ailesbury, Cts of, accompanied by, **39**. 219
—— tells HW nothing about, **39**. 206
Calais visited by, **6**. 165
Cambis, Mme de, friend of, **6**. 240, 241
charming, **32**. 49
death of, **33**. 261
Du Deffand, Mme, inquires about, **6**. 282
—— sends compliments to, **6**. 158
——'s opinion of, **6**. 104, 108, 134–5, 142, 155,
160, 190
engagements of, rumoured, **6**. 190, 240, 241
expected in Paris, **30**. 264
father accompanied by, to Paris, **39**. 186, 195n
Foley marries, **39**. 215n
Fontainebleau to be visited by, **6**. 106
—— visited by, **6**. 112
HW's gout benefits from wishes of, but her
father's does not, **39**. 237
HW's opinion of, **6**. 173
HW writes to Mme du Deffand about, **6**. 124
health of, swelled face, **39**. 215
Liotard to depict, **37**. 355
Luxembourg, Mme de, likes and is liked by,
6. 101, 104, 115
Marie-Antoinette gracious to, **6**. 127
marriage of, **6**. 245, 269
marriage planned for, **32**. 49

Mirepoix, Mme de, likes and is liked by, **6**.
101, 115
mother and husband and, meet Mrs Damer,
32. 314n
(?) mother to tour France with, **39**. 261
Paris left by, **6**. 156, 240
—— reached by, from Spa, **39**. 269
—— visited by, **6**. 99, **39**. 215n, 539
print of, as 'Court Beauty,' **32**. 49n
silent, **6**. 134–5, 235
social relations of, in Paris, **6**. 106, 110, 229,
232, 235, 240
Stormont attentive to, **6**. 134, 147, 160, 170,
175, (?) 265
—— escorts, from Paris, **6**. 156
—— said to have been rejected by, **6**. 179,
186, 200, 203, 240
Versailles visited by, **6**. 127
Viry, Contessa di, to be visited by, **6**. 106
Stanhope, Hon. Henry Fitzroy (1754–1828),
army officer; M.P.:
baptism of, **9**. 163
bequest to, from Lord Harrington, **33**. 97
father accompanied by, to Paris, **39**. 141
wife of, **12**. 33n, 136n
Stanhope, Hon. Mrs Henry Fitzroy. *See* Falconer
or Faulkner, Elizabeth
Stanhope, Lady Isabella (1748–1819), m. (1768)
Charles William Molyneux, 8th Vct Molyneux, 1759; cr. (1771) E. of Sefton:
at Mrs Boyle Walsingham's ball, **42**. 222n
Christian VII dances with, **35**. 327n
club at Almack's founded by, **10**. 305
Guines, Duc de, gives supper for, **32**. 277
HW visits, **33**. 203
Hobart, Mrs, entertains, at play at Ham
Common, **33**. 370
Holck, as Christian VII's protégé, refused
by, **39**. 108
—— woos, **35**. 407–8
Liotard to depict, **37**. 355
politics of, admirable, **33**. 348
quadrille danced by, at Duc de Guines's ball,
32. 110
Stanhope, James (1673–1721), cr. (1717) Vct
and (1718) E. Stanhope:
pension of, **18**. 178
Port Mahon capture brings peerage to, **21**.
52, **43**. 273
Walpole, Horatio (1678–1757), secretary to,
in Spain, **36**. 28n
Stanhope, John (d. 1621), cr. (1605) Bn Stanhope:
Cavendish assaulted by, **37**. 477
Stanhope, Hon. John (1705–48), M.P.:
Admiralty post assigned to, **19**. 463, **20**. 12
(?) Blandford, Lady, entertains, **37**. 51
Chesterfield inherits villa at Blackheath from,
22. 164n
—— requests Admiralty post for, **19**. 463n
——'s inheritance from, **20**. 12
death of, **20**. 12, 19

Sandwich succeeded by, in Admiralty post, **19**. 464n

witticism by, on Curzon's drippy nose, **20**. 12

witty, **24**. 90

Stanhope, Lady Lucy (1714–85):

Theodore of Corsica, 'admirer' of, **18**. 192, 207–8, 221, 229

Stanhope, Mary (ca 1686–1762), m. (1707) Charles Fane, 1st Vct Fane:

death of, **22**. 74, **38**. 167

nervous disorders of, **22**. 74

Stanhope, Philip (1584–1656), cr. (1628) E. of Chesterfield:

HW's ancestor, **1**. 375n

Stanhope, Philip (ca 1634–1714), 2d E. of Chesterfield, 1656:

Derbyshire estates bought by, from Darcy sisters, **40**. 72

print of, **9**. 118n

Stanhope, Philip (1673–1726), 3d E. of Chesterfield, 1714:

son of, **9**. 72n

Stanhope, Philip (1714–86) 2d E. Stanhope, 1721:

brother of, **17**. 356

Euclid deserted by, for matrimony, **19**. 19

father's pension ends soon, **18**. 178

Geneva residence of, **6**. 29

HW orders medals from, **38**. 535

mob incited by, **17**. 390

Paris visited by, **6**. 29

Parliamentary address against use of Hanoverian troops proposed by, **18**. 158, 178

Parliamentary speech by, on Habeas Corpus, **37**. 529

social relations of, in Paris, **6**. 39

son not permitted by, to powder hair, because of expense, **39**. 183–4

son of, **24**. 52n, 67

Voltaire not seen by, **6**. 29

Stanhope, Philip (1732–68), diplomatist; natural son of 4th E. of Chesterfield:

allusion to 'graces' in father's letters to, did him no good, **25**. 337

(?) at Chesterfield's assembly, **37**. 326

father's letters to, *see under* Stanhope, Philip Dormer, 4th E. of Chesterfield

Florence and Rome visited by, **20**. 174n

HW's opinion of, **6**. 36

Harte, Walter, tutor to, **20**. 174n

MS of Chesterfield's *Characters* lent to, **28**. 145

Niccolini entertains, at dinner, **20**. 174

Parliamentary Address debated by, **37**. 415

remained an unlicked cub, **28**. 146–7

Steavens meets, in Venice and Vienna, **20**. 175n

tutors of, **6**. 36

Venice rejects, as English Resident, because of illegitimacy, **23**. 325

widow of, **28**. 144n

Williams's 'Ode on the Death of Matzel' written for, **30**. 115n, 318

Stanhope, Philip (1755–1815), 5th E. of Chesterfield, 1773:

ambassador to Spain, **33**. 430

HW criticizes appointment of, **36**. 215

heir of 4th Earl, **32**. 112

portrait in possession of, **16**. 323n

Stanhope, Mrs Philip. *See* Peters, Eugenia

Stanhope, Philip Dormer (1694–1773), 4th E. of Chesterfield, 1726; M.P.:

Académie des Inscriptions' letter from, on his election, **37**. 408

Admiralty post and colonelcy requested by, for John and George Stanhope, **19**. 463n

age and deafness incapacitate, **23**. 263n

agrees with HW about Robertson's treatment of Mary, Q. of Scots, **15**. 62n

Allen, Lady, introduced by, to Mme de Tencin, **35**. 94n

Amelia, Ps, offered house by, **9**. 314

anecdotes of Jervas told by, **15**. 144

aphrodisiac blamed by, for Sir C. H. Williams's decline, **21**. 183n

assembly by, for opening of Chesterfield House: **20**. 302; (?) guests at, listed, **37**. 325–7

bad actors and authors patronized by, **20**. 142

ballad by Pulteney, E. of Bath, and, **31**. 415n

Barnard's relations with, at Tunbridge, **19**. 404

Bath visited by, **19**. 463

Bath, E. of, makes witticism to, on being lean and deaf, **37**. 474

Boufflers writes 'envoi' under name of, for Mme du Deffand, **6**. 462

Boughton Malherbe once owned by, **20**. 166

brother calls on, at Blackheath, **22**. 164

brother leaves Blackheath villa to, **22**. 164n

brother of, **2**. 368, **17**. 279n, **19**. 463, **21**. 417n, **22**. 521n

brother's bequest to, **20**. 12

brother's correspondence with, **20**. 472

bust of, at Stowe, **10**. 154n, **41**. 6n

Bute attends ministerial conference at suggestion of, **21**. 97n

Case of the Hanover Forces by, **18**. 123, **35**. 49

Catherine II gives box to, in return for compliments to her ambassador, **23**. 376

Chancery bill filed by, against George II, **2**. 125, 127

character of, superficially brilliant, **28**. 147

Characters of Eminent Personages of his own Time by: **6**. 465; badly written and unjust, **28**. 302–3; Cambis, Mme de, translates, **6**. 461–2, 465; MS of, supposedly burnt but first copied, **28**. 145

Cholmondeley answers, **17**. 230

Churchill attributes stale jokes to, **18**. 131

Chute's house near that of, **35**. 110

Claude Lorrain painting bought by, **23**. 466

[Stanhope, Philip Dormer, *continued*]
coalition ministry promoted by, **18.** 550n
Congratulatory Letter to a Certain Right Honourable Person upon his Late Disappointment supposedly by, **18.** 231n, **30.** 316n
coughs asserted by, to be controllable, **38.** 155
Crébillon's letter to, about Voltaire, **35.** 587–8
——'s *Sopha* put on sale by, at White's, **17.** 334
Dalrymple's memoirs disgust, **28.** 145
Dayrolles friend of, **28.** 288n
—— says, unwilling to accept any place, **20.** 207n
——'s relations with, **19.** 404, **30.** 308n
death of, **5.** 413, **23.** 471, **32.** 112
Derby election financed by, **20.** 19
Devonshire, D. of, succeeded by, as lord lieutenant of Ireland, **18.** 550
Dodd forges signature of, **2.** 34n, **32.** 360n
—— former tutor of, **32.** 360n
Dublin gentleman praises 'humility' of, **19.** 189–90
Dutch negotiations of, unlikely to succeed, **19.** 68–9
epigram on Hervey attributed to, **30.** 25
everything attributed to, at first, **30.** 25
Fleury to be threatened by, **17.** 371
Fox, Henry, discusses D. of Newcastle with, **20.** 502
France said to be visited by, **17.** 371
—— visited by, **17.** 133n
Frederick, P. of Wales, impelled by, against Sir Robert Walpole, **17.** 329
—— persuaded by, to seek chancellorship of Cambridge, **20.** 10n
Frederick Augustus II's candidacy supported by, **19.** 7n
French, the, imitated by, **28.** 136
French invasion feared by, **24.** 391
French reception of, **17.** 232
French war not expected by, **20.** 472
gallantry of, **32.** 32
George II begrudges audience to, **18.** 564
—— forces, to demand Newcastle's election as chancellor of Cambridge, **20.** 10n
——'s levee attended by, **18.** 102
Gisors appraises, **31.** 3n
government attacked by, for neglecting Maria Theresa, **17.** 230n
Guasco intimate with, **22.** 530
HW asks, if family and friends approve of publication of his letters, **31.** 173
HW asks opinion of, concerning Mme du Deffand's 'Sévigné' letter, **31.** 119
HW disparages, **9.** 40
HW expects more from Pulteney's paper than from that of, **20.** 374
HW identifies, **16.** 348
HW inferior to, as author, **31.** 173
HW in same Paris hotel with, **13.** 11n
HW mocks, in epilogue to *Braganza*, **6.** 152
HW not a disciple of, **16.** 268

HW parodies, **13.** 49, **35.** 572
HW says, has 'little title to fame,' **20.** 166
HW's correspondence with, **40.** 72–3
HW sends message to, by Anne Pitt, **10.** 219
HW should include, in future *Royal and Noble Authors*, **40.** 159
HW's letter to, in character of Cts of Suffolk's maid, **31.** 132, 431–2
(?) HW's letter to Rousseau approved by, **31.** 111
HW's 'morsels of criticism' ridicule system of, **31.** 281
HW's objection to writing preface to letters of, **31.** 173–4
HW's opinions in *Royal and Noble Authors* endorsed by, **9.** 218–19
HW's political opinions to be followed by, **10.** 219
HW's relations with, **31.** 173
HW thinks wit of, inferior to Winnington's, **30.** 70
HW to be reported by, as nuisance, **10.** 2
HW visited by, at SH, *Public Advertiser's* verses on, **43.** 338
Hague, The, gives cool reception to, **26.** 10
—— visited by, **18.** 564
Halifax rejects proposal of, of meeting with Newcastle, **21.** 111n
Hamilton and Elizabeth Gunning entertained by, **20.** 302–3
Hammond, favourite of, **17.** 275n, 451
Hanoverian dynasty attacked by, **17.** 230, **18.** 123–4
Hardinge, despite maxims of, does not return HW's visit, **35.** 570
Harrington may be succeeded by, as secretary of state, **19.** 326
hay probably made fashionable by, **35.** 370
health of: attacks in head and stomach, **37.** 474; deaf, **9.** 215, **20.** 207; restored by 'old disorder,' **40.** 364
Hervey 'lives shut up with,' **17.** 275
Holland and then Ireland to be visited by, **18.** 562
Houghton lantern bought by, **13.** 112n
house of, in South Audley St, **23.** 471n
humour lacked by, **35.** 647
Irish lord lieutenancy given to, **18.** 102n
Jones described by, to HW, **20.** 214
——'s *Earl of Essex* revised by, **20.** 214n
laughter deplored by, **28.** 153
Leicester, E. of, to be visited by, **30.** 70
letter from, **9.** 367n
letter of, read by Conway, in Holdernesse's hands, **38.** 30
letters of: **16.** 347; interest HW, **17.** 1n; lack wit, **24.** 91; parodied by HW, **32.** 202; should not have been printed, **42.** 121–2
Letters to His Son by: **25.** 337n, **43.** 96; conditions under which publication of, was permitted, **28.** 144–5; Delany, Mrs, criticizes, **41.** 275n; Dodsley to publish, **28.** 115; Du Deffand, Mme, wants, **6.** 40–1; enter-

taining but repetitious, **28.** 146–7; French translation of, improbable, **6.** 37; grammatical error in, **28.** 156; HW declines request to write preface to, **28.** 115; HW's opinion of, **6.** 36–8; Hardinge quotes, **35.** 586; Mason 'improved' by, **28.** 157–8; moral code in, dubious, **28.** 154; returned by HW to Mrs Delany, with comment, **41.** 275–6; sale of, pleases Dodsley, **28.** 216; wit infrequent in, **28.** 154

Lyttelton defends, **17.** 232

Mallet addresses poem to, **28.** 41n

—— and Flobert meet at house of, **21.** 377

Mallet's poem improved by, **14.** 36n

Mann astonished by, **17.** 133

—— doubtful about stability of, in office, **19.** 338

—— fears cunning of, **18.** 557

—— introduces HW's verses as those of, **18.** 372

—— receives commissions from, **19.** 422–3

Mann, Galfridus, buys Boughton Malherbe manor from, **13.** 29n

Marchmont advanced by, **20.** 5

—— supposed to have written apology for resignation of, **20.** 6

Marlborough, Ds of, leaves legacy to, as 'patriot,' **18.** 540

Marshall, Mrs, sends play to, **1.** 301n

Mason, not HW, wrote verses mocking, **43.** 98

Milton translation by Mme du Boccage praised by, **20.** 142

Miscellaneous Works of: **6.** 423, 427, 438; discussed by Hardinge, **35.** 586; Du Deffand, Mme, wants translation of, **6.** 427, 429; HW's comments on, **28.** 289–92, 294, 295; Noailles's *Mémoires* are the counterpart of, **28.** 296; to be published, **28.** 131, 136, 140

Monconseil, Marquise de, corresponds with, **3.** 123n, **6.** 423

mother-in-law leaves nothing to, **18.** 231

Murray examined before, **19.** 391n

naval investigation proposed by, in Parliament, **18.** 400

Newcastle, D. of, may be jealous of, **19.** 413

—— persuades George II to discard, as secretary of state, **40.** 88

——'s quarrel with, **19.** 463

—— unlikely to be defended by, **35.** 224

New Ode, A, mentions, **18.** 52

newspapers print farewell speech of, **19.** 52

Nivernais's eulogy of, **5.** 413

Nugent, Mrs, asks, to urge her husband to speak in Parliament, **17.** 254–5

Old Pretender's people exult in retirement of, **19.** 475

Opposition still includes, **18.** 102

Orford, Cts of (Bns Walpole), amuses, by mistakes in her letters to him, **19.** 70

—— corresponds with, **17.** 409, **19.** 61, 70

—— hopes to secure Clinton barony through **17.** 360, 409

—— receives intelligence from, **17.** 371

—— would never be content with, **20.** 439

Orford, 2d E. of, sells Houghton lantern to, **20.** 163

Ormond visited by, at Avignon to tell Pretender to persuade Jacobites to vote against Sir Robert Walpole, **17.** 133n, 232n, **19.** 68–9

paintings bought by, **32.** 102

Paoli presented to, **23.** 150n

Parliamentary address of thanks moved by, **28.** 479n

Parliamentary speeches by, **9.** 18, **17.** 230, 232, **18.** 356

peace articles prepared by, **19.** 441n

pedigree of, **20.** 181, 195

Pelham must bring in, **18.** 537

Pembroke, E. of, addressed by, 'in the Thames,' **31.** 402, **42.** 178

pension for Lady Frances Shirley requested by, **19.** 463n

Phipps, Mrs, called on by, **19.** 190

Pitt, Anne, talks with, **10.** 219

—— to invite, to SH, **31.** 111

Pope's alterations to Bolingbroke's *Letters* reported by, **20.** 61

Poulett's motion opposed by, **35.** 224

presidency declined by, **20.** 207

private letter of, printed by, **1.** 301

prophecy in Ezekiel found by, promising victory over France, **35.** 218–19

Pulteney's *Epistle* in Lovel's name to, **37.** 82

Ranelagh absorbs, **37.** 164

rebus mentions, **30.** 42

reference of, to the Graces, **25.** 337, **32.** 202

resignation of, as secretary of state: **19.** 463; rumoured because Newcastle may be jealous **19.** 412–13

returns from Holland, **19.** 52

Richecourt and Bns Walpole hope to manage English relations with Tuscany through, **17.** 387

Richelieu reminds HW of, **39.** 35

riddle by Mme du Deffand baffles, **31.** 83

Robinson's correspondence with, preserved, **28.** 297

St-Germain intimate with, **26.** 21

Sandwich, E. of, may succeed, **19.** 413, 422

——'s instructions questioned by, **19.** 289n

Saxe sends book to, through D. of Cumberland, **9.** 52

saying attributed to, **1.** 330n

secretaryship of state predicted for, by Gage, **17.** 296

Shirley, Lady Frances, subject of verses by, **24.** 401n, **42.** 489, 490

Siena marble procured for, **19.** 423

simper only allowed by, **34.** 171

sister of, **24.** 90–1

son and godson of, under Dunoyer's tutelage, **9.** 29n

son did not benefit by allusions to *the Graces* in letters of, **25.** 337

[Stanhope, Philip Dormer, *continued*]
son (natural) of, **23.** 325, **30.** 318
song supposedly by, **28.** 412n
Stanley reads Gray's *Odes* to, **9.** 215
Stowe visit brings memories of, to HW, **10.** 314
titles of works of, **28.** 121
valet sent by, to bid at art sale, **32.** 103n
Venice to receive minister selected by, **19.** 453
verses attributed to, **37.** 82
verses commended by, **9.** 8n
Vindication of a Late Pamphlet, A, by, **18.** 141, **35.** 49
Wade's house commented on by, **9.** 56
Waller instructs, in public accounts, **17.** 332n, **30.** 291n
Walpole, Sir Robert, greeted by, at House of Lords, **17.** 338
—— opponent of, **2.** 122n, **31.** 173
—— quotes, **17.** 232
—— subject of account by, **2.** 126
—— talks to, at George II's levee, **18.** 102
war ignored by, to play picquet at Bath with Moravian baron, **35.** 258
Westminster election bragged about by, to Lovel, **17.** 272
'When Fanny blooming fair' by, celebrates Lady Fanny Shirley, **24.** 401n, **42.** 489, 490
Whitefield's preaching heard by, **9.** 74
wife of, **2.** 123n, **24.** 283n, 412n, **25.** 248n
Williams, Sir C. H., receives goldfish from, **40.** 86n
—— satirizes, **30.** 314
—— thinks, lacks wit, **30.** 70
—— thought by, to be mad, **21.** 190n
—— writes ode to, **30.** 318
will of, **32.** 112
Winnington's witticism on turncoat politics of, **18.** 540
wit of, **17.** 270, **20.** 507, **30.** 70
witticisms of: **32.** 102–3, 112; concerning ancestors, **16.** 334; on Carteret's marriage, **18.** 424; on England's being invaded at home, while victorious overseas, **38.** 154–5; on George II and Q. Caroline at deserted opera, **38.** 123; on giving Hanover to Pretender to make him unpopular in England, **18.** 123–4; on Henry Jones, **20.** 214, 218; on Mrs Fitzroy as 'striking beauty,' **32.** 104n; on Norfolk visit, **30.** 70–1; on Pembroke's conduct at Bridge Committee, **20.** 108; on Talbot's parsimony, **10.** 32; on the Pelhams, **20.** 214; on the presidency, **20.** 214; on the Viscontina, **17.** 197; on Waller, **30.** 291n; preserved by Mrs Piozzi, **12.** 92–3; to Anne Pitt, on Pitt's speaking in a horizontal posture, **23.** 177; to sister, when she invited him to Methodist 'seminary' in Welsh mountains, **24.** 91
words carefully selected by, **28.** 156
World contributions by, **3.** 93n, **7.** 319, **9.** 178, 195, **20.** 374, 395n, 400n, **35.** 199, 257, 258, 339, 586, **37.** 420

Stanhope, Philip Henry (1781–1855), styled Vct Mahon; 4th E. Stanhope, 1816:
mother of, **11.** 260n
Stanhope, Spencer. *See* Spencer Stanhope, Walter
Stanhope, Sir Thomas (d. 1770), Kt, 1759; naval Capt.:
defeated in Derby election, **20.** 19
Derby Whigs oppose Rivett to, as Devonshire's and Chesterfield's candidate, **20.** 19n
Du Quesne and officers courteously treated by, **21.** 255
Du Quesne put on *Swiftsure* of, instead of Hervey's ship, **21.** 193n
ships would have been taken by, if he could have kept station in Malta channel, **21.** 249n
Stanhope, Walter Spencer. *See* Spencer Stanhope, Walter
Stanhope, William (ca 1683–1756), cr. (1730) Bn Harrington, (1742) E. of Harrington; M.P.:
alleged lover of Mme de Tencin, **28.** 291
Anglo-Prussian convention signed by, **19.** 95n
(?) at Chesterfield's assembly, **37.** 326
biographical information about, corrected, **43.** 237
brother of, **20.** 110
circular letter of, to Trevor, **17.** 180n, 281
Cope promoted by, **19.** 117
Cox bought off by, despite Bristow's and Frankland's opposition, **20.** 156–7
daughter of, **22.** 484
deathbed visit of, to House of Lords, **37.** 458
Dorset, D. of, replaces, in Ireland, **20.** 202
—— succeeds, as lord president, **18.** 550
earldom given to, **17.** 333
Frederick, P. of Wales, makes Elizabeth Chudleigh write to, for warrant as secretary at war, **19.** 175
—— tells footman not to give letter to, except in Yonge's presence, **19.** 175
Garter might be expected by, **20.** 84
George II displeased with, **20.** 202
—— does not make, K. G., **20.** 72–3
—— offended by refusal of, to coalesce with Granville and Bath, **19.** 326n
——'s favour abandoned by, to please D. of Newcastle, **21.** 100
——'s return to London announced by, **19.** 92n
Granville (Carteret) less civil than, to Mann, **18.** 363
—— said to resign Seals to, **18.** 556
——'s victims not to be reassured by, **9.** 116
Hanover visit of, with George II, **17.** 113n, **18.** 363
Hardwicke and Pelham visited by, to ask how he has offended George II, **20.** 207n
Holdernesse's experience compared with that of, **21.** 100
Irish appointment of, preserves harmony, **19.** 327n

Irish lord lieutenancy or presidency of the Council may be offered to, **19**. 327

Ligonier plays whist with, at Petersham, **19**. 166

lord lieutenant of Ireland, **20**. 156n, **21**. 100n

Mann asked by, to aid Nomis, **18**. 110

—— directed to send dispatches to, **17**. 113n

—— hears from, of neutrality, **17**. 181

—— informed by, of George II's intention of going to England, **19**. 99

—— receives letter from, giving George II's approval, **19**. 86

—— sends news to, of Young Pretender's departure, **17**. 113, 115, 119, 208

——'s letter to, predicts alliances, **17**. 208n

mob assaults, at Dublin, **20**. 156

Murray, Sir John, examined by, **19**. 288n

Newcastle, D. of, attacks, **26**. 10

—— corresponds with, about French invasion, **19**. 78n

—— disagrees with, about orders to be sent to Sandwich, **19**. 326n

—— may quarrel with, **20**. 326

peace with France urged by, **30**. 109n

president of the Council, **17**. 333

regent, **18**. 209n

resignations instigated by, **20**. 207

Sandwich's instructions from, at Breda, **19**. 289n

secretaryship of state given back to, **18**. 537

secretaryship of state resigned by, **19**. 211, 326

son of, **19**. 43n, 294n, **30**. 325n

Stanislas I's candidacy supported by, **19**. 7n

Suares recommended by, for preferment, **18**. 455

Tabuerniga family receive pension through, **17**. 278

Stanhope, Hon. Sir William (1702–72), K.B., 1725; M.P.:

brother called on by, at Blackheath, **22**. 164

brother's correspondence with, **20**. 472

daughter informed by, of his remarriage, **35**. 298

daughter of, **11**. 41n

daughter's marriage alienates, **19**. 485

deed for Shirley's separate maintenance to be carried by, from Florence to England, **20**. 569

Frederick, P. of Wales, cool to, for his behaviour at Carlton House, **17**. 279

HW publishes speech, in name of, **9**. 72n, **13**. 21

heir not begotten by, **22**. 418

Henry Frederick, P., mistaken by, for wax doll, **19**. 175

Herbert, Mrs, shocked by, at Ps of Wales's reception, **19**. 175

house and entertainment of, seem Florentine, **19**. 485

house of: in Dover St, **19**. 485n, **22**. 164n; in Twickenham, **2**. 368, **12**. 158n, **21**. 417–18, **25**. 177–8, **42**. 481

jealous, **22**. 170, 418

Mann told by, in Florence, about trials of deafness, **21**. 177

Naples to be visited by, **21**. 550

—— visited by, **22**. 418

Parliamentary debates hardly heard by, with ear trumpet, **22**. 183

Parliamentary memberships of, corrected, **43**. 242

Parliamentary speech of, against Grenvilles, interrupted, **13**. 21

Petersham, Lady Caroline, entertained by, at ball, **19**. 485

Petershams may inherit property from, **19**. 485

Pope's house and garden altered by, **21**. 417–18, **25**. 177–8

——'s villa bought by, **2**. 368, **12**. 158n

returns to England, disgusted by Naples, **22**. 418

Rigby to visit, **9**. 72

Rome visited by, **20**. 472n

son-in-law advises, **21**. 417

Talbot's treatment of Knights of the Bath resented by, at George III's Coronation, **9**. 389

wife of, **9**. 260n, **22**. 521n

wife parts with, at Blackheath, **22**. 164

wife's relations with, **22**. 164, 170

Wilkes chiefly intimate with, at Naples, **22**. 292

witticisms by: on ear-cropping, **22**. 183; to young wife on wedding night, **22**. 164

witty, **24**. 90

Stanhope, William (1719–79), styled Vct Petersham 1742–56; 2d E. of Harrington, 1756:

Almack's frequented by, **32**. 191

daughter of, **28**. 403n

death and will of, **33**. 97

'debilitated and premature old age' of, **32**. 191n

dresses in pink and green, **32**. 191

Du Deffand, Mme, has social relations with, **6**. 118

expected in Paris, **30**. 264

family of, **30**. 325n

George II dismisses, **10**. 153n

Grafton unsuccessfully promoted, as M.P. for Sudbury, **30**. 331n

Guines's ball attended by, **32**. 96n

HW mentions, **18**. 374

HW's 'The Beauties' describes, as more blessed than Paris, **30**. 326

HW wishes daughter would transfer her swelled face to, **39**. 215

'harem' of, **33**. 97

health of, gout uncured by daughter's wishes, **39**. 237

heir displeases, **39**. 141

Hesse, Landgraf of, does not interfere in marriage of, **9**. 27

house of, in Stable Yard, St James's, robbed, **38**. 259, 265

house taken by, **9**. 30

[Stanhope, William (1719–79), *continued*]
  marriage of: 9. 27, 19. 294; arranged, 9. 30
  misfortune at house of, 37. 387, 388
  Paris reached by, from Spa, 39. 269
  —— to be left by, 6. 240
  —— to be visited by, with son, taking Hertford's letter to HW, 39. 141
  —— visited by, 39. 215n
  shambling gait of, 9. 107
  Stanhope, Sir William, may leave property to, 19. 485
  Stormont friend of, 6. 118, 120
  White's Club attended by, just before earthquake, 20. 140
  wife no longer loved by, 37. 359
  wife of, 9. 19n, 17. 184n, 274n, 25. 508n, 28. 403n
  wife rudely treated by, 9. 107–8
  wife wakes, after earthquake, 20. 140
  wounded at Fontenoy, 19. 43, 36. 12

Stanhope, Durham:
  Keene gets living of, from Sir Robert Walpole, 20. 346
  —— rector of, 2. 371n, 20. 346n

Stanhope family:
  aristocratic ugliness of, 9. 260
  name of, becomes popular as Sir Robert Walpole's declines, 17. 270
  pedigree of, 20. 181, 195
  publication of Chesterfield's letters opposed by, 28. 144–5
  Stanhope's rejection at Derby a blow to, 20. 19
  wit of, 20. 12, 24. 90

Stanhope St, Berkeley Sq., London:
  Beauchamp writes from, 39. 249
  Caracciolo lives in, 10. 216n
  Selwyn addressed in, 30. 262

Stanislas I (Leszczyński) (1677–1766), K. of Poland 1704–9, 1733–6; D. of Lorraine and Bar 1737–66:
  Beauvau asks, to transfer Lorraine guards to French regiment, 18. 267n
  Boufflers chided by, 4. 361
  —— sent to Ps Christine by, 3. 40, 53
  ——'s witticism on picture of, 39. 219
  Boufflers, Marquise de, mistress of, 20. 236, 22. 243, 270n
  —— ridicules, in letters to husband, 20. 236
  career of, 22. 402–4
  chancellor of, *see* Chaumont, Antoine-Martin de, Marquise de la Galaisière
  Charles XII of Sweden wishes election of, 22. 403n
  Conway sees palace of, at Lunéville, 39. 539
  Craon favoured by, 20. 236
  ——'s correspondence with, 19. 467
  —— watched by, in illness, 20. 92
  Craon, Princesse de, given Queen's apartment by, 20. 116
  —— may displace her daughter in affections of, 20. 26
  —— may wed, 20. 116, 126, 132

Craons courted by, 19. 467
daughter visits, at Nancy, 7. 259, 39. 9n
death of: 7. 304, 356, 397, 22. 402–3; daughter dying of grief for, 30. 219
France cannot put, on Polish throne, 42. 494, 496
Frederick Augustus II, former rival of, 22. 403
funeral orations for, in Paris, 3. 68, 69, 71, 74, 76, 86, 93, 22. 403–4, 31. 111
George II sees objections to candidacy of, for Emperor, but Harrington and Granville support him, 19. 7n
granddaughters permitted to visit, when treasurer says expense is justifiable, 22. 403
HW calls, 'best of beings,' 22. 254
living when Churchills were at Nancy, 33. 419
Lorraine Guards assigned to, 17. 11n
parliament of Paris's condolences to Louis XV on death of, 39. 56
Peter the Great and Charles XII prepared the way for, 22. 404
Poland too stupid to reelect, 22. 402
Pomfret, E. of, 'nicknamed K. Stanislas' after, 18. *501*
smokes a pipe, 19. 467, 20. 26
still alive in Stanislas II's reign, 7. 356, 22. 253, 404
verses by Porquet for bust of, 4. 325
virtues of, 7. 356
wealth and bequests of, 22. 403
witticisms by: on daughter's gift of a nightgown, 22. 403; on Marquise de Boufflers's intrigue with La Galaisière, 22. 244, 246; to lady who burned her arm, 22. 403

Stanislas II (Stanislas Augustus Poniatowski) (1732–98), K. of Poland 1764–95:
  arrested in England, 11. 243
  attack upon, must alarm other monarchs, 23. 359
  brother of, in London, 11. 242
  Catherine II strips, of power, 31. 371
  ——'s ultimatum to, 31. 371n
  chosen instead of Czartoryski, 22. 248n
  Clairon, Mlle, to play for, 3. 268
  Confederation of Targowicz joined by, 34. 159n
  Conway knew, 22. 248
  Craven, Bns, asked by, about HW, 34. 36n
  —— shows HW's letter to, and he translates it into French, 25. 632–3
  Czartoryski's cousin and friend, 22. *248*, 25. 633
  England visited by, 25. 633n
  English books desired by, 11. 243
  English fleet might restore, 23. 475
  Frederick II urges Catherine II to make, abdicate in favour of P. Henry of Prussia, 25. 44–5
  Geoffrin, Mme, fond of, 3. 178n, 4. 214n
  —— friendly with, 6. 296n
  —— invited by, to Poland, 31. 101–2
  —— praises Mme d'Egmont to, 3. 42n

George III, Frederick II, Adolf Fredrik, and Christian VII make treaty with, protecting Polish Dissidents, **22.** 574n
Gordon, Ds of, woos, **35.** 82
great-grandmother of, a Gordon, **35.** 82
HW acquainted with, in England, **22.** 253, **38.** 281
HW asked by, for *Anecdotes of Painting*, **36.** 238, 281, **42.** 161–4
HW's *Anecdotes* to be brought to, by Potocki, **42.** 163
HW's correspondence with, **36.** 281, **42.** 162–4
HW thanked by, for *Anecdotes of Painting, Catalogue of Engravers*, and *Modern Gardening*, **42.** 164
handsome, **35.** 82
Joseph II's letter to, **5.** 346n
kingdom of: may be more manageable after its partition, **23.** 440; may be partitioned, **23.** 419
letter by, shown by Potocki, **42.** 162
letters of: **3.** 109n; to Broglie brothers, **3.** 102–3, 109
Lind taken by, as preceptor to nephew, **23.** 565
made K. of Poland, **22.** 253
Müntz in service of, **12.** 263
Nivernais's *Jardins modernes* given to, **12.** 260
Noyon, Bp of, nominated for cardinalate by, **3.** 102–3
Ogiński incited by France against, **33.** 511n
Polish minister at Rome reports Young Pretender's alleged Polish trip to, **23.** 352
Russians may depose, **36.** 281
Stanislas I alive during reign of, **7.** 356, **22.** 253, 404
Sulkowsky's competitor, **33.** 279–80
Thomatti, Mme de, refuses, **3.** 349n
unhappy, **23.** 352
(?) Voltaire calls, best of kings, **8.** 165
Stanley, Bn. *See* Smith Stanley, Edward (1752–1834)
Stanley, Bns. *See* Hamilton, Lady Elizabeth (1753–97); Holroyd, Maria Josepha (ca 1771–1863)
Stanley, Mr:
SH visited by, **12.** 241
Stanley, Mrs. *See* Hoby, (?) Elizabeth
Stanley, Anne (ca 1725–1803), m. (1765) Welbore Ellis, cr. (1794) Bn Mendip:
brother's bequest to, **33.** 161–2
Clifden, Lady, dies at house of, **11.** 328n
cribbage liked by, **12.** 167
grapes at Prado's mentioned by, **32.** 208
grotto of, **12.** 140, **33.** 105, **39.** 327–8
guests of: Agars, **12.** 202; HW, **12.** 202, 204, **34.** 62; Johnstons, **12.** 202; Williams, **12.** 202
HW asked by, for flags (iris) for her grotto, **39.** 327–8
husband of, **11.** 41n
plump, **12.** 12

Richmond expects return of, **12.** 141
sister of, **12.** 58n
SH visited by, **12.** 238
SH visitors sent by, **12.** 233
Stanley, Lady Charlotte (1728–76), m. (ca 1751) Gen. John Burgoyne:
biographical information about, corrected, **43.** 84, 301
Burgoyne runs away with, **28.** 336
Carmontelle's water-colour of Mme de Choiseul will disappoint, **41.** 137
Choiseul, Duchesse de, friend of, **3.** 243n
—— writes to, **41.** 110
Du Deffand, Mme, asks for news of, **5.** 272
HW sends news of, **6.** 282
health of, is reason for husband's recall from America, **41.** 314n
Stanley, Hans, writes to Duchesse de Choiseul about, **3.** 243
Viry, Contessa di, sends regards to, **41.** 203
Stanley, Edward (1689–1776), 11th E. of Derby, 1776:
Burgoyne marries daughter of, **28.** 336
daughter of, **3.** 243n, **28.** 336
regiment raised by, **19.** 128
son of, **21.** 199n, 552n, **23.** 313n, **30.** 302n
Stanley, Edward Smith. *See* Smith Stanley, Edward
Stanley, Lady Elizabeth Henrietta (1779–1857), m. (1795) Stephen Thomas Cole:
birth date of, corrected, **43.** 155
Dorset father of, **33.** 79n
HW to send ticket to, for SH, **12.** 159
SH visited by, **12.** 161, 249
Twickenham resident, **42.** 485
Stanley, George (d. 1734), Hans Stanley's father:
daughter of, **11.** 41n
suicide of, **7.** 201, 442, **29.** 5, **33.** 162
Stanley, Mrs George. *See* Sloane, Sarah
Stanley, Hans (1721–80), politician; M.P.:
adjournment of House advocated by, **38.** 317
Admiralty changes expected by, **22.** 326
army left by, **30.** 71
Bedford's dismissal affects, **22.** 326–7
biographical information about, corrected, **43.** 105, 120, 189, 259, 305, 313, 328, 352
Blaquiere resembles, **5.** 137
Buckinghamshire tells, about duel, **9.** 319
Bussy's exchange with, **38.** 89–90
Caswall told by, about duel, **9.** 319
Chanteloup to be visited by, **5.** 270
Chesterfield hears Gray's *Odes* read by, **9.** 215
Choiseul, Duc de, much with, because of Mme de Gramont, **38.** 427
—— no longer cares about, **4.** 461
Choiseul, Duchesse de, inconvenienced by, **3.** 251
—— receives letter from, **3.** 243
Churchill or Craufurd hears from, of Conway's trip to Bath, **39.** 317
Conway visited by, in Flanders, **37.** 167

[Stanley, Hans, *continued*]

Corsican rebels said to concern, **22.** 326n

costume of, when calling on Conway in Paris, **37.** 308

Dalrymple given letter of introduction by, **28.** 368n

Du Deffand, Mme, inquires about embassy of, **3.** 251

—— mentions, **4.** 242

Dyson succeeds, as cofferer, **28.** 143n

(?) election given up by, **14.** 197

English courier sent to, with news of Pondicherry's capture, **21.** 515

Fontainebleau to be left by, for Paris, **38.** 452

footman thrashed by, for insolently barring theatre box, **37.** 433

Fox, Henry, jokes about excessive visits of, to HW, **30.** 71

France visited by, to discuss peace terms, **9.** 389n

frigate awaits, at Leghorn, **22.** 326

German war supported by, in debates on foreign estimates, **21.** 553n

good-humoured, **37.** 167

Gray's *Odes* attributed to, **9.** 215

Grenville ministry's offer spurned by, **22.** 327n

HW asks Bns Hervey to thank, for attentions in Paris, **31.** 53

HW calls, 'dove,' **31.** 30

HW learns anecdote about D. of Newcastle from, **31.** 11

HW may get postscript from, to Conway's letter, **37.** 167

(?) HW mentions, **7.** 368, **10.** 224

HW reads poem by, at Bns Hervey's, **29.** 8

HW recommends, to Mann, **22.** 292, 300, 304

HW sails with, **7.** 324

HW's correspondence with, **41.** 116–17, 126–30

HW sees, at opera, and hears Hertford praised, **38.** 466

HW sends letter by, **7.** 376

HW's letter to be sent by, **31.** 53

HW's relations with, **30.** 71

HW taken by, to see archives in Paris, **7.** 266

HW warns Mann about conversation with, **22.** 300, 304

Halifax entertains, at Horton, **10.** 194

house of, in Paris, **3.** 24, 358, 372

(?) Hungary visited by, **39.** 182–3

Isle of Wight's governor, **38.** 418

Italy to be visited by, **22.** 293, 300

Kames tries to send MS to HW through, **40.** 229

Lauzun imitates, **3.** 239

lord of the Admiralty, **22.** 292

Mann encloses letter to, to Paris, **22.** 340

—— entertains, **22.** 313, 326

may be ambassador to Russia, **22.** 444

(?) Montbazon and Townshend talk at house of, **37.** 545

Newcastle's social relations with, **31.** 11

Paris mission of, **21.** 504, 514, 515, 536, **22.** 92–3, 300

Paris visit by, rumoured, **31.** 30

Paris visited by, **31.** 49, **35.** 230, **37.** 307–8, **38.** 427

peace negotiations of, **21.** 526n

plan of Bubb Dodington's house drawn by, for HW, **30.** 71

popularity of, in Paris, **31.** 49

recalled from Paris, **38.** 128

Rome but not Naples to be visited by, on way to Paris, **22.** 327

Russian embassy of: appointment of, cruel to Macartney, **30.** 233; George III promises to limit, to two years, **30.** 233; Hertford, Cts of, told by him of dislike for, **30.** 233; salary and allowances for, **30.** 233

St James's Palace visited by, **9.** 319

Scarbrough succeeded by, as Cofferer, **22.** 473

secretary at war's post may be sought by, **39.** 93

sister of, **11.** 41n

social relations of, in Paris, **4.** 461, **7.** 261, 265, 266, 316, 318, 322, 442

suicide of, **7.** 201, 442, **29.** 5, **33.** 161

Treasury offer spurned by, but Admiralty and Isle of Wight governorship retained, **43.** 280

Treasury post rumoured for, **22.** 37n

trunk of, opened on way to England, and books sent to London customs, **38.** 483–4

Usson mimics, **7.** 297

Virrette released by influence of, with Holdernesse, **19.** 182n

waddles, **39.** 183

Wilkes drinks health of, at Paris, **38.** 484

will of: **33.** 161–2; leaves Cadoxton estate to Rice, **41.** 117n

works in MS left by, **29.** 8

Stanley, Hans Sloane. *See* Sloane Stanley, Hans

Stanley, Harriet. *See* Smith Stanley, Hon. Henrietta

Stanley, Henrietta Mary (1630–85), m. (1655) William Wentworth, 2d E. of Strafford: husband's inscription to, on tomb, **35.** 268

Stanley, Hon. Henrietta Smith. *See* Smith Stanley, Hon. Henrietta

Stanley, James (1664–1736), 10th E. of Derby, 1702:

apartment built by, at Halnaker House, **12.** 200

Stanley, James (1717–71). *See* Smith Stanley, James

Stanley, Sir John (ca 1663–1744), Bt:

catalogue of Charles I's collection in hands of, **16.** 290n, **42.** 354n

Stanley, Sarah (ca 1726–1821), m. (1765) Christopher D'Oyly:

brother's bequest to, **33.** 161–2

Churchills visit, **12.** 105

HW hears of Lady Westmorland's illness from, **12.** 63–4

HW likes to visit, **12.** 58

HW visits, **12.** 103, 105, 121

illness of, **12.** 146–7

marriage date of, corrected, **43**. 352
officers from London visit, **12**. 121
Sloane, Mrs, to visit SH with, **12**. 146–7
SH visited by, **12**. 158, 249
Twickenham resident, **42**. 485
Stanley, Sir Thomas (ca 1435–1504), cr. (1485)
E. of Derby:
Bourchier's commission to, as Edward IV's
executor, **41**. 124
position of, at Henry VII's Court, **2**. 365
Stanley, Hon. Thomas (? 1753–79), M.P.; army
officer:
birth date of, **43**. 62
Ewin's controversy with, **1**. 362
(?) Hungary visited by, **39**. 182–3
Stanley, Venetia Anastasia (1600–33), m. (1625)
Sir Kenelm Digby, Kt:
Argonne's book mentions pictures of, **16**.
205–6
children of, **10**. 332
HW's miniature of family of, **28**. 180
miniature of, by Oliver, after Van Dyck, **2**.
43, 159, 176
miniature portrait of, with family, **1**. 358
name of, corrected, **43**. 38
paintings of, **15**. 205
portrait busts of, **1**. 9, 27–8, **2**. 43
portraits of: at Gothurst, **10**. 332; at Mr
Skinner's, **1**. 29; at Windsor, **1**. 29; in man-
ner of Van Dyck, **1**. 26, 27, 29
print of: by Hollar, **1**. 181; wanted by HW,
42. 18
print of bust of, **2**. 43
Stanley family:
arms of, **1**. 27
Stanmer, Sussex, Thomas Pelham's seat:
Pelham, Mrs, at, **10**. 338
Dodd and Whaley to dine at, **40**. 6
Stanmore, (? Middlesex):
Parr's school at, **15**. 215n
Stanmore. See also Stainmore
Stannaries:
Morice was lord warden of, **21**. 389n
Waldegrave, warden of, **22**. 126n
Stanno. See Stanhoe
Stanstead Park, Sussex:
Conway may have seen, **39**. 309
HW recommends, to Mary Berry, **12**. 206
HW visits, **4**. 455n
Halifax at, **10**. 246
—— inherits, **10**. 205n
Stansted House, Sussex:
(?) Northumberlands build at, **20**. 341
Stansted. See also Stanstead
Stanton, Charlotte (ca 1766–1830), m. (1787)
Thomas Goodall; actress:
acts in *The Beaux' Stratagem*, **11**. 101
Stanton, Miles (1676–1753), conduct at Eton:
(?) Montagu mentions, **10**. 309
Stanton. See also Staunton
Stanway, Glos:
Tracy of, **14**. 18n, 199n

Stanwick Park, Yorks:
Smithsons' ancestral estate, **20**. 341n
'Stanzas on the Death of a Bullfinch Killed by
a Cat.' *See under* Williams, Sir Charles Han-
bury: 'Ode on the Death of Matzel'
Stapleford Abbots, Essex:
Day of, **2**. 207n
Staples, Hon. Henrietta. *See* Molesworth, Hon.
Henrietta
Staples, (?) John (d. 1789), lawyer:
Dingley assaulted by, **23**. 98
Stapleton, Chevalier de, Württemberg's min-
ister to England:
Hertford asks about, **38**. 507
Stapleton, Mrs:
SH visited by, **12**. 234
Stapleton, Catherine (ca 1732–1802), m. Sir
James Wright, Kt, 1766; cr. (1772) Bt:
George III's picture done by, for Mann, and
shown to Q. Charlotte, **22**. 501, 503
Venice visited by, on way to Rome and
Naples, **21**. 457n
Stapleton, Catherine (1734–1815), dau. of
James Russell Stapleton of Bodrhyddan,
Flintshire:
birth date of, corrected, **43**. 338, 352
Blandford, Lady, attended by, **31**. 197
—— nursed by, **33**. 121
Digby miniatures acquired from, by HW,
43. 297
fortune of, **33**. 121
Grenville, George, entrusts children to, **31**.
198n
Grenvilles did not deserve, **31**. 198
HW compliments, on birth of Lady Wil-
liams's son, **31**. 170
HW receives offer of miniatures through, **41**.
269
HW's regard for, **31**. 198
HW to be helped by, to see Digby minia-
tures, **41**. 253
ill-usage of, **31**. 198
Stapleton, Elizabeth (1740–1825), m. (1767)
Watkin Williams:
Digby miniatures owned by, **43**. 62
HW acquires miniatures through, **43**. 297
Stapleton, Frances (1741–1825):
Digby miniatures sold by, to HW, **41**. 253,
43. 297
Stapleton, Lady Georgiana Maria. *See* Fitzroy,
Lady Georgiana Maria
Stapleton, Col. James Russell (d. 1743) of
Bodrhyddan:
family of, **41**. 253n
Stapleton, Mrs John Horace Thomas. *See* Fitz-
roy, Lady Georgiana Maria
Stapleton, Penelope (b. 1732):
Digby miniatures sold by, to HW, **41**. 253n,
43. 297
Stapleton, T.:
print of, **40**. 237
Stapleton, Sir Thomas (1727–81), 5th Bt; M.P.:
(?) club at house of, **32**. 361

[Stapleton, Sir Thomas, *continued*]
Oxford corporation tries to sell Parliamentary seat to, **22**. 584n

Stapleton, Thomas (d. 1821), of Carlton, Yorks:
(?) club of, **32**. 361

Stapleton, Walter (d. 1746), Brig.-Gen. in French service:
Kilmarnock's severity opposed by, **19**. 285
Perth aided by, **19**. 259

Stapleton, Walter Valentine (d. 1746), Irish officer in French service:
fatally wounded at Culloden, **37**. 240

Stapleton, William (d. ?ca 1826), army officer:
goes to West Indies with the Guards, **11**. 119
wife of, **7**. 53n, **10**. 206n, **11**. 119n, **28**. 445n

Stapleton, Mrs William. *See* Keppel, Anna Maria

Stapleton:
Young, Sarah, of, **16**. 125n

Stapletons, manor in Norfolk:
HW's will mentions, **30**. 368

Stapylton. *See* Stapleton

Star, Mrs Edmund. *See* Jennings, Mary

'Star, the' (? tavern):
Deards, William, has shop at, at end of Pall Mall near St James's, Haymarket, **21**. 296n
See also Star and Garter

'Star,' inn:
near Newmarket, **18**. 315n

Star; stars:
astronomers' theory about, **19**. 71, **21**. 85
Cowper orders, from London, **25**. 568
Herschel's discoveries about, **15**. 187, **33**. 475
'millions of coveys of worlds' among, **15**. 187
newly discovered, **15**. 187, **25**. 614, **33**. 475
silver, embroidered on gown, **10**. 198

'Star and Garter,' tavern in Pall Mall:
Byron kills Chaworth in duel at, **22**. 284, **38**. 501, 503
cricket club formed at, **23**. 495n
George IV joins freemasons at, **34**. 23n
Johnson exhibits at, **35**. 290n

Star and Garter (insignia):
Vorontsov, Cts, wears, **22**. 193

Starch:
in neckcloth, **35**. 124

Star Chamber:
England seems as if fined in, **22**. 274
HW's verses mention, **33**. 204

Starhemberg, Fürstin von. *See* Arenberg, Louise Franziska (1764–1838); Salm-Salm, Maria Franziska von (1731–1806)

Starhemberg, Georg Adam (1724–1807), Graf; cr. (1765) Fürst; Austrian ambassador to France:
Austrian-Dutch quarrel discussed by, at Paris, **25**. 561
Bernis tells, that France cannot send troops to Moravia, **20**. 589n
Choiseul pressed by, not to negotiate with England, **21**. 360n

dances at ball in honour of Dauphin's marriage, **4**. 410
HW describes, **21**. 498n
HW informed by, of courier from Spain, **39**. 63
Hertford and, the only ambassadors at Fontainebleau, **38**. 464
Louis XV consents to demand of, to marry Maria Isabella to Archduke Joseph, **21**. 323n
Maria Theresa orders Mercy-Argenteau and, to have French troops near Austrian Netherlands, **24**. 520n
—— sends, to Paris, **21**. *498*
Pompadour, Mme de, gets letters from Maria Theresa transmitted by, **21**. 258n
recall of, arouses fear of war in France, **22**. 404
social relations of, in Paris, **7**. 267, 301, 312

Stark, Brig.-Gen. John, American army officer:
Baume defeated by, at Bennington, **24**. 340n

Starkey, Hugh (d. 1500), gentleman usher:
buried at Over, **1**. 251

Starkey, Sir Oliver (d. 1588), Kt of Malta:
accounts of, **1**. 250–1
books of, **1**. 249

Starkey family:
arms of, **1**. 251

State; states (chair of state):
Mary, Q. of Scots', at Hardwick, **9**. 297

Statement of Facts, in Answer to Mrs Gunning's Letter, A. See under Bowen, Capt. Essex

Staten Island, New York:
Howe, Adm., and Hotham join Gen. Howe at, **24**. 241n
Howe, Gen., lands on, **24**. 229, 241
Sullivan, Gen., raids, **24**. 331n

State of Parties. See St John, Henry (1678–1751), Vct Bolingbroke: *Letters*

State Paper Office, London:
Astle examines parchments in, **28**. 238

State Papers. See under Hyde, Edward (1609–74), E. of Clarendon: *State Papers*; Yorke, Philip (1720–90), E. of Hardwicke: *Miscellaneous State Papers*

States general, Dutch. *See under* Holland

States general, French. *See* États généraux

'Statesman, The.' *See under* Williams, Sir Charles Hanbury

State Trials. See Complete Collection of State Trials, A

Stationer; stationers. *See* Woodmason, James

Stationers Company:
Baskerville's agreement with, for Psalms and Prayer Book, **40**. 275
Beecroft, master of, **2**. 81n
HW jokes about SH Press being opened by, **35**. 98

Stationers' Hall:
book entered at, **29**. 141n
HW jokes about entry book at, **31**. 226–7
Mason's bookseller neglects to enter works at, **28**. 150

Stationery:
HW's accounts for providing, for Exchequer Office, 24. 29–33, 34, 42. 29–30
Mann's expense allowance for, 18. 516
'Statira' (alternate name for Alexander the Great's wife, Barsine; heroine of La Calprenède's *Cassandre*):
HW had no youthful passion for, 11. 362
HW uses name of: for Lady Caroline Fitzroy, 37. 196; for 'Perdita' Robinson, 33. 354; for Mrs Strawbridge, 33. 556
Orford, Cts of, signs herself 'Stitara' after, 20. 248
See also under Lee, Nathaniel: *Alexander the Great*
Statistical Account. See under Sinclair, Sir John
Statius, Publius Papinus (ca 61–96), Latin poet:
ranting style of, 29. 223, 256
secretary of militia reads, aloud, to E. of Orford's guests, 24. 295
soldiers would despise war poetry of, 16. 269
Sylvæ by: HW might have compared *Georgics* to, 13. 198; HW quotes from, 13. 224; West paraphrases, 13. 91, 92
Statuary:
Barrett Lennard fond of, 35. 184
in Piccadilly, 32. 342
in wax, 38. 198–9
ruins of, make one regret not seeing it intact, 42. 507
See also Sculpture; Statue
Statue; statues:
ancient, show character, not passion, 35. 445
antique, of Saturn going to eat Jupiter, 32. 169
at: Casa Feroni, 17. 33; Dublin, 9. 401; Easton Neston, 20. 390; Elizabeth Chudleigh's, 9. 277; Florentine Duomo, weep on catafalque, 22. 367; Herculaneum, 16. 89; Kedleston, 10. 230; Lichfield, 9. 224, 294; Park Place, 39. 550; Rochester Cathedral, 40. 213, 221; Stowe, 10. 315, 35. 76; Wilton, 40. 8; Wilton, adorned with charcoal, 25. 178
casts of, to be exhibited in D. of Richmond's garden room, 21. 173
Charles II's, 9. 294
Churchill might knock down Britain's foes with, 38. 188
colossal: of Guy of Warwick, 32. 353n; of Venus, 22. 583
Corinthian, Roman sailors to replace, if lost, 19. 264, 37. 102
Damer, Mrs, may want to copy, at Florence, 25. 184
Del Nero's, 18. 308, 326, 338, 347
Druid's, at the Vyne, 35. 642
export of, from Tuscany, forbidden, 20. 465
for Chatsworth bridge, 9. 296
Francavilla's, bought by Mann for Frederick, P. of Wales, *see under* Francavilla
HW discusses, with Stanley, 30. 71

HW's: bought at Rome, 26. 7; Mann distressed by accidents to, 19. 13
HW to get, at Lichfield, 9. 224
in Capitol at Rome, 20. 470
in Florentine loggia, 22. 123–4
in Melrose Abbey, 42. 68
in Tribune of Florentine Uffizi, 24. 527
in Uffizi gallery, 24. 527, 25. 170, 35. 55
ivory, in Sicily, plundered by Verres, 37. 432
La Borde's, 31. 80
Leicester to obtain, from Rome, 20. 104
Louis XVI orders, of balloon æronauts, 25. 450
Lyttelton orders gesse of, 20. 539, 547, 554, 21. 40
Mann advises Botta about placing, 22. 124
modern, at Wentworth Castle, 35. 267
Monck's, in Westminster Abbey, 38. 126
of Apollo, *see under* Apollo
of *bergamote* and biscuit porcelain, 31. 100
of Cicero, in Pomfret collection, 20. 390
of diamonds, in *Arabian Nights*, 38. 88
of Elgin, Cts of, on tomb, 39. 139
of Ganymede, 18. 153, 178, 303, 329, 561
of George II, at Stowe, 35. 76
of George III, by Mrs Damer, 43. 167
of gesso, *see under* Gesso
of Henri IV, 24. 19, 36, 31. 99, 34. 176
of Hermaphrodite, *See* Hermaphrodite
of James IV, 42. 12n
of Leda and the Swan, 20. 547
of 'Livia.' *See under* Livia
of Louis XIV in Place Vendôme, destroyed in French Revolution, 31. 372, 39. 473
of Louis XV, at Bordeaux, 17. 125
of Lucius Antonius, thought to be of Cicero, 16. 300
of Mercury, *see under* Mercury
of Morpheus, 18. 153, 178, 303, 329, 561
of St Ignatius, 23. 513
of Saxon king, found under Westminster Hall, 16. 198
of slave in chains, at Cirencester, 40. 11
of Venus, 'colossean,' 22. 583
of Venus, extracting a thorn, 20. 547
of Venus, *see also under* Venus
on monument in Trinity Hospital, Greenwich, 16. 88–9
Pisans may erect, to Leopold, 23. 95
Pomfret's, presented to Oxford, 20. 390n, 470, 562n, 579
Pygmalion's, of Galatea, 35. 343–4
Radnor's garden full of, 35. 175n
removed from Tribune in Uffizi gallery, 25. 170
Roman, appear to Chute like those at Hyde Park Corner, 35. 58
Walpole, Sir Robert, needs, at Houghton, 18. 326
Wilton's, 20. 397–8
William III's, 9. 401
Statuta hospitalis Hierusalem, ed. Rondinelli:
Farmer sends, to Cole, 1. 257–8

Statute of lunacy:
  HW and Sir Edward Walpole not to take out,
    for E. of Orford, **24**. 294, **25**. 126
Staunton, Francis (d. after 1627):
  family of, **38**. 125
Staunton, Mrs Francis. *See* Caulfeild, Lettice
Staunton, Sir George Leonard (1737–1801), cr.
  (1785) Bt:
  *Authentic Account of an Embassy from the
  King of Great Britain to the Emperor of
  China, An*, by, **12**. 191n
  Du Deffand, Mme, gives Necker mémoire by,
    for Macartney, **7**. 210
  ——'s social relations with, **7**. 206
  —— to have parcels sent by, **7**. 213
  —— urged by, to ask for Macartney's ex-
    change, **7**. 211
  Holland may be visited by, **7**. 213
  Macartney friend of, **7**. 206
  ——'s correspondence with, **7**. 211
  SH visited by, **12**. 234
Staunton family:
  Howard and Seymour families not related to,
    38. 133
Staveley, Thomas (1626–84), antiquary:
  HW asks for portraits of, and wife, from
    Bibliotheca topographica Britannica, **42**.
    289
Staveley, Mrs Thomas. *See* Onebye, Mary
Stavely, W. (d. after 1805), painter:
  Cadogan, Bns, painted by, **24**. 320n
  (?) Mason sends memorial to Conway in be-
    half of, **39**. 136
  SH visited by, **12**. 223, 241, **42**. 364n
Staves. *See* Staff
Stavordale, Bn. *See* Fox Strangways, Henry
  Thomas (1747–1802)
Stawel, Mary (1726–80), m. 1 (1750) Henry
  Bilson Legge; m. 2 (1768) Wills Hill, 2d E.
  of Hillsborough; she was cr. (1760) Bns
  Stawel, s.j.:
  Bristol's proposal refused by, **30**. 241
  marriage of, **9**. 53n
Stay; stays (corsets):
  colour of binding of, denotes classes at St-Cyr,
    10. 293
  diamond hooks for, offered to Mrs Scott by
    Sir Edward Walpole, **10**. 329
  Geoffrin, Mme, does not wear, **31**. 59n
  HW dresses as old woman with, **17**. 359
  Richecourt, Comtesse de, wears, in England,
    20. 365
  Rochford, Cts of, dances without, **35**. 213
Staymaker; staymakers:
  Lombard, Peter, said to have been, **23**. 435
  Ray is, in Holywell St, **33**. 98n
  wife of, consulted by Susannah Owens, **9**. 75
Steane, Northants:
  chapel and manor-house at, **35**. 74
  chimney-piece from, **9**. 156
  Thanet and Douglass hunt near, **9**. 201

Steare, Staples, bookseller and publisher in
  Fleet St:
  North Briton published by, **23**. 28n
  prosecuted as Wilkes's publisher, **23**. 29
Steavens, Miss:
  Mann recommends, to Hamiltons at Naples,
    24. 337n
Steavens, (?) Mary (d. 1747 *or* 1748), wife of
  Sir Thomas Steavens:
  death of, **20**. 175
Steavens, Sarah (d. 1799), m. (1738) James
  West:
  husband and brother of, **20**. 371n
  husband's MSS promised by, to Ds of Port-
    land, but sold to E. of Shelburne, **41**. 253
Steavens, Thomas (ca 1728–?59):
  critically ill in Padua, **20**. 175n
  HW recommends, to Mann, **20**. 371
  Mann's correspondence with, **20**. 379
  mother mourned by, **25**. 175n
  Stanhope and Harte met by, in Venice and
    Vienna, **20**. 175n
  West's brother-in-law, **20**. 371
  Williams, Sir C. H., friend of, **20**. 175n
  witticism of, to Signora Capello, **20**. *175*
Steavens. *See also* Steevens; Stephens; Stevens
Stebbing, Henry (1687–1763), D.D.:
  Middleton's reply to, **15**. 297
  Observations on the Introductory Discourse
    by, **15**. 197
Stecchi, Giovanni Batista, printer:
  Pignotti's *Shakespear* printed by, **24**. 536n
Stedman, Mrs John. *See* Moders, Mary
Steel:
  buckles of, *see under* Buckle
  from Woodstock, **17**. 302
  HW sends, to Mann, **17**. 302
  machine of, **20**. 203
  of agate, mirror of, **32**. 323
  scissors of, **31**. 76, 84–5
  suit and sword of, **25**. 667n
Steele, Mrs:
  objections raised to, as guardian for Miss
    Nicoll, **14**. 207
Steele, Elizabeth (d. 1782), m. John Trevor, 3d
  Bn Trevor:
  genealogy of, **10**. 352
Steele, Sir Richard (1672–1729), Kt; essayist;
  dramatist; M.P.:
  Conscious Lovers, The, by: HW prefers, to
    Moore's *Foundling*, **19**. 465; performed at
    Drury Lane, **18**. 538n
  daughter of, **10**. 352
  Fortune Tellers by, performed at Drury Lane,
    18. 538n
  Funeral, The, by: Delane acts in, **13**. 96n;
    Foote threatens to revive, as attack on Ds
    of Kingston, **28**. 218; Foote may act 'Lady
    Brumpton' in, **39**. 252
  Pinkerton tells HW an anecdote about, **16**.
    287

Tender Husband, The, by, 'Biddy Tipkin' in, **21**. 438, **33**. 527, **38**. 100
see also under *Spectator, The*
'Steel waters':
HW jokes about Lady Mary Coke and, **31**. 25
Steelyard (balance):
S. Lysons acquires, **15**. 202
Steene. *See* Steine
Steenkerke, battle of:
Conway and Scott visit site of, **39**. 536
Mackay killed at, **15**. 59n
'oiseaux de,' *see* Steinkerque, oiseaux de
Steenwyck, Hendrik van (ca 1580–1649), Flemish painter:
painting by, of St Peter, in Mead's collection, **16**. 155
painting of church interior attributed to, **40**. 369
Steeple; steeples:
visible from Wichnor, **38**. 71
Steevens, George (1736–1800), editor:
a fellow-commoner of King's, **2**. 294–5
Biographical Anecdotes of William Hogarth by Isaac Reed, and, **41**. 448
carries letters for Cole, **2**. 334, 338
Chatterton to be published by Percy and, **2**. 114n
Cole dissuaded by, from editing, **2**. 335, 338
—— may have received Malone's pamphlet from, **2**. 296n, 305
——'s correspondence with, **43**. 75
——'s opinion of, **2**. 285, 286, 290, 295
disbelieves in Ireland's MSS, **15**. 321
Dramatic Works of Shakespeare published by, **11**. 357, **28**. 116n, **33**. 546n
Farington aided by, in compiling list, **15**. 321
Fielding and Walker encouraged by, to seek Lort's patronage, **16**. 177
HW converses with, about Malone's *Cursory Observations*, **42**. 3n
HW permits Lort to show letter about Chatterton to, **16**. 226
HW's civility to, **2**. 287, 290, 292–3, 294–5, 300
HW's correspondence with, **43**. 75
HW's *Mysterious Mother* described by, **33**. 578n
Hogarth's prints collected by, **43**. 73
Hogarth's unpublished plates sought by, **2**. 273
in Cambridge, **2**. 335
Johnson suspects, of writing *Archæological Epistle*, **29**. 212, 218
Lort tells, of HW's letter about Chatterton, **16**. 225
Malone's correspondence with, **42**. 3
Mason defends allusion to *Macbeth* against, **29**. 212
—— possibly alludes to, **29**. 182n
Percy aided by, on Surrey's poems, **42**. 367n
print by, of Willis, **2**. 285, 287
reply to Milles and Bryant expected from, **29**. *183*

Ritson attacks, **2**. 335n
Rowley poems' authenticity discussed by, **2**. 290
Steevens. *See also* Steavens; Stephens; Stevens
Stefanucci, Orazio (1706–75), S.J.; authority on canon law:
imprisoned at Rome, **23**. 516n, 517n, 526
treatise attributed to, **23**. 517, 526–7
Steinberg, Baron:
(?) Princes examined by, at George II's command, **9**. 58
Steinberg, Georg Friedrich von:
Münchhausen conveys George II's orders for D. of Cumberland to, at Hanover, **21**. 136n
Steine. *See under* Brighton
'Steinkerque, les oiseaux de.' *See* Alsace-Hénin-Liétard, Gabrielle-Françoise-Charlotte d', Mme de Cambis; Beauvau, Marie-Françoise-Catherine de, Marquise de Boufflers; Boufflers, Louise-Julie de, Mme de Boisgelin
Steinwick. *See* Steenwyck
'Stella.' *See* Johnson, Esther
Stella:
discussion about, in *giuoco della sibilla*, **20**. 477
Stella (fl. 1670):
dedication to, **16**. 371
Stella, Jacques (1596–1657), painter:
(?) paintings by, at Carmelites', **7**. 264
Stendardi, ——, Tuscan consul at Algiers:
Bey expels, **20**. 472n
Stent, Peter (fl. 1640–67), engraver:
Overbury's portrait said to be engraved by, **16**. 64
print by, of Bp Montaigne, **1**. 149
Stephan (servant):
Orford, Cts of, accompanied by, to England, **19**. 50
—— to be accompanied by, **19**. 46
Pomfret, Cts of, had, as valet-de-chambre, **19**. 46
Stephan's Inn:
at Naples, **22**. 292n
Stephen, St, of Hungary:
order of, *see* Order of St Stephen
Stephen (ca 1097–1154), K. of England 1135–54:
cost of garments of, **34**. 224
nephew of, **2**. 182
wife of, dies at Hedingham Castle, **9**. 67
Stephen's, St, chapel. *See* Parliament: House of Commons
Stephens, Mr, Chatterton's editor:
Chatterton's letter to, **16**. 129n
Stephens, Catherine (1794–1882), m. (1838) George Capel-Coningsby, 5th E. of Essex:
husband of, **11**. 238n
Stephens, Mrs Joanna (d. 1774):
medicine of: Parliament rewards, **40**. 275–6; stone, the, cured by, **4**. 133, **5**. 285; Victoire, Mme, cured by, **22**. 164; Walpole, Sir Robert, takes, **18**. 552

Stephens, Rev. Michael Pye (ca 1752–1822):
  (?) Boycott, Louisa, baptized by, 11. 195
Stephens, Peter (d. ?1775), artist:
  drawings printed by, at Rome and given to Mann, 20. 427–8
  Florence and Rome visited by, 23. 427
  HW gets engraving of, 23. 423
  mad, 23. 423
  Mann has never seen prints by, 23. 427
  ——'s house said to have been frequented by, 23. 423
  prints by, not to be had in Rome, 23. 429
  views by: HW sees, at Lord Ossory's, 23. 422–3; HW wants, from Mann, 23. 422–3
Stephens, Sir Philip (1723–1809), cr. (1795) Bt; M.P.:
  biographical information about, corrected, 43. 303
  (?) Conway with, at Chatham, 38. 33
  Eliott's and Murray's dispatches to, 25. 136n
  Keppel notified by, of Palliser's letter, 24. 427n
  secretary to the Admiralty, 28. 408
Stephens, Samuel (ca 1695–1764), actor:
  'button-maker,' 13. 63n, 97
  death date of, corrected, 43. 174
  praised by inebriate, 13. 63–4
Stephens, William (fl. 1736–73), engraver:
  Henshaw's instructor, 1. 294n, 296
  retired to Yorkshire, 1. 296
Stephens. See also Estienne; Steavens; Steevens; Stevens
Stephenson, Mr:
  HW's social relations with, in Paris, 7. 288
Stephenson, Edward:
  widow of, 11. 238n
Stephenson, John (? 1709–94), M.P.:
  Fox, Henry, and D. of Bedford support, 13. 26n
Stephenson, Sir William (d. 1774), Kt, 1759; lord mayor 1764–5:
  Élie de Beaumont visits, 38. 461
Stephenson, William, undertaker, in the Strand:
  Lovat buried by, 37. 267n, 268
Stephenson. See also Stevenson
Stepney, George (1663–1707):
  William III orders, to sound out George I on giving up Hanover, 7. 362
Stepney, Sir John (1743–1811), Bt; M.P.:
  Berlin embassy of, as envoy to Prussia, 25. 314n, 33. 336n
Stepney, London:
  robbery near, 29. 60n
Sterborough, Surrey:
  Cobham of, 14. 75n
Sterling Castle, English ship:
  Cooper, commander of, 19. 64n
  Saunders writes to Pitt from, 21. 336n
Sterndale, John, printer:
  House of Commons questions, 23. 555
Sterne, Rev. Laurence (1713–68), novelist:
  Burton, Dr John, satirized by, 16. 25n
  'capricious pertness' of, 2. 301

HW not amused by, 40. 386
HW reads Letters of, 28. 229, 233
Life and Opinions of Tristram Shandy by:
  copies of, autographed, 28. 150; dramatization of, 29. 291; HW sends, to Mann, 21. 407; HW's opinion of, 10. 255, 15. 66, 16. 44; Mann's opinion of, 21. 446, 520–1; Roxburghe lends, to Mann, 21. 520–1
Modène, Hôtel de, lodging of, in Paris, 6. 330n
Paris visited by, 40. 386
Patch's caricature of, 23. 5, 27, 33, 37
preaches in Hertford's chapel, 38. 353
Sentimental Journey, A, by: Du Deffand, Mme, owns, 8. 33n; French character described, 31. 45n; HW's opinion of, 10. 255; Montagu sends for copy of, 10. 256; tiresome but good-natured and picturesque, 14. 183
Sherlock imitates, 2. 301
success and fame hurt, 15. 66
Warburton calls, English Rabelais, 15. 67
Sternhold, Thomas (d. 1549), translator; versifier of Psalms:
  James I's version of Psalms outdoes that of, 16. 366
  metre of, compared to Home's, 32. 101
  Waller's diction compared with tunes of, 30. 291–2
Stert, Arthur (d. 1755), M.P.:
  (?) HW has less chance of being liked than, 17. 270, 43. 241
Stert, Sophia (ca 1769–1829), m. (1785) Hon. Robert Walpole:
  does not attend Lady Craven's wedding, 34. 133
Stettin (Germany):
  Frederick II's artillery was to have prevented fall of, 22. 12
Steuart, Agnes (d. 1778), m. (1739) Henry David Erskine, 10th E. of Buchan:
  HW sees, at Methodist chapel, 35. 119
  Rich, Mary, asked by, about HW, 35. 119
Steuart, William (1686–1768), M.P.:
  (?) HW has less chance of being liked than, 17. 270, 43. 241–2
Steuart. See Steward; Stewart; Stuart
Stevenage, Herts:
  HW stops at, 28. 36n
Stevens, Capt. and Mrs:
  Othello said to be acted by, 20. 230n
Stevens, Mrs, of (?) Kingston:
  SH ticket not used by, 12. 224n
Stevens, George Alexander (1710–84):
  'Nancy Dawson' ascribed to, 39. 3
Stevens, Maj.-Gen. Humphry (d. 1791):
  SH visited by, 2. 236
Stevens, Dr (?) Sacheverel (d. 1768):
  England called a 'mobocracy' by, 21. 138
  Norfolk St, home of, 21. 138n
  Travels Through France written by, 21. 138n
Stevens. See also Steavens; Steevens; Stephens

Stevenson, Mr (fl. 1778):
Keene's remark to, **2**. 86
Stevenson, Mr:
Ossory's social relations with, in Paris, **7**. 283
Stevenson, Mr:
SH visited by, **12**. 226
Stevenson, Mrs, of Richmond:
SH visited by, **12**. 229
Stevenson, Ann, m. (1760) Christopher Pemberton:
husband of, **1**. 287n
Stevenson, John, Cole's friend:
daughter of, **1**. 287n
Stevenson, John (1737–1829):
(?) Keene, Bp, speaks to, **2**. 86n
Stevenson, John Hall (1718–85):
HW grateful for verses of, **40**. 208
Makarony-Fables by, **14**. 169
Stevenson, Matthew (fl. 1654–85), poet:
Florus Britannicus by, **1**. 173
Stevenson, Robert (1734–92):
(?) Keene, Bp, speaks to, **2**. 86n
Stevenson, St George, army officer:
(?) in Grafton St, Dublin, **37**. 332
Stevenson, Samuel, mayor of Maidstone:
Holdernesse's letter to, **21**. 34
Stevenson, William (1736–1815):
(?) Keene, Bp, speaks to, **2**. 86n
Stevenson. *See also* Stephenson
Steward, ——:
Mann presents, to Leopold, **23**. 527n
Steward, Capt. [? James *or* William Stewart]:
Ireland to be visited by, to enter Parliament, **23**. 1
Irish gentleman, **23**. 27
Mann sends caricature and paper on Tuscany through, to HW and Shelburne, **23**. 27–8
—— sends letter through, to HW, **23**. 1
Steward, John, sea captain:
Sally, ship of, **21**. 16n
Steward. *See* Steuart; Stewart; Stuart
Steward; stewards. *See under* Servant
Stewart, ——:
arrested in Covent Garden bagnio, **17**. 505
Stewart, Alexander (ca 1454–ca 1485), cr. (? 1456) D. of Albany:
biographical information about, corrected, **43**. 188
HW in error about, **14**. 182
Stewart, Archibald (1697–1780), M.P.: provost of Edinburgh:
Argyll's terror of prison described by, **7**. 360
arrested, **19**. 181
birth date of, **43**. 259
HW sees, at Tower, **9**. 46
trial and acquittal of, **19**. 181n
Wade with, **19**. 175–6
Stewart, Archibald James Edward. *See* Douglas, Archibald James Edward
Stewart, Lady Catherine, m. (1752) James Murray of Broughton:
husband leaves, for Grace Johnston, **33**. 489n

Stewart, Charles, of Jamaica:
Somerset, slave of, freed, **35**. 566
Stewart, Lt Charles:
hostage in Marátha war, **24**. 510
Stewart, Hon. Charles (1681–1741), Vice-Adm.; M.P.:
(?) on board the *Blenheim*, **40**. 8
Stewart, Charles (d. 1764), 5th E. of Traquair:
arrest of, **19**. 288
Barrymore, Cotton, and Williams converse with, about Old Pretender's affairs, **19**. 381
evidence expected from, about plot, **19**. 381, 391
HW sees, at Tower, **9**. 46
Lovat's body paraded before dungeon of, **19**. 387
released from Tower, **19**. 381n
Stewart, Lady Charlotte (d. 1818), m. (1759) John Murray, 4th E. of Dunmore:
Du Deffand, Mme, has social relations with, **4**. 283, **6**. 284
—— to send letter by, **4**. 371, 374
pleases, at Coronation, **38**. 127
Stewart, Hon. Elizabeth. *See* Molesworth, Hon. Elizabeth (d. 1835)
Stewart, Frances Theresa (1647–1702), m. (1667) Charles Stuart, 3d D. of Richmond and 6th D. of Lennox:
portrait of, at Hagley, **35**. 147–8
sister of, **1**. 181n
Stewart, James (ca 1531–70), cr. (1562) E. of Moray and E. of Mar; Regent of Scotland 1567–70:
HW wishes to see life of, **15**. 182
portrait of, **15**. 182
Stewart, Hon. James (ca 1699–1768), army officer; M.P.:
birth date of, **43**. 273
conduct of, to be probed, **21**. 23
Gibraltar resolution signed by, **20**. 560n
Panmure said to be replacing, **20**. 562
recall of, from Gibraltar, recommended, **20**. 561n
Stewart, John (ca 1380–1424), 3d E. of Buchan; Constable of France:
HW inquires about, **15**. 182
Stewart, John (d. 1536), 2d D. of Albany, ca 1505; Regent of Scotland:
painting represents, **15**. 139n
Stewart, John (called John Roy) (1700–52):
death of, rumoured, **37**. 230
(?) Strath Bogie defended by, **37**. 229n
Stewart, Hon. John (ca 1709–96), M.P.:
Parliamentary membership of, corrected, **43**. 245
voted for, as commissioner, **17**. 438
Stewart, John (1736–1806), styled Lord Garlies 1746–73; 7th E. of Galloway, 1773:
Balgonie, Lord and Lady, visited by, **12**. 113
Blandford, Lord, to marry daughter of, **11**. 348–9
daughter of: **11**. 104n; dances Scotch reels, **12**. 113

[Stewart, John (1736–1806), *continued*]
Pecquigny almost duels with, at Milton's ball, **38**. 295
second marriage of, **38**. 369
Stewart, John, F.R.S.:
'Account of . . . Tibet' by, **25**. 15n
Stewart, John (d. after 1788), cr. (1784) titular Bt; valet to Young Pretender:
Young Pretender accompanied by, to France, **19**. 319n
—— attended by, **23**. 318
—— sends, to Paris for daughter, **25**. 513
Stewart, John Shaw:
withdraws as Parliamentary candidate, **41**. 279n
Stewart, Hon. Keith (1739–95), naval officer; M.P.:
naval disasters reported by, **33**. 245
Parliamentary membership of, corrected, **43**. 353
Stewart, Mary (d. 1751), m. (1741) Kenneth Mackenzie, styled Vct Fortrose:
rebels joined by, **19**. 233
Stewart, Mary (d. 1769), m. James O'Hara, 2d Bn Tyrawley:
husband of, **17**. 104
Lobkowitz and Signora Capello accompanied by, **37**. 289
Stewart, Capt. Robert:
Braddock rescued by, **20**. 495
Stewart, Robert (1739–1821), cr. (1789) Bn, (1796) E., and (1816) M. of Londonderry:
Seymour-Conway, Lady Sarah, to wed, **39**. 71, 72
wife of, **4**. 440n
Stewart, Hon. Robert (1769–1822), styled Vct Castlereagh 1769–1821; 2d M. of Londonderry, 1821:
Hertford visited by, at Sudbourne, **39**. 444, 445
wife of, **12**. 5n
Stewart, Mrs Robert. See Pratt, Frances (ca 1751–1833)
Stewart, Lady Sarah Frances. See Seymour-Conway, Lady Sarah Frances
Stewart, Lady Susan (1767–1841), m. (1791) George Spencer, styled M. of Blandford; 4th (5th) D. of Marlborough, 1817:
Blandford, Lord, to marry, **11**. 348–9
Dashwood, Sir Henry, contrives match of, **11**. 349
husband of, **11**. 104n
marriage of, **11**. 352, 366, **34**. 125
Stewart, Lady Susanna (ca 1731–1805), m. (1768) Granville Leveson Gower, 2d E. Gower, 1754; cr. (1786) M. of Stafford:
(?) arranges marriage of Lord and Lady Warwick, **32**. 295–6, 347
Augusta, Ps, attended by, at private Court ball, **38**. 143
birth date of, corrected, **43**. 124, 151, 350
daughter of, **11**. 244n

family of, **1**. 196n
Guines's ball attended by, **32**. 96n
HW dislikes, **12**. 113n
HW mentions, **9**. 402, 403
Karl Wilhelm Ferdinand offers seat to, at opera, **38**. 289
lady-in-waiting to Ps Augusta, **9**. 321
(?) 'Lady Notable,' **32**. 296
leaves Dunstable as HW enters, **32**. 291
'Machiavellian aunt,' **32**. 347
match-making of, **11**. 349, (?) **32**. 295–6, 347
places disposed of by, **32**. 317
royal ball for Christian VII attended by, **23**. 57n
solicitations by, **32**. 317n
Stewart, William (fl. 1731–43), paymaster of pensions:
Jeffries said to succeed, **17**. 494
Stewart. See also Steuart; Steward; Stuart
Steyning, Sussex:
West expects HW to represent, **13**. 235
Stick; sticks (walking-):
French do not ridicule one's, **31**. 89
George II walks with, **21**. 256
HW able to walk without, in less than a month after attack of gout, **24**. 70
HW falls by not using, **31**. 298
HW may be forced to use, **31**. 72
HW no longer needs, **35**. 340
HW uses, for gout, **10**. 180, 266, **31**. 197, **38**. 66
of office, see Staff
Stanley carries, long, **37**. 308
Stick, white (of government offices). See Staff
Stiell, Alexander (d. 1792), page, clerk, and steward to D. of Gloucester:
Adair's letter to, about D. of Gloucester, **36**. 139
Bryant's letter to, about D. of Gloucester, **36**. 138, 139
Gloucester, D. of, orders, to send Edward Walpole game and venison, **36**. 324
Gloucester family's return makes, joyful, **36**. 155
letter from D. of Gloucester's surgeon shown to HW by, **32**. 378
Waldegrave, Lady Elizabeth Laura, revived by good news from, **36**. 149
Stier, Chevalier de:
SH visited by, **12**. 236
Stiffkey, Norfolk:
monument to Sir Nathaniel Bacon at, **1**. 23
Stile:
HW and Mary Rich tumble from, **35**. 275–6
Stiletto; stiletti:
Italians no longer wield, **22**. 254
Jacobins have, **15**. 221
Still; stills:
distillery burnt by head of, flying off, **37**. 153
Stillingfleet, Benjamin:
Windham's letter from, about visiting Brown in Norwich, **43**. 49

Stillington, Robert (d. 1491), Bp of Bath and
Wells:
Masters finds fault with, **2.** 240n
Stillwater, battle of:
Burgoyne defeated at, **6.** 486n
Stilo ('Stillo'), Italy:
earthquake damages, **25.** 376
Stilt; stilts:
Blandford, Lady, would use, in Paris, **31.** 49
man on, peers through second-story windows
in London, **17.** 399
Stilton, Hunts:
Bell Inn at, **1.** 363
Dodd and Whaley to visit, **40.** 17
Gray sees Wharton at, **14.** 58n
Thornhill's ride to London from, **1.** 363
Stinsanacone (Italy):
earthquake account mentions, **25.** 376
Stiozzi-Ridolfi, Palazzo. *See* Ridolfi, Palazzo
Stiria. *See* Styria
Stirling, Capt.:
Rodney's letters to Admiralty brought by, **25.**
139n
'Stirling, E. of.' *See* Alexander, William
Stirling, Walter:
Gunnersbury House bought by, **33.** 535n
Stirling, Mrs William Moray. *See* Douglas, Hon.
Frances Elizabeth
Stirling, Scotland:
Conway stationed at, **37.** 254–7, 259–60, 263–4
—— to be in winter quarters at, **37.** 253
Falkirk near, **19.** 214
fit only for 'the old, the poor, and the dull,'
37. 256
London's example followed by, with regard
to Pitt, **21.** 546
moralizing at, **37.** 257
Stirling Castle, Scotland:
Barré dismissed as governor of, **22.** 189n, **38.**
255
—— succeeded by Campbell as governor of,
38. 255
Cumberland, D. of, may relieve, before it is
captured, **19.** 204
Hawley sent to relieve, **19.** 201n
Stirrup; stirrups:
Joseph II unlikely to hold, for Clement XIII,
22. 555
'Stitara.' *See* 'Statira'
Stiver, Dutch coin:
value of, **38.** 101n
Stoch. *See* Stosch
Stock, Rev. Richard (ca 1569–1626), Puritan
divine:
Commentary on Malachy by, **16.** 66n
engraving of, **16.** 66
Stockbridge, Hants:
Dodd and Whaley pass through, **40.** 8
election at, Powerscourt defeats Hay in, **21.**
73n
Fox, Henry, undermines Hay's leadership in,
9. 204, **21.** 23

Hay loses seat for, **21.** 73
Stockdale, John (ca 1749–1814), bookseller:
London Courant published by, **29.** 157
Stock exchange:
House of Commons described in terms of,
38. 1
See also Change Alley
Stockgrove, Bucks:
Hanmer of, **2.** 266n
Stockholm:
Barthélemy secretary of embassy at, **5.** 96n
French troops may go to, **5.** 338
Gustav III's portrait at, **7.** 339n
incendiaries from, said to have tried to burn
Copenhagen arsenal, **23.** 470
Usson ambassador at, **3.** 253n
Vergennes ambassador at, **24.** 17
Stockholm Castle:
balloon imitates, **39.** 419
Stockings:
beaver, worn by HW and Gray in crossing
Alps, **13.** 189
cabriolets embroidered on, as clocks, **20.** 483
cerulean, worn by Chandos in Van der Myn's
portrait, **30.** 61
Conti's, rolled in outmoded style, **38.** 221
Doncaster, Craon wears, as sleeves, **18.** 109
grey, worn by Lady Mary Wortley Montagu,
22. 3
HW's, thin, **34.** 20
HW's use of thinner, brings rheumatism, **33.**
278
Hervey, Mrs, had holes in knees of, before
marriage, **30.** 116
ladies', cost of, **18.** 281
Lee invents loom for weaving, **16.** 36
red, worn by Brissac, **30.** 205
thread, to be worn outside bootikins, **24.** 494
white, thief thought to be wearing, **38.** 259
white silk, **21.** 399n
worsted, worn by Stanley, **37.** 308
Young Pretender's troops make, at Perth, **19.**
105
Stocking trimmer:
fire damages back of house of, in Phoenix
Court, Newgate St, **38.** 168n
Stocking-weaver:
at Nottingham, **25.** 104n
Stock-jobber; stock-jobbers:
Charles III's abdication may be rumour
spread by, **39.** 237
emissaries sent by, to Frankfurt to send false
news, **39.** 512
HW's reflections on, **25.** 287
lies circulated by, **24.** 412
Stock-jobbing:
'patriots' involved in, **22.** 498
Stockport, Cheshire:
Prescot rector of, **2.** 23n
Stocks:
affected by false American reports, **32.** 396,
33. 60

[Stocks, *continued*]

affected by war rumours, **32.** 301

American news affects, **39.** 250

American war not reflected in, **28.** 211

bolstered, so that they are no longer fortune's weather-glass, **24.** 464

Brest fleet's sailing causes, to sink, **39.** 306

Chancery trust money keeps up, **41.** 315

Chute thinks of withdrawing his money from, **24.** 210

—— to talk about, with Sir Robert Brown, **35.** 86

East India, *see under* East India Co.

English newspapers concerned with, **22.** 174

English-Russian war, effect of, on, **11.** 247, 256, 297, 336

English-Spanish peace, effect of, on, **11.** 134

fall: **21.** 74; as peace hopes wane, **38.** 178; in Dutch war, **33.** 272; on American-French alliance news, **24.** 348, 364; on American war prospects, **24.** 213; on French war prospect, **24.** 179, 282, 361; on news of peace failure, **22.** 81; on report of Frederick II's death, **30.** 156; on Spanish war prospect, **23.** 239, 250, 282; on war news, **39.** 306; on Young Pretender's invasion of England, **19.** 186

fall of, expected, **28.** 391, **39.** 211

false peace news forged to manipulate, **34.** 213n

fluctuate: **29.** 101; according to manufactured American news, **32.** 388; during English-Spanish negotiations, **39.** 478–9

French may buy, in England to profit by rise at peace news, **25.** 357

French money brought to England raises the price of, **34.** 69

Gazette news does not raise, **29.** 137

HW advises Lady Ossory not to buy, on basis of rumours, **33.** 276

HW does not understand, **38.** 310

HW does not want to sell, to buy house in town, **39.** 289

HW prefers a bronze to a fortune in, **21.** 558

HW saves £45 by rise of, **33.** 67

HW sells, **33.** 67

invasion of Ireland and Jamaica would lower, **21.** 558

invasion threats scarcely affect, **18.** 393

level of, affects payment of HW's legacies, **15.** 337–8

Louis XVII's rumoured restoration affects, **12.** 119

'low-spirited,' **29.** 162

Lunardi invests in, **25.** 543

Mann's legacy from father invested in, **21.** 54–5, 61

Martinique's capture by English raises, **12.** 91

newspapers alter prices of, by false news, **39.** 512

not affected by rumours of French war, **33.** 109

'not of the heroic majority,' **28.** 374

peace not indicated by level of, **25.** 354

peace treaty fails to raise, **19.** 511

peace would raise, **21.** 497

Pompadour, Mme de, buys, in England, to profit by rise at peace news, **25.** 357

price of, absorbs coffee-house patron, **42.** 503

Pulteney said to increase, **18.** 91

rise and fall on news from Spain, **23.** 250

rise of: **28.** 448, **29.** 118, **33.** 60; indicates hopes of Spanish neutrality, **24.** 463–4; on news of peace with Spain, **36.** 184; shows hope of peace, **19.** 483, **21.** 504, **22.** 38

rise six per cent, **25.** 139

Selwyn makes money in, **17.** 330n

Shorter estate might be put into, in trustees' hands, **40.** 79

Spanish treaty boosts, in England, **20.** 198

Spanish war, rumours of, do not affect, **24.** 98

talk of peace is expected to prop, **28.** 380

trading in, at Jonathan's, **23.** 134n

unaffected by martial rumours, **11.** 257

Stocks Alley. *See* Change Alley

Stocks Market:

in Stratford's tragedy, **29.** 223

See also under Bucklersbury

Stockwood, Dorset:

Crawley, Miss, lives at, **10.** 348

'Stoic,' E. of Orford's race horse:

HW sells, **23.** 497, **32.** 133

Stoic; stoics:

HW does not imitate, **23.** 365

HW is not, about gout, **32.** 211

HW refers to himself as, **33.** 68

indifference of, **37.** 198

Lucas has greater sangfroid than, **25.** 307

Stoicism:

HW's distresses sometimes distract him from his, **24.** 327

Stoke, Notts:

battle of, **2.** 364, **42.** 255n

Stoke, near Chichester, Sussex, Lord George Lennox's seat:

HW may visit, **31.** 175

Lennox, Lady George, addressed at, **31.** 353–6, 366

—— anxious to return to, **31.** 118

Stoke Gifford Park, near Bristol, Ds of Beaufort's seat:

Berkeley of, **35.** 288

HW inquires if Miss Williams is at, **31.** 333

More, Hannah, to visit, **31.** 335

—— visits, **31.** 281, 320

Stoke Mandeville, Bucks:

HW's letter goes to, by mistake, **14.** 60

Stoke Manor House, Bucks:

Gray's sketch of: **14.** 59; improved by Bentley, **35.** 185

Stoke Poges, Bucks:

Garricks visit Lady Cobham at, **14.** 99n

Gray at, **14.** 25, 30, 43, 59, 86, 95, **35.** 91, **43.** 191

—— buried at, **1.** 230–1, 232

—— may be visited at, by Garrick, **40.** 97

——'s cenotaph at, 11. 159n
——'s poor health since arrival at, 14. 83n
Gray, Mrs, buried at, 14. 66n
HW asks Montagu to find tomb at, 9. 102–3
HW mentions, 9. 100
HW prefers Westminster Abbey to, for Gray's monument, 28. 276
mis-spelling of, 43. 115
Salter family of, 14. 25n
Stoke Poges Park:
West End cottage in, 14. 25n
Stoker, B.:
Jephson's portrait by, 42. 409n
Stokes, ——, Conway's factotum:
Conway loses, 39. 445–6
Stokes, Adrian (ca 1533–85):
portrait of, by Lukas de Heere, bought by HW at E. of Oxford's sale, 17. 373–4
Stokes, Mrs William Richard. See Scott, Ann Dorothea
Stolberg-Gedern, Ps of. See Hornes, Élisabeth-Philippine-Claudine de
Stolberg-Gedern, Christian Karl (1725–64). Prinz von; army officer:
Finck encircled by, at Maxen, 21. 354n
Stolberg-Gedern, Gustav Adolf (1722–57), P. of:
daughters of, 25. 427n, 538n
wife of, 5. 218n
Stolberg-Gedern, Karoline Auguste of (1755–1829), m. 1 (1771) Charles-Bernard-Pascal-Janvier Fitzjames, Marquis de la Jamaïque, 4th D. of Berwick (attainted), 1785; m. 2 (1793) Dominique, Duque de Castelfranco:
England visited by, 25. 427
marriage of, corrected, 43. 94
sister of, 5. 218, 23. 402
Stolberg-Gedern, Luise Maximiliane of (1752–1824), m. (1772) Charles Edward Stuart, the Young Pretender; called Cts of Albany:
Ailesbury, Cts of, entertains, 11. 280, 42. 326n
Ailesburys related to, 11. 258, 270
Alfieri may wed, 33. 438–9
——'s affair with, 25. 397, 535, 538n
—— teaches and tempts, 25. 106–7
ancestry of, 23. 402, 25. 538n
appeal of, for financial aid from England, 11. 343
beauty of: rivalled by Cts Cowper's, 24. 245; vastly faded, 24. 480
Berry, Mary, identifies, 11. 258n
Blanchette convent the temporary refuge of, 25. 101–2, 108n
breakfast often taken by, with husband and Mme Orlandini, 25. 101
brother-in-law and Pius VI invite, to convent at Rome, 25. 106
brother-in-law consulted by, about leaving husband, 25. 101
brother-in-law protects, in Rome, 25. 108n, 150, 26. 47–8
brother-in-law publishes intrigues of, with Alfieri, 25. 397

brother-in-law to lend coach to, 25. 107
calls not returned by, at Florence, 25. 535
Coke in love with, and is given her picture, 39. 180
convent can seldom be left by, in husband's lifetime, 25. 107
convent entered by, 33. 260
Cosway child's godmother, 42. 233n
Damer, Mrs, entertains, at supper, 11. 307
England left by, 11. 343
—— may be visited by, to wed Alfieri, 26. 48
English relationships of, 43. 147
erudition of, 25. 106
Fitzherbert, Mrs, introduced to, 11. 284–5
George III's box at opera occupied by, 11. 272
goddaughter of, 11. 285n
Grenville and other English lords in love with, 24. 102
Gustav III discouraged by, at Rome, from aiding her husband, 25. 475
HW describes, 11. 280
HW entertains, at breakfast, 11. 302, 303
HW's comments on, 11. 270, 304
HW to see, 11. 258
HW wants print of, 23. 422, 427, 429
House of Lords visited by, 11. 296
husband abhorred by, 11. 270
husband bars all access to room of, save from his own, 24. 245
husband blames his impotence on potion given him by, at Mann's instigation, 25. 102
husband does not conceal his stench and temper from, 24. 480
husband guards, jealously, lest legitimacy of heirs be dubious, 24. 94, 137, 245
husband ill-treats, 25. 100–1, 108n, 150, 538n
husband insists on royal honours for, against her wishes, 23. 406
husband meets, at Loreto and conveys her to Macerata and Rome, 23. 406
husband separated from, 25. 100–1, 108n, 150, 396–7, 538n, 26. 47–8
husband's recovery from illness will disappoint, 25. 395
husband tenderly treated by, 24. 137
income of, after separation from husband, 25. 536
invited to Pitti Palace gala, 25. 50n
'late Queen of England,' 11. 294
Leopold, protector of, against husband, 25. 101–2, 108n
London visited by, 11. 270
Louis XVI gives pension to, 25. 150, 536
Louise, Princesse, may have produced, 23. 399
Maltzan, Baronne de, companion to, 25. 522
Marie-Antoinette's gracious letter to, 25. 150
marriage of, 5. 218, 23. 398–9, 402, 405–6
Orsolene convent at Rome to be occupied by, 25. 106

[Stolberg-Gedern, Luise, *continued*]
'pinchbeck Queen Dowager of England,' **11.** 258

pitied in Florence at the time of her separation from husband, **25.** 396

Pius VI to give half of husband's pension to, **25.** 107

presented to Q. Charlotte, **11.** 270, 271

probably at Paris, **24.** 102

probably not a Protestant, **23.** 402

Roman visit of, called imprisonment by HW, **25.** 115

seals of, with royal arms, **11.** 272

Seymour attached to, with husband's consent, **24.** 94, 102

sister of, **25.** 402, 427

stepdaughter's arrival may cause, to repent of her elopement, **25.** 535

Stormont leaves Paris to avoid meeting husband and, **6.** 160n

SH visited by, **12.** 238

visitors call on, in husband's theatre box, **24.** 245

'titular Queen of France,' **11.** 302

Wales, P. of (George IV), to entertain, at dinner, **11.** 284

Walkinshaw, Clementina, pleads with, for daughter, **26.** 47

Stole, Groom of. *See* Groom of the Stole

Stolowicze, battle of:
Ogiński defeated at, **33.** 511n

Stomach:
bleeding from, probably not caused by gout, **25.** 560

complaint in, **39.** 449

cramp in, **39.** 513n

disorder in, **35.** 319

Fox's, 'gone,' **30.** 176

HW's, *see under* HW: health of

Mann attributes HW's illness to, **22.** 114

organic disorder of, **21.** 217

pain in, **10.** 47, 115, 119

sickness of, **24.** 244, **40.** 388

See also Disorder in stomach and bowels; Dropsy in the stomach; Indigestion; Vomiting; Water in the stomach

Stomacher; stomachers:
Charlotte, Q., has: of diamonds, **21.** 529; sumptuous, **38.** 116

diamond, **21.** 529, **31.** 125, **37.** 442

HW jokes about making, of crystal, **31.** 158

Northumberland, Cts of, wears diamond, **31.** 125

Stone, Miss:
SH visited by, **12.** 222

Stone, Andrew (1703–73), undersecretary of state; M.P.; George III's sub-governor:
address to George II said to demand dismissal of, as George III's tutor, **20.** 370

Argyll praises, for treatment of two Scotch place-seekers, **20.** 366

Augusta, Ps of Wales, has, as treasurer, **23.** 538n

Barnard consoled by, **35.** 166

Bedford, D. of, and others vote for motion against, **20.** 366n

'begotten by Bolingbroke and begot Markham,' **29.** 72

biographical information on, corrected, **43.** 233

Birtles's dispatches betrayed by, **20.** 364

Bolingbroke's creature, **20.** 343n

brother of, **20.** 315, 505

Charlotte, Q., includes, in Household as treasurer, **9.** 377, **21.** 517–18, **38.** 96

Christ Church people flatter, **20.** 261

Chute's jingle hints at, **35.** 261

death of, **23.** 538

Dorléans book disclaimed by, **20.** 344

Fox, Henry, sends letter from, to HW, **30.** 107

George III's sub-governor, **19.** 347n, **20.** 246, 323

HW advises Mann not to give presents to, **18.** 137

HW asks Mann for Roman gossip about, **20.** 360

HW hints at Jacobitism of, **30.** 91–2, **35.** 21

Harcourt calls, a Jacobite, **20.** 344

—— fit to be a cipher to, **20.** 246, 345

—— refuses to act with, **20.** 343–4

Hayter and Harcourt oppose, over George III's tutorship, **20.** 323, 343–4

House of Commons calls no re-election for, **20.** 247n

'humours' of, over Lovat's execution, **37.** 267

Johnson, Bp, contemporary with, **20.** 345

Letter to, **35.** 68

Mann astonished at account of, **18.** 381

—— hopes for payment of his arrears through, **18.** 516–17, **19.** 56, 221, 490

—— neglected by, **19.** 474, 483–4, 490, **20.** 195

—— pays, for 'protection,' **23.** 538

——'s credentials perhaps delayed by, **17.** 24n

——'s present to, useless, **18.** 115

—— tells, of his poor state of health, **17.** 97n

Mann, Galfridus, says, is unfriendly to Mann, **18.** 115

Monitor, The, attacks, **21.** 39n

Murray examined before, **19.** 391n

—— urges Bp Hayter to promote, **20.** 345

Newcastle, D. of, consults, **19.** 347

——'s confidant, **35.** 21

——'s favourite, **20.** 505

——'s secretary, **17.** 6, 137n, **19.** 347n, **23.** 538n

Oswald brings fans to, **17.** 6

Ravensworth accuses, of toasting Old Pretender and Dunbar, **20.** 360–1, 364

snuff-box for, **17.** 29, **18.** 115, 330, 445, 496

town calls, a Jacobite, **9.** 144

treasurer: to Augusta, Ps of Wales, **23.** 538n; to Q. Charlotte, **9.** 377, **21.** 517–18, **38.** 96

unpopularity of, **20.** 345

Whigs disown, **20.** 345

York, D. of, consults, **22.** 437n

Stone, Mrs Andrew. *See* Mauvillain, Hannah

Stone, Dr George (ca 1708–64), Bp of Ferns and Leighlin 1740–3, of Kildare 1743–5, of Derry 1745–7; Abp of Armagh 1747–64:

Bedford, D. of, rejects overtures of, 21.154

Boyle's strife with, in Ireland, 9. 130, 157n

—— to be married by, to Catherine Ponsonby, 38. 235

brother of, 20. 315, 505

'cardinalesque' inclinations of, 20. 315

controls patronage, 10. 110n

Conway instigates dropping of, from Irish regency, 20. 503n

credit of, decays, 20. 505

Cuninghame aide-de-camp to, 20. 315

—— brought by, into Irish parliament, 20. 316

death of: 10. 145; 28. 252n; from drunkenness, 22. 269, 275

Devonshire, D. of, appeased by support of his son's opposition to, in Ireland, 37. 409

Dorset, D. of, asked by, to promote Cuninghame, 20. 316n

Dorset family would make, sole regent, 20. 316

epigram handed to, at dinner at Dublin Castle, 20. 316, 318

exclusion of, from Irish regency, demanded, 35. 235–6

HW jokingly calls, 'primate of Novogorod,' 10. 40

Halifax leaves, as lord justice in Ireland, to retrieve reputation in England, 38. 147

Hamilton, William Gerard, on bad terms with, 10. 110, 38. 251n

—— unendurable to, 38. 393n

Hartington confers with, 37. 393n

——'s policy towards, 37. 403n

——'s resolutions against, 37. 399

health of, dropsy in the breast, 38. 469

Irish administration to give up, 35. 254

Irish dissensions reported by, 20. 455n

Irish House of Commons not influenced by, 21. 154n

Irish unrest provoked by, 21. 154, 474

Kildare presents manifesto to George II protesting administration of, in Ireland, 20. 440

—— under pressure to oppose, until Stone is dropped, 37. 409

Leixlip the house of, near Dublin, 37. 342

lord justice in Ireland, 20. 426, 38. 28n

lord justice's position not to go to, 37. 404

Lorraine, Primate of, compared with, 20. 316, 22. 269

member of D. of Dorset's party, 20. 402n

Montagu calls: 'chief person at the Castle,' 10. 110; (?) 'Sangrenuntio,' 9. 409

(?) —— defends Halifax to, 9. 409–10

(?)—— entertained by, 9. 409

—— hears stories from, about Bentley, 9. 393

—— visits, 9. 396

Newcastle's abandonment of, surprises Mann, 20. 505

——'s correspondence with, 43. 266

Pembroke's tennis games with, stopped because of blasphemy, 20. 109

Ponsonby and Devonshire administration denounced by, in Dublin, 37. 463

removal of, a 'peace-offering,' 20. 503

ring of, includes Cts of Northumberland's voided stone, 10. 132

Sackville's disgrace will not help, 38. 28

St Patrick's Cathedral visible from windows of, 9. 396

Syon House visited by, looking old and broken, 38. 429

to be sacrificed for Ireland's tranquillity, 35. 242

Stone, Henry (1616–53), *and* John (1620–67), stonemasons:

father of, 1. 7n

monument erroneously attributed to, 2. 256n

Stone, Nicholas (1586–1647), stonemason:

account-book of, 43. 38

monument by, in Trinity Hospital, Greenwich, 16. 87–9

monument erroneously attributed to, 2. 256, 258

monuments by, 1. 7, 7n

portrait attributed to, 35. 148n

St Albans's portrait attributed to, 35. 228n

sons of, 1. 7n, 2. 256n

Sutton's tomb and Law's monument by, 16. 48

Stone, Nicholas (1618–47), stonemason:

father of, 1. 7n

monument erroneously attributed to, 2. 257n

Stone, Staffs:

Cumberland, D. of, awaits rebels at, 19. 173, 178

Stone, the (disease):

cutting-gorget facilitates operation for, 9. 185

Du Muy operated upon for, 24. 133

in bladder, suspected, 37. 543n, 547n, 549

Mackenzie may have, 31. 288

Montagu, Lady Mary Wortley, wants her enemies to suffer from, 35. 489

Northumberland, Cts of, voids, in Dublin, 10. 132

occurrences of: 3. 236, 4. 85, 86, 118, 133, 135–6, 257, 300, 6. 178, 291, 10. 132, 18. 140, 538, 552, 566, 19. 16, 22, 29, 510n, 20. 418, 21. 259n, 22. 27, 164, 28. 61, 34. 210, 37. 256, 39. 92n, 40. 268

operation for, 4. 300

treatments for, 4. 114n, 119n, 133, 136, 285, 18. 552, 22. 164

Walpole, Horatio (1678–1757), cured of, by Dr Whytt, 19. 510n

Whalley uses charm against, 15. 315

worst evil, 7. 210

Stone; stones:

artificial: gate piers of, 23. 311; HW gets, from Mrs Coade, 41. 227–9; used in Carlton House, 42. 274n

[Stone; stones, *continued*]

black, of Dr Dee, 23. 286–7, 301, 33. 323–4, 43. 389

bridge of: at Henley, *see under* Henley; over Serpentine, 37. 560

chimneys of, 35. 71

deluge, Holbach thinks Pall Mall paved with, 30. 208

Democritus's experiments on, 35. 196

do not bear transplanting, 39. 195

French build landscapes of chalk and, 31. 55

HW jokes about Lady Ailesbury giving him fish instead of, 38. 100

hard: box of, 22. 241, 243; Craon and Mann discuss, 18. 207

imported to Ireland from England, for Marino, 9. 400

Medusa should turn SH into, 35. 420

new road through Paddington proposed to avoid, 37. 452

snuff-box of, 17. 48

stair-cases should be built of, 22. 143

with vases, in Stosch's collection, 21. 201

Yorkshire roads 'mended' with, 35. 269

See also Gem; Jewel

Ston Easton, Somerset:

Coxe of, 11. 122n, 333n, 42. 161n

Stone-cutter:

Churchill seduces daughter of, 38. 234

Stone-cutter's shop:

SH resembles, 35. 231

Stonehenge:

Charleton and Inigo Jones might have described, 39. 460

Conway's temple a miniature of, 39. 460

Dodd and Whaley visit, 40. 8

HW visits, 38. 25

Park Place imitates, 34. 14

Park Place's temple 'but a chapel of ease' to, 35. 396

Stonehewer. *See* Stonhewer

Stonehouse, Penelope (d. 1734), m. 1 (1723) Sir Henry Atkins, 4th Bt; m. 2 (1733) John Leveson Gower, 2d Bn Gower; cr. (1746) E. Gower:

family of, 30. 328n

Stonehouse family:

beauty of members of, 30. 328

Dashwood family closely related to, 30. 328n

Stoneland Lodge, Sussex:

Sackville, Lord George, inherits, 40. 386n

Stoneleigh Abbey, Warwickshire:

Leigh of, 12. 128n

Stone-mason. *See* Carr, Joseph; Stone, Henry; Stone, John; Stone, Nicholas; Stone, Nicholas, jr

Stone pines:

HW to send, to Montagu, 9. 177

Stone-pippin. *See* Pippin

'Stone-water':

Omai's name for ice, 24. 175

Stoney, Andrew Robinson (1747–1810). *See* Bowes

Stoney Lane, Horsely Down, Southwark:

fire near end of, 25. 577n

Stonhewer, Richard (ca 1728–1809), undersecretary of state 1765–6; auditor of excise 1772–89; friend of Gray and Mason:

(?) Burnet's *History* to be examined by, 28. 451

Euston visited by, 28. 60

(?) extract from Knight's poem sent to Mason by, 29. 334

Grafton, D. of, asked by, to appoint Langstaff, 33. 238n

——'s divorce intentions announced by, to Ds of Grafton, 33. 333n

—— sends message by, for Lady Ossory, 33. 15–16

Gray receives pianoforte from, 1. 233

—— sends for, 1. 231

——'s friendship with, 41. 216–17

——'s legacy to, 1. 232

——'s letters to, excellent, 28. 64

——'s monument partly paid for by, 2. 101n, 28. 439n, 41. 387n

——'s picture by Tyson should be inscribed to, 1. 236

——'s professorship obtained for him by, from D. of Grafton, 39. 106, 41. 164

HW and, consider Mason indiscreet, 28. 314

HW and Mason exchange books and parcels through, 28. 18, 21, 23, 26–7, 32, 37, 111, 114, 116, 138, 140, 149, 151, 271, 313, 363, 29. 66, 100, 119, 137, 197, 204, 226

HW applauds Lady Ossory's letter to, 33. 238

HW inquires of, about Mason, 29. 38, 61

HW's correspondence with, 41. 216–17, 267–8

HW sends method of aquatinta to Gilpin through, 29. 112

HW sighs with, 35. 519

HW's social relations with, 28. 250, 29. 16, 116, 148, 161

HW to consult, about 2d edn of Hoyland's *Poems*, 28. 17

HW visited by, 33. 332

Heroic Epistle not listed as being given to, 28. 56n

ill with influenza, 29. 254

Jersey, Lady, tells, to ask for cure for insanity, 33. 380

Mason gets writing-paper from, 28. 398

—— hopes to visit SH with, 29. 274

—— rambles with, 28. 106

—— refers HW to, 28. 343–4

——'s correspondence with, 28. *11*, 37, 44, 60, 148, 152, 29. 166–7, 280, 291, 298, 321, 366

——'s Dufresnoy given to Reynolds by, 29. 91, 93

——'s letter forwarded to HW by, 41. 216

——'s memoir of Gray sent by, to HW, 41. 267

—— visits, in London, 28. 272–3, 340

Middleton visited by, 41. 217

name of, corrected, 43. 56, 67

Ossory, Lady, avoids, 33. 332

Pantheon praised by, **28**. 102
Wharton attended by, to SH, **29**. 16
Stony Point, on the Hudson:
Americans capture, **24**. 519
English capture, **24**. 500
Stony Stratford, Bucks:
as Virgil would have described it, **13**. 86
Stool; stools:
Bayreuth, Margravine of, provides few of, for Florentine visitors, **24**. 164
loo players sit on, **9**. 337
new, at Windsor Castle, **11**. 363
Richecourt and Stampa dispute over, **20**. 320
sold out of Palazzo Vecchio, **25**. 231
Stopford, Vcts. *See* Scott, Lady Mary
Stopford, Hon. Edward (1732–94), army officer:
(?) Pembroke's correspondence with, **10**. 15
Stopford, James (1731–1810), 2d E. of Courtown, 1770:
Beauvau asks about family of, **41**. 332
Stopford, James George (1765–1835), styled Vct Stopford; 3d E. of Courtown, 1810:
marriage of, **11**. 121
SH visited by, **12**. 239
wife of, **10**. 281n
Stoppani, Giovanni Francesco (1695–1775), cardinal, 1754; nuncio:
Benedict XIV's nuncio at Emperor's Court, **19**. 3n
Falkirk news sent to Rome by, **19**. 214
'Stoppart, Mr':
Conway's Irish friend, **37**. 434
Stopper:
golden, for Q. Caroline's crystal hunting-bottle, **25**. 464
Stop-watch. *See under* Watch
Storace, Anna Selina (1766–1817), soprano; m. (ca 1784) John Abraham Fisher:
in Paisiello's *Il re Teodoro*, **33**. 587
Storace, Stephen (1763–96), composer:
music by, for *No Song No Supper*, **12**. 79n
Störck, Dr:
Maria Theresa's physician, **24**. 201n
Storer, Anthony Morris (1746–99), M.P.; collector:
antiquarian interests of, **33**. 273–4
antiquarian turn of, surprising in a Macaroni, **35**. 359
appointed to Board of Trade, **33**. 314
Carlisle may promote, in Ireland, **35**. 359
comment by, on *Jekyll*, **11**. 34n
disbelieves in Ireland's MSS, **15**. 321
Guilfords entertain, at dinner, **11**. 114
HW sees, at Selwyn's, **33**. 236
HW's publications collected by, **33**. 362n
HW's social relations with, **7**. 342
HW visited by, **33**. 373, **35**. 359–60
Hobart, Mrs, entertains, at play at Ham Common, **33**. 370
if long-lived, will complain about youthful airs and hours, **35**. 352
losses of, from hurricane, **33**. 266
Nivernais's *Jardins modernes* given to, **12**. 260

Paris secretaryship of embassy may go to, **42**. 73n
quadrille danced by, at Duc de Guines's ball, **32**. 111
Richmond House play praised by, **33**. 563n
secretary at English embassy in Paris, **33**. 420
SH visited by, **12**. 225, **35**. 359–60
Storer, Rev. Bennet:
Newcastle's neglect by clergy, at his retirement, lamented by, **22**. 37n
Storer, Sidney (d. 1793), m. (1753) Sir John Hawkins, Kt, 1772:
HW buys cup, saucer, and plate for, **7**. 409
Storer, Thomas (ca 1717–93), father of A. M. Storer:
losses of, from hurricane, **33**. 266
Storer, Thomas James (ca 1748–92), brother of A. M. Storer:
Hobart, Mrs, entertains, at play at Ham Common, **33**. 370
losses of, from hurricane, **33**. 266
quadrille danced by, at Lord Stanley's ball, **32**. *115–16*
Storer, William (fl. 1777–85), inventor:
camera of, **16**. 235
'delineator' invented by: **39**. 293; brought to SH, **28**. *329*; HW cannot work, **28**. 335; HW's description of, **28**. 328–9, **29**. 371–2; improved, **28**. 339; Mason asks HW to lend him, **28**. 338, 339; Mason is sceptical of, **28**. 333–4; Reynolds approves of HW's description of, **29**. 371, 372
HW's correspondence with, **41**. 366
Syllabus to a Course of Optical Experiments by, **16**. 235n, **28**. 329n
Store-ship:
English forced to burn, in attack on Charleston, **24**. 236
Stork; storks:
kite's fight with, in clouds, will be reproduced by rival aviators, **25**. 543
Storm; storms:
Berry, Mary, frightened of, **12**. 161
HW's former delight in, **12**. 161
Stormont, Vct. *See* Murray, David (ca 1689–1748); Murray, David (1727–96)
Stormont, Vcts. *See* Bunau, Henrietta Frederica von (d. 1766); Cathcart, Hon. Louisa (1758–1843); Scott, Marjory (d. 1746)
Story, —— (fl. 1677), sculptor:
monument of Lord Crofts by, **2**. 256, 258
Story, Capt.:
Prince of Orange packet-boat commanded by, **24**. 302n
Story, Edward (d. 1503), Bp of Carlisle 1468–77, of Chichester 1478–1503:
Bourchier's commission to, as Edward IV's executor, **41**. 124
Chichester cross erected by, **28**. 214n
chooses builders, **1**. 17
Story of Sinful Sally, The:
in 'Cheap Repository Tracts,' **31**. 396n

Story's Gate, St James's Park, London:
pamphlet vendor at, 9. 41

Stosch, Bn. *See* Muzell (later Stosch), Heinrich
Wilhelm (1723–82); Stosch, Philipp von
(1691–1757)

Stosch, Heinrich Sigismund (1699–1747):
birth date of, 43. 261
Mann sends corpse of, to Leghorn, 19. 358

Stosch, Philipp von (1691–1757), Baron; 'John
Walton'; 'Cyclops'; English agent in Italy:
amours of, 17. 164n
arrears of pension sought by, 20. 53
Bentinck and Raymond make offers to, for
'Gladiator' and 'Meleager,' 17. 264
brother of, dies, 19. 358
Buonaccorsi and Mann executors to, 21. 149
Buonaccorsi inherits picture from, 21. 149
cameos of: France buys, 21. 201; Mann inherits, 21. 149, 25. 650; numerous, 21. 151;
sent to HW by Mann, 26. 56; to be sold
separately, 21. 186
cats described by, 17. 434
cats of, 17. 164, 181, 434, 462
Chute gets from, a rare print by 'Marc Antonio' after Raphael, 23. 432
collection of: Benedict XIV might have
bought, for Instituto at Bologna, 21. 434;
Botta to send account of, to Francis I, 21.
149n; contains tracts about the Medici, 21.
278; Frederick Augustus II covets, 21. 434;
George II's death may facilitate sale of,
21. 445; HW desires items from, 21. 188–9;
HW's medals from, 15. 278; marble fragment in, 21. 192; nephew must sell estate's
debts out of, 21. 149n; nephew probably
comes to England to sell, 21. 427; nephew
to sell, intact, 21. 186; nothing yet sold
from, 21. 192; offered to Francis I, 21. 149,
151; overrated, 25. 651; Richecourt may in-
corporate, by edict, 21. 475; stones with
vases not to be separated from, 21. 201;
Strodtmann's *Das neue gelehrte Europa* describes, 21. 151n; would be more valuable
if kings could compete for it, 21. 434
correspondence of, with learned men at
Perugia interrupted by Inquisitor on suspicion of freemasonry, 30. 11–12
Dalton buys modern medals from collection
of, 21. 478
death of, 21. 149, 151
Del Nero does not employ, as English agent
for his pictures, 18. 308
Description des pierres gravés by, 20. 157n
drawings and prints of, 21. 189, 202
Duncannon buys 'Gladiator' from, 21. 151
—— corresponds with, about 'Meleager,' 20.
159
—— gets intaglio by paying pension arrears
of, 17. 212n, 20. 70, 159, 43. 240
Electress's wealth falsely reported by, 18. 206
England's spy on Old Pretender, 17. 164n
English government pays, for reports, 18. 225n

English secret service at Rome managed by,
21. 149
English visitors shown collection of, 18. 41, 62
engraved cornelian from collection of, 30. 11n
Frederick II acquires intaglii of, 21. 186n
—— buys map collection of, 21. 187n, 25. 651
—— feared by, 18. 308
freemason lodge in Florence attended by, 19.
364n
freemasons gather at house of, 17. 404n
Galla Placidia medal offered by, to HW, 20.
53, 70
Galli, Contessa, jokes about, 17. 445
Gavi offered sum by, for Homer intaglio, 19.
489
gazettes relied on by, for news, 18. 308
Gazzetta letteraria exposes, 17. 381–2
George II alone believes tales of, 18. 225
'Gladiator' intaglio of, 17. 212n, 264, 302,
18. 369, 20. 157, 159, 21. 151
Greek medals procured by, through Albani
and Mann, from estate of deceased Roman,
18. 478
HW could pity, for edict restricting sale of
his collection, 21. 475
HW expects to be overcharged by, for Virgil
gem, 30. 11
HW mentions, 21. 168
HW not indebted to, 17. 439
HW offended at, for selling 'Gladiator' to
Duncannon, 20. 157, 159
HW's letter from, about pension arrears, 20.
36, 53
HW's transactions with, 17. 416, 439, 18. 347
HW suggests giving Maltese cats to, to pay
postage, 17. 452
HW wants 'Gladiator' intaglio and 'Meleager'
of, 17. 212n, 264, 302
HW wants items from collection of, 21. 178,
189, 201–2
HW writes about, 37. 53
health of: apoplexy, 21. 149; cut for the piles,
17. 112, 404; inflammation of the bowels,
21. 149
Houghton views coveted by, in return for
carriage of medals and postage, 17. 416
Ilay resembles, 17. 420
intaglii cornered by, 20. 104
intaglii of: collected systematically, 21. 186;
numerous, 20. 149
intaglio praised by, 19. 476
Kaunitz gets present from, by claiming relationship, 17. 48–9
library of: 21. 187; HW asks about state
papers and letters in, 21. 278; sold to Vatican, 21. 284
London Gazette gets false news from, 18. 206
Mann asked by, to punish editors of *Gazzetta
letteraria* for insulting him, 17. 382
—— called on by, 18. 308
—— congratulated by, on not having apoplexy, 19. 477

—— consults, about Cicciaporci's drawings, **18.** 313

—— executor to, **21.** 149, 151

—— inherits cameo from, **21.** 149, **25.** 650

—— sends news of HW's illness to, **17.** 51

—— thanked by, for sending brother's corpse to Leghorn, **19.** 358

—— to tell, of Oxford's sale, **17.** 378

—— wants the former appointments of, as English secret agent, **21.** 149

—— will speak to, about Galla Placidia medal, **20.** 70

MSS of: auctioned at Florence, **21.** 284n; MSS of Q. Christina stolen by, from the Vatican, **21.** 284n

maps collected by, **21.** 186

maps of: Benedict XIV not to buy, **21.** 186; catalogue printed of, **21.** 192

medals carried by, from Rome for HW, **17.** 416

medals of: bawdy, **21.** 160; bought by Dalton for George III, **21.** 231; HW insists on paying for, **21.** 215; HW receives prices of, **21.** 227; HW thanks Mann for, **21.** 203; sent by Albani, **18.** 478

'Meleager' and 'Gladiator' might be given up by, to escape criminal charges, **18.** 369

'Meleager' of, **17.** 212n, 264, 302, **20.** 159

Natter's correspondence with, through HW, **19.** 243

Neapolitan troop movements reported by, **17.** 265n

nephew heir to, **21.** 149, 151

nephew of, **21.** 348n

nephew recalled by, from army, **21.** 149, 434

Newcastle, D. of, might have heard from, of HW's and Mann's illnesses, **17.** 51

—— receives information from, about Modena, **18.** 228n

Old Pretender's movements to be reported by, to England, **17.** 9–10

pension of, **17.** 212n, **20.** 53

Prideaux discusses collection and 'heathenish' remarks of, with HW, **17.** 378, 404

Prussian, **17.** 164n

Richecourt probably made edict against export of antiquities in order to get collection of, **20.** 465

Roman correspondent of, dies, **18.** 380

Rome expels, **17.** 164n

soul said by: to be located in anus, **17.** 112, 404; to resemble glue, **17.** 378, 404

Valenti makes offer to, through Albani, **21.** 192

—— offers to buy map collection of, **21.** 186

'Walton, John,' code name of, **18.** 225n, 380n

weekly letters written by, about Young Pretender, **20.** 333

will of, **21.** 149, 151, 380

Young Pretender believed by, to be dead, **20.** 333, 508

——'s departure not known to, **18.** 380

youth mistreated by, **18.** 369

Stosch, William; 'Stoschino'. *See* Muzell, Heinrich Wilhelm (1723–82)

Stothard, Thomas (1755–1834), painter:
SH visited by, **12.** 243

Stott, (?) John (d. ca 1777), capt. of the *Juno*:
Plymouth reached by: after receiving Falkland Islands from Spain, **32.** 68n; in 40 days from Port Egmont, **23.** 359n

Stoughton's drops:
Du Deffand, Mme, orders, from England, **6.** 226, **7.** 26, 40, 43, 120, 125, 135, 170

—— receives, from HW, **7.** 131, 180, 226, 240, 431

——'s digestion aided by, **7.** 170

—— takes, **6.** 222, 223, 240, **7.** 125, 170

—— takes 6 drops of, a day, **7.** 180

HW to send, to Mme du Deffand, **36.** 168, 169

Livingston procures, for Mme du Deffand, **7.** 172, 427

Stour, river:
tides on, at Mistley, **30.** 87

Stourbridge, Worcs:
rioters lower food prices at, **22.** 460n

Stourbridge Fair:
Cambridge students' attendance at, compared to Dublin diversions, **10.** 11

Cole dines at, **2.** 27

Mawdesley's servants 'keep,' **1.** 273

Stourhead, Wilts:
HW visits, **40.** 251

Hoare of, **10.** 123n

paintings at, **21.** 208n

Stourton, Charles (b. between 1518 and 1524, d. 1557), 8th Bn Stourton:
Hartgill murdered by, **40.** 252n

Stourton, Charles Philip (1752–1816), 17th Bn Stourton, 1781:
Norfolk's bequest to, **32.** 384, **36.** 151

Stourton, William (1704–81), 16th Bn Stourton, 1753:
bequest to son of, **32.** 384

Stove; stoves:
at opera house, **38.** 289

Bianchi's, for washing linen, sets fire to Uffizi gallery, **22.** 67n

Buzaglo's, **32.** 407n

Choiseul, Duc and Duchesse de, have, in their gallery, **6.** 378

Clement, Jane, has maid to clean, **36.** 319

Dutch, at Syon House, **38.** 60

earthenware for, **25.** 645

German: Botta's room heated by, **21.** 370; Pitti palace furnished with, **22.** 291, 576

Germans miss, in Florence, **22.** 576

Westminster Hall heated with, **37.** 454n

Stow, John (ca 1525–1605), chronicler:
Annales . . . of England by: Gray quotes from, **14.** 71; HW consults, **42.** 218; Warbeck's proclamation not in, **14.** 176, 180

Annales of Scotland by, cited by Vertue about Mestrell, **16.** 159

[Stow, John, *continued*]
 future imitators of, **20**. 58
 London's factions would tire patience of, **23**. 330
 Richard III's appearance described by, **2**. 153, 155
 Shakespeare turns, into verse, **41**. 294
 Survay of the Cities of London and Westminster by: **43**. 68; Carte's history compared with, **18**. 480; Strype's edition of, **2**. 145
 Strype's life of, **2**. 153, 155
Stow Bardolph, Norfolk:
 Hare of, **42**. 437n
Stowe, Mary Anne, m. (ca 1784) Sir Simeon Stuart, 4th Bt:
 (?) SH visited by, **12**. 227
Stowe, Bucks, E. Temple's seat:
 alto-relievo at, **9**. 64n
 arch at, for Ps Amelia, erected by Temple, **10**. 315, **31**. 146
 Bedford, D. of, makes overtures at, **7**. 367
 Boston patriots not to be enshrined at, **31**. 94
 Brown, Lancelot, landscaper at, **9**. 121n
 castle at, **10**. 315
 Coke, Lady Mary, will write about house-party at, **35**. 338
 cold and damp, **10**. 314
 column at, **39**. 127
 connections of, with Chesterfield, Christian VII, Cobham, Congreve, Frederick (P. of Wales), Gibbs, Glover, Grenvilles, Kent, Lytteltons, Pope, Vanbrugh, the West family, and Wilkes, **10**. 314
 drawing-room at, **10**. 312, 313
 'Elysian Fields' at, **10**. 314, 315
 fishing at, **10**. 313
 garden at: Amelia, Ps, and guests walk and drive in, **10**. 313; crowds in, to see 'Vauxhall,' **10**. 314
 garden edifices enrich the 'insipid country' of, **39**. 436
 Gray hears verses on, **13**. 143
 grotto at: **39**. 127; guests sup in, after 'Vauxhall,' **10**. 315; illuminated, **10**. 314; inappropriateness of, for supper party, **10**. 315
 guests at, **4**. 439n; *see also under* visitors to
 HW describes, **4**. 432, **35**. 75–7
 HW describes house-party at, for Ps Amelia, **10**. 313–16, **39**. 127–8
 HW does not prefer D. of Cumberland's lodge to, **10**. 43
 HW does not wish to visit, **10**. 310–13
 HW enjoys breakfast at, **9**. 155
 HW often studies plan of, **39**. 436
 HW's meditations at, **10**. 313–14
 HW thinks Temple would be happier at, **10**. 168
 HW to visit, **38**. 434
 HW writes from, **35**. 69
 haycocks at, **10**. 315
 Hervey's behaviour at, **30**. 51–2
 illumination at, inadequate, **10**. 314
 inn at, Berwicks stay at, **10**. 132

 landscape effects at, **10**. 44, 313–15
 Lovell's work at, **9**. 183n
 Marble Hill's poetic rivalry with, **40**. 366
 Mason hopes to visit, **28**. 45
 Montagu prefers D. of Cumberland's lodge to, **10**. 42
 monuments at: Chatham's, **10**. 314; show folly of erecting monuments to living people, **10**. 154; statues, **10**. 315
 music at, inadequate, **10**. 314
 orange trees at, **10**. 315
 Palladian bridge at, **10**. 315
 Rigby sees Grenville and Temple at, **22**. 538n
 road to, bad, **9**. 155
 stairs at, **39**. 127
 'Temple of Friendship' at, **41**. 6
 temples at, **10**. 314, **39**. 127
 Temple's seat at, **2**. 119n
 Towne, archdeacon of, **15**. 302n
 Twickenham does not vie with pomps of, **33**. 473
 'Vauxhall' acted for guests at, **10**. 314–15
 visitors to: Ailesbury, Cts of, **9**. 152, **37**. 369; Amelia, Ps, **10**. 310, 311, 313–16, **22**. 247, **31**. 146–7, **35**. 338n, **39**. 127–8; Berwicks, **10**. 131–2; Bessborough, E. of, **10**. 313–16; Bridgwater, Ds of, **22**. 247; Coke, Lady Mary, **10**. 313–16, **31**. 146–7; Cole, **2**. 119n; Conway, **9**. 152, **37**. 366, 369; Élie de Beaumont, **38**. 461; Grenville, James, **35**. 75; HW, **4**. 432–3, 445n, **9**. 122, 151–2, 155, 156, **10**. 126, 310, 311, 313–16, **31**. 146–7, **35**. 338–9, **37**. 369, **38**. 434; Howard, Lady Anne, **10**. 313; Lyttelton, Sir R., **22**. 247; Middleton, Catharine, **10**. 313; Miller, Sanderson, **9**. 156
Stowe. See under Seeley, B.
Stowell, Bn. *See* Scott, William
Stowell Park, Glos, Chedworth's seat:
 Chedworth invites Bn Walpole to, **40**. 60
Stowe Nine Churches, Northants:
 Lady Danvers's tomb in St Michael's Church at, **1**. 6–7, 6n
Straaten; Stratten. *See* Van der Straaten
Strabo (ca 63 B.C.–A.D. 21), geographer:
 Falconer's proposed edition of, **28**. 198, 209
Strachey, Henry, undersecretary of state:
 preliminary peace articles taken to England by, from Paris, **25**. 342n
Strada del Pò, Anna (fl. 1729–38), singer:
 diverts attention from Conti's mouth, **13**. 102
Strada Felice, Rome:
 Chambers, Patch, and Vierpyl live in, **20**. 392n
Stradbroke, E. of. *See* Rous, Sir John
Strafford, Cts of. *See* Campbell, Lady Anne (ca 1720–85); Johnson, Anne (ca 1684–1754); La Rochefoucauld, Henrietta de (d. 1732); Stanley, Henrietta Mary (1630–85)
Strafford, E. of. *See* Wentworth, Sir Thomas (1593–1641); Wentworth, Thomas (1672–1739); Wentworth, William (1626–95);

Wentworth, William (1722–91)

Strahan, Rev. George (1744–1824):
Johnson's *Prayers and Meditations* edited by, 33. 493

Strahan, William, bookseller:
Hume instructs, to send copy of *Exposé* to HW, 41. 44n
Johnson's *Journey to the Western Islands* to be published by, 32. 225n
son of, 33. 493n

Strahan, W., and T. Cadell; booksellers:
Gibbon's *Decline and Fall* published by, 31. 255n
Hawkesworth's book to be published by, 28. 86
Keppel's court martial printed by, 24. 427n

Strait-jacket; strait-jackets:
Orford, E. of, wears, 36. 119, 335
See also under Strait-waistcoat

'Straits, The.' *See* Gibraltar

Strait-waistcoat:
Chatham does not wear, 39. 115
madwoman asks for, 33. 233

'Straizes,' Comte de:
England visited by, 25. 409

Stralsund:
Frederick II orders Dohna and Manteuffel to drive Swedes from Mecklenburg to, 21. 258n
—— to besiege, 21. 265

Strand, The, London:
Adelphi bounded by, 28. 102n
Bathoe bookseller in, near Exeter Exchange, 10. 102n, 14. 121n, 22. 10n, 40. 290n
Beaufort Buildings in, 23. 56, 43. 275
Bell bookseller in, 35. 508n
Bingley, publisher, opposite Durham Yard in, 23. 28n
Blamire in, 29. 278
Buckingham St near, 42. 5
Cadell and Davies in, 15. 283
Campbell, bookbinder in, 25. 192
Catherine St in, 10. 349, 350, 13. 103n
conversation heard on, 37. 438
Coutts's bank in, 25. 355n
Craven St in, 14. 51n
Crown and Anchor Tavern in, 34. 172n
engravers of book illustrations get models from, 42. 271
Essex St in, 42. 348n
Exeter Change in, Bathoe, Mrs, succeeded by John Bell as bookseller near, 23. 418n
fire in, viewed by HW and ladies, 32. 109
Fountain, tavern in, 17. 429n
HW envisages trapes in, 33. 313
Hodsoll, banker in, 40. 221n
Holyland Coffee House in, 42. 384
Lyttelton picks up girls in, 28. 480
Montagu mentions, 10. 170
Northumberland House in, 20. 507n
Payne, bookseller in, 1. 255n
precautions in, during Gordon riots, 33. 188

puppet show at Exeter Change in, 25. 174n
Somerset House in, 14. 111n
Stephenson, undertaker in, 37. 267n, 268n
Surry St near, 21. 514n
Talbot, The, in, 21. 199n
Vaillant, French bookseller in, 9. 283n, 21. 400
Vanderburgh, bookseller at Exeter Change in, 22. 216n
Wilson, David, bookseller in, 42. 283n
windows broken in, on Bastille Day, 11. 314

Strange, Bn. *See* Smith Stanley, Edward (1752–1834); Smith Stanley, James (1717–71)

Strange, Bns. *See* Hamilton, Lady Elizabeth (1753–97)

Strange, E. *See* Murray, John (1755–1830)

Strange, ——, merchant at Cadiz:
ship of, 21. 269

Strange, Edmund (d. 1756), naval officer:
Savona blockade by squadron under, 43. 261

Strange, Sir John (ca 1696–1754), Kt, 1740; Master of the Rolls; solicitor-gen. 1737–42; M.P.:
biographical information about, corrected, 43. 242
chief justiceship may be given to, 17. 494
daughter of, 12. 21n
death of, 17. 494n
Frederick, P. of Wales, proposes opponent for, 17. 299
Indemnity Bill supported by, 17. 429
Master of the Rolls, 17. 494n
moves to revive Secret Committee, 18. 118n
Murray succeeds, as solicitor-gen., 17. 494, 18. 118
named in Secret Committee lists, 17. 384
resigns because of ill health, 18. 118

Strange, John (1732–99), English Resident at Venice 1773–88:
article by, 2. 164n
conduct of, in Venice, justified by his long tedious letters which were unanswered, 24. 298
letters of, to Mann and Lynch about D. of Gloucester's recovery are transposed, 24. *140*
Mann's correspondence with, about D. of Gloucester, 24. 135–6, 140, 329
papers on Roman antiquities by, 15. 179n
Rochford should have been told by, about D. of Gloucester's health, 24. 136

Strange, Lucy (d. 1800), m. (1762) Rev. Charles Wheler, 7th Bt, 1799:
HW visited by, 12. 21, 105
Johnston, Lady Cecilia, entertains, 12. 100
Richmond visited by, 12. 21
SH visited by, 12. 228

Strange, Sir Robert (1721–92), Kt, 1787, engraver:
Albano pilgrimage may be made by, 21. 404
Bute after quarrel with, allegedly sets up Dalton as rival, 21. 478n

[Strange, Sir Robert, *continued*]
—— turns against, for Jacobitism, **21**. 404n
drawings by, **21**. 470, **22**. 108
drawings engraved by, **21**. 470, **22**. 108
HW recommends, to Mann, **21**. *404*, 448, 461, **22**. 108
HW sends letter to Hertford through, **38**. 428, 439
HW's social relations with, in Paris, **7**. 262, 314
house of, in Castle St, Leicester Fields, **24**. 24n
Italy to be visited by, **21**. 404
Jacobite, **21**. 404, 461
Mann encloses letter to, **24**. 24
—— presented by, with copy of Strange's works, **21**. 461n
—— promised by, to be prudent at Rome, **21**. 470
——'s advice from, about collecting virtu for George III, approved by HW, **21**. 497
—— tells: to deal with lady at Barberini palace for Guido's Magdalen, **21**. 532–3; to look for art purchases at Rome and Naples, **22**. 115
(?) Mariette sends drawing to HW by, **3**. 389
method invented by, for drawing in colours, **22**. 108
permission granted to, to draw in Florentine palaces, **21**. 448
probably lives in St Martin's Lane, **24**. 24
sale of, at Christie's, **32**. 102n
sale of pictures of, **23**. 466n
Sampieri, Valerio, asked by, to allow the engraving of Guercino's 'Hagar' and Guido's 'Sts Peter and Paul,' **21**. 231n
Strange, Sarah (d. 1799), m. (1764) Edward Robert Nassau Chapeau:
HW visited by, **12**. 105
Strangeways, Lancs:
Reynolds of, **9**. 184n
Strangeways (surname). *See* Strangways
Strangury:
occurrences of, **7**. 44, 46, **28**. 410, **36**. 117
Strangways, Lady Catherine. *See* Gordon, Lady Catherine (d. 1537)
Strangways, Elizabeth Horner. *See* Horner, Elizabeth Strangways
Strangways, Susanna (1689–1758), m. (1713) Thomas Horner:
Caroline, Ps, said to be 'cuckolded' by, with Hervey, **30**. 27
Fox, Henry, kept by, until she quarrels with him, **30**. 313
(?) HW mentions, **17**. 475
Hervey betrays Fox's courtship of Ds of Manchester to, **30**. 313
—— recipient of largesse of, **30**. 313, **43**. 313
wealth of, **30**. 313
Strangways. *See also* Strangeways; Fox Strangways
Strangways Horner, Elizabeth. *See* Horner, Elizabeth Strangways

Strasbourg, Bp of. *See* Leopold Wilhelm (1614–62); Rohan, Armand-Gaston-Maximilien de (1674–1749); Rohan-Guéménée, Louis-René-Édouard de (1734–1803)
Strasbourg:
Cholmondeley will miss Gloucester family at, **36**. 132
clergy of, protest, **34**. 71n
Conway writes from, **39**. 195
fall of, expected, **12**. 53
military division of Alsace, **6**. 322
visitors to: Beaune, **7**. 427; Conway, **39**. 195, 538, 539; Craufurd, **4**. 428; Gloucester, Ds of, **33**. 419n; Gloucester, D. and Ds of, **24**. 134, **35**. 532; Scott, **39**. 538, 539
Stratclyde. *See* Strathclyde
Stratfield, Mr, of Kingston:
SH visited by, **12**. 248
Stratford, Agnes:
Lord Russell printed for benefit of, **29**. 223n
Stratford, Edward Augustus (ca 1740–1801), styled Vct Amiens, 1777; 2d E. of Aldborough, 1777; M.P.:
busy in politics and improving estate, **33**. 376
Essay on the True Interests . . . of the Empire, An, 'foolish and contemptible,' **33**. 421
wife of, **16**. 277n
Stratford, Mrs Edward Augustus. *See* Herbert, Barbara (1742–85)
Stratford, Rev. Thomas (1735–86), writer:
Fontenoy, a Poem: HW aids publication of, **29**. 234; sent by HW to Mrs Bouverie, Mrs Garrick, and Hannah More, **42**. 40
HW's account of, **29**. *233–5*
Lord Russell, a Tragedy by: Cumberland adapts, for stage, **29**. 225, 233, 273, **33**. 356; frenzy of, **33**. 356; HW's account of, **29**. 223–5; Mason assumes Sherlock is author of, **29**. 228–9, 233; to be performed at Drury Lane, **29**. 273
'Whig to the marrow,' **29**. 235
Stratford-upon-Avon, Warwickshire:
Coke, Lady Mary, goes to Ragley by way of, **37**. 564–5
corporation of, repaints Shakespeare's bust, **9**. 120
HW visits, **9**. 120
Shakespeare festival to be held at, under Garrick's care, **10**. 287, 298
Shakespeare jubilee at, **4**. 287n
tombs in church of, **9**. 120
Stratford Place, London:
Blair lives in, **15**. 199n
Herbert helps build, **33**. 376n
Strathallan, Vct. *See* Drummond, James Francis Edward
Strathaven, Lady. *See* Cope, Catherine Anne
Strathaven, Lord. *See* Gordon, George (1761–1853)
Strath Bogie, Scotland:
Bland to attack rebels at, **19**. 233n
English expedition against rebels in, **37**. 227, 229–30

Strathclyde, Kingdom of:
  HW praises Pinkerton's treatment of, **16**. 303
Strathfieldsaye, Hants:
  Pitt, George, of, **13**. 233n, **17**. 468n
  Trapp, rector of, **17**. 63n
Strathmore, Cts of. *See* Bowes, Mary Eleanor
  (1749–1800); Cheape, Marianne (ca 1773–
  1849); Cochrane, Susan (d. 1754)
Strathmore, E. of. *See* Bowes, John (1769–
  1820); Lyon, Charles (1699–1728); Lyon,
  John (1737–76); Lyon, Patrick (1643–95)
Strathnaver, Bn. *See* Leveson Gower, George
  Granville (1786–1861)
Stratton, Mrs, of Twickenham:
  SH visited by, **12**. 222, 223, 248
Stratton, George:
  trial of, at Westminster Hall, for deposing
  Pigot, ordered by House of Commons, **25**.
  12n
Stratton St, Piccadilly:
  Bull, Richard, addressed in, **41**. 467n, **42**. 237
  Walpole, Thomas jr, addressed in, **36**. 276
Straw, Jack, rebel:
  Dalrymple identifies, with Wat Tyler, **15**. 123
Straw:
  bed of, **35**. 244
  bricks without, **32**. 166, **33**. 523
  County Gaol lacks, **40**. 308n
  Gage loses, **39**. 232
  hat of, **20**. 430
  streets strewn with: **31**. 189; to deaden noise
    outside windows of women who lie in, **23**.
    323
  used in drawing lots, **10**. 188, 191
  young men at St Alban's Tavern have streets
    littered with, **23**. 323
  See also Jack-straws
Strawberry; strawberries:
  at SH, 'Tonton' likes to eat, **11**. 29
  beds of, at SH, **37**. 338
  (?) conundrum on, **32**. 330
  cup and saucer with, **36**. 182
  disagree with Mme du Deffand, **4**. 244, 252,
    5. 81, 371
  Du Deffand, Mme, eats, with cream after
    supper, **39**. 269
  —— tempted by, **4**. 244, 252
  HW hears of, in October, **9**. 249
  HW hopes for, at Marble Hill, **31**. 40
  HW 'kills,' **28**. 162
  HW promises, to Mason, **29**. 263
  HW regrets missing, at Marble Hill, **31**. 37
  HW's parched, **39**. 499
  HW thanks Mason for warning him against,
    28. 420
  HW will choose, as regimental badge, **38**. 41
  Mason asks if Rousseau died from eating,
    28. 418
  Petersham, Lady Caroline, and guests eat,
    9. 109–10
  poem about, mistakenly attributed to Spenser
    by HW, **10**. 85
  served at Elizabeth Chudleigh's ball, **35**. 301

St-Évremond's remark about, **10**. 34
supper-room at Bath knights' ball crowded
  for, **39**. 322
'Strawberry, Counts of':
  armorial achievements of, **20**. 200
'Strawberry Committee':
  Belhus not up to standards of, **35**. 183
  cypresses would be inserted by, at Tun-
    bridge, **35**. 135
  Strafford erects building designed by, **35**. 297
  Vyne chapel's embellishment voted by, **35**.
    185
  Williams, Frances Hanbury, should be
    thanked by, **35**. 177
'Strawberry Courant':
  HW describes his gossip as, **32**. 70
Strawberry Hill (SH); HW's seat at Twicken-
  ham:
  abbeys' and cathedrals' gloomth imparted to,
    20. 372
  additions and improvements to: **1**. 11–12, 145,
    4. 251n; **9**. 102, 146–7, 149–51, 160, 168,
    170, 248, 292, 304, 360, 368–9, 379, 385, 398,
    10. 26, 53–4, 57, 61, 64, 72, 84–5, 91, 92, 94,
    120, 274, 304, 307, **13**. 17, 31. 297; expen-
    sive, **38**. 90; inquired about by Mme du
    Deffand, **4**. 104, 105, 147, 251, 255
  'African mole-hill outshines,' **42**. 117
  Africa's mole-hills outshone by, **39**. 430
  Agincourt wishes to engrave architect's de-
    signs for, **42**. 103
  Ailesbury, Cts of, and Mary Rich to visit,
    35. 98
  Ailesbury, Cts of, does worsted-work land-
    scape for, **38**. 438
  —— fails to visit, **39**. 159
  —— to visit, in October, **39**. 252
  —— works fire-screen for, **37**. 505
  air and tranquillity of, are HW's requisites,
    25. 257
  'all brick and mortar,' **20**. 368
  'all gold, and all green,' **35**. 225
  'almost the last monastery left,' **1**. 325
  altar at: HW falls against, **11**. 19; (?) HW
    mentions, **10**. 10, 64
  Amelia, Ps, dislikes, **35**. 227
  —— praises, **9**. 331
  'amusements des eaux de, les,' **11**. 83
  animals at, **4**. 439, **9**. 51, 77, 134, 155, **10**. 94,
    108, 127
  Anne Boleyn's 'walk' at, **35**. 142
  annuity for Maria Colomb charged on estate
    of, **30**. 363
  'ark,' **31**. 24
  Armoury at: **9**. 146n, **11**. 25n, **20**. 375n, 381,
    396, 400; added, **20**. 348n; bows and arrows
    in, **11**. 25; completed, **9**. 150; Fitzpatrick,
    Richard, gives (? bullet) for, **33**. 146–7;
    Francis I's armour for, **32**. 66; HW jokes
    about contents of, **31**. 26; shields to hang
    in, **35**. 421
  arms in windows of, **1**. 254, 377, 378

[Strawberry Hill, *continued*]

assemblies at, to show Gallery, **10.** 102, 106, 107

assembly at, for HW's nieces, **33.** 61

Astle invited by HW to call on him at, **42.** 148

—— invited by HW to dine and sleep at, **41.** 95

attempted robbery at, foiled, **31.** 298

attracts too many people, **33.** 411–12, 413

auction may soon be held at, **35.** 516

Augusta, Ps of Wales, would like keys of, for visit, **39.** 116

autumnal beauties of, **35.** 521

'baby-house, full of playthings,' **42.** 285

backstairs of, window on, **9.** 385

baked for a week for HW, **33.** 81

ball at, described, **28.** 445–8

balloons not to imitate, **39.** 419

barn at, blown down, **32.** 76

Barrett Lennard's Gothic interior to, **35.** 183

Bath, E. of, celebrates, in ballad, **9.** 168–9, 189, **35.** 236–7

battlements at: **9.** 102, 149, 292, 379, **35.** 161; HW may mount pop-guns on, **21.** 311; to be reared, **20.** 199

beans, peas, roses, and strawberries at, all parched, **39.** 449

bears away the bell 'for wit and cheerfulness and humour,' **41.** 366

Beauclerk, Lady Diana, and Mrs Damer enrich, **35.** 385

Beauclerk Closet at: **2.** 13n, 28n, **5.** 392n, **10.** 53n, **11.** 29n, 82n; built to hold Lady Diana Beauclerk's illustrations for HW's *Mysterious Mother*, **24.** 524; Coke, Lady Mary, admires, **31.** 297; Conway and family have not seen, **39.** 294; designed by Essex, **2.** 13, 28n; HW shows to Mary Hamilton, **31.** 206, 216; HW puts Portland purchases in, **39.** 443

Beauclerk Closet and Tower at, **32.** 294, 304, 320, 322, 326, 358, 364

Beauclerk Tower at: **1.** 12n, 178n, 338n, 344n, **2.** 13n, 16n, 58n, **6.** 337n, 348, 349n, 352, **9.** 93n, 244n; added in 1776, **1.** 12n; almost finished, **28.** 315; bills for work on, **2.** 58n, 61, 66; building of, **2.** 24; designed by Essex, **1.** 178n, 338n, **2.** 15, **39.** 275–6; HW describes, **28.** 275, 318–19; HW pleased with, **2.** 41; HW writes in, **29.** 71; Mason longs to see, **28.** 317; tower copied from Thornbury Castle, **1.** 344n

beauty of, compared with Osterley Park, **32.** 127

Beauty Room at: **39.** 275–6; *see also* Yellow Bed-Chamber *below*

Bedchamber, HW's, *see* Red Bedchamber *below*

bedchamber in Round Tower at, to be hung with brocatelle, **21.** 420

Bedford, Ds of, suggests that HW give ball at, **38.** 335

bell at gate of, **9.** 304, **35.** 331

Bentley and workers untrained in architecture when they built, **42.** 220

Bentley expected at, **35.** 177, 226

—— 's decline after leaving, **10.** 243

(?) —— 's drawing of, **9.** 212, 213, 217

—— 's landscape painting of Jersey at, **35.** 207n

—— 's plan for Chinese building at, **35.** 177–8

—— 's view of, HW sends, to Mann, **20.** 368, 377, 379, 386–7, 390

—— thought, dreary at first sight, **35.** 265

Berry family hopes to see Pinkerton at, **16.** 381

billiard sticks at, **39.** 294

bird-cherry trees burnt because of caterpillars, **33.** 340

bird collection at, **1.** 56n

birds at, **3.** 76, 80, 105, **4.** 77, 239; *see also* nightingales at

Blue bedchamber at: **2.** 274n, **10.** 106n, **20.** 381, 387; activity on roads before, **34.** 195–6; added, **20.** 348n; Bentley's chimneypiece in, **35.** 173–4; Berry, Agnes, to occupy, **11.** 71; bow-window of, **11.** 86, **33.** 82, **35.** 173–4; Bransom, Ann, to delay visitors in, **12.** 168; Churchill's portrait in, **13.** 183n; flooded, **35.** 228; furniture in, **35.** 173–4; HW able to walk from his bedchamber to, **34.** 105; HW chiefly lives in, **33.** 273; HW in, in fit of gout, **33.** 81, 408; HW in winter shifts from Red Room to, **39.** 317; HW sits in, **11.** 178; mentioned, **11.** 177; over supper parlor, **35.** 173–4; stairs to, **33.** 435; storm threatens, **12.** 143; windows in, undamaged by explosion, **39.** 152

Blue Breakfast-Room at: HW finds letter in, **28.** 443; HW sits in window of, **28.** 405; portraits in, **28.** 39, 196, **29.** 45; Prince Yusupov to see, **28.** 269; Roberts's copy of Opie's 'Hannah More' in, **31.** 279n

blue room at: Cowley portrait to be in, **42.** 203; HW lies on couch in, **10.** 320; HW longs to chat with Chute and Montagu in, **10.** 202; under HW's bedchamber, **35.** 279

books at: **20.** 382; to be rearranged, **15.** 215; *see also under* Library *below*

Boufflers, Cts of, considers, unworthy of English solidity, **22.** 270

Boughton Park has tower copied from, **35.** 279

'Bower': Cole commends idea of, **1.** 85; erected and planted, **1.** 85; plans for, **1.** 90–1

'bower of tuberoses,' **32.** 137

bowling green at, **35.** 177, **39.** 403

bow-window at, **10.** 29; HW writes in, **20.** 46, 48

'bow window room' at, *see* Blue Bedchamber

Boyle Walsingham, Mrs, to bring Cowley portrait to, in chaise, **42.** 203

breakfast party at, **11.** 280

Breakfast Room at: **2.** 373, **4.** 30n, 305n, **9.** 124n, **15.** 191n, 281n, **20.** 382, **28.** 405n; added, **19.** 486n; dark, **32.** 409; Grignan, views of, in, **35.** 600n; ivory carving of Virgin and Child in, **35.** 513n; portrait of Lady Ossory in, **33.** 17; print of Fontenelle in, **31.** 137; 'this blue room,' **33.** 17; *see also* Blue Breakfast Room *above*

Brentford election keeps HW from, **23.** 73

bridge for, designed by Essex, **2.** 79

Bristow and Lady Hervey praise, to E. of Bath, **35.** 236

Bristow praises, **9.** 169

'brown and parched,' **33.** 212

Burney, Dr, to call at, **42.** 173, 299

Burney, Fanny, may not leave Windsor for, **42.** 170, 173

cabinet and gallery at: Pitt, Thomas, draws Gothic ornaments for, **22.** 25; to be finished in summer, **21.** 18

Cabinet ('Chapel,' 'Tribune') at: **1.** 11n, 22n, 325n, **2.** 274n, **4.** 251n, **5.** 417n, **9.** 83n, 276n, 304n, 385n, **10.** 64n, **11.** 5n, 19n, **15.** 16nn, 17n, 190n, 191n, 270n, **16.** 284n; Ailesbury, Cts of, to tell Conway about, **38.** 175; altar in, **10.** 64, **28.** 446; Amelia, Ps, pleased with, **10.** 82; building of, **1.** 11n, 145n; cabinet of enamels in, **9.** 83; Caligula's bust in, **22.** 523, **25.** 89, 90; cameo in, **25.** 89; carpet in, **10.** 64; carpenters' strike delays, **22.** 49; construction of, halted, 9, 398, **22.** 49; cost of, **21.** 514; 'delineator' transfigures, **28.** 329; Devonshire, D. of, wants to give incense pot to, **38.** 362; Edwards's drawing of, **2.** 274; Fenns recollect, with pleasure, **42.** 97; grated door of, mistaken in dark for dungeon, **33.** 403; gilded by sun for Ds of York's visit, **12.** 10; glass case in, **25.** 90; HW calls, 'chapel,' **10.** 64; HW calls, work of fancy, **12.** 137; HW hopes for sunshine to illumine, **10.** 101; HW to consult Chute about, **9.** 385; HW to dedicate Cellini coffer in, **23.** 425; HW to impart 'Catholic' air to, **21.** 306, **22.** 136; HW trips on carpet in, **11.** 19; HW wants Crébillon's and Marivaux's portraits for, **20.** 324; Hardinge, Mrs, draws in, **35.** 627; ivory statues, carved by Verskovis, in, **19.** 420n; kingwood ('rosewood') cabinet in, **9.** 83, **18.** 277n, **34.** 208n, **42.** 111n, 262n; Mann to enrich, with medal, **24.** 470; materials for, arrive, **9.** 385; mentioned, **12.** 27; miniatures in cabinet in, **31.** 170, 216; Montagu mentions, **10.** 66; Nivernais takes off his hat in, **22.** 136; Rosalba's portrait of Lady Brown in, **18.** 166n; sunshine in, compared to 'glory of popery,' **10.** 168; Theodore's Corsican relics in, **21.** 45n; to be built, **21.** 238, **35.** 298; valuables in cabinet at, **1.** 275; Van Dyck's 'Soldiers at Cards' in, **17.** 343n; views of Grignan for, **35.** 600; visitors charmed with, **10.** 72; windows in,

10. 64, 72; windows in, undamaged by explosion, **39.** 152

cabinet by HW's bedside at, **35.** 373

carpenters at: make repairs, **11.** 71; stop work, **1.** 11n, 14, 21, **9.** 398, **22.** 49, **35.** 315

cascades at, **35.** 324, **39.** 133

Castle of Otranto largely set in, **1.** 91n

catalogue of collections at, **32.** 216; *see also* *Description of . . . SH*, by HW

catalogue of HW's books at, **42.** 6

'Cat's Vase' at, used to store goldfish, **39.** 404

cattle at, **4.** 267, 394; *see also* cows at

cellars of, have four feet of water, **35.** 264

chapel in garden at: **2.** 249n, **15.** 271; altar doors to be placed in, **2.** 221; Beaufort, Ds of, visits, **33.** 279, 280; building of, **1.** 243–4, 256, 275, 325, **2.** 370; Bury altar tablets to be on sides of shrine in, **16.** 184; Cole could be inaugurated in, **1.** 328, 332; Cole's account of, **2.** 370; contains shrine sent by Hamilton, **35.** 421; copied from Salisbury Cathedral tomb, **41.** 420; Donatello's bas-relief in, **23.** 450n, 456, 499, **24.** 15; finished, **24.** 15; foundations of, to be dug, **28.** 28; HW uses stick to go to, **33.** 279; prints of, **2.** 251; sarcophagus from Rome would adorn, **24.** 462; Sulkowsky gives gratuity to gardener at, **33.** 280; tomb, or shrine, of Capoccio in, **1.** 244, 256, **2.** 221, 370, **15.** 271–2, **43.** 284; 'Tonton' and 'Rosette' buried at, **34.** 45; window in, procured by Lord Ashburnham for HW, **1.** 244, 256, **2.** 370, **32.** 197

Charlotte, Q., approaches, in coach, **38.** 418

—— arranges her visit to, **35.** 544–5

—— curious to see new room at, **36.** 323

'cheeses' made at, **9.** 168

Chenevix, Mrs, the seller of, **35.** 140

Chesterfield may disapprove of, **31.** 111

chickens at, **3.** 80, 105, 107

'child' of HW, **32.** 241

chimney fire at, **23.** 201

chimney-pieces at: Bentley designs, **35.** 644; imitated from Canterbury Cathedral, **12.** 105

China Closet; China Room at: **2.** 274n, **4.** 302n, **15.** 16nn, 318, **20.** 382, 387; ceiling copied from that at little Borghese villa, **21.** 471; escapes in explosion, **32.** 76, **37.** 152; Gloucester Cathedral tiles laid in floor of, **36.** 39; HW shows, to guests after dinner, **31.** 206, 216; Harcourt gives paving tiles to, **35.** 537; Montagu hopes Ps Amelia saw, **10.** 84; old kitchen converted into, **35.** 259; porcelain specimens from all countries in, **25.** 591

Churchill, Lady Mary, admires, **5.** 34

Chute and Gray to visit, **35.** 177

Chute avoids, in autumn, for fear of gout, **35.** 115

—— pursued to, by gout, **35.** 259

——'s bedchamber at, **20.** 381

—— the presiding genius of, **24.** 209

[Strawberry Hill, *continued*]
—— to accompany HW to, in post-chaise, **35**. 69
—— to bring Müntz back to, **35**. 89
—— to describe, to Mann, **19**. 497
—— to visit, **35**. 65
Clive, Mrs, makes, sultry, with her red face, **32**. 360
cloister and Holbein Chamber added to, **21**. 238
Cloister at: **21**. 238, **40**. 255; chairs for, bought at Bateman's auction, **32**. 242, 245–6; Chute's design for, praised by HW, Bentley, and Müntz, **35**. 110–11; extends, **21**. 506; finished, **36**. 39; HW seeks old chairs for, **1**. 90; Montagu family portraits temporarily in, **10**. 103; music in, **10**. 71, 127; paving of, **9**. 385
closet, glazed, in Great North Bedchamber at, **23**. 432
closet next to HW's bedchamber in attic at, **43**. 155
coal hole at, **40**. 150
Coke, Lady Mary, praises, **31**. 299
—— praises contents of, **31**. 168
Cole praises, **1**. 34, 42, 67, 80, 113, 125, 254, 254n, **2**. 276
collection at, itemized in Lysons's *Environs*, **15**. 270–1
collection of birds at, **1**. 56n
columbarium intended for, **21**. 157
Combe calls, pretty, **15**. 321–2
committee at, on taste, *see* 'Strawberry Committee'
Comyn's house near, rejected by Conway, **37**. 304
construction at: delayed by rain, **31**. 23–4; done slowly, **10**. 304; expenses of, **21**. 420, 514
'contains more verdure than all France,' **1**. 112
contents of, bequeathed by HW to remain with the house, **30**. 351–3
Conway and wife to visit, **37**. 366, 367–8, 374
Conway and wife want daughter taken to, by HW, **37**. 330
Conway calls, HW's 'new tub,' **37**. 277
—— describes, to Mann, **20**. 290–1
——, Hertford, and Beauchamp to dine at, **38**. 74
Conway sends coachmaker's apprentice to HW at, **23**. 284, 286
—— to show, to Johnstones, **35**. 535
Conway, Anne Seymour (Mrs Damer), to visit HW at, **37**. 334
'cool as a grotto,' **33**. 171
Coombe Bank competes with, for antiquities, **37**. 460
copper-plates from, **9**. 170
corbeilles to be introduced at, **31**. 54
Cottage at: **4**. 147n, 268n, **10**. 148n, **15**. 16n, 215n; added to estate, **10**. 147–8; decorated in pea-green, **4**. 268; Du Deffand, Mme,

charmed by account of, **4**. 268; Du Deffand, Mme, inquires about, **4**. 147, 251, 255; Gothic style not to be forced upon, **10**. 168; HW builds, **23**. 128; HW shows, to Chute and Cowslade, **10**. 168; lead stolen from door pediment of, **39**. 416
Cottage Garden (Flower Garden) at: **2**. 249n; area of, **1**. 151n; planting of, **1**. 85, 151; print of, **2**. 251, 254
couple, but not a patriarchal family, can be housed at, **37**. 289–90
cows at, **19**. 414, **20**. 380, **25**. 532; *see also* cattle at
Cowslade to visit, **41**. 420
Craon, Princesse de, would be pleased by, **20**. 387
crowds at: **34**. 50, 62; force Cts of Hertford into kitchen, **10**. 106
curiosities at: **9**. 304, **15**. 316; packed for winter, **33**. 60
Czartoryska, Ps, three times denied admission to, **42**. 307
damage from water at, **33**. 117
Damer, Mrs, bequeathed life occupancy of, **30**. 349
—— bequeathed money for maintenance of, **15**. 336, **30**. 354
—— may be burdened by expense of keeping up, **15**. 337–8
——'s works at, **12**. 271–2
dampness of: disagrees with HW, **24**. 277–8; may give rheumatism to HW, **22**. 456–7; worries Mme du Deffand, **5**. 294, 416, **6**. 17, 63, 98, 197, 271, 281, 384, 401
Delineator, The, adapted to, **39**. 293
'Description' of: almost finished, **25**. 531; *see also Description of the Villa of Mr Horace Walpole* (by HW)
destruction of cypress and laurustinus at, **1**. 133
dinner excursions to, **35**. 173
dinner guests at, come early to see house, **40**. 363
Drawing-Room at, pictures in, **31**. 206
drought at, **1**. 14, 21, **9**. 82, **10**. 38, **38**. 165
Du Deffand, Mme, asks about location of, **7**. 52
—— cannot visit, because of blindness, **10**. 289
—— comments on, **3**. 306
—— compares HW to, **5**. 34
—— inquires about construction at, **4**. 104, 105, 147, 251, 255
—— inquires if Grosvenor Bedford is at, **4**. 123
—— lacks a, **5**. 117
—— mentions: **3**. 21, 26, 27, 45, 75, 78, 101, 104, 105, 109, 118, 165, 167, 169, 191, 195, 199, 207, 226, 238, 275, 338, 340, 353, 354, **4**. 82, 137, 140, 141, 147, 221, 239, 253, 275, 455, **5**. 82, 139; in parody, **3**. 28, 40
—— prefers HW at, rather than London, **4**. 394, **6**. 85

—— says, belongs in *Thousand and One Nights*, 4. 248

—— threatens to visit, 4. 66, 69

—— to ask questions about, 4. 266

—— worried by HW's being alone and ill at, 4. 148, 150, 151, 160, 5. 294, 6. 281

—— worries about dampness of, 5. 294, 416, 6. 17, 63, 98, 197, 271, 281, 384, 401

—— would like to be at, 4. 345

Durham, Bp of, wishes to see, 10. 203

eating-room and library to be built at, 20. 382

Edwards employed at, 2. 274n

Elliot compliments, 10. 94

Ellis requests ticket for, for Fisher family, 42. 224–5

elms at, lost in hurricane, 2. 135

entail of, 30. 349–51

expense of entertainment at, 10. 127, 278

festino at, 10. 278–9

fête at, 4. 234, 236–8, 246, 7. 78

field at, mentioned by *Public Advertiser* as needing drainage, 25. 146

fields at, fenced, 23. 128n

Fiesole hill compared with, 20. 193, 203

filled with portraits, 10. 53–4

'finished,' 39. 187

finished except for Great North Bedchamber, 23. 340

fire at, 10. 262

five acres only belonged to, at first, 37. 270n

floods surround, 9. 195

floors laid at, 10. 26

flowers at: 9. 364, 10. 69, 127, 156, 188, 208, 304, 31. 36; 'Arabian,' 39. 299

footman hangs himself at, 11. 369, 370

foreigners about to leave England to dine on Sunday at, 42. 449–50

foreign visitors to England are all sent to, 28. 269

foreign visitors to, admitted without ticket, 33. 280

France may capture, 9. 168

Frenchmen's opinion of, 23. 312

fruit lacking at, 39. 416

full of Mann's gifts, 23. 425

full of pictures, 16. 54, 320

furniture at: altar, 10. 61, 64; basin, 9. 155; bed, 10. 320; bench, 9. 237, 10. 93, 168; cabinet of enamels, 9. 83; (?) candlesticks, 9. 295; canopies, 10. 53; carpet, 10. 64; chairs, 9. 384; clock, 9. 304; (?) commodes, 10. 207; couch, 10. 167, 320; decanter, 9. 155; grate, 9. 161; lantern, 9. 150–1; pail, 9. 155; paintings and miniatures, 9. 304, 379; tea-strainer, 9. 155; transported from Arlington St, 10. 43, 193

gallery and cabinet at, delayed by labour strike, 22. 49

Gallery at: 1. 11n, 22n, 133, 151n, 2. 274n, 3. 405n, 4. 251n, 13. 232n, 14. 68n, 15. 16n, 17nn, 167, 21. 238, 31. 46, 147, 206; advances, 21. 497, 506, 558, 22. 18; 'all sun

and gold,' 10. 224; all the earth begs to see, 38. 108; almost complete, 10. 84; Amelia, Ps, does not look at pictures in, 31. 147; arms in window of, 1. 378; assembly to show, 10. 102, 106, 107; begun, 9. 360, 369–70, 33. 403; Bentley's 'Mont Orgeuil' in, 35. 243n; Bromwich and Peckitt decorate, 40. 312n; bronze of Ceres in, 33. 479; building of, 1. 11n, 34, 44, 161n; canopies in, 10. 53; carpenters' strike delays, 22. 49; ceiling of, 10. 53; ceiling of, 'richer than the roof of paradise,' 28. 446; Chantilly gallery inspired, 31. 46; Chiffinch's and St Albans's portraits in, 35. 228n; chimney of, catches fire, 38. 175; Cole will peep into, 1. 79; completed, 38. 207; construction of, halted, 9. 398; cost of, 21. 514; damaged by water, 33. 117; 'delineator' transfigures, 28. 329; eagle and Vespasian bust to adorn, 21. 461; eagle, marble in, 12. 11n, 42. 387; explosion damages, 39. 152; Falkland's picture in, 42. 106; 'fine apartment,' 10. 85; 'finished,' 1. 151; finished but unfurnished, 10. 92; foreigners, about to leave England, to dine on Sunday at, 42. 449–50; foundations of, in progress, 16. 44; gilded by sun for Ds of York's visit, 12. 10; gilding delays completion of, 10. 57, 91; grows too magnificent for HW's humility, 22. 152; guests had not seen, 38. 362; HW and Thomas Pitt arrange, 10. 94; HW installs pictures in, 9. 379; HW invites Montagu to visit, 10. 118; HW mentions, 10. 81, 11. 168, 12. 168; HW serves beverages in, 10. 127, 279; HW's guests meet Ps Amelia in, 31. 147; HW will give no balls to bring dust and dirty candles into, 38. 335; HW writes in, 22. 219; lighted for entertainment of Churchills, 33. 355; lit with candles, 10. 279; made splendid by presence of HW's nieces, 32. 382; might become ark after deluge, 35. 316; Montagu fears foreigners would not appreciate, 10. 74; Montagu mentions, 9. 396; Montagu praises, 10. 281; Montagu would like to see, complete, 10. 84; painting and gilding at, 40. 288; Peckitt's windows for, 1. 145; pictures in, 31. 206; 'radiant,' 10. 168; Richmond dwellers to come to see, 10. 281; Rosalba's portrait of Law in niche in, 42. 386–7; Sandby, T., makes drawing of, 2. 274, 41. 189; servants' hall under, 38. 175; to be added, 21. 238; to be on site of old printing-house, 35. 296, 298, 309; visitors throng to see, 10. 98, 106, 109; visitors unimpressed by, 10. 72; West inquires about artists of ceiling, glass, and wainscoting in, 40. 312; windows in, undamaged, 39. 152; workmen quit, 35. 315

garden, gardens at: 3. 367, 10. 215, 306, 12. 74, 199; altar to adorn recess in, 20. 325, 368–9, 372; cat's ossuarium to be placed in,

[Strawberry Hill, *continued*]
10. 155; clove-carnations in, killed, 33. 567; HW able to creep about in, 31. 345; HW able to traverse, only twice in summer, 39. 493–4; HW cannot walk whole circuit of, 33. 561; HW 'crawls' around, 10. 167; HW kept from, by excessive heat, 35. 98; HW's improvements at, 40. 61; HW supervises servants lopping trees in, 24. 48; HW unable to make circuit of, 39. 447; HW walks in, at night, 10. 156; Mann supposes, to be Gothic, 20. 368, 372; 'new,' 23. 128n; poplars, Lombardy, in, 33. 480; sepulchral altar installed near wood in, 20. 388; shrubs for, 21. 113; *see also* flowers at; HW's planting at; Prior's Garden at; Privy Garden at; verdure at
gardener reduces, to barren Highlands, 35. 480
gate; gates at: 9. 304, 10. 274, 278; bell at, 9. 304, 24. 211, 35. 331; 39. 176; by Essex, 1. 178–9, 184, 190, 193, 196, 197; for garden, 23. 128n; Gothic, in garden, 23. 311, 43. 54; Gothic, robbery near, 11. 283
gateway at, of artificial stone, 41. 227
Giberne restrained from calling at, 20. 97, 98
'gloomth' of, 10. 307
Gloucester, Ds of, hopes that HW will leave, to her family, 36. 161n
Golconda not more magnificent than, 12. 65
goldfish at: disappear, 39. 403, 404; suffer from drought, 10. 38; *see also under* Goldfish
goldfish pond at: 20. 188, 21. 361, 33. 292; *see also under* Po-Yang
Gothicism of, keeps up idea of haunted walks and popish spirits, 31. 316
Gothic museum to be added to, 30. 176–7
Gothic pretensions of, 20. 362
Gothic style of, 'true,' 31. 216
'Gothic Vatican of Greece and Rome,' 12. 261, 33. 529
Gough and Nichols to visit, 42. 28–9
gout said to pursue Chute to, 35. 259
Grandison, Vcts, unable to attend dinner at, 10. 306
Gray to visit, 14. 30–1, 83, 84, 92, 102
Great Bed at: Coke, Lady Mary, sees, 31. 179; HW wishes George III and Q. Charlotte to see, 31. 169
Great North (State) Bedchamber at: 1. 256n, 305n, 313n, 2. 249n, 5. 65n, 116n, 9. 223n, 11. 94n, 15. 191n, 16. 284n, 28. 339n; Bentley designs ostrich plumes for, 20. 375n; building of, 1. 256, 23. 240; Cellini's chest to be in glass closet in, 23. 432; Charlotte, Q., wants to see, 32. 195n; chimney-back for, 20. 396; Coke, Lady Mary, sees, 31. 179; 'delineator' transfigures, 28. 329; ebony cabinet in, 43. 378; finishing touch to SH, 23. 432; HW delighted with, 28. 42; HW has portrait of Frances Jennings in, 39. 294; HW to air, for Campbells, 39. 295;

ivory carving of Venus and Cupid in, 33. 513n; minchiate and tarocco cards in, 17. 193n; nearing completion, 28. 28; print of view from, 2. 251; 'proceeds fast,' 23. 311; royal portraits in, 33. 472; table in, bequeathed to HW by Bns Hervey, 31. 137; tapestry bed in, 28. 446
Great Parlour (Refectory) at: 2. 274n, 11. 370n, 20. 382; breakfast in, 10. 71; crowded, 10. 127; dinner served in, 10. 279; fire-screen in, 34. 15n; frieze at, to be like that at Wroxton, 35. 73; furniture for, 35. 233n; Gothic chairs for, 35. 181–2; HW adds, 20. 380n; HW seeks granite for sideboard in, 35. 178n; HW to descend to, after gout, 39. 238; Harris wedding feast served in, 35. 217; nearly finished, 35. 174; passage windows to, damaged by explosion, 39. 152; plasterers at work on, 35. 79–80; Thames agitation visible from, 10. 93; vase on chimney-piece of, 26. 4n
'great tower' of, *see below under* tower of
Green Closet at: 2. 32n, 7. 417n, 9. 146n, 304n, 12. 144n, 15. 191n, 43. 202; bas-relief of Benedict XIV in, 21. 105n; damaged by rain, 33. 402; HW breakfasts in, 12. 144; Hoadly's head in wax in, 17. 502n; Stavely's portrait of Bns Cadogan in, 24. 320n; visitors may overflow, 12. 27; windows in, undamaged by explosion, 39. 152
greener than Elysian Fields, 32. 132
Grignan drawings heirlooms at, 35. 649
Grosley's *Londres* describes, inaccurately, 28. 269
grove at, increases, 35. 173
'grows near a termination,' 20. 368
Guilford unable to attend dinner at, 10. 306, 308–9
HW adding to, 38. 59
HW adds to acreage of, 20. 16
HW admits Lady Tyrconnel to, with 3 guests only, 42. 472
HW allows Bindley a ticket for 5 visitors to, 41. 440–1
HW alone at, 38. 94, 155, 187, 39. 119
HW always makes, agreeable to his company, 31. 147
HW apologizes for not asking Pinkerton to, 16. 310
HW asks Conway to send poplar-pines to, by Henley barge, 39. 133
HW assumes 'Burlington air' for, 20. 361
HW at: 11. 97, 142, 145, 246, 254, 279, 283, 293, 12. 51, 63; 'constantly,' 20. 324; for change of air, 20. 119; 24. 432, 436, 25. 284; for Easter, 21. 75; for rest of season, 19. 435; for some days, 22. 98; for summer, 20. 422; in mid-winter, to safeguard orange trees and goldfish, 21. 361; in summer, 15. 73; till after Christmas, 32. 64; to be near Galfridus Mann, 20. 525; twice in June 1772, 33. 336; when told of James Mann's death, 22. 225–6

HW better in London than at, **22.** 451, 456–7, **24.** 288, **35.** 375

HW brings parties from London to dine at, **35.** 173

HW brought to, after severe illness, **42.** 439

HW builds 'little Gothic castle' at, **20.** 111

HW busy with, **20.** 371, 396

HW calls: 'abbey,' **10.** 127; 'baby house,' **42.** 99, 285; 'castle,' **37.** 406–7; 'charming villa,' **19.** 497; 'convent,' **10.** 127, 167; 'country palace,' **25.** 262; 'extreme pretty place,' **30.** 113; his 'Castle of Bungey,' **37.** 406, 407, 411; his 'Kingsgate,' **30.** 182; "immortal Strawberry,' **32.** 220; 'loveliest of all places,' **35.** 333; 'nutshell,' **37.** 406, **39.** 180; 'Otranto,' **23.** 350; 'Tempe,' **10.** 316; 'Versailles,' **10.** 297; 'Woden,' 'Thor,' and 'Gothic Lares,' **21.** 433

HW calls himself 'seneschal' of, **30.** 282

HW cannot miss lilacs at, **22.** 289

HW cannot stir from, without armed servants, **35.** 367

HW collects arms at, **20.** 375, 396

HW cool and comfortable at, **30.** 199

HW 'could not presume to send' ticket to, to Archduke and Archduchess of Austria, **33.** 529

HW declines Beloe's offers to compliment, **15.** 228, 229–30

HW declines Mme du Deffand's offer of cabaret for, **4.** 312

HW describes: **20.** 379–82, **25.** 532, **30.** 113–14; in oriental imagery, **28.** 446

HW detained at, by company, **30.** 161

HW directly supervises work at, **10.** 84

HW disparages, after visits to Ilchester's seats, **40.** 251

HW does not expect Montagu to revisit, **10.** 306

HW does not like to be alone at, **35.** 391

HW does not like to keep money at, **42.** 198

HW does not spend Christmas at, **10.** 241

HW does not visit, because of Brentford elections and high water, **23.** 73

HW dreams some one in future will walk about, and talk of Lady Ossory, **33.** 43

HW encloses ticket for, with visitors' rules, to Hon. Thomas Fitzwilliam, **42.** 195–6

HW exhausts hoards and collections at, **23.** 432

HW expects company to dine at, **30.** 173

HW expects to be robbed at, **20.** 188, **39.** 416

HW finds sketch of Charles VI's head at, in Vertue's MSS, **42.** 217

HW first dates a letter from, **37.** 287

HW flees from, for fear of gout, **35.** 524

HW foresees ruin of, **28.** 406

HW gives himself airs of an old baron in, **37.** 406

HW gives only a transient glance to, **20.** 163

HW goes to: **30.** 125, 172; to avoid celebrations of George III's recovery, **31.** 293; to avoid squibs and crackers, **33.** 95; to

collect his works for Hannah More, **31.** 229; to correct workmen's mistakes, **31.** 315; to cure cold, **38.** 522; to recuperate, **33.** 157, 159

HW hardly has a chance to go to, **21.** 101

HW has been five days at, **32.** 124

HW has completed: 'almost,' **20.** 110; 'these 3 years,' **24.** 100

HW has Hollar's prints of 'Dance of Death' at, **16.** 156–7

HW has 'set of company' at, **42.** 115

HW hopes, will not be carried to Paris, **35.** 235

HW hopes Lort will visit, **16.** 157

HW hopes to find the grass green at, **25.** 497

HW hunts at, for treillage paper, **35.** 483–4

HW hurries carver, painter, and paper-hanger at, **35.** 173

HW hurries to, from London, **32.** 84

HW improves, into 'charming villa,' **19.** 497

HW in September stows away small pictures and curios at, **41.** 441, **42.** 401

HW invites Berrys to, **11.** 61, 355, 360, 373

HW invites Bewley to, **42.** 457

HW invites Blandford, Lady, to, **31.** 406

HW invites Browne, Lady, to, **31.** 406, 407

HW invites Burneys to, **42.** 149–50, 331–2

HW invites Chute to, **35.** 85, 91

HW invites Coke, Lady Mary, to, **31.** 23

HW invites Conway and Cts of Ailesbury to, **39.** 128, 391–2

HW invites Fitzwilliams to, **42.** 53

HW invites Genlis, Comtesse de, to, **31.** 233

HW invites Harcourt to, **35.** 453, 454, 488

HW invites Jerseys to, **35.** 454, 471

HW invites Lady Harcourt to, **35.** 471, 488

HW invites Lodge and Nicol to, **42.** 315

HW invites Misses Clarke, Mary Hamilton and Mrs Vesey to, **42.** 99

HW invites Mrs Garrick and Mrs Montagu to breakfast at, **42.** 83

HW invites More, Hannah, to, **31.** 211

HW invites Pinkerton to, **16.** 252, 267, 273, 290–1, 293, 316, **42.** 110

HW invites Pitt, Anne, to, **31.** 41

HW invites Thomas Walpole jr to, **36.** 276–7

HW invites Unknown to, **42.** 474

HW invites Wyatt to stay at, **42.** 261

HW invites Zouch to, **16.** 40

HW jokes about, as being in a distant county, **30.** 117

HW jokes about transporting, to Paris, **31.** 93

HW keeps Christmas at, **20.** 16, 212, **21.** 558, **24.** 55

HW keeps no dress-coat nor sword at, **39.** 441

HW leases: **19.** 414; and later purchases it, **13.** 17; from Mrs Chenevix, **19.** 414n, **37.** 269–70

HW leaves, because of bad weather, **31.** 214

HW likely to be pleased with, because of alterations to be made, **30.** 114

HW lives at, in tranquillity and idleness, **25.** 608

[Strawberry Hill, *continued*]

HW makes alterations at, **19.** 486

HW may add gallery, tower, larger cloister and cabinet to, **21.** 238, 306

HW mentions, **31.** 109, 250

HW mentions house for Montagu near, **10.** 242

HW moves philosophy and tea-things from Windsor to, **37.** 270

HW must linger in London before going to, **22.** 416

HW must return to, from Paris, **39.** 50

HW never stays long at, in wet weather, **24.** 288

HW never wants amusement at, **24.** 283

HW not to leave, to Hertford, **42.** 424

HW offers bed and breakfast at, to one busy with 'presentations,' **42.** 364

HW offers to lend, to Beauchamp after Lady Beauchamp's death, **39.** 153–4

HW pays Philip at, **7.** 410

HW permits Montagu to take guests to, without asking leave, **10.** 205

HW plans chimney-piece at, imitating Edward the Confessor's tomb, **35.** 406

HW plans retirement to, **10.** 147

HW plans 'terreno' at, **20.** 131

HW prefers: to 'almost everything,' **32.** 238; to Anne Pitt's ball, **32.** 52; to lands on the Ohio, **21.** 306

HW reads little at, **12.** 58

HW refuses no visitors to, **42.** 284

HW refuses tickets for, to Lady Lansdowne and Marchioness Grey, **33.** 502

HW regrets that he cannot show, to Mann, **20.** 53, **24.** 103, **25.** 532

HW reproached by applicants because of his restrictions on tickets to, **42.** 144

HW returns to 'headquarters' at, **16.** 290, **32.** 239

HW's absorption in, **3.** 331, **4.** 267, 283, **5.** 268, **6.** 183

HW's additions to, will not be interrupted by the French, **21.** 310

HW said to have been rescued by man who asked for a perpetual ticket to, **34.** 201

HW says glories of, verge towards setting, **10.** 126

HW's bed at, to be heated, and shared with 'Tonton,' **39.** 420

HW's bedchamber at: built over Blue Room, **35.** 259; Patapan's portrait in, **18.** 220n; Waldegrave, Cts, occupies, **10.** 63

HW's books at: **16.** 25; inaccessible from London, **41.** 355; *see also below under* Library at

HW's breakfast at, for D. of Bedford's 'court,' **35.** 225

HW's Christmas at, **35.** 200, 201

HW's Christmas party at, **9.** 267, 332, 417, **38.** 276

HW's collection at, cannot be perpetuated, **42.** 424

HW's collection of prints after Guido Reni at, **30.** 217

HW's completion of, expected, **40.** 82

HW's contentment at, unusual in England, **24.** 100–1

HW's delight in, doubted by the Foxes, **30.** 111

HW's departure for, in *Public Advertiser*, **43.** 362

HW's descendants not to ruin, **9.** 349

HW's *Description* of: **28.** 101, **29.** 150; to aid housekeeper in exhibiting, to visitors, **42.** 39; would make visitors too inquisitive, **33.** 575; *see also Description of the Villa of Mr Horace Walpole*

HW's early additions to, **30.** 114

HW's Easter party at, **9.** 183, 186, (?) 277, 417, **10.** (?) 53, 121, **37.** 459,

HW sees balloon from, **25.** 579

HW's farming at, **9.** 134, 168; *see also above under* animals at, *and below under* hay at

HW's fêtes at: for French visitors, **4.** 234, 236–8, 246; for his nieces, **7.** 78, **35.** 494

HW's first alterations to, **20.** 64n

HW's first letter written from, **30.** 113–16

HW's fondness for, **28.** 232

HW's goldfish at, **40.** 85

HW's heirs will condemn, and pull it to pieces, **24.** 27

HW's hospitality at: **3.** 264–5; limited, **9.** 77

HW's housekeeper at, *see* Bransom, Ann; Young, Margaret

HW's joy at revisiting, after long absence, **23.** 554–5

HW's Lares at, **42.** 202

HW's legacy to Mrs Damer for keeping up, **15.** 336, **30.** 354

HW's letter-writing improves at, **20.** 53

HW's letter written in solitude and silence of, **25.** 226

HW's 'little cockboat shall waft' him to, **22.** 311

HW's MSS at, **36.** 310–16

HW's melancholy reflections on future of, **32.** 241

HW's notes on Shakespeare kept at, **42.** 137, 138

HW's occupations when alone at, **38.** 94

HW's 'out-of-town' house-parties at: for Christmas, **9.** 267, 332, 417, **38.** 276; for Easter, **9.** 183, 186, (?) 277, 417, **10.** (?) 53, 121

HW spends time at, to be near Galfridus Mann, **37.** 436

HW's planting at: **9.** 79, 103, 136, 168, 176–8, 197, 385, **10.** 148, 224, **37.** 301; 'vast,' **20.** 53–4; *see also above under* flowers at; garden at, *and below under* verdure of

HW's sketches for additions to, **37.** 402

HW's sketch of, given by Edwards to Baker, **42.** 71n

HW's tranquillity at, overbalances the detrimental air, **39.** 290

HW's travels between Berkeley Square and, **33.** 318

HW supervises construction at, **20.** 371, **37.** 352

HW's verses on Berrys' visit to, **12.** 94

HW's visit to, in May 1766, corrected, **43.** 280

HW takes furniture to, from Arlington St house, **10.** 43, 193

HW 'takes the veil' at, **41.** 5

HW thinks, less brilliant after Berkeley Square, **39.** 342

HW theatens to send, to Mann, **23.** 450

HW tires of neighbourhood of, **10.** 130–1

HW to bring Galfridus Mann to, **20.** 525–6

HW to bring print from, for Ducarel, **40.** 120–1

HW to come to, once a week, **39.** 342

HW to 'concentre my few remaining joys' at, on return to England, **22.** 359–60, 365

HW to enjoy roses but miss lilacs at, **42.** 245

HW to find data at, on Rousseau controversy, **41.** 26

HW to fold sheep on lawn at, **30.** 116

HW to fortify, against invasion, **35.** 255

HW to give dinner at, to Foxes and Kildares, **35.** 229

HW to go to: **11.** 222, 281, 289, 293, 307, 372–3, **12.** 41, 47, 189–90, 215n, **30.** 194, 195, 229, 233; if Parliament is dissolved, **25.** 461; unless Pitt arrives in London, **31.** 122

HW to invite Mrs Abington to, **42.** 450

HW to leave, **31.** 127, 140

HW to move to, **9.** 57

HW to offer, for royal nursery, **9.** 314

HW to read romances at, **24.** 117

HW to receive company at, **25.** 401

HW to regard Mme de Forcalquier as old window-pane of, **41.** 94

HW to return to, **31.** 209

HW to spend Christmas at, **10.** 298, **42.** 202

HW tormented by visitors to, **25.** 423

HW to 'trifle' at, **23.** 145

HW unable to make gardener produce flowers and fruit at, **35.** 479

HW unable to stand to show, **34.** 49

HW unwell at, **15.** 325

HW warms, for January visit, **39.** 317

HW wishes Dickensons would take house near, **31.** 400–1

HW wishes poplars for, **39.** 133, 134

HW wishes stained glass for, **20.** 111

HW wishes to retire to, **22.** 359–60, 365, **25.** 22, 33–4

HW wishes to stay at, **10.** 183, 228, 231, 290

HW would leave, if gout demanded, **31.** 75

HW would preserve Aymer de Valence's tomb at, if discarded from Westminster Abbey, **38.** 110

HW would sacrifice, to his country or principles, **40.** 336–7

HW would send, to Duchesse de Choiseul, **3.** 79

HW writes at: from bow-window, **20.** 46, 68; from China Closet, **20.** 382; from Gallery, **22.** 219; from Round Drawing-Room, **23.** 315

HW writes Wilkes's symbol on gates of, **10.** 274

Hall and Staircase added to: **20.** 348n; wallpaper for, **35.** 150

Hall at: **9.** 146n; Bentley's design for, **35.** 171; decked with saints and called Paraclete, **20.** 372, 381; Gothic lantern in, **35.** 233n; music in, **10.** 71; paper for, painted by Tudor under Bentley's direction, **9.** 150

Ham House contrasted with, **10.** 307

—— visible from, **34.** 61

Hamilton's gifts at, **35.** 431

——'s Gothic shields shame, **35.** 420

Hamilton, Mary, describes contents of, **31.** 206, 216

Hamiltons to visit, **35.** 411, 429

Hampton Court, if King's residence, would draw crowds to, **34.** 50

——'s proximity to: attracts visitors, **41.** 441; may make it a royal amusement park, **9.** 314

Hampton Court Park near, **24.** 315

Hanover troops may bring crowds to, **9.** 189

Harcourt calls, 'Caprice Hill,' **29.** 357

——'s gifts to, **35.** 477, 515–16

Hardinge asked by HW to bring his legal gown to, **35.** 602

—— dares not forsake Westminster Hall for, **35.** 578

—— hopes to visit HW at, **35.** 554, 555

——'s guests not admitted to, because unannounced, **35.** 634–5

—— to bring bride to, to sleep in same bed he occupied alone, **35.** 591, 598

—— to call on HW at, **35.** 567, 589

—— to spend day at, **35.** 623

—— tries to call on HW at, but does not want him to call back yet, **35.** 625

—— unable to visit, because of Parliament's dissolution, **35.** 612

—— visits, in HW's absence, **35.** 590, 591, 647

—— wants ticket to, for friends, **35.** 574

—— wants to call on HW at, **35.** 554, 555, 570, 574, 577–8

—— wants to dine and sleep at, **35.** 633

—— would gladly exchange Ragman's Castle for, **35.** 633

Hardinges to dine with HW at, **35.** 598, 628

Hawkins tries to call on HW at, **40.** 227

hay at, **9.** 372, **10.** 156, 217–18, 262, **39.** 416, 497

hay-making at, **39.** 276

height of, **11.** 1, **12.** 121

Henry VII's chimney-back at, **20.** 395, 396

Hertford hopes HW will soon leave Paris for, **39.** 25

—— may visit, **38.** 177

Hertfords and Lady Mary Coke to dine at, **38.** 86

[Strawberry Hill, *continued*]

Hervey, Bns, discouraged from visiting, 31. 13

Holbein Chamber at: 1. 191n, 2. 117, 200n, 249n, 274n, 9. 124n, 10. 64n, 11. 370n, 15. 190n, 16. 265n; Abp of Canterbury enthroned in purple chair in, 32. 156; chimney-piece of, 1. 191n, 2. 150, 254; complete, 9. 248, 35. 296; ebony furniture of, 1. 94n; HW occupies, 10. 63–4; HW oversees workmen from, 10. 64; HW's construction of, 38. 15–16; HW serves tea in, 10. 168; HW wants Strafford to approve of, 35. 298; housekeeper's room over, 33. 476; Montagu offers sofa for, 9. 247–8; portrait of Ds of Suffolk in, 17. 373n; print of, 2. 254; (?) screen for, 40. 150; windows of, undamaged by explosion, 39. 152

horses at, 20. 380

hothouse being built at, 32. 216

Houghton inspires HW to beautify, 23. 499

——'s decay makes HW want to sell, 28. 103

housekeeper at, might exhibit Bentley's pictures, 35. 243

ice house at: 23. 128n; being built, 12. 163, 176

Ireland requests ticket for, 42. 175

island opposite, 34. 207

Jerningham to spend night at, with Conway and Lady Ailesbury, 42. 252

—— to visit, 42. 109, 303

jonquils at, 1. 311n

kings and queens in neighbourhood of, 10. 127

King's College Chapel more beautiful than, 28. 306

Kingston Fencibles salute, 12. 144

kitchen at: 10. 106; moved, 19. 486n

labour troubles at, 1. 11n, 14, 21, 9. 398, 22. 49, 35. 315

landscape effects at, 20. 53–4, 380, 386, 23. 315, 555, 25. 532

lane between Thames and, flooded, 24. 47

Languedoc resembled by, 31. 36

lantern at: 40. 150; designed by Bentley, 35. 644

large enough to hold all the people HW wishes to see, 30. 114

lawn at: a lake, 35. 228; HW sits on, 12. 202; suffers from drought, 10. 36–7

leads of, 35. 373

lease of, 19. 486

Lee Priory compared to, 12. 111, 134, 137

—— 'fathered' by, 11. 98

Library at: 2. 249n, 334n, 15. 23n, 191n, 215n; Bentley's design for ceiling of, 35. 643–4; Bentley's designs inferior to Chute's for book-cases in, 35. 157; best room in the house, 16. 206; book-cases in, 43. 292; ceiling of, to be designed by Bentley, 35. 164, 171; ceiling of, to be painted by Clermont, 35. 79–80, 171; chimney-piece of, to frame 'Marriage of Henry VI,' 35. 158,

164; Chute and HW decide on plan for, 35. 164; Chute searches, 20. 64; delightful, 35. 184–5; finished except for painting, 35. 185; grows finished, 35. 174; HW adds, 20. 380n; HW and dogs retire to, 22. 257; HW in, does not hear sounds of robbery, 33. 476; HW lives chiefly in, 16. 206; HW places books in, 35. 200; HW's grandfather's account-book kept in glass closet in, 17. 505n; HW shows, to guests after dinner, 31. 206; HW to place books in, 20. 456; Müntz might paint, 35. 186; passage windows to, broken by explosion, 39. 152; print of, 2. 254; to be built, 20. 382; Williams, Sir C. H., intends to reproduce, at Coldbrook, 30. 147; Wollstonecraft, Mary, works by, excommunicated from, 31. 373

lighting at, 32. 208

lilacs at: 1. 109, 113, 2. 318, 38. 554, 39. 62, 368; scent even SH's interior, 39. 411

lilac-tide at, HW anxious to return for, 30. 218

Little Parlour at: 9. 146n, 11. 112n; added, 20. 348n; 'Death of Cardinal Wolsey' hung in, 11. 113; flooded, 35. 228; location of, 33. 273; 'monuments of female genius' in, 11. 248; re-papered, 11. 111–12, 121, 125, 248; stained glass in, 30. 136n; visitors may overflow, 12. 27

loo played at, 31. 179

Lort declines HW's invitation to, 16. 182

—— hopes to see HW at, 16. 172, 188

Louis dies at, 10. 241

lower pond at, 9. 197

luxuriant leafage from wet summer at, 33. 355

Lysons guesses, will be left to Ds of Gloucester for her life, 15. 335

Lyttelton, Bns, considers, cold, 39. 167

made of paper, 33. 43, 38. 110

Mann advises HW not to visit, in winter, 22. 456–7, 24. 285

—— and Hamilton discuss, 22. 260

Mann congratulates HW on safe return to, 20. 42, 22. 562

—— envies, 20. 146, 443

—— expects HW to be at, 22. 411–12

—— fears that charms of, will keep HW from Florence, 20. 349

—— longs to see, 20. 377

—— must call 'Strawberry Hill' and not 'Twickenham,' 19. 486

—— sends ivy seeds to HW for, 21. 457–8

——'s gifts convert, into a *Galleria Reale*, 25. 531

——'s letters at, 23. 73, 25. 185

——'s presents in every chamber of, 24. 15

——'s presents to be entered in catalogue of, 25. 90, 531

—— unable to collect ornaments for, except altar, 20. 365

—— urges HW not to retire to, 25. 33–4

—— will prefer Parliamentary news to that of, 20. 30

—— will share his melancholy with HW if he visits, **21**. 512

Mann, Horace II, and Lady Lucy may dine at, **23**. 408

Mann, Horace II, has presumably sent HW's letters to, **25**. 417

—— may call on HW at, **25**. 659

Marble Hill's poetic rivalry with, **40**. 366–7

Marlboroughs breakfast at, **39**. 418

Mason to visit, **28**. 272, 273, **29**. 93, 260, 274, **35**. 520

meadow, meadows at: **10**. 93, **25**. 497; flooded, **35**. 264, **39**. 187

medals at, **15**. 278, 285

melancholy completely absent from, **20**. 64

Milbourn, John, draws at, **11**. 113–14

Miller's castle at Hagley worthy of, **35**. 148

miniature at, of Comtesse de Grignan, **10**. 12

Montagu calls: cold, **10**. 146; unwholesome, **10**. 110; 'Tusculum,' **10**. 122

——'s portraits to be brought to, from Hampton Court, **10**. 67

—— thanks HW for thinking of house near, **10**. 242

Montagu, Charles and George, to visit, **35**. 177

More, Hannah, calls 'Castle of Otranto,' **31**. 116

—— inquires whether Mary Hamilton has visited, **31**. 216

—— looks forward to visiting, **31**. 295

Morice lives near, **25**. 159

Müntz's services to, **35**. 91

—— stays at, **21**. 239

——'s views of, **30**. 370, **35**. 232

—— to be sent to, **35**. 89, 91

—— to leave, at once, **40**. 169–70

—— to enlighten HW at, on military events, **35**. 103

name of, chosen, **19**. 486, 490

nearness of, to London, probably helps HW's delight in, **30**. 111

Necker describes, **8**. 213

neighbourhood of, **25**. 532

neighbours of, gossip about admittance of HW's visitors, **42**. 143–4

never looked so Gothic, **32**. 75

Newcastle, D. of, to call on HW at, **40**. 361–4

Nicol's friends to visit, **42**. 401

nightingales at, **9**. 364, **10**. 29, 34, 188, 279, 281, **39**. 3

Nivernais's paintings of four seasons deemed unworthy of, **10**. 57

Noble's book kept at, **42**. 128, 140

North pleased with, **10**. 319

not shown after October, **33**. 501

not to be a 'cheesecake house,' **10**. 33

nursery at, **9**. 176–8

Offices at: **1**. 178n, 339n, **15**. 215n, **28**. 93n; being built, **11**. 74, 84; building of, postponed, **2**. 75, 173, 246; built, **1**. 339n; built by Wyatt, **28**. 31n; construction of, delays HW's settling at SH, **31**. 315; Essex designs,

1. 178n, 338, **2**. 13, 75, 150; prints from Berkeley Sq. house may be put in wardrobe in, **30**. 374; Wyatt to design, **42**. 261

old hall at, might become columbarium, **36**. 39

old kitchen at, made into China Room, **35**. 259

'old, old, very old castle,' **28**. 28

Onslow to visit, **40**. 98

opening of, as 'cake-house,' **39**. 381

orange trees at, **10**. 224

Oratory at: floor-plan of, **38**. 107; HW begins, **9**. 379

Ossory, Lady, has not visited, for 3 years, **34**. 5

—— to visit, **32**. 113

owls, three, at, **1**. 321n

ownership of, disputed, **9**. 83

paint, 'commodity' of, **9**. 170

painted glass at, *see below under* stained and painted glass at

painting of marriage of Henry VII desired for, **20**. 390

'paper,' **33**. 43, **38**. 110

Paris contrasted with purity of, **31**. 45

Park Place compared with, **37**. 366, 379

Parliamentary bill for purchase of, **9**. 82–3

parlour at, **20**. 380, **31**. 406; *see also* Great Parlour; Little Parlour

Pars does views of, **24**. 135, 144, **26**. 48, **35**. 424

parsonage resembled by, before HW bought it, **35**. 186

peach-coloured hangings unsuitable to solemnity of, **21**. 471

pedigree explaining portraits and arms at, **2**. 47, 48

Penny, Mrs, writes poem on, **16**. 182

pictures and curiosities of, packed away in winter, **2**. 40–1

pictures at, please Lady Mary Coke, **31**. 179

pictures, drawings, and busts by Lady Diana Beauclerk at, **31**. 206, 216, 297

Pinkerton to receive order for visitors' admission to, **42**. 197

—— to visit, when Conway and family have left, **42**. 111–12

Pitt, Anne, brings French horns to, **35**. 225

—— has unlimited power of inviting to, **31**. 111

Pitt, Thomas, 'surveyor' of 'Board of Works' at, **40**. 273

plan of, **1**. 178n

plantations at, HW busy with, **30**. 117

politics keep HW from lilacs at, **38**. 554

portrait at, of Cts of Exeter, **1**. 149–50

post leaves, early, **16**. 277

post to, from London, **40**. 134

powder-mills' explosion damages, **39**. 152

Po-Yang, pond at: **9**. 134; Catherine whispers to reeds in, **35**. 227; drained, **39**. 403, 404; fish in, poisoned by salt water, **35**. 206; goldfish from, given to Perron, **35**. 225–6; named by HW, **35**. 158n; popular, **35**. 225;

[Strawberry Hill, *continued*]

robbed of goldfish by herons, **35.** 158–9, 184

press at, *see* Strawberry Hill Press

printing-house at: **40.** 255; begun, **35.** 296; damaged by storm, **12.** 175; finished, **35.** 298; *see also* Strawberry Hill Press

prints convey solemnity of, without the gaiety of the scenery, **25.** 532

prints in trunk at Berkeley Sq. to be sent to, **30.** 373–4

prints of: for *Description of SH*, **1.** 379, **2.** 249, 254, 274, **43.** 72; given to Cole, **1.** 52–3, 61, **2.** 47, 48, 251, 253–4, 255; subjects of, **2.** 251, 253–4

prints of marble eagle at, best memorandum of HW and SH, **31.** 263

Prior's Garden at: **2.** 249n; print of, **2.** 254

Privy Garden at, begun, **9.** 385

proposed highway near, **3.** 313–14, 316

prospective visitors to: Blandford, Lady, **31.** 406; Browne, Lady, **31.** 406, 407; Chabrillan, **30.** 244; Coke, Lady Mary, **31.** 23; Compton, Lady Margaret, **31.** 406; Conolly, Lady Anne, **31.** 406; Coyer, **30.** 179; Craufurd, **30.** 259; Du Châtelet, **30.** 244; Fagnani, Maria, **30.** 282; Genlis, Comtesse de, **31.** 233; Howard, Lady Caroline, **30.** 281; Keppel, Lady Caroline and Lady Elizabeth, **30.** 136; Lauraguais, **30.** 179; LeNeve, Isabella, **30.** 133; Malpas, Vcts, **31.** 406; March, E. of, **30.** 166; More, Hannah, **31.** 211; Ossory, Lord and Lady, and their 'court', **30.** 259; Pitt, Anne, **31.** 41; Ravensworth, Lady, **33.** 435; Rena, Contessa, **30.** 166; Sarsfield, **30.** 179; Scott, Lady Jane, **31.** 406; Selwyn, **30.** (?) 118, 150, 166, 179, 244, 259, 282; Williams, Sir C. H., **30.** 114, 118; Williams, G. J., **30.** 166

purchase of land for, **32.** 271

purchase from Mrs Kennon's sale to be deposited at, **37.** 440

quiet at: HW carried by, through attack of gout, **39.** 198; HW's best and sole medicine, **31.** 41

Raftor, James, lives with HW at, **31.** 238n

'Raspberry Plain' to be counterpart of, **36.** 201

Red Bedchamber at: **9.** 146n, **10.** 57n, **20.** 381, **43.** 271; added, **20.** 348n; Bentley's and Müntz's 'Elizabeth Castle' in, **35.** 207n, 243n; chintz bed in, **39.** 285; HW able to walk from, to Blue Room, **11.** 177, **34.** 105; HW, in winter, shifts from Blue Room to, **39.** 317; HW lives in, during fit of gout, **11.** 72, **33.** 81; rained into, **33.** 102; Sophia Dorothea's copied portrait in, **42.** 180n; to be occupied by Mary Berry, **11.** 72

Refectory at, *see above under* Great Parlour of

Richmond Park's disputes near, **20.** 322–3

road to Ragman's Castle from, unsafe, **35.** 633

Robinson, John, may call at, **41.** 326

Robinson, William, original designer of, **19.** 487n, **20.** 375n

Roehampton near, **10.** 187

roof of, leaks into Blue Bedchamber and Little Parlour, **35.** 228

rooms added to, to make it habitable, **30.** 114

roses and orange-flowers at, **39.** 176

roses at: **39.** 3, 497; on *treillage*, **39.** 316

Round Chamber at: Archduke and Archduchess entertained in, **33.** 529; building of, **4.** 104, 105, 251; vase in, broken by visitor, **33.** 522

Round Drawing-Room at: **1.** 151n, **2.** 274n, **4.** 251n, 260n, **7.** 181n, 287, **28.** 102n; building of, **1.** 151; chimney-piece and hearth in, by Richter, **35.** 407n; chimney-piece of, **2.** 370; 'delineator' transfigures, **28.** 329; Du Deffand, Mme, mentions, **4.** 248; fire-screen in, **34.** 15n; furnishings of, **4.** 249, 260n; HW sends books to Adam for ceiling and fireplace designs of, **41.** 39; hung with crimson Norwich damask, **21.** 458n; pane of glass in, demolished by explosion, **39.** 152; Steenwyck's church interior hung in, **40.** 369n; Van Dyck painting over mantel of, **21.** 420n; York, Ds of, drinks chocolate in, **12.** 11

Round Tower ('Great Tower') at: **1.** 151, **15.** 215n, **40.** 255; Bianca Cappello's portrait to hang in, **21.** 420; construction of, advanced, **10.** 304; cost of, **21.** 514; does not fall down, **35.** 303; erected, **9.** 292; finished, **23.** 311; finished and whitened, **35.** 173; finishing, **23.** 128; French prisoners might be confined in, **21.** 310; HW in field near, **39.** 423–4; HW wants stained glass for, **16.** 40–1; HW writes in bow-window of, near Bianca Cappello's portrait, **23.** 315, **35.** 329; Montagu to deposit Comtesse de Gramont's miniature in, **10.** 15; owl hooted in, **32.** 193; portraits to be placed in, **10.** 54; prints from Berkeley Sq. house may be placed in library in, **30.** 373–4; storm threatens, **12.** 143; to be added, **21.** 238; to be furnished when Gallery is complete, **21.** 497; to replace foundations of old printing-house, **35.** 296, 298; Vasari's portrait of Bianca Cappello hung in, **20.** 398n

rules for visiting: **12.** 219–20, **31.** 236, **35.** 634–5, **43.** 162–5; HW to suspend, for Malone, **42.** 96, 143, 144; HW to suspend, for Mrs Abington, **41.** 413; printed, **33.** 435–6; strictly enforced, **29.** 270, **42.** 384

Saint-Cyr admittance order from Bp of Chartres to be preserved at, **10.** 292

screen for (?) Holbein Chamber at, **40.** 150

screens at, **40.** 255

seeds from, sent to Bentley, **35.** 185

Selwyn disappoints party at, **30.** 151

servants at, *see under* Servant

servants' hall at, **38.** 175

settees at, **20.** 382, 387

(?) Sévigné, Mme de, patron saint of, **10.** 187

Seward wants to visit, **16.** 189

sheep at: **4.** 394, **19.** 414, **20.** 380, **25.** 532; killed by dogs, **10.** 94

shell bench at, **9.** 237, **10.** 93, (?) 168

showing of, a grievance, **11.** 57

shown to visitors from May 1 to Oct. 1 only, **42.** 337

shrine in chapel at, *see above under* chapel in garden at

shrubs at, delight HW, **23.** 555

shrubs from, for Cole's garden at Milton, **1.** 194, 195

Shuvalov likes, as belonging to prime minister's son, **10.** 157

Simco to have ticket to, **42.** 258

simplicity of: **20.** 382; disappearing, **10.** 84–5

size of, due to increase in HW's collection, **10.** 85

skylight at: **35.** 228; rain beats upon, **32.** 315

smallness of, **30.** 114

small pictures and curiosities at, always locked up for winter, **41.** 441, **42.** 401

snow prevents Montagu and Bp Trevor from visiting, **10.** 210

softens the decays of age, **24.** 103

'solitude,' **31.** 126

'source of elegancy and erudition,' **21.** 253

spring bloom at, **2.** 318

stained (and painted) glass at: **1.** 21n, 145, 201n, **4.** 439, **9.** 102, 146–7, 150–1, 385, **10.** 61, 64, 72, 120, 274, 307, **11.** 82, **31.** 216, **35.** 494; broken by explosion, **1.** 254, **5.** 172, 184n, 224, 235, **23.** 365, **32.** 75, **39.** 152–3; from Bexhill, **1.** 244, 256, **2.** 370; HW collects, **20.** 111, 119, 371–2; 'long saints' in, **20.** 372; Mann does not know where to find, **20.** 119; painted by Pearson, **1.** 201n; painted by Price, **1.** 201n; Palmer glazier for, **20.** 396; pane of, from Lady Brown, **40.** 89; red ivy would look well through, **21.** 457–8; sun makes, 'gorgeous,' **25.** 532

staircase at: **9.** 146n, **20.** 361, 368, 381, **35.** 644; Bentley designs, **35.** 644; Bentley's Gothic lantern in, **9.** 150; Cumberland, D. of, likes, **35.** 161; damaged by water, **33.** 117; Medusa's shield on, **33.** 518; paper for, painted by Tudor under Bentley's care, **9.** 150; repainted, **12.** 243n

Stanhope to escort Vcts Townshend to, **40.** 100

Star Chamber at: **1.** 90n, **4.** 333n, **9.** 146n, **10.** 64n, **12.** 27, 111n, **15.** 17nn; damaged by water, **33.** 117; mahogany cabinet in, **33.** 403n; obscured to raise Gallery, **33.** 403; 'pink room,' lock in, **40.** 150; stairs to, **33.** 435; wallpaper in, pink, **40.** 150n

State Bedchamber at, *see above under* Great North Bedchamber at

statue of Cupid at, **2.** 373

Stevenson, John Hall, should avoid mentioning, in his verses, **40.** 208

stone-cutter's shop resembled by, **35.** 231

Strafford to visit, **35.** 313

Suffolk, Cts of, HW's only sensible friend at, **22.** 544

Sunday alone at, HW's chief entertainment, **32.** 279

supper-parlour of, **35.** 173

swans at, **25.** 532

table at, well served, **31.** 206

taste of, **4.** 41, **8.** 213

terrace at: **10.** 93, 127, **20.** 16; print of view from, **2.** 251

tickets of admission to: **10.** 98, 109, 151, 158, 215, **11.** 57, 74, **12.** 27, 167, 221–52, **15.** 199, 267, **29.** 268, 270, **31.** 236, **35.** 574, 635, **40.** 345, **41.** 441, **42.** 96, 144, 384, **43.** 162–5; addressed to Ann Bransom, **43.** 164, 165; addressed to Margaret Young, **43.** 163; discussed, **33.** 51, 122; requested, **33.** 196; sent to Fitzwilliam, **42.** 195–6; wanted by Ireland, **42.** 175

tiles for, from Gloucester Cathedral, **35.** 151–2

too much written about, **15.** 272

'too slightly built for duration,' **15.** 228

too unfinished to entertain San Severino, **20.** 372

towers at: arise, **21.** 506; 'Lilliputian,' **35.** 390; to be added, **21.** 238

trees at: 'blue' and 'green,' **20.** 54; felled by storm, **12.** 175; HW delights in, **23.** 555; may be injured by wind, **20.** 24; orange trees, **21.** 361, 369; trimming of, **23.** 315, **24.** 48

treillage and fountains to be introduced at, **31.** 46

treillage paper may be at, **35.** 483

Tribune at, *see above under* Cabinet at

turf at, affected by drought, **31.** 36

turkeys at, **4.** 394

valuables at, kept in private recess, **15.** 284

verdure at, **10.** 93, 127, 130, 132, 156, 168, 224, 281, 298

verses on, by Y, **2.** 78, 79n

view from: **10.** 168, **19.** 496, **20.** 16, 380, 382, **23.** 315, 491, **25.** 532; blocked, **11.** 287; delightful, **30.** 114

views of, at the Vyne, **35.** 640

vignette of, on title-page of *Bishop Bonner's Ghost*, **31.** 316

visitors overrun, **35.** 531

visitors' rules at, *see above under* rules for visiting

visitors to (general references): **4.** 439; 'almost drive me, out of my house,' **32.** 295; anecdote about, **11.** 25; annoyance from, **1.** 166, 373–74, **2.** 275; between 70 and 80 groups, **34.** 62; break off eagle's bill, **11.** 293; detain HW in his bedchamber, **31.** 202; Du Deffand, Mme, says HW is pleased by, **4.** 249, 260; Frenchmen, who whisk through it, **25.** 423; French people, who consider it one of the sights, **25.** 427; HW

[Strawberry Hill, *continued*]

detained by, in his bedchamber, **31**. 202; HW tormented by, **39**. 106, 440; limited to 4 on same day, **42**. 96; lists of, in 1784, **12**. 221–2; lists of, in 1785, **12**. 223–4; lists of, in 1786, **12**. 224–7; lists of, in 1787, **12**. 227–9; lists of, in 1788, **12**. 229–32; lists of, in 1789, **12**. 232–5; lists of, in 1790, **12**. 235–7; lists of, in 1791, **12**. 237–40; lists of, in 1792, **12**. 240–2; lists of, in 1793, **12**. 243–5; lists of, in 1794, **12**. 245–7; lists of, in 1795, **12**. 247–9; lists of, in 1796, **12**. 250–2; Malone applies for tickets for, **42**. 96; most in May, **2**. 75; numerous, **35**. 396–7; 'quality' of Hampton and Richmond, **31**. 392; three groups on same day, **11**. 317; troublesome, **32**. 295, **33**. 435, 575; usually limited to four at a time, **1**. 315

visitors to (specific): actress, **10**. 107; Abington, Mrs, **41**. 413; Addington, Mr, **12**. 241; Adhémar, Comte d', **12**. 221, **33**. 403; Agar, Diana, **12**. 158, 249; Agar family, **15**. 327; Ageno, Francesco Maria, **12**. 222; Agincourt, **39**. 291, **42**. 102; Aikin, A. L. (Mrs Barbauld), **32**. 197; Ailesbury, Cts of, **9**. 237, **10**. 99, 100, 133, 260, **31**. 142, **33**. 104, 142, 281, **34**. 57, **35**. 217, 275–6, 283, **37**. 468, 491, 492, **38**. 175, 207, **39**. 328, **42**. 111–12; Albani, Principe and Principessa, **33**. 530; Albany, Cts of, **12**. 238; Albemarle, Cts of, **12**. 226; Alexander, Mr, of Teddington, **12**. 233; Alexander, Mrs, **12**. 230; Alfieri, Vittorio, **12**. 238; Althorps, **39**. 390; Alvensleben, Philipp Karl, **12**. 233; Amelia, Ps, **10**. 82, 84, **12**. 225, **31**. 147, **35**. 227; Amelia, Ps, servants of, **42**. 96; Ancram, Cts of, **39**. 104; Anderson, Francis Evelyn, **12**. 244; Andrews, Miles Peter, **12**. 231; Anstruther, Sir John, **12**. 234; Araujo de Acebedo, Antonio de, **12**. 233; Archdeacon (Archdeakon), Mr, **12**. 245, 250; Arden, Bn and Bns, **12**. 251; artists, **12**. 232, 234; Ashburnham, **32**. 197, **38**. 276; Ashburton, Bns, **12**. 232; Ashmore, Mrs, **12**. 237; Ashwell, Mr, **12**. 242; Astle (son), **12**. 231; Astle, Thomas, **12**. 225, 231, **41**. 399; Astley, Lady, **12**. 231, 237; Astley, Miss, **12**. 227; Athawes, Mrs, **12**. 248; Atherton, Mr, **12**. 223, 245; Atterbury, Mr, of Teddington, **12**. 239; Attonville, M. d', **12**. 237; Auriel, Mrs, **12**. 239; Austria, Archduke and Archduchess of, **12**. 227, **33**. 529–31; Aylmer, Mr, of Whitton, **12**. 227, 229, 234; Aylmer, Mrs, of Whitton, **12**. 227, 229, 246; Ayton, William, **15**. 338, **42**. 175n; Baker, Mr, **12**. 249; Banks, Lady, **12**. 243; Banks, Sir Joseph, **12**. 226, 243; Banks, Thomas, **12**. 236; Bannerman, Mr, **12**. 225, 241; Baring, Mr, **12**. 235; Barker, Lady, **12**. 248; Barker, Mr, **32**. 208; Barker, Mrs, of Richmond, **12**. 232, 250; Barnard, Mr, **12**. 227; Barnard, Mrs Anna, **12**. 227; (?) Barnardiston, Mr, **12**. 251; Barrett (Barret) Thomas, **12**. 203; Barrington, Hon, Shute, **12**. 240; Barrow, Joseph Charles, **12**. 222, 234; Barrymore, Cts of, **12**. 228; Barthélemy, François, **12**. 228; Bartolozzi, Francesco, **12**. 252; Basset, Sir Francis, **12**. 222, 225, 229; Bateman, **10**. 306; Bath, E. of, **35**. 236; Bathurst, E. and Cts, **12**. 221; Batt, John Thomas, **12**. 232n; Baynes, Mrs, of Kingston, **12**. 248; Beauchamp, Lady, **12**. 232; Beauchamp, Lord, **12**. 223; Beauchamp, Mr, **12**. 222, 226, 228, **39**. 453; Beauclerk, Lady Diana, **6**. 460, **15**. 320, **32**. 242, 365, **39**. 276; Beauclerk, Topham, **15**. 320, **32**. 242, 365, **39**. 276; Beaufort, Dr, **12**. 236; Beaufort, Ds of, **33**. 278–9; Beaulieu, Cts (Manchester, Ds of), **10**. 100, 106, 107; Beaulieu, E. of, **10**. 106, 107; Beaumont, Lady, **12**. 233; Beaumont, Sir George, **12**. 227, 233, 243; Beaune, Vicomte de, **12**. 240; Beauvert, Comte de, **12**. 249; Beaver, Mrs, **12**. 239; Beazley, Mr, **12**. 231; Beckford, Mrs, **12**. 229; Bedford, D. and Ds of, **35**. 225; Bedford, Charles, and 2 sons, **12**. 229, **43**. 163; Béhic, Monsieur, **12**. 238; Bekel, Monsieur de, **12**. 222; Bell, Mrs, **12**. 246; Bellamy, Mr, **12**. 224; Bellew (? Pellew), C., **12**. 228; Bellingham, Mrs William (later Lady), **12**. 223; Beloe, Rev. William, **12**. 242; Beloe family, **12**. 243; Bentley, Misses, **12**. 248; Bentley, Richard, **9**. 105, 134, 216; (?) Beresford, **33**. 60, 117; Berry, Robert, **12**. 230, **15**. 318; Berry sisters, **12**. 230, 237, **15**. 318; Bertrand, Mr, **9**. 83; Berwick, D. and Ds of, **10**. 129; Berwick, Lord, **12**. 248; Berwick, Mrs Joseph, of Worcester, **12**. 239, **43**. 162; Billingsley (Billingsly), Mr, **12**. 224, 225; Bindley, **41**. 440–1; Binning, Lady, **12**. 243, 245; Birch, Mrs, **12**. 245; Birch, William, **12**. 244; Biron, Duchesse de, **12**. 235; bishops, **10**. 107; Blackstone, Mr, **12**. 229; Blagden, Sir Charles, **12**. 198, 246; Blair, Colonel, **12**. 231; Blair, Mr, **12**. 235; Blake, Captain, **12**. 250; Blake, Mrs, **12**. 221; Blake, John, **12**. 237, 240; Blake, Robert, **12**. 184; Blakeney, John, of Twickenham, **12**. 224; Blakiston, Mr, **12**. 228; Blanchard, Mrs, **12**. 239; Bland, Miss, **9**. 215–16; Blandford, Lady, **31**. 147; Blome, Otto, **12**. 229; Blomfield, Captain, **12**. 221; Blot, Mme de, **39**. 292; Blount, Colonel, **12**. 246; Blowes, Mrs, **12**. 239; Boisgelin, Monsieur de, **12**. 237; Boissier, Monsieur **12**. 231; Bolingbroke, **39**. 104; Bonnel, Mr and Mrs, of Whitton, **12**. 229; Boone, Mrs, **12**. 234; Boscawen, Mrs Edward, **12**. 228, 231, **31**. 342; Boscawen, Hon. George, **9**. 161; Boscawen, Mrs George, **9**. 161; Boswell, James, **12**. 223n; Boswell, Veronica, **43**. 161–2; Boteler, Mrs, **12**. 242; Boufflers, Comtesse de, **10**. 70–1, **12**. 236, 237, **22**. 270, **39**. 473; Boufflers, Amélie de, **12**. 236, 237, **39**. 473; Bourges, Archbishop of, **12**. 245; Bouteiller, Monsieur, **12**. 238; Bouverie, Mrs, **32**. 244, **39**. 74–5; Bowater, Edward, **12**. 221; Bowater, Mrs Edward, **12**. 230; Bowdler, Mr ? John, and family, **12**. 237; Boyd, Sir Robert, **12**. 230; Boydell, John and Josiah, **12**. 236; **42**. 283; Boyle, Charlotte, **31**. 206; Bradshaw, Mrs, **12**. 226; Bramstone, Mr and Mrs, **12**. 229; Brand, John, **12**. 226, **43**. 160; Brand, Thomas, **37**. 471; Bray, Mrs, **12**. 224; Brazier, Mr, **12**. 222; Bright, Mr, **12**. 232; Brigstockes, Mrs, **12**. 237; Briscoe, John, **12**. 226, 239, 240; Briscoe, Mrs John, **12**. 242; Bristol, E. of, **31**. 147; Bristol, Lady, **12**. 246; Bristow, **35**. 236; Brook, Mrs, **12**. 244; Brougham, Rev. Mr, **12**. 245; Broughton, Lady, **12**. 223; Brown, Mr, **12**. 238; Browne, Lady, **12**. 224, **31**. 147, 297; Browne, Mr and Mrs Isaac Hawkins, **12**. 235; (?) Bruce, (?) Mrs, **12**. 229; Brusby, Mr, **12**. 226; Bruyn, Mr de, **12**. 242; Brydges, Sir Samuel Egerton, **12**. 240; Brydson, Mr, **12**. 251; Buccleuch's servants, **12**. 246; Buckingham, M. and Marchioness of, **12**. 240; Buckinghamshire, Cts of, **10**. 93; Buckinghamshire, E. of, **9**. 237, **12**. 223; Buckland, Mr, **12**. 236; Bucknall, Mr, **12**. 222; Budé, Jacob de, **12**. 11; Budgen, John Smith, **12**. 231, 236; Bukaty, Franciszik, **12**. 231; Bulkeley, Vcts, **12**. 235; Buller, Mrs James, **12**. 227, 228, 241; Bunbury, Mr Henry William, **12**. 234; Burgoyne, Miss, **12**. 236; Burke, Richard, **31**. 206; Burney, Charles, **12**. 203, **33**. 498; Burney, Frances, **12**. 222, **33**. 498, **42**. 293; Burrell, Lady, **12**. 236; Burrell, Sir Charles Merrik, **12**. 236; Burrell, Sir William, **12**. 236; Burroughs, Captain, **12**. 246; Burt, Rev. Robert, **12**. 233, 239; Burt, Mrs Robert, **12**. 251; Burton, Mr, **12**. 222, 252; Burton, Mrs, of Richmond, **12**. 247; Bury, Mr, **12**. 250; Bush, Mr, **12**. 141, 239, 249; Bute, Cts of, **12**. 241; Byng, Miss, **12**. 246; Byres, James, **12**. 237; Cadell, Thomas, **12**. 225, (?) 248; Cadogan, Lady, **33**. 565; Cadogan, Lord, **12**. 223, **33**. 565; Caldecott, Mr, **12**. 221; Cambis, Mme de, **12**. 5, 203, 235, **35**. 532, **39**. 403–4; Cambridge, George, **12**. 20; Cambridge, R. O., **42**. 297; Campbell, Miss, **12**. 232; Campbell, Mrs, **12**. 232; Campbell, Mrs, of Whitton, **12**. 246; Campbell, Caroline, **39**. 295; Campbell, Lady Frederick, **12**. 238, **31**. 142; Campbell, Lord Frederick, **12**. 238, **31**. 142, **35**. 283; Campbell, Lady William, **33**. 104, **39**. 295; Campbell, Lord William, **39**. 295; Caraman, Comte de, **10**. 156, **12**. 229, **31**. 36; (?) Carlisle, **4**. 249; Carpue, Mr, **12**. 246, 251, 252; Carr, Lady, **12**. 222; Carr, Mrs, **12**. 235; Carr, Rev. Colston, **12**. 225, 232, 242; Carr, Henry, **12**. 251; (?) Carrion, **10**. 127; Carter, Elizabeth, **12**. 229; Carysfort, Bns and Cts of, **12**. 229; Castille, **6**. 444; Cave, Mr, **12**. 245; Cavendish, Lord John, **12**. 246;

Cay, Mr, **12**. 228; Cayley, Sir George, **12**. 244; Cecil, Lady Anne, **12**. 230; Chabrillan, Comte de, **3**. 306; Chadwick, Mr, **12**. 227, 230; Chalais, Prince de, **12**. 244; Chamberlaine, Mrs, **12**. 237; Chamberlaine, John, **12**. 241, 243; Chamberlayne, Mr, **12**. 221; Champignelles, Madame de, **12**. 250; Chandler, Mrs, **12**. 224, 226, 230, 234; Chapeau, Mrs Edward Robert Nassau, **12**. 105; Chapman, Mrs, **12**. 236; Charlotte, Q., **12**. 144, 248, **22**. 426, **39**. 510–12; Chartres, Duc de, **33**. 402, **35**. 531; Chastellux, **23**. 468; Châteaugiron, Monsieur de, **12**. 233; Cheap, Mr, **12**. 231; Cheap, Mrs, **12**. 233; Chenevix, Mrs, **9**. 83; Chester, Mrs, **12**. 251; Chesterfield, **43**. 338; Chewton, Lord, **33**. 540; Chichester, Mrs, **12**. 238; Child, Mrs Robert, **12**. 222; Chimay, Princesse de, **12**. 242; Choiseul, Mme de, **12**. 244; Cholmeley, Francis, **12**. 247; Cholmondeley, George James (b. 1749), **12**. 115; Cholmondeley, George James (b. 1752), **32**. 388; Cholmondeley, Hon. Mrs Robert, **12**. 238; Cholmondeley, Rev. Hon. Robert, **12**. 230; Churchill, Charles, **12**. 29, 38, 104, 105, **16**. 302, **32**. 124, 357, **33**. 355, 565, **34**. 57, **35**. 217, 225, **37**. 289, **38**. 27, **39**. 276; Churchill, Horace, **12**. 243; Churchill, Lady Mary, **12**. 29, 38, 104, 105, **16**. 302, **32**. 124, **33**. 565, **34**. 57, **35**. 217, 225, **37**. 289, **38**. 38, **27**, **39**. 276; Churchill, Mary, **37**. 378; Chute, John, **10**. 168, **19**. 435, 442, 497, **20**. 361, 381, 382, 456, **22**. 257, 265, **23**. 284, 310, 350, **24**. 103, 209–10, **35**. 177, **38**. 453; Chute, William John, **12**. 227, 228; Clarges, Lady, **12**. 243, 252; Clarke, William, **12**. 247; Claussonette, **10**. 156; clergyman, **12**. 232; Clerke, Lady, **12**. 233; Clermont, Cts of, **12**. 236; Clifden, Lord, and son, **12**. 231; Clifford, Mr, **12**. 226, 237; Clitherow, James, **12**. 224; Clive, Mrs, **35**. 454n, **41**. 365; Codrington, Miss, **12**. 244; Coke, Lady Mary, **10**. 70, **31**. 127, 129, 139, 142, 147, 168, 179, 297, 299, 347, **32**. 207, **35**. 225, 319n, **39**. 104; Colbert de Seigneley, François, **12**. 250; Cole, Miss, **12**. 239; Cole, Mr, **12**. 233; Cole, Reverend Mr, **12**. 230; Cole, Lady Elizabeth Henrietta, **12**. 161, 249; Cole, Stephen Thomas, **12**. 161, 249; Cole, Thomas Rae, **12**. 225; Cole, Rev. William, **1**. 28n, 30n, 48, 145n, 151n, 176–77, 178n, 185, 263, 306n, 307n, 348, **2**. 368–9, 370–75, **10**. 135, 136; Combaud, Mrs, **12**. 243; Comings, **2**. 39, 40–41, 42; Compton, Lady Elizabeth, **33**. 278–9; Compton, Lady Margaret, **31**. 297; Conant, Mr, **12**. 235; Conolly, Lady Anne, and daughters, **38**. 73; Conway, Hon. Henrietta Seymour, **38**. 46; Conway, Henry Seymour, **10**. 99, 100, 133, 260, **12**. 105, 106, **22**. 322, 432n, **31**. 142, **32**. 10–11, 124, **33**. 23–4, 142, **34**. 57, **35**. 217, 275–6, 361, **37**. 468, 558, **38**. 207, **39**. 289, 295, **42**. 111–12; Conway's family,

[Strawberry Hill, *continued*]
39. 295; Conyers, Lady Harriot, 11. 57, 12. 232n, 234; Conyers daughters, 11. 57, 12. 234; Coote, Mr and Mrs, 12. 225; Corbett, Mrs, 12. 250; Cornwallis, Abp, 32. 156; Cornwallis, Mrs, 12. 246, 32. 156; Correa, M., 12. 232; Cosby, Mrs, 9. 134; Cosway, Richard, 12. 203, 228; Cosway, Mrs Richard, 12. 222, 228; Cotgrave, Mr, 12. 237; Cotterel, Mrs, 12. 232; Cotton, Mr, of Kingston, 12. 247; Cotton, Mrs, of Ham Common, 12. 238; Cotton, Sarah, 2. 316; Cotton, Sir Robert, 12. 221; countesses, 10. 107; Court, John, 12. 227; Courtenay, 42. 143n; Coutts, Thomas, and family, 12. 243; Coventrys, 9. 237; Cowe, Mr, 12. 243; Cowper, Mr, from Temple, 12. 243; Cowper, Mrs, of Cold Green, 12. 247; Cowslade, 10. 168; Cox, Mr, 12. 233; Cox, Mr, 12. 250; Coxe, Rev. William, 12. 182, (?) 223; Cozens, John Robert, 12. 237; Cramer, Wilhelm, 12. 228; Cramer, Mrs Wilhelm, 12. 228; Cranch ('Crank'), John, 12. 234, 43. 161; Crawford, Mrs, 12. 231; Crespigny, Mr and Mrs, 12. 246; Crewe, Mr and Mrs, 12. 225; Crewe, Mrs, 12. 248; Crewe, Mrs John, 39. 74–5; (?) Crewes, Mrs, 12. 228; Crosby, Mr, 12. 246; Crowle, Mr, 12. 248; Crussol, Duchesse de, 12. 248; Cruttenden, Mr, jr, 12. 236; Cruttenden, Edward Holden, 12. 236, 242, 249, 250, 251; Cruttenden, Mrs Edward Holden, 12. 242; Culverden, William, 12. 226, 237; Culverden, Mrs William, 12. 224; Cumberland, Mr, 12. 229; Cumberland, William, D. of, 35. 161; Cummings, Captain, 12. 248; Cunynghame, Lady, 12. 236; Currie, Miss, 12. 231; Curtis, Mr, 12. 251; Czernin von Chudenitz, Comte and Comtesse, 12. 230; Dacre, Bn and Bns, 9. 231, 24. 103; Dakin, Mr, 12. 246; Dalbi, 12. 237; Damas d'Antigny, Marquise de, 4. 176–7, 10. 278–9; Damer, Mrs, 12. 49, 51, 166, 167, 31. 142, 33. 142, 34. 57, 166, 37. 334–343, 378n, 492, 38. 207, 39. 403–4; Dance, George, 12. 243, 15. 316; Danes, 12. 225; Daniel, Mr, 12. 238; Daniel, Mr, of Thames Ditton, 12. 230, 240; Dansie, Mrs, 12. 225; D'Aranda, Rev. Peter, 12. 238; Darby, Lt-Col. William John, 12. 228; Darell, Mrs, 12. 244; Darrel, Mr, 12. 225; Dashkov, Ps, 203; Dashwood, Lady, 12. 249; Dashwood, Mr, 12. 241; Davenport, John, 12. 239; Davidson, Mrs, 12. 228; Davis, Mr, 12. 251; Davis, Mr, of Teddington, 12. 221; Davison (Davidson), Mr, of Twickenham, 12. 239, 240, 242, 246; Davison, Mrs, of Isleworth, 12. 239; Davison, Mrs, of Twickenham, 12. (?) 227, 241, 250; Day, Mr, of Richmond, 12. 234; Day, Sir John, 12. 234, 246; Dayrell, Mrs Marmaduke, 12. 244; Dayrolles, Mrs Solomon, 12. 234; Deards, John, 222; Debrett (Debret), John, 12. 246;

Dedel, Solomon, 12. 227, 246; Delany, Mrs, 10. 306; Delaval, John Hussey, 12. 251; Deluc, Mr and Mrs Jean André, 12. 237; Demainbray, Rev. Stephen, 12. 227; Demidov (Demidoff), Count, 12. 236; Devereux, Mr, 12. 228; De Vesci, Vct and Vcts, 12. 227; De Visme (de Vismes), M., 12. 251; Devonshire, Ds of, 33. 21; Devonshire, D. of (4th), 38. 362; Devonshire, D. of (5th), 12. 251; Dewitz, 38. 418; Dickenson, John, 12. 226, 229; Dickenson, Mrs John, 12. 229; Digby, 32. 197; Dilkes, Juliana, 12. 175; Divett, Mrs, 12. 221; Dixon, Mr, 12. 227; Dobbs, Mr, 12. 243; Dobson, Mrs, 12. 230; Dobson, William, 12. 223; doctor of physic, 10. 107; Dolichos, the, 12. 239; Donne, Mr, 12. 225; Douce, Mr, 12. 234; Douglas, Bns, 12. 135, 226, 248; Douglas, Mr, 12. 222; Douglas, Mr, of Teddington, 12. 223, 245; Douglas, Lady Catherine Anne, 12. 164, 229, 235; Douglas, John, 12. 240; Douglas, Sylvester, 12. 164, 235; Down and Connor, Bp of, 12. 225; Downe, Vcts, 12. 236; Downes, Mr, 12. 222; D'Oyly, Mrs Christopher, 12. 158, 249; Drake, Dr, 12. 225; (?) Dray, Mr and Mrs, of Cross Deep, 12. 240; Dromore, Bp of, and family, 12. 241; Du Châtelet, Comte, 10. 278–9; Du Châtelet, Comtesse, 4. 176–7, 10. 278–9; Ducie, Bn and Bns, 12. 221; Duclos, 10. 70–1; Dudley, Vct, 12. 228; Duncannon, Vct, 12. 232; Dundas, Mrs David, 12. 231, 247; Duppa, Mr, 12. 247; Dutchman, 12. 227; Dutton, Miss, 12. 236; Dutton, Mr, 12. 244; Dysart, Cts of, 9. 237, 369, 10. 63, 32. 382, 38. 196; Dysart, E. of, 9. 369, 10. 63, 32. 382; East Indians, 10. 107; Eden, Sir Frederick, 12. 242; Edgcumbe, 9. 186, 35. 200; Edmonds, Mrs, 12. 232; Edmonstone (Edmondson), Sir Archibald, 12. 252; Edwards, Captain, 12. 239, 242; Edwards, James, 12. 223, 224, 244, 247; Edwin, Lady Charlotte, 31. 147; Egerton, Lady Caroline, 35. 225; Einsiedel, Comte and Comtesse, 12. 238; Élie de Beaumont, 30. 176, 38. 461n; Elizabeth, Ps, and 2 sisters, 39. 510–12; Elliot, Gilbert, 10. 94; Ellis, Mr and Mrs Welbore, 12. 238; Ellis's servants, 12. 241; Elmsley, Alexander, 12. 234; Elphinstone, Bns, 12. 234; Englefield, Lady, 12. 230; Englefield, Sir Henry Charles, 12. 223, 230, 31. 236; Englefield, Teresa Ann, 12. 230; Éon, 10. 70–1; Equino (? Eguino), Monsieur d', of Kingston Hill, 12. 240; Erroll, Cts of, 12. 223; Essex, James, 1. 215, 222, 2. 13n, 15, 17, 18, 66, 32. 294; Evans, Dr, 12. 227; Ewart, Mrs Joseph, 12. 11; Ewer, Mr, 12. 233; Ewin, 1. 158, 161, 165; Fagnani, Maria, 33. 347; Falconet, Mr, 12. 238; Fanshawe, Mrs Simon, 12. 223; Farington, Joseph, 12. 194, 243, 244, 15. 240, 316, 317, 319, 327, 333, 43. 162; Farington, Mrs Joseph, 12. 244, 15. 240, 317; Farington, William, 12. 222; Farren, Elizabeth, 12. 228; Farren, Mrs George, 12. 228; Fasset, Thomas, 12. 248; Fauquier, Mr and Mrs, 12. 232n; 234; Fauquier, Jane Georgiana, 35. 454n; Fawkener, William Augustus, 12. 250; Fenns, 42. 97, 100; Ferguson, Mrs, 12. 247; Ferrers, Mr, 12. 228; Fieldhouse, Mr, 12. 249; Findlater (Finlater), Cts of, 12. 233; Fisher, John, and family, 12. 231, 43. 161; Fittler (Fitler), James, 12. 231, 234; Fitzherbert, Mrs Thomas, 12. 248; Fitzpatrick, Hon. Richard, and children, 32. 51; Fitzroys, 10. 129, 278–9; Fitzwalter, Mr, 12. 248; Fitzwilliam, E. and Cts, 12. 247; Fitzwilliam, Thomas, 12. 246, 250; Fleetwood, Sir Thomas, 12. 248; Fletcher, Mrs, 12. 222, 223; Fletcher, Rev. Henry, 12. 239, 241; (?) Fleury, 10. 70–1; Fleury, M. de, 12. 226; Fliess, Mme de, 12. 242; Floyer, Mr, 12. 224; Fonnereau, Mrs, 12. 242; Fontana, Madame, 12. 241; Foote family, 12. 236, 39. 475; Forbes, Mr, 12. 248; Ford, Mrs, 12. 228; Ford, Samuel, 12. 230; Fortescue, Captain, 12. 249; Fortescue, E. and Cts, 12. 235; Forth, Mrs, 12. 227; Foster, Mr, 12. 227; Foster, Lady Elizabeth, 12. 251; Fountaine, Mr, 12. 221, 240; Fox, Hon. Caroline, 12. 232n; Fox, Lady Caroline, 30. 114, 35. 229; Fox, Henry, 30. 114, 35. 229, 37. 497; Foyle, Mr, 12. 235; Franks, Miss, 12. 224; Franks (? Vranks), M. and Mme, 12. 228; Franks, Aaron, 2. 373, 12. 224; Franks, Mrs Phila, 12. 222; Freeman, Mr, 12. 250; French, Mrs Jeffrey, 12. 229, 230; French people, 10. 69–72, 127, 129, 156, 215, 278–9, 12. 27, 221, 223, 224, 227, 230, 231, 236, 240, 241, 242, 243, 244, 245, 247, 249, 25. 423, 427, 32. 355, 357; Frere, Mr and Mrs, 42. 97, 100; Fuhr, Mrs, 12. 242; Furtado, Mr, 12. 250; Fury, Mrs, 12. 229; Gale, Mr, 12. 238; Gallitzine, 12. 234; Galloway, Mr, of Twickenham, 12. 239; Garden, Mr, 12. 224; Gardiner, Mr, of Hampton Green, 12. 241; Gardiner, Mrs, of Hampton Green, 12. 248; Garrick, David, 39. 276, 41. 365; Garrick, Mrs David, 31. 216, 392, 39. 276, 42. 83, 99n; Garrick, Mrs George, 12. 246; Gascoyne, Mr, 12. 233; Gee, Mr, of Ireland, 12. 251; Gell, Mrs, 12. 250; Genlis, Mme de, and Pamela, 33. 482–3; Georg August of Mecklenburg, 38. 418; George III, 22. 426; George III's three daughters, 12. 248; Gerard, Miss, 12. 226; German people, 12. 223, 225, 236, 244, 39. 440; Gibbon, 43. 100; Gilbert, Mrs, 12. 250; Gilchrist, Mrs, 12. 249; Gilchrist, George, 12. (?) 244, 249; Gildart, Mr, 12. 232; Gilpin, Rev. William, and son, 12. 239; Glasse, Mr, 12. 251; Gleichen, 4. 360; Gloucester, Ds of, 6. 329, 12. 21, 115, 36. 328; Glynn, Mr and Mrs, 12. 236; Glynn, Robert, 1. 372, 373–74; Goodenough, Mr, 12. 233; Goodenough, Mrs, 12. 235; Good-

enough, Mrs William, 12. 243; Goodere, Lady, 12. 227; Goodwin, Mr, of Richmond, 12. 247; Gorman, Mr, 12. 238; Gosling, Miss, 12. 226; Gosling, Mrs Anne, 12. 223, 234, 251; Gosling, Mr and Mrs George, jr, of Whitton, 12. 241; Gough, Richard, 2. 325, 327, 331, 333, 29. 270; Gould, Mr, 12. 240; Gower, E. and Cts, 35. 225; Grafton, Ds of (3d), 10. 70–1; Grafton, D. of (2d), 35. 217; Grafton, D. of (3d), 10. 70–1; Grand, Monsieur, 12. 223; Grandison, Vcts, 10. 72, 99–100; Granger, 1. 177n; Graves, Mr, 12. 225; Gray, Robert, of Twickenham, 12. 223, 225, 227; Gray, Robert, Bp of Bristol, 12. 233; Gray, Thomas, 1. 134, 9. 364, 35. 100, 177, 43. 185, 187; Greatheed, Mr and Mrs Bertie, 12. 229; Green, Mr and Mrs, 12. 227; Greenway, John, of Twickenham, 12. 230; Greenway, Mrs John, 12. 223, 232, 235, 237, 240, 244, 247; Greenwich, Bns. 31. 147, 297; Gregory, Dr, of Richmond, 12. (?) 245; Gregory, Rev. Mr, 12. 243; Grenville, Hester, 12. 235; Grenville, William Wyndham, 12. 248; Greville, C. F., 6. 379; Grey, Marchioness, 12. 226; Grey de Wilton, Bn, 12. 232; Griffchop (? Griffinhoope), Mr, 12. 251; Griffin, Mr, of Piccadilly, 12. 243; Griffith, Mr, of Ireland, 12. 238; Grose, 12. 235; Grose, Mrs, 12. 224; Guerchys, 10. 127, 215, 38. 402, 403; Guilford, Cts of, 12. 164; Guillanez, Mr, 12. 225; Guillemard, Mrs, 12. 248; Guines, Duc de, 23. 311, 312–13, 33. 403, 35. 369, 531; Guines's daughters, 33. 403, 35. 369, 531; Gundry, Mr, 12. 245; Haddington, E. of, 12. 245; Hall, Mrs, 12. 222; Haller, Mme, 12. 227; Hamilton, Captain, of Twickenham, 12. 236; Hamilton, Ds of, 9. 237; Hamilton, Miss, 12. 233; Hamilton, Catherine, Lady, 23. 339; Hamilton, Emma, Lady, 12. 228; Hamilton, Mary, 31. 206, 215–16, 217; Hamilton, Sir William, 12. 239, 23. 339, 31. 217; Hamilton, William Gerard, 9. 377–8, 10. 36; Hammond, Richard, of Twickenham, 12. (?) 234, (?) 242, 249; Hamond, Horace, 15. 318; Hancarville, 33. 479; Handcock, Mrs, 31. 206; Hane, Count d', 12. 231; Hanoverian people, 12. 251; Harding, Silvester, 12. 229; Hardinge, George, 12. 166, 239, 244, 247, 249 35. 647; Hare, Mrs, James, 12. 222; Harley, Mr, 12. 244; Harrach, Comte, 12. 245; Harris, Mr, 12. 230; Harris, Mr and Mrs John, 35. 217; Harrison, Mr and Mrs, 12. 247; Harrowby, Bn and Bns, 12. 230; Hart, Emma, 12. 239; Harvey, Mr, 12. 238; Hastewell, Mrs, 12. 248; Hatsell, Mr, 12. 230; Haverfield, Mrs, 12. 225; Hawker, Mr, 12. 247; Hawkins, Henry, 12. 249; Hawkins, James, 12. 244; Hawkins, John Adair, 12. 241; Hayfeld, Count d', from Mains, 12. 229; Hayley, Mrs, 12. 250; Hemming, Rev.

[Strawberry Hill, *continued*]

Samuel, 12. 247; Hénin, Princesse d', 12. 41, 240, 243; Herbert, Lady Caroline, 12. 223; Herbert, Hon. Charles, 12. 223; Herbert, George Augustus, 33. 403; Herbert, Lady Henrietta Antonia, 39. 284, 285, 286; Hereford, Vcts. 12. 244; Herries, Lady, 11. 81, 12. 230, 236, 39. 475; Herries, Sir Robert, 12. 230; Hertford, Cts of, 10. 106, 31. 179, 180, 297, 32. 207, 301n, 35. 217; Hertford, E. of, 10. 70–1, 31. 297, 35. 217; Hertford family, 39. 284, 285, 286; Hervey, Bns. 35. 236, 37. 537; Hervey, (?) Augustus, 31. 147; Hervey, Elizabeth, 12. 238; Hervey, Mrs William Thomas, 11. 280, 12. 238; Hesketh, Lady, 12. 231; Heslop, Mr, 12. 245; Hessenstein, 33. 413–14, 39. 403; Hessian barons, 12. 221; Hewetson (Huitson), I. P., 12. 235, 241, 248, 250; Hewett, Mr, 12. 226; Hewett, Mrs, of Richmond, 12. 232; Hierons, Mr, 12. 223; Hildyard, Sir Robert Darcy, 12. 233; Hill, Mr, 12. 236; Hinchliffe, 2. 156n; Hinton, Rev. Anthony, 12. 167–8, (?) 222, (?) 235, 249; Hoare, Mr, 12. 234, 238; Hobart, Hon, Mrs George, 12. 229; Hodginson, Mr, 12. 226; Holcroft, 42. 226, 227; Holdernesse, Cts of, 10. 72–3, 278–9, 31. 139, 297, 39. 104; Holdernesse, E. of, 10. 72–3, 278–9; Holland, 3d Bn, 34. 88–9; Holroyd, Maria Josepha, 12. 229; Hopetoun, E. of, 12. 237; Hopkins, Mr, 12. 239; Hornby, Mr and Mrs, 12. 232; Hotham, Henrietta Gertrude, 10. 93, 12. 102, 249; Howard, Mrs, 12. 240; Howe, Hon. Mrs Caroline, 31. 179, 180, 32. 207; (?) Huber (? Auber, ? Archer), Rev. Mr, of Twickenham, 12. 252; Hughes, Mr, 12. 235; Hume, David, 31. 139, 39. 104; Humphreys, Mrs, 12. 222; Hunter, John, 12. 230; Hunter, Mrs John, 12. 230, (?) 233, 236; Huntingtowers (*see* Dysart *above*); Hurdis, Rev. James, 12. 244, 43. 165; Hurdis, Jane Elizabeth, 12. 244, 43. 165; Hurs, Palmer, 12. 226; Hurter (? Hunter), Mr, 12. 222; Hutchesson, Mann, 12. 242, (?) 250; Hutchins, Mr, 12. 224; Ingilby (Inglesby), Sir John, 12. 227; Inglis, Mr, 12. 242; Ingram, Mr, 12. 232; Ingram, Mr, of Teddington, 12. 251; Ingram, R., 12. 228, 241; Ireland, Samuel, 12. 226, 15. 338, 42. 175n; Irish people, 10. 107, 12. 225, 249; Ironside, Colonel, of Upper Brook Street, London, 12. 230; Ironside, Edward, 12. 225, 228, 237; Isham, Mrs, 12. 248; Isham, Edmund, 12. 248; Italian people, 11. 125, 12. 223, 237; Jamaica, M. of, 10. 129; Jamaica's tutor, 10. 129; Jamaican people, 12. 235; Jannagan, Mr, 12. 237; Jardine, Major, 12. 245; Jarnac, Comte de, 12. 247, 249; Jeffreys, John, 12. 241; Jeffreys, Mrs John, 12. 225, 228; Jennings, Miss (? Susannah), 39. 328; Jephson, Robert, 12. 232; Jerningham,

Charles, 35. 531–2; Jerningham, Edward, 12. 223, 235, 39. 436; Jerningham, Frances, Lady, 12. 243; Jerningham, Mary, Lady, 35. 534; Jersey, Cts of, 29. 72–3, 35. 454n; Jersey, E. of, 35. 454n; Jessup, Mr, 12. 242; Jewish people, 10. 107; John (? Johnes), Mr, 12. 247; Johnson, Lady, 12. 245; Johnston, Lady Henrietta Cecilia, 12. 51, 143, 196, 41. 366; Johnston, Mrs Henry George, 12. 51, 196; Johnston, Gen. James, 12. 51, 31. 297, 41. 366; Johnstone, Gov. and Mrs, 35. 535; Jones, Mr, of Emmanuel College, Cambridge, 12. 245; Jones, George Lewis, 12. 234; Jones, John, 12. 231; Joye, Mrs, 12. 222; Juliac (? Juillac), Mme de, 10. 156, 31. 36; Keate, George, 12. 240; Keate, Mrs George, 12. 240; Keene, Whitshed, 31. 179, 32. 207; Keene, Mrs Whitshed, 12. 230; Kemble, Mr and Mrs John Philip, 12. 229; Kemble, Joseph, 12. 241; Kemp, Mr, 12. 250; Kendal, General, 12. 249; Kent, Mr, 12. 221; Keppel, Anna Maria, 32. 382, 36. 150; Keppel, Hon. Frederick, 9. 369, 10. 63, 93, 22. 128, 32. 382, 36. 150; Keppel, Hon. Mrs Frederick, 9. 369, 10. 63, 93, 12. 224, 225, 31. 297, 32. 382, 36. 150, 38. 109, 196; Kerrich, Thomas, 2. 120, 128, 129, 12. 240; Kildares, 35. 229, 230–1; Killaloe and Limerick, Bp of, 12. 243; Kinderley, John, 12. 241; Kinnaird, George, 12. 229; Kippis, 2. 117; Knight, (?) Samuel, 12. 244, 43. 162; Knox, Mr, of Apps Court, Surrey, 12. 239; La Basque (Labascque), Comte de, 12. 240; La Borde, Monsieur, 12. 240; Lally-Tollendal, Trophime-Gérard de, 12. 41, 243; (?) Lambrière, Marquis de, 12. 252; Lane, Mrs, 12. 224; Lane, Thomas, 12. 229; Langdale, Mrs, 12. 229; Langley, Rev. Thomas, 12. (?) 229, 251; La Noue, Mme de, 12. 241; La Rochefoucauld-d'Anville, Duc de, 4. 226; La Rochefoucauld-Liancourt, Duc de, 10. 278–9; Las Heras, Señor de, 12. 242; La Tonelli, 12. 246; Laurence, Miss, 12. 247; Lavagna, 10. 127; La Vaupalière, Marquise de, 10. 278–9; La Villebague, Mme de, 12. 230; Lawless, Mr, of Ireland, 12. 242, 248; Lawless, Mrs, of Ireland, 12. 242; Lawrence, Sir Thomas, 12. 248, 15. 333; Legge, Miss, 12. 224; Legge, Mrs, 12. 229; Leicester, Lord and Lady, and family, 12. 236, 43. 162; Leicester, Mr, 12. 236; Leigh, Mr, 12. 239; Leigh, Lady Caroline, 12. 239, 240, 246; Leman, Mr, 12. 229; Lesarne (? Leserve), Mr, 12. 234; Lestrange, Mr, 12. 238; Le Texier, 39. 276, 41. 366; Leveson Gower, Hon. Baptist, 35. 229; Leveson Gower, Mrs John, 12. 231, 247; Lewes, Sir Watkin, 12. 231, 232; Lewis, Mr, of Moulsey (1), 12. 231; Lewis, Mr, of Moulsey (2), 12. 231; Lewis, Mrs, of Moulsey, 12. 231; Lillebonne, 3. 42; Lisieux, Bp of, 12. 248; L'Isle, 4. 246, 10. 278–9; Lisle, Misses,

12. 102; Lister, Miss, 12. 243; Lister, Mrs, 12. 228, 243; Lister, Lt-Gen. Henry, 12. 222, 223; Lloyd, Mr, of Carnarvonshire, 12. 243; Lloyd, Rachel, 32. 242; Lobb, Mr, 12. 242; Lock, Mr and Mrs William, and William, jr, 12. 232, 43. 161; Lodge, Edmund, 12. 239, 243; Lonsdale, Cts of, 12. 222; Lorenzi, 1. 105n, 20. 87, 89; Lort, 2. 375; Loutherbourgh (Louterbourg), Philip James de, 12. 236; Lowry, Miss, 12. 248; Lubomirska, Ps, 12. 228, 39. 453, 42. 196–7; Lucans, 39. 390; Lucchesi-Palli, Ferdinando, 12. 228; Lushington, Mrs, of Kingston, 12. 249, 251; Lusignan, 33. 406, 35. 532; Luxembourg, 33. 406, 35. 532; Lynden van Blitterswyk, Dirk Wolter van, 12. 228; Lysons, Rev. Daniel, 12. 29, 183, 194, 207, 239, 15. 201; Lysons, Mary, 12. 227; Lysons, Rev. Samuel, 12. 233; Lysons, Samuel, 12. 57, 244, 15. 316, 317, 319, 327, 333, 43. 162; Lysons, Mrs Samuel, 12. 233; Lyttelton, Bn, 35. 85, 37. 551; Lyttelton, Bns, 10. 133, 156, 260, 31. 142; 35. 85, 38. 102, 207, 39. 167; Lyttelton, Bp, 37. 551, 38. 362; Macartney, Bn and Bns, 12. 235; Macdonald, Sir Archibald and Lady Louisa, 12. 238, 34. 156; Mackenzie, Mr, of Teddington, 12. 239, (?) 250; Mackinson (? Mackinnon), Mr, 12. 251; Macnamara, Mr, 12. 238; Mailly, Duchesse de, 12. 242; Malden, Vct and Vcts, 12. 233; Malone, Catherine, 42. 143n; Malone, Edmond, 12. 221, 223, 232, 42. 96, 143n; Malone, Henrietta, 42. 143n; Mandeville, 9. 233; Mann, Miss, 12. 222; Mann, Edward Louisa, 19. 503, 20. 63, 64, 456; Mann, Galfridus, 19. 503, 20. 63, 64, 456; Mann, Sir Horace II, 12. 233, 24. 490, 493, 497, 25. 154, 532; March, E. of, 10. 127, 32. 197, 38. 175; March, Mrs, of Hampton, 12. 237; Marchant (Marchand), Nathaniel, 12. 178; Markham, Mr, 12. 247; Marlborough, Ds of, 11. 82, 12. 221, 33. 11, 39. 418; Marlborough, D. of, 11. 82, 12. 221, 39. 418; Marsh, Mr and Mrs, 12. 236; Mason, 1. 134, 9. 364, 28. 162, 33. 96, 275, 35. 370, 524; Masserano, 10. 127, 278–9, 23. 311, 38. 402, 403; Masserano's secretary, 10. 127; Masterman, Mrs, 12. 233; Masters, Mrs, 12. 232; Matthew, Mr, 12. 229; Matthews, Dr, 12. 247; Matthews, Mrs, of Richmond, 12. 237; Mawhood (? Maud, ? Maude), Col., 31. 179, 32. 207; (?) May, Mrs, of Twickenham, 12. 244; May, John, 12. 248; Maysey, Mrs, of Richmond, 12. 240; Mechel, Mr, 12. 242; Melbourne, Vcts, 35. 532, 39. 403–4; Melo e Castro, 10. 278; Mercier, 42. 226; Meux, Richard, 12. 251; Meux, Mrs, Richard, 12. 249; Mierop, Mrs, van, 12. 231; Miles, Edward, 12. 242; Miller, Rev. James, 10. 99; Milles (Mills), Mr, of Twickenham, 12. 228, 232, 246; Milman, Dr Francis, 12. 228; Milner, Dr, 12. 246;

Milner, Mr, 12. 229; Milward, Mrs, 12. 231, 239, 249; Molesworth, Richard Nassau, 12. 221; Molinedo (Molinero), Chevalier, 12. 232; Molteno, Mr, 12. 237; Montagu, Mr and Mrs, 12. 240; Montagu, Charles, 9. (?) 231, (?) 233, 35. 184, 37. 388, 38. 27; Montagu, Mrs Elizabeth, 42. 83; Montagu, Frederick, 10. 306; Montagu, George, 4. 345, 9. 52, 111, 165, 10. 36, 122, 207, 225, 226, 35. 161, 184, 37. 388, 38. 27, 453; Montagu, Henrietta, 9. 167; Montagu, John, 9. (?) 231, (?) 233, 374, 10. 99, 135, 224, 225, 304; Montboissier, Messrs de, 12. 223; Montesquieu, Bn de, 33. 408; Montfort, 33. 406; Moore, Colonel, 12. 232; Moore, Mrs, 12. 242; Morande, Charles Thévenot de, 12. 227; Moranville, Comte de, 12. 236, 39. 473; Mordaunt, Mr, 12. 238; Mordaunt, Lady Mary Anastasia Grace, 12. 21; More, Mr, 12. 246; More, Hannah, 12. 229, 235, 31. 211, 395, 36. 285–6; Moreland, Mr, 12. 225; Morris, Mr, 12. 232, 237; Morrison, 9. 304; Mount Edgcumbe, Cts of, 12. 203, 232n; Mount Edgcumbe, E. of, 12. 232n; Mountmorres, Vct, 12. 236, 241; Mount Stuart, Vcts, 12. 233; Müntz, 9. 187, 190, 216, 35. 100, 226, 265; Mure, Mr, 12. 243; Murray, Lady Anne, 12. 20, 250; Murray, Lady Marjory, 12. 20, 250; Musgrave, Mr and Mrs, 12. 242; Musgrave, George, 12. 242; Musgrave, Sir William, 39. 104; Muzell (Stosch), 21. 427, 433; Nadaillac, Marquise de, 12. 244; Nangis, Mlle de, 10. 127; Narbonne-Lara, Louis-Marie-Jacques-Amalric, 12. 243; Nares, Robert, 12. 236, 242, 243; Nassau de Zuylestein, George, 12. 221; Nassau-Weilburg, P. of, 9. 189; Necker, M. and Mme, 6. 292, 296, 334, 8. 213; Nelthorpe, Sir John, 12. 233; Newcastle, D. of, 38. 445; Newcomes, 1. 44; Newport, Mr, 12. 245; Newport, Sir John, 12. 250; Newton, Mr, 12. 249; Nichols, 12. 236; Nichols, John, 2. 331, 29. 270; Nichols family, 12. 234; Nicol, George, 12. 239, 243, 42. 283, 284; Nicol, Mrs George, 42. 283, 284; Nicholson, Mr, 31. 126; Nightingale, Mr, 12. 229; Nivernais, 22. 136; Noailles, Marquis de, 32. 357; Noble, Mark, 33. 468; Noé, Louis Pantaléon, 12. 247; Norfolk, D. of, 12. 238, 248; Norford, 43. 162, 164–5; Norford, Mr, jr, 12. 240; North, Bn, 9. 174, 10. 319, 320, 12. 225, 32. 156; North, Bns, 32. 156; North, Lady Anne, 12. 164, 229, 335; North, Lady Charlotte, 12. 164, 229; North, George Augustus, 12. 232; Northcote, James, 12. 229; Northmore, Mr, 12. 238; Offley, 10. 70–1; Ogiński, 12. 226, 35. 386; Olier, Mrs, 12. 231; Onslow, Bn, 12. 5, 228, 32. 156; Onslow, Bns, 12. 5, 32. 156; Onslow, Arthur, 38. 95; Onslow, Thomas, 12. 245; Orange, Ps of, 12. 248, 39. 511–12; Orde family, 12. 244; Orford, 35. 217; Orléans, Duc d', 12. 235; Osbaldeston, Mrs George,

[Strawberry Hill, *continued*]

12. 245; Osborn, Sir George, 12. 243; Osborn, Lady Heneage, 12. 243; Ossory, Lady, 12. 232n; Ossory, Lady, and daughters, 34. 49; Ossory, Lord, 11. 229; Otley, Mr, 12. 235; Otto, Mr, 12. 225; Owen, Mrs, 12. 234; Page, Mr, 12. 245; Palmerston, Vct and Vcts, 12. 236; Panton, Paul, 43. 164; Paoli, Pasquale, 12. 222; Park, Mr and Mrs Thomas, 12. 229; Parr, Mr, 12. 249; Parsons, Mrs, 12. 249; Parsons, William, 12. 229; Partridge, Mrs, (1), 12. 249; Partridge, Mrs (2), 12. 249; Pavie, M. de, 12. 231; Paxton, Mrs, 12. 226; (?) Payne, Lady, from Mortlake, 12. 251; Payne, Sir Ralph and Lady, 12. 224; Payne (Paine), Thomas, 12. 247; Peachey, Mrs, 12. 229; Pelham, Frances, 12. 5; Pelham, Henry, 12. 224; Pemble, Mrs, 12. 229; Pembroke, Cts of, 4. (?) 249, 33. 403, 39. 276, 447; Pembroke, E. of, 39. 276; Pembroke, Mr, 12. 249; Penn, Granville, 12. 246; Penn, Lady Juliana, 12. 231, 34. 14; Penn, Mr and Mrs Richard, 12. 242; Penneck, Rev. Richard, 12. 238; Pennicott, Rev. William, 12. 224, 232, 238, 239, 251; Penrose, Mr, 12. 234; Pentland, Mr, 12. 231; Pentycross, Rev. Thomas, 12. 207, 15. 287; Pepys, W. W., 31. 206, 327; Perkins, Dr, of Hampton, 12. 233; Perkins, Mr, 12. 222; Perry, Mr and Mrs, 12. 229; Perryn, Lady, 12. 224; Perryn, James, 12. 224; Persse, Mr, 12. 237; Pether, Abraham, 12. 251; Petrie, Mr, 12. 221; Petrie, Robert, 12. 222; Pettiward, Mrs Roger Mortlock, 12. 244; Phelp, Mr, 12. 241; Phelps, Mr, 12. 248; Philipe, Mr, 12. 250; Philipps, Catharine, 12. 232n; Philipps, Joyce, 12. 232n; Philipps, Mary, 12. 232n; Phillips, Molesworth, 12. 243; Phyn, Mr, 12. 243; Picard, Thomas, 12. 245; Pigou, Frederick, 12. 241, 249; Pindemonte, Ippolito, 12. 235; Pinkerton, 29. 358, 359, 42. 197–8, 225; Pinto, Mme, 32. 372; Piozzi, Mrs, 12. 242; Pirski, Mr, 12. 233; Pitcairn, Dr David, 12. 248; Pitt, Anne, 10. 127, 31. 139, 35. 225, 39. 104; Playfair, Mr, 12. 244; Pleydell, Mrs, 12. 227; Plumer (Plummer), Mrs, 12. 229, 230; Pocock, Admiral George, 31. 202; Pocock, Sir George, 12. 248; Pocock, Nicholas, 12. 239; Poissonnier, 5. 381; Poix, Prince de, 12. 243; Polhill, Charles, 12. 239; Polignac, Comtesse Diane de, 12. 227; Polish people, 12. 224, 233, 33. 502; Pomeroy, Miss, 12. 247; Ponsonby, Lady Elizabeth, 12. 240; Ponsonby family, 12. 246; Pont, Miss, 12. 244; Pool, Mrs, 12. 251; Pope, Mr, 12. 228; Pope, Mr and Mrs Alexander, 12. 237; Pope, Jane, 12. 224; Porter, Mr, 12. 232n; Porteus, Bp, 12. 232n, 233, 16. 222, 31. 312; Porteus family, 12. 232n, 233, 16. 222; Portland, Ds of, 10. 306; Portman, Mr, 12. 226; Pott, Mr, 12. 242; Potts and ladies, 43. 164; Pougens, Marie-Charles-Joseph de, 12. 231; Powis, Cts of, 31. 147, 32. 301n, 39. 284, 285, 286; Pownall, Thomas, 12. 225; Preston, Mr, 12. 250; Price, Mr, 12. 225; Prime, Samuel, 12. 224, 249; Pritchard, Miss, 12. 229; Probyn, Mrs, 12. 221; Prussian people, 12. 246; Pry, Mrs, 12. 242; Purchis, Mr, 12. 237; Queensberry, Ds of (3d), 35. 454n, 42. 469–70; Queensberry, D. of (3d), 35. 454n, 42. 469–70; Queensberry, D. of (4th), 12. 240; Rae, Mr, 12. 235; Raftor, James, 2. 373, 12. 225, 41. 366; Raikes, Thomas, 12. 237, 43. 162; Railton, Mr, 12. 225, 230; Ramsay, Mr, 12. 237; Ranusi, Prince, 12. 222; Rawlinson, 1. 161, 165; Rawstone, Mr, 12. 238; Ray, Mr (1), 12. 232; Ray, Mr (2), 12. 244; Raynal, 32. 357; Read, Mr and Mrs Henry, 12. 222; Reader, Mr, 12. 249; Reeve, Mr, 12. 234; Remonville, M. de, 12. 237; Rena, Contessa, 23. 107, 38. 175; Repton, Humphry, 12. 243; Reveley, Willey, 12. 232n; Rezzonico, Carlo Gastone della Torre di, 12. 229; Rhodes, Mr, 12. 245; Rice family, 9. 134, 161; Rich, the Misses, 12. 241; Rich, Mary, 10. 260, 35. 275–6, 283, 37. 492; Richardson, William, 12. 233; Richmond, Ds of, 9. 237; Richmond, D. of, 22. 322, 432n; Roach, Mrs, 12. 249; Rochford, Cts of, 9. 215–16; Rochford, E. of, 12. 221; Roe, Mr, 12. 234; Roffey, Mr, 12. 224, 228, 249; Rogers, Mr and Mrs, 12. 232; Rogers, Mrs (1), 12. 222; Rogers, Mrs (2), 12. 222; Roman Catholics, 10. 107; Roncherolles, M. de, 12. 235; Roope, Mr, 12. 236; Rospigliosi, Prince and Princess, 12. 230, 15. 198; Rowley, Lady, 12. 239; Rowley, Mr, 12. 225; Ruden, Mr, 12. 250; Russel, Mr, 12. 226, (?) 237, 33. 523; Russel, Mrs, 12. 226, 33. 523; Russell, Lady Caroline, 35. 225; Russell, Lord John, 12. 243; Russian person, 12. 236; Rycroft, Sir Nelson and Lady, 12. 241; Ryland, Mr, 12. 248; Sackville, (?) Lady John Philip, 31. 147; St Asaph, Vct, 12. 241; St Aubyn (St Aubin), Sir John, 12. 221; Saint-Chamans, Marquis and Vicomte de, 33. 408; Saint-Gervais, Comte de, 12. 222; St Helens, Bn, 12. 241; Saltonstall, Mrs, 12. 242; Saltykov, Count and Countess, 33. 362; Sandby, Mr, of Teddington, 12. 230; Sandby, Paul, 12. (?) 221, 15. 338, 42. 175n; Sandby (son), 12. 234; Sandwich, Lord, 33. 468; Sarsfield, 3. 286n; Sayer, Mr, 12. 224, 225; Scawen, Miss, 12. 224; Schall, Comte de, 12. 237; Schaub, Lady, 10. 156; Schnebellie, Jacob, 43. 162; Schomberg, 39. 292; Schutz, Mr, 12. 234; Schwarz (Schwartz), Frederik, 12. 243; 'scientific lady,' 33. 522–3; Scott, Mr, 12. 231; Scott, Mrs (1), 12. 231; Scott, Mrs (2), 12. 241; Scott, Lady Jane, 31. 147; Scottish people, 10. 107; Scrafton, Mr, 12. 251, Sebright, John, 35. 225, 42. 326; Se-

bright family, 11. 286, 12. 238, 42. 326; Seckendorff, Baron von, 12. 225; Sedgwick, Mr and Mrs, 12. 222; Sefton, Cts and E. of, 12. 248; Seilern, 23. 311; Selby, Henry Collingwood, 12. 241; Selwyn, George Augustus, 4. 249, 6. 64n, 9. 186, 417, 10. 127, 12. 229, 237, 32. 197, 33. 347, 427, 468, 34. 49, 35. 200, 38. 276, 39. 104; Sévery, Monsieur, 12. 229; Seyer, Mrs, from Richmond, 12. 245; Seymour, Lady George, 12. 169; Seymour, Lady Hugh, 12. 158, 160, 169; Seymour-Conway, Hon. George, 39. 284, 285, 286; Seymour-Conway, Hon. Henry, 39. 74–5; Seymour-Conway, Hon. Hugh, 39. 502; Seymour-Conway, Lady Isabella, 39. 284, 285, 286; Seymour-Conway, Hon. William, 39. 284, 285, 286; Shakerley, Mrs Peter, 12. 241; Sharp, Mrs, 12. 247; Sheffield, Bn and Bns, 12. 229; Sheppard, Mr, 12. 231; Sherriff, Mr, 12. 252; Shirley, Mrs, 38. 102; Shuvalov, 10. 156–7; Shuvalov, Comtesse, 12. 226; Siddons, Mr and Mrs William, 12. 229; Simco, John, 12. 234, 241, 43. 161; Simons, Dr, 12. 232; Simpson, Lady Anne, 12. 228; Sloane, Mrs, 12. 158, 249; Sloane, Hans, 12. 223; Smart, Mr, 12. 246; Smith, Mr, 12. 225, 251; Smith, Mr, of Twickenham, 12. 228; Smyth, Lady Georgiana, 12. 223; Smythe, Mrs Walter, 12. 231; Soame, Mrs Henry, 12. 230, 43. 160; Soderini, 33. 530; Soltau, Mr, 12. 226, 227; Somers, Bns, 12. 250; Somerset, Ladies, 12. 247; Somerton, Bns, 12. 249; Spence, Miss, 12. 248; Spencer, Lady, 33. 21; Spencer, Mr and Mrs, 12. 246; Spencer, Lord Robert, 33. 403; Spyers, John, 12. 221; Stafford, Cts of, 37. 537; Stainforth, Mr, of Weybridge, 12. (?) 233, 246; Stainforth, Mrs, 12. 238; Stampa, Marquis di, 12. 231; Stanhope, Cts, 12. 232; Stanley, Mr, 12. 241; Stapleton, Mrs, 12. 234; Starhemberg (Staremberg), Ps of, 12. 252; Staunton, Sir George Leonard, 12. 234; Staveley, W., 12. 223, 241; Stevens, Maj.-Gen. Humphry, 12. 236; Stevenson, Mr, 12. 226; Stevenson, Mrs, of Richmond, 12. 229; Stier, Chevalier de, 12. 236; Stone, Miss, 12. 222; Stonhewer, Richard, 29. 16, 161; Stopford, Vct and Vcts, 12. 239; Storer, Anthony Morris, 12. 225, 35. 359–60; Storer, William, 28. 329, 39. 293; Stormont, Vct, 12. 247; Stothard, Thomas, 12. 243; Straffords, 38. 362; Stratfield, Mr, 12. 248; Strathnaver, Lord, 34. 156–7; Stratton, Mrs, 12. 222, 223, 248; Streatfield, Mrs, 12. 229, 231; Stretch, Rev. Laurence M., 12. 222; Stuart, Lady, 12. 227; Stuart, Sir Simeon, 12. 233; Stuart, William, 12. 241; Stuart Mackenzie, Lady Elizabeth, 12. 5, 177, 31. 127, 129, 35. 319n, 39. 467; Stuart Mackenzie, James, 12. 5, 39. 467; Suckling, Mr, 12. 167–8, 249; Suffolk, Cts of, 31. 129, 35. 319n; Suffolk, E. of, 12. 248; Suffrein, M.

and Madame de, 12. 237; Sulivan, Mr and Mrs, of Sunbury, 12. 228; Sulkowskys, 33. 280; Sullivan, Richard Joseph, 12. 246; Sunderlin, Lady, 42. 143n; Sutherland, Elizabeth, Cts of, 12. 242, 34. 156; Sutton, Mr and Mrs Thomas, 12. 249; Swan, Miss, 12. 247; Swanton (Swainton), Mrs, of Richmond, 12. 234, 240, 241; Swedish people, 12. 225, 243; Swinburne, Mrs Henry, 12. 226; Symonds, Mr, of Twickenham, 12. 238; Synnot, Sir Walter, Lady, and Miss, 12. 243; Tavistock, 35. 225; Taylor, Dr, of Isleworth, 12. 233; Taylor, Mr, of London, 12. 106, 247; Temple, Mr, 12. 246; Temples, 10. (?) 126, 35. 454n; Tennant, Mr, 12. 248; Thackeray, Joseph, 12. 243, 247; Thackeray, Mrs Joseph, 12. 239; Thomas, Miss, 12. 240; Thornhill, Mrs John, 12. 246; Thrale, Hester Maria, 12. 234; Tighe, Mrs, 12. 237; Tolly, Mrs, 12. 236; Toulmin, Messrs, 12. 222; Toundrow, Mr, 12. 235; Tour and Taxis, 2 Princes of, 12. 229; Tourney, Rev. Mr, 12. 236; Towers, Dr, 12. 222; Towneley, Mr, 12. 223; Towneley, John, 33. 408; Townshend, Miss, 12. 228; Townshend, Miss, 33. 197; Townshend, Vcts, 9. 215–6, 35. 186, 40. 100; Travers, Mr, 12. 227; Tresham, Henry, 12. 237; Treves, 33. 565; Trevor family, 9. 161; Trigge, Col. Thomas, 12. 234; Trossarelli, Mr, 12. 246; Trower, Mr, 12. 224; Trumbull, John, 12. 229; Turner, Captain, 12. 235; Turner, Mrs, of Teddington Common, 12. 238; Turpin, Comte de, 12. 240; Twining, Mr, 12. 224; Tynte, Mr and Mrs, 12. 237; Tyrconnel, Cts of, 12. 246; Tyson, 1. 215, 222; Udny, Mr and Mrs Robert, 12. 236; Upper Ossory, E. of, 11. 229; Usson, Comtesse d', 10. 70–1; Uzès, Duc d', 12. 248; Vaillant, Paul, 12. 237, 241; Vaughan, Miss, 12. 224; Vaughan, the Misses, 12. 244; Vaughan, Mrs, 12. 224; Vaughan, Mrs, of Richmond, 12. 236; Vaughan, Dr and Mrs Henry, 12. 251; Vere, Bn and Bns, 9. 151; Vere, Mr, of Kingston, 12. 244; Vernon, Miss, 12. 252; Vernon, the Misses, 12. 229; Vernon, Mr, of Devonshire, 12. 251; Vernon, Mrs, 12. 252; Vernon, Hon. Caroline, 35. 454n; Vernon, Lady Henrietta, 31. 147; Vernon family, 10. 121–2; Vesey, Mr and Mrs, 31. 206, 215–16; Vesey, Maj. George, 12. 237; (?) Vigne, Comtesse de, of Richmond, 12. 252; Villebois, Mr and Mrs, 12. 222; Villegagnon, Marquise de, 10. 278–9; Villiers, 10. 70–1; Villiers, Mrs, 12. 249; Vorontsov, Semen Romanovich, 12. 228, 234; Vougnys, 12. 240; (?) Voyer, 10. 278; Wade, Watson, 12. 221; Waldegrave, Cts, (Maria Walpole), 9. 233, 237, 369, 10. 59, 93, 127, 22. 127–8, 38. 73, 109, 196; 43. 185; Waldegrave, Lady, Anna Horatia, 12. 225, 24. 315, 32. 382, 33. 210, 279, 283, 34. 199; Waldegrave, Lady Char-

[Strawberry Hill, *continued*]
lotte Maria, 24. 315, 32. 382, 33. 210, 275, 279, 283; Waldegrave, Lady Elizabeth, 35. 225; Waldegrave, Lady Elizabeth Laura (Lady Chewton; Cts Waldegrave), 10. 63, 12. 50, 51, 209, 24. 315, 32. 382, 33. 210, 279, 283, 534, 540, 34. 53, 191, 36. 234, 240, 247, 290, 330; Waldegrave, George E., 33. 534, 540, 34. 53, 36. 234, 240, 247; Waldegrave, James, E., 9. 215–16, 233, 237, 369, 417; Waldegrave, Lady Maria Wilhelmina, 12. 50, 51; Waldegrave, William, 33. 210, 279; Walker, Joseph Cooper, 12. 242; Walpole, Bns, 12. 240; Walpole, Hon. and Mrs Horatio, 16. 302, 34. 57; Walpole, Hon. Richard, 32. 366–7; Walpole, Hon. Thomas, 33. 352, 36. 243; Walpole, Thomas, jr, 36. 212, 213; Walsingham, Mrs, 31. 206; Walter, John, 12. 250; Walter, Mrs John, 12. 235; Walton, Mr and Mrs, 12. 246; Warren, John, Bp of Bangor, 12. 227; Warren, Sir John Borlase, 12. 232; (?) Warwick, Lady, 34. 199; Wathan, Mr, 12. 230; Watson Wentworth, Lady Charlotte, 12. 20; Way, Mr, 12. 221; Weatherall, Mrs, 12. 234; Webb, Captain, of Hampton, 12. 233; Webb, Mr, of Twickenham, 12. 242; Wegg, Mrs Samuel, 12. 234; West, James, 20. 371n, 40. 311–12; West Indian people, 10. 107; Westmorland, Cts of, 12. 225; Wettenhall, 9. 231, 233, 10. 121–2; Wettenhall, Mrs, 9. 231, 233; Weyland, Mark, 12. 235; Wharton, Dr Thomas, 29. 16; Wheate, Mrs, 12. 240; Wheatfield, Mrs, 12. 233; Wheler, Sir Charles, 12. 21, 228, 233; Wheler, Mrs Charles (later Lady), 12. 21, 105, 228; Whitaker, Mrs, 12. 228, 236; Whitbread, Miss, 12. 224; White, Benjamin, jr, 12. 247; Whiteside, Mrs, 12. 249; Whithed, 19. 442; Wickham, Mr, 12. 235; Wilberforce, William, 12. 224; Wilbraham, Mr, 12. 223; Wilkes, Mary, 12. 248; William IV's household, 12. 244; Williams, Sir Charles Hanbury and Frances Hanbury, 35. 177; Williams, George James, 9. 186, 417, 12. 223, 250 bis, 15. (?) 327, 30. 176, 32. 197, 35. 200, 38. 276; Willock, Mr, 12. 231; Willoughby de Broke, Lord, 12. 221, 250; Wilmot, Sir John Eardley, 12. 222; Wilson, Lady, 12. 239; Wilson, Christopher, 12. 236; Winslow, Thomas, 12. 230; Winter, Miss, 12. 228; Wiseman, Mr, 12. 245; Wollaston, Dr, 12. 226; Wombwell, Lady, 12. 240; Woodward, Mr, 12. 250; Worcester, Marchioness and M. of, 12. 238; Worseley, Mr and Mrs, 12. 247; Wray, Mrs Daniel, 12. 224, 228; Wrench, Jacob, 12. (?) 246, 251; Wrighte, Mrs, 12. 222; Württemberg, D. of, 28. 258; Wyat, Mr, 12. 227; Wyatt, Benjamin Dean, 12. 247; Yates, Mrs, 12. 221, 223, 225, 229, 230, 239, 240, 241; Yonge, Mrs, 31. 127; York, Ds of, 12. 6, 9, 10–11, 13, 24, 245, 248, 39. 501n, 510–12;

York, Edward, D. of, 9. 304, 34. 20–1; York, Frederick, D. of, 12. 231, 34. 20–1, 23, 35. 397; Yusupov, Prince, 28. 269; Zeerleder, Mr, 12. 246

Waldegrave, Cts, declines HW's offer of, as home, 10. 69

wallpaper at: on hall and staircase, copied from P. Arthur's tomb at Worcester, 35. 150; painted by Bromwich's man, not Bentley, 35. 191

walnut tree at, 11. 159

Walpole, Sir Edward, mentions, 36. 22

Walpole family pictures at, described by HW, 36. 160–2

Walter, Mr, takes villa near, 12. 139

Warton could see Gothic designs at, 40. 255

Wentworth to have admittance to, 16. 55

West Drayton near, 10. 256

wet, 6. 24

wet and cold, 34. 142

whimsical indulgence of HW's imagination at, 31. 111

William III's spurs given to, by Harcourt, 35. 477–8, 488

Wilmot, Mrs, wishes tickets for, 10. 158

Williams, Frances Hanbury, draws views of, 35. 177

Williams, G. J., fears he and Selwyn may lose Christmas at, 30. 177

windows at: liked by D. of Cumberland, 35. 161; *see also above under* stained (and painted) glass at

wood at: French horns placed in, 35. 225; Montagu might gather laurels in, 35. 102; thinned, and fields planted with trees, 35. 259

woodwork at, illustrates art history, 42. 103

workmen at: 20. 348, 22. 49; slow in finishing, 35. 68; *see also* labour troubles at, *above*

Yellow Bedchamber at: 2. 274n, 9. 146n, 15. 190n, 191n, 20. 381; added, 20. 348n; becomes Beauty Room, 32. 294, 33. 273, 39. 276; chimney-piece of, 33. 273; Hermaphrodite statue in, 17. 213n; painting in, of P. Arthur and Catherine of Aragon, 42. 215n

Young, Margaret, escorts visitors through, 39. 106

Zouch's letters at, 16. 56

'Strawberry-Hill, A Ballad.' *See under* Pulteney, William, E. of Bath

Strawberry Hill, Little. See Little Strawberry Hill

Strawberry Hill Press:
Anecdotes of Painting from: 16. 41; given to Stanislas II, 36. 238, 281; price of, 2. 319; second edn of, being printed, 40. 367–8; third edn, printed elsewhere, 42. 20; Vol. IV of, being printed, 31. 154

apprentice to be instructed at, 40. 164

Barthélemy asks for book from, 3. 268, 272, 293n, 295, 297, 312 'beautiful negligence' of productions of, 28. 88

Bentley's *Lucan* published by: 1. 35n, 2. 188, 21. 472, 29. 10, 35. 644; delayed by poor printers, 16. 33; presented by HW to Hénault, 41. 28, 107

Bentley's verses to HW on beginning of, 35. 643

Bishop Bonner's Ghost printed at: 31. 302, 314, 34. 52, 53, 54, 39. 469, 42. 250, 253; plate of SH for, printed in London, 34. 53

books from: given to Bibliothèque du Roi, 3. 260n, 262–3, 268, 297, 36. 280–1; HW would send, to Albani in exchange for Herculaneum book, 21. 262; HW would send, to Charles of Naples in exchange for Herculaneum book, 21. 131; prized by collectors, 31. 244, 313; rarity of, 21. 278, 33. 573; sent to Dalrymple, 15. 37; usually quartos, 29. 364

Bute-Chatham papers should be printed at, 33. 64

Castle of Otranto not printed at, 35. 436

Cole's encomiums on, 1. 295, 296

constantly at work, 21. 239

Conway asks about opening of, 37. 500

—— praises, 37. 578

Cornélie vestale printed at, 3. 376, 385–6, 4. 24, 32, 73, 84, 88, 99, 103, 41. 106–7

Dalrymple declines honour of being printed at, 15. 36

—— wishes productions of, were uniform, 15. 103

Danish prince regent asks HW for books from, 36. 281–2

difficulty with printer at, 1. 12, 16. 27

Drumgold hopes that his comparative study of French and English languages will be printed at, 40. 304

——'s 'productions' printed at, 40. 303–4

Du Deffand, Mme, asks for book from, 3. 112–13

—— asks for book from, for Pont-de-Veyle, 3. 264, 272, 295, 297, 312

—— mentions, 4. 99

elegy on Caroline Campbell not printed at, despite attributions, 6. 158n

erected, 13. 28, 14. 97

Essay on Modern Gardening: 16. 275; *see also below under* Nivernais's translation of

fallow for some time, 31. 306

Farmer's agreement with HW for, 40. 164

financial profit not wished by HW, but he must meet the expenses of printing, 1. 300

Fitzpatrick's *Dorinda* printed at, 31. 182, 35. 470, 39. 249

Forrester, apprentice at, 40. 164n

Fugitive Pieces, Whitworth's *Account* and Spence's *Parallel* printed at, 37. 552

Gramont's *Mémoires* printed at, *see under* Hamilton, Anthony

Gray's *Odes* to appear at opening of, 13. 28, 16. 206, 35. 98–9, 43. 191

Greek not to be printed at, 16. 275

Grenville ministry's censorship makes HW fear for liberty of, 38. 446

HW adds to Ayton's collection of imprints of, 15. 338

HW an 'honest printer' at, 31. 309

HW begins new printing-house for, 35. 296

HW declines to print Sir Dudley Carleton's *Letters* at, 41. 283–4

HW disappointed that Mason's *Gray* is not to be printed at, 28. 87–8

HW gives editions from: to Bibliothèque du Roi at Paris, 3. 72, 260n, 262–3, 268, 297, 36. 280–1, 41. 57–9, 64; to Dr William Hunter, 41. 422; to Mrs Anderson, 42. 146; to Nivernais, 10. 57; to Pinkerton, 16. 274

HW has laid down, 2. 116, 245–6

HW has no time to attend to, 29. 193

HW hopes to print Gray's MSS at, 28. 19–20

HW hopes to print Mason's verses at, 29. 183, 189

HW hopes to publish treasures at, 35. 104

HW hopes to send Chute a specimen from, 35. 100

HW jokes about printing works by Lady Mary Coke at, 31. 143, 154

HW lists numbers of copies printed of publications at, 43. 79, 358

HW offers: for Gray's MSS, 1. 229, 336; for Hamilton's publications, 35. 419; to Lyttelton for his *Henry II*, 40. 96; to Mason, 28. 162, 164, 166, 29. 253, 310, 312

HW offers edns from, to Nash, 43. 384

HW paraphrases Pope's 'Essay on Criticism' apropos of, 32. 298

HW parodies Pope in alluding to, 35. 101

HW's collected works to be printed by, 1. 150–1

HW's copies of imprints of, uniformly bound, 41. 467

HW seeks materials for, 1. 255, 294

HW sends copies of imprints at, to Mrs Anderson, 42. 146

HW's *Letter from the Honourable Thomas Walpole* printed at, 36. 204n

HW's motives in selecting products for, 31. 305n

HW's preoccupation with, 38. 16

HW's reflections on publishing at, 32. 45–6

HW's relative wants a bulky work printed at, 41. 284

HW's resolution not to publish his own writings at, broken, 15. 60

HW's verses to Berrys, at, 34. 26–7

HW to send books from: to Duchesse de Choiseul, 5. 316; to Hannah More, 31. 231

HW will not print Voltaire's and Wyndham's letters at, 42. 121

HW will print only gift books at, 21. 131

[Strawberry Hill Press, *continued*]

HW wishes Mann to have complete set of editions of, **21**. 278

HW wishes to print Cts Harcourt's verses at, **35**. 459, 471, 486, 491–2, 521

HW wishes to print letters of Ninon de Lenclos at, **31**. 7

Harcourt, Cts, should be ashamed to approach, **35**. 471

Hardinge asks about next imprints from, **35**. 584

Hardinge, Nicholas, said to have wanted verses printed at, **35**. 605

Hentzner's *Voyage* printed at, **35**. 643, **42**. 49

imprints of: bring ridiculous prices, **36**. 238, 281, **42**. 20; scarce, **21**. 278, **33**. 573

Jerningham's tribute on *Bishop Bonner's Ghost* too flattering to be printed at, **42**. 257

Jones's *Muse Recalled* printed at, **35**. 362

Letters from King Edward VI to Barnaby Fitz-Patrick printed at, **32**. 45

Letter to the Editor of the Miscellanies of Thomas Chatterton printed at, **2**. 138, **41**. 396

Life of Edward Lord Herbert of Cherbury printed at: **1**. 69, **28**. 3, **30**. 175, **32**. 45, **40**. 287, 355, 356–60, 368; given by HW to Pitt, **40**. 356

likely to flourish, **31**. 12

list of prints from, **1**. 195n

lists of imprints of, printed, **33**. 574, 575, 578, **43**. 79, 358

Lucan printed at, *see above under* Bentley's *Lucan* printed at

Mann instructed not to give books from, to Firmian, **21**. 278

—— receives *Fugitive Pieces* and *Royal and Noble Authors* from, **21**. 339

—— thanks HW for Spence's *Parallel* from, **21**. 289

—— will get ode from, if he captures a town, **21**. 266

Mason denies having had offer of, **29**. 363

Miller's verses printed at, **29**. 7

Miscellaneous Antiquities discontinued because of low sales, **1**. 300

miscellany of verses perhaps to be printed at, **15**. 58

Montagu asks about, **9**. 208

—— glad of popularity of publications of, **10**. 142

—— mentions, **10**. 84

—— praises 'offspring' of, **10**. 134

More, Hannah, proud to be published at, **31**. 307–8

Mysterious Mother printed at, **4**. 84n, **41**. 427, **42**. 309n, 351, 352

Nivernais compliments HW on *Fugitive Pieces* printed at, **41**. 20

——'s translation of *Essay on Modern Gardening* printed at, **16**. 275n, **33**. 496, **35**. 635, **42**. 169

nothing more for the public to be printed at, **28**. 166

nothing new at, **39**. 187

not let out for hire, **2**. 109

objects of, **31**. 305

old printing-house for, **35**. 296, 298

opening of, **9**. 214

operations of, have turned against HW, **1**. 300

Ormesson thanks HW for gift of editions from, to Bibliothèque du Roi, **42**. 357

Ossory, Lord, to have complete set of editions of, **33**. 552, 573

out of order, **15**. 145–6, **34**. 53

paper used at: **40**. 117; 'magnificent,' **31**. 316

Pearce congratulates HW on 'learned authors' printed at, **38**. 111

Pinkerton recommends work for, **16**. 275

politics and satire never printed at, **29**. 253

Postscript to the Royal and Noble Authors printed at, in 40 copies only, **42**. 184

Pratt, William, a printer at, **40**. 289

prefaces to editions of, **16**. 259

price of *Anecdotes* printed at, **2**. 319

printers at: listed, **35**. 303n; well paid, **15**. 55–6

printing-house for, finished, **35**. 298

printing of, 'nice,' **31**. 316

proceeds 'soberly,' **9**. 215

productions of, sometimes charitable, **28**. 23–4

revived, **10**. 260

Robinson, printer at, **21**. 120–1

Rochester, Bp of, compliments HW on publications of, **40**. 202

rolling press out of order at, **34**. 53

Royal and Noble Authors hastily written to provide work for, **16**. 206

—— printed in small edition at, **40**. 127

(?) Royston receives book from, **21**. 538n

rumour of robbery at, **29**. 281

Sleep-Walker, The (Le Somnambule) adapted by Lady Craven, issued by, **2**. 111, 112, 119, **28**. 443, **33**. 39

slowness of, **15**. 98

small editions cause fame of, **31**. 309

Spence's *Parallel* printed at, **35**. 107, **37**. 552

Spence wishes, 'may flourish and abound,' **40**. 116

stopped by Robinson's flight, **16**. 27

stopping of, releases Kirgate for other work, **12**. 163

Strafford has all the publications of, **35**. 362

SH visitors' regulations printed at, **33**. 435–6

title-pages printed at, for etchings by noble amateurs, **28**. 195

Townshend, Vcts, visits, **40**. 100

two or three things to appear from, before *Anecdotes of Painting*, **37**. 551

typesetter's possible mistakes in printing *Anecdotes of Painting*, **40**. 325–6

value of publications from, **2**. 109, 188, 248–9, 319

verses printed at, for foreign visitors, **10.** 69, 71, 73, 74, 127, 279

Voyer given complete publications of, **4.** 264

See also under Kirgate, Thomas; Printer, HW's

Strawberry Hill Sale, 1842. *See introductions to individual correspondences*

'Strawberry King at Arms.' *See* Chute, John

Strawbridge, Mrs (d. 1742), Bubb Dodington's mistress:

Bubb Dodington and Rowe said to have written song to, **9.** 169n

Bubb Dodington gives bond to, not to marry anyone else, **33.** 556

——'s ballad on, **33.** 556, **34.** 262-3

death of, releases Bubb Dodington from his bond, **18.** 105n

HW remembers E. of Warwick better than, **33.** 559

house of, on Vigo Lane and Old Bond St, **33.** 556n

Rowe said to have written ballad on, **9.** 169n, **35.** 237

Straw man; straw men:

cannon use, for target practice, **38.** 410

Strayler, Alan (fl. *temp.* Henry III), painter:

Cole's note on, **1.** 17, **2.** 282

Streamer; streamers:

gondola decked with, at Ranelagh, **20.** 47

in postilions' hats, for Zorndorf victory, **37.** 566-7

Streatfield, Mrs, of Long Ditton:

SH visited by, **12.** 229, 231

Streatham, London:

Bedford, D. of, had expected to live at, to be near George III, **38.** 423

Streatham Park, Mrs Piozzi's residence:

fête at, attended by Daniel Lysons, **11.** 106

Street, Ann (1734–1801), m. 1 (1754) William Dancer; m. 2 (1767 *or* 8) Spranger Barry; m. 3 (1778) Thomas Crawford; actress:

biographical information on, corrected, **43.** 354

refuses part in *Count of Narbonne*, **33.** 302, **41.** 447

Vitellia's chief rôle not suited to, **41.** 361

Street; streets:

French unpave, in towns, **37.** 502

Ghent people live in, **37.** 124

London's: dirty, **19.** 317; newly added, **24.** 228, **39.** 498; repaved in summer, **21.** 427

neatness of, in Bruges, **37.** 118

present age prefers riding about, to roads or turf, **25.** 317

Raftor enraptured by rows of lamps on, **39.** 133

Rotterdam's, **37.** 134

Street cries:

in London, **21.** 154

'oysters,' **9.** 318

Street robbers:

gang of, **35.** 230

Street signs:

medieval head-dresses would brush against, **35.** 249

See also Sign

'Streets of London,' work proposed by HW:

Cole sends notes for, **1.** 137-8, 148

HW plans, **1.** 134, 194

Street Walker, The. See under Berkeley, Elizabeth, Bns Craven

'Street walker':

HW's simile, **29.** 168, **33.** 313, **43.** 308

Streetwalker; streetwalkers. *See* Whore; whores

Strehlen (Germany):

Frederick II receives peace conditions at, **17.** 121n

Strelitz (Germany):

Charlotte's marriage a sensation at, **21.** 525 **38.** 400

Yertzin, Mme de, wears costume unusual at, **38.** 400

'Strephon':

'Chloe' restricted by Parliament in matching with, **37.** 361

'Strephon II':

Conway signs himself as, **37.** 3

'Strephon's Complaint,' by HW:

Conway dislikes format of, **37.** 103

to tune of 'Il est dans le voisinage,' **39.** 521-2

Stretch, Rev. Laurence M. (ca 1737–1813); master of academy at Twickenham:

SH ticket not used by, **12.** 222n, 228

SH visited by, **12.** 222

Stretham, Cambs:

Brown, rector of, **1.** 290n

Stretton, Rutland:

Plumptre, rector of, **2.** 154n

Stretton Hall, Staffs:

Conolly's seat, **31.** 199n

Stretzer, Thomas:

New Description of Merryland attributed to, **37.** 82n

Strickland, Elizabeth (d. 1821), m. (1781) Strickland Freeman, of Fawley Court, Bucks:

Conway's neighbour, **25.** 576

Damer, Mrs, models head from, **25.** 576

——'s sculpture suggested by, **11.** 75n

Strickland, William (1714–88), M.P.:

story told by, in Parliament, **18.** 355

Strictures on Female Education. See under More, Hannah

Strictures upon a Pamphlet Entitled Cursory Observations. See under Greene, Edward Burnaby

Strigoil, E. of. *See* Marshal, William

Strike; strikes (labour):

at SH, **1.** 11n, 14, 21, **9.** 398, **22.** 49, **35.** 315

Stringer, ——, (?) Yorkshire bookseller:

Ware, Mrs, corresponds with, **16.** 43

Strode, Mrs:

Mann and Mrs Morehead entertained by, **19.** 477

Strode, Mrs Samuel. *See* Richbell, Anne

Strode, Maj.-Gen. William (? 1698–1776):
    Bedford, D. of, receives letter from, 21. 373n
    Jennings, Lt-Col., serves under, 21. 373n
Strodtmann, J.C.:
    Neue gelehrte Europa, Das, by, describes Stosch's collection, 21. 151n
Strogonov, Cts. *See* Troubetskoi, Catherine Petrovna; Vorontsova, ——
Strogonov, Alexander Sergeievich (1734–1811):
    St-Ouen visted by, 6. 229
    social relations of, in Paris, 6. 228, 7. 346, 347, 349
Strohmfeld, Maj., Baron; gentleman of the Chamber to D. of Östergötland:
    (?) Mann sends HW's letter to Ds of Gloucester by, 24. 247
Stroke; strokes (apoplectic *or* paralytic):
    facial, 39. 278, 279, 280–1, 283
    Montagu dreads, 10. 164
    occurrences of, 9. 300, 322, 10. 164, 348, 21. 15, 21, 27, 29, 232, 234, 252, 432, 22. 72, 23. 43, 70, 455, 24. 5, 55, 86–7, 230, 237, 283, 32. 36n
    'palsy' causes, 35. 350–1, 39. 197
'Strolling Actresses Dressing in a Barn.' *See under* Hogarth, William
Strolling players. *See under* Theatre
Strong, Edward (ca 1652–1723), master mason:
    attends, as master mason, the laying of last stone of St Paul's lantern, 40. 350n
    Wren saved by, from falling, 40. 350–1
Strong, Thomas (d. 1681), master mason:
    attends, as master mason, the corner-stone laying at St Paul's, 40. 350n
Strong box:
    Charles II leaves papers (concerning his faith) in, 31. 323
'Strong man, the':
    HW may be solicited by, for patronage, 9. 306–7
    performance of, in HW's newspaper parody, 9. 126, 127n
Strongoli, island of (Italy):
    earthquake account mentions, 25. 376
    earthquake destroys, 33. 397
'Strong woman, the':
    exhibition of, recorded in HW's newspaper parody, 9. 126
Strowan, Perthshire:
    Murray of, 29. 53n
'Strowell, Mrs':
    Lincoln and Spence to receive compliments of, 30. 19
Strozzi, Principessa. *See* Strozzi, Giulia (1726–85); Strozzi, Teresa (1682–1748)
Strozzi, Ferdinando (1719–69), Principe:
    marriage of, 19. 350
Strozzi, Filippo (1700–63), Duca di Bagnolo:
    assembles adherents, 15. 278n
    mother disowns, 19. 350
    mother's museum probably robbed by, 19. 350

Strozzi, Girolamo (1724–81):
    Bagnesi's duel with, 18. 133
Strozzi, Giulia (1726–85), m. (1747) Principe Ferdinando Strozzi:
    marriage of, 19. 350
Strozzi, (?) Isabella (ca 1757–83):
    (?) brother offered, as wife, to Mozzi, 25. 130, 498
Strozzi, Lorenzo (d. 1802), Duca di Bagnolo:
    sister offered by, as wife, to Mozzi, 25. 130, 498
    York, D. of, to have Roman house of, 22. 215
Strozzi, Luigi:
    medals collected by, 19. 350n
Strozzi, Ottavia (1709–48), m. (1728) Principe Filippo Corsini:
    daughter of, 18. 121
Strozzi, Pietro:
    Rozzo Strozzi's closest relative, 18. 146n
Strozzi, Roberto (1717–80):
    (?) Bocchineri's duel with, prevented, 17. 111
Strozzi, Rosso (d. 1743), introduttore degl' ambasciadori at Florence:
    Baldocci deputy to, 18. 146, 182
    (?) ball given by, 18. 60, 166
    death of, 18. 145
    distant relatives heirs to, 18. 146
    estate mismanaged by, 18. 145–6
    Francis I's birthday to be celebrated in gala announced by, 18. *113*
    Frescobaldi, Mme, cicisbea of, 18. 145
    grandmaster of ceremonies and introducer of ambassadors, 18. 146
    homage to Francis III received by, 17. 449n
    horses of, numerous but underfed, 18. 146
    servants of, obliged to borrow sheets and shirts for him, in last illness, 18. 146
Strozzi, Teresa (1682–1748), m. (1699) Principe Lorenzo Francesco Strozzi:
    HW pities, 19. 361
    museum of, robbed, 19. 349–50, 361n
    sons of, 19. 350
Strozzi, Teresa (1747–1816), m. (1766) Giuseppe Luigi Riccardi:
    (?) wedding dinner for, 22. 458
Strozzi, Casa, at Florence:
    family fracas in, over robbery, 19. 349
Strozzi, Palazzo, at Florence:
    balls held at, 13. 201
    concert not to be held in, 17. 316
Strozzi family:
    collation of MSS of, sent by Mann to Dr Kennicott, 22. 477n
    collection of, 14. 239
Struensee, ——, brother of Dr Struensee:
    imprisoned, 23. 374n
Struensee, Johann Friedrich (1737–72), Greve; physician; Danish Court favourite:
    arrest of, 23. 373, 385
    beheaded, 5. 178n, 23. 392, 401, 409
    Caroline Matilda's affair with, 4. 420n, 28. 58n

Christian VII and Caroline Matilda ruled by, **23**. *273*

imprisoned for affair with Caroline Matilda, **5**. 183

opponents to accuse, of drugging Christian VII, **23**. 380

probably a French tool, **23**. 273

'Struldbrug'; 'Struldbrugs'. *See under* Swift, Jonathan: *Gulliver's Travels*

Struldbrugism:

HW's, **42**. 229

Strutt, Lady Charlotte Mary Gertrude. *See* Fitzgerald, Lady Charlotte Mary Gertrude

Strutt, John (1727–1816), M.P.:

bill by, for increasing Parliamentary qualifications, **29**. 49, 50

Strutt, Joseph (1749–1802), antiquary; artist:

(?) Bull's books extra-illustrated by, **33**. 376n

Compleat View of the Manners . . ., A, by, **1**. 351, **2**. 175, **43**. 61

drawings by: formerly Bull's, **43**. 220; from Ives's pictures, **1**. 351–2

Regal and Ecclesiastical Antiquities, The, by: **42**. 38, **43**. 220; has print of Humphrey, D. of Gloucester, **16**. 187; Saxon MSS mentioned in, **42**. 67

Strutt, Samuel (d. 1785), clerk assistant to House of Lords:

Chatham carried to house of, **24**. 371

Struve, Burkhard Gotthelf (1671–1738):

Bibliotheca antiqua by, **1**. 258

Strype, John (1643–1737), historian:

Annals of the Reformation in England by, **2**. 145, 349

Baker aids, **2**. 349

—— asked by, to solicit subscriptions for his Stow's *Survey*, **2**. 145

——'s letters to, **2**. 144–5, 358

Burnet's *History of the Reformation* aided by, **2**. 348–9

Ecclesiastical Memorials by, cited, **1**. 220, 262, **43**. 49

History of the Life and Acts of . . . Edmund Grindal, The, by, cited, **1**. 273

Knox's letters to, **2**. 134, 140

print of, **2**. 352

Stow's life by, **2**. 153, 155

Stuard. *See* Stuart

Stuart, Lady. *See* Stowe, Mary Anne

'Stuart, Mr':

Bute's pseudonym, **23**. 103

Stuart, Alexander:

HW sends letters by, **7**. 278

social relations of, in Paris, **7**. 279, 284

Stuart, Andrew (1725–1801), lawyer; M.P.:

birth date of, **43**. 294

HW's letter to Conway taken by, to England, **39**. 35

'junto' includes, **11**. 197n

Letters to the Right Honourable Lord Mansfield by: **32**. 89–90; (?) cited by Hardinge, **35**. 614; HW calls, well-bred abuse, **28**.
61–2; Mason and Holdernesse discuss, **28**. 82; Mason asks HW to send, to him, **28**. 62–3; Mason's indignation aroused by, **28**. 83; privately printed, **28**. *79*; seditious, **28**. 67

Mason mistakenly calls, 'Sir,' **28**. 62, 67, 73

Thurlow duels with, after opposition in Douglas case, **32**. 90n

Stuart, Lady Anne (1746–ca 1819), m. 1 (1764) Hugh Percy, styled Bn Warkworth 1750–66 and E. Percy 1766–86 (divorced, 1779), m. 2 (1780) Friedrich Karl Hans Bruno, Baron von Poellnitz:

(?) Buckingham House ball attended by, **38**. 290

grandfather's bequest to, **21**. 473

husband's separation from, rumoured, **14**. 141

marriage of, **22**. *302n*

mother's remark about, **24**. 378

pregnant and to be divorced, **24**. 378

uncle not told of disgrace of, **24**. 381

weak, **24**. 378

Stuart, Lady Arabella (or Arbella) (1575–1615), m. (1610) William Seymour:

Basire's engraving of, **42**. 313n

portrait of, at Welbeck Abbey, and HW's copy of it, **15**. 160, 163, 191, 209

print of, scarce, **15**. 160–1

Stuart, Lady Augusta (1749–78), 4th dau. of 3d E. of Bute, m. (1773) Capt. Andrew Corbet:

dies of putrid sore throat, **28**. 354

Findlater supposedly to marry, **23**. 312

grandfather's bequest to, **21**. 473

marriage of, rumoured, **33**. 55

Stuart, Capt. Benjamin:

(?) Mann's letter taken by, to HW, **25**. 42, 49

(?) Murray sends, as courier from Minorca, **25**. 42

(?) quarantined, **25**. 42

Stuart, Lady Caroline (1750–1813), m. (1778) Hon. John Dawson, styled Bn Dawson 1776–9, 2d Vct Carlow, 1779; cr. (1785) E. of Portarlington:

grandfather's bequest to, **21**. 473

homely, **32**. 48

Macartney seen by, at Dawson Court, **33**. 548n

Pitt, Anne, plans match for, **32**. 48

Stuart, Charles (1666–7), D. of Kendal:

heraldic arms not those of, **41**. 451

Stuart, Hon. Sir Charles (1753–1801), K.B., 1799; army officer; M.P.:

capture of, in America, rumoured, **33**. 57

grandfather's bequest to, **21**. 473

letters brought by, from America, **33**. 76

Stuart, Charles Edward (the 'Young Pretender'). *See* Charles Edward

Stuart, Charlotte (1753–89), dau. of Young Pretender; cr. (1784) Ds of Albany:

appearance of, resembles father's, **25**. 535

calls to be returned by, **25**. 535

[Stuart, Charlotte, *continued*]
educated in Paris convent, **25.** 512, **26.** 47
father acknowledges, as his daughter and sole heiress, **25.** 512–13, 516n, **33.** 438
father creates, Ds of Albany, **33.** 438
father gives private balls to amuse, **25.** 549n
father joined by, just in time to reap inheritance, **25.** 549
father registers, at Paris and Florence, as Ds of Albany, **25.** 512–13, 516n, 521–2
father sends Stewart to Paris to fetch, to Florence, **25.** 513
father's intended bequest to, **25.** 512–13, 522
father's jewels worn by, **25.** 536
father's only child, **26.** 47
father summons, to Florence, and has her called Ds of Albany, **25.** 538n
father to marry, to Florentine cavaliere, **25.** 513, 522
Fitzjames family do not acknowledge, lest they have to support her, **25.** 516, **26.** 47
Fitzjames family will be caused no expense by, **25.** 522
Florence expects, soon, **25.** 521
—— reached by, **25.** 535, 538
Florentine ladies leave cards at door of, **25.** 535
Florentine theatres visited by, in father's jewels, **25.** 536
French Court said to grant tabouret to, as Duchess, **25.** 537
Gem, Dr, attends, at Paris, **25.** 516, **26.** 47
grandfather offers to provide for, **26.** 47
HW wants to hear more about, **25.** 520
inheritance of, may lure Swedish princes, **33.** 449–50
Maria Louisa has not yet received, **25.** 537
mother of, **33.** 442
mother would disgrace, **25.** 522
O'Donnel, Mrs, and Nairne accompany as *dame de compagnie* and *écuyer*, **25.** 536
on way to Florence, escorted by 2 ladies and 2 gentlemen, **25.** 524
Pius VI allows father of, to make her a duchess but her uncle does not, **25.** 552–3
—— writes congratulatory answer to letter of, **25.** 550
Rohan, Abp, often visited by, **25.** 513
stepmother may repent after arrival of, **25.** 535
uncle does not answer letter of, **25.** 549–50
uncle will not give jewels to, **25.** 525–6
Stuart, Hon. Frederick (1751–1802), M.P.:
grandfather's bequest to, **21.** 473
Stuart, Gilbert (1742–86):
Henry attacked by, **15.** 169n
Stuart, Henry (1545–67), styled Lord Darnley; 2d husband of Mary, Q. of Scots:
cenotaph of, **15.** 158n
Mary, Q. of Scots' passion for, **15.** 42
mentioned in Mackenzie's account of Ruthven, **15.** 35
mother of, **15.** 139n, 233n, **42.** 11

niece of, **15.** 160n
portrait of, at Hardwick, **9.** 298
Robertson exaggerates faults of, **15.** 62
supposed portrait of, **2.** 44
Stuart, Henry (1640–60), D. of Gloucester. *See* Henry (Stuart) 1640–60
Stuart, Henry Benedict Maria Clement, Cardinal York. *See* Henry Benedict Maria Clement
Stuart, James (1708–67), 8th E. of Moray:
rebel lords' condemnation shunned by, **19.** 284
Stuart, James (1713–88), 'Athenian'; architect and archæologist:
frieze of, at Nuneham, **29.** 268
Hogarth's 'Five Orders of Perriwigs' portrays, **9.** 401
Montagu erroneously attributes design of Kedleston and authorship of *Ruins of Palmyra* to, **10.** 230
Montagu House built by, **29.** 184n
Nuneham church altered by, **35.** 460n
(?) Virrette talks to, at opera, **38.** 307
Stuart, Hon. Col. James:
Boswell sketches, **33.** 462n
Stuart, James (d. 1793), army officer:
Pigot arrested by, after dinner, **35.** 486
Stuart (later Stuart Wortley Mackenzie), James Archibald (1747–1818):
date of name-change by, corrected, **43.** 276
grandfather leaves reversion of estates to, on condition of taking name of Wortley, **21.** 473
Ossory, Cts of, said to be having affair with, **33.** 79n
Stuart, James Francis Edward (the 'Old Pretender'). *See* James Francis Edward
Stuart, Lady Jane (1742–1828), m. (1768) Sir George Macartney, Kt, 1764; K.B., 1772; cr. (1776) Bn, (1792) Vct, and (1794) E. Macartney:
(?) Buckingham House ball attended by, **38.** 290
Court ball attended by, **9.** 406, **38.** 143
family of, **32.** 280
grandfather's bequest to, **21.** 473
HW does not visit, **33.** 132
HW mentions, **9.** 402, 403
HW visits, **33.** 548
house of, in Curzon St, **33.** 548
husband not accompanied by, to Madras, **33.** 257
husband of, HW intercedes for, **33.** 126
letter of, seen by HW, **33.** 132
Lyttelton's improper conversation before, **15.** 330
Macartney marries, **23.** 586
Middlesex, Ellis, and Macartney suitors for, **38.** 406
popularity of, changes with father's status, **38.** 476
son of, **12.** 94n
SH visited by, **12.** 235

Stuart, John (Young Pretender's valet). See Stewart, John

Stuart, John (1713–92), 3d E. of Bute, 1723; prime minister 1762–3:

accused of all, and in panic, 39. 100

acts in Queensberry House Theatre, 19. 468n

Adam begins Shelburne House for, 33. 125n

—— vents discontent of, 28. 481n

Adam brothers patronized by, 28. 102n

administration of: cannot endure at same time with two others, 21. 465; commission of accounts may not be amenable to, 38. 193; Rockingham denounces, 38. 180; to have majority in everything but numbers, 38. 186

age of, 11. 160

Akenside deserts Aristides and Cato for, 35. 566

Amelia, Ps, jokingly suggested as wife for, 9. 209–10

—— surrenders rangership of Hampton Court and keepership of Richmond Park to, 20. 29n

Ampthill manor's reversion obtained by, 38. 433–4

appearance of: altered, and looks old, 23. 103; emaciated and looks older, 23. 312

Argyll's Scotch patronage to be inherited by, 9. 358, 21. 527n

artistic propensities of, 16. 42

Augusta, Ps of Wales, gets doves and parrot from, provoking satire, 38. 462

—— implied by satiric print to be having affair with, 21. 487

—— said to send express to, 38. 315–16

——'s alleged affair with, 9. 202n, 237, 305, 343n, 12. 262, 21. 6n, 487, 22. 53n, 33. 242, 37. 438–9

—— tells, to announce to Mann the P. of Saxe-Gotha's impending visit, 23. 328

Barèges to be visited by, 23. 152n, 161n

—— visited by, 7. 367

Bedford, D. of, and George Grenville joined by, in wanting troops sent to America, 22. 401

Bedford, D. of, calls, his 'bitter enemy' and accuses him of breaking promise, 30. 185

—— courts, 38. 354–5

—— preferred by, as lord privy seal, 21. 541n, 38. 132n

—— rejects offer by, 22. 130n

Bedford faction and Grenville opposed by, on Poor Bill, 38. 528–9

Bedford faction ignores, but Gower courts him, 38. 534

Bedford faction may conciliate, 9. 341

Bedford faction may triumph over, 38. 561

behaves moderately, despite recent good fortune, 21. 527

Bentley appointed by, commissioner of the Lottery, 10. 72, 35. 645

—— flatters, in prologue to The Wishes, 35. 645

(?) —— may choose, for hero, 10. 113

—— may write panegyric to, 9. 417

—— mentions, in Patriotism, 10. 154

—— uses, as character in Philodamus, 9. 414

Bolingbroke's influence on, 28. 416

Bothmer attends levee of, 10. 35

brother considers Mann's delay in getting Bath ribbon a reflection on, 23. 52–3

brother may be involved in resignation of, 22. 133

brother of, 9. 86n, 11. 35n, 21. 212, 22. 302n, 24. 401n

brother's dismissal enrages, 30. 184

Brudenell's joke about, 10. 35

Bubb Dodington calls, 'Pollio,' 28. 242

Buckingham House private levee attended by, 36. 40n

Cabinet Council includes, 21. 443

Campbell, Lord Frederick, received place for life from, 30. 184

Canterbury, Abp of, attends levee of, 10. 35

cards of, labelled 'Mr Stuart,' 23. 103

caricature of, 21. 93

Carmarthen omits, from dinner, 33. 554n

chapel not seen by HW in absence of, 32. 84

Chatham's relations with, 3. 120

——'s 'treaty' with, 33. 64

Chesterfield mentions, 6. 37

Chudleigh, Elizabeth, retorts to Ps of Wales about, in satiric print, 9. 338

Cider Tax causes downfall of, 21. 129, 132

Clement XIII might be succeeded by, 23. 92

clergyman given rich living by, to get possession of Lady Mary Wortley Montagu's letters, 22. 85n

Clerk, though court-martialled, a favourite of, 37. 582n

Coke, Lady Mary, receives buck from, 31. 179

Cole indifferent about, 1. 86

Conway's request for return to England dodged by, 38. 190n

Cumberland, D. of, would hardly attend, in illness, 38. 344

Cumberland, Richard, writes verses to, 9. 373, 35. 645

Dalton ordered by, to buy medals for George III, 21. 478

—— said to be set up by, as rival to Strange, 21. 478n

daughter, daughters of, 14. 141n, 21. 416, 527, 531, 22. 302n, 586, 23. 312, 24. 378, 38. 290

death of, 34. 205

Denbigh, E. of, a tool of, 28. 81n

Devonshire, D. of, thinks himself forced out to make room for, 22. 97n

divorce jokingly suggested for, 9. 209

drawings in the hands of, 2. 238n

Dukes of Cumberland, Bedford, Newcastle, and Devonshire unite against, 38. 186

Dyson asked by Wilkes to remind, of play dedication, 10. 52

—— a tool of, 28. 143n

[Stuart, John (1713–92), *continued*]
East India affairs distract attention from, 38. 368

Edwards dedicates book to, 9. 270

Eglintoun friend of, 21. 460n, 465n

Egremont chosen by, for secretary of state, 21. 540n

—— said to have been sent to George III with resignation plans of, 10. 64–5

Elliot might aid, in difficulties, 38. 431–2

enemies made by, over Lord Frederick Campbell's place, 30. 184

England reached by, 23. 312

——'s subsidy to Prussia opposed by, 22. 8n

—— thrown by, into confusion, 38. 417

English disputes blamed on, 23. 83

English victory or defeat would make Pitt seem preferable to, 22. 48

Éon's alleged letter to, 22. 248n, 38. 507n

epigram on, 39. 100

Erskine favourite of, 9. 318n

faction of: 3. 22n; Conway's retention as Cabinet councillor and House of Commons's manager advised by, 22. 571n

falls from cliff, 11. 160

father-in-law's death benefits, 21. 527

first lord of the Treasury, 32. 372

Fletcher's promotion ascribed to, 38. 432n

Florence visited by, 23. 103, 107n

Fox, Henry, recommends Gower to, 41. 67n

—— shocked and angry at Grenville ministry's treatment of, 30. 190

——'s understanding with, 38. 195

—— will embarrass, 22. 93

—— will not easily be removed by, 38. 194

friends of: assert recall of Pitt entirely the responsibility of Northington, 30. 222; indignant over Ps of Wales's exclusion from ministry, 22. 297; listed by Martin, 21. 465n; might be removed from power, 41. 85; support Pitt-Grafton ministry, 30. 243; to compose new administration, 22. 521; warm, 22. 496

Garter installation of, at Windsor, 22. 37, 79

Garter knighthood of, 10. 32, 44

Garter not worn by, 23. 91, 96, 103

George II's death benefits, 21. 527

——'s followers expected to break with, 10. 26

George III advised by, to dismiss ministers, 22. 301–2

—— constantly seen by, 38. 286

——, Court, and House of Lords visited by, 38. 354

—— 'determined' for friends of, 41. 23n

—— gives gold medals to doctors for cure of, 38. 58

—— grants offices to friends of, 22. 307

—— makes, prime minister, 32. 60

—— may be afflicted by resignation of, 10. 63

—— might be saddled by, with Grenville ministry, 22. 396

—— names, Cabinet councillor, 9. 313

—— not to be alienated from people by unpopularity of, 38. 195

—— offers to repudiate, 10. 99n

—— refuses request of, for dukedom of Cardigan, 30. 247

—— 'sacrifices,' 22. 172, 23. 221

——'s coronation attended by, 9. 389

——'s favour retained by, 22. 129

——'s Groom of the Stole, 21. 6, 13

—— should not have been involved by, in deep measures, 22. 134

——'s love for Fox's sister-in-law alarms, 21. 517n

——'s marriage blamed upon, 22. 53, 43. 277

——'s offer of Francavilla statues declined by, 25. 94

——'s private meetings with, hinted at, 39. 61

——'s speech said by Wilkes to have been written by, 22. 136n

(?) —— to be influenced by, 9. 313

—— told by, that E. of Orford bets on his having a child, 21. 530–1

German asks HW to procure place for him from, 38. 176

German war opposed by, 22. 31n

Graeme, friend of, 28. 131n, 32. 183n

(?) Gray inquires about activities of, at Court, 14. 136

——'s name suggested to, for professorship at Cambridge, 28. 79n

——'s paragraph about, should be removed from Gray correspondence, 28. 78–9

Grenville, George, and Halifax insist on removal of, 22. 168

Grenville, George, hopelessly offends, 22. 490

—— makes abject advances to, 22. 419

—— may be removed by, to make Northumberland prime minister, 38. 429, 497

—— must be jealous of, 38. 355

—— probably embarrassed by return of, 38. 355

—— reconciled to, 38. 283–4

——'s enmity with, 22. 92n, 38. 533

—— would have been preferred by, to Fox, as manager of House of Commons, 22. 92

Grenville administration affronts, by Regency Bill, 22. 299–300

Grenville administration demands exclusion of, 38. 562–5

Grenville administration forbids George III to consult, 22. 302

Grenville administration may be supported by, 38. 363

Grenville administration partly reconciled with, 38. 286

Grenville administration's affront to, does not increase their popularity, 30. 187

Groom of the Stole's position may be resigned by, 30. 162

Grub Street papers about, printed in Vienna court gazette, 22. 178

guard given to, at Barèges, 7. 367

HW asked by, to write a history of manners, **1.** 139n, **2.** 307, **14.** 122

HW asks, for payment of Exchequer orders, **40.** 277

HW believes North to be attached to, **10.** 215n

HW compares: to Granville, **9.** 315; to Mme de Pompadour, and imagines D. of Cumberland tending his sick-bed, **38.** 344

HW disclaims desire of preferment from, **13.** 38

HW does not want to show, to Fleury, **22.** 135

HW esteemed by, **23.** 103

HW fears making faux pas before, **9.** 305

HW glad he had no letter from, **23.** 107

HW identifies, **16.** 350

HW informs, of campaign conditions on Spanish-Portuguese border, **40.** 240

HW intercedes with, for Brett, **40.** 194–6

HW jokes about exile of, to Orkneys, **10.** 39

HW judges temper of, by friends' behaviour, **30.** 184

HW might have received reversion of collectorship of Customs from, **10.** 317

HW not to make, jealous, **9.** 269

HW's correspondence with, **40.** 184–6, 187–9, 194–6, 209–12, 239–40, 277, 278

HW sends catalogues of royal collections to, for George III, **40.** 187–9

HW's verses on 'fuction' of, **21.** 7n

HW's *World* seems to hint at affair of, with Ps of Wales, **37.** 438–9

HW thanked by, for *Anecdotes*, **40.** 209–11

HW thinks, should enlist under Pitt to punish 'traitors and wretches,' **38.** 553

HW to arrange with, for presentation to George III, **40.** 184–5

HW told to write to, **9.** 306

HW unacquainted with, **30.** 184

HW wants to preach to, at Houghton, **9.** 349

HW would have received letter from, from Otranto, **23.** 103, 107n

HW writes to, about Court presentation, **9.** 311

Halifax adjourns House of Lords before friends of, arrive, **22.** 297n

—— may ask, for office, **10.** 238

——'s witticism on Fox's overtures from, **22.** 93n

Hardinge, Mrs, makes witticism about George III's choice of, **21.** 459–60

Hardwicke and Newcastle advise, to be secretary of state, **21.** 488

Hardwicke and Newcastle join, against Pitt, **21.** 539n

Harrogate visited by, **38.** 206

health of: broken past recovery, **23.** 302; continental journey made for, **23.** 42, 152; disorders in stomach and bowels, **23.** 103; epidemic fever and sore throat, cured by Duncan and Middleton, **38.** 58; extremely ill, **23.** 152; fever and sore throat, caught from daughter, **21.** 416; gallstones, **32.** 119; good, **23.** 312; Mann sees little hope for, **23.** 162; Naples air bad for, **23.** 96; political aspect of, **23.** 152; retirement caused by, **22.** 128; said to be recovered, **23.** 83; thought to be in great danger, **31.** 193

Hertford consults about attending George III's marriage, **38.** 98, 113

—— entertains, **9.** 237

—— said not to be favoured by, **38.** 283

Hertford, Cts of, complimented by, **38.** 113

'Highland Seer' satirizes friendship of, with Augusta, Ps of Wales, **22.** 53n

Hill favoured by, **28.** 199n

Holdernesse succeeded by, as secretary of state, **9.** 340, **21.** 487, **30.** 162

—— to be appeased by, **21.** 487n

Home secretary to, **9.** 209n

house of, in South Audley St: **21.** 531n; **23.** 312n; attacked by mob, **23.** 7

House of Commons would, if possible, be managed by, in person, **22.** 92

House of Lords filled by, with country bobs, **38.** 159

incognito of: **23.** 91, 96, 103, **28.** 294; (?) satirized, **35.** 471

Italy visited by, **28.** 294

itinerary of, **23.** 103

Jenkinson favourite of, **28.** 71n

—— receives reversion of collectorship of Customs from, **10.** 317

——'s appointment to please, **22.** 472n

—— secretary to, **22.** 91n

—— the 'creature' of, **29.** 322n

Johnston recalled from Minorca for dismissing brother-in-law of, **38.** 394

Le Despenser, follower of, **22.** 473n

Lee jealous of favour of, with Ps of Wales, **21.** 104

Legge's correspondence with, about Hampshire election, **38.** 474

Leicester House believed by, to come to terms with Newcastle, **21.** 75n

—— presses for employment of, about Ps of Wales, **20.** 570n

Lethieullier-Frederick diary may be owned by, but his drawings are not, **2.** 238–9

letters against, **42.** 505

levee of: **10.** 35; not the path of fortune, **38.** 194

Lincoln vacillated between Pitt and, **30.** 179

London calls, 'Sir Eustace,' **37.** 438

—— opposes, **9.** 320

——'s petitions hasten downfall of, **22.** 129

luck of, will not long keep him in power, **38.** 183

Luton Hoo bought by, **22.** 172n, **35.** 332n

—— not opened by, to visitors, **32.** 84n

—— the seat of, **14.** 184n

Luttrell backed by, in Parliamentary election, **32.** 77

Macartney member of family of, **30.** 274

Mallet praises, **28.** 41n

[Stuart, John (1713–92), *continued*]

(?) 'man-mountain,' **14.** 136

(?) Mann asks questions of, about Wilkes's election, **23.** 110

—— offers his house to, **23.** 53, 96, 103

—— sends invitation to, through brother, **23.** 42, 53, 103

marriage of, managed by Lady Mary Wortley Montagu, **13.** 244

Martin favoured by, **34.** 264

—— gets reversion of Customs post from, **28.** 71n

—— ordered by, to pay Exchequer orders, **40.** 277

—— secretary of the Treasury under, **22.** 183n, **28.** 75n

match planned for 5th daughter of, **32.** 48

may fall into Grenville's hands, **22.** 489

may go abroad, **22.** 168

Melcombe carries Bentley's *Wishes* to, to be shown to George III, **9.** 381n, **36.** 645

—— entertains, **9.** 373

Melo seeks English military aid through, **21.** 559n

ministerial changes attributed to influence of, **22.** 431

ministerial conference attended by, at Chesterfield's suggestion, **21.** 97n

ministerial office of, may protect him from House of Commons, **9.** 341

minister in power, though out of office, **22.** 133

ministry of, cannot endure at same time with two others, **21.** 465

mob hangs, in effigy, **38.** 512

mob hisses and pelts, **22.** 102

Montagu pleased by resignation of, **10.** 62

(?) —— wishes George III freed from teaching of, **9.** 309

Mortimer and D. of Suffolk compared with, **22.** 53

Müntz's paintings bought by, **12.** 263

'Murray' the pseudonym of, **23.** 91, 96

Musgrave charges, with receiving bribes, **7.** 367n

musical interests of, **23.** 96n

Naples visited by, **23.** 91, 96

negotiates with both sides, **38.** 342

Newcastle, D. of, coldly treated by, on retirement, **22.** 37n

—— conciliates, **9.** 341

—— informed by, that George III permits choosing a new Parliament, **21.** 444n

—— probably dismissed by, because peace seemed certain, **22.** 38

—— reports aversion of, to peace, and preference for Pitt's war measures, **21.** 527n

—— settles changes with, **21.** 487n

—— to win over, **21.** 86n

newspaper epigrams on doves and parrot given by, to Ps of Wales, **38.** 462

Nivernais dines with, **22.** 82

North Briton accuses, of making George III tell a lie, **22.** 136

—— attacks, **35.** 328

obliging attitude of, **21.** 484

opponents of, unite, **9.** 315–16

Opposition includes, **29.** 322

—— joined by former followers of, **22.** 381n

—— may be courted by, **38.** 328

—— may realize Grenville ministry is more detestable than, **30.** 185

——'s boasts alarm, **22.** 508

Opposition view of, **10.** 52n

organ invented by, **23.** 96n

out of Parliament, **36.** 184

Oxford Tories disgusted with, **38.** 159

Paris to be visited by, **4.** 127

Parliamentary debate on Poor Bill avoided by, **38.** 528

Parliamentary speech by, on making peace, **32.** 22n

Parliamentary support not secured by, **9.** 315

party of, receives reinforcements, **32.** 19

peace must be hastened by, **38.** 163

peace plans outlined by, to Viry and Mansfield, **22.** 30n

peace rumoured to be chosen by, **38.** 159

Pembroke's correspondence with, **10.** 14–15

'persecuted,' **22.** 395

Pitt (Chatham) and D. of Newcastle reconciled by, **21.** 97

Pitt (Chatham) attacks, **22.** 395

—— disagrees with, about Clerk, **37.** 574n

—— does not receive keys from, **22.** 130

—— hopes to oust, **7.** 273

—— may approach, closer, **22.** 490

—— may become unpopular when allied with, **22.** 433

—— may dispute leadership with, in state department, **9.** 340

—— may negotiate with, through Shelburne, **38.** 334

—— might join Newcastle to oust, **22.** 102n

—— or Grenville suggested by, to George III, to head ministry, **22.** 431n

Pitt (Chatham) promises to aid friends of, **22.** 436

—— rejects junction with, **22.** 93n

—— said to be treating with, **38.** 533

—— said to insist on George III's separation from, **38.** 210–11

——'s alliance with: **22.** 473; suggested, **22.** 78n

——'s friendship with, would please George III but alienate the people, **22.** 440

——'s interview with, after Egremont's death, **22.** 159n, 160n

——'s ministry advised by, from fear, **22.** 159–60

——'s negotiations with, worry Bedford faction, **38.** 405

——'s relations with, **3.** 120, **10.** 39–40, 45, 222

——'s Spanish war proposal opposed by, **38.** 131n

—— the chief rival of, at George II's death, **23.** 152

—— treats with, **33.** 64, **38.** 334, 355

Pitt, Anne, friend of, **24.** 378

—— gets pension through, **31.** 40n

political annihilation of, **10.** 153

political unpopularity of, **10.** 222

Pomfret defends against secretaries of state's attack, **30.** 182

Portland's violence against, softened, **30.** 187

private levee at Buckingham House attended by, **38.** 354n

Privy Purse resigned by, **22.** 172n

Prussian subsidy opposed by, **22.** 32n

reappearance of, **36.** 40–1

Regency Bill's inclusion of Ps of Wales affects, **38.** 541, 544, 553

Regency may be object of, **38.** 355

regency measure pressed upon, **22.** 294

regents not likely to be resisted by, **10.** 154

regime of, probably ending, **22.** 93

'Repeal, The,' caricatures, **22.** 400

resignation of, as prime minister, **10.** 59–60, 62, **15.** 88n, **22.** 128–9, **38.** 194–5

resort near Venice revisited by, for health, **23.** 161

returns to London, **22.** 219

reversions of offices granted by, to followers, **10.** 65

Rigby's reference to 'Stuart principles' perhaps aimed at, **38.** 501

Robinson said to owe archbishopric to influence of, **22.** 276

Rockingham ministry's opposition to, will counteract Pitt's concessions to him, **22.** 436

Rockingham, Portland, and Cavendishes think England has no enemies but Dyson and, **38.** 100

Roe, Rev. Stephen, may choose, for hero, **10.** 113

Rome visited by, **23.** 83, 91, 96

royal family chiefly at Richmond with, **38.** 418

Russian affairs eclipse, in HW's interest, **10.** 39

Sackville dissatisfied with, **38.** 498n

satirical print of, **28.** 45n

Scotsmen not preferred by, **21.** 465, **22.** 295

Scott attacks, **22.** 410n, **28.** 465n

secretaries of state hint that mob is fomented by, **30.** 182

secretary of state's position may have been accepted by, in order to make a popular peace, **21.** 488

Selwyn attends levee of, **10.** 35

—— jokes about family name of, **9.** 321

shameful French negotiations of, **29.** 65

Shaw would make Newcastle jealous by dosing, **38.** 83

Shelburne employed by, to negotiate for Pitt's return, **14.** 128n

—— flatters, **38.** 248n, 255n

Society of the Antiquaries of Scotland elects, president, **15.** 150n, **29.** 107

sole minister for a day or two, **21.** 448

son-in-law not helped by, **32.** 280

son of, **25.** 336n, 398n

Squire, Dr, believes, is Ps of Wales's lover, **21.** 6n

Stamp Act repeal may be opposed by, in House of Lords, **41.** 9

statue decorated by, **32.** 91

Strange discarded by, because of Jacobitism, **21.** 404n

Stuart supported by, in Hampshire election, **38.** 474n

successors named by, **10.** 60

suppers may be given by, as George III's mother's paramour, **37.** 458

sycophants of, ungrateful, **10.** 157

'system' of absolutism by, **29.** 267

taciturnity of, **30.** 274

(?) Talbot, Cts, would find no charms in, **9.** 343

Talbot, E., complains to, about diplomatic measures, **9.** 389

Temple objects to people of, in administration, **22.** 308n

Terrick deserts D. of Devonshire for, **30.** 209n

Tories lean more to Grenville than to, **30.** 187

'totters,' **10.** 45

Townshend, Hon. Charles, connects with, **38.** 502

—— 's witticism about, **35.** 93

Townshend, George, Vct, friend of, **22.** 549n

Treasury accepted by, **10.** 32

—— headed by, **22.** 37, **32.** 372

—— resigned by, **10.** 59–60, 62, **15.** 88n, **22.** 128–9, **38.** 194–5

—— would have been given by, to Henry Fox, **22.** 134

Treaty of Paris and, **32.** 22

turbulence stirred up by, **22.** 209

unpopularity of, **12.** 262

Vansittart, Miss, said to lend sedan chair to, for visits to Ps of Wales, **38.** 462n

Venice left by, for England in poor health and spirits, **23.** 297, 302

Vesuvius climbed by, **23.** 91n

Waldegrave did not like, **10.** 64, **22.** 128

Walpole, Sir Edward, makes pun about, **10.** 60

weekly papers abuse, especially for being Scotch, **22.** 42

Weston receives benefits from, **13.** 4n

Whisperer and *Parliamentary Spy* attack, **39.** 124n

wife of, **9.** 338n, **12.** 42n, **13.** 36n, **28.** 164n

Wilkes talks to Dyson about play dedicated to, **10.** 52

[Stuart, John (1713–92), *continued*]
—— writes *North Britons* against, **22.** 60n
Worsley a creature of, **9.** 343n
Wortley the Yorkshire seat of, **28.** 164n
would be in panic at Mme Schwellenberg's being prime minister, **32.** 168
Yarmouth, Cts of, notices coolness between Pitt and, **21.** 13n
York, D. of, allies, with Bedford and Grenville, **22.** 402
Yorke family may upset control of, **22.** 98
Stuart, John (1744–1814), cr. (1776) Bn Cardiff; styled Vct Mount Stuart 1744–92; 4th E. of Bute, 1792; cr. (1796) M. of Bute:
ambassadorship to Spain promised to, **25.** 345–6
appearance of: **10.** 237; handsome, **32.** 19
arrives in London, **25.** 354
Beauchamp may stay with, **39.** 154
book of prints sold to, **1.** 183n
Bull's collection bought by, **15.** 161
Bute's party reinforced by, **32.** 19
Carmarthen omits, from dinner, **33.** 554n
Cole approached by Gulston to sell prints to, **1.** 335, **43.** 60
Cole's prints bought for, **1.** 335, 354, **2.** 307
collector, **1.** 313n
Dutens employed by, in Turin embassy, **25.** 625n
envoy to Turin, **25.** 336
Ewin sells prints to, **2.** 27
'fracas of gallantry' may have caused departure of, from Turin, **25.** 336, 346
Granger accompanies, on tour, **2.** 12n
——'s papers bought by, **2.** 12
Gulston accompanied by, at Cambridge, **2.** 27
—— dines with, **1.** 313n
HW mentions, **5.** 126
handsome, **32.** 19
house of, in Audley St, **25.** 354n
Madrid may be post of, **25.** 363, 398
manifesto of, **33.** 65
Mann receives accounts from, of destruction of floating batteries, **25.** 325
—— receives letter of *congé* from, **25.** 345
marriage of, **22.** 465
Northington may succeed, at Turin, **25.** 336, 354
Paris visited by, **33.** 134
peerage of, corrected, **43.** 129
portrait-frenzy of, **2.** 12
return of, to England, known by HW before Mann, **25.** 354
reversion of auditorship granted to, **10.** 65
servants dismissed by, and equipages sold, **25.** 345
sister-in-law of, **22.** 480
Turin left by, **25.** 336n, 345–6, 354
wife of, **10.** 237
Wilkes avoided by, **22.** 292n
Stuart, Lady Louisa (ca 1757–1851):
Alison, Mrs, described by, quoting HW, **43.** 356

grandfather's bequest to, **21.** 473
HW jokes with, about Lady Mary Coke, **31.** 186–7
HW's paternity questioned by, **17.** 403n
Montagu, Lady, receives letter from, about memoirs, **43.** 371
Parsons, 'Nancy,' described by, **43.** 375
Stuart, Ludovic (1574–1624), 2d D. of Lennox; cr. (1623) D. of Richmond:
HW's portrait of, **16.** 191
peerages of, corrected, **43.** 44
wife of, **1.** 24n
Stuart, Mary, Q. of Scots. *See* Mary (Stuart) (1542–87)
Stuart, Lady Mary (1740–1824), m. (1761) Sir James Lowther, 5th Bt; cr. (1784) E. of Lonsdale:
Coke, Lady Mary, called on by, **31.** 168
grandfather's bequest to, **21.** 473
HW sees, at Lady Bute's, **12.** 69
Hobart, Mrs, entertains, at play at Ham Common, **33.** 370
marriage of, **21.** 527, 531, **35.** 312
peerage of husband of, corrected, **43.** 362
royal ball for Christian VII attended by, **23.** 57n
SH visited by, **12.** 222
Stuart, Matthew (1516–71), 13th E. of Lennox, 1526; Regent:
wife has golden heart made after murder of, **42.** 12n
Stuart, Roy. *See* Stewart, John Roy
Stuart, Sir Simeon (ca 1721–79), 3d Bt, 1761, of Hartley Mauditt, Hants; M.P.:
biographical information about, corrected, **43.** 122
Bolton's duel with, **9.** 281
Carnarvon, Bute, and P. of Wales support, in Hampshire election against Legge, **38.** 474n
Hampshire election contested by, **9.** 281
Jervoise succeeds, **28.** 488n
library of, sold at auction, **32.** 323n
Stuart, Sir Simeon (d. 1816), 4th Bt, 1779:
SH visited by, **12.** 233
Stuart, Sophia (d. ca 1716), m. Henry Bulkeley:
print of, **1.** 181
Stuart, Lady Susan. *See* Stewart, Lady Susanna
Stuart, Lt-Gov. William:
report from, about Dominica, **24.** 421n
Stuart, William, bookseller in Paternoster Row:
SH visited by, **12.** 241
Stuart, Hon. William (1755–1822), Bp of St David's, 1793; Abp of Armagh, 1800:
grandfather's bequest to, **21.** 473
wife of, **11.** 6n
Stuart. *See also* Stewart
Stuart dynasty ('House of Stuart'):
adherents of, decry Q. Elizabeth, **24.** 415
Albany, Cts of, gets nothing from, **25.** 536
arbitrary acts of, hurt the people, **42.** 78
Atkyns praises, **35.** 146
Barnard and Stone might switch to, **35.** 166

Benedict XIV might have exiled Virgin with, to Albano, **22**. 227

Carlisle garrison has to swear never to fight against, **19**. 166

conclusion of, 'wretched,' **25**. 108

Critical Review abuses HW for disliking, **13**. 30

France tells Holland not to oppose, **19**. 134

Guglielmi a former dependent of, **22**. 392

HW's ideas on legitimacy of, **37**. 63

HW's verses mention, **33**. 204

historians may now forget, unless Cardinal York becomes pope, **25**. 106

House of Hanover should learn from example of, to avoid despotism, **24**. 140

Hume and Bolingbroke apostles of, **28**. 72

Hume laughs at, **35**. 214

——'s and Smollett's histories 'whiten,' **16**. 30

Jewish customs might be imitated by, **25**. 115

Lennox, Lady Sarah, descended from, **21**. 531

less harmful to England than Pelhams and Patriots are, **19**. 456

put name of Charles into fashion, **2**. 104

Rome to entertain D. of York under very nose of, **22**. 177

Selwyn's joke on, **9**. 321

Sophia Matilda of Gloucester born on holiday of, **23**. 483

strange termination of, **22**. 325

Stuart, Charlotte, one of last chapters in history of, **25**. 538

Stuart Mackenzie's death would prevent pollution of noble blood of, **30**. 59

topographers praise, **16**. 26

'tyranny' of, deplored by Lynn electors, **41**. 91

Walpole daughters marry into, **21**. 285

weak and unfortunate, **37**. 263–4

York, Cardinal, might marry to continue line of, **25**. 115

York, D. of, must vex, by his welcome at Rome, **22**. 237

Stuart Fitzjames. *See* Fitzjames

Stuart Mackenzie, Lady Elizabeth. *See* Campbell, Lady Elizabeth (ca 1722–99)

Stuart Mackenzie, Hon. James (? 1719–1800), politician; M.P.:

acts at Queensberry House theatre, **19**. 468n

Amelia, Ps, entertains, **22**. 579

Argyll to be succeeded by, in Scotland, instead of going to Venice, **21**. 511n

Barbarina's affair with, **17**. 358n, **30**. 59

Berry, Mary, identifies, **11**. 35n

Besançon news received by, in letter, **12**. 13

biographical information about, corrected, **43**. 82, 140, 281, 313

Brighton visited by, **12**. 203

Bristol to be visited by, with George Pitt, **30**. 59

Bute's resignation may involve, **22**. 133

Campbell, Lord Frederick, succeeds, despite obligations to Bute, **30**. 184

Charlotte, Q., to receive Mann's box of essences through, **22**. 241, 243

couriers to, have long since departed, **21**. 465

Douglas, Lady, visited by, **12**. 117

Dundas dines with, **12**. 39

Dutens chaplain to, **25**. 625n

—— employed by, in Turin embassy, **25**. 625n

——'s letter to, shown to HW, **11**. 35

England reached by, **24**. 401

fans might be sent by, from Turin, **21**. 462

finances of, **30**. 184n

Florence to be visited by, on way to Naples for health, **23**. 337

—— visited by, **23**. 401

Fox, Henry, shocked and angry at Grenville ministry's treatment of, **30**. 190

George III buys Smith's collection at recommendation of, **22**. 107n, 115

—— promised privy seal of Scotland to, for entire reign, **30**. 184

—— promises to, to give Bath order to Mann, **22**. 580, **23**. 3, 5

—— required to dismiss, **10**. 152n

——'s appointment of, to Venetian envoyship, **21**. 471–2, 508

Gordon rioters pick pockets of, **25**. 54, **33**. 175

Grafton's dealings with, about Mann's Bath knighthood, **22**. 580, 587, **23**. 41

Grenville ministry demands dismissal of, as lord privy seal for Scotland, **22**. 302, **38**. 564, 565

HW and Hon. Charles Townshend entertained by, **38**. 502

HW called on by, at SH, with letter from Dutens, **39**. 467

HW considers, 'a man of strict honour,' **22**. 111

HW entertains, at dinner, **10**. 5

HW learns of battle from, **31**. 27

HW may intercede for Mann through relatives of wife of, **21**. 452

HW mentions, **9**. 211

HW sees, about Mann's Bath ribbon, **22**. 579–80

HW sees letter received by, about D. of Brunswick's victory, **39**. 506

HW shocks, **9**. 86–7

HW talks with, about Mann, **24**. 412

HW tells Mann to write to, **22**. 111, 580, **23**. 42, 49

HW told by, that Dick will bring Mann his Bath ribbon, **23**. 41, 52

(?) HW unsuccessfully urged restitution of, to office, **31**. 108

health of: **31**. 288; love-sick and spits blood, **30**. 59; rheumatism, **12**. 203

Hertford persuades Conway to restore, **22**. 431n

Hyndford sends, from Berlin, **30**. 58–9

—— sends back to England, at Ilay's request, **17**. 358n

Italy may be visited by, **23**. 53

[Stuart Mackenzie, Hon. James, *continued*]
Lee said to be succeeded by, as treasurer to Ps of Wales, **21.** 104–5, 110
Louis XVII's restoration doubted by, **12.** 119
Lyttelton may succeed, at Turin, **21.** 507–8
Mann corresponds with, about Francavilla statues, **23.** 583
—— corresponds with, about getting Bath order, **22.** 235–6, 314, 317, 469–70, 486, 582, **23.** 1, 3, 4, 5, 14, 52, 53
—— hears from, of Boscawen's victory, **21.** 330n
—— might be helped by, to get Neapolitan post, **22.** 107, 111
—— might offer services to, for collecting virtu for George III, **21.** 452
—— offers Bute a lodging through, **23.** 53, 103
——'s delay in getting Bath ribbon considered by, a reflection on Bute, **23.** 53
——'s friendship with, **21.** 212, 462, **22.** 107, 111, **24.** 381, 401
——'s pretensions not to be compared to those of, **21.** 472, 483
——'s protector, **24.** 160
—— visited by, in Florence on way to Venice, **24.** 381
—— would be warned by, of any danger, **22.** 115
—— writes to, but does not mention Bath ribbon, **22.** 580
Mount Edgcumbe, Lady, visited by, **10.** 39
Muzell's correspondence with, **21.** 413n
niece's disgrace not known by, **24.** 381
Northumberland House dinner reached by, late, **38.** 530
only child of, dies, **38.** 24
out of Parliament, **36.** 184
'patriot,' **9.** 87
Petersham, home of, **31.** 287–8
Pitt and Temple differ about, **41.** 23n
Privy Seal of Scotland awarded to, **3.** 104, **22.** 133n, 444, 453
—— lost by, **10.** 153
reinstatement of, suggested, **22.** 308n
Richmond visited by, **11.** 148
Rockingham ministry shows civilities to, **22.** 431
Shaw, Elizabeth, said to have flirted with, at ridotto, **19.** 27
Smith's intermediary in selling library to George III, **22.** 107n
SH breakfast not attended by, **31.** 127
Temple asks whether Pitt is to aid, **30.** 226
Townshend, Vcts, visited by, **30.** 58
Turin post to go to, **21.** 212, 218
Vauxhall visited by, **9.** 86–7
Venetian appointment not notified to, **21.** 511
Venice rejects, **23.** 325
vice-chamberlain's post rumoured for, **21.** 452
wife of, **9.** 37n
Stuart McKinsy. *See* Stuart Mackenzie

Stuart Wortley Mackenzie, Hon. James Archibald. *See* Stuart, James Archibald
Stubbs, George (1724–1806), animal-painter and anatomist; A.R.A.:
horses and bull painted by, **23.** 211n
invention of, **29.** 137
Stucco:
at Hagley, **35.** 104
ceiling design may be executed in, **31.** 106
Conway's, mixed by nightingale, **39.** 505
gilt, used to ornament room in Uffizi gallery, **25.** 170
in Great Parlour frieze, at SH, **35.** 79–80
new French room at Florence built of, **33.** 286
polished, in Paris dining-room, **32.** 261
should be invented for concealing thoughts, **33.** 365–6
tomb in, imitating marble, **41.** 103
Stud House, Hampton Court:
Keppels at, **33.** 346
Studiati, Dr Cesare:
Lady Orford's death certificate signed by, **43.** 288
Studley Royal, Yorks:
Aislabie of, **28.** 37n
Stuff; stuffs:
gold, given by Delaval to Lady Susan O'Brien, **38.** 379
gold and silver, to enliven London, **22.** 196
Irish, Conway wishes HW would send for, **37.** 420
Stukeley, Rev. William (1687–1765), antiquary:
Byrom's verses mention, **2.** 162n
Cole's copy of 'Escape of K. Charles I' by, **2.** 296, 297
——'s life of, **2.** 226n
Conway's temple will be offered mistletoe by, **39.** 460
Philosophy of Earthquakes by, attributes earthquake to electricity, **20.** 154, 158
sale of, **15.** 195n
'Stumpity.' *See* Lysons, Daniel
Stura, valley of:
Austrians and Sardinians meet at, **19.** 432
campaign of, **18.** 466n
Sturbridge, Mary. *See* Truebridge, Jane
Sturbridge. *See also* Stourbridge
Sturgeon, Agnes, m. Pierre-Jacques La Chesnaye:
mother settles property on, **38.** 456n
Sturgeon, Charles Alexander (d. 1845):
mother settles property on, **38.** 456n
Sturgeon, Charlotte, m. (1789) Capt. James Edwards:
mother settles property on, **38.** 456n
Sturgeon, Lady Henrietta. *See* Watson Wentworth, Lady Henrietta
Sturgeon, Henry Robert (d. 1814), army officer:
mother settles property on, **38.** 456n
Sturgeon Thomas William (d. 1823), naval officer:
mother settles property on, **38.** 456n

Sturgeon, William (1741–1831), footman:
Watson Wentworth, Lady Henrietta, elopes with, **38**. 456
Sturgeon:
Clement XIII's fondness for, **22**. 327, 331, 380, **23**. 4
——'s major-domo gives, to D. of York, as Tiber product, **22**. 229
orange juice with, as 'remove,' **19**. 357n
Sturges, Rev. Charles, Vicar of Ealing:
Loveday's letter from, about visit to Bp Porteus at Fulham, **43**. 342
Sturgis ('Sturgiss'), Rev. Samuel (ca 1701–43), fellow of King's College, Cambridge 1723–36:
academician promised English paints by, **17**. 462
'black wig' of, **17**. 461
'blind' coffee-house frequented by, **17**. 462
clothes of, in Bns Walpole's cases, **17**. 224
Dashwood's correspondence with, **17**. 125
death of, **18**. 197–9, 210, 217
Geneva and Aix inquired about by, **17**. 95
health of, jaundice, **18**. 197–8
identification of, corrected, **43**. 179
Leghorn merchants tell lies to, **17**. 462
Mann fears he may have to bury, **18**. 198
Pannoni's avoided by, **17**. 462
Pasquale, not Cocchi, physician to, **18**. 198
registrar of warrants in Customs, **17**. 71n
sent to Leghorn: **17**. 95, 107; for burial, **18**. 199
Swiss coffee-house frequented by, **17**. 406
Walpole, Bn (2d E. of Orford), friend of, **17**. 70n
Walpole, Bns (Cts of Orford), banishes, for debts, **17**. 95, 461
—— has, as lover, **13**. 227n, **15**. 325, **17**. 70, 89–90, 461
—— has, tell lies at coffee-house, **17**. 406, 462
—— houses, **17**. 70–1
—— richer because of death of, **18**. 217
—— tired of, **18**. 198
Walpole, Sir Robert, denounced by, **17**. 406
Sturrock, William (d. 1765):
Beauchamp's tutor, **18**. 510n
biographical information about, corrected, **43**. 255
Hertford, E. and Cts of, inform, that they will provide for him for life, **18**. 544
Sturt, Capt. See Stuart, Benjamin
Sturt, Mr:
Critchill the seat of, **12**. 188n
Sturt, Diana (d. 1805), m. (1776) Sir William Mordaunt Milner, 3d Bt, 1774:
Berry, Mary, identifies, **11**. 141n
Farren, Mrs, exchanges visits with, **11**. 64n, 141
Sturt, Mrs, writes to, **11**. 141–2
Sturt, Mrs Humphrey Ashley. See Woodcock, Mary
Sturt, John (1658–1730), engraver:
engraving wrongly attributed to, **16**. 67

Sturt, Mary (d. 1800), m. (1749) Hon. George Shirley:
(?) Chalfont visited by, **9**. 284–5
(?) HW accompanies, to Bois Prévu, **35**. 115
HW entertains, at dinner at SH, **38**. 102
(?) HW mentions, **14**. 120
(?) HW sends letters by, **7**. 379
(?) HW sends snuff-box by, **7**. 404
(?) social relations of, in Paris, **7**. 277, 291, 293, 298
Stutterheim, Otto Ludwig von (1718–80), army officer:
Frederick II orders, to join D. of Württemberg to cover Berlin, **21**. 441n
Stuttering:
dinner for people afflicted with, **33**. 554
Stuttgart (Germany):
Vestris goes to, **38**. 483
Style:
literary: clergyman's, **30**. 183; Eastern, **30**. 288; good, as common as a good print, **15**. 56; HW's reflections on, **16**. 52, 269; mechanization of, **16**. 52; Voiture's, formerly admired, **30**. 75; *see also under names of authors*
Styles, Benjamin (d. 1739):
Moor Park owned by, **30**. 62n
Styptic:
newly-discovered, is to be tested by highwayman, **22**. 147
Styria:
Venice may be menaced by army in, **20**. 176
Styx:
bootikins resemble water of, **39**. 206
Catherine II's shedding of blood will make a, **34**. 146
HW imagines Mexicans and Peruvians on shores of, **25**. 109
HW jokes about, **32**. 74, **33**. 538
HW mentions, **10**. 232
Suabia. *See* Swabia
Suard, Jean-Baptiste-Antoine (1733–1817), journalist:
Académie française's election of, vetoed by Louis XV, **5**. 234
Aiguillon ruins, **7**. 341
censor of plays, **29**. 323n
documents in Hume-Rousseau quarrel translated by, **3**. 128n, *158*
Du Deffand, Mme, does not know, **6**. 317
English journal edited by, **6**. 396
epigram on, **6**. 131
Gazette de France taken from, for calling Lady Waldegrave the wife of D. of Gloucester, **5**. 93, **7**. 340
Harcourt, Earl, makes no complaint against, **5**. 93, **7**. 341
Hume's *Autobiography* translated by, **6**. 425
Louis XV angry at article by, **5**. 92
—— dislikes liaisons of, **5**. 234
—— vetoes election of, **5**. 234

[Suard, Jean-Baptiste-Antoine, *continued*]

Montagu, Mrs, retorts to, at meeting of Académie française, **24.** 267

Redmond wants punishment for, **7.** 341

secretaryship to dukes and peers sought by, **5.** 142

social relations of, in Paris, **7.** 263, 299

(?) suggested as translator for HW's *Historic Doubts,* **4.** 18, 28–9, 32

Variétés littéraires by: Du Deffand, Mme, owns, **8.** 32; *Éloge de Richardson* in, **6.** 251

Suarès; Suarès d'Aulan. *See* Suarez; Suarez d'Aulan

Suares ('Suarez') de la Concha, Mme. *See* Valvasone, Maria Anna

Suares de la Concha, Baldassare (1692–1758), balì; postmaster-general:

daughter says her suitors are older than, **18.** 197

HW's correspondence with, **17.** 49

Scarperia dinner in honour of Modenese princess attended by, **17.** 56

son ordered by, to visit grandparents, **17.** 70

wife's illness patiently borne by, **19.** 226

Suares de la Concha, Ferdinando (1718–99), balì:

Friulian lady said to be engaged to, **17.** 416

mother's illness does not disturb, **19.** 226–7

Suares de la Concha, Francesco (1720–77), cavaliere ('Cecco'; 'Cecchino'):

arrival of, at Florence, in disobedience of parental orders, **17.** 69–70

cane heads inquired about by, **17.** 117

carries letter from HW to Mme Grifoni, **17.** 78

'Cecca' *or* 'Cecchina, la,' pursued by, **17.** 70, 121, 128, 156, **35.** 29

Chesupiades shared by, with Pepi, **18.** 345

Chute and Whithed invited by, to music at villa, **35.** 5

Demetrio not to be acted by, **17.** 99

Federici, Contessa, wooed by, **18.** 345

Florentine gates guarded by, during plague, **18.** 288, 295

grandfather to be visited by, at Friuli, **17.** 70

(?) Gray's odd behaviour with, **17.** 50

HW gives cane to, **17.** 117, 456

HW gives flutes to, **18.** 12–13

HW may be visited in England by, **18.** 108–9

HW might have given cane heads for, to Chute at Venice, **35.** 6

HW's correspondence and friendship with, **17.** 72, 74, 103, 115, 147, 181, 456, **18.** 108–9

HW's news of, pleases his mother, **17.** *39*

HW to receive 'services' of, **35.** 5

HW travels with, from Reggio to Venice, **43.** 170

Harrington through Robinson recommends, for preferment, **18.** 455

Mann called on by, **18.** 108–9

—— discusses Agdollo with, **17.** 149

—— discusses HW with, **17.** 72, 73

—— entertains: at concert, **18.** 12–13; at supper, **17.** 104

—— expects letter of thanks from, for HW, **17.** 456

—— hears news of HW through, **17.** 50

——'s correspondence with, **17.** 52

—— seldom sees, **17.** 147

——'s opera box entered by, **17.** 81, 149

mother's brothers may aid, **17.** 161

mother's embarrassment explained by, **17.** 137

mother's illness does not disturb, **19.** 226–7

Pepi's child attributed to, **18.** 345

Pistoia visited by, **17.** 103

Serristori rebukes, **17.** 149

sister of, **22.** 491

sun-burnt, **17.** 69

to play flutes at concert, **18.** 12–13

Valvasone visit of, **17.** 70, 156, 181

Suares de la Concha, Giuseppe (d. 1755), Bp of San Miniato 1735–55:

bishopric resigned by, **18.** 40

nieces' marriages to Richecourt and Rucellai suspected by, in ravings, **18.** 40

nieces receive no dowries from, **17.** *138*

Richecourt's and Rucellai's persecutions make, mad, **18.** 40

(?) Rucellai's persecution of, **18.** 63

Ruspanti include, **17.** 273n, **18.** 40n

San Miniato left by, **18.** 40

sister-in-law shown 'bawdy matters' by, **18.** 40

Suares de la Concha, Maria Teresa (1723–1809), ('Teresina'), m. (1746) Conte Bernardo Pecori:

convent life contemplated by, **18.** 138

Dal Borgo entertains, **18.** 85

Demetrio to be acted by, for Modenese princess, **17.** 99, 100, 101

disappointed not to have Mann's opera box, **17.** 81

elderly suitors rejected by, **18.** 197

grows beautiful, **18.** 85

Guicciardini might marry, **18.** 138

HW compliments family on engagement of, **19.** 161

husband jealous of, **19.** 311

husband not yet found for, **18.** 526

Mann entertains: at concert, **18.** 12–13; at supper, **17.** 104

——'s opera box to be occupied by, **17.** *69*

marriage of, **19.** 227, 238

Maynard regrets that only Italian is spoken by, **18.** 372

mother wants to marry, to Roberto Pandolfini, **17.** 137, 171, 202

Panciatichi may marry, **18.** 197

Pecori to marry, **19.** 136

—— will make, happy, **19.** 145

Rosalba's studio visited by, **18.** 243n

Salimbeni constantly with, **17.** 101

sister's marriage no longer to be postponed in hopes of a match for, 19. 84

uncle fears marriage of, to Richecourt or Rucellai, 18. 40

uncle has no dowry for, 17. 138

uncle's madness may hinder marriage of, 18. 40

Suares de la Concha, Maria Vittoria (1725–1806), m. (1744) Pierfrancesco Carducci; 'Vittorina':

beauty and costume of, 35. 29

Carducci to wed, 18. 439, 526, 19. 84, 136

Demetrio to be acted by, for Modenese princess, 17. 99, 100, 101

disappointed not to have Mann's opera box, 17. 81

Grand Duchess represented by, at ceremony of the *doti*, 18. 196n, 22. 491

Grand Duchess's lady of honour, 17. 38n

HW compliments family on marriage of, 18. 540

health of, measles, 17. 444, 445

husband jealous of, 19. 145, 311

husband of, 17. *38n*

Mann entertains: at concert, 18. 12–13; at supper, 17. 104

——'s opera box to be occupied by, 17. 69

marriage of, 19. 145

Molinari woos, 18. 29, 138, 197

poverty of, 19. 145

pretty, 18. 29

Rosalba's studio visited by, 18. 243n

Salimbeni constantly with, 17. 101

to sing at concert, 18. 12

uncle fears marriage of, to Richecourt or Rucellai, 18. 40

uncle has no dowry for, 17. 138

uncle's illness may hinder marriage of, 18. 40

Suares de la Concha family:

Bologna visited by, 17. 444, 445

Demetrio given by, for Modenese princess, 17. 65, 99, 100, 101, 104

Florence revisited by, 17. 55, 444, 456, 35. 29

HW sends box and cane to, 17. 416

HW sends compliments to, on daughter's marriage, 18. 540

HW suspects loyalty of, to Mann, 17. 419

lotteries appropriate for, 18. 351

Mann entertains: and gives necklaces to them, 17. 484; at *conversazioni*, 30. 8; at farewell dinner, 17. 161; at dinner, 18. 251

—— to give HW's compliments to, on daughters' espousals, 19. 161

Munich may be sought by, 17. 161

Pisa visited by, 19. 227

uncle mourned by, 18. 439

Venice and Valvasone visited by, 17. 156, 161, 171, 202

villa of: Carducci to wed Teresa Suares at, 19. 136; Chute and Whithed invited to opera at, 35. 5; Dal Borgo villa near, 18. 85; dancing after theatrical performance at,

17. 104n; Mann and Chute see *Demetrio* performed at, 17. 120

Suarez, Denis-François-Marie-Jean de (1729–90), Marquis d'Aulan, Mme du Deffand's nephew:

Aulan, Marquise d', fetched by, 7. 132

—— loved by, 7. 72

—— to be brought to Paris by, 7. 71, 72

Avignon home of, 7. 79, 219

—— to be visited by, 7. 219, 225, 227

biographical information about, modified, 43. 143

claim to Mme du Deffand's papers given up by, 36. 193

Du Deffand, Mme, accompanied by, 7. 64, 71, 73, 198

—— bored by, 7. 212

—— gives tapestry chairs to, 7. 430

—— mentions, 7. 81

—— names, as her executor, 8. 5, 8, 11, 47

——'s bequest to, 8. 5n

——'s correspondence with, 7. (?) 440, 455–7, 459, (?) 461

——'s expenses augmented by, 7. 115–16, 117, 123, 125

——'s opinion of, 7. 71–2, 120–1, 167, 219

——'s residuary legatee, 8. 8

—— to have, as companion: 6. 487, 488, 490, 7. 8, 14, 16, 46, 47, 51, 53–4, 62, 64, 75, 79, 85, 94, 115–16, 120–3; against HW's advice, 7. 125–6

—— visited by, 6. 492

HW to write to, 36. 183

hanged by French mob at Avignon, 11. 76, 84, 91, 31. 357

Juilly visited by, 7. 450

marriage of, 7. 71n

Nicolet attended by, 7. 66

Panthémont to be visited by, for news of Maria Fagnani, 7. 148

(?) Paris visited by, 3. *400*

Plombières to be visited by, 7. 53, 219

—— visited by, 7. 235, 454

Selwyn procures razors for, 7. 131

social relations of, in Paris, 7. 66, 131, 135, 136, 138, 162, 427, 429, 431, 448

Versailles visited by, 7. 451

Suarez, Henri de (b. 1704), Bailli d'Aulan:

Paris visited by, 3. 366

Suarez; Suarres. *See also* Suares de la Concha

Suarez d'Aulan, Anne-Gabrielle-Françoise de (b. 1726); Abbess of St-Sauveur at Marseille:

Du Deffand, Mme, leaves annuity to, 8. 7

——'s correspondence with, 7. 440

Suarez d'Aulan, Étienne-Anne-Marie-Bernard-Régis de (b. 1767):

leaves for school, 7. 431

Paris visited by, 7. 426

Suave mari magno turbantis æquora ventis:

HW's 'old tune,' 24. 48

Subdeacon:

York, Cardinal, becomes, 19. 499

Sublet d'Heudicourt, Charlotte-Alexandrine (b. 1722), m. (1737) Antonin-Armand de Belsunce; Marquis de Castelmoron:
HW likes, **3.** 346
Hénault describes virtues of, **4.** 348n
Lauraguais's answer to Maurepas told by, **3.** 370
social relations of, in Paris, **3.** 346, **7.** (?) 323, (?) 325
Sublime, The:
Greek artists alone attain, **35.** 432
Sublime Society of the Steaks. *See* Beefsteak Club
Subscription; subscriptions:
for French émigré clergy, **31.** 383
for Mrs Yearsley, **31.** 222
HW dislikes being named in, **31.** 222, 383
Subscription book:
HW's London parish circulates, **19.** 167
Subterranean passage:
at Park Place, **39.** 549
Success, English ship:
boatswain of, killed, **21.** 210n
Succession, Act of. *See under* Parliament: acts of
Succinct Genealogies of the noble and ancient houses of . . . Mordaunt. See under Mordaunt, Henry
Suckling, Catherine (1725–67), m. Rev. Edmund Nelson:
father of, **9.** 153n
Suckling, Sir John (1609–42), poet:
engraving of, prefixed to his *Fragmenta aurea,* **16.** 66
Suckling, Rev. Dr Maurice (ca 1675–1730):
marriage of, **9.** 153
squire thrashed by, **9.** 153
Suckling ('Sucking'), Maurice (1726–78), naval Capt., 1755; comptroller of the Navy, 1775; M.P.; HW's cousin:
Fox tells Mann about, **18.** *152*
Mann sends messages to, by Fox, **18.** 182
on board *Newcastle* at Leghorn, **18.** 152, 182
Walpole, Sir Robert, great-uncle of, **18.** 152, 182
will of, names HW and others, **36.** 162
Suckling, Mrs Maurice. *See* Turner, Anne (fl. 1700–30); Walpole, Hon. Mary (1726–64)
Suckling, William (1730–98), deputy collector of Customs; HW's cousin:
address of, in New North St, Red Lion Sq., **24.** 209
brother's executor, **36.** 162
Customs collectorship may temporarily go to, **41.** 325
Customs place described by, **26.** 53–4
HW called on by, **41.** 389
HW does not receive Customs House document from, **24.** 361
HW has not seen, **36.** 156
HW hears about Hon. Thomas Walpole's law suit from, **36.** 204
HW's and Sir Edward Walpole's cousin, **24.** *178*

HW's correspondence with, **42.** 46–7
HW tells, to give exact account of customhouse operations, **42.** 46–7
HW tells Mann to write to, with instructions to execute Collector's duties, and pay HW and Sir Edward Walpole, **24.** 231
Mann's correspondence with, about Customs place, **24.** 231, 237, 243, 252
——'s place in Customs House to be filled by, **24.** 178, 184
—— to insert name of, in letter of attorney, **24.** 209
Rogers can be informed by, of HW's illness, **42.** 389
(?) SH visited by, **12.** 167–8, 249
Walpole, Sir Edward, gets money from, **36.** 328
Suckling, William, jr (1762–1833); army officer:
father buys cornetcy for, **42.** 47
Sudborn. *See* Sudbourne
Sudbourne Hall, Suffolk, Hertford's estate:
HW and Cts of Hertford do not admire, **39.** 263
(?) HW may visit, **6.** 137
HW visits, **35.** 247
Hertford may move Taplow furniture into, **38.** 26
——, Richards, and Hon. Henry Seymour-Conway at, choosing Orford mayor, **39.** 265
Hertford to go to, **38.** 29
—— to visit SH after, **38.** 177, 179
—— writes from, **39.** 314–15, 422, 426, 427, 431–4, 443–4, 457, 463–4
Hertford, Cts of, to go to, **39.** 260, 263
Hertfords return from, **39.** 264–5
—— to be at, **39.** 263, 286
Seymour-Conway, Lady Horatia, visits, with her son, **39.** 463–4
Stewart, Robert, visits Hertford at, **39.** 444, 445
Sudbroke. *See* Sudbrook
Sudbrook ('Sudbroke'), Surrey; D. and Ds of Argyll's villa:
Argyll, 2d D. of, builds, **35.** 282n
Coke, Lady Mary, leaves, **35.** 282
—— permitted to live at, **23.** 538n
—— to visit, **39.** 94
Greenwich, Bns, lives at, **31.** 147, **39.** 90, 94
—— 'the blatant beast' of, **11.** 63
groves of, HW hopes to meet Lady Mary Coke in, **31.** 22
HW sends card to Lady Mary Coke at, **31.** 129
near Petersham, **9.** 61n
visitors to: Coke, Lady Mary, **31.** 129, 147, 314; HW, **31.** 27, 133; (?) Sackville, Lady John, **31.** 147
Sudbury, Derbyshire, Bn Vernon's seat:
Montagu visits, **10.** 227, 229
Venables-Vernon dies at, **29.** 73n
Vernon of, **22.** 31, **29.** 75n
Sudbury, Suffolk:
borough of, advertises for a purchaser of election, **21.** 484

card from mob of, to Bury mob, about election, **35**. 196

Chapman, archdeacon of, **15**. 297n

——'s charge to archdeaconry of, **15**. 304

election petitions concerning Rigby's election at, **30**. 331n

Fonnereau the Court candidate at, **30**. 331n

Frederick, P. of Wales, offered financial aid to Rigby to contest, in his interest, **30**. 331n

Gooch archdeacon of, **1**. 354n

Grafton in vain promoted Harrington's candidacy for, **30**. 331n

populous town, **30**. 331

Rigby may lose election at, **9**. 51

—— M.P. for, **30**. 330n

——'s successful campaign at, **30**. 331

Robinson's friends oppose Rigby at, **30**. 331n

Sudeley, Lord. *See* Boteler, Sir Ralph (d. 1473)

Sudeley, Glos:

Montagu's farm at, **9**. 361n

Sudeley Castle, Glos:

Berrys visit, **12**. 165

Gothic chapel at, **42**. 113–14

Montagu visits, **10**. 285

Parr, Catherine, buried at, **10**. 285

—— exhumed at, **42**. 112–17

print of chapel at, **12**. 165

Rivers owns, **42**. 113

Seymour owns, **10**. 285

spelling of, corrected, **43**. 143

Sudely. *See* Sudeley

Sudermania. *See* Södermanland

Sudley, Vct. *See* Gore, Sir Arthur (1703–73); Gore, Arthur Saunders (1734–1809)

Sudley, Vcts. *See* Annesley, Catharine (d. 1770)

Suer. *See* Suard

Suera, Baron, Russian official:

Orlov receives peace treaty from, **24**. 40

Suetonius Tranquillus, Caius (A.D. ca 69–ca 141), historian:

Lives of the Cæsars by, quoted by Bentley, **10**. 17

translation of: HW comments on, **4**. 487; sent to Mme du Deffand by HW, **4**. 482, 484

Sueur, Le. *See* Le Sueur

Suez:

English caravan from, captured by Arabs, **24**. 510

Suffield, Bn. *See* Harbord, Hon. William Assheton

Suffield, Bns. *See* Hobart, Lady Caroline

Suffocation:

Orford, Cts of, suffers from, **25**. 112

Suffolk, Cts of. *See* Finch, Lady Charlotte (1754–1828); Graham, Catherine (d. 1762); Hampden (Trevor), Hon. Maria Constantia (1744–67); Hobart, Henrietta (ca 1688–1767); Inwen, Sarah (1714–76); Knyvett, Catharine (after 1563–after 1638)

Suffolk, Ds of. *See* Brandon, Lady Frances (1517–59); Chaucer, Alice (ca 1404–75); Elizabeth (Plantagenet) (1444–? 1503); Mary (Tudor) (1496–1533)

Suffolk, D. of. *See* Brandon, Charles (ca 1484–1545); Pole, John de la (1442–91); Pole, William de la (1396–1450)

Suffolk, E. of. *See* Howard, Charles (1675–1733); Howard, Edward (ca 1671–1731); Howard, Hon. George (ca 1625–91); Howard, Henry (1707–45); Howard, Henry (1739–79); Howard, Henry Bowes (1687–1757); Howard, John (1739–1820); Howard, Theophilus (1584–1640); Howard, Lord Thomas (1561–1626); Howard, Thomas (1721–83); Pole, William de la (1396–1450)

Suffolk, Marquess of. *See* Pole, William de la (1396–1450)

Suffolk:

anti-American address from, **39**. 270n, **41**. 311n

Barrow in, **16**. 203

Broome, William, in, **2**. 259

Bunbury and Grafton friends in, **39**. 2

Bungay in, **41**. 96

Charlotte, Q., arrives on coast of, **21**. 528, **35**. 311, **38**. 115–16

Cole's informant comes from, after seeing Nasmith, **2**. 73

draining of fens in, **1**. 132

Gage removes chimney-piece to, **1**. 171

Gipps's MS concerning, **1**. 377, 386, **2**. 221

Gray visits, **14**. 158n

Green, Rev. Edward, clergyman in, **15**. 309

HW writes to Mason in, **28**. 194

Hertford and Richards to go to, **39**. 261

Hertford may be in, **36**. 87

—— may visit, **39**. 129

——'s manorial courts in, **38**. 25–6

—— to go to, **33**. 371, **39**. 163

Hertfords to go to, **39**. 313

Holt has estate in, **19**. 106

invasion may land in, **18**. 401

Keppel chosen M.P. for, **36**. 174

—— declines election offer from, **25**. 86

Mistley Hall overlooks part of, **9**. 15

poor men from, eligible for Trinity Hospital, **16**. 90

West Norfolk regiment encamped on coast of, **42**. 334n

Suffolk, Countesses of:

buried in Saffron Walden Church, **33**. 387

Suffolk, Earls of:

Audley End belongs to, **13**. 88

buried in Saffron Walden Church, **33**. 387

HW queries relationship of, to Dukes of Norfolk, **23**. 485n

Suffolk House:

White's formerly called, **42**. 380n

Suffolk St, London:

Anhalt, P. of, lodges in, **22**. 437

bawdy-house in, **17**. 331

Berwicks stay in, **38**. 406

Bussy takes house in, **21**. 514n, **35**. 308, **38**. 97

foreigners frequent, **22**. 437n

[Suffolk St, London, *continued*]
La Condamine lodges in, **22.** 146
La Rochefoucauld arrives in, **4.** 187n
Nivernais wrongly expected to live in, **38.** 172
Nolcken's house in, **6.** 281n
Saxe-Gotha, P. of, lodges in, **17.** 331
Suffrein. *See* Suffren de St-Tropez
Suffren, —— de, French Adm.:
Trincomalee captured by, **25.** 393n
Suffren de St-Tropez, Marquise de. *See* Choiseul-Meuse, Mlle de
Suffren de St-Tropez, Pierre-Marie (1753–1821), Marquis de:
(?) SH visited by, **12.** 237
Sugar:
and water raised in tanner's bark and peach skins, **35.** 473
Beckford concerned with price of, **22.** 39
Carlisle citadel reproduced in, **19.** 174–5
Dutch brig carries, **33.** 272n
from Jamaica, **33.** 138
HW's gifts of candied, **6.** 235
HW should use, sparingly on stewed fruit, **22.** 114
mechanical cultivation of: (?) Clarkson, (?) Ramsay, and Wilberforce think, practical, **31.** 328; HW delighted to find, practical, **31.** 331; HW suggests, **31.** 324–5
negroes employed chiefly in cultivating, **31.** 260n
sotilties of, **16.** 47
tax on, **22.** 489
West Indian, not preferable to Oriental booty, **33.** 315
Wilton bridge modelled in, **9.** 363
Sugar-boiler:
Hertford is attacked in writings by, **39.** 71
Sugar cane:
hurricane damages, **20.** 331
Sugar-dish:
HW has, of Venetian glass, **17.** 73n
water for tea served in, at Wellingborough inn, **10.** 89
Sugar-figures:
for dessert, castrated by Bns Münchhausen, **20.** 125, 144
Sugar-loaf:
French male head-dress resembles, **30.** 215
Sugar of mercury:
Du Deffand, Mme, takes, **7.** 458
Sugar plantations:
non-owners of, may abolish slave trade, **31.** 324
Sugar planters:
slavery preserved by, **31.** 284
Sugar-plums:
at Florentine wedding, **13.** 230
HW proposes to surfeit schoolboys with, **32.** 316
sugar 'citadel' pelted with, **19.** 175
Sugden, Rev. William (? 1748–1820), Cole's curate:
votes for Dean Milles's son, **2.** 228

Suger, Abbé (ca 1082–1152):
eulogy of, received by Mme du Deffand, **7.** 426
'Suicide.' *See under* Blackett, Mary Dawes
Suicide:
Condorcet's, **31.** 397
crossroads burial of, **36.** 134
Crowley's, **35.** 236
Damer's, **39.** 281–2
Drumlanrig's, **35.** 202–3
Edgcumbe would like to commit, **30.** 36
English trait: **3.** 50, **5.** 321, **6.** 6, **25.** 385–6, 407, **32.** 183, **35.** 236, 256
French dragoons ape English fashion in, **32.** 183
Goodenough's, **33.** 308n
HW calls, 'death *à l'anglaise*,' **25.** 385–6
HW considers, a philosopher's affectation, **39.** 79
HW jokes about committing, **10.** 111–12
HW's reflections on, **20.** 461
Hesse's, **31.** 267
insurers entertained by man intending to commit, **35.** 203
July supersedes November as month for, **10.** 166–7
Keyt's, **30.** 23
life insurance invalidated by, **35.** 203
man who attempted: HW promises Hannah More two guineas for children of, **31.** 338; More, Hannah, cares for, **31.** 337; More, Hannah, solicits HW for aid to family of, **31.** 337
Montfort's, **35.** 201–3
occurrences of, **13.** 147, **17.** 296n, **23.** 420, **25.** 386, 407
old customs concerning perpetrators of, **31.** 267
Orford attempts, **23.** 495, 505, **24.** 293
out of fashion, **19.** 229
Perry's, **30.** 137
popular in Paris, **5.** 175, 205, **7.** 62
Powell's, will convince French visitors of English fondness for self-murder, **25.** 407
Say and Sele's, **31.** 267
Scarbrough's, **30.** 313
will not invalidated by, **35.** 203
World, The, discusses, **31.** 265, 267
See also under Bradshaw, Thomas; Clive, Robert; Damer, Hon. John; Fitzherbert, William; Hay, Sir George; Stanley, Hans
Suidas (fl. 970–1000), lexicographer:
misinterpretations of, **13.** 240
Suin, Mme. *See* Vriot, Marie-Denise
Suit; suits (clothing):
Beauclerk's, at tailor's in Paris, **36.** 192, 196
black (?) velour, **39.** 50–1
crimson velvet, worn by Pomfret, **20.** 390
Du Deffand, Mme, makes: for Conway, **6.** 149; for HW, **6.** 11, 15, 34, 41
English should wear, of sackcloth and ashes, **37.** 437
English steel, **25.** 667n

for Birthday, **17.** 185, **37.** 105, 116
Francis I's, **19.** 58–9
fur-lined, **19.** 420n
HW's: embroidered, worn to fire, **35.** 210; of silver stuff for George III's wedding, **23.** 285
HW sends, to Bp of Mirepoix, **6.** 235, 243, 246–7, 251–3, 255, 257, 258, 263
Holdernesse's, for Birthday, **37.** 116
Mann orders, from Lyon, **22.** 357
of mourning, to be ready in 8 hours, **35.** 159
plain, worn by Hon. Richard Walpole, **20.** 342
price of, **6.** 243, 246–7, 252, 258
silver-laced, **17.** 183
summer, made for Ashburnham, **19.** 420
Suite de la correspondance entre M. le Chancelier . . . See under Pidansat de Mairobert, Mathieu-François
Sukey, English sloop:
Gage sends dispatches by, **24.** 110
Sulgrave, Northants:
enclosure of, proposed in Parliament, **9.** 336
ladies own manor of, **9.** 336
Sulivan, ——:
Mann escorted by, **23.** 60n
Sulivan, Mr and Mrs, of Sunbury, Middlesex:
SH visited by, **12.** 228
Sulivan, Laurence (ca 1713–86), deputy chairman of East India Co.; M.P.:
Ashburton to be borough of, **36.** 47
Barré intended by, for Bengal, **38.** 378
Clive bribes East India Co. director away from, **38.** 378
——'s enemy, directed by Chatham, **22.** 497n
East India Co. elects choices of, as directors, **38.** 371
——'s deputy chairman, **43.** 317
——'s new proposals influenced by those of, **22.** 508n
East India Judicature Bill brought in by, **23.** 399n
Fox supports, against T. Walpole, in Ashburton election, **30.** 169n
HW tired of, **38.** 368
mob attacks, by mistake for Onslow, **23.** 288
Opposition's voting for, **22.** 507n
proposals by, **22.** 497n
Rous enemy of, **38.**378
Sulivan, Lt Philippe:
captured at Velletri, **18.** 492
Sulivan. *See also* O'Sullivan; Sullivan
Sulkowsky, Mme. *See* Mniszech, Louise
Sulkowsky, August Casimir (1729–86), D. of Bielitz, 1762:
parsimony of, **33.** 280
Stanislas II competes with, for Polish crown, **33.** 279–80
SH visited by, **33.** 280
Sulla, Lucius Cornelius (138–78 B.C.), Roman dictator:
ape of, might call himself Brutus, **15.** 131
Walpole, Sir Robert, compared to, **42.** 79

Sullivan, Lady Henrietta Anne Barbara. *See* Hobart, Henrietta Anne Barbara
Sullivan, Maj.-Gen. John (1740–95):
Long Island defeat of, **24.** 249
naval operations reported by, **24.** 419n
Staten Island attacked by, **24.** 331n
Sullivan, Luke (d. 1771), engraver:
print by, after Hogarth, in Clubbe's *Physiognomy*, **16.** 173
Sullivan, Richard Joseph, of Thames Ditton:
SH visited by, **12.** 246
Sullivan. *See also* O'Sullivan; Sulivan
Sully, Duc de. *See* Béthune, Maximilien de (1559–1641)
Sully, Duchesse de. *See* Baylens de Poyanne, Henriette-Rosalie de
Sully, Hôtel de, Paris:
Hénault meets Mme de Flamarens at, **3.** 144n
Sulphur:
Mann, Lady Lucy, might go to Puzzuolo to breathe, **24.** 190
ointment of, **23.** 460, **36.** 332
Sulpice, St, church of. *See* St-Sulpice
Sultan; sultans:
handkerchief flung by, in harem, **9.** 91n
print of George III as, **33.** 159
Sultan, English ship:
Howe to be joined by, **24.** 411
Sultana; sultanas:
Joseph II might free, **42.** 183–4
'Sultane, la.' *See* Bécu, Jeanne, Mme du Barry
Sultaness. *See* 'Scheherazade'
Sultan of Turkey. *See under* Turkey
Sulzbach, Elector of. *See* Karl Theodor
Sulzbach, Pfalzgräfin von. *See* Eleonore (1712–59)
Sumach:
box of, from Ampthill, for HW, **34.** 44
Summer; summers:
English: coal mines and verdure substitutes for, **34.** 143; coal mines provide, **36.** 282; deplorably wet, **25.** 312; does not ripen, **33.** 561, **34.** 52; HW ridicules, **10.** 262; HW's observations on, **1.** 177, 328; hot and dry, **20.** 188; 'made to be felt and enjoyed,' **33.** 334; marriages and deaths unfashionable in, **22.** 251–2; warmer than in Ireland, **21.** 121; worst ever, **34.** 170
HW dreads, in wartime because of danger to friends, **24.** 529
HW stores knowledge during, **21.** 368
Summer Assizes:
Aylesbury's contest with Buckingham over, **20.** 449n
Summer Hill *or* Somerhill, Kent:
Gramont's 'Princess of Babylon' lived at, **35.** 135–6, **39.** 310
HW and Chute visit, **35.** 135–6
HW finds, a mere farm-house, **39.** 310
Summer house; summer houses:
at Heath Lane Lodge, Twickenham, **43.** 363
at La Trappe, **35.** 302
at Orford House, Chelsea, **37.** 126

[Summer house; summer houses, *continued*]
at the Vyne, **35**. 640
Mr May's 'Cupid' blown from, **12**. 157
Radnor's, in Chinese style, **20**. 382
Selby's, at Twickenham, **11**. 60
Wren should have confined his building to, **40**. 349
Summer Islands:
English weather as gorgeous as, **12**. 152
Summer's Tale, The. See under Cumberland, Richard
Summons. See under Dugdale, Sir William
Sumner, Jane (d. 1766), m. (1764) William Skrine:
brother of, gives her a fortune on her marriage, **38**. 394
death of, at Rome, **7**. 397, **22**. 398, 402
Sandwich, E. of, 'bestowed on the public,' **22**. 402
Sumner, William Brightwell (b. ca 1730):
sister given fortune by, on marriage, **38**. 394
Sumorokov, ——:
Hamlet translated by, into Russian, **22**. 426n
Sun:
Jupiter supposedly moves the earth towards, **20**. 119–20, 143
Louis XIV and, story of, variations on, **43**. 153
Mann fond of, **20**. 143
Sunbury, Middlesex:
balloon descends near, **39**. 424
good private houses with gardens at, **2**. 200
Montfort has house at, **2**. 115
robbery at, **35**. 315
Sunday:
English clergyman refuses to attend opera on, **18**. 162–3
joint and pudding doubled for dinner on, **32**. 191n
Macaronies run races in evenings on, **23**. 491
Methodists do not play cards on, **20**. 34
—— object to opera attendance on, **20**. 86
newspapers do not come on, **35**. 378
observance of, by royal proclamation, **34**. 25n
religious people turn, into fast day, **31**. 435–6
SH visitors give no holiday on, **33**. 523
See also Sabbatarianism
Sunday schools:
Horsley, Bp, opposes, **31**. 396n
Sunderhausen, Germany:
Soubise's victory at, **9**. 254n
Sunderland, Cts of. *See* Churchill, Lady Anne (1683–1716); Sidney, Lady Dorothy (1617–84); Tichborne, Judith (d. 1749)
Sunderland, E. of. *See* Spencer, Charles (ca 1674–1722); Spencer, Charles (1706–58); Spencer, Robert (1641–1702); Spencer, Robert (1701–29)
Sunderland, John, of Clare Hall, Cambridge:
(?) Ashton's verses on death of, **14**. 235
Sunderland estate:
Spencer, John, entails, on Pitt, **9**. 34, **22**. 277n
Sunderland, Durham:
iron works at, **16**. 77n

Sunderlin, Bns. *See* Rooper, Philippa Elizabeth Dorothy
Sundermania. *See* Södermanland
Sundon, Bn. *See* Clayton, William
Sundon, Bns. *See* Dyve, Charlotte
Sun Fire Insurance:
Houghton fire damage estimated by, **34**. 88n
Sunninghill ('Sunning Hill'), Berks:
(?) Bellenden and Coke meet at, **9**. 60
Churchills visit, **37**. 289
Clarke, Anna Maria, thought to be at, **31**. 326
Coke and Lady Mary Coke at, **37**. 288
HW jokes about waters of, **31**. 96
Hervey, Bns, benefited by waters of, **31**. 90
—— calls, *fontaine de jouvence*, **31**. 81
—— visits, **31**. 81, 119
Milles writes from, **2**. 227
mineral waters of, **31**. 81n
Pitt, Thomas, to drink waters of, **22**. 73
wells of, Cumberland, D. of, closes road to, **13**. 22n
Sun Tavern Fields, Shadwell:
rioters hanged at, **23**. 39n
Superb, English ship:
Hervey, William, commands, **17**. 275n
Vernon dispatches, **17**. 276n
Superbe, French ship:
Roquefeuil dies aboard, **18**. 423n
sunk, **21**. 351
Superstition; superstitions:
avoidance of unlucky days, **22**. 465n
Coventry attributes, to disappointment in love, **9**. 7
HW's belief in, **33**. 25, 340
HW's housekeeper's, **32**. 76
HW wishes, still alive, **33**. 8
Mann's reflections on, **18**. 59, **20**. 429–30
misfortune the mother of, **35**. 261
religious times would interpret casualties as portents, **33**. 335
Supper; suppers:
after Elizabeth Chudleigh's ball, **35**. 301, **38**. 205
after Florentine opera, avoided, **18**. 303
after loo party at Cts Waldegrave's, **38**. 371
agreeable at Park Place, **38**. 100
Aiguillon gives, for English prisoners, **21**. 251
Aiguillon, Duchesse d', invites HW to, **41**. 8
Albemarle dies after, **35**. 201
Amelia, Ps, gives, for Christian VII, **23**. 48
Arenberg entertained only at, **18**. 97
assemblies followed by, **35**. 213
at Almack's, **38**. 512n
at Anne Pitt's ball, **38**. 335
at Bedford House, **35**. 217, 225
Athenry, Bns, gives, **37**. 442
at Holdernesse's ball, **35**. 162
at 9 P.M. in Paris, **38**. 238
at 1 A.M. in Florence, **37**. 78
at Oxford tavern, **30**. 330n
at Pantheon fête, **39**. 330

at Paris: excessive, **38.** 267; on Ash Wednesday, **41.** 2
at Richmond, end at midnight, **11.** 163–4
at Stowe, **10.** 313
Bedford, Ds of, gives, in opposition to Cts of Lincoln, **37.** 454
Berkeley's, on eve of joining army, **37.** 530
brawn only for, **2.** 180
Choiseul, Duchesse de, gives, **35.** 335–6
Chute eats veal at, **35.** 21
cold, at Haymarket entertainment, **39.** 382
constant, at Compiègne, **38.** 408
Conti's, at Isle-Adam, **31.** 45
Conway and wife give, in Warwick St, **38.** 142
Conway enjoys, in Ireland, **37.** 442
Corsi gives, for Eszterházys, **20.** 350
Court ball ends without, **38.** 143, 290
Craon's: **17.** 194; for English captains, **18.** 98
Craon, Princesse de, provides, nightly, **37.** 69
—— takes, at midnight, **18.** 122
cricket players have, **40.** 6
Derby's cook resents serving, at 3 A.M., **24.** 310
Du Barry, Comtesse, gives, **23.** 115
Du Deffand, Mme, and guests sit around fire after, **41.** 42
Du Deffand, Mme, entertains Mme de Forcalquier at, **41.** 162
—— gives: for Choiseul's adherents, **41.** 194–5; to ungrateful circle, **41.** 4
—— in a passion with her cook over, **39.** 269
—— may give up, **6.** 118, 133
—— places, among the four ends of life, **7.** 138–9
——'s established: a score of frequenters of, **6.** 207; Friday, **3.** 12, 205, 229, 278, **4.** 38, 110, **7.** 13, 102, 166, 168; New Year's, **4.** 324, **6.** 3; Saturday, **5.** 5, 13, 27; Sunday, **3.** 5n, 19, 64–5, 170, 173, 191, 205, 206, 244, 303, **4.** 37, 38, 46, 69, 80, 112, 140, 163, 191, 205; Thursday, **6.** 200–1, 240, 267–8, 353; twice weekly, **6.** 200–1, 240, 267–8, 353, **7.** 13, 102, 166, 168; Wednesday, **6.** 134, 200–1, 240, 267–8, 353, **7.** 13, 102, 166, 168
—— should take dinners instead of, **36.** 58
——'s menu for, **5.** 73
—— takes, at home: alone, **5.** 122; rarely, **5.** 180; scarcely twice a week, **5.** 13; usually, **7.** 80; with a few guests, **5.** 73, 83, 351
—— will send, to HW's hotel, **3.** 342
English begrudge invitations to, **31.** 4
Ferdinand of Naples gives, at Caserta, without tables, **23.** 191
for Cts of Yarmouth, **37.** 458
for lady dancers at Robinson's ball, **37.** 115
Foxes have, with D. and Ds of Richmond, **30.** 112
Frederick, P. of Wales, gives, after son's christening, **19.** 174–5
French eat, with doors open, **31.** 93

—— leave windows open till, **35.** 343
—— play before and after, **38.** 238
George II takes, with family, **20.** 539
Gloucester, D. of, to have been entertained at, in Pisa theatre, **23.** 357
Good's, **37.** 14
HW busy with, **38.** 312
HW deserts, in order to finish letter, **38.** 371
HW diverted by Lincoln's account of Mme de Matignon's, **30.** 30
HW does not wish raw beef for, **30.** 260
HW enjoys, in Paris, **10.** 175
HW gets to bed at 2 or 3 o'clock after, **39.** 258
HW has, twice a week with Mme du Deffand, **30.** 204
HW might eat stewed fruit for, **22.** 114
HW's, at 12:30 A.M., **38.** 371
HW serves, cold, at SH, **10.** 279
HW substitutes for dinner, in France, **22.** 396
HW takes: at 1 A.M. in Florence, **37.** 78; in company, **21.** 368; with Mrs Clive, **35.** 239
HW takes hartshorn and pears at, **22.** 110, 114
HW to leave ball before, **25.** 22
Hertford, Cts of, learns to like, in Paris, **39.** 46
—— to return to Paris after, at Isle-Adam, **31.** 45
Hertford may forgo dinners in favour of, **38.** 271
——'s, for Mme de Praslin, **38.** 253
—— to give, in Paris, **38.** 246
Hertfords': for Englishmen at Paris, **38.** 516; to be directed by Duchesse de Mirepoix, **38.** 217
Holland, Bn, never stays for, **38.** 337
hour of: **3.** 280, 387, **4.** 66, 153, 314, **6.** 178, **7.** 13; at SH, **31.** 179; in country, **4.** 447; in Paris, **31.** 48; More, Hannah, and Mary Hamilton have, between 10 and 11 P.M., **31.** 229
in Mann's opera box, on ball nights, **20.** 75n
in Paris, frequent, **38.** 337
Italian opera subscribers to have, **10.** 138
Leopold and Maria Louisa do not restrict guests at, **23.** 191
Leopold and Maria Louisa take, at 9 P.M., **22.** 354
Leopold and Maria Louisa to give, at Great Theatre, for D. and Ds of Cumberland, **25.** 645
Louis XV's expenses not all swallowed up by, **20.** 500
Lucca serves, of 60 covers, for D. of York, **22.** 222
Mann and Horace Mann II walk in moonlight before, **24.** 517
Mann finds, too expensive, **18.** 281
—— regularly entertains Pelham with Englishmen at, **20.** 115
——'s diet at, **17.** 78

[Supper; suppers, *continued*]

Masserano's, in London, **38.** 399–400

Montagu enjoys, because of HW's letter, **10.** 165

Montfort orders, despite intended suicide, **35.** 202

Northumberlands give, for Cts of Yarmouth, **21.** 191

Parisian: consist of three courses and a dessert, **31.** 48; HW eats, **31.** 93; HW has, in dressing-room, **31.** 67; HW has, in two or three societies, **31.** 78–9; Hayes, Mrs, invites HW to, **31.** 65; Luxembourg, Mme de, gives, in paved and vaulted hall, **31.** 112–13; Rochefort, Comtesse de, gives, at Luxembourg Palace, **31.** 54; seldom lively, **31.** 137; sole events, **31.** 137

Petersham, Lady Caroline, gives, at tavern, **35.** 222–3

'reformed' in France, **35.** 126

Richmond, D. of, gives, at Whitehall, **31.** 35–6

Robinson's, for lady dancers, at 12, **17.** 185, **37.** 115

Rohan, P. Camille de, gives, at Leghorn, for Leopold, **22.** 556

St John prepares, at Craon's, **21.** 533

Sansedoni, Mme, gives, for D. of York, **22.** 224

served on waiting tables, **37.** 115

small, are Paris's only Lenten diversion, **38.** 485, 504

Stair's, **37.** 149

Strafford stays, till after midnight for Conway and D. of Cumberland, **37.** 212

Suffolk, Cts of, takes, in chamber with Lord Chetwynd, **22.** 544

Townshend, Vcts, takes, in silver saucepan to Brompton lodging, **30.** 70

Tuscan Court gives, weekly, at Pisa, **23.** 171, 191, 262

Whitehead's, at 'Bedford Head,' **17.** 211

Williams, G. J., has, with HW, **30.** 125

winter's, to consist of autumnal harvests, **35.** 474

Supplement, A. See under Granger, James

Supplément à la correspondance de M. le Duc d'Aiguillon. See under Vignerot du Plessis-Richelieu, Emmanuel-Armand

Supplément à la Gazette de France. See under Gazette de France

Supplement to the Historic Doubts, by HW:

Cole refers to, **2.** 6n

HW printed, but did not publish it, **16.** 266

Hardinge makes suggestions for, **35.** 608, 610

Pinkerton's opinion of Hume's history concurs with that of, **16.** 266

published in 1798, **1.** 134n, 219n

shown to Hume, **1.** 134n

Supplement to the Miscellanies of Thomas Chatterton. See under Chatterton, Thomas

Supporter; supporters:

armorial, heraldic, **35.** 93

Surat, India:

hurricane and flood reported at, **25.** 428

Spencer's letter to S̲h̲āh 'Ālam about defence of, **23.** 381n

Surbois. *See* Royer de Surbois

Surcoat, herald's:

Cts of Shrewsbury's costume compared to, **10.** 337

Surfeit water:

Nugent takes, at night, **17.** 271

Surgeon; surgeons:

Acquaviva's, **19.** 136

at Pisa, **11.** 235

Beaufort's potency examined by, **18.** 185

Benedict XIV's, *see* Ponzio

Bentley needs, instead of apothecary, **35.** 221

Capponi treated by, **18.** 183

Chetwynd's wound dressed by, **18.** 192

Clement XIV's, *see* Laboussiere

commission on Felipe Antonio's imbecility consults, **21.** 329

Downe tells, to disregard pain, **21.** 466

English, for D. of Gloucester, throws Italian prescriptions away, **23.** 393

Ferrers's body to be delivered to, **21.** 388, 403

French, **12.** 25

French and German, Panciatichi not cured by, **20.** 36

Greek, Cocchi's book on, **20.** 179, 189, 437

HW attended by, **31.** 237, 298

HW has to have, for gout in arm, **25.** 618

HW in hands of, **15.** 284

HW's, wants him to take the air too soon, **25.** 617

HW's, *see also* Gilchrist, Stirling (d. 1791); Huitson, I.P.; Watson, Henry (d. 1793)

HW's finger dressed by, **12.** 76, **29.** 337

HW to be treated by, **17.** 52

HW told by, about effects of castration, **18.** 565

HW unwell while absent from, **15.** 325

HW urged by, to take the air, **25.** 626

Hawley asked by, for corpse of spy to dissect, **19.** 201

in country, ill-treats Vct Townshend, **38.** 346

injured performers call for, **13.** 113

Irish, picked up at Tunbridge by Ds of Bolton who makes will in his favour, **21.** 365

Italian, distrusted by HW, **11.** 261

Lobkowitz accompanied by, **18.** 564

Mann given false encouragement by, **25.** 567

——'s: alarmed by Mann's swollen feet, **24.** 79; believes his rheumatism to be gout in head, **24.** 479; feeds him ice creams and uses bleedings and senapisms, **25.** 560; Mann tells, that he must get well, to entertain the Hollands, **22.** 467; tells him that chalkstones are painful, **25.** 626; *see also* Benevoli, Antonio

murderers' bodies delivered to, **21.** 388

ordinary correspondents like unskilful, when they condole, **37.** 31

papal, *see* La Bossier *or* Laboussiere, Carlo

Parisian, fails to cure Panciatichi's knee, **20.** 36

poison found by, in dead race-horse, **41.** 6

royal family used to be attended by, when out hunting, **35.** 107

St-Aignan's: Mann thinks, might be valet-de-chambre, **17.** 81; St-Aignan recommends, to Mann, **17.** 81

'sensible young,' in D. of Gloucester's suite, **26.** 50

survival of twice-pierced victim expected by, **37.** 253

Tencin in vain dissuaded by, from trip to Rome, **17.** 481

Wilkes may have additional, **38.** 273

See also Benevoli, Antonio; Charlton, John; Cocchi, Antonio; Davenport, R.; La Peyronie; Mick; Nesi, Francesco Maria; Obrian, Dennis; Pasquale, Gaetano; Patch, James

See also under Page-surgeon

Surgeon-page. *See* Page-surgeon

Surgeon's Hall, London:
Ferrers's body dissected at, **21.** 403
hanged Jews dissected at, **32.** 68n

Surgères, Comte de. *See* Granges de Puiguyon, Louis-Armand-François de (ca 1744–67); La Rochefoucauld, Jean-François de (1735–89)

Surgères, Comtesse de. *See* Chauvelin, Anne-Sabine-Rosalie

Surgères, Marquise de. *See* Fleuriau d'Armenonville de Morville, Jacquette-Jeanne-Thérèse

Surgical instruments:
Benevoli lacks, **17.** 89, 341
Gloucester, D. of, presents, to hospital at Rome, **24.** 129
See also Cutting-gorget

Sur la destruction des Jésuites. See under Alembert, Jean le Rond d'; Voltaire

Sur la législation et le commerce des grains. See under Necker, Jacques

'Sur la poule au pot':
Du Deffand, Mme, quotes, **6.** 93

Surplice; surplices:
Gray swears to wear a clean, **13.** 59
Mason's, **28.** 147

Surprise, English frigate:
Quebec reached by, **24.** 215n

Surprise. See also *Surprize*

Surprise de l'amour, La. See under Marivaux, Pierre Carlet de Chamblain de

Surprises de l'amour, Les. See under Bernard, Pierre-Joseph; Rameau, Jean-Philippe

'Surprising History of a Late Long Administration, The':
(?) Conway thinks, stupid, **37.** 228

Surprize, American privateer:
Prince of Orange captured by, **24.** 302

Surprize. See also *Surprise*

Surrenden Dering, Kent:
Dering of, **10.** 40n

Surrey, Cts of. *See* Fitzroy Scudamore, Frances

Surrey, E. of. *See* Howard, Charles (1746–1815); Howard, Henry (ca 1517–47); Warenne, William de (d. 1089)

Surrey:
bridge built across Thames from Woolstaple, Westminster, to, **20.** 108n
Brixton Causeway in, **42.** 491, 492
Conway and Cts of Ailesbury visit in, **37.** 304–5
counter-protests signed in, **25.** 10
earthquake causes powder-mill explosion in, **17.** 278n
election ends in, **36.** 177
'Gillian of Croydon' lives in, **13.** 149
grand jury of, indicts keepers of Richmond New Park, **20.** 322n
high sheriff of, *see* Saunderson, Edward
house in, too near London, **37.** 304
Keppel accepts election offer from, **25.** 86
—— ousts Onslow as M.P. for, **36.** 174
Kingston celebrations proclaim Keppel's election for, **36.** 178
Mann family's estate possibly in, *see under* Sussex
Oatlands the pride of, **35.** 237
Onslow elected for, **30.** 290
petitions from, **35.** 334
Stanley's villa in, **24.** 14

Surrey Road:
George St in, **42.** 448

'Surrey Wonder.' *See under* Vertue, George

Surry. *See* Surrey

Surry St, the Strand, London:
Becket and De Hondt at Tully's Head near, **21.** 514n

Surtout; surtouts:
heraldry on, **40.** 225

Survay of London. See under Stow, John

Surveillante, French ship:
Yorktown surrender news brought by, **25.** 211n

Survey; surveys:
HW's letters will be less dull than, **35.** 146

Survey of the Cathedral Church of Worcester. See under Thomas, William

Survey of the Doctrine and Argument of St Peter's Epistles. See under Whitaker, John

Surveyor-general of the Works:
Benson succeeds Wren as, **40.** 346–7
Wren as, held Exchequer lease on Hampton Court house, **40.** 4

Surveyor of Mercers' Company:
monument to be examined by, **16.** 89

Surveyor of the Forests:
Legge succeeds Whitworth as, **17.** 493

Surveyor of the Gardens:
Vernon's place as, held for him by Dickinson, given to Cadogan, **38.** 377

Surveyor of the King's Pictures:
Grafton asks Hertford to give reversion of, to Sandby, **39.** 114n

Surveyor of the Roads:
  Finch succeeds Erskine as, **9**. 318
  Legge becomes, **19**. 457n
  See also Phillipson, John (d. 1756); Walker, Thomas (d. 1748)
Surveyor of the Royal Gardens. *See* Hervey, Hon. Thomas (d. 1775)
Surveyor of the Woods:
  Devonshire, D. of, revokes promise to Henry Fox of, for Hamilton, **30**. 130n
  See also Phillipson, John
Susa, Vittorio Francesco (1692–1762), Marchese di:
  captured, **18**. 436
  English captains entertained by, **18**. 360
  Villefranche commanded by, **18**. 360
Susa (Italy):
  governor of, Viry ordered to report to, twice a day, **24**. 328
  HW and Gray pass through, **13**. 190
  Viry arrested at, **6**. 474, **24**. 328
Susanna:
  Lely's painting of, **10**. 346
Suspicious Husband, The. See under Hoadly, Benjamin (1706–57); Hoadly, John (1711–76)
Sussex, Cts of. *See* Hall, Hester (ca 1736–77); Palmer, Anne (1662–1722); Sidney, Frances (ca 1531–89)
Sussex, D. of. *See* Augustus Frederick (1773–1843)
Sussex, E. of. *See* Lennard, Thomas (1654–1715); Radcliffe, Thomas (ca 1525–83); Yelverton, George Augustus (1727–58); Yelverton, Henry (1728–99)
Sussex:
  army camps to be formed in, **35**. 255
  Brest fleet near coast of, **18**. 402
  Burrell's collections for history of, **1**. 162n
  ——'s drawings for, **15**. 203
  Conway familiar with, **39**. 309–10
  counter-protest signed in, **25**. 10
  discomforts of travel in, **9**. 96
  Dodd and Whaley tour, **40**. 5–6, 8
  Egremont, Cts of, returns to, **40**. 324
  election for, **41**. 73
  Gibbon goes to, **32**. 341
  Gideon visits Gage in, **2**. 118
  HW and Chute tour, **9**. 96, **35**. 131–46
  HW recommends sights in, **39**. 309
  HW visits, **1**. 66, **4**. 445n, 455n, **9**. 96, **35**. 131–46
  Harcourts visit, **28**. 404
  Kent competes with, at cricket, **40**. 6
  Lennox, Lord George, elected M.P. for, **30**. 242n
  Mann family estate allegedly in, **18**. 307, **20**. 307n, **24**. 168, 173, 176, 181
  Middlesex opposed by Sergison in by-election for, **30**. 20
Montagu compares himself to inhabitants of, **10**. 158
  —— jokes about residents of, buying armour, **10**. 287
  —— travels in, **9**. 286
  mutton from, **38**. 256
  Newcastle, D. of, kisses men of, at troop review, **19**. 495
  —— might be begging France for post in, **21**. 499
  Peachey loses election in, **39**. 207
  Richmonds pleased by election in, **30**. 242
  Seymour-Conway, Lord and Lady Hugh, visit Bathursts in, **36**. 288
  Silver Hill overlooks, **35**. 141
  South Downs in, **39**. 550
  Stanmer in, **10**. 338
  Taaffe to build prison in, **9**. 159
  Temple, Mrs, in, **20**. 180
  wrecking of ships in, **10**. 158
Sutherland, Cts of. *See* Maxwell, Mary (ca 1740–66); Sutherland, Elizabeth (1765–1839); Wemyss, Lady Elizabeth (d. 1747)
Sutherland, Ds of. *See* Sutherland, Elizabeth (1765–1839)
Sutherland, D. of. *See* Leveson Gower, George Granville (1758–1833); Leveson Gower, George Granville (1786–1861)
Sutherland, Capt.:
  Cumberland, D. of, entertains, at Calais ball, **23**. 351n
Sutherland, Elizabeth (1765–1839), Cts of Sutherland, s.j., 1766; m. (1785) George Granville Leveson Gower, styled Vct Trentham to 1786 and E. Gower 1786–1803; 2d M. of Stafford, 1803; cr. (1833) D. of Sutherland:
  arrest of, at Abbeville, **34**. 156n
  eldest son of, **34**. 156–7
  HW visited by, at SH, **12**. 242, **34**. 156
  Marie-Antoinette and Louis XVII get disguises from, **34**. 156n
  returns from Paris, **34**. 156
  Wales, Ps of, rumoured to be attended by, **12**. 123
Sutherland, James (ca 1731–91), Judge of the Vice-Admiralty Court of Minorca:
  Mann sends packet through, to HW, **25**. 81, 87, 93
  Minorca left by, for England after rift with Murray, **25**. 81
  Murray sued by, **43**. 287
  Scarniccia well known to, **25**. 199n
  suicide of, **43**. 287
Sutherland, Scotland:
  rebels go towards, **37**. 233
Sutherland, English ship:
  expected at Port Mahon, **17**. 285
Sutherland clan:
  Coke, Lady Mary, would like to lead, against French, **38**. 17
Sutler; sutlers:
  Conway may outlast, in army service, **38**. 128

Suttermans, Justus (1597–1681), painter:
(?) masquerader costumed like portrait by, **17.** 338
Sutton, Daniel (ca 1735–1819), inoculator:
brother may have been confused with, **24.** 3n
European princes might be saved by, **22.** 562
prominent inoculator, **6.** 75n
Sutton, Evelyn (d. 1817), naval officer:
Johnstone accuses, of cowardice, **29.** 146
(?) Parker's dispatches brought by, **25.** 21n
Sutton, Lady George. *See* Peart, Mary
Sutton, Lord George. *See* Manners, Lord George
Sutton, Richard (1674–1737), Lt-Gen.; M.P.:
Walpole, Sir Robert, when shaving, accompanied by, **38.** 55
Sutton, Robert (1662–1723), 2d Bn Lexington, 1668:
Manners inherits estate of, **9.** 97n
Sutton, Sir Robert (ca 1671–1746), K.B.:
wife of, **34.** 258
Sutton (formerly Manners), Lord Robert (1722–62), M.P.:
death date of, corrected, **43.** 115
French capture, at Laeffeld, **37.** 273n
Norfolk, Ds of, entertains, to divert from arsenal, **9.** 97
Robinson entertains, **17.** 222
safe on parole after Laeffeld battle, **40.** 58
Worksop arsenal to be revealed to, **9.** 97
Sutton, Robert (? ca 1731–97), inoculator:
(?) Lauzun, Duchesse de, inoculated by, **6.** 75
rumoured to be at Paris, **24.** 2
Stormont said to have been asked to take, to Louis XV, **24.** 2
Sutton, Thomas (1532–1611), founder of the Charterhouse:
engraving of, **16.** 65
tomb of, by Stone, **16.** 48
Sutton, Thomas:
Onslow, Denzil, replaces, as commissioner of salt, **20.** 518n
Sutton, Sir Thomas (ca 1755–1813), cr. (1806) Bt:
Berrys attend ball at house of, at Hampton Court, **12.** 157
HW calls, 'civilest of men,' **12.** 157
Hotham, Miss, visited by, **12.** 154
SH visited by, **12.** 249
Sutton, Mrs Thomas (later, Lady). *See* Smith, Lucy Assheton
Sutton, Surrey:
(?) Crane, rector of, **9.** 399n
Mason of, **1.** 181n
Sutton Friars, Canterbury:
Layard of, **11.** 255n
Sutton Park, Beds:
Burgoyne of, **9.** 360n, **10.** 295n
Suttons' powders:
taken during inoculation for smallpox, **6.** 75
Suvorov, Gen.:
Oginski defeated by, **33.** 511n
Turks defeated by, **24.** 29n

Suze, Comte de:
L'Hôpital, Marquis de, accompanied by, to St Petersburg, **21.** 53n
Suze. *See also* La Suze; Susa
Swabia:
Mindleheim in, **11.** 197n
portrait of James II of Scotland found in, **15.** 157
Swaffham, Norfolk:
Edgar of, **42.** 333
Orford, 3d E. of, supports coursing meeting at, **43.** 151
Saham Toney near, **28.** 329n, **29.** 372, **41.** 366
Seward at, on way to Houghton, **16.** 189
Swaffham Coursing Society:
Orford, 3d E. of, founds, **42.** 333n
'Swagger, General.' *See* Burgoyne, John
Swainton. *See* Swanton
Swale, Richard (b. ? ca 1562), warden of Trinity Hospital, Greenwich:
appointed first warden of Greenwich hospital, **16.** 90n
Hillier mistakes Griffith for, **16.** 89
Swale, river:
Smelt lives on banks of, **29.** 287
Swallow, English ship:
Howes' dispatches come on, **24.** 331n, 334n
news by, **32.** 392n
Swallowfield, Berks, Dodd's seat:
Dodd of, **2.** 229n, **13.** 100n, **30.** 371
HW to visit, **17.** 253
HW visits and praises, **30.** 26
Swallow St, London:
fire endangers, **9.** 363
Swalwell, near Newcastle:
Crowley moves to, **16.** 77n
Swan, Miss, of Kingston:
SH visited by, **12.** 247
Swan, Alice (1737–after 1769), m. Rev. Henry Hoggart:
(?) escapes from fire, **35.** 210
Swan, Anne, m. (after 1769) James Yates:
(?) escapes from fire, **35.** 210
Swan, Elizabeth (1739–after 1769):
(?) escapes from fire, **35.** 210
Swan, English sloop:
Wilson, Capt., brings express from St-Malo in, **21.** 212n
Swan; swans:
at Marble Hill, **32.** 31
Bennet, Lady Camilla, as a, **30.** 295
Cooper's geese are, **33.** 539
death song of, **33.** 41
double-beaked, **6.** 297
HW compares himself to, **10.** 298
HW hopes to get, for Chute, **35.** 89–90
in print of Richmond Palace, **16.** 73, 79
Racine comparable to, **16.** 271
song of, too trite for verse, **39.** 470
visible from SH. **25.** 532
See also 'Leda and the Swan'

Swanevelt, Herman (b. 1620), painter:
  Hôtel de Lambert has panels by, **7**. 337
Swan Inn, Bedford:
  designed by Holland, **34**. 188n
Swansea:
  tomb in St Mary's Church in, **41**. 116, 126–9
Swansfield, Northumberland:
  Selby of, **11**. 17n
Swanton, Mrs, of Richmond:
  SH visited by, **12**. 234, 240, 241
Swanton, Robert (d. 1765), naval officer:
  ships brought by, to Point Lévis, **21**. 419n
Swan-upping:
  City companies perform, **9**. 42
Swares. *See* Suares de la Concha
Sweating draught:
  Gilchrist gives HW, for sciatica, **31**. 205
Sweating sickness:
  occurrences of, **35**. 100
Sweats, cold:
  occurrence of, **36**. 138
Swede; Swedes:
  Du Deffand, Mme, has social relations with,
    7. 187
  SH visited by, **12**. 225, 243
Sweden, K. of. *See* Adolf Fredrik (1710–71);
    Charles XII (1682–1718); Fredrik I (1676–
    1751); Gustav III (1746–92); Gustav IV
    (1778–1837); Gustavus (Vasa) I (1496–1560);
    Gustavus Adolphus (1594–1631); Karl XIII
    (1748–1818)
Sweden, P. of. *See* Adolf Fredrik (1710–71)
Sweden, Q. of. *See* Christina (1626–89); Louisa
    Ulrica (1720–82); Ulrica Leonora (1688–
    1741)
Sweden:
  Adolf Fredrik heir to crown of, **18**. 203n, 219,
    275n, 278
  ambassadors from and to, *see under* Ambas-
    sador
  Annual Register prints article on, **28**. 101
  arms of, **15**. 112
  army of: Fermor tells, to meet him near
    Stettin, **21**. 247n; Johns, Mlle Julie, said to
    have married officer of, **21**. 183n
  Austrian alliance with, **17**. 446, **22**. 564
  Barthélemy, Marquis de, secretary of French
    embassy in, **6**. 183, 198
  Campbell to seek alliance and to hire troops
    in, for England, **37**. 497–8, 500
  captains from, at Leghorn, *see* Anckarloo,
    David; Fleetrood
  Catalogue of French Books, A, satirizes, **18**. 53
  Catherine II of Russia quarrels with, **36**. 251
  ——'s warfare with, **35**. 397, 400
  Chambers, Sir William, born in, **28**. 450
  Choiseul 'buys,' **23**. 133
  copper money abundant in, **11**. 350
  Danish prince proposed as future king of, **18**.
    203n
  Daun and Fermor may be joined by troops of,
    21. 247

Du Deffand, Mme, acquainted with visitors
    from, **6**. 395
  earthquakes in, **35**. 265
  England insults, **28**. 455
  English fleet may transport troops to, **5**. 338
  envoys from and to, *see under* Envoy
  fleet of: Russians defeated by, **39**. 462n; to
    enter Mediterranean, **25**. 59
  France encourages revolution in, **23**. 436n
  —— informs, that she must make peace, **21**.
    498
  —— makes treaty with, to guarantee Treaty
    of Westphalia, **21**. 96n
  —— may aid, against Russia, **4**. 203
  —— may intervene in revolution in, **5**. 338
  —— might be aided by, in invasion, **21**. 296n
  ——'s ally, **20**. 571
  ——'s efforts in, may aid Turks, **23**. 470n
  Frederick II menaced by, **21**. 119, 247, 258, 327
  French baffled in, **23**. 157
  French subsidy to, **42**. 495
  French troops said to be going to, in English
    men of war, **23**. 466
  HW's ignorance of, **15**. 32
  HW would be glad to see revolution in, **32**.
    184
  hesitant, **21**. 502
  history of, recommended to Robertson, **15**.
    56–7
  in danger at home, **34**. 32
  Loutherbourgh from, **24**. 93
  Maria Theresa's alliance with, **22**. 564
  ministers from and to, *see under* Minister
  Peter III heir to crown of, **10**. 39
  princes of, *see* Adolf Fredrik; Gustav IV;
    Karl XIII
  Raynal's account of, **5**. 211
  reform Diet in, **23**. 157n
  revolution in, **5**. 267, 338, **23**. 438, **28**. 47
  right of convoy claimed by, in war between
    England and Holland, **21**. 269n
  royal family of, smallpox deaths in, **17**. 255
  Russia agrees with, about K. of the Romans,
    42. 496
  —— draws, on her shoulders, **34**. 32
  Russian army imitated by that of, **21**. 312
  Russia's war with, **39**. 462–3; *see also* War:
    Russian-Swedish
  St-Priests go to, **11**. 256n
  seamen of, on Prussian privateer, **21**. 349
  secretary of legation of, at Rome, *see* Basquiat
  secret committee in, **23**. 436n
  Senate of, to choose bride for Adolf Fredrik,
    18. 305
  ship of, captured by Prussian privateer, **21**.
    330n; see also *Esperance*
  Thurot may enlist troops of, **21**. 347
  troops of: approach Berlin but are repulsed,
    21. 247; Frederick II orders Dohna to drive,
    out of Mecklenburg, **21**. 257n, 258n; Wedell
    and Bevern defeat, at Tornow and Fehr-
    bellin, **21**. 247n

Ungern-Sternberg assembles force in, **21.** 119n

Vergennes appointed ambassador to, **5.** 46, 48

Wroughton minister to, **4.** 241n

Young Pretender said to be visiting, **20.** 44

—— to be aided by, **19.** 311

Swedenborg, Emanuel (1688–1772), philosopher:

disciples of, multiply, **34.** 51, 83

proselytes of, **16.** 227

Swedish Curate, The. See under Jerningham, Edward

Sweepstakes:

at Huntingdon, **38.** 109

HW searches newspapers for accounts of, **23.** 497

HW talks of, **32.** 131

Sweet bags:

Anne of Denmark's, **32.** 225

Sweetbreads:

as hors d'œuvre, **19.** 356n

Sweeting's Alley, Royal Exchange:

Ellicott's shop in, **21.** 293n

Sweetmeats:

HW's relatives send, **11.** 194

Mann sends, to Mathews, **18.** 195

York, D. of, presented with, **22.** 221n

Sweet peas:

Chudleigh, Elizabeth, wears, **10.** 245

HW sticks, in his hair, **10.** 94

'Sweet William's Farewell.' *See* Gay, John: 'All in the Downs'

Swelled face:

occurrences of, **30.** 7, **36.** 57, **42.** 203

Swelling. *See* Swollen ankles; Swollen body; Swollen feet; Swollen legs

Swerford, Oxon:

Travell of, **14.** 201n

Swetenburg. *See* Swedenborg

Swiegel. *See* Schwichelt

Swift, Jonathan (1667–1745), dean of St Patrick's Cathedral, Dublin; satirist:

amusing though vitriolic, **42.** 499

Atterbury, correspondent of, **11.** 20n

'Ballad on Quadrille' attributed to, quoted, **32.** 96

Bathurst's correspondence with, is said to have been burnt, **28.** 239

'Battle of the Books' satirized by, **29.** 294n

Bickerstaffe satirized by, **28.** 277n

Bolingbroke and Pope urge, to burn history of Anne's reign, **21.** 184

Bolingbroke insolently treated by, **7.** 354

——, Pope, Q., and, flatter one another, **35.** 568

Boyle's *Occasional Reflections* satirized by, **16.** 138n

Burnet's *History* annotated by, **35.** 496n

Caroline, Q., would have been praised by, as much as Q. Anne, if she could have helped him, **25.** 8

Charteris's immorality celebrated by, **19.** 148n

church service of, at Laracor, is dialogue with his clerk, **30.** 237

Complete Collection of Genteel and Ingenious Conversation by, puts Gray to sleep, **13.** 153

Cork's *Remarks on the Life* of, **20.** 454n, 457, **21.** 194, **37.** 360

correspondence among Bolingbroke, Arbuthnot, Pope, and, published, **30.** 24

correspondence of, with Bolingbroke, Gay, and Bathurst read by HW, **25.** 6–8

Cutts, Bn, subject of epigram by, **9.** 252

Damer, subject of elegy by, **10.** 233n

Dennis satirized by, **13.** 65n

epitaph by, for himself, **10.** 11

Fountaine a friend of, **16.** 153n

Germain, Lady Elizabeth, correspondent of, **10.** 218

—— friend of, **28.** 208n

'Grand Question Debated' by, mentions Hamilton's Bawn, **37.** 66n

Gray's mistaken allusion to, **13.** 62

Gulliver's Travels by: Arbuthnot and Pope had no part in writing, **34.** 259; Brobdingnags in, **12.** 23, **33.** 365, 446, **37.** 439; Desfontaines's translation of, dedicated to Mme du Deffand, **7.** 237; fire at Lilliput in, **9.** 55; Gough's *Sepulchral Monuments* suited for, **34.** 227; HW alludes to, **6.** 47, 49, **13.** 142, **18.** 495, **28.** 160, 186, 347, 391–2, 397, 467, **29.** 283, **31.** 100, **35.** 390; HW alludes to Struldbrugs in, **22.** 110, **24.** 219, **39.** 254, 415; HW compares D. of Cumberland to Gulliver in Lilliput, **35.** 161; HW composes sequel to, **32.** 71–3; HW contrasts Brobdingnag and Lilliput in, **35.** 182; HW jokes about Bigendian heresy in, **35.** 212; HW jokes about Lilliput and Brobdingnag in, **35.** 184, 201, 267; HW mentions Lilliput in, **37.** 347; HW seeks Latin name for Lilliputians in, **39.** 460; Houyhnhnms in, **33.** 418, **34.** 64; Lilliputians in, **33.** 127; More, Hannah, alludes to 'flapper' in, **31.** 272; solemnity of, equalled by modern rumours, **24.** 519; Struldbrugs dispensed from making visits, **33.** 461; Struldbrugs in, **28.** 186, **42.** 229; Struldbrugs include HW, **32.** 364, **33.** 463, 464, **34.** 13, 64, 205; Struldbrugs in France, **32.** 260; Struldbrugs not known by Swift when he drew the character, **33.** 464; Struldbrugs proclaimed by youth as, **32.** 316; Temple compared to Struldbrugs in, **30.** 272

HW calls: 'malignant,' **25.** 6; 'wild beast,' **25.** 8

HW interested in letters of, **17.** 1n

HW quotes, in *Lesson for the Day*, **17.** 493n

HW said to quote, **9.** 199, **13.** 142

Hamilton and guests discuss, at Bushey Park, **9.** 380

history by, of Q. Anne's last years: HW discusses, **21.** 184–5; Lucas the editor of, **21.** 200–1; Mann attributes, to Lord Cork, **21.** 194; Mason alludes to, **28.** 208n

impotence of, alleged, **10.** 219

[Swift, Jonathan, *continued*]

Johnson, Esther, correspondent of, **10**. 219

Johnson, Dr Samuel, dislikes, **11**. 277

Letters of: cited, **2**. 96, 343, 344; disagreeably mention Lady Suffolk, **22**. 524, 543n, **25**. 8; Du Deffand, Mme, asks about, **3**. 133; HW comments on, **14**. 183; HW describes, **10**. 218–19; HW discusses, with Selwyn, **10**. 219; HW interested in, **17**. 1n; HW objects to inclusion in, of letters of living persons, **10**. 218; Meinières, Mme de, wishes to translate, **4**. 335; Montagu enjoys, **10**. 223, 239; quotation from, **12**. 256

Love Song ('Mild Arcadians') by, imitated in *Arno Miscellany*, **25**. 507

Lyttelton's *Dialogues of the Dead* mentions, **21**. 408

Marlborough attacked by, in *The Examiner*, **42**. 503n

Memoirs . . . of Martin Scriblerus by, characters in, **20**. 214, **43**. 247

Mohocks terrify, **10**. 219

Montagu asks HW to send writings of, to Mme Roland, **10**. 174, 182

monument to, in St Patrick's Cathedral, **9**. 404, **10**. 11

new-coined words irritate, **25**. 538

Oxford, E. of, a friend of, **2**. 144n

—— insolently treated by, **7**. 354

pamphlet attributed to, **16**. 370n

Pilkington, Letitia, friend of, **14**. 13n

Pomfret, Cts of, condemns humour of, **17**. 477

Pope in awe of, **25**. 6

prices of works of, in France, **10**. 180

Project for the Advancement of Religion by, **25**. 8n

Queensberry, Ds of, friend of, **9**. 61n

—— mentioned in letters of, **19**. 195n

St Patrick's Deanery occupied by, **9**. 396

Schomberg's epitaph by, **10**. 11

Sheridan, Thomas, wished the piles by, as mark of health, **20**. 334n

short verses of, **33**. 501

stammering squire and, **35**. 30

style of: **31**. 224; excellent but without grace, **16**. 269

Suffolk, Cts of, friend of, **10**. 118n

—— disagreeably mentioned in letters of, **22**. 524, 543n, **25**. 8

Tale of a Tub by: HW alludes to, **39**. 455; Mason alludes to, **28**. 158; St-Simon's translation of, **35**. 241, **40**. 82–3

Vanhomrigh, Esther, probably mistress of, **10**. 218–19

Wilkes contrasts HW's comment on the Scots with those of, **13**. 37n

witticism by, about Holland, **24**. 523

Swift, Theophilus (1746–1815):

Lennox's duel with, **11**. 25n

Swiftsure, English ship:

Monmouth supported by, **21**. 193

Stanhope, captain of, **21**. 193n

Swillington, Yorks:

Zouch rector of, **16**. 1n

Swimburn. *See* Swinburn; Swinburne

Swimmer. *See* Swymmer

Swimming:

Pembroke, E. of, addicted to, **42**. 178

Roman youths' usual exercise, **37**. 8

Swinbrooke, Oxon:

Fettiplace of, **9**. 140n

Swinburn, William (d. 1755), HW's deputy as Usher of the Exchequer:

active in vestry of St George's, Queen Sq., **40**. 84n

Bedford, Grosvenor, succeeds, in Exchequer deputy ushership, **42**. 491

death of, **40**. 84

Swinburne, Henry (1743–1803), traveller:

Florence left by, **25**. 65

letter to, from wife in Paris, **11**. 52

Mann sends rock crystals through, to HW, **25**. 65

Neapolitan and Roman news from, **24**. 451n

Travels in the Two Sicilies by, made obsolete after earthquake, **33**. 397

Travels through Spain by, **2**. 149, 151, **16**. 180, **43**. 68

Swinburne, Mrs Henry. *See* Baker, Martha

Swinburne, Henry, jr:

mother of, **11**. 52n

Swinford. *See* Swynford

Swing; swings:

HW in, in Venice, **35**. 27

Swinging:

Mann to use, for exercise, **18**. 558

navy uses, for exercise, **18**. 558

Swinny, Owen Mac (d. 1754), playwright:

bankruptcy and exile of, **17**. 296n

George II's message to Frederick, P. of Wales, to be read by, **17**. 296

HW relates anecdote told by, **28**. 274

playhouse director, **17**. 296n

Robinson's ball attended by, though not of 'first fashion,' **37**. 114

witticism by, on Cambric Bill, **18**. 192

Swinton, Samuel:

Courier de l'Europe published by, **25**. 71n

Swiny. *See* Swinny, Owen Mac

Swiss:

at Wilkes's Paris hotel, **38**. 280

Louis and Favre are, **38**. 418

maladie du pays of, **22**. 198

murdered in Paris, **31**. 372–3

pen brought to HW under conduct of two, **37**. 67

Swiss clergyman:

HW receives *Mémoires littéraires* from, **13**. 44

Swiss coffee-house. *See under* Coffee-house

Swisserland. *See* Switzerland

Swiss Guards:

Florentine: captain of, accompanies Dumesnil to Electress, **17**. 236; Francis I orders sent, from Florence, **19**. 82

French: Artois received as general of, **5.** 209; Artois said to command, **5.** 161; Choiseul deprived of command of, **5.** 155, 165–7, **23.** 322, 363; Choiseul may lose, **41.** 200; command of, not decided, **5.** 159, 161; Louis XVI's, massacred, **34.** 152n, **39.** 492; secretaryship of, **4.** 9–10, 12, **5.** 155, 168; Soissons visited by, **3.** 117

Swithin (Swithun), St (ca 800–62), Bp of Winchester:
biographical information about, corrected, **43.** 140

correspondence discouraged by, **35.** 388
cricket match interrupted by, **36.** 251
'diabetes' of, **35.** 239
HW expects rain from, **39.** 499
party at Fulham kept indoors by, **11.** 45
proverb about, based on fact, **35.** 388, **39.** 469
rains in England attributed to, **11.** 37
summer should begin after deluges of, **12.** 153
urn of, dry on 15 July 1793, **34.** 182

Swithin's Lane, Lombard St, London:
Clive's house in, **21.** 429n
Kemble, grocer in, **12.** 241

Switzer, Christopher, German wood-engraver:
(?) print by, **43.** 382–3

Switzerland:
Berrys consider returning through, **11.** 146, 173, 174, 189
——' friends in, **11.** 172, 359
Beylon from, **40.** 214
Bocard regiment of, in French service, **40.** 92
Buignon from, **25.** 517n, 523
Burdett, Charles, drowns in, **12.** 54
Burnaby raises troops in, **18.** 215
Choiseul oppresses, **23.** 130
Colomb's sisters in, **42.** 297
Condorcet rumoured to be in, **12.** 66
English travellers swarm in, **25.** 618
French ambassador alarms, with news of P. Charles's invasion, **18.** 290
French treaty with, **42.** 496
Gloucester, D. of, to visit, **24.** 123
Grimm a native of, **16.** 181n
guards from, *see* Swiss Guards
HW advises Berrys to return through, **11.** 139, 354
HW admires attachment of, to liberty, **41.** 354
HW mentions, **11.** 9, 16
HW's servant Louis from, **20.** 554
Hardinge to learn French for visit to, **35.** 581
—— to tour, **35.** 579
London servants from, form a regiment, **18.** 409
Louis XVI's recapture arouses rejoicings in, **11.** 335–6
mercenary voting in, **17.** 470
ministers from and to, *see under* Minister
Montagu, Lord, drowns in, **12.** 54
mountains of, a fine sight, **35.** 427
Müntz from, **21.** 239, **35.** 185n

Natter trained in, **16.** 299n
Northamptons die in, **10.** 288n
officials of, join Young Pretender, **19.** 259
Palmerston's travels in, with Pars, **26.** 48
Pars draws views of, for Palmerston, **35.** 424
Pennsylvania's immigrants from, may form regiment, **20.** 531
porters from, kept by Northumberlands, **20.** 341
Prévost to visit relatives in, **23.** 554
regiments from, **38.** 77n
revolutionary spirit of, **11.** 85, 335
Richecourt said to visit, **17.** 125
Rousseau and Voltaire endanger religion and government in, **35.** 583–4
Rousseau expelled from, **39.** 43
servants from, *see also under* Servant
Shorter's servant from, **35.** 159n
Tollendal emigrates to, **11.** 286n
troops of: at Rome, **18.** 532; object to crossing Rhine into Germany, **21.** 94n
Villettes afterwards minister to, **19.** 456n
—— sends courier through, **18.** 385
Viry, envoy to, **9.** 406n
visitors to: Boisgelin, Comtesse de, **6.** 281; Boufflers, Marquise de, **6.** 281; Mirepoix, Mme de, **6.** 281; Sillery, Mme de, **12.** 66; Young Pretender, **21.** 59n
Voltaire in, **21.** 51
Webster, Lady, ill-used on frontier of, **11.** 331
See also Berne; Geneva; Grisons; Lausanne; Zurich

Swollen ankles:
occurrence of, **24.** 280

Swollen body:
occurrence of, **25.** 394

Swollen feet:
occurrence of, **25.** 593, **40.** 388

Swollen leg:
occurrences of, **23.** 355, 369, **24.** 137, 244, **25.** 266, 442, **36.** 138, 139, 141, **40.** 388

Sword; swords:
Alexander's, better used on Gordian knot than on war, **34.** 111
Balaam's, **35.** 33
Birmingham hopes to make, for American war, **24.** 77
black, for Court mourning, **32.** 102n
Brescia has trade in, **17.** 324n
broadsword portrayed in stained glass, **40.** 224
Conway busy with, **37.** 336, 358
(?) —— mentions, **37.** 332
——'s, left behind, to be returned by HW's nephew, **38.** 72
damascene, price of, **5.** 114
diamond-studded: Catherine II gives, to Gunning, **23.** 508; Clive gives, to George III, **22.** 540n; Mathews receives, **18.** 370
duel fought with, **30.** 264
flaming, of angels, **35.** 209
Flobert guards mistress's house with, **21.** 386

[Sword; swords, *continued*]
Frederick II gives, to Chernyshev, **22.** 62n
garden, to be used as scythes, **39.** 499–500
George II lays, on his signature to war declaration, **20.** 556n
——'s, at Garter ceremony, **22.** 79n
Gunter designs handles for, **42.** 107n
HW gives, to Monaco princes, **5.** 172
HW has to send to town for, to dine with Ps Amelia, **39.** 441
HW hopes not to wear, when receiving Q. Charlotte, **35.** 545, **39.** 510
Henry, P. of Wales, draws, to kill stag, **35.** 73
Herbert of Chirbury's, **42.** 43
Highlanders use, at Culloden, **37.** 239
Irish Catholics forbidden to carry, **20.** 289
Italian wears, in portrait at Drayton, **10.** 342
James IV's, taken at Flodden Field, **42.** 421n
lady in Pope's elegy did not die from, **42.** 123
lord mayor's, **38.** 121
Marlborough's, **18.** 248
of Calais, used to behead Anne Boleyn, **17.** 233n
of St Paul, **37.** 15
pandours carry, **37.** 142
Parliament members might use, in Gordon Riots, **33.** 177
regulation of, in ecclesiastical costume, **41.** 223
Rinaldo's, **10.** 346
rioters seize, in Genoa, **19.** 338
sailor tosses, to unarmed opponent, **24.** 543
steel, **25.** 667n
Walpole, George, wants, **37.** 73
See also Claymore; Sword of state
Sword of state:
forgotten, at Coronation, **38.** 121
Sackville should carry, at Thanksgiving, **38.** 200
Swymmer, Anthony Langley (ca 1724–60), M.P.:
birth date of, corrected, **43.** 271
(?) Florence visited by, **20.** 376
(?) Rome visited by, **20.** 376n
Swymmer, Mrs Anthony Langley. *See* Astley, Arabella
Swynford, Lady. *See* Roet, Katharine
Swynnerton family:
Essington and Hilton manors united in, **41.** 77n
Sybil; sybils. *See* Sibyl
Sycamore:
at Knole, **35.** 132
Sydall, Thomas:
execution of, **19.** 287n
Sydenham, Humphrey (1694–1757); M.P.:
Book of Common Prayer dominates mind of, **30.** 292n
HW's 'character' of, **30.** 292
motion to resume sentence against Murray opposed by, **20.** 286n

Parliamentary debates by: on amendment to the Address, **26.** 23; on Scotch Bill, **26.** 31
Syderstone (*or* Systern), Norfolk:
advowson of, **30.** 368
HW's will mentions, **30.** 344, 368
Sydney, Bn. *See* Sidney, Robert (1563–1626); Townshend, Thomas (1733–1800)
Sydney, Bns. *See* Powys, Elizabeth (1736–1826)
Sydney, Vct. *See* Sidney, Hon. Henry (1641–1704); Townshend, Thomas (1733–1800)
Sydney, Vcts. *See* Powys, Elizabeth (1736–1826)
'Sydney, Algernon':
letter-writer's nom-de-plume, **42.** 505
Sydney. *See also* Sidney
Sykes, Lady. *See* Tatton, Elizabeth
Sykes, Arthur Ashley (ca 1684–1756), D.D.:
Two Questions Previous to the Free Inquiry by, **15.** 299, 303
Sykes, Mrs Christopher. *See* Tatton, Elizabeth
Sykes, Decima Hester Beatrix (1775–1843), m. (1795) John Robinson Foulis:
contingent heiress of Samuel Egerton, **33.** 168–9
Sykes, Sir Francis (1732–1804), cr. (1781) Bt; M.P.; East India Co. official:
excessive table allowance of, **23.** 451–2
HW says: was formerly a footman, **29.** 122–3; was formerly a tavern waiter, **11.** 295n, **25.** 141
Haidar 'Alī Khān thinks he has as much right as, to Indian diamonds, **25.** 141
Raynal fits HW to talk about, **39.** 168
Sykes, William (ca 1659–1724), picture-dealer:
Pomfret, E. of, buys painting from, **40.** 215–16, 219
Sylla. *See* Scylla; Sulla
Syllabub; syllabubs:
at Oxford coffee-houses, **38.** 46
definition of, **43.** 118
HW's, at SH, **9.** 134, **10.** 127
Oxford Loungers discuss ministers and Sackville over, **38.** 46
Pelham, Frances, serves, at Esher party, **10.** 73
'under the cow,' **32.** 234
Sylph; sylphs:
in Darwin's *Botanic Garden,* **42.** 269, 271
Sylphe, Le:
presented before Christian VII, **4.** 166
Sylva. See under Heathcote, Ralph
Sylvæ. See under Statius
Sylvester, John:
London's petition read by, **24.** 89n
Sylvester, Rev. Matthew (? 1636–1708), nonconformist divine:
Reliquiæ Baxterianæ by, **2.** 64
Sylvestre, ——:
D. of Montagu's son tutored by, **10.** 34n
'Sylvia':
Berkeley, Lady Henrietta, and Vcts Belfield both use, as nom-de-plume, **18.** 220

See also under Farquhar, George: *Recruiting Officer*

Sylvie. See under Laujon, Pierre

Symeon, Elizabeth (d. 1634), m. (1619) John Hampden:
Hardinge asks if wedding gloves belonged to, 35. 597–8

Symeonis monachi Dunhelmensis libellus . . .:
Bedford's edition of, 2. 356

Symes, Henrietta (d. 1816), m. (1773) William Dickson, Bp of Down and Connor 1783–1804:
Beauclerk, Lady Diana, and Lady Holland visited by, 32. 407

Symmetry:
in landscape effects, 42. 165

Symonds, John, of Twickenham:
SH visited by, 12. 238
Twickenham resident, 42. 482

Symonds, John (1730–1807), LL.D.; professor of modern history at Cambridge:
La Rochefoucauld brothers lodge with, at Bury, 16. 225–6
(?) SH visited by, 12. 232
succeeds to Gray's professorship, 13. 137n

Symonds, Richard (1617–ca 1692), royalist; antiquary:
MSS of, in Mead's library, 16. 154

Symonds. *See also* Symons

Symons (*or* Symonds *or* Simmonds), George:
respited, 38. 15

Symons (Simons), Ralph (fl. 1584–1612), architect:
portrait of, at Emmanuel College, 14. 114

'Symphony' (unidentified ? Etonian):
HW alludes to affair of, 13. 219

Symphony:
during Battle of Ivry, in Farmain de Rozoi's *Henri IV*, 39. 218

Symphysis:
operation on, 7. 424

Sympson, Thomas (fl. 1740–50), antiquary; master of the works at Lincoln Cathedral:
biography of, 43. 38, 39
on Richard de Gaynisburgh, 1. 10, 13n
son has antiquarian writings of, 40. 233

Sympson, Thomas (ca 1726–86), prebendary of Lincoln 1759–86:
information from, 43. 38, 39
Lyttelton presumably saw, at Lincoln, 40. 233
Richardson informed by, about inscription at Lincoln, 40. 234–5

Symptomatic fever. *See under* Fever

Symson, Rev. Peter (ca 1708–? 80), (?) assistant at Mayfair Chapel:
sermon by, 20. 241, 243
Tracy and Susanna Owens married by, 9. 76

Synagogue; synagogues:
English and German, in Jamaica, 32. 217n
in Duke's Place, 32. 217n

Synge, Nicholas (d. 1771):
succeeds as Bp of Killaloe, 14. 9–10n

Synnot, Lady. *See* Seton, Jane

Synnot, Maria, dau. of Sir Walter Synnot:
SH visited by, 12. 243

Synnot, Sir Walter, of Ballymoyer; Kt, 1783:
son of, 12. 88n
SH visited by, 12. 243
wife of, 12. 124n

Synnot, Walter (d. 1850), army officer, cousin of Berry sisters:
Amherst appoints, to ensigncy, 12. 88

Synod of Dort:
Carleton's dispatches chiefly concerned with, 1. 380n

Synonymes français:
second edition of, owned by Mme du Deffand, 8. 25

Synopsis apocalyptica. See under Mackenzie, George (1630–1714)

Synopsis Palmariorum Matheseos. See under Jones, William (1675–1749)

Syon Hill, Isleworth, E. of Holdernesse's seat:
Coke, Lady Mary, visits, 31. 169
courier brings Zorndorf news to, 37. 563
dinner party at, 31. 139
dressing-room of Cts of Holdernesse at, 38. 60
Dutch stoves at, 38. 60
fossé at, 35. 308
(?) Gray alludes to, 14. 51
HW alludes to, 11. 128, 28. 162
HW dines at, 38. 36
HW, Haszlang, and Lady Mary Coke entertained by Holdernesses at, 38. 36
HW hears at, of satiric verses on Bedfords, 38. 462
HW to dine at, 39. 390
HW visits, with Lady Hertford's loo party, 32. 160
Holdernesse entertains at, 38. 461, 462
——'s seat at, 14. 51n
—— writes from, 40. 180
Holdernesse, Cts of, entertains at, 43. 304
—— has life use of, 33. 13
—— injured in fall at, 28. 111
—— loses, 29. 303
lease of, to be settled with Northumberland, 28. 399
Marlborough's seat at, 11. 82n
Marlboroughs probably at, 11. 201n
Robinson's house at, 41. 325
visitors to: Alderson, 28. 150; Gunning, Miss, 11. 217; Harcourt, Mrs, 28. 470; Marlboroughs, 11. 82; Mason, 28. 1; Riddell, Sir John, 11. 217

Syon House, Isleworth; D. of Northumberland's house:
Adam's gateway and screen for, lace and embroidery, 28. 102
ball at, 35. 330–1
bridge at, designed by Adam, 28. 108
gate of endangered, 32. 213
'great Sion,' 32. 160
HW declines dinner at, 39. 101
HW visits and describes, 38. 429

[Syon House, Isleworth, *continued*]
lamps in garden at, **35.** 331n
Northumberland House paintings taken to, **20.** 329n
Northumberland's seat, **28.** 399n
Northumberlands build at, **20.** 341
Percys and Seymours of, must envy Osterley Park, **32.** 125
plates of, by Adam brothers, **28.** 101n
road, paddock, and bridge built at, **35.** 331
Somerset, D. of, leaves furniture of, to E. of Hertford, **20.** 10n
SH compared with, **9.** 169, **35.** 237
'the great Sion,' **32.** 160n
visitors to: Bowlbys, **38.** 429; HW, **38.** 429, 461; Pitt, Mrs George, **38.** 461; Stone, Abp, **38.** 429

Syon Lane:
HW meets Cts of Holdernesse and daughter in, **38.** 60

Syracuse, Bp of. *See* Testa, Francesco Maria (d. 1773)

Syren, English ship:
merchant ships convoyed from Leghorn by, **21.** 69n
naval engagement of, **24.** 216n

Syrène, French frigate:
news of Montcalm's siege of Ft Orange comes by, **21.** 229n

Syria:
La Condamine visits, **22.** 147n
Lucian born in, **14.** 20
travellers from, perform quarantine, **35.** 521
Wortley Montagu visits, **22.** 113n

Syringa:
at SH, **9.** 149, 162, **10.** 156, **31.** 36
Conway's double-flowering, blooms single, **37.** 528

Syringe; syringes:
Ponzio uses, on Benedict XIV, **21.** 37
templars take, to theatre, **19.** 469

Syringe-baths:
Gloucester, D. of, takes, **23.** 334

'Sysigambis':
HW's name for Augusta, Ps of Wales, **38.** 315

System; systems:
HW averse to, **10.** 184, **32.** 79, 345

Systema naturæ. See under Linnæus

Systematists:
weakness of, **3.** 250

Système de la nature. See under Thiry, Paul-Henri

Systèmes, Les. See under Voltaire

Szabó, David Baróti (1739–1819), poet:
(?) Hungary's Ovid, **39.** 182

Szembeck, Barbe-Madeleine-Élisabeth de (ca 1709–62), m. 1 Jean Clément, Comte de Branicki; m. 2 (1736) Ulrik Frederik Woldemar Løvendal, Comte de Lowendal:
Coventry, Cts of, gives fan to, and is forced to take it back, **20.** 338

T

T ——, Miss:
HW mentions, **20.** 292

Taaffe, John (d. 1773):
death of, **5.** 404
'demoiselle' of, *see* Lespinasse, Julie-Jeanne-Éléonore de
Du Deffand, Mme, offers lodging to, **5.** 231, 242, **8.** 3
——'s correspondence with, **3.** 12, 13, **5.** 1n
——'s opinion of, **5.** 231
executor of, pays HW money for Mme de Mirepoix, **6.** 136
HW tells Mme du Deffand not to give lodging to, **5.** 242, 253, **7.** 395
Lespinasse, Mlle de, not to be seen by, **5.** 231, 253
Mirepoix, Mme de, corresponds with, **5.** 231
—— leaves E. W. Montagu's note with, **5.** 434
—— seeks letter of, **6.** 16, 19

Taaffe, Theobald (ca 1708–80), M.P.:
Albemarle bails, but makes no defence for him, **20.** 294
biographical information about, corrected, **43.** 117, 118, 263, 351
Bland's death caused by, **9.** 172
burgundy smuggled by, **20.** 289
Coke's witticism about Parliamentary membership of, **20.** 289
Englishmen worthy only to be directed by, **35.** 187
expected return of, to England, in HW's newspaper parody, **9.** 126
faro-banker for Duchesse de Mirepoix, **20.** 288
Fort l'Évêque to be reproduced by, in Sussex, for Henry Fox, **9.** 159
French Court receives, **21.** 473
galleys may be punishment of, **20.** 288, 294
gout of, cured by Buzaglo, **32.** 407
imprisoned with Wortley Montagu at Fort l'Évêque, Paris, for robbing Payba, **19.** 450n, **20.** 288, **21.** 473, **43.** 263
Lincoln receives truffles from, in HW's newspaper parody, **9.** 126
Newcastle, D. of, accompanied by, to Lewes races, **20.** 289
——'s connection with, **9.** 159
Parliamentary membership of, **19.** 450n, **20.** 289
Payba accuses, of cheating at cards, **19.** 450n
—— claims, extorted notes from him, **20.** 288n
Pompadour, Marquise de, receives turtles and pineapples from, **20.** 289
religion forsaken by, to fight a duel in Ireland, **20.** 289
Taaffe, John, confused with, **3.** 12n
White's Club does not include, **20.** 289
Woffington, Margaret, makes bet with, **20.** 289

Tabachiera. *See* Snuff-box

Tabby; tabbies:
  ladies to wear, for Court mourning, **32**. 101n
  York, D. of, wears, at ball, **35**. 300
Tabbycoat; tabbycoats:
  Lobkowitz's, sky-blue watered, with gold buttonholes, **37**. 289
Tabernacle; tabernacles:
  by Donatello, *see under* Donatello
  in Palazzo Pitti oratory, **20**. 489
Tabernego. *See* Tabuerniga
Table; tables:
  Adam's frames for, brittle, **28**. 102
  at: Blenheim, **9**. 289; Burghley House, **10**. 347; Castle Ashby, **10**. 336; Elizabeth Chudleigh's, **9**. 277; Greatworth, **10**. 133; Hardwick, **9**. 297; Mamhead, **30**. 67; Navestock, **9**. 244; Wanstead, coveted by HW, **35**. 238
  black and white (? marble), **26**. 7
  charge for casing, **26**. 4
  faro, **30**. 6
  fly, Vyne parlour to have, **35**. 639
  for E. O., **35**. 101n
  granite, **26**. 3, 7
  great chair at, used for royal guests, **20**. 466n
  HW falls against, **31**. 303
  HW's: covered with gazettes, **35**. 103; in Round Chamber at SH, **33**. 522; with drawers, in Arlington St, **23**. 285
  HW wants granite for, **35**. 191, 208
  HW writes on, **31**. 64
  Hervey, Bns, bequeaths, to HW, **31**. 137, **43**. 88–9
  La Borde's, of granite, **31**. 80
  length of, for Bastille Day jubilee, **11**. 78
  library, sent to Bns Hervey by Comtesse d'Egmont, **38**. 279, 340, 358, 373, 379
  marble: at Gorhambury, **40**. 194; in Coventry's dining-room, **38**. 348; offered by Tylney to HW, **35**. 238
  mosaic: ancient, **26**. 7; given by Hamilton to HW, **35**. 408
  Newcastle, D. of, takes, to Germany, **19**. 484–5
  octagon, in Uffizi, removed, **25**. 170
  oriental alabaster, **26**. 7
  Pitt, Anne, arranges, in alehouse fashion, **38**. 335
  plain, for Methodist altar, **35**. 119
  porphyry, **26**. 7
  Rowley gives, to Mann, **19**. 9
  scagliola, *see under* Scagliola
  silver, left by Electress to Rinuccini, **18**. 169
  sold out of Palazzo Pitti, **25**. 231
  trou-madame, **32**. 201
  velvet, at Knole, **35**. 132
  waiting, supper served on, **37**. 115
  Wren's, sold, **40**. 348
  See also Card table; Hazard table; Loo table; Scagliola; Wainscot
Tableau de la ville de Paris. See Jèze, ——: *État ou tableau de la ville de Paris*
Tableau de Paris. See under Mercier, Louis-Sébastien

Tableau parlant, Le. See under Anseaume, Louis
Tableau philosophique de l'esprit de Voltaire. See under Sabatier de Castres, Antoine
Table Bay:
  Guardian brought into, **11**. 92n
Table d'hôte:
  Conway converses with, at Marseille, **37**. 312
Table of consanguinity. *See under* Church of England
Table of English Silver Coins. See under Folkes, Martin
Tablet; tablets:
  marble, carved by Charlotte Boyle, **35**. 390
Tablette. *See* Pocket-book
Tablette chronologique. See under Lenglet du Fresnoy, Nicolas
Tablettes dramatiques:
  Du Deffand, Mme, owns, **8**. 26
Tabor; tabors:
  and pipe, HW's term for M. and Mme Necker, **39**. 258
  at Haymarket entertainment, **39**. 382n
  militiaman plays, badly, at Stowe, **10**. 314
  people dance to, around maypole, **20**. 47
  played at Bedford House, **9**. 369
Tabor, Mt, in Palestine:
  Ossory, Lady, resembles Deborah on, **33**. 25
Taboureau des Réaux, Louis-Gabriel (1718–82):
  Louis XVI names, controller-general of finance, **6**. 369, **24**. 254n, 255n
  resigns, **6**. 454, 455
Tabouret; tabourets:
  at French Court: Mirepoix, Mme de, does not have, **20**. 28, 92, 144; Mirepoix, Mme de, regains, **20**. 280–1; Stuart, Charlotte, said to have, **25**. 537
  HW has, for gouty feet, **31**. 67
Tabuerniga, Marquesa de. *See* Fuentes, ——
Tabuerniga, ——, brother of Marqués de Tabuerniga:
  Carteret and his daughter shelter, **17**. 278
  flees from Spain after offending Elizabeth Farnese by supporting her stepson, **17**. 277–8
  Harrington procures pension for, **17**. 278
  returns to Spain to rescue fiancée, **17**. 278
Tabuerniga, Marqués de (d. 1753):
  Carterets protect, **17**. 278, **30**. 47
  duplicity of, **17**. 278n
  Fermor, Lady Sophia (Bns Carteret) retorts to, about Lord Lincoln, **18**. 483, **30**. 47
  flees from Spain after offending Elizabeth Farnese by supporting her stepson, **17**. 277–8
  Harrington procures pension for, **17**. 278
  Newcastle, D. of, employs, to report on Leicester House, **17**. 277n, **19**. 360n
  Pomfret, Cts of, calls on, **17**. 277
  Ranelagh visited by, **18**. 483, **30**. 47

[Tabuerniga, Marqués de, *continued*]
returns to Spain after Philip V's death, **17.** 277n

Tacitus, Publius Cornelius (ca 55–ca 117), historian:
Agricola by: HW compares Mason's *Gray* to, **28.** 185; La Bletterie's translation of, **4.** 75
Alembert's translations from, **41.** 53, 62
Annals of: account of Nero in, **15.** 173, 236; Gordon translates, **15.** 293, **20.** 167n; La Bletterie's translation of, discussed by Mme du Deffand and HW, **4.** 59, 62, 75, **7.** 141, **8.** 152; Peter III's murder makes, seem more credible, **22.** 65; Voltaire's rudeness over translation of, **4.** 105
collected sayings of, **16.** 309n
Gray's Latin inscription to be in style of, **20.** 407
HW contrasts Gibbon with, **28.** 243
(?) HW quotes, **19.** 78
HW quotes passage in, about mutineers, **20.** 125
maxim of, that night favours the reckless and the timid, **19.** 266n
'speaks daggers,' **28.** 402

Tackle (? harness):
on rented chaises, **37.** 40

Tactique, La. See Guibert, Jacques-Antoine-Hippolyte de: *Essai général de Tactique*; *see also under* Voltaire

Taffanel, Clément de (1706–95), Marquis de la Jonquière, French naval officer:
Anson's battle with, **19.** 402n, **20.** 38, **40.** 284

Taffeta:
as court-plaster: **4.** 49, 67–8, 70, 73; price of, **4.** 68
cradle-mantle lined with, **32.** 325
Du Deffand, Mme, buys dress of, **7.** 456

'Taffeties, old':
Jacobite peeresses wear, **9.** 24

Tagliacozzi, Gaspare (1545–99), Bolognese plastic surgeon:
Hervey, Bns, encloses extract reminiscent of, **31.** 60
severed nose first repaired by, **31.** 60n

Tagliamento, Italian river:
overflowing of, **21.** 134

Tagus, river in Spain and Portugal:
victualling fleet blockaded in, **18.** 477n

Tahiti ('Otaheite'), Q. of. *See* Beriea

Tahiti ('Otaheite'):
Banks and Solander brought 'our abominable passions' to, **2.** 225
forgotten, **24.** 21
inhabitants of, fortunate to have no gold mines, **32.** 359
living with the young is like living in, **25.** 538
macaw from, **32.** 111
not exploited because it has no wealth, **25.** 545
Omai native of, **24.** 175

rites of love in, **32.** 128

Tail; tails:
Monboddo's theory about, **33.** 363

Tailor; tailors:
Albemarle ruins, **20.** 270
at Paris, *see* Le Duc, ——
Boutin's garden like paper patterns of, **39.** 213
Colomb's debt to, **42.** 297
Conway's, should make him a purple domino, **38.** 206
domino to be made by, **40.** 284
English: promote 'French' fashions, **32.** 182; rush to France at peace, **37.** 297
French furnish, to the age, **22.** 15
goose of, in Swift's *Tale of a Tub*, **35.** 241
HW's, in Paris, **31.** 44
Hill, Robert, is, at Birmingham, **21.** 289n
in Drury Lane farce, **20.**
in Soho, harbours Theodore of Corsica, **21.** 45
Italian, brought to London by Vaneschi, **17.** 191
journeymen: clothes made by, for figure burnt in effigy, **10.** 23; go on strike, **23.** 30–1; marriage proposed by, in letter, **10.** 22–3
'Kitten's' relations with, **30.** 66
Montagu, D. of, places, on Great Wardrobe payroll, **20.** 79
pattern papers of, **35.** 125, **39.** 213
riot of, predicted, **30.** 181n
Thanet asks, to make suit in 8 hours, **35.** 159
See also Delage, ——

Taintarier (? Tinturier), D.:
print of, **40.** 237

Tait, John (d. 1800) of Harvieston, Midlothian; Writer to the Signet, 1763:
Craufurd addressed in care of, **41.** 277

Tait. *See also* Tate

Talard. *See* Tallart

Talaru, Louis-François (1729–82), Vicomte de:
made member of Ordre du St-Esprit, **6.** 199

Talbot, Bns. *See* Beauchamp, Lady Margaret (d. 1467); De Cardonnel, Mary (ca 1719–87)

Talbot, Cts. *See* De Cardonnel, Mary (ca 1719–87); Hill, Charlotte (1754–1804)

Talbot, Lady. *See* Cavendish, Mary

Talbot, ——:
HW mentions, **37.** 472

Talbot, Lady Alathea (d. 1654), m. (1606) Thomas Howard, 14th E. of Arundel, cr. (1644) E. of Norfolk:
Arundel Collection formed by husband and, **15.** 114n
Hollar's print of, **16.** 153

Talbot, Barbara (ca 1671–1763), m. (1689) Henry Yelverton, 15th Bn Grey; cr. (1690) Vct de Longueville:
charity of, **10.** 339
death and grave of, **10.** 339
grandson aided financially by, **10.** 339
jointure of, **10.** 339
Yelverton library in possession of, **15.** 115

Talbot, Barbara (d. 1759), m. (1742) James Aston, 5th Bn Aston of Forfar:
Boulogne visited by, 17. 140

Talbot, Catherine (ca 1646–1726), m. 1 Walter Littleton; m. 2 (1684) Lancelot Blackburne, Abp of York:
husband's mistress allegedly resented by, 15. 143

Talbot, Lady Cecil (1735–93), m. (1756) George Rice (? m. 2 Robert Wilson); Bns Dinevor, s.j., 1782:
father's barony to revert to, 25. 86
genealogy of, 10. 352
marriage of, expected, 9. 190

Talbot, Charles (1660–1718), 12th E. of Shrewsbury, 1668; cr. (1694) D. of Shrewsbury:
HW confuses ancestor with, 42. 286
Montagu, D. of, supposed to own papers of, 42. 286
portrait of, 10. 338
wife of, 10. 88n, 338, 20. 203n

Talbot, Charles (1685–1737), cr. (1733) Bn Talbot; lord chancellor, 1733–7:
brother of, 9. 20n
death of, 37. 11, 70
explosion in Westminster Hall amuses, 13. 104
son of, 9. 181n, 17. 385n
Walpole, Sir Robert, quarrels with, over bishopric of Gloucester, 13. 83n

Talbot, Charles (ca 1722–66):
Boulogne visited by, 17. 140

Talbot, Charles (1753–1827), 15th E. of Shrewsbury, 1787:
pays for ferrying Roman Catholics to his chapel, 34. 195

Talbot, Lady Eleanor. See Butler, Lady Eleanor

Talbot, Elizabeth (d. 1507), m. John de Mowbray, 6th D. of Norfolk:
at Henry VII's Court, 2. 364

Talbot, Lady Elizabeth (ca 1581–1651), m. 1 (1601) Henry Grey, styled Lord Grey, 8th E. of Kent, 1623; (?) m. 2 John Selden:
birth date of, corrected, 43. 45
Choice Manuall . . . , by, 1. 39
HW's knowledge of, 1. 41
portrait of, 10. 338
print of, 1. 39, 182, 188, 190

Talbot, Ely or Elizabeth, m. Capt. Thomas Cornwall:
Cornish's 'patent' to 'qualify,' 10. *190*
HW does not understand Montagu's reference to, 10. 193
HW forgets husband of, 10. 193
Montagu's opinion of, 10. 190
stepmother of, dies, 9. 161

Talbot, Francis (1727–1813):
Boulogne visited by, 17. 140
student at Douai, 17. 140n

Talbot, George (ca 1522–90), 6th E. of Shrewsbury, 1560:
birth date of, corrected, 43. 149

Elizabeth, Q., corresponds with, 15. 209n, 42. 286n
HW wants prints of portrait of, 42. 313
Lodge publishes papers of, 42. 286
son of, 11. 278n
son's letter to, 11. 278
wife inherits property of, 9. 298, 40. 182
wife of, 42. 313

Talbot, George (1719–87), 14th E. of Shrewsbury:
Boulogne visited by, 17. 140
Bulstrode tutor to, 17. 11n, 140n
Craon, Princesse de, attends tenebræ with, 17. 4
Dashwood ridicules Roman Catholicism of, 18. 79
Mahony, Comtesse, to be accompanied by, 17. 28
Rome visited by, 17. 4
servant of, talks with Smyth about Young Pretender's departure, 17. 14

Talbot, Hon. Mrs George. See Fitzwilliam, Hon. Mary

Talbot, Gilbert (1552–1616), 7th E. of Shrewsbury:
daughter of, 1. 39n, 182n, 16. 153n
house of, in London, 1. 148
letter of, to father, 11. 278

Talbot, Henry (1700–84), 'the man Tiger':
cottage adorned by, with spire, 9. 88
daughter of, 10. 190
HW and Montagu may visit, 9. 71
Jekyll, Lady Anne, visits, 9. 20
Montagu visits, 9. 20
wife of, dies, 9. 161

Talbot, Mrs Henry. See Clopton, Catharine

Talbot, James (1726–90), Bp of Birtha:
Boulogne visited by, 17. 140
student at Douai, 17. 140n

Talbot, John (ca 1384–1453), 7th Bn Talbot; cr. (1442) E. of Salop, known as E. of Shrewsbury, (1446) E. of Waterford:
biographical information about, corrected, 43. 183
HW praises, 18. 357
in Margaret of Anjou's escort, 14. 72, 74
portrait of, 10. 337, 41. 220, 251
print of, in Pennant's *Journey*, 42. 16n
second wife of, 10. 337
squint-eyed, 10. 337
wife of, 14. 73n

Talbot, John (d. 1751):
Boulogne visited by, 17. 140

Talbot, Hon. John (ca 1712–56), M.P.:
birth date of, 43. 244
(?) HW's friend, 19. 176
Indemnity Bill supported by, 17. 429
lord of trade, 9. 181, 20. 517
named in Secret Committee lists, 17. *385*, 391
Parliamentary vote by, on privately-raised regiments, 26. 19
(?) steward of Cheshire estate ordered by, to burn stock if rebels approach, 19. 176

Talbot, Lucy (d. 1787):
Boulogne visited by, **17.** 140
Talbot, Marie-Madeleine-Sophie, m. (1765) Charles-François-Fidèle, Marquis de Vintimille:
social relations of, with Contessa di Viry, **7.** 350
Talbot, Mary (d. 1650), m. (1604) William Herbert, 3d E. of Pembroke:
portrait of, **10.** 4n
Talbot, Mary (d. 1676), m. 2 Sir William Armine or Armyne:
print of, **1.** 181
Talbot, Mary (1723–53), m. (1749) Charles Dormer, 8th Bn Dormer:
biographical information about, corrected, **43.** 237
Boulogne visited by, **17.** 140
Talbot, Richard (1634–91), cr. (1685) E., and (1689) D. of Tyrconnel:
marriage of, **41.** 469, **42.** 89
peerage of, corrected, **43.** 303
print of, **1.** 182
wife of, **5.** 222n, **11.** 94n, **28.** 387n
Talbot, Richard Francis (1710–52), 3d E. of Tyrconnel:
Vintimille, Marquise de, daughter of, **7.** 350
Talbot, Thomas Joseph (1727–95), Bp of Acon, 1766:
Boulogne visited by, **17.** 140
student at Douai, **17.** 140n
Talbot, William (1710–82), 2d Bn Talbot, 1737, cr. (1761) E. Talbot:
Bath knights and Cinque Ports barons denied dinner by, **38.** 133
Beaufort pities, for ill-tempered mistress and wife, **17.** 486
—— sues, **18.** 185
Beaufort, Ds of, commits adultery with, **17.** 453
Beckford and Cinque Ports barons complain to, about City's treatment at Coronation, **9.** 389
becomes Earl, **21.** 489, 490
becomes lord steward, **21.** 489
Bedford's motion against Stone voted for by, **20.** 366n
Bubb Dodington supported by, **20.** 39
Bute gets complaint from, about diplomatic measures, **9.** 389
Chesterfield jokes about parsimony of, **10.** 32
daughter of, **9.** 190n
Dinevor title conferred on, to go to daughter's heirs, **25.** 86
Ferrers's trial attended by, **9.** 280
'Fountain' meeting attended by, **17.** 336
George III's Coronation attended by, as lord high steward, **9.** 388–9
Gower may succeed, as lord steward, **24.** 526n
Grenville ministry does not satisfy, **38.** 286
Grenville ministry may proscribe, **38.** 565–6
HW agrees with, in debate on the Address, **37.** 416
HW considers, mad, **9.** 280

HW jokes about pugnacity of, **10.** 44
Halifax to be succeeded by, in Board of Trade, **21.** 486
Henley may be succeeded by, as lord president, **41.** 73
horse backed by, down Westminster Hall at Coronation, **9.** 388–9, **38.** 128
Keppel, Mrs, praises, for rudeness to D. and Ds of Gloucester, **36.** 326
lacking in dignity at Coronation, **38.** 126
law suit will deprive, of wealth acquired by marriage, **18.** 199
may become Groom of the Stole, **30.** 163n
mob breaks lord steward's wand in hand of, **23.** 98–9
Murray's testimony interrupted by, **19.** 381
Newcastle, D. of, advised by, on Pitt's resignation, **21.** 540
Nugent-Irvine quarrel appeased by, **37.** 447
Parliamentary speech by, on Habeas Corpus, **37.** 529
'patriot feats' of, in youth, **10.** 274
peerage for, **36.** 174
Pitt, Elizabeth, mistress of, **20.** 507n
prophecy by, about Ferrers, **9.** 272–3
Regency Bill opposed by , **20.** 248
riot quelled by, **10.** 274
Rutland succeeded by, as lord steward of the Household, **9.** 343
wife separated from, **17.** 486
Wilkes fights duel with, **9.** 389n, **22.** 137, 163, **38.** 229
witticism by, about D. of Newcastle, **22.** 79
Talbot, William (d. 1811), chancellor of Salisbury; fellow of Clare Hall, Cambridge:
(?) Gray a friend of, **10.** 170
(?) Montagu describes, **10.** 170
(?) —— told by, about Cambridge election of high steward, **10.** 170
(?) Osborn's farm inhabited by, during vacation, **10.** 170
'Talbot, the,' tavern in the Strand:
dromedary and camel shown at, **21.** 199n
Talbot family:
genealogy of, brings them no advantages, **20.** 408
HW praises, **18.** 357
Halifax's intentions known to, **9.** 351
Lodge publishes correspondence of, **11.** 277–8
MSS of, discovered by Lodge, **15.** 209
motto of, **20.** 475
(?) Rice, Mrs, hears from, of Montagu's appointment, **9.** 351
Talbot Inn:
Waldegrave sisters take refuge in, in shower, **35.** 634
Talent; talents:
'an affectation,' **37.** 526
More, Hannah, discusses, **31.** 249
See also Parts
Tale of a Tub. See under Swift, Rev. Jonathan
Talerand; Taleron. See Talleyrand
Tales in Verse. See under Pinkerton, John

Tales of the Fairies. See under Berneville, Marie-Catherine-Jumelle de

Taliaris, Carmarthenshire:
Seymour-Conway of, 9. 225n

Talien. *See* Tallien

Talisman:
HW's bronze, 15. 13, 17

Tallard, Mme de:
Sauvé, Dame, informs, of plot to throw things into D. of Burgundy's cradle to injure Louis XV, 20. 287n

Tallart, Comte de. *See* Hostun, Camille d'

Talleyrand, Baron de. *See* Talleyrand-Périgord, Louis-Marie-Anne de

Talleyrand, Baronne de. *See* Montigny, Louise-Fidèle-Sainte-Eugénie de

Talleyrand, Comtesse de. *See* Damas d'Antigny, Alexandrine-Victoire-Éléonore

Talleyrand, Archambaud-Joseph de (1762–1838), Vicomte de Périgord; Duc de Talleyrand-Périgord:
marriage of, 7. 92

Talleyrand, Augustin-Louis (b. 1739), Chevalier de:
chevalier d'honneur to Mesdames Victoire and Sophie, 4. 442
(?) social relations of, with Marquise de Damas d'Antigny, 7. 338

Talleyrand, Charles-Daniel (1734–88), Comte de:
made member of Ordre du St-Esprit, 6. 199
social relations of, in Paris, 7. 325, 338
son of, marries, 7. 92

Talleyrand, Élie-Charles de (1754–1829), Prince de Chalais; Duc de Périgord:
SH visited by, 12. 244

Talleyrand, Gabriel-Marie de (1726–95), Comte de Périgord:
governor of Languedoc, 7. 340

Talleyrand, Henri de (1599–1626), Comte de Chalais:
Du Deffand, Mme, reads account of execution of, 4. 471

Talleyrand-Périgord, Duc de. *See* Talleyrand, Archambaud-Joseph de

Talleyrand-Périgord, Duchesse de. *See* Olivier de Sénozan de Viriville, Madeleine-Henriette-Sabine

Talleyrand-Périgord, Charles-Maurice de (1754–1838), Bp of Autun; cr. (1806) P. of Benevento:
in England but little noticed, 34. 138
responsibility of, for French Revolution, 31. 385

Talleyrand-Périgord, Louis-Marie-Anne de (1738–1809), Baron de Talleyrand:
Chanteloup visited by, 8. 202

Talleyrand-Périgord, Marie-Jeanne de (1747–92), m. (1762) Louis-Marie de Mailly d'Haucourt, Marquis (later Duc) de Mailly:
dame d'atour, 6. 401, 7. 216
dances at ball in honour of Dauphin's marriage, 4. 410

Tallien, Jean-Lambert (1767–1820), revolutionary:
assassination of, attempted, 12. 125–6
Louis XVII falsely reported to have been proclaimed by, 12. 118

Tallmadge, Maj. Benjamin (1754–1835):
Washington reassured by, about spies, 33. 239n

'Tall-Match.' *See* Tollemache

Tallow:
cheap in Florence, 18. 281

Tallow candles. *See under* Candle

Tallow-chandler; tallow-chandlers:
break windows for Revolution Society's jubilee, 11. 314
HW attributes rioters' window-breaking to glaziers and, 25. 343
mob of, riots in London, 23. 200

'Tall woman, the':
HW may be solicited by, for patronage, 9. 306–7

Talmach; Talmache. *See* Tollemache

Talman, John (d. 1726) of Hinxworth, Herts:
codicil revokes bequest of, to Trinity College, Cambridge, 42. 458

Talman, William:
Chatsworth designed by, 9. 292
Dyrham Park designed by Hauduroy and, 40. 11n

Talmond, Prince de. *See* La Trémoïlle, Antoine-Charles-Frédéric de

Talmond, Princesse de. *See* Jablonowska, Marie-Louise

Talon, Françoise-Madeleine (1730–67), m. (1746) Président Étienne-François d'Aligre:
Conti's friendship with, 3. 395–6
death of, 3. 395, 395–6
Lespinasse, Mlle de, befriended by, 3. 395

Tamar. See Tamer

Tambour; tambours:
bobbins for Lady Ossory's, 32. 250
vest, given to HW by Lady Ossory, worked partly in, 32. 220

Tamburini, Fortunato (1683–1761), cardinal, 1743:
Benedict XIV makes, cardinal, 18. 302n

Tamburro notturno. See under Rucellai

Tamer or *Tamar*, English ship:
Winchilsea returns with Capt. Mason on, 32. 308n

'Tameridge, Cosin':
Lincoln and Spence to receive compliments of, 30. 19

Tamerlane. See under Rowe, Nicholas; Sacchini, Antonio

Tamerlano. See under Bernasconi, Andrea; Pioveno, Conte Agostino

Taming of the Shrew. See under Shakespeare, William

Tamworth, Staffs:
Prinsep of, 13. 109n
Townshend, G., and Weymouth quarrel over election for, 30. 193

[Tamworth, Staffs, *continued*]
Townshend, G., reportedly backs Luttrell against Weymouth's candidate at, **30.** 193
Tamworth Castle, Staffs:
paintings formerly in, **2.** 165
proposed repairs at, **2.** 135, 146
Tanara, Alessandro (1680–1754), cardinal, 1743:
Benedict XIV makes, cardinal, **18.** 302n
Tanaro, Italian river:
Charles Emmanuel III and Austrians behind, **19.** 84
Spaniards dislodge Charles Emmanuel III from posts along, **19.** 120
Tancred, Sir Thomas (d. 1784), 5th Bt:
acting by, at Winterslow House, **32.** 176n
Tancred. See Voltaire: *Tancrède*
'Tancred and Sigismonda':
Sir Cauline resembles story of, **40.** 374
Tancred and Sigismunda. See under Thomson, James
Tancrede, Cavaliere [? Sir Thomas Tancred]:
Mann escorted by, **23.** 60n
Tancrède. See under Voltaire
Tancredi, Cavaliere [Sir Thomas Tancred]
Pembroke, E. of, accompanied by, to Corsica, **23.** 138n
Tandeau, ——:
attends session of parliament of Paris, **8.** 173
Tangier, Bay of:
St Esprit may have sunk in, **19.** 82
Tanjore, 'King' (*or* Rajah) of. *See* Tuljajī
Tanjore ('Tanjour'), India:
capture of, **23.** 561
Tankard; tankards:
milkwomen borrow, for May Day, **33.** 463
Tankersley, Yorks:
Zouch, rector of, **16.** 1n
Tankerville, Cts of. *See* Astley, Alicia (1716–91); Colville, Camilla (1698–1775)
Tankerville, E. of. *See* Bennet, Charles (1697–1753); Bennet, Charles (1716–67); Grey, Ford (1655–1701)
Tanner, Jonathan (d. 1769), merchant:
(?) Coates talks with, **30.** 230
Tanner, Thomas (1674–1735), Bp of St Asaph; antiquary:
Bibliotheca Britannico-Hibernica by: **43.** 57; HW misled by, **16.** 4n; Hoccleve's portrait of Chaucer mentioned in, **14.** 109; quoted, **1.** 272
Cole's note on, **2.** 257
letter from Anne of Denmark owned by, **15.** 74
Notitia monastica by: arms might be found in, **33.** 427; Cole consults, **2.** 277; Nasmith edits, **1.** 268n
Willis's prefatory epistle to, **2.** 351
Tanner's bark:
and peach skins, **35.** 473
See also under Bark
Tant mieux pour elle:
Crébillon thought to have written, **38.** 57

Tanucci, Bernardo (1698–1783), statesman:
Charles of Naples confides in, **21.** 330
Cocchi, schoolmate and friend of, **21.** 495n
dissertation by, advocates a king of Italy, **21.** 494–5
Dissertatione del dominio antico de' Pisani sulla Corsica by, **21.** 494n
Ferdinand not intellectually oriented by, **35.** 432n
Firmian informs, that Maria Josepha's engagement with Archduke Joseph is broken, **21.** 323n
Floridablanca blamed by, for rumours of Clement XIV's poisoning, **24.** 42n
Gray, Sir James, to get billet from, **21.** *160*
—— told by, that Naples and Charles III want neutrality, **22.** 5–6
Hamilton, Sir William, not on good terms with, **22.** 547
Jesuits opposed by, **26.** 49
La Ensenada called by, fomenter of riot, **39.** 64n
Neapolitans clamorous against, **21.** 329–30
Pitt's letter to, about Sir James Gray's Bath investiture, **21.** 507n
professor of jurisprudence at Pisa, **21.** 495n
Tuscan government hated by, **22.** 448
Wilkes neglected by, **22.** 292
Tanzaï et Néodarné. See under Crébillon, Claude-Prosper Jolyot de
Tape; tapes:
HW furnishes, **9.** 117n
red, notes tied up with, **30.** 289
Taper; tapers:
heat from, at Jewish wedding, **37.** 312
lighted, (?) carried by prisoners, **9.** 192
Tapestry; tapestries:
Ailesbury, Cts of, makes, for Mme du Deffand, **6.** 228
Arnaldi's, **17.** 56
at: Bayeux, **40.** 213, 221; Blenheim, **9.** 18; Burghley House, **10.** 345; Chatsworth, **9.** 296; Exchequer House, **37.** 454n; Hardwick, **9.** 297; Hinchingbrooke, after cartoons, **40.** 283; House of Lords, **1.** 10–11, 13, **9.** 18, **23.** 242, **34.** 84–5; Knole, **35.** 133; Norfolk House, **37.** 438; Standon, **40.** 198–9
Charles III may declare war from horse of, **23.** 245
—— said to have flogged horse in, **23.** 230–1
—— shoots at, **23.** 237–8
—— should be left to enjoyment of, **23.** 254
—— slaughtered animals in, **23.** 241
cost of, **1.** 22, 25
Crane's interest in, **1.** 2, **43.** 38
Cumberland, D. of, receives, at Rome, **23.** 566
Ferdinand VI tries to mount horses in, **23.** 241
Ferdinand of Naples's pastimes worse than shooting birds or thrashing horses in, **23.** 254
French, chairs covered with, **23.** 285

from Cheveley, 1. 169
from Raphael's cartoons: Alba's at Madrid, 16. 169; at Rome, 16. 169; in England, 16. 147, 157; said to be at Burghley House, 16. 159
Gobelin, at Osterley, 34. 237, 238
HW and Lady Mary Churchill buy, 7. 335
HW gives maps of, to Harcourt, 35. 539–40
in Ducarel's book, 15. 123
La Savonnerie, 6. 449
Mereworth has bed of, 35. 143
obsolete in France, 35. 123
of Armada's destruction, in House of Lords, 1. 10–11, 13, 9. 18, 23. 242, 34. 84–5
of Charles Brandon's history, 32. 325
of Crusades, near House of Commons, 40. 213
Palavicini's interest in, 1. 2
Paris shop for, visited by HW, 7. 305
portrait in, 35. 269
purchased for HW, 4. 428, 437, 439, 452
worsteds in, 40. 278
York, D. of, receives, at Rome, 22. 229, 232
See also Bed; Damask; Gobelin; Hangings; Sheldon maps
Tapestry Hangings of the House of Lords. See under Morant, Philip; Pine, John
Tapeworm:
Elliot suffers from, 7. 213
Taploe. See Taplow
Taplow, Bucks:
Conway writes from, 37. 384, 538
Conway, Hon. Anne Seymour, visits E. of Hertford at, 37. 385
dryness of, 38. 26
HW to dine at, and be picked up by Conway, 37. 470
Hertford hopes to see HW at, 38. 26
visitors to: Conway and wife, 37. 538; (?) Harris, Mrs, 38. 29; Pembroke, Cts of, 37. 538
Tappia, Conte:
San Remo deputy, 19. 123
Tapping (for the dropsy):
Saxe subjected to, 19. 91
Tar:
Norway, 18. 452n
sailor mends wooden leg with, 24. 283–4
Southwark magazines of, catch fire, 25. 577
Tarantula. See under Lyne, Richard
Tarantula; tarantulas:
music said to cure bites of, 35. 425
Tarare. See under Beaumarchais, Pierre-Augustin Caron de
Tarascon. See Richard de Tarascon
Tarbat, Vct of. See Mackenzie, George (1630–1714)
Tarente, Princesse de. See Hesse-Cassel, Amelie von (1625–93)
Target, Gui-Jean-Baptiste (1733–1806):
Lettres d'un homme à un autre homme, by, 5. 104

Tariff. See Protecting Duties
'Tarinity':
Henley preaches on, 18. 465
Tarleton, Sir Banastre (1754–1835), cr. (1815) Bt; army officer; M.P.:
Cornwallis dispatches, to South Carolina, 33. 298n
defeated in America, 25. 141, 29. 124, 128
French war opposed by, in Parliament, 39. 508n
news of, in London Gazette, 29. 110
Sheridan's witticism on, 29. 188–9
Tarleton, John (1755–1820), merchant; M.P.:
More, Hannah, interrupted by arrival of, 31. 297
slavery to be defended by, as Liverpool delegate, 31. 297
Tarnow (Galicia):
Wedell and Bevern defeat Swedes at, 21. 247n
Taro, Italian river:
armies of Austria and Spain separated by, 19. 245
Imperial army awaits Gages on banks of, 19. 236
Taroc (tarot):
game played with tall cards, at Turin, 13. 191
HW has Florentine cards for playing, 17. 193n
Tarpaulin; tarpaulins:
preferable to Mrs French's pavement, 35. 389
Tarporley, Cheshire:
Allen rector of, 1. 4n, 14. 78n
Crewe, Sir John, buried in, 1. 4n
(?) painting Gray wants to see is at, 14. 78
Tarquin, Roman king, 7th or 6th cent. B.C.:
value of, as member of society, 33. 158
Tarquinius Priscus (d. ? 578 B.C.), K. of Rome:
Servius Tullius gets Greek influence from Court of, 14. 21
'Tarred and feathered':
Mahon described as, 39. 184
Tarsis et Zélie. See under Le Vayer de Boutigny, Roland
Tart; tarts:
Austrobritons should eat plain, not French, 35. 36
currant: HW advises Berrys against, 12. 145; Mann serves, to Contessa del Benino, 17. 68
entremets of, 19. 357n
gooseberry: Hobart and Mann consume, 19. 261; Mann has, for dinner in garden, 21. 10; Mann lives on, 17. 57, 61; Mann sends, to Princesse de Craon, 19. 402; 'wooden,' 9. 130
of duke cherries, 20. 260
of spinach, 17. 218
Tartan, English cutter:
Marlborough's letters brought by, 21. 210
Tartan; tartans (vessels):
English use, as fire-ships, 18. 301
French, captured by English, 17. 408

[Tartan; tartans, *continued*]
French ship to be escorted by, back to Tripoli, **23**. 24
Genoese, burnt to prevent plague, **18**. 252n
Norris captures, **18**. 455

Tartar; Tartars:
Churchill, Lady Mary, resembles princess of, **39**. 146
Crimean, Khan of, **23**. 116n
Dashkov, Anastasia, is, **33**. 172
Dashkov, Ps, brings, to SH, **33**. 203
—— is, **23**. 248
Frederick II tries to represent, as intending to break union with Russia, **30**. 321
Greeks said to have borrowed from, **33**. 479
HW wishes Montagu resembled, **10**. 262
Montagu roams like, **35**. 70
—— with his caravan will resemble chief of, **10**. 253
See also Tartary

Tartar, East India ship:
Fiott captain of, **24**. 246n

Tartar, English frigate:
Johnstone arrives in, **24**. 419n

Tartar, English merchant ship:
pirates chased by, **25**. 480n, 493n

Tartar, English ship:
Brown, captain of, **23**. 226n

Tartar, English tartan:
sails to Minorca, **25**. 249

Tartar:
salt of, makes green ink out of privet, **35**. 204

Tartary, Khan ('Cham') of:
Craven, Lady, may be in tent of, **42**. 177
Russians allegedly defeated by, **23**. 160n

Tartary:
Craven, Lady, crosses, **42**. 176
forces of, oppose Frederick II, **21**. 327
Frenchman and Englishman would seem fellow-countrymen if they met in, **25**. 555–6
Ireland could be of interest only to, **37**. 75
ownership of portions of, inconsequential, **23**. 420
Pomerania worth more than, **22**. 11

Tart Hall:
Arundel of, **15**. 114n

Tartini, Giuseppe (1692–1770), violinist:
HW unable to answer West's questions about, **13**. 233
Nardini, pupil of, **22**. 537n

Tartuffe. See under Molière

Tar-water:
Berkeley's *Siris* popularizes, **18**. 452, 464–5, **29**. 282
Mann, Galfridus, takes, **21**. 30, 36
newspapers print verses on Berkeley and, **18**. 505
Orford's only medicine, **36**. 124

Tassa. *See* Tassi

Tassels:
gold: gown trimmed with, **10**. 198; on chairs at Boughton House, **10**. 341

on Ds of Buckingham's funeral canopy, **18**. 193

Tassi *or* Tassa, Nicolli *or* Nicholas, notary or lawyer:
attestation by, to Lady Orford's will, **43**. 287, 288
(?) Mann consults, **25**. 120
(?) —— opens Cts of Orford's will in presence of, **25**. 114, **43**. 289

Tassie. *See* Wedgwood and Tassie

Tasso, Torquato (1544–95), poet:
Conway wants to read, **37**. 73
Este, Leonora d', said to be mistress of, **35**. 409, 412
frontispiece to *Life of Edward Lord Herbert of Cherbury* reminds Montagu of, **10**. 134
Gerusalemme liberata by: **29**. 262, **40**. 245; Armida in, **33**. 61; HW finds, wearisome, **29**. 256; HW quotes, **13**. 190; HW to write another, for Leonora d'Este, **35**. 421; Rinaldo in, **13**. 60n, **38**. 126, **40**. 245; West and Gray read, **13**. 133
Hoole translates, **15**. 261n

Tassoni, Alessandro (1565–1635):
Considerazioni sopra le rime del Petrarca by, **40**. 116

Taste:
and genius, HW's reflections on, **40**. 352
English, in gardens, **11**. 168
French, in small ornaments, surpasses English, **25**. 635
HW jokes about marriage to City fortune as source of, **30**. 87
HW's reflections on: **39**. 120, 296; as responsible for ill-advised alterations, **25**. 177; differ from Alison's essay, **42**. 273–4
HW's reflections on change in, **10**. 262
HW's reflections on schools of, **30**. 114
improvement in, **31**. 251
in beauty and wit, alters, **25**. 308
madmen overwhelm, **35**. 127
More, Hannah, reflects on truth in, **31**. 224
not hereditary in families or in places, **35**. 430
reason inferior to, **11**. 22
refined, Pope's garden spoilt by, **25**. 177
spoilt by criticism and comparison, **11**. 22
Strafford's, praised, **11**. 66

'Taste À-La-Mode,' satiric print:
Fitzroy, Lady Caroline, may be satirized in, **37**. 228

Taster; tasters:
'cups of assay' for, **32**. 324

Tate, Mr:
HW sends letter by, **7**. 396

Tate, Sir Bartholomew (d. 1533), Kt:
arms of, **2**. 220, 222
Bury St Edmunds and, **2**. 220, 221–2
portrait of, **2**. 220–1

Tate, Sir John (d. 1515); lord mayor of London 1496–7:
arms represent marriage of, **16**. 185n

name of, corrected, **43**. 220

Tate, Nahum (1652–1715), dramatist:
Duke and No Duke, A, by, 'Trappolin' in, played by Woodward, **38**. 544

Tate. *See also* Tait

Tatler, The:
character in, **9**. 16n
spurious edition of, **10**. 238n

Tattersal, —— (d. 1795), horse-dealer:
Orford's dogs to be sold by, **39**. 490

Tatton, Elizabeth (d. 1759), m. (1741) Henry Flower, 2d Bn Castle-Durrow; cr. (1751) Vct Ashbrook:
son of, **10**. 210

Tatton, Elizabeth (d. 1803), m. (1770) Sir Christopher Sykes, 2d Bt, 1783:
heir of Samuel Egerton, **33**. 168

Tatton, Katharine (d. 1729), m. 1 (1724) Edward Nevill, 15th Bn Abergavenny; m. 2 (1725) William Nevill, 16th Bn Abergavenny:
buried in Kensington Church, **20**. 182
daughter of, **19**. 63

Tatton, Neville (d. 1792), Gen.:
Churchill, Mrs, mistress of, **7**. 374

Tatton, Rev. William (1720–82):
death of, **2**. 304

Tatton, Mrs William. *See* Egerton, Hester

Tatton Egerton. *See* Egerton, William Tatton

Tattooing:
modern Englishmen might revert to, **32**. 359

Tattoo of drums:
English royal family enjoys, **17**. 410

Taube, Gräfin von. *See* Hoym, Gisela Erdmuth von

Taube, Evert Vilhelm (1737–99), Freiherre; Swedish army officer:
(?) Mann sends HW's letter to Ds of Gloucester by, **24**. 247

Taunton, Somerset:
address from, against Americans, **24**. 132n, **39**. 270n, **41**. 311n
Maxwell, M.P. for, **20**. 441

Taureau blanc, Le. See under Voltaire

Tauris:
archbishopric of, in Turkish hands, **22**. 196

Taurus, Mt:
Voltaire mentions, **35**. 413

Tavannes, Cardinal de. *See* Saulx, Nicolas

Tavannes, Comte de. *See* Saulx, Charles-François-Casimir de

Tavannes, Comtesse de. *See* Lévis-Châteaumorand, Marie-Éléonore-Eugénie de

Tavanti, Signora. *See* Cocchi, Beatrice

Tavanti, Angelo (1714–82), Tuscan financier:
government post given to, **23**. 294
Mann granted permission by, for Zoffany to paint picture of Tribune, **23**. 430n

Taverham, Norfolk:
Micklethwait of, **12**. 50n

Tavern; taverns:
American agitation descends from Parliament to, **24**. 86
Argyll, Ds of, dines at, at 76, **35**. 297, 299

at Ghent, **37**. 119

at Oxford, **30**. 88n, 330n

Carteret and Winchilsea never dine at, **17**. 335

Cock Lane séances profitable to, **10**. 6

Conway and friends go from opera to, **37**. 54
—— visits, in dream, **37**. 17

dinners at, for Parliamentary candidates, **17**. 243

Flattery's, in Dublin, **39**. 421n

Fuller's murals for, in London, **42**. 380n

future dukes will frequent, **20**. 155

Hamilton frequents, **20**. 155

hats hang on pegs in, **28**. 206

in Newgate St, **25**. 386n, **36**. 210n

in Pall Mall, adorned with Townshend's caricatures, **37**. 444

in Piccadilly, **19**. 387n

Norsa keeps, **19**. 284

Petersham, Lady Caroline, gives supper at, **35**. 222–3

Pitt might be satirized in sign for, in London, **38**. 137

Rigby, Selwyn, and Sir C. H. Williams sup at, at Oxford, and riot ensues, **30**. 330n

Rockingham's friends and George Grenville dine at, **23**. 115

Rumbold and Sykes formerly waiters at, **25**. 141

Selwyn drinks out of popish chalice at, **30**. 89

'Three Tuns,' at Cambridge, **14**. 91n

would-be suicide entertains his insurers at, **35**. 203

See also Angel, The; Bedford Arms; Bedford Head; Crown; Crown and Anchor; Duke's Head; Fountain; Horn Tavern; King's Arms, Palace Yard; London Tavern; Mitre, The; St Alban's Tavern; Salutation; Ship Tavern; Star, The; Star and Garter; Talbot, The; Three Tuns, The; Vine Tavern

See also under Inn; *and under* Twickenham

Tavernier, ——:
attends session of parliament of Paris, **8**. 173

Tavernier, ——, watchmaker:
watch made by, left by Mme du Deffand to Mlle Couty, **8**. 27

Tavernier, Jean-Baptiste (1605–89), Baron d'Aubonne, 1670:
Six Voyages by, (?) HW reads of temple in, **24**. 433

Tavernier de Boullongne, Catherine-Jeanne (ca 1750–1838), m. (1765) Mathieu-Paul-Louis, Vicomte (later Comte) de Montmorency-Laval:
admitted to suppers at little château at Compiègne, **4**. 441
dances at ball in honour of Dauphin's marriage, **4**. 410

Provence, Comtesse de, dismisses, **7**. 439

Tavern-keeper; tavern-keepers:
English, rush to France at peace, **37**. 297

Tavistock, Marchioness of. *See* Keppel, Lady Elizabeth (1739–68)

Tavistock, M. of. *See* Russell, Francis (1739–67); Russell, Francis (1765–1802)

Tavistock, Devon:
burgess for, **16**. 65

Tavora, Francisco d'Assis de (1703–59), Marqués de Tavora:
alleged plot by, **21**. 250
daughter-in-law of, was José I's mistress, **21**. 250n
limbs of, broken alive, **21**. 267n

Tavora, Dona Leonor de (1700–59), m. Francisco d'Assis de Tavora:
alleged plot by, **21**. 250
beheaded, **21**. 267n
executed for attempted murder of José I, **21**. 250n
Tavora, Marqués de, marries, **21**. 250n

Tavora, Dona Teresa de (1723–94), m. (1742) Dom Luis Bernardo de Tavora, Marqués de Tavora:
Portugal, K. of, has intrigue with, **31**. 9–10

Tax; taxes:
called heavy, in House of Lords, **18**. 158
cider: **10**. 57–8, **22**. 277n; George III promises Pitt to alleviate, **30**. 188
coach, HW's, **41**. 432
country gentry want, low, **36**. 221
Craon to pay, on future daughter-in-law's fortune, **19**. 23
Eden's pamphlet discusses, **28**. 484
embargo may be mistaken for, **35**. 320
England expects additions to, **24**. 448
—— levies, on American colonies, **35**. 571, **38**. 508–9
—— may levy, deeper, to extricate herself, **35**. 363
—— may see folly of imposing on America, **24**. 208
Ferrara's and Romagna's, **18**. 344
Florentine: as high as they can be, **22**. 254; on decedents' estates, **21**. 149, 151
French: of ten percent, **17**. 115; on land, proposed, **42**. 346; unpaid, **39**. 485
Genoa does not levy, **18**. 555
HW instructs Bedford to pay, pending clarification from Legge, **40**. 153–5
HW's reflections on, **29**. 42
Haarlem riot over, **37**. 286
House of Commons considers, **25**. 566, 573, 583
India subjected to, by East India Co.'s servants, **23**. 451–2
inheritance: in Tuscany, acquittance needed for, **25**. 521; on legacies, in Tuscany, **25**. 666
Irish: absentee, **23**. 524, 531, **32**. 159, 161, 164, **35**. 348, 464; on pensions, **23**. 174n
land: Buckingham grand jury thanks Parliament for lowering, **22**. 494; cattle distemper makes, more serious, **42**. 497; continued, **17**. 390; diminution of, not irreparable, **22**. 501; diminution of proves

unpopular, **22**. 494; English country gentry oppose, **34**. 20; English country gentry try to avoid, by piling up public debt, **25**. 506; joke about, **10**. 116; London opposes country squires' attempt to lower, **22**. 487–8; ministry defeated in attempt to preserve, **22**. 487–9; reduced, **30**. 243n; remonstrants may refuse to pay, **23**. 197; Townshend refuses to pay, **23**. 346
Legge speaks on, **37**. 444–5
Londoners ignore, **25**. 243
malt tax, **39**. 482
Mason's reflections on, **4**. 39
merchants thrive by, **21**. 549
Meredith's pamphlet mentions Greek republics' resistance to, **39**. 318
ministry dispenses with, for Scotland, **20**. 311
Minorcans do not pay, to England, **37**. 311
new, in England, **11**. 173, **25**. 506, 566
North's peace terms disclaim levying of, **24**. 354
—— to lay, before House of Commons, **25**. 254
on bread, in Spain, **39**. 60–1, 63
on coaches, Bedford to pay, for HW, **41**. 432
on Electress's pensions to servants, **19**. 23–4
on houses, windows, and wrought plate, **21**. 199n
on Irish absentee landlords, **23**. 524, 531, **32**. 159, 161, 164, **35**. 348, 464
on oil, in Spain, **39**. 63
on places, HW concerned with, on his Exchequer place, **40**. 153–5
on plate, **37**. 451
on plate, bricks, tiles, cards, and dice, **37**. 445
on post horses, **28**. 459, **29**. 39, **33**. 108
on servants, **41**. 432, 433
on tea, proposed, **18**. 141–2
on tobacco, at Florence, **20**. 389
on tradesmen's bills, **20**. 183
Orford, Cts of, averse to, **20**. 504–5
Parliamentary opposition to, **38**. 273
Parliament debates new, because of armament against Spain, **11**. 173
—— debates over, **19**. 458
—— should heap, on advocates of American war, **24**. 133–4
Pitt, William II, has trouble with, **39**. 482
place tax: debated in House of Commons, **21**. 199; HW's, on his Exchequer place, **40**. 153–5
Portuguese officer prosecuted for not paying, **23**. 166
proposed excise on wine and tobacco, **13**. 59
Pulteney said to increase, **18**. 91
Rouen parliament wants power to levy, **38**. 299
Scottish, **20**. 311
size of, in England, **17**. 401
Smelt recommends raising, **28**. 491–2
Spanish army levies, on Italian towns, **18**. 344

Tuscan collectors of, more diligent than under the Medici, **22**. 254-5

Tuscan quarantine creates, **18**. 297

war's sole fruits, **35**. 361

window tax: **4**. 75, **21**. 199n; Clive, Mrs, pays, **35**. 468

See also Cider tax; Sugar tax, etc.

See also under France: finances of

Taxal, near Chapel le Frith, Derbyshire, Dickenson's seat:

Dickenson, Mrs, addressed at, **31**. 335, 344

HW not to visit, **31**. 345

Taxier. *See* Le Texier

Tay, river:

'poetical banks of,' **37**. 217

Taylor, ——:

(?) HW's correspondence with, **38**. 555

Taylor, ——, of Ashton:

rioters demolish house of, **31**. 361n

Taylor, Capt.:

Isabel commanded by, **25**. 665n

Taylor, Mr (visitor to Paris):

HW sends letter by, **7**. 380

HW sends letters by servant of, **7**. 377

Taylor, Mr, of London:

Berry, Mary, describes, **12**. 106n

HW visited by, **12**. 106

SH visited by, **12**. 247

Taylor, Mrs:

HW sends compliments to, **40**. 200

Taylor, Brook:

Contemplatio philosophica, HW thanks Seward for, **42**. 388

HW wants duplicate of print of, **42**. 388

Taylor, Clement (d. 1804), M.P.:

election of, **25**. 86n

Taylor, Elizabeth (1729–1801), m. (1747) Sir William Young, cr. (1769) Bt:

Florence visited by, **20**. 327

from Kent, 'refined' in France, **20**. 327

Taylor, George:

print of, **40**. 236

Taylor, Henry (d. 1758), of Charles St, Westminster; Conway's regimental agent:

Conway to write to, **37**. 254

Taylor, Jeremy (1613–67), Bp of Down and Connor; writer:

Holy Living and Holy Dying by, **28**. 311n

Mason calls, 'my friend,' **28**. 311

Taylor, John (1580–1653), the 'water-poet':

To the Honour of the Noble Captaine O'Toole, satire by, **1**. 62n

Taylor, John (1703–72), quack oculist, known as 'Chevalier Taylor':

calls himself 'Chevalier,' **21**. 252

Florentine oculist outdoes, **18**. *240*

HW calls, quack, **20**. 461n

HW's epigram on, **21**. 252, 255, **31**. 11

Kilmorey, Vcts, recommends, to Albani, **20**. 458

King's mock eulogy on, in Latin, **31**. 11n

Walpole family's patronage boasted of by, at Rome, **20**. 458, 461

Taylor, John (1704–66), LL.D.; Fellow of St John's College, Cambridge; F.R.S.; F.S.A.; archdeacon of Buckingham:

Cole expects visitation by, **1**. 47

opinion by, about portrait at St John's, **14**. 115

Taylor, John (ca 1745–1806), landscape-painter:

(?) HW gets method of aquatinta from, **29**. 112

Taylor, Mary (fl. ca 1751–3), housekeeper at Hampton Court:

visitors conducted by, **20**. 272

Taylor, Robert (1710–62), physician:

Frederick, P. of Wales, attended by, **20**. 232

Taylor, Sir Robert (1714–88):

Cornewall's monument by, **37**. 271n

Taylor, Thomas (1758–1835), Platonist:

Euclid published by, **31**. 273n

Philosophical and Mathematical Commentaries of Proclus, by, HW's contempt for, **34**. 82–3

Taylor, William (ca 1753–1825), proprietor of King's Theatre, Haymarket:

biographical information about, corrected, **43**. 146

Concise Statement of Transactions and Circumstances respecting the King's Theatre, in the Haymarket, A, by, attacks Salisbury, **11**. 191

publishes advertisement against Salisbury's injustice, **11**. 227

Taylor. *See also* Taylour

Taylour, Mrs. *See* Cholmley, Anne

Taylour, Joseph (d. ? 1790), LL.D., of Isleworth:

(?) SH visited by, **12**. 233

Taylour. *See also* Taylor

Taymouth, Perthshire:

'black book' of, **40**. 264

Campbell seat at, contains Jamesone portraits, **40**. 264–5

portrait of James IV at, **16**. 321n

Tchesmé, Asia Minor:

battle of, **23**. 226–8, 232–6

Russians do not follow up successes at, **23**. 331

Turkish fleet burnt in harbour of, **23**. 234–5

Te, Palazzo del, at Mantua:

Giulio Romano designs, **35**. 4n

Tea:

Amelia, Ps, serves, in Gunnersbury dairy, **33**. 517

Americans are ordered to drink, **28**. 217

at 6 P.M., **1**. 88

Beauvau, Princesse de, orders, from Hon. T. Walpole, **7**. 233

beggars drink, **7**. 258

booths for, at Ranelagh, **20**. 47

[Tea, *continued*]

Bostonians dump, in harbour, **23**. 550, **24**. 13

camœdris infused like, **6**. 384

Cholmondeley, Mrs, at HW's request, urges Mme du Deffand to forsake, **36**. 57–8

Cole never tastes anything after taking, **2**. 180

—— sends to London for, **2**. 148

contraband, **9**. 105

Conway takes, **39**. 280

—— wants to serve, to HW, **37**. 93

delivered to Mme du Deffand, **4**. 73

dinner guest leaves SH after, **34**. 186

dish of, taken by Sir Edward Walpole, **25**. 463

drinking of, **1**. 299, **2**. 22n, 51, 147, 180, 311, **3**. 224, 316, 323, 343, **4**. 165, 200, 272, 299, 309, 339, **5**. 54, 62, 160, 208, 237, 243, 350, 370, 417, 418, 424, 430, **6**. 27, 245, **7**. 72

Du Deffand, Mme, benefited by, **4**. 332, 334, **5**. 353

—— orders, **4**. 28, 35, 39, **5**. 28, 305–7, 311, 317, 331, 342, 351, 353, **6**. 128, 132, 134, 302, 334, 408, 489, 494, **7**. 125, 128, 135, 226

—— receives gift of, **3**. 87, **5**. 429, **6**. 56, 317, 423, 425, 438, 495, **7**. 28, 29, 131, 240, 423

—— takes, weak, with milk, **4**. 332

—— takes, while awaiting horses, **41**. 196

—— thanks HW for, **4**. 307, 309

Dutch skippers drink, in Conway's cabin, **37**. 209

duty on, proposed by English ministers, **18**. 141–2

East India Co. buys, at Ostend, to cheat smugglers, **25**. 577–8

——'s stock of, at Southwark, catches fire, **25**. 577–8

East Indian, **33**. 138

English army drinks, when invading France, **37**. 541, 547

English have not drunk, under Cherbourg's cannon, **39**. 526

for breakfast, **7**. 258, **30**. 132n

French, inferior to English, **6**. 492

French Customs will confiscate, **37**. 40

George II to hold cup for, at subscription masquerade, **20**. 49

green, ordered by Mme du Deffand, **3**. 308, 317

HW avoids, **23**. 76

HW benefits by leaving off, **14**. 142

HW drinks: at Houghton, **9**. 349; at Paris, **35**. 124; outdoors at Fitzroy Farm, **32**. 121–2; with Mme de Mirepoix, **31**. 93

HW forbidden, by gout, **31**. 75

HW leaves off, to cure stomach sickness, **39**. 30

HW longs for, in France, **39**. 7

HW mentions, **20**. 326

HW prepares, for Archduke and Archduchess of Austria, **33**. 529

HW receives, from Mann, **17**. 12, 17, 19

HW's: at SH for Selwyn, Bolingbroke, and

Musgrave, **39**. 104; used by Mme du Deffand, **4**. 332–3

HW sends, to Mme du Deffand, **6**. 258

HW serves, at SH, **10**. 69, 127, 168, 279, **31**. 206, 216, **38**. 362

HW's things for, moved from Windsor to SH, **37**. 270

HW suggests that Mme du Deffand give up, **6**. 133

HW to provide himself with, for journey, **9**. 118

HW to send, to Mme du Deffand and Mme de Cambis, **36**. 168, 169

HW wants boiling water for, at Welling-borough inn, **10**. 89

Hertford serves, on George III's birthday, **38**. 398

hour for, **1**. 88, **4**. 319, 442, **5**. 160, 164, 430, **6**. 178n

Mann, Chute, and Whithed take, **17**. 428

Mann serves, to Vorontsov family, **22**. 193

—— takes, under orange trees, **17**. 104

—— to take, with Chute and Whithed, **17**. 161

—— unable to get, for HW, **17**. 59

Mirepoix, Mme de, drinks, **31**. 55

—— orders, from Hon. T. Walpole, **7**. 233

—— receives, from Hon. T. Walpole, **7**. 226

—— toasts HW in, **39**. 7

—— wants, from England, **36**. 168

Newcastle, D. of, to take, with HW at SH, **40**. 361

New York rejects, **24**. 13

Nivernais serves, with dinner, **7**. 341

plants of, thrive in green-houses around London, **18**. 183n

ratsbane not to be put in, by Mlle Morphy and Mme de Pompadour, **35**. 173

Raynal discusses, **39**. 168

seed of: Ginori content with small quantity of, **18**. 235; Ginori thinks, is in Botanic Garden at Chelsea, **18**. 183; HW to get, through brother at Chelsea, **18**. 250; Mann wants, **18**. 323; to be sought in Chelsea botanical garden, **18**. 216; Walpole, Sir Edward, forgets to get, **18**. 284

served: at Bushey Park, **9**. 380; at Cambridge, **10**. 92; at Esher, **10**. 73; at Kimbolton, **10**. 77; at Robinson's ball, **17**. 185; at Stowe, **10**. 313; at SH, **10**. 69, 127, 168, 279, **31**. 206, 216, **38**. 362; in summer-house at La Trappe, **35**. 302; in Wroxton library, **35**. 72

smuggled: found, **33**. 178; found in Hasz-lang's house, **25**. 55; Gray alludes to, **13**. 156

tax on, proposed, **18**. 141–2

universal use of, **18**. 142

Venice well stocked with, **17**. 59

Walpole, Hon. Robert, sends, to Mme du Deffand, **5**. 130

See also Camomile tea; Elderflower tea

Tea canister; tea canisters:
cherry brandy kept in, **37**. 22
Teacup; teacups:
escape a falling chimney-stack, **39**. 481
HW knows face of every, in French shops,
39. 145
strawberries and cream served in, **31**. 40
Tea dealer; tea dealers ('tea-man'; 'tea merchant'):
licence tax on, **25**. 254n
Mawhood, James, son of, **39**. 250
Walpole, Hon. Robert, recommends, **5**. 231
Teakettle; teakettles:
Boufflers, Comtesse Amélie de, desires HW
to get, for her, **6**. 9, 13, 33, 39, 42
Couty to buy: for Comtesse Amélie de Boufflers, **6**. 9, 13, 39; for Comtesse de Boufflers,
5. 418
Du Deffand, Mme, asks for another, **5**. 177,
182, 193, 200, 205, 206, 207, 211
—— receives, **5**. 223
HW secures, for Comtesse de Boufflers, **5**.
417–18, 425, 433, 436, **6**. 2, 4, 7–9
incrustation by water on, **42**. 406
lamp of, only light in Cts of Coventry's sick-
room, **21**. 451
Mirepoix, Mme de, to receive, **5**. 160, 162, 197
ormolu, sold at auction, **23**. 211–12
Teano, Principe di. See Gaetani, Michelangelo
(ca 1689–1760)
Teapot; teapots:
Monmouth's white china, given by Harcourt
to HW, **35**. 477n
Sally, Mrs, procures, for HW, and brings
them to The Hague, **38**. 129
'Tears of Scotland, The.' See under Smollett,
Tobias George
Tea service:
of Chelsea china, **22**. 121–2
Teaspoon; teaspoons:
Marlborough abandons, in retreat from St-
Malo, **21**. 221
——'s, returned by Aiguillon, **37**. 544, 547
silver, prize for horse race, **37**. 311
Tea strainer; tea strainers:
HW fishes with, **9**. 155
Tea tongs:
English may try to batter Calais with, **21**. 221
Teatro degl'Intrepidi (called Teatro della Palla
a Corda), Florence:
Mann serves sherbets before opening of, **25**.
585, 592
masked balls given free at, for Archduke and
Archduchess of Milan, **25**. 50
new theatre, opened with show about Amerigo Vespucci, **24**. 514
open in June, 1785, **25**. 585
(?) Young Pretender decorates box in, **25**.
536
Teatro del Borgo de' Greci, at Florence:
used in Lent for concerts and poetry readings, **23**. 458n

Teatro del Cocomero, Florence:
Accademia degli Immobili founded, **17**. 56n
admission price to, **20**. 357
Andromaca in prose given at, **18**. 128
bad opera at, **18**. 555
Bagnano not to give operas in, **17**. 56
burletta in, **17**. 128, **19**. 356, 476
Fumagalli almost inaudible in, **17**. 423
Gloucester, D. of, attends, with Leopold and
Maria Louisa, **23**. 405
Iphigenia at, **18**. 128, 134
Lee, Charles, strikes Laugier in, **20**. 363n
Leopold frequents, **22**. 477
(?) little opera at, **17**. 80
Mann serves sherbets before opening of, **25**.
585, 592
Medici, Filippo, impresario at, **18**. 178
name of, corrected, **43**. 238
opening of, **23**. 458n
open in June 1785, **25**. 585
opera not to be given at, **17**. 56
operas at, **17**. 284
Pepi, Francesco Gaspero, impresario at, **18**.
41n
Pertici at, **18**. 198n
Ughi family proprietors of, **17**. 163n
Vanni, Gobbo, impresario at, **18**. 527n
Via della Pergola in opposition to, **19**. 356
Teatro del Falcone. See under Genoa
Teatro della Pergola, at Florence:
Accademia degli Immobili owns, **18**. 439n,
19. 355n
Accademia dei nobili to give celebration at,
22. 367
accademici deny use of, to Filippo de' Medici,
18. 439
admission fee for, **23**. 458
bad opera at, **17**. 128, 155
ball at, **19**. 8, 115, 364, **22**. 486
balls, masked, at: **23**. 456, 458n; given free
for Archduke and Archduchess of Milan,
25. 50
balls discontinued at, when masking is forbidden, **20**. 219
Botta wants opera at, in autumn, **22**. 166
boxes at, hung with damask, **17**. 60
Chimenti, Margarita, sings at, **18**. 361n
Coke, Lady Mary, saw Botta in, **23**. 552
Craon, Princesse de, attends opera in Francis I's box in, **17**. 83
—— takes curtain-raising at, as compliment,
19. 358
—— to have attended, in mask, **19**. 8
crowded because of masks, **18**. 372
Cumberland, D. and Ds of, eat ices at Mann's
before going to, **25**. 644
deserted, **18**. 139, **20**. 357
doormen of, inspect pies, **20**. 219
empty without masking, **20**. 216
English do not wear gala at, from pique at
Richecourt's neglect, **21**. 9
fat pies and meat dishes forbidden at, **20**. 219

[Teatro della Pergola, *continued*]
Francis I's box at, **17.** 60, 83
Fumagalli ineligible for, **17.** 423
Galli, Mme, has box in, **19.** 505
Gloucester, Ds of, Joseph II, and Leopold drive to, **23.** 112
Gloucester, Ds of, to be attended at, by Mann's servants with ice refreshments, **24.** 291
HW imagines himself in, **18.** 149
Hobart starts riot in, **19.** 478
Holt and Monro attend, masked, **19.** 400
illuminated, **19.** 355
intermezzi worse than those of, **20.** 210–11
Joseph II attends, **23.** 108, 112
Karl Alexander visits ladies in boxes at, **20.** 376
Mann becomes cicisbeo in order to attend, **22.** 180
—— indifferent to maskings in, **20.** 404
—— mistakenly takes Richecourt's box in, **17.** 394
——'s box at: **17.** 48, 51, 60, 69, 81, 111, 136, 149, 239, 240, 394, **18.** 29, 128–9, **19.** 311; changed for Richecourt's, **17.** 240, 394, **18.** 129, 139; Feroni, Mme, and Suares family conflict over, **17.** 81; Knight to use, **19.** 462; lined and matted to exclude cold, **18.** 128–9; Salins, Mme de, orders supper every ball night in, **20.** 75n; shared by a lady, **22.** 180; *see also under* Theatre: Florentine: Mann's box in
—— sees Mme Venturini at, **18.** 392
—— sees Young Pretender at, **25.** 467
—— serves sherbets before opening of, **25.** 585, 592
—— takes Morice to, to hear Marchesi, **25.** 435
—— to get second box at, for Mrs Garrick, **22.** 180
masks to be permitted in, **18.** 364
Medici family's private theatre originally, **17.** 48n
Meroni, Maria, ballerina at, **20.** 219n
(?) open after Lent, **22.** 224
opening of, **23.** 458n
open in June 1785, **25.** 585
operas in, **18.** 134, 555, **19.** 356, **20.** 357, **22.** 477, **35.** 16, 28; *see also under* Opera
Pinacci, impresario at, **18.** 361n
Ridolfi, impresario at, **17.** 104n
San Vitale tells directors of, to arrest the Tesi's insulter, **18.** 368
Sauveterre dances in, **19.** 355–6
second opera in, to be improved by Manzuoli to attract Grand Duke, **22.** 477
to be scene of *bal masqué* and supper for D. and Ds of Cumberland, **25.** 644–5
Young Pretender often sick in corridor of, **24.** 244
——'s box at: frequented by visitors to his wife, **24.** 245; furnished with couch, **24.** 244; lined with crimson damask, with vel-

vet gold-laced cushion, **25.** 536; Young Pretender sleeps in, **24.** 244–5
Teatro della Piazza di Santa Maria Novella, at Florence:
opening of, **23.** 458n
Teatro del Lavoro:
formerly Teatro Mediceo, **17.** 202n
puppet show at, **17.** 202n
Teatro del Vangelista, at Florence:
Metastasio's *Ciro* at, **23.** 458n
Teatro di Porta Rossa, at Florence:
used in Lent for concerts and poetry readings, **23.** 458n
Teatro di Via Santa Maria, at Florence:
opening of, **23.** 458n
Sacchini's *Armida* at, **23.** 547n
Teatro Mediceo. *See* Teatro del Lavoro
Teatro Sant 'Angelo, at Venice:
Pertici at, **18.** 294n
Teatro Santo Casciano, at Venice:
Camilla at, **18.** 294n
Giramondo, Il, at, **18.** 294n
'Teazle, Lady.' *See under* Sheridan, Richard Brinsley: *School for Scandal*
Tebaldi, Signora. *See* Ganganelli, Porzia
Techen. *See* Teschen
Tecla Haimanout II, K. of Abyssinia:
accident to, **28.** 249n
thorn-bush strips, of outer clothing, **39.** 476
Teddington, Middlesex:
avenue leading to, **9.** 386n
Bentley lives at, **9.** 301
Berrys at, **34.** 85
—— take house at, **11.** 54, 55, 56, 58, 62, 71, **12.** 177, **31.** 325, **34.** 68
brick-making on common field at, **43.** 155
Chandler of, **9.** 53n
Dudley's landscape effects at, **35.** 389
Franks dies at, **2.** 373n
—— of, **16.** 182n
HW finds house at, for Berrys, **31.** 325
Hammond sells estate at, **35.** 499
house at, tumbling down, **11.** 103
manor-house at, **11.** 30n
Prescotts' marital difficulties at, **33.** 424–5
Sibley, Ann, lives at, **30.** 362
SH visitors from, **12.** 221–52 *passim*
Thames agitation near, **10.** 93
Udny lives at, **11.** 89n, **12.** 154n
vicar of, *see* Cosens, John
Walter, John, retires to villa at, **12.** 139n
Woffington, Mrs, lives at, **30.** 52
Teddington Lane:
Royal Horse Guards wade through floods in, **9.** 195
Tedeschi, Caterina, Italian singer:
Delaval flogs, on finding Guadagni in her bed, **20.** 41, 55, **23.** 278
——'s mistress, **20.** 41
flogging of, would shock Florentines, **20.** 55
Venetian career of, **20.** 41n
Tedeschino [? Giovanni Tedeschi], singer:
Salimbeni imitated by, **17.** 284

Te Deum; Te Deums:
abundance of, to celebrate alleged victories, 21. 246
at Florence, for Francis I's election, 19. 115
Austrians sing, at Campo Santo, 18. 163
Botta does not order singing of, 21. 317
—— does not sing, 21. 435
Charles Emmanuel III has, sung for his recovery, 19. 324n
England sings, for Frederick II, 21. 319
English political parties sing, for alleged victories, 38. 324
English victories hard to crowd into a single, 21. 333
Florentine, for Joseph II's coronation, 22. 237n
Florentine Regency attends, at the Annunziata, 18. 241n
for Maria Theresa's coronation, 17. 100
for Prague coronation (of Maria Theresa), 18. 240, 241–2
France sings, for insignificant successes, 21. 502
Francis I orders, to be sung in Tuscany, 21. 112
Frederick II does not sing, for trivial victories, 33. 124
French and Spanish supporters sing, for alleged victory, 19. 268
Gages's victory celebrated with, 18. 161n
HW quotes from, 33. 319
Incontri, Abp, and attendants whisper, in coach, 21. 151–2
in St Paul's Cathedral, 32. 389, 33. 552
Leopold's arrival not to be celebrated by, in Florentine Duomo, 22. 334
Lorenzi has, sung in French convent for Dauphin's wedding, 19. 114
Mann may sing, in his chapel, 24. 216
Mantua sings, for Daun's defeat, 21. 463
on Dettingen victory, 35. 39
Paris celebrates with, for victory in Germany, 22. 90
Richelieu's army sings, on landing at Ciudadela, 20. 567
Spain not to sing, for victories in Naples, 18. 486
Spaniards sing, for supposed victories, 18. 161
sung at Florence for Maria Theresa's recovery, 22. 532
sung at Florence, Leghorn, Siena, and Pistoia, 21. 112
sung at Madrid and Port Mahon, for Spanish landing on Minorca, 25. 189
sung for Estaing's victories, 7. 173, 174, 428
sung in Florentine church, 17. 100
Tuscan singing of, followed by orders of neutrality, 21. 114
Teerlinc, Mrs George. See Bening [Benninck], Levina
Teeth. See Tooth; teeth; see also Roots for the teeth

Tehidy, Cornwall:
Basset of, 11. 351n
Teissonière. See Dayrolles
'Telemachus':
Cumberland's Calypso includes, 2. 150
HW's name for: Christian VII, 35. 329; George III, 32. 89, 250; Holland, 3d Bn, 33. 257
Télémaque. See under Salignac de la Mothe Fénelon, François de
Telescope; telescopes:
Chenevix's library at SH has, without lenses, 37. 270
comet to be viewed through, 10. 290
diminishing end of: HW in old age looks through, 25. 616; SH should be viewed through, 25. 532
discoveries made by, 15. 167–8
HW draws, on Pam card, 38. 89
Herschel's, 33. 360–1, 569, 42. 270
Vere's, found after robbery, 35. 315
Telesephorus:
Mann might be compared to, 19. 383
Middleton's figure of, 15. 16
Téligny, seigneur de. See La Noue, Odet de
Teller of Exchequer. See under Exchequer
Tellier, Le. See Le Tellier
'Telypthorus.' See 'Thelyphthorus'
Temistocle. See under Metastasio, Pietro; Porpora, Niccolò Antonio
Temora. See under Macpherson, James
Tempe:
England, rural, surpasses, 10. 298
SH is, in 'gay solitude,' 10. 316
Tempera:
varnished, resembles oil painting, 42. 65
Temperance:
HW recommends, to Montagu, 10. 276, 277
HW's gout shows unreliability of, as gout preventive, 38. 68
Tempest, Henrietta (d. 1795), m. (1784) Marmaduke Dayrell:
SH visited by, 12. 244
Tempest, The. See under Shakespeare, William
Tempi, Marchesa. See Bentivoglio, Elisabetta (ca 1696–1771); Capponi, Maria Laura (1726–77)
Tempi, Marchese Ferdinando:
Mann corresponds with, about Bitcher, 20. 219n
(?) Richecourt's orders to, about theatre, 20. 219
Tempi, Leonardo (1685–1752), Marchese:
ball to be given by, 18. 435
daughter-in-law pleases, 18. 438–9
death of, 20. 298
Dini, Mme, has, for cicisbeo for 30 years, 20. 298
health of, apoplexy, 20. 298
(?) villa of, near Leghorn gate in Florence, visited by Ds of Modena and daughter, 18. 227–8

Tempi, Luca Melchior (1688–1762), nuncio at Brussels 1737–44, at Lisbon 1744–54; cardinal:
Clement XIII summons, to advisory congregation, 21. 308n
Riccardi to send gems to, to be sold in Portugal, 19. 94, 259, 349
Tempi, Luigi (1721–63), Marchese:
marriage of, 18. *435*, 438–9
(?) Salviati family related to, 18. 520
(?) Tesi, the, pursued by, 18. 520
wife pleases his father more than, 18. 438–9
Tempi, Maria Maddalena (d. 1798), m. (1739) Niccolò Martelli:
ball given by, for brother's marriage, 18. 435, 438
Tempi family:
bereavement excludes, from Carnival diversions, 20. 298
Carteret wedding too simple for, 18. 445
Tempio della Gloria, Il. See under Cocchi, Gioacchino
Templar; templars (residents of Inner and Middle Temples):
attempt to kiss Ps of Wales and Lady Middlesex on stairs, 30. 95
Foundling upheld by, 19. 469
HW's story of, 37. 14
syringes taken by, to theatre, 19. 469
Temple, Cts. *See* Chambers, Anne (ca 1709–77); Nugent, Lady Mary Elizabeth (d. 1812); Temple, Hester (ca 1690–1752)
Temple, E. *See* Grenville, George (1753–1813); Grenville Temple, Richard (1711–79)
'Temple, Idole du.' *See* Campet de Saujon, Marie-Charlotte-Hippolyte de, Comtesse de Boufflers
Temple, Lady. *See* Halsey, Anne (d. 1760)
'Temple, Le.' *See* Bourbon, Louis-François de, Prince de Conti
'Temple, Lord':
Young Pretender said to have dispatched, to his father, 19. 87
Temple, Mr:
SH visited by, 12. 246
Temple, Lady Elinor:
print of, 40. 236
Temple, Henry (ca 1673–1757), cr. (1723) Vct Palmerston:
daughter-in-law of, 20. 180n
Limerick gets reversion from, 17. 492
Temple, Henry (1739–1802), 2d Vct Palmerston, 1757:
Batheaston's verse contributions by, 32. 225
Beauclerk, Topham, visited by, 32. 292–3
Boswell sketches, 33. 462n
brother-in-law of, 12. 237
Carter, Mary, travels with, 42. 405n
Du Deffand, Mme, sends parcel by, 5. 401, 410
—— sends to HW by, a brochure, 5. 419n
Garrick to accompany, from Genoa to Florence, 22. 180

Hertford's letter to be taken to HW by, 38. 484–5
Hobart, Mrs, entertains, at play at Ham Common, 33. 370
Italy visited by, 12. 59
lord of the Admiralty, 24. 135, 144
noise of, in trying to talk, 32. 292–3
Ossory, Lady, visited by, 33. 434
Pars does volume of washed drawings for, 24. 135
—— draws Swiss views for, 35. 424
—— former valet of, 6. 236
——'s patron, 24. 135, 144, 26. 48
SH visited by, 12. 236
Switzerland visited by, 26. 48
verses by: 39. 241; for Batheaston miscellany, 32. 225; on Ds of Devonshire, 28. 202; praised by Tickell, 28. 384
Temple, Henry John (1784–1865), 3d Vct Palmerston, 1802:
Italy visited by, 12. 59
Temple, Hester (ca 1690–1752), m. (1710) Richard Grenville; Vcts Cobham, s.j., 1749; cr. (1749) Cts Temple:
apparition haunts house of, 9. 128
Grosvenor St residence of, 9. 128
Temple, Jane Martha (1672–1751), m. 1 (1692) John Berkeley, 3d Bn Berkeley of Stratton; m. 2 (1700) William Bentinck, 1st E. of Portland:
George I makes, governess to his granddaughters, 34. 260
Pembroke treats, indecently in law suit, 20. 109
Remenham bequeathed to, for life, by daughter, 30. 115
Temple, John (1732–98):
Whately's duel with, 32. 167
Temple, Sir Richard (1675–1749), 4th Bt; cr. (1714) Bn and (1718) Vct Cobham; field marshal; M.P.:
Blandford, Lady, entertains, 37. 51
Brown gardener to, 9. 121n
bust of, at Stowe, 10. 154–5n
Churchill's regiment acquired by, 19. 62
considered sensible because of his sensible nephews, 30. 62
(?) death of, expected, 9. 57
dragoons of, at Culloden, 37. 240
faction of: disbanded, 19. 194; may be dismissed, 19. 188
field marshal in command of troops in England, 17. 457
Frederick, P. of Wales, impelled by, against Sir Robert Walpole, 17. 329
French Court obliged to, and his nephews, 37. 201
Glover friend of, 37. 19
Hervey visits, 30. 51n
nephews of, 9. 84, 10. 314, 18. 98
New Ode, A, satirizes, 18. 50
Pope deified by, at Stowe despite quarrel, 35. 76

——'s allusion to, 35. 556

Powlett, Lord Harry, says, would be ashamed of George Grenville, 38. 500

regiment of, 17. 457n

resignation of, 18. 356

Stowe commemorates quarrels of, 35. 75–6

—— visit brings memories of, to HW, 10. 314

Walpole, Sir Robert, meets with ingratitude from, 17. 329n

—— opposed by, 9. 64n

Wharton, Lady, loved by, 34. 256

wife of, 14. 60n

William III promotes, 26. 14

Temple, Hon. Richard (ca 1726–49), M.P.:
death date of, 43. 267
wife of, 20. 180n

Temple, Mrs Richard. See Pelham, Henrietta (1730–68)

Temple, Sir William (1628–99), cr. (1666) Bt; statesman and writer:
anecdote about 'sun' compliment by, 12. 93n, 43. 153
aphorism by, 35. 614
Fox, Henry, may follow example of, 30. 130
Memoirs of What Passed in Christendom from the War Begun 1672 to the Peace Concluded 1679 by, paraphrased by Fox, 30. 130
Norwich, E. of, said by, to have outlived his reputation as a wit, 25. 308, 34. 39
'On Health and Long Life' by, mentions Cts of Desmond, 40. 108
'Sharawaggi' first attributed by, to Chinese, 20. 127n

Temple, Rev. William Johnson (1739–96), Boswell's friend:
Gray's 'character' by, adopted by Mason, 28. 209

Temple; temples:
at: Castle Howard, 30. 257; Horton, 10. 334; Stowe, 10. 44, 313–15, 35. 75–7, 39. 127; Wentworth Castle, 9. 295, 35. 267; Wentworth Woodhouse, 35. 280; Wroxton, 35. 74
Bentley's, for Wentworth Castle, 35. 279, 282, 306
——'s Gothic, for Strafford's menagerie, 35. 279–80, 282, 297, 306
circular, at Hagley, 35. 148
'Druidic': at Park Place, 11. 75, 35. 395, 396; presented to Conway by Jersey, and brought to Park Place, 39. 460–1
Edward, D. of York's emblem, 38. 204
Garrick builds, to Shakespeare, 35. 242
Gothic or Chinese, in English landscape effects, 20. 166
in corn-fields at Wentworth Woodhouse, 35. 267
Indian, richly decorated, has old baboon in shrine, 24. 433
manufacture of, advertised, 33. 97
Merlin's, in stage scenery, 39. 134
octagon, at Mereworth, 35. 143
of Hymen, 11. 26
of the Jews, 33. 119

of Venus, Drury Lane Theatre called, 12. 56

Sicilian, plundered by Verres, 37. 432

Solomon's, 39. 182

Temple, The, in London:
(?) Cowper, Mr, from, visits SH, 12. 243
denizens of, disregard monarchs, 23. 497
Goldsmith's chambers in, 32. 193n
HW inquires about fashions at, 13. 238
Hardinge invites HW to breakfast at, 35. 575
—— of, 32. 307
—— rides from, to Kingston, 35. 549
——'s mail will be forwarded from, 35. 594
—— writes from, 35. 549, 550, 552, 553, 554, 557, 559, 560, 562, 564, 565, 567, 570, 571, 573, 578, 580, 590
Hull attorney in, 24. 78, 200
Inner Temple: Bootle's chambers in, visited by P. of Wales and Breton, 30. 94; Capper called to bar at, 14. 196n; Dalton of, 9. 113n; Gray admitted to, 13. 115n; West admitted to, 13. 143n, 167n, 244n
literary judgments heard at, ridiculed by Gray, 14. 37
Lysons, S., of, 15. 316, 43. 152
Malcolm, Sarah, washerwoman at, 19. 460n
Middle Temple, Hardinge of, 32. 307
Paper Buildings in, Hardinge's address, 35. 582
Secret Committee to sit in hall of, 17. 386n
Seymour-Conway sends letter to T. Tighe at, 25. 608
Sherlock, Bp, at, 15. 307
—— master of, 20. 133n
Tighe of, 25. 608, 32. 230n

Temple, The, in Paris:
asylum for criminals, 31. 89n
Conti's home, 3. 41n, 7. 288, 41. 7
——'s opera may be given at, 4. 217
Des Alleurs, Mlle, to live in, after marriage, 4. 106
Du Deffand, Mme, invited to, 3. 68, 69, 111–12, 245
—— sups at, 3. 248, 4. 130, 440
French royal family imprisoned at, 31. 372n, 34. 152n, 39. 498
HW attends concert at, 7. 308, 43. 107
HW to sup with Conti at, 30. 215
HW uses name of, when indicating Conti, 31. 101
HW visits, 7. 306, 314
Herbert, Lady Mary, sheltered at, 7. 288
Hertford retrieves HW's letter and *Anecdotes* from, 38. 328
Luxembourg, Mme de, enjoys, 3. 91
—— jokes about, 4. 12
—— sups at, 4. 130
—— unable to sup at, 4. 47
Marie-Antoinette in, 39. 498
——'s son torn from her at, 39. 498
Mirepoix, Mme de, goes to, 6. 27
occupants of, mentioned, 3. 267
'pagode, la grande,' 4. 188
Rousseau at, 31. 89

[Temple, The, in Paris, *continued*]
Sartine searches Conti at, **23.** 453
Tavistock sups with Conti at, **38.** 359–60
Temple, The, Jewish:
'Athalie' in, **41.** 154
when it totters, perverse Jews scold, **33.** 119
Temple, Rue du, at Paris:
Astley's amphitheatre in, **33.** 515n
Soubise, Hôtel de, near, **7.** 283n
Temple Bar, in London:
Crassus the richest man on other side of, **21.** 558
Dick's Coffee-House near, **13.** 167n
HW jokes about Glover's chariot at, **9.** 398
Hat and Hatter at, **37.** 332
London and House of Commons must be pacified by, **23.** 283
mob intercepts merchants at, **23.** 98
riot at, **10.** 273
tavern near, **9.** 158n
Temple de Terpsychore, Paris:
Guimard, Mlle, builds, **23.** 322–3, **35.** 343
Temple Garden, London:
HW advises West to read in, **13.** 167
Templenewsam, Yorks, near Leeds; Lady Irvine's seat:
Gordon, Lord William, goes to, *en famille*, **33.** 213
'Temple of Caledonian Fame.' *See under* Erskine, David Steuart
'Temple of Concord':
HW's satiric term for House of Commons, **35.** 260, **38.** 187
'Temple of Friendship.' *See under* Stowe
Templeogue, Dublin:
Domvile of, **9.** 403n
Templetown, Bn. *See* Upton, Clotworthy (1721–85)
Templetown, Bns. *See* Boughton, Elizabeth
Tempsford Hall:
Payne of, **12.** 252n
Tenant; tenants:
Cole's loss through failure of, **1.** 213
——'s relations with, **1.** 15, 59, 60, 97
——'s voting, **1.** 198n
Townshend, Vct, drinks hard with, thrice weekly, **30.** 33
Ténay, Chevalier Marc-Jean de (1700–87), later Marquis de St-Christophe:
(?) social relations of, with Mme du Deffand, **7.** 340
'Tench, Mr':
Old Pretender's name for Sir Robert Walpole, **17.** 479
Tencin, Cardinal de. *See* Guérin de Tencin, Pierre
Tencin, Marquise de. *See* Guérin, Claudine-Alexandrine
Ten Commandments:
England does not strangle, **22.** 91
HW's reflections on, **31.** 261, 365, 434–7
Hervey cites, **40.** 19

Montagu jokes about, **10.** 297
parody of, **17.** 313
Tender; tenders:
English capture Adm. Péroz's, **17.** 380–1
Martin commands, **18.** 15n
Townshend's, **19.** 325
Tender Husband, The. See under Steele, Sir Richard
Tendon; tendons:
Townshend, Vcts, breaks, **37.** 383
Tendring Hall, Suffolk:
Williams of, **9.** 66n
Tenducci, Giusto Ferdinando (ca 1736–ca 1800), singer:
England long despises, **23.** 353
—— to be revisited by, **23.** 353
Ezio acted by, **38.** 467
Gloucester, D. of, hears, in Florence, **23.** 353
Lyttelton, Bns, writes love letters to, **38.** 14n
Tenebræ:
Craon, Princesse de, and Lord Shrewsbury attend, **17.** 4
HW and Chute celebrate, in Chute's chapel, **9.** 164, 166
Tenedos:
Elphinston sent to, to blockade Dardanelles, **23.** 228
Teneriffe:
ship from, **12.** 189n
Tenham. *See* Teynham
Ten Hove, Nicolaas (1732–82), statesman and writer:
Mémoires généalogiques de la maison de Médici, by, **15.** 275n
Roscoe's 'character' of, applied by HW to Roscoe himself, **15.** 275
Teniers, David (1610–90), painter:
box decorated by, **4.** 3n
Burgess says, was in England, **40.** 239
figures after, on flowerpots, **7.** 402
HW buys prints by, **7.** 402
HW wishes he knew nothing of, **18.** 218
Hôtel de Bouillon has painting by, **7.** 317
Julienne has paintings by, **7.** 286
Monaco, P. of, has paintings by, **7.** 335
painting after, **30.** 371
painting by, at Waldershare, of gallery, **40.** 5
pictures by, at Blackheath, **33.** 137
Praslin has paintings by, **7.** 353
Thiers has views of Brussels by, **7.** 373
Van Dyck's painting in the manner of, **7.** 286, **17.** 373
views of Brussels by, **5.** 148n, **7.** 373
Tenison, Thomas (1636–1715), Abp of Canterbury, 1694:
drawing of, by Bp Greene, **1.** 162
Ossory, Lady, sends HW four lines of Latin of, **33.** 568
portrait of, by Mrs Beale, **1.** 171
removal of monument from Dover Castle permitted by, **16.** 86

Ten Minutes Caution:
  HW recommends, **15**. 232
Tennant, Mr, of Dover St, London:
  SH visited by, **12**. 248
Tennis:
  Du Deffand, Mme, explains phrase from, **4**. 494
  Pembroke and Primate of Ireland play, **20**. 109
  Selwyn's witticism on players of, **20**. 155
Tennis ball:
  Frederick, P. of Wales, injured by, **20**. 240
Tennis court:
  French National Assembly's oath in, **34**. 50n
Tent; tents:
  American, destroyed, **24**. 309n
  Braitwitz demands, **17**. 293
  Cham of Tartary's, **42**. 177
  English army strikes, **37**. 135
  for army camp, **37**. 121
  French lose, at Crefeld, **35**. 101n
  Goldsmiths' Company dine in, **39**. 311
  in Mann's garden, **21**. 10
  Leghorn officers live in, **17**. 303
  prepared at San Martino for Leghorn troops, **18**. 76
  Turkish, captured by Russians, **23**. 478–9
Tent-bed:
  Downe offers, to Cts of Coventry, **20**. 324
Tenterden St, Hanover Sq., London:
  Bromley, Robert, writes from, **2**. 154
Tentore, Queen's County, Ireland:
  Ossory's seat, **32**. 159n
Tenures:
  purchase of, to secure election, **20**. 435–6
  See also Burgage-tenures
Teodoli Palace. *See under* Rome
Teodosia, Abp of. *See* Manciforte Spinelli, Giovanni Ottavio
Teologo. See Theologian
Teraille. *See* Du Terrail
Terence (Publius Terentius) (ca 194–ca 158 B.C.), dramatist:
  Andria by: **18**. 334n; cited by Mme du Deffand, **5**. 17–18; Steele's *Conscious Lovers* based on, **19**. 465n
  Colman translates, **16**. 265n, **41**. 401n
  Conway paraphrases, **37**. 90
  Eunuchus, quoted by Conway, **37**. 102
Teresa (1515–82), St:
  Du Deffand, Mme, cites, **3**. 175
  Huntingdon, Cts of, compared to, **21**. 398
  Maria Theresa's day, **19**. 439
  opera performed on day of, **22**. 558–9
Teresa, American privateer:
  captured by English, **6**. 452
Teresa, Spanish ship:
  in Spanish fleet, **17**. 286
Ternay ('Terney'). *See* Arzac de Ternay; *see also* Ténay, Chevalier Marc-Jean de
Terne, Christopher:
  print of, **40**. 236

Terpsichore, French frigate:
  in Thurot's fleet, **21**. 372
Terra Australis cognita:
  HW's copy of, **43**. 49
Terrace; terraces:
  at Park Place, **39**. 3
  HW's new, at SH, **20**. 16
Terra-cotta:
  bust in, **32**. 282, **43**. 155
  Damer, Mrs, models kittens and bridge keystones in, **25**. 576
  HW has cast in, of 'Livia' statue, **22**. 107
  model of statue in, **18**. 179, 190, 197, 200, 210
  Proctor's model in, of Ixion, **25**. 577
  sleeping dogs modelled in, **35**. 385
Terradellas ('Terradeglias'), Domingo (1713–51), Spanish composer:
  birth date of, corrected, **43**. 181
  music by, to *Mitridate*, **14**. 10n
  rehearsal of *Mitridate* by, **43**. 181
Terra del Sole, Italy:
  Lobkowitz to pass through, **19**. 11
Terræ filius, or Harlequin Candidate, by HW:
  Gray asks about success of, **14**. 21
Terræ filius. See also under Amhurst, Nicholas
Terrail. *See* Du Terrail
Terray, Joseph-Marie (1715–78), abbé; controller general:
  age of, **4**. 329
  appointed controller-general, **4**. 325–7, **23**. 164
  banished, **24**. 34–5
  bankruptcy advocated by, **4**. 449
  Béringhen's death aids reforms of, **4**. 362
  Boutin's correspondence with, **8**. 161
  Choiseul discusses La Balue closing with, **4**. 373
  —— intercedes with, for Mme du Deffand's pension, **4**. 375–6
  —— may be attacked by, **4**. 372–3
  —— opposes reforms of, **4**. 365, 378n
  —— opposes war plans of, **23**. 258
  —— proves that war funds cannot be raised by, **39**. 135
  —— reluctant to petition, **4**. 358
  ——'s budget to be cut by, **4**. 372
  ——'s enemy, **4**. 464n
  ——'s standing with, not yet known, **4**. 329
  Choisy to be visited by, **6**. 53–4
  Condé's reconciliation with Louis XV said to be negotiated by, **5**. 296
  dismissal of, expected, **5**. 74, 107
  Du Barry, Mme, courted by, **4**. 371
  Du Deffand, Mme, mentions, **4**. 352, 379, 394
  ——'s opinion of, **4**. 372–3
  ——'s pension under control of, **4**. 334, 353–4, 358, 359, 364, 375–6
  economy plan to be presented by, **6**. 54
  exiled to La Motte, **6**. 87, 93, **32**. 205
  financial reforms of, **4**. 363n, 365n, 378n, **5**. 100n, **23**. 192, **32**. 54
  Forcalquier, Mme de, exalts, **4**. 382
  income of, **4**. 326

[Terray, Joseph-Marie, *continued*]
influence of, **4.** 341, 371, 464
Invault succeeded by, **4.** 321n
La Balue closing follows edict of, **4.** 373
La Borde consults, about payment of obligations, **8.** 161
La Garde, Baronne de, mistress of, **5.** 107
—— sacrificed by, **23.** 339
La Vallière entertains, **4.** 472
Louis XV made a despot by, **34.** 73
ministry of marine temporarily supervised by, **5.** 5
offices of, **4.** 325, 326
outcry against, **4.** 356, 373, 374
public rejoicing at exile of, **6.** 93
resignation and subsequent reinstatement of, rumoured, **23.** 284
resignation of, expected, **5.** 35
Rosières, brother of, **4.** 442
ruins everybody but his mistress's protégés, **39.** 144
St-Florentin to speak to, for Mme du Deffand, **4.** 359
thought to be insecure, **5.** 45
Tourville intercedes with, for Mme du Deffand, **4.** 353–4, 358
treasury controlled by, **4.** 334n
verses on, **6.** 194, 243
Walpole, Hon. T., said to be favoured by, **5.** 107
Terray, Pierre (1712–80), seigneur de Rosières; Terray's brother:
made chancellor of Comte de Provence, **4.** 442
'Terreens.' *See* Tureens
Terreno. See under Mann, Horatio (1706–86): house of
Terrible, English sloop:
cruises off Porto Spezia, taking prizes, **19.** 277n
French fired on by, **19.** 336n
involved in war, **19.** 235–6, 277, 336
Proby, Capt., commands, **19.** 235n
Terrible, English war ship:
destroyed, **25.** 194
Domingo-men captured by, **24.** 464n
Keppel awaits, **39.** 307
Rodney detaches, **25.** 24n
Terrible, La, French ship:
Kempenfelt encounters, **25.** 221n, **33.** 315n
Terrick, Elizabeth (ca 1729–1804), m. (1762) Nathaniel Ryder, cr. (1776) Bn Harrowby:
Conway and wife visited by, at Park Place, **39.** 419n
SH visited by, **12.** 230
Terrick, Richard (1710–77), D.D.; Vicar of Twickenham 1749–64; Bp of Peterborough, 1757, of London, 1764:
anti-Catholic activities of, **30.** 209, **31.** 94
bishopric conferred on, **38.** 392
brother of, **10.** 347
death of, **28.** 298
Devonshire, who got him Peterborough see, deserted by, for Bute, **30.** 209n

English Roman Catholics persecuted by, **22.** 394, **30.** 209, **31.** 94
George III sends, to examine proofs of Gloucester's and Cumberland's weddings, **23.** 483, **36.** 92
—— unable to heed plea of, against Soho ball, **23.** 193
Gloucester, D. of, advised by, to marry again, **23.** 484n
HW disparages, **28.** 49
HW feared, would be archbishop, **39.** 104
HW hopes Rousseau will quarrel with, **31.** 94
HW's rudeness to, **2.** 374
HW to be reported by, as nuisance, **10.** 2
ingratitude of, **30.** 209
Newton's planned promotion to London bishopric discomforts, **38.** 364–5
pastoral letter of, **28.** 293
Roman Catholic chapel permitted by, at Twickenham, **30.** 209
Sturges visited Fulham in time of, **43.** 342
Terrick, Samuel (ca 1708–61), prebendary of Durham:
death of, from apoplexy at Peterborough, **10.** 347
tomb of, **10.** 347
Terrington, Norfolk:
Fenwick of, **11.** 286n
Terror, English sloop:
French ships engaged by, **37.** 246
Tersac. *See* Faydit de Tersac
Tertian fever:
ascribed to nerves, **5.** 352
double, **4.** 124, **5.** 179, 395, **6.** 94, 95
occurrences of, **5.** 352, 358, **6.** 92–5, 353, 358, 460
treatment of, **5.** 352
Terwhit. *See* Tyrwhitt
Terziarii:
of Jesuits, **23.** 503–4, **24.** 50
Teschen (Silesia):
peace congress to meet at, **24.** 454
peace of: **7.** 2, 67n, **28.** 382n; signed, **7.** 132
Teshu Lama. *See* dPal-ldan ye-šes (1737–80)
Tesi, Vittoria (1700–75), m. (ca 1743) Giacomo Tramontini; actress; contralto singer:
acting resumed by, **19.** 355
applauded by audience, **19.** 452
biographical information about, corrected, **43.** 234, 313
Chute and Mme Suares quarrel with, **18.** 322
Corsi and Tempi pursue, **18.** 520
costume of, **17.** *40*, **18.** 263, 302, 361
Craon gives banishment notice to, **18.** 520–1
—— criticizes acting of, **18.** 302
—— envies costume and coiffure of, **18.** 263
engaged for the Carnival, **18.** 322
fashion brought by, from Reggio, **17.** 110
fee of, for singing, **18.** 281
gendarmes insult, at opera, **18.** 368
HW agrees with Princesse de Craon's opinion of, **18.** 318

HW and Mann invited by, to (?) Dashwood's *accademia*, **40**. 33

HW cannot get dog for, **18**. 280, 293, 334, 351, 368

HW discourages English projects of, **19**. 289, 293–4

HW mentions, **17**. 43

HW occupies box with, at Florentine opera, **30**. 14

HW's correspondence with, **40**. 33

HW urged by, to make her a prima donna in England, **19**. 277

Hildburghausen led by, as her hero, at Vienna, **21**. 194

Juvrecourt scolds, for applying to Richecourt and not to him, **18**. 368–9

libels against, **18**. 391

Mann called on by, **18**. 281

—— dares not convey HW's messages to, **19**. 304

——discourages, from going to England, **19**. 305

Neapolitan cantata to include, **19**. 438

opera for, rehearsed in Mann's house, **18**. 294

opera in Florence ruined by ostentation of, **18**. 361

opera of: in Venice, a failure, **18**. 280–1; in Florence, successful, **18**. 302–3

Parigi, the, 'creature' of, **18**. 302

'passed the bloom of her wrinkles,' **21**. 194

Petrillo a dependant of, **17**. 130

return of, to Florence, **18**. 263

Richecourt's amours revealed by, **17**. 45

rôle of, in *Ipermestra*, **18**. 281n

San Vitali breaks with, **18**. 391

—— brings coach horses and servants for, **18**. 263

—— dismissed by, **18**. 520

——, 'dying lover' of, gives presents to her, **17**. 70

—— may buy Niccolini's jewels for, **17**. 135

——'s jewels worn by, **18**. 263

Suares, Mme, tries to promote opera for, **18**. 280–1

to sing at Venice, **18**. 520–1

Walpole, Bns, tells, that HW will forget to send her a dog, **18**. 334

Walsegg ['Walseck'] escorts, to burletta, **17**. 130

Williams's former flame, **21**. 194

Tessé, Comte de. *See* Froulay, René-Mans de

Tessé, Comtesse de. *See* Noailles, Adrienne-Catherine de

Tessier. *See* Le Texier

Test, The, weekly paper:

Bubb Dodington said to be author of, **21**. 38

Fox founds, and Murphy conducts it, **21**. 38n

HW disparages, **9**. 203

Pitt (Chatham) attacked by, **21**. 38

Pitt, Elizabeth Villiers, sends brother's letters to, **21**. 46

Testa, Francesco Maria (d. 1773), Bp of Syracuse 1748–54; Abp of Monreale 1754–73:

Charles III sends, to Malta as ecclesiastical visitor, **20**. 405n

Malta refuses visitation from, **20**. 405

Test Act:

French equivalent of, **4**. 424

See also under Parliament: acts of

Testament politique, Le. See Du Plessis, Armand-Jean, Cardinal de Richelieu: *Maximes d'État*

Testament politique de M. de V——. See under Marchand, Jean-Henri

Testament politique du Chevalier Walpoole, Comte d'Orford:

attributed to Maubert de Gouvest, **43**. 173

Du Deffand, Mme, sends, to HW, **3**. 200, 201, 207, 209–10, 212, 223

—— will not mention, again, **3**. 225

HW's letter commenting on, **3**. 220

HW writes 'detection' of, **13**. 42

not translated into English, **13**. 42

reviewed in Fréron's *Année littéraire*, **3**. 209

Testaments politiques:

HW calls, generally spurious, **31**. 278

Testas, Maria Anna (1715–95), m. Jan Nicolas Floris, Rijksgraaf van Nassau, Heer van Ouwerkerk:

Cowper not allowed by, to use Auverquerque title, **24**. 370

Tester; testers:

beds in Italian inns lack, **18**. 315

Mann anxious to hear that Louis XV has installed Mme du Barry under, **23**. 90

of HW's bed, **39**. 127

two beds under one, **31**. 180

Testimonies to . . . Sir Joshua Reynolds. See under Felton, Samuel

Teston, Kent:

Bouverie, Elizabeth, of, **42**. 40n

Testoon; testoons:

Florentine currency, **18**. 348

HW seeks, for Cts of Pomfret, **17**. 4

Tête naissante:

Mesman exhibits, despite graying hair, **24**. 243–4

Tetley, Elizabeth, m. (before 1775) George Garrick, treasurer of Drury Lane Theatre:

SH visited by, **12**. 246

Teutonic Order:

preferment in, purchasable, **40**. 18

Teutschmaister:

regiment of, **18**. 164

Tevahine Airorotua i Ahurai i Farepua (ca 1722–7 – ca 1775–6), Q. of Otaheite (Tahiti); called Purea, Oberea, Oberiea, *or* Berea:

Hawkesworth describes, **32**. 127–8

misfortunes of, should interest Lady Mary Coke, **31**. 162

Tewkesbury, Glos:

borough of, trusts Gage, **17**. 255

church at, **2**. 240

[Tewkesbury, Glos, *continued*]
Edward's (1453–71) coffin discovered at, **30.** 275
Texel:
Dutch fleet at, **25.** 281, 311
Texier. *See* Le Texier
Textiles:
Irish, **37.** 420
See also Cloth
Teynham, Bns. *See* Lennard, Anne (1684–1755)
Thackeray, Joseph (d. 1807), of Isleworth:
SH visited by, **12.** 243, 247, *bis*
Thackeray, Mrs Joseph (d. 1827):
SH visited by, **12.** 239
Thackeray, Thomas (1736–1806), surgeon:
Cotton's body examined by, **2.** 281
Thackray. *See* Thackeray
Thaïs, mistress of Alexander the Great:
breast of, pressed by Cupid, **30.** 324
fame of, **31.** 21
HW would not distinguish between Frede-gonde and, **24.** 35
Thalestris, Q. of the Amazons:
HW jokes about Alexander the Great and, **31.** 160
HW's name for: (?) Catherine II, **33.** 179; Dashkov, Ps, **33.** 172; Fitzroy, Mrs, **32.** 106; French fishwomen, **31.** 332
Thalia:
gives ease to sketch of vest, **32.** 220
Thamas Kouli Kan, French ship:
Admiralty court to adjudge detention of, at Plymouth, **24.** 365n
Noailles claims, after English seize it, **24.** 366
'Thame':
Damer, Mrs, does mask of, for Henley bridge, **25.** 576, 613, **33.** 485, **34.** 15, **35.** 385, 386, 395
Fitzpatrick has not rechristened, **33.** 469
mask of, not inserted in Combe's *Thames*, **15.** 319
Thames, River:
Adelphi bounded by, **28.** 102n
agitation in, **10.** 93
Americans of future will find, small, **28.** 234
Arno compared with, **37.** 49, 72
as broad as Danube, **39.** 187
at Nuneham, must be brimfull, **35.** 521
Avon inferior to, **39.** 76
banks of: compared with Avon's, **31.** 131; dry, **35.** 357; fireworks on, **33.** 182–3; HW jokes about meeting Lady Mary Coke on, **31.** 27; HW urges Mary Berry to stay on, **11.** 86, 336; More, Hannah, compared with weeping willow on, **31.** 347
Berry, Mary, should not prefer ocean to, **12.** 103
bridge over, at Henley, **25.** 576, 613, **39.** 386
cannot be crossed at Richmond, **24.** 47
Cascines compared to meadows on, **11.** 337
Chesterfield addressed letter to Pembroke in, **31.** 402, **42.** 178

Chevreuse, Ds of, swims across, **1.** 183n, **15.** 265, **42.** 235–6, 238–9
Chute's trip on, from SH to London, **19.** 497
Clifton recalls beauty of, **35.** 279
Cole's pleasure in, **1.** 113
Combe's *History* of, **12.** 185, 187, **15.** 217, 319
'Cupid' blown from Mr May's summer-house into, **12.** 157
Dignam sentenced to work on, **28.** 288n
drought affects, **35.** 282
dry, **35.** 533
dry and low, like HW, **35.** 374
dry spell impairs, **39.** 381
Dublin's views surpass those on, **9.** 400
Du Deffand, Mme, mentions, **3.** 248
Dudley's canal near, **35.** 389
Dutch troops arrive in, **30.** 97
east wind on bank of, **35.** 391
England's Brenta, **19.** 497
Farington does series of views on, **35.** 542
fireworks on banks of, **33.** 182–3
fish in: forced by heat to bury themselves in mud, **20.** 166n; killed by falling tree, **12.** 177
Fitzpatrick has not renamed, **33.** 469
fleets could almost sail up, to Twickenham, because of deluges of rain, **25.** 306
flooded, **24.** 47, **31.** 180, **35.** 542
floods in, imitate Rhone, **35.** 264–5
fogs on, at Christmas, **31.** 362
French, Mrs, builds marble pavement near, **35.** 389
frozen: **9.** 267; at Kingston, **32.** 342n
full, at SH, **12.** 11
goldsmiths' barge in, **33.** 47
Goodere, water-bailiff of, **11.** 124n
Grafton, Ds of, wishes house on, **32.** 30
HW and guests collide in, with boat, **33.** 47
HW and Lady Browne escape ferry-boat acci-dent on, **41.** 278–9
HW, Campbells, and Mrs Damer embark on, to see Henley bridge, **35.** 386
HW feels like swan returning to, **10.** 398
HW jokes about flinging himself into, **12.** 164
HW prefers, to grotto at Oatlands, **34.** 8
HW refers to, as portent, **32.** 214
HW separated by, from Ds of Queensberry, **37.** 269
HW's goldfish might be mixed with gud-geons in, **37.** 370
HW should have flung money into, instead of losing it to Mrs Howe, **28.** 230
HW sighs for, **23.** 491
HW's new terrace overlooks, **20.** 16
HW's parties on, **37.** 157
HW urges Mary Berry to stay on, **11.** 86, 336
HW walks by, **21.** 238
Hagley makes HW forget, **35.** 1
Ham House near, **10.** 306
——'s view of, opened by storm, **33.** 82
Hardinges' 'constant object,' **35.** 631
—— to see HW 'upon the banks of,' **35.** 598

Hay, Dr, drowns himself in, **33**. 59
heat of, in hot spell, **20**. 166
hot enough to bathe in, in February, **24**. 442
houses on, **2**. 368–9
in print of Richmond Palace, **16**. 73
island in, opposite SH, **34**. 207
Italian gardens compared to those on, **11**. 168
Jacobites expect French expedition to go up, **18**. 433
Jones, John Paul, should sail up, **35**. 497
lane between SH and, flooded, **24**. 47
Linton hardly needs, **21**. 129
'little turbulent ocean,' declaring its independence, **25**. 306
London City's barge horses for, **33**. 207
London Gazette would celebrate capture of an ait in, **33**. 123
Maltese cats to be drowned in, **17**. 482
masquerade to be held on, **24**. 86
Monkey Island in, **9**. 20n
monkey-worship on banks of, **33**. 399
Montagu should spend rest of his life on, 'in gaiety and old tales,' **10**. 258
Nile unlike, **39**. 381
North, Lady, and children promenade on, **33**. 338
not easily crossed at Richmond in high water, **23**. 73
not visible from Ham House, **10**. 307
nude bathing in, **35**. 302
overflows, **35**. 279
Park Place near, **33**. 480
—— the finest place upon, **39**. 549
Peru's treasures diverted to, **38**. 188
prospect of, from SH, **2**. 368–9, 373
races on, **9**. 57, 58n
rains swell, **39**. 187
regatta on, **6**. 354n, **32**. 237
regatta to be held upon, **24**. 112
Rhone and, compared, **33**. 355, **35**. 264–5
Richmond's fireworks on, **20**. 56, **22**. 148–9
Robinson's letter mentions, **21**. 121
ruined castle should enhance, **40**. 252
Senauki swims, **42**. 236
ships frozen in, **22**. 579n
'silver,' **30**. 303
Somerset House must be seen from middle of, **29**. 138
SH on an elbow of, **25**. 532
SH overlooks, **2**. 368–9, 373, **19**. 414
Suffolk, Lady, lives on, **30**. 171
swollen, **10**. 108
Tiber less beautiful than, **33**. 524
Trinity Hospital, Greenwich, faces, **16**. 85
Twickenham on banks of, **29**. 292
Vanneck's house on, bought by family, **28**. 405
view of: from D. of Montagu's garden, **11**. 106; from Sir E. Walpole's villa, **34**. 195–6; from SH, **2**. 368–9, 373, **19**. 414, **20**. 380, **25**. 532; near Park Place, **34**. 15
Waldegrave, 5th E., drowned in, **36**. 286
water in, low, **33**. 57
Whitehall gardens slope to, **20**. 56

Thames, English ship:
French capture, **21**. 414–15
Howe, captain of, **24**. 216n
Thames Ditton, Surrey:
Boyle Farm at: **31**. 216, 233, 251, **35**. 390; has Charlotte Boyle's chimney-piece, **33**. 573
Boyle Walsingham, Mrs, buys Hertford's house at, **39**. 416
—— gives ball at, **35**. 391
gardens opposite, **12**. 13n
HW sends letter to Conway in care of Hertford at, **39**. 339
HW to dine at, **39**. 335
HW to visit, **36**. 177
HW unable to dine at, **39**. 341
Hertford sells house at, to Mrs Boyle Walsingham, **39**. 416
——'s house at: **39**. 339n; HW sends servant to, to inquire for grandson, **30**. 272; too damp for Lady Hertford, **33**. 370
—— writes from, **39**. 340, 343, 344, 396
visitors to: Conway, **33**. 305–6; HW, **33**. 214, 283, 289, 305–6, 346; Waldegraves, **33**. 283
West, Lady Cecilia, to entertain HW at, **39**. 390
See also Boyle Farm
Thames St, London:
Ferdinand as popular as if born in, **21**. 227
'Thamyris':
HW's name for Miss Pelham, **32**. 106
Thane, John (1748–1818), engraver and printseller:
British Autographs by, **42**. 246n
print of HW's supposed portrait of Humphrey, D. of Gloucester, made by, **42**. 246
Thanet, Cts of. *See* Sackville, Mary (1746–78); Saville, Lady Mary (1700–51)
Thanet, E. of. *See* Tufton, Nicholas (1631–79); Tufton, Sackville (1688–1753); Tufton, Sackville (1733–86); Tufton, Thomas (1644–1729)
Thanet, Isle of, Kent:
Berry, Mary, describes riding in, **12**. 124
European war has no effect on, **12**. 114
toured by Whaley and Dodd, **40**. 4
Thanet House, Aldersgate St, London:
print of, **43**. 383
Thatched House Tavern, near St James's St, Westminster:
Catch Club at, **33**. 424n
Frere, master of, **32**. 103n
Lord Mayor's guests escorted from, to Mansion House, **23**. 200
musical meeting at, **33**. 30n
Rockingham faction dines with Grenville at, **23**. 115
Thavies Inn, Holborn:
Gray seeks Periam in, **13**. 143
The, Palazzo del. *See* Te, Palazzo del
Theatre; theatres:
admission fee to, **9**. 70
at Ampthill, for Lady Ossory, **33**. 552
at Bruges, French, **38**. 4
at Brussels, **10**. 344

[Theatre; theatres, *continued*]

at Cambridge, *see* Senate House

at Chambéry, 11. 140n

at Dublin, 37. 412; Arne puts operas on at Theatre Royal at, 37. 412n; compared to London's, 41. 410; Hertford attends, weekly, 39. 39; surpasses Bath's, 37. 412

at Ghent, 37. 124

at Hanover, attended by Richelieu in George II's box, 30. 137–8

at Kingston, admissions fee to, 9. 70

at Lyon, 11. 140n

at Richmond, 9. 74

at Richmond House, 35. 391n

at Valenciennes, manager of, offers play, 34. 186

Barrymore, Lord, converts Squibb's auction-room into, 11. 95, 101

'boxing-match' in, 11. 9

Boyle, Miss, does designs for, 42. 204

Clive, Mrs, acts to crowded audiences in, 40. 61

comedies, old, offensive, 31. 296

common sense's pulpit, 7. 361

Conway thinks, vulgar diversion, 37. 232

Danish, Schwarz from, visits SH, 12. 243

Danish Court, Christian VII sees Comédie française at, 23. 385n

Dublin's, compared to London's, 41. 410

English: HW calls, 'bear-garden,' 41. 404; too sanguinary for Paris, 15. 220; *see also under* London, *below*

English mania for, 24. 435

excesses not acceptable in, 33. 265

Florentine: closed for a year of mourning, 22. 340; closed on account of mourning, 18. 558; deserted, 18. 139; Florence unsociable during closing of, 19. 476–7; Gloucester, D. of, to attend, in Mann's coaches, 24. 291; Leopold amuses himself with masks at, in the Carnevalino, 24. 343; Leopold disgusted with poor performances in, 22. 477; manager of, wants to give passion play in Lent, 23. 459; Mann accompanies Lady Mary Coke to, 31. 177; Mann does not attend, because of excessive cold, 25. 248; Mann enjoys evenings alone more than, 21. 49; Mann's boxes at, decorated for D. and Ds of Cumberland, 25. 644; Mann's boxes at, offered to D. of Gloucester, 24. 291; Mann's boxes at, used by Lady Mary Coke, 23. 543; Mann's boxes at, Windham to use, 25. 33; Mann's boxes at, *see also under* Teatro della Pergola; Mann's servants forbidden to go to, after his death, 25. 670; Maria Louisa attends, nightly, 22. 581; Maria Louisa dances at, 22. 491; masks everywhere in, 18. 391; masks not permitted in, 18. 139; not to open for a year, 22. 354; open, 25. 33; opening of, expected, 18. 113; 'smallest theatre,' Leopold attends low farces in, 22. 477; 'smallest theatre,' *nobili* act in, 22. 393;

Stuart, Charlotte, appears at, in father's jewels, 25. 536; to be opened, but Leopold and Maria Louisa will not be allowed to go to them, 22. 407; Young Pretender wants to decorate his boxes in, 25. 536; *see also* Teatro degl'Intrepidi; Teatro del Borgo de' Greci; Teatro del Cocomero; Teatro della Pergola; Teatro della Piazza di Santa Maria Novella; Teatro del Lavoro; Teatro del Vangelista; Teatro di Porta Rossa; Teatro di Via Santa Maria

French, *see under* Paris, *below*

Genoese, French plays at, 30. 1

HW never expects to die in, 25. 649

HW reflects on pleasure of success in, 28. 53, 54

HW regards contemporary events as scenes in, 25. 387

HW's memory of, 32. 233

HW thinks of kings and empresses as playing in, 25. 552

Hamilton, Lady, should steal plumes from, 35. 428

Irish, 42. 253

Italy's increased taste for, 23. 458

Leghorn: Langlois insulted in, 19. 365–6, 374; only theatre in Tuscany to be open for a year, 22. 354

London: accident at Covent Garden, 13. 113; actors in, poor, 30. 26; audience at, noisy, 30. 26; audiences at, pelt candle-snuffers while waiting, 24. 348, 39. 371; Barry, Elizabeth, wears clogs and Mrs Bracegirdle pattens to, 17. 435; Clive, Mrs, harangues audience at, for pelting her, 30. 26; deserted, 19. 177; England in 1778 like half-hour before play begins in, 24. 348; Frederick, P. of Wales, attends, at Queensberry House, 19. 468–9; French players at, provoke riots, 20. 100; George III and Q. Charlotte coldly received at, 38. 288; George III and Q. Charlotte seen by crowds at, 38. 123; George III attends, 21. 461; George III never applauded at, and Q. Charlotte slightly, 38. 276; George III's attempted assassination to have been carried out in, 12. 118; Gordon, Ds of, attends, 11. 273; Gray describes stagecraft of *Atalanta* in, 13. 102; Gray describes stagecraft of *King Arthur* in, 13. 97–8; Gunning sisters draw mobs to, 20. 311–12; HW attends, only twice in first five months of 1786, 25. 648; HW attends, twice in week, 12. 83; HW compares Garrick with other actors in, 38. 524–5; HW does not visit, often, 39. 387; HW not to attend, 30. 26; Hervey, Bns, unable to visit, 31. 83; Jerningham's benefit for *Siege of Berwick* at, 12. 70; Licensing Act to restrain, 37. 25–6; lord chamberlain's authority over, 39. 222; low state of, 28. 131; national calamities make no difference to attendance at, 25. 110; new, to be erected for people of fashion, **25**. 317; Oldfield, Mrs, leaves, in chair, **17**. 435; pantomimes may be expelled from, **18**. 538; patriots groan at, **37**. 449; Pertici wants engagement in, **18**. 198; Petersham, Lady Caroline, has footman guard her box in, **37**. 432–3; 'pit, box, and gallery' in, **28**. 183, 367; pit of, in Selwyn's riddle, **28**. 102; riots at, **28**. 112, **37**. 419, **38**. 273; royal family postpone attendance at, **12**. 42; scenery for Dryden's *King Arthur* in, **31**. 152, **39**. 133–4; scenery for *Mother Shipton* in, **31**. 152; scenery in, for Haymarket entertainment, **39**. 382n; shut because of epidemic disorder, **25**. 284; stage box in, occupied by George II, **20**. 290; subject of dinner conversation, **38**. 530; upper galleries in, riotous before opening, **39**. 371; very active, **14**. 15; Walpole, Sir Edward, promises to take Mrs Scott to, three times a week, **10**. 329; Westminster, used by D. of York, Lady Stanhope, and Delaval family, **22**. 521; wild dukes in, **19**. 317; *see also* Covent Garden Theatre; Dorset Garden Theatre; Drury Lane Theatre; Haymarket: King's Theatre in; Haymarket: Little Theatre in

modern, HW's opinion of, **10**. 298

Paris: actresses in, ugly, **31**. 48; allows no indecencies, **33**. 543; Biron, Duchesse de, attends, **11**. 175; Dauphin's death closes, **31**. 92, 93; Dauphin's death would close, **31**. 47; drama, French, criticized by HW, **31**. 255; HW comments on decline of, **10**. 175; HW's opinion of, **39**. 212–13; HW to see, **10**. 171; knowledge of, needed for conversation, **38**. 238; mad foreigner wears ribbons of every order at, **25**. 572; Marie-Antoinette's *accoucheur* has freedom of, **33**. 318; officer addresses pit in, as 'canaille,' **10**. 49; plays ceaseless at, **38**. 574; Saurin's *Orpheline léguée* at Théâtre-français at, **31**. 77n; *Siège de Calais* not given at, because of actors' dissension, **38**. 538; Simonet, Mlle, first dancer in Théâtre Italien at, **25**. 575n; *Tarare* at Théâtre-français at, **31**. 255n; two gentlemen (who later disappear) often open tragedy in, **34**. 80

Pisan: ball and supper to have been given at, for D. of Gloucester, **23**. 357; impresario of, has burletta performed, **23**. 171; Mann to attend, **23**. 72; new, **23**. 353

plays at: dullness, greatest fault in composition of, **31**. 335; French, at Genoa, **30**. 1; HW denounces English, **30**. 26; HW packs up volumes of, **30**. 68; More, Hannah, indifferent to fate of, **31**. 295; More, Hannah, criticizes modern, **31**. 295; thrive in London, **31**. 152

Richelieu attends, at Hanover, in King's box, **30**. 137–8

Roman: furbished up by Benedict XIV, **20**. 98; Pius VI rejects proposal to close, **25**.

383; to reopen after Old Pretender's burial, **22**. 385

Roman, to be built at the Vyne, **35**. 640

Russian, head of, translated *Hamlet*, **22**. 426

Scottish nobility and Cts of Dalkeith form, in Queensberry House, **19**. 468

Sienese: burnt, **18**. 46; new, **20**. 391; York, D. of, hears cantata at, **22**. 232

strolling players make, in barns, (?) **9**. 72, **24**. 371, **39**. 493

Viennese, to be closed for a year, **22**. 340

Warton's account of revival of, **28**. 385

See also under Actor; Comedy; Dramatic criticism; Opera; Play; Show; Tragedy, *and under names of theatres*

Theatre, Cambridge. *See* Senate House

Théâtre à l'usage des jeunes personnes. See under Ducrest de St-Aubin, Stéphanie-Félicité, Mme de Genlis

Théâtre anglais. See under La Place, Pierre-Antoine de

Théâtre de La Noue. See Sauvé, Jean-Baptiste: *Œuvres*

Théâtre des grecs. See under Brumoy, Pierre

Théâtre espagnol. See under Linguet, Simon-Nicolas-Henri

Theatre of . . . Great Britaine. See under Speed, John

Theatricals, amateur or private. *See under* Ampthill Park; Blenheim; Chanteloup; Queensberry House; Richmond House; Wynnstay

Thebes, Abp of. *See* Borromeo, Vitaliano

Thebes:
Amphion's lyre raises walls of, **39**. 505
Conway quotes Horace on, **37**. 81
harp of, described by Bruce, **28**. 249

Thedwestre Hundred, Suffolk:
Burwell family moves to Rougham in, **1**. 377

Theft:
of HW's portmanteau at Chantilly, **1**. 98
See also Robbery

Thellusson, Georges-Tobie (1728–76), banker: house of wife of, **7**. 9, 11

Thellusson, Mme Georges-Tobie. *See* Girardot, Marie-Jeanne

Thellusson, Peter (1737–97), merchant and banker:
decides against purchase of Park Place, **12**. 176

Thelyphthora. See under Madan, Martin

'Thelyphthorus':
HW signs himself as, **11**. 12

Thémines. *See* Lauzières de Thémines

Themiseul, Chevalier de. *See* Cordonnier, Hyacinthe

Themistocles (ca 514–449 B.C.):
Greece, home of, **8**. 163

Thenford, Northants:
Wodhull of, **10**. 151n

Theobald, James (d. 1759), F.S.A.; F.R.S.:
account of Canynges's donation exhibited by, to Society of Antiquaries, **16**. 176

Theobald, Lewis (1688–1744), editor and writer:
Orpheus and Eurydice by: pantomime, **43.** 146; serpent in, **29.** 3–4
prefaces by, to Shakespeare, **24.** 267n
Thirlby gives notes to, for Shakespeare edition, **20.** 215n
West dreams about edition of, **13.** 131
Theobalds, Herts:
James I, not James II, owned, **42.** 131
Prescott builds new house at, **42.** 131n
Theocritus (3d cent. B.C.), pastoral poet:
'piping' of, **31.** 264
probably not known in 15th century, **16.** 335, 343
Theodora (d. 548), wife of Justinian:
HW might substitute portrait of, for Bns Craven's, **29.** 362
Theodore, 'King' of Corsica. *See* Neuhoff, Théodore-Antoine, Baron de
Théodore, Mlle. *See* Crépé, —— (d. 1798)
Théodore, Mme:
HW buys ruffles from, **7.** 404
Theodore and Honoria:
story of, **25.** 247
See also under Dryden, John: *Fables*
Theodosius (346–95), Roman emperor:
Maximus defeated by, **9.** 69n
Theodosius, or the Force of Love. See under Lee, Nathaniel
Theologian; theologians:
Lami is, to Francis I, **22.** 13
Maria Theresa gives Giustiniani a patent as, **22.** 465
Theological Remarks on Ordinary Discourse. See under White, George
Théologie portative, La:
Voltaire criticizes, **8.** 152
Theology:
HW dislikes 'fractions' of, **42.** 221
Theophila. See under Benlowes, Edward
Theophilus (fl. 12th century), monk:
Schedula diversarum artium by: Raspe discovers and transcribes, **29.** 5; Raspe's edition of, **15.** 145–6
Theophrastus (ca 372–ca 287 B.C.), philosopher:
Virgil borrows from, **14.** 20
Wilkes thanked by HW for edition of, **42.** 263
Theoric fund:
Athens sets aside, for festivals, **28.** 393n
Theorie der Gartenkunst. See under Hirschfeld, Christian Cajus Lorenz
Théorie des jardins. See under Morel, Jean-Marie
Théorie des lois civiles. See under Linguet, Simon-Nicolas-Henri
Theory of Moral Sentiments. See under Smith, Adam
Theresa, St. *See* Teresa
Therese (1723–43) of Bavaria:
Electress's bequest to, **18.** 171

Thérèse (b. ca 1759), Marquise de Boufflers's servant:
Huber paints, **5.** 298
Thérèse, Rue, in Paris:
Despueches in, **13.** 184n
Thérèse de St-Augustin. *See* Louise-Marie, Princesse
Thérèse de Savoie, Princesse. *See* Marie-Thérèse (1756–1805) of Savoie
Therfield, Herts:
Etough rector of, **14.** 42n
Therm; therms:
of jasper, **23.** 569n
Thermometer; thermometers:
clinical: **3.** 397; sent to HW by Mme du Deffand, **3.** 374
eclipse causes lowering of, **38.** 372
Thermopylæ (Greece):
battle of, **29.** 296, **37.** 19
Parliamentary opposition compared to defenders of, **38.** 315
Peruvians should not have to traverse Paris to find liberty at, **28.** 301
straits of, witticism on, by Ds of Northumberland, **38.** 526
Théroigne de Mericourt, Anne-Josèphe (1762–1817), revolutionary:
Wallace, Lady, worthy to be aide-de-camp to, **12.** 87
Thésée. See under Cassanea de Mondonville, Jean-Joseph; Lulli, Jean-Baptiste; Quinault, Philippe
Thésée, French ship:
sunk, **21.** 351, 357
Theseus, mythical king of Athens:
Bacchus consoles maid abandoned by, **11.** 65–6, **12.** 269
Cumberland, D. of, might explain his death to, **38.** 512
Dryden's, Lady Diana Beauclerk's drawing of, **11.** 247
Luxborough, Lady, lacks, **11.** 65–6
Thessaly:
'herbalized' in John May's verses to HW, **12.** 96
Thetford, Norfolk:
attacked, **7.** 368
Beauclerk, Aubrey, to be M.P. for, **31.** 18
Beauclerk, Lord Henry, succeeds Lord Augustus Fitzroy as M.P. for, **37.** 104
borough of, Grafton gives, not to Conway but to Fitzroy and Scudamore, **39.** 194
Conway loses seat for, **6.** 177n
—— M.P. for, **22.** 238n
—— might be M.P. for, **37.** 104
—— to visit, **38.** 458
corporation of, sends address to Conway drafted by HW, **39.** 528
election at, **7.** 368
Euston Hall near, **5.** 244n
Grafton's electoral interest at, **31.** 18, **39.** 194
HW mentions, **5.** 244

Martin's *History* of, **2**. 163, 176, 191

Wales, Frederick, P. of, to go shooting at, **9**. 67

Thetis, English frigate:

Great Duchess of Tuscany pursued by, **25**. 480n, 493n

Thetis, English man of war:

Mann receives news of Spanish fleet from, **22**. 19

Moutray commands, **22**. 12n

news brought by, **33**. 216n

Thétis, French ship of India Co.:

captured off Cape Finisterre, **19**. 410

Thévenart, Gabriel-Vincent (1669–1741), opera singer:

Du Deffand, Mme, enjoyed, **7**. 15

Thévenot (*or* Théveneau) de Morande, Charles de (1748–1803):

Anecdotes sur la vie de Mme du Barry wrongly attributed to, **6**. 273n

SH visited by, **12**. 227

Vie privée du Duc de Chartres, La, by, **33**. 46n

Thianges, Marquis de. *See* Damas, Jean-Pierre de

Thianges, Marquise de. *See* Le Veneur de Tillières, Michelle-Pétronille

Thiard, Claude de (1721–1810), Comte de Bissy:

(?) Chesterfield mentions friendship of, with Duchesse de la Vallière, **6**. 37

Thiard, Henri-Charles (1722–94), Comte de:

(?) Chesterfield mentions friendship of, with Duchesse de la Vallière, **6**. 37

social relations of, with Mme de Luxembourg, **7**. 352

tries to unlock Marquise de Beuvron's secretary, **3**. 61–2, 63, 72

Valentinois, Comtesse de, friend of, **6**. 71

verses by, for Mme de Mirepoix, **3**. 129–30

Thiard, Marie-Claudine-Sylvie de, m. (1768) Jean-Charles, Marquis de Fitzjames:

Valentinois, Comtesse de, leaves diamond to, **6**. 71

Thibault Dubois, Georges-Julien-François (d. 1768), 1st commissioner of war:

apoplexy of, **3**. 376, **4**. 9

Du Deffand, Mme, characterizes, **3**. 376

death of, **4**. 9, **5**. 155n

Thibaut de Chanvalon, Jean-Baptiste (ca 1725–85):

sentence of, **7**. 320

Thibaut de Chanvalon, Mme Jean-Baptiste:

sentence of, **7**. 320

Thibert du Martrais, Marie-Madeleine (d. 1780), m. 1 Jacques-Alexandre Briçonnet d'Auteuil; m. 2 (1769) Henri-Claude, Comte d'Harcourt:

will of, **7**. 451

Thibouville, Marquis de. *See* Herbigny, Henri Lambert d'

Thicknesse, Philip (1719–92), writer and traveller:

Orwell abused by, **7**. 315

Sketches and Characters of the Most Eminent and Most Singular Persons Now Living by, HW is assumed in, to be dead, **28**. 47

wife of, **9**. 338n

Thicknesse, Mrs Philip. *See* Ford, Ann

Thief; thieves:

gentlemen attacked by, in grounds near Greatworth, **10**. 120

HW calls Algiers the metropolitan see of, **39**. 420

house-dogs sometimes poisoned by, in Twickenham, **31**. 185

Thiériot, Nicolas-Claude (1696–1772):

death of, **5**. 340

epigram on, **5**. 340

Voltaire mentions, **5**. 340

Thierry, St. *See* St-Thierry

Thierry, Marc-Antoine (d. 1792), Dauphin's valet-de-chambre:

Du Barry, Mme, former occupant of apartment given to, **6**. 57

Thiers, Baron de. *See* Crozat, Louis-Antoine

Thiers, Hôtel de, in Paris:

HW and Sir Joshua Reynolds visit, **7**. 338, **43**. 107

Thigh; thighs:

Conway should not produce tight, rose-coloured, **38**. 206

Montagu's, broken in battle, **37**. 192

Thil (in Burgundy):

HW and Gray at, **13**. 180n

Thimbleby, Lady Elizabeth. *See* Savage, Lady Elizabeth

Thimbleby *or* Thimelby, Elizabeth, m. Hon. Henry Lumley:

(?) Ossory, Lady, asks about, **33**. 288

Thinking:

a headache to a man of quality, **7**. 360, **22**. 415

Thirlby, Styan (? 1686–1753), fellow of Jesus College, Cambridge:

career and publications of, **20**. 215n

King's Waiter in Port of London, **20**. 215n

Montagu thinks he saw, **9**. 20

pamphlet attributed to, **13**. 19n

papers left by, to Sir Edward Walpole, **20**. 215n

Ralph accuses, of writing *Letter to the Tories*, **43**. 170

Theobald gets notes from, for Shakespeare edition, **20**. 215n

Walpole, Sir Edward, friend of, **15**. 2n

—— gets Customs place for, **20**. 215n

—— shares house with, **9**. 14

—— wants, to write Sir Robert Walpole's life, **20**. 215

Whiston attacked by writings of, **20**. 215n

Thiroux d'Arconville, Mme. *See* Darlus, Marie-Geneviève-Charlotte

Thiroux de Crosne, Louis (1736–93), intendant des finances at Rouen; intendant de police at Paris:
death date of, corrected, **43.** 107
HW asked by, at Mme de Choiseul's, about English and Scottish roads, **35.** 335–6, 337
London arrival of, **11.** 55
report (false) of beheading of, **11.** *40*, 55
(?) social relations of, in Paris, **7.** 321, 328–9
Thirty-nine Articles, of Church of England:
clergy's adherence to, debated in Parliament, **23.** 366, 376, **28.** 71–2
HW laughs at, **2.** 61
subscription to, discussed in House of Commons, **28.** 71–2
Wyvill's tract on removing subscription to, **29.** 25, 26
Thirty-Three Plates of English Medals. See under Snelling, Thomas
Thirty Tyrants:
uncertainty about, **7.** 358
Thiry, Paul-Henri (1723–89), Baron d'Holbach; encyclopedist:
circle of, **5.** 65
credited with *Exposé succinct* regarding Hume and Rousseau, **3.** 158
Duni sings at house of, **7.** 304
HW and Raynal dine with, **39.** 212
HW at house of, **28.** 420n
HW entertained by, **10.** 176
HW mentions, **3.** 341
HW's relations with, **30.** 208
HW visits, with Diderot, **34.** 181
Hume and Wilkes entertained by, **38.** 280n
Hume's letter to, attacking Rousseau, **3.** 89, 91, **41.** 6on
Pall Mall believed by, to be paved with lava or deluge stones, **30.** 208
protégés of, bore HW, **30.** 208
social relations of, in Paris, *see index entries ante* **8.** 528
Système de la nature by, **4.** 454
'Thisbe.' *See* Gunning, Mary, Cts of Coventry
'Thisbe':
Coventry, Cts of, mispronounces, **20.** 367
Thistle; thistles:
Scottish, baneful, **39.** 272
thornless, **10.** 223
Thistle, crown of:
all crowns are, **37.** 256–7
Thistle, Order of the:
Carlisle, E. of, invested with, by Charles Emmanuel III, **23.** 59
——— obtains, **22.** 554, **23.** 14, 502
———'s election to, to wait till he is of age, **30.** 246
Cowper covets, **22.** 555, **23.** 502, 508, 511, 513
Dumfries receives, **20.** 311
foreigner at Paris displays, **24.** 361, **25.** 572
Hyndford gets, **17.** 497
more than two Englishmen never receive, at one time, **22.** 555

Northington receives, **23.** 508, 511, 513, **25.** 398n
not given to men under age, **30.** 246
ribbon of, green, **30.** 246
Selwyn seeks, for Carlisle, **39.** 97
Thistlethwaite, James (fl. 1775–80), poetaster; Chatterton's friend:
Chatterton imitated by, **16.** 130n
Consultation, The, by, copies Bentley's *Patriotism,* **16.** 353
Thistlethwayte, Alexander (? 1717–71), M.P.:
bankrupt, **22.** 268
brother leaves Norton estate to, **20.** 238
brute, **20.** 237, 246
(?) Chute and Edward Louisa Mann write to, **22.** 316
Chute urges, to pay Sophia Lucchi's fortune, **22.** 268
Dagge authorized by, to write note to Galfridus Mann, **22.** 265, 267
——— calls on, to get his signature to Lucchi paper, **21.** 420
——— engages, to pay Sophia Lucchi's fortune, **21.** 413
——— represents, as ready to pay Sophia Lucchi, **22.** 278
——— threatens, with law suit, **22.** 268
election of, **14.** 197
HW expects delays and evasions from, **21.** 421
inhuman, **20.** 243
Lucchi, Angiola, gets annuity from, **20.** 312n, **22.** 265, 278–9
Mann writes to, about the Lucchi, **20.** 330
Mann, Galfridus, more acceptable than Chute to, **20.** 312
Whithed's bequest to Sophia Lucchi withheld by, **20.** 246, 254, 312, **22.** 265, 268, 278–9, 288–9
———'s co-heir, **14.** 49
Thistlethwayte, Robert (1690–1744), D.D., 1724; Warden of Wadham College, Oxford 1724–39:
expulsion of, **30.** 89
Thistlethwayte, Rev. Robert (ca 1721–67):
brother dragged out by, to hunt, **20.** 237
brother's bequest to, **20.** 238
brute, **20.** 237, 246, 288
(?) Chute and Edward Louisa Mann write to, **22.** 316
Chute urges, to pay Sophia Lucchi's fortune, **22.** 268
Dagge authorized by, to write note to Galfridus Mann, **22.** 265, 267
——— calls on, to get his signature to Lucchi paper, **21.** 420
——— engages, to pay Sophia Lucchi's fortune, **21.** 413
——— represents, as ready to pay Sophia Lucchi, **22.** 278
——— threatens, with law suit, **22.** 268

HW expects delays and evasions from, **21.** 421

inhuman, **20.** 243

legal devices of, to avoid paying Sophia Lucchi's fortune, **22.** 288

Lucchi, Angiola, gets annuity from, **20.** 312n, **22.** 265, 278–9

Mann, Galfridus, more acceptable than Chute to, **20.** 312

money will be paid by, to Sophia Lucchi, **21.** 421

not docile, **22.** 268

Whithed's bequest to Sophia Lucchi withheld by, **20.** 246, 254, 312, **22.** 265, 268, 278–9, 288–9

——'s co-heir, **14.** 49

Thistleworth. *See* Isleworth

Thois, Marquis de. *See* Gouffier, Jean-Timoléon

Thois, Marquise de. *See* Penancoët de Kérouaalle, Henriette-Mauricette de

Tholsel, the. *See under* Dublin

Thom, Mr:
HW said by, to be unjustly calumniated about Chatterton, **43.** 218

Thomæ Gemini Lysiensis compendiosa totius Anatomes delineatio:
copperplate illustrations in, **40.** 306n

Thomas, St (apostle):
figure of, in painting of Henry VII's marriage, **20.** 390n

HW needs assurance from, before believing news, **12.** 47

Titian's painting of, **10.** 334

Thomas (1300–38) of Brotherton, cr. (1312) D. of Norfolk:
HW does not forget, **42.** 422

Thomas (Plantagenet) (1355–97) of Woodstock, son of Edward III; cr. (1385) D. of Gloucester:
ambitious of supplanting Richard II, **15.** 172

descendants of, **16.** 234n, **33.** 454

HW's ancestor, **1.** 375n

widow of, **42.** 139

Thomas (Plantagenet) (b. ca 1450), brother of Edward IV and Richard III:
birth of, unregistered, **1.** 320

Thomas, Miss:
SH visited by, **12.** 246

Thomas, Anne (d. 1788):
Jeffreys, Miss, to be accompanied by, to Hampton Court ball, **10.** 166

Thomas, Antoine-Léonard (1732–85), writer:
À la mémoire de Mme Geoffrin by, **6.** 494, 497

Arnaud resembles, **6.** 366

Du Deffand, Mme, writes verses on, finished by HW, **6.** 495, 497

Éloge de Marc-Aurèle by, **6.** 177, 181, 185, 247, **43.** 98

Essai sur le caractère . . . des femmes, by, disliked by Mme du Deffand, **5.** 202

Essai sur les éloges by: Caracciolo admires, **5.** 358; Du Deffand, Mme, dislikes, **5.** 357–8

French of, inferior, **35.** 635

Geoffrin, Mme, leaves annuity to, **6.** 484

'gros Thomas' of the wits, **5.** 202

HW's correspondence with, **7.** 384

HW speaks irreverently of, **32.** 259

HW to send *Lucan* to, **7.** 415

Jumonville by, **41.** 147

Moulin-Joli visited by, **6.** 459

Necker's style influenced by, **5.** 400

social relations of, in Paris, **7.** 261, 267

style of, disliked by HW and Mme du Deffand, **33.** 496

Thomas, Don Domingo:
Saragossa mob scattered by, **8.** 120

Thomas, Sir Edmund (1712–67), 3d Bt, 1723; M.P.:
becomes lord of Trade, **21.** 490

petition against, **17.** 318

treasurer to Augusta, Ps of Wales, **21.** 105n, **43.** 274

Thomas, Elizabeth (1677–1731), poet and adventuress:
Luxborough, Lady, compared with, **32.** 244

Thomas, Gertrude Mary (d. 1820):
Jeffreys, Miss, to be accompanied by, to Hampton Court ball, **10.** 166

Thomas, Rev. Hugh ((1707–80):
Lort and Shepherd dine with, **2.** 226

Lort to preach for, **2.** 97

offers dwelling to Cole, **1.** *146*

statue of Henry VII in possession of, **1.** 282

Thomas, Jean (d. 1757), quack doctor:
charlatan, **3.** 250, **5.** 202

Thomas, John (1691–1766), Bp of Lincoln, 1744; of Salisbury, 1761:
Carteret makes, bishop, **18.** 537–8

Keene dines with, when told of new bishopric, **20.** 347

Walpole, Sir Robert, called on by, **18.** 537

Thomas, John (1696–1781), Bp of Peterborough, 1747, of Salisbury, 1757, of Winchester, 1761:
George III's tutor, **20.** 348

read prayers to George II at Leicester House, **20.** 348

Thomas, John (1712–93), Bp of Rochester 1774–93; Dean of Westminster 1768–93:
Amelia, Ps, has use of gallery of, in Westminster Abbey, **25.** 648

HW dines with, at George Onslow's, **32.** 156

HW entertains, at breakfast, **32.** 156

HW is consulted by, about altar-piece for Westminster Abbey, **2.** 185, **28.** 214

HW mentions, **6.** 202

Thomas, John (1724–76), American Gen.:
(?) appointed director of minute-men, **39.** 239–40

Thomas, John (fl. 1739–77), army officer:
(?) HW mentions, **37.** 186

Thomas, Mary (d. 1832), m. (ca 1772) John Zoffany:
marriage of, perhaps bigamous, **24.** 539

Thomas, Sir Noah (1720–92), M.D., 1753; Kt,
1775:
Chute treated by, 24. 210
consulted in Rockingham's last illness, 25.
287
Thomas, R., publisher:
Original Letters to an Honest Sailor printed
for, 19. 459n
Thomas, Lady Sophia. *See* Keppel, Lady Sophia
Thomas, Sophia, dau. of Lady Sophia Thomas:
Jeffreys, Miss, to be accompanied by, to
Hampton Court ball, 10. 166
Montfort, Lady, visited by, 1. 287
Thomas, William (d. 1554), scholar:
character of, 1. 273
Pilgrim, The, by: Cole's notes on, 1. 272–3,
274; HW wants, 1. 271
Thomas, William (18th cent.):
Survey of the Cathedral-Church of Worcester
by, depicts Arthur's tomb, 35. 150n
Thomas, English ship:
New York news brought by, 24. 334n
'Thomas le Grand' (quack). *See* Thomas, Jean
Thomatti ('Tomatesse'; 'Tomatis'), Mme:
Craufurd attracted by, 3. *349*
—— friendly with, 5. 374n
virtuous, handsome, and refused K. of Poland
and 6000 ducats a year, 3. 349n
Thomond, Comte and Maréchal de. *See*
O'Brien, Charles
Thomond, Cts of. *See* Seymour, Lady Elizabeth
(1685–1734)
Thomond, E. of. *See* O'Brien, Henry (1688–
1741); Wyndham O'Brien, Percy (? 1723–74)
Thomond, Marchioness of. *See* Palmer, Mary
Thomond, M. of. *See* O'Brien, Murrough
(1726–1808)
Thompson, Mr:
HW's social relations with, in Paris, 7. 344,
348, 349
Mariette's sale visited by, 7. 350
Thompson, Rev. Anthony (d. 1756), English
chargé d'affaires at Paris; Dean of Raphoe
1744–56:
Amelot notifies, of France's declaration of
war against England, 18. 422
France's answer to, about Young Pretender,
18. 409
HW to hear Mann's news explained by, 17.
115
Irish dean, 18. 422n
Mann informs, of Young Pretender's de-
parture, 18. 373n
——'s correspondence with, 18. 397, 404
——'s letters forwarded by, 18. 380, 397, 412
politeness expected from, despite war with
France, 18. 283
Waldegrave's chaplain, 18. 422n
Thompson, B. B., mayor of Kingston-upon-
Hull 1779–80:
(?) Orford, E. of, thanked by, 25. 355
Thompson, Charles, English naval capt.:
Boreas commanded by, 32. 321n

Thompson, Edward:
wife of, intrigues with brother-in-law, 33.
223n, 34. 257
Thompson, Edward (1696–1742), M.P.:
voted for, as commissioner, 17. 437
Thompson, Edward (ca 1736–86), naval officer
and writer:
extract from preface by, 28. 120, 123
(?) *Hyæna* commanded by, 25. 17n, 24n
Shadwell's *Fair Quaker* revised by, 28. 110,
120
Trincalo's Trip to the Jubilee by, 39. 120
Thompson, Mrs Edward. *See* Dunch, Arabella
Thompson, George (ca 1620–ca 1679), M.D.:
engraving of, 16. 66
Thompson, Gregory. *See* Thompson, George
Thompson, Henrietta (d. 1764), m. Lt-Gen.
Henry Wolfe:
son of, killed, 9. 253
Thompson, Richard, printer:
arrested, 23. 280
Crosby refuses to arrest, 14. 189n
Thompson, Thomas (d. 1763), quack physician:
Burton's disagreement with, satirized in *Dis-
cord,* 37. 162, 165
nerves treated by, 20. 389
Winnington 'murdered' by, 9. 66, 19. 249
Thompson. *See also* Thomson; Townson
Thompson, English ship:
Jones, John Paul, burns, 24. 377n
Thomson, James (1700–48), poet:
Agamemnon by, 13. 151, 40. 27
Alfred by Mallet and, 16. 296n, 28. 110n
beneath even Voltaire's envy, 28. 278
blank-verse tragedies of, 33. 501
Buchan's jubilee for, 11. 353
Frederick, P. of Wales's protégé, 13. 249
HW calls, 'silly fellow,' 30. 105
HW criticizes, 31. 211
'Hymn to Liberty' seems to imitate, 16. 375
Johnson, Dr Samuel, admires, 29. 97, 111
Lyttelton tries to convert, 20. 52n
More, Hannah, likes, 31. 211
popularity of, 9. 215
Rosedale, villa of, bought by Mrs Boscawen,
11. 34n, 32. 335n
Seasons, The, by: 29. 97n; HW jokes about,
31. 348; HW prefers Lee to, 19. 27; HW's
opinion of, 11. 353
song by, 16. 296n
Tancred and Sigismunda by: 19. 27; acted at
Drury Lane, 19. 27n
Yearsley, Mrs, unacquainted with, 31. 218
Thomson, James (d. 1767), of Portlethen:
Jamesone's self-portrait owned by, 41. 266,
269
Thomson, Paton (?1750–after 1821):
illustrations to *Scotland's Skaith* engraved by,
42. 432n
'Thomson, Uncle':
epitaph on, 37. 568

Thomson, William (1746–1817):
Cunningham's *History of Great Britain* translated by, **15.** 193n, **29.** 360n, **33.** 562n
Thomthwaite, J., engraver:
print by, of Mrs Siddons, **33.** 377n
Thomyris. *See* Thamyris
'Thor':
Christian VII watched over by, **35.** 326
HW's term for SH, **21.** 433
Thorel de Campigneulles, ——:
Voltaire imitation ascribed to, **21.** 514n
Thoresby, John (d. 1373), Abp of York; lord chancellor:
York Minster choir begun by, **16.** 49
Thoresby, Ralph (1658–1725), antiquary:
Ducatus Leodiensis by: describes his museum, **35.** 179–80; HW makes use of, **16.** 1n
museum of: **10.** 278n; auction at, **38.** 340n; HW asks about, **16.** 10; James I's gloves from, **35.** 598n, **38.** 340n
Thoresby, Richard:
genealogy of, **10.** 352
Thoresby, Mrs Richard. *See* Montagu, Elizabeth (b. 1680)
Thoresby Lake:
ships in, **31.** 289n
Thoresby Park, Notts, D. of Kingston's seat:
fire at, **20.** 321
HW is not tempted to stop at, **28.** 42
HW's opinion of, **32.** 375
Kingston, Ds of, returns from, **28.** 224
—— said to be selling, **35.** 347
Kingston, D. of, carries milliner to, **38.** 473
Ossory admires, **32.** 375
Thorkelin, Grimur Jonsson (1752–1829), antiquary; editor:
Banks would appoint, to succeed Planta at British Museum, **16.** 294–5
Essay on the Slave Trade, An, by, **31.** 280n
HW esteems, **15.** 343
suggests that Dempster correspond with Pinkerton, **16.** 306n
Thorn; thorns:
at Glastonbury, *see under* Glastonbury
Thornbury:
Holwell vicar of, **1.** 345n
Thornbury Castle, Glos:
'Buckingham's Plotting Closet' at, like tower at SH, **32.** 322
HW copies tower from, **1.** 344n
HW to visit, **1.** 341n
HW visits, **1.** 343, 344–5, 346, **6.** 83n, **28.** 167, **39.** 179
Thorndon Hall, Essex:
HW and Barrett Lennard visit, **35.** 184
Thorney Abbey, Cambs:
arms in, of Catherine of Aragon, **1.** 242
Thorngate Hundred:
Whithed inherits estates in, from mother, **20.** 238n
Thornhill, ——, dau. of Sir Robert Thornhill:
death of, **9.** 233

Thornhill, Cooper (d. 1759), innkeeper:
daughter of, **1.** 363
ride of, from Stilton to London, **1.** 363
Thornhill, Sir James (1675–1734), Kt, 1720; painter; M.P.:
book abuses, **9.** 366
daughter may provide information about, **40.** 76
daughter of, **2.** 273n, **9.** 365
Germans praise, **9.** 366
HW cannot find material on, in Vertue's MSS, **41.** 17–18, 76
HW has materials for life of, **40.** 382
HW leaves, to last vol. of *Anecdotes of Painting,* **40.** 310, 381
HW sends account of, to Hutchins, **41.** 205
historical painting introduced by, into England, **9.** 366
Hogarth defends, to HW, **9.** 365–6
Hutchins calls, 'English Raphael,' **40.** 382
print of, **14.** 190
Thornhill, Jane (?1709–89), m. (1729) William Hogarth:
father of, **9.** 365
HW's account of Hogarth displeasing to, **2.** 273, 276
HW's correspondence with, **41.** 416–17
HW sends 4th vol. of *Anecdotes* to, **41.** 416–17
HW wishes to spare feelings of, **28.** 149n
husband's works to be published by, **41.** 451
Hutchins might ask, for information about her father, **41.** 76
lives at Golden Head, Leicester Fields, **41.** 76
Livesay lodges with, in Leicester Fields, **42.** 153
Thornhill, Mrs John, of Berkeley Sq.:
SH visited by, **12.** 246
Thornhill, Mary, m. Allen Hopkins:
print of, **1.** 363
Thornhill, Susannah, m. John Beverley:
marriage of, **1.** 363
Thornton, Bonnell (1724–68), satirist:
City Latin by, satirizes bridge inscription, **21.** 449n
HW disparages poetry of, **14.** 169–70
son of, gives 'Marcella' story to Hayley, **34.** 7n
translation project for Latin comedies begun by, **41.** 401n
Thornton, Jane (1757–1818), m. (1784) Alexander Leslie, styled Lord Balgonie, 9th E. of Leven and 6th E. of Melville, 1802:
Berrys dine with, at Broadstairs, **12.** 113
Thornton, John (fl. 1405–8):
window in York Minster executed by, **16.** 47n
Thornton, Thomas (1757–1823), sportsman:
Orford's falcons to be under care of, **32.** 355
Thornton, William (? 1712–65), M.P.:
Parliamentary debate by, on Scotch Bill, **26.** 32
Thornton, William, East India Co. director:
withdraws at East India Co. election, **38.** 378n
Thornton, near Malton, Yorks:
Hill of, **9.** 153n

Thornton Watlass:
Dodsworth of, **28.** 492n
Thorold, Charles:
Roman Catholicism abjured by, at St Martin's, London, to secure inheritance, **22.** 380
Thorold, Sir George (ca 1666–1722), cr. (1709) Bt; lord mayor of London 1719–20:
Pope alludes to, **39.** 150
Thorold, Jane (d. 1759), m. Col. Daniel Leighton; Bedchamber woman to Augusta, Ps of Wales:
biographical information about, corrected, **43.** 259
warrant request not signed by, **19.** 175
Thorold, Sir John. *See* Thorold, Sir George
Thorold, Sir Nathaniel (d. 1764), cr. (1741) Bt:
dies at Naples, **22.** 380
Thorough-bass:
of drums and trumpets, will be needed by Pitt, **10.** 222
political events compared to, by HW, **10.** 153
Thorpe, Ethelinda Margaret, m. Cuthbert Potts, jr:
marriage of, **43.** 164n
SH to be visited by, **43.** 164n
Thorpe, John (ca 1565–1655), 'surveyor' and architect:
biographical information about, corrected, **43.** 353, 364
book of plans by, **33.** 248–9, 256, **35.** 412
drawings by, owned by E. of Warwick, **42.** 20
HW adds, to *Anecdotes of Painting*, **42.** 20
Thorpe, John (1682–1750), M.D., F. R. S.:
Cole acquires *Registrum Roffense* by, **1.** 159n
collection of, **1.** 159n
royal statues at Rochester discovered by, **40.** 213
Thorpe, John (1715–92), F. S. A.:
father's *Registrum Roffense* published by, **1.** 159n, **40.** 213
Thorpe, Rev. John:
Arundell's and Stone's letters from, about search of Jesuit archives, **23.** 533n
Thou, Jacques-Auguste de (1553–1617), 'Thuanus'; Baron de Meslai; historian:
Canterbury, Abp of, quotes, **17.** 301
Histoire universelle by, **4.** 405, 427, **5.** 151, **43.** 91
Historiarum sui temporis, by: **1.** 60n, **17.** 301n, **43.** 46; HW buys, **38.** 340n
tomb of, **7.** 282
Thou, Mme Jacques-Auguste de. *See* Barbançon, Marie de (d. 1601); La Chastre, Gasparde de (1577–ca 1617)
Thoughts in the Form of Maxims. See under Byron, Isabella, Cts of Carlisle
Thoughts on Comedy, by HW:
HW has no time to put, in shape, **41.** 363
Thoughts on Hunting. See under Beckford, Peter

Thoughts on Money, Circulation and Paper Currency. See under Murray, Patrick
Thoughts on the Cause of the Present Discontents. See under Burke, Edmund
Thoughts on the Difficulties and Distresses. See under King, John (ca 1753–1823)
Thoughts on the Importance of the Manners of the Great. See under More, Hannah
Thoughts on the Letter of Edmund Burke. See under Bertie, Willoughby
Thoulier, Pierre-Joseph (1682–1768), Abbé d'Olivet:
Voltaire's letter to, on prosody, **3.** 251
Thoulouse. *See* Toulouse
Thousand and One Days, The. See under Pétis de la Croix, François
Thousand and One Nights. See *Arabian Nights*
Thoyras, sieur de. *See* Rapin, Paul de
Thrace:
'dauphin' of, **35.** 336
Thrale, —— (d. 1790), pastry-cook:
Lort stays with, **16.** 164
Thrale, Henry (ca 1729–81):
Baretti, friend of, **28.** 97n
——'s quarrel with, **42.** 245n
great brewer, **25.** 633n
mistress of, **10.** 40n
party at house of, **16.** 178n
Seward, friend of, **16.** 189n
Southwark election won by, **39.** 197n
villa of, **11.** 106n
wife of, **11.** 21n, **25.** 611n, 633n
Thrale, Mrs Henry. *See* Salusbury, Hester Lynch
Thrale, Hester Maria (1764–1857), m. (1808) George Keith Elphinstone, cr. (1797) Bn and (1814) Vct Keith:
Baretti, language-teacher to, **42.** 245n
Burney, Frances, describes SH to, **42.** 149n
SH visited by, **12.** 234
Thrapston, Northants:
Cole and HW visit, **10.** 343
Thread; threads:
Charles III pulls wigs off with, **23.** 238
papers for, **16.** 356
Threadneedle St, London:
Colebrooke, money-scrivener in, **30.** 114n, **37.** 243n
Neal, James, Fordyce, and Down, bankers in, **23.** 418n, **39.** 156n
Thread stockings. *See under* Stocking
'Three children sliding on the ice':
'collection of blunders,' cited by HW, **35.** 386
'Three Firing Glasses,' lodge of Vienna freemasons:
Francis I sponsors, **18.** 208n
Three Hours after Marriage. See under Pope, Alexander
Three Kings, Biblical:
Radicofani and, **37.** 66–7
Three Letters to the Whigs, by HW:
editions included in, **43.** 170–1

Three-livre piece, French:
value of, **37**. 39
Three Primates. *See Tre Primati*
Three Princes of Serendip, The, fairy tale:
'serendipity' derived from, **20**. 407–8, **26**. 34–5
Three Sisters, English ship:
Tryon sends news by, **24**. 185n
'Three Tuns,' in Chandos St, Covent Garden, London:
Finch stabbed at, **19**. 389n
'Three Vernons, The,' by HW:
HW shows, to Cambridge by mistake, **32**. 203
HW's picture of Carolina Maria Vernon in, **34**. 226
HW writes, **13**. 49n
read inadvertently to D. of Grafton, **32**. 208
reprinted incorrectly, **34**. 58
Three Weeks after Marriage. See under Murphy, Arthur
Thrift St, Soho Sq., London:
Capello's house in, **18**. 244n, **19**. 17n, 134n
Throat. *See* Sore Throat
Throckmorton, Lady. *See* Carew, Anne
Throckmorton, Elizabeth (1565–1647), m. (1592) Sir Walter Ralegh:
portrait of, **33**. 272
Throckmorton, Sir Nicholas (1515–71), Kt; diplomatist:
family of, **38**. 125
Throckmorton, Sir Robert (1662–1721), 3d Bt:
Cole on name of, **1**. 40
Throckmorton, Sir Robert (1702–91), 4th Bt:
Browne, Lady, addressed at house of, **31**. 237
Cole on name of, **1**. 40
house of, at Coughton, **9**. 224–5
Throckmorton family:
coats of arms of, in stained glass, **9**. 224–5
Throgmorton, ——:
Mann sends books to England by, **23**. 430n
Throgmorton. *See also* Throckmorton
Throne; thrones:
at Windsor Castle, gaudy and clumsy, **11**. 363
bishop's, at Peterborough, **12**. 347
Bristol, E. of, revived by prospect of, **22**. 450
Charlotte, Q., stands under, **21**. 531
Mogul's, of gold, **25**. 545
Throsby, John (1740–1803), antiquary:
Memoirs of the Town and County of Leicester, The, by, **2**. 195, 199, 201, **43**. 70
Thrower, Hester:
Conway hears of Mrs Whaley from, at Mrs Grosvenor's, **37**. 62
Thrush (disease):
Albemarle, Lady, recovers from, **34**. 63
Mann does not know meaning of, **20**. 242
occurrences of, **19**. 250, **20**. 232, **30**. 155
Thrush; thrushes (birds):
HW deprived of, by bad summer, **32**. 359
jerboa resembles, **9**. 142
Lort wants, in garden, **16**. 190
Twickenham militia learning exercise on, **33**. 8

Thuanus. *See* Thou, Jacques-Auguste de
Thubières. *See* Tubières
Thucydides (d. ca 400 B.C.), historian:
Boston may produce counterpart of, **24**. 62
HW compares Monckton's letter to histories by, **10**. 22
'Thucydides, Dame':
HW's name for Mrs Macaulay, **33**. 84
Thugny (France):
Choiseul, Duchesse de, visits, **4**. 192–4, 198, 205
—— writes from, **41**. 171
Thugut, François-Marie (1734–1818), Baron de:
Maria Theresa's peace proposals brought by, to Frederick II, **24**. 398n
Paris visited by, **7**. 442
Thuilleries. *See* Tuileries
Thulemeyer, Baron de, Prussian envoy to England:
Frederick II's demands to Holland presented by, **33**. 384n
Thumasin, ——, Maj.:
captured at Velletri, **18**. 491
Thumb, Tom:
imitation of, **35**. 33, **37**. 228
to ride three horses, **32**. 174
'Tory' seized like, **37**. 43
Thumb; thumbs:
bishop's, worn flat from turning over Bibles, **37**. 35
Thun, Josef Maria von (d. 1763), Bp of Gurk, 1741; of Passau, 1761; Austrian minister at Rome, 1740:
Acquaviva obtains Young Pretender's passports from, **18**. 378
auditor of the Rota, **17**. 201n
Benedict XIV hears news from, **17**. 201n, 282
—— rebukes, at audience, **17**. 201
——'s memorial from, fictitious answer to, **17**. 442, 445–6
Braitwitz communicates with, at Rome, **17**. 282
——'s correspondence with, **18**. 42
English captain does not know how to address, **18**. 461
English captains dine with, **19**. 12
Gages seizes letters of, **18**. 359n
Licanian captures estimated by, **18**. 460
Mann flattered by, **18**. 461
—— informed by, of Young Pretender's escape from Rome, **18**. 373, 380
—— receives courier from, **18**. 453
—— satisfies demand of, for English naval help, **18**. 471
——'s correspondence with, **18**. 474, 476
Mathews's friendship to Austria doubted by, **18**. 476
Pontano claimed by, from prison, **18**. 56
Traun and Vienna to receive couriers from, **18**. 56
Vienna refers letters of, to Lobkowitz, **18**. 515
Young Pretender's departure prophesied by, **17**. 101

Thunder and lightning:
Italian feature, 37. 72, 73
Thunderer, English ship:
Dutch contraband seized by, 25. 3n
Keppel joined by, 39. 307
Thundersley Hall, Essex:
Molineux of, 2. 207n
'Thunder-ten-tronck':
HW refers to Ham House as, 10. 307
in Voltaire's *Candide*, 38. 418, 473
Thuret, ——, director of the Opéra:
Gesvres and Carignan receive rent from, 13. 165n
Thürheim, Ludwig Franz, Graf; commander at Schweidnitz:
surrender of, to Lt-Gen. Tresckow, 21. 198n
Thuringia:
Soubise commands French and German army in, 21. 137n
Thurlborne, Elizabeth (1731–90), m. James Essex:
invited to dine with Cole, 1. 217
returns from Margate, 2. 26
Thurloe, John (1616–68), statesman:
spurious portrait of, 1. 208, 43. 55
Thurlow, Edward (1731–1806), cr. (1778) Bn Thurlow; attorney-gen. 1771–8; lord chancellor, 1778–92:
administration might have been wrecked by, to satisfy Opposition, 24. 447
amendment proposed by, to anti-Papist bill, 25. 67n
attorney disqualified by, 11. 243
attorney-general, 23. 269
Bath and Tunbridge visited by, 33. 173n
Bathurst succeeded by, as lord chancellor, 7. 47n, 49n, 24. 385
Boswell sketches, 33. 462n
brother of, may be Bp of Salisbury, 33. 116
'bully,' lacking true courage, 36. 222
Burke calls, 'iron Pluto,' 25. 684
——'s quip on tears shed by, 34. 41n
chancellorship designated for, 28. 401
chancellorship retained by, 29. 207
chief justice of Chester, 39. 136n
cicisbeo to Lady Craven, 29. 235
coalitions of, HW indifferent to, 29. 314, 317
constitutional bills opposed by, 29. 214
counsel for the prosecution at Ds of Kingston's trial, 28. 261–4, 266
(?) Craven to sue, for affair with wife, 36. 210
deanery of St Paul's requested by, for brother, 29. 192
discontent of, 29. 128, 129
dispatch of, in law, 33. 116
Dutch ships' searching advocated by, 33. 156n
elected for Tamworth, 30. 194n
Enclosure Bill opposed by, in speech, 29. 128n
faction of, blames Opposition's intemperance, 24. 534n
Fox and North will get able opposition from, 29. 314n

Fox's altercation with, in House of Commons, 32. 402
George III blamed by, for insisting on new army, 33. 433
—— confers with, 25. 683, 684, 685
—— consults, about C. J. Fox and George IV, 25. 381–2
—— insists on keeping, as chancellor, despite opposition of North and D. of Portland, 25. 381
—— refers Ds of Kingston's *nolle prosequi* to, 24. 162
—— said by, to be impeachable if not parting with army, 34. 331
——'s progress reported by, 34. 43n
——'s wishes to patch up administration seconded by, 25. 379
—— told by, to put George IV and C. J. Fox in Tower, 25. 382n
—— writes to, about Pitt, 25. 685n
Gibbon writes mémoire justificatif to France at request of, 24. 531n, 33. 303n
Gloucester, Ds of, may borrow from, for daughters, 36. 327–8
government to be assumed by, 25. 683
Great Seal may be given back to, 25. 460
Grenville to aid, in House of Lords, 11. 151
(?) HW calls, a 'black ace,' 28. 479
HW complains to office of, about Bisshopps, 36. 166n
HW's and Mason's opinions not to be changed by utterances of, 29. 66
HW's Berkeley Sq. house subject of complaint to, 34. 250
HW thinks, will not succeed Rockingham, 25. 289
HW will not go to Court unless fetched by, 35. 511
Hastings trial's cessation favoured by, 11. 269
health of: precarious, 33. 173; thought to be dying, 29. 47
Ireland meets with firmness from, 33. 173
Irish secretaryship rumoured for, 38. 568
Jersey, Lord and Lady, get remonstrance from, 12. 150
Johnson's letter to, 12. 22n
Kingston, Ds of, opposed by, at trial, 24. 193, 196
Kingston trial under authority of, 24. 192n
'little faction' of, with Gower and Weymouth, 24. 534n
lord chancellor, 25. 460n
Loughborough's salary grant not signed by, 33. 332
Mann's brother's will to be inspected by, 24. 258
Mason's counsel, 28. 322n
merits of, unrewarded, 36. 285
North vainly asked by, for St Paul's deanery for brother, 39. 388
Parliamentary reform resisted by, 25. 273
Pitt administration's more respectable member, 36. 222

Planta denied permission by, to go abroad, **16.** 294–5
praised by all sides, **29.** 65
prime minister's office offered to, **36.** 209
remains as lord chancellor, **25.** 262
resignation of: **15.** 216n; rumoured, **11.** 152; shows his 'virtue' 'dragged through the kennel,' **33.** 405
ridiculous in House of Lords, **25.** 407
Rockingham and Grafton betrayed by, **33.** 95n
Rockingham approached by, to form ministry, **25.** 256
Roman Catholic toleration disliked by, **25.** 66–7
rumoured to be prime minister, **33.** 391
severe on divorce, **36.** 210
Shelburne administration may include, **25.** 260n
son of, supposed illegitimate, **33.** 406n
Stuart duels with, after opposition in Douglas case, **32.** 90n
swarthy complexion of, **28.** 477n
testimony by, at Kingston trial, **24.** 88n
thieves steal Great Seal from, **25.** 481
Waldegrave, Cts, sees, in London, **36.** 284
Waldegrave children to be aided by, **36.** 284
ward's marriage to Gordon opposed by, **33.** 213n
weeps when with George III, **25.** 684
Thurlow, Thomas (1737–91), Bp of Lincoln 1779–87, of Durham 1787–91:
brother asks North for St Paul's deanery for, **29.** 192n, **39.** 388
brother gets deanery for, despite North's opposition, **33.** 339n
death of, **11.** 288n
Gordon rioters ill-treat, **33.** 174, 175
may be Bp of Salisbury, **33.** 339
Thurlow. *See also* Thurloe
Thurlow (village). *See* Little Thurlow
Thurmond, Mrs John. *See* Lewis, Sarah (fl. 1715–37)
Thurn-Valsassina, Gräfin. *See* Reischach, Gabriele
Thurn-Valsassina, Anton (1723–1806), Graf; army officer; Tuscan Grand Maître 1771–90:
Albrecht's death notified by, **24.** 23n
Barbantane writes to, **24.** 394
brother and Leopold accompanied by, **22.** *350*
captain of the *garde noble*, **22.** 398
captain of the *garde noble* and *Grand Maître*, **23.** 253
Gloucester, D. of, receives, **23.** 352
Leopold accompanied by, to Rome, **23.** 91n
Mann told by, about sales of grand ducal furniture, **25.** 231
Thurn-Valsassina, Franz (*or* Johann Franz Joseph) (1718–66), Graf; Tuscan Grand Chamberlain 1765–6; army officer:
Botta at odds with, **22.** 398
brother of, **22.** 350

death of: HW admires Leopold for mourning, **22.** 404; increases Lenten solemnity in Florence, **22.** 400; soon after his marriage, **22.** 398
diplomatists call upon, at Florence, **22.** *337*
Leopold's former governor, **22.** 398
Lorenzi and Viviani excluded from antechamber of, **22.** 346
Mann escorts Murray to apartment of, **22.** 350
Thurot, François (1727–60), French naval capt.:
Boys, Commodore, expected to pursue, **21.** 346n
—— pursues, towards Aberdeen, **21.** 346n, 352n
cutter of, cruises off Wingo, **21.** 346n
departure of, from Dunkirk: **21.** 315n, 328n, 336n, 338n; said to indicate beginning of invasion, **21.** 349
first goes to sea as penniless ship's surgeon, **21.** 328n
fleet of: captures Carrickfergus, **21.** 371–4; carried to Isle of Man, **21.** 376; English frigates capture, in Irish Channel, **21.** 376, 385–6; Gothenburg reached by, **21.** 346–7; Ostend said to be visited by, **21.** 349; raids Islay, **21.** 371–2; said to set sail, **21.** 338; Scotland threatened by, **21.** 328, 352
HW asks about, **9.** 254
HW glad that Mann has got letter about, **21.** 389
Hall, Lt, told by, of voyage, **21.** 371n
Jennings might be carried off by, **21.** 381
killed, **21.** 376
newspapers describe birth and apostasy of, **21.** 381–2
orders of, to invade Ireland or Scotland, **21.** 315n
re-embarkation of, from Carrickfergus, **21.** 376
rumour of English birth denied by, at Gothenburg, **21.** 381n
Swedish troops might be enlisted by, **21.** 347
Tinker, Capt. Bladen, discovers, off Newport Gat near Ostend, **21.** 338n
Thursby, ——:
Dolben's motion substituted for that of, at Northampton meeting, **25.** 10n
Thursday nights:
Mann's assemblies on: garden incident discredits, **19.** 497–9, **20.** 447; Mann cured by, of fever, **18.** 300; Mann gives up, **19.** 501; Mann's entertainments to be confined to, **18.** 285–6; Mann's terreno illuminated on, **19.** 490; opened by a concert, **19.** 421; popular, **18.** 289, 297, **19.** 279
Richecourt gives assemblies on, **20.** 446
Thuxtons, manor in Norfolk:
HW's will mentions, **30.** 368
Thwaite, Suffolk:
Dixon settles at, **41.** 97
Thyme:
used in tincture for the eyes, **18.** 365n

Thynne, Hon. Charlotte (1761–4):
  birth of, **38**. 143
Thynne, Frances (ca 1673–1750), m. (1690) Sir
  Robert Worsley, Bt:
  HW's account of, **29**. 288
  Pope's friend, **29**. 285
Thynne, Frances (ca 1699–1754), m. (1715)
  Algernon Seymour, styled E. of Hertford; 7th
  D. of Somerset, 1748:
  Bootle woos, **20**. 183
  Cowslade with, **9**. 251n
  Dalton and Lady Luxborough friends of, **32**.
    283
  daughter of, married, **20**. 183n
  death of, will give her a chance to explore
    spiritualism, **35**. 179
  HW imagines presents that would be given to,
    according to Italian custom, **18**. 141
  house of, in Grosvenor Sq., **20**. 183n
  husband's letter to George II resigns pension
    of, as lady of Bedchamber to Q. Caroline,
    17. 346
  Luxborough, Lady, informed by, of verses,
    43. 298
  Pomfret, Cts of, corresponds with, **14**. 248
  son's death distresses, **18**. 522
  Sturrock's correspondence with, **18**. 544
  (?) Wyndham, George O'Brien, said to be
    godson of, **9**. 126
Thynne, Francis, Lancaster Herald:
  *Discourse on the Dutye and Office of an
    Heraulde*, by, **40**. 178
Thynne, Lady Henrietta (1762–1813), m. (1799)
  Philip Stanhope, 5th E. of Chesterfield:
  grandmother maintains, **38**. 567
Thynne (Carteret after 1776), Hon. Henry
  Frederick (1735–1826), cr. (1784) Bn Car-
  teret; M.P.:
  'dumb beggar' but gets peerage, **36**. 223
  elder brother of, **33**. 140
  HW mentions, **10**. 7
  Harris's post to go to, **22**. 569n
  house of, in Curzon St, **33**. 548
  ill-informed on fleet movements, **33**. 140
  not a man of curiosity, **15**. 77
  portrait owned by, **15**. 139, 155
Thynne, Sir John (d. 1580), Kt; secretary to
  D. of Somerset:
  Longleat built for, **14**. 111, **28**. 302
  MSS of the time of, **15**. 77
Thynne, Lady Louisa (1760–1832), m. (1781)
  Heneage Finch, 4th E. of Aylesford, 1777:
  at Mrs Boyle Walsingham's ball, **42**. 222n
  grandmother maintains, **38**. 567
  marriage of, **36**. 205
  Waldegrave family hospitably treated by, **34**.
    75, **36**. 260, 265, 268, 270, **43**. 387
Thynne, Lady Mary. *See* Villiers, Lady Mary
Thynne, Sophia (1763–91), m. (1784) George
  Ashburnham, styled Vct St Asaph; 3d E. of
  Ashburnham, 1812:
  children of, **11**. 244
  death of, **11**. 244
  grandmother maintains, **38**. 567

Thynne, Thomas (ca 1640–1714), 1st Vct Weymouth:
  alleged widow of, **34**. 255
  daughter of, **29**. 285n
  pine trees introduced by, **9**. 177
Thynne, Thomas (1648–82), M.P., of Longleat:
  Northumberland, Lady, not responsible for
    death of, **42**. 395
Thynne, Thomas (1734–96), 3d Vct Weymouth;
  cr. (1789) M. of Bath:
  Adair and Jebb send bulletins to, about D.
    of Gloucester, **36**. 130
  administration might have been wrecked by,
    to satisfy Opposition, **24**. 447
  afraid of remaining secretary of state, **24**.
    526n
  Almodóvar gives Spanish rescript to, **24**. 483n,
    33. 102n
  Amelia, Ps, entertains, **32**. 307–8
  American department offered to, **23**. 424n
  Bedford, D. of, seeks paymastership for, **22**.
    463n
  Cabinet may be re-entered by, **23**. 424
  Cabinet meeting called by, on French war
    declaration, **24**. 399n
  Calais-Dover mails to be stopped by, **24**. 496n
  circular letter of: about French provocation
    and George III's messages to Parliament,
    24. 373–4; about loss of 3 mails from Italy,
    24. 468; about P. Octavius's birth and Eng-
    lish victories, **24**. 454
  Conway said to decline resigning in favour of,
    22. 578n
  —— succeeded by, as secretary of state, **3**.
    407n
  —— to be succeeded by, as secretary of state,
    22. 569, 571, 578
  cowardice of, **33**. 93, 141
  daughter of, **11**. 244n
  Dorset's house in Arlington St taken by, **10**.
    271
  employment demanded for, **30**. 236n
  forced to illuminate his house, **33**. 93
  Fox, C. J., drinks with, **33**. 93n
  —— with, at White's, **35**. 520
  France the refuge of, from debt, leaving
    family with mother-in-law, **38**. 567
  Garter for, **7**. 49n, **24**. 386n, **32**. 381n
  George III adds, to Bedchamber, **9**. 324, **21**.
    460
  —— offers lord presidency to, **24**. 526n, 533n
  Gibbon asked by, to write mémoire justificatif
    to France, **24**. 531n, **33**. 303n
  good-natured, **22**. 578
  Grafton's meeting attended by, **7**. 367
  HW called on by, daily, when ill, **35**. 331
  HW mentions, **10**. 7
  HW's letters may be opened during secretary-
    ship of, **22**. 570
  HW willing to resign empire to, **32**. 176
  habits of, **9**. 236

Hertford asked by, to consult HW about deputy lieutenants for Hertford's militia, **39.** 297

—— asks, about Jersey attack, **24.** 471n

——'s letter from, about protecting Channel Islands, forwarded by, to HW for Cts of Ailesbury, **39.** 319–20

Hillsborough succeeds, as secretary of state, **24.** 533, 534

ill-informed, **33.** 140

Irish lord lieutenancy of: infuriates Irish in London, **30.** 188; resigned by him, **22.** 311; suggested for, **38.** 545, 557, 563, 565, 567, 572, 575, **41.** 86

lacking in spirit even when drunk, **33.** 93

letter of, illegally printed, **23.** 77

'little faction' of, with Thurlow and Gower, **24.** 534n

Longleat the seat of, **1.** 25n, **28.** 302n

—— visited by, **24.** 534

lord presidency of the Council may go to, **24.** 526n

Madrid embassy considered for, **22.** 463n

Mann, Horace II, intercedes with, for Whitham, **24.** 353n

MSS owned by, **15.** 77

marriage compared by, to hanging, **9.** 236

Murray's letters dispatched to, by Mann, **24.** 380, 443

—— told by, that his secrets can be ciphered by Mann and conveyed by post, **25.** 42

Newcastle House meeting attended by, **22.** 541n

Noailles notifies, of American-French treaty, **24.** 363–4, **28.** 370–1

Northumberland, D. of, to be succeeded by, as lord lieutenant of Ireland, **22.** 303

Pitt thought to be in league with, **23.** 259

'poltroon,' but gets peerage, **36.** 223

'poltroonery' of, **29.** 207

Pomfret replaces, as Ranger of the Parks, **20.** 226n

presents George III's request to Parliament, **7.** 40n

prime ministry suggested for, **24.** 447n

Privy Seal coveted by, **23.** 310

Proby's instructions from, **23.** 244n

regimental returns laid by, before House of Lords, **24.** 351n

resignation of, as secretary of state: rumoured, **33.** 134; takes place, **23.** 255, **24.** 534, **28.** 478, 479, 485, **33.** 141; threatened, **28.** 474

Richmond names, for viceroy of Ireland, **41.** 86

Rochford succeeded by, as secretary of state for southern province, **24.** 142

Rockingham and Grafton betrayed by, **33.** 95n

Rockingham refuses Shelburne's request to ask Cabinet post for, **25.** 261

Sandwich succeeds, as secretary of state, but in northern province, **23.** 255

Seals resigned by, **23.** 255, **24.** 534

Selwyn jokes with, on pun, **9.** 236

Shelburne administration may include, **25.** 260n

Shelburne succeeded by, as secretary of state, **23.** 62

son-in-law 'marries,' **36.** 205

Spanish rescript and Almodóvar's recall notified by, to Lords, **24.** 483n

speaks in House of Lords, **28.** 373n

Tamworth candidate of, said to be opposed by Luttrell with G. Townshend's backing, **30.** 193

Villiers not to be re-elected by, **30.** 193

warrant forged in name of, **28.** 288n

Thynne, Thomas (1765–1837), 2d M. of Bath, 1796:

grandmother maintains, **38.** 567

wife of, **12.** 107n

Thynne, William (d. 1546):

Chaucer edition published by, **29.** 163n

'Thyrsis':

Fleury, Duc de, called, **12.** 30

Thyrsis:

Gray's verses on, **38.** 144–5

Tiara:

cardinals accept, though about to die, **24.** 432

Charlotte, Q., has, of diamonds, **21.** 529, **38.** 116

papal, may be discredited by Galluzzi's history, **25.** 80

Tibbald. *See* Theobald, Lewis

Tiber, River:

Atrisco tries to cross, **18.** 443–4

Avon paltry enough to be, **39.** 76

Borghese's valet drowns in, **19.** 444

bridge at Henley worthy of, **39.** 76

bridge over, demolished, **18.** 444, 525

fight at Ponte Molle on, **18.** 531–2

HW calls, 'nasty foul thing,' **30.** 5

Julius II crosses, **37.** 15

Lobkowitz to bridge, **18.** 437

mouth of, closed to ships to prevent plague, **18.** 252n

Pius VI cannot cleanse Ds of Kingston with all the holy water in, **24.** 126

Spaniards control, **18.** 533

sturgeon from, **22.** 229

Tiberius (Tiberius Claudius Nero Cæsar) (42 B.C.–A.D. 37), Roman emperor A.D. 14–37:

bust of, among HW's antiquities, **37.** 111

Charles II said to resemble, **16.** 48–52

divorce of, from Vipsania Agrippina, **13.** 117

Giovanni Gastone de' Medici the counterpart of, **17.** 273n

La Bletterie writes notes on, **8.** 152

Linguet writes about, **8.** 180

name of, on MS, probably indicates former ownership by Cottonian library, **40.** 305–6

Trojan ambassadors answered by, **36.** 280

Tibet, Lama of. *See* dPal-ldan ye-šes; *see also under* Dalai Lama

Tibetot. *See* Tiptoft

Tibia:
HW wants *Sappho* to be accompanied by lyre and, **28.** 347

Tibullus (Albius Tibullus) (ca 54–18 B.C.), poet:
De sulpicia by, HW translates, for Spence, **40.** 68–9
grace of, **16.** 270
West translates elegy of, **13.** 120, **14.** 15

'Tibullus':
character in *Ballet de la Paix*, **18.** 496

'Ticchi Micchi':
HW's name for his boar pig, **37.** 347, 349, 350

Tichborne, Betty (d. 1752):
Edgcumbe attached to, **34.** 258

Tichborne, Judith (d. 1749), m. 1 (1717) Charles Spencer, 3d E. of Sunderland; m. 2 (1749) Sir Robert Sutton:
family of, **34.** 258

Tichborne. *See also* Titchborne

Tichfield. *See* Titchfield

Tickell, Richard (1751–93), poet and satirist:
Anticipation by: **12.** 55, **16.** 186n, **43.** 152; drafts of speeches that would probably be made were printed in, **24.** 528n
Cassette verte de Monsieur de Sartine, La, and *Opposition Mornings* by, **39.** 326
Epistle from the Hon. Charles Fox by: HW criticizes, **33.** 145; 'hodgepodge of partridges and House of Commons,' **28.** 487
HW admires writings of, **12.** 55
lines of *Jekyll* attributed to, **11.** 34n
Project, The, by, as good as *The Wreath of Fashion,* **28.** 384
Rolliad contributor, **25.** 613n
Short Review attributed to, **33.** 557n
suicide of, at Hampton Court Palace, **12.** 55
Wreath of Fashion, The, by, satirizes sentimental poets, **28.** 384

Tickell, Mrs Richard. *See* Ley, Sarah

Tickell, Thomas (1685–1740), poet:
Addison's friend, **12.** 55n, **28.** 384
'Fragment of a Poem on Hunting, A,' by, quoted, **12.** 260
poems of, in Dodsley's collection, **14.** 35
verses on painting of Charles I owned by, **16.** 48

Ticket; tickets:
Bunbury's, for Wynnstay theatre, **34.** 4n
Conway obtains, for *lit de justice* at Paris, **39.** 224
for Bath installation, **30.** 79, 81, 83
for Conway's *False Appearances,* **31.** 263–4
for (?) Coronation, HW unable to get, **40.** 205
for Dublin ball, **37.** 413
for Garter installation, **38.** 177
for Hastings's trial, **11.** 9–10, **31.** 265, **35.** 541
for Hyde and St James's Parks, **41.** 350

for Lincoln's gallery in House of Lords, **30.** 160, 177–8
for Marie-Josèphe's funeral oration, not required, **31.** 138
for Richmond House masquerade, **40.** 284
for Richmond's ball, **22.** 149n
for SH visitors, *see under* Strawberry Hill lottery, *see under* Lottery
opera, *see under* Opera
(?) theatre, HW thanks Henderson for, **42.** 5
to St James's Park, **35.** 549, 550, 557

Tickhill, Yorks:
Sandbeck Park near, **15.** 139n

Ticonderoga, N.Y.:
Americans said to be besieged in, **24.** 261
Amherst takes, **9.** 248n, **21.** 326, 333
—— threatens, **21.** 301n
Burgoyne captures, **6.** 470, 472, **24.** 323, 329, **32.** 374
—— may have taken, **32.** 370
English defeat at: **21.** 233, 241, 246, **37.** 560, 563; Paris fireworks to celebrate, **21.** 246
HW jokes about spelling and pronunciation of, **30.** 148
Howe and others killed at, **30.** 148
loss of, **32.** 400
more success than, needed, **32.** 380
Townshend, Hon. Roger, killed at, **9.** 32n, **13.** 34

'Ticonderogicus':
Amherst should be called, **35.** 294

Tide-waiters:
Newcastle, D. of, restores, to office, **22.** 323

Tidone (Italy):
battle of, **19.** 291, 302

Tieleners. *See* Tilenus, Daniel

Tiepolo, Alvise, Venetian ambassador to Rome:
Florence visited by, **24.** 113n

Tieremhausen, Gen.:
captured at Zorndorf, **37.** 562n

Tiers état, French:
courier from D. of Devonshire pretends to have been sent by, **11.** 36

Tie wig. *See under* Wig

Tiger; tigers:
Arabian deserts thought to have, **37.** 130
at Horton, **10.** 334
cows at Mrs Barnard's resemble, **33.** 568
Crammond's, **37.** 383
element of, in human composition: **23.** 192, 194, 201, 387; suggested by Voltaire, **43.** 283
England's 'Asiatic' government will produce, **33.** 97
exhibited at York, **28.** 91
fable about, **9.** 270
ferocity of, **31.** 114
French revolutionists resemble, **31.** 372, **34.** 148, **39.** 491
HW sees D. of Cumberland's, at Windsor, **37.** 383

HW's metaphor of, **15.** 236
Hasan Effendi gives, to Francis I, **20.** 127n
Indian screen depicts killing of, **35.** 445
in Tower of London: **34.** 62, 122; whelped, **31.** 114
'mounting tiger,' **34.** 194
Rapin's term for Jeffreys and Kirke, **20.** 194n
tame, HW jokes about, **37.** 293
Zanetti's intaglio of: HW covets, **21.** 562; Mann often reminds Murray about, **22.** 116; Murray has not found, **22.** 14
'Tiger, the man.' *See* Talbot, Henry
Tighe, Mrs:
SH visited by, **12.** 237
Tighe, Edward (fl. 1759–97), Irish M.P.; playwright:
HW asked by, to write epilogue to Jephson's *Braganza*, **41.** 287
HW's *Mysterious Mother* read aloud by, **31.** 216
Irish House of Commons diverts, from theatrical management, **41.** 458n
Irish pension of, **32.** 230n
Jephson zealously supported by, **41.** 458
London left by, to attend Irish parliament, **41.** 458n
to read parts of Jephson's *Braganza*, **32.** 229–30
Tighe, T., of the Temple:
Seymour-Conway's letter sent to, with abbreviated address, **25.** 608
Tiglath-pileser, K.:
Rich, Lady, does not allude to, **35.** 78
Tignonville, Guillaume de (d. 1414):
Dictes and Sayings translated by, **40.** 119
Tigrane, opera:
Haymarket theatre opens with, **32.** 29n
'Tigress,' the. *See* Clopton, Catherine
Tilbury, Tom, landlord of Red Lion Inn at Bagshot:
Northington nicknamed after, **30.** 246n
Tilbury, English ship:
Portsmouth reached by, **30.** 112n
Tile; tiles:
Dutch: HW jokes about origin of, **31.** 326; wallpaper at SH imitates, **20.** 382
from Gloucester Cathedral, purchased for SH, **35.** 151–2, **36.** 39
from Pipwell Abbey Church, given by Harcourt to HW, **35.** 537
from William I's kitchen in Normandy, received by HW from Churchill, **1.** 65n, **36.** 38–9
HW sends to Lynn for, **32.** 143
London streets littered with, after storm, **10.** 14
made from native red clay, **35.** 151–2
red and yellow, in Malvern Priory, **35.** 151
road strewn with, after storm, **33.** 81
storm injures, on New Year's Day, **24.** 431
tax on, **37.** 445

Tilenus, Daniel (1563–1633), Protestant divine:
Canones Synodi Dordracenæ by, **14.** *129*
Gray cannot identify, **14.** 128
—— identifies, **14.** 129–30
Speculum Antichristi by, **14.** 129
Tillemont. *See* Le Nain de Tillemont
Tilliburdin. *See* Tullibardine
Tillières, Comte de. *See* Le Veneur, Alexis-Paul-Michel
Tillières, Comtesse de. *See* Verdelin, Henriette-Charlotte de
Tillières, Marquis de. *See* Le Veneur, François-Jacques-Tannegui
Tillières (France):
Jonzac, Marquise de, to visit, **20.** 211
Tillot. *See* Du Tillot
Tillotson, John (1630–94), D.D.; Abp of Canterbury, 1691:
Birch's life of, **14.** 62, **20.** 282n, **28.** 30
country clergy use sermons of, **28.** 117
in Stratford's tragedy, **29.** 224
Mysterious Mother's events thought to happen in time of, **39.** 102–3
Russell's letter from, shows he regards resistance to authority as a sin, **2.** 359
Russell, Lady Rachel, urges, to accept archbishopric, **20.** 282n
Whitefield as popular as, **13.** 249–50
Tilly, François-Bonaventure de (ca 1701–75), Marquis de Blaru; lieutenant of the bodyguard:
hunts with Louis XV, **3.** 291
Tilly, John (ca 1715–90), attorney:
HW expects, concerning purchase of house in Berkeley Sq., **33.** 67
HW gets letter from, about purchase of house, **33.** 115–16
Tilney, Norfolk:
bequests to churches in, **15.** 2n
Tilney. *See also* Tylney
Tilney St, London:
Chute's house in: **9.** 330; coveted by Mrs Grenville, **35.** 105, 108; near Chesterfield's, **35.** 110
Tilson, ——, writer:
World contributions by, **20.** 400n
Tilson, Charlotte (d. 1798), m. (1738) Sir Robert Deane, 5th Bt:
(?) Paris visited by, **4.** 271
Tilson, Christopher (1670–1742), M.P.:
death of, ascribed to examination by Secret Committee, **18.** 33
Fane succeeds, **18.** 33
Tilson, Elizabeth Anne (d. 1821), m. (1779) Charles Henry Coote, 2d Bn Castle Coote, 1802:
(?) SH visited by, **12.** 225
Tilson, Lady Frances. *See* Brudenell, Lady Frances
Tilson, Rev. George (ca 1713–78), army chaplain:
(?) HW mentions, **37.** 186

Tilson, (?) Oliver (ca 1717–88):
  HW's correspondence with, 41. 405
  HW to give *Essay on Modern Gardening* to,
    41. 405
Tilt Yard, The, London:
  conversation at, 26. 14
Timber:
  France needs, for navy, 25. 4
  French hope to get, from Corsica, 23. 47
  French vessels laden with, captured, 19. 230n
  See also Tree; Wood
Timbrune de Valence, César-Jean-Baptiste de
  (1719–ca 93), Marquis de Timbrune:
  made governor of École Royale Militaire, 5.
    431, 435
Time (clock):
  Italian way of computing: 17. 32n; changed
    at Florence to French, 20. 26
Time; times:
  'a great philosophizer,' 32. 274
  HWs lessons from, 24. 301
  HW's reflections on, 31. 143
  'make men, not men times,' 23. 514
Times, The, London newspaper:
  Cambridge's verses in, 34. 87
  HW and George IV mentioned in, 12. 112
  HW's alleged bequest reported in, 42. 424n
  obituary notice of Lady Ravensworth to be
    inserted in, 34. 198
  paragraphs transcribed from, 11. 84
  Park Place described in, 39. 549–52
  Twickenham storm to be reported in, 12. 176
  Walter inserts paragraphs in, about HW's
    will, 12. 139, 140, 141, 143
  —— publishes, formerly *Daily Universal Reg-
    ister*, 31. 265n
  witticism in, about HW's *Royal and Noble
    Authors*, 12. 201
Times, The (poem). *See under* Churchill,
  Charles (1731–64)
Times, The (translation of Goldoni's *Bourru*).
  See under Griffith, Elizabeth
Timeur Marquise de. *See* Chauvelin, Louise-
  Philippe de
'Timion,' E. of Orford's horse:
  Burlton acquires, 32. 131n
Timms, Richard (d. 1785), Lt-Col.; amateur
  actor:
  HW admires acting of, 33. 369
Timoni, Louis, Imperial commissary:
  Algiers reached by, from Tunis, with Al-
    gerian-Tuscan peace proposals, 25. 270n
Timon of Athens. See under Shakespeare, Wil-
  liam
Timothy:
  St Paul addresses, 32. 385
Tims. *See* Timms
Timwhiskey (carriage):
  apprentices take, to Epsom, 39. 106
Tin:
  case of, with *éloge* of deceased, put into
    tombs in Italy, 21. 170

cases of, for money, 38. 259n
  See also Tin mine
'Tinca nera.' *See* Pertici, 'Tinca Nera'
Tincture of spleenwort:
  Hill sells, 28. 199
Tindal, Matthew (ca 1653–1738), deist:
  Bolingbroke to be classed with, 20. 454
  House of Commons condemns writings of,
    20. 454n
Tindal, Rev. William (1756–1804), antiquary:
  History and Antiquities of . . . Evesham by,
    15. 253–4
Tingry, Prince de. *See* Montmorency-Luxem-
  bourg, Charles-François-Christian de
Tingry, Princesse de. *See* Des Laurents, Éléo-
  nore-Josèphe-Pulchérie
Tinker, John Bladen (d. 1767), naval Capt.:
  Thurot discovered by, off Newport Gat near
    Ostend, 21. 338n
Tinker; tinkers:
  Clement XIV son of, 23. 117
  new National Assembly to be full of, 34. 124,
    39. 487
Tin mines:
  in Cornwall, 33. 499
Tinsel:
  Damer, Mrs, picks out of silks, 38. 198n
  HW compares glory to, 24. 327
  on Twelfth-cakes, 34. 231
  royal velvet and ermine might just as well be
    actor's, 25. 624
  worn by humbler Florentine ladies, 25. 175
Tintagel, Cornwall:
  Montagu's estate at, 21. 472n
Tintoretto (Jacopo Robusti) (1512–94),
  painter:
  Monaco, P. of, has paintings by, 7. 335
  paintings by: at the Escurial, 16. 180n;
    bought from England by Cárdenas, 16.
    154–5
Tintori, Corso de', at Florence:
  Teatro Mediceo in, becomes Teatro del
    Lavoro, 17. 202n
  Ubaldini's apartment in, 17. 146n
Tip; tips:
  actors at Calais expect, 23. 519–20, 32. 150–1
  Amalia of Modena's, 17. 64–5
  at christening, 24. 199, 219
  Bromfield gives, to groom of chambers at
    Petworth for list of pictures, 40. 318
  for French postilions, 37. 41
  HW's, in Paris, 7. 399, 407, 408, 409, 412
  Pulteney family niggardly about, 19. 443
  servants' vails, 20. 89n
  Sulkowsky's, at SH, paltry, 33. 280
  York, D. of, gives, to Lucchese servants, 22.
    222
  Young, Margaret, receives, from Ps Amelia,
    10. 82
  See also Tipping; Vail
'Tipkin, Biddy.' *See under* Steele, Sir Richard:
  Tender Husband

Tipperary, Ireland:
  Montagu's lace must come from, 10. 1
  'Peach in Brandy, The,' mentions, 32. 60
  Whiteboys in, 22. 24n
Tippet; tippets:
  fur, worn by Princesse de Craon, 18. 109
  HW sends, to Pandolfini, 17. 45, 47, 52
  white, worn by St-Cyr pensioners, 10. 293
Tipping, Lady. See Cheeke, Anne (d. 1728)
Tipping, Catherine (d. 1754), m. (1726)
    Thomas Archer, cr. (1747) Bn Archer:
  Hertfords' visit to, 39. 131
Tipping, Letitia (d. 1779), m. (1725) Samuel
    Sandys, cr. (1743) Bn Sandys:
  conundrum on 'queer arse' of, 19. 28
  Downing St former residence of, 30. 74
  HW evicted by, from Downing St, 9. 24
  HW mentions, 17. 475
  HW's sarcasms on, 30. 74
  husband of, 9. 35
  Orford title of great-uncle of, 17. 333
  Walpoles notified by, to quit house at Down-
    ing St, 17. 478
  Wilmington offers Downing St house to, 17.
    478
Tipping:
  at brothel, 24. 413
  English custom of, imitated by Duc and
    Duchesse de Mirepoix, 20. 89
  of ships' officers, 1. 101
  women of fashion never practise, 20. 89
  See also Tip; tips
Tippoo Saheb. See Tipu Sultan
Tiptoft or Tibetot, John (1427-70), 2d Bn
    Tiptoft, cr. (1449) E. of Worcester:
  Caxton's comment on execution of, 28. 48
  HW wishes to have letters of, copied, 13. 104
  Wood's Historia includes, 40. 298
Tiptoft or Tibetot family:
  property of, at Eversden, Cambs, 1. 140
Tipu Sultan (1750-99), ruler of Mysore, 1782;
    Padshah, 1787:
  biographical information about, corrected,
    43. 146
  Cornwallis's victory over, 34. 146
  England at war with, 11. 186, 251, 256
  Maxwell saved from, by Medows, 34. 108n
  reported to have sued for peace, 11. 350
Tirand des Arcis, Mme René-François. See
    Aumont de Mazarin, Louise-Félicité-Victoire
    d'
Tiran le Blanc:
  Du Deffand, Mme, cites, 3. 270, 280
Tircis. See Thyrsis
Tirconnel. See Tyrconnel
Tire-boudin, Rue, in Paris:
  Du Barry, Mme, assigned to, in joke, 8. 181
Tirelarigot:
  verses to air of, 6. 406
Tirell. See Tyrell; Tyrrel; Tyrrell
'Tiresias, blind':
  Reynolds's painting of, 33. 571-2

Tirewomen:
  medieval milliners surpass, 35. 249
'Tiribasas' (? R. O. Cambridge):
  monopolizes conversation, 12. 266
Tirkner, John:
  Surrey lands of, 24. 168n
Tirol. See Tyrol
Tiroux d'Arconville, Mme. See Arlus, Marie-
    Geneviève-Charlotte d'
Tirrel. See Tyrell; Tyrrel; Tyrrell
Tischbein, W.:
  Hamilton's Collection of Engravings edited
    by, 35. 442n
Tisdal, Philip (1703-77), Irish politician; at-
    torney-gen. of Ireland:
  accustomed to open budget in Parliament,
    32. 161
  member of D. of Dorset's party, 20. 402n
Tisio, Benvenuto (1481-1559), called Garofolo
    Garofolo:
  paintings by, sold by Francis III to K. of Po-
    land, 19. 314n
'Tisiphone':
  applied to: Catherine II, 34. 144, 39. 180;
    Greenwich, Bns, 33. 457-8, 485; Mann, Mrs
    Galfridus, 21. 129; Maria Theresa, 21. 498;
    Montagu, Ds of, 33. 299
  East India Co. should be corrected by, 23. 442
  HW's verses mention, 31. 120
Tisséranderie, Rue de la:
  Boudot in, 6. 72n
Tissot, Simon-André (1728-97), Swiss physician:
  Beauvau attended by, 7. 235, 241, 453, 458
  Carlisle, Cts of, advised by, to go to Rome,
    23. 447
  Du Deffand, Mme, has social relations with,
    7. 437
  Herbert, Lady Charlotte, to have consulted,
    at Lausanne, 25. 493
  Lausanne visited by, 7. 241
  Morice's motions directed by, 25. 435
Tissue; tissues:
  Craon's reception of toison d'or characterized
    by, 17. 20
  Edward I's, found perfect in his grave, 24. 4
  Erroll's costume of, for George III's wedding,
    9. 388
  for Coronation robes, 38. 100
'Titania':
  Choiseul, Duchesse de, called, 10. 198
Titchborne, Mrs:
  Cowslade to visit, at Englefield Green, 41.
    420
Titchfield, Marchioness of. See Scott, Henrietta
Titchfield, M. of. See Bentinck, William Henry
    Cavendish (1738-1809); Cavendish Scott Ben-
    tinck, William Henry Cavendish (1768-
    1864)
Titchfield, Hants:
  Abbey at: 43. 183-4; Margaret of Anjou mar-
    ried in, 14. 72
  Place House at, 10. 102n

'Tite-Live,' race horse:
'Noir et tout noir' to run against, **31.** 112
Titery:
Bey of, in army at Algiers, **24.** 122n
Tithes:
Mason's, **28.** 231
parson sues HW's tenants for, **39.** 494
surveys are full of, **35.** 146
Talbot takes, in kind, **19.** 176
Titi, Julia. *See* Julia
Titian (Tiziano Vecellio) (1477–1576), painter:
alleged 'Danæ' by, bought by Young from Hugford, **20.** 330
Barbiellini prints letter from, **7.** 355
Barry includes, in allegorical painting, **29.** 301
Cambis, Mme de, resembles, **6.** 430
'Concert,' attributed to, **22.** 179, 246, 291
'Ecce Homo' by: Buckingham sells, to Archduke Leopold, **16.** 153–4; Hollar's print of, **16.** 153
England does not yet outdo, **24.** 92
Félibien and Dufresnoy praise colours of, **30.** 325
female beauty inspired, **30.** 325
Furnese has pictures by, **21.** 172n
Guido's colours compared to those of, **11.** 150n
HW objects to *New Oxford Guide's* spelling of, **35.** 462
HW's and Mrs Damer's opinions of, **11.** 266
Jackson's prints imitate, **20.** 381
'Lord's Supper' by, in Pierson's sale, **23.** 570n
Monaco, P. of, has paintings by, **7.** 335
Oliver imitates, **10.** 345
Ossory's alleged copy by, disparaged by Reynolds but restored by Van der Gucht, **33.** 538n
paintings by: at Devonshire House, **38.** 455n; at Escurial, formerly Charles I's, **16.** 168, 180n; at Marigny's, **39.** 15; in Colebrooke's sale, **23.** 569n; in Pitti palace, banished because the sitter's back is turned, **22.** 179; of 11 Cæsars, bought by Cárdenas from England, **16.** 155; of 11 Cæsars, sold by Francis III to the K. of Poland, **19.** 314n; of St Peter, **15.** 335; of St Thomas, **10.** 334; of Venus, **7.** 313; of Venus, ill-copied in Zoffany's painting of Tribune, **24.** 527; of Venus, would not please Q. Charlotte, **24.** 540
Philip II addressed as K. of England by, **7.** 355
Pope's epigram mentions paintings by, **30.** 5
(?) portrait by, of Cesare Borgia, **9.** 414
Spence attributes Rubens's 'Prometheus' to, **10.** 78
Vasari's portrait of Bianca Cappello worthy of, **20.** 407
West asks for list of works of, in England, **40.** 312
works of, at Venice, blackened, **11.** 266

Titi Livii Foro-Juliensis vita Henrici Quinti:
cited, **1.** 262
Title; titles:
HW's reflections on futility of, **25.** 583
HW's reflections on succeeding to, **31.** 364
National Assembly abolishes, in France, **11.** 76
See also Nobility
Title-deed; title-deeds:
Conolly, Lady Anne, lets HW see, **42.** 418
Title-page; title-pages:
Smith's reading does not go beyond, **17.** 467
Titley, Walter, English representative in Denmark:
Fenwick tells, at Copenhagen about Thurot, **21.** 346n
Williams, Sir C. H., said by, to be in poor health, **21.** 183n
Tito, Santo di (1526–1603), painter:
Mann has 'Last Supper' by, copied for Chute's chapel, **9.** 216, **20.** 529
Tito Manlio, opera:
at Siena, **20.** 391n
Titon, ——:
attends session of parliament of Paris, **8.** 173
'Titus':
character in Racine's *Bérénice*, **41.** 154
Titus (Titus Flavius Sabinus Vespasianus) (A.D. 40–81), Roman emperor A.D. 79–81:
(?) arch of, **33.** 54
Berenice and, **31.** 155
daughter of, **15.** 12n
Fox, C. J., compared with, **32.** 166
Herculaneum restored in time of, **13.** 222
Jerusalem besieged by, **33.** 133
Jewish war of, **28.** 92–3
Jews enjoy their Ranelagh, when their Knightsbridge is occupied by, **25.** 317
regret by, for any day not well employed, **42.** 163
sometimes lost a day, **35.** 338
Titus, Catherine (d. 1732):
Ramsey Abbey bequeathed by, to servants, **12.** 257
Titus Andronicus. See under Shakespeare, William
'Tivoli, Rosa di.' *See* Roos, Philipp Peter
Tivoli (Italy):
Atrisco halts near, **18.** 444
HW and Gray visit, **17.** 26
HW compares Twickenham to, **20.** 16
Modena, D. of, has house at, **18.** 335n
Patch's 'girl' at, **23.** 275n
sea-coal fires inappropriate at, in summer, **10.** 315
temple at: copied at Wentworth Castle, **35.** 267; copied for frieze of Houghton picture gallery, **18.** 63
Twickenham to be as famous as, **35.** 234
Tizzard, Edward:
rewarded for voting in Weymouth election, **17.** 421n
Toad; toads:
Argyll's interest in, **37.** 150

Ireland exposed to, **35**. 478
Toad-eater; toad-eaters:
dowagers usually accompanied by, **19**. 298
Robinson, 'long' Sir Thomas, leader of, **35**. 579
Selwyn's witticism on Pelham's plate eaten off by, **35**. 220–1
Toadstool; toadstools. *See* Mushrooms
Toast; toasts:
Hamiltons never make, to those beneath the rank of earl, **20**. 339
Mann's, at Leghorn, **19**. 151, 152
out of fashion, **28**. 216, **33**. 356
Passionei, Cardinal, gives, to the Pope, in English manner, **12**. 266
Price's, to National Assembly, **11**. 135
Westmorland, Lady, and, **33**. 356
Toasting-fork:
Du Deffand, Mme, uses, **39**. 219
Toasting-grate:
HW sends, to Mme du Deffand, **39**. 219
Toast-rack:
(?) Du Deffand, Mme, orders, **6**. 128, 132
HW sends, to Mme du Deffand by Mrs Damer, **6**. 101, 102
Tobacco:
at Houghton, **13**. 104
at Peterhouse, **13**. 63
Cole wishes for, to amuse him in evenings, **2**. 34n
Conway avoids, at Sluys, **38**. 6
country gentlemen addicted to, **37**. 107
dealings in, **5**. 107
Dodd and Whaley armed with, to explore Wokey Hole, **40**. 10
Dutch brig carries, **33**. 272n
duty on, at Florence, **20**. 389
English addiction to, **19**. 272
farmers smoke, at inn, **35**. 135
French customs will confiscate, **37**. 40
furnished at election at King's Lynn, **9**. 350
German artist smells of, **37**. 103
justices of the peace addicted to, **10**. 89
pigtail, used by Ferrers on way to execution, **21**. 401
sparks from, might explode a bomb, **21**. 155
tax on, **25**. 254n
Tuscan trade in, **20**. 389
Walpole, Hon. Thomas, and Vanneck have contract for, with French *fermiers généraux*, **38**. 545–6, 556–7
Walpole opponents drown feuds in, **37**. 90
Wellingborough inn bedroom smells of, **10**. 89
Tobago (West Indies):
Macartney voted salary by, **32**. 386n
peace negotiations include, **21**. 526n
taken by French, **25**. 172, **33**. 295n
Tobia (Tobiu; Tupia; Tupaia) (d. 1770), Tahitian priest:
Beriea's lover, **31**. 162
death of, at Batavia, **31**. 162

Tobit:
Castiglione's painting of, *see under* Castiglione, Benedetto
tapestry of, **40**. 198
'Toby':
HW's signature, **42**. 502, 505
Tocha, La, ship:
in Spanish fleet, **17**. 286
Tocsin:
at Monte Santa Maria, **20**. 423
Todd, Capt.:
General Barker commanded by, **25**. 119n
Todd, Elizabeth:
Critical Review criticizes novels of, **31**. 274n
Todd, John (d. 1736), actor:
injured, **13**. 113n
Toft, Mary (ca 1701–63), 'rabbit-woman':
Hogarth's prints of, **16**. 73
'modest impostor' compared to Cock Lane ghost, **10**. 6
no successors to, **18**. 124
Tofts. *See* Toft
Toilet; toilets:
Finch, Lady Charlotte, displays, at accouchement, **19**. 442
gold, **18**. 170
Toilette. *See under* Gay, John
'Toilette, or the Morning.' *See* Williams, Sir Charles Hanbury: 'Isabella or the Morning'
Toilette; toilettes:
Roland, Mme, has, **10**. 246
Suffolk, Cts of, has, **10**. 113
Toinette, Mme du Deffand's servant:
daughter born to, **7**. 439
Du Deffand, Mme, gives 'pet-en-l'air d'indienne' to, **7**. 451
(?) —— shares lottery ticket with, **7**. 422, 455
——'s legacy to, **8**. 6
fears customs office has seized Mrs Cholmondeley's goods, **4**. 488, 496
wages of, **8**. 46
Toison d'or (Order of the Golden Fleece):
Choiseul and Fuentes receive, **21**. 560
Craon receives, **17**. 11, 16, 20
Leopold II gives, to son, as Joseph II's deputy, **23**. 55, 59
—— thinks that English honours are as common as, **23**. 502
Maria Theresa bribes Gen. Brown with, **21**. 72
secretary of, *see* Nenny, Cornelius van
secretary to bring, from Vienna to Florence for Francis II, **23**. 1
Tokay (wine):
Chudleigh, Elizabeth, offers, to D. of Kingston, **35**. 301
Foote's witticism on small bottle of, **28**. 189
Wortley Montagu's only indulgence, **35**. 268
Toland, John (1670–1722), deist:
Bolingbroke to be classed with, **20**. 454
House of Commons condemns writings of, **20**. 454n
Life of Milton by, edited by Hollis, **29**. 18n

Tôle:
gift of, 4. 313
Toledo, Abp of. *See* Lorenzana y Butrón, Francisco Antonio (1722–1804); Ximenes de Cisneros, Francisco (1436–1517)
Toledo (Spain):
'cardinalino' of, *see* Luis Antonio
Toll, Rev. Frederick (ca 1708–65):
Church's reply to, 15. 301
Defence of Dr Middleton's Free Inquiry by, 15. 298
Dodwell's reply to, 15. 302
Sermon Preached at the Visitation at Basingstoke, A, by, 15. 302
Some Remarks upon Mr Church's Vindication of the Miraculous Powers, by, 15. 301
Tollemache, Lady:
Little Marble Hill, Twickenham, occupied by, 42. 484
Tollemache, Lady Bridget. *See* Henley, Lady Bridget
Tollemache, Lady Elizabeth. *See* Murray, Lady Elizabeth (ca 1628–98)
Tollemache, Lady Frances:
brother's marriage wished by, 36. 328
Tollemache, Hon. George (1744–60):
drowned, 32. 398
godparents of, 18. 431
Tollemache, Hon. John (1750–77), English naval capt.:
death of, in duel, 32. 398
marriage of, 35. 467
'Mr Tall-match,' 32. 164
wife of, 32. 398
Zebra commanded by, 32. 165n
Tollemache, Lionel (ca 1497–1571), *or* Lionel (ca 1545–75), *or* Sir Lionel (1562–ca 1620), cr. (1611), Bt:
(?) Pennant sees portrait of, 16. 285
Tollemache, Sir Lionel (1624–69), 3d Bt:
not a general, 16. 285
wife of, 10. 306n
Tollemache, Lionel (1708–70), 4th E. of Dysart:
appearance of, 9. 301
death of, 10. 306n
HW jokes about death of, 9. 312
Ham House gates opened by, only for Granville, 10. 307
—— the residence of, 21. 438n
meadow of, 35. 388–9
son denied money by, to get married, 21. 438–9
son's relations with, 9. 301, 312
wife of, 9. 171n
Tollemache, Lionel (1734–99), styled Lord Huntingtower 1740–70, 5th E. of Dysart, 1770:
antiquity of Ham House to be preserved by, 10. 306–7
appearance of, 9. 301
Beauclerks visited by, 36. 328
brother-in-law of, 28. 429n
brother of, drowned, 32. 367

Clement, Anne, visits, at Ham House, 36. 268
—— to accompany, in his bereavement, 36. 268–9
Clement, Jane, visits, at Ham House, 36. 63
elms of, blown down at Ham, 33. 82
father's relations with, 9. 301, 312
financial expectations of, 9. 301
Gloucester, D. and Ds of, visit, at Ham, 36. 79–80
grandfather's advice to, 9. 301
HW calls, 'hog' and compares him to dragon of Wantley, 31. 191
HW lacks picture of, 36. 160
HW mentions, 10. 7
HW to entertain, at SH, 9. 369
HW to receive compliments of, 36. 80
HW visited by, at SH, 10. 63, 32. 382
Mann guesses that appearance of, outweighs his poverty, 21. 446
marriage of, 9. 301, 21. 438–9
meadow of, 11. 337, 341, 35. 388–9
portrait of Cts of Carlisle owned by, at Ham, 41. 443
remarriage possible for, though he may be impotent, 36. 328
Scott, Lady Jane, fined by, for inheritance at Twickenham, 31. 185
storm destroys trees of, 12. 175
succeeds father, 10. 306n
Waldegrave girls brutally treated by, 36. 327
wife mourned by, 34. 63
wife of, 9. 13n, 11. 56n, 16. 310n
wife's affection for, 32. 398
wife's memory cherished by, 36. 268–9
Tollemache, Lady Louisa, m. John Manners:
sister-in-law of Lady Dysart, 28. 93n
Tollemache, Wilbraham (1739–1821), 6th E. of Dysart, 1799:
HW hears good reports of, 32. 398
Tollemache, Hon. William (1751–76):
Courtenay, Miss, loved by, 32. 147, 152, (?) 187
drowned, 32. 367, 398, 36. 131
Dysart, Cts of, friendly with, 36. 131
(?) love affair of, 32. 186–7
Tollemache family:
HW jokes about seeing ghosts of, at Ham House, 10. 306
inflexibility of, 10. 307
Tollendal, Baron de. *See* Lally, Thomas Arthur (1702–66)
Tolley, ——, hosier:
fire at house of, opposite Salisbury St in Strand, 32. 109n
Toll-houses:
on Blackfriars Bridge, 33. 188
Tolly, Mrs, of Richmond:
SH visited by, 12. 236
Tollymore Park, co. Down, Ireland:
Clanbrassill's seat, 42. 381n
Tolmache. *See* Tollemache
Tolomei, Celso:
Jesuit college founded by, 13. 204n

Tolstoi, Count Peter:
Magnan secretary to, 18. 548n
Tom, Conway's servant:
Helvétius announced by, as 'Helvoetsluys,' 38. 359
'Tom, HW's old.' See Barney, Tom
Tomatesse; Tomatis, Mme. See Thomatti, Mme
Tomb; tombs:
Addison describes, at Bolsena, 15. 22
at Hurstmonceaux, 35. 139
Celestines' church crowded with, 39. 201
clumsy, in early times, 2. 301
Condé's, at Great Jesuits Church, 39. 203
Egyptian or Turkish, 15. 19
Elgin, Cts of, occupies, in Bruce mausoleum, 39. 139
Fitzalan family's, 39. 310
Gothic, at Winchester, 35. 250
HW's reflections on, as 'lasting mansions,' 35. 250
HW's witticism on, 32. 22
in Westminster Abbey, subject of curiosity to foreigners, 30. 176
Italian, contain éloges, 21. 170
kings', HW's reflections on, 39. 230–1
Mary, Q. of Scots's, 15. 113, 139
painting in HW's Blue Room of Gray's, 28. 196
picture cut from wall of, 15. 16
Pitt wishes his sentiments to be written on, 37. 441
Roman, found in England, 15. 179
sepulchral altar-, see under Altar
William of Hatfield's, 28. 42–3
See also Monument; Tombstone
Tombstone; tombstones:
Corelli has favourite jig engraved on, 37. 442
face from, 37. 345
Fox's witticism to Pitt on epitaphs on, 37. 426, 429, 441–2
HW bids against Gen. Campbell for, 37. 460
Wood's, at Putney, to be designed by HW, 41. 245–9, 254–5, 307–8, 317–18
Tom Jones, comic opera:
at Covent Garden, 23. 82n
See also under Danican, François-André; Fielding, Henry; Poinsinet, Antoine-Alexandre-Henri
Tom Jones, novel. See under Fielding, Henry
Tomkins, P. W., engraver:
Palmer's portrait of Louisa engraved by, 33. 490n
Tomkyns, ——:
Gloucester, Ds of, sends money to, through Ned Roberts, 36. 72n
Tomochichi (d. 1739), chief of the Yamacraw Indians:
Oglethorpe brings, from Georgia, 42. 236
Tompion, Thomas (1639–1713), watch and clock-maker:
'clockwork as old as,' 28. 407
'To Mr Conway,' by HW:
HW transcribes, to Conway, 37. 522–3

'To Mr Garnier and Mr Pearce of Bath.' See under Williams, Sir Charles Hanbury
'To Mr Pitt,' verses by HW:
HW quotes, 12. 259, 38. 41
'To Mrs Crewe.' See under Fox, Hon. Charles James
Tom's Coffee-house, London:
Edwin and Gage at, 17. 296
Hogarth's tavern drawn from, 17. 296n
Spectator mentioned by man at, 19. 565
West, Capt. Thomas, landlord of, in Russell St, 17. 296n
Tom Thumb:
HW might copy, 35. 33
See also Thumb, Tom
Tom Thumb the Great. See under Fielding, Henry
'Tom Tilbury.' See under Henley, Robert
Tom Tower. See under Christ Church, Oxford
Tondertentronk. See Thunder-ten-tronck
Tonduti, Joseph-Pierre-François de, Marquis de Malijac, or Jacques-Jean-Baptiste de (b. 1712), Baron de Malijac:
Simiane, Mme de, succeeded by, at Belombre, 34. 85n
Tonelli. See La Tonelli
Tonge Castle, Salop:
Stanley of, 1. 9n
Tonghes. See Tongs
Tongres (Belgium):
Conway and Scott visit, 39. 537
Tongs, fire- :
Ussé leaves, to Mme Rondé, 5. 276
Tongs, Kent, Halifax's seat:
Bentley to visit Montagu at, 9. 105
HW may visit Montagu at, 9. 118
Tongue; tongues:
Vane's, monstrous, 30. 303n
Ton humeur est, Catherine:
verses to air of, 5. 353, 365
Tonley, Aberdeenshire:
Byres retires to family estate at, 42. 63n
Tonnant, Le, French ship:
unreported, 25. 1n
Tonnay, Geoffroy de:
wife of, loved by Rigaut de Barbezieux, 21. 169
'Tonneau,' Mme du Deffand's hooded chair:
Choiseul, Duchesse de, supplies, at Chanteloup, 5. 79
Gustav III would have liked to have, for Mme du Deffand, 5. 39
Mme du Deffand's: notaries have difficulty naming, 5. 28; verses on, 4. 289–91, 295, 305, 454; verses on, by Mme du Deffand, 4. 290, 5. 39
Tonnelier, Le. See Le Tonnelier
Tonnerre, Maréchal de. See Clermont-Tonnerre, Gaspard de
Tonnerre, M. de. See Clermont-Tonnerre, Charles-Henri-Jules, Comte de
Tonnerre (France):
Éon ordered to go to, 6. 474

Tonsilitis:
occurrences of, 6. 299
Tonson, Jacob (ca 1656–1736), printer:
grandnephews of, 15. 57n, 20. 165n
Kit-Cat portraits commissioned by, 42. 249n
Tonson, Jacob jr (d. 1767), *or* Richard (d. 1772), M.P.; booksellers:
Ashton's books sold by, 20. 165
Baskerville threatened by, 40. 275n
HW gets paper from, for printing, 40. 117
HW meets, at Onslow's, 20. 165
Percy asked by, to edit Wyatt and Surrey, 41. 320n
——'s Surrey and Buckingham editions unfinished at death of, 42. 366
printer for HW found by, 15. 57
SH Press's opening attended by, 35. 98
Tonson (formerly Hull), William (1724–87), cr. (1783) Bn Riverdale; Irish M.P.:
peerage of, 25. 433
Tonsure:
abbé receives, 17. 62
Tontine:
ball to be named, 36. 232
proposed as means of raising money for Ireland, 32. 161
'Tonton' (1773–89), Mme du Deffand's (later HW's) black spaniel:
affection of, for Mme du Deffand, 5. 426, 6. 67, 98, 135, 206, 238, 240, 243, 253, 259, 376, 447, 449
as despotic at SH as at St Joseph's convent, 39. 370
Barrymore, Lady, attacked by, 30. 265, 39. 258
Bauffremont gives, to Mme du Deffand, 5. 422
bites no more, 7. 253
bites seldom, 36. 205
bons mots of, HW might compile, 33. 385
Boufflers's verses on, 7. 2
charade on, 35. 525, 526
Crabbe's comment on dogs true of, 33. 288
death of, 12. 265, 34. 45
'Druid' to receive compliments of, 35. 523
Du Deffand, Mme, bequeaths, to HW, 2. 251n, 29. 145
—— envies, 7. 235
—— hopes that HW will see, 6. 72
—— infuriates, by raging at her cook, 39. 269
—— irritated by, 6. 74, 83–4
—— names, 5. 425
—— reduced to society of, 6. 353, 367, 476
——'s affection for: 5. 428, 433, 6. 2, 30, 67, 83–4, 103, 135, 167, 194, 206, 238, 253, 334, 376, 401, 410, 430, 447, 7. 174, 235; HW comments on, 6. 410
——'s greatest pleasure, 6. 190
——'s servants like, 6. 98
——'s verses to, 6. 103
enemies of, 6. 447
English not understood by, 39. 370
faults of, 6. 447
friends of, 6. 447

gold snuff-box, with portrait of, left by Mme du Deffand to HW, 33. 235
grows fat, 6. 295
HW almost knocked down by, 33. 375
HW asks for, to be sent to him, 33. 235
HW insists on confinement of, after 5 P.M., 39. 258
HW no better informed than, 29. 288
HW receives, from France, 2. 270, 271, 39. 367, 370
HW's cat exiled by, 39. 370
HW's devotion to, 36. 202
HW's dog attacked and bitten by, 39. 370
HW shares bed with, at SH, 39. 420
HW's only remaining link with France, 29. 306
HW takes the air with, 29. 356
HW to meet, 6. 212, 215
HW to take, after Mme du Deffand's death, 6. 2, 5, 7. 201, 11. 13n, 29. 145
HW will not take, to Ampthill, 33. 281
HW wishes to have, 36. 190
health and spirits of, 36. 242
health of, 6. 233, 238, 240
invited to attend HW, 33. 285
jealous, 6. 98, 103
La Harpe's verses on, 7. 2, 8
naughty only when near Mme du Deffand, 7. 253
Necker astonished at not being bitten by, 8. 213
Ossory, Lord, bitten by, 33. 464
pismires deluged by, 33. 367
portrait of, on snuff-box: 36. 182, 43. 105; given to Mme du Deffand, 7. 2, 201; left to HW by Mme du Deffand, 7. 201, 8. 26, 33. 235
Selwyn calls, 'god-dog' of Berrys' 'Tonton,' 11. 13
shows HW's vulnerability to bribery, 33. 277
sleeps on Mme du Deffand's arm, 7. 118
sleeps well, 6. 447
Sophia, Ps, invites, to Pavilions, 33. 276–7
Straffords' lambs to receive regards of, 35. 368
vomits objects, 6. 323
Walpole, Hon. T., to take, to HW, 7. 253
Walpole, Thomas jr, delivers, to HW, 36. 196
Wiart to be told about, 36. 207
'wife' desired by, 6. 177, 206, 278
'wife' escapes from, 6. 201
'Tonton,' Berry family's dog:
beard of, 11. 29
good-tempered and quiet, 11. 50
HW describes, 11. 13
HW mentions, 11. 18
HW pampers, 11. 51
left in HW's care, 11. 13n
nose of, long, 11. 13, 29, 50
prefers footboy to HW, 11. 50–1
strawberries liked by, 11. 29
Tonyn, ——, gov. of Florida:
Clinton's letter from, about d'Estaing, 24. 544n

Tooanahowi ('Tooanohowy'), Cherokee Indian 'prince':
  HW calls Young Pretender, 30. 94
Tooke, Rev. John Horne (1736–1812), M.P.; politician and philologist:
  arrested, 12. 119n
  dines at Shakespeare Tavern, 11. 319n
  election petition of, fails, 11. 194
  Fox, C. J., and Hood oppose, in Westminster election, 39. 472n
  HW calls, 'philosophizing serpent,' 31. 373
  hissed at Bastille Day celebration, at Crown and Anchor, 11. 89n, 35. 399n
  House of Commons accuses, of attacking Norton, 23. 555–6
  Kennedy's pardon opposed by, 30. 254n
  Lansdowne suspected of connection with, 11. 78
  London apt to produce, 11. 208
  nobility condemned by, 11. 78
  Norton, Sir Fletcher, attacked by, 28. 135n
  Onslow's suit against, 35. 553n
  unlikely to give England better representatives, 15. 131
  Wilkes defeats, 23. 314
  —— quarrels with, 23. 263, 274, 31. 151
  —— triumphs over, 32. 52
Tooke, William (d. 1802):
  involved in law suit, 28. 135n
Tool; tools. See Burglar's tools; Chisels
Toole. See O'Toole
Tooley Park:
  Clopton of, 12. 201n
Tooley St, Southwark:
  fire in, 25. 577n
Tootel, Hugh. See Dodd, Charles
Tooth; teeth:
  Ailesbury, Cts of, jokes about pulling out Mme Mingotti's, 37. 477
  alum for, 10. 276, 39. 106
  artificial, 18. 289n
  bells used, to soothe cutting of, 30. 308
  black, 24. 295, 35. 300
  Catherine Parr's, perfect, 42. 113
  Churchill loses, 17. 271
  Chute loses, 10. 204
  Clement XIV's, fall out, 24. 43
  Conway's, fine, 37. 261
  Craon, Princesse de, loses, 6. 213
  Desmond, Cts of, cuts, three times, 40. 112n
  false, 18. 289
  gnashing of, 37. 67
  Goldsworthy, Maria Carolina, to cut, 17. 351
  Gondi, Mme, loses, 18. 86–7
  Grosvenor, Ann, preserves, 10. 276
  HW has lost all, 35. 352
  HW's, well-preserved, 34. 55–6
  HW uses alum to prevent loss of, 10. 276
  man draws out, and puts them in again, 20. 291–2
  Montagu loses, 10. 275
  Newcastle, D. of, loses, 9. 363

  Nivernais picks, at embarrassing moment, 22. 83n
  Norton's, pulled, 25. 40
  of Gévaudan beast, 39. 14
  Oglethorpe's, gone, 25. 570
  Richards may safely clean, 39. 261
  roots for, 39. 267–8
  sacred, listed, 37. 320
  Salimbeni loses, 17. 116
  ——'s, fast again, 17. 132
  Selwyn loses, 9. 52
  transplanting of, 18. 324
  Turk, Martha, has, black, 24. 295
  William Frederick, P., cuts, 24. 315
  See also Dentistry; HW: health of
Toothache:
  gout sounds as harmless as, 39. 162
  HW jokes about, 30. 55
  Macaronies fear, 38. 401
  occurrences of, 18. 324, 20. 87, 33. 286
  Vorontsov, Mme, pretends to have, 21. 248
Tooth-cutting:
  children's complaint, 17. 351, 42. 412
Toothdrawer. See Lodomie, ——
Toothpick; toothpicks:
  HW's gift of plants resembles, 9. 180
  use of, introduced from Spain, 33. 246
Toothpick case, cases:
  at Elizabeth Chudleigh's, 9. 277
  'boat no bigger than,' 33. 47
  HW does not want, from Ireland, 9. 398
  new ones, not available in Paris, 32. 54
Tooth powder:
  HW sends, to Mme du Deffand, 5. 387
  Lodomie's dispute about, 37. 355
Tooting, Surrey:
  Thrale's villa near, 11. 106n
Topaja, Villa della:
  Craon to take Mann, Chute, and Whithed to, 17. 443
Topaz; topazes:
  George II gives, to maids of honour, 20. 112
  Mann has seal cut on, for Rowley, 19. 9
  ring sent to Robert Child, 32. 361
Topham, Edward (1751–1820), journalist; engraver; editor of The World:
  epilogue by, 33. 369n
  HW jokes about Hannah More's quoting, 31. 268
  More, Hannah, criticizes style of, 31. 265
  prints by, 1. 210, 212, 213, 216
Topham, John (1746–1803), antiquary:
  Description of an Antient Picture in Windsor Castle, A, by, 2. 308
Toplin, ——, George III's footman:
  George III aided by, 34. 11n
Topographer; topographers:
  HW's low opinion of, 16. 25
Toppaia. See Topaja
Torbay, Devon:
  Arbuthnot to join convoy at, 39. 320
  Brest fleet near, 18. 398, 407
  Darby reported at, 25. 186

[Torbay, Devon, *continued*]
—— returns to, 25. 182
——'s fleet at, 29. 151
HW dreams French land at, 33. 338
Hardy's fleet at, 24. 500
Howe's inactivity at, 12. 18, 24
Martinique ships at, 33. 209
Norris reaches, 13. 226n
——'s squadron unable to sail from, 13. 230
Torbay, English ship:
Conflans's alleged letter to St-Florentin attributed to officer of, 21. 356n
Norris obtains court martial aboard, 19. 55n
Torch; torches:
at George II's funeral, 9. 321-2
Bentley depicts light of, well, 35. 243
Florentines use, to watch floods, 19. 131
footmen bear, 37. 288
Neapolitan cardinals forbidden by Spain to light, for Francis I's election, 19. 183
priests carry, at Electress's funeral, 18. 173
wax: Lorenzi illuminates windows with, 19. 14; Neapolitans told to use, in carrying out San Gennaro, 24. 541; Old Pretender does not use, to celebrate Francis I's election, 19. 184
Torchi, Angiolo, Neapolitan composer:
Rubinelli's part in *Virginia* composed by, 25. 646n
Torcy, Comtesse de (d. 1777):
(?) social relations of, in Paris, with Contessa di Viry, 7. 350
Torcy, Marquis de. *See* Colbert, Jean-Baptiste (1685-1746)
Torcy, Marquis de (d. 1788):
(?) social relations of, in Paris, 7. 332, 350
Torcy:
bloodstone, 35. 86
Torfæus, Thormodus (Thormador Torfason) (1636-1719), antiquary:
Scotland lacks, 16. 379
Torgau (Prussia):
battle of, 9. 323, 21. 452, 456, 459, 463
Daun defeated at, 9. 323n
Frederick II dismisses Stormont at, 21. 2n
Tories. *See* Tory; Tories
Tornabuoni, Via de', at Florence:
Corsi house in, 17. 122n, 137n
Palazzo Viviani in, 17. 137n
Strozzi palace in, 17. 316n
Tornaquinci, Abate Giovanni Antonio (1680-1764), Tuscan secretary of state:
aged 80 and very weak, 21. 62
childish from old age, 21. 107
custom house to be ordered by, to release HW's picture, 17. *162*
Electress leaves annuity to, 18. 169
Francis I's letter from, omits vowels, 21. 62, 85
health of, put to bed and bled, 21. 62
incapable of business, 21. 84-5
Mann asks, about Silva's authority, 17. 180

—— hears from, about Leghorn earthquake, 17. 293
—— presents Antinori with memorial in absence of, 20. 276n
—— protests to, about *Oxford's* quarantine, 18. 309n
—— receives apologies from, for letter, 20. 146
——'s correspondence with, about Wright, 21. 20n
——'s dispute with, over citizenship of English at Leghorn, 20. 266-7
office of, 17. 57
Pucci writes to, of English earthquake, 20. 143
Regency member, 17. 162n, 21. 107n
Richecourt dictates letter to, calling British merchants at Leghorn subjects of Francis I, 20. 267n
—— forces, to write severe letters to Mann, 20. 146
—— formerly abused by, to Mann, 20. 267
——'s opposition to Mann discussed by, with Rinuccini and Braitwitz, 18. 10
secretary of state and third of Regency, 21. 62
valet-de-chambre of, used to get ten-paul-pieces for issuing passports, 21. 482
Vienna neglects, 21. 107
Torporley. *See* Tarporley
Torre, La. *See* La Torre
Torre, ——, merchant in Paris:
Bassan's account of, 6. 269
(?) —— suggests sending portrait by, 20. 245
Torre di Mezza Via (Italy):
camp at, 18. 531
Torreggiani, Marchesa. *See* Capponi, Maria Settimia
Torreggiani *or* Torriggiani, Luca (d. 1770), Marchese:
marriage of, 19. 506
Torreggiani, Luigi Maria (1697-1777), cardinal, 1753:
Almada's paper attacks, 21. 423
book burnt by order of, 21. 476-7
Bourbon Courts would exclude, from Papal councils, 23. 16
Clement XIII aided by, against anti-Jesuit champions, 21. 475
—— summons, to advisory congregation, 21. 308n
congregation orders, to bid prelates pay no royal honours to Young Pretender, 22. 392
Corsini subject of complaints of, to Clement XIII, 21. 425
courier from Lisbon expected by, 21. 430
dying, 20. *463*
epitaph for, 21. 436-7
foreign courts offended by, 23. 119
French, Neapolitan, and Spanish ministers refuse to negotiate through, 23. 35
Jesuits befriended by, 21. 436
—— threaten to withdraw pension from, if he does not make Clement XIII yield, 21. 425

José I's brief from, given to Almada at Aix, **21**. 340n

plot allegedly instigated by, with Acciaioli and bastard brothers, against Portuguese king, **21**. 475

Portuguese king offended by, **21**. 348, 425

Portuguese rupture with, permanent, **21**. 437

St-Odile refuses to wait in ante-chamber of, **22**. 573

York, Cardinal, receives billet from, **22**. 388, 391

Torreggiani. *See also* Torrigiani

Torres y Morales, Rodrigo (ca 1687–1755), Adm.; Marqués de Matallana:

Cartagena abandoned by, with fleet and treasure, on Vernon's approach, **17**. 71

Havana reached by, with ships and treasure, **17**. 71n

treasure said to have been taken by, to Cadiz, **17**. 83

Torri, Flaminio (1621–61), painter:

Guido's pupil, **17**. 268, **18**. 214

intaglios, made by, **17**. 268n

'Magdalen' by: Chute likes, **17**. 268; companion to Guido's head, **17**. 241, **18**. 214; Penny sends, to Mann for HW, **17**. 268

paintings by, sold by Francis III to K. of Poland, **19**. 314n

Torriano, Lady. *See* Mann, Eleanor (d. 1789)

Torriano, Sir John (d. 1778), Kt, 1755:

caveat entered by, against James Mann's will, **22**. *240*, 241–2, 245, 247, **24**. 271

father-in-law excludes, **23**. 51, 112

Mann family quarrels with, **22**. 245

wife of, **22**. 242n

Torrigiani *or* Torrigiano, Pietro (1472–1528), sculptor:

busts attributed to, **2**. 174, 177

Gray sends name of, to HW, **14**. 117

Henry VII's tomb executed by, **2**. 174

identification of, **43**. 47

name of, corrected, **43**. 184

religion of, **1**. 81

Torrigiano. *See also* Torreggiani; Torrigiani

Törring-Jettenbach, Ignatius Felix Joseph (ca 1679–1763), Graf von; Gen.:

capture of, rumoured, **17**. 289

relief force of, dispersed, **17**. 289

Torrington, Vct. *See* Byng, Sir George (1664–1733); Byng, George (1740–1812); Byng, John (1743–1813); Byng, Pattee (1699–1747)

Torrington, Vcts. *See* Boyle, Lady Lucy (1744–92); Forrest, Bridget (d. 1823)

Torso:

Gaddi's, in Uffizi gallery, **25**. 170

Tort de la Sonde, Barthélemy (1738–1818), Guines's secretary:

(?) Du Deffand, Mme, to send furniture by, **5**. 139, 148

Guines, Duc de, sued by, **6**. 24n, 142n, **8**. 200, **24**. 90n, 100

—— writes *Mémoire* against, **30**. 264n

mémoires of, suppressed, **8**. 200

Premier mémoire contre le Comte de Guines by, **6**. 160, 175

second mémoire by, **6**. 168, 173, 179, 181

sentenced, **6**. 196, 200, **8**. 200

(?) third mémoire by, **6**. 183

Tortoise:

Cumberland, D. of, compared with, **20**. 121

HW as nimble as, **36**. 282

HW walks like, **35**. 366

Tortoise-shell:

armoires decorated with, **31**. 80

case of, **35**. 429–30

snuff-boxes of, **25**. 501, **30**. 219, **31**. 146n

Tortola (British West Indies):

lands in, claimed by Mann family: Allet tells Mann about, **24**. 168, 200, 220; Duane and Hull seek new grant for, **24**. 200; HW never heard of, **24**. 176; Mann, Edward, had grant of, **24**. 168, 199–200; Mann, Edward Louisa, had no right to alienate, from family, **24**. 173; Mann, Edward Louisa, inherits, from Edward Mann, **24**. 173; Mann, Edward Louisa, leaves, to Mary Mann, **24**. 168, 202; Mann, Horace II, consults Duane about, **24**. 181; Mann, Mary, applies for grant of, **24**. 264; probably worthless during American Revolution, **24**. 206–7; revert to the Crown, **24**. 202, 206, 264; visitor to, tells Mann of value of, **24**. 169, 200

Tortona ('Tortonne'), Italy:

besiegers set fire to parts of, **19**. 100

Charles Emmanuel III insists on evacuation of, **19**. 279

—— to besiege, **19**. 262n

Gages approaches, **19**. 41, 84, 292

Genoese galleys try to supply provisions for, **19**. 344

HW and Gray at, **13**. 192n

La Mina abandons, **19**. 292n

siege of: Charles Emmanuel III does not raise, **19**. 100; French and Spaniards may begin, **19**. 36, 75, 84; Maillebois announces, **19**. 89

Spaniards may retire to, **19**. 267

surrender of, **19**. 78n, 100

Torture:

Corsican patriots racked on the wheel by the French, **23**. 148

Damiens subjected to, **21**. 59, 79–80, **22**. 147

French army officers at Metz broken upon wheel, **21**. 382–3

Portuguese, **21**. 267n

use of, in Scotland, **16**. 376

Tortworth Court, Ducie's seat:

(?) HW hoped to visit, **30**. 150

'Tory,' HW's black spaniel:

HW at Houghton swallowed up like, **37**. 178

HW laments absence of, on travels, **37**. 49

ode on death of, **1**. 379

wolf devours, in Alps, **13**. 189–90, 196, **17**. 257, **37**. 43, 47

Tory; Tories (English):

adherents gained by, in Parliament, **19**. 4

administrations of, disgrace the country, **2**. 84

'afraid of their own success,' **29**. 23

[Tory; Tories (English), *continued*]

Akenside and Dyson become, **35.** 566n

appointed to the Admiralty, **17.** 356, 363, 366

Argyll pleases, **17.** 366

army increases opposed by, in Parliament, **17.** 410

at Cambridge, **13.** 58

at Oxford, deplore rumoured peerages as removing property-holders from Commons, **38.** 159

Beaufort's defection may affect, **23.** 174

Berkeley, Norborne, is, **21.** 460

Blenheim altered the situation of, **40.** 12

consistency of, **35.** 561

Country Girl, The, mentions, **17.** 24

country squires of, defeat land tax, **22.** 489

Court aided by clergy and, to infatuate England, **24.** 491

——'s partiality to, **38.** 200

Dalrymple thinks every public man of, deserves hanging, **35.** 555

Deerhurst betrayed by, **17.** 211

defection of, from Court, temporary, **29.** 27, 29, 39

defenders of James II's expulsion denounced by, on principle, **35.** 613

Denbigh is, **20.** 409n

Egmont not forgiven by, for desertion, **20.** 32

English invasion of Flanders 'laid down' to please, **37.** 553

Fazackerley is, **22.** 42

Fox, C. J., might by violence provoke, against himself and North, **25.** 379

Fox, Henry, and Pitt hated by, **20.** 510

Fox, Henry, not surprised that Grenville ministry is supported by, **30.** 189

—— will alienate, **22.** 93

Frederick, P. of Wales, leagued with, **20.** 3

George II rejects, **17.** 363, 365

George III appoints, to Bedchamber, **21.** 460, 460n, 465n

Gower treated with deference by, **18.** 141

Grenville rather than Bute supported by, **30.** 187

HW and Ps Amelia discuss, **10.** 49–50

HW describes differences between Whigs and, **28.** 411–12

HW impartial towards, **15.** 94

HW is, in friendship, **35.** 490

HW's verses mention, **31.** 15

Haddock would anger, if he let Spanish fleet escape, **17.** 219

Hanoverian troops not discussed by, in House of Lords, **18.** 141

Huber's views are, **35.** 583

indoctrination by, **42.** 403

in House of Commons, **19.** 4

in Oxfordshire election voting, **35.** 192

insolence of, **35.** 496

investigation of Port Mahon's capture languidly pursued by, for fear of uniting D. of Newcastle and Henry Fox, **21.** 56

Labour in Vain mentions, **18.** 20

ladies indicate preference for, by patching, **16.** 258

Letter from Cocoa Tree to make rift between Opposition and, **22.** 102n

Mathews opposed by, in Mediterranean investigation, for opposition to them in Monmouthshire election, **19.** 33

meeting of, at Horn Tavern, votes against Parliamentary report, **35.** 215–16

Middleton leaves, **15.** 292

Minorcan investigation to be used by, against ministry, **21.** 77

Morton's motion inspired by Bute and, **22.** 299n

national interests neglected by, for private faction, **35.** 215

Newcastle, D. of, gives positions to, **9.** 329

——'s court abuses, **9.** 329

Newdigate attended by, in Grosvenor Sq., on way to Brentford election, **18.** 25

new Opposition not liked by, **19.** 370

newspaper of, **18.** 33

Norfolk, do not sign petitions, **33.** 166

Northey is, **21.** 460

North followed by, against Shelburne, **25.** 379

——'s conciliatory bills shame, **28.** 359

not reconciled to House of Hanover in time of George II, **29.** 22

old-fashioned, preferable to modern Whigs, **35.** 604

opposition from: expected, **18.** 564; in Parliament, **19.** 202

Opposition joined by several, **28.** 350

—— made destruction of, fundamental point, **30.** 190

——'s triumph must surmount attacks from, **35.** 617

Oxfordshire and Staffordshire the strongholds of, **33.** 347

Parliamentary voting avoided by, **18.** 383, **25.** 19

Patriots join, in opposition to Sir Robert Walpole, **17.** 231n

Pelham must bring in, **18.** 537

—— neglects Whigs to court, **13.** 19

Pitt (Chatham) abandoned by, in demand for review of Spanish negotiations, **21.** 553

—— promises, that he will shun House of Commons, **22.** 101n

—— rejects exclusion of, **22.** 102n

—— supported by, in attempt to oust Hessian troops, **21.** 33–4

—— supports safety of, under Grenville ministry, **30.** 190

Pitt, George, is, **21.** 460

positions refused by, **18.** 550

Pownall thinks, represent England's Norman heritage, **42.** 78n

preferment of, may upset government, **21.** 465

prerogative supported by, **24.** 492

Prowse leads, **20.** 32

public measures not opposed by, **17.** 390

Pulteney pretends to join, **18**. 49
rancour of, hoodwinks English people, **24**. 491
Regency Bill's modification to include Ps of Wales might be sought by, **38**. 548
revolution of 1688 represented by, as unique, **39**. 395
Rosseter is, **32**. 40n
royal prerogative would speak only to, **38**. 200
Sandys acts with, **17**. 250n
—— opposed by, in election, **17**. 250n
Somers humoured, to preserve 1688 settlement, **35**. 613–14
Strange usually votes with, **20**. 32
subsidiary treaties opposed by, in House of Commons, **20**. 300
Thanet, 7th E. of, was, while M.P. for Appleby, **20**. 435n
Thomson celebrates Whigs' triumph over, **16**. 379
too contemptible to hold office, **22**. 295
treachery of, to Lord Holland, **29**. 30
Wales, Ps of, suggested by, as Regency member, **22**. 299
Walpole, Sir Robert, not to be persecuted by, **17**. 336
—— opposed by, **37**. 90
—— resented by, **17**. 363
——'s accident 'comes of dining' with, **18**. 277n
Whigs and, succeeded by new parties, **38**. 140–1
Whigs contend with, **38**. 417
—— may detain Hessian troops to thwart, **21**. 33–4
—— say, no longer exist, **17**. 337, 363
William III betrayed by, **28**. 387
Williams, Sir C. H., disliked by, **30**. 312
Wray supported by, at Westminster election, **36**. 231n
Tory; Tories, American (loyalists):
Carlisle, E. of, disapproves of sacrifice of, at peace treaty, **25**. 365
Cornwallis's surrender terms said to protect, **25**. 211
English invasion of Carolina might be aided by, **24**. 157–8
Toscanella, Orazio:
Dictionarium Latinum et Italicum by, owned by HW, **20**. 196n
Toscanelli, Francesco Antonio:
Dissertatio super controversiis . . . Cybo, by, **17**. 34
Tosh, Isabella, m. George Jamesone:
husband provides for, in will, **40**. 285
husband's portrait of, **40**. 266
Tosier. See Tozier
To the Author of a Libel:
HW binds, in volume of tracts, **20**. 65n
'To the Earl of Bath.' See under Williams, Sir Charles Hanbury
'To the Fountain Blandusia.' See under West, Richard

'To the Honourable Horace Walpole.' See under Berry, Mary
'To the Printingpress at Strawberry hill.' See under Bentley, Richard (1708–82)
Tothill, Robert (d. 1753):
Chatham sued by, **8**. 162
will of, **3**. 64n
Tothill, William Daw:
(?) 'petit garçon de quinze ans,' **3**. 64
Tothill Fields Bridewell:
Mason, confectioner, committed to, **16**. 204n
Totila (d. 552), K. of the Ostrogoths:
Jackson's prints seem coeval with, **20**. 381
Totnes:
mayor of, forwards to Sir Robert Walpole a letter from Frederick, P. of Wales, recommending candidate, **17**. 299
Wills's death necessitates by-election at, **17**. 299n
Totness, E. of. See Carew, Sir George (1555–1629)
Toto, Anthony. See Del Nunziata, Antonio
Tottel's Miscellany:
lyric in, **28**. 191n
Tottenham, Middlesex:
London dies at, **2**. 200n
Townsend returns to Bruce Castle at, **23**. 346n
Tottenham Court Road, London:
Langlois of, **10**. 207n
Tottington, Norfolk:
Norton attacked for enclosing lands at, **23**. 555n
Tottleben, Gottlob Kurt Heinrich, Graf; Gen. in Russian service:
Berlin menaced by, **21**. 441n
Touche, La. See Gervaise de la Touche
Touchet, ——, baigneur at Paris:
Joseph II to have lodged with, **6**. 435
Touchet, ——, 'broken' London merchant:
Holland shown by, the Ds of Gloucester's letter, **36**. 71
Touchet, 'young Mr':
HW's social relations with, in Paris, **7**. 327
Touillet. See Trouillet
Toulmin, Messrs:
SH visited by, **12**. 222
Toulon (France):
armament of, supposedly to aid Spain against Algiers, **24**. 179
Belle-Isle plans to attack Port Mahon from, **20**. 528n
Bompar, Comte de, commander at, **21**. 297n
Boscawen might be forbidden to bombard, **21**. 302
——s fleet cruises near, **21**. 297
—— writes from Namur, off, **21**. 307n
capture of, unlikely, **19**. 358
Catalonian troops to embark at, **18**. 93n
Clement XIV's ship takes D. of Cumberland to, **23**. 566
convoy of, escapes, **19**. 277
Corsica well situated to overlook, **21**. 37

[Toulon (France), *continued*]

Cumberland, D. and Ds of, visit, **23.** 566n

Elliot, Sir Gilbert, appointed civil commissioner of, **12.** 19

Elphinstone's victory at, over French, **12.** 7, **39.** 504n, 505

English capture French fleet at, **12.** 8, 89

English fleet should have blocked the French at, **20.** 564–5

English invasion might threaten, **21.** 223

fleet of: **28.** 460n; alarms HW for Mann's safety, **18.** 384; blown back, **24.** 383; Boscawen demolishes, **21.** 326; Boscawen may engage in battle, **21.** 318; Boscawen to bottle up, **21.** 292; Court commands, **18.** 370n; destination of, **33.** 8; England said to be destination of, **21.** 328; English fleet should have destroyed, **20.** 564; English preparations against, **23.** 478; estimated, **17.** 286, **18.** 396; France alarmed lest Byron and Howe encircle, **24.** 394; gets no treasure, **17.** 36; Gibraltar straits not yet passed by, **33.** 9–10; goes to America, **24.** 386; Hawke watches, **20.** 583; Mann surprised to see himself quoted on sailing of, **24.** 380; Mathews said to have injured, **18.** 402, 403; may be bound for Minorca, **24.** 375, 380–1; may have gone to America to attack Howe, **24.** 381; may intercept ship to Leghorn, **22.** 88; may try to reach West Indies, **21.** 318; Philip, Don, may be accompanied by, **17.** 215; preparation of, **20.** 540–1, 545, 558, **21.** 263–4, **23.** 261; prepares to attack Russian fleet, **23.** 474; reaches Barcelona, **17.** 190; recalled, **5.** 349; returns, **17.** 46, **20.** 581; said to have sailed, **24.** 376; Saunders pursues, from Malta towards the Levant, **21.** 431; size of, unknown, **28.** 396; Spanish fleet joined by, **17.** 269; threatens to expel Hawke from Mediterranean, **20.** 587; to be kept in reserve instead of attacking Boscawen, **21.** 303; to join Brest fleet, **18.** 393, 396, 404, 423; Townshend avoids, **19.** 324–5; *see also under* La Clue

France does not make war preparations at, **23.** 244

—— orders, to give provisions to English Mediterranean fleet, **20.** 513n

French and Spanish fleets at, **18.** 93

French and Spanish fleets plan Italian invasion from, **18.** 370–1

French and Spanish fleets preparing to leave, **18.** 359

French and Spanish fleets said to go to, from Spezia, **17.** 322–3

French assemble expedition at, **18.** 106

French fleet goes to, from Hyères, **17.** 309

French force English and Spanish troops from, **39.** 508n

French may try to reach Corsica from, **20.** 588

French send army against English at, **12.** 89

French transports at, **20.** 545

Fronsac brings news of St Philip's surrender, to, **20.** 572

HW not sanguine about English forces at, **12.** 88

HW visits, **13.** 11

Hood directs attack on, **12.** 50n

—— obtains surrender of, **12.** 18n, **39.** 502

La Clue naval commander at, **21.** 188n

—— reaches, **21.** 199

La Fayette detained at, **6.** 435

La Galissonnière's squadron returns to, **20.** 587n

Lage's fleet at, **19.** 253

Lauzun ordered to await Chauvelin at, **4.** 135

letters from, received at Leghorn, **24.** 461

Mathews approaches, **18.** 447

—— bottles up French fleet at, **18.** 15

—— may attack Court at, **18.** 443

—— threatens, **18.** 463

Medley leaves ships near, **19.** 334

Mirepoix's letters from, **21.** 141

Neapolitan troops heroic at, **12.** 53

Noel goes to, to spy on French, **20.** 536

O'Hara to command at, **12.** 7, 18, 57, 67, 158n

Osborne's fleet menaces, **21.** 135

plague at, **18.** 271n

Richelieu at, **20.** 576n

royalists march to, **12.** 40n

safety of, reported, **12.** 42, 49

second squadron sails from, **24.** 397

Spanish vessels at, commanded by Navarro, **18.** 371n

Stormont to visit, **23.** 25

Townshend may command squadron off, **19.** 376

trade at, interrupted, **21.** 123

Toulon, Battle of:

account of, **18.** 410n

Mathews's fleet at, **18.** 396n

Norris, Capt., absconds after, **17.** 471n

Toulongeon, Comte de. *See* Chavignard, Anne-Théodore

Toulongeon, Marquise de. *See* Aubigné, Marie-Joséphine-Marguerite de

Toulouse, Abp of. *See* Loménie de Brienne, Étienne-Charles de

Toulouse, Comte de. *See* Raymond VI

Toulouse, Comtesse de. *See* Noailles, Marie-Victoire-Sophie de

Toulouse (France):

Fitzjames governor at, **38.** 271

—— recalled from, **38.** 301

HW calls, theatre of fanaticism, and compares it to Bristol, **31.** 276–7

insurrection at, over militia levy, **39.** 66

vicar-general of, **6.** 222n

visitors to: Buccleuch, **31.** 79n, **38.** 337; Caraman, **6.** 373; Fitzjames family, **38.** 217; HW, **13.** 11; Mann, Horace II and Lady Lucy, **24.** 239, 251; Smith, Adam, **31.** 79n

Toulouse, Hôtel de, in Place des Victoires, Paris:

Forcalquier, Mme de, staying at, **3**. 114
HW visits, **7**. 302
Toulouse, parliament of:
Aiguillon menaced by arrêts from, **4**. 449n
Aix parliament upholds, **38**. 301
Beauvau thought to be improper person to suppress, **23**. 321–2
Fitzjames imprisons members of, for refusing to register edicts, **38**. 300
——'s arrest ordered by, **38**. 271, 301–3
Mirepoix, Bp of, to attend, **6**. 304, 374
reformed, **5**. 106
Toulouse, Abp of, to attend, **6**. 374
Toundrow, Thomas, of Twickenham:
(?) SH visited by, **12**. 235
Tounson, Robert:
Customs place granted to, **26**. 52
Tounson. *See also* Townson
Toupée *or* toupet:
Charlotte, Q., refuses to curl, **21**. 528, **38**. 116
French fashion for, **39**. 271
gray, elderly soldiers cover, with helmets, **9**. 269
Tour, La. *See* La Tour; Serres de la Tour
Touraine, D. of. *See* Douglas, Archibald (ca 1370–1424)
Tour and Taxis. *See* La Tour and Taxis
Tourette. *See* Toinette
Tour from Downing to Alston-Moor, A. See under Pennant, Thomas
Tourier; touriers:
Court preceded by, with baggage, **23**. 108
Tour in North Wales. See under Pennant, Thomas
Tournai (Flanders):
Agincourt and Crécy incongruous with, **37**. 200
Austrian soldiers captured at, later killed, **34**. 141n
Austrians retreat towards, **15**. 227–8n
battle of, since called battle of Fontenoy, **19**. 42n
citadel of: holds out, **36**. 13; surrenders, **37**. 199
Conway and Scott visit, **39**. 536
Dutch engineer at, defects to French, **37**. 201
English capture, **19**. 52, **37**. 194
English march on, planned, **18**. 500n
French besiege, **19**. 39
French capture, **19**. 61
governor of, *see* Dorth
spelling of, corrected, **43**. 359
Tournai, Battle of. *See* Fontenoy, Battle of
Tournament; tournaments:
England celebrates with, **20**. 71
Florence plans, for Maria Josefa, **22**. 525
HW to dream about, **35**. 421
of bears, at Hanover, **20**. 20
Surrey's, at Florence, **42**. 421
Temple not fond of, **21**. 346
Tournay, Rev. Thomas (d. 1795), of Yate, Glos:
(?) SH visited by, **12**. 236

Tournay, Flanders. *See* Tournai
Tournelle, La. *See* La Tournelle
Tournemine, La. *See* La Tournemine
Tourneur, Le. *See* Le Tourneur
Tournon, Louis-François-Paul (d. 1787), Vicomte de:
death of, reported, **7**. 436
Tournon, Rose-Marie-Hélène de (ca 1757–82), m. 1 (1773) Jean-Baptiste (called Vicomte Adolphe) du Barry; m. 2 (1782) Jean-Baptiste-Marc-Antoine de Tournon, Marquis de Claveyson:
beauty of, admired at ball, **5**. 425
brother of, dies, **7**. 436
Châteauroux, Duchesse de, said to resemble, **5**. 386
Damer, Mrs, accompanied by, to England, **7**. 184
—— meets, at Spa, **33**. 71n
—— said to accompany, **7**. 88
family of, **5**. 374
husband of, **5**. 147n
Louis XVI banishes, **6**. 52
marriage of, **5**. 374, 376, 378, 381, 382
Paris visited by, **7**. 88
Rueil visited by, **6**. 48
St-Joseph's convent to be occupied by, **7**. 184, 434
social relations of, with Mme du Deffand, **7**. (?) 434, 435, 439, 443
Tournon, Rue de, in Paris:
Tréville, Hôtel de, in, **6**. 440n
Tourreil, Jacques de (1656–1715), classical scholar:
(?) *Œuvres* by, owned by Mme du Deffand, **8**. 35
preface by, to translation of Demosthenes, **16**. 370
Tours, Abp of. *See* Boisgelin de Cucé, Jean-de-Dieu-Raymond de (1732–1804); Conzié, Joachim-François-Mamert de (1736–95); Du Chilleau, Jean-Baptiste (1735–1824); Rosset de Ceilhes de Fleury, Henri-Marie-Bernardin de (1718–81)
Tours (France):
Aiguillon's country seat near, **4**. 253n
Barthélemy praises bridge at, **8**. 201
Du Deffand, Mme, buys dress of silk from, **7**. 446
Helisberg, Mlle, dies near, **11**. 218n
Hertford's son ill at, **38**. 246
Joseph II visits, **6**. 453, **8**. 201
Marmoutier near, **5**. 241
St Martin's Church at, scene of Margaret of Anjou's proxy marriage, **14**. 71, 72
Tour Through Normandy. See under Ducarel, Andrew Coltee
Tour Through Sicily and Malta . . . , A. See under Brydone, Patrick
Tourton et Bauer, Messrs, bankers at Paris:
Foljambe's address, **28**. 50

Tour to the East, A. See under Calvert, Frederick

Tourves, Marquis de. *See* Valbelle-Oraison, Joseph-Alphonse-Omer de

Tourville, Chevalier de. *See* Villicy, Jean-Baptiste-Nicolas-Louis de

Tous les hommes sont bons:
   verses to air of, **5.** 226

Toussaint, F. V.:
   Mœurs, Les, and *Éclaircissement sur les mœurs* by, **38.** 402, 443, 447, 451, 476, 477

Toussaint, Franz Joseph (d. 1762), Freiherr von ('All Saints'; 'All the Saints'):
   Acton, John, comes to Florence with, **20.** 99n
   bigot, **20.** 445
   Dumesnil accuses, of heresy for avoiding Mass, **19.** 491
   father-in-law of, **17.** 406
   Florence suddenly visited by, to confer with Acton and Mill, **20.** 97–8
   Francis I and Richecourt reconciled by, **17.** 235, 490
   Francis I's favourite, **17.** 189n, (?) 328, **19.** 7, **20.** 97
   Mill recommended by, **19.** 407
   ——'s scheme to destroy East India Co. quashed by, **20.** 101
   orders from, to fire on Florence in case of insurrection, **17.** 349
   Richecourt favoured by, **17.** 189n, 235, 490, **18.** 363
   Tuscany to be temporarily administered by, **21.** 107
   Uguccioni hopes for preferment through, **18.** 455, **35.** 53
   Walpole, Bns (Cts of Orford), said to court, through Richecourt, **18.** 210
   Wasner instigated by, to plead for Bns Walpole, **18.** 194

Toutsain. *See* Toussaint

Tout va cahin-caha:
   verses to air of, **7.** 214

Towcester, Northants:
   Pomfret's seat near, **9.** 122

Tower (wig):
   HW wears, **9.** 355
   Montagu wishes, **9.** 355

Tower; towers:
   at Lady Suffolk's Gothic Farm, **35.** 644
   Vyne, The, to have, **35.** 640

Tower at SH. *See under* Strawberry Hill

Tower Hill, London:
   Bethell's house next to the scaffold on, **19.** 299n
   Ferrers to be executed on, **9.** 272
   Giberne, Isaac Louis, employed on, **17.** 190n
   Mann hopes that Young Pretender will be hanged on, **18.** 421

Tower of Babel:
   Bryant's *New System* reminds HW of, **28.** 146

Tower of London:
   act of attainder against D. of Clarence found in, **15.** 171, 175, 176, **41.** 323

Argyll dreads, **7.** 360

armoury in, has (?) Q. Elizabeth's pistol, **35.** 373

artillery being assembled at, **28.** 460

Balmerinoch returns to, **9.** 38

Bastille no longer resembled by, **22.** 312

Belle-Isle might be confined in, **18.** 563

Brackenbury unlikely to have been dismissed from, for not murdering princes, **41.** 113

Burke imagines animals being loosed from, **28.** 355

—— says he deserves to be sent to, **23.** 170

Capel's letter from, **16.** 139

Carlisle, Bp of, fears Walpoles will go to, **28.** 48

chaplain of: **9.** 283; said to have slain Q. Joan's confessor, **42.** 220n; *see also* Harby, Rev. Edward (ca 1700–61); Humphreys, Rev. Cornelius

Cherbourg cannon carried to, **37.** 571

Clancarty escapes from, **19.** 160n

clock at, **2.** 334

constable of, *see* lieutenant of

Conway gets Sampson a place in, **22.** 588n, **33.** 584n

—— walks from, **39.** 348

curiosities of, **17.** 233

deputy lieutenant of, *see* Williamson, Adam

ditch at, dead dogs thrown into, **35.** 306n

Dorcas, Mrs, to spend night at, **7.** 47

Elizabeth, Q., in, **16.** 208, **33.** 111

gentleman gaoler of, *see* Fowler, Abraham

George III to be shut in, by plot, **6.** 230

Gordon, Lord George, not worthy of, but no other prison remains, **35.** 354

'governor' of, *see* lieutenant of

Granville might be sent to, under another upheaval, **19.** 213

guards at: **23.** 12n; disperse London mob, **23.** 7

guns of: celebrate d'Estaing's defeat, **24.** 545; fired for celebrations, **38.** 105n; fired for Q. Charlotte's arrival, **35.** 314n; fired for St Eustatius's capture, **36.** 192; fired for Torgau victory, **21.** 452n; HW jokes about, **9.** 222, 378; Mann expects to hear, in honour of Eliott and Howe, **25.** 340; proclaim P. Ferdinand's victory, **35.** 101

HW fears Bastille more than, **30.** 141

HW jokes about being sent to, **17.** 233

HW might be sent to, for publishing *Xo Ho*, **9.** 207

HW visits, **9.** 46

Henry VIII's codpiece in, **17.** 233

——'s statue at, **9.** 70, **17.** 233n, **38.** 379

hyena in, **34.** 62

Kelly escapes from, **19.** 153n

Lansdown and Sir Robert Walpole imprisoned in same room in, **32.** 276

Lansdown's verses at, **31.** 193–4

lieutenant and constable of, *see* Cornwallis, Charles (1700–62); Cornwallis, Charles (1738–1805)

lions and tigers whelped at, **31**. 114
lions in: **9**. 28n, **17**. 233, **22**. 135; object of curiosity to foreigners, **30**. 176; were to be loosed in Gordon riots, **33**. 197
Lion Tower in, **2**. 244n
Llywelyn's head fixed on rails of, **34**. 95
London officials may be put in, for remonstrance, **23**. 197
Lovat buried in, **19**. 386n, **37**. 267
madman sent to, instead of Moorfields, **36**. 187
M.P.s can be sent to, if House so votes, **30**. 299n
menagerie at, visited by Cts of Ailesbury, **37**. 396
Minories between Aldgate and, **9**. 112n
mobs carry Sir Robert Walpole's effigy to, **17**. 390
Murray, Sir John, examined at, **19**. 288n
'Nero,' lion in, **38**. 203
Northesk takes daughter to, **35**. 373
peers, when arrested, usually held at, **35**. 229
Pennant's account of beasts in, **34**. 122
Pitt might aspire to seize, **38**. 131
princes murdered in, **14**. 179
prisoners from *Soleil* taken to, **19**. 180n
prisoners in: Balmerinoch, Bn, **19**. 281, 282, 296, 299; Cameron, Archibald, **20**. 373n, 384; Cecil, William, **18**. 408; Cromarty, E. of, **19**. 272, 281; Crosby, Brass, **14**. 189n, **23**. 291; Derwentwater, E. of, **19**. 180–1; Edward V, **14**. 179; (?) Elizabeth, Q., **16**. 208, **33**. 111; Ferrers, E., **9**. 272, 279, 283, **21**. 374, 388, 397–9, 408; Gordon, Lord George, **2**. 224, **25**. 62, 64, 90–1, **33**. 194, **35**. 354; Howard, Lord Thomas and wife, **42**. 11n; Kelly, George, **19**. 153n; Kilmarnock, **19**. 281, 299; Kynnaird, Vct, **19**. 241; Lansdown, **32**. 276; Laurens, Henry, **25**. 91, 212, **36**. 179; Lovat, **19**. 380, 387; Marlborough, **35**. 153; Oliver, Richard, **23**. 288; Pomfret, E. of, **25**. 98, **36**. 187n; Richard, D. of York, **11**. 347, **14**. 179, **33**. 504; Sayre, **24**. 138, **28**. 227, 229; Traquair, E. of, **19**. 381n, 387; Tullibardine, M. of, **19**. 106n, 254n; Walpole, Sir Robert, **9**. 207, **22**. 26, **31**. 194, **32**. 276; Warwick, E. of, **2**. 364; Wilkes, **25**. 136, **38**. 197, 199
record at, about Windsor chapel, **40**. 220
records in, **41**. 141
Richard III unlikely to have murdered his nephews in, **41**. 113
Richard, D. of York, supposedly murdered in, **11**. 347, **14**. 179, **33**. 504
Richardson says that Sayre tried to bribe him to betray, **24**. 138
Rigby's mistake regarding time of procession's arrival at, **30**. 54
Rooke, keeper of records in, **15**. 1n
Scrope does not dread, **17**. 458
Shah-Goest placed in, **21**. 378
shut at 7, **19**. 138

Spanish treasure paraded to, **30**. 53n
Stair said to have patent from, **18**. 224
Temple refused admittance to Wilkes in, **38**. 199
Thurlow suggests that George IV and C. J. Fox be put in, **25**. 382n
tigers and hyena at, **34**. 62
tigers whelped at, **31**. 114
Tyrwhitt, Lady, presents book of prayers to Q. Elizabeth at, **16**. 208
undertaker of, *see* Allingham
(?) village near, **40**. 199
Wales, P. and Ps of, embark at, **17**. 451
Walpole, Horatio (1678–1757), may go to, **17**. 299
Walpole, Sir Robert, may go to, **17**. 233, 299
—— refuses to send Sir William Wyndham to, **23**. 289
warden's duties at, **19**. 301n
warders of, pass stable boy over to Vcts Townshend, **37**. 268
Yorke advises that Wilkes be committed to, **38**. 325
Towers, Rev. Joseph (1737–99), LL.D.; nonconformist divine:
Barrington's life by, **33**. 470n
Examination into the Nature and Evidence of the Charges Brought against Lord William Russel and Algernon Sidney, by Sir John Dalrymple, An, by, **28**. 85n
Kippis aided by, in *Biographica Britannica*, **2**. 196n
(?) SH visited by, **12**. 222
Thoughts on the Commencement of a New Parliament by, **11**. 169n
Towers, William (ca 1681–1745), D.D.; master of Christ's College, Cambridge:
Cornwallis's fellowship opposed by, **13**. 155
Tower Street, London:
Mark Lane off, **6**. 269n
Town; towns:
new, rise every day in England, **39**. 498
Town and Country Magazine:
Chatterton asks HW to send MSS to, **16**. 113, 175
——'s contribution to, **16**. 175
—— took story of HW and Mrs Clive from, **16**. 345–6
Fox, C. J., and Mlle Heinel in, **32**. 91n
'Tête-à-Tête' of HW and Mrs Clive in, **2**. 330
Town crier. *See under* Crier
Towne, John (ca 1711–91), archdeacon of Stowe:
Argument of the Divine Legation of Moses, The, by, **15**. 302
Town Eclogue, by Fitzpatrick. *See* Fitzpatrick, Hon. Richard: *Dorinda*
'Town Eclogue,' by HW:
Churchill discussed in, **30**. 289n
Vane, Lady, described in, **30**. 295n
Town Eclogues. See under Pierrepont, Lady Mary (Lady Mary Wortley Montagu)

Towneley, Charles (1737–1805), collector:
  Buchan recommends John Brown to, **15.** 189
  HW laughs at 'systematizing plan' of, **15.** 318–19
  mentioned in memorandum, **12.** 258n
  (?) SH visited by, **12.** 223
  uncle of, **33.** 407
Towneley, Francis (1709–46), Jacobite officer:
  execution of, **19.** 287n
  head of, on Temple Bar, **9.** 46
  rebels joined by, **19.** 179
Towneley, John (1697–1782), Jacobite:
  Hudibras translated into French by, **28.** 259
Towneley, John (1731–1813):
  HW's correspondence with, **31.** 204
  HW sees, at the Grove, **33.** 407–8
  HW visited by, at SH, **33.** 408
Towneley. *See also* Townley
Town hall:
  Winchester Palace resembles, **35.** 249
'Towneley, Lady'; 'Townley, Lord.' *See under*
  Cibber, Colley, *and* Vanbrugh, Sir John:
  Provok'd Husband
Townley, Sir Charles (1713–74), Garter prin-
  cipal king of arms, 1773:
  at Lenton Abbey, near Nottingham, **41.** 93
  Edmondson asks HW to forward 'table' to,
  41. 93
Townley, James (1714–78), dramatist:
  High Life Below Stairs by: acted at Ampthill
  Park, **34.** (?) 1n, 4; acted at Cassiobury
  Park, **32.** 180n; acted at Winterslow House,
  32. 176n; Selwyn's bon mot on, **31.** 14
Townley. *See also* Towneley
Town Malling, Kent:
  Nightingale dies at, **1.** 238n
Townsend, Francis (ca 1749–1819), herald:
  believes in Ireland's MSS, **15.** 321
Townsend, Isaac (ca 1685–1765), Adm.; M.P.:
  Martinique fleet defeated by, in West Indies,
  19. 186
Townsend, James (1737–87), alderman; sher-
  iff; lord mayor; M.P.:
  Bordeaux, Paris, and London visited by, **6.**
  352, 354, 355
  elected alderman, **39.** 114
  George III disrespectfully treated by, **23.** 196
  goods of, seized because he refuses to pay
  land tax, **23.** 346
  HW first meets, at Lady Shelburne's, **32.**
  153–4
  House of Commons's conduct charged by, to
  Ps of Wales's influence, **23.** 289
  London's remonstrance avowed by, **23.** 198
  memorials by, in newspapers, **23.** 339
  Middlesex election may be entered by, **32.**
  213n
  Montagu jokes about, **10.** 309
  name and dates of, corrected, **43.** 100, 137
  Oliver carried by, in London election, **39.** 196
  Opposition alderman, **35.** 334n
  Public Advertiser blames election of, as lord
  mayor, on Oliver, **23.** 441n
  social relations of, with Mme du Deffand in
  Paris, **6.** 352, 354, 355
  weavers pacified by, **23.** 163
  Wilkes contends with, for Middlesex election,
  24. 47
Townsend, Mrs James. *See* Du Plessis, Henri-
  etta Rosa Peregrina
Townsend, John (*or* James) (ca 1759–1832),
  Bow Street runner:
  conspirators against George III seized by, **12.**
  115–16
Townsend, Robert, American spy:
  Washington gets intelligence from, **33.** 239n
Townsend. *See also* Townshend
Townshend, Lady. *See* Vere, Hon. Mary (ca
  1611–69)
Townshend, Marchioness. *See* Montgomery,
  Anne (d. 1819)
Townshend, M. *See* Townshend, George (1724–
  1807)
Townshend, Vct. *See* Townshend, Charles (1675–
  1738); Townshend, Charles (1700–64); Town-
  shend, George (1724–1807)
Townshend, Vcts. *See* Compton, Lady Charlotte
  (d. 1770); Harrison, Etheldreda *or* Audrey
  (ca 1708–88); Montgomery, Anne (d. 1819);
  Walpole, Dorothy (1686–1726)
Townshend, ——:
  dances at Robinson's ball, **37.** 115
Townshend, Capt.:
  Hopson's aide-de-camp, brings dispatches, **21.**
  277n
Townshend, 'Master':
  HW has, at Bedford's house, for Coronation,
  38. 123n
Townshend, Mr:
  Foljambe's travelling-companion, **28.** 150
Townshend, Albinia (ca 1731–1808), m. (1752)
  George Brodrick, 3d Vct Midleton; Selwyn's
  niece:
  HW may have persuaded, that Fagnanis plan
  to poison Selwyn, **30.** 266
Townshend, Hon. Audrey (d. 1781), m. (after
  1756) Capt. Robert Orme:
  Conway pities, on elopement, **37.** 480
  family disapproves of marriage of, **20.** 495n
  HW should inspire passion in, for Prince
  Eszterházy, **40.** 47
  Lennox, Lord George, pursued by, **9.** 188
Townshend, Hon. Augustus (1716–46); East India capt.:
  Augusta commanded by, **19.** 277n
  captain of an Indiaman, **17.** 173
  death of, **9.** 32, **19.** 277
  HW's cousin, **13.** 3n
  imports of, from China, destroyed by fire,
  40. 45
  playthings liked by, **36.** 1
  'skipping and hollowing' before HW, **40.** 47
  Townshend, Vcts, hates, **9.** 34
  Walpole, Lady Mary, supposedly loved by,
  40. 47
  well, and wants nothing, **36.** 2

Weston, tutor to, **36**. 2n
will of, **9**. 34
Winnington's duel with, **17**. 172–3, 207, **37**. 112
Townshend, Caroline (d. 1809), m. (1759) Frederick Cornwallis, D.D., Abp of Canterbury:
dined at Onslow's and breakfasted at SH, **32**. 156
HW calls: 'Archbishopess of Canterbury,' **33**. 313; 'Madam the Metropolitan,' **32**. 156
soirées of, **11**. 217n
SH visited by, **12**. 246 *bis*
whist played by, **33**. 313
Townshend, Charles (1675–1738), 2d Vct Townshend; secretary of state; M.P.:
daughter of, **37**. 202n
George I's death reported to, **2**. 124
guards sent by, to keep crowds away from plague house in London, **25**. 423
HW receives instructions at house of, **13**. 4
HW's christening paid for by, **13**. 3n
marriage of, **25**. 423n
offer of, to pay for George I's statue, **13**. 119–20
secretary of state, **21**. 516n, **22**. 211n, **25**. 423
Selwyn in the confidence of, **13**. 14n
son's education neglected by, **19** 169
sons of, **2**. 217, **9**. 32n, **19**. 320n, **21**. 138n, 516n, **22**. 47n, 211n
sons of, accompanied by HW to Bexley, **13**. 3
Townshend, Charles (1700–64), 3d Vct Townshend; 1738; M.P.:
Bath visited by, **36**. 41n, **38**. 319, 346
Bedford's motion against Stone voted for by, **20**. 366n
death of: **22**. 211; at Raynham after Bath visit, **38**. 346; expected, **9**. 181
drinks hard with his tenants thrice weekly, **30**. 33
dying at Bath, and sends for son, **38**. 319
grandson's godfather, **37**. 550
HW would inform wife of, if death threatened, **40**. 47
housekeeper probably afraid to ask, about identity of portraits, **30**. 81
housemaid bears three children to, and inherits his money, **22**. 211
long hair worn by, **21**. 138
mistress hurries, away from family and is said to have got his money, **38**. 346
mob raised, and papers posted by, against Militia Bill, **21**. 138
not dead yet, **38**. 327
Poyntz tutor to sons of, **20**. 208n
scurrilous papers written by, against son, **30**. 142
son opposes, about Militia Bill, **30**. 142, **35**. 286
son's marriage plans thwarted by, **37**. 363
sons of, **14**. 36n, **19**. 468n, 566, **20**. 33, **21**. 104n, 138, 552n, **25**. 392n

Walpole, Sir Robert, asked by, to intervene for George Townshend, **36**. 7
wife of, **9**. 16n, **13**. 34n
wife separated from, **17**. 173
(?) wife's portraits burnt by, at Raynham, **30**. 1
wife's witticism on vote of, at rebels' trial, **19**. 285
will of: **38**. 346; omits younger son, **36**. 41
Townshend, Hon. Charles (1725–67), M.P.; chancellor of the Exchequer:
administration to have been betrayed by, to Opposition, **22**. 552
Admiralty appointment of, cancelled because of presumptuous request, **10**. 69, **20**. 517
Admiralty to be headed by, **22**. 130
Ailesbury, Cts of, might invite Dutch people and Jews instead of, **38**. 100
American taxes supported by, in Parliamentary speech, **38**. 508
appointment of, as chancellor of the Exchequer, **30**. 227, 228
arguments supplied by, against national debt, **9**. 86
autopsy on, **39**. 90–1
autopsy reveals fatness of, **22**. 551n
Barré's opposition to, **30**. 244, **38**. 508, 552
Barrington succeeded by, as secretary at war, **21**. 490
Beckford accuses, of 'diarrhœa of words,' **38**. 499
Breda conference might be attended by, as Leicester House candidate, **21**. 355n
Brocklesby, Dr, defended by, attacking North and Grenville, **38**. 273–4
brother brags that pay office was accepted by, at his urging, **30**. 188
brother influences, **31**. 39, **39**. 46
brother of, **21**. 553n
brother pushes, into knavery, **22**. 493
brother's caricature furnished by, with inscription, **21**. 78
brother's Irish post and wife's peerage given to attract, **22**. 549n
brother's opinion of Pitt-Newcastle ministry shared by, **30**. 135
brother's quarrel with, temporarily healed by mother, **38**. 407
Cambridge visited by, to support Hardwicke's candidacy, **38**. 341
chancellor of the Exchequer, **22**. 443, 494, 498, 549
children of, provided for, **39**. 91
Churchill longed to satirize, **22**. 261, 304
clerks employed by, to search records, **38**. 243
coarse, **37**. 450
Conway and Pitt feared by, **38**. 502
Conway has offer from, to move question on officers' dismissal, **38**. 498–9
—— influenced by, against Pitt's plans for East India Co., **22**. 493

[Townshend, Hon. Charles (1725–67), *cont.*]
—— inquires if Grafton wants him to act jointly with, **39**. 84
—— joins, in trying to appease Lyttelton, **38**. 311
—— might shift to Exchequer to make room for, **22**. 310n
——'s preferment hurts, **22**. 493
——'s speech makes, jealous, **38**. 309
—— wants to share Commons leadership with, **39**. 84
—— wonders at silence of, on Address, **37**. 419
Court ascribes to, rumours of changes on Bn Holland's resignation, **38**. 377
Dalkeith, Cts of (Bns Greenwich), about to marry, **9**. 171
—— marries, **35**. 236, 308
Dashwood succeeds, as treasurer of the Chambers, **21**. 490
death of, **7**. 319, 398, **10**. 249n, **22**. 551–2, **31**. 135, **39**. 88, 89, 90–1, 91, 94
Defence of the Minority, A, by, about general warrants: Hunter probably sent, to Hertford, **38**. 429; to be sent by HW, **38**. 422
dismissal claimed by, **22**. 494
dismissed, **9**. 181
Dowdeswell answered by, in naval estimates debate in Parliament, **38**. 496
Earthquake by, **38**. 31
East India Co. dispute settled by, **22**. 478n
East India Co. inquiry supported by, **41**. 65n
East India Co. speculations of, **39**. 81
East India Co.'s proposals acceptable to, **30**. 240n, 244n
East India Co. stock owned by, **22**. 498
Egmont attacked by, in Parliamentary debate, **35**. 195n
epigram by, on 'poor Sal,' **43**. 185
ex-ministers receive promises from, **30**. 193
family of, considerate to his wife, **9**. 171
father of, not dead yet, **38**. 327
father's deathbed shunned by, **38**. 319
father's death confines, **22**. 211
father's will disappoints, **36**. 41, **38**. 426
father thwarts marriage plans of, **37**. 363
finances of, **39**. 91
fits discussed by, at Lady Townshend's, **35**. 80
Fox, Henry (Bn Holland), pleased at conduct of, in Pay Office, **30**. 191
——'s appointees continued by, **30**. 191
——'s sacrifice to, displeases Bns Holland, **38**. 572
—— succeeded by, as Paymaster of the Forces, **22**. 304
friends alone can be injured by, **22**. 492
Garter installation attended by, at Windsor, **22**. 86
George III threatened by, through Conway, with resignation if wife does not get peerage, **39**. 94
—— visited by, **31**. 39
German war supported by, in debates on foreign estimates, **21**. 553n

Grenville, George, attacked by: **38**. 285, 307; on navy bills, **38**. 307; over Wilkes's complaint on privilege, **38**. 292
——'s amendment opposed by, **22**. 381n
——'s appointment and George III's refusal of place for wife resented by, **38**. 142n
——'s devotion from, may bring no preferment, **38**. 497, 498
——'s wing again shelters, **38**. 499
—— to be succeeded by, **10**. 60
HW admires, **32**. 327, 360
HW cares not about politics of, **38**. 511
HW dines with, at Stuart Mackenzie's, hearing Grenville ridiculed, **38**. 502
HW hears from: about Lady Mary Wortley Montagu's MSS, **22**. 85–6; of Conway's speech on Qualification Bill, **38**. 49
HW mentions, (?) **9**. 211, **37**. 443
HW might consult, about politics, **40**. 386
HW's couplet on Opposition's being deserted by Charles Yorke and, **38**. 496–7
HW's opinion of, **10**. 254
HW's witticism on his speaking well of himself, **38**. 552
Hamilton's kindness from, HW congratulates Fox on, **30**. 188
Hardwicke recommends, to George II as treasurer of the Chambers, **21**. 104n
health of: epilepsy, **35**. 308; fever, putrid, **22**. 551; fit, **37**. 444; inflammation in bowels, **39**. 91; nervous complaint, **39**. 90
Hertford distrusts, **39**. 85
—— writes to, about Conway's possible winter quarters in Germany, **38**. 190
Hillsborough to be succeeded by, as treasurer of the Chambers, **21**. 26
independence will unloose parts and presumption of, **35**. 236
inheritance from father expected by, **38**. 319
Irish secretaryship desired by, **9**. 396
jokes on deathbed, **22**. 551
land tax's continuance proposed by, **22**. 488n
Legge and, **37**. 465
London to be left by, **30**. 135, 193
lying, **38**. 471
Lyttelton, Sir Richard, approached by, in affair against Johnston, **38**. 311
Marriage Bill opposed by, **9**. 147
marriage of, **9**. 171, **35**. 236, 308n
Montbazon tells, at Stanley's, of Rochefort's defence, **37**. 545
more volatile than entire French nation, **38**. 203
mother-in-law mocked by, **37**. 429–30
mother of, **9**. 32n, **21**. 24n
mother quotes, **38**. 27–8
North and Forrester answered by, in debate on Wilkes, **38**. 309
North compared to, **39**. 88
—— declines to succeed, as secretary of state, **22**. 552
Onslow's wrangle with, in Commons on Regency Bill, **38**. 552

Opposition aided by, in Parliament, **9.** 180

—— may be joined by, when Yorkes do so, **38.** 285

opposition tendencies of, alienate brother, **38.** 407n

pamphlet attributed to, **16.** 39n

Paris peace treaty now applauded though formerly opposed by, **38.** 496

Parliamentary activity of, tempestuous, **37.** 444

Parliamentary Address may be opposed by, **20.** 509n

Parliamentary debate on East India Co.'s petition avoided by, **22.** 495

Parliamentary division over dubious words in question of, **21.** 86n

Parliamentary speeches by: **10.** 242; on seizure of Wilkes's papers, **22.** 208; opposing Clandestine Marriages Act, **37.** 362–3; praised, **38.** 325; promised but undelivered, **38.** 243; when brilliantly drunk, **22.** 512

Parliament to be avoided by, on motion for officers' dismissals, **38.** 502

paymaster, **10.** 153, **38.** 565, 572, **43.** 366

paymastership to go to, **38.** 496

Pay Office instead of Exchequer accepted by, **30.** 188n

pays for statue, **13.** 120n

Pitt (Chatham) bids, to be chancellor of Exchequer, not paymaster, and then shifts, **22.** 439–40, 442

—— meets, at Newcastle House, **30.** 136

—— names, for secretary of state, **22.** 161

—— opposed by, on East India affairs, **30.** 243–4

—— resented by, for making him chancellor of the Exchequer, **22.** 493

——'s ally, **38.** 142

——'s future speeches mimicked by, at sister-in-law's, **38.** 28

——'s half-ally, disgruntled at Grenville's advancement, **21.** 553

——'s interview with, **30.** 134

——'s remark to, about union with D. of Newcastle, **30.** 136

——'s speech supported by, **38.** 319

—— visited by, at Hampstead, **30.** 227

politically undependable, **38.** 285–6

Poyntz tutor to, **20.** 208n

pranks may be played by, at Versailles, **38.** 380

Ramsay to call on, to discuss portrait, **40.** 150

re-election of, will be sign for HW to re-attend House of Commons, **30.** 238

relations of, with Conway, Pitt, Bute, Vct Townshend, Grenville, Sackville, and Charles Yorke, **38.** 502

retires to country in a rage, **21.** 104

Robertson's *History of Scotland* admired by, **15.** 42

Rockingham ministers receive applications from, **30.** 193

Rockingham ministry delayed by indecision of, **31.** 39

Rockingham ministry supported by, but with dissatisfaction, **39.** 46

Rockinghams may be led by, **22.** 495

Rockingham's offers refused by, but he tries to aid G. J. Williams and Buller, **30.** 193n

rumours of Holland's resigning paymastership may be invention of, **38.** 377

Sackville's appointment resented by, **21.** 104

St Alban's Tavern meetings attended by, **21.** 553

Scarborough visit of, for health, **30.** 58n, **40.** 47

secretaryship of state proposed for, **22.** 302n, 310n

Sewell ridiculed by, **35.** 560

Shelburne to succeed, **10.** 60

silent: in debate on *North Briton*, **38.** 226; in debate on privilege, **38.** 243, 250; in Parliament, **38.** 258

Smith, Adam, chosen by, as D. of Buccleuch's travelling companion, **40.** 321

successor of, will not speak so well in Commons, **39.** 90

Suffolk, Cts of, has note from, about Havana, **38.** 181

to be secretary at war, **21.** 486

treasurership of the Chambers to be retained by, unconnected with Pitt-Newcastle ministry, **30.** 135

uncertain about Rockingham ministry, **39.** 40

vacillations of, **31.** 92, **32.** 193, 228, 243–4

vanity of, **32.** 12

waits for Yorkes to join Opposition, **38.** 285

Wedderburn entertained by, **10.** 32

Whitehead's verses to, **14.** 36

wife of, **11.** 63n, **19.** 468n, **28.** 447n

wife's peerage reported to be a bribe to, **39.** 94

wife thought not to be in despair over death of, **39.** 94

'wild, romancing, indiscreet manner' of, **22.** 494

witticisms by: about Temple's asking for Garter, **9.** 271; at Vauxhall to Lady Mary Coke, on moon, **37.** 557; HW prefers, next to Selwyn's, **30.** 208; on Anson, **37.** 527; on being governed by Newcastle or Bute, **35.** 93; on bill for increasing judges' salaries, **9.** 235–6; on Ds of Newcastle's beard, **35.** 256; on Elizabeth Chudleigh, **9.** 318; on Miss Draycott's tonnage and poundage, **38.** 310; on Sewell's thinking in bed, **35.** 560; on Vcts Falmouth's stomach, **37.** 429, 442; to d'Abreu about asking George II to send for foreign ministers instead of foreign troops, **37.** 474; to mother about Bns Anson's virginity, **21.** 66; to wife at E. of Strafford's dinner, **37.** 430; to wife instructing her about his absence, **10.** 33

Yarmouth cannot re-elect, **21.** 26

Townshend, Charles, writer:
Every Man His Own Letter-Writer by, advertised, 33. 378
Townshend, Charles (1728–1810), of Honingham; cr. (1797) Bn Bayning; M.P.:
HW persuades, to abstain from voting on Regency Bill, 38. 548
Spanish position of, 25. 392n
treasurer of the Navy, 25. 392
Townshend, Charlotte, m. Thomas Fauquier:
(?) SH visited by, 12. 232n, 234
Townshend, Hon. Dorothy (ca 1714–76), m. (1743) Rev. Hon. Spencer Cowper:
Conway sorry for, 37. 137
Townshend, Hon. Edward (ca 1719–65):
Conway sorry for, 37. 137
HW's cousin, 13. 3n
playthings liked by, 36. 1
well and wants nothing, 36. 2
Weston tutor to, 36. 2n
Townshend, Hon. Elizabeth (d. 1785), m. (1722) Charles Cornwallis, 5th Bn Cornwallis; cr. (1753) E. Cornwallis:
HW mentions, 38. 555
Reynolds buys miniature from, 33. 539n
Townshend, Hon. George (1715–69), naval officer; HW's cousin:
acquittal of, 19. 376
Admiralty lords suspend, 19. 324
Admiralty scolded by Charles Emmanuel III for court-martialling, 19. 332
Bastia bombarded by, 19. 157, 162, 169
Bedford taken to England by, 19. 374n
Botta's peace terms condemned by, 19. 312
brother of, 19. 277
Cambridge receives mummy from, 15. 17–18
captains' prizes shared by, at Leghorn, 19. 277
Charles Emmanuel III pleased by conduct of, 19. 325
—— seeks cooperation of, against Genoa, 19. 292
——'s headquarters visited by, after landing at Vado Bay, 19. 292n
—— to confer with, 19. 297
conferences of Corsican malcontents unknown to, 19. 183
Corsican rebels to have been aided by, 20. 274, 385, 21. 37
Corsica's capture expected of, 19. 245
court martial of, 19. 245, 324, 325n, 332, 359–60, 361, 373, 378–9
disgrace of, 19. 324
eagle recommended by, at Port Mahon, 19. 268
eagle to be conveyed by, 19. 253
eagle would be thrown overboard by, 19. 263–4
education of, neglected, 19. 169, 190, 269
failure of, in Mediterranean, 20. 274, 43. 269
Florence to be visited by, 19. 42
French squadron should be demolished by, 19. 265
Genoese harmed by, 19. 157

—— to be harassed by, 19. 245, 292
—— to be threatened by, to save Corsican rebels, 19. 260
George II said to favour, 19. 374
HW comments on stupidity of, 19. 190
HW's cousin, 13. 3n
HW thanks Mann for news of, 19. 390
health of, impaired by confinement, 19. 324n
informed of nothing, 19. 171
Lage's fleet to be attacked by, near Genoa, 19. 253
——'s ships avoided by, 19. 324–5
Leghorn visited by, 19. 156, 169, 277
letter of, used as evidence against him, 19. 324
Liechtenstein congratulated by, 19. 269
Mann advises, to write to D. of Newcastle, 19. 375–6
—— confers with, about eagle, 19. 253
—— gives exact description of Corsica to, 21. 37
—— indirectly responsible for command being given to, 19. 146–7
—— regrets having recommended, to Sardinians, 19. 169–70
——'s correspondence with, 19. 42, 147, 156, 169–70, 216, 245, 292, 374
—— seeks further information about, 19. 350
—— to confer with, at Leghorn, 19. 183
—— tries to impel, towards Corsica, 19. 163
—— will ask, about pedestal for eagle, 19. 427
Mathews to be surpassed by, 19. 253
Medley not a friend to, 19. 374
—— not the prosecutor of, 19. 359
playthings liked by, 36. 1
'plenipotentiary' in Corsica, 19. 182
Port Mahon visited by, 19. 207, 216
Rivarola does not assist, 19. 157
—— to be landed by, on Corsica, 19. 146
Rowley tells, to conquer Corsica, 19. 146
Sandwich causes court martial of, 19. 332, 361, 374
'Sebastian' in Dryden's *Don Sebastian* resembled by, 19. 190n
ship of, returned to him, 19. 375
ships left by, near Corsica, 19. 207
ships to be sent by, to Riviera di Ponente, 19. 292
snuff-box for Stone sent by, to England, 18. 445, 477
squadron of, near Genoa, 19. 253
squadron off Marseille and Toulon may be commanded by, 19. 376
storm drives, from Corsican coast, 19. 215n
Toulon convoy missed by, 19. 277
Villettes's correspondence with, 19. 183, 245
—— seeks interview with, 19. 292
well, and wants nothing, 36. 2
Weston tutor to, 36. 2n
Townshend, Hon. George (1724–1807), 4th Vct Townshend, 1764; cr. (1787) M. Townshend:
absurdity of, encourages Irish opposition, 23. 362
Albemarle challenged by, to duel, 9. 318

Anecdotes of Painting does not discuss, **9.** 326

army joined by, too late for Fontenoy, **37.** 196

arrival of: from Germany awaited, **21.** 552; in London, **40.** 52

Art of Political Lying attacks, **21.** 78, **37.** 473n

assembly postponed on account of, **32.** 97

bad company endangers, **36.** 7

Bedford, D. of, dislikes rumoured marquisate for, **38.** 392–3

Bellamont's duel with, **32.** 93

Bristol, E. of, replaced by, as lord lieutenant of Ireland, **22.** 549, **30.** 246

brother influenced by, **31.** 39, **38.** 502, **39.** 46

brother pushed by, into knavery, **22.** 493

brother said by, to have accepted Pay Office at his urging, **30.** 188

brother's loss felt by, **39.** 94

brother's quarrel with, temporarily healed by mother, **38.** 407

Buckinghamshire, E. of, taken by, as second in duel, **9.** 319

Bute's friend, **22.** 549n

Campbell, Lord Frederick, goes to Ireland as secretary to, **22.** 549

captain of horse in 7th Dragoons in Flanders, **18.** 566n

card caricatures by, **9.** 195

caricatures by, of political figures: **21.** 77–8, 90, 93, **43.** 365; in Pall Mall taverns, **37.** 444; sent to Strafford by HW, **35.** 280

carpenter and 'low fellows' live with, **23.** 380

Caswall arrests, **9.** 319

changes sides in voting on Wilkes and warrants, **38.** 309

Conway's army conduct possibly reported by, **38.** 146

—— shunned by, for wanting troop augmentation, **23.** 156n

—— speaks to, about Ordnance, **39.** 83

—— succeeds, as lieutenant of Ordnance, **22.** 549

—— to get instructions from, about militia, **37.** 568

'Cotillon, The,' by, satirizes Irish, **23.** 380

Court supported by, from self-interest, **38.** 285

creditors fled by, **41.** 260

Cumberland, D. of, attacked by, **20.** 33

—— disliked by, **39.** 46n

—— has, as aide-de-camp, **20.** 33

Daily Advertiser's advertisement by, about Quebec, **38.** 56–7

debts contracted by, before he went to Ireland, **41.** 260n

declines son's request that he take title of Leicester, **15.** 330

depicted on design for Wolfe's monument, **21.** 422

Dettingen service of, **36.** 7

disappointed at not becoming marquess, **22.** 493

elevation of, **10.** 252n

father of, not yet dead, **38.** 327

father opposed by, over Militia Bill, **30.** 142, **35.** 286

father's bequest to, **38.** 346

Fawkener's letter sent to Poyntz by, **40.** 58

Fitzroy, Lady Caroline, has affair with, **30.** 84, **37.** 194, 196–7

Flood opposes administration of, in Ireland, **35.** 467n

Foote's letter from, **32.** 97

Fox, Henry, hated by, **30.** 169n

——'s presence resented by, **21.** 104

Gardiner, Mrs, should inform mother about, **40.** 46

George II not to be told of objection of, to Fox, **30.** 135

George III and Conway agree with, about Conway getting Ordnance, **39.** 83–4

George III praised by, **38.** 489

——'s wishes might be communicated by, to E. of Orford, **39.** 298

—— urges, to persuade brother to take Exchequer, **31.** 39n

—— visited by, **31.** 39

Gordon rioters threaten, **25.** 53, **33.** 175

Grenville ministry's ties with, alienate brother, **38.** 407n

HW hears, is out of humour at not becoming lord lieutenant of Ireland, **30.** 188

(?) HW mentions, **9.** 211

HW said to be related to, **39.** 111

HW's correspondence with, **41.** 260–1, **42.** 332–7, 343–5

HW sends Orford's dogs and horses to, **41.** 261

HW tells nephew to consult, **36.** 27

HW thanks, for solicitude at Houghton for E. of Orford, **42.** 335–6

HW thinks, may grow impatient for regiment, **37.** 572

Hague, The, visited by, **18.** 566

Harcourt to replace, in Ireland, **39.** 163

Hardwicke recommends, to George II for employment, **21.** 104n

Hyde supported by, in election, **2.** 167

investigation of Port Mahon's fall languidly pursued by, for fear of uniting D. of Newcastle and Henry Fox, **21.** 56

Ireland lingered in by, to face challengers, **39.** 163

—— to be visited by, as lord lieutenant, **39.** 90, 94

Irish Parliament prorogued by, **23.** 166, 170

Irish post given to, to win brother, **22.** 549n

Irish Revenue Board promoted by, **23.** 380n

Irish will be imposed upon by, at first, **22.** 549

'King's Arms' visited by, **9.** 86

libels attacked by, forgetting his own caricatures, **38.** 489

lives with low associates, and satirizes chief Irishmen in ballad, **23.** 380

London to be left by, **30.** 135

[Townshend, Hon. George (1724–1807), *cont.*]
lord lieutenant of Ireland, **22.** 549, **23.** 362n,
39. 90, 94
'low woman' accompanies, at Dublin, **23.** 362
Luttrell reportedly backed by, for Tamworth
election, **30.** 193
Marquessate may be given to, **38.** 392
Marybone visited by, **9.** 318–19
Master of the Ordnance, **25.** 53
Militia Bill promoted by, **21.** 137–8, **37.** 444
militia schemes of, worthy to be in his caricatures, **37.** 573
militia service of, **37.** 575
militia's restorer, **21.** 552
Molesworth's case should be referred to, **39.**
111
mother apprehensive about, **35.** 295, **38.** 27
mother gives ball for, on his coming of age,
19. 18
mother of, **9.** 32n, **21.** 24n
mother's illness would distress, **30.** 121
mother's Jacobite tendencies counteracted by
transfer of, to D. of Cumberland, **36.** 7n
mother's protégé not to be revealed to, **37.** 268
(?) 'Motion, The,' by, **37.** 96n
nephew's godfather, **37.** 550
Newcastle's neglect nettles, **30.** 193n
nobility said by, to have turned into recruiting sergeants, **37.** 446
Ordnance may be given to, **39.** 160n, 163,
164n
Orford, E. of, caricatured by, **43.** 365
—— governed by, **30.** 169n
—— influenced by, against Henry Fox, **30.**
169n
—— invited by, to recuperate at Raynham,
42. 334, 336
——'s funeral attended by, **42.** 339n
—— should be prevented by, from quartering
militia, **39.** 298
Parliamentary Address debated by, **37.** 414,
415, 419
Parliamentary Address moved by, in House of
Lords, **38.** 489
Parliamentary Address opposed by, **20.** 510n
Parliamentary debate by, advocating enlistment of Irish papists, **41.** 213n
Parliamentary motion of, in House of Commons, **20.** 229n
picture of, **30.** 84
'Pillars of State, The,' satiric print by: **37.**
473–4; (?) HW sends, to Strafford, **35.** 280
Pitt (Chatham) might be urged by, to storm
Rochefort with militia, **37.** 572–3
—— sent news of Quebec capture by, **21.** 337n
——'s interview with, **30.** 134–5
——'s offer of office refused by, **30.** 135
Pitt-Newcastle ministry disapproved by, **30.**
134–5
Poyntz tutor to, **20.** 208n
Quebec command assumed by, **9.** 253n
Quebec expedition led by, **21.** 266–7

Quebec no more lost than won by, **38.** 57
——'s conqueror, **35.** 297
—— surrenders to, after Wolfe's death, **22.**
16n
—— victory shared by, unharmed, **40.** 168
regiment to be raised by, for Dutch service,
18. 566
retires to the country in rage, **21.** 104
Rockingham ministry opposed by, **30.** 193
scurrilous papers written by, against father,
30. 142
sister of, **20.** 495n
son of, **2.** 167n, **15.** 330, **25.** 392n, 612n
'Treaty, The,' equals caricatures of, **21.** 93
Vernon saved by intervention of, **30.** 193n
Walpole, Sir Robert, wants Conway and
Churchill to befriend, **36.** 6–7
Weymouth quarrels with, over Tamworth
election, **30.** 193
wife's letter from, **40.** 168n
witticisms by: **33.** 83; on Hastings's trial, **35.**
391–2
'wrongheadedness' of, **21.** 267
Townshend, George (sometime Elleker) (1753–
1811), 4th Bn Ferrers, 1770; cr. (1784) E. of
Leicester; 2d M. Townshend, 1807; F.R.S.;
F.S.A.:
ancestry the passion of, **2.** 135–6, **15.** 330, 334
antiquarianism of, **29.** 360
a rising herald, **2.** 146, 148, 153
arms identified by, **2.** 220
barony of Basset and championship of England claimed by, **15.** 330
Cole owns pedigree of family of, **2.** 153–4, 155
dines with HW, **2.** 165
dubious right of, to Earldom of Leicester,
33. 465
HW to be consulted by, on repairs for Tamworth Castle, **2.** 135, 146
HW told by, of heraldic claims, **34.** 28
Hamilton's dedication to, **35.** 442n
joint postmaster-general, **12.** 118
King resigns in favour of, **2.** 245n
peerage creation for, **39.** 410n
peerage of, corrected, **43.** 213
Penshurst's purchase wished by, **34.** 28
—— visited by, **34.** 28
Sidney ancestry of, **43.** 68
SH visited by, **12.** 236, **43.** 161
Tallien, false news of, received by, **12.** 118
Whig meeting attended by, **29.** 261
Townshend, Hon. Georgiana (1761–1835):
Churchill, Lady Mary, succeeded by, as house-
keeper of Windsor Castle, **43.** 132
(?) SH visited by, **12.** 228
Townshend, Henry (1736–62), army officer;
M.P.:
death of, **22.** 47
HW mentions, **10.** 7, (?) **37.** 467
killed at Wilhelmsthal, **38.** 161
witticism by, on Sylvester Smith, **37.** 530
wounded, **9.** 379, **21.** 516, **35.** 310

Townshend, Hon. Horatio (d. 1751):
daughter carries out will of, 9. 184
nephew of, 9. 184n
Townshend, Hon. Horatio (ca 1717–64):
HW's cousin, 13. 3n
playthings liked by, 36. 1
well, and wants nothing, 36. 2
Weston, tutor to, 36. 2n
Townshend, Hon. (afterwards Lord) John (1757–1833); M.P.:
HW votes for, in Westminster election, 34. 11, 13
debts of, 30. 270
Jekyll: a Political Epilogue by, 11. 34–5, 43. 140, 203
lord of the Admiralty, 25. 392
naval volunteer, 30. 270
ode attributed to, 33. 465n
Rolliad and other verses by, 25. 612n
stands for Cambridge University, 2. 167, 168
turned out of coach by Lady Granby, 2. 167n
Townshend, Letitia (ca 1726–56), m. (1748 or 9) Brownlow Cecil, styled Lord Burghley, 9th E. of Exeter, 1754:
death and will of, 9. 184
husband of, 10. 344
Townshend, Hon. Mary (ca 1720–76), m. (1753) Lt–Gen. Hon. Edward Cornwallis:
'abominable hermitage' of, 37. 205
Ailesbury, Cts of, to visit, at Ewhurst, 37. 317
—— will ask, to look at Eversley, 37. 305
bereavement of, 9. 32
biographical information about, corrected, 43. 112
Conway agrees with HW about, 37. 179–80
—— and wife may be visited by, at Park Place, 37. 350
Conway and wife to console, for husband's expulsion from Bedchamber, 38. 470
Conway loves, 'excessively,' 37. 206–7
—— sends compliments to, 37. 195, 199, 205
(?) Cornwallis's return to be hailed by nosegays bought by, in Covent Garden, and laurel at pastry-cooks', 37. 197
dances at Robinson's ball, 37. 115
HW may plot with, to eschew the world for religious life, 37. 206
(?) HW mentions, 37. 175
HW's correspondence with, 37. 310, 40. 44–6
HW to be welcomed by, in Bruton Street, 40. 46
(?) HW to receive respects of, 37. 34
HW urges, in Conway's name, to forsake country life, 37. 206
(?) Hampshire, home of, 37. 305
health of, recovered, 37. 235
husband of, dismissed, 38. 435
London visited by, 9. 37
unhappy, 9. 37
Walpole, Lady Mary, to visit, at Muffetts, 37. 202
well, at Raynham, 40. 47

Townshend, Mary, Selwyn's niece:
(?) Selwyn to consult, 4. 68
Townshend, Mary, dau. of Hon. Edward Townshend:
(?) HW's cousin, a stranger to him, 33. 197
ticket for, to visit SH, 33. 197
Townshend, Robert (ca 1708–91), recorder of Chester:
Hertford hears speech by, 39. 18
Townshend, Sir Roger (ca 1596–1637), cr. (1617) Bt; M.P.:
marriage of, 9. 68
Townshend, Hon. Roger (ca 1731–59), Lt-Gen.:
Adam uses Breton's relief for monument for, in Westminster Abbey, 21. 421n
(?) Amherst's spyglass sought by, 9. 248
buried at Chislehurst, 13. 4n
death of: 9. 248, 38. 27, 40. 165–6; at Ticonderoga, 35. 294–5
HW designs monument for, 40. 166–7
HW's epitaph for, unused, 13. 34
monument to, in Westminster Abbey, 43. 172
(?) Townshend, Hon. Augustus, accompanied by, 9. 32
Townshend, Hon. Thomas (1701–80), M.P.:
at point of death, 2. 217
Exchequer tellership of, son wants reversion of, 39. 99
Exeter, Cts of, leaves money to, 9. 184
Frognal, house of, 30. 261n
Gray, Sir James, aided by, in diplomatic career, 19. 444, 453
HW and Selwyn may dine with, at (?) Frognal, 30. 261–2
(?) HW hears from, about his pets, 36. 1
HW opposed by, in House of Commons, 13. 20
HW persuades, to abstain from voting on Regency Bill, 38. 548
half-brother of, 15. 18n
marriage of, to Selwyn's sister, 13. 3n, 30. 261
M.P. for Cambridge University, 2. 219
Parliamentary activity of, on Regency Bill, 38. 548, 551
Parliamentary speech by, 29. 123n
solicits subscriptions for Life of Cicero, 15. 6–7
son of, 9. 379n, 21. 516n, 22. 47n, 39. 99
teller of Exchequer, 21. 516n, 39. 99
Townshend, Thomas (1733–1800), cr. (1783) Bn and (1789) Vct Sydney; M.P.:
advertisement by, in Northampton Mercury for detection of Ampthill arsonist, 34. 4n
announces that peace is near, 33. 379
Dundas's motion stopped by, 25. 35n
Fox's resignation condemned by, 35. 518n
George III receives bulse with diamond from, 33. 568n
——'s emissary at death of Ps Amelia, 33. 535
Germain's second, in duel, 23. 255n

[Townshend, Thomas (1733–1800), continued]
Grafton alienates, by removing him from Pay Office, 23. 186n
Grenville denounced by, 38. 499
Grenville ministry's conduct on warrants attacked by, 38. 488
HW persuades, to abstain from voting on Regency Bill, 38. 548
Holroyd's motion opposed by, 25. 29n
House of Commons divided by, 38. 224
House of Lords ejects, 23. 256n
lord mayor's letter from, about peace negotiations, 25. 347n
may continue in office, 35. 518
North rebuked by, for slandering Opposition, 25. 35n
Parliamentary motion by, for Renunciation Bill, 33. 382n
Parliamentary speech by, on East India Co.'s purchase of seats in Parliament, 33. 244n
peace notified by, to City of London, 25. 355n
Pitt gets overtures through, at Bath, 22. 413n
proposed as speaker of House of Commons, 23. 180
report by, of Godolphin's death, misinterpreted, 25. 583
resigns on Rigby's appointment, 39. 98–9
reversion of father's Exchequer tellership wanted by, 39. 99
Rockingham's emissary to Pitt, 22. 395n
Sandwich attacked by, in Parliamentary debate, 38. 499
secretary at war, 25. 264n
secretary of state, 25. 295n, 300n, 355n, 460n, 583
Selwyn reclaims Cleveland Court house from, 33. 236n
Shelburne may succeed, as home secretary, 25. 487
Townshend, Thomas Charles (1758–82), army officer:
baptism of, 37. 550
Townshend, Hon. William (1702–38), M.P.; army officer:
HW may visit, 13. 4n
HW succeeds in Exchequer, 13. 7
son of, 25. 392n
Townshend. See also Townsend
Townshend family ('The Family'):
barbarous dialect of, 30. 73
Campbell family to be rivalled by, 38. 36
Castle Rising borough might go to, 36. 14, 16
Conway warns Mary Townshend against, 37. 235
Ferrers, Bn, of, 2. 135
gambling losses of, 30. 69
HW calls, Sauromatæ, 30. 73
HW criticizes childishness of, 30. 50–1
HW persuades, not to vote against Ps of Wales in Regency dispute, 38. 548
Ludgershall inherited by, 11. 184n
Norfolk home of, 10. 344

Orme's elopement with Lady Audrey Townshend not approved by, 20. 495n
Selwyn offends, by revealing their faro playing, 30. 69
Townshend, Vcts, breaks with, 17. 173
—— does not resemble, in treatment of friends, 40. 371
Tunbridge Wells visited by, 30. 69
untruthfulness of, 38. 346
Walpoles on dangerous ground when dealing with, 36. 7
Williams, Sir C. H., might extract amusement from, 30. 50
Townson, John (? 1725–97), merchant; M.P.:
birth date of, 43. 309
contract of, investigated, 29. 191–2
profits of, 39. 388
Townson, Robert (1575–1621), Bp of Salisbury:
Fuller on, 2. 101n
Towry, Mr:
SH ticket not used by, 12. 226
Toy, inn at Hampton Court:
pistols discharged at, as HW's nieces were going by, 33. 370
waiter at, makes pedantic remarks on violinist, 34. 173
Toy; toys:
dolls' houses, 20. 187
Du Quesne has, on shipboard, 21. 255
from Paris, at Leghorn fair, 22. 423
go-cart, 32. 30
Pius VI's nephew receives, in France on Princess's birth, 24. 470
top, 32. 30
Toyman; toymen. See Chenevix, Paul Daniel; Deard, —— (Mrs Bertrand); Deard, Elizabeth (Mrs Chenevix); Deard, John; Deard William; Gray, Robert
Toynbee, Mr and Mrs Paget:
HW's letters edited by, 26. 38, 39; see also Introductions to Vols 1, 3, 9, 11, 13, 15, 16, 17, 28, 30, 31, 32, 35, 36, 37, 40
HW's 'Paris Journals' printed by, in extracts in Blackwood's Magazine, 43. 105
'To Zelinda, from Florence,' by HW:
Conway thanks HW for, 37. 81
Fermor, Lady Sophia, not meant by, 37. 84–5
Tozier, Grace (d. 1753), tavern-keeper:
Wales, P. and Ps of, visit tavern of, 17. 451
Tozzetti, Francesco, Florentine physician:
autopsy on Dr Cocchi's body performed by, 21. 162n
Trace; traces (harness):
long, on Electress's coach, 19. 370
Trachshuit. See Trekshuit
'Tractate on Education.' See Milton, John: 'Of Education'
Tracte Containing the Artes, A. See under Lomazzo, Giovanni Paolo
Tracts by Warburton and a Warburtonian. See under Parr, Samuel

Tracy, —— (d. 1763), m. John Travell; John Chute's niece:
Chute, Ann, mentions, in will, 43. 189
son of, 14. 201
Tracy, Anthony (d. 1767):
Chute's nephew, 14. 95n
Tracy, Mrs Ferdinando. See Keck, Katherine
Tracy (formerly Keck), Hon. Henrietta Charlotte (d. 1817), m. (1774) Edward Devereux, 12th Vct Hereford, 1760:
SH visited by, 12. 244
Tracy, John (d. 1735), of Stanway:
wife of, 14. 18n
Tracy, John (1706–73):
Chute's nephew, 14. 95n
Tracy, John (1722–93), 7th Vct Tracy, 1792; D.D.:
nominated for living, 14. 201
Tracy, Mrs John. See Atkyns, Anne
Tracy, Mary (1581–1671), m. Bn Vere of Tilbury:
print of, 1. 183
Tracy, Robert, 'Handsome Tracy':
butterwoman's daughter pursued by, married, and taken to France, 9. 75–6
Tracy, Robert (1706–67); M.P.; Chute's nephew:
Chute, Anthony, prejudiced against John Chute by, 14. 211
—— revokes nomination of, as Miss Nicoll's guardian, 14. 200
Chute, John, uncle of, 14. 95n
fortune of, depleted, 14. 201–2
HW and Chute affront, 14. 227
HW pleased by opposition to, at Worcester election, 35. 150
HW pleased that Chute was not ousted by, 35. 85
Nicoll guardianship lost by, 14. 229
solicits friends' interest for support in Nicoll affair, 14. 202
source of story about Richard Walpole, 14. 224
Walpoles accused by, of plot against Miss Nicoll, 14. 215
wife offered by, as guardian for Miss Nicoll, 14. 199
Tracy, Mrs Robert. See Hudson, Anna Maria; Owens, Susannah
Tracy, Thomas (? 1716–70), M.P.:
Chute's nephew, 14. 95n
(?) death of, reported, 7. 398
Parliamentary debate by, over Scotch Bill, 26. 31
Tracy, Thomas Charles (1690–1756), 5th Vct Tracy:
son of, nominated for living, 14. 201
Tracy Atkyns. See Atkyns
Tracy family:
Chute inheritance may be claimed by, 9. 161
Chute may be courted by, for estate, 35. 86
Chute wishes to prevent visit of, 14. 95

Trade:
American, restricted by act of Parliament, 28. 179
board of, see Board of Trade; Trade and Plantations, Commissioners of
despotism incompatible with, 33. 103
England loses, by American war, 25. 506
——'s loss of, 28. 175
French, see under France
HW calls, 'modern religion,' 31. 269
HW does not understand, 33. 545
See also Commerce
Trade and Plantations, Commissioners of:
Nova Scotia lands granted by, 20. 40n
Trade Bills. See under Parliament: acts of
Tradesman; tradesmen:
bills of, may be taxed, 20. 183
Chudleigh, Elizabeth, has scaffolds for, at fireworks, 38. 204
Chute would cheat, to buy paintings, 35. 38
Fox, C. J., pays, with faro winnings, 39. 369
imprisoned for debt, perhaps aided by HW, 40. 345n
Louis XV's, ruined, 39. 143
luxury of, in England, 22. 455
lying is merely an expletive for, 25. 298
sign used by, after removal, 33. 195
York, Ds of, invites, to husband's birthday, 39. 493
Tradrums ('trawdrums'):
high Court, Serristori, Giovanni, wears, at baptism, 17. 473
Suares, Vittoria, in, 35. 29
Traduction de quelques ouvrages de Tacite. See Tacitus, Publius Cornelius: Annals of: La Bletterie's translation of
Traduction du poème de Jean Plokof . . . . See under Voltaire
Traetta, Tommaso Michele Francesco Saverio (1727–79), composer:
Olimpiade, L', by, 22. 558, 39. 119
Trafalgar:
Gravina dies at, 12. 53n
Tragedy; tragedies:
astonishment essential to, 41. 297
at Drury Lane Theatre, ill-played, 23. 82
Bayreuth, Margravine of, composes, 20. 478
delay never impairs, 41. 362
fables contrasted with, 3. 119
French, given once a week at Fontainebleau, 38. 451
French rules for: Garrick defers to, in alteration of Hamlet, 29. 368–70; observed by Mason, 29. 321, 323, 326
HW's thoughts on, 41. 289–98
incest not the business of, 28. 16
Jephson's 'vocation,' 41. 288
modern, HW's opinion of, 10. 260
Pertici undeserving of Garrick's praises for, 20. 357
Roman nobility act, at Frascati, 20. 481
terribleness easy in, 41. 297

[Tragedy; tragedies, *continued*]
'the world is . . .' *See under* World
tragédie bourgeoise now prevalent in, **41**. 374
Walpole, Bns, prefers, **18**. 128
See also Greek drama
Tragedy of King Saul, The. See under Trapp, Joseph
Tragopodagra. See under Lucian
Traicté des chiffres. See under Vignère, Blaise de
Trail, Rev. James (1725–83), D.D.; Hertford's chaplain; Bp of Down and Connor, 1765:
  baptism started by, before infant is brought, **37**. 430
  bishopric given to, through Hertford, **39**. 19
  HW to receive compliments of, **38**. 44
  'Scottish Presbyterian,' yet reads Anglican liturgy in Hertford's chapel, **38**. 347n, 352
  Wilkes must make the mention of sin difficult to, in embassy sermons, **38**. 279
Train; trains (to clothing):
  Craon, Princesse de, wears, at ceremony of the *doti*, **18**. 196
  Cumberland, D. of, wears, at George II's funeral, **9**. 322
  lady's, in Paris, carried by hat-wearing servants, **35**. 112
  long, at Versailles ball, **32**. 255
  Maintenon, Mme de, wears, long, in portrait by Ferdinand, **10**. 294
  of black crêpe: Kingston, Ds of, wears, **23**. 556, **39**. 272; might be worn by Ds of Kingston at trial, **24**. 187
  St-Cyr nuns wear, long, **10**. 293
  trapes with long, **33**. 313
Train-bearer; train-bearers:
  Beauchamp one of George III's, at Coronation, **38**. 122
Train-oil:
  Eskimos wish for, **32**. 357
Traité de la goutte:
  HW owns, **43**. 83
Traité de l'orthographe françoise. See under Le Roy, Cl.
Traité des différentes sortes de preuves. See under Griffet, Henri
Traité des pierres gravées. See under Mariette, Pierre-Jean
Traité du poème épique. See under Le Bossu, René
Traité méthodique . . . de la goutte. See under Paulmier, François
Traité pratique sur la goutte et sur les moyens de guérir cette maladie. See under Coste, Dr, jr
Traitta *or* Trajitta. *See* Traetta
Trajan (Marcus Ulpius Trajanus) (ca 53–117), Roman emperor 98–117:
  Danube bridged by, **8**. 201–2
  good emperor, **35**. 127
  HW praises: **33**. 479; despite private vices, **15**. 50–1
  Hervey's epigram mentions, **15**. 3

(?) medal of, **17**. 12
medal of father of, **26**. 7
medal of forum of, **26**. 7
Pliny's praise of, mentioned in Hervey's epigram, **40**. 22
Porquet alludes to, **4**. 325
Voltaire mentions, **35**. 413
Tramontini, Signora. *See* Tesi, Vittoria
Tranquillity:
  advantages of, HW's reflections on, **23**. 367
  HW on, **4**. 426
'Tranquilus':
  popular signature for letters to newspapers, **42**. 500
Trans, Abbé de. *See* Villeneuve, Alexandre-Marie de
Trans, Marquis de. *See* Villeneuve, Louis-Henri de
Trans, Marquise de. *See* Chamillart-la-Suze, Anne-Madeleine de
Transactions of the Society . . . for the Encouragement of Arts, Manufactures, and Commerce:
  HW reads in, of Lord Ossory's medal and gardener, **33**. 480
Translation; translations:
  HW distinguishes between types of, **29**. 103, 106, 117
  HW's opinion of, **10**. 298
  West thinks, should be close, **13**. 101
Transmigration of souls:
  HW jokes about, **21**. 7
  HW speculates about, **35**. 356
Transport; transports (vessels):
  Americans capture, **24**. 229
  Cowes reached by, for embarkation to Rochefort, **37**. 503
  Dutch, escape English seizure, **25**. 9
  English: detained in the Downs, **21**. 130; Newcastle, D. of, hires, to take him to Holland, **19**. 484; Rodney sends, to Gibraltar, **25**. 16; sail to America, **35**. 230; sinking of, rumoured, **35**. 196
  expense of, to Boston, **41**. 313
  Fitzjames's, captured, **19**. 209n
  for Rochefort expedition, awaited, **37**. 495, 499, 501
  French: at Dunkirk, **18**. 407, **19**. 103; at Toulon, **20**. 545; Boscawen to 'swallow up,' **20**. 483; captured by English privateers, **19**. 230; French send, to Toulon from Minorca for more troops, **20**. 552; Norris to burn, at Dunkirk, **18**. 402; Parker defeats, **25**. 21; take English troops to Gibraltar, **20**. 581; to be disarmed, **21**. 352n
  Hanoverian troops to be taken away in, **21**. 13
  lost in storm at Portsmouth, **25**. 115
  Medley sends ships to protect, in Adriatic, **19**. 206n
  Neapolitan, escape with artillery, **19**. 82
  Pringle hostage for, **25**. 309
  Spaniards hire, at Genoa and Leghorn, **19**. 304
  Theodore's, dispersed, **18**. 174

tonnage prices raised by demand for shipments to America by, **41**. 313n

Transportation:

breakage in, **2**. 47

Calais to Paris, **5**. 229

cost of: **5**. 233, **6**. 257, **17**. 130, 257; between London and Cambridge, **1**. 225n, 263n, 281

London-Paris trip made in 3 days despite delays at sea, **38**. 360

London to Dover, **5**. 307

noblemen often fail to defray charges of, **17**. 474

of criminals: **9**. 256; HW suggests, as punishment for Haynes, **43**. 381

of goods: **3**. 92; tax on, **25**. 254n

of Montagu's pictures, **10**. 67, 81, 123

of parcels, **1**. 101

packing for, **3**. 297, **5**. 125, 233, 317, **6**. 13, 14

Salisbury improves means of, **10**. 348

water route: Paris-Chanteloup-Barèges, **5**. 352, 352–3; Rouen-England, **6**. 411

See also Ark; Balloon; Barge; Bark; Berlin; Boat; Body-coach; Cabriolet; Calash; Cambridge coach; Cambridge fly; Cambridge wagon; Canal; Carriage; Carrier; Carrosse; Cart; Chair; Chaise; Chariot; Coach; Courier; Curricles; Diligence; Dray; Equipages; Ferry; Fly; Frullone; Furniture purchased by HW, transportation of: Gigs; Gocart; Gondola; Hack; Hearse; Horse-litter; Landau; Lighter; Litter; Mail-coach; Merlin: chair of; Mules; Packet-boat; Phaeton; Post-chaise; Privateer; Procaccia; Roads; Sedan chair; Ship; Sloop; Stage-coach; Timwhiskey; Vettura; Vis-à-vis; Voiture; Wagon; Wheelbarrow; Wheelchairs; Whiskies

Transport Office:

Derwentwater the first prisoner to be taken to, **19**. 299n

Transteverini; Transtiverains. *See* Trasteverini

Transubstantiation:

Maguire cannot swallow, **17**. 420

Transylvania:

Austrians may be marching to, **37**. 296

Trant, Mr (fl. 1684):

to pay bill for Nell Gwyn, **1**. 350

Trapaud, Cyrus (ca 1714–1801) army officer:

house of, at Twickenham, **10**. 247, 248, 252, 253

Montagu to look at house of, **10**. 253

—— wishes HW to talk with, about rent, **10**. 248

Trapaud, Mrs Cyrus (ca 1733–1803):

(?) HW accompanies, to horse race, **7**. 304

Trap-ball:

Frederick, P. of Wales, plays, **20**. 240n

Trapes, street-walker:

in the Strand, England compared to, **33**. 313

Trapp, Joseph (1679–1747), D.D.; poet; pamphleteer; professor of poetry at Oxford:

son of, **17**. 70

Tragedy of King Saul, The, by, ascribed to Orrery, **16**. 21, **43**. 216

translation of Virgil by, quoted, **13**. 87

Trapp, Rev. Joseph (ca 1716–99), rector of Harlington and Strathfieldsaye:

Bouverie pays travelling expenses of, **17**. 70

Chute's fan displeases, **17**. 116–17

Florence visited by, **17**. *63,* 67, 70

languages not known by, **17**. 70

Mann entertains, **17**. 70, 116–17

—— ridicules behaviour and costume of, **17**. 132

——'s little house occupied by, **17**. 67, 146, 154

Pisa visited by, **17**. 67

Rome to be visited by, **17**. 154

silent, **17**. 67, 70, 116

Trappe, La, French monastery:

Drumlanrig's death enough to send one to, **37**. 389

epistle concerning, **3**. 286, 295

HW and Mme du Deffand might dispute at, **3**. 390

Trappe, La, Hammersmith:

Bubb Dodington's villa, **20**. 54n

marble floor of sculpture gallery of, surpasses that of Barberini palace, **20**. 54n

'Trappolin.' *See under* Tate, Nahum: *Duke and No Duke*

Trapps, Joyce (Jocosa) (1531–87), m. 1 (before 1558) Henry Saxey; m. 2 William Frankland: portrait of, at Emmanuel College, **14**. 113

Traquair, E. of. *See* Stewart, Charles (d. 1764)

Traschieto. *See* Treschietto

Trasteverini (Roman slum-dwellers):

Albani might arouse, **19**. 114

Clement XIII's nephews may be stoned by, **22**. 229

ready to rebel, **18**. 462

Trattato dei diletti e delle pene. See under Bonesana, Cesare

Trattato della pubblica felicità. See under Muratori

Traun, Otto Ferdinand (1677–1748), Graf von Abensberg-Traun; Austrian field marshal:

accounts, of battle, not received from, **18**. 154

Alberoni's lands in the Plaisanterie seized by, **18**. 199

Austrian-Sardinian negotiations awaited by, **18**. 263

Bologna scene of military preparations of, **18**. 55

—— threatened by army of, **17**. 500

—— to be occupied by, **18**. 199

Bosville to join army of, **18**. 309

Braitwitz hears from, that Spaniards will invade Tuscany when P. Charles invades France, **18**. 285

—— ordered by: not to obey Francis I's orders, **18**. 128; not to risk battles with Spaniards, **18**. 295; to send troops to San Martino, **18**. 85

Buon Porto, station of, when rejoined by Faenza detachment, **18**. 66

Cesena visited by, **18**. 13

[Traun, Otto Ferdinand, *continued*]
Charles Emmanuel III checks ardour of, **18**. 13
—— joins, at Piacenza, **17**. 312n
——'s and George II's intercessions might save, **18**. 285
courier from, **18**. 175
Craon's letter from, **18**. 164–5
Dettingen victory exaggerated by, **18**. 269
Faenza visited by, **18**. 3
Gages may be forced to give up Bologna to, **18**. 108
German troops withdrawn by, from Tuscan borders, **18**. 134
Lobkowitz to replace, **18**. 279–80, 285, 302
Lombardy to be defended by, **18**. 263, 295
Lorraine's recovery expected by, **18**. 285
Mantuan abbeys seized by, **18**. 55n
Maria Theresa to get remonstrances from, to orders, **18**. 128
Mathews wants, to coop up Spaniards in Tuscany, **18**. 108
Milanese abbeys seized by, **18**. 55
money demanded by, **18**. 199
money shortage prevents, from marching against Spaniards, **18**. 257
Montemar fears, **17**. *341*
—— to be attacked by, with aid of Sardinian troops, **17**. 350
nephews of, captured by Spaniards, **18**. 154
Panaro not to be crossed by, **18**. 66
—— not to be left by, **18**. 76
Ponte del Reno visited by, **17**. 500
regiment of, **18**. 164
Spaniards deterred by fear of, from invading Tuscany, **18**. 58
—— may be dislodged by, **18**. 58, 253, 257, 271
Thun sends courier to, **18**. 56
troops of, too weak to make promised attack on Spaniards, **18**. 127
Tuscany not to be defended by, **18**. 295
—— warned by, of Spanish invasion from Bologna, **18**. 76
Zambeccari may be seized by, **18**. 257
Trautmansdorf, Count:
Belgioioso might be succeeded by, at Brussels, **39**. 456n
Travancore, Raja of:
Tippoo Sahib's attacks on, **11**. 186n
Travel; travels:
benefit of, discussed by HW, **11**. 358
Berrys choose injudicious months for, **11**. 173
dangers and inconveniences of, **11**. 84–6, 87–8, 90–1, 96–7, 103, 158, 161
expenses of: Dover-Calais boat, **7**. 399, 407, 409, 412; London to Paris, **7**. 399, 405, 407, 410, 413; Paris to London, **7**. 401, 412
HW dislikes writing about, **30**. 95
HW not fatigued by, **11**. 97
Penthièvre, Duc de, takes only two posts a day, **20**. 466

time of: Amiens to Abbeville, **3**. 2; Chanteloup to Paris (15 hours), **4**. 110; London to Paris, **3**. 342, **6**. 226, **7**. 258–9, 315–16, 324, 333–4, 342–3; Paris to Chanteloup, **3**. 289; Paris to Chantilly, **3**. 1; Paris to London, **3**. 213, **4**. 345, **6**. 228, **7**. 314, 324, 333, 342, 353
weapons needed as precaution for, **20**. 312
See also Post; Transportation
Travell, Ferdinando Tracy (d. 1808):
connected with Tracys, **14**. 201n
Travell, Francis (ca 1728–1801), of Swerford, Oxon:
(?) nominated for living, **14**. 201
Travell, Mrs John (*née* Tracy) (d. 1763). See Tracy, ——
Traveller and the dove, the:
verses on, **9**. 7–8
Travellers:
English: get no benefits at Naples, **35**. 440; in France, **11**. 331, 359; in Italy, **11**. 263
HW's reflections on, **20**. 180
Irish in Italy, **11**. 263
Traveller's Pocket Companion:
letters might become supplement to, **13**. 192
Travels and Adventures of Three Princes of Serendip. See under Chetwood, William
Travels in Greece. See under Chandler, Richard
Travels in the Two Sicilies. See under Swinburne, Henry
Travels into Poland, Russia, Sweden and Denmark. See under Coxe, William
Travels of Mr John Gulliver, The. See under Lockman, John
Travels through Different Cities . . . . See under Drummond, Alexander
Travels through France. See under Stevens, Dr Sacheverel
Travels through Portugal and Spain. See under Twiss, Richard
Travels through Spain. See under Swinburne, Henry
Travels to Discover the Source of the Nile. See under Bruce, James
'Travendahl, Comte de':
Christian VII's assumed name, **23**. 43n
Travers, Mr:
SH visited by, **12**. 227
Traversay, Jean-François Prévost de. See Prévost de Traversay, Jean-François
Traverse for brushing clothes:
fire-screen resembles, **42**. 315
Trayford, Sussex:
manor of, **1**. 376
Treason:
counsel for persons impeached for, **19**. 395n, 397n
Skinner's speech defining, **19**. 282n
Treasonable Practices Bill. *See under* Parliament: acts of
Treasurer; treasurers:
Court, reform of, **7**. 423

Stone, Andrew, to be, to Q. Charlotte, **38**. 96

Treasurer of the Chambers *or* Chamber:

appointment of, **9**. 33, 181

Arundel replaces Cotton as, **19**. 256

Cotton replaces Hobart as, **18**. 551, **30**. 303n

Dashwood succeeds Charles Townshend as, **21**. 490

Elliot becomes, **22**. 38

Hardwicke recommends Charles Townshend to George II as, **21**. 104n

Hillsborough succeeds Arundel as, **20**. 517

Townshend, Charles, to remain, unconnected with Pitt-Newcastle ministry, **30**. 135

—— to succeed Hillsborough as, **21**. 26

See also Arundel, Richard; Cotton, Sir John Hind; Hobart, John (1723–93), E. of Buckinghamshire; Vice-treasurer

Treasurer of the Household:

Bateman receives white stick as, **37**. 481

—— succeeds Berkeley as, **21**. 25

Berkeley succeeds Fitzwalter as, **20**. 518

Clifford's staff as, **35**. 148

Egmont declines appointment as, **35**. 195n

—— may succeed Fitzwalter as, **35**. 195

joke about office of, **10**. 116

Shelley succeeds Edgcumbe as, **22**. 470

Stone becomes, to Q. Charlotte, **21**. 517–18

Treasurer of the Navy. *See under* Navy

Treasurer of the Opera:

plot against, **35**. 230

Treasury:

adjournment of, in Sir Robert Walpole's absence, **43**. 174

Ancel at, **41**. 119

appointments to: **9**. 33, 180, **10**. 32, 60, **35**. 517–18; rumoured, **9**. 72, 202

Bedford, Grosvenor, might lose place because of, **40**. 41

Bedford faction willing to let Grafton keep place in, **22**. 538

board of: Cavendish, Lord John, assumes Grafton would not want a Cavendish on, **30**. 232; Legge opposes Hessian subsidy at meeting of, **20**. 501; meets at Sir Robert Walpole's house, **17**. 391n; receives Customs commissioners' complaint, **41**. 325–9

Bradshaw secretary to, **24**. 56

Bubb Dodington a member of, **30**. 292n

—— resigns as lord of, **17**. 257n

Bute may substitute Northumberland for Grenville as head of, **38**. 429, 497

—— to be first lord of, **22**. 37

—— would have given, to Fox, **22**. 134

Carteret covets place in, **18**. 265–6, 277

—— said to allow George II no power in, **18**. 81

Cavendish, Lord John, leaves, **22**. 444

changes in: **17**. 332, **18**. 350, 551, **19**. 211, 256, **20**. 517, **21**. 24, 25, **25**. 392; planned, **38**. 370

commissioners of, tell Rose to ask HW for stationery accounts for 1780, **42**. 29–34

Compton appointed to, **17**. 337

Conway's office in Ordnance perhaps incompatible with, **39**. 93–4

Devonshire, D. of, first lord of, **21**. 17, 24, 74

Earle is lord of, **17**. 242n, 250n

Edgcumbe may get post in, **18**. 356–7

Elliot succeeds James Grenville in, **21**. 490

Exchequer dependent on, **39**. 94

Fane made clerk of, **18**. 33

first lord of: Exchequer auditorship controlled by, **20**. 233n; Exchequer chancellorship separated from, **20**. 422n; Hardwicke or Newcastle may become, **35**. 165; ignorant and must rely on chancellor of Exchequer, **39**. 108; salary of, **17**. 333n; to be chosen, **18**. 265, 277

Fox, C. J., dismissed as lord of, **23**. 557

—— in, **34**. 253

Fox, Henry (Bn Holland), may succeed Pelham as lord of, **20**. 411, 419

—— to be lord of, **18**. 350, 356

—— wishes Northumberland to replace Grenville as head of, **38**. 429

Furnese lord of, **20**. 517, **21**. 172n, **35**. 263

—— succeeds Legge as secretary of, **17**. 492–3, **30**. 305n

George II, Lady Yarmouth, and Hardwicke expect Henry Fox to decline, **30**. 128

George II wants to dismiss people from, **18**. 232

Grafton becomes head of, **22**. 439, 443

—— believed to be head of, **30**. 227

Grenville, George, replaces Middlesex as lord of, **19**. 419

—— to be first lord of, **22**. 130

Grenville, James, commissioner of, **21**. 346n

Grenvilles propose poor relief by, **30**. 235

—— want Newcastle not Rockingham to head, **41**. 86

—— will not waive, to Rockingham, **23**. 181

HW cannot guess who will have, **30**. 226

HW hopes that Henry Fox will not decline, **30**. 128

HW jokes about Mann's essences sweetening, **18**. 292

HW proposes Dorset as head of, **21**. 98n, **37**. 487n

HW's duties pertaining to, **14**. 256–7

HW's money may be withheld by, as political reprisal, **38**. 415

HW's patent place in, **32**. 281, 288–9

HW unconcerned about family's loss of, **30**. 39

HW will not connive with people at, for private profit, **41**. 206–7

(?) Hampton Court lodgings now administered by, **39**. 314

Hertford offers to compensate HW for losses from, **38**. 430–1

Hessian treaty arrives at, **20**. 493

Jeffries secretary to, **18**. 321, 365

[Treasury, *continued*]

junior lords of, cultivated by D. of Newcastle, **40.** 88

Legge, lord of, **19.** 256, 457n

—— replaced in, by D. of Newcastle, **21.** 103

—— secretary of, **17.** 492, **19.** 457n

letter for HW's Exchequer payments not prepared by, for Martin's signature, **40.** 277–8

lords of, Mann, Mary, might apply to, for grant of Tortola lands, **24.** 264

Lyttelton a lord of, **30.** 303n

—— at, announces 'business at the House,' **19.** 168

Mann does not understand Newcastle's position in, **20.** 422

Martin secretary to, **21.** 25, **22.** 183n

—— writes from, **40.** 277

Middlesex to continue in, **19.** 370

—— to join, **18.** 365

money of, hoodwinks English people, **24.** 491

Murray may succeed Pelham as first lord of, **20.** 411, 419

Newcastle, D. of, has Nugent appointed commissioner of, **20.** 425n

—— proposes himself as first lord of, **21.** 86n

—— rumoured to succeed Devonshire as first lord of, **21.** 91n

—— takes charge of, **20.** 417, 422

—— to be head of, **35.** 168

New Ode, A, satirizes, **18.** 50

North and C. J. Fox propose Portland as first lord of, **25.** 377, 379

Nugent a lord of, **17.** 254n, **21.** 24

Oxenden, lord of, **33.** 222

Pelham, as first lord of, controls Exchequer auditorship, **20.** 233n

—— first lord of, **18.** 299, 313, **20.** 233n, **25.** 20n

—— may get post in, **18.** 147, 265–6, 277

—— resigns as first lord of, **19.** 211

—— resumes first lordship of, **19.** 212

Pitt (Chatham) asks Newcastle to confine himself to, **21.** 91

—— blames Newcastle and Legge for mismanagement of, **21.** 290n

—— may succeed Pelham as first lord of, **20.** 411, 419

—— wants Temple as head of, **22.** 161, 307, 433

Pitt, William II, may become first lord of, **25.** 460

Portland, D. of, resigns post in, **25.** 460n

—— succeeds Shelburne as first lord of, **25.** 391, **36.** 208–9

promotions in, talked of, **30.** 162

Pulteney, E. of Bath, covets post in, **18.** 265, 277, 299, **19.** 211, 212

—— refuses post in, **18.** 72, **19.** 212

——'s appointees in, called 'dish clouts,' **18.** 350

Rockingham becomes first lord of, **25.** 261–2

—— succeeds George Grenville as first lord of, **22.** 310

salary of commissioner and of lord of, **17.** 333n

Sandys in, **18.** 103

Scrope, secretary to, **17.** 467

Sharpe, John, solicitor to, **20.** 547n

Shelburne resigns as first lord of, **25.** 377

——'s accession as first lord of, produces resignations, **25.** 293–4

Stanley spurns Grenville's offer of place in, **43.** 280

Temple refuses to become first lord of, **22.** 307–8, **30.** 225

Treby, lord of, **17.** 332, 333n

vacancies in, **22.** 38

Vane lord of, **20.** 39, 72

Villiers covets post in, **19.** 458

Waldegrave might be first lord of, **21.** 98

Waller refuses lordship in, **17.** 332, **30.** 291n

Walpole, Lady, has house adjoining, **15.** 326

Walpole, Sir Robert, first lord of, **22.** 26–7

—— would not return to, **18.** 142

West, secretary to, **20.** 371n, **21.** 25

Westcote gets place in, **32.** 354

Wilmington's impotence in, satirized in ballad, **18.** 83

—— to head, **17.** 319, 332

Treasury, Irish:

appointments in, rumoured, **9.** 181, 320

Treasury Bench:

Grenville, George, not defended by, **38.** 500

Townshend confounds, **37.** 444

Treasury Chambers:

Martin writes from, **40.** 277

Treasury warrants:

(?) Legge refuses to sign, **43.** 272

Treatise Concerning Civil Government, A. See under Tucker, Josiah

Treatise of the Natural Grounds and Principles of Harmony. See under Holder, William

Treatise on . . . Civil Architecture. See under Chambers, Sir William

Treatise on Miracles. See under Le Moine, Abraham

Treatise on the Roman Senate, A. See under Middleton, Conyers

'Treaty, The' (satiric print). *See* 'Treaty or Shabear's Administration, The'

Treaty; treaties:

Mann's reflections on, **24.** 374

See under War; *see also under* names of treaties and under names of countries

'Treaty-dictionary':

Walpole, Horatio (1678–1757), called, **17.** 243n

Treaty of Navigation and Commerce, English-French:

HW does not understand, **33.** 545–6, 548–9

'Treaty or Shabear's Administration, The' ('The Turnstile'), satiric print:

HW describes, and sends it to Mann, **21.** 93

HW sends, to Montagu, **9.** 210, 211

Trebbia River, the, in Italy:
Charles Emmanuel III joined by Austrians at, 19. 269
HW and Gray cross, 13. 192n
Trebeck, Andrew (ca 1681–1758), D.D.; rector of St George's, Hanover Sq.:
(?) Hamilton-Gunning marriage not performed by, 20. 303
Trebizond:
Erekle II said to have taken, 22. 420n
Trebur (Hesse):
Pernklö reaches, 37. 159
Treby, George (ca 1684–1742), M.P.; lord of the Treasury, 1741:
post in Treasury lost by, 17. 332
salary of, as lord of Treasury, 17. 333n
Trechsel, Kaspar and Melchior:
Simulachres et historiées faces published by, at Lyon, 42. 432n
Trecothick, Barlow (? 1718–75), M.P.; alderman of London:
London's election candidate, 23. 5
——'s petition accompanied by, 23. 132n
——'s remonstrance avowed by, 23. 98
Trecothick, Mrs Barlow. *See* Meredith, Anne
Tredegar, Monmouthshire:
Gould of, 2. 219n
Morgan of, 23. 174
Tredille:
eighteen-penny, played by HW with Ds of Newcastle and Lady Browne, 39. 187–8
HW plays, 33. 200
played at Ds of Richmond's, 38. 400
Tree; trees:
Abercorn's, had nothing to do but grow, 33. 478
aeronauts land in, 33. 458
Amelia, Ps, to receive, from France, 38. 279, 339–40, 345, 358, 366, 373, 379
amours of, 34. 123
at: Anne Pitt's house at Knightsbridge, 31. 55, 68; Bath, not faded in October, 31. 130; Esher, 10. 72; Ham House, 10. 306; Hanworth, cut down, 11. 287; Knole, sacrificed by Dorset, 23. 83; Livry, 10. 212; Rotterdam, 37. 134; Scawen's Park, 33. 111; Twickenham, damaged by storm, 12. 175; Vauxhall, do not inspire HW to poetry, 30. 100
Bentley draws, well, 35. 243
——'s, in landscape, criticized by HW, 35. 208
—— sends, to HW, 35. 207
clumps of: at Holkham, HW will not be dragged to see, 30. 37; HW interested in, only in Grosvenor Sq., 30. 37
Conway plants, in all weathers, 37. 350
cut for firewood in Dresden garden, 21. 361n
Dutch, are in rows, 37. 134
English, are often in full leaf by end of April, 25. 497
'fish-bearing,' 37. 117
foreign, England imports, 10. 262
forty, in Onslow's wood, 30. 292n
French: clipped, 31. 45, 49; excessively trimmed, 10. 201; 'maimed' along roads, 39. 251; 'royal timber' when over 30 years old, 35. 336; short-lived, 10. 212
French 'educate,' by lopping them off, 35. 336
fruit, in Dauphiné, killed by frost, 22. 514n
growth of, measures their planters' decay, 37. 303
HW's, at SH: broken by storm, 9. 134; golden, 12. 65; grow too slowly for HW, 37. 292; HW's servants lop, 24. 48; HW thins, 23. 315; HW thins, from woods, and puts them in fields, 35. 259; plantations of, 30. 117; wind may injure, 20. 25
HW's acquaintance limited to, 35. 341
HW sends, to Bentley, 35. 204–5
HW's interest shifts to, from china, 20. 53–4, 70
HW to plant, with rain, 37. 348
HW used to want lamps on, as at Vauxhall, 39. 133
in Netley Abbey ruins, 35. 251
Islip's rebus, 35. 132
lamps in, for ball decorations, 35. 391
lanes full of, near Worcester, 35. 152
'loose,' at St John's, Oxford, 33. 57
Marsac's, massacred near Park Place, 39. 550
Minorca lacks, 37. 310
Moone's collection of, rare, 32. 135n
Müntz depicts, 35. 232
Northington orders cutting of, to spite his son, 23. 368
olive, 37. 551
on old Boulevard at Paris, 32. 261
Pantheon's subterranean apartment planted with, 39. 330
Park Place's view not obstructed by, 37. 350
Radnor's, ruin his prospects, 37. 348
road strewn with, after storm, 33. 81
Roland, Mme, makes, of green paper, in La Malle plan, 10. 196
storm injures, on New Year's Day, 24. 431
whirlwind at Rome injures, 20. 69
See also Acacia; Almond tree; Aloe tree; Apple tree; Apricot tree; Arbor vitæ; Arbutus; Ash; Beech; Bullen tree; Cedar; Cedar of Lebanon; Cherry orchard; Cherry tree; Chestnut tree; Cypress; Cytisus; Elm; Evergreen; Fig tree; Fir; Fir-grove; Forest; Fountain tree; Glastonbury thorn; Holly tree; Horsechestnut tree; Ironwood; Laburnum; Larch; Laurel tree; Lignum vitæ; Lime tree; Lombardy pine; Mulberry tree; Oak; Olive tree; Orange tree; Palm tree; Peach tree; Pinaster; Pine; Pippin tree; Plant; Pomegranate tree; Poplar; Spanish brooms; Spindle tree; Spruce fir; Sumach; Sycamore; Thorn; Timber; Verdure; Walnut tree; White pine; Willow; Wood; Yew
Treffonds. *See* Paris de Treffonds

Trefoil; trefoils:
HW criticizes design of, on Harcourt tomb, **35**. 487
in Gloucester cloister, **35**. 154
on P. Arthur's tomb, **35**. 151
Trefusis, Robert Cotton St John (1787–1832), 18th Bn Clinton, 1797:
Cholmondeley and Mrs Damer sue, **25**. 148n
Trefusis, Robert George William (1764–97), 17th Bn Clinton, 1791:
Callington borough inherited by, **13**. 11n
Clinton barony goes to, **25**. 151n, 165n
HW never saw, **42**. 377
HW offers burgage tenures to, **42**. 376–8
HW sells burgage-tenures to, **34**. 184n
Orford's heir in Devonshire, **42**. 377–8
Tregony, Cornwall:
(?) Trevanion promises to secure election of Edmund Nugent for, **30**. 332n
Tréguier, Bp of. *See* Cheylus, Joseph-Dominique de
Treillage:
arbor of, at Bushey Park, **9**. 380
at Colisée, **39**. 145
at Drayton, **10**. 90
flowers on, painted by Lady Diana Beauclerk, **42**. 490
HW plants roses against, at SH, **39**. 316
HW's cottage to have, on outside, **1**. 90
HW to bring, from Paris for new cottage, **10**. 168
HW to introduce, at SH, **31**. 46
Sutton, Mrs, has gallery painted in, **12**. 157
Treillage paper. *See under* Wallpaper
Trekh-ierarkhov. *See* Tre-Primati
Trekshuit; trekshuits (Dutch canal *or* river boat):
Ailesbury, Cts of, might give dog to master of, **38**. 132
Conway and Frenchmen travel on, **38**. 4
Trelawnay, Col.:
49th Foot regiment of, **19**. 69n
Trelawney; Trelawney. *See* Trelawny
Trelawny, Sir Jonathan (1650–1721), 3d Bt; Bp of Bristol, 1685, of Exeter, 1689, of Winchester, 1707:
one of seven imprisoned bishops, but swore like a trooper, **38**. 202
Trelawny, William:
West Looe elects, instead of Burrell, **21**. 89n
Tremaine. *See* Tremayne
Tremayne (fl. 1747), painter of kings at Chichester:
kings' pictures repainted by, at Bp Mawson's expense, **1**. 23
Trembleurs, Les:
verses to air of, **5**. 413, **6**. 405
Trémoïlle. *See* La Trémoïlle
Trenchard, George (ca 1684–1758), M.P.:
Wolfeton House long in family of, **37**. 491
Trenchard, John (1668–1723), M.P.:
Cole says, committed suicide, **15**. 311
letters signed 'Cato' written by, **15**. 293

widow of, marries Gordon, his co-author in 'Cato' letters, **20**. 167
wife of, **15**. 293n
Trenchard, Mrs John. *See* Blackett, Anne
Trenchard, Mary (ca 1717–1806), m. (1740) Richard Owen Cambridge:
beauty of, unfaded, **11**. 16
Cambridge calls, 'Venus' but seldom sees her, **15**. 332
card-playing opposed by, **11**. 305
Clarence, D. of (William IV), disliked by, as neighbour, **11**. 63, 70
Fitzherbert, Mrs, to be neighbour of, **12**. 138
gossiping of, **11**. 305, **12**. 17
HW calls, 'nymph of the cherry-tree,' **12**. 32
HW mentions, **12**. 61
HW visits, **12**. 15, 177
husband and, resolve not to grieve for grandson, **15**. 332
illness of, **12**. 26, 32
prudishness of, **12**. 17
Twickenham resident, **42**. 484
Trencher; trenchers:
in Q. Elizabeth's collection, **32**. 324
Trenck, Franz, Baron von:
pandours commanded by, **17**. 144n
pandours organized by, **9**. 206n
pandours the local troops of, in Croatia, **30**. 73n
Prussian army defeated by pandours of, **19**. 62n
Trent (Italy):
couriers from Germany pass through, twice a week, **24**. 321
Gloucester, Ds of, writes from, **36**. 126, 128, 135, 141
mail not received from, **32**. 376, 377
Ursulines of, prayed for D. of Gloucester, **32**. 389
visitors to: Adair, Robert, **36**. 130, 139, 141, 142; Cholmondeley, **24**. 319, **36**. 132, 134, 135, 137; Gloucester, D. and Ds of, **6**. 467n, 477n, **24**. 317, 319, 321–3, 325–6, 329, 336–7, **26**. 50, **32**. 362–3, 364–5, 373, 376–7, 389, **36**. 128–45; Heywood, Col., **24**. 317, 321, 337; Heywood, Mrs, **24**. 323; Jebb, Richard, **36**. 130, 133, 135, 136, 138, 141, 142; Pitt, Anne, **24**. 389
Winckelmann murdered at, **23**. 113
Trent (? Dorset):
Wyndham of, **1**. 48n
Trent, river:
bridge over, **40**. 43
HW sees, at Wichnor, **9**. 294
Wichnor Park overlooks, **38**. 71
Trent, Council of:
inspiration needed by, **32**. 373
Trente et quarante (game):
gambling at, at White's, **38**. 469
losses at, **4**. 54
popularity of, **6**. 393
Trentham, Vct. *See* Leveson Gower, Granville (1721–1803)

Trentham, Vcts. *See* Egerton, Lady Louisa

Trentham, Staffs:
Bedford, D. and Ds of, to visit Gower at, 38. 423, 433
Bedford, D. of, visits, 38. 433
Cumberland, D. of, at, 38. 19
Lloyd, Rachel, to visit, 39. 131
party moves from, to Ragley, 38. 64

Trento, Antonio da. *See* Fantuzzi da Trento, Antonio

Trenton, N. J.:
Americans encamped at, 29. 112n
battle of: 28. 287n; Hessians defeated in, 24. 285–6; won by Americans, 6. 415n, 417n
Hessians at, 28. 282n

Trepanning:
performed on Lord Temple, 28. 463
Tavistock undergoes, 22. 497

Trepid, English ship under Capt. Young:
almost sunk, 20. 591
letter from, discredits Byng, 20. 591

Tre-Primati, Russian ship:
at Leghorn, 23. 191
(?) Greig commands, 23. 227n

Treschietto, Marchese di. *See* Nay, Emmanuel-François-Joseph-Ignace de

'Treschietto':
Richecourt's new title, 19. 385, 394

Tresckow, Joachim Christian von (1698–1762); Lt-Gen.:
Harsch besieges, at Neisse, 21. 254n
Thürheim, Count, surrenders Schweidnitz to, 21. 198n

Tresconi (country dances):
Florentines offended by interruption to, 19. 365

Tresette *or* Tré-sept (game):
Karl Friedrich's only game, 20. 148–9
played at Choiseul's, 6. 161

Tresham, Henry (ca 1749–1814), painter:
SH visited by, 12. 237
SH visitors sent by, 12. 237

Tresmes, Comtesse de:
social relations of, with Mme Geoffrin, 7. 277

Tresmes, Duc de. *See* Potier, Louis-Léon (1695–1774); Potier de Gesvres, François-Bernard (1655–1739)

Tresmes, Duchesse de:
(?) social relations of, with Comtesse de Brionne, 7. 295

Tressan, Comte de. *See* La Vergne, Louis-Élisabeth de

Tressemanes de Brunet, Gaspard de (1721–84), Bp of Glandèves 1755–72:
Dauphin's safety assured in dream to, 7. 285, 31. 79
Marie Leszczyńska reassured by, that her son will be preserved, 7. 284, 39. 33

Tres Tabernæ on Appian Way, Italy:
waiters from, 11. 295

Trevalyn ('Trevallin'; 'Trevallyn'), Denbighshire:

Boscawen and Trevor families of, 9. 112n, 10. 295n, 352
spelling of, corrected, 43. 137

Trevanion, John (ca 1740–1810), M.P.:
Dover election won by, 39. 197

Trevanion, William (1727–67), M.P.:
birth date of, corrected, 43. 326
Frederick, P. of Wales, opposed by, at (?) Tregony, 30. 332n
ministry secured election of, under age, 30. 332n
Nugent obtains appointment of, as groom of Bedchamber to Frederick, P. of Wales, 30. 332n
Nugent, Edmund, promised election by, 30. 332n

Trevecca House, Talgarth, Wales:
Hotham, Lady Gertrude, invites Chesterfield to, 24. 91

Trevelyan, John (1761–1846), 5th Bt, 1828:
Gunning, Miss, allegedly refuses to marry, 11. 202

Treves, Pellegrine (1733–1817), 'the Jew':
Cadogan and George, P. of Wales (George IV), fond of, 33. 565
George IV said to be pushed by, towards Mrs Fitzherbert, 33. 565n
HW entertains, at SH, 33. 565

Trevigar, Rev. Luke (1705–72), Fellow of Clare Hall, Cambridge:
benefice of, 2. 372
Cole's tutor, 2. 371
HW hears lectures of, 12. 208n, 13. 6
HW's tutor in mathematics at Cambridge, 12. 208, 21. 353
HW told by, about Mrs Daye, 2. 371

Trevigi. *See* Pennacchi da Trevigi

Tréville, Hôtel de, in Paris:
Joseph II's suite lodges at, 6. 440
Leinster, Ds of, at, 7. 14
Luxembourg, the, near, 7. 14

Trevilyan. *See* Trevelyan

Trevis. *See* Treves

Trevisani, Angelo (1669–?1753), painter:
Correggio painting copied by, 26. 7
Vendôme's portrait by, 35. 509

Tre Visi, Villa di. *See* Palmieri, Villa

Trevor, Bn. *See* Hampden, Hon. Robert (1706–83); Trevor, John (1695–1764); Trevor, Thomas (1658–1730); Trevor, Thomas (ca 1692–1752)

Trevor, Bns. *See* Burrell, Elizabeth (d. 1734); Serle, Elizabeth; Steele, Elizabeth (d. 1782); Weldon, Anne (d. 1746)

Trevor, Miss, 'sister of Lord Hampden':
legacy said to have been made by, to Lady Diana Beauclerk's daughter, 30. 275

Trevor, Anne (d. 1760):
genealogy of, 10. 352

Trevor, Anne (1710–83), m. (1743) Hon. George Boscawen; 'Mrs Muscovy':
childbirth of, 9. 141
genealogy of, 10. 352

[Trevor Anne (1710–83), *continued*]
HW asked by, to write to Montagu, 9. 112
HW calls on, 9. 12, 141
HW sends message through, 9. 87
HW to entertain, at SH, 9. 161
HW to see, 9. 49
Montagu's cousin, 9. 93n
——'s jasmine interests, 9. 79
Rice, Mrs, and Lucy, to receive letters from, 9. 12
son of, 10. 295n
Trevor, Arabella (d. 1734), m. 1 (1707) Robert Heath; m. 2 Brig.-Gen. Edward Montagu; George Montagu's mother:
genealogy of, 10. 352
Montagu hears from, about Bns Cutts's portrait, 9. 252
—— son of, 1. 36n
monument to, at Horton, 10. 333
Trevor, Arabella (1714–89):
genealogy of, 10. 352
sisters of, may sometimes be confused with her, 9. 141n
Trevor, Arthur:
Wynn's election petitioned against by, 18. 392n
Trevor, Diana (1744–78):
genealogy of, 10. 352
Trevor, Elizabeth (1683–1706), m. (1702) David Polhill:
genealogy of, 10. 352
Trevor, Elizabeth (1703–20):
genealogy of, 10. 352
Trevor, Hon. Elizabeth (d. 1761), m. (1732) Charles Spencer, 2d (3d) D. of Marlborough:
death of, 9. 392, 38. 133, 134
genealogy of, 10. 352
Hague, The, to be visited by, 18. 209
(?) inseparable from husband, 39. 3
laundry-maid of, reveals alleged plot, 35. 230
mother of Lady Diana Beauclerk, 16. 280n
Pembroke disliked by, when he was making love, 10. 20
steward of, to write to Montagu, 9. 245
Trevor, Gertrude (1713–80), m. (1744) Hon. Charles Roper:
genealogy of, 10. 352
Trevor, Grace (b. 1706, living at Bath, ? 1792):
(?) Bath visited by, 10. 229, 231
genealogy of, 10. 352
(?) HW calls on, 10. 230–1, 234
(?) HW fears he may not recognize, 10. 229
(?) HW finds, altered, 10. 234
(?) HW to call on, 10. 229
(?) house of, at Bath, 10. 231
(?) Montagu sends compliments to, 10. 230
sisters of, may be confused with her, 9. 141n
Trevor, Sir John (d. 1672), secretary of state; M.P.:
genealogy of, 10. 352
Trevor, John (ca 1652–86), of Plas Tag, Flints:
genealogy of, 10. 352

Montagu's grandfather, 9. 191n
wife of, 9. 191, 191n, 252
Trevor, John (1695–1764), 3d Bn Trevor; M.P.:
genealogy of, 10. 352
Trevor, John (? 1717–43), M.P.; lord of the Admiralty:
Admiralty appointment of, 17. 366
genealogy of, 10. 352
lacks estate and parts, 17. 366
Pelhams' relative, 17. 366
Phillipson replaces, in Admiralty, 18. 349n
Trevor, Hon. John (1749–1824), 3d Vct Hampden, 1524; minister to the Diet at Ratisbon 1780–3; envoy extraordinary at Turin, 1783:
former German employments of, 25. 398
genealogy of, 10. 352
HW asks Lady Diana Beauclerk to get poems of father of, 42. 397–8
Turin post of, 25. 398, 595n
wife of, 25. 595n
Trevor, Mrs John. *See* Burton, Harriet (ca 1751–1829); Clark, Elizabeth (ca 1655–93)
Trevor, John Morley (1681–1719), of Glynde:
daughter of, 9. 12n, 10. 229n
genealogy of, 10. 352
Trevor, Mrs John Morley. *See* Montagu, Lucy
Trevor, Lucy (d. 1720):
death of, 9. 134n
references not to, 9. 141n
Trevor, Lucy (b. 1705), m. (1722) Edward Rice:
Boscawen, Mrs, to write to, 9. 12
genealogy of, 10. 352
HW consults, about Montagu's address, 9. 161
(?) HW mentions, 37. 425
HW sends compliments to, 9. 12
Montagu promises to lend copy of *Life of Edward Lord Herbert of Cherbury* to, 10. 143
——'s correspondence with, 9. 351, 352, 10. 143
(?) Talbot family tell, of Montagu's appointment, 9. 351
Trevor, Margaret (1711–69), 'Peggy':
Boscawen, Anne, attends, 10. 302
carriage accident of, 10. 135
death of, 10. 300
Frogmore visited by, 10. 135
genealogy of, 10. 352
HW informed by, of Montagu's movements, 9. 174
HW meets, at Mrs Boscawen's, 9. 141
HW sends to Montagu condolences on death of, 10. 300
(?) HW to meet, 9. 152
HW wished by, to intercede for servants at Windsor, 10. 137
Montagu asked by, to have HW intercede for servants at Windsor, 10. 137
—— brings, to Frogmore, 10. 135
—— comforted by, in bereavement, 9. 176

—— mourns, **10.** 302

——'s correspondence with, **10.** 137

—— to be visited by, **9.** 174

Windsor Castle, home of, **10.** 135, 142n

Trevor (after 1754 Hampden), Hon. Maria Constantia (1744–67), m. (1764) Henry Howard, 12th E. of Suffolk:

death of, **22.** 484

marriage of, **38.** 334

name of, corrected, **43.** 130

Trevor, Mary (1708–? 80):

genealogy of, **10.** 352

sisters of, may be confused with her, **9.** 141n

Trevor, Hon. Dr Richard (1707–71), Bp of St David's, 1744, of Durham, 1752:

armour given by, to Montagu, **10.** 301

armour rescued by, from braziers, **10.** 287

Bentley's designs for palace of, **35.** 644

Bishop Auckland altered by, **9.** 310

Canterbury archbishopric may go to, **21.** 185, **40.** 125

Carlton House visited by, **10.** 301

Cumberland to convey Bentley's apologies to, **9.** 343

death of, **23.** 313

'fat-bellied,' **10.** 257

genealogy of, **10.** 352

Gosset's portrait of, **9.** 213

guests of: Abercorn, E. of, **10.** 210; Carlisle, Bp of, **10.** 210; Cumberland, **9.** 343; Manchester, D. of, **9.** 310; Montagu, George, **10.** 210; Trevor, Bn, **10.** 210; Trevor, Richard, **10.** 210

HW's conversation with, **10.** 301

Manchester, D. of, talks with, **9.** 310

Montagu does not visit, **10.** 245

—— identifies pictures of, **10.** 80

——'s opinion of, **10.** 257

—— to visit, **10.** 243, 244

Pelhams give Durham bishopric to, **20.** 323n

prints of, **2.** 27, 28, 29, **41.** 350–1

SH visit of, prevented by snow, **10.** 210

SH visit requested by, **10.** 203

Trevor, Richard (d. 1775), deputy secretary in lord chamberlain's office:

(?) deafness preserves, from Bp of Carlisle's eloquence, **10.** 210

death of, **7.** 398

(?) Durham, Bp of, entertains, **10.** 210

Trevor, Hon. Robert. *See* Hampden, Hon. Robert

Trevor, Hon. Mrs Robert. *See* De Huybert, Constantia

Trevor, Ruth (1712–64):

genealogy of, **10.** 352

sisters of, may be confused with her, **9.** 141n

Trevor, Thomas (1658–1730), chief justice of Common Pleas; 1st Bn Trevor; M.P.:

genealogy of, **10.** 352

Trevor, Thomas (? b. ca 1682):

genealogy of, **10.** 352

Trevor, Thomas (ca 1692–1753), 2d Bn Trevor:

genealogy of, **10.** 352

Trevor (afterwards Hampden), Thomas (1746–1824), 2d Vct Hampden, 1783; M.P.:

genealogy of, **10.** 352

Mann receives attentions from, at Florence, **25.** 592

wife of, **25.** 592, 595n

Trevor family:

HW entertains, at SH, **9.** 105, 161

portrait of Bns Cutts not obtained by, **9.** 259

Welsh origins of, **9.** 112

Trévoux, ——:

Louis XV's conversation with, **7.** 364

Theodore of Corsica's nephew, **7.** 364

Trews:

Young Pretender wears, **19.** 320n

Treyford. *See* Trayford

Treyssac de Vergy, Pierre-Henri (d. 1774):

Argental's dialogue with, **22.** 262n

Éon, Chevalier d', attacks, **22.** *190*

—— liberates, from prison, **22.** 262

—— now makes affidavit for, **38.** 467

—— promises not to fight, **38.** 244n

Guerchy accused by, **22.** 262

—— said to have hired, to murder d'Éon, **38.** 466

Mann astonished by story of, **22.** 273

Trial, Mme. *See* Milon, Marie-Jeanne

Trial, Bristol privateer:

San Zirioco captured by, **19.** 134, 138

Trial, English sloop:

Dutch intercepted by, **22.** 71

Trial; trials:

Orford, Cts of, deserves place only in collection of bawdy, **30.** 93

See also under Chancery; Court martial; Court of Common Pleas; Court of King's Bench; 'Rebel Lords'; *and under names of defendants*

Trial of Selim the Persian. See under Moore, Edward

Triand, Marquis de:

social relations of, with Marquise de Monconseil, **7.** 297

Trianon, at Versailles:

HW and Gray 'slubber over,' **13.** 168

in disrepair, **17.** 127

Joseph II entertained at, **6.** 443

—— to be entertained at, **6.** 441

Louis XV gives, to wife, **17.** 127

—— proposes visit to, **4.** 195

Marie-Antoinette at, **7.** 129

Mirepoix, Mme de, at, **5.** 98

See also Petit Trianon

Tribune; tribunes (Roman officials):

comparable to English wagoner, **38.** 120

Tribune; tribunes (galleries):

Du Deffand, Mme, has, in convent chapel, **39.** 233

Tribune, at SH. *See* SH: Cabinet at

Tribune, in Uffizi Gallery at Florence, *see under* Uffizi

'Tribune at Florence' (painting). *See under* Zoffany, John

Trichonium, Bp of. *See* La Ville, Jean-Ignace de

Tricolour cockade. *See under* Cockade; cockades

Tricot:
made from Mme du Deffand's effilage, **5.** 284, **6.** 34, 41

Tric-trac (game):
Fox, C. J., loses at, **4.** 324
played, **5.** 120, **6.** 161, 378, **11.** 250

Trident, English ship:
Adm. Dennis's ship, **23.** 353
Gloucester, D. of, to entertain Grand Duke and Duchess of Tuscany on, **23.** 353
survives Jamaica hurricane, **39.** 353n

Triennial Act. *See under* Parliament: acts of

Trier, Abp and Elector of. *See* Klemens Wenzel (1739–1812)

Trieste (Austria):
Austrian army to embark at, for Naples, **18.** 3
corn must be shipped from, from Hungary to Italy, **22.** 448
declared a free port to improve relations with Tuscany, **20.** 98n
English attack expected at, **21.** 134
Florentine goods sent from Leghorn to, **17.** 380
German reinforcements to embark at, **19.** 206, 220
Louis XVI's aunts die at, **11.** 208n
Maria Theresa's maritime power established at, **20.** 98, 102
——'s subsidy carried to, from England by Forrester, **18.** 107
Venice to be eclipsed by, **20.** 102

'Trifaldin'; 'Trifaldine, Cts.' *See under* Cervantes, Miguel de: *Don Quixote*; *see also* 'Trufaldin'

Trifles:
as important and less harmful than serious things, **39.** 409
HW prefers, to serious things, **10.** 171–2

Trigge, Thomas (d. 1714), K.B., 1801; army officer:
Mann consigns packet to, **24.** 380
——'s express sent by, **24.** 377n
Rome left by, for Florence on way to England, **24.** 380
SH visited by, **12.** 234

Trille (game):
Louis XV plays, **38.** 268
played, **7.** 265, 273

Trim, County Meath, Ireland:
Rivertown near, **41.** 248

Trimlestown, Bn. *See* Barnewall, Nicholas

Trimnell, Charles (1663–1723), Bp of Norwich and of Winchester:
drawing of, by Bp Greene, **1.** 162

Trincalo. *See* Trincolo; Trinculo

'Trincolo':
applied to Capt. Prescott, **33.** 424
See also under Shakespeare, William: *Tempest*

Trincolo's Trip to the Jubilee. See under Thompson, Edward

Trincomalee, Ceylon:
English capture, **25.** 277, **34.** 212
French said to have retaken, **25.** 393

'Trinculo, Duke':
HW's name for D. of Newcastle, **20.** 502
HW's name for sea captains, **18.** 117

Tring, Herts:
Gore of, **2.** 239n

Trinità, bridge of, at Florence. *See* Ponte a Santa Trinità

Trinità del Monte, at Rome:
Palazzo Medici on, **19.** 113

Trinité, La. *See* La Trinité

Trinity, the:
Berkeley's *Siris* discusses, **18.** 452, 465
Charlotte, Q., George IV, and William Pitt II called, by HW, **25.** 680
Hume, Richardson, and whist popular as, in Paris, **30.** 208–9
Hutchinsonians consider York Buildings Waterworks a symbol of, **35.** 156
Italian painter includes Madonna in, **23.** 459
Maguire cannot swallow doctrine of, **18.** 420
pope's tiara symbolizes, **19.** 358

Trinity College, Cambridge:
Ashton's brother a fellow of, **43.** 189
Bentley buried in chapel of, **15.** 20n
—— Master of, **20.** 368n, **23.** 365n
(?) *Castle of Otranto's* setting taken from, **6.** 145
Cole invited to dine in Hall of, **1.** 267n
Dale, Dr, of, **43.** 186
dinner in Hall and Master's Lodge of, for D. of Newcastle's installation as chancellor, **20.** 71n
divided in election, **2.** 167n
elms of, damaged, **2.** 136
former students at: Halifax, E. of, **10.** 334; Montagu, Christopher, **10.** 333; Montagu, George, **10.** 333; Orwell, **10.** 334; Osborn, Sir George, **9.** 248
HW's coming to, erroneously reported in newspapers, **13.** 78
HW visits, **1.** 32n, **6.** 145
Hollis, benefactor of, **1.** 360n
Lort leaves, for summer excursion, **16.** 141
MS in, **15.** 146
Master's Lodge at, treasures in, **15.** 19
Middleton, fellow of, **15.** 291, 305
—— educated at, **15.** 305
Middleton, Mrs, attempts settlement in lodge at, **15.** 313
Newton's statue in chapel of, **2.** 330
painted glass at, **1.** 30–1
Parne of, **15.** 315
Porter, David, seeks patron in, for son, **16.** 217–18

Porter, Stephen, advised by Lort to defer entering, **16**. 224
Postlethwaite the new master of, **16**. 218
Senior Fellow of, *see* Allen, John
students at, are rakes, **13**. 58
Talman revokes bequest to, **42**. 458
translation of Loredano's book in library of, **16**. 371
See also under Middleton, Conyers
Trinity College, Dublin:
Hartington welcomed by, **37**. 393n
Hertford's compliments from, **39**. 26
Trinity College, Oxford:
founder of, **35**. 73
Huddesford president of, **20**. 579n
Tindal, fellow of, **15**. 253
Trinity Hall, Cambridge:
Dickins, Dr, of, **13**. 6
picture of Bp Gardiner in lodge at, **2**. 171n
Trinity Hospital. *See under* Greenwich: Trinity Hospital at
Trinity House, Tower Hill, London:
Sandwich toasts Palliser at, **29**. 47
Trinity Monday:
Trinity Hospital accounts audited on, **16**. 81, 82
Trinity Sq., London:
Catherine Court becomes, **19**. 299n
Trino, near Turin (Italy):
Charles Emmanuel III at, **19**. 156
Trinquemale. *See* Trincomalee
Triomphe de l'amitié, Le, ou l'histoire de Jacqueline et Jeanneton. *See under* Guichard, Octavie
Triomphe du sentiment, Le. See under Bibiena, Jean Galli de
Trionfo d'amore, Il, one-act pastoral opera:
HW attends, **32**. 106
Triple alliance:
Dunkirk to be demolished under terms of treaty of, **19**. 481n
English fleet relies on, **18**. 339
mis-spelling of, **18**. 336, 339, 544
tricolour cockade for, **18**. 336, 522, 544
Tripod; tripods:
at Kedleston, **10**. 230
Tripoli:
ambassadors from and to, *see under* Ambassador
dey of, *see* Ali I (d. 1796) Karamanliya; Mehemmed Pāshā Karamānlī (d. 1754)
French demands refused by, **20**. 319
French ship returns to, **23**. 24
French ships may go from Malta to, **20**. 320
La Condamine visits, **22**. 147n
ministers from and to, *see under* Minister
Sicard becomes Mohammedan at, **20**. 319n
Trip to Calais, A. See under Foote, Samuel
Trismegistus. *See* Hermes Trismegistus
Tristes regrets, Les. See under La Place, Antoine de
Tristia. See under Ovid
Tristram Shandy. See under Sterne, Laurence

'Tristram Shandy':
Patch's caricature of: HW sure he has thanked Mann for, **23**. 33; Mann sends, to HW by Capt. Steward, **23**. 27; Mann's reasons for asking about, **23**. 37
Triton, cartel ship:
English prisoners from France arrive on, **21**. 249, **37**. 502n
Triton, English ship:
(?) Arbuthnot captain of, **20**. 280n, 284n, **43**. 270
(?) Minorca reached by, from Portugal, **20**. 280n
Triton, French war ship:
in Mediterranean, **21**. 249
Triton; tritons:
Berrys' vessel 'whisked' by, **11**. 120
English, are humane to women, **12**. 195
Ossory, Lady, will please, when bathing, **33**. 206
state coach adorned with, **22**. 104
Triulzi, Ps. *See* Archinto, Maria
'Triumph of Bacchus.' *See under* Carracci, Annibale
Triumph of Flora. See under Darwin, Erasmus
Triumph of Liberty and Peace with America:
Conway praised in, **43**. 290
Triumphs of Owen. See under Gray, Thomas
Triumphs of Temper, The. See under Hayley, William
Triumvirate, Le. See under Crébillon, Prosper Jolyot de
'Triumvirate':
HW's and Montagu's, at Eton, **9**. 4
Troad de Beaulieu, Sieur:
L'Heureux commanded by, **19**. 317n
Troarn, Abbé de. *See* Vaux de Ciry de St-Cyr, Claude-Odet-Joseph de
Trocadéro, at Paris:
Mme du Deffand's picture exhibited at, **8**. 215
Trochaics:
HW does not admire, **34**. 91
Troil, Uno von (1746–1803), Swedish scholar and divine:
Letters on Iceland by, quoted by HW, **29**. 30–1
Troilus and Criseyde. See under Chaucer, Geoffrey
Trois dialogues. See Robinson, Elizabeth, Mrs Montagu: *Dialogues of the Dead*
Trois empereurs en Sorbonne. See under Voltaire
'Trois exclamations, Les':
Conway praises, but does not send it to HW, **39**. 243
epigram on Suard, **6**. 131, 137
Trois imposteurs, Épître à l'auteur des. See under Voltaire
Trois siècles de notre littérature. See under Sabatier de Castres, Antoine
Trois sultanes. See Marmontel, Jean-François: *Soliman II*

'Trojan horse':
Belle-Isle compared to, **18**. 564n
Mathews's horse called, **18**. 453
Trojan War:
paintings of, at Mantua, **35**. 5
Pythagoras claimed to have been in, **12**. 33
Trolle, Swedish frigate:
Leghorn reached by, from Malaga, **25**. 16n, 24n
Trollope, William (ca 1707–49), fellow of Pembroke College, Cambridge:
'Characters of the Christ-Cross Row' by, **28**. 74, 76, 79
Mason sends letters of, to HW, **28**. 174
(?) verses by, **14**. 27–30
Trollopee. *See* Andrienne
Trombetta, ——, husband of Colomba Mattei:
Haymarket Theatre managed by, with wife, **35**. 287n
Tromp, Cornelius van (1629–91), *or* Martin Harpertzoon (1597–1653), Dutch admirals:
supposed drowning of, **30**. 11
tortoise-shell case belonging to, **35**. 430–1
winter weather not braved by, **9**. 268
'Trompeurs, trompés, trompettes':
Mme du Deffand's witticism on, **8**. 66
Trompeur trompé, Le. See under Vadé, Jean-Joseph
Tron, Andrea (1712–85), procurator of St Mark; Venetian ambassador to Austria:
dismissal of, from Vienna, depends on Benedict XIV's parley with Rezzonico, **20**. 190n
Ulfeld threatens, **20**. 190
Tronchin, Jean-François (b. 1743):
Rousseau's fellow-lodger, **3**. 97
Tronchin, Jean-Robert (1702–88):
Lettres écrites de la campagne by, answered by Rousseau, **14**. 138n
Tronchin, Théodore (1709–81), Swiss physician:
Académie des Sciences elects, **7**. 12
certainly a quack, **22**. 154
charlatan, **22**. 152
inoculation method of, **10**. 294n
Northampton may consult, at Geneva, **22**. 150, 152
patients of: Beauvau, Princesse de, **3**. *114*; Colonna, **7**. 99; La Rochefoucauld, Duchesse de, **5**. 95, 96; Lennox, Lady Cecilia Margaret, **4**. 292n; Luxembourg, Mme de, **4**. 446, **6**. 304, **7**. 205, 207, 208, 444; Voltaire, **7**. 22, 24, 26
social relations of, with Duchesse d'Anville, **7**. 311
son of, **3**. 97n
Tronson-Ducoudray, Guillaume-Alexandre (1750–98), counsel for Marie-Antoinette:
HW calls, 'monster' allotted to her as a defamatory spy, **12**. 48
Tronto, the, river in Italy:
Austrians cross, **18**. 419, 438
Spaniards retreat to Naples by way of, **18**. 412

Trooper; troopers:
De la Warr's, predicts earthquake, **20**. 137, 147, **23**. 261
Trossarelli, Gaspare (1763–1825), *or* Giovanni; painters:
SH visited by, **12**. 246
Troti, Angiolo (1503–63), called Bronzino; painter:
fresco by, only authentic portrait of Bianca Cappello, **20**. 398n, **43**. 128
portrait by, bought from Laurenzo by Mme Suares, and given to Mann to be sold, **17**. 128
Vasari's portrait of Bianca Cappello attributed to, **20**. 399
Trott, John:
Patriot Unmask'd by, **43**. 125
Trotti, Joachim-Jacques (1705–99), Marquis de la Chétardie; French ambassador to Russia 1739–42, 1743–4:
Anne of Russia said to have imprisoned, **13**. 217, **17**. 20
disgrace of, due to Bestuchev, **18**. 494n
Elizabeth of Russia demands her presents back from, **18**. 495
Russia said to have dismissed, **18**. 466, 495
Troubadour; troubadours:
HW's low opinion of, **31**. 254
history of, *see under* La Curne de Ste-Palaye, Jean-Baptiste de
poetry of, **40**. 303–4
Troubetskoi, Catherine Petrovna (1744–1815), m. (ca 1770) Alexander Sergeivich Strogonov:
St-Ouen visited by, **6**. 229
social relations of, in Paris, **6**. 228, **7**. 346, 349
Trouillet. *See* Raffron du Trouillet
Trou-madame (game):
HW would not have table of, without a king and queen, **32**. 201
Trousers:
nankeen, Diomède lacks, in medallion, **39**. 254
Orléans, Duc d', wears, **34**. 164
price of, **5**. 233
red, English disputes should not be settled by, **25**. 5
Trousset. *See* Du Trousset
Trout rivers:
HW's treatise will descant on convenience of, **37**. 293
Trouvé, Dom François, Abbé de Cîteaux 1748–82:
(?) Cholmondeley daughter's expulsion demanded by, **4**. 400
Trowel; trowels:
Gothic, **40**. 288
Trower, Mr:
SH visited by, **12**. 224
Troy, Jean-François (1679–1752), painter:
paintings by: at Ste-Geneviève, **7**. 305; at Sceaux, of Duc and Duchesse du Maine, **7**. 322

Troy (Asia Minor):
Anchises carried out of, **33**. 108
HW hopes to see taking of, **35**. 218
HW will not hobble like Nestor to siege of, **25**. 296
Ovid's line about, **9**. 26, **33**. 397, **34**. 86
siege of, compared with sieges of Valenciennes and Mainz, **34**. 182
SH nearly as ruined as, **23**. 365
Tiberius answers ambassadors from, **36**. 280
See also Trojan Wars
Troyes, Bp of. *See* Barral, Claude-Martin-Joseph de
Troyes (France):
Scellières near, **7**. 48
'Troy town':
HW quotes Ovid on, **9**. 26, **33**. 397, **34**. 86
Troy weight:
Legge only man in Parliament who has learnt, **37**. 445
Trubridge, Mary. *See* Truebridge, Jane
Truchenu, Marquise de. *See* Adhémar de Monteil de Grignan, Françoise-Pauline d'
Truckle-bed; truckle-beds:
servant sleeps on, **16**. 368
Trudaine, Daniel-Charles (1703–69):
death of, **4**. 189
Hénault's social relations with, **7**. 305
(?) intermediary for HW, **3**. 113
Trudaine de Montigny, Charles-Michel (ca 1766–94):
birth of, **3**. 57n
Trudaine de Montigny, Jean-Charles-Philibert (1733–77), director of bridges and causeways:
address of, sent to HW, **3**. 50
Castle of Otranto for, **4**. 100, 102, 114, 115
Châtillon visited by, **7**. 331
circle of, **4**. 100
Clairon, Mlle, acts for, **4**. 30
death of, **6**. 466
Du Deffand, Mme, acquires spy-glass through, **4**. 36
—— consults, about: son of Mme Dumont, **3**. 49; Voltaire and *Castle of Otranto*, **4**. 99, 100
—— grateful to, **3**. 406, **4**. 77, 100
——'s boxes taken out of customs by, **5**. 3
——'s correspondence with, **5**. 160, 161, 301
——'s intermediary, **3**. 113
——'s opinion of, **4**. 30, 77, 100
——'s packages sent to, **4**. 30, 31, **6**. 257
—— wishes HW to know, **4**. 266
—— wishes to avoid bothering, **5**. 205
father of: **3**. 113n; dies, **4**. 189
HW's *Gramont* given to, **5**. 268, 299, 305
HW to send parcels through, **4**. 74, 77, **5**. 128, 156, 160, 162, 163, 171, 212, 301, 436, **6**. 2, 9, 85, 117, 128, 132, 181, 246
in pitiful state, **4**. 310
lettre de cachet expected by, **5**. 48

Lyon, Avignon, and Montpellier visited by, **4**. 310
offers to translate HW's *Historic Doubts*, **4**. 11, 19
Paris left by, **4**. 253
Paris residence of, **5**. 162
Sanadon arrangements made by, **3**. 406
social relations of, in Paris, *see index entries ante* 8. 532
Suard said by, to write well, **4**. 32
Trudaine de Montigny, Mme Jean-Charles-Philibert. *See* Bouvard de Fourqueux, Anne-Marie-Rosalie de
True Account of . . . Trinity College, A. See under Middleton, Conyers
True and Authentic Account, A. See under Frey, Andrew
True and Faithful Account of . . . Munpferdt the Surprising Centaur. See under Bentley, Richard (1708–82)
True and Faithful Relation, A. See under Dee, John
True and Genuine Account of the Two Last Wars. See under Carleton, Capt. George
Truebridge, Jane, HW's housekeeper at Arlington St:
HW corrects Montagu's mistake about, **9**. 375
(?) handwriting of, **10**. 40
Montagu praises, **9**. 374, 375, **10**. (?) 199
True Briton, The (periodical):
Allied losses announced in, **12**. 135
HW mentioned in, **12**. 108
HW refers to, **12**. 7, 23, 33, 63, 66, 67, 121
Howe's news given in, **12**. 76
Marie-Antoinette's death reported in, **12**. 41
Maubeuge siege's raising reported in, **12**. 43
obituary notice of Lady Ravensworth to be inserted in, **34**. 198
Saxe-Coburg, P. of, reported in, as winning victory, **12**. 44
True Copy of the Last Will and Testament of her Grace Sarah late Duchess of Marlborough. See under Jennings, Sarah, Ds of Marlborough: will of
'Trueman, Thomas':
name used by HW in 'Noble Jeffery,' **32**. 85
'Truepenny, Old':
HW's name for the gout, **33**. 106
True Remembrances. See under Boyle, Richard
'Trufaldin.' *See* Gleichen, Carl Heinrich; *see also* 'Trifaldin'
Truffle; truffles:
description of, in Darwin's *Botanic Garden*, **31**. 293
Trumbull, John (1756–1843), American painter:
SH visited by, **12**. 229
Trumbull. *See also* Turnbull
Trump, Van. *See* Tromp
Trumpet; trumpets:
Cumberland, D. of, likes, **19**. 20
English army marches without, **37**. 136n
for Dettingen victory, **35**. 39

[Trumpet; trumpets, *continued*]
George II's fondness for, **21**. 238
HW suggests that Mason experiment with, **28**. 195
in open boat, **37**. 289
in regatta concert, **32**. 237n
Pitt's, **35**. 89
—— will need the thorough-bass of drums and, **10**. 222
played at *Old Woman's Oratory*, **9**. 131
Prussians blow, prematurely, at Kunersdorf battle, **21**. 331
scarlet represents sound of, to blind Sanderson, **41**. 292
See also Ear trumpet; Speaking trumpet

Trumpeter; trumpeters:
Austrians accompanied by, when entering Berlin, **21**. 445n

Trumpington, Cambs:
Cole calls on Pemberton at, **1**. 287
Pemberton of, **13**. 146n

Trumpinton. *See* Trumpington

Truncheon; truncheons:
Conway thinks expedition has too many, for small successes, **37**. 527

Trunk; trunks:
Austrobritons should get, without embroidered linings, **35**. 36
Berrys', ransacked at Bourgoin, **11**. 137, 139
chaise's capacity for, **37**. 40
French officer and wife unload, at Calais, **10**. 283
HW's: full of masquerade costumes, **23**. 193; opened at Calais, **17**. 142, 161
James II's, saved in shipwreck, **32**. 390
Mann sends, to Cts of Pomfret, **17**. 129
Mozzi unpacks, **25**. 435
Pomfret family's, **35**. 7
prints in, **30**. 373-4
silver, for perfumes, **26**. 56
Stanley's, searched on return to England, **38**. 483-4
Uguccioni writes to Cts of Pomfret about, **17**. 170
Walpole family papers in, **30**. 372

Trunk-makers:
printers consign cancelled sheets to, **42**. 368

Trunk shop:
at Charing Cross, opposite Northumberland House, **32**. 322, 322n

Truro, Cornwall:
Frederick, P. of Wales, quarrels with Falmouth over candidate for borough of, **17**. 451

Trusseralla. *See* Trossarelli

Trusty, English ship:
Francis II dines on board, **25**. 499n

Truth:
dearer to HW than his life, **36**. 77
'died a virgin,' **11**. 307, 347, **12**. 45, 266
difficulty of establishing, in England, **24**. 63-4
Du Deffand, Mme, finds, only in HW, **3**. 92, 203

—— on charm of, **4**. 489
——'s love of, **4**. 67
genius needed to convey, **4**. 489-90
HW discusses fugitive nature of, **32**. 78-83
HW mentions, **11**. 30, 37, **12**. 115, 116, 176
HW on, **2**. 155
HW's aphorisms on, **12**. 104, 263
HW's love of, **2**. 143, **3**. 162, 189-90, **37**. 197
HW's reflections on, **21**. 167
humanity not born to distinguish, certainly, **32**. 348
in politics, difficult to obtain, **32**. 10
lacking, these four years, **33**. 115
natural to youth, **33**. 550
needs no poetry, **5**. 72
not a leaf to be had in London, **33**. 133
Pilate and Dr Beattie not sure of, **34**. 43
rare in Paris, **3**. 68
said to lie at bottom of well, **34**. 38
seems to have taken flight, **34**. 169
source of unhappiness, **7**. 357

Tryal, English packet boat:
Madras news comes by, **25**. 149n

Trye, near Gisors, France:
Rousseau at, **3**. 314n, 317n

Tryon, Mary:
guest at private Court ball, **9**. 402, 403, **38**. 143

Tryon, William (1729-88), colonial governor; army officer:
Connecticut magazines destroyed by, **24**. 309, **32**. 354
Montgomery's victory over Carleton reported by, **24**. 156
Washington accused by, of burning New York, **24**. 256n

Tryton. See Triton

Tuam, Abp of. *See* Hort, Josiah (? 1674-1751)

Tub; tubs:
bath, Paris procession carries Marat's, **31**. 388
Belgioioso said to escape from Brussels in, **39**. 455-6
fir trees planted in, at Ranelagh, **20**. 47
HW orders, at Hammersmith for Cts of Ailesbury, **38**. 198
HW's, in which his cat drowned, **28**. 101
HW's name for his house at Windsor, **37**. 258, 259, 269, 273

Tubal (Biblical):
Ossian might be claimed to antedate, **29**. 38

Tube; tubes:
silver, used to ventilate bed, **20**. 203

Tuberculosis. *See* Consumption

'Tubero, Orasius.' *See* La Mothe le Vayer, François de

Tuberose; tuberoses:
at SH, **32**. 137
England has to import, **33**. 561
roots of, HW sends, to Bentley, **35**. 161

Tubi, Giambattista (1635-1700), sculptor:
assists in Mazarin's tomb, **13**. 165n
marbles by, at Sceaux, **7**. 322

Tubières de Grimoard de Pestel de Levy, Anne-Claude-Philippe de (1692–1765), Comte de Caylus; archæologist:
collection of, sold at auction, **7.** 271, 275, **43.** 106
encaustic method of, **21.** 239
encaustic painting studied by, **28.** 300
HW's acquisitions from collection of, **16.** 284n, **39.** 32
Stosch's cameos coveted by, **21.** 434
wax painting invented by, **13.** 34
Works of, Cole asks Gulston for, **1.** 291n
Tubières de Grimoard de Pestel de Levy, Charles de (ca 1698–1750), Marquis de Caylus:
Barnett defeats, **18.** 15
English men of war exchange presents with, **18.** 15n
governor of Martinique, **18.** 15n
Turkish ambassador entrusted to, **18.** 15
Tuccoli, ——, Italian physician:
Gloucester, D. of, attended by, **23.** 334, 337, 341, 342, 393
Tuchet, James (1723–69), 7th E. of Castlehaven; 7th Bn Audley:
costume of, at Ferrers's trial, **9.** 281
dances at Robinson's ball, **37.** 115
Tuchomirschitz, (?) Austria:
Austrians hold council of war at, **21.** 95n
Tucker, Mr, Calais importer:
HW sends boxes through, **7.** 414
Tucker, Gertrude (d. 1796), m. 1 (1747) William Warburton; m. 2 (1781) Martin Stafford Smith:
Allen's niece, **10.** 228n
marriage of, **40.** 228n
Potter said to be lover of, **22.** 184n
Tucker, Rev. Josiah (1712–99), D.D.; Dean of Gloucester 1758–99:
Case of Going to War, by: *Critical Review* attributes, to HW, **10.** 75; Walpole, Sir Robert, lauded by, **10.** 75
HW cannot read tracts of, **28.** 233
Humble Address and Earnest Appeal, An, by, **28.** 233n
Jenyns satirizes American views of, **32.** 287n
Mason expects, to be made a bishop, **29.** 246
—— satirizes in *The Dean and the 'Squire*, **29.** 248n
sends ear of Italian wheat to Greaves, **1.** 282
'Thoughts' by, **28.** 452n
Treatise Concerning Civil Government, A, by: bishops approve, **29.** 132; HW agrees to read one sentence of, **29.** 134; Locke attacked in, **29.** 125–6, 131–2; Mason offended by, **29.** 241n
Tucker, Richard, receiver of hawkers and pedlars:
turned out of office, **17.** 420
Tucker; tuckers:
Gramont, Comtesse de, wears, in Lely's miniature, **10.** 12
St-Cyr pensioners wear, **10.** 293

Tuckfield, Margaret (ca 1678–1754), m. 1 (1704) Samuel Rolle; m. 2 John Harris, of Hayne:
bequests of, **20.** 418, 424
brother leaves fortune to, **20.** 482n
Conway, Anne Seymour, gets letter from, **37.** 338
daughter accuses, of having 'sold' her, **20.** 439
daughter announces coming visit to, **19.** 60
daughter coolly received by, **19.** 139
daughter offered house by, **19.** 104
daughter receives allowance from, **19.** 224
daughter's education neglected by, **25.** 121
daughter's jewels supposed to have belonged to, **25.** 144, 148
daughter tells, about Walpole family, **19.** 139
daughter wounds, by her misconduct, **19.** 39
death of, **20.** 418
grandson slights, **20.** 482
grandson's losses could be alleviated by, **14.** 50
HW's narrative of Nicoll affair is addressed to, **14.** 193
London visit of, postponed till daughter is out of the way, **19.** 60
marriages of, **17.** *486*, **20.** 418n, 482n
'poor weak woman,' **19.** 104, 132
second husband and, gouty in wheel-chairs, **33.** 525
Tuckfield, Roger (? 1685–1739), M.P.:
sister inherits from, **20.** 482n
Tuddenham, Sir Thomas:
Warwick, E. of, asks to borrow money from, **42.** 192n
Tudor, ——, painter:
paper for hall and stair at SH painted by, **9.** 150
Tudor, Arthur, P. *See* Arthur (1486–1502), P. of Wales
Tudor, Edmund (1430–56), cr. (1452) E. of Richmond:
body of, transferred to St David's, **42.** 20
family of, **42.** 19–20
Henry VII's father, **16.** 233n
Tudor, Henry. *See* Henry VII; Henry VIII
Tudor, Jasper (1431–95), cr. (1453) E. of Pembroke and (1485) D. of Bedford; Henry VII's uncle:
family of, **42.** 19–20
peerage of, corrected, **43.** 77
position of, at Court, **2.** 365
red rose might well be worn by, **16.** 234
relationships of, **2.** 363, 364
Tudor, Ps Margaret. *See* Margaret (Tudor) (1489–1541)
Tudor, Ps Mary. *See* Mary (Tudor) (1496–1533); Mary (Tudor) (1516–58)
Tudor, Owen (d. 1461), 2d husband of Q. Catherine (of Valois):
Catherine's romance with, obscure, **42.** 19
perhaps beheaded in Wars of the Roses, **42.** 19
wife's love for, **28.** 318
wives and sons of, **42.** 19–20

Tudor, Owen (d. 1501):
  monk at Westminster, **42.** 20
  perhaps beheaded in Wars of the Roses, **42.** 19
Tudor, Mrs William. *See* Cole, Harriet
Tudor family:
  Catherine of Aragon out of place in painting of, **40.** 319
  rigorous discipline characteristic of, **11.** 278
Tuer, —— (b. ca 1688), Cole's uncle:
  Baker and Orchard, godfathers to, **2.** 351
Tuer, —— (1686–1773), Cole's aunt:
  dies insane, **2.** 321n
Tuer, Rev. Abdias (d. ? 1627), vicar:
  Cole's great-great-grandfather, **1.** 50, 73
  vicarage date of, **43.** 47
Tuer, Anne, m. Joseph Cock:
  Cole's maternal aunt, **1.** 83n
Tuer, Catherine (ca 1683–1725), m. William Cole; William Cole's mother:
  Cole's mother, **1.** 35n, 83n
  family of, **2.** 378
Tuer, Herbert (fl. 1640–75), painter:
  Cole's account of, **1.** 50–1, 70, 73–4
  HW mislays account of, **1.** 72
  HW's account of, **1.** 77n, 78, 82
  Jenkins's *Life* mentions, **1.** 114
  ——'s portrait painted by, **1.** 72, 74
  picture of, for *Anecdotes of Painting*, **1.** 74, 82–3, 83, 85, 87
  prints of, given to Cole by HW, **1.** 127, 127–8, 129
Tuer, Mrs Herbert. *See* Gameren, Mary Van; Heymenbergh, Elizabeth Van
Tuer, Rev. John (1567–1621):
  Cole's ancestor, **1.** 73
Tuer, John (fl. 1680), son of Herbert Tuer:
  settled at Nimuegen, **1.** 51, 73
Tuer, Theophilus (fl. 1625), William Cole's great-grandfather:
  George Herbert's niece married to, **1.** 70, 73
  picture of, **1.** 87
Tuer, Theophilus (fl. 1640–90), soldier; merchant; William Cole's grandfather:
  Cole's account of, **1.** 50, 51, 70, 73, 74–5, 81, 114
  daughter of, **2.** 378
  genealogy of, **1.** 70n
Tuer, Mrs Theophilus. *See* Dix, Mary (fl. 1660–90); Vaughan, Catharine (fl. 1625)
Tuffnall, Charles, Capt., 1759:
  health of, camp fever and bloody flux, **40.** 144
Tuffnall. *See also* Tufnell
Tufnell, Col. (d. 1765), 'Capt.':
  death of, **7.** 397
Tufnell, George Foster (1723–98), M.P.:
  speaks in House of Commons, **28.** 294n
Tufnell, John Jolliffe (1720–94); M.P.:
  (?) Florence visited by, **17.** 106
  name of, corrected, **43.** 237
Tufton, Lady Anne (1693–1757), m. (1709) James Cecil, 5th E. of Salisbury, 1694:
  Clifford title not left to, **18.** 144

Tufton, Lady Catharine (1693–1734), m. (1709), Edward Watson, styled Vct Sondes:
  Clifford title not given to, **18.** 144
Tufton, Lady Charlotte (1728–1803):
  Bellenden reconciles sister to, **9.** 359
  Bristol's proposal refused by, **30.** 241
  Dacres' social relations with, in Paris, **7.** 330
Tufton, Hon. George (1650–70):
  Elector Palatine rescued by, **2.** 1–2
Tufton, Lady Isabella (d. 1764), m. 1 Lord Nassau Powlett; m. 2 Sir Francis Blake Delaval:
  Foote arranges second marriage of, **20.** 231
  —— kept by, **20.** 231
  mad, **20.** 231n
Tufton, Sir Lewis de (fl. 1346):
  at Crécy and Calais, **2.** 5
Tufton, Lady Margaret (1700–75), Bns de Clifford, s.j., 1734; m. (1718) Thomas Coke, cr. (1728) Bn Lovel, and (1744) E. of Leicester:
  Clifford barony bestowed on, **18.** 144
  family of, mad, **19.** 457
  HW ignorant of, **34.** 260
  son's marriage arranged by, **9.** 37
Tufton, Lady Mary (1701–85), m. 1 (1718) Anthony Grey, styled E. of Harold; m. 2 (1736) John Leveson Gower, 2nd Bn Gower; cr. (1746) E. Gower:
  dies from burns, **33.** 460, **36.** 232, 233
  (?) HW mentions, **20.** 326
  husband's resignation denied by, **20.** 417n
  letter of, about hangings and weddings, **37.** 339, 341–2
  Mason visits, at Bill Hill, **33.** 407n
  Montagu, Mrs Charles, entertained by, at Bill Hill, **10.** 306
  mourned by 132, **36.** 233
  nephew's marriage arranged by, **9.** 37
  niece of: dies, **38.** 530; presented by her, to Frederick, P. of Wales, **19.** 447
  remark by, about Frederick, P. of Wales's musical clock, **19.** 447
Tufton, Lady Mary (1723–1806), m. (1763) Dr William Duncan, cr. (1764) Bt:
  Badini's abusive exchange with, **11.** 307–8
  Bellenden reconciles sister to, **9.** 359
  Florence visited by, **24.** 105
  great-aunt displeased by marriage of, **38.** 457
  Gunnings replaced by, in town talk, **11.** 307
  HW to visit, **11.** 153
  Hotham, Miss, entertains, **12.** 154
  husband leaves all to, recommending his nephew to her, **24.** *41*
  Mann to tell, that English ladies weep no more, **24.** 112
  marriage of: a mésalliance, **38.** 367; perhaps platonic, **24.** 41, 48–9; Selwyn's witticism on, **9.** 360, **24.** 49
  Pacchierotti admired by, **29.** 174
  tears of bereavement cause, to leave her callers, **24.** 105

Tufton, Nicholas (1631–79), 3d E. of Thanet:
HW thinks 'Milord Janet' might be a mistake for, 9. 118
Tufton, Sackville (1688–1753), 7th E. of Thanet, 1729; M.P.:
daughters of, 9. 359n, 11. 153n
death of, 35. 159
Lee and Honywood candidates of, at Appleby, 20. 435n
tailor asked by, to make suit within 8 hours, for brother-in-law's mourning, 35. 159
Tory, while M.P. for Appleby, 20. 435n
wife of, 9. 28n
Tufton, Sackville (1733–86), 8th E. of Thanet, 1753:
(?) aloofness of, provokes attacks on his horsemanship, 9. 201
(?) Douglass hunts with, near Steane, 9. 201
father of, Tory while M.P., 20. 435n
feat of an ancestor of, 2. 1–2
land belonging to, 1. 382
Lowther contests Appleby election with, 20. 435
(?) ministry may include, 9. 201, 203
Paris visited by, 35. 230
(?) Rochford, Cts of, receives ruby ring from, 35. 215
sensible of wife's merit, 33. 59
sister of, 24. 48n
voting shunned by, 22. 508n
'young Crœsus,' 20. 435
Tufton, Thomas (1644–1729), 6th E. of Thanet:
daughter of, 20. 231n
Tufton family:
eagle of, 2. 5
land granted to, 1. 382, 2. 1
madness in, 19. 457
Tugny. See Thugny
Tuilerie, La. See La Tuilerie
Tuileries, at Paris:
Bretons march to pont tournant of, 11. 99
Dauphin's garden on terrace of, 11. 100
Grande Écurie near, 6. 162n
HW has not walked in, 13. 165
lacks verdure, 35. 533
Le Nôtre designer of gardens at, 28. 30n
Louis XVI and Marie-Antoinette at, 11. 300n
Louis XVI and Marie-Antoinette escape from, 34. 113n
Louis XVI and Marie-Antoinette move to, 34. 72n
Marie-Antoinette's female attendants murdered at, 31. 372
mob invades, 31. 372n
mobs assemble in, 11. 215
outrages in, 34. 143–4
Petworth remodelled in style of, 9. 97
pond at, provides fashionable circuit, 8. 208
prisoners said to have been massacred at, 15. 237
Salm insulted by Lanjamet at, 6. 279
Théroigne, Mlle, flogged in, 12. 88n

visitors to: Alembert, 7. 54; HW, 7. 308, 318; Wiart, 7. 54
Yertzin, Mme de, hissed at, 38. 401
Tuite, Nicholas:
Copt Hall occupied by, 35. 346n
Tulip; tulips:
at SH, 10. 69
HW would make a rainbow of, 11. 29
in convent garden, 13. 169
oaks will be moved as easily as, by posterity, 37. 292
transitory, 35. 461
'Tulipe,' Mme du Deffand's dog:
banished, 4. 25
Carmontelle portrait shows, 4. 27
Choiseul, Duchesse de, applies verses to, 3. 60
Du Deffand, Mme, loved (but everybody else hated) by, 3. 225
—— mentions, 3. 15, 45, 173
——'s love for: 3. 212; mediocre, 4. 25; not equal to HW's for his dogs, 3. 365
Tuljajī (d. 1787), Raja of Tanjore:
father of, made English-guaranteed treaty with Nawab of Arcot, 23. 562n
HW could learn about, 25. 117
Pigot and Madras council dispute over Tanjore payments before restoration of, 24. 288n
tribute refused by, to Nawab of Arcot, 23. 561n
Tull, Jethro (1674–1741):
Horse-hoing Husbandry, The, by, read by Conway, 37. 576
Tullamore, Bn. See Moore, Charles (1712–64)
'Tullibardine, Marchioness of':
Strafford, Cts of, to entertain, 9. 24
Tullibardine, M. of. See Murray, William (1689–1746)
Tullie, Isabella (d. 1800), m. (1766) Lionel Darell, cr. (1795) Bt:
Berry, Agnes, and Juliana Dilkes visit, 12. 175
HW calls, 'Lady Dancinda Darrell,' 12. 183
Wales, P. of (George IV), to dine with, at Richmond, 12. 183
Tullie, Joseph (d. 1774), deputy usher of the Exchequer (under HW):
Bedford, Grosvenor, succeeded by, as HW's deputy in the Exchequer, 41. 206n, 42. 491
death of, 6. 115, 32. 217–18
estate of, in Yorkshire, 23. 498
HW's correspondence with, 7. 379
Yorkshire farmer refuses to accept new guineas from, 23. 498
Tullie, Thomas (d. 1742), rector of Aldingham, Lancs:
death of, 40. 37
Tullus:
quotation about, from Horace, 42. 272
Tully. See Cicero
Tullybardine. See Tullibardine

Tully's Head, near Surry St, the Strand:
Becket & De Hondt at, **21**. 514n

Tulsk, Roscommon:
Cunninghame replaces St George Caulfeild as
M.P. for, **20**. 316n

Tumbler; tumblers:
HW has, of Venetian glass, **17**. 73n

Tumour; tumours:
occurrences of, **4**. 5, 13, **5**. 133, **7**. 247
on the brain, **38**. 450

Tumour *or* boil:
bark for, **2**. 337
Cole's, **2**. 335–8
dispiriting, **2**. 336

Tumuli:
ancient, near Dorchester, **37**. 491

Tunbridge Wells, Kent:
Amelia, Ps, talks about acquaintances at, **38**. 344
Bolton, Ds of, picks up Irish surgeon at, **21**. 365
Buxton Wells compared with, **40**. 16
Carteret, Bns, to visit, **18**. 501
Chesterfield tries to establish Barnard as a wit at, **19**. 404
Conway to settle wife at, to take waters, **37**. 345
—— writes from, **37**. 346–7
Dacres leave suddenly, for Paris, **38**. 273
exodus to, **38**. 273
fecundity supposedly increased by visits to, **18**. 501
Gilchrist ill at, **11**. 369
Gramont's characters ride to, **35**. 136
HW compares Reggio fair to, **13**. 242
HW may visit, **17**. 452
HW might prefer, to Paris, **22**. 492
Hertford writes from, **39**. 312
Holdernesse abused for playing blindman's buff at private room at, **20**. 346
horses from, **35**. 135
market at, **35**. 135
Marlborough and Comyns meet at, **7**. 362
Mason to come to London from, **14**. 90
Pantiles at, **12**. 151
Penshurst near, **34**. 28
Pinchbeck's great room at, **33**. 127
Selwyn writes from, **7**. 458
Vesey, Mrs, might be at, **31**. 250
visitors to: Amelia, Ps, **32**. 7, **38**. 344, 421; Bath, E. of, **30**. 92; Bolton, Ds of, **21**. 365; Carteret, E. and Cts, **43**. 255; Chute, **19**. 436, **35**. 135, 140; Clanbrassil, **38**. 421; Comyns, **7**. 362; Conway and wife, **37**. 346–7; Craster, Mrs, **38**. 421; Dacres, **10**. 290, **38**. 273; Fergusons, **32**. 16; Fermor, Lady Charlotte, **43**. 255; Gilchrist, **11**. 369; Grafton, Ds of (Lady Ossory), **32**. 11; HW, **35**. 135, 140; Harrington, Cts, **38**. 421; Hertford, **39**. 304; Holdernesse, **9**. 145, **20**. 346; Hope, **38**. 421; Johnstons, **11**. 89; Keenes, **12**. 164; Leicester, E. of, **34**. 28;

Lincoln, Cts of, **12**. 158; Marlborough, **7**. 362; Newhaven, Lady, **33**. 127; Norfolk, Ds of, **35**. 270, 280; Norfolk, D. of, **35**. 270; Percy, Bp Thomas, **42**. 369; Pomfret, E. and Cts of, **43**. 255; Selwyn, John, **37**. 80; Thurlow, **33**. 173n; Townshend, Vcts, **30**. 121, **37**. 347; Townshend family, **30**. 69; Vane, Frederick, **38**. 421; Vesey, Mrs, **33**. 127; Waldegrave, Cts, **38**. 421; Whithed, **19**. 436

waters of, drunk by Vcts Townshend, **30**. 121

Tunis, Bey of. *See* Ali II; Ali ben Muhammad ben 'Ali (d. 1756); Husain ben 'Ali (d. 1735); Muhammed ben 'Ali (fl. 1756); Yunus Bey (d. 1756)

Tunis:
bey's son revolts in, **20**. 319
La Condamine visits, **22**. 147n
revolutions in, **20**. 318n
Spanish fleet may have its hands full at, **24**. 120
Theodore of Corsica chooses Agostini to carry instructions to, **20**. 379n

Tunny fish:
Leopold to watch catching of, at Porto Ferrajo, **23**. 131

Tunstall, Catherine (d. 1807), m. 1 (1789) Rev. Thomas Chamberlayne; m. 2 (1806) Horatio Walpole, 2d E. of Orford, n.c.:
husband of, **2**. 316n

Tunstall, Rev. James (ca 1708–62), D.D.:
daughter of, **2**. 316n
Epistola ad virum eruditum Conyers Middleton, by, attacks Middleton, **15**. 10n, 11
Melmoth seems to agree with, about Cicero's epistles to Brutus, **15**. 304
Middleton replies to attack by, **15**. 10–11
——'s life of Cicero disparaged by, **15**. 8n, 296
——'s translations of Cicero's and Brutus's epistles attacked by, **15**. 296
Observations on the Present Collection of Epistles between Cicero and M. Brutus, by, answers Middleton, **15**. 10n

Tunstead, Norfolk:
HW's will mentions, **30**. 344

Turban; turbans:
Grosvenor, Bns, wears, **39**. 18

Turbot; turbots:
Chapman dies of eating, **28**. 154
Dutch usurp the territory of, **35**. 392
Mason treats Bp Markham to, **28**. 316
post-chaise takes, to Powis Castle, **32**. 302n
with sorrel sauce, **19**. 357n

Turchine:
monks of, **19**. 123

Turcotti, Maria Giustina (1720–ca 1800), singer and impresario:
Arminio chosen by, **17**. 80
Mann's conversation with, **19**. 317

Tureen; tureens:
at Elizabeth Chudleigh's, **9**. 277
from Chelsea china set, **43**. 278

Turenne, Maréchal Vicomte de. *See* La Tour d'Auvergne, Henri de (1611–75)

Turenne, Prince de. *See* La Tour d'Auvergne, Godefroy-Charles-Henri de (1728–92)

Turenne, Princesse de. *See* Lorraine, Louise-Henriette-Gabrielle de (1718–84)

Turenne, Vicomte de. *See* La Tour d'Auvergne, Henri de (1611–75)

Turenne, Hôtel de, at Paris:
Abington, Mrs, stays at, **41**. 215

Turf, the:
present age prefers riding about streets to riding on, **25**. 317
See also Race; races

Turgot (d. 1115), Bp of St Andrews; historian:
Chatterton may have read, **16**. 336–7, 341, 343
diary by, **42**. 2

Turgot, Chevalier:
'considerable sea officer,' **24**. 26n

Turgot, Anne-Robert-Jacques (1727–81), Baron de l'Aulne; French controller-general:
'absolute,' **6**. 295
Albert protected by, **6**. 184–5, 300
Amelot's replacing Malesherbes enrages, **24**. 207n
Angiviller friend of, **6**. 299
attempts by, to mitigate monarchy and relieve the French people, **32**. 266
Boynes replaced by, **24**. 26
Caracciolo admires, **6**. 314
Clugny replaces, **6**. 311, 326
confident, **6**. 278
controller-general, **6**. 87, 95
corvées suspended by, **28**. 221, 226
dismissed, **24**. 140n, 208
Du Deffand, Mme, gives opinion of, **6**. 278, 321–2, 341–3
economical, **32**. 257
economy of, restrains Ps of Piedmont's wedding festivities, **39**. 255
edicts of, awaited, **6**. 261
Fontainebleau visited by, **6**. 235, 236
Guines opposed by, **6**. 263n
——'s rift with, **24**. 178n
HW admires, **6**. 296, 318, 341–2, 342, **24**. 133, 140, 208, **41**. 345
health of, **6**. 235, 236, (?) 238, 240
Joseph II converses with, **6**. 443
Lespinasse, Mlle de, friend of, **6**. 77, 95, 155
lit de justice managed by, **24**. 102
Malesherbes induced by, to interview Marie-Antoinette, **6**. 321
Marie-Antoinette restrained from imprisoning, **24**. 208n
Maurepas jealous of, **24**. 207
——'s friendship with, **6**. 77
minister of finance, **32**. 205
Necker attacks policy of, **6**. 183n
——'s supposed letter from: Du Deffand, Mme, reads, **7**. 450; Necker libelled by, **7**. 225, 227
Paris jurisdiction may be given to, **6**. 300

patriotic plans of, **6**. 193n
philosophical leanings of, **6**. 154–5
Plan de Paris by, **8**. 3–4
popular expectations about, **6**. 95, 154–5, 272
reforms of: Du Deffand, Mme, makes witticism about, **30**. 264; intended, **6**. 277n; Voltaire praises, **8**. 197–8
satire against, **6**. 325n
secretary of state for the marine, **6**. 77, **32**. 200
sister of, family of, **6**. 342
social relations of, in Paris, **6**. 443
Terray succeeded by, as controller-general of finance, **24**. 26n
tottering, **39**. 270–1
Toulouse, Abp of, friend of, **6**. 277, 299
verses on, **6**. 193, 194

Turgot, Hélène-Françoise-Étiennette (1729–84), m. (1757) Paul-Hippolyte de Beauvillier, Duc de St-Aignan:
Jansenist, **6**. 342

Turin:
academy at, Davison attends, **19**. 407
Adélaïde and Victoire, Princesses, set out for, **11**. 208
Albani's messenger goes to, **19**. 2
Bartolommei to send news from, **17**. 342
Beauchamp to visit, **38**. 448
Bedford, D. of, chooses Rochford over Williams as envoy at, **20**. 58n
Berrys disappointed at lack of mail at, **11**. 142, 162
——' lodgings at, **11**. 143, 158
—— to arrive at, **11**. 111
Birtles to send Genoese courier to, **18**. 375
Bristol, E. of, has no successor at, **21**. 191, 202–3
—— makes post at, too expensive for Mann, **21**. 175, 195
—— minister at, **2**. 321n, **19**. 372n
—— prepares to leave, **21**. 195
Broglie wishes to visit, to pay court to Victor Amadeus III, **5**. 402, **23**. 521
Carlisle, E. of, might be envoy at, **24**. 36
Charles Emmanuel III leaves, **18**. 59, **19**. 432
—— to return to, **19**. 353
Chauvelin ambassador at, **5**. 433n
Coke, Lady Mary, to visit, **31**. 177
—— well received at, **23**. 560
Conti menaces, **18**. 504
courier arrives at, almost naked, **19**. 334
courier from: about Genoese campaign, **19**. 451; arrives, **19**. 358; awaited, **19**. 335; just arrived, **19**. 440; to Florence, discontinued, **19**. 131
couriers sent to, **18**. 411
Court of: awaits England's example in answering Leopold's letter, **22**. 378; contributes patents only, to Corsican revolt, **20**. 274; Corsican rebels should be protected by, **19**. 258; English negotiations with, may be upset by Minorca's capture, **20**. 576; expected Corsican conquest, **19**. 215;

[Turin, *continued*]

French overtures to, **19**. 218; Mann negotiates with, over Corsican rebels, **19**. 276; Stuart Mackenzie's mission to, **11**. 35n; to welcome D. of York, **22**. 201; Townshend's appointment will please, **19**. 147; Vienna Court at odds with, **19**. 478; Vienna Court negotiates with, **19**. 400–1; wants Mann to borrow money, **19**. 215, **20**. 386; wears tricolour cockade, **18**. 544; Young Pretender not recognized at, **19**. 143

Cumberland, D. of, avoids, because of English minister, **23**. 525

dispatches deciphered at, **19**. 12

dispatch from, sent by Mount Stuart, **25**. 325

Dutens employed in English embassy at, **25**. 625n

English visitors flock to Florence after festivities at, **20**. 159, 160, **24**. 131

express from, to carry battle news to England, **18**. 436

fever in, prevalent, **19**. 477

Florence communicates with, only through the Grisons, **19**. 214

Fox, Henry, wants C. H. Williams to have post at, **19**. 16

'fracas' at, may have caused Mount Stuart's departure, **25**. 336

French army to march upon, **19**. 304

Fuentes ambassador at, **9**. 338n

Fumagalli to be sent to England from, **18**. 97

Genoa siege's raising rumoured at, **19**. 422

Greville, secretary of legation at, **21**. 124n

Guasco brothers leave, **22**. 529

HW anxious to hear of Berrys' arrival at, **11**. 113, 118, 122, 129, 134, 139

HW describes, **13**. 190–1

HW lists letters sent to, **11**. 123, 134, 157

HW mentions, **11**. 116, 117, 138

HW receives Mary Berry's letters from, **11**. 142

Hamilton abandons Mme de St-Gilles at, **20**. 309

Hedges envoy at, **9**. 66n

house rent at, **21**. 175

lady from, entertained by Mann, **19**. 499

letter from, with news of Gibraltar, **19**. 329

letters from, about Bergen-op-Zoom, **19**. 440

letters to, report Anson's victory, **19**. 415

Lobkowitz's son to bring father's dispatches to, **18**. 486–7, 491

Lombardy poplar brought from, **11**. 146n, **39**. 133n

Lynch is English minister at, **23**. 272, **24**. 36

Lyttelton refuses to succeed Stuart Mackenzie at, **21**. 507–9

Mann hears from, of English-French peace negotiations, **22**. 89

—— hopes to hear of Bristol's successor at, **21**. 197

—— might be envoy at, **21**. 166, 175, 191, 195, 202, **22**. 500

—— might visit, incognito, **21**. 266

——'s letters sent through Germany from, **18**. 412

—— to decipher dispatch from, **17**. 428

—— writes to, for orders for Sardinian galleys to put to sea, **19**. 236

Maria Theresa sends Bartolommei to, **17**. 196

messenger from Naples to, **20**. 576

ministers from and to, *see under* Minister (*from and to* Sardinia; Savoy)

ministers of, at Paris and London, help in peace of Paris, **22**. 105

Montagu, Lady Mary Wortley, searched by customs officer at, **14**. 245

Montemar may visit, **17**. 198

Noailles temporarily replaces Chauvelin at, **20**. 497n

Northington may succeed Mount Stuart as envoy at, **25**. 336, 354

Orford, E. of, covets ambassadorship at, **20**. 420n

—— declines post at, **21**. 195, 206

Perrone takes goldfish to, **35**. 226

Pitt, George, envoy at, **21**. 548, **22**. 2n, 500

—— to take Grafton's house at, **22**. 2

Richecourt, Comtesse, returns to, after husband's death, **20**. 45n

Richelieu said to visit, **20**. 576

Rochford, Cts of, to go to, **20**. 58

Rochford, E. of, envoy at, **20**. 58, 420, 426

—— returns to, without increase in rank, **20**. 420n

——'s new appointment vacates post at, **20**. 461

sea engagement not reported from, **18**. 403

Spaniards may besiege, **19**. 120

Spanish invasion of Lombardy apprehended at, **18**. 295

Stormont said to have bribed Contessa di Viry to reveal negotiations at, **6**. 474n

Stuart Mackenzie envoy at, **9**. 86n, **11**. 35n, **21**. 212, 218

—— may send fans from, **21**. 462

——'s infant dies at, **38**. 24

theatre in, **13**. 191

Townshend's instructions to come from, **19**. 245

Trevor envoy at, **25**. 398, 595n, **42**. 397

Trino near, **19**. 156

Villettes, English minister at, **18**. 60n, **19**. 150, 183, **20**. 76

—— sends courier from, through Germany, **18**. 389, 397

——'s post at, more important than Mann's at Florence, **19**. 431n

Viry's secret correspondence at, **24**. 328n

visitors to: Almada, **21**. 436; Ansbach, P. of, **20**. 370n; Artois, Comte d' (Charles X), **11**. 39n; Artois, Comtesse d', **11**. 96n; Baden-Durlach, Margrave of, **20**. 148n; Bartolommei, **17**. 195–6; Beauchamp, **38**. 482; Blythe, **43**. 178; Bute, **23**. 103; Chetwynd, **43**. 178; Coke, Lady Mary, **23**. 543, 545, 553, 556, 559, 560; Conway, **20**. 293,

304; Cordon, **11.** 87n; Cuzzens [? Cosins], **22.** 41n; Dundas, **22.** 41n; Ferdinand of Naples, **25.** 586; Fox, C. J., **34.** 31n; Fumagalli, **18.** 97; Gloucester, D. of, **23.** 370, **24.** 252; Goguel, **22.** 41n; Grafton, D. and Ds of, **21.** 537, 554, 557, 565n, **22.** 2, 34, 39n; Gray, **13.** 9, 190–1, **17.** 51n, **30.** 1n; HW, **13.** 9, 190–1, **17.** 51n, **30.** 1; Karl Wilhelm Ferdinand, **22.** 457n; Kendrick, **22.** 41n; Lincoln, E. of, **17.** 51n, **30.** 1; Mann, Horace II, **24.** 129; Mathews, Adm., **18.** 215, 360, 370; Mellican, **22.** 41n; Money, **19.** 12; Montagu, Lady Mary Wortley, **14.** 245, **17.** 91; Orford, Cts of, **23.** 120; Pembroke, E. of, **23.** 138n, 152n; Penthièvre, **20.** 466; Phelps, **22.** 112; Philipps, **17.** 138; Pratt, Mrs, **43.** 247; Raper, **17.** 138; Richecourt, **17.** 95; Richecourt, Comte and Comtesse de, **20.** 45; Rochford, E. and Cts of, **20.** 370n; Spence, **17.** 51n, **30.** 1n; Wallmoden, **22.** 327n; Wentworth, **19.** 401, 406; York, D. of, **22.** 193, 201, 204, 244

wedding, royal, at, **20.** 159

Williams, Sir C. H., may succeed Villettes as minister at, **19.** 347, 456, 465, 466, **30.** 319–20

—— on Newcastle's list for appointment to, **19.** 456n

—— prefers, to Warsaw, **20.** 16n

Wright would probably want post at, if Mann rejects it, **22.** 503

Turinetti, Ercole (1717–81), Marchese di Priero e Pancalieri, imperial envoy to Rome: Benedict XIV sends for, **19.** 157

Viennese couriers awaited by, **19.** 158

Turinetti, Giovanni Antonio (1687–1757), Marchese di Priero e Pancalieri, imperial ambassador to Venice:

Maria Theresa's letter to, threatens Venice with diplomatic break, **20.** 190

memorial delivered by, to Venice, **20.** 161

Turino, Giovanni *and* Lorenzo:

statue designed by, **13.** 204n

Turk, Martha ('Patty') (ca 1737–91), 3d E. of Orford's mistress:

age of, forty, **24.** 295

appearance of, fat, coarse, and old, **42.** 333n

biographical information about, corrected, **43.** 96

death of, **42.** 333

Du Deffand, Mme, interested in history of, **5.** 436, 438, **6.** 4, 14

Eriswell, place of death of, **42.** 333n

HW calls, 'housemaid,' **25.** 133

HW describes, **24.** 295

HW persuades, to let E. of Orford go to London, **36.** 118–19

HW prevents doctors from separating, from E. of Orford, **42.** 336

HW's attention to, in E. of Orford's former illness, **24.** 294

HW urged by, not to remove E. of Orford from Eriswell, **24.** *293*

keeper retained for E. of Orford at request of, **24.** 296

Orford, E. of, accompanied by, **36.** 335

—— has slept with, for 20 years, **24.** 295

—— helps, to chicken, **36.** 122

—— joins his forehead to, every evening at table, **24.** 295

—— praises Dr Monro to, **24.** 372

——'s bequest to, **15.** 324, **42.** 333n

——'s mistress, **28.** 92n, **43.** 151

Piddletown manor intended by Orford to go to, **25.** 148n

Walpole, Sir Robert, made plans which are baffled by, **25.** 133

Turk; Turks:

believe that fools are inspired, **33.** 103

Caprara's trophies taken from the, **13.** 194

Catherine II compels HW to sympathize with, **23.** 116

—— may want to conquer, **33.** 562

—— threatens, **11.** 226, 233

Charles V's wars with, **15.** 46

Crawford fights against, in Hungary, **20.** 110

fortune's pranks among, **37.** 221

George I's, taken in Hungary, **20.** 110

HW hopes that Catherine II and Joseph II will be defeated by, **35.** 392

HW hopes that Catherine II will be punished by, **39.** 146

Joseph II baffled by, **34.** 32

—— reported to have declared war on, **2.** 309

kinder to animals than Christians are, **40.** 257

Lorraine, Primate of, defends amorous practices of, **17.** 273

Louis XV negotiates with, **18.** 543

Ottoman, at first deserved defeat but modern Turks do not, **35.** 392

pagan, HW prefers, to Catherine II and Joseph II, **34.** 19

St Stephen knights to win prizes from, to pay for church, **22.** 259

Turkey, Sultan ('Grand Signior') of. See Abdul Hamid I (1725–89); Achmet (*or* Ahmed) III (1673–1736); Mahmoud I (1696–1754); Murad I, II, III, and IV (fl. 1359–1640); Mustafa III (1717–74); Osman III (1696–1757)

Turkey, Sultana of:

pregnant, **21.** 494

Turkey:

ambassadors from and to, *see under* Ambassador

anti-Russian grumbling of, more audible in England than in Italy, **25.** 436

archbishopric of Tauris in hands of, **22.** 196

armaments prepared by, **21.** 493

armaments will be abandoned by, if Sultana produces an heir, **21.** 494

army of, in wretched condition, **23.** 173

Austria and Russia may dismember, **25.** 399

Austria, Prussia, and Russia may combine against, **25.** 359, 436

barbarism of, in Greece, **42.** 507

[Turkey, *continued*]

beads from, **22.** 523n

Catalogue of French Books, A, satirizes, **18.** 53

Catherine II and Joseph II said to have been mollified by compliance of, to their demands, **25.** 409–10

Catherine II attacked by, at Choiseul's instigation, **23.** 133–4, 143

—— duped by, **23.** 438

—— may give, to son, **23.** 236

—— may turn from, to Denmark, **23.** 273

——'s destruction of, would harm the faithful, **23.** 169

——'s war against, miscarries, **23.** 157

—— to defend usurpations in, **25.** 436

cavalry of, to have been remounted, **23.** 160

Choiseul might espouse quarrel of, **24.** 11

—— must abandon or aid, **23.** 202

——'s intrigues a disadvantage to, **23.** 259

Christians at Smyrna cruelly treated by, **23.** 233, 235

Constantinople's approaches fortified by, **23.** 331

costume of, **20.** 362, **22.** 148

courier from India travels to port in, **21.** 523

Craven, Lady, corrects Lady Mary Wortley Montagu's accounts of, **42.** 183

—— should lead Catherine II and Joseph II to free captives of, **42.** 183–4

despotism of, depopulated the land, **34.** 192

Edgcumbe exiled to, **30.** 115n

England angers, by letting Russian fleet cross the English Channel, **23.** 479

—— will be glad of diverting news of, **23.** 121

English intervention against France will distress, **23.** 479

Fane said to be ambassador to, **19.** 99–100

fleet of: Elphinston attacked by, at Napoli di Romania, **23.** 234; Ibrahim commands, **23.** 234; Russians destroy, **23.** 226–8, 232–5, 236, 239, 249; said to be burnt at Lemnos, **23.** 319

France incited, against Russia, **23.** 307, 338

—— may aid, against Austria, Prussia, and Russia, **25.** 359

—— may incite, against Joseph II, **25.** 46

—— said to threaten Joseph II if he makes war on, **25.** 415

—— tries to embroil Russia with, **33.** 14

—— unpopular in, as cause of war with Russia, **23.** 202

Francis I to have commanded Charles VI's armies against, **37.** 97n

French merchant ships intercepted by Russians on way to, **23.** 307

French to assist, with advisers and technicians, **23.** 185

frigates of, *see under* Frigate

galley slaves of, escape from French galleys to Leghorn, **20.** 206n

Giovanni Gastone's collection sent to, **19.** 437

girls from, *see* Girls: Turkish

Golitsyn defeated by, **23.** 140

Great Admiral of, **20.** 480n

Greeks do not aid Russia against, **23.** 222

—— flee to Venice to escape vengeance of, **23.** 226

—— will be sacrificed to, by Russians, **23.** 212

Grotius and Puffendorf will be taught to people of, **23.** 88

HW asks about, and compares it to Babylon, **23.** 212

HW desires revolution in, **4.** 405

HW prefers Grand Signior of, to Catherine II, **23.** 195

janizaries of, may precipitate war, **25.** 360

Kücük Kainardje treaty not observed by, **24.** 278n

Louis XV and French ministers vainly encourage, **23.** 331

Malta fears, **21.** 493–4

man *or* men of war of, *see under* Man of war

Maria Theresa forbids Knights of Malta to fight, **21.** 505

—— need not fear, **21.** 494

Mazarin aids Pope in making war on, **4.** 324n

Orlov, Alexis, the scourge of, at sea, **24.** 114

Orlov, Grigorii, conducts Russian negotiations with, **23.** 441

ornament from, **40.** 89n

paradise of, **35.** 32

pipes from, **37.** 439

pirates from, feared by Pope's seamen, **17.** 16

Pitt might encourage, to be impertinent in order to use armament, **21.** 537

Polish confederates not aided by, **23.** 319

religion forces Roman Catholic countries to oppose, **18.** 428

revolutions in: HW desires, **4.** 405; surpassed by Russian ones, **10.** 39; Voltaire desires, **4.** 405

Rome prays for, in war with Russia, **23.** 140

Russia attacked by, **23.** 133–4, 143

—— battles with, over Bender, **23.** 154–5, 160, 245

—— may be too preoccupied with, to aid England, **39.** 304

Russian fleet might frighten, into peace, **23.** 149, 192

Russian fleet to attack, **23.** 148–9

Russian invasion of, disliked by France, **23.** 204

Russian negotiations with, **23.** 469–70

Russian relations with, **21.** 247–8

Russians capture military chest and tents from, **23.** 479

Russians defeat, before Golitsyn's recall, **23.** 146

Russians force, from Moldavia and Volakia, **23.** 154–5

Russians haggle with, over villages in the Morea, **23.** 224

Russian squadron may move to Malta to scare, **23.** 189

Russia's clash with, stirred up by France, **33.** 14n

——'s war with, *see under* War: Russian-Turkish

—— unlikely to wrest Holy Land from, **23.** 194–5

sedition in, possible, **23.** 155, 159–60

slave of, **35.** 206

Spain's treaty with, **25.** 415n

Tuscany's treaty with, **19.** 437

Venice threatened by, **21.** 494

war or peace in, intermittent, **23.** 432

See also under Turk; Turks

Turkey; turkeys:

at SH, **4.** 394

come from the Orient, **25.** 609n

cups in shape of, **33.** 325

eggs of, **41.** 108, 110

English capture in France, **19.** 327

entremets of, **19.** 354n

geese to race with, **21.** 7

HW does not eat, at Christmas, **19.** 16

Leneve, Isabella, counts, after Houghton dinner, **25.** 609

small: HW thinks, should be called 'turkey-pouts,' **25.** 609n; served as second course at dinner but seldom eaten, **25.** 609

verses mention, **31.** 191

Turkey carpet. *See under* Carpet

Turkey cock:

Orford, Cts of, resembles, **19.** 224

Turkey Company:

Wright's offers from, **21.** 21

See also Levant Company; Turkey merchants

Turkey handkerchiefs. *See under* Handkerchief

Turkey leather. *See under* Leather

Turkey merchants (English merchants trading with Turkey):

Clephane's correspondence with, about Cartagena, **17.** 71

Laws, Capt., tells, of English loss at Cartagena, **17.** 71

Turkish china. *See under* China

Turkish opium. *See under* Opium

Turkish slave. *See under* Slave

Turkish Spy. See Letters Writ by a Turkish Spy

Turkish tomb:

mummy dug out of, **15.** 19

Turk's Island:

French seizure of, **22.** 252, **38.** 428, 432, 441

Hertford gets satisfaction from French Court about, **38.** 441

—— tired of hearing of, **38.** 447

Turlis, Thomas (d. 1771); hangman 1752–71:

North Briton burnt by, with link instead of faggots, **38.** 256

Turlough, Mayo:

Fitzgerald of, **9.** 150n

Turmenyes, —— de, garde du Trésor royale:

receipt by, **8.** 30

Turnbull, Rev. George (ca 1703–48), LL.D.:

health of: poor, **19.** 232; possible consumption, **19.** *184–5*; probably hopeless, **19.** 132

Old Pretender's movements to be watched by, **19.** 184n

'pandle,' **19.** 232

Rome to be visited by, **19.** 232

Walpole, Horatio (1723–1809), accompanied by, to Italy as tutor, **19.** 184–5, 192

Turner, Lady. *See* Leigh, Cassandra (1723–70); Walpole, Mary (1673–1701)

Turner, ——, china merchant:

large price asked by, for jar cracked by earthquake, **20.** 155

Turner, Capt.:

SH visited by, **12.** 235

Turner, Mr:

Kentish's partner, **16.** 70n

Turner, Mrs:

SH ticket not used by, **12.** 226n

Turner, Mrs, of Teddington Common:

SH visited by, **12.** 238

Turner, Anne, m. Rev. Dr Maurice Suckling: husband of, **9.** 153

Turner, Rev. Baptist Noel (1739–1826):

(?) picture belonging to, **16.** 202

Turner, Cassandra (1746–1813), m. (1771) Martin Bladen Hawke, 2d Bn Hawke, 1781:

Julia de Gramont by, Hannah More knows no one who has read, **31.** 273

Turner, Sir Charles (ca 1665–1738), cr. (1727) Bt:

daughter of, **9.** 153n, **14.** 198n

son-in-law of, **9.** 153n

wife of, **18.** 182

Turner, Charles (ca 1726–83), cr. (1782) Bt, of Kirkleatham, Yorks; M.P.:

candidate for York, **28.** 173n, **39.** 179n

chariot of, damaged in Gordon riots, **25.** 54, **33.** 177

Gordon derided by, in House of Commons, **33.** 177n

Gordon rioters rob, **33.** 186

Lowther's legacy to, **9.** 184

York election won by, **39.** 197n

Turner, Mrs Charles. *See* Walpole, Mary (1673–1701)

Turner, Charlotte (1749–1806), m. (1765) Benjamin Smith; poet and novelist:

Desmond by, might be answered by HW, **34.** 155

Turner, Cholmley (1685–1757), M.P.:

election of, **17.** 295n

named in Secret Committee lists, **17.** 384

Secret Committee not attended by, **17.** 401

Turner, Christiana (1623–94), m. Samuel Cooper:

Pope's aunt, **29.** 279

Turner, Edith (1642–1733), m. Alexander Pope; mother of Alexander Pope, the poet:

birth date of, corrected, **43.** 247

birth of son of, satirized in *New Lesson for Pope*, **17.** 34

Mason is misled by HW's account of, **29.** 278, 279

[Turner, Edith, *continued*]
Spence fondles old mother in imitation of Pope and, **20.** 189
——'s mother's ghost will be pursued by that of, **20.** 189
Turner, Sir Edward (1719–66), 2d Bt, 1735; M.P.:
candidacy of, for Oxfordshire, **37.** 371n
Parliamentary membership of, corrected, **43.** 238
petition about Oxford election presented by, **20.** 435n
Spanish privateer said to have captured, between Dover and Calais, **17.** 153
Turner, Elizabeth (d. 1763), m. John Fowle; HW's cousin;
connection of, with Nicoll affair, **14.** 198, 199
Lely portrait given by, to uncle, **41.** 98
Lely portrait given to, by Mrs Dixon, **41.** 98
Turner (after 1775 Page Turner), Sir Gregory (1748–1805), 3d Bt, 1766; M.P.:
great-uncle leaves fortune to, **39.** 252n
Mann to be accompanied by, at investiture, **23.** 60
Turner, Hannah (d. 1759), m. (1722) Rev. Dr John Gardiner:
biographical information about, corrected, **43.** 255
(?) gallantries of, **18.** 522n
Orford, 2d E. of, unlikely to have been lover of, **43.** 68
son of, not by Bn Walpole, **18.** 522
Townshend, Vcts, should have heard from, about her children, **40.** 46
Turner, Sir John (ca 1712–80), 3d Bt; M.P.:
Grenville's follower, **39.** 96n
HW mentions, **10.** 220
King's Lynn electors dislike stand by, on general warrants, **41.** 90
King's Lynn suffers from, **39.** 96
writ for HW's election to be settled by, **36.** 33
Turner, Richard, London steward to D. of Newcastle:
Hurdis's letter from, **40.** 343n
Turner, Robert:
prints of, **40.** 236, 237
Turner, Shallet (1692–1762), LL.D.; fellow of Peterhouse:
death of, **28.** 79n
Gray alludes to, in connection with fellowship election, **14.** 1, 2, 4, 41
Piazza assistant to, **13.** 6n
professorship of, **13.** 137
Turner, William (1597–1665), Pope's grandfather:
Mason mentions, **29.** 278
Turner, William (ca 1698–1790):
death of, at Richmond, **11.** *15*
Nicholls, Rev. Norton, and mother, heirs to, **11.** 152
Turner. *See also* Garth Turnour; Turnor; Turnour

Turner; turners:
Montagu to stay with, in Mayfair, **10.** 253
Turnham Green, Middlesex:
Conway might meet daughter at, **39.** 404
Dunkeron's house at, **10.** 154
HW jokingly refers to American privateer on, **33.** 21
highwaymen at, **42.** 109
man at, advertises 'ready-made temples,' **29.** 99
Mirepoix lives at, **10.** 154
robbers infest, **31.** 234–5
sign at, **33.** 97
Turnip; turnips:
Chute lives on, **18.** 100
fields of, **30.** 72
HW not interested in, **18.** 47
in Ludgershall, **33.** 228
in Norfolk, **43.** 247
Rigby talks language of, **30.** 80
West's letter about, **13.** 84
Turnkey; turnkeys:
at Newgate, **20.** 312
Turnor, Edmund (ca 1755–1829), M.P.:
HW recommends, as friend of Thomas Walpole jr, to Mann, **24.** 488
Turnor, Sir William, Kt, 1686:
Wright friend of, **17.** 423
Turnor. *See also* Garth Turnour; Turner; Turnour
Turnour, Elizabeth (d. 1754), m. (1709) Thomas Lewis:
Ashton living at house of, **13.** 176, **43.** 180
Grosvenor, Mrs, living at house of, **13.** 220–1
Turnour. *See also* Garth Turnour; Turner; Turnor
Turnpike; turnpikes:
at Bournbridge, **1.** 363
Bedford and Grafton dispute over, **20.** 549
Brown, Sir Robert, avoids fees for, **25.** 609n
Cole's horses clear, **2.** 180
English controversies over, astonish the French, **37.** 456–7
House of Commons busy about, **31.** 5
Irish Parliament's bills about, for Clonmell and Mallow, **37.** 426, 428
letters for Cole left at, **2.** 118, 133, 181
messengers numerous upon, after Parliament's dissolution, **24.** 45
tolls on, **20.** 112n
Turnpike Bill. *See under* Parliament: acts of
Turnpike gate:
at Hyde Park Corner, **30.** 144
'Turnstile, The.' *See* 'Treaty or Shabear's Administration, The'
Turnur. *See* Garth Turnour; Turner; Turnor; Turnour
Turócz (Hungary):
Conway and Scott visit, **39.** 538
Turpentine:
Southwark magazines of, catch fire, **25.** 577

Turpin, ——, French lawyer:
Necker suggests, as Hon. Thomas Walpole's lawyer, 36. 177n
Turpin, Henri-Roland-Lancelot-Joseph (b. 1754), called Comte de Turpin:
(?) SH visited by, 12. 240
Turpin, Richard ('Dick') (1706–39):
leader of highwaymen in Epping Forest, 13. 79n
Turret; turrets:
at Holland House and Houghton Park, 39. 140
at Houghton, inspired by Osterley, 34. 237
Turriano, Orazio, secretary of the senate of Messina:
deaths from plague reported by, 18. 252n
Türrschmidt, Karl (1753–97), player of French horn:
HW hears, 33. 471
Turtle; turtles:
Egremont looks forward to dinners of, 22. 159
feast of, 35. 70
HW's jokes about, 11. 106
Taaffe brings, to Mme de Pompadour, 20. 289
'Turtle and the Sparrow, The.' See under Prior, Matthew
Turtledove; turtledoves:
foolishness of, 9. 140
HW's name for Ds of Bedford, 38. 178
Venus's, Andersons compared to, 11. 57
See also Dove; doves
Turton, John (1735–1806), M.D.; physician:
alarmed about Morice, 25. 202
asks receipt of HW's diet drink, 2. 292
Delany, Mrs, attended by, 31. 261
Dickenson, Mrs, consults, 31. 368
Dysart, Cts of, attended by, 34. 61n
Morice attended by, 25. 202, 33. 300
Turvile Park, Bucks:
Perry of, 10. 122n
Tuscan architecture. See under Architecture
Tuscan Council, at Vienna:
Alberti appointed to, 20. 220
Tuscan language. See under Italian language
Tuscan vases. See under Vase
Tuscan verse:
HW's verses mention, 31. 96
Tuscany, Grand Duchesses of:
Allegrini's prints of, see under Allegrini, Francesco
See also Ludovica (1773–1802); Marguerite-Louise (1645–1721); Maria Louisa (1745–92); Maria Theresa (1717–80); Martelli, Camilla (d. 1590)
Tuscany, Grand Dukes of:
gallery of, see Uffizi Gallery
See also Cosimo I (1519–74); Cosimo II (1590–1621); Cosimo III (1642–1723); Ferdinando I (1549–1609); Ferdinando II (1610–70); Ferdinando III (1769–1824); Francesco I (1541–87); Francis I (1708–65);

Giovanni Gastone (1671–1737); Leopold II (1747–92)
Tuscany:
Acquaviva tells Montemar to invade, 17. 266
Algeria makes peace with, 20. 472, 25. 270
Algerian corsairs prey on trade of, 20. 472–3
Algerian war with, 20. 472, 487–8
ancient people of, addicted to divination, 20. 477
Antinori rules, 21. 90
antiquities from, collected by Hamilton and brought to England, 32. 70
Aranjuez preliminary treaty guarantees territorial integrity of, 20. 294n
army of: Franchini drummed out of, 21. 510; leaves for Austrian service, 21. 179–80; see also Tuscany: troops of
art shipments from, must have export licences, 20. 465, 21. 208
Austria dominates, 25. 505, 554
—— forgets the money accumulating in, 21. 102
Austrian artillery permitted to pass through, 18. 541–2
Austria's connection with, to increase, 25. 128
Bandini and Old Pretender's underling pass through, from Rome, 18. 380
bankruptcies in, 17. 61n
Barbary states the only official enemies of, 21. 349
Benedict XIV reconciled with, 20. 446
—— to settle disputes about, with St-Odile, 20. 305
Berrys might be informed by ministers of, 11. 230
Betange and Cocchi discuss government of, 35. 16
Bientina lake protected by dykes from overflowing into, 20. 515
borders of, manned under pretence of guarding against plague, 18. 270, 285
Botta commands troops in, for Francis I, 21. 471n
—— to govern, 21. 125
Braitwitz commands Grand Duke's troops in, 17. 49n
bread shortage in, 22. 448, 25. 318
Capponi sent by, to remonstrate with Montemar, 35. 22–3
Charles III and Gages threaten, 18. 509
Charles III may declare war on, 19. 65
—— once acknowledged as Great Prince of, 21. 494–5, 22. 406
Charles, P., possibly to rule, 18. 2, 30, 331, 336, 21. 556
Charlotte, Ps, may govern, 19. 49, 207, 20. 29, 178, 355
china factory in, 25. 598, 635, 645
Clement XIII bullied by, about ecclesiastical immunities, 22. 449
cloth unobtainable in, save from England, 20. 205

[Tuscany, *continued*]
coastal towers and forts of, in disrepair, **20.** 472n

corn expensive in, **22.** 452

corn plentiful in, but money is not, **22.** 486

corn sought by, in England and Hungary, **22.** 446, 448

Corsica may be ceded to, **23.** 469n

Corsican news depresses, **23.** 130

Corsican women banished to, **23.** 245

Corsica receives notice from, by felucca, **18.** 263

council of, in Vienna, **20.** 220

Court of: *accesso* a dignity conferred by, **22.** 531; at Pisa, **22.** 417, 422, 511, 515, **23.** 149, 325, 352, **24.** 188, **25.** 334, 436; at Porto Ferrajo, **23.** 131; attends two playing societies, **22.** 393; Barbantane does not acknowledge pretensions of habitués of, **22.** 481; Beaufort, Ds of, and family, favoured by, **23.** 406; Botta explains altered ceremonies of, **22.** 378; Boufflers's friends not so well received as he by, because no foreign minister presented them, **22.** 474; Charlotte's brother well received by, **22.** 437–8; Coke, Lady Mary, complains of neglect at, **31.** 176; Coke, Lady Mary, thinks virtues no recommendation at, **31.** 180; Cumberland, Ds of, may embarrass, **23.** 501–2; drawing-room at, for Archduke and Archduchess of Milan, **25.** 50; drawing-room not held in, **25.** 340; drawing-rooms and public table not held at, **31.** 176; English visitors at, served punch, **22.** 430; English visitors irritated by procedure of, **22.** 482, 483; etiquette of, **22.** 367, 378, **25.** 334, 340; etiquette of, at Pisa, **23.** 171, 191, 262; etiquette of, excludes Dick, **23.** 395; etiquette of, too much for untitled visitors, **22.** 467; fine clothes not required at, **25.** 340; gala *appartement* at, **25.** 301; gala at, **22.** 467; gala day routine of, **22.** 367; Gloucester, Ds of, received by, before any other court did so, **22.** 297; grandees of, must all be invited to meet visiting sovereigns, **24.** 164; Guasco accepted by, **22.** 531; Herveys well received by, **22.** 430; Holy Week ceremonies of, worthy of Vienna, **22.** 412; Huntingdon favoured by, **23.** 406, 446; imitates that of Vienna, **22.** 390; Kingston, Ds of, may shun, **24.** 398; Kingston, Ds of, sends respectful message to, **24.** 7; Lappeggi preferred by, to Castello and Petraia, **22.** 412; Leghorn's preparations for, **22.** 417, 422; Leghorn to be visited by, **22.** 417; less exacting than any other in Europe, **25.** 340; Mann does not follow, to Pisa, **25.** 334; Mann goes to, only to deliver letters or present strangers, **25.** 340; Mann presents Lord Robert Manners at, **25.** 282; Mann's truculence to, would be backed by Pitt, **22.** 483; Mann to accompany, to Pisa and perhaps to Siena,

22. 511; Mann to present English visitors at, **24.** 250–1; Maria Josefa's wedding to be celebrated by, **22.** 556; mourns for Ps Charlotte, **23.** 533; no longer follows Francis I's ceremonies, **22.** 378; no public days, levees, or drawing-rooms at, **25.** 340; Pisa shows for, uninteresting, **22.** 515; Poggio a Caiano the residence of, **23.** 296; Poggio a Caiano to be visited by, **23.** 325; Rena must be excluded by, **23.** 119; resides at Poggio Imperiale, **24.** 7, **25.** 301; returns from Vienna, **24.** 250; returns to Pisa from Leghorn, **23.** 80; Salviati made Grand Chambellan by, **22.** 467; Siena may be visited by, **22.** 511; Sienese shows please, **22.** 515; Spanish minister attends, at Pisa, **25.** 334; Suares, Mme, 'bred up' at, **17.** 39n; to visit Vienna, **23.** 214; Vienna Court prescribes etiquette to, for Maria Louisa's churching, **22.** 486–7; Vienna to regulate mourning for, **22.** 337, 340; Vienna will lecture, for extravagance, **23.** 134–5; will soon find travelling too expensive, **23.** 134

Craons may help Old Pretender's sons across, **17.** 15

Cristiani may rule, **20.** 335

crops in, destroyed by drought, **25.** 314, 318

Cumberland, D. of, may visit only Leghorn in, **23.** 53

Cuneo's capture would endanger, **18.** 513

Del Monte banditti terrorize, **20.** 446

desertion expected from, **18.** 120

disloyalty of, caused by dislike of Richecourt, **19.** 11

divination popular in, **20.** 477

edict of, for Del Montes' arrest or death, **20.** 446

Electress's death frees Francis I from interference in, **18.** 160

England given credit by, for coming independence, **22.** 123

—— opposed by, despite trade benefits, **20.** 581

—— quarrels with, over Wright, **21.** 20–1

—— reported to have resigned, to Spain, **17.** 182

—— would prefer, to be independent of Spain or Austria, **18.** 2

English china compared to that of, **25.** 635

English cloth contraband in, **20.** 205

English-commanded ship of, rescued from Prussian privateer, **21.** 349

English corn kept from, by embargo, **22.** 460, 462

English fleet to go to, **21.** 114

English fleet to protect, **18.** 27, 37–8, **19.** 10

English fleet well received by, **21.** 128

English privateers almost provoke, to war, **21.** 335

English relations with, may be guided by Richecourt and Bns Walpole through Chesterfield, **17.** 387

English ships carry flag of, when carrying French goods, **21**. 269, 273–4

English trade beneficial to, **20**. 581, **21**. 36, 108, 269

envoys from and to, *see under* Envoy

Etruscan vases said to have been discovered in, **22**. 561

famine expected in, from heat and drought, **25**. 314, 318

fathers in, post notices that they will not pay sons' debts, **24**. 237

finances of, loan sought from Jews at Leghorn, **22**. 448

first minister of, Rosenberg to replace Botta as, **22**. 447–8, 453–4

flag of, **21**. 269, 273, 278

fleet of, consists of three ships, **20**. 487

Fleury about to permit Spanish invasion of, **18**. 42

—— assures Stainville of safety of, **17**. 205n

—— said to oppose Spanish invasion of, **17**. 197–8, 205, 230

Flobert banished from, **21**. 377

floods in, **17**. 109, **20**. 220, **21**. 359n, **23**. 274, 378, 383

Foligno gives access to, **17**. 261

France guarantees safety of, **17**. 120, 198n, 205, 206, 214, 229, 230, 281, 288, 290, **18**. 502, 509, **35**. 14

—— orders Lorenzi to protest to, against hospitality to English ships, **21**. 36n

—— said to have ordered Gages not to invade, **19**. 7

—— to keep Francis I in, away from German influence, **17**. 152

Franchini banished from, **21**. 511

Francis I and Leopold vainly try to drain marshy tract in, **24**. 343

Francis I denudes, of troops, **17**. 180

—— does not want troops of, at Leghorn, **19**. 11

—— exchanges Lorraine for, against mother's wishes, **37**. 97n

—— may get Naples instead of, **18**. 331

—— may visit, on way to Naples, **18**. 3

—— neglects, **21**. 90

—— not alarmed over, **17**. 216

—— orders, to prepare, **18**. 364

—— orders Braitwitz to keep Spaniards out of, **18**. 66, 127, 134

—— orders Te Deums to be sung in, **21**. 112

—— reproves, for method of chastising Del Monte family, **20**. 437

—— said to have excluded English ships from ports of, **17**. 36

——'s interests in, endangered by Richecourt's opposition to English fleet, **18**. 329

——'s only interest in, is to get money, **17**. 406

——'s troops sent to borders of, to preserve neutrality, **18**. 541

—— to lose, to Don Philip, **17**. 196

—— trusts France's guarantee of neutrality of, **18**. 509

—— uncertain about France's guarantee of, **17**. 288

—— unlikely to relinquish, **20**. 178

—— will still get revenue from, even when son reigns at Florence, **22**. 255

Francis III of Modena may invade, **18**. 295

French guarantee of, may cease if England joins with Austria, **17**. 288

French propaganda in, **24**. 416

Gages crosses, **19**. 40–1

—— may call Francis I to account for mobilization in, **18**. 127

—— may invade, **18**. 509, 556, 559, **19**. 35–6, 38

—— prepares invasion of, while awaiting new orders from Madrid, **19**. 10

—— promises not to invade, **19**. 38

——'s march to Genoa may endanger, **19**. 53

—— to enter Lombardy to isolate, **19**. 31

galleys and war ships lacked by, **22**. 259

Genoa receives disavowal from, of captain's action, **18**. 263

George II assures, of protection, **17**. 281

——'s intention to protect, known to Regency Council, **18**. 27, 38

George III might not consider, worthy of a minister plenipotentiary, **23**. 293

German troops sent from, **17**. 154, 214, 229

German wars not to involve, **21**. 112

Giovanni Gastone governs, through Giuliano, **21**. 62

Goldsworthy says that Francis I, Mann, and Regency Council belittle danger of, **18**. 106–7

government of: may be taken away from Richecourt, **18**. 310; poor, **30**. 5; posts in, never vacated, **20**. 210

grenadiers to be contributed by, to Austrian army, **21**. 15

HW can escape from in 10 hours, **40**. 36

HW hopes secretaries of state in, do not open letters, **24**. 38

HW may ask Sandwich to defend, **18**. 561

Hancarville proposes to furnish, with fresh fish, **23**. 448

Hanoverian negotiations said to be concerned with, **20**. 178

harvest in, **25**. 318

health magistrates of, **18**. 270

Hervey, Bn, envoy to, **11**. 129n

Hervey, Bp, 'hovers around,' **25**. 561

horses in, all employed by new Court, **21**. 336

imperial fiefdom of, makes it liable to contribute troops, **21**. 15

influenza in, **25**. 304

Inquisition to be re-established in, **20**. 420, 445, 446, 448

Jesuits' revenues in, small, **23**. 508

—— suppressed in, by Leopold, **23**. 508, 512–13

Joseph II favours, **25**. 137

[Tuscany, *continued*]
—— to renounce, to brother, **22.** 123
'Julianism' of, **21.** 62
Karl Joseph expected by, as Grand Duke, **20.** 178, 295, **21.** 556
lack of defences and of money exposes, to any enemy, **19.** 120
law courts in, more lax than in England, **25.** 131
laws of: Act of Succession, **20.** 466; edict against export of antiquities, **20.** 465, **21.** 208
Leopold (Peter Leopold; Leopold II) inherits, instead of Milan, **20.** 393n
—— officially takes possession of, **22.** 412
—— proclaimed as Grand Duke of, **22.** 329, 330
—— rides around, as a private gentleman would on his estate, **24.** 343
—— to be ruler of, **21.** 556, **22.** 123, 125
Lestock ordered to defend, **17.** 405
Lobkowitz cannot save, and aid Charles Emmanuel III too, **18.** 512
—— leaves artillery with, **18.** 529–30
—— may enter, **18.** 339
—— may retreat through, **18.** 508
—— not to retreat through, **18.** 520
—— ordered by Vienna to bring his army into, **19.** 11
—— preserves, **18.** 343
——'s retreat to Lombardy may expose, **18.** 502, 508
Lorraine faction depend on Francis I's favours to people of, **21.** 125
Lorrainers hated by, **20.** 581
Lorrainers probably introduced French practice of branding criminals in, **20.** 144n
Lucca could conquer, **19.** 120
—— may be flooded by, **20.** 514–15, 521–2
Madrid treaty expected to aid, **20.** 294
Mann advised by HW not to quit post at, **20.** 409
—— disputes in, over prizes from the Levant and French West Indies, **21.** 280–1
——'s disputes with, over seizure of English ships carrying Tuscan flag, **21.** 269, 273
——'s MS account of, for George III, sent to Shelburne through Capt. Steward, **23.** 27–8, **25.** 230
Maria Theresa may send troops to, **20.** 320
—— may want a few troops from, **21.** 175
——'s army protects, **18.** 352
—— wants aid from, **18.** 359
—— will lose, **18.** 521
Martin's squadron to protect, from invasion, **18.** 26
Mathews does not understand situation in, **18.** 98
—— may land marines in, **18.** 26
—— to defend, **18.** 296
—— wants Charles Emmanuel III and Traun to coop up Spaniards in, **18.** 108

Migazzi gets orders from, to oppose Dumesnil's consecration, **19.** 492
Milan may be exchanged for, **17.** 290
minister of, to France, warned by Fleury, **17.** 290
ministers from and to, *see under* Minister
mobilization in, under pretence of guarding against the plague, **18.** 285
Montemar demands passage through, **17.** 226, 228, 280, 289–90, **18.** 46
—— may invade, **18.** 16
——'s army may leave garrison in, **17.** 228–9, 289
Murray cannot get aid from, **25.** 196–7
Naples and Rome shut off from, for fear of plague, **18.** 270
navy of, Mann opposes English sailors' enlisting in, **20.** 472
Neapolitan ambitions of Viennese Court may endanger, **18.** 390
Neapolitan cavalry to return through, **19.** 297
Neapolitan troops may invade, **18.** 295, **19.** 346
Neapolitan troops rumoured to be invading, **19.** 364
neutrality of: disputed at Leghorn, **18.** 438; follows singing of Te Deum, **21.** 114; Francis I preserves, **17.** 456, **18.** 92, 339, 361, 541, **21.** 114; has hitherto protected it, **18.** 361; irritates Mathews, **18.** 339, 361; preserved even after Charles VI's death, **21.** 112; Richecourt proclaims, in spite of his probable distrust, **18.** 513; will be preserved, **21.** 176
Niccolini allowed to return to, **20.** 145n
—— banished from, **20.** 2
nobility of: classified, **22.** 350–1, 360n; inferior to English M.P.s, **22.** 483; to be classified as *patrizi* and *nobili*, **20.** 192–3
orders awaited by, from Vienna, **21.** 85
Paris embassy of, run by chargé d'affaires, **20.** 192n
passports for: invalid, **21.** 482; Modena, Ds of, wants, **18.** 223; Montemar and Castellara want, **18.** 44; Young Pretender gets, **18.** 378
peeress of, given niggardly present by husband on giving birth to heir, **24.** 233
people of: cross, **30.** 5; may aid Spanish army, **19.** 11, 31
Philip, Don, might become Grand Duke of, **17.** 196, 380, 389
pickets of, **18.** 100
Pisa baths are Mann's favourite place in, **20.** 158
plague precautions of, futile, **18.** 295
Port Mahon packet-boat almost destroyed by government of, **24.** 416
post office of, **25.** 564
Protestant girls in, converted by priests, **22.** 249–50

publication rules of, violated by edition of Montesquieu's letters, **22**. 295

quarantines in, futile, **18**. 295

rainfall in, excessive, **20**. 149

Regency administers affairs of, **17**. 40n

revolutionary disturbances in, **11**. 84, 91, 103

Richecourt carries away money of, **19**. 115

—— has Cavaliere Pecci examine finances of, **20**. 327n

—— manages finances of, **19**. 394n

—— muzzles discontent in, **20**. 77

——'s letters intercepted by Spaniards may endanger neutrality of, **18**. 516

—— will leave, in a state of Julianism, **21**. 62

Rome does not yet treat, severely, **20**. 458

——'s agreement with, **20**. 420–1

——'s authority in, resisted, **23**. 504

Rosenberg's debts in, not paid, **23**. 294

ruined, **30**. 5

Russian fleet awaited by, **23**. 159

St-Odile secretary of Inner Council for, at Vienna, **20**. 305n

secretary of state of, *see* Secretary of state, Tuscan

secretary of war of, *see* Secretary at war, Tuscan

ships fly colours of, for self-protection, **21**. 269

ships of: brought into Leghorn by *Glasgow* and *Ambuscade*, **21**. 273n, 288n; English men of war capture, **21**. 269; load French goods for the Levant, **21**. 273; Prussian privateer captures, **21**. 330, 349; respected by all but Algerians, **25**. 270; to carry books to HW, **25**. 138

Spain notifies, that goods sent to England will be confiscated, **25**. 509

—— orders Naples to send food to, despite Tanucci's dislike, **22**. 448

—— suspects, of intercepting courier, **18**. 85–6

Spaniards and Neapolitans march across, to join Gages, **19**. 65

Spaniards cannot help knowing preparations of, **18**. 359

—— may cross, to join Don Philip, **19**. 2

—— may enter: **19**. 24–5; from Genoa, **18**. 454; from Perugia, **19**. 10

—— may exchange Lombardy for, **17**. 206

—— may invade, when P. Charles invades France, **19**. 285, 295

—— may invade Genoa by way of, **19**. 36

—— to cross Pietra Santa in, **19**. 35

—— unlikely to molest, **18**. 58

Spanish aid hoped by, **17**. 144

Spanish army crosses, at Pietra Santa, **19**. 40

Spanish invalids from Viterbo to cross, to join Gages, **19**. 47, 55, 58

Spanish invasion diverted from, to Lombardy, **19**. 22

Spanish invasion of: depends on Don Philip's success, **18**. 312; prevented, **18**. 108

Spanish invasion threatens, **17**. 41n, 179–81, 192–3, 195, 196, 197–9, 204–5, 207, 213–15, 226, 228–9, 230, 238, 259, 261–2, 265–7, 269, 280–2, 288, 289–91, 314, 322–3, 349, 427, **18**. 16, 26, 27, 37, 58, 76, 92, 98, 100, 105, 127–8, 129, 175–6, 295–6, 297, 312, 361, 454, **19**. 10–11, 24, 25, 35–6, 53, 245

Spanish troops negotiate with, **17**. 228–9

Stainville may rule, **20**. 29, 192n

state jewels of, **18**. 170n

state papers of, of Medici period, not accessible, **21**. 284

taxes in, *see under* Tax

Theodore wants English newspapers in, **20**. 378

titles of, not acknowledged by Barbantane, **22**. 481

tobacco trade in, **20**. 389

Toulon squadron may threaten, **17**. 190

Toussaint to administer, temporarily, **21**. 107

Traun not to defend, **18**. 295

—— warns, **18**. 76

—— withdraws German troops from borders of, **18**. 134

tribute may no longer be paid by, to Barbary states, **22**. 259

Trieste declared free port to improve relations with, **20**. 98n

troops for, said to assemble in Lombardy, **20**. 320

troops of: at Cortona, **20**. 437; desert, **18**. 100, **20**. 424; Francis I orders, to keep active, **18**. 100; Frederick II's witticism about, **21**. 224; Leghorn to be guarded by, **18**. 530, **19**. 2; Lobkowitz to be joined by, **19**. 11; mobilized for defence, **18**. 530; Prato and Pistoia to be stations of, **18**. 98, 100; to join Austrian army, **21**. 15; to stay in garrison at Vienna, **21**. 195–6; to take oath to Maria Theresa at Linz, **21**. 180

Turkey's treaty with, **19**. 437

Vienna connections of, must interest it in events on the Scheldt, **25**. 544

Vienna ministers neglect, **21**. 102

villas of, disparaged by HW, **20**. 165–6

Viviani expects Spaniards to conquer, **17**. 129

vulnerable, **18**. 435

Wachtendonck commands imperial troops in, **17**. 40n

war preparations of, will be halted by non-cooperation of English fleet, **18**. 370

war ship of, at Leghorn, **23**. 108

war ships of, cruise with Pope's and Genoese against Algerians, **20**. 473n

woods of, Cargil and Hamilton live in, **21**. 457

Wright may seek appointment to, **22**. 499

York, D. of, tours through, in coach, **22**. 220–5

Young Pretender crosses, **18**. 378

—— may retire to, **20**. 93

—— to cross, **17**. 13, 15

Tusculum, Cicero's villa:
  Montagu compares SH to, **10**. 122
Tusmore, Oxon, Fermor's seat:
  Browne, Lady, at, **31**. 192–3, 198–9, 286
  Fermor writes from, **42**. 112, 115
Tussaud, Mme. *See* Gresholtz, Marie
Tutet, Mark Cephas (1732–85), merchant and antiquary:
  ancient cards owned by, **15**. 195, **43**. 202
Tuteur dupé, Le. See under Cailhava d'Estandoux, Jean-François
Tuthill, Henry, Thomas Gray's friend:
  possible reference to, **14**. 4n
Tuting, Sarah:
  Panton's mistress, **24**. 500n
Tutor; tutors ('governors'). *See under* Servant
'Tuum, Abp of':
  character in 'The Peach in Brandy,' **32**. 62
  (?) Dacre's bishop the counterpart of, **35**. 572
Tuyman and Baker, London merchants:
  packet boat of, stopped, **24**. 365n
Tver, Abp and Bp of. *See* Levshin, Petr Georgievich (1737–1812)
Tweed, river:
  Buchan is HW's new connection north of the, **29**. 107
  ——'s house on, **15**. 193n
  Harcourt alludes to, **29**. 358
  Mason alludes to, **29**. 373
  'poetical banks of,' **37**. 217
Tweedale. *See* Tweeddale
Tweeddale, Marchioness of. *See* Carteret, Hon. Frances (d. 1788)
Tweeddale, M. of. *See* Hay, John
'Tweedside':
  Veracini always plays air of, when Mann is present, **20**. 148
Twelfth-cake; twelfth-cakes:
  decked with comfits, **33**. 429
  on shop boards of pastry-cooks, **34**. 231
Twelfth Night:
  'All-Gamesters-Day,' **37**. 443, 447
  Bland and Offley gamble at, **35**. 204
  George II plays hazard on, **35**. 204n
  hazard played at Court on, **18**. 565, **35**. 204n, **39**. 79
  Winchilsea gambles at Court on, **18**. 565
  See also Epiphany
Twelfth Night. See under Shakespeare, William
Twelfth Night King. *See* Roi de la fève, le
Twelve-sol piece, French:
  value of, **37**. 39
Twenty-four-sol piece, French:
  value of, **37**. 39
Twickel. *See* Wassenaer Twickel
Twickenham, curate of, *See* Disturnell, Josiah; Lacy, James
Twickenham, vicar of. *See* Costard, George; Terrick, Richard
Twickenham, Middlesex:
  actors at, **9**. 70
  'à la bouches' at, **9**. 53

Ashe, nurseryman at, **35**. 157n
attorney's wife at, has guns fired at night, **9**. 74
auctions at, **21**. 121–2
Baiæ and Tivoli rank with, **35**. 234
Beauclerk, Lady Diana, comes to, **34**. 56
—— moves from, **35**. 506n
beauty of, **15**. 247
Berry, Mary, suggests stay at, **11**. 372
Berry, Robert, looks for house in, **11**. 7
Berrys spend 3 weeks in Montpelier Row in, **11**. 79n
—— visit, **11**. 79, 189
Berwick asks HW for route to, **10**. 129
book on gardens of, **1**. 361, 367
bridge to Richmond from, **39**. 176, 187
Browne, Lady, leaves, **34**. 472
Bunburys seek place at, **42**. 316
burglars at, **9**. 132–3
Cage (jail) at, Light Horse confined in, **38**. 34
Cambridge retails only scandals to be heard in, **33**. 171
'campaign' in, dull as in Flanders, **37**. 292
'carnival' at, from Michaelmas on, **35**. 524
celebrated inhabitants of, **35**. 234
Charles III of Spain might clear thieves from, **39**. 420–1
Church at: **2**. 368; attended by HW, **31**. 359, **39**. 173–4; has hard pews, and psalms squalled to a hand-organ, **34**. 115; Lort to preach at, **2**. 97; Montagu to avoid, **9**. 376; parsonage of, **42**. 482; Porteus, Bp, preaches charity sermon at, **31**. 359; vicar and churchwardens of, trustees under HW's will, **30**. 364–6
churchyard at, full of apprentices and footmen, **34**. 115
Chute and Whithed visit HW at, **19**. 442
Chute to visit, **19**. 435
climate of, healthy, **9**. 171
coaches at, said to outnumber all France's, **35**. 234
'cold and comfortless,' **35**. 81
Cole and HW accidentally meet at, **1**. 37
Cole visits, **2**. 370
Conolly, Lady Anne, sends abstract of title-deeds to her property at, **42**. 416
Conway visits sister at, **37**. 21
Conway, Hon. Jane, visits, **37**. 23
'Crown,' inn at, **29**. 59
dowagers at: in HW's circle, **33**. 200, 344, 354; like M.P.s, have not moved from town yet, **39**. 415; 'roost,' **10**. 259
dried up, and barren as Westphalia, **35**. 315
drought at, **10**. 38
Duane is HW's neighbour at, **25**. 216
—— to settle in, **33**. 200
ferry at, **12**. 74
Finett's house at, **1**. 184
fleets could almost sail to, in floods, **25**. 306
footpads near, **42**. 109
Forbes leases house at, **31**. 287
Forrester, John, gardener at, **40**. 164n

Fox Lane, Lady Bridget, enlivens, **32.** 132
Francklin is HW's tenant at, **20.** 374
French conquerors might give SH to 'intendant' of, **9.** 168
Giles is HW's neighbour at, **24.** 247, 255n
glass broken during cartage to, **2.** 47
Gray asks about location of, **14.** 30, 32
Greenwich, Bns, news-monger of, **30.** 270
Greenwich Park superior to, **35.** 234
HW a burgess of, **34.** 147
HW and Townshend cousins at, **13.** 4n
HW avoids, because of severe weather, **33.** 431
HW considers houses in Montpelier Row at, for Berrys, **11.** 103
HW constantly on road from, to London, **38.** 115
HW 'drowned out of,' **35.** 348
HW has no better gazettes than, **39.** 250
HW hears but one cuckoo at, **34.** 52
HW jokes about Mme Necker directing flat-bottomed boats to, **39.** 292
HW mentions, **11.** 43, 54, 283, **12.** 98, 162
HW mentions ornaments of, **32.** 31
HW not to lead militia of, **21.** 300, 307, **24.** 98
HW not to raise regiment in, **9.** 303
HW's and Lady Ossory's letters pass at, **34.** 54
HW's apothecary at, **11.** 369, **34.** 199
HW's artificial stone piers erected at, **41.** 229
HW's bequest to poor of, **30.** 364–6
HW's carriage accident talked about at, **39.** 454
HW's coachman reports news from, **33.** 196
HW sells house at, **40.** 62
HW sends servant to, **31.** 37
HW sends to, for apothecary, **34.** 199
HW settles in, **19.** 414
HW's house at, mentioned by Sir Edward Walpole, **36.** 22
HW's landscaping at, *see under* Strawberry Hill
HW's 'metropolis,' **19.** 496
HW's news from, not fresh, **33.** 10
HW's stay at, enables him to see Galfridus Mann, **19.** 442
HW's verses not worthy of, **29.** 312
HW takes SH at, **13.** 17, **37.** 269–70
HW tires of, **10.** 130–1
HW unable to go to, **15.** 284
HW writing the history of, **32.** 199
Ham House near, **10.** 307, **21.** 439n
Hamilton lives in Montpelier Row at, **33.** 218n
Hardinge to bring wife to, **35.** 593
Hawkins writes from, **40.** 227
highwaymen beset, **29.** 273n, **32.** 309, 352–3, **35.** 367, 525
highwaymen isolate, **35.** 525
illness at, general, **33.** 333–4
inhabitants of, glad of death of Haidar 'Alī **33.** 408
inn at, *see* 'Crown'; 'George'
Ironside's *History* of, **11.** 1n
Jerningham, Edward, visits, **33.** 41

justices robbed at, **33.** 445
Kew pagoda visible from Montpelier Row at, **35.** 308
Kneller's 'Cave' at, **18.** 36
land scarce and villas abundant at, **20.** 16
lane at, flooded with water, **24.** 47
lawlessness in vicinity of, **29.** 273n
letter mailed from London arrives day sooner than one from, **39.** 448
Lewis's survey of, **42.** 477
lies reach newspapers before they reach, **30.** 270
life at, resembles that in army at Flanders, **37.** 292
Lort's gift to be forwarded to, from Berkeley Sq., **16.** 196
—— to preach at, **2.** 97
Mann must not use name of, for SH, **19.** 486
manor of, owned by Vct Bolingbroke, **12.** 257
Marble Hill at, **3.** 331n, **13.** 41n
Mawhoods discussed at, **39.** 250–1
meadows at: HW annoyed by crowds in, **9.** 154; HW meets Ellis in, **10.** 83
military preparations at, **24.** 512
militia at, **33.** 88
Montagu considers taking house at, **10.** 216, 246–8, 251–3, 258–9
—— receives views of, from HW, **9.** 404
Montpelier Row at: Kew pagoda visible from, **35.** 308; occupants of, **42.** 484
natives of, unchanged, **15.** 269
'neighbourhood composed chiefly of gossiping old women,' **36.** 227
news at, repeats London's, **33.** 520
old gentlewomen HW's only company at, **25.** 530
old ladies' old news is HW's only information at, **35.** 316
'old market-women' of, **33.** 413
Ossory, Lady, perhaps caught cold at, **32.** 58
—— to visit, **32.** 127
Ossory, Lord, takes villa at, **32.** 46, 57, 76
Ovid's *Metamorphoses* has passage applicable to, **10.** 38
Pitt, Thomas, deserts 'Palazzo Pitti' at, **40.** 288
—— receives call at, from Strathmore, **22.** 152
—— takes house at, **22.** 18, 25
poor of: aided by SH edition, **28.** 23; HW's bequest to, **30.** 364–6
Pope, Alexander, is the last to wear laurel in, **33.** 465
——'s garden at, **21.** 417, **25.** 177
——'s house at, **9.** 72n, **10.** 83n, **15.** 319, **28.** 400, **29.** 130
——'s lines on grotto at, travestied by Ashton, **14.** 235
——'s residence at, mentioned in *New Lesson for Pope*, **18.** 35–6
postal arrangements at, **33.** 566
postal difficulties at, **16.** 219, 296
post at: arrives at 11 A.M., **31.** 234; leaves early, **31.** 346

[Twickenham, Middlesex, *continued*]
powder mills explode near, 23. 365, 39. 153
Pritchard, Mrs, has house at, to be used by Cts Waldegrave, 40. 282
Probyn dies at, 31. 199
provisions unobtainable at, 39. 404
Radnor buried at, 2. 368n
——'s garden at, 35. 174–5
rents of houses at, 10. 247, 252
residents at: Brown, Lady, 29. 160n, 31. 147, 188, 190, 209; Buller, Mrs, 11. 333; Cambridge, George, 12. 180; Cambridge, R. O., 11. 31n, 32. 192; Catherlough, Lady, 11. 65; Chenevix, Mrs, 9. 32, 83; Franks, 33. 81; Hamilton, Charles, 33. 218; Hamilton, Sir Patrick and Lady, 33. 218; Hawke, Hon. Chaloner, 32. 381; Hénin, Princesse d', 12. 14; Macclesfield, 10. 36; Meynells, 32. 192; Montagu, Lady Mary Wortley, 9. 119, 33. 255; Pitt, Mrs, 7. 397; Pitt family, 9. 263; Prado, 2. 373n; Pritchard, Mrs, 10. 69; Radnor, 9. 53, 21. 1n; Shelburne, Cts of, 10. 216, (?) 12. 268; Shirley, Lady Frances, 10. 7; Shirley, George, 14. 120n; Stafford, Cts of, 9. 119; Strafford, E. and Cts of, 32. 192; Suffolk, Cts of, 10. 118, 15. 152; Trapaud, 10. 247, 253; Waldegrave, Cts, 10. 69; Westmorland, Lady, 33. 260; Wharton, D. of, 9. 119; Whitchurch, 33. 81; *see also* Hawkins, Sir John; Pereira, Ephraim Lopez; Raftor, Catherine (Mrs Clive); Raftor, James; Scott, Samuel, *and under* Little Marble Hill; Little Strawberry Hill; Marble Hill; Strawberry Hill
residents at, listed, 42. 480–7
Richmond House near, 10. 216n
rivulet at, 2. 79n
road from Bletchley to, 1. 37–8
road not mended by, 35. 468
robberies in, 32. 213
Robinson's letter mentions, 21. 121
Roman Catholic chapel permitted at, 30. 209
Shirley builds 'Spite Hall' at, 35. 358
——'s field at, scene of goldsmiths' dinner, 39. 310–11
spring slow at, 39. 407
storm damage at, 33. 81–2
Stowe's pomps not rivalled by, 33. 473
Strafford's house in: at other end of, from HW, 38. 362; bow window inserted in, 35. 347; coach overturns near door of, 35. 279; new offices for, 35. 293
SH in parish of, 30. 349, 352
SH 'just by,' 30. 113
SH view posted at, to go to Florence, 20. 379–80
Swift's *History of the Four Last Years of the Queen* read at, by Pope and Bolingbroke, 21. 184n
Terrick, vicar of, 2. 374n
thieves sometimes poison house-dogs at, 31. 185
to be abandoned after October, 31. 180

Tuscany as ignorant as, of Dutch events, 25. 544
Twickenham Manor includes, 42. 417n
'Twitnamshire,' 32. 137, 207
unauthentic accounts at, of George III's illness, 34. 31
'unpolitical village,' 25. 589
views of: from SH, 20. 380, 25. 532; sold, 38. 340n
Vincent, Mrs, to leave, 31. 199
visitors to, 12. 221–52, *passim*
Waldegrave, Cts, takes house at, 22. 136
Wales, P. of (George IV) to succeed HW as attraction at, 12. 108, 112
wall built next to Lord Strafford's by Lady (?) Denbigh, 35. 307–8
Walnut Tree House at, 30. 366
Weekes carpenter at, 35. 221n
Whitmore, Lady, buried at, 16. 324n
windows at, shattered by explosion, 39. 153
York Farm (*or* House) at: 33. 81n, 42. 417n; rent of, 42. 417n; Whitchurch lives at, 42. 482
Yorkshire as far as, from news sources, 35. 349
See also Cross Deep Lodge; George Inn; Heath Lane Lodge; Little Marble Hill; Little Strawberry Hill; Marble Hill; Poulett Lodge; Ragman's Castle; Strawberry Hill; Twickenham Park
Twickenham Common:
Gunning, Gen., rents Lady Tweeddale's house on, 34. 17
postman drops letter on, 42. 293
'Twickenham Daily Post':
HW's name for his letter, 12. 176
Twickenham Lane:
HW and Lady Browne robbed in, 33. 295–8
Twickenham Manor:
Bolingbroke owned, 12. 257
history of leases of, 42. 417–18
Twickenham Meadows:
Cambridge lives in, 17. 282n
improved by Cambridge, 9. 154n
Twickenham Park, Middlesex, seat of Ds of Montrose:
Bacon receives, as recompense, from E. of Essex, 42. 489
Cambridge's house at, 11. 16n
Cavendish, Lord Frederick, inherits, 11. 50n
—— succeeds Ds of Montrose at, 36. 252
Compton, Lady Margaret, to visit, 31. 203
HW and Lady Browne frequent, 35. 365, 373
HW and Lady Browne suffer at, from Northesk's talk, 35. 373
HW at, 29. 160, 33. 234, 412
HW, Lady Browne, and Lady Anne Conolly return from, with guard, 35. 355
HW often sees Mrs Noel at Ds of Montrose's at, 25. 187, 312, 319, 320
HW to accompany Lady Browne to, 31. 218
HW unable to accompany Lady Browne to, 31. 202, 205–6
Montrose, Ds of, lives at, 15. 181n

Mountrath, Lady, bequeaths, to Lord Frederick Cavendish subject to life occupancies, **30.** 223, **31.** 123
—— lives at, **9.** 135n
Newcastle, Ds of, has little company at, **35.** 349–50
occupants of, **42.** 484
visitors to: Browne, Lady, **31.** 407–11; HW, **31.** 236, 407–11
See also under Manners, Lady Lucy, Ds of Montrose
Twickle. *See* Wassenaer, Unico Wilhelm
Twig; twigs:
Democritus's experiments on, **35.** 196
Twilight:
English should screen off, except in September and October, **35.** 474
Twining, Thomas (1735–1806), classical scholar:
(?) SH visited by, **12.** 224
Twiss, Richard (1747–1821), traveller and writer:
Travels through Portugal and Spain by: belittled by HW, **28.** 191; satirized by Preston, **41.** 434n
Twistleton, Thomas (ca 1735–88), 7th Bn Saye and Sele:
barony of Saye and Sele adjudged to, **25.** 165
suicide of, **31.** 267
'Twitcher'; 'Jemmy Twitcher.' *See* Montagu, John (1718–92), E. of Sandwich
'Twitcher, Jemmy':
Fox's name for Calcraft, **38.** 200
Sandwich's nickname, **38.** 363
'Twitcherites':
Sandwich's followers known as, **38.** 363
Twitnam; Twittenham. *See* Twickenham
Two Dissertations upon the Mint and Coins of . . . Durham. See under Fenn, Sir John
Two Dithyrambic Odes. See under Pinkerton, John
'Two Hunters and the Stag, The,' (? HW's) fable:
quoted in HW's 'Paris Journals,' **7.** 361
Two Letters Addressed to a Member. See under Burke, Edmund
Two Misers. See under O'Hara, Kane
Two Questions Previous to the Free Inquiry. See under Sykes, Arthur Ashley
Two Sicilies, K. of. *See* Ferdinand IV (I) of Naples
Two Sicilies, Kingdom of:
Montemar conquers, **17.** 427
protest against nomination of king of, **21.** 330
See also Naples; Sicily
Twyne, Brian (? 1579–1644), antiquary:
Account of the Musterings of the University of Oxford by, **2.** 347n
Antiquitatis academiæ Oxoniensis apologia by, **2.** 347n
Archæologia eulogizes, **2.** 347
Twysden, Frances (1753–1821), m. (1770) George Bussy Villiers, 4th E. of Jersey:

beauty of, in miniature, **25.** 411
Bedchamber appointment of, to Q. Charlotte, **12.** 138n
Bognor Rocks visited by, **12.** 204
bon mot on Ps of Wales and, **12.** 142
Charlotte, Q., supposed to favour, **12.** 186
conduct of, in intercepting letter, **15.** 327–8
daughter of, **32.** 247
daughter's house shelters, **12.** 188
fears assault by mob, **12.** 200
George IV's mistress, **34.** 142n
HW entertains, at dinner at SH, **35.** 454n
HW invites, to SH, **35.** 454, 471
HW meets, at Lady Diana Beauclerk's, at Richmond, **35.** 506
HW's correspondence with, **41.** 184–5
HW to call on, **41.** 185
insult to, at opera, **12.** 186
Jerningham a friend of, **12.** 155
Johnston, Lady Cecilia, gossips about, **12.** 143
news told by, probably apocryphal, **29.** 75
Nuneham visited by, **32.** 247
Paris to be visited by, **25.** 411
pregnancy of, at Brighton, **12.** 142
pretty foreteeth of, **33.** 82
resignation or dismissal of, rumoured, **12.** 188, 193
son of: **29.** 329; dies, **12.** 188
Stonhewer asked by, to ask HW for cure for insanity, **33.** 380
SH visited by, **29.** 72–3
Tyrwhitt reproaches, **12.** 149, 155
verses given by, to Mrs Delany, **29.** 175
Wales, Ps of, does not banish, **12.** 138
Warwick St house of, **12.** 150
Tyber. *See* Tiber
Tyburn, London:
Cameron dislikes ignominy of, **20.** 384
Derwentwater to be hanged at, **19.** 181
Ferrers executed at, **9.** 283, **13.** 35n, **21.** 402–3
Gibson hanged at, **1.** 134n
Gregory executed at, **13.** 87n
HW to send servant to, to ransom his watch, **40.** 64
Hackman hanged at, **2.** 156n
Holles fined and imprisoned for conference at, with Weston, **16.** 163
housebreakers incur risk of, **23.** 301
Methodists fail to convert at, **9.** 284
Townshend, Vcts, enjoys hangings at, from her villa nearby, **22.** 165
Wesket executed at, **38.** 490
'Tydeus':
Eton and King's man, **13.** 94
West inquires about, **13.** 92
Tyers, Jonathan (d. 1767):
Vauxhall Gardens managed by, **13.** 102n
Tyghe. *See* Tighe
Tyler, Wat (d. 1381), rebel:
Dalrymple identifies, with Jack Straw, **15.** 123
Walworth kills, **23.** 6n
'Tyler, Wat':
Conway's nickname for HW, **18.** 539, 559

Tylney, E. See Child, Richard (1680–1730);
Tylney, John (1712–84)

Tylney (before 1734, Child), John (1712–84),
2d E. Tylney, 1750:
Abano visited by, to avoid nephew's death
throes, 24. 22
brother of, 20. 483n
brother's misfortune shocks, 20. 355–6
card-playing of, 25. 534n
codicils probably to be cancelled by, 24. 23
Conway and HW shun, with his family, 37.
309
death of, greatly affects Mann, 25. 533–4, 537
dinner given by, for Mann's investiture, 23.
60, 63–4
embarks at Calais, but driven ashore at Ostend, 37. 325
Florence to be visited by, 24. 23, 312
—— visited by, 20. 355–6
Florentine house to be re-occupied by, 23. 468
French of, deficient, 37. 309
Fuentes, Conde and Condesa de, do not attend ball given by, at Wanstead, 21. 417
HW entertained by, at ball at Wanstead, 21.
417, 35. 238
HW offered marble tables by, but accepts
venison only, 35. 238
HW praises, 21. 417
HW tries to get pheasants from, for Lady
Strafford, 35. 275
health of, nose-bleed, 24. 145
heir wanted by, 24. 182
house of, in Piazza del Carmine, 23. 468n
invited to Pitti Palace gala, 25. 50n
Jermy, as his banker, leaves legacy to, 25.
206
jewels bought from Lady Orford by, and
given to his niece, 25. 144
legacies of, to Mann and Chase, 25. 534
Leopold receives, 22. 345n
—— 's comptroller has beer and punch served
to, 22. 379
lives in pompous style, 24. 312
Longs accompany, 24. 312
Mann accompanied by: at investiture, 23. 60;
to receive Karl Alexander, 20. 376
—— intimate with, for years, 25. 533, 537
—— tells, that HW caused his promotion,
22. 376
Neapolitan possessions of, to be sold for servants' benefit, 25. 534
Neapolitan visit deferred by, 24. 145
Orford, Cts of, occupies Florentine house of,
23. 468
Paris visited by, with Mr Wynn, 37. 309
Patch's conversation piece depicts, 43. 281–2
Rome visited by, 37. 324–5
servants devour, 25. 534n
servants of, have new laced clothes, 23. 60,
63–4
sister left inconsolable by, 37. 309
spacious fine house occupied by, at Naples,
24. 280

Wanstead the seat of, 15. 143n
will of, courier takes, to nephew and heir,
25. 533
Wilton does statue of Bacchus for, 20. 397–8
Tympany:
Conway's big goldfish has, 37. 476
Pomfret, Cts of, beats time on, 20. 584
—— exhibits, 20. 579
Tyndall, Thomas (d. ca 1766), antiquary:
Ducarel's friend, at Doctor's Commons, 40.
221
Lethieullier's MS bought by, 40. 221
Tyne, river:
HW moves to 'old goody' on, 30. 171
Tynemouth, Northumberland:
Rainsford governor of Cliff Fort at, 25. 271n
Tynte, Sir Charles Kemys (1710–85), 5th Bt;
M.P.:
Mathews defeats, at Glamorgan by-election,
43. 257
peerage rumoured for, as voting bribe, 38.
159n, 326, 328
Tynte, J. K. (ca 1737–1806) of Hill St, Berke-
ley Sq., and Mrs J. K.:
(?) SH visited by, 12. 237
Type, printer's:
Florentine, 25. 507
small, in Onslow's Popery Unmasked, 30. 57
Typhus fever:
jail fever a form of, 40. 308n
occurrences of, 22. 154n
Typographical Antiquities. See under Ames,
Joseph; Herbert, William
Typography:
Nicol improves, 42. 286
Tyrannick Love. See Dryden, John: Tyrranick
Love
Tyranny:
HW detests, but would not shed blood to act
against it, 34. 119
HW's reflections on, 23. 100, 452
Mann's reflections on, 23. 518
Tyrant; tyrants:
consciences lacked by, 35. 398
deified by pensioned authors, 7. 287
HW comments on, 25. 214
HW considers, a proof of an hereafter, 24.
103–4
only successful when they reign in the hearts
of the people, 23. 100
statesmen become, 37. 176
Tyrawley, Bn. See O'Hara, James
Tyrawley, Bns. See Stewart, Mary
Tyrconnel, Cts of. See Delaval, Sarah Hussey
(1763–1800); Jennings, Frances (ca 1647–
9—1731); Manners, Lady Frances (1753–92)
Tyrconnel, Ds of. See Jennings, Frances
Tyrconnel, E. of. See Carpenter, George (1723–
62); Talbot, Richard (1630–91); Talbot,
Richard Francis (1710–52)
Tyrconnel, Vct. See Brownlow, Sir John (d.
1754)

Tyre, Abp of. *See* Baiardi, Ottavio Antonio (1694–1764)

Tyre, Mrs Charles Bradon. *See* Lysons, Mary

Tyre:
Arlington St's resemblance to, **20.** 469

Tyrell, Sir James (1445–1502), Kt, 1471:
attainder act against, sought for HW, **41.** 92
commissioned to murder princes, **14.** 180, 182–3
Henry VII makes, ambassador, **41.** 113
More and, **43.** 188
murder of princes denied by, **41.** 113

Tyrell, James (fl. 1752):
Ralph Howard's letter from, **43.** 178, 233

Tyrell, Richard (d. 1766), Capt. of the *Buckingham*:
dispatches from Martinique brought by, **21.** 277n

Tyrell. *See also* Tyrrel; Tyrrell

Tyringham, Bucks:
HW not acquainted with portraits at, **41.** 252
portrait of Backwell at, **10.** 301n

Tyrol:
German troops to march to, **17.** 154
Gloucester, D. of, must traverse, in litter, **36.** 129

Tyrone (Ireland):
French, Jeffrey, of, **9.** 113n
subdued, **33.** 349

Tyrranick Love. See under Dryden, John

Tyrrel, ——:
Old Pretender's private agent, **18.** 87n

Tyrrel, Dr Thomas, of Florence:
Boswell treated by, **43.** 248
Gondi, Mme, not treated by, **18.** 87, **43.** 248
mercurial unctions administered by, for scurvy, **18.** 87

Tyrrel. *See also* Tyrell; Tyrrell

Tyrrell, ——, Lt-Gen.:
regiment of, **17.** 300n

Tyrrell, Christobella (1695–1789), m. 1 John Knapp; m. 2 John Pigott; m. 3 (1753) Richard Fiennes, 6th Vct Saye and Sele:
biographical information about, corrected, **43.** 125
black wig worn by, over white hair at Coronation, **9.** 388, **38.** 127

Tyrrell, Sir John (ca 1728–66), 5th Bt:
(?) Drury, Mary Anne, accompanied by, **9.** 309
HW hopes, did not catch cold at fish pond, **40.** 200
(?) Isted talks with, **9.** 309

Tyrrell. *See also* Tyrel; Tyrrel

Tyrwhitt, Lady. *See* Burgh, Elizabeth

Tyrwhitt, Thomas (1730–86), classical commentator:
antiquity of Rowley poems not denied by, **28.** 281–2
Appendix, Containing Some Observations upon . . . the Poems Attributed to Rowley, by, owned by HW, **16.** 357

Bryant and Milles answered by, **2.** 287–8
Bryant and Milles to be attacked by, **28.** 176n
Chattertonian writings of, **33.** 319n
Chatterton's forgery convincing to, **2.** 82–3, 85, 90, 92
——'s debt to Skinner's glossary asserted by, **16.** 179
Chaucer edited by, **2.** 82
——'s *Canterbury Tales* given tedious notes by, **28.** 191
enters Rowley controversy, **2.** 294n
nephew of, **12.** 149n
Porter intimate with, **16.** 217
Rowley poems edited by, **2.** 83n
Rowley poems no longer considered authentic by, **28.** 424
Rowley poems published by, **28.** 281, 292, **29.** 374
Vindication of the Appendix to the Poems Called Rowley's, A, by: **35.** 522–3, **43.** 74, 198; completely victorious, **15.** 165; HW's notes on, **16.** 358–9

Tyrwhitt, Sir Thomas (1763–1833), M.P.; Kt, 1812:
Jersey, Lady, reproached by, **12.** 149
Wales, P. of (George IV), wrongly reported to have dismissed, **12.** 149–50, 155

Tyson, ——, master of ceremonies at Bath:
minuet of, **33.** 572n

Tyson, Michael (1740–80), antiquary and artist:
account by, of an antiquarian ramble, **2.** 174–5, 177
Account of an Illuminated Manuscript in the Library of Corpus Christi College, Cambridge, An, by, **1.** 199, 202–3, 304
arms painted by Freeman for, **2.** 171–2
Boteler note sent to HW by, **1.** 318
Charles Carter praised by, **43.** 294
Chigwell inhabited by, **2.** 101
Cole called on by, **1.** 217, 264
—— calls on, **1.** 203, 290
—— commends, **1.** 169
—— copies MS for, **2.** 226
—— dines with, **1.** 167n, 193, 202, 267, **2.** 97
—— gives print to, **1.** 355n
—— receives Monsey print from, **1.** 364
—— receives new publications from, **2.** 148, 174
——'s life of, **2.** 226n
——'s portrait desired by, **2.** 112–13
——'s regret for, **2.** 212
—— told by, of agate-handled knives, **2.** 12n, 14, 16
—— writes to, **2.** 118
copies by, of: picture in Ely Cathedral, **1.** 160, 161n; portrait of St Etheldreda, **1.** 185; portrait of Willis, **2.** 285; print of Wyatt, **1.** 189n, 261; statue of Henry VII, **1.** 278–9, 282
Cullum, Sir John, friend of, **2.** 222
dies very poor, **29.** 40–1

[Tyson, Michael, *continued*]

drawings by, for Society of Antiquaries, 16. 181

drawings by, of: Baker, 1. 142; Butler, 1. 142; Gray, 1. 235, 236; Lagden, Mrs, 1. 364; Sebert, 2. 183

engraving discontinued by, 1. 386

Farmer, Cole, Masters, and Chettoes entertained by, 2. 119n

Gothic architecture's history to involve, 1. 191–2, 203–4, 206

Gough's letter from, 43. 286, 294

—— sorts papers of, 2. 226, 296

—— writes to, about drawing by Sherwin, 2. 8

Gray has not seen, 14. 187

Gundred's epitaph sent by, to Cole, 2. 6

HW hopes for print and visit from, 1. 280, 282

HW inquires after, 1. 379

HW mentions, 14. 188

HW receives packet from, 1. 202

HW's compliments to, 1. 183

HW thanks, for prints and notes, 1. 190

HW to receive prints from, 1. 193, 196, 197, 198, 200

HW to receive receipt from, 2. 74

HW wishes joy to, 2. 99, 101

HW writes to, 1. 203

history by, of fashions and dresses, 1. 191–2, 204

illness and death of, 2. 211, 212

Lambourne living presented to, 2. 77, 101

London visited by, 1. 216, 2. 74

marriage of, 2. 97, 97n, 101

Mason tells, of seeing Rowley MSS at HW's, 16. 126n

Masters's *Some Remarks*, printing of, discussed by, 1. 290

notes of, on *Anecdotes of Painting* and *Catalogue of Engravers*, 1. 169–76

plate by, of 'Jane Shore,' 1. 142, 144, 149, 150

print of E. of Cumberland lent to, 1. 355, 357

print of Theodore Haveus to be made by, 2. 77

prints by: 1. 144n; Cowper, J., 2. 302, 307–9; Dalton, 1. 193, 196, 362–3; Etough, 1. 193, 196; fish, 1. 282; Lagden, Mrs, 1. 363, 2. 307; Parker, 1. 193, 196; wheat, 1. 282; Winchester, M. of, 1. 213, 216

tapestry depicting Henry VI discovered by, 14. 166

vignette by, for Gough's *British Topography*, 2. 183, 191

Tyson, Mrs Michael. *See* Wale, Margaret

Tytherley, Hants:

Thistlethwayte rector of, 14. 49n

Tytler, James:

balloon experiment by, at Edinburgh, 25. 527n

Tytler, William (1711–92), historian:

Poetical Remains of James I, King of Scotland by, 15. 178, 181–2

U

Ubaldini, Contessa. *See* Antaldi, Lavinia

Ubaldini, Monsieur ——:

(?) Chute and Whithed occupy 'dull' apartment of, 17. 146

Ubaldini, Maria Ottavia (d. 1744), m. (1702) Pier Filippo Uguccioni; Electress's mistress of the Household:

dies about a year after Electress, 19. 23

Electress discusses her health with, 18. 172

——'s bequests to, 18. 169–70, 19. 23

son of, 18. 170

Ubaldini, Petruccio (?1524–?1600), illuminator; scholar:

Cole offers print of, to HW, 1. 130

HW declines Dalrymple's offer of work of, 15. 94–5

HW's copies of works of, 43. 196

Vita delle donne . . ., Le, by, offered to HW, 1. 2, 12

Vita ed i fatti di sei donne illustri, Le, by, 1. 1–2

Ubaldo (*called* Mignon *or* Velluti) (d. 1750), rector of the college of Scolopi:

(?) Medici bastard, 18. 39

Ubertini, Francesco (1494–1557), painter:

price of painting by, 19. 392n

'Ucalegon' in Virgil's *Æneid*:

allusions to, 23. 34n, 28. 25, 454, 33. 180

HW compares himself to, on Selwyn's death, 11. 183

Uccellatori, Gli. See under Gassmann, Florian; Goldoni, Carlo

Uccello, Paolo (1396–1475), painter:

Hawkwood's portrait by, 23. 428n

Udine, the (Italy):

Benedict XIV creates archdiocese of, 20. 173n, 191

Venice offers to transfer patriarchate to, 20. 206

Udney. *See* Udny

Udny, John (1727–1800), English consul at Venice ca 1761–76, at Leghorn 1776–ca 1800:

Berry, Mary, confuses, with his brother, 12. 160n

Dick succeeded by, as consul at Leghorn, 24. 233, 251

dispatches from Gen. Murray brought to Florence by, 25. 233

finances of, diminished by Leghorn's dwindling trade, 24. 437n

Greek proposes to, to raise Slavonians and Greeks to aid Minorca, 25. 196n

house of, Mann's body lies in chapel of, 25. 665n

Mann hears from, of Crillon's expedition to Minorca, 25. 174n

—— receives dispatches from, 25. 196n

——'s accounts with, relating to Minorca's siege, 25. 303, 429–31

——'s letter from, about D. of Gloucester, 24. 311

——'s post coveted by, **25.** 660n
—— tells: to collect provisions at Florence for Minorca, **24.** 380; to send express about naval actions near Gibraltar, **25.** 9
Mann, Horace II, to leave uncle's official papers with, **25.** 676n
—— turns over envoy's duties to, **25.** 676
Parker to be asked by, about Murray's correspondence with Crillon, **25.** 208n
Pleydell writes to, about D. of Gloucester, **24.** 311
Tuscany demands satisfaction from, in case of Port Mahon packet-boat, **24.** 417
unable to aid Murray, **25.** 197
Venetian consulship exchanged by, for one at Leghorn, **24.** 233
vouchers by, for money supplied by Mann, **25.** 204n
Udny, Mary (d. after 1811), m. (1785) Sir William Augustus Cunynghame, 4th Bt:
Hotham, Miss, entertains, **12.** 154
SH visited by, **12.** 236
Udny, Robert Fullarton (1722–1802), merchant; art-collector; HW's neighbour:
Berners St the address of, **42.** 165
Berry, Agnes, attends concert at house of, **12.** 198
Berry, Mary, confuses, with his brother, **11.** 90n, **12.** 260n
Bristol visited by, **12.** 210
Cosways visit, **12.** 203
daughter of, **12.** 154n
Elgin, Lady visits, **12.** 160
HW congratulated by, on purchase of missal, **33.** 519n, **39.** 442, **42.** 165
HW exchanges visits with, **11.** 89, **12.** 160
HW might be shown pictures acquired by, **42.** 165
HW's correspondence with, **42.** 165, **43.** 378
HW sends venison to, **12.** 160
'old and decrepit,' **11.** 105
SH ticket not used by, **12.** 225n
SH visited by, **12.** 236
Teddington, house at, occupied by, **12.** 160n
Udny, Mrs Robert Fullarton. See Jordan, Margaret
Udny Castle, Aberdeenshire:
Udnys of, **11.** 90n
Uffington, Lincs:
Bertie's seat at, **1.** 171
Uffizi Gallery, at Florence:
Act of Accession provides against scattering the treasures of, **21.** 466
(?) Archduke Leopold's gallery mistaken for, **40.** 5
armoury converted into bad rooms for, **25.** 170
Bianchi, keeper of, **17.** 213n
—— sets fire to, and robs it of a gold foot, **25.** 65
bronzes in, fill several rooms, **25.** 170
Bruce, Miss, offended by pictures in, **20.** 145
'Cabinet de Madame' in, **25.** 170

Cellini's alleged artifacts stolen from, **23.** 407n
Charles III's tour of, **21.** 500
china in, rearranged, **25.** 170
Cicero bust in, **20.** 86
Cocchi, Raimondo, an antiquarian in, **21.** 152
Conway introduced to Bianchi in, **20.** 290
—— sees, **37.** 319
corridors in, resemble upholsterer's shop, **25.** 171
crowded with modern painters' portraits, **25.** 170
drawings of, executed for HW at Mann's order, **17.** 36n, 58, 68, **18.** 133, 181, 202, 214, 291, 303
fire at, **22.** 67–8, 71, **25.** 65
Francis I has not yet stripped, **19.** 83
Gaddi torso in, **25.** 170
Giovanni Gastone's bust in, **25.** 170
HW and Gray neglect, **13.** 230
HW feels no emotion in, **13.** 199
HW's description of, entices Conway, **37.** 73
HW's lodging faces, **37.** 68
HW to forsake, for Parliament, **37.** 93
HW unwilling to leave, **37.** 49
HW would be glad to have longer account of, when it appears, **25.** 531
Jamesone's portrait in, **40.** 267
Laocoön in, **22.** 67, 71, **25.** 171
Leopold disperses Niobe group in, **25.** 170–1, 203, 530–1
—— increases contents of, **25.** 230
Mann's old apartment near, **17.** 381
—— tired by, though carried up stairs, **25.** 171
medals in: Conway studies, **20.** 290, 297; remain unchanged, **25.** 170
new staircase made to, from loggia, **22.** 123, **25.** 169–70
Pitt, Anne, considered a connoiseuse at, **23.** 457
proposal to plunder, **17.** 193
Richecourt fears that the Spaniards may rob, **18.** 295
scaffali (bookcases) in, taken away, **25.** 170
Siries's rooms in, **25.** 169
statues in, **20.** 547n
Teniers painting supposedly of, **40.** 5
transformation of, **25.** 169–71
treasures of, not removed, **17.** 380
Tribune in: Chute dreams of Venus's marriage in, **35.** 54; Crew to take designs of, to HW, **18.** 274; crystal vase from, **25.** 169, **26.** 56; HW deplores violation of, **25.** 177; HW prouder of Harcourt's goodness than of, **35.** 516; 'improved' by Leopold, **33.** 286; Mann wishes to give, to HW, **17.** 324; perforated, **25.** 170; rock crystal and other 'rubbish' sold from, **25.** 65; Venus in, **20.** 331, **35.** 52; Zoffany sent to do view of, **23.** 430, 436n, 519, **24.** 33–4, 539–40; Zoffany's painting of, criticized by HW, **24.** 526–7; Zoffany's painting of, will record its former

[Uffizi Gallery, at Florence, *continued*]
state, **25.** 177; Zoffany's view of, crowded with portraits of English travellers then in Florence, **24.** 34; Zoffany transferred paintings to, from Pitti, **24.** 540
visitors to: Brand, **20.** 471; Bruce, Miss, **20.** 145; Charles III, **21.** 500; Conway, **20.** 290; Damer, Mrs, **25.** 203; Huntingdon, **20.** 457; Pitt, Thomas, **21.** 500–1; Vorontsov and postmaster, **21.** 249
Walpole, Sir Robert, would enjoy, **18.** 212
Wilton guides Huntingdon in, **20.** 457
Zoffany had right to take down any painting in, **24.** 540
Ufton Court, Berks:
Perkins of, **12.** 206n
Ughi, Maria Minerva (1731–1822), m. (1750) Luigi or Louis Roland, Conte Lorenzi:
Louis XV reverenced by, when playing kings at cards, **20.** 276
Madonna di Loreto visited by, to induce pregnancy, **20.** 437
marriage of, to take place, **20.** *192*
'Paris doll,' **21.** 501
Ughi, Scipione (1670–1746) *or* Piero (1676–1744):
Modenese princess told by, that he had danced with her, **17.** 66
Ughi, Palazzo:
Accademia degli Immobili founded in, **17.** 56n
Ughi family:
Teatro del Cocomero owned by, **17.** 163n
Ugo. *See* Franchini, Ugo
Ugolino della Gherardesca (d. ca 1288), statesman, of Pisa:
Carlisle's translation of passage on, in the *Inferno*, **28.** 35
Uguccione. *See* Uguccioni
Uguccioni, Signora. *See* Ubaldini, Maria Ottavia
Uguccioni, ——:
confirmed as a nun, **18.** 45
Uguccioni, Giovanni Battista Maria (1710–82), senator, 1761; 'Bistina':
abbé writes epithalamiums for, **18.** 510
alarm of, over possible reception of his poem and presents, **18.** 553–4
Alamanni, friend of, **18.** 127
believes Cts of Pomfret's boast about her ancestry, **20.** 78
Bosville, Mrs, aided by, **18.** 242, 251
brothers of, leave Mann to tell him of Cts Granville's death, **19.** 151
canary birds coupled by, at Casa Cannonoci, **18.** 446
cantata and epithalamium sent by, to England, **18.** 510, 545
Carteret's marriage gives hope of preferment to, **35.** 52–3
Carteret's wedding shocks, by its simplicity, **18.** 445

compliments expected by, on Carteret wedding, **18.** 446
diamond-studded picture of Cts Granville expected by, **18.** 554
English visit of, would flatter Bns Cartetet and Cts of Pomfret, **18.** 467
epithalamium of, must be rewritten, **18.** 522
expense of shipping Cts of Pomfret's furniture will ruin, **17.** 130
Fermor, Lady Juliana, and Miss Shelley will be loved by, **20.** 70
Fermor, Lady Sophia (Cts Granville) corresponds with, **19.** 151
—— tells, about matrimonial plans, **20.** 70
—— will shock, by her death, **19.** 133, 148
Fermor, William, missed by, at Leghorn, **18.** 509–10
Fermor family idolized by, **18.** 509
Granvilles' gifts from, **18.** 553
HW's correspondence with, **40.** 32–3
Lestevenons repulse, **17.** 217
Mann contradicts guess of, about Cts of Orford, **19.** 75
—— may entertain HW, Dini, and, at faro, **40.** 32
—— sees Cts Granville's letters to, **19.** 151
—— to get Chute and Whithed introduced by, at Baronessa Ricasoli's, **17.** *129*
—— told by, that Cts of Pomfret wishes her furniture sent on to her, **17.** 129
—— to tell, that Cts Granville still holds conversazioni, **18.** 537
mother's inheritance mentioned by, **18.** 170
Orford, Cts of (Bns Walpole) has affair with, **17.** 448, **43.** 271
—— recommends Guise and Valtravers to, **20.** 393
—— will probably ask, to get her a house, **20.** 393
poems of, would provide Pomfrets with household paper, **18.** 510, 554
Pomfret, Cts of, corresponds with, **17.** 129, 170, 217, **18.** 126, 196, **19.** 61
—— gives silver standish to, **18.** 126
—— to translate mottos by, for pictures, **18.** 545
—— will not be welcomed by, **20.** 102
Pomfret family's return to Florence wished by, **20.** 70
Pomfret family will keep, busy, **20.** 97
Pomfrets friendly with, **18.** 467n
preferment hoped by, through Carteret's marriage to Lady Sophia Fermor, **18.** 455, 554, **35.** 52–3
religion might be changed by, to get English preferment, **18.** 554
ruspanti member, **17.** 273n
Ugurgieri Malavolti, Signora. *See* Chigi Zondadari, Cecilia
Uhbrichts Dahl:
Swedish Court at, **40.** 214
Uhlefeld *or* Uhlefeldt. *See* Ulfeld

Uist. *See* South Uist

Ulcer; ulcers:
Bertin has, **6.** 97
Gloucester, D. of, thought to have, in large intestine, **23.** 337

Uldall, ——, Danish councillor:
Caroline Matilda notified by, **23.** 409n

Ulfeld, Corfiz Anton (1699–1760), Graf; Austrian statesman:
Aix treaty negotiated by, **20.** 400n
Francis I to discuss English difficulties at Leghorn with, **20.** 277n
Magnan sent by, to Francis I, **18.** 564
Tron told by, that his dismissal from Vienna depends on Benedict XIV's parley with Rezzonico, **20.** 190n
Venetian ambassador told by, that Maria Theresa demands change in their policy, **20.** 189–90

Ulla. *See* La Ulla

Ulm (Germany):
Conway and Scott visit, **39.** 538–9

Ulrica Leonora (1688–1741), Q. of Sweden 1719–41:
death of, puts English into mourning, **17.** 255
smallpox prevalent in family of, **17.** 255

Ulrick:
young Hungarian in George I's service, **34.** 260

Ulster, E. of. *See* Edward Augustus, D. of York

Ulster, K. of. *See* O'Neill, Hugh (d. 1230)

'Ulysses':
Conway as remote as, **39.** 320
policy of, **37.** 37
Putello acts part of, **19.** 355

Umberslade, Warwickshire; Archer's seat:
HW visits, **9.** 121
Hertford dines at, **38.** 69

Umble pie. *See* Pie, umble

Umbrella; umbrellas:
French servants use, instead of hats, **35.** 112
servant carries, **31.** 215
silk, Hertford, Cts of, wishes HW to bring, from Paris, **39.** 267

Umbria:
Lobkowitz to go to, **18.** 529

'Uncle, the':
Grafton, Ds of, sorry to leave, **38.** 89

Uncles:
HW's reflections on, **25.** 331

Unconnected Whig's Address to the Public, An:
HW comments on, **32.** 383
HW recommends, **28.** 337
Mason inquires about, **28.** 333

Unction:
Dumesnil receives, as bishop, **19.** 492
extreme: Benedict XIV receives, **21.** 37, 81; Botta receives, **22.** 13; Dauphin's, **22.** 364; Electress has, **18.** 160; Old Pretender receives, **21.** 391, 392, **22.** 379; Pompadour,

Mme de, receives, **38.** 372; Richecourt's daughter has, **21.** 43; Young Pretender receives, **25.** 468, 482n
mercurial, **18.** 87

'Undecimillia,' St. *See* Ursula, St

Under-actors:
Murphy's *All in the Wrong* opened by, at Drury Lane, **38.** 87

Underdoorkeeper of House of Commons:
insolence of, **17.** 245

Under Mr Milton's Picture. See under Dryden, John

Under-petticoat; under-petticoats:
beaver, lined with scarlet shag, given by Braitwitz to Mme Vitelli, **18.** 333
Eve's, eaten by goat in Noah's ark, **39.** 294
HW wears, as old woman, **18.** 359
Salisbury famous for, flannel for, **40.** 8

Undersecretary of state, English. *See* Stone, Andrew (1703–73); Wood, Robert (?1717–71)

Undersecretary of state for foreign affairs, English:
HW wishes cousin to succeed Maddison as, **42.** 73

Undersecretary of state, Tuscan. *See* Antinori Calderini, Cavaliere Gaetano

Undertaker; undertakers:
Brown, Sir Robert, bargains with, over daughter's funeral, **10.** 68, **25.** 609n
Cameron not disturbed by, **20.** 384
escutcheon placed by, on Mrs Edwards's door, **20.** 4
Ferrers's scaffold hung with black by, **9.** 283, **21.** 402
HW's term for Daun, **21.** 432
of Tower of London, *see* Allingham
See also Stephenson, William

Undertakers (political):
for petitions, in English counties, **23.** 163

Underwaistcoat:
Mason recommends, to HW, **28.** 182

Unembarrassed Countenance, The. See under Williams, Sir Charles Hanbury

Ungern-Sternberg, Mattias (1689–1763), Friherre von; Swedish army officer:
force assembles under, in Sweden and Pomerania, **21.** 119n

'Unhappy England, Still in Forty-One.' *See under* Williams, Sir Charles Hanbury

Unhappy Favourite, The. See under Banks, John

Unicorn, English ship:
Lippe sails from Falmouth on, **22.** 48n

Uniform; uniforms:
blue and red, laced, worn by Mill and Davison, **19.** 407
country squires wear, **21.** 312
English ladies wear their husbands', **24.** 384
for calcio at Leghorn, **22.** 423
Joseph II wears, without ensigns, **23.** 108
Masserano's gentlemen wear, light blue with silver arras lace, **38.** 399n

[Uniform; uniforms, *continued*]
of Jacobite forces, **19.** 299
scoured, worn by camp-followers, **35.** 509
Voltaire's disrespect for, **34.** 209
whimsical, worn by English at Venice when
attending opera at Padua, **21.** 513
white, worn by troops at Bologna border, **18.**
85–6
Unigenitus Dei filius (papal bull):
Benedict XIV's senility exhibited in, **21.** 44–5
HW jokes about, **9.** 152
HW might amuse himself with, in Paris, **21.**
337
HW on, **5.** 12
Louis XV's assassin may have been motivated
by, **21.** 48
Union, French bark:
capture of, with Campoflorido's servants and
baggage, **19.** 383n
Union Coffee-house, London:
riot's encouragement from, prompts Egmont
to demand that the mistress testify, **38.** 257
Union Court, Broad Street, London:
Chevalier of, **7.** 205n
See also under Old Broad Street
Union flag. *See under* Flag
Union of the two noble and illustre fameties.
See under Hall, Edward
'Uniquity':
HW's reflections on, **31.** 313–14
Unitarianism. *See under* Socinianism
'United Provinces:
Conway might form, from Channel Islands,
39. 299
United Provinces of the Netherlands. *See under*
Holland
United States of America. *See under* America,
United States of
Universal Advertiser:
Cox directs 'patriot' attacks in, on Harting-
ton, **37.** 393n
Universal Etymological English Dictionary, An.
See under Bailey, Nathan
Universal History. See under Voltaire
Universalist:
Clarke is, **42.** 448
Universal Passion, The. See under Young, Ed-
ward
Universe:
creation of, discussed in Erasmus Darwin's
Botanic Garden, **42.** 270–1
Université, Rue de l', in Paris:
Aiguillon, Hôtel d', in, **6.** 5n
Beaupréon, Hôtel de, in, **7.** 267
Brancas, Hôtel de, in **38.** 305n
Hambourg, Hôtel d', in, **6.** 383
Soyecourt, Hôtel de, in, **4.** 367n
University; universities:
Bingham, Hon. Richard, too young for, at 15,
24. 462
books have imprimatur of, **18.** 480
British, should teach English constitution,
42. 403

HW scoffs at degrees taken at, **25.** 316
King, Dr William, in oration deplores decay
of, under Hanoverians, **20.** 50n
University of Paris:
Parliament of Paris orders report by, on inoc-
ulation, **22.** 153n
See also Sorbonne
Unknown Frenchman:
HW's correspondence with, **42.** 473
Unknown individuals:
HW's correspondence with, **40.** 29, 181, 207,
208–9, 237–9, 279, **41.** 1, 111–15, 399–401,
42. 62, 151, 337, 364, 386, 402–4, 414–15,
472, 474
Untrustworthiness:
Conway's reflections on universal prevalence
of, **37.** 176
Uomo nero:
Conway diverted by, **37.** 320
HW asks meaning of, **20.** 291, 298
Upholsterer; upholsterers:
Ailesbury, Cts of, fears she treats HW as if
he were, **37.** 466
at Nuneham, **35.** 521
crowds of, at sales at Palazzo Pitti, **25.** 231
Gibson is, **20.** 224
price of, for pier-glasses, **32.** 115
working in Gallery at SH, **10.** 84
Upholsterer's shop:
corridors in Uffizi Gallery resemble, **25.** 171
Upholstering:
Lund's remark on painting and, **30.** 62
Uppark, Sussex, Fetherstonhaugh's seat:
Chartres visits, **33.** 483n
HW calls, 'splendid seat,' **12.** 206
HW visits, **4.** 455n
Upper Brook St. *See* Brook St, Upper
Upper Grosvenor St. *See* Grosvenor St, Upper
Upper Ossory, Bn. *See* Fitzpatrick, Sir Barnaby
Upper Ossory, Cts of. *See* Leveson Gower, Hon.
Evelyn (1725–63); Liddell, Hon. Anne (ca
1738–1804)
Upper Ossory, E. of. *See* Fitzpatrick, John
(1745–1818)
Upper Seymour St, Portman, Sq., London:
Northmore, Thomas, of, **12.** 238
Upper Wimpole St, London:
Newcome, George William, dies in, **2.** 265n
See also Wimpole Street
Upton, ——:
Mann presents, to Leopold, **23.** 527n
Upton, Mrs ——:
Braddock ill-treats, for not giving him enough
money, **20.** 492–3
Upton, Clotworthy (1721–85), cr. (1776) Bn
Templetown:
New York lands granted to, **38.** 421n, 422
Upton, Mrs Clotworthy. *See* Boughton, Eliza-
beth
Upton, John (d. 1740), Irish M.P.:
death of, **37.** 74n

Upton, Thomas (d. before 1796), watchmaker:
implicated in plot to assassinate George III,
12. 115, 118
Upton, Warwickshire, Child family's seat:
to be kept as in Mr Child's lifetime, **12**. 72
Upton-on-Severn, Worcs:
church at, half-ruined, **35**. 152
HW visits, **35**. 152
Upway, Dorset:
Lisle of, **12**. 200n
Upwell, Norfolk:
Bell of, **1**. 10n
Urania. See under Sidney, Mary, Cts of Pem-
broke
Uranus, planet:
Brobdingnags inhabit, **33**. 365
discovery of, **33**. 360, 365, 367
Herschel names, 'Georgium Sidus' for George
III, **15**. 188
orbit of, **33**. 365
Urban II (Odo *or* Eudes) (ca 1042–99), pope
1088–99:
Charles III's Maltese claims based on bull of,
20. 406n, **43**. 272
Urban IV (Jacques Pantaléon) (d. 1264), pope
1261–4:
HW in *Anecdotes of Painting* mistakes, for
Urban V, **42**. 66–7
Urban V (Guillaume de Grimoard) (1310–70),
pope 1362–70:
HW in *Anecdotes of Painting* mistakes Urban
IV for, **42**. 66–7
Urban VIII (Maffeo Barberini) (1568–1644),
pope 1623–44:
Galluzzi condemns Galileo's ill-treatment by,
25. 224n
great-grandnephew of, **13**. 214n
Urbino seized by, from Grand Duchess Vit-
toria, **18**. 169n
Urbino (Italian duchy):
Clement XIV from, **23**. 117
Court of, **15**. 53
St-Odile, Barone di, arranges sale of Medici
estates at, to Benedict XIV, **20**. 306n
Urban VIII seizes, from Tuscany, **18**. 169n
Urfé, Honoré d' (1568–1625), writer:
Astrée, L', by: 'Celadon' the hero of, 13.65n;
Du Deffand, Mme, compares, with *Bajazet*,
3. 294; Du Deffand, Mme, mentions, **4**. 71;
Du Deffand, Mme, owns, **8**. 33n; HW to
resemble shepherd in, **19**. 414
philosophes a compound of Diogenes and,
39. 292
Urfey, Thomas d' (1633–1723), dramatist:
song by, **13**. 201n
Wonders in the Sun by, quoted by HW, **12**.
33, **43**. 152
'Uriah's Letter.' *See under* Franciabigio
Urinal; urinals:
Luke, St, depicted as holding, **35**. 133
Tesi seems to be using, **18**. 361
Urination:
Indians', extraordinary, **35**. 187

ladies perform, in front of footmen, **34**. 257
Orford's unconscious, a sign of insanity, **36**.
122
Urine, suppression of:
occurrences of, **22**. 380n, **24**. 39
Urn; urns:
alabaster, *see under* Vase
antique Roman sepulchral, *see under* Altar
at the Vyne, **35**. 640
cherry brandy 'distilled' from, **37**. 22
Etruscan, HW's, **15**. 13
French, with Greek motifs, **31**. 99
funeral, **15**. 16
glass, bought by HW, **26**. 7
HW buys, at Rome, **26**. 7
HW's sepulchral, for Galfridus Mann's monu-
ment: designed by Bentley, and placed in
Linton church, **21**. 128, 142, 157, 249–50;
Mann frames design of, for his bedside,
21. 253
HW's sepulchral for Horace Mann, placed in
Linton church, **25**. 666, 668, 670, 671, 678
HW's sepulchral, for Montagu family, **10**. 333
HW's sepulchral, with indecent decoration,
15. 22
La Borde's, of porphyry, **31**. 80
Mann presents, to Ds of Gloucester, **24**. 453
—— procures, for Sir Robert Walpole, **17**. 24
—— sends, to E. of Lincoln, **35**. 23
marble: in monument, **35**. 644; in St John's
College, Oxford, contains Rawlinson's
heart, **42**. 239n
Middleton describes, **15**. 19
of Clodia, bought by HW, **26**. 7
on monument at Horton, **10**. 333
on monument at Peterborough, **10**. 347
on tomb, **35**. 149
Roman: from Great Chesterford, **1**. 210; in-
scription on, **15**. 13
Wood's tombstone might be, **41**. 308
Urquhart, Chevalier Adam:
Young Pretender drives, away, **26**. 47
Urquhart, Sir Thomas (1611–60), translator:
Ἐκσκυβαλαυρον by, sent to HW by Lort, **16**.
163–4
Urre d'Aiguebonne, Anne-Marie d' (ca 1633–
1724), m. François de Rostaing, Comte de
Bury:
HW seeks print of, **6**. 344, 346, 347, 368
Urrutia, Don Rodrigo, capt. of the *Poder*:
rescue of, **18**. 414
Urry, Capt.:
Havana news brought by, **38**. 174n
Urry, John (1666–1715), editor of Chaucer:
confused account by, of Chaucer's portrait,
14. 109
Ursins, Comtesse des. *See* Mérode, Joséphine-
Monique-Mélanie
Ursins, Princesse des. *See* La Trémoïlle, Anne-
Marie de
Ursula, St:
Sévigné, Mme de, may be eclipsed by, **35**. 393

Ursula (Plantagenet) (b. 1455):
birth of, 1. 320
Ursuline; Ursulines:
convent of, at Rome, entered by Mary Wortley Montagu, 22. 113
nuns of, *see under* Nun
of Trent, prayed for D. of Gloucester, 32. 389
Uruguay, South America:
Jesuits said to endanger Portuguese sovereignty in, 21. 217n
Usage des Romains:
Du Deffand, Mme owns, 8. 34
Use and Intent of Prophecy. See under Sherlock, Thomas
Use and Intent of Prophecy and the History of the Fall. See under Bate, Julius
Usez. *See* Uzès
Ushant (Ouessant), French island off Brittany:
battle of, 29. 48n
English fleet may land near, 37. 530
fleets clash west of, 28. 422n
Keppel's fleet off, 39. 313
skirmish off, 28. 425n
Usher, Anne (d. 1759), m. (1748) Hon. Richard Fitzpatrick:
husband to introduce, to Ds of Bedford, 37. 289, 291
Usher, Capt. Arthur (d. 1763):
death of, in fire, when visiting sister on return from Jamaica, 22. 138, 38. 201
negroes of, suspected of starting fire, 22. 141
Usher, Mary Jenney (ca 1723–63), m. (1744) Richard Molesworth, 3d Vct Molesworth:
burnt to death in fire at house in Upper Brook Street, 22. 138, 139, 140, 143, 145, 25. 242, 38. 201
family of, 37. 356
husband persuaded by, to give annuity to his brother, 22. 140
Usher. *See also* Ussher
Usher of the Black Rod. *See* Bellenden, Hon. Sir Henry (d. 1761); Edmonstone, Sir Archibald (1717–1807); Molyneux, Sir Francis (before 1737–1812); Montagu, George (ca 1713–80); Robinson, Sir Septimus (1710–65)
Usher of the Black Rod in Ireland. *See* Dayrolles, Solomon
Usher of the Exchequer. *See under* Exchequer
Usquebaugh:
Montagu brings, from Dublin, 10. 119
—— jokes about, 9. 346
—— offers, to HW, for stomach pain, 10. 119, 120
Ussé, Marquis d'. *See* Bernin, Louis-Sébastien
Ussé. *See also* Uzès
Ussel, Marc-Antoine, Marquis d':
(?) Mme du Deffand mistakes another for, 4. 493
Ussher, James (1581–1656), Abp of Armagh:
letters of, may tell of Dionysius publication, 16. 11
Usson, Comte d'. *See* Usson de Bonac, Pierre-Chrysostome d'

Usson, Comtesse d'. *See* Poll, Margarethe Cornelia van de
Usson, Charles-Armand d' (ca 1731–1811), Marquis de Donnezan; amateur comedian:
acts at Chanteloup, 5. 382n
social relations of, in Paris, 3. 24, 100, 6. 404, 7. 297, 301, 303, 304, 306, 308, 309, 347, 351, 430
Stanley mimicked by, 7. 297
verses on, 6. 407
Usson, François-Armand d' (1716–78), Marquis de Bonac; French ambassador to Holland 1751–6:
death of, 7. 140
Rouillé writes through, to Henry Fox, 20. 524
Usson de Bonac, Jean-Louis d' (1734–1821), Abbé de Bonac; Bp of Agen 1767–90:
Du Deffand, Mme, gives opinion of, 5. 98
Paris visited by, 7. 452
Pontchartrain to be visited by, 5. 98
Rueil visited by, 7. 335
social relations of, in Paris, 5. 97, 98, (?) 145, 7. 335–6, 338, 340, 342
Usson, brother of, 7. 335
Usson de Bonac, Louise-Pétronille d', m. (1768) Jean-Paul, Marquis d'Angosse:
Du Deffand, Mme, corresponds with, 7. 442
(?) ——'s opinion of, 6. 475
——'s social relations with, 6. (?)474, 7. 131, 431, 432, 460
family calamities of, 7. 139–40
Paris left by, 7. 433
—— visited by, 7. 431
St Joseph's convent occupied by, 6. 474–5, 7. 131
Usson de Bonac, Pierre-Chrysostome d' (1724–82), Comte d'Usson, French ambassador to Sweden 1774–82:
acts at Chanteloup, 5. 382n
appointed ambassador to Sweden, 6. 87, 89
arrival of, in England, 22. 135
biographical information about, corrected, 43. 84
envoy to Sweden, married to Dutchwoman, 22. 135n
good-humoured country gentleman, on good behaviour after debauch, 38. 203
(?) HW mentions, 3. 341
HW's party at SH missed by, 10. 71
HW to sup with, in Paris, 39. 16
health of, fever, 10. 71–2
Hertford sups with, at Fontainebleau, 38. 218
Hervey, Bns, often entertains, 22. 135
Polish embassy may be given to, 31. 102, 39. 24
social relations of, in Paris, *see index entries ante* 8. 534 (erroneously listed *sub* Usson, Victor-Timoléon)
Swedish embassy of, revoked, 5. 48
Usurer; usurers:
caution should be taught to, in money-lending to noblemen's sons, 24. 237

HW confuses, with jockeys, **32**. 131
interest reduction opposed by, **20**. 111
Mann has little pity for, **20**. 242
rapine by, in England, **24**. 231
Usury:
Walker's, **19**. 511n
Utensil; utensils:
from Pompeii and Herculaneum should be
listed by Hamilton, **35**. 419
Utica:
Pomfret, Cts of, mistakes Attica for, **20**. 579
Scipio's confinement at, **10**. 256
Utkinton, Cheshire:
Sir John Crewe's library at Utkinton Hall
at, **1**. 4
Utopia. See under More, Sir Thomas
Utrecht:
Bloemaert of, **7**. 355
Conway at, **37**. 134
De Jong burgomaster of, **13**. 50n
English church at, **4**. 52n
Ligonier, Edward, writes from, **21**. 314n
Maclaine, Rev. Archibald, at, **20**. 193n
Tuer, Herbert, at, **1**. 73–4
Utrecht, Gazette d'. See Gazette d'Utrecht
Utrecht, Treaty of:
Aix treaty has Dunkirk demolished according
to terms of, **19**. 481, **21**. 527
Bath's anecdote about, **7**. 354
Catalonians' treatment under, **23**. 212n
Dunkirk's demolition prescribed by, **19**. 481,
21. 527, **30**. 53
Dutch do not forget, **19**. 68
English and not French allowed by, to build
forts among the Iroquois, **35**. 212n
English conquests 'refunded' by, **33**. 215
English M.P.s accused of trying to re-enact,
26. 10
France has not forgotten, **29**. 65
—— insists on solution of colonial question
according to, **20**. 541n
—— questions validity of, **20**. 468n
French profess willingness to abide by, **35**.
208n
HW calls, 'scandalous peace,' **34**. 230
Holland obliged by, to supply troops if Prot-
estant succession is threatened in England,
19. 103n, **21**. 298n
Pynsent opposed to, **22**. 277, 284
—— quits the world because of, **38**. 493
Tickell's poem on, **14**. 35
Utrecht Gazette. See Gazette d'Utrecht
Uxbridge, E. of. *See* Bayly, Henry (1744–1812);
Paget, Henry William (1768–1854)
Uxbridge, Middlesex:
'King's Arms' at, Brackley carrier starts from,
10. 87
Latimers near, **37**. 299
Montagu family portraits to be called for at,
by Montagu's wagoner, **10**. 67
Montagu family portraits to be sent to, **10**.
67, 81, 85

on road between Bletchley and SH, **1**. 2n
road through, **1**. 37
Uzerches (France):
Barbarina misbehaves at, **30**. 20
Uzès, Bp of. *See* Béthizy, Henri Benoît-Jules de
Uzès, Comte d'. *See* Crussol, Pierre Marie de
Uzès, Duc d'. *See* Crussol, François-Emmanuel
de
Uzès, Duchesse d'. *See* Pardaillan de Gondrin,
Madeleine-Julie-Victoire de
Uzès, Hôtel d', at Paris:
Caracciolo at, **5**. 140n

V

Vacation, long:
Londoners used to be lively after, **25**. 558
Vachel, Mr:
Hardinge to be addressed to, in Chesterfield
St, **35**. 595
Vachel. *See also* Vachell
Vachel family:
Hampden's second wife said to belong to,
35. 598
Hardinge connected with, through wife, **35**.
598
Vachell, Lady. *See* Knollys, Letitia (d. 1666)
Vachell, Lucy, m. (1755) Rev. Richard Long:
ancestry of, **35**. 610n
'Vachette.' *See* 'Rosette'
Vacquières. *See* Du Roy de Vacquières
Vadbeaure, Mr:
HW mistaken for, **7**. 266
Vadé, Jean-Joseph (1719–57), dramatist:
Trompeur trompé, Le, by, **7**. 319
Vado (Italy):
Ambrose to bring squadron from, to Leghorn,
19. 2n
English ships at, **19**. 10
Mathews at, **18**. 438
Medley takes house at, **19**. 432
Osborn, Commodore, visits, on the *Essex*,
19. 10n
Vado Bay:
English fleet to be open to, **20**. 588
France said to have demanded, of Genoa, **20**.
277
Townshend, Capt., lands at, **19**. 292n
Vado Hospital:
rum used in embalming at, **19**. 434n
Vail; vails:
prime ministers entitled to, **43**. 119
servants at best houses receive, of 10 *s.* to a
guinea, or two, **20**. 89n
See also Tip; tips
Vaillant, Paul (ca 1715–1802), bookseller;
sheriff:
Ferrers converses with, before execution, **9**.
283
HW patronizes, **21**. 400
HW's correspondence with, **21**. 400
sheriff at Ferrers's execution, **21**. 400–2

[Vaillant, Paul, *continued*]
Sheriff's Account of Earl Ferrers's Behaviour by, 21. 400–2
Strand shop of, thronged with curiosity-seekers, 21. 400
SH visited by, 12. 237, 241
Twickenham resident, 42. 486
Vainqueur, Le, French ship:
Gwynn, Richard, captures, 21. 123n
Vairasse, Denis (fl. 1665–81):
Histoire des Severambes, L', by, 21. 552n
Val, Le. *See* Le Val
Valance; valances:
on hats, fashionable in 1791, 11. 273
Valantano, Madonna di. *See* Madonna
Valbelle, Marquise de. *See* Bouthillier, Gabrielle-Pauline
Valbelle, Marguerite-Delphine de, m. (1723) André-Geoffrey de Valbelle, Marquis de Rians:
(?) social relations of, with Duchesse de Praslin, 7. 349
Valbelle-Oraison, Joseph-Alphonse-Omer de (1729–78), Marquis de Tourves:
death of, 7. 87
Du Deffand, Mme, gives opinion of, 7. 87
Valck, Gerard (1652–1726):
engravings by: after Van der Werff's James IV, 42. 12n; of Margaret, Q. of Scotland, 15. 123n
Valdagno (Italy):
Mann, Horace II, and Lady Lucy visit, 24. 114–15, 118, 122–3
Schio near, 24. 122
waters of, agree with Lady Lucy Mann, 24. 122
Valdagou, MM. de, surgeons. *See* Dumont de Valdagou
Val-de-Grâce, church in Paris:
convent of, may be destroyed by French reformation, 10. 167
HW visits, 7. 265
Hamilton, Lady Archibald, might be buried at, 35. 68
Marie-Antoinette said to be confined at, 11. 300
worth a glance, 39. 202
Valence, Comtesse de. *See* Brulart de Genlis, Edmée-Nicole-Pulchérie
Valence, Aymer de (ca 1270–1324), called E. of Pembroke, 1307:
tomb of, in Westminster Abbey, may be moved, 38. 110, 40. 201
Valence. *See also* Valencia; Valenza
Valencia (Spain):
Maella from, 16. 170
Valencia de Alcántara (Spain):
English troops capture, 22. 78
Valenciennes (France):
Boufflers, Mme de, visits, 11. 76n
difficult for Allies to capture, 12. 67
lace from, *see under* Lace

Louis XV and Noailles at, 18. 441
surrender of, 12. 34n, 34. 182, 185, 186
Valentano, Madonna di. *See* Madonna
Valentano, 'Prophetesses' of. *See* Poli, Anna Teresa; Renzi, Bernardina
Valenti, ——, dancer:
England visited by, 19. 455
Narni dances with, 19. 455
Valenti, Silvio (1690–1756), called Valenti Gonzaga; cardinal, 1738; papal secretary of state 1740–56:
Albani induces, to release statues for Leicester, 20. 104n
Benedict XIV assembles cardinals in apartment of, 18. 444
—— consults, about Young Pretender, 20. 22
—— governed by, under Acquaviva's tuition, 19. 114, 158, 330
—— indemnifies, for loss of abbeys, 18. 55
—— said to be betrayed by, to France, Spain, and Austria, 19. 492
——'s secretary of state, 18. 55, 19. 144
Colonna may become *camerlingo* after death of, 20. 589
Conclave entered by, 37. 57
death of, expected, 20. 463
Mann translates English addresses for benefit of, 19. 144
Maria Theresa's general seizes abbeys of, 18. 55
—— will blame, for Pontano's arrest, 18. 56
paralyzed, 20. 463
St-Odile asks, about Benedict XIV's claim to Monte Santa Maria, 20. 428
Spanish sympathies of, 19. 114
statues for Leicester impounded by, 20. 104n
Stosch receives offer from, for map collection, 21. 186, 192
translations of Cts of Pomfret's letters sent to, 18. 558
Venetians reject, for low birth, until he becomes Gonzaga, 20. 409, 23. 325
Young Pretender urged by, to settle in Bologna, 20. 44n
Valentia, Vct. *See* Annesley, Arthur (1744–1816); Annesley, George (1771–1844)
Valentia, Vcts. *See* Lyttelton, Lucy Fortescue (1743–83)
Valentini, Regina (1722–1808), m. (1747) Pietro Mingotti; opera singer:
Ailesbury, Cts of, writes to, in Italian, about opera boxes, 37. 476–7
benefit for, Cts of Ailesbury puts off party for, 38. 12
biographical information about, corrected, 43. 120, 273
Brown, Dr John, sings *Stabat Mater* with, 9. 219
capriciousness of, provokes hissing, 35. 257
Carlisle, Cts of, entertains, 9. 219
Churchill, Lady Mary, to withhold reply to, about opera box, 37. 477–8

Cumberland, D. of, favours, **20**. 557
disliked, when Giardini forces her on town, **38**. 250
good humour of, may not last, **37**. 427
HW praises, **35**. 192
hissing might not harm, **35**. 220
Madrid visited by, **20**. 557n
Ricciarelli's quarrel with, **35**. 256–7
secretary of state obtains substitute for, **35**. 257
son born to, **20**. 557n
to sing in London, **38**. 233
Vaneschi disputes with, **20**. 557
——'s operas rivalled by, under D. of Cumberland's patronage, **37**. 459n

Valentinian. See under Fletcher, John

Valentinois, Comtesse de. *See* Rouvroy de St-Simon, Marie-Christine-Chrétienne de

Valentinois, Duc de. *See* Goyon-de-Matignon de Grimaldi, Honoré-Aimé-Charles-Maurice

Valentinois, Duchesse de. *See* Aumont de Mazarin, Louise-Félicité-Victoire d' (1759–1826); Poitiers, Diane de (1499–1566)

Valenza (Italy):
Charles Emmanuel III to besiege, **19**. 237
Sardinians capture, **19**. 253, 258
Spaniards threaten, **19**. 120, 137

'Valere,' character in Italian comedy:
Lincoln, E. of, resembles, **18**. 103

Valerian (Publius Licinius Valerianus) (d. 269), Roman emperor:
(?) reign of, **16**. 210n

Vale-Royal Abbey, Cheshire:
Cole at, **1**. 251

Vale-Royall of England. See under King, Daniel

Valet; Valet-de-chambre. *See under* Servant

Valetort. *See* Valletort

Valet-secretary, Mann's, *see* Palombo, Domenico

Valetta, Malta:
plan of, **1**. 257

Valette, La. *See* Lavalette

Valiant, English ship:
Dutch contraband seized by, **25**. 3n
La Belle Poule approached by, **24**. 395n

Valière. *See* La Vallière

Valk, Gerard. *See* Valck, Gerard

Valk, Dutch ship:
Feilding captures, **25**. 3n

Vallabriga y Rozas, María Teresa de (b. 1758), m. (1776) Luis Antonio de Borbón, Infant of Spain:
Charles III regulates marriage of, **36**. 308

Valladolid, University of:
Mercado, professor of medicine at, **14**. 126–7

Vallancey, Charles (1721–1812), soldier; antiquary:
Collectanea de rebus Hibernicis by, includes Pownall's letter, **29**. 130–1
Montagu gives HW's *Anecdotes of Painting* to, **10**. 66n

Vallancy. *See* Vallancey

Valle, Andrea. *See* Valle, Filippo

Valle (*or* Della Valle), Filippo (1697–1770), sculptor:
birth date of, corrected, **43**. 171
HW dissatisfied with 'Livia' statue executed by, **18**. 292, 303
'Livia' or 'Pudicitia' statue by: made for Lady Walpole's cenotaph in Westminster Abbey, **13**. 26, **17**. 212n; payment for, **26**. 5; to be done, **17**. *317*; to be varnished, **18**. 116
Mann's communications with, about statue, **18**. 161, 175, 177, 214, **22**. 107, 114–15
——'s payment to, for statue, **18**. 175, 177, 214
model by, for statue: HW's, decays, **22**. 98; Valle may sell, **18**. 178–9
mould for statue by: HW wishes another cast from, **22**. 98; Mattei, Duke, receives, **22**. 115–16
Parker not trusted by, **18**. 152
—— to threaten, to get statue finished, **17**. 317
slowness of, enrages Mann, **18**. 127
statue not to be sent by, till paid for, **18**. 152

Vallee, La. *See* Valle

Vallesantoro, Marqués de. *See* Gregorio, Leopoldo de

Valletort, Vct. *See* Edgcumbe, Richard (1764–1839); Edgcumbe, William Richard (1794–1818)

Valletort, Vcts. *See* Hobart, Lady Sophia (1768–1806)

Valley Forge, Pennsylvania:
American losses at, **28**. 422n

Valli. *See* Valle

Vallière. *See* La Vallière

Vallombrosa ('Valombroso'), Italy:
Berrys disappointed at not seeing, **11**. 357
Hugford at, **17**. 482, **19**. 427n, **20**. 23
Mann has never visited, **20**. 329
Milton's mention of, arouses English interest, **11**. 357, **20**. 317
Paoli, Clemente, at, **23**. 130, 159
print of: HW sees, at Barrett Lennard's, **20**. 317; Mann to send, to HW, **20**. 320, 329
scagliola tables to be sent from, **20**. 23
snow imported from, for sherbets, **20**. 25

Vallory. *See* Valori

Vallotton, Charles (d. 1793), Capt.:
Conway to ask, about Henry Ibbot, **42**. 41

Valltravers. *See* Valtravers

Val Montone (Italy):
Neapolitan troops at, **18**. 447

Valmy (France):
battle of, **12**. 2n, **15**. 225n

Valois dynasty:
Richelieu avenges defeats of, **35**. 277

Valombrosa; Valombroso. *See* Vallombrosa

Valory, Mlles de:
(?) La Live's social relations with, **7**. 295

Valory, Guy-Louis-Henri (1692–1774), Marquis de; French minister to Prussia:
Bestuzhev seizes letters of, **18**. 495n
Frederick II wishes, as minister, **20**. 541–2
(?) La Live's social relations with, **7**. 295

Valory, Jules (*or* Louis)-Hippolyte (1696–1785), Chevalier de:
(?) La Live's social relations with, **7**. 295

Valory. *See also* Valle
Valour:
  made a virtue by some ambitious general, **7.**
  361
'Valpolhausen, Horatius':
  HW's nom-de-plume, **9.** 222
Valtravers, (?) Johann Rudolf (fl. 1747–64),
  diplomatist:
  Florence visited by, **20.** 393
  Guise's 'governor,' **20.** 393
  Orford, Cts of, recommends, to Uguccioni,
  20. 393
  Palatine legation councillor in London, representing Tuscany and Baden, **20.** 393n
  tutor to Graf von Loss, **20.** 393n
Valvasone, Contessa di. *See* Verità, Eurizia
Valvasone, Carlo Luigi di (1698–1773):
  nephew may be aided by, **17.** 161
  nephew to see, **17.** 70
Valvasone, Clemente Giuseppe di (1699–1744),
  Col.:
  death of, **18.** 439
  nephew may be aided by, **17.** 161
  nephew to see, **17.** 70
Valvasone, Ferdinando di (1702–49), and Gabriele Carlo di (1705–85):
  nephew to be aided by, **17.** 161
  nephew to see, **17.** 70
Valvasone, Maria Anna (1697–1773), m. (1716)
  Balì Baldassare Suares de la Concha:
  Amorevoli negotiates with Mann through, **17.**
  101, 112
  antiquated head-dress of, **20.** 148
  appearance of: once handsome, now horrible,
  23. 306; 'shrunk,' **35.** 29
  ball to be given by, **17.** 56
  'Bronzino' bought by, from Laurenzo and sent
  to Mann to be sold, **17.** 128–9
  brother-in-law shows 'bawdy matters' to, **18.**
  40
  brother-in-law's madness concealed by, **18.** 41
  brothers of, to help her son, **17.** 161
  Cerchi, Cavaliere, related to, **17.** 123
  Charles Albert may be sought by, **17.** 161
  Chute and Mann entertained by, at play, **17.**
  120
  Chute greeted by, in HW's box, **35.** 29
  Chute, Mann, and Whithed secured by, to
  back Tesi's opera, **18.** 280–1
  daughter's dowry worries, **17.** 137
  daughter's match expected by, **18.** 138
  daughter's match imagined by, **17.** 202
  daughter's suitor may be cloyed by, **18.** 29
  daughter wanted by, to marry Roberto Pandolfini, **17.** 137, 171, 202
  Demetrio performed at house of, **17.** 65, 100,
  104, 120
  'easy of access,' **19.** 84
  Electress's funeral procession passes house of,
  18. 173
  emerald earrings of, in pawn, **17.** 484
  family of, at Valvasone, **17.** 202

Florentines all flock to, **17.** 101
Frederick Augustus II buys pictures from,
  19. 392
HW asks about, **17.** 402
HW questions loyalty of, to Mann, **17.** 419
HW sends news about son and sister of,
  17. *39*
health of: issue of blood, **19.** 226, 238, 243;
  toothache, **18.** 324
Hobart may be enjoyed by, **19.** 63
jewels pawned by, **17.** 137, 484
ladies to be brought by, to Mann's garden,
  17. 498
Mann expects letter of thanks from, for HW,
  17. 456
—— gives news of HW to, **17.** 39
—— goes to Electress's funeral from house of,
  18. 173
—— hears from, about Salimbeni, **17.** 116, 132
—— receives mistaken news from, **19.** 75
——'s emerald earrings seized by, **17.** 484
——'s guests counted by, **18.** 1
——'s opera box sometimes occupied by, **17.**
  69, 81, **18.** 29, **19.** 311
——'s relations with, strained, **17.** 81, **18.** 242
——'s social relations with, **17.** 101, 104, 120,
  484, **18.** 1, 98, 275, 281, 353
—— visited by, with diversions, in his illness,
  17. 101
Maynard talks French with, **18.** 372
—— to be introduced to, by Mann, **18.** 367
Modenese princess gives étui and snuff-box to,
  17. 64
Modenese princess to be treated at villa of,
  with comedy, **17.** 65
Modenese princess ushered in by, **17.** 56
Orford, Cts of, said by, to have received husband's letter, **19.** 47
papers sought by, **18.** 29
parties avoided by, because her jewels are in
  pawn, **17.** 137
Pisan lady conducted by, **18.** 353
Richecourt said by, to have received letters
  from Cts of Orford, **19.** 64
ruspanti member, **17.** 273n
Salimbeni and Amorevoli brought by, to
  Mann, **17.** 101
Salimbeni's accident described by, **17.** 116, 132
Scarperia dinner in honour of Modenese princess attended by, **17.** 56
sister of, **17.** 39n, **18.** 25n, 246n, **30.** 7
son ordered by, to visit her parents at Friuli
  and wait for her there, **17.** 70
son presents 'la Cecca' to, **17.** 128
son's offer of preferment refused by advice of,
  18. 455
Tesi quarrels with, **18.** 322
——'s opera may be produced through efforts
  of, **18.** 280, 281
Verona ladies served by, **18.** 286
Villio buys pictures from, **19.** 392
Violante, Principessa, patroness of, **17.** 161n

—— subject of stories of, **19**. 311

Walpole, Horatio (1723–1809) enjoys, **19**. 84

Worsley cicisbeo to, **21**. 460

Valvasone, Maria Cristina di (1705–47), m. (1721) Marchese Orazio Francesco Pucci:

(?) Chute and Whithed to be polite to, **17**. 42

family of, **18**. 25n

Florence visited by, **30**. 7

Giovanardi accompanies, **17**. (?) 42, **18**. 273

—— advises, **17**. 46

—— aids, and is aided by, **18**. 54

—— may give refuge to, at Bologna, **17**. 158, 171

—— visited by, near Modena, **18**. 54

HW asks if Ds of Modena is to take, to France, **18**. 246

HW commends Mann's advice to, **17**. 171

HW describes, **30**. 8

HW inquires about fate of, after fall of Modena, **18**. 31

HW mentions, **17**. 42

HW not in love with, **30**. 8, 12

HW politely treated by, **17**. *39*

HW's correspondence with, **18**. 25, 31, 54, 68

HW sends silks to, **17**. 159, 222, 416, **18**. 112

HW to receive compliments of, **17**. 158

Lincoln acquits HW of love for, **30**. 12

Mann's correspondence with, **17**. 158, 416

—— sends compliments to, **17**. 42

Modena, Ds of, not accompanied by, **18**. 273

Modena visited by, **18**. 112

Modena Duchess's Bedchamber woman, **18**. 25n, 246n

Modenese Duke and Duchess quarrel with, **17**. 158

namesake of, **18**. 212

raffle of china won by, **17**. 159

Rangoni rejected by, as cicisbeo, **17**. 46

success of, at Reggio, **17**. 46

Valvasone, Massimiliano di (b. 1708):

nephew may be aided by, **17**. 161

nephew to see, **17**. 70

Valvasone, Nicolò Cesare (1666–1745), Conte di:

daughters of, **18**. 25n

grandson to have visited, at Friuli, **17**. 70

Valvasone, Valenzio di (1703– between 1746 and 1760):

nephew may be aided by, **17**. 161

nephew to see, **17**. 70

Valvasone, near Friuli, Italy:

Suares family visits, **17**. 202

Valvasone family:

estates of, **17**. 156n

Valverde, Duca di. *See* Gravina, ——; Reggio e Branciforte, Don Luigi

Vampire; vampires:

George II believed in, **33**. 508

Van, Charles (d. 1778), M.P.:

Wilkes's expulsion from Parliament to be moved by, **39**. 225

Van, Glamorgan, Wales:

Lewis of, **13**. 176n

Van Belcamp, John (d. 1653), painter:

Knole paintings perhaps copies by, **35**. 132–3

Van Berckel; Van Berghen. *See* Berckel

Vanbrugh, Charles (d. 1745), Ensign:

mortally wounded at Fontenoy, **19**. 43, **36**. 12

Vanbrugh, Giles Richard (d. 1746), naval Capt.:

Antelope commanded by, **19**. 232n

drowned, **19**. 378–9

Goldsworthy's brother-in-law, **19**. 379

letter delivered by, to Rivarola, **19**. 276n

storm drives, from Corsican coast, **19**. 215n

Vanbrugh, Sir John (1664–1726), Kt, 1714; dramatist; architect:

Blenheim designed by, **9**. 289

—— predicted by, to become 'glorious ruins,' **40**. 350

Bubb Dodington's house at Eastbury built by, **40**. 9

Castle Howard's façade by, clashes with Robinson's, **30**. 257

——'s workmanship by, without ponderosity, and shows taste in extent and cupolas, **30**. 257

Cholmondeley Castle altered by, **10**. 96n

Clermont built by, **9**. 71n

Compton House perhaps designed by, **10**. 286n

'excellent,' **33**. 492

Francavilla statues wanted by, for Blenheim, **21**. 480n

genteel comedy of, **33**. 563

HW praises plays of, **41**. 374

HW ridicules architecture of, **24**. 93

Nivernais and Drumgold translate scenes by, **7**. 281

Opera House built by, **11**. 14n, **28**. 362n

Provok'd Husband, The, by Cibber and: **2**. 250; acted at Cassiobury Park, **32**. 180n; acted by amateurs, **32**. 342; approached by *School for Scandal*, **41**. 363; came out when HW was at Eton, and never since surpassed, **35**. 350; Cibber's preface to, **23**. 132n; Garrick as 'Lord Townley' in, **33**. 87, **38**. 525; HW quotes Townley's remark in, **23**. 210, **25**. 476; HW's liking for, **33**. 514

Provok'd Wife, The, by: **7**. 281; 'Brute, Sir John' in, **43**. 240; Christian VII attends performance of, **23**. 57; Cibber acts in, **17**. 222n; Garrick as 'Sir John Brute' in, **33**. 88, **38**. 525; Quin in, **19**. 342n, **38**. 525; quotation from, **18**. 292n

Relapse, The, by, **14**. 145, **42**. 158n

Stowe visit brings memories of, to HW, **10**. 314

Stratford unfamiliar with, **29**. 234

Vanbrugh, Philip (1682–1753), naval Capt.; naval commissioner:

daughter to live with, at Plymouth, **18**. 158

Vanbrugh, Philippia (ca 1716–77), m. (1734) Burrington Goldsworthy, consul at Leghorn 1736–54 and at Cadiz 1754–62:

absurdities of, **17**. 351

[Vanbrugh, Philippia, *continued*]
Albizzi, 'the little,' calls on, **17.** 316
Barrett Lennard, Mrs, will be tired by, **20.** 93
children misinformed by, **17.** 351
Chute irritated by, **17.** 372
—— 's joke about, **17.** 351, 373, **20.** 93, 298
concert to be attended by, **17.** 316
Craon calls on, **17.** 314
Craon, Princesse de, exchanges calls with, **17.** 316
Del Benino, Contessa, calls on, **17.** 316
'droppings of nonsense' by, **35.** 25
England may be visited by, with her children, **17.** 262
—— to be visited by, **18.** 13, 31
father to be visited by, at Plymouth, **18.** 158
Galli, Contessa, helps, **17.** 351
Grifoni, Mme, calls on, **17.** 316
HW commends Mann's kindness to, **17.** 334
HW disliked by, **17.** 146
HW meets, at Ds of Richmond's, **18.** 158, 188
HW misses, at Bedford House, **22.** 17
HW's apartment at Mann's house occupied by, **17.** 314
HW thinks English journey of, useless, **18.** 31
Horton escorts, to Villefranche, **18.** 13n
husband's gout encourages, **20.** 335
Italian learnt by, at Leghorn, **21.** 353n
Leghorn house of, prepared, **17.** 381
—— situation described by, **17.** 313
maids of, misbehave, **17.** 395
malapropism of, **35.** 34
Mann calls, 'horrid fool,' 'unconnected,' and 'fiddle faddle,' **17.** 316
—— leaves, with Chute and Whithed, **17.** 313
—— longs for departure of, **17.** 316, 351, 362, 371, 381
—— pays court to, in Leghorn theatre, **17.** 260
—— 's house left by, **17.** 395, 401–2
—— 's letter from, **17.** 395, 420, **20.** 335
—— to be visited by, **20.** 93
—— to shelter, at Florence, **17.** 293, 306
—— visited by, **17.** 313, 343, 381
—— would wish for husband of, to receive a good post to deter him from Florentine promotion, **18.** 13–14
'pert little unbred thing,' **18.** 158
Pomfret, Cts of, corresponds with, **17.** 420
Port Mahon visited by, **18.** 13n
Richmond, Ds of, invites, for a visit, **18.** 158
—— 's companion, **17.** 186, 334n
Richmonds to be urged by, to intercede for her husband, **18.** 13
servants of, **17.** 306, 313
verbs disliked by, **21.** 353n
Wachtendonck cicisbeo to, **17.** 146–7, 186n
—— leaves coach and horses to, **17.** 110
—— pays, **17.** 147, 186
—— praised by, **17.** 105
—— relinquishes picture of, at priests' demand, **17.** 109
—— 's death may make, anxious to leave, **17.** 138

Wager, Sir Charles, said to be uncle of, **17.** 302n
—— will aid, **18.** 13, 31
Walpole, Bns (Cts of Orford), tells rumour to, **17.** 361
Whithed escorts, to *accademia*, **35.** 23
'young fellows' call on, **17.** 314
'Vanbrugh Castle,' Greenwich:
Goldsworthy, Mrs, lived near, when Richmonds rented it, **17.** 186n
Vanburgh. *See* Vanbrugh
Vance, Abbé de:
Lorenzi tells story about irregular baptism of, to Mann, **17.** 62
Vandal; vandals:
authors swarm like, **29.** 295
Penshurst tomb worthy of, **35.** 142
Sauromatæ sometimes stands for, **30.** 73
spawned by 'Académies de Sciences et de Belles Lettres,' **34.** 173
Tribune at Florence demolished by, **33.** 286
See also Goths and Vandals
'Vandalmania,' D. of. *See* Charles XIII of Sweden
Vandelli, Joseph:
captured at Velletri, **18.** 493
Van den Berghe, Ignatius Joseph (1752–1824), engraver:
print by: of Mrs Middleton, **16.** 324; of Richelieu, **16.** 323
Van den Hove, Frederik Hendrik (ca 1628–98), engraver:
engravings by, **16.** 65
Van de Pass, Crispin (1561–1627), engraver. *See* Pass, Crispin van de
Vandeput, George (d. 1800), naval Capt.:
Carysfort commanded by, **23.** 108n
Vandeput, Sir George (ca 1717–84), 2d Bt:
Crowle counsel for, **20.** 224
HW calls, Egmont's puppet, **20.** 224n
HW suggests, as godfather to P. Frederick, **9.** 104
High Bailiff grants scrutiny in Westminster election, as demanded by, **20.** 108n
petition of, presented by Egmont, **20.** 224
petition withdrawn by, for Westminster election, **20.** 223n
Trentham accused by, of Jacobitism, **20.** 107n
—— opposed by, in Westminster election, **20.** 107n
Wales, Frederick, P. of, supports, **20.** 223n
Vanderbanck (*or* Vandrebanc), Peter (1649–97), engraver:
prints by: of Bn Dartmouth, **1.** 181, 182n; of Tenison, **1.** 171; of Waller, **16.** 67
Vanderbank, John:
print attributed to, **41.** 452n
Vanderbergh, S., bookseller in Exeter Change, the Strand, London:
Éon's *Lettres* published by, **22.** 216n
Van der Does, Johan (1545–1604), poet:
Glover extols, **13.** 197

Van der Doort ('Dort'), Abraham (d. 1640):
*Catalogue and Description of King Charles
the First's Capital Collection* by, **1**. 173, **16**.
142n, **43**. 54, 226; sent by HW to George III,
40. 187-9
head by, at Houghton, **43**. 54
name of, corrected, **43**. 219
portrait of, **1**. 171

Van der Goes, Hugo (d. 1482), painter:
double portrait of James II and wife attributed to, **16**. 322

Van der Gucht, Benjamin (d. 1794), painter
and picture-dealer:
HW recommends picture in collection of, **15**.
321
Hamilton sells alleged Correggio to, **32**. 70n
Ossory's alleged Titian cleaned by, **33**. 538n

Van der Gucht, Gerard (1696-1776), engraver:
prints by: of Fortescue, **35**. 628n; of Sir Lionel
Jenkins, **1**. 72

Van der Gucht, John (1697-1776), engraver:
Hogarth's frontispieces to Molière engraved
by, **16**. 173n
Law's portrait engraved by, **42**. 387n

Van der Gucht, Michiel (1660-1725), engraver:
(?) Addison's portrait by, after Kneller, left
by Cts Harcourt with HW who will return
it, **35**. 515-16
Hollar's print of Richmond Palace copied
by, for *Surrey*, **16**. 78

Van der Leeuw, Jan (b. ca 1680), engraver:
engraving by, of Cowley, **16**. 67

Vandermeer. *See* Montvandermeer

Vandermeulens. *See* Meulen, Adam Frans van
der

Van der Myn (Van der Mijn; 'Vandermine'),
Herman (1684-1741), Dutch painter:
portrait by, of D. and Ds of Chandos, **30**. 61

Van der Straaten, Hendrik (ca 1665-1722),
landscape painter:
HW ignorant of, **40**. 310

Van der Werff, Adriaen (1659-1722), painter:
Abishag painted by, **43**. 124
James IV's portrait by, **42**. 12n
Margaret (Tudor) 's portrait by, **15**. 123n
Page, friend of, **33**. 137n
paintings by: at Page's, spoiled by sun, **33**.
137; Louvre, the, purchases, **33**. 137n

Van de Velde, Adrian (1639-72), Dutch painter:
paintings by: at Julienne's, **7**. 287; Furnese
owns, **21**. 172n

Van de Velde, Willem (1633-1707), the younger;
marine painter:
seapieces by, at Hinchingbrooke, **40**. 283

Vandières, Marquis de. *See* Poisson, Abel-Fran-
çois

Van Dorth. *See* Dorth

Vandrebanc. *See* Vanderbanck

Van Dyck, Sir Anthony (1599-1641), Kt;
painter:
Abercorn, E. of, dresses in style of, to sit for
portrait, **9**. 207
Anne of Denmark's grant to, **16**. 35

Arundel family group by, at Antwerp, **41**.
168, **42**. 420n
cat in style of, **17**. 495
Cipriani's paintings to replace those of, at
Houghton, **25**. 316
'Clinton's' portrait attributed to, **25**. 151, 227,
240, 292, 298, 304, 501, 504
costumes of, imitated at masquerades, **17**.
339, **23**. 193
Dorset's portrait by, **33**. 223n
Elector Palatine's paintings by, **39**. 537
Exeter's portrait in style of, at Burghley
House, **10**. 345
galleys to have been fate of, **7**. 371
Gloucester Cathedral tombs attributed to, **35**.
153
HW attributes painting of Prometheus to, at
Kimbolton, **10**. 78
HW compares Reynolds to, unfavourably,
29. 284-5
HW signs himself as, **30**. 335
HW will not list further works of, **15**. 95
Hogarth emulates, **9**. 365
Hudson inferior to, **39**. 32
Jamesone's paintings resemble those of, **40**.
263-4
—— studies with, at Antwerp under Rubens,
40. 263
Jode engraves after, **1**. 23n
Jonson van Ceulen said to have lost popu-
larity on arrival of, **16**. 149-50
Julienne has paintings by, **7**. 286, 287
Leman, Mrs, medallion of, copied from paint-
ing by, **7**. 325
—— painted by, **7**. 287
Lens's copies of, **2**. 222n
Lombart's prints after, **35**. 174n
Long family said to have original sketch by,
of Count Arenberg's portrait, **35**. 594
lost painting by, **9**. 114n
Lucan, Bns, copies, **41**. 418n
Macaronies to revive costume of, **35**. 419
Madonna allegedly by, owned by Pierson,
35. 428
Madonna and Child by, for sale, **32**. 289
Malone sends note about, to HW for *Anecdotes*, **41**. 465
Mariette finds anecdote about, **7**. 371
miniatures after, **2**. 43n
musician's portrait by, **43**. 167
Oliver's miniature after, of Digby family, **28**.
180
Orford, Cts of, owned alleged portrait by,
25. 151n
Orford, 3d E. of, complained of having too
many pictures by, **25**. 418
painting attributed to, **15**. 205
painting at Buckden in manner of, **1**. 280, 281
painting of two of Charles I's children attributed to, for sale by Scarlett, **30**. 149
paintings by: **10**. 78n, 79n, **28**. 197n; at
Althorp, **9**. 299; at Clifton Hall, **35**. 279;
at Cornbury, **9**. 5, **40**. 12; at Ham House,

[Van Dyck, Sir Anthony, *continued*]
  10. 306; at Horton, of Mrs Smyth, 10. 335;
  at Kimbolton, 10. 78; at Penshurst, 35. 141;
  at SH of Ladies Leicester and Carlisle,
  10. 123, 21. 420n, 41. 443; at the Grange,
  9. 222–3; at Wrest, 39. 139n; of a Cæsar,
  brought by Cárdenas from England, 16.
  155; of Charles I and Henrietta Maria,
  16. 166; of Cts of Exeter, 1. 149–50; of
  Gerbier, 1. 25n; of Henrietta Maria, 1.
  180n; of Mrs Smyth, HW's copy of, 10. 335;
  purchased by K. of Poland from Francis
  III of Modena, 19. 314n; said to be in
  Scotland, 16. 51
  picture of, would make Chatterton affair
  more absurd, 42. 3
  pictures by, to be sold by auction at Brussels,
  33. 487
  portrait after, 15. 191n
  portrait in manner of, 40. 283
  portrait of Lady Digby in manner of, 1. 26,
  27
  portraits attributed to, at Knole, 35. 153
  prices of, found in office-book of the E. of
  Pembroke's lord chamberlain, 41. 465n
  prints after, 1. 182n, 183n
  quarantine refused by, 7. 371
  Rubens's novelty of loose dresses imitated by,
  16. 149
  Russel's copies of, 15. 205
  sale of pictures by, 38. 340n
  'Soldiers at Cards' by: 7. 286; bought by HW
  at E. of Oxford's sale, 17. 343
  Strafford and Mainwaring painted by, 35.
  267–8
  Walpole, Sir Robert, had pictures by, 2. 168,
  169
  —— purchased pictures by, at Winchendon
  House, 30. 371
  Walpole family's full-length portraits by, sold
  for a song, 20. 261
  West asks for list of works of, in England,
  40. 312
Van Dyke. *See* Van Dyck
Vane, Vcts. *See* Hawes, Frances (ca 1718–88)
Vane, Hon. Anne (1705–36):
  portrait of, would be unlike Anne Boleyn's,
  41. 451
Vane, Lady Anne (d. 1776), m. 1 (1746) Hon.
  Charles Hope Weir (divorced, 1757); m. 2
  Hon. George Monson:
  elopement of, 37. 232
  son of, 38. 421
Vane, Hon. Frederick (1732–1801), M.P.:
  convert to Opposition, 38. 318
  (?) Harrington, Cts of, berates, for complain-
  ing of footman's impertinence, to him,
  38. 421
  Meredith's motion seconded by, 38. 318
  Pulteney's legacy to, 22. 560
Vane, Mrs Frederick. *See* Meredith, Henrietta
Vane, Gilbert (1678–1753), 2d Bn Barnard:
  son of, 20. 39n, 30. 303n

Vane, Hon. Gilbert (d. 1772), Ensign, 1732;
  Lt-Col., 1745:
  German officers will not serve with, unless
  he fights duel with Rich, 17. 486
Vane, Sir Henry (1589–1655), Kt, 1611:
  Dalrymple's interest in, 15. 77
  print of, 1. 183
  Wentworth enrages, by taking Raby title,
  17. 333n
Vane, Sir Henry (1613–62), Kt, 1640; M.P.:
  Lely's portrait of, 42. 125–6
Vane, Hon. Henry (ca 1705–58), 3d Bn Barnard,
  1753; cr. (1754) E. of Darlington; M.P.:
  afterwards E. of Darlington, 18. 8n, 20. 39n
  Bath, E. of, gives position to, 18. 72n
  ——'s 'creature,' who had him made joint
  vice-treasurer of Ireland, 30. 303n
  ——'s 'toad-eater,' 17. 487, 20. 39
  'centurion of their spies,' 14. 56
  Cholmondeley succeeds, as vice-treasurer of
  Ireland, 18. 551
  confusion of, 20. 4
  coronet of, in gamblers' coat of arms, 9. 186
  Country Girl, The, satirizes, 18. 23
  dismissed as lord of the Treasury, 20. 517
  earldom of Darlington predicted for, 9. 150
  Edgcumbe may be succeeded by, as Irish paymaster general, 17. 487, 492
  HW mentions, 14. 56
  HW's opinion of, 20. 39
  HW's satiric epigram on, 14. 56
  HW's verses on appointment of, as joint
  paymaster, 14. 87–8
  joint paymaster, 9. 180, 20. 517, 35. 263, 37.
  424
  Labour in Vain satirizes, 18. 18–20
  monstrous tongue of, 30. 303
  New Ode, A, satirizes, 18. 51
  Pelham the guardian angel of, 35. 165
  Potter succeeds, as joint paymaster, 21. 25
  predicted, jokingly, as future prime minister,
  9. 210
  salaries and fees collected by, 18. 19n, 20n
  Selwyn's witticism on Newcastle's getting paymaster's place for, 35. 263
  ——'s witticism turned into an epigram on,
  perhaps by HW, 30. 125
  Stone comforts, with hint about Stuarts, 35.
  166
  toasts drunk by, 9. 110
  tongue of: droops, 35. 166; monstrous, 30.
  303
  Treasury appointment of, 20. 39
  Treasury duties of, interrupted by care of
  Ds of Newcastle's pig, 20. 72
  Walpole, Sir Robert, gives Lely's portrait of
  Vane to, 42. 125–6
  Williams, Sir C. H., satirizes, 18. 321
Vane, Henry (1726–92), 2d E. of Darlington:
  brother of, 38. 318
  Cleveland's bequest to, 23. 5
  Lely's portrait of Vane probably owned by,
  42. 126

Petersham, Lady Caroline, accompanied by, to theatre, 37. 433
—— coupled with name of, 20. 140
—— has affair with, 9. 104n, 43. 116, 267
—— includes, in Vauxhall party, 9. 107
—— no longer loved by, 37. 359
Pulteney's legacy to, 22. 560
Vane, Hon. Raby (1736–69), M.P.:
Pulteney's legacy to, 22. 560
Vane, William Holles (1714–89), 2d Vct Vane, 1734:
advertises for eloped wife, 37. 1n
Churchill's remark to, 17. 139
entail of Newcastle estate broken by, 17. 209–10
wife idolized by, 17. 459
wife of, 10. 228n, 14. 48n, 20. 230n
wife's divorce from, wished by Berkeley, 17. 459
wife tells, of her affair with Shirley at time of her marriage to, 20. 439n
wife to be received by, 37. 2
wife wanted back again by, 17. 209–10
Vane family:
paintings at Raby Castle owned by, 42. 126n
Vaneschi, ——, son of Francesco:
(?) arrested for alleged plot, 35. 229
HW thinks, is a child, 35. 229
Vaneschi, Mme ——:
Amorevoli used to keep, 18. 210
Holdernesse entertains, 18. 131
marriage of, 18. 210
Vaneschi, Abate Francesco (fl. 1732–56), opera manager:
arrested for alleged plot, 35. 229, 230
Bonducci reports English success, operas, cheating of Lord Middlesex, change of religion, and marriage by, 18. 198
—— wishes to succeed, 18. 198
Calais visited by, 17. 141
Cumberland, D. of, disputes with, over opera house, 20. 557
death of, reported, 18. 198, 210
excessive charges by, 17. 191, 216
German policy of, will revive opera, 38. 2
HW travels with, 17. 141
Hardwicke intimate with, 35. 229
Holdernesse entertains, 18. 131
London opera to discard, 17. 358
low Englishwoman married by, 18. 210
lyrics for Alexander in Persia adapted by, 17. 184n
Middlesex and Raymond cheated by, at Lucca, 17. 216
Mingotti and Ricciarelli dispute with, 20. 557
Mingotti sets up rival opera against, 37. 459
opera by, parodied by Crudeli, 17. 200
opera directors dominated by, 17. 191
opera managed by, 9. 157n
tailor brought by, from Italy, 17. 191
yacht visited by, 17. 141
'Vanessa.' See Vanhomrigh, Esther

Van Eyck, Huybrecht or Hubert (ca 1366–1426), painter:
(?) collaborator in discovery of oil painting, 29. 5n
Van Eyck, Jan (ca 1390–1441), painter:
HW suspects, did not discover oil colours, 29. 5
manuscripts prove, did not discover oil painting, 15. 145
oil painting perhaps invented by, 16. 106, 42. 65–6
Van Gameren, Mary:
daughter of a 'procurer' of Utrecht, 1. 78n
Van Goyen, Jan Josephsz (1596–1656); painter:
Chesterfield buys landscape by, 32. 103n
Vanguard, English ship:
Point Lévis reached by, 21. 419n
Van Heck, Daniel (fl. 1697–1750), postal director at Leyden:
dates of, corrected, 43. 259
delays caused by, sending letters through, 19. 145–6, 257
Van Helmont. See Helmont
Van Hoe. See Van den Hove
Van Hoey, Abraham (1684–1766), Dutch ambassador to France:
clemency for Young Pretender urged by, 19. 264n
Dutch minister at Paris, 19. 264n
Dutch troops at Fontenoy said by, to do nothing, 36. 13n
England antagonized by letter of, favouring Jacobites, 9. 31, 19. 116n
Holland asked by, if he should celebrate French victories in Flanders, 19. 91
Kilmarnock spurns intercessions of, 19. 285
letters of: HW asks about, 18. 337; printed in English press, 19. 271
Paris visited by, 19. 264
Vanhomrigh, Esther (1690–1723), 'Vanessa':
Swift's correspondence and relations with, interpreted by HW, 10. 218–19
Van Honthorst. See Honthorst
Van Hove, Frederick Hendrick (1628–98), engraver:
prints by: of Bns Vere, 1. 183; of Lady Armine, 1. 181
Van Huysum, Jacob, painter:
Walpole, Sir Robert, employed, at Chelsea, 36. 238n
Van Huysum, Jan (1682–1749) or Justus (1659–1716), painters:
Beauclerk, Lady Diana, surpasses 'finical' work of, 36. 238
brother of, 36. 238n
Julienne has paintings by, 7. 287
Vanities:
HW receives, because he never seeks them, 25. 68
Vanity:
aggravates every fault, 33. 18
Du Deffand, Mme, on, 5. 187
HW abhors, in authors, 33. 537

[Vanity, *continued*]
HW ashamed of wearing livery of, **33.** 2
HW frightened of, **32.** 23
HW has no more, than hypocrisy, **33.** 1, 18
HW's: **33.** 584, **34.** 100; compared to Charles Townshend's, **32.** 12
HW's reflections on, **31.** 254, **32.** 203, 220, **33.** 38, 53
HW's reflections on difficulty of avoiding, **16.** 275
Leopold II's, **33.** 286
Mann considers, essential to Court life, **22.** 407
——'s reflections on, **20.** 150
'thin crust of pride,' **35.** 561
Van Keppel. *See* Keppel
Van Lennep, Cornelia Jacoba (d. 1839), m. (1785) Hon. William Waldegrave, cr. (1800) Bn Radstock:
HW asks about, **36.** 273
Van Lewen. *See* Lewen
Van Linge, Bernhard (fl. 1622–32), Dutch glass-painter:
window by, at Wroxton, **35.** 73
Vanloo, Carlo (1705–65), painter:
dying Magdalen painted by, **7.** 280
paintings by: at Augustins' in Paris, **7.** 282; over doors in French houses, **31.** 88
Van Loo, Jean-Baptiste (1684–1745), painter:
death date of, corrected, **43.** 66
Eccardt, pupil of, **30.** 324n
mezzotint of 1st E. Gower after, **10.** 224n
Montagu, Lady Mary Wortley, writes lines on Churchill's portrait by, **14.** 246
portraits by, of: Hertford, Cts of, **37.** 385n; Montagu, George, **9.** 35n; Townshend, Vcts, **17.** 174; Walpole, Sir Robert, **2.** 57, **42.** 249
Van Miereveld. *See* Miereveld
Vanneck, Elizabeth (d. 1760), m. (1750) Hon. Thomas Walpole:
death of, from fever and sore throat, **21.** 416
marriage of, **12.** 150n
Vanneck, Gerard (d. 1750), merchant:
legacies of, to Schutzes, **9.** 112
Vanneck, Sir Gerard William (?1743–91), 2d Bt, 1777; merchant; M.P.:
alleged daughter of, **21.** 416n
house of, depreciates in value, **28.** 405–6
Vanneck, Gertrude (d. 1798), Privy Purse to Ps of Wales:
Brighton visited by, **12.** 150
'Lady Loverule' compared with, **12.** 150
Vanneck, Sir Joshua (d. 1777), cr. (1751) Bt:
daughter of, **9.** 105n, **12.** 150n, **21.** 416n
house of, on Thames, **28.** 405–6
Walpole, Hon. Thomas, and, have tobacco contract with French *fermiers-généraux,* **38.** 545–6
Vanneck, Margaret (d. 1818), m. (1758) Hon. Richard Walpole:
husband of, **14.** 57n
marriage of, **12.** 150n

Vanneck family:
Ailesbury, Cts of, may invite HW's relatives of, **38.** 100
HW not to marry into, **9.** 105
Vannes (France):
Aiguillon to leave, in Hawke's absence, **21.** 337n
Conflans sails to, to embark Aiguillon's troops for Scotland, **21.** 350n
Duff blockades, **21.** 336n, 350n
Sombreuil shot at, **12.** 152n
Vanneschi. *See* Vaneschi
Vanni, Gobbo:
Babi paid by, for Florentine appearance, **18.** 526
impresario at Cocomero theatre, **18.** 527n
impresario of *La semplice spiritosa,* **19.** 356n
Vannini, Attilia *and* Giovanni, inn of, at Florence:
Elector Palatine receives Leopold's visit at, **24.** 164
(?) Young Pretender stays at, **23.** 225
Vannini, Signora Maria, Florentine inn-keeper:
inn of: Elector Palatine stays at, **24.** 164n; Gloucester, D. of, stays at, **23.** 333n, 355n; Saxony, Electress of, stays at, **24.** 164n
Van Nost, John (d. 1780):
statue by, **9.** 391n
Van Oost, Jacob (1601–71):
portrait by, **1.** 182n
Van Rensselaer, Col. John:
Holland, Bn, and E. of Ilchester contest New York land grants by, **38.** 422n
Van Rijn, Rembrandt. *See* Rembrandt van Rijn
Van Riske. *See* Van Risquet
Van Risquet, ——; painter:
painting by, at Horton, **10.** 334–5
Van Riswick, Deric (fl. 1650–3), engraver:
(?) engraving by, **16.** 166
Van Robeis, ——:
woolen factory of, at Abbeville, **37.** 41
Vansittart, Miss, Ps of Wales's attendant:
Bute said to use sedan chair of, in visiting Ps of Wales, **38.** 462n
Vansittart, Henry (1732–?70), gov. of Bengal:
Bengal Council rebels against, **38.** 310
ship of, lost, **23.** 282
Van Somer, Paul (1576–1621), painter:
Northampton's portrait probably by, **16.** 92
portraits by: (?) of Henry Frederick, P. of Wales, **10.** 102; of Lord Falkland, **1.** 88; **42.** 106n
Van Stratten. *See* Van der Straaten
Van Trump. *See* Tromp
Van Veen. *See* Veen
Vanvitelli, Luigi (1700–73), architect:
Aquedotto Carolino designed by, **21.** 379n
Dichiarazione dei disegni del reale palazzo di Caserta by: awaits shipment at Leghorn, **21.** 318; HW acquires duplicate of, **21.** 363n; HW receives, **21.** 363; HW thanks Mann for, **21.** 327; Hamilton might be jealous of Mann over, **22.** 547; Mann gets,

and hopes to get further ones, 22. 547; Mann sends bill of lading for, to HW, 21. 324, 22. 545, 547, 555, 559, 561, 562; Mann trying to get, for HW, 21. 272

Doria's palazzo converted by, 23. 109n

Van Voerst, Robert (1596–1636), engraver:
Aurelius's portrait engraved by, 16. 64
print by, of Charles I and Henrietta Maria, 16. 166

Vapeur:
charade on, 33. 508

Vapours (physical or mental ailments):
occurrences of, 3. 185, 256, 297, 363, 372, 4. 13, 332, 415, 5. 12, 35, 76, 81, 236, 6. 101, 246, 247, 262, 264, 295, 300, 360, 425, 463, 7. 73, 78, 122, 130, 154, 182, 191, 206, 35. 585

Var, *or* Varo, Italian river:
Austrian crossing of: accomplished, 19. 336; Genoese should have been disarmed before, 19. 345; in retreat, 19. 363; Maillebois will make Austrians regret, 19. 334; Mann awaits news of, 19. 330
Charles Emmanuel III said to have defeated the Spaniards near, 18. 466
—— urges Austrians to drive French across, 19. 436
English ships at mouth of, 19. 336
French crossing of: Austrians would be embarrassed by, 19. 367; Boufflers predicts, 19. 406; in retreat, burning bridges, 19. 323; may not be possible, 19. 405–6; to intercept Austrian expedition for Genoa, 19. 374, 376; under Belle-Isle, 19. 363, 409; would encourage Neapolitan advances, 19. 378
Spanish cavalry to repass, 19. 51

Varagne-Gardouch, François de (1725–1807), Marquis de Bélesta:
Examen de la nouvelle histoire de Henri IV de M. de Bury by, 4. 94–5, 158–9, 163, 171
Voltaire sends letter of, to Mme du Deffand, 4. 182

Varchi, Benedetto:
Topaja, Villa della, bestowed on, 17. 443n

Varcy. *See* Vesey

Vardes, Marquis de. *See* Du Bec-Crespin, François-René

Vardie, de la. *See* Del'Averdi

Varelst. *See* Verelst

Varenne, Rue de, in Paris:
Broglie, Hôtel de, in, 38. 340
Monaco, Hôtel de, in 4. 438n

Varennes, Marquis de:
Choiseul, Duchesse de, invests money with, 8. 36–7
See also Pelée de Varennes

Varennes (France):
French royal family's flight to, 11. 96n, 298n, 12. 61n, 31. 402n, 34. 112–13

Varese (Italy):
revenues of, 22. 331
Simonetti, Contessa, becomes princess of, 22. 331

Varey, Rev. William (ca 1712–94):
(?) Hertfords visited by, at Ragley, 38. 70

'Varice.' *See* Bulkeley, Charlotte

Varicour. *See* Rouph de Varicour

Variétés littéraires. See under Arnaud, François; Suard, Jean-Baptiste-Antoine

Variety, a Tale for Married People. See under Whitehead, William

Varillas, Antoine:
Histoire de François Ier by, 30. 55n

Varnish:
French spoil paintings with, 35. 425, 429
Jamesone uses, in painting, 40. 264
pictures covered with: 35. 344, 39. 202; at Elizabeth Chudleigh's, 9. 277
tempera, covered by, resembles oil painting, 42. 65

Varnon. *See* Vernon

Varo, Italian river. *See* Var

Varranes:
'fire' of, 43. 75

Varro (M. Terentius Varro Reatinus) (116–28 B.C.), Roman writer:
Spence relies on, as authority, 14. 19n

Varvel (for hawk):
(?) HW finds, in mother's patch-box, 43. 64

Vasari, Giorgio (1511–74), biographer; architect; painter:
Cavallini's alleged work at St Paul's mentioned by, 42. 67
HW imitates, 35. 207
invention of oil painting attributed by, to Van Eyck, 29. 6
portrait by, of Bianca Cappello: 14. 67n; HW installs, in Arlington St house, 20. 407; HW thanks Mann for, 20. 403; HW to frame, with Latin inscription and grand ducal coronet, 20. 407; HW used to admire, at Casa Vitelli, 20. 398, 402–3, 404; Mann hangs, in his bedchamber, 20. 398; Mann sends, to HW, 20. 398, 402–3, 404, 407, 414, 26. 56
Uffizi, the, built by, 13. 199n, 25. 169n
Vite de' più eccellenti pittori, scultori e architetti by, includes story of Antonio da Carpi, 16. 96–7

Vase; vases:
alabaster, from Volterra; Conway's, procured by Mann, 20. 321, 329; Dashwood's, procured by Mann through HW at Dashwood's request: 17. 249, 287, 351, 369, 18. 214; export permit for, 17. 24n; Fox's, for Holland House, procured by Mann, 20. 569, 582, 21. 49, 97, 118, 123, 132, 134, 139, 148, 155, 178, 187, 189, 212, 218; HW's, for Wolterton, procured by Mann, 18. 47; Hyde's, arrive, 22. 13; Hyde's, ready and awaiting shipment from Italy, 21. 524; Lyttelton's, procured by Mann, 20. 539, 547, 554, 557, 582; Mann gets, weekly, 17. 394–5; Westminster Hall decorated with, used as lamps, 37. 454n
alabaster, owned by Nivernais, 7. 341

[Vase; vases, *continued*]

alabaster pieces seldom big enough for four-foot vases, **20.** 582

antique: bought by HW, **26.** 4; HW loves form of, **35.** 443

at Elizabeth Chudleigh's, **9.** 277

at Park Place, **39.** 550

at SH, broken by visitors, **33.** 522

bronze: HW buys, at Mead's sale, **20.** 470n; HW buys, at E. of Oxford's sale, **17.** 374

Cardigans', **38.** 357

crystal: at Burghley House, **10.** 91, 345; at Kedleston, **10.** 230; *see also* Rock crystal

Etruscan: alleged discovery of, in Tuscany, **21.** 561, **22.** 6; at Osterley, **34.** 238; blackness of, **33.** 410; brought to England by Hamilton, **32.** 70; Fullarton gives, to Mme du Deffand, **7.** 81; Hamilton compiles book about, **26.** 46; Hamilton's collection of, purchased for British Museum by Parliament, **26.** 46; reproduced in Staffordshire, **23.** 211

Etruscan or Greek, inexpressive, **35.** 445

Ferdinand of Naples might have, of lava, in Portici garden, **35.** 433

Frascati, in Mrs Miller's *Poetical Amusements*, **32.** 222

from Ginori's factory in Tuscany: HW receives, from Mann, **25.** 635, **26.** 56; Mann orders, for HW, **25.** 598; take 4 months to make, **25.** 645

gilt, at Burghley House, **10.** 346

Gray's poem celebrates, **33.** 522

HW buys, at Rome, **26.** 7

HW's, at SH: broken by visitors, **33.** 522; for goldfish, **39.** 404

HW's gift of, to Mme du Deffand: 4. 307, 334, 336, 343, 404, 428, 430; Choiseul, Duchesse de, to inherit, **4.** 428; covers for, **4.** 307, 334, 336, 343, 404, 408, 422, 423, 428

HW to buy at Mead's sale, **20.** 470

Hamilton's, in Ds of Portland's collection, **36.** 237

——'s books on, *see under* Hamilton, Sir William

—— to bring, **35.** 415

La Borde's, **31.** 80

of citrons, **17.** 322

of flowers, for nosegays, **35.** 301

of petrified water, **10.** 12

of rock crystal, *see under* Rock crystal

on eagle's pedestal, **19.** 122

on Stosch's sculptured gems, **21.** 189, 201

Portland: bought by D. of Portland, **39.** 442; criticized by HW, **35.** 444; Darwin's *Botanic Garden* mentions, **42.** 267; history of, **33.** 485n; owned by Ds of Portland, **33.** 485–6, 489–90

prize cups at races might develop into, **16.** 298

Raphael's china, price of, **10.** 345

Roman, to receive Millers' poetic contributions, **39.** 241

silver, at Knole, **35.** 132

Tuscan: **37.** 379; HW's, **29.** 360; *see also* Etruscan

Wedgwood, **36.** 168, 169

white: HW's, **7.** 402; Mme du Deffand's, **7.** 402

Vasil'chikov, Alexander Semenovich: Catherine II's new favourite, **23.** 441, 444

Vaslet, Louis: Mason's portrait by, **28.** 39n, **29.** 290n, **43.** 57

Vassal, Elizabeth, m. Hon. Gen. John Barrington: (?) Kingston, Ds of, attended by, **24.** 192

Vassal. *See also* Vassall

Vassal; vassals: allusion to, in HW's *Letter from Xo Ho*, not understood by Fox, **30.** 133; always belong to Crown or nobles, **30.** 133

Vassalage, feudal: privately-raised regiments will help to restore, **26.** 15

Vassali, Francis, stuccoist: ceilings by, at Ragley, **38.** 62–3; (?) stucco work by, at Hagley, **35.** 104n

Vassall, Elizabeth (ca 1770–1845), m. 1 (1786) Sir Godfrey Webster, 4th Bt, 1780 (divorced); m. 2 (1797) Henry Richard Fox, 3d Bn Holland, 1774: Brompton Park home of, till divorce and remarriage after son's birth, **34.** 222n; ill-used on Swiss frontier, **11.** 331

Vassall. *See also* Vassal

Vassall Fox, Henry Richard. *See* Fox, Henry Richard (1773–1840)

Vassari. *See* Vasari

Vassé, Marquise de. *See* Broglie, Louise-Auguste-Philippine-Charlotte-Françoise de

Vassé, Alexis-Bruno-Étienne (1753–1820); Marquis and Vidame de: (?) Broglie, Comte de, quarantines himself with, **7.** 443; (?) has smallpox, **7.** 443; marriage of, **7.** 223n

Vassé, Jules de (1780–ca 1800): birth of, **7.** 460

Vassinhac, Marie-Louis-Charles de (d. 1786), Vicomte d'Imécourt: Chanteloup visited by, **8.** 207; marriage of, **5.** 431n

Vassor. *See* Le Vassor

Vatas, Mme: wishes to go to London, **36.** 325

Vatel, ——, maître d'hôtel to the Great Condé: HW thinks of, when revisiting Chantilly, **31.** 46

Vatican, the: air of, pestiferous in hot months, **24.** 462; Albani, librarian of, **17.** 9n; Apamea, Abp of, prefect of library at, **17.** 48n; Austrians occupy heights near, **18.** 533; balcony of, Benedict XIV gives public benediction from, **21.** 103

Charles of Naples dines at, **18**. 533

Chartreuse of Paris must yield to, **35**. 126

Clement XIII at, during D. of York's visit to Monte Cavallo, **22**. 228

Clement XIV poisoned at, **24**. 49

—— 's body brought to, **24**. 43

HW asks whether, is hung with sackcloth, **25**. 237

HW's Gothic, 'of Greece and Rome,' **33**. 529

Mann has the library at, searched for Richard I's poem, **21**. 157, 169–70, **40**. 115

—— should threaten Florentines with thunder of, if they do not welcome Garrick, **22**. 177

—— to get copies of paintings at, **20**. 328

Ottoboni collection at, Passionei buys Stosch's MSS for, **21**. 284n

paintings at Boyle Farm copied from, **42**. 205n

Passionei, Cardinal, librarian of, **21**. 170n

Petrarch's and Bembo's notes on MS at, **21**. 169

possesso procession from, to St John Lateran, **24**. 136n

Raphael's loggias in, **23**. 298

—— 's paintings in, damaged through 'veiling', **20**. 328n

—— 's sculpture in gallery of, **28**. 472n

secret archives of, **15**. 186

Stosch's library bought by, **24**. 284

—— steals MSS from, **21**. 284n

Vauban, Marquise de. *See* Puget de Barbantane, Henriette de

Vaubecourt, Marquis de. *See* Nettancourt, Charles-Jean-François de

Vaucanson, Jacques de (1709–82), inventor; mechanic:

automatons of: Du Deffand, Mme, alludes to, **4**. 235; verses mention, **6**. 406

Vaudemont, Prince de. *See* Lorraine d'Elbeuf, Marie-Joseph de

Vaudemont, Princesse de. *See* Montmorency, Louise-Auguste-Élisabeth-Marie-Colette de

'Vaudeville'; 'vaudevilles' (ballads):

HW sends, to West, **13**. 171, 173

ladies make, against Mme du Barry, **39**. 143

Vaudois. *See* Waldensians

Vaudreuil, Comte de. *See* Rigaud, Joseph-Hyacinthe-François de Paule de (1740–1817); Rigaud, Louis-Philippe de (ca 1691–1763)

Vaudreuil, Mme de. *See* Le Clerc de Fleurigny, Louise-Thérèse

Vaudreuil, Marquis de. *See* Rigaud, Louis-Philippe de (1724–1802); Rigaud, Pierre-François de (1698–1765)

Vaudreuil, Marquise de. *See* Fleury de la Gorgendière, Louise-Thérèse; Guyot de la Mirande, Marie-Claire-Françoise; Le Moine de Sérigny, Catherine-Élisabeth

Vaudreuil, Vicomtesse de. *See* Riquet de Caraman, Pauline-Victoire de

Vaudreul. *See* Vaudreuil

Vaudrey, Jeanne-Gabrielle-Catherine de, m. Patrick Wall, called Comte Patrice de Wall: social relations of, in Paris, **7**. 297, 298

Vaugeois, ——, furniture-maker:

Du Deffand, Mme, has receipt from, **8**. 41

Vaughan, Miss, dau. of Maj. (?Daniel) Vaughan:

SH visited by, **12**. 224

Vaughan, the Misses:

SH visited by, **12**. 244

Vaughan, Mrs, of Richmond:

SH visited by, **12**. 236

Vaughan, Mrs (d. 1803) of Twickenham; widow of Maj. (?Daniel) Vaughan:

SH visited by, **12**. 224

Vaughan, Lady Anne (d. 1751), m. (1713) Charles Powlett, 3d D. of Bolton:

ugliness of, **2**. 328–9, 330

Vaughan, Catharine (fl. 1625), m. Theophilus Tuer; William Cole's great-grandmother:

George Herbert's niece, **1**. 70, 73

picture of, **1**. 87

Vaughan, George (fl. 1730–47), sedan-chair-maker:

Frederick, P. of Wales, dismisses, for voting for Trentham, **20**. 122

witticism by, on Frederick, P. of Wales's chair, **20**. 122, 144

Vaughan, Hannah (1711–68), m. (before 1733) William Pritchard; actress:

acts in *Jane Shore*, **32**. 145–6

(?) Christie auctions effects of, **32**. 124n

epilogue by HW to *Tamerlane* spoken by, **9**. 48n, **13**. 16, **19**. 333n

famous Twickenham resident, **35**. 234

Farren, Miss, inferior to, as 'Beatrice', **11**. 64

'fat,' **32**. 145

Garrick jealous of, **33**. 88

HW invites, to dinner, **9**. 70

HW's dinner attended by, **9**. 73

HW's *Mysterious Mother* written for, but not performed, **11**. 247n

HW takes house of, for Cts Waldegrave, **10**. 69, **40**. 282

HW would like, to play in *Mysterious Mother*, **10**. 259

Kingston play to be attended by, **9**. 70

last appearance of, corrected, **43**. 135

'Maria' in the *Nonjuror* acted by, **33**. 87

Montagu mentions, **10**. 297

Much Ado About Nothing's 'Beatrice' as played by, surpasses Garrick's 'Benedick,' **33**. 88

plays acted by, **19**. 342

Ragman's Castle, Twickenham, bought by, **35**. 234, **40**. 282n

—— occupied by, **11**. 86n, **42**. 483

retirement of, from stage, expected, **10**. 259

soul of, needed for *Pigmalion*, **28**. 183

Whitehead's *Creusa* acted by, **35**. 79n

Vaughan, Henry (d. 1775), of Twickenham:

death of, **7**. 398, **39**. 262

gouty, **39**. 251

Vaughan (after 1809, Halford), Henry (1766–1844), M.D.; cr. (1809) Bt:
SH visited by, **12.** 251
Vaughan, Mrs Henry (widow of Henry Vaughan, d. 1775, of Twickenham):
HW should no longer tell story about, after husband's death, **39.** 262
(?) Raftor talks to, about Mawhood's marriage, **39.** 251
Vaughan, Mrs Henry. *See also* St John, Hon. Elizabeth Barbara
Vaughan, Sir John (ca 1731–95), K.B., 1792; Lt-Gen., 1782:
Burke moves for inquiry into conduct of, at St Eustatius, **36.** 199n
Dutch colonies capitulate to, **25.** 145n
ingratitude of George III and Lord North towards, **25.** 218
report by, on Barbados hurricane, **25.** 109n
St Eustatius captured by, **25.** 139n, **36.** 192n
Tobago's capture reported by, **25.** 172n
Vaughan, Owen, of Llwydiart, Wales:
Cole's ancestor, **1.** 70n
Vaughan, Lady Rachel. *See* Wriothesley, Lady Rachel (ca 1637–1723)
Vaughan, Robert (d. 1667), engraver:
print attributed to, **16.** 64n
print by, of tomb, **1.** 174
rare print by, **2.** 170n
Vaughan, Sir Thomas (d. 1483):
beheaded at Pontefract, **35.** 269
Vaughan, Hon. Wilmot (ca 1730–1800), 4th Vct Lisburne, 1766; cr. (1776) E. of Lisburne:
(?) footman tries to bar, from theatre box, **37.** 433
Gloucester, D. and Ds of, visit, in Devonshire, **25.** 203n
HW's correspondence with, **42.** 376–8
Keppel, Mrs, intercedes with HW to get burgage-tenures for, **42.** 376–7
Vaugirard, Rue de, in Paris:
Bauffremont writes from, **41.** 415
Chartreux near, **13.** 169n
convent in, **15.** 219n
Sandwich, Cts of, dies in, **1.** 89n
Vaugirard barrière:
Walpoles rent house at, **4.** 211, 212
Vauguion; Vauguyon. *See* La Vauguyon
Vaujour, Duchesse de. *See* Crussol, Anne-Julie-Françoise de (1713–93)
Vaulserre des Adretz, Marie-Olympe de (ca 1701–82), m. 1 (1730) Louis-Alexandre de Sallers de Montlor; m. 2 (1738) Louis de la Tour-du-Pin, Comte de Montauban:
social relations of, with Comtesse de la Marche, **7.** 298
verses by, to Mme de Luxembourg, **5.** 394
Vaulting:
by Accademia dei nobili, **22.** 365
Vaumal, Abbé:
discourse read by, **7.** 460
social relations of, with Mme du Deffand, **7.** 455, 460

Vaupalière. *See* La Vaupalière
Vaure, du. *See* Du Vaure
Vauvillars, Marquis de. *See* Clermont-Tonnerre, Gaspard de
Vaux, Comte de. *See* Jourda, Noël de (1705–88)
Vaux, —— de:
Boufflers's verses on P. de Beauvau and, **39.** 212
Vaux, Ann (d. 1767), m. 1 (1737) William Penn; m. 2 (1767) Alexander Durdin:
Burdett accompanies and abandons, in Paris, **20.** 20
Vaux, Sir Nicholas (ca 1460–1523), cr. (1523) Bn Vaux of Harrowden:
HW's discussion of, **16.** 366n
Holbein's portrait of, **40.** 126
poetry attributed to, **40.** 373
Vaux, Thomas (1509–56), 2d Bn Vaux:
biographical information about, corrected, **43.** 231
Percy's observation on poetry attributed to father of, **40.** 373
sonnet by, **16.** 366
Vaux (place). *See* East Ruston Vaux; Netherhall Vaux
Vaux de Giry de St-Cyr, Claude-Odet-Joseph de (ca 1694–1761), Abbé de Troarn:
Catéchisme et décisions de cas de conscience by, owned by Mme du Deffand, **8.** 35n
Vauxhall, London:
ballads at: equal to Lord Lyttelton's, **33.** 501; sung, **39.** 182
Beauclerk, Lady Diana, does drawing of, **29.** 354
boats ply to, **9.** 308
children's saying at, **9.** 17
Colisée resembles, **7.** 350n
Conway and wife to attend party at, **37.** 489
Cumberland, D. of, gives ball at, **9.** 42
diversions at, must be curtailed by inclement weather, **20.** 69
Du Deffand, Mme, mentions, **4.** 239
entertainments at, **39.** 322
gatekeeper at, *see* More, Mrs
Gunning sisters pursued at, by mobs, **20.** 260
HW amuses himself at, **37.** 157
HW avoids, **17.** 434, **37.** 533
HW evades question about going to, **28.** 48
HW jokes about re-establishing, when Walpole family again is fashionable, **30.** 62
HW on way to, stops under Marble Hall's trees, **37.** 288
HW prefers, to Ranelagh because of water approach and better garden, **17.** 434
HW takes party to, **30.** 62
imitated, for guests at Stowe, **10.** 314–15
lamps on trees at, **39.** 133
link-boys' saying at, **20.** 91
Mann's garden compared to, **18.** 478, 485, 497, **20.** 427
Newcastle's dessert imitates, **20.** 126
operas eclipsed by, **17.** 421

painting at, of Henry VIII and Anne Boleyn, **41.** 451

Parsons, Nancy, might be courted by bishops at, **39.** 105

pattern of events at, **38.** 273

Petersham, Lady Caroline, gives party at, **9.** 106–10

popularity of, as 'Spring Garden' will be transitory, **13.** 102–3

price of admission to *ridotto al fresco* at, **10.** 279

Ranelagh eclipses, **37.** 164

—— to rival, **17.** 401

ridotto al fresco at, described by HW, **10.** 279

trees at, do not inspire HW to poetry, **30.** 100

visitors to: Ashe, Elizabeth, **9.** 106–10; Beauclerk, (?) Caroline, **9.** 107–10; (?) Carrion, **10.** 127; Cathcart, **9.** 42–3; Christian VII, **23.** 41; Coke, Lady Mary, **37.** 557; Conway, **10.** 279; Furnese, Selina, **9.** 85; Granby, **9.** 108–10; Guerchys, **10.** 127; HW, **9.** 86–7, 106–10, **10.** 279, **17.** 450; Kingston, D. of, **9.** 107–10; Lavagna, **10.** 127; Lloyd, Mrs Gresham, **9.** 108; March, E. of, **9.** 107–10; Masserano, **10.** 127; Nangis, Mlle de, **10.** 127; Neale, Mrs Elizabeth, **9.** 109; Norsa, Hannah, **9.** 109; Orford, 2d E. of, **9.** 109; Pelham, Frances, **37.** 557; Petersham, Lady Caroline, **9.** 106–10; Pitt, Anne, **10.** 127; Rice, George, **9.** 85; Selwyn, **10.** 127; Sparre, Amelia, **9.** 107–10; Stuart Mackenzie, **9.** 86–7; Townshend, Hon. Charles, **37.** 557; Vane, **9.** 107–10; Waldegrave, Cts, **10.** 127; Walpole, George, **17.** 450; Whithed, **9.** 107–10

Vauxhall, at Paris:

balls at, **38.** 404

HW and Richmonds visit, **7.** 328

Vauxhall; Vauxhalls:

elderly English frolic at, in Paris, **38.** 404

Irish counterparts of, **37.** 336

Vauxhall Affray. See under Bate, Henry

Vaux-Praslin, near Melun, France:

Praslin banished to, **23.** 257n, **39.** 134n

Vavassor, Miss:

'ecclesiastic processes' of, in (?) Doctors' Commons, **35.** 181

HW's alleged letter to Seward probably a fabrication by, **35.** 181

(?) overtures to be made to, in Bentley's behalf, **35.** 219

(?) 'Mrs Tisiphone,' **43.** 119

Vayer, Le. *See* Le Vayer

Vayres, Marquise de. *See* Lamoignon, Olive-Claire de

Veal:

Chute's gout aggravated by, **35.** 21

Veal cake; veal cakes. *See under* Cake

Vecchiarelli, Isabella (ca 1681–1761), m. Scipio Publicola, Principe di Santa Croce:

Craon, Princesse de, met by, **17.** 3

Vedaine, M. *See* Vedel-Montel, François de

Vedel-Montel, François de:

censured, **6.** 439

Richelieu to pay, **6.** 439

Veen *or* Venius, Otto van (1556–1629), artist:

Henry VIII family group attributed to, **42.** 248

Rubens's master, **42.** 248

Veers, Daniel Diederick (b. ca 1718), impostor:

borrows from bankers in Paris, Lyon, Marseille, and Genoa, **19.** 507, 510n

Niccolini not present to detect, **20.** 7

Onslow's son impersonated by, in Florence, **19.** 505, 510n

signatures forged by, **19.** 507

Veezy. *See* Vesey

Vega, Martínez de la. *See* Martínez

Vegetable; vegetables:

English grow, at Gibraltar, **25.** 340n

Mann, Horace II, has diet of, **25.** 353

Pembroke, E. of, lives on, **20.** 109

Vegetable Staticks. See under Hales, Stephen

Vegha, Conte, of Rome:

Young Pretender accompanied by, at Florence, **23.** 225n

Veglia:

'Grogrum' gives, **18.** 333

'Vehicle':

apothecaries' term, **35.** 263

Vehla, Gen.:

Austrian corps under, invades Dalmatia, **24.** 11n

Veigel, Eva Maria (1724–1822), dancer, called 'Violette'; m. (1749) David Garrick:

Adelphi residence of, **31.** 211

Batt, Charles, reported by, to HW, as having died, **11.** 322

Batt, John visits, **11.** 33

Beauclerk visited by, **32.** 170

Beaumont, Lady, has 'warm words' with, **11.** 253

Bedford House visited by, **9.** 28

biographical information about, corrected, **43.** 112, 140, 184, 310, 338, 348, 361

Boyle Walsingham, Mrs, with daughter and Mary Hamilton, visits, **39.** 416n

Bristol visited by, **31.** 345

Burlington, Cts of, chaperones, **9.** (?) 79–80, 81

—— encourages, **9.** 28

—— gives mortgage to, **20.** 74n

—— leaves nothing to, **9.** 226n

—— may have spoiled, **22.** 180

Bury causes riot to get more dances from, **20.** 74n

Cadogan, Dr, visits, **11.** 33

career of, **20.** 74n

Chiswick House visited by, **9.** 28

Christmas spent by, with Hannah More, and Mrs Boyle Walsingham, **42.** 205

Chute and Whited dislike dancing of, **19.** 342

company disliked by, **31.** 228

[Veigel, Eva Maria, *continued*]

Conway's *False Appearances* attended by, **31.** 293

costume of, at her début at the Haymarket, **19.** 293n

Coventry said to be married to, **9.** 79

death of, **12.** 148n

Devonshire, D. of, pays interest to, on mortgage, **20.** 74n

fame of, increases, **9.** 28

Frederick, P. of Wales, displeased with, **9.** 29

——'s offer to, refused, **19.** 294n

Garrick marries, **20.** 34n, 74

—— ogles, **9.** 81

Gray said by, to understand dancing, **40.** 101, 105

HW, Boyle Walsinghams, and Mary Hamilton dine with, **35.** 384–5

HW called on by, at SH, with Mrs Montagu, **42.** 83

HW dares not give *Bishop Bonner's Ghost* to, **31.** 309

HW dines with, **11.** 310, 329

HW inquires for, **31.** 344

HW invites: to Berkeley Sq., **31.** 242, 393; to breakfast at SH, **42.** 83

HW learns of Hannah More's health from, **31.** 293

HW meets, at theatre, **31.** 293, 296

HW praises, **35.** 244

HW rarely sees, **31.** 374

HW receives fruit from, **31.** 374

HW's correspondence with, **42.** 40, 211, 410, 426–7, 434

HW seeks place in theatre box of, for Malone to see *Vortigern*, **42.** 434

HW sends *Bishop Bonner's Ghost* to, **31.** 313

HW sends compliments to, **31.** 212

HW sends Stratford's *Fontenoy* to, **42.** 40

HW suspects, would be glad to end winter visits from Hannah More, **31.** 348

HW thanks, for fruit, **42.** 410

HW to visit, **31.** 217

HW visited by, at SH, **39.** 276

HW visits, **11.** 33, 249, **12.** 148, **31.** 259, 351

HW wishes Hannah More would persuade, to settle earlier in London, **31.** 284

HW writes to, at Hampton Court, to bring deed to town, **42.** 211

Hamilton, Mary, and Sir William Hamilton to dine with, at Hampton Court, **31.** 217

Hartington asked by, about ministry, **35.** 165

health of, **31.** 345–6, 392

Hilverding's pupil, **19.** 293n

hip hurt by, on road, **22.** 203

Italy to be visited by, **22.** 164

Malone seeks Shakespeare's deed owned by, **42.** 426–7

—— to receive deed from, **42.** 211

Mann's expectations from, **22.** 170, 191

—— to get second theatre box for, **22.** 180

—— will be embarrassed to present, to Florentine nobility, **22.** 170, 180

masquerade attended by, **9.** 79–80

Middlesex, E. of, belittles performance of, **19.** 294n

Monboddo's proposal rejected by, **29.** 271, **33.** 363

Montagu, Mrs, visits, at Hampton Court, **42.** 83

More, Hannah, lives with, **31.** 211 *et passim*

——'s relations with, **31.** 348

—— visited by, at Cowslip Green, **31.** 321

Naples visited by, **22.** 203

Nardi's quarrel with, **19.** *293*

Newcastle, D. of, concerned about, **20.** 74n

Nicholl, Mrs, visits, **11.** 33

nieces visit, at Hampton Court, **12.** 148

Paris visited by, looking much altered, **38.** 478

plays danced in by, **19.** 342

'Pomona,' **31.** 374

Porteus, Bp, entertains, at dinner, **11.** 291

—— visited by, **11.** 253

Porteuses visit, **11.** 33

Richmond's fireworks attended by, **9.** 81

Sabbatini asks about, **9.** 81–2

social relations of, with: Boyle, Charlotte, **31.** 206, 228, **35.** 384–5, **39.** 416n; Boyle, Richard, **35.** 384–5; Boyle Walsingham, Mrs, **31.** 206, 213, 217, 228, **35.** 384–5, **39.** 416n; Burney, Dr Charles, **31.** 213; Burney, Frances, **31.** 213; Cardigan, Cts of, **9.** 28; Carter, Elizabeth, **31.** 228; HW, **31.** 206, 213, 228, **35.** 384–5, **42.** 83; Hamilton, Mary, **31.** 206, 228, **39.** 416n; Hamilton, Sir William, **35.** 384–5; Herries, Lady, **31.** 229; Jenyns, Mr and Mrs, **31.** 213; Johnstons, **11.** 310, 329; Montagu, Mrs, **31.** 228; Ord, Mrs, **31.** 213; Pepys, W. W., **31.** 206, 213, 228; Pepys, Mrs W. W., **31.** 213; Rothes, Cts of, **31.** 213; Shipley, Bp and Mrs, **31.** 213; Smelt, Mr and Mrs, **31.** 228; Vesey, Mrs, **31.** 214

Stoke visited by, **14.** 99

SH may be visited by, **31.** 295

SH not to be visited by, **31.** 400

SH to be visited by, **31.** 262

SH visited by, **31.** 216, 392, **42.** 99n

Thanet, Cts of, encourages, **9.** 28

Vertue engraves benefit tickets for, **20.** 74n

will be called 'the Violetta' in Florence, **22.** 180

Veii:

borough of, unimportant, **39.** 121

Veil; veils:

and mantle, **1.** 7

beguine's, **40.** 226

black: figure wears, on monument at Easton Maudit, **10.** 339; Waldegrave, Cts, wears, **23.** 193

black crêpe, worn by Ds of Kingston, **24.** 6, 187, **32.** 146, **39.** 272

crêpe, worn by St-Cyr nuns, **10.** 293

lion skin used as, **9.** 414

Madonna della Impruneta covered by seven, **30.** 4

red, worn by Mrs George Pitt at masquerade, **20.** 49

Salins, Mme de, wears, **20.** 75n

white-laced, Bisham church monument depicts, **9.** 101

'Veiling' (copying paintings by coating them, and taking impressions):

Charles III refuses Mann permission to use, in copying paintings, **20.** 328n

Raphaels at the Vatican injured by, **20.** 328n

Veillard, —— (d. 1780):

(?) Rousseau's *Émile* used for education of son of, **7.** 287

(?) social relations of, with Crébillon, **7.** 287

Velasquez de Silva, Diego (1599–1660):

paintings by, sold by Francis III of Modena to K. of Poland, **19.** 314n

Veldt-marshal:

HW jokes about Conway becoming, **39.** 178

Veletri. *See* Velletri

Velleius Paterculus Gaius (ca 19 B.C.–after A.D. 30):

story by, about Mummius, **37.** 102

Velletri (Italy):

Charles of Naples at, **18.** 447, 454, 487, 489, 490, 504

—— retires to, **18.** 533

Clement XIV's entertainment at, for D. of Gloucester, **23.** 388n

false news from, **37.** 160

Francis III of Modena at, **18.** 454, 487

Lobkowitz blamed by Mann for Charles's escape at, **18.** 514–15

——'s attack on, **18.** 486–94, 504, 514

Spaniards and Neapolitans fortify, **18.** 454

Spaniards fear repetition of attack on, **18.** 533

'victory' at, **35.** 51

York, cardinal-bishop of, **17.** 10n

Vellinghausen:

battle of, **9.** 379

Vellum:

Barrett shown leaves of, by Chatterton, **16.** 176

Castle of Otranto, Bodoni edn, partly printed on, **15.** 213

drawings copied on, **22.** 233n

HW wishes Irish bindings in, **9.** 418, **10.** 13, 16, 18

leaves of, in pocket-book, **17.** 194

MS book of, of Campbell genealogy, **40.** 264

Velluti, Ferdinando (1681–1763), Barone del Galluccio:

Montemar to confer with, **17.** 228, 314, 323

Spaniards' route to be protested by, **17.** 341

Velluti. *See also* Filippo; Ubaldo

Velmonte. *See* Val Montone

Velour:

(?) suit of, black, **39.** 50–1

Velvet:

Beauclerk, Lady Diana, paints on panels of, **42.** 490

black: cap of, **18.** 85; Florentine husband gives 'coupon' of, to wife on birth of heir, **24.** 233; gown of, worn by Bagnolese, **18.** 128; hangings of, **9.** 297

blue: chairs covered with, at Boughton House, **10.** 341; mantle of, **42.** 180n; Montagu wears, **10.** 1

breeches of, **18.** 334

brocade of, **18.** 169

carpet of, **25.** 536

coffin of, **22.** 216

crimson, Pomfret wears suit of, **20.** 390

cushion of, **25.** 536

disrespect shown to wearers of, **21.** 94

Edward I's, found perfect in his grave, **24.** 4

green: at Osterley, **34.** 237; bag of, used by secretaries of state and lord treasurer, **18.** 225; ballroom floor and ceiling to be covered with, **37.** 412; in Mereworth gallery, **35.** 143

hangings of, **42.** 314n

horse caparison of, **32.** 325

in Brandon's supposed codpiece, **35.** 360

Italian, **8.** 22

leather box lined with, **35.** 477n

muffeteens of, **22.** 3

purple, canopy of, at George II's funeral, **9.** 321

purses of, **10.** 116

red: bed of, at Hinchingbrooke, **40.** 283; Buckingham, Ds of, has robes of, **17.** 254; coffer of, **37.** 439n; figure of Siena dressed in, for St John's Day celebration, **18.** 251; may cover Jack Pudding, **35.** 400; on fire-screen, **42.** 314–15

royal garments of, might just as well be buckram and tinsel, **25.** 624

spotted, Ionic columns of, **39.** 139

tables of, at Knole, **35.** 132

Utrecht, **8.** 12, 15, 18, 21

violet-coloured mantle of, **21.** 529, **38.** 116

yellow: fire-screens of, at Hardwick, **9.** 297; Montagu, Lady Mary Wortley, wears, **22.** 17

Velvet cup:

girl wishes to drink from, **7.** 358

Vamberght, Mrs Mary Reda. *See* Reda, Mary

Venables Vernon, Hon. Elizabeth (1746–1826), m. (1765) George Simon Harcourt, styled Vct Nuneham 1749–77; 2d E. Harcourt, 1777:

Addison's portrait left by, with HW who returns it, **35.** 515

Amelia, Ps, entertains, at Gunnersbury, **33.** 463

brother of, **28.** 443n

charade to be guessed by, **35.** 525

Chewton wedding attended by, **29.** 245n

Clio to rejoin, in Wales, **35.** 465

Court appointment of, **29.** 330n, 332, 348, 359

Craven, Bns, attended by, at Drury Lane, **29.** 43

—— improperly refers to, **35.** 538

Dublin visited by, **28.** 109n, **35.** 457n, 459n, (?) 469n

erysipelas of, **12.** 189

[Venables Vernon, Hon. Elizabeth, *continued*]
faro punter, 39. 377n
father-in-law avoided by, because of his possible re-marriage, 39. 267
father-in-law to be visited by, in Ireland, 35. 457
father of: 29. 73n; dies, 35. 506
father to be visited by, 29. 73, 35. 506–7
Gloucester, Ds of, pleased by kindness of, to her daughter, 35. 494
Gloucester, D. and Ds of, arouse solicitude of, 35. 472, 474
'goodness itself, and has a wicked husband,' 35. 453
HW accepts dinner invitation from, 35. 485
HW condoles with: on father-in-law's death, 35. 476; on her father's death, 35. 506; on her sister's death, 35. 470
HW corresponds with, about getting a place for Harcourt, 35. 511–13
HW dines with husband and, at Mrs Montagu's, 29. 184
HW does not wait on, since he also avoids Lady Hertford's, 35. 511
HW exchanges calls with, 35. 544
HW excuses himself from calling on, 35. 482, 489, 511
HW expects, to act as if she were at Court, 33. 463
HW forgets dinner engagement with, 35. 455
HW gives compliments of, to D. and Ds of Gloucester, 28. 340
HW gives *Mysterious Mother* to, 35. 493
HW inquires after health of, 29. 361
HW invites, to SH, 35. 471, 488
HW jokingly calls, George III's 'Montespan,' 33. 498
HW might be immortalized by, 35. 466
HW's correspondence with, 29. 332, 35. 511–13
HW sent regards from, 29. 275
HW's indebtedness to, 35. 505, 515–16
HW's nieces entertained by, at Nuneham, 35. 496
HW suspected by Mason and, of addressing anonymous verse letter to her, 29. 363–4
HW's verses from, 35. 646
HW's verses replying to those of, 35. 461
HW thanks, 35. 458
HW to call on, 35. 456, 483, 504
HW to meet, at Leicester House, 35. 463, 465, 467
HW to visit, 33. 211
HW to visit, at Nuneham, 35. 470–1, 489, 506–8, 524, 531
HW unable to visit, 28. 445
HW visits, 33. 234, 417
HW visits, at Nuneham, 35. 458–9, 469–70, 490–2
HW wishes, were invisible at Mrs Vesey's, 35. 495
handwriting of, illegible, 29. 353
hothouses of, not envied by HW, 35. 473

husband may find verses of, in her dressing-room, 35. 469
husband not good enough for, 35. 453
Ireland visited by, 35. 463–4, 465
Irish and Mrs Montagu praise, 35. 495
Irish pleased by, 35. 467
Irish visit keeps, too busy for poetry, 35. 465
(?) Jephson persuaded by, to give *Count of Narbonne* to Sheridan, 33. 300–1
London visited by, 29. 175
Mason and Wentworth Castle should be visited by, 35. 361
Mason sends compliments of, to HW, 28. 407, 29. 275
—— silent to, about ode, 29. 189
'may frisk and vagary anywhere,' 35. 480
modesty of, concerning literary talents, 29. 45
Montagu, Mrs, borrows *Mysterious Mother* from, 35. 493n
Nuneham's flowers immortalized by, 35. 461
—— visited by, 12. 188–9
poetic talents of, 35. 459
poetry rather than animals occupies, 35. 474
SH ticket requested by, for Wilmot, 29. 268, 270
taste of, 35. 361
Thurlow subject of remark by, 29. 235
verses by: 32. 136; HW hopes to print, at SH, 28. 443, 29. 183, 193, 263, 270, 312, 35. 459, 471, 486, 491–2, 521; Mason might improve, 35. 493–4; may be read in her dressing-room, 35. 469; on Ds of Kingston, 35. 491; on husband's birthday, 35. 491; secret, 28. 105, 106; shown to HW by Cts Temple, 35. 465
'Vice-Queen of Ireland,' 35. 459
Waldegrave, Lady Elizabeth Laura, invited by, to Nuneham, with HW as her escort, 35. 492–3
Wales to be traversed by, from Ireland, 35. 465
Whitehead and Miss Fauquier with, at Nuneham, 35. 531
William III's spurs should be visited yearly by, at SH, 35. 478
Venables Vernon (formerly Vernon), George (1710–80), cr. (1762) Bn Vernon; M.P.:
birth date of, corrected, 43. 127, 278, 307, 353
daughter of, 12. 189n, 28. 105n
death of, 29. 75n, 33. 220, 35. 506
Harcourts to visit, at Sudbury Hall, 29. 73, 35. 507
Montagu visits, 10. 227, 229–30
peerage granted to, 10. 26, 22. 31
son of, 29. 81n
wife of, 28. 443n
Venables Vernon, Mrs George. *See* Fauquier, Jane Georgiana
Venables Vernon (formerly Sedley), Henry (1747–1829), 3d Bn Vernon of Kinderton, 1813:
Harcourt visits, 29. 81
wife of, 10. 190n

Venaissin, Comtat:
France to annex, **34**. 120n
Vence, Marquise de. *See* Simiane, Madeleine-Sophie de
Vence (France):
French forces at, **19**. 336
Vendée, La, department in France:
struggle between republicans and royalists in, **12**. 51, 53, 66, 71, 84, 89
Vauban serves in, **7**. 139n
Vandelwelden, Capt. (d. 1779), Capt. of Danish ship:
Arabs waylay, **24**. 510n
Vendôme, François de (1616–69), Duc de Beaufort:
Montagu thinks, abler than Newcastle, **9**. 333
Vendôme, Louis-Joseph (1654–1712), Duc de:
(?) Petitot's miniature of, **39**. 32n
Philip V aided by, **6**. 429
Vendôme, Philippe (1655–1727), Chevalier de:
Anderson's tribute to wit and spirit of, **35**. 509
Mignard's portrait of, given by HW to Harcourt, **35**. 508–9, 535n
Trevisani's portrait of, at Dacre's, shows his deterioration, **35**. 509
Vendôme, Place, in Paris:
Capuchins' church near, **7**. 281n
Feuillants' and Capuchins' gates make vistas to, **7**. 282
Foire Ste-Ovide in, **10**. 289n
HW examines house in, **7**. 266
Louis XVI and Marie-Antoinette taken to, to see ruins of Louis XIV's statue, **31**. 372
Venereal disease:
Keysar's pills to cure, **24**. 451n
occurrences of, **17**. 444, **18**. 104n, **20**. 36, 447, **22**. 551
Venerosi Pesciolini, Signore Michele:
(?) Santa Maria faction led by, at Pisa, **25**. 582
Venetian; Venetians:
Cerretesi taken by, to Oxford and Blenheim, **18**. 166
freemasonry said to have been introduced by, to Europe, **39**. 158
'Venetian ambassadress.' *See* Colalto, Eleonora
Venetian glass. *See under* Glass
Venetian Gothic. *See under* Architecture: Gothic
Venetian mask. *See under* Mask
Venetian noble:
Catalans seek to capture, **17**. 132
Venetian prints:
Jackson's, at SH, **20**. 375, 380–1
Venetian song:
Salimbeni and Amorevoli sing, in Mann's garden, **17**. 240
Venetian windows:
(?) Newstead Abbey to be furnished with, **9**. 299
Veneur. *See* Le Veneur
Vengeance, English war ship:
escapes to Ireland, **25**. 152

in danger, **21**. 350
Nightingale, Gamaliel, capt. of, **21**. 350n
Vengeances divines, Les. See under Drouin, Daniel
Venice:
air of: asthma cured by, **17**. 77n; (?) HW benefits by, **17**. 77; nauseous, **24**. 314; pestilential, **11**. 287, **34**. 245
airs of, *see* Airs, Venetian
ambassadors from and to, *see under* Ambassador
Aquileia's suppression and new patriarchate at Udino urged by, **20**. 206n
arsenal at: **17**. 76n, **22**. 241; busy preparing regatta for D. of York, **22**. 241
Ascension Day festivities at: Beauchamp to attend, **38**. 531; Craons to attend, **17**. 25, 20. 29; Cumberland, D. of, to attend, **23**. 559; England might copy, **24**. 112; English visitors to flock to, **22**. 292n, **23**. 296–7; Gloucester, D. and Ds of, to attend, **24**. 291; Gray visits Venice for, **13**. 9–10; Joseph II and Leopold II to attend, **23**. 108, 111, 24. 95, 105; Maria Louisa to attend, **23**. 205; Pitt, Thomas, to attend, **21**. 500; regatta on, **22**. 241n; to be rivalled at Florence on St John's Day, **18**. 462; York, D. of, to attend, **22**. 204, 224, 232
Austrian corps invades Dalmatian areas of, **24**. 11n
Austrian minister to, named by Guadagni, **23**. 272
barcaroles of, **20**. 177, **23**. 249
baths near, **4**. 428
Bavarian troops said to be visible from, **17**. 108
beheading at, of man who stole a cup from a church, **17**. 85
Benedict XIV abused even by boatmen of, **20**. 177
—— demands complete submission from, **20**. 206
—— quarrels with, over Attems's appointment to Aquileia, **20**. 160–1, 163, 165, 173, 176, 177, 189–91, 198
Berrys to visit, **11**. 367, 371
—— write from, to HW, **11**. 368, 372
Bethel's asthma cured at, **18**. 65, 117
Bonaichi flees to, **17**. 148
Bonaventuri flees from, to Florence, **20**. 414
Boothby to get passports at, **21**. 481
bride of, abducted by Pembroke, **23**. 152
Brown, Sir Robert, gets fortune as merchant at, **9**. 16n, **25**. 609
Capello recalled by, from Rome, **20**. 161, 176
Cappello, Bianca, made daughter of the Republic by, **20**. 399, 415
carnival at, **17**. 134
Chesterfield to select minister to, **19**. 453
Chute suggested by Mann for post at, **19**. 444, 448, 458
Clement XIII's election as pope will heal Rome's breach with, **21**. 219

[Venice, *continued*]

——'s family honoured by, **21**. 230

——'s ridiculous letters to, **21**. 236–7

Compagni and Libri's correspondent at, **17**. 422

consuls from and to, *see under* Consul

Cornaro daughter made daughter of the Republic by, **20**. 399, 415

Council at: Grimani, sage of, **17**. 75n; poor nobles entitled to vote in, **17**. 75n

courier from India to, **21**. 523

Craon, Princesse de, would dislike fleeing to, **17**. 178

Craven, Lady, writes from, to HW, **42**. 176

custom-house officer in, **17**. 64

dialect of, heard at Reggio fair, **13**. 242

Dixon in service of, **23**. 296

doge and senate of, told by Lady Mary Wortley Montagu that she will reconcile them with George II, **17**. 98

doge; doges of: dies, **22**. 142n; rule harmlessly, **21**. 105, 126; salary of, **17**. 75; *see also* Foscarini, Marco (1695–1763); Grimani, Pietro (d. 1752); Pisani, Luigi (1663–1741)

Du Tillot may succeed Montallegre at, **23**. 325

edict of, against Rome, **23**. 56

election at, for doge and procurator, **17**. 75–7

Eleonora, Ps, dies at, **18**. 62n

Elisi sings at, **20**. 86n

England severs diplomatic relations with, **17**. 98n

——'s friendship with, **37**. 98

—— to receive delegates from, to congratulate George II, **21**. 508–9

English peer demanded by, as Resident, **23**. 325

English trade with, **15**. 81

English visitors to, soon to come in crowds to Florence, **22**. 41

fanali from, desired, **17**. 59, 73, 76, 87

Ferrara may be garrisoned by, **17**. 380

fireworks at, for doge's election, **17**. 76

floods in territory of, **21**. 134, 359n

Florence full of letters from, **18**. 553

Florentine opera lures Sir James Gray from, **19**. 433

foreign ministers left isolated at, **10**. 141

France tries to influence, against Francis III and Maria Theresa, **20**. 400n

Francis I's agent at, sends rumours of English-French war, **18**. 44

Francis III and Don Philip said to have retreated to, **19**. 269

Francis III may finish Carnival at, **18**. 161

French ambassador at, sent to Naples, **21**. 333n

Gaetani at, collects notices of great men, **22**. 14, 35

George III buys art collection from Smith at, **22**. 107, **25**. 93

——'s letter to, accrediting Northampton, **22**. 150

——'s portrait to be sent from, to Mann, **22**. 501

Giovanelli not confirmed as patriarch of, **24**. 189n

glass of, **37**. 439n; *see also under* Glass

Gloucester, D. of, made ill by heat and nauseous air of, **24**. 314

—— not to take house at, **24**. 252

—— to visit, **23**. 370

—— writes from, **36**. 308

gondoliers at, **17**. 64, **20**. 177

Gradenigo, ambassador from, **3**. 147n

Gray, Sir James, feigns illness before departure from, **20**. 370

—— said to have accepted post at, with reluctance, **19**. 472

—— stays in, in hope of shift to Berlin, **19**. 444

—— temporarily leaves, **19**. 433, 438

—— will not leave, **19**. 457

Greek refugees flee to, **23**. 226, 235, 236n

HW mentions, **17**. 43

HW's letter comes by way of, **19**. 348

HW writes to Ds of Gloucester at, **7**. 396

Hartington and Smyth set out for, **17**. 23

Henri IV induces Paul V to compromise on excommunication of, **20**. 198n

Holbein painting at, **14**. 165

Holdernesse not improved by stay at, **19**. 435

—— to leave Sir James Gray at, as Resident, **18**. 431–2, **19**. 41

Holdernesses expect child at, **19**. 41

Inquisition at, **20**. 198, 420

Jackson of, **11**. 112n

Joseph II invades, **24**. 37

Laschi sings at, **20**. 41n

Law, John, buried at, **15**. 180

letters from: reach Florence on Wednesdays only, **24**. 136; report D. of Gloucester's death, **24**. 136

library of St Mark at: Chute has seen, **18**. 63; to be copied for ceiling of Houghton picture gallery, **18**. 63

Loredano of, **16**. 371

Løvendal not to enter service of, **20**. 176n

manifest prepared by, for circulation in European courts, **20**. 176

Mann hears rumour from, of Murray's transfer to Constantinople, **22**. 356

—— hopes Cts of Orford will prefer, to Florence, **19**. 369

—— hopes not to be sent to, **18**. 244

—— receives letter from, **17**. 108

—— regrets that HW's portrait was not painted for him at, **18**. 243

—— will write to, about Zanetti cameo, **22**. 6

Mantuan duke might be bullied by, **20**. 409

Maria Theresa may arouse France by threats to, **20**. 176

—— negotiates with, **20**. 189–90

—— suspends Batthyány's orders to invade, **20.** 173n

—— threatens, but does not harm it, **20.** 173

—— told by Benedict XIV not to attack, **20.** 177

—— wishes, to accept Attems, **20.** 160–1

Marieschi's views of, **30.** 370

Mari leaves, **17.** 226

Marlborough said to have bought Zanetti's gems at, **21.** 561, **22.** 6

masking at, **17.** 77

masquerade at, imitated at Ranelagh, **20.** 46

Methodists would have been gondoliers at, singing hymns, **20.** 177

Middlesex may be ambassador to, **18.** 289

mineral specimens from, **11.** 95n

ministers from and to, *see under* Minister

minister to be sent by, to England, **18.** 244

mirrors from, bought by Yasous II of Abyssinia, **39.** 476

Modenese ducal family to flee to, **17.** 442

Montagu, Lady Mary Wortley, gives copies at, of her letters, **22.** 141

—— leaves her clothes at, **22.** 4

—— meets Conti in, **14.** 246n

—— 's indiscreet behaviour at, **14.** 245

Murray usually takes company from, to opera at Padua, **21.** 513

neutrality promised by, **17.** 226

Niccolini may live at, **20.** 24

Northampton leaves, for Geneva, **22.** 150, 154

—— 's official entry at, **22.** 142, 150, 154

—— to go to, as minister, **21.** 505

nunciature and dataria shut up by, **20.** 173

nuncio at, *see under* Nuncio

Old Pretender not recognized by, **20.** 332n

opera scene depicts, **17.** 302

Orford, Cts of, has house at, **19.** 50

—— may settle at, **19.** 46, 50

Orlov receives courier from, **23.** 204

Pasquali at, seeks books on music for HW, **21.** 477, 482

patriarchate might be transferred by, to the Udine, **20.** 206

Paul V's quarrel with, **20.** 198

Pertici, Laschi, (?) Guadagni, and Fanti usually appeared with wives in performances at, **20.** 4n

pictures at, black, **11.** 266, **15.** 335

Pierson brings pictures from, **24.** 570

Pius VI threatens, with interdiction, **24.** 189

Pope's lines on, in the *Dunciad*, **16.** 272

post from, to Florence, **17.** 88, 190, **19.** 439

Prussian minister at, desires peace, **17.** 483

quarantine on borders of, **18.** 122

Querini sent from, to Rome to aid Capello, **20.** 190n

Raphael died at, **16.** 147

residents from and to, *see under* Resident

Richecourt may visit, **19.** 47

—— sends valuables to, **18.** 513

rôle of, in *La Passion des Jésuites*, **5.** 315

Rome and Vienna receive couriers from, **20.** 190

Rome gets no more money from, for benefices, **20.** 173

——'s quarrels with, **20.** 160–1, 163, 165, 173, 176, 177, 189–91, 198, 206, 420, **21.** 219, 230, **23.** 56, **24.** 189

rumour of Austrian-Prussian peace comes from, **17.** 134

St Mark's library at: **18.** 63; ceiling of, **32.** 141n

Salviatis, bankers at, **14.** 67n

San Barnaba, poor nobles at, **17.** 75

senate of: Benedict XIV distrusts, **20.** 206; candle-snuffers at Drury Lane Theatre represent, **32.** 115; censures Capello, **20.** 177; costume worn by, **17.** 75n; dismisses nuncio, **20.** 173, 176; Grimani's family loses votes in, **17.** 76; Louis XVIII reported to receive pension from, **12.** 118–19; Mann to send memorial to, **20.** 198; Wotton's relations with, **20.** 198

Shakespeare's shift of scene to or from, **33.** 553

ship of: captured by English, **19.** 81; gives information to Cornish, **18.** 414

Shirley's letters from, **15.** 79–82

Smith, Joseph, 'merchant' of, **18.** 465

——'s collection at, packed by Dalton, **22.** 107, 115

—— tries to hire Pertici and 'tinca nera' at, for English theatre, **18.** 198

'snug,' for love affairs, **17.** 108

Stanhope rejected by, as England's Resident, because of illegitimacy, **23.** 325

Stowe pillar reminiscent of, **35.** 77

Strange justifies his conduct at, in letters, **24.** 298

SH's view resembles, **19.** 497

Stuart Mackenzie gets equipment for embassy at, **21.** 508

—— said to be rejected by, **23.** 325

Suares family to visit, **17.** 156, 161, 171

tapestry from, bought by Henry VIII, **16.** 147

tea plentiful in, **17.** 59

Tedeschi, Caterina, sings in, **20.** 41n

Tesi performs in opera at, **18.** 280, 520–1

theatres in, *see* Teatro Sant'Angelo; Teatro Santo Casciano

Titian's works at, blackened, **11.** 266

Trieste to eclipse, **20.** 102

Turkish threat incites, to prepare for war, **21.** 494

Udny transferred from, to Leghorn, **24.** 233

Ulfeld sends courier to, **20.** 190

unwholesome place, **34.** 245

Valenti rejected by, for low birth, **20.** 409, **23.** 325

vessel of, with English engineers, intercepted by French frigate off Corsica on way from Leghorn to Minorca, **24.** 476–7

[Venice, *continued*]

Vienna Court threatens, for defying Benedict XIV, **20**. 176

visitors to: Bagot, Richard, **22**. 150n; Beauchamp, **38**. 531; Bethel, **18**. 65, 117; Botta, **22**. 454n; Brown, Lady, **25**. 246; Burney, **13**. 64n; Bute, **23**. 103, 161, 297, 302; Carter, Mary, **42** 405–6; Cholmondeley, 4th E., **23**. 349, **36**. 137; Chute, **17**. 74, 101, **19**. 257, 268, **35**. 4, 21, 27; Craven, Bns, **25**. 632, 654, **42**. 176; Dalton, **22**. 107, 115; Damer brothers, **22**. 287; Dick, Mr and Mrs, **22**. 142, 154; Earl Marischal, **19**. 379; Elcho, **19**. 148, 379, **30**. 16; Eleonora, Ps, **17**. 74, 77; Fordwich Vct (3d E. Cowper), **21**. 543n; Francis III of Modena, **18**. 222, **20**. 76; Gloucester, D. and Ds of, **24**. 125, 130, 134, 305, 314–15, **34**. 245; Gray, Thomas, **13**. 9, **17**. 43, 59n, 82, 445, **28**. 69, **43**. 169–70; HW, **11**. 287, **13**. 10, 243, **15**. 335, **17**. 54, 58, 59n, 64, 72, 74–7, 84–5, 86, 88, 94, **30**. 14, 16, 17, **35**. 6, 21, 27; Harte, **20**. 175n; Hervey, **19**. 148; Karl Wilhelm Ferdinand, **22**. 457n; Lee, Capt., **20**. 364; Lincoln, E. of, **17**. 41, 61, 72, 86, **30**. 14, 17; Magnan, **19**. 563; Modena, Ds of, **18**. 222; Montagu, Lady Mary Wortley, **14**. 245, **17**. 92, 98; Murray, Lord George, **19**. 379; Niccolini, **20**. 24; Pembroke, E. of, **23**. 119; Penny, **35**. 19; Pitt, Thomas, **21**. 512; Pomfret family, **17**. 35, 41; Richecourt, **17**. 195; Rochfords, **20**. 376n; Schulenburg, **19**. 50–1; Spence, **17**. 86; Stanhope, Philip, **20**. 175n; Steavens, Thomas, **20**. 175n; Stuart Mackenzies, **24**. 381; (?) Walpole, Bns (Cts of Orford), **17**. 71n, 107, 115, 125, 134; Whithed, **17**. 74, 101, **19**. 257, 268, **35**. 4; Wright, Sir James and Lady, **21**. 457n; Württemberg, D. of, **22** 41n; *see also under* Ascension Day; festivities of

Voltaire's *Candide* mentions deposed kings at, **33**. 587

Walpole, Bns (Cts of Orford), wears costume of, **17**. 317

Walpole, Sir Robert, to be subject of panegyric in work to be published at, **22**. 14, 35

Wright, Sir James, takes post at, **22**. 499

York, Cardinal, *persona non grata* at, **20**. 332n

Young Pretender said not to be well received at, **17**. 98

—— said to be coming to, incognito, **20**. 84n

Zatta said to be publisher in, **21**. 476n

Venice Preserved. See under Otway, Thomas

Veni Creator Paraphrased:

House of Lords votes, a breach of privilege, **38**. 229n

Venise. *See* Venice

Venison:

Bedford people may poach, **34**. 210

Clive, Mrs, invites HW to dine upon haunch of, **31**. 127

—— receives, **10**. 236, 238, 240, 241

Coke, Lady Mary, sends haunch of, to HW, **31**. 179

Conway offers haunch of, to HW, **39**. 84

Cosby, Mrs, receives, **10**. 238, 240

doe: digestibility of, **10**. 268; season for, **10**. 235; warrant for, **10**. 235

Glass goes to Northampton to get, **10**. 296

Gloucester, Ds of, sends, to Sir Edward Walpole, **36**. 324

(?) Grafton, D. of, to give, to Mrs Cosby, **10**. 240

HW accepts haunch of, from Tylney, **35**. 238

HW compares curacy to, **15**. 199

HW overwhelmed with, from Houghton, **12**. 164

HW receives, **10**. 235, 236, 238–41, 268

HW sends, to Udnys, **12**. 160

HW sends warrant for, to Cts Waldegrave, **36**. 289

HW serves, at SH, **20**. 89

HW to send, to Lady Ossory, **32**. 67

Harcourt gives, to Mrs Clive, **35**. 533

Italian contempt for, **20**. 83

Johnstons thank HW for, **12**. 196

large entremets of, **19**. 357n

leaner, in cold weather, **10**. 236

Lorenzi says, is as good as beef, **20**. 89

(?) Lort mentions, **16**. 216

Lyttelton dies after eating fish and, **28**. 480

Montagu's perquisite as deputy ranger of Rockingham Forest, **10**. 214

Newcastle, D. of, procures, from New Park, **17**. 506

pasty of, **22**. 322

Rockingham Forest keeper to send, to HW, **10**. 241

slaves get, from Pisa forest, **20**. 83

See also under Game

Venison Club:

annual, at Cambridge, **1**. 272n

Venius. *See* Veen, Otto van

Venn, Rev. Richard (1691–1740):

Gibson's creature, **15**. 296

Middleton's letter to, **15**. 295

Rundle's promotion prevented by, **15**. 296

Venner, Tobias (1577–1660), physician:

print of, **1**. 179, **40**. 237

Ventem:

HW mentions, **35**. 65

Ventimiglia (Italy):

Ambrose blockades, **19**. 37

Austrians and Piedmontese retreat towards, **19**. 409

French capture castle of, **19**. 422

Leutrum to besiege, **19**. 436–7, 441

Spanish stores at, destroyed by Charles Emmanuel III's troops, **19**. 58

Ventletrap:

price of, **21**. 173

Vento, Mattia, composer:

Leucippo by, **38**. 288

Ventriloquist:

Lukins said to be, **31**. 276n

Venture, ——, seacaptain:
Hannah commanded by, **24**. 410n
——, sloop of, brings dispatches, **33**. 52n
Venturelli, Gregorio:
Dissertatio super controversiis . . . Cybo by, **17**. 34
Venturi, Neri (1702–58), senator, 1734:
new Regency member, **21**. 107n, 125
Venturi Gallerani, Ottavia, m. (1716) Ottavio Sansedoni:
(?) dying, **20**. 429
Venturini, Signora. See Behan, ——
Venturini, Leonardo (fl. 1738–59), bookseller and publisher at Lucca:
Baronius's Annales ecclesiastici published by, **18**. 391n
England visited by, **18**. 391
Mabillon's Annales ordinis S. Benedicti has dedication to Cardinal Rezzonico by, **18**. 392n
wife met by, at Boulogne, and brought to Lucca, **18**. 392
Venus:
and Adonis: Oliver's, at Burghley House, **10**. 345; Titian's and Reynolds's paintings of, **33**. 538n
armour brought by, to Æneas, **32**. 220
Aylesford's marriage serves Bacchus instead of, **36**. 205
Bacchus shares empire with, in Ireland, **37**. 35
bed at SH suitable for, **28**. 42
bronze statue of, bought by HW, **26**. 7
bust of, in Nuneham garden, **35**. 484n
chooses pattern for HW's vest, **32**. 219
Churchill's invocation to, in Williams's verses, **37**. 76
Cupid, son of, **32**. 263
Darwin's Botanic Garden mentions, **42**. 267
drawing of: Hoare, Miss, does, **33**. 512; Ossory, Lady, clothes, **33**. 516
Elizabeth, Czarina, and Maria Theresa said to resemble, **16**. 148
English at Florence prefer brothels to statues of, **35**. 52
Francavilla's statue of, **22**. 583
Gordon, Ds of, as, **35**. 82
Grafton, Ds of, compared to, in verses, **38**. 89
Greeks said to have borrowed, from mummies and idols, **33**. 479
HW compares Lady Mary Coke to, **38**. 83
HW mentions, **10**. 274
HW's name for the Tedeschi, **20**. 41
HW swears by, **32**. 32
HW tired of, in verses, **39**. 243
HW would sacrifice to, **32**. 64
Lennox, Lady Emilia, compared to, **30**. 105
Maria Theresa compared with, **16**. 148, **30**. 321, **37**. 353
Mars and, **32**. 252
mentioned, **11**. 57, 295, **12**. 157, 294, **30**. 290, 294, 324
Ovid's Heroides mentions, **33**. 209
Pope refers to, **32**. 33

statues of: at Easton Neston, **9**. 5; at Stowe, mentioned in HW's verses, **10**. 315–16; destroyed in Uffizi fire, **22**. 68n; expression in, **11**. 338; extracting thorn from foot, **20**. 547; see also 'Venus Callipygus,' 'Venus de' Medici'
Titian's, **7**. 313, **24**. 527, 540
waves calmed by, **38**. 83
Venus (planet):
Bošković to observe passage of, across sun, **22**. 527n
ear-trumpet to hear sounds on, **33**. 365
transit of, **38**. 89
Venus, English war ship:
Cumberland, D. of, capt. of, **23**. 50n
Gloucester, D. of, sends baggage by, **23**. 407n
in danger, **21**. 350
'Venus and Adonis.' See under Venus
'Venus Callipygus' (statue):
casts of, **12**. 268
'Venus, Cupid, and Satyr.' See under Cambiaso, Luca
'Venus de' Medici':
Chute dreams of marriage of, **35**. 54–5
compared to alleged Titian, **20**. 331
does not 'take the air' at SH, **32**. 29
gesso of: HW seeks, **19**. 34; Mann to get, for Lyttelton, **20**. 539, 547, 554
Gray's mention of, inspires West's elegy, **28**. 97, 99
Harwood copies, for Northampton, **25**. 93n
Milton's 'Eve' comparable to, **16**. 270
not indebted to Egyptians, **33**. 479
Wilton copies, for Rockingham, **20**. 397
Zoffany's painting of the Tribune omits, **24**. 527
'Venus Disarming Cupid.' See under Cambiaso, Luca
Venusta Monumenta, by Society of Antiquaries:
HW mentions, **37**. 349
Venuti, ——, Papal antiquary:
dismissal of, for giving export permit for statues, **20**. 104n
Venuti, Ridolfini:
Stephens's Italian views have remarks by, **23**. 428n
Ver. See Le Ver
Vérac, Marquis de. See St-Georges, Charles-Olivier de
Veracini, Francesco Maria (1690–1768), musician and composer:
Adriano in Siria by, expires, **13**. 95
death date of, corrected, **43**. 175
London visited by, **20**. 148n
sonata performed by, **20**. 148
theme from Gay's Polly borrowed by, **20**. 148n
Veragua, Ds of. See Silva, Maria Teresa de
Veragua, D. of. See Fitzjames, James Francis Edward Stuart
Verard, A.:
'Dance of Death' published by, **40**. 220n

'Verax':
popular signature for letters to newspapers, 42. 500
Verazano. *See* Verrazzano
Verb; verbs:
Goldsworthy, Mrs, ignorant of, 21. 353
Verberil. *See* Rigaut de Barbezieu
Vercelli (Italy):
robbery near, 19. 334
Vercellini, Frans, Lt:
captured at Velletri, 18. 493
Verdala, Hugh Loubenx de (d. 1595), cardinal:
prints of, 1. 257
Verd antique:
panels of, in Paris dining-room, 32. 261
pillars painted like, at Mereworth, 35. 144
Verdea:
wine of, *see under* Wine
Verdelin, Marquise de. *See* Brémond d'Ars, Marie-Louise-Madeleine de
Verdelin, Henriette-Charlotte de (1757–1834), m. (1778) Alexis-Paul-Michel le Veneur, Vicomte le Veneur; Comte de Tillières:
marriage of, 7. 50
social relations of, with Mme du Deffand, 7. 338
Verden (Germany):
French to occupy, 21. 136n
Verdier. *See* Du Verdier
Verdière d'Hem, Charles (ca 1729–94), Lt-Gen.:
(?) Macartney exchanged for, 7. 190
Verdigris:
beer and porter contaminated by, 40. 257
Mann's 'accident' from, 24. 8, 15
Verdun, Bp of. *See* Nicolaï, Aimar-François-Chrétien-Michel de
Verdun (France):
Choiseul imprisoned at, 11. 301n
Verdure:
at SH and Little Strawberry Hill, 12. 11, 16, 26, 74, 96, 99, 101
HW would like to transport, to Paris, 31. 93
in London, 12. 152
Vere, Bn. *See* Beauclerk, Aubrey (1740–1802); Beauclerk, Lord Vere (1699–1781); Vere, Horace (1565–1635)
Vere, Bns. *See* Chambers, Mary (d. 1783); Ponsonby, Lady Catherine (1742–89); Tracy, Mary (1581–1671)
Vere, Lady. *See* Courtenay, Joan (b. ca 1411)
Vere, Mr, of Kingston:
SH visited by, 12. 244
Vere, Alberic de. *See* Vere, Aubrey de (d. 1194)
Vere, Anne Stafford de. *See* Stafford, Anne
Vere, Aubrey de (d. 1194), cr. (ca 1142) E. of Oxford:
Matilda, Q., dies at castle of, 9. 67
Vere, Aubrey de (1626–1703), 20th E. of Oxford:
children of, impoverished, 9. 63
portrait of, at Windsor, 37. 242
Vere, Charles de:
death of, in miserable cottage, 9. 63

Vere, Lady Diana de (d. 1742), m. (1694) Charles Beauclerk, cr. D. of St Albans:
(?) beauty of, her only means of support, 9. 63
father of, 9. 63n
Hampton Court painting of beauties includes, 17. 295n
sons attend funeral of, at Windsor, 17. 295
Vere, Lady Henrietta de (ca 1682–1730):
(?) beauty of, her only means of support, 9. 63
father of, 9. 63n
Vere, Horace (1565–1635), cr. (1625) Bn Vere of Tilbury:
daughter of, 9. 68
wife of, 1. 183n
Vere, John de (1408–62), 12th E. of Oxford, 1417:
heir-apparent of, 2. 38n
Vere, John de (d. 1540), 13th E. of Oxford:
HW sees tomb of, 9. 63
Henry VII fines, 9. 63n
wife of, 2. 365n
Vere, Hon. Mary (ca 1611–69), m. 1 (ca 1628) Sir Roger Townshend; m. 2 (1638) Mildmay Fane, 2d E. of Westmorland, 1629:
birth date of, 43. 114
'Horace' becomes a Townshend family name through, 9. 68
Wilkinson delivers goose to, 40. 77
Vere, Lady Mary de (1681–1725):
beauty of, her only means of support, 9. 63
Vere, Richard de (ca 1385–1417), 11th E. of Oxford:
burial of, at Colne Priory, 43. 114
Vere, Robert de (1362–92), 9th E. of Oxford; D. of Ireland:
death and burial of, 9. 68, 78
HW's portrait of, 2. 324, 325
Richard II confers dukedom on, 9. 68
titles of, 2. 327
tomb of, at Earl's Colne, 9. 67, 68
Vere, Susan de (1587–1629), m. (1604) Philip Herbert, 4th E. of Pembroke:
Eusebia of, 16. 27
Vere, Walter de (d. 1210 *or* 1211):
(?) HW mentions, as founder of Drayton, 10. 90
Vere family:
arms of, used in Gothic lantern at SH, 9. 151
Collins's account of, 42. 313
Gough's collections on, 2. 325
HW cannot trace his ancestry to, 9. 67–9
pedigree of, 20. 181
portraits of, at Welbeck, 35. 270
poverty of, 9. 63
tombs of: at Earl's Colne, 9. 63–4, 67, 68, 78; said to be in Addington Church, 10. 343
Tyson's drawings of, 2. 175
Verelst, Harry (1733–85), gov. of Bengal; Mason's cousin-by-marriage:
Bengal governor, 28. 63n, 321n
Clive asked by, to come to London, 32. 218

fourth part of Aston bought by, **28**. 172, 231
Holdernesse estate partly bought by, **28**. 91n
house of, in St James's Sq., **28**. *63*, 322, 333
Indian prints owned by, **28**. 63
influenza brought to Aston by, **28**. 230
London visited by, **28**. 363
Mason on bad terms with, **29**. 186
—'s *Epistle to Dr Shebbeare* received by, **28**. 321
servant of, **28**. 128
Verelst, Simon (1644–?1721), painter:
flower picture by, at Welbeck, celebrated by Prior, **35**. 271
two pieces by, **1**. 171
Véret (France), Duc d'Aiguillon's seat:
Aiguillon, Duc d', at, **5**. 48
—— not to go to, **6**. 200
—— said to be going to, **6**. 196
—— to go to, **6**. 67
Aiguillon, Duchesse d', at, **4**. 270
—— to go to, **4**. 253, 256, 265
visitors to: Boucault, Mme, **4**. 146, 270; Chabrillan, Comte de, **4**. 146; Irwin, **4**. 146
Vergennes, Comte de. *See* Gravier, Charles (1718–87)
Verges, ——, advocate-gen.:
requisitoire of, **5**. 203–4
Vergès, Marie-Madeleine de (1762–1837), m. (1779) Antonin-Louis de Belsunce, Marquis de Castelmoron:
marriage of, **7**. 109
Vergil (Latin poet). *See* Virgil
Vergil, Polydore (ca 1470–?1555), historian:
Anglicæ historicæ libri by, **42**. 255n
Vergne, La. *See* La Vergne
Vergniaud, Pierre-Victurnien (1753–93):
execution of, **15**. 248n
Vergniaux, ——:
Debry's proposal to National Assembly attacked by, **35**. 447n
Vergy. *See* Treyssac de Vergy
Verhulst, Peter (1751–1809):
painting by, **15**. 321n
Véri, Joseph-Alphonse de (1724–99), abbé; auditor of the Rota:
(?) Bouret, subject of anecdote by, **7**. 274
Guasco excluded by, **22**. 575
(?) HW converses with, **7**. 274
(?) social relations of, in Paris, *see index entries ante* **8**. 536
Verimas:
meaning of, **1**. 36
Véritable grandeur d'âme, La. See under Magnanne, Marquis de
'Veritas':
popular signature for letters to newspapers, **42**. 500
Vermigli, Pietro Martire (1500–62), called Peter Martyr; regius professor of divinity at Oxford:
bones of, wrongly said to have been burnt at Oxford, **29**. 107

Vermilion:
Maryland bought with, from Indians, **35**. 241
Modenese duke wears, **33**. 531
Vermin:
Conway's name for Jacobites, **37**. 238
—'s partridges devoured by, **37**. 476
French, **39**. 255
Vermond, Charles-Thomas, Marie-Antoinette's accoucheur:
Hunter, Dr, might be sent on mission to, **33**. 318
Verna, La ('the Vernia'):
Paoli, Clemente, seeks retreat at, **23**. 130
Vernacci, Mme. *See* Brandi, Gaetana
Vernaccini, Abate Francesco (fl. 1783–5), Neapolitan agent in Tuscany:
news received by, **25**. 375
Spanish letters to, about Gibraltar attack, **25**. 174n
Vernaccini, Abate Ranieri (d. 1759), Spanish agent in Tuscany 1741–59:
Castellar tells, to threaten Regency with blockade, **17**. 349
Craon pressed by, for answer, **17**. 280
—'s letter from, **17**. 241–2
Gages's correspondence with, **18**. 324
Montemar sends courier to, **17**. 226
—— sent news by, **17**. 238
—— to receive pistols from, **17**. 207
Regency council receives Neapolitan memorial from, about allodials, **18**. 177
Salas communicates with, **17**. 215
Vienna Court sends packet to, by Craon, **19**. 292–3
Vernaci. *See* Del Vernaccia
Vernaci, Mme. *See* Brandi, Gaetana
Vernage, Michel-Louis (1697–1773), physician:
patients of: Hénault, **3**. 371, **4**. 13n, 50, 342; Marie Leszczyńska, **3**. 5; Toulouse, Comtesse de, **3**. 112
poisoning of Mme de Châteauroux denied by, **14**. 153n, **18**. 552n
social relations of, in Paris, **3**. 5, 124, 300
treatment by, of gout, **3**. 124–5
Vernage, Mme Michel-Louis (d. 1817):
social relations of, with Hénault, **7**. 300
Vernaroli, Ipolite, Col.:
captured at Velletri, **18**. 493
Vernet, Joseph (*or* Claude-Joseph) (1714–89), painter:
Guibert, brother-in-law of, **30**. 251n
HW buys cup and saucer decorated by, **7**. 414
Louvre has paintings by, **7**. 339
Patch studied under, **23**. 275
social relations of, with Mme Geoffrin, **7**. 283, 304, 345
wife of, **17**. 82n
Verneuil, Marquise de. *See* Balzac d'Entraigues, Catherine-Henriette de
Verney, George (1674–1728), 12th Bn Willoughby de Broke, 1711; Dean of Windsor:
HW wishes copy of sermon of, **16**. 21

Verney, Isabella (fl. 1440):
　received into fraternity of Bury Abbey, **2**. 38
Verney (later Peyto Verney), John (1738–1816),
　14th Bn Willoughby de Broke, 1752:
　family portraits of, **10**. 286
　Gordon rioters attack, **25**. 53–4, **29**. 52, **33**.
　　175
　Montagu's conversation with, **10**. 286
　—— to call at seat of, **10**. 286
　SH visited by, **12**. 221, 250
　Yeomen of the Guard may be headed by, **25**.
　　241n
Verney, Ralph (1714–91), 2d E. Verney, 1752;
　M..P.:
　petition on Buckinghamshire election brought
　　in by, after defeat there, **25**. 572n
Verney, Sir Richard (d. ca 1490):
　Compton House built by, **10**. 286n
Verney, Richard (1693–1752), 13th Bn Wil-
　loughby de Broke, 1728:
　verses by, **16**. 21
Verney family:
　portraits of, **10**. 286
Vernio, Conte di. See Bardi, Carlo
Vernon, Bn. See Venables Vernon, George
　(1708–80); Venables Vernon, Henry (1747–
　1829)
Vernon, Bns. See Fauquier, Jane Georgiana (d.
　1823)
Vernon, ——:
　dances at Robinson's ball, **37**. 115
Vernon, Miss:
　SH visited by, **12**. 252
Vernon, the Misses:
　SH visited by, **12**. 229
Vernon, Mr, of Devonshire:
　SH visited by, **12**. 251
Vernon, Mr and Mrs:
　Hertfords entertain, at dinner, at Ragley, **39**.
　　131
Vernon, Mrs:
　SH visited by, **12**. 252
　See also Poitier, Miss
'Vernon, Mrs':
　character in Pinkerton's play, **16**. 253, 256
Vernon, Hon. Caroline (1751–1829), maid of
　honour to Q. Charlotte:
　ball delayed till arrival of, **32**. 110
　biographical information about, corrected,
　　43. 145
　HW entertains, at dinner at SH, **35**. 454n
　Handel oratorio attended by, **32**. 110
　loses £200 at faro, **11**. 184–5
　Martindale tricked by, **11**. 185
　quadrille danced by, at Duc de Guines's ball,
　　32. 110
　Reynolds depicts, as 'Sabra,' **32**. 316n, 337n
Vernon, Caroline Maria (1761–1833), m. (1797)
　Robert Percy Smith; Lord Ossory's half-sister:
　Ampthill would miss, **32**. 374
　beauty of, **32**. *117*
　Bedford, Ds of, might take, abroad, **33**. 208
　—— presents, at Court, **33**. 208n

birth date of, corrected, **43**. 173
Guines's ball attended by, **32**. 117
HW advises, to go abroad, **33**. 254
HW has not seen, **33**. 200
HW last saw, 'as charming' as in 'the Three
　Vernons,' **34**. 225–6
HW's affection for, **22**. 291
HW's 'gracious message' from, **34**. 225–6
HW's sympathy for, in illness of Lady Hol-
　land, **33**. 26
HW's verses on, see 'Three Vernons, The'
HW wishes, in allegorical painting, **32**. 182
health of: delicate, **33**. 170; improved, **33**.
　267; poor, **33**. 241, 254; precarious, **33**. 265
Keppel, Mrs, entertains, at Isleworth, **33**. 481
'nymph of the first water,' **33**. 46
one of 'the Graces,' **32**. 291, 298
one of the 'nymphs of Ampthill,' **32**. 281
Ossory, Lady, and Ampthill forsaken by, **32**.
　178
Ossory, Lady, keeps, in country, **32**. 345, 347
——'s affection for, **33**. 46
——'s match-making for, **32**. 296
Reynolds includes, in 'Bedford family,' **32**.
　337, 354
to drink tea with HW, **32**. 291
unaware of Lord Ossory's activity, **33**. 482
Wakefield Lodge to be visited by, **32**. 313
Vernon, Hon. Catherine (1749–75):
　death of, **35**. 470
Vernon, Charles (1719–1810), Gen.:
　army promotions of, corrected, **43**. 319, 333
　Conway's letter delivered by, to HW in Paris,
　　39. 42
　footman tries to bar, from theatre box, **37**.
　　433
　Granby's intervention saves, from dismissal,
　　30. 192–3
　HW receives scissors from, **31**. 95
　Paris visited by, **30**. 215
　(?) social relations of, in Paris, **7**. 294, 298,
　　299, 310
Vernon, Edward (1684–1757), Adm., 1745; M.P.:
　absurdities of, **30**. 76
　American war may produce successor to, **20**.
　　449
　arrives at house in Jermyn St, **18**. 143n
　Ascanio, Père, disparages, **17**. 86
　Biblical quotation by, **35**. 29–30
　birthday of, **13**. 236, **17**. 196, 211, **21**. 171
　bust of, at Wimbledon, **9**. 120
　Cartagena failure of, **30**. 29, 35
　——'s forts taken by, **17**. 68n
　—— should not have been relinquished by,
　　17. 96
　—— to surrender to, **17**. 71n
　coast patrol organized by, **19**. 110
　Cuban conquests of, **30**. 29
　Cumberland, D. of, remembers vanished pop-
　　ularity of, **36**. 186
　disgrace of, **19**. 188, 244, 253
　election of, **17**. 220n

England protected only by 6-ship fleet of, **30.** 92

Estevenon, Mme, discusses, **17.** 200

false report of successes of, **17.** 27n

Fonnereau gets, to present petition against Rigby, **30.** 331n

forgotten in England, **17.** 390

Genoese remonstrances to be answered by England through, **35.** 63

George II receives, **18.** 143n

'Gossips-Toast, The,' song on, transcribed by Conway, **37.** 82–4

Gray congratulates, **13.** 211

HW characterizes, **14.** 51, **30.** 303n

HW expects his endurance to be tried by, **30.** 81

HW knows inside information of, about West Indies, **19.** 494

HW parodies, **17.** 76

HW's Parliamentary speech denouncing, **30.** 331n

habeas corpus suspension opposed by, **18.** 408

head of, unpopular on signs in Rochester, **30.** 29, **35.** 11

Ipswich near home of, **19.** 494n

letters to, published by him, **19.** 459, 472

Mann curious to hear about reception of, in England, **18.** 151

Martin to succeed, **19.** 188

Mathews may be succeeded by, **18.** 312

medals honouring, **13.** 226, **17.** 229n

merchant knocks down, **18.** 143

name of, removed from list of admirals, **19.** 244, 253, 459n

Newcastle's letter from, **17.** 76n

Ogle, Adm., joins with, **17.** 36n

Original Letters to an Honest Sailor published by, **19.** 459n

Ormonde's head replaced by that of, and then replaced by D. of Cumberland's on signs, **37.** 266, 272

Panama governor told by, that Q. of Spain is 'Italian madwoman,' **37.** 53

Parliamentary Address debated by, **37.** 414, 415

Parliamentary speeches of, extravagant, **30.** 303

Philipps receives letter of complaint from, about provisions, **19.** 168

places named by, **17.** 175

Porto Bello captured by, **9.** 235, **17.** 5n, **30.** 331

portrait of, on ale-house signs, **18.** 423, **19.** 255

privateers pursued by, **19.** 173

Pulteney's letter to, on Porto Bello's capture, **19.** 459

returns to England, no longer popular, **18.** 135

revered by seacaptains, but hated by army officers, **18.** 151

Rigby quarrels with, over Sudbury election, **30.** 331

Rome depreciates success of, **17.** 7

Santiago to be attacked by, **17.** 75

Some Seasonable Advice, and *A Specimen of Naked Truth* attributed to, **19.** 459n

(?) speech by, reported in *Berne Gazette,* **18.** 206

Superb dispatched by, from Cuba, **17.** 276n

Torres pursued by, at Cartagena, **17.** 71

unpopularity of, **9.** 52

unpopular with Mediterranean fleet, **18.** 312

Vernon, Henry, boasts of relationship to, **17.** 126, **20.** 305

victory of: not repeated, **17.** 466; should please George II and Sir Robert Walpole, **17.** 7; Walpole party's victory instead of, **17.** 362

Walpole, Sir Robert, and followers, disparage conquests of, **30.** 29

Walpole, Sir Robert, opposed by, **17.** 211n

Warren as absurd as, **20.** 33

Wentworth's quarrel with, **17.** 175, **18.** 143

West and East Indies may be captured because of fondness of, for global war, **37.** 249

Wilkes compared with, **23.** 8

Vernon, Elizabeth, m. (1598) Henry Wriothesley, 3d E. of Southampton:

portrait of, at Boughton House, **10.** 340

Vernon, Elizabeth (1762–1830), Lord Ossory's half-sister:

Ampthill would miss, **32.** 374

beauty of, **32.** *117*

Bedford, Ds of, may take, abroad, **33.** 208

birth date of, corrected, **43.** 173

Cowslade commends, **33.** 170

Guines's ball attended by, **32.** 117

HW has not seen, **33.** 200

HW's affection for, **32.** 291

HW's sympathy for, in illness of Lady Holland, **33.** 26

HW's verses to, see 'Three Vernons, The'

HW wishes, in allegorical painting, **32.** 182

Keppel, Mrs, entertains, at Isleworth, **33.** 481

'one of the Graces,' **32.** 291, 298

one of 'the nymphs of Ampthill,' **32.** 281

Ossory, Lady, and Ampthill forsaken by, **32.** 178, 181

Ossory, Lady, keeps, in country, **32.** 347

——'s affection for, **33.** 46

——'s match-making for, **32.** 296

to drink tea with HW, **32.** 291

Vernon, Francis (ca 1715–83), cr. (1762) Bn Orwell, (1776) Vct Orwell, (1777) E. of Shipbrook; M.P.:

painting by Van Risquet includes, **10.** 334

Thicknesse abuses, **7.** 315

Trinity College, Cambridge, attended by, **10.** 334

Vernon, George Venables. See Venables Vernon, George

Vernon, Mrs George Venables. See Fauquier, Jane Georgiana

Vernon, Lady Harriet *or* Henrietta. See Wentworth, Lady Henrietta

Vernon, Lady Henrietta (d. 1828), m. 1 (1764) Richard Grosvenor, 1st Bn Grosvenor, cr. (1784) E. Grosvenor; m. 2 (1802) George Porter (after 1819 de Hochepied), Bn de Hochepied:
ball at Chester attended by, in turban, **39.** 18
brother of, **7.** 372n
Chatterton calls, 'Lady Harriet Grosvenor, **16.** 347
coach of, has glass broken by mob, **39.** 560
Cumberland, D. of, has affair with, **23.** 165, 345n
gossip about, **4.** 310, **5.** 131
Grosvenor Sq. conducive to adultery of, **33.** 80n
HW smiles at headgear of, **38.** 509–10
husband discards, **23.** 165
Vernon, Henrietta (1760–1838), m. (1776) George Greville, 2d E. Brooke; E. of Warwick; Lord Ossory's half-sister:
Ampthill would miss, **32.** 374
beauty of, **32.** *117*
charming at Birthday, **32.** 345
fable and verses sent by, to HW, **32.** 221
Fox, Caroline, adopted by, **33.** 63
—— worries, by illness, **33.** 130n
Guines's ball attended by, **32.** 117
HW calls on, **32.** 330
HW meets, at Lady Bute's, **34.** 199
HW met, at Ampthill, **34.** 203
HW's affection for, **32.** 291
HW's good opinion of, **34.** 203
HW's sympathy for, in Lady Holland's illness, **33.** 26
HW's verses to, *see* 'Three Vernons, The'
HW wishes, in allegorical painting, **32.** 182
HW wishes to borrow Thorpe's book from, **33.** 248
Hamilton, Sir William, should be charmed with, **32.** 321
health of, prolonged recovery expected, **33.** 170
Isleworth villa of, **34.** 195, 199
Leveson Gower, Catherine, remembers, in will, **32.** 173
marriage of, pleases HW, **32.** 295–6
miscarriage of, **32.** 359
not in town, **32.** 330
not yet married, **32.** 293, 301
one of 'the Graces,' **32.** 291, 298
one of 'the nymphs of Ampthill,' **32.** 281
Ossory, Lady, and Ampthill forsaken by, **32.** 178, 181
Ossory, Lady, fond of, **33.** 46
—— to visit, **32.** 352
to drink tea with HW, **32.** 291
Warwick, E. of, gives party for, **32.** 296
wishes to see SH, **34.** 199
Vernon, Henry (fl. mid-16th cent.), of Sudbury:
Essington and Hilton manors acquired by, by marriage, **40.** 77n

Vernon, Henry (1718–65), of Hilton Park; M.P.:
at Boughton Park, **37.** 212
Bolingbroke introduces, to Duchesse du Maine, **17.** *126*
candidate for Brackley, **9.** 171n
Cotton travelled with, **18.** 342
daughter of, **11.** 184n
joke to, about 'uncle,' **17.** 126, 135, **20.** 305
marriage of, **18.** 342
money squandered by, on clothes and opera girl, **17.** 126
Paris visited by, **13.** 166, **17.** 126
Parliamentary membership of, corrected, **43.** 177, 237
relationship to Adm. Vernon claimed by, **17.** 126, **20.** 305
subscriber to Middleton's *Cicero*, **43.** 177
wagers laid by, on Cartagena's capture, **17.** 126
wife of, **6.** 364n
Vernon, Henry (1748–1814):
Craven, Bns, has adventures with, **25.** 632
—— said to be cousin of, **25.** 632
interference of, in Bns Craven's quarrel with Horace Mann II, **25.** 616
Vernon, Henry Venables. *See* Venables Vernon, Henry
Vernon, Jane (d. 1805), sister of the Hon. Caroline Vernon:
quadrille danced by, at Duc de Guines's ball, **32.** 110
Vernon, Matthew, mercer:
alleged Jacobite toasts at house of, **20.** 361
Caldecott, Borrodale, partners with, in Ludgate St, **20.** 361n
Fawcett related to, **20.** 360n, 361n
Jacobite, **20.** 361n
Murray, William, inherits estate from, in Cheshire and Derbyshire, **20.** 361n
Vernon, Richard (1726–1800), sportsman; M.P.; Lord Ossory's stepfather; 'father of the turf':
Bedford, D. of, desires place for, **30.** 232
—— visited by, at Woburn, **20.** 301
blackballed by his friends at White's, **20.** 300–1
clerk comptroller of the Green Cloth, **38.** 377
daughters of, **13.** 49n, **32.** 359
Dickinson held place for, of Surveyor of the Gardens, **38.** 377
HW jokes about racing interests of, **30.** 218
Jockey Club member, **20.** 300n
mistress accompanies, to visit Lord Montfort, **1.** 194n
news of Saltykovs conveyed to Lady Ossory by, **33.** 353
offers to live at Houghton, **28.** 93
Waldegrave, Cts, may be married to, by Ds of Bedford, **38.** 396
Vernon, William (d. 1771), Capt.:
(?) death of, **7.** 372, 398
Vernon. *See also* Venables Vernon

Vernon (France):
mutton sent from, **7**. 436
Vernon family:
HW not known by, **10**. 122
of Derbyshire, arms of, **1**. 27–8
SH praised by, **10**. 121–2
Wettenhall, Mrs, does not join, on excursion to SH, **10**. 123
Vernon's Glory:
Gossips-Toast, included in, **37**. 82n
Veroli, ——, opera singer:
sings at musical accademia, **23**. 405n
Veroli, Giacomo:
accademia by, **23**. 64n
Verona (Italy):
Barzizza succeeds Barbarigo as mayor of, **17**. 196n
Bellotto's views of, attributed to Canaletto, **23**. 298–9
Dunbar said to visit, **17**. 113
Gloucester, D. of, to leave family at, **36**. 309
Leopold to meet Joseph II at, **24**. 105
Maffei writes from, **17**. 150
Mann entertains ladies from, **18**. 286
Podestà of, has son who has affair with Bns Walpole (Cts of Orford), **17**. 196
Richecourt and Bns Walpole (Cts of Orford) to meet at, **17**. 107
seizure of, jokingly suggested, **37**. 98
visitors to: Gloucester, D. and Ds of, **24**. 314, **26**. 50, **32**. 363, **34**. 245–7; Louis XVIII, **42**. 406n; Macartney, **12**. 190n; Walpole, Bns (Cts of Orford), **17**. 107, 134, 150
Young Pretender said to visit, **17**. 113
Veronese, Paolo (1528–88), painter:
paintings by: at Escurial, **16**. 180n; at Quatre Nations, Paris, **7**. 276; sold by Francis III of Modena to K. of Poland, **19**. 314n
two pictures by, **2**. 168–9
Veronica, St:
handkerchief of, **13**. 210
Verpillier, La (France):
HW and Gray at, **13**. 181n
Verracini. *See* Veracini; Vernaccini
Verrazzano, Neri da' (1683–1745), senator, 1736:
Electress's executor, **18**. 168
Verre, La. *See* La Verre
Verres, Gaius *or* Caius (d. 43 B.C.), Roman magistrate:
Catherine II's collection resembles loot of, **34**. 217
Clive compared with, **23**. 530
future imitator of, will despoil Henley bridge, **33**. 524
Knowles compared with, **37**. 432
Verrio, Antonio (ca 1639–1707), painter:
Marriot, Mrs, painted by, as a Fury, **20**. 212
paintings by, at Burghley House, **10**. 345, 346
Versailles:
album of portraits of Court ladies of, annotated by HW, **43**. 106

American-French treaty of alliance signed at, **24**. 362
apartment at, assigned to Mme Victoire, **3**. 286
ball at: **6**. 162, **7**. 343; Houdetot's indiscretion at, punished by Marie-Antoinette, **39**. 244n
balloon ascent at, **25**. 527n, **39**. 419n
bal paré at, **32**. 254–6
Beauvau addressed from, about Cholmondeley's passport, **22**. 211
Berrys to visit, **11**. 122n
bread riot at gates of, **24**. 106
Brest courier brings bad naval news to, **25**. 286n
Breton parliament attends Louis XV at, **38**. 521
Brissac is shot at, **5**. 107n
Broglie and royalists encamped before, **11**. 41
Bureau des Interprètes at, HW to send *Historic Doubts* to, for Voltaire, **41**. 146
cabinet of, upholds William Pitt II, **25**. 485
château of, disappoints HW, **13**. 167–8
Chaville near, **5**. 363
Choiseul, Duchesse de, writes from, **41**. 108
Clement XIV's treatment of threats from, **23**. 221
council of: **4**. 458; Tencin urges cause of Young Pretender at, **18**. 379n
Court absent from, **1**. 96
—— at, **5**. 71, **6**. 478
—— of: carts Clement XIII, **23**. 32; Joseph II perhaps rebuffed by, **24**. 278; should wait for end of campaign before making peace, **21**. 504–5; willing to make peace, **21**. 360; *see also* France: Court of
—— removes to, **7**. 287
—— to go to, **5**. 84
Deane openly countenanced at, **24**. 253
Dillon a favourite at, **35**. 369
Dillons appeal to Louis XV at, **3**. 33
Du Barry, Mme, eclipses beauties and duchesses of, **23**. 75
Du Châtelet's conduct may offend, **23**. 127
Du Deffand, Mme, proposes to sup at, **4**. 362, **6**. 191
Dunn in favour at, **22**. 7
earthquake felt at, **20**. 531n
Egmont, Mme d', gives balls at, **38**. 505
Ellis a favourite at, **35**. 569
England might have been captured and sent to, **21**. 300
English Court lacks Herculaneum and, for sumptuous publications, **14**. 123
English-French naval disarmament pact concluded at, **24**. 299n
English people fashionable at, **35**. 369
envoys at, **5**. 7
epigrams exhaled at, **25**. 496
festivities at, for Ps of Piedmont's wedding, **39**. 256

[Versailles, *continued*]

foreign ambassadors' wives allowed privileges of duchesses at, **20.** 144n

Fort l'Évêque close to, **21.** 473

fountains at, **11.** 120, **13.** 168

Fox, C. J., has partisans at, **25.** 495

Franklin reads English newspapers at, **33.** 30–1

—— received at, as ambassador, **28.** 373

French cardinals send an express to, protesting against Cavalchini's appointment, **21.** 224

garden at, designed for a 'great child,' **13.** 168

gendarmes at, the only martyrs for Louis XVI, **39.** 486

Genoese doge and senate go to, **19.** 312–13, **21.** 386

Gloucester, D. and Ds of, refuse Louis XVI's invitation to, **36.** 114n

gout specialist at, **6.** 197

guard at, **34.** 67n

guards at, die of heat, **20.** 166

Guibert's *Connétable de Bourbon* to be given at, **6.** 215

Guines writes from, **41.** 423

HW and Lady Mary Coke attend theatre at, **31.** 182

HW embarrassed by his letter being exhibited at, **41.** 33, 34

HW has not yet visited, **13.** 165

HW need not go to, to meet Choiseul, **41.** 75

HW prevented by gout from going to, **10.** 180

HW sees Beast of Gévaudan at, **22.** 289n, **31.** 52, 56, 61

HW sees Mme du Barry at, **11.** 294

HW's name for SH, **10.** 297

HW's thanks to Mme de Choiseul for 'Sévigné' letter would cause ridicule at, **31.** 119

HW visits, for presentation at Court, **31.** 52, 56

HW wishes to see foliage at, **10.** 201

Hertford, Cts of, to be presented at Court at, **38.** 220

—— to visit, **38.** 236

Hertford, E. of, awaits business from, **38.** 304

—— expected by Wilkes to hear at, about Webb's indictment, **38.** 297

——'s negotiations at, **38.** 269

——'s post-chaise overturns when coming from, **38.** 387

—— to attend wife to, for her presentation, **38.** 236

—— to visit, **38.** 236, 304

Hervey, Bp, declines to go to, as peace delegate, **25.** 454

Holdernesse, Cts of, presented at Court at, **38.** 252

Holland, Bn, to visit, **38.** 314

Hunter, Dr, might go on mission to, **33.** 318

inn at, *see* Belle Image

La Chalotais's trial at, **23.** 206

La Tournelle, Mme de, has apartment at, **18.** 103n

Le Nôtre designs park at, **28.** 30n

lit de justice at, **4.** 183–4, 429, 493, **5.** 60, 61, 66, **8.** 168

Louis XIV requests copy of Correggio Madonna for, **18.** 338n

Louis XV attends council at, after assassination attempt, **21.** 44n

——, Comtesse du Barry, and Maupeou almost alone at, **23.** 298

Louis XV has young girls kept at, **38.** 350

—— orders registers of parliament of Paris sent to, **31.** 109

——'s return to, depends on partridges at Compiègne, **38.** 404

—— stabbed at, **14.** 152n

Louis XVI and Marie-Antoinette leave, for Tuileries, **34.** 72n

Louis XVI and Marie-Antoinette married at, **4.** 406–7

Louis XVI and Marie-Antoinette might flee to England from, **39.** 468

Louis XVI besieged at, by mob, **24.** 112

——'s ministers at, **20.** 67

Luxembourg, Mme de, deprived of lodging at, **5.** 129

machine at Marly conveys water to, **21.** 354n

Marie-Antoinette carried to, after attempted escape, **12.** 120

——'s accouchement expected at, **7.** 90

Marigny's house at, with unhung royal collection of pictures, **39.** 15, 201

massacre at, **12.** 28n, **15.** 237n

Maurepas dies at, **25.** 212n

menagerie at, visited by HW, **7.** 334

ministers' wives usually at, **38.** 246

Mirepoix, Mme de, arrives at, **20.** 280n

—— finds it unnecessary to go to, **5.** 51

—— has no tabouret at, **20.** 144

—— to take Mrs Damer to spectacles at, **42.** 230

Morphy, Mlle, lodged at, **35.** 173

news report from, **19.** 259

paintings at, over-varnished, **35.** 425

paintings from Chartreuse to be taken to, **35.** 430

'parade and poverty' at, **7.** 357, **35.** 112

Paris gossip soon heard at, **38.** 305

parliamentary deputation waits on Louis XV at, **20.** 293n

parliament of Paris meets at, **8.** 168

parliament of Paris to compromise with, **23.** 265

peace negotiations at, end in deadlock, **19.** 271n

peace of, *see* Versailles, Treaty of

Petit Trianon at, **6.** 57, 60, **7.** 334

play at, for Mme Clotilde's wedding, **39.** 256

Pompadour, Mme, de, interrupts diversions of, by her illness, **38.** 338

Potter gets passport renewed at, **21.** 557n

Poussin paintings surpassed in size only by those at, **21.** 209

presentations at, require forms not easily submitted to, by English and Germans, 38. 252
pride and meanness of, 23. 142
Queen's ante-chamber at, displays Beast of Gévaudan, 31. 52, 56, 61
Raphaels and other paintings at, neglected, 35. 344
Richelieu sends courier to, for aid, 23. 329
—— to be in charge of diversions at, 38. 465
riot at, 6. 184
Royal Chapel at: 1. 146; French cardinal talks of, 13. 209; HW sees royal family at Mass at, 10. 291–2
St-Esprit, Ordre du, has ceremony at, 6. 127
St-Simon's *Mémoires* locked up in Dépôt des Papiers at, 34. 29
theatre at: Guibert's *Connétable de Bourbon* to be acted at, 32. 257; HW at, 7. 334, 344, 31. 182; marvellous, 4. 407
the heaven of French ministers, 33. 273
'tottering roof' of, 35. 9
Townshend, Hon. Charles, may be playing tricks at, 38. 380
treasures from the Louvre taken to, 14. 145
Trianon at, *see under* Trianon
victims massacred at, 12. 28n
(?) view of, in Ferdinand's portrait of Mme de Maintenon, 10. 294
Villars, Duchesse de, dies at, 5. 106n
Viry, Mme de, dazzles, 41. 343
visitors to: Aiguillon, 5. 165; Aiguillon, Duchesse d', 3. 65; Ailesbury, Cts of, 6. 127, 148; Artois, Comte d' (Charles X), 6. 450, 7. 29; Barthélemy, 4. 6, 9, 169; Beauvau, 4. 404, 5. 210, 256, 350, 6. 434, 7. 219–20; Beauvau, Princesse de, 4. 404, 5. 210, 256; Bourbon, Duc and Duchesse de, 7. 29; Bourbon-Busset, Comtesse de, 5. 357; Choiseul, Duc de, 4. 86, 253, 360, 383, 6. 127, 162, 383, 35. 422, 42. 194; Choiseul, Duchesse de, 4. 6, 173, 174, 190, 308, 310–11, 324, 335, 337, 360, 360–1, 380, 404, 486, 488; Cholmondeley, Mrs, 4. 402, 10. 291–2; Coke, Lady Mary, 7. 343, 39. 256; Conway, 6. 127, 148; Craufurd, 5. 285; Damer, Mrs, 6. 127, 148; Deane, Silas, 24. 253n, 254n, 28. 277; Du Châtelet, 5. 165; Du Deffand, Mme, 3. 17, 27, 29, 50, 4. 245, 404, 5. 78, 6. 48, 192; Forcalquier, Mme de, 5. 357; Franklin, 6. 383, 28. 373; Gibbon, 6. 445; Gramont, Duchesse de, 4. 195; Grave, 10. 291–2; Guines, 6. 274, 277, 283, 284, 290; HW, 7. 266, 295, 297, 298, 316, 330, 334, 343, 344, 10. 291–2, 39. 12–14, 44; Harcourt, Earl, 5. 74; Hart, Mrs, 10. 291–2; Hertford, E. of, 38. 483, 571; Holland, Bn, 38. 314; Joseph II, 6. 435–6, 443; La Fayette, 7. 113; Louis XV, 3. 122, 292, 4. 169, 196, 458, 5. 36, 84; Louis XVI, 6. 54, 60, 67, 195, 277, 38. 218; Lucan, Bns, 6. 349; Luxembourg, Mme de, 3. 376, 6. 192; Marchais, 6. 49, 56; Marchais, Mme de, 6. 56, 247; Marie-Antoinette, 38. 218; Maximilian, Archduke, 6. 156; Miller,

5. 74; Mirepoix, Mme de, 5. 49, 51, 198, 260, 421, 6. 191, 192, 38. 237; Monin, 38. 314; Necker, 11. 26, 27; Paoli, 23. 31; Pope, Mrs, 9. 189; Quane, Mrs, 9. 189; Richmond, Ds of, 39. 44; Richmond, D. of, 6. 460; Roland, Mme, 10. 211; St-Florentin, 38. 483; Scheffer, 5. 36; Sévigné, Mme de, 39. 13n; Stanhope, Lady Harriet, 6. 127; Swedish royalty, 5. 36; Vernage, 3. 5
Voltaire wishes to visit, 7. 21
waterworks at, 32. 383
Versailles, Treaty of:
Colloredo makes excuses for, 20. 568n
completion and terms of, 20. 565, 570, 578, 582, 21. 229
France and Austria renew Treaty of Westphalia with, 21. 96n
France guaranteed Bavarian and Württemberg troops by, 21. 147n
French try to modify, about Irish linens, 39. 439–40
Louis XV bound by, to guarantee and defend territories of Maria Theresa, 21. 229n
Russia to accede to, 21. 53n
signing of, 20. 589n
'Vers à sa Majesté Louis XVI sur l'édit du 31 mai 1774.' *See under* La Harpe, Jean-François de
'Vers de M. de Voltaire à Mme la Marquise du Deffand.' *See* Voltaire: Lullin, Mme, verses to, by
Verse; verses:
alliterative prose worse than alliteration in, 31. 350
blank: HW dislikes, 31. 211; HW jokes about Hannah More's fondness for, 31. 348; learning necessary for, 31. 220; More, Hannah, likes, 31. 211; needs high colouring to be distinguished from prose, 31. 219–20
by 'persons of honour' in 'the last age,' criticized by Hannah More, 31. 273–4
distichs, epigram on Jadot's complaint to Lami about length of, for Charles VI's catafalque, 30. 9
HW's criticism of Lady Mary Coke's, sent to him, 31. 404–5
Jacobite: 30. 125–6; criticized by HW, 30. 127
See also Bout rimé; Poetry
'Verses on his Grotto.' *See under* Pope, Alexander
'Verses Sent to Lady Charles Spencer,' by HW: (?) HW reads, to Montagu, 43. 131
Vershauffen, ——, Papal antiquary:
appointment of, 20. 104n
statue for Lord Leicester not released by, 20. 104n
Verskovis, James Francis (d. ca 1750), Flemish carver:
HW employs, 19. 420–1
HW's arms carved by, 19. 421n
returns to Rome to carve for the English, 19. 421

Versoix (France):
Choiseul tries to rival Geneva's commerce by that of, 3. 392–3, 23. 130n
Voltaire's mail comes by way of, 41. 151
——'s verses on, 4. 396–7
Vers présentée à Sa Majesté le Roi de Suède. See under Crussol de Florensac, Anne-Charlotte de, Duchesse d'Aiguillon
Verten. *See* Verton
Verton, Philippe-Louis de (b. 1707):
(?) HW replaced by, at cavagnole, 5. 101
(?) social relations of, with Mme du Deffand, 5. 101
Vertot, René-Aubert de (1655–1735), abbé; historian:
Ambassades de Messieurs de Noailles en Angleterre by, 1. 186–8, 192
English ministerial changes resemble *Révolutions* of, 19. 213, 22. 158, 169
French Revolution would be enjoyed by, 31. 329
HW praises Hannah More's reflections on, 31. 332
HW reads *Histoire de la conjuration de Portugal* by, 19. 213n, 43. 91
Histoire des chevaliers hospitaliers de St Jean de Jérusalem, L,' by: Du Deffand, Mme, comments on, 5. 6, 17; Du Deffand, Mme, inquires about, 4. 482; Du Deffand, Mme, owns, 8. 34; Du Deffand, Mme, unable to finish, 5. 6, 77; HW comments on, 4. 478–9, 5. 12; HW likes, 5. 77, 78; HW recommends, 4. 478–9, 482, 492
Histoire des révolutions . . . de la République romaine by: Du Deffand, Mme, owns, 8. 35n; HW has read, 4. 479, 43. 91; Linguet's continuation of, 4. 488n
More, Hannah, discusses, 31. 329
piety of, 31. 329
revolutions in Sweden by, owned by HW, 43. 91
state convulsions the subjects of, 31. 329
Vertue, ——, m. —— Chandler; George Vertue's sister:
servant of, repeats Vertue's story of Greenwich Palace, 16. 74–5
Vertue, George (1684–1756), engraver and antiquary:
account by, of crosses, 15. 203
Anecdotes of Painting based on notes of, 31. 428, 40. 288
——'s faults not to be blamed on, 40. 309, 354
Bacon's monument described by, 1. 25
Baker's likeness drawn by, as commission, 2. 144, 352, 361
benefit tickets for Eva 'Violette' designed by, 20. 74n
Buckingham House, drawings at, traced by, on oil paper, 41. 320n
candour of, 16. 166
catalogue of Charles I's collection prepared by, 1. 173n, 16. 290n
cautious, 2. 350

Cavallini said by, to have decorated Edward the Confessor's chapel, 42. 67
Charles VI's head, sketched, found by HW in MSS of, at SH, 42. 217
Chatterton calls, ignorant of Saxon history, 16. 115
Chaucer twice engraved by, 14. 109, 16. 134
copies identified by, 15. 95n
copies made by, of paintings: of Lady Arabella Stuart, 15. 160, 209; of Mary Q. of Scots, 15. 190n, 16. 284n; of Philip II and Mary I, 9. 124
Cromwell's funeral described in notes by, 42. 127
'Dance of Death' at Basel doubted by, 40. 254
Danvers's name mistaken by, 1. 7
Description of the Works of . . . Hollar by: Hollar adequately treated in, 16. 68; readers of, will be grateful that HW revised Vertue's MSS, 16. 142
drawings by: of crosses, 15. 203; of Greenwich Palace, 16. 75; of painting in Hungerford Chapel, Salisbury, 16. 156; of Richmond Palace, 16. 73–4, 78–9; owned by HW, 2. 292n
Ducarel's information from, about painting of Henry VII's marriage, 40. 215–16, 219, 222
engravings by: 2. 341n, 9. 114n, 197n, 15. 96n; of Bess of Hardwick, 42. 313–14; of Chaucer, 14 109; of Chaucer and Lydgate, 16. 134; of Flamsteed, 2. 352; of Henry VII and his family, 2. 323; of Lady Jane Grey, 32. 353n; of Middleton, 15. 303; of Q. Elizabeth's visit to Hunsdon, 9. 101; of Spence, 14. 14n; of Strype, 2. 352; of Warham, 1. 81
engravings by Faber and, 9. 114n
'Explanations of Historic Prints' by, 42. 459n
eyes of, failed in old age, 42. 314
Freeman, at desire of, brings Van Voerst engraving to Society of Antiquaries, 16. 166
Gabburri's collection described by, in note-books, 35. 47n
Graham an acquaintance of, 29. 288n
Gravelot's drawings discussed by, 2. 239–40
HW cannot find account of Thornhill in MSS of, 41. 17–18, 76
HW examines MS catalogue of, without finding its origins, 42. 354
HW labels information from, which may be doubtful, 41. 97
HW merely saved what had been collected by, 42. 302
HW not answerable for everything alleged by, 2. 322, 324
HW owns copy by, of Margaret, Q. of Scotland's portrait, 40. 365
HW's *Anecdotes of Painting* renders compilations of, interesting and amusing, 38. 151
HW's information about artists comes from note-books of, 42. 206

HW's mistake about Atkyns's book may be due to, **16.** 158

HW's sponsor at Society of Antiquaries, **13.** 28n

HW's use of researches of, **34.** 244

Harleian collections of, **28.** 180n

head and tail-pieces to Waller's works designed by, **17.** 358n

Heads of Illustrious Persons of Great Britain, The, by, **1.** 81, 171, 207

historical prints and map of London by, published by Society of Antiquaries, **2.** 8, 11, **16.** 166

Holbein portrait thought by, to be Mary Tudor, **40.** 365

Johnson, Maurice, receives letter from, **43.** 219

Laniere, Nicholas, discussed by, **1.** 25

manuscripts of: **1.** 381, 383, 384, **15.** 72, 198, 29. 279, **43.** 310; confused and in diminutive handwriting, **16.** 299; forty years spent in collecting, **16.** 51; Gray answers HW's queries about, **14.** 108–16; HW buys, **9.** 366, **13.** 33, **16.** 26; HW indexes, three times, **10.** 307; HW indexes, twice, **41.** 18; HW in no hurry for, **16.** 274; HW invites Pinkerton to search, **16.** 299; HW's editing of, for *Anecdotes of Painting*, **16.** 29, 36, 46, 156; large quantity of, **16.** 41; on coins, **12.** 256n; provide data on painters from Henry VIII's time, **16.** 37; reveal little architectural history, **16.** 27; search for, **16.** 134; used by HW for *Anecdotes of Painting*, **13.** 34

Maratti's having painted Roscommon probably based on note by, **42.** 159

Mary, Q. of Scots's portrait at Chiswick doubted by, though he engraved it, **42.** 321

Mary Tudor's portrait engraved by, **40.** 365

Medals, Coins, Great Seals, Impressions from the Works of Thomas Simon by: readers of, will be grateful that HW revised Vertue's MSS, **16.** 142; Simon, Abraham and Thomas, mentioned in, **40.** 238; Simons and Mestrell mentioned in, **16.** 159; painter's bill said to have been transcribed by, **16.** 133

miniature engraved by, **15.** 112

Northumberland House gateway ascribed by, to Christmas, **41.** 106

notebook of, **14.** 107

Oliver's picture of Mary, Q. of Scots, doubted by, though he engraved it, **42.** 320

painter's bill copied by, **42.** 3n

Perrot portrait at Pakington's noticed by, **40.** 271

Petitot's portrait of Ds of Richmond discussed by, **1.** 24

picture list may have been extracted by, from Fairfax's, **42.** 354

print and water-colour by, of Henry VII and family, **43.** 76

Richard III and his Queen drawn by, **41.** 132

Richard III engraved by, for Rapin's history, **41.** 132

Roman Catholicism of, rigid, **14.** 107

Scotland probably not visited by, **16.** 51

'sedulous and faithful,' **2.** 300

servant of, repeats tale of Greenwich Palace's founding, **16.** 74–5, 81

sister of, **16.** 74

'Surrey Wonder' drawn by, attributed to Hogarth, **16.** 173

thoroughness of, **1.** 62

Van der Gucht 'master' of, **16.** 78n

Van Voerst's engraving of Charles I and Henrietta Maria retouched by, **16.** 166

verses sought by, in MSS, **16.** 134

Vogelsanck mentioned in notes by, **15.** 143

wife of, **14.** 120n

Wimbledon's portrait mentioned by, **40.** 142

Zincke's miniature of Sir Robert Walpole engraved by, for *Ædes Walpolianæ*, **42.** 249n

Vertue, Mrs George. *See* Evans, Margaret

Vertue, James (fl. 1726–51), engraver:

'Surrey Wonder' engraved by, attributed to Hogarth, **16.** 173

Vertumnus:

and Pomona, **35.** 459

Chudleigh, Elizabeth, seems to be kept by, **35.** 301

Vertus, Comtesse de. *See* Charette de Montebert, Marie-Madeleine-Élisabeth

Verulam, Bn. *See* Bacon, Sir Francis

'Verus':

letter-writer's nom-de-plume, **42.** 500

Vervant, Marquis de. *See* St-Hermine, Henri-René-Louis de

Veryard, Ellis:

Account of Divers Choice Remarks by, describes epitaph, **41.** 309

Verzenay (France):

Gray and HW pass through, **13.** 180n

Vesci, De. *See* De Vesci

Vescovich, Count Antonio, Dalmatian leader:

Mann confers commission on, **25.** 249

Vesey, Agmondesham (d. 1785), Irish M.P.:

Burke nominates, for Club, **30.** 51n

Clarges St house left by, to widow, **31.** 230n

death of, **31.** 230

(?) HW bored by, **30.** 51

HW's intelligence about Money Bill confirmed by, **38.** 138

HW to give private party for, **42.** 86

health of, **31.** 222–3

mistress's legacy from, **31.** 230n

Stephens, friend of, **23.** 423n

SH visited by, **31.** 206, 215–16

(?) Walpole, Mr and Mrs, entertained by, **12.** 270n

wife of, **10.** 16n, **29.** 36n

Vesey, Mrs Agmondesham. *See* Vesey, Elizabeth

Vesey, Elizabeth (ca 1715–91), m. 1 William Handcock; m. 2 (before 1746) Agmondesham Vesey:

bluestocking parties of: 31. 213–15, 227–8, 33. 269; spoiled by too many great ladies, 31. 228, 243

carriage can be afforded by, 31. 230n

characteristics of: benevolent, 31. 228, 234, 247, 249, 258; forgetful, 31. 243; impetuous, 31. 234; sweet-tempered, 31. 228; unpunctual, 31. 216

Clarges St residence of, 31. 222, 223, 247, 255, 336

deafness of, 29. 356, 31. 222

death of, desirable, 31. 345

HW attends assembly of, 35. 495

HW enlisted in 'academy' of, 32. 229–30

HW, Hannah More, and Elizabeth Carter have regular 'assignations' at house of, 31. 242–3

HW hears from, about prices of Irish paintings, 10. 16

HW inquired after by, 39. 48

HW inquires about husband's provision for, 31. 230

HW inquires for, 31. 228, 230, 231

HW invites, to SH, 42. 99

HW might visit, 31. 235

HW misses Hannah More at house of, 31. 244

HW's attentions to, 31. 249

HW's correspondence with, 42. 99

HW to give private party for, 42. 86

HW to invite, to SH, 31. 232

HW visited by, with Hannah More, 31. 242n

HW 'will never disobey,' 31. 214

HW wishes to visit, 31. 233

Hamilton, Mary, sends Spectator portrait to, as resemblance to HW, 31. 256

Handcock, Mrs, attends, 31. 252

Harcourt finds HW in circle of, 29. 356

health of: deafness, 29. 356, 31. 222; weakness, 31. 222

Hertford's morning visitor, at Dublin, 39. 48

houses of, in Bolton Row and Clarges St, 32. 229n

Jones, Sir William, presented by, to HW, 29. 36

Lucan, Lady, imitates bluestocking parties of, 29. 104

Margate may be visited by, 33. 438

mental decay of, 31. 249, 252, 255, 257–8, 277, 336, 345

Miller, Mrs, as sophisticated as, 39. 241

Montagu, Mrs, one of chief stars at parties of, 33. 269

More, Hannah, compared with, 31. 247

—— concerned for, 31. 266

—— dedicates Bas Bleu to, 31. 212n, 33. 512n

—— loves, 31. 249–50

Newhaven, Lady, sarcastically informed by, at Tunbridge Wells, 33. 127

niece of, 31. 252

social relations of, with: Burke, Edmund, 31. 214, 242; Burke, Richard, 31. 214, 33. 466; Burney, Frances, 31. 247; Carter, Elizabeth, 31. 242–3; Garrick, Mrs, 31. 214; Gunning, Elizabeth, 31. 215; HW, 31. 210, 213, 214–15, 223, 228, 242–3, 247, 336, 33. 466; Hamilton, Mary, 31. 214–25; Jenyns, Soame, 31. 213; Montagu, Mrs Elizabeth, 31. 215; More, Hannah, 31. 210, 213, 214, 228, 242–3, 244; Oglethorpe, 31. 214; Reynolds, Sir Joshua, 33. 466; Townshend, Vcts, 31. 228; (?) Walpole, Mr and Mrs, 12. 270n; Walsingham, Mrs, 31. 214

'sounded trumpet' in quarrel between Dr Johnson and Mrs Montagu, 29. 115

SH visited by, 31. 206, 215–16

'Weesey, Mrs,' 32. 229

Vesey, Maj. George (after 1754–ca ?1793):

reports of Mrs Vesey's mental decay confirmed by, 31. 252

(?) SH visited by, 12. 237

Vesey, Mrs, aided by, 31. 230n

Vesey, Sir John Denny (ca 1709–61), 2d Bt; cr. (1750) Bn Knapton; M.P.:

peerage granted to, 20. 136

Vesey, Thomas (d. 1804), cr. (1776) Vct De Vesci:

SH visited by, 12. 227

Vesey, Mrs Thomas. See Brooke, Selina Elizabeth

Vesoul (France):

explosion near, 11. 52n

Vespa, Giuseppe (1727–1804), cr. (1802) Freiherr von Vespa; Court physician to Maria Louisa of Tuscany:

Leopold and Maria Louisa accompanied by, 23. 220

Maria Louisa may choose, as physician, 22. 460

—— sends for, to Vienna, 24. 240n

Vespasian (Titus Flavius Sabinus Vespasianus) (A.D. 9–79), Roman Emperor 69–79:

bust of: 15. 12, 35. 217, 37. 111; bill of lading for, 26. 6; bill of lading for pedestal of, 21. 521, 533, 538; bought at Ottoboni's sale, 13. 232–3, 15. 12, 35. 217, 37. 111; Caligula's bust superior to, 22. 523; casing expense for, 26. 4; considered the fourth or fifth best bust in Rome, 22. 523; HW hopes that Spaniards do not capture ship carrying pedestal for, 21. 559; HW likes pedestal for, 22. 17–18, 25; HW's eagle confronts, 19. 420, 21. 461; HW seeks altar as pedestal for, 21. 461, 471, 514; HW wishes to know price of pedestal for, 22. 9; large, 21. 471; Mann fears that HW does not like pedestal for, 22. 20; Mann seeks altar for pedestal for, 21. 470, 482, 512; Mann surprised to hear that pedestal for, has not arrived, 22. 6; Parker sends, 26. 4; pedestal for, approved by HW, 21. 525; pedestal for, being repaired by workmen, 21. 521; pedestal for, in same

ship with Hyde's vases, **22**. 13; pedestal for, on shipboard awaiting convoy, **21**. 524; price of, **43**. 262
son of, **15**. 12n
Vespasiano, Carlo, (?) abbé:
(?) HW hears reading by, of Italian sonnets, **7**. 264
Vespers:
at St-Cyr, **10**. 293
Vespucci, Amerigo (1415–1512), Italian navigator:
Florentine theatre opens with show about return of, from conquest of America, **24**. 514
Vessel. *See* Ship
Vest; vests:
ducal, Venetian senate wears, purple, **17**. 75n
Jonzac, Mme de, sends, to HW, **4**. 24
See also Waistcoat
'Vesta, Temple of':
HW's name for Anne Pitt's house, **24**. 15
Vestal, English frigate:
Mercury captured by, **25**. 91n
Vestal or *La Vestale*, French ship:
Bellona brings, into Portsmouth from Martinique, **21**. 277n
Vilaine entrance defended by, **21**. 351
Vestal virgin; vestal virgins:
tea-makers in white habits of, **32**. 115
urn of, **26**. 8
Vestibule:
at the Vyne, **35**. 642
'Vestiges':
Bromfield's hints about, **40**. 316
'Vestimento':
Scarlatti, Signorita, has, **17**. 53
Vestment; vestments, ecclesiastical:
discovered in D. of Cumberland's baggage, **19**. 242
embroidered, Mann hopes to exchange, for Correggio picture, **17**. 199
Vestr'Allard. *See* Vestris, Marie-Jean-Augustin
Vestris, Mme Angiolo. *See* Gourgaud, Françoise-Rose
Vestris, Gaetano Apolline Baldassare (1729–1808), dancer:
benefit for, delays Parliamentary business, **29**. 109
'Grand Entertainment' by, at Haymarket, fails, **39**. 381–2
HW lacks agility of, **39**. 434
HW suggests, as dancing teacher to Lady Anne Fitzpatrick, **33**. 268
HW supposes print of, teaching HW to dance, **33**. 282
name of, corrected, **43**. 290
Paris opera left by, for Stuttgart, **38**. 483
public attention absorbed by, **35**. 381
'reigning bubble' in England, **25**. 134
son of, **11**. 218n
Storer's visit does not make HW a disciple of, **35**. 359
trial of Lord George Gordon may obliterate, **29**. 102

vogue of, **29**. 114, 122, 283
wife of, **5**. 154n, **28**. 142n
Vestris, Mme Gaetano Apolline Baldassare. *See* Heinel, Anne-Frédérique
Vestris, Maria Teresa Francesca (1726–1808), actress:
biographical information about, **43**. 265
Walpole, Horatio (1723–1809), described by, **20**. 22
Vestris, Marie-Jean-Augustin (1760–1842), called Vestr'Allard; dancer:
Allegranti applauded more than, **25**. 243
benefit for, better attended than opera for hurricane-sufferers, **25**. 134
dancing of, at opera house in London, **11**. 218
'Grand Entertainment' by, at Haymarket, fails, **39**. 381–2
HW sees performance of, **33**. 271
HW the last, **33**. 285
HW will see, later, **33**. 257–8
'reigning bubble' of London, **25**. 134
Ricimero performance of, praised, **33**. 254–5
successful in London, **29**. 102n
'Vesuve, Comte de':
Mann may be given title of, **18**. 484
Vesuvius, Mt, near Naples:
Bute climbs, **23**. 91n
English politics compared to, **22**. 567
English weather worthy of, **35**. 415
eruption(s) of: **28**. 475, **31**. 279, **35**. 436–7; Damer, Mrs, misses, **7**. 175–6; **39**. 339; HW surprised that Mann does not mention, **24**. 515; Hamilton announces, **33**. 509; Hamilton describes, **23**. 339n, **24**. 529, 541, **26**. 46; Herculaneum buried by, **13**. 222; sketch of, sent to HW by Mann, **24**. 514, 520, 541
HW compares Frederick II and Joseph II to, **24**. 38
HW lives as if at the foot of, **33**. 106
HW to subscribe to Hamilton's work on, **35**. 427
Hamilton, Sir William, burnt by, to a cinder, **23**. 339
—— not to dive into caverns of, **35**. 415
—— should send, to England, **35**. 408
lava of, like chalk eruptions in HW's hand, **33**. 325
'out of humour,' **22**. 422
Spencer, Lord and Lady, ascend, **33**. 509
upsetting the world, **34**. 2
Veteran, English ship:
Nugent, captain of, **12**. 82n
Vettura (carriage *or* fly):
slow conveyance, **25**. 677
Veuve de Malabar, La. See under Lemierre, Antoine-Marin
Via de' Banchi. *See under* Banchi
Via de' Bardi. *See under* Bardi
Via de' Ginori. *See under* Ginori
Via del Giardino. *See under* Giardino
Via de' Renai. *See under* Renai
Via de' Rondinelli. *See under* Rondinelli
Viaggiatori felici, I. See under Anfossi, Pasquale

Viaggiatori ridicoli tornati in Italia, I. See under Guglielmi, Pietro
Vial, ——, maître d'hôtel:
    Mme du Deffand's receipt from, **22.** 42
Via Larga, at Florence:
    Botta reviews troops in, **21.** 179
Viale, ——, Genoese agent:
    Theodore of Corsica's assassination to be arranged by, **18.** 187n
Vialis, Sieur de:
    Gracieuse commanded by, **24.** 397n
Vianc, Mme, painter. *See* Rebout, Marie-Thérèse
Viar. *See* Wiart
Viareggio (Italy):
    Montemar visits, **18.** 59
Viaticum:
    Marie Leszczyńska receives, **30.** 219
    Voisins receives, **41.** 17
    York, Cardinal administers: to Old Pretender, **21.** 390; to Young Pretender, **25.** 627
    See also Unction, extreme
Vibraye, Comte de. *See* Hurault, Louis
Vibraye, Marquis de. *See* Hurault, Louis (1733–1802); Hurault, Paul-Maximilien (1701–71)
Vibraye, Vicomte de. *See* Hurault, Charles-François
Vic, Louis-Antoine de (d. 1805)
    (?) Caraman, Comte and Comtesse de, recommend, **6.** 29, 34
    (?) Du Deffand, Mme, does not know, **6.** 34
    (?) —— gives letter of introduction to HW to, **6.** 29, 34
    (?) —— sends parcel to HW by, **6.** 29, 34
Vic, Mme Louis-Antoine:
    (?) Caraman, Comte and Comtesse de, recommend, **6.** 28, 32, 34
    (?) Du Deffand, Mme, does not know, **6.** 28, 32, 34
    (?) —— sends parcel to HW by, **6.** 28, 32, 34
'Vicar of Bray':
    HW to be ready to imitate, **33.** 339
    Mason quotes, **29.** 132
Vicar of the Conclave, at Rome. *See* Colonna, Marcantonio
Vicars, Robert, Lt:
    captured at Velletri, **18.** 492
Vice; vices:
    HW has no regard for, **33.** 479
    'orthodox' are drinking and avarice, **20.** 134
Vice-Admiralty Court:
    at Gibraltar, **21.** 273
Vice-chamberlain:
    Cantelupe is, **38.** 143
    Finch, Hon. William, is, **17.** 468n, **19.** 389n
    —— succeeds Lord Sidney Beauclerk as, **17.** 493–4
    Stuart Mackenzie may become, **21.** 452
    to Q. Charlotte, Charles Fitzroy becomes, **23.** 66
    Villiers succeeds Hon. William Finch as, **22.** 311

See also Robinson, Thomas (1738–86), 2d Bn Grantham
'Vice-chancelier, Le,' *See* Hue de Miromesnil, Armand-Thomas (1723–96); Maupeou, René-Charles de (1688–1775)
Vice-Chancellor of Cambridge; of Oxford. *See under* Cambridge University; Oxford University
Vice-chancellorship of Santa Chiesa, at Rome:
    Archinto receives, **20.** 590
    Benedict XIV appoints Colonna to, **20.** 589
    Old Pretender wishes son to have, **20.** 589–90, **21.** 8
Vice-legate:
    at Avignon, *see* Acquaviva, Pasquale
    at Bologna, *see* Molinari, Giovanni Carlo
Vicentino, Valerio (Valerio Belli) (1468–1546), engraver of jewels:
    bust by, of Q. Elizabeth, **9.** 414
    heads of Q. Elizabeth supposedly by, **16.** *148–9,* 157
Vicenza, Bp of. *See* Priuli, Michele
Vicenza (Italy):
    Cerigati house at, pleases Chute, **35.** 4
    Villa Rotonda at, **35.** 143
Vice-treasurer:
    Q. Charlotte's, James Grenville resigns as, **23.** 180
Vice-treasurer of Ireland. *See under* Ireland: joint vice-treasurership of; vice-treasurer of
Vichy, Marquise de. *See* St-Georges, Claude-Josèphe-Marie de
Vichy, Abel-Claude-Marie-Goeric-Cécile de (1765–1832), Comte de Champrond; Mme du Deffand's grandnephew:
    Du Deffand, Mme, visited by, **6.** 188
Vichy, Abel-Claude-Marthe-Marie-Cécile de (1740–93), Marquis de Vichy; Comte de Champrond; Mme du Deffand's nephew:
    Champrond, Abbé de, visited by, **7.** 225
    Du Deffand, Mme, corresponds with, **7.** 430, 455
    —— visited by, **6.** 188, 283
    Paris visited by, **4.** *464–5,* **6.** 188, 283, **7.** 225, 450
    will of Mlle de Lespinasse seen by, **6.** 327–8
Vichy, Anne de (1706–69), m. Jean-François de Suarez, Marquis d'Aulan; Mme du Deffand's sister:
    apartment of, beneath Mme du Deffand's, **4.** 65, **8.** 3
    brother-in-law of, **3.** 366n
    death of, **4.** 229
    Du Deffand, Mme, affectionate towards, **3.** 330
    ——'s opinion of, **4.** 229
    ——'s social relations with, **7.** 270, 274–5, 282, 303
    health of, **3.** 330, 338
    Luynes, Duchesse de, leaves property to, **8.** 36
    Marie Leszczyńska sees, **3.** 382, 383
    son of, **11.** 76n
    to return to Avignon, **3.** 376, **4.** 65, 69

Vichy, Gaspard de (d. 1736), Comte de Champrond; Mme du Deffand's father:
daughter's scepticism alarms, 8. 54
wife of, 4. 284n, 5. 225n

Vichy, Gaspard-Claude-Félix (1767–ca 1802), Comte de: Mme du Deffand's grandnephew:
Du Deffand, Mme, visited by, 6. 188

Vichy, Gaspard-Nicolas de (1699–1781), Comte de Champrond; Mme du Deffand's brother:
Albon connected with Mme du Deffand through, 6. 26
Choiseul, Duchesse de (his grandmother), leaves money to, 8. 36
Du Deffand, Mme, has annuity from, 8. 40–1
——'s correspondence with, 7. 440, 455
illegitimate daughter of, 3. 290n
lives in Burgundy, 4. 228n
Luynes, Duchesse de, leaves property to, 8. 36
Puigautier represents, at Mme du Deffand's inventory, 8. 11, 46–7
son of, 7. 225

Vichy, Nicolas-Marie de (d. 1783), Abbé de Champrond; Mme du Deffand's brother:
Choiseul, Duchesse de (his grandmother), leaves money to, 8. 36
Du Deffand, Mme, leaves silverware and china to, 8. 7, 12–13, 28–9
Luynes, Duchesse de, leaves property to, 8. 36
Montrouge, summer home of, 7. 123
Puigautier represents, at Mme du Deffand's inventory, 8. 11
social relations of, in Paris, see index entries ante 8. 538

Vichy, Marquis de, visits, 7. 225

Vichy-Champrond, Marie de (1696–1780), m. (1718) Jean-Baptiste-Jacques-Charles du Deffand de la Lande, Marquis de Chastres: called Marquis du Deffand:
See vols 3 – 8 passim
age of: 7. 368, 30. 263; corrected, 43. 72
Ailesbury, Cts of, pleases, more than Conway does, 39. 200–1
—— suggests to HW, medallions as presents for, 39. 254
—— to get letter from, about accident, 39. 257
Alembert may attack HW as friend of, 41. 49, 55–6, 61–2
—— seldom mentioned by, 41. 55
Amant indécis, L', by, 8. 77
apartment of, see St-Joseph, Convent of
asks to know tune to which poem is to be sung, 33. 423–4
Auteuil visited by, 31. 183
aversions of: to philosophes, 39. 190; to politics, 39. 189
Barrymore, Cts of, bitten by dog of, 39. 258
Barthélemy friend of, 16. 281n
Bauffremont accompanies, from Mme de Choiseul's, 41. 196
—— friend of, 36. 180
Beauvau leaves picture of, to HW, 12. 14, 15

—— defrauds HW of papers after death of, 12. 14, 15
—— not to have letter from, 41. 199
—— will withdraw compromising pieces from papers of, 41. 423
bedroom grate of, has arms of Mme de Montespan, the former occupant, 39. 233–4
Biblical misreading recounted by, 32. 258
birth date of, corrected, 43. 72
birthday of, 6. 479, 7. 368
Bishop befriended by, at HW's instance, 36. 106–7
books of, 8. 32–5, 43. 108–9
Boufflers's verses to be given by, to Choiseuls, 39. 236
Boulevard to be visited by, 10. 289
Bret's Mémoires sur . . . Mademoiselle mentioned by, 39. 242
burial of, 7. 252
Carmontelle's water-colour of, see under Carrogis, Louis de
characteristics of: cannot bear to have stated occupations, 30. 267; eager about daily events, 30. 204; frank and clever, 39. 189; impatience, 38. 257; never loves friends by halves, 38. 257; overflowing heart, 39. 210
charity of, 7. 425, 8. 42
Choiseul gives porcelain to, 41. 197
—— meets Franklin and Deane at house of, 24. 273n
——'s adherents entertained at supper by, 41. 194–5
Choiseul, Duchesse de, entertains, 41. 194, 196
—— intimate with, 39. 135–6
—— is called 'grand'maman' by, 41. 192
—— prevented by, from answering HW, 41. 179
——'s correspondence with, 41. 194, 196, 43. 91, 92
Choiseuls associated with, 15. 134n
——'s return will gratify, 39. 223
Cholmondeley, Mrs, mentions 4th E. of Cholmondeley to, but he never comes, 39. 219
—— not to have letter from, 41. 198
—— urges, in HW's name, to forsake tea, 36. 57–8
—— will console, 36. 54–5
Clive, Mrs, jokes about, 10. 216
Coke, Lady Mary, does not mention HW to, 31. 178
—— introduced to, 31. 134
—— praises, 31. 134
Collé's Partie de Chasse attended by, 39. 216–17
company and suppers enjoyed by, on deathbed, 36. 171
confession of, not completed, 7. 252
conversation of, contains good sense and good humour, 39. 218
Conway and wife may have been thrust upon the Choiseuls too fast by, 39. 236

[Vichy-Champrond, Marie de, *continued*]

Conway can hear from, of HW's quarrels over Rousseau, **39**. 231

—— could get to hear Mlle Clairon through, **39**. 213

—— said by, to be soon returning, **39**. 242

—— scolds HW on behalf of, **39**. 249

—— to be shown by, the picture of Mme de Prie, **39**. 215, 234, 243

—— to explain to, HW's fear of getting gout in Paris, **39**. 199

—— to get from, admission order to kings' effigies at St-Denis, **39**. 203

Craufurd admired by, **31**. 91

——'s generosity to servants of, angers her, **41**. 4

——'s letter consoles, **41**. 3

——'s numerous visits to, **30**. 262

—— speaks of Voltaire to, **22**. 40n

Craufurds liked by, **32**. 392

Creutz receives HW's medallions from, **41**. 340

Dalrymple tells, of Ds of Gloucester's beauty, **36**. 131

death of: **7**. 250, **12**. 76, **25**. 90, **29**. 83, **33**. 229–31, 233, 235; expected, **33**. 229–30, **35**. 507–8; HW knows nothing of French politics after, **36**. 249

dinners better for, than suppers, **36**. 58

dog of, *see* 'Tonton'

Élie de Beaumont seldom sees, **41**. 173

eloquence disliked by, though she was eloquent, **34**. 71

enemies of, take English people to Mlle de Lespinasse, **39**. 191

English people patronized by, despite persecution, **30**. 218

family of, 'détestable,' **4**. 240

fans wanted from England by, for Mme de Marchais, **39**. 257

finances of: **4**. 91, 349, 351, 392, **5**. 5, 281–2, 295, **7**. 115–16, 123, **8**. 5–47; budget, **4**. 386–7; cash on hand at death, **8**. 29, 44–5; concealed assets, **4**. 379; HW's offers to supplement, **4**. 358–9, 364–6, 375, 379, 403, **5**. 7; pension may be endangered, **39**. 136, 189; watched over by Duchesse de Choiseul, **3**. 388, **4**. 79, 86, 91, 97, 103, 289, 315, 361, 362, 365, 375; *see also under* Pension

Foire Ste-Ovide to be visited by, **4**. 289

Forcalquier, Mme de, friendly with, **41**. 162

Gennevilliers to be visited by, with HW, for supper, **35**. 121

Geoffrin, Mme, enemy of, **14**. 150, **39**. 190

Gleichen first met HW at house of, **24**. 171

Gloucester, Ds of, hopes to see, **36**. 142

—— will not see, **36**. 132

grandmother takes, to see Mme de Coulanges, **41**. 259

Grave follows sentiments of, regarding HW, **41**. 143–4

—— friend of, **34**. 82

guests of, at 1 A.M., listed, **39**. 271

HW announces Pitt's overture to, **39**. 245

HW answers inquiries of, about his Berkeley Sq. house, **30**. 272

HW asks, to aid Macartney, **33**. 123, 126, 132

HW asks Conway to bring back HW's correspondence with, **39**. 190, 234

HW asks Mme de Choiseul's consent to his 'marriage' to, **7**. 321

HW attends midnight Mass in tribune of, **39**. 233

HW attends 'tragedy' with, **33**. 543

HW attributed Mme de Genlis's visit to, **33**. 483

HW called on by, at his hotel, **39**. 255

HW calls: 'delicious,' **30**. 204; his and Selwyn's 'good old friend,' **30**. 267; his 'poor dear old woman,' **31**. 118; 'old blind debauchee of wit,' **39**. 12; 'Star in the East,' **30**. 263

HW can be kept in Paris only by, **35**. 128

HW cares for 'Tonton' for sake of, **34**. 45

HW compares, to his mother, **10**. 290

HW could visit, more often but for his curiosity about Paris and its sights, **30**. 204

HW dares not ask, about Mme de Choiseul's health, **41**. 100

HW describes, **10**. 289–90, **14**. 150–1

HW discusses, with Mary Hamilton, **31**. 215

HW does not expect to visit, again, **30**. 268

HW does not inform, of Lady Mary Coke's visit, to Paris, **31**. 182

HW does not want her transmission of news to him to be known publicly, **39**. 190

HW fears he may never see, again, **10**. 290

HW finds, better than 4 years before, **39**. 255

HW first sups with, meeting Hénault, **39**. 12

HW glad that death of, occurred before French Revolution, **31**. 357

HW goes to Paris only to see, **35**. 342

HW hears from, of Choiseul's peril, **39**. 119

HW incapable of writing to, **30**. 261

HW instructs Conway and wife about seeing, **39**. 188–91

HW intends to see, once more, **39**. 223

HW jokes about marrying, **7**. 321, **31**. 156

HW jokes with, about Craufurd, **31**. 91

HW loved by, better than all France, **39**. 189

HW met Bauffremont at salon of, **41**. 415

HW might hint to, that there is corn at Genoa and Naples, **24**. 106

HW not told enough by, about Cts of Ailesbury, **39**. 209

HW nurses, **31**. 183

HW overwhelmed with social engagements made by, **39**. 257

HW peruses papers of, **39**. 385

HW plays cavagnole with old ladies at party of, **30**. 220

HW prefers company of, to Sir John Cust's, **30**. 220

HW procures drawing through, **2**. 195n

HW proud of his wisdom in visiting, **30.** 263

HW receives commissions from, for Hon. Thomas Walpole to fetch, **36.** 168–9

HW receives letter from, through Conway, **39.** 220

HW receives Mme de Choiseul's note by means of, **41.** 16

HW receives news of sea battle from, **33.** 23

HW receives packet from, **31.** 179

HW said by: to have *le fou moquer*, **30.** 208; to love Conway above all, **39.** 271

HW's arrival desired: by Mme de Choiseul and, **41.** 75; by Mme de Forcalquier and, **41.** 94

HW's bounty to Echlin administered by, **41.** 398n

HW's civilities from Mme de Choiseul described by, **41.** 42

HW scolded by, for his poor French, **28.** 96

HW's concern for, doubled by difficulty in communicating with her, **30.** 268

HW's correspondence with: vols 3 – 8 inclusive, **25.** 90, **28.** 259, **31.** 119, **41.** 192–200, **43.** 80; dishonourable to him, **35.** 648; facilitated by Hon. Robert Walpole, **36.** 48–9; HW asks Selwyn to provide proper address for, **30.** 266–7; interrupted by stoppage of packet-boats, **30.** 271; interruption of, will vex her, **30.** 267; MSS of, **36.** 310, 312; posthumous publication of, **4.** 279; secret, **3.** 3, 16, 18, 46, 82, 86, 90, 98, 149; to be preserved, **3.** 33; *see also* Walpole, Horatio, (1717–97): letters of, to Mme du Deffand

HW's decline dedicated to 'raking' with, **30.** 263

HW sees Bp of Arras at house of, **11.** 144

HW sends medallions to, for Shuvalov, **41.** 348

HW sends news to, **31.** 182

HW's farewell from, **7.** 243

HW's first meeting with, **7.** 261

HW's frequent visits to, **1.** 124, 196, 358, **30.** 262

HW's friendship with, **25.** 90, **28.** 51, 159

HW's *Gramont* dedicated to, **1.** 293n

HW's grate replaces toasting-fork of, **39.** 219

HW's kind reception by, **32.** 253

HW's last letter from, **36.** 170

HW's last Paris visit a sacrifice to, **39.** 252

HW's legacies from: **2.** 251, **36.** 181–96, 202, 204, 216, **43.** 72; gold snuff-box, **33.** 255; her MSS, **8.** 7, 44, **12.** 14–15, **16.** 198–9, **29.** 167–8, 306, **33.** 235, 292, 567, **41.** 423, 424, 425–6; 'Tonton,' **11.** 13n, **29.** 145

HW's letter from, under name of Mme de Sévigné, *see under* Rabutin-Chantal, Marie de

HW's letters to: kept or burnt, **36.** 171; to be returned through Conway, **39.** 190–1, 198, 234

HW's sole remaining link with France, **2.** 233

HW's relations with, vols 3 – 8 *passim*; **10.** 290, 292

HW's rift with Barthélemy after death of, **16.** 281

HW sups with: frequently, **31.** 75; twice a week, **30.** 204

HW tells: how well Elliot imitates Pitt, **39.** 13; to write, **5.** 199–200, 215

HW tells Mme de Forcalquier to teach English to, **41.** 34

HW thanks Conway for goodness to, **39.** 210

HW thanks Selwyn for introduction to, **30.** 203–4

HW thinks, more worth visiting than ever, **30.** 262–3

HW told by, of Frenchmen's opinions of SH, **23.** 312

HW too long absent from, **41.** 171

HW too tired to see, on first reaching Paris, **35.** 124

HW to receive St-Lambert's *Saisons* from, **36.** 49

HW to revisit Paris to see, **10.** 247, **22.** 484, **23.** 311, **24.** 130, **30.** 238, **35.** 471

HW to send description of Bedfordshire militia to, **33.** 13

HW to send tea and Stoughton's drops to, **36.** 168, 169

HW to write to, **36.** 56

HW transmits news from, to Mason, **28.** 408, 418

HW united with, by congenial talents and mutual vanity, **35.** 648

HW urged by: to revisit Paris, **24.** 120; to take apartment in convent of St-Joseph, **30.** 220

HW will be thought neglectful of, **30.** 268

HW wishes iris roots for, **23.** 323

HW wishes to dedicate a few lines to, **30.** 261

HW would like to bring, to England, **10.** 208

HW writes to, about nothing, **36.** 54

HW writes to Mme d'Aiguillon for sake of, **32.** 50

habits of: at Chanteloup, **5.** 243, 255; diet, **4.** 332, **5.** 138, 345, 353, 371, **6.** 108, 219–21, 224, 269–70, 371, **7.** 119, 243–5, 247, 249; dinners, Monday, **4.** 131, 165; drives about boulevard till 2 A.M., **35.** 121; established in 'tonneau' at 4 P.M., **5.** 6; hours of coming home, **4.** 122, 315–16; hours of going out, **4.** 491, **5.** 6, 35, 43, 311; occupations, **4.** 436; pays no calls, **5.** 6, 17; reading hours, **4.** 471, **5.** 190; rising and retiring hours, **4.** 121–2, 140, 180, 182, 216, 254, 316, 318, 327, 332, 376, 428, 458, **5.** 43, 126, 161, 163, 182, 409, **6.** 265; sings and composes songs, **10.** 289; tea, hour for, **5.** 160, 164; toilette, hour for, **4.** 381; visits, hour for receiving, **6.** 268; whispers in company, **32.** 267; wishes to drive around Paris at 1 A.M., **30.** 263; *see also under* Effilage; Supper

[Vichy-Champrond, Marie de, *continued*]

handwriting of, **3.** 2, 5n, 80, 145, 176, 177, 223, **4.** 218 250

health of: (1766) **3.** 23, 35, 40, 41, 52, 54, 99, 131, 145, 183, 185, 188, (1767) 244, 251, 258, 282, 304, 310, 319, 383, **7.** 319, (1768) **4.** 5, 136, (1769) 178, 228–9, 248, 327, (1770) 331, 334, 356, 364, 393, (1771) **5.** 3, 42–3, 44, 83, 87, (1775) **7.** 350, **31.** 183; aphasia, **5.** 208–9; (?) apoplexy, **5.** 208–9; better, **35.** 121; blindness, **3.** 19n, **10.** 216, 289, **12.** 14, **14.** 144; 150, **31.** 75, 91, 215, **33.** 229; boils, **7.** 88; cassia taken, **41.** 195; catarrh, (1766) **3.** 93, 106, 163, 185, (1767) 304, 306, 327, 330, 338, 400, (1768) **4.** 109, (1771) **5.** 120, (1774) **6.** 45; colds, (1766) **3.** 4, 9, 76, 93, 211, (1767) 402, (1769) **4.** 207, 228, 322, **7.** 328, **8.** 159, (1774) **6.** 45, 81, 98, 119, (1775) 192, 236, (1776) 274, (1778) **7.** 68, 71, (1779) 198, 199; colic, **3.** 185, 392; deafness, **5.** 120, **7.** 51, 90, 94, 123, 140, 149, 189, 226, 230, 252, **30.** 268, **33.** 229; delicate, **10.** 289; fainting, **3.** 292, **4.** 322, 332; faintings from cassia, **36.** 58; fall and subsequent pains, **6.** 255–9, 261, 298, 300; feebleness, **6.** 330–2, 336, 465, **7.** 200, 242–5, 247, 248; fever (1766) **3.** 29, 33, 170, (1767) 280, 400, (1769) **4.** 219, (1774) **6.** 99–101, 105, (1775) 244, (1777) 444, 450, (1778) **7.** 71, 73, (1780) 243–9, **33.** 228; fidgets, **6.** 74; flux, **3** 185, **5.** 120; fluxion, **3.** 168, **4.** 136, 224; gout, **6.** 454; grippe, **3.** 400, **6.** 245, 247; HW detained in Paris by, **39.** 269, 271–2; HW's concern for, **3.** 167, 265, **4.** 332; headache, (1769) **4.** 219, (1771) **5.** 120, 128; heart, oppression of, **7.** 242; illness, **32.** 267; indigestion (1766) **3.** 137, (1767) 251, 256, 292, 295, (1768) **4.** 13, 29, 122, 136, 165 (1769) 219, 244, 247, 252, 287, 304, 322, (1770) 332, 348, 394, 415, (1771) **5.** 76, 81, 94, 109, (1772) 176, 208–9, (1774) **6.** 48, 74, (1776) 339, 341, (1778) **7.** 68, (1779) 119, 170, 195, 437, (1780) 198, 200; insomnia, **3.** 174, 245, 328, **4.** 304, 420, 436, **6.** 223, (1766) **3.** 2, 21, 25, 34, 36, 68, 80, 107, 124, 137, 140, 173, 175, 185, (1767) 203, 223, 226, 228, 231, 251–3, 256, 259, 274, 276, 280, 295, 297, 300, 304, 312, 338, 343, 346, 363, 378, 386, 389, 392, 400, (1768) **4.** 13, 19, 28, 29, 68, 83, 85, 86, 88, 93, 131, 136, 165, 167, 168, 170, (1769) 177, 179, 182, 183, 198, 218, 223, 224, 233, 250, 252, 254, 261, 268, 269, 276, 278, 281, 282, 288, 310, 327, (1770) 332, 336, 338, 345, 346, 348, 394, 415, 417, 428, 448, 464, 491, (1771) **5.** 27, 33, 35, 43, 76, 79, 80, 91, 94, 97, 98, 100, 109, 118, 126–7, 133, 138, 140, 149, 150, (1772) 178, 181–2, 190, 191, 197, 210, 236, 239, 279, (1773) 311, 312, 345, 353, 371, 378, 380, 394, 401, 402, 404, 434, 436, (1774) **6.** 2, 7, 82, 92, 93, 105, 108, 110, 121, (1775) 198, 218–20, 222, 232, 233, 240–2, 246, 247, 250, (1776) 256, 257, 266, 267, 269, 271, 274, 281,

360, 371, 373, (1777) 393, 402, 445, 447, 468, 479, (1778) **7.** 58, 68, 69, 71, 93, (1779) 101, 116, 118, 119, 122, 143, 162, 172, 176, (1780) 200, 203, 204, 208, 217, 235, 238, 242–4; last illness, **2.** 233, **7.** 243–53, **36.** 170–3, 176–8; legs not good, **7.** 230, 242; loss of voice, (1766) **3.** 29, (1776) **6.** 254–5, **7.** 242; medicine taken, **4.** 400, **5.** 93–4 (*see also* Cassia; Stoughton's Drops); noise in the head, **6.** 78; not well, **10.** 290; physician refuses to use James's medicine for, **33.** 229–30; regimen, **5.** 27, 138, 236; stays in bed, **6.** 235; tea beneficial to, **36.** 58; tumour, **5.** 133, **7.** 247; vapours, **3.** 185, 256, 297, 363, 372, **4.** 13. 332, 415, **5.** 12, 35, 76, 81, 236, **6.** 101, 246, 247, 262, 264, 295, 300, 360, 425, 463, **7.** 73, 78, 122, 130, 154, 182, 191, 206; varying, **41.** 331; weak, **3.** 312, **5.** 29, 43

Hénault's former mistress, **39.** 12

'Herculean weakness' of, susceptible to strawberries and cream after supper, **39.** 269

Hervey, Bns, may know, **31.** 75

hours of, **10.** 289–90; *see also under* habits of

impetuosity of, typical of bygone French, **24.** 498

indelicate remark by, **14.** 144

inventory of effects of, **8.** 10–47 (*see also under individual items*)

James's powders should be given to, **36.** 172–3, 176

justice of, to the English, unique in France, **12.** 14

La Fontaine idolized by, **28.** 420

La Harpe and Thomas unintelligible to, **33.** 496

Lennox, Lady George, asked by HW to visit, **31.** 118

letters from living persons to, returned to their writers, **41.** 425

Lort hopes that HW will do justice to the memory of, **16.** 200

Luxembourg, Mme de, informs, of d'Alembert's suspicions of her, **41.** 62n

Maurepas and Nivernais may be feared by, **39.** 189

Mirepoix, Mme de, old friend of, **41.** 192

—— warns, of Choiseul's fall, **41.** 193–4

modern French not understood by, **25.** 538, **33.** 496

Montagu mentions, **10.** 297

——'s relations with, **10.** 285, 289, 296

nephew of, murdered, **11.** 76, **31.** 357

nightmare of, **4.** 83, 85

'one can be but what one is born' a saying of, **32.** 267

papers of: **8.** 35–45; Beauvau's controversy with HW over, **36.** 183, 185–6, 188–94, 196, 202, **41.** 423, 424, 425–6; catalogue of MSS bequeathed to HW, **8.** 7, 44; financial, **8.** 35–45; HW examines, **16.** 198–9; inventory of, **8.** 7, **41.** 424; marriage contract, **8.** 30; marriage register, **8.** 30; separation contracts, **8.** 30–1, 44; *see also under* HW's legacy from

Petitot miniature sought by, for HW, **39.** 198, 208, 215

politics abhorred by, **30.** 271

politics would not be revealed by, **30.** 271

Pont-de-Veyle friend of, **2.** 111n

——'s death no great loss to, **41.** 279

—— tells, of Choiseul's fall, **41.** 195–6

'portraits' by, of herself and members of her circle, **8.** 48–9, 60–1, 71–7, 78–87, 91–5, 102–3, 104–6, 108–11, 113–16, **43.** 109

portraits painted of: **3.** (?) 129, **4.** 35, **8.** 215–17, **28.** 39; Carmontelle's, *see under* Carrogis, Louis

'portraits' written of: **8.** 48–70; HW's, **3.** 190, 194, 199, 216, **4.** 275, 286, **6.** 109–10, **8.** 54–6

protégé of, writes piece for puppet-show, **35.** 121

Raucourt, Mlle, described by, **39.** 212

Regent's mistress for a fortnight, **14.** 144, 150

reminiscences may be written by, **6.** 393, 398–9

riddles by: attempts to solve, **31.** 83; HW sends, to Bns Hervey, **31.** 75

Roissy visited by, **32.** 260, **34.** 77–8

Rousseau not admired by, **28.** 420

——'s *Confessions*, preface to, sent by, to HW, **28.** 426n

St-Cyr abbess asked by, to show HW the convent, **10.** 292

St-Simon's *Mémoires* read by, **34.** 30

salon of: members of, dull, **30.** 204; vacancies in, recruited for, **30.** 265

satirical ballads sung by, **7.** 289

self-analysis by, **3.** 48, 265, **4.** 239, **5.** 414–15, 425, **6.** 203, 285–7, 335, 356, 366–7, 432–3, **7.** 120, 132

Selwyn's correspondence with, **43.** 81

——'s letters described by, **33.** 55–6

——'s message to, delivered by HW, **30.** 262

——'s probable return pleases, **30.** 218

——'s promised Paris visit would please, more if she believed it, **30.** 262

—— to have copy of Carmontelle's portrait of, **30.** 252

Sens, Abp of, 'nephew' of, **34.** 19

Sévigné, Mme de, compared with, **10.** 289

——'s letter chosen by, for HW, **41.** 109

social relations of, with: Ailesbury, Cts of, **39.** 218; Arras, Bp of, **11.** 144; Barrymore, Cts of, **31.** 183; Boufflers, **39.** 219; Broglie, **39.** 191; Caraman, Comte and Comtesse de, **32.** 260, **34.** 77–8; Choiseul, Duc de, **39.** 269; Cholmondeley, Mrs, **36.** 57; Cholmondeleys, **36** 49; Clairon, Mlle, **10.** 175n; Coke, Lady Mary, **31.** 134, 182–3; Denis, Mme, **28.** 153n; Elliot, **39.** 13; Fitzroys, **41.** 41; Forcalquier, Mme de, **39.** 13; Franklin, Benjamin, **32.** 344; Gleichen, **24.** 171; HW, **24.** 171, **31.** 134, 183, **39.** 12; Hénault, **39.** 12; Hessensteins, **33.** 413–14; La Vallière,

Duchesse de, **30.** 263, **39.** 13; Lennox, Lady George, **31.** 125; Mirepoix, Mme de, **31.** 183; St-Antoine abbess, **34.** 77–8; Ségur, Comtesse de, **30.** 220–1; Virys, **39.** 219; Voltaire, **28.** 366; *see also ante* **41.** 192–200, *and index entries ante* **8.** 219–561 *under names of individuals*

SH visit of, prevented by blindness, **10.** 289

style of writing of: Du Deffand, Mme, comments on, **3.** 199; HW criticizes, **5.** 316, 319; HW praises, **4.** 141, **7.** 236; Selwyn criticizes, **5.** 316, 319

suppers in country attended by, **10.** 289

suppers of, eaten by ungrateful 'friends,' **41.** 4

'Tonton's' faults encouraged by, **39.** 370

verses by: for Carmontelle portrait, **3.** 394, 405, **4.** 6, 14; for Choiseul, **4.** 178, 183, **6.** 122–3; for Choiseul, Duchesse de, **4.** 175–6; for HW, **4.** 29; for Luxembourg, Mme de, **5.** 225–6, 232, 298, 431, **6.** 249, **8.** 186; 'Malgré la fuite des amours, **4.** 307; on Colmant, **4.** 19–20; on Forcalquier, Comtesse de, **4.** 20, 302, 308, 310; on HW's handshake, **3.** 348; on old age, **5.** 413; on 'Tonton,' **6.** 103

verses on Shuvalov sent to HW by, **12.** 254n

Voltaire's correspondence with: **39.** 385–6, **41.** 199; to be printed, with HW's consent, **41.** 425

——'s death described by, **28.** 410

——'s style admired by, **28.** 420

will of: **8.** 5–11; Beauvau permitted by, to copy Mme du Deffand's MSS, **3.** 5n, **8.** 8; codicil to, **7.** 461, **8.** 8–11; HW to receive Mme du Deffand's MSS by, **5** 1–2, **7.** 54, 201, **8.** 7; making of, **5.** 28, **7.** 201, 442, **8.** 5

wills of, **7.** 201n

wit of: **3.** 215; praised by HW, **4.** 440

witticisms of: (?) on Hume-Rousseau quarrel, **30.** 238; on Mme d'Olonne, **32.** 282; on Turgot's reforms, **30.** 264; on Voltaire, **28.** 468

writes only of her own circle, **32.** 312, 320, 363

youthful spirits of, **10.** 289–90

'Vicinage':

Chatham, E. of, said to have coined, **11.** 348

Vickers, Christopher, HW's gardener:

assistant of, finds footman's body, **11.** 369

HW's bequest to, **30.** 362

lavender plants distributed by, around Little Strawberry Hill, **12.** 36

Strawberry Hill shown by, **12.** 249

Vicomte du Rumain de Coëtanfao. *See* Le Vicomte du Rumain de Coëtanfao

Victoire-Louise-Marie-Thérèse (1733–99), Princesse; 'Madame Victoire'; dau. of Louis XV:

apartment of, **3.** 286

ball at Versailles attended by, **32.** 255

Beauvillier scratched by, from party list, **23.** 115–16

Bernis receives, **11.** 4n

[Victoire-Louise-Marie-Thérèse, *continued*]
Boisgelin, Comtesse de, tells anecdote about, **7.** 121
Choisy visited by, **6.** 50, 55
Du Barry, Comtesse, to be presented to, **4.** 191–2, **23.** 78
Du Deffand, Mme, mentions, **3.** 360
English might reduce, to shift and no rouge, **37.** 535
escapes from France, **11.** 215
expense of coffee and rouge for, **20.** 500
father devoted to, **22.** 164
father nursed by, though she had never had smallpox, **6.** 50, **24.** 1–2
father's alleged relations with, **9.** 152
Gatti's reply to, **7.** 281
HW describes, **35.** 113
HW not spoken to by, at Versailles, **39.** 14
HW presented to, **7.** 266
HW watches, at dinner at Versailles, **10.** 292
Hertford, Cts of, well received by, **38.** 261
household of, **4.** 442
Louis XVI to see, at Compiègne, **6.** 60
Marie-Antoinette governed by, **23.** 321
(?) Marie-Josèphe's funeral oration attended by, **7.** 318
meals of, public spectacles, **10.** 292
mother and sisters not addressed by, across father at dinner, **20.** 340
Orléans, Bp of, talks with, and she betrays him to her father, **23.** 321
poissardes detain, in Paris, **11.** 207
Poyntz, Mrs, cures, of stone by Mrs Stephens's medicine, **22.** 163–4
Rome to be visited by, **11.** 222
sets out for Turin, **11.** 208
smallpox of, **6.** 55, 57, **24.** 1–2
Stanislas I visited by, **22.** 403
stiff, **38.** 221
well-behaved, **38.** 218
Victoires, Place des, at Paris:
Augustins' church in, **7.** 282
Toulouse, Hôtel de, in, **7.** 302n
Tourton et Bauer, bankers in, **28.** 50
Victor Amadeus II (1666–1732), K. of Sardinia 1718–30:
morganatic marriage of, **22.** 144
Raphael painting would have been bought by, **18.** 235
Victor Amadeus III (1726–96), styled D. of Savoy, 1730; K. of Sardinia, 1773:
Adélaïde, Mme, said to be marrying, **19.** 218–19
Berry, Mary, describes, **11.** 138n
Broglie, Comte de, wishes to pay court to, **5.** 402, **23.** 521
burning of his minister's chapel in London may alienate, **29.** 52–3
Chambéry should be revisited by, **11.** 138
Corsica may go to, **24.** 26
daughter of, **11.** 303n
death of, **34.** 223

French send army against, **12.** 89
George III persuades, to pardon Viry, **24.** 328n, **35.** 522n
Mann praised by, through Gorsegno, **19.** 170
Milan coveted by, **23.** 469
Napoleon forces, to sign treaty, **12.** 191n
Sardinian army directed by, **19.** 344
son of, **12.** 191n
Viry exiled by order of, **24.** 328n
wedding of, **20.** 159
Victor Emmanuel I (1759–1824), K. of Sardinia:
Charles Emmanuel IV abdicates in favour of, **12.** 191n
Victoria (1819–1901), Q. of England 1837–1901:
father of, **11.** 145n
Victoria. *See also* La Victoria
Victory, English ship:
expense of, **18.** 521
Faulknor capt. of, **24.** 399n
lost, with Sir John Balchen and crew, **18.** 521, 543
mizzen-mast of, lost in storm, **18.** 407n
Norris's flagship, **13.** 226n
Victory:
peace preferable to, **22.** 85
Victualling fleet:
Hardy convoys, **18.** 447n
Victualling Office:
Cooper a commissioner of, **19.** 64n
Vidimus:
meaning of, **43.** 45
Vie d'Agricola, La. See under La Bletterie, Jean-Philippe-René de
Vie de Cicéron, La. See Middleton, Conyers: *History of . . . Cicero*
Vie de Cromwell:
Du Deffand, Mme, owns, **8.** 34
Vie de François Ier. See Gaillard, Gabriel-Henri: *Histoire de François Ier*
Vie de l'empereur Julien l'apostat. See under La Bletterie, Jean-Philippe-René de
Vie de Mlle Lenclos. See Bret, Antoine: *Mémoires sur la vie de Mlle de Lenclos*
Vie de Marianne, La. See under Marivaux, Pierre Carlet de Chamblain de
Vie de Marie de Médicis, La. See under Arlus, Marie-Geneviève-Charlotte d'
Vie de M. d'Orléans de la Motte, La. See under Proyart, Liévain-Bonaventure
Vie de Philippe. See under Leti, Gregorio
Vie de Richelieu. See under Leclerc, Jean
Vie de St-Louis, La. See under Joinville, Jean; Promontorio, Nicolas
Vie des saints:
Mme du Deffand may read, **5.** 282
Vie du Cardinal Duc de Richelieu, La. See under Leclerc, Jean
Vie du Dauphin. See under Proyart, Liévain-Bonaventure
Vie du Maréchal Duc de Villars. See under Villars, Claude-Louis-Hector, Duc de

Vie du Pape Clément XIV, La. See under Caraccioli, Louis-Antoine de

Vieilles Audriettes, Rue des, at Paris:
Trudaine lives in, **5.** 162

Vien, Joseph-Marie (1716–1809), painter:
social relations of, with Mme Geoffrin, **7.** 345

Vien, Mme Joseph-Marie. *See* Rebout, Marie-Thérèse

Vienna:
account from, of Dettingen, belittles English army, **35.** 40
Albani's messenger goes to, **19.** 2, 114
Althan to go to, with Lobkowitz's dispatches, **18.** 486, 489, 491
ambassadors from and to, *see under* Ambassador
America is connected with, by ignorant Florentines, **21.** 236
Antinori neglected by, **21.** 107
Argyll, Ds of, may visit, **33.** 288
Austrian army complains to, of lack of artillery carriages, **19.** 406
Austrian-Prussian peace not reported from, **17.** 134
Bagard's dismissal ordered by, **17.** 368, 406
balls allowed at, despite mourning for Madame Royale, **19.** 14
bank of, Francis III ensures money in, **22.** 144
Barthélemy, Marquis de, to be secretary of embassy at, **6.** 184, 198
Bartolommei former minister at, **17.** 195
Bavarian elector expected to besiege, **17.** 143, 151, 155
—— writes letter to, **18.** 55
Botta goes to, **21.** 424, **22.** 87
—— leaves Brussels for, **20.** 320n
—— ordered by, to give precedence to nuncio, **22.** 44
——'s credit at, secure, **22.** 254
——'s plea to Francis I may not reach, in time, **22.** 267
——'s proposals rejected by, **22.** 13
——'s retirement finally approved at, **22.** 448
Braitwitz sends remonstrances to, **18.** 128
Breteuil made ambassador to, **5.** 93n
'brother at,' *see* Joseph II
Catherine II's manifesto reaches Florence from, **22.** 74
ceremonial for Maria Louisa's churching established at, **22.** 486–7
Chandos, Ds of, proposes to go to, **33.** 291–2
Charles III sends courier to, with message to Joseph II and Maria Theresa, **23.** 446
——'s neutrality statement to appease, **21.** 271
Charles, P., invites James to, for Joseph II's wedding, **21.** 462
—— retires to, **17.** 430
Charles Emmanuel III awaits answers from, **19.** 393
—— sends courier to, **19.** 312
Choiseul, in letter, disparages his post at, **21.** 242, 307

Cholmondeley, 4th E., should visit, **36.** 134
Coke, Lady Mary, returns from, **5.** 69n
Conclave sends courier to, to complain of Bourbon cardinals, **24.** 79
convent of Saliciennes to be founded at, by French ladies, **20.** 333–4
Conway to visit, **39.** 175
Corsican disappointment depresses, **23.** 130
council of war at, gives orders to Daun, **21.** 96
councils held in, **21.** 72
courier from: awaited, **18.** 168, **19.** 313, 455; dispatches of, not divulged, **18.** 182; forbids Leopold to negotiate with Spain, **25.** 46; to England, with peace news, **17.** 472
couriers to: about Dumesnil's arrest, **19.** 492; from Rome, **19.** 158; seeks Francis I's orders, **19.** 298
court gazette of: Mann to show mourning notice in, for George II, to Botta, **21.** 463; reprints Grub Street papers, **22.** 178
Court of: alarmed, **21.** 195; Albani's and Thun's letters referred by, to Lobkowitz, **18.** 515; apprehensive about Peter III, **22.** 14; Brown may be told by, not to press the French, **19.** 436; Catherine II's accession disliked by, **22.** 75; Charles of Naples unlikely to allow, to take Naples from him, **21.** 280; Charles Emmanuel III cannot be expected by, to be too loyal, **19.** 156; Coke, Lady Mary, no longer suspects, **23.** 560; commissaries might be appointed by, to suppress Jesuits, **23.** 135; contributes patents only, to Corsican revolt, **20.** 274; Corsican conquest expected by, **19.** 215; Corsican rebels trusted promises of, **19.** 258; Cumberland, Ds of, may embarrass, **23.** 502; dislikes Russian invasion of the Morea, **23.** 204–5; England should have joined, to keep Corsica out of French hands, **24.** 437; England still treats, politely, **21.** 462; English Court unlikely to complain to, about Niccolini, **19.** 19; Europe organized by, to destroy Prussia, **21.** 5; France may appease, by Sardinian concessions, **20.** 576; France may give less aid to, **21.** 187; French Court may be overshot by, **21.** 141; HW shuns, **33.** 503; hears of Peter III's dethronement before express arrives, **22.** 62–3; ignores Lobkowitz's weakness, **18.** 515; instigates Martin's ultimatum to Charles III, **22.** 565; Jesuits' dissolution may be delayed by, to secure total suppression, **23.** 477; Kaunitz inclines, towards Bourbons, **23.** 54; Lorenzi scolded by, **21.** 475; Neapolitan conquest desired by, **18.** 390; not so sure of Catherine II's friendship, **22.** 75; observes no law but that of pride, **22.** 395; Parma suspects, of trying to usurp it, **22.** 379; Peace of Füssen concealed by, **19.** 38; Rodt supposed to bring secret of, to Conclave, **21.** 215; Russian revolution foreseen by, **22.** 63n; shame-

[Vienna, *continued*]

proof, **22.** 2; spreads report that English will attack Trieste, **21.** 134–5; Tesi's banishment from Florence ordered by, **18.** 520; threatens Venice for defying Benedict XIV, **20.** 176; Turin Court's relations with, **18.** 228, **19.** 400–1, 478; unwilling to make peace till Silesia is regained, **21.** 360; will seek to advance to Naples, **19.** 306; wishes Mann to borrow money, **20.** 386; woos Ferdinand VI, **19.** 292; would be edified by Holy Week in Florence, **22.** 412; would spend its last florin rather than yield to Frederick II, **22.** 87

Cowper to go to, from Frankfurt, **25.** 661

Craon receives courier from, **19.** 292–3

—'s disavowal of Richecourt's enmity to Ginori to impress Court of, **18.** 216

—'s medical excuse to visit Pisa to be reported to, **17.** 342

Craven, Bns, to go to, **25.** 655, **42.** 176

Cristiani summoned to, **20.** 335

Dal Pozzo, Mme, avoids, **17.** 80

daughter's birth to Leopold and Maria Louisa disappoints, **22.** 481

Daun's defeat causes consternation in, **21.** 456

—'s retirement reported from, **21.** 470

devil more feared at, than anywhere else, **20.** 334

dispatches sent to, about English at Leghorn, **20.** 277

dispensation sent to, for P. Charles's wedding, **18.** 330

Du Châtelet's haughtiness at, **23.** 127

Durfort goes to, as ambassador, **39.** 65

England may substitute Prussia for, as an ally, **19.** 238

English-French peace hoped by, to be deferred, **22.** 87

English march on Rhine rumoured from, **18.** 290

etiquette of, does not allow early announcement of pregnancy, **22.** 427

experiments with diamonds at, **31.** 158

express from, to England, announcing Young Pretender's departure, **18.** 404

Florence gets information from, **17.** 40, 121, 143, 151, **18.** 553, **19.** 441, **21.** 90, 107, **22.** 10, **24.** 454

Foljambe on way from, to Paris, **28.** 50

Francis I announces from, that Botta will rule Tuscany, **21.** 125

—— blamed by people of, **17.** 143

—— invites Craons to, **20.** 25

—'s ministers ignore affairs of, **17.** 155

Francis II to be educated at, **25.** 474, 499

Frederick II may threaten, **18.** 512, **21.** 95

freemasons suppressed at, **18.** 226

French minister expected at, **17.** 151

French rejoice in the destruction of Lyon as if it were, **34.** 192

French treaty with, *see* Versailles, Treaty of

Gavi's prosecution transferred to, **17.** 491

—'s release ordered from, **17.** 368

Genoese doge and senate to go to, **22.** 312–13

George II's death to be mourned by, **21.** 462

German gazetteers told to get all military news from, **21.** 310

Germans at, would faint at Joseph II's and Leopold II's informality, **23.** 112

Germans find Florentine climate as bad as that of, **22.** 575

Ginori's mission to, **17.** 395, 406, 490, **18.** 122, 138

—— to replace Bartolommei at, **17.** 395, 406, 490

Gradenigo, ambassador at, **3.** 147n

Grantham ambassador at, like his father, **25.** 296n

Grune's rumoured appointment to, **17.** 144, 151

Guadagni omnipotent at, through Francis I's cicisbea, **23.** 272, 278–9

HW averse to any detachment from, **22.** 333

HW if commander-in-chief would dash to, to make peace, **21.** 285

HW not to make pilgrimage to, **31.** 155

hope in, about war's success, **21.** 519–20

Ingenhousz inoculates archduchesses at, **23.** 91

inhabitants of, would stone Wraxall, **25.** 138

Irish Lorrainer goes to, to protest to Francis I, **21.** 125

Jesuits remain at Court in, **22.** 517n

Joseph II intends, to be capital of Europe, **33.** 524

—— sends courier to, **23.** 111

—— taken from, **17.** 155

—— to return to, **22.** 556, **24.** 312

Kaunitz orders James to leave, **21.** 462

—'s alleged stud of horses at, **17.** 49

Keith ambassador at, **9.** 45n

—— minister to, during Robinson's absence, **20.** 16n

—— signs convention for Modenese succession at, **20.** 393n

Khevenhüller to defend, **17.** 151

Kingston, Ds of, rebuffed at, **24.** 398

Kinsky brings Order of Marie-Thérèse to Leopold from, **22.** 362

Langlois affair sent to, by courier, **19.** 374

Leghorn governor tells, of Saunders's approach, **21.** 507

Leopold and Francis II visit, **25.** 505

Leopold and Maria Louisa avoid burletta for fear of reprimand from, **22.** 393

Leopold and Maria Louisa may be forbidden by, to attend theatre, **22.** 407

Leopold asks permission from, for trip to Rome, **23.** 91

—— awaits instructions from, **22.** 337, 350, 353, 356

—— hears from D. of Gloucester at, about marriage, **23.** 308

—— hopes for remission from, of orders to go to Parma, **23.** 413

—— probably told by, how to receive D. of Gloucester, **24**. 129

—— receives private messenger from, every fortnight, **25**. 44

letters patent from, signed by Bartenstein for Maria Theresa, and by Gorsegno for Charles Emmanuel III, **19**. 215n

Lobkowitz ordered by, to enter Tuscany, **19**. 11

——'s army not reinforced by, **19**. 22

——'s expedition promised from, **18**. 271

Lorenzi hears English news from, **17**. 325

Louis XV overcomes Neapolitan opposition at, to Maria Isabella's marriage, **21**. 323n

—— said to get troops from, **37**. 570

Louisbourg's capture probably causes sensation at, **21**. 235

Lucca sends emissary to, to complain of floods, **20**. 515

Magnan sends letters to, by courier, **19**. 220

—— sent to, by George II, **18**. 564

——'s plan for Corsican rebellion submitted to, **20**. 274, 386

Mann, Horace II, to visit, **24**. 374

Maria Theresa orders Francis I to return to, **17**. 316

masking to be allowed in Florence if there is no bad news from, **22**. 559

mass said at, for those killed in whole campaign, **21**. 333

Mathews to send couriers to, **18**. 325

Mauduit's *Considerations* appear at, **21**. 469

Maximilian Joseph of Bavaria sent to, **26**. 10

Migazzi gets orders from, to oppose Dumesnil's consecration, **19**. 492

minister of, at Florence, is plenipotentiary, **23**. 293

minister at odds with, **21**. 102

mob of, tries to honour Paoli on proposed visit, **23**. 140

Modenese treaty with, **20**. 393–4, 400

mourning at, for Duchesse de Lorraine, **19**. 14

mourning directions expected from, on Electress's death, **18**. 175

mourning rigorously enforced at, **22**. 354

Newcastle replaces Villiers's name with Keith's for, **20**. 16n

Niccolini may be visiting, **19**. 7

Niccoli's iniquity discovered at, **20**. 335

nuncio may be dismissed from, **17**. 56

nuncio's status at, **22**. 319

orders awaited from, about Electress's effects, **18**. 176

orders may have been received from, about announcing Leopold's accession, **22**. 345

Orford, Cts of, may visit, **19**. 48

Orsi disappointed at French not capturing, **17**. 481

Osnabrück and Hanover closer to, than Brabant is, **34**. 90

panduri to be placed outside of, **17**. 144

Paris, Abp of, asked to send nuns to, **20**. 333–4

Pius VI asks leave of Joseph II to visit him in, **25**. 239

—— proposes to visit, **2**. 306

——'s visit to, **25**. 250, 384

Pompadour, Mme de, might visit, **21**. 258n

Prague disaster concealed at, **21**. 242

preparations for defence of, **17**. 143–4

Priero to go to, **19**. 158

Protestant girls' case contested in, **22**. 250

Pucci's letter mentions no orders from, **21**. 116

report from, **11**. 91

Richecourt blamed for Tuscany's poor relations with, **20**. 267

—— complains to George II through, **18**. 328

—— dies on way back to, **20**. 335n

—— permitted to visit, whenever he pleases, **20**. 392

—— prepares for trip to, **20**. 327, 334

—— refused leave to visit, **20**. 252

——'s brother dies on way to, **20**. 335n

—— sends courier to, **18**. 314

—— shines dimly at, **19**. 219

——'s influence at, said to have declined, **20**. 463

——'s intrigues at, **19**. 322

——'s rebuffs from, **20**. 284

——'s return from, will be awaited by Cts of Orford, **19**. 144

—— summoned to, **17**. 89, 95

—— to refer Mann's letter about jurisdictions to, **19**. 1

—— wants money to take to, **20**. 488

Richecourts of Turin to visit, **20**. 45

Richmond, Mrs, sends to, **19**. 290

Robinson, Sir Thomas, English minister to, **17**. 497n, **20**. 202, 417n, **25**. 296n

Roe ambassador to, **15**. 93n

Rosenberg visits, to get his debts paid, **23**. 220

rumours from, of Russo-Turkish peace, **39**. 180

Russian manifesto forwarded from, to Florence, **22**. 74

St Joseph's Day at, **22**. 371

St-Odile opposes Richecourt in, **20**. 305, 308

—— secretary of Inner Council for Tuscany at, **20**. 305n

Sankt Pölten near, **17**. 194

Seckendorf discloses plan to, **21**. 266

secretary of *toison d'or* to come to Florence from, **23**. 1

Seilern chief justice in, **10**. 139n

siege of, represented in dance at Florentine opera, **25**. 360, 361n

Simonetti, Mme, makes plan at, for Modenese heiress, **22**. 201

Spanish hospital at, **22**. 459n

Stainville has no place at, **20**. 29

Stanislas II sends letter to his 'sister' at, **25**. 633

Stormont to have post at, **22**. 130

—— to return to, **23**. 18, 25

[Vienna, *continued*]
Te Deum sung at, **21**. 246n
theatres at, closed for a year for mourning, **22**. 340
Thun sends courier to, **18**. 56
Thurn, Comtesse, left at, **23**. 253
Tornaquinci neglected by, **21**. 107
Toussaint sends orders from, **17**. 349
Treaty of, **18**. 53n
Tron's possible dismissal from, **20**. 190n
Tuscan Council in, **20**. 220
Tuscan Court awaits orders from, before admitting visitors, **22**. 337, 340
Tuscan Court imitates, **22**. 390, 412
Tuscan Court will be lectured by, for extravagance, **23**. 134–5
Tuscan regency defends Langlois case to, **19**. 366
Tuscan regency mentions to, Mann's reported promotion, **22**. 346
Tuscan regency sends couriers to, **20**. 423
Tuscan regents neglected by, **21**. 107
Tuscan troops to form garrison at, **21**. 195–6
Tuscany awaits orders and officials from, **21**. 85
——'s link with, entails interest in Scheldt dispute, **25**. 544
Venice sends couriers to, **20**. 190
Villiers may become minister to, **19**. 16–17
Villierses to visit, **39**. 261
visitors to: Botta, **22**. 245n, 246; Chute, **19**. 207, 279; Coke, Lady Mary, **23**. 553, **31**. 148–50, 154, 155, 160–7, 175, **32**. 251; Conway, **39**. 537–8; Craon, Princesse de, **22**. 324; Craven, Bns, **42**. 84n; Derby, Cts of, **33**. 288; Dumesnil, **19**. 491; Forrester, **18**. 107; Gloucester, D. of, **23**. 332; Hamilton, Sir William and Lady, **23**. 448; Harte, **20**. 175n; Hasan Effendi, **20**. 127n; Hildburghausen, **21**. 194; Kingston, Ds of, **24**. 398n; Lee, **24**. 390; Leopold, **11**. 355n; Leopold and Maria Louisa, **23**. 205, 214, 220, 332, **24**. 240, 250, 370, 389, 409; Löwenstein, **19**. 306; Magnan, **18**. 564; Mill, **19**. 407, 454; Old Pretender, **42**. 10n; Pius VI, **25**. 283, 384; Richecourt, **17**. 89, 95, **19**. 144, 192, 219, 290, 322, **20**. 327, 334, 335, 392n, 421, 488, **21**. 80; Schulenburg, **19**. 50; Scott, **39**. 537–8; Scottish gentlemen, **19**. 290; Simonetti, Contessa, **22**. 126, 201; Stanhope, Philip, **20**. 175n; Steavens, **20**. 175n; Tesi, **18**. 521, **21**. 194; Vespa, Dr, **24**. 240n; Villiers, Lord and Lady, **32**. 251; Vorontsov, **22**. 180; Wharton, **42**. 10n; Whithed, **19**. 207, 279
Walpole, Bns (Cts of Orford), might follow Richecourt to, **17**. 89, 95, 125
Williams's distich on Maria Theresa admired at, **37**. 354
Williams sent on unofficial mission to, **30**. 321
Vienna Gazette:
Mauduit's pamphlet printed in extracts in, **21**. 469n

Vienne, Abp of. *See* Lefranc de Pompignon, Jean-Georges
Vie privée du Duc de Chartres, La. See under La Fite de Pellepore, Anne-Gédéon; Thévenot de Morande, Charles
Vieri, Abbé. *See* Véri, Joseph-Alphonse de
Vieri, Girolamo (d. 1742), Auditor:
daughter supported by, **17**. 473
death of, from falling picture, **17**. 473, 481
Vieri, Maria Maddalena (d. 1794), m. (1731) Conte Giovanni Francesco del Benino:
Buckingham's story would be enjoyed by, **18**. 307
Del Monte comforts, **17**. 473
——'s affair with, **17**. 33, 123, (?) 156, 473
father of, dies, **17**. 473, 481
father supports, and keeps her from husband's ill-treatment, **17**. 473
Goldsworthy, Mrs, called on by, **17**. 316
HW to receive compliments of, **17**. 37, 68
husband of: a beast, **17**. 473; put under *pupilli*, **17**. 122
Mann entertains, at coffee, **17**. 33
—— serves currant tarts to, **17**. 68
——'s party not to be attended by, **17**. 498
Vierpyl, Simon (ca 1725–1810), sculptor; art dealer:
(?) Chute employs, to purchase eagle, **19**. *101*
(?) Mann employs, to get sepulchral *ara*, **20**. 352
—— helped by, at Rome, in finding art objects, **20**. 391
Strada Felice, Roman address of, **20**. 392n
Vierville, Marquise de. *See* Fresnel, Françoise-Élisabeth de
Vies des pères:
Lorraine, Primate of, suggests, as title for *Le Portier des Chartreux*, **17**. 274
Vies des . . . poètes provensaux, Les. See under Notredame, Jean de
Vieumenil. *See* Viomenil
Vieuville, Comte de la. *See* La Vieuville, Charles-Marie
Vieuville, Mme de:
social relations of, with Comtesse de Maurepas, **7**. 296
Vieux Colombier, Rue du, in Paris:
Miséricorde convent in, **26**. 47
'View from the Thatched House, The.' *See under* West, Richard
View of the Controversy, A:
pamphlet in miracles controversy, **15**. 297
View of the Expediency and Credibility of Miraculous Powers, A. See under Chapman, John
View of the Internal Evidence of the Christian Religion, A. See under Jenyns, Soame
Vigenère, Blaise de (1523–96):
Traicté des chiffres by, **40**. 250
Vigier. *See* Du Vigier
Vigilant, English ship:
Keppel awaits, **39**. 307
—— mentions, **28**. 415n

Vigna, Casa. *See* Pisa: Mann's house at
(?) Vigne, Comtesse de, of Richmond:
SH visited by, **12.** 252
Vignerot du Plessis, Louis-François-Armand
(1696–1788), Duc and Maréchal de Richelieu; first gentleman of the Bedchamber at
the French Court:
Adélaïde, Mme, advised by, to receive Mme
du Barry, **23.** 87
Aiguillon, Duc d', not expected by, to over-
take D. of York, **7.** 366
Aiguillon, Duchesse d', may bring, to Mme
du Deffand's, **3.** *154*
Aller crossed by troops of, **21.** 167n
army under: aids Soubise, **21.** 137, 146, 159;
embarrasses Frederick II's strategy, **21.**
146; may attack Minorca, **20.** 545; may
invade England, **19.** 187, 509; reassembled
at Celle after Soubise's defeat at Rossbach,
21. 158n
bagwig of, **7.** 370
Barrymore, Cts of, provided by, with opera
box, **32.** 55
Bastille confinement of, **6.** 38
Beauvau replaces, as governor of Guyenne,
22. 342n
becomes Maréchal, **19.** 510
Belle-Isle discredits, with Louis XV, **21.** 172n
Bourgogne, Duchesse de, said by Chesterfield to have had affair with, **6.** 38, 41
Byng's behaviour not to be evaluated by, **21.**
61
——'s squadron cannot stop land operations
of, **20.** 558
Charles Emmanuel III to be visited by, at
Turin on way to France, **20.** 576
Chesterfield praises, **6.** 37
Choiseul, Duc and Duchesse de, enrage, by
visiting his château, **6.** 463
Choiseul, Duc de, makes remark to, on Mme
du Barry, **7.** 369
——'s joke on Mme de Mirepoix answered
by, **7.** 369
Ciudadela magistrates surrender on board
ship of, **20.** 552
Cour des Aides brought order of suppression
by, **5.** 58–9
daughter of, **3.** 42n, **31.** 79
Dauphin's entrée given to, **4.** 444
Du Barry the pimp of, **23.** 75
Du Barry, Comtesse, entertains, at supper,
23. 115
——'s presentation at Court involves, **4.** 191–
3, 196, 200
—— wins from, **4.** 250–1
Dubois's daughter has him forced into theatre by, enraging other actors, **38.** 538–9
Du Deffand, Mme, thinks, not greatly to be
feared, **4.** 234
Egmont, Comtesse d', summoned to be the
consolation of, **7.** 287
embarkation orders received by, **20.** 541n

Estrées succeeded by, in army command, **37.**
497n
Ferdinand, P., denounces Convention of
Klosterzeven even to, **21.** 153n
——'s convention with, **21.** 153n
financial misconduct of, attacked, **21.** 172,
193–4, 195
first gentleman of the Bedchamber, **4.** 191n,
31. 64
garden and pavilion of, at Paris, **7.** 284
Genoa expects arrival of, **20.** 576n
—— to be evacuated by, **19.** 510
George II's box at Hanover occupied by,
after victory, **30.** 137–8
Germans force, to fight in winter, **21.** 158,
176
Gibraltar reinforcements spur, to desperate
attack on Minorca, **20.** 576
graces of, **32.** 13
grandson and son of, **34.** 109
HW compared with, by Mme Geoffrin, **31.**
74, 82
HW compares: to Lt-Gen. Charles Churchill,
10. 181; with Chesterfield, **39.** 35
HW curious to see, **38.** 470
HW describes, **35.** 114
HW inquires about lawsuit of, **6.** 445, 449
HW jokes about his resemblance to, **31.** 58,
74
HW sups with, and calls him 'old piece of
tawdry,' **39.** 34–5
HW will imitate, **32.** 246
Hanover electorate plundered by, **21.** 172n,
23. 329
health of, **7.** 230
itinerary of, from Minorca to Paris, **20.** 576n
Jesuits said to have been restored by, **23.** 316
Klosterzeven convention concluded by, with
D. of Cumberland, **21.** 136n
La Vauguyon told by, to notify Mme Adélaïde
of Mme du Barry's presentation, **23.** 85n
Lixin killed by, in duel, **28.** 290
Louis XV asked by, to permit Comtesse du
Barry's presentation, **23.** 115
—— laughs at reply by, concerning Comtesse
du Barry, **4.** 250–1
—— should permit, to give balls and fêtes,
38. 469
Maillebois opposed by, **6.** 323
Maintenon, Mme de, describes first appear-
ance of, **35.** 277
marriage of, **7.** 204, 208, 215, 220, 443
Maurepas's disgrace plotted by, **20.** 51n
'Mémoire contre M. de Maurepas' by, attacks
naval mismanagement, **20.** 51n
'Methusaleh,' **32.** 13
Minorcan expedition of, **37.** 462
Mirepoix, Mme de, joins, **4.** 256n
—— leagued with Mme du Barry and, against
Choiseul, **41.** 192
—— reconciled with, **7.** 369
operas ordered by, for Fontainebleau, **31.** 56,
64

[Vignerot du Plessis, Louis, *continued*]

Parallèle de la conduite du Roi contains P. Ferdinand's letter to, **21.** 235n

Paris, Abp of, forbids marriage of, **7.** 204

parliament of Bordeaux intimidates, **23.** 329

Parma expects arrival of, to conclude treaty with France, **20.** 576n

pavilion built by, with his Hanoverian spoils, **21.** 172n, **23.** 329

Port Mahon captured by, **20.** 552

pretence by, of still having mistresses, **10.** 181

Prussia negotiates with France through, **21.** 153n

red heels worn by, **31.** 79

retreats to Fronsac, and sends to Versailles for help, **23.** 329

Rueil visited by, **7.** 335

St-Vincent, Présidente de, accuses, **6.** 157–8, 160, 168, 289, 291, 292

—— loses lawsuit against, **6.** 439, 440, **30.** 263

Savona attacked by, **19.** 476n

social relations of, in Paris, *see index entries ante* **8.** 540

son-in-law of, sent by him to Madrid, **20.** 572

son of: **3.** 237n; boasts of father's amours and lack of Latin, **20.** 339; sent to Paris with news, **20.** 572

Te Deum sung by, on landing at Minorca, **20.** 567

Valois defeats avenged by, **35.** 277

Versailles Court entertainments to be under care of, **38.** 465

Voltaire sends to Byng a letter of, **21.** 51, 61

winter quarters must be left by, to aid Soubise, **21.** 158

wrinkles of, **23.** 329

York, Cardinal, rebuked by, **19.** 509–10

York, D. of, receives letter from, **7.** 366

——'s arrival at Bordeaux not announced to, **7.** 365

Zoll reached by, **21.** 137n

Vignerot du Plessis-Richelieu, Armand-Désiré (1761–1800), Duc d'Agenois:

marriage of, arranged, **7.** 453

reversion of colonelcy of chevau-légers given to, **7.** 440

Vignerot du Plessis-Richelieu, Armand-Emmanuel-Sophie-Septimanie (1766–1822), Comte de Chinon; Duc de Fronsac, 1788; Duc de Richelieu, 1791:

arrives in London, **11.** *256*, 259, **34.** 109

grandfather and father of, **34.** 109

late gentilhomme du chambre du Roi, **11.** 259

returns to Paris, **11.** 259

Vignerot du Plessis-Richelieu, Emmanuel-Armand (1720–88), Duc d'Aiguillon; gov. of Brittany:

affair of, no longer talked of, **4.** 438

Aiguillon, Duchesse d' (dowager), forced by, to entertain Comtesse du Barry, **5.** 110

—— lives with, **5.** 13

Aiguillon visited by, **6.** 199, 200

ambassador to England to be named by, **5.** 116

Arnaud and Suard dismissed by, **7.** 341

Avignon may not be relinquished by, **23.** 527

Avignon parliament's restoration not wanted by, **23.** 527n

becomes prime minister, **23.** 314

Bernis ordered by, to support Azpuru's efforts at Rome, **23.** 373n

books on: **4.** 429, 493–4; sent by Mme du Deffand to HW, **4.** 378–80, 425, 427–9

Bordeaux visited by, **7.** 336

Breton difficulties of, **3.** 118, 302, **4.** 259n, **8.** 167, 168

Brittany governed by, **21.** 221n

—— not to be visited by, **3.** 370

Broglie, Comte de, an adherent of, **23.** 283

——'s correspondence with, **5.** 402

——'s quarrel with, **23.** 521

cabinet post to go to, **23.** 265

Chaulnes replaced by, **7.** 370

chevau-légers commanded by, **7.** 370

chevau-légers excessively costly to, **4.** 340

chevau-légers kept by, **6.** 67, 251

Choiseul may be succeeded by, **23.** 79, 84n, 85, 258

——'s enemy, **3.** 349n, **4.** 196–7, 464n

——'s resignation demanded through, **5.** 165–7

—— succeeded by, **11.** 44n

Condé opposes, **5.** 5, 45

—— said not to like, **5.** 5

——'s reconciliation with Louis XV not negotiated by, **5.** 296

Conflans to convoy transports of, from Vannes, **21.** 350n

Correspondance de Monsieur le Duc d'Aiguillon by: **7.** 173, 175–9, 188; received by Richmond from HW, **41.** 299

correspondence in Guines's case published by, **24.** 90

country seat of, **4.** 253n

Craufurd to consult, **5.** 285

customs barriers, proposed alteration of, in ministry of, **7.** 375

daughter of, **3.** 130n

Dauphin's entrée granted to, **4.** 444

death of only daughter of, **6.** 332, **32.** 298

dinner given by, **5.** 86–7

diplomatists entertain, **5.** 108

dismissal of, expected, **6.** 59

Du Barry, Comtesse, aids, and is aided by, **4.** 169n, 196–7, 339–40, **5.** 45, 48, 69, **39.** 144

—— often visited by, **23.** 321

—— on good terms with, **4.** 372

—— receives patent of, **7.** 370

—— retires to estate of, at Rueil, **24.** 2

—— said to have been betrayed by, **24.** 12

Du Châtelet negotiates Choiseul's resignation with, **5.** 165–6

—— receives letter from, **5.** 165

Du Deffand, Mme, gives opinion of political status of, **4.** 340

—— thinks, not greatly to be feared, **4.** 234, 464

—— tired of, **4.** 434

England or Ireland may be destination of, **21.** 346n, 351n

England told by, that French fleet is countermanded, **23.** 475n

English prisoners entertained by, at supper, **21.** 251, 255

'Épigramme' on, sent by Mme du Deffand to HW, **4.** 494, **8.** 180

expedition to Scotland to be led by, **21.** 296n, 328n, 346n, 350n, 351n

faction of, promises peace, **39.** 135

fête given by, **5.** 324, 338

Forcalquier, Mme de, accuses Mme du Deffand of opposing, **4.** 382

foreign affairs ministry of, announced, **32.** 49

foreign affairs secretaryship resigned by, **32.** 195–6

French prime minister, **35.** 342

friends of, imply that Choiseul wanted war, **23.** 258

Gazette article on Cts Waldegrave discussed by, **5.** 92–3

Goëzmann protected by, **6.** 35

Guines's expulsion threatened by, **7.** 341n

Gustav III aids, **5.** 48

HW disparages, **4.** 433, 434

HW mentions, **4.** 423

HW's interest in, **3.** 65, **4.** 429, 434

HW's opinion of, **23.** 323

HW to address envelope to, **5.** 114

HW to send *Fugitive Pieces* to, **7.** 416

jaundiced by vexation, **23.** 207

Jesuits may be befriended by, **23.** 260

—— no longer protected by, **5.** 213

La Chalotais drives, to demand a trial, **23.** 206–7

—— opposes tyranny of, **3.** 109n, **11.** 43

——'s pension and arrears restored by, **39.** 144

Lambert's toast must have made bad impression on, **21.** 255

Louis XV confers with, on Choiseul's fall, **41.** 193

—— does not favour, much, **23.** 321

—— quells Breton opposition to, **8.** 167, 168

—— supports, against parliament, **4.** 427, 429–30, 449n, 459, **8.** 169–70, 173–5

Louis XVI and Marie-Antoinette dislike, though Viennese Court wishes to keep him, **24.** 10n

Louis XVI forces, to resign, **28.** 221

——'s attitude towards, conjectured, **24.** 18

——'s consecration not to be attended by, **6.** 196

Mann asks about, **24.** 10

Marie-Antoinette intercedes for, **32.** 298

—— obtains return of, **6.** 323, 332

Marlborough's teaspoons returned by, **21.** 221, **37.** 544, 547

marriage of, **3.** 302n

Maupeou foe of, confers with Louis XVI, **24.** 10n

—— opposes, **5.** 213, 285, **23.** 453

——'s contest with, **39.** 144

Maurepas advises, to resign, **24.** 10n, 18n

—— demands return of, **6.** 314, 315

——'s nephew, **6.** 251, 314, 315

——'s possible colleague, **6.** 397

ministry of foreign affairs expected by, **5.** 5, 8, 18, 29, 48, 67, 69, 72, 80

ministry of foreign affairs given to, **5.** 82, 86

ministry of war given to, **6.** 12, 20

Monteynard succeeded by, **6.** 10n

mother lives with, **5.** 13

mother of, **8.** 81n, **22.** 524n, **28.** 51

mother told by, to visit Mme du Barry, **5.** 110, **23.** 338, **41.** 193

Orléans and other Princes of the Blood forbidden to enter controversy over, **8.** 166

pacific policy of, his only virtue, **24.** 11

parliamentary investigation asked by, **4.** 196–9

parliament of Bretagne restored in spite of, **23.** 134

parliament of Paris's investigation of: **4.** 425, 427, 429–30, 459, 470; judgment in, **4.** 430, **8.** 168–9; Louis XV reverses decision and suppresses documents in, **4.** 427–30, 449n, 459, **8.** 167, 169–70, 173–5

parliaments detest, **23.** 259

Praslin favours investigation of, **4.** 197

—— rumoured to be succeeded by, **39.** 65

prime ministry expected for, **39.** 134

Princes of the Blood to be reconciled by, to spite Maupeou, **23.** 399

proceedings against, **4.** 449n

public hostile to, **4.** 203, 378, 380

public interest in, **4.** 425, 427, 429

Redmond a favourite of, **3.** 295

removal of, popular, **35.** 422

resigns, **6.** 60, 64n

reward to be given to, **4.** 427, 428, 450

social relations of, in Paris, **4.** 288, 472, **5.** 40, 92, 194, 324, 338

Sorba gives dinner for, **5.** 83

Spain's negotiations with, over Jesuits, **23.** 306n

spoken of, for King's regiment, **3.** 349, 354, 356–7

Stormont confers with, **5.** 345

SH makes HW pity, **23.** 315

Suard and Arnaud dismissed by, **7.** 340n, 341

Supplément à la correspondance de M. le Duc d'Aiguillon by, **6.** 181

supporters of, **4.** 196–7, 202, 428

Thurot's diversion to allow, out of Vannes in Hawkes's absence, **21.** 337n

Véret, country seat of, **4.** 146

—— said to be destination of, **6.** 196

—— to be visited by, **6.** 67

—— visited by, **5.** 48

Vergennes replaces, as prime minister, **24.** 17

verses on, **6.** 194, **8.** 180

Voltaire praises, **28.** 153, **32.** 50

[Vignerot du Plessis-Richelieu, Emmanuel-Armand, *continued*]

Walpole, Hon. Robert, sees, **5**. 83

York, D. of, converses with, **7**. 366

—— overtaken by, **7**. 366

Young Pretender's Polish project explained by, **23**. 338n

Vignerot du Plessis-Richelieu, Jeanne-Sophie-Élisabeth-Louise-Armande-Septimanie (1740–73), m. (1756) Casimir Pignatelli d'Egmont, Comte d'Egmont:

Aiguillon, Duchesse d', visits, **3**. 130

attends supper in her night-cap, **32**. 27

balls given by, at Versailles, **38**. 505

beauty of, **14**. 156, **31**. 47, 79, 91

beauty prize given to, at Mirepoix ball, **3**. 221

Brunswick, P. of, flirted with, by, **3**. 42

dances at Mirepoix ball, **3**. 217

Du Deffand, Mme, mentions, **3**. 318

HW describes, **32**. 26–7

HW entertained by, but Mme de Brionne is away, **39**. 42

HW jokes about his 'love' for, **31**. 79

HW's admiration for, **3**. 42

HW's correspondence with, **7**. 382

HW's present to, **3**. 142

Hertford, Cts of, left by, after supper, **38**. 517

Hertford, E. of, glad that HW is in love with, **39**. 45

——'s party attended by, **38**. 517

honeywater requested by, **31**. 104

Molé benefit urged by, **3**. 230

Monaco, Princesse de, surpasses, **39**. 45

relatives of, **31**. 79, 91

Richelieu summons, for consolation at news of Dauphin's death, **7**. 287

social relations of, in Paris, *see index entries ante* **8**. 541

York, D. of, admires, **3**. 341, **7**. 365

Vignerot du Plessis-Richelieu, Louis-Antoine-Sophie (1736–91), Duc de Fronsac:

attends session of parliament of Paris, **8**. 172

Coigny fights duel with, **7**. 444

Compiègne visited by, **20**. 572n, 574n

conveys letters for Mme du Deffand and Duchesse d'Aiguillon, **3**. 255

Dubois's daughter said to be mistress of, **38**. 538n

father's amours and lack of Latin proclaimed by, **20**. 339

first gentleman of the Bedchamber, **4**. 191n

HW mentions, **3**. 341

Hervey, Bns, unable to aid, **3**. 277

London visited by, **3**. 237, 251

marriage of, **3**. 226n

news of St Philip's surrender brought by, from Minorca to Toulon and Paris, **20**. 572

Orford, E. of, assists, **3**. 277

protests illegal parliament, **5**. 61

social relations of, in Paris, **7**. 267, 293, 319, 320

son different from, **34**. 109

wife of, **3**. 226n

Vignerot du Plessis-Richelieu d'Aiguillon, Innocente-Aglaé (1747–76), m. (1766) Joseph-Dominique de Guigues de Moreton, Marquis de Chabrillan:

death of, **6**. 323n, 332, **32**. 298

Du Deffand, Mme, hears answers to Princes' protest read by, **5**. 72

marriage of, **3**. *130*, 183

social relations of, in Paris, **3**. 342, **5**. 138, 145, 183, 194, **7**. 280, 283, 285, 291, 323, 340

son born to, **3**. 382

Vigneul-Marville, M. de. *See* Argonne, Noël d'

Vignolles, Marie-Charlotte de, m. Charles Sarrazin:

cannon reverberations from Modena allegedly heard by, **17**. 443

Chute discusses smallpox with, **17**. 498

Craon and friends banish, from quadrille médiateur games, **18**. 329

Craon's guests told by, not to mention his son's death, **17**. 463

Craon, Princesse de, discussed by, with Mann, **18**. 175

—— entertains, **17**. 414, 498

—— has, as companion, **17**. 436n

—— tired of compliments of, **18**. 362

—— tires, by illnesses, **18**. 122

Craons dismiss, **18**. 361

daughter in Lorraine to take care of, **18**. 361

daughter of, **19**. 452

faro played by, **18**. 318

HW asks if Princesse de Craon's suppers make, impatient for cards, **19**. 161

HW imagines comment of, on Mrs Bosville, **18**. 298

income of, **18**. 361

India ink praised by, **17**. 414, 436

Juvrecourt son-in-law of, **17**. *193*, **18**. 368

'Lorraine Lady,' **17**. 436n

Mann, Chute, and Whithed forced by, to play quadrille médiateur, **18**. 132, 148

quadrille médiateur craved by, **18**. 122, 148, 329, 361

to retire to Lorraine, **18**. 361

wig of: clawed aside during gambling, **18**. 318; HW remembers, **19**. 452; will suffer after her dismissal, **18**. 361

Vignoris (France):

HW and Gray pass through, **13**. 180n

Vigo:

Watson reports action at, **21**. 297

Vigo Lane, London:

Queensberry's house in, **38**. 502

Strawbridge, Mrs, has house in, **33**. 556n

Vilaine River, France:

French ships driven up, **21**. 351, 359

Vilana Perlas, Gräfin von. *See* Seilern, Maria Anna von

Vilett, Jack (d. 1779):

Customs clerkship unsuitable for, but Pells place may be found, **36**. 89–90

Gloucester, Ds of, seeks Ordnance post for, through HW and Conway, **36**. 79–80

Vilette ('Villette'), Mme de. *See* Des Champs de Marcilli, Marie-Claire

Vilette, Seigneur de. *See* Le Vallois, Philippe

Villa; villas:
architecture of, around Florence, **20**. 166, 191
Italians never spend both spring and summer in the same, **22**. 456
Mann hankers for, **20**. 25, 160, 193
views of, HW receives and dislikes, **19**. 185, **20**. 166
See also under names of individual villas

Villa Bromhamensis. See under Hampden, Robert

Villafranca (Villefranche):
battle at, **18**. 435–7, 441
Charles Emmanuel III to attack, **19**. 313
English batteries protect, **17**. 408n
French blockade of, **21**. 264
frigate sails from, to pursue pirates, **25**. 480
garrison of, **19**. 323
Goldsworthy, Mrs, escorted to, by Rev. Thomas Horton, **18**. 13n
Lobkowitz to avenge loss of, by taking Naples, **18**. 437
Mathews arrives at, **17**. 361n
—— to leave, **18**. 360
Medley receives letter at, from Townshend, **19**. 359
——'s fleet at, **19**. 334
men sent to, could have discovered location of French fleet, **20**. 587n
Noel goes to, to spy on French, **20**. 536
one of England's last available Mediterranean ports, **20**. 575
Philip, Don, to attack, by land, **18**. 371n
Sardinians abandon, **18**. 436
sea engagement not reported at, **18**. 403–4
seaman at, reports victory to Florence, **17**. 471
Susa commander of, **18**. 360

Village, The. See under Crabbe, George

Village Politics. See under More, Hannah

Villain; villains:
HW's reflections on, **15**. 172–3

Villa Medici. *See under* Medici

Villa Negroni. *See under* Negroni

Villa Patrizzi. *See under* Patrizzi

Villa Petraia. *See under* Petraia

Villaret de Joyeuse, Louis-Thomas (1750–1812), Comte; vice-adm.:
fleet under, **12**. 18n
Howe defeats fleet of, **34**. 197n

Villarias, (?) Marqués de, Spanish official:
Ferdinand VI retains, in his Court, **19**. 278n

Villars, Duchesse de. *See* Noailles, Amable-Gabrielle de (1706–71)

Villars, Maréchale de. *See* La Rocque de Varengeville, Jeanne-Angélique de (d. 1763)

Villars, Claude-Louis-Hector (1653–1734), Duc de; Maréchal de France:
Eugene, P., defeated by, at Denain, **34**. 173n
French army commanded by, against Austrians in Italy, **20**. 159n
minuet danced by, supported by aides-de-camp, **20**. 159
pun by, on Milan, **20**. 159
vain and insolent, **34**. 173
Vie du Maréchal Duc de Villars by: **33**. 439; borrowed from HW by Hardinge, **35**. 633

Villars, Honoré-Armand (1702–70), Duc de:
ball given by at his country seat, **7**. 365, **22**. 553
social relations of, in Paris, **3**. 9, 111, **4**. 154, **7**. 308, 309, 314
wife of, **5**. 106n
York, D. of, entertained by, **7**. 365, **22**. 553

Villars-Brancas, Duc de. *See* Brancas, Louis de (1714–93)

Villars-Brancas, Duchesse de. *See* Mailly-Nesle, Diane-Adélaïde de

Villa Suares, near Florence:
Mann does not wish to spend the night at, **18**. 333
Modenese princess to be entertained at, **17**. 99, 100

Villa Viçosa, headquarters of House of Braganza:
José I attacked at, **4**. 329

Ville, Antoine (1596–1656), Chevalier de:
Marly machine invented by, **21**. 354n

Ville, La. *See* La Ville

Villebague. *See* La Villebague

Villebois, Mr (d. before 1801):
SH visited by, **12**. 222

Villebois, Mrs. *See* Read, Miss

Villebrune. *See* Lefebvre de Villebrune

Ville de Paris, La, French ship:
De Grasse's ship, taken by Rodney, **25**. 278

Villefort. *See* Bachois de Villefort

Villefranche. *See* Villafranca

Villegagnon, Marquis de. *See* Durand, ——

Villegagnon, Marquise de. *See* Batailhe de Montval, Jeanne-Marguerite

Villegaignon. *See* Villegagnon

Villeggiatura; villeggiature:
Clement XIV passes, at Castel Gandolfo, **23**. 526
Florence deserted during, **18**. 64, 329
Florentines prolong, till St Martin's Summer, **20**. 451

Villeinage:
laws about, **35**. 565

Ville-Issey, Bn de. *See* Jadot, Jean-Nicolas (1710–61)

Villemur, Marquis de; Lt-Gen.:
officers sentenced by, **21**. 382n

Villeneuve, Marquise de. *See* Simiane, Madeleine-Sophie de

Villeneuve, Alexandre-Marie de (b. 1748), Abbé de Trans:
censured, **6**. 439
Richelieu to pay, **6**. 439

Villeneuve, Julie de (ca 1731–78), m. (1746) Jules-François de Fauris de St-Vincent; 'Présidente de St-Vincent':

[Villeneuve, Julie de, *continued*]
Richelieu accused by, **6.** 157–8, 168, 289, 291, 292
—— wins lawsuit brought by, **6.** 439, 445, **30.** 263
Sévigné, Mme de, great-grandmother of, **30.** 263
Villeneuve, Louis-Henri de (b. 1739), Marquis de Trans:
social relations of, with Marquis de Brancas, **7.** 298
wife of, **4.** 410n
Villeneuve. *See also* Dufour de Villeneuve
Villeneuve-Flayosc, Abbé de:
censured, **6.** 439
Richelieu to pay, **6.** 439
Ville Patour, ——, army officer:
(?) made maréchal de camp, **7.** 147n
Villequier, Duc de. *See* Aumont, Louis-Alexandre-Céleste d'
Villeroy, Duc de. *See* Neufville, Gabriel-Louis-François de (1731–94); Neufville, Louis-François-Anne de (1695–1766)
Villeroy, Duchesse de. *See* Aumont, Jeanne-Louise-Constance d'
Villeroy ware:
HW sends, to England, **7.** 407
Villers-Cotterêts, Duc d'Orléans's seat:
crowded, **39.** 143
entertainments at, **3.** 340
Paris robbed of good company by, **4.** 440, **5.** 82, **6.** 80, 84
spelling of, corrected, **43.** 91
verses from fête at, **3.** 121, 129
visitors to: Beauvau, Princesse de, **3.** 114, 123; Cambis, Vicomtesse de, **6.** 342, 462, 466; La Marche, Comtesse de, **3.** 330, 334; Luxembourg, Mme de, **5.** 380, 382, 394, **6.** 342, 462, 466; Tronchin, **3.** 114
Villette, Marquise de. *See* Des Champs de Marcilli, Marie-Claire (1675–1750); Rouph de Varicour, Reine-Philiberte (1757–1822)
Villette, Charles (1736–93), Marquis de:
Beaune, Rue de, home of, **7.** 17
Du Deffand, Mme, gives opinion of, **7. 20,** 35
Ferney visited by, **7.** 12
Raucourt, Mlle, insulted by, **6.** 157
verses on, **7.** 23
Voltaire accompanied by, to Paris, **7.** 17
—— aided by, in conversation, **7.** 21
—— to be brought to Paris by, **7.** 12
Villette. *See also* Rétaux de Villette; Vilette
Villette de Murçay, Marthe-Marguerite de (1673–1729), m. (1686) Jean-Anne de Tubières de Pestel de Levy, Marquis de Caylus:
Mann quotes, **23.** 406
Villettes, Arthur (ca 1702–76), English secretary of embassy at Court of Savoy 1734–41; Resident 1741–9; minister to Switzerland 1749–62:
Birtles's correspondence with, **19.** 65
Botta's peace terms condemned by, **19.** 312
Charles Emmanuel III persuaded by, about Corsican rebels, **19.** 260

——'s account of battle to be forwarded by, to England, **18.** 155
——'s attitude reported by, to be favourable, **17.** 265
—— sends, to confer with fleet, **19.** 64
——'s intentions doubted by, **17.** 312
——'s picture given to, **20.** 76
—— summons, to approve his evacuation of Chambéry, **18.** 142
—— to be notified by, of Young Pretender's departure, **17.** 14
—— urged by, to coordinate plans for invasion of Provence, **19.** 323n
Chute and Whithed laugh at, **18.** 279
cipher not used by, **18.** 385
Cooper assured by, **19.** 81
Corsican rebellion approved by, **19.** 276
courier cannot be sent by, through France, **18.** 385
couriers of: carry incomplete news, **19.** 335; dispatched at every opportunity, **19.** 436; go faster than Mann's, **19.** 305; reaches England, **18.** 417; sent from Turin through Germany, **18.** 389, 397; will disappoint England, **19.** 363
courier's robbery concealed by, **19.** 334
England hears little of, **18.** 293
—— visited by, before settling at Berne, **20.** 76, 90
English fleet off Genoa to be visited by, **19.** 64
English minister at Turin, **18.** 60n, **19.** 456n
fleet's movements not announced to, **19.** 334
Florence visited by, **19.** 64
Fumagalli's capture at Turin requested of, **18.** 96–7
Genoa capitulation dispute mishandled by, **19.** 312n
Genoa visited by, **18.** 271
Genoese news reported by, **19.** 367, 436
Gorsegno's conduct upheld by, **19.** 478
—— tells, at Charles Emmanuel III's quarters, about English captain's disloyalty, **19.** 150
HW attributes Mann's illness to tiring qualities of, **18.** 60
HW has nothing to do with, **20.** 90
Hyères visit refused by, **18.** 271
illness of, at Turin, prevents Gorsegno from consulting him, **19.** 150
letters of: immoderately long, **18.** 508, **19.** 237, 245, 312, 426, 465, 466; pompous, **18.** 279, 385, **19.** 183, 476; quoted by Mann, **19.** 237; use ciphers, **18.** 59, 97
Lombard victories to be reported by, **19.** 291
Mann angry with, for diverting courier, **18.** 404
—— asked by, to borrow money from Leghorn merchants, **19.** 215
—— awaits return of, with orders for Cooper, **19.** 81
—— communicates with, about Young Pretender, **17.** 13n
—— confers with, **19.** 64

—— corresponds with Gorsegno since visit of, to fleet, 19. 150

—— dislikes possible replacement of, by Williams, 19. 466

—— expects to hear from, 17. 342

—— informed by, of prospect of winter campaign, 18. 59n

—— informs, of Young Pretender's departure, 18. 373n

—— involved by, in Corsican intrigues, 19. 260–1

—— may assist, at fleet conference at Leghorn, 17. 443

—— mistakenly writes name of, for Villiers, 18. 25

—— plagued by, 18. 293

—— receives from, a letter from Nice, 18. 413

—— receives news of fleet from, 18. 403n

——'s correspondence with, 18. 16, 59, 79, 385, 404, 413, 19. 237, 374

—— sends letters through, 18. 385

——'s jealousy of, 19. 431n

——'s plan for Corsican conquest forwarded by, to England, 20. 386

—— to notify, of Young Pretender's departure, 17. 13–14

—— will enjoy Williams's letters more than those of, 19. 465

Mathews may be summoned by, 18. 16

—— not to act too suddenly on advice of, 18. 26–7

——'s correspondence with, 18. 26, 37

—— sees, at Genoa, 18. 271

——'s treaty with Genoa aided by, 18. 271, 455, 529

—— to confer with, 18. 240–1

minister to Switzerland, 19. 456n

Money's dispatches said by, to assure English fleet's continuing to threaten Genoa, 19. 12

Montagu, Lady Mary Wortley, praises, 17. 98n

Montemar's motives interpreted by, 18. 16

Newcastle, D. of, thinks well of, 19. 431n

Piacenza visited by, 17. 392n

plans to be announced by, 19. 353

Port Mahon reached by, on way to see Rowley, 19. 81

Rochford to meet, in Paris, 20. 76

San Lazaro victory may be announced by, 19. 265

Savona attack will be described by, 19. 476

secret instructions to, about Don Philip, 19. 278n

servant of, takes news to England, 19. 431

solemnity of, 20. 76

Spaniards commented on by, 18. 279

successor to Wentworth desired by, 19. 451

Townshend, Capt., corresponds with, 19. 183, 245

—— to be interviewed by, 19. 292

Turin left by, 20. 76

Turin post of, more important than Mann's at Florence, 19. 431n

Turin-Vienna convention reported by, 19. 401n

war operations shunned by, 19. 402n

Wentworth's mission advised by, 19. 401–2

Williams, Sir C. H., may succeed, at Turin, 19. 347, 456, 465, 466

Villevieille, Marquis de. *See* Pavée de Villevieille, Philippe-Charles

Villiars. *See* Villiers

Villicy, Jean-Baptiste-Nicolas-Louis de (b. 1709), Chevalier de Tourville:

(?) affairs of Hon. T. Walpole known to, 5. 116

(?) Du Deffand, Mme, friend of, 4. 78–9, 165, 388

(?) ——'s opinion of, 4. 374

(?) HW inquired after by, 5. 382, 6. 384

(?) HW praises, 4. 358, 365, 374

(?) HW sent regards by, 5. 139

(?) HW's *Gramont* not to be given to, 5. 308

(?) HW told to give *Gramont* to, 5. 299

(?) HW to meet, 5. 86

(?) health of, 6. 384

(?) pension of, reduced, 4. 353–4

(?) *Roi et le fermier, Le*, attended by, 7. 320

(?) social relations of, in Paris, 3. 393, 404, 4. 165, 6. 384, 7. 295, 297, 298, 312, 316, 332, 338, 340, 352

(?) Terray interceded with by, for Mme du Deffand, 4. 353–4, 358

Villiers, Bn. *See* Mason Villiers, George (1751–1800)

Villiers, Vct. *See* Mason Villiers, George (1751–(1800); Villiers, George (1592–1628); Villiers, George Bussy (1735–1805)

Villiers, Vcts. *See* Fane, Lady Sarah Sophia (1785–1867); Seymour-Conway, Lady Gertrude (1750–93)

Villiers, ——:

attends session of parliament of Paris, 8. 173

Villiers, Mrs:

SH visited by, 12. 249

Villiers, Lady Anna Barbara Frances (1772–1832), m. 1 (1791) William Henry Lambton; m. 2 (1801) Hon. Charles William Wyndham:

French bonnet 'aristocrate' drawn by, in lottery, 34. 142

Jersey, Lady, moves to new house of, 12. 188

mother of, 12. 188n

Villiers, Anne (d. 1654), m. (1627) Robert Douglas, 8th E. of Morton; governess to Ps Henrietta:

portrait of, 30. 370

Waller alludes to, 30. 370

Villiers, Barbara (1641–1709), m. 1 (1659) Roger Palmer, cr. (1661) E. of Castlemaine; m. 2 (1705) Robert Feilding; cr. (1670) Ds of Cleveland, s. j.; Charles II's mistress:

Dixon's portrait of, 41. 97

Fitzroy, Lady Caroline descended from, 30. 326n

granddaughter of, 25. 508

[Villiers, Barbara, *continued*]
Hamilton, Lady Archibald, contrasted with, **9.** 16
—— to accompany, in death, **35.** 68
Lely's portrait of: as Pallas, **30.** 326; at Julienne's, **7.** 287
Nonsuch Palace placed in trust for, **2.** 150n
portraits of, **7.** 287, **30.** 326, **40.** 284, **41.** 97
print of, **16.** 323
Rose, gardener to, **2.** 200n, **29.** 45n
son of, **1.** 350n
Yarmouth, Cts of, the successor of, **20.** 90
Villiers, Lady Barbara (d. 1761), m. 1 (1725) Sir William Blackett, 2d Bt; m. 2 (1729) Bussy Mansell, 4th Bn Mansell:
death of, expected, **9.** 345
Villiers, Caroline Elizabeth (1774–1835), m. 1 (1795) Henry William Paget, later M. of Anglesey (divorced); m. 2 (1810) George William Campbell, 6th D. of Argyll:
husbands of, **11.** 108n, 187n
Villiers, Catherine (d. 1772), m. John Craster:
death of, vacates Winchester Tower, Windsor, **36.** 323
(?) footman of, dismissed for impertinence, **38.** 421
Villiers, Lady Charlotte (1721–90). *See* Capel, Lady Charlotte
Villiers, Lady Charlotte (1771–1808), m. (1789) Lord William Russell:
at Nuneham, with her mother, **32.** 247
Villiers, Lady Charlotte Barbara (b. 1761):
at Mrs Boyle Walsingham's ball, **42.** 222n
Villiers, Edward (?1656–1711), 1st E. of Jersey:
picture of, **2.** 341
Villiers, Elizabeth (d. 1733), m. (1695) George Hamilton, cr. (1696) E. of Orkney; William III's mistress:
meeting of, with other royal mistresses at Windsor, **33.** 528–9, **34.** 260
Villiers, Lady Elizabeth (d. 1782), m. 1 (1739) Aland John Mason; m. 2 (1763) Gen. Charles Montagu; cr. (1746) Vcts, (1767) Cts Grandison, s. j.:
assembly of, **10.** 206
Barrymore dies at house of, **32.** 139
Beaulieu, Cts, would have told, of seeing Williams's portrait, **10.** 107
Chute to receive compliments of, **10.** 136
daughter-in-law forced by, to travel with husband, **39.** 261
death of, at Spa, **33.** 334
Ditton Park visited by, **10.** 100
Dublin to be visited by, **10.** 66, 215
father's wealth to be inherited by, **10.** 215, 217
'formal, proud, and weak,' **36.** 76
Frogmore residence of, **10.** 74–5, 83, 210
genealogy of, **10.** 352
Gloucester, Ds of, formerly courted by, **36.** 76
HW to entertain, at breakfast, at SH, **10.** 99–101

HW to receive compliments of, **10.** 100, 103, 131, 135, 136
Hertford advises, not to call on Ds of Gloucester, **36.** 76–7
Hertfords entertained by, **39.** 281
Ireland to be visited by, **10.** 66, 75, 215
London visited by, **10.** 194
marriage of, arranged, **10.** 51
Montagu, George, asked by, for Eccardt's portrait of Charles Montagu, **10.** 132
—— entertained by, **10.** 206
(?) —— mortified by, **10.** 173, 267
—— promised by, a copy by Eccardt of portrait of Charles Montagu, **10.** 132
—— to be visited by, at Greatworth, **10.** 83
—— to visit, **10.** 75
—— visited by, at Greatworth, **10.** 131, 132
(?) Oxford visited by, **10.** 41–2
parents to be visited by, **10.** 66
peerage of, not to be extended to husband, **10.** 240
second husband of, dies, **36.** 134
son of, **10.** 43n, **23.** 323
son of, marries, **1.** 236
Townshend, Vcts, entertained by, **10.** 206
Waldegrave, Cts, entertained by, at Frogmore, **10.** 246
wealthy Irish peeress, **23.** 323
(?) Welderen, Countess van, praised by, **39.** 266
Villiers, Lord Francis (d. 1648):
death of, **16.** 154n
Villiers, Sir George (d. 1606):
HW jokes about ghost of, **10.** 282
Villiers, George (1592–1628), cr. (1616) Vct Villiers, (1617) E. and (1623) D. of Buckingham; James I's favourite:
Anne of Denmark's letter to, **15.** 74
educational progress a credit to, **16.** 152
Eglisham's book, attacking, **1.** 62
father of, **10.** 282n
HW interested in letters of, **17.** 357n
HW satirizes, **18.** 357
indecent expression of, **15.** 87
James I calls, 'Steenie,' **15.** 341
——'s letters to, **15.** 339–42, **17.** 357
Johnson's portrait of, **40.** 226
letters of, printed by Dalrymple, resemble those in British Museum, **15.** 84–5
member of House of Lords' committee on education, **16.** 151
mother of, **10.** 341
nephew of, **16.** 27n
print of, **1.** 179
Rubens's alleged portrait of, **34.** 239
son sells pictures formerly owned by, **16.** 153–4
Vertue's extract from letter of, **14.** 107
wife of, **15.** 341n
Villiers, George (1628–87), 2d D. of Buckingham, 1628; poet; dramatist:
Antwerp the refuge of, during English rebellion, **16.** 153–4

catalogue of collection of, **13**. 28

china manufactured by, **10**. 345

Clifford, friend of, **16**. 5n

'Ecce Homo' sold by, to Archduke Leopold, **16**. 153–4

Knole's associations with, **33**. 223

Marcus Brutus by, **35**. 478n

Percy's edition of: **42**. 366–70; not completed, **41**. 321n; undertaken for Tonson, to be finished by Percy's nephew, **42**. 368

portrait of, at Windsor, **37**. 242

Protestant miracles affirmed by, to James II's emissary, **18**. 306

Rehearsal, The, by: **43**. 62; Belsham's 'Strictures' discusses, **31**. 294; *Champion, The,* quotes, **18**. 33; Charlotte, Q., attends, at Drury Lane, **38**. 127; Conway alludes to, **37**. 221; Conway quotes, **37**. 249; 'Drawcansir' in, **1**. 361, **29**. 86, **31**. 117, **41**. 321; Garrick acts in, **17**. 435n; Garrick and Cibber as 'Bayes' in, **33**. 88, **38**. 525; HW alludes to, **9**. 9, 22, 394; HW compares Garrick to 'Bayes' in, **28**. 286; HW praises, **31**. 294; HW refers to two kings in, **35**. 324; half of merit of, is in the notes, **33**. 159; Hardinge refers to 'Bayes' in, **35**. 557; 'King Phiz' in, **32**. 143; Mason quotes from, **28**. 183, 367; Raftor dances hays in, **35**. 468; revolution in, **30**. 222; revolutions should be as bloodless as in, **23**. 236; *Royal and Noble Authors* discusses, **31**. 294; troops dance in, **37**. 297; 'universal ballet' in, **35**. 213; wet brown paper in, **43**. 257; Williams, G.J., quotes 'Bayes' in, assessing HW's plan to add Gothic museum to SH, **30**. 177

relation concerning entertainment of, in France, **38**. 158

'rogue,' **28**. 72

seat of, mentioned by Pope, **29**. 178

successor of, may have been imitating him, **16**. 15

witty but unprincipled, **33**. 223n

Villiers (later Child Villiers), George (1773–1859), styled Vct Villiers; 5th E. of Jersey, 1805:

Harcourt gives Brutus ring to, **29**. 329, 348

mother of, **12**. 204n

wife of, **12**. 68n

Villiers, Mrs George. *See* Beaumont, Mary

Villiers, George Bussy (1735–1805), styled Vct Villiers 1742–69; 4th E. of Jersey, 1769:

Admiralty post lost by, **22**. 109n

becomes lord of the Admiralty, **21**. 490

complains to George III, **15**. 328

daughter of, **11**. 108n, 187n, **32**. 247

dismissed by administration, **32**. 405

Finch, Hon. William, succeeded by, as vice-chamberlain, **22**. 311

Gloucester, D. of, mentioned by, **36**. 144

HW entertains, at dinner at SH, **35**. 454n

HW invites, to SH, **35**. 454, 471

(?) HW mentions, **38**. 555

Hyde, brother of, **23**. 313n

resigns as vice-chamberlain to George III, **39**. 122

seat of, **28**. 44n

Warton might be aided by, **41**. 164

Warwick St house not to be occupied by, **12**. 150

Weymouth refuses to re-elect, **30**. 193

Whitehead tutor to, **32**. 247n

wife of, **12**. 138, **15**. 327n, **25**. 411n

Villiers, Lady Gertrude. *See* Seymour-Conway, Lady Gertrude

Villiers, Mrs Henry. *See* Fowke, Mary

Villiers, John (ca 1615–59), 3d Vct Grandison: verses by, in first folio edition of Beaumont and Fletcher, **16**. 27

Villiers, John (ca 1684–1766), 5th Vct Grandison; cr. (1721) E. Grandison; M.P.:

daughter and son-in-law to visit, at Dublin, **10**. 66

death of: **10**. 216, 217; expected, **10**. 215

Montagu, Charles, may inherit from, **10**. 216

wealth of, **10**. 215

Villiers, Lady Mary (d. 1735), m. 1 Thomas Thynne; m. 2 (1711) George Granville, cr. (1712) Bn Lansdown:

marriages and gallantries of, **34**. 255

Villiers, Thomas (1709–86), cr. (1756) Bn Hyde, and (1776) E. of Clarendon; n.c.:

Admiralty lord, **19**. 458n, **20**. 17

Admiralty post may be obtained by, **20**. 12

Admiralty post taken from, **21**. 25

Berlin post refused by, **19**. 458

character of, **19**. 458, **20**. 17

Frederick II said to have requested, as English minister, **20**. 541

——'s letters from, printed, **20**. 171

—— succeeds with, at Dresden treaty, **20**. 541

Frederick Augustus II makes peace through, **17**. 499

'gazetted,' **20**. 17

Granville hampers negotiations of, by anti-Prussian policies, **19**. 223n

——'s conversation with, **20**. 17

Gray, Sir James, congratulated by, **19**. 444, 453

Guerchys entertain, at dinner, **38**. 510

HW discusses election with, at Granville's, **20**. 17

HW entreats, to care for relics at Kenilworth, **32**. 356

HW to tell, that his alabaster vases are ready and awaiting shipment from Italy, **21**. 524

Madrid embassy considered for, **22**. 463n

Mann mistakenly writes 'Villettes' for, **18**. 25

Newcastle, D. of, replaces name of, by Keith's, for Vienna post, **20**. 16n

Recueil de quelques lettres by, Frederick II orders Néaulme to publish, at The Hague, **20**. 17n

son of, **2**. 167n

superseded as postmaster, **22**. 311

to be chancellor of the Duchy of Lancaster, **23**. 313

[Villiers, Thomas (1709–86), *continued*]
  Treasury post coveted by, **19**. 458
  vases for: arrive, **22**. 13; ready and awaiting shipment, **21**. 524
  Vienna post may go to, **20**. 17–18
  witticisms by: about Treaty of Breslau, **35**. 32; on P. Charles's victories, **17**. 499, **18**. 25
Villiers, Thomas (1753–1824), styled Lord Hyde; 2d E. of Clarendon, n.c., 1786; M.P.:
  stands for Cambridge University, **2**. 167, 168
Villiers, Mrs Thomas. *See* Capel, Charlotte (1721–90)
Villiers, William (ca 1712–69), 3d E. of Jersey, 1721:
  brother of, **19**. 458n
  death of, **7**. 398
  Ferrers's trial deserted by, **9**. 279
  Ford, Ann, writes letter to, **9**. 338–9
  HW mentions, **9**. 278
  Halifax succeeds, as chief justice in eyre, **9**. 33
  Irish pension given to, **9**. 33
  Middleton built by, as hunting-lodge, **35**. 71–2
  Selwyn jokes about, **9**. 339
  son of, **22**. 311n
  wife of, **34**. 259
Villiers. *See also* Coulon de Villiers; Poitevin de Villiers
Villinghausen, battle of:
  French defeated at, **21**. 515, **35**. 309–10
Villio, Amilius, Graf; Polish ambassador to Venice 1712–63:
  Florentine pictures sought by, for K. of Poland, **19**. 392
Vilmanstrand (Finland):
  Russian-Swedish battle at, **17**. 155
Vilshoven (Bavaria):
  Austrians capture, **17**. 288
Vilvorde (Brabant):
  Conway and D. of Cumberland leave, **37**. 210
  Conway encamped at, **37**. 203–8
Vilvorde (*or* Willebroek) Canal:
  English fortify, **37**. 204–5
Vimeur, Donatien-Marie-Joseph de (1750–1813), Vicomte de Rochambeau:
  O'Hara exchanged for, **12**. 7n
Vimeur, Jean-Baptiste-Donatien de (1725–1807), Comte de Rochambeau:
  Arbuthnot alleged to have fought with, **25**. 150
  expected arrival of, encourages Americans, **25**. 70
  Lauzun sent by, to Paris with news of Yorktown, **25**. 208n
  (?) made maréchal de camp, **7**. 147n
  Washington agrees with, for La Fayette's relief, **25**. 150n
Vincennes (France):
  castle of, prisoners in, **4**. 449n
  Du Barry, Comte, imprisoned at, **6**. 52
  Young Pretender imprisoned at, **20**. 8, 22, 44

Vincens de St-Michel, Louis-Fouquet de (1737–1813), Marquis d'Agoult:
  Condé requests resignation of, as captain of guards, **7**. 438
  ——'s duel with, **7**. 438
Vincent, Lady. *See* Astley, Arabella
Vincent, ——:
  HW must remember, **18**. 111
  Lorraine, Primate of, ruins, **18**. 111
  Nomis accompanied by, **18**. 111
Vincent, Mrs, of Chelsea:
  painting of, at Cannons, **30**. 61n
Vincent, Augustine (ca 1584–1626), herald:
  'leaves' from, **43**. 200
  MS baronage by, quoted by HW, **20**. 138, **43**. 267
Vincent, Nicholas, naval officer:
  misbehaviour of, **21**. 296
Vincent, Mrs Philip. *See* Pocock, Sarah
Vincentino. *See* Vicentino
Vincenza. *See* Vicenza
Vinci, Jacopo, lawyer:
  Electress's will attested by, **18**. 173
Vinci, Leonardo (1690–1730), composer:
  Gray collects compositions by, **13**. 233n
Vinci, Leonardo da (1452–1519), artist:
  Drawings of . . . at Windsor Castle, **43**. 167
  George III owns drawings by, **12**. 263
  Monaco, P. of, has painting which HW attributes to, **7**. 335
  paintings by, at Marigny's, **39**. 15
  pictures by, at Devonshire House, **38**. 455n
  portrait by, **2**. 238n
Vinckeboons, David (1578–1629), painter:
  painting of palace attributed to, **16**. 75n
Vindication of a Late Pamphlet, A. See under Stanhope, Philip Dormer, E. of Chesterfield; Waller, Edmund
Vindication of Natural Society. See under Burke, Edmund
Vindication of Robert III, King of Scotland, A. See under Mackenzie, George (1630–1714)
Vindication of Some Passages in the . . . Decline and Fall of the Roman Empire. See under Gibbon, Edward (1737–94)
Vindication of the Appendix. See under Tyrwhitt, Thomas
Vindication of the Free Inquiry, A. See under Middleton, Conyers
Vindication of the Literal Account of the Fall. See under Le Moine, Abraham
Vindication of the Miraculous Powers. See under Church, Thomas
Vindication of the Rights of Man; Vindication of the Rights of Women. See under Wollstonecraft, Mary
Vine, English ship:
  Franklin brings, to Nantes, **32**. 337
'Vine, the.' *See* Fitzroy, Lady Caroline
Vine, the, John Chute's country seat. *See* Vyne, the

Vine; vines:
Florentine vineyards', injured by floods and cold, 21. 510
frost said to have killed, in France and Italy, 22. 514
hailstorm injures, at Geneva, 37. 104
Mann's lamp standards covered with, 18. 479
planting of, a 'civil act,' 35. 335–6
See also Ivy; Woodbine
'Vinegar, Mr and Mrs':
tale of, applied to Pitt and wife, 38. 131
Vinegar:
Arabians and Venetians use, to fumigate houses, 18. 271n
Berry, Mary, washes nose with, 11. 235
Lorraine officials sell, at Florence, 18. 270
used against plague, 18. 270
Vinegar Yard, London:
odd character at Cambridge must have come from, 13. 73
Viner, Sir Robert (1631–88), 1st Bt; lord mayor: print of, 1. 179
Vinerian Professorship of Common Law, at Oxford:
Milles stands for, 2. 228
Wooddeson elected to, 2. 228n
Vine Tavern, near Dover St, Piccadilly, London:
master of, murdered in 1756 by Capt. Ogle, 38. 168n
Vineyard, the. See Vyne, the
Vineyard; vineyards:
absent from neighbourhood of Arras, 7. 315
Hooker's, at Tunbridge, 35. 135
Spaniards destroy, in Italy, 18. 344n
Vinfen. See Wimpffen
Vingt-et-un (game):
Gloucester, D. of, plays, with entourage, 23. 352
grand, 4. 315
played in Paris, 4. 191, 315, 317, 324, 327, 337, 352, 381, 393, 461, 5. 10, 7. 325, 331, 336, 340
Vingtième (French tax):
joke about continuation of, 4. 184
Vins, Joseph Nicolaus de (1732–98), Freiherr; Austrian Maj.-Gen.:
Prussians defeat, 24. 403–5
Vintimiglia. See Ventimiglia
Vintimille, Marquise de. See Mailly-Nesle, Pauline-Félicité de (1712–41); Talbot, Marie-Madeleine-Sophie
Vintimille, Charles-Emmanuel-Marie-Madelon de (1741–1810), Marquis de Luc:
birth of, 17. 125
Vintimille. See also Ventimiglia
Vintner; vintners:
French, get Englishmen's money, 37. 172
Vinto, Giovan Battista:
note on, 1. 8
Violante, ——; Italian athlete:
death of, from broken neck, 25. 451
descent of, from St Martin's steeple, 25. 450

Violante Beatrix (1673–1731) of Bavaria, m. (1689) Ferdinando de' Medici, Grand Prince of Tuscany:
Saletti, 'virtuoso' of, 30. 14n
Suares, Mme, lady of honour to, 17. 39n, 19. 311n
—— protégée of, 17. 161n
—— tells stories of, 19. 311
Violence:
is never justified, 29. 81
Violet; violets:
daisies are weeds compared to, 42. 273
Harcourt to pluck, in September, 28. 408
'qui se cachoit sous l'herbe,' 33. 473
Stanley spangled with, 32. 116n
'violet-tide,' 32. 25
'Violetta' or 'Violette.' See Veigel, Eva Maria
Violin; violins:
barge full of, 37. 289
Buller, John, plays, 12. 18
Craon distracted by, from his cards, 17. 417
Dudley's bridge resembles that of, 35. 389
figure of old man playing, in Bristol Cathedral, 16. 174
Giardini's, 28. 354
harpsichord combined with, in celestinette, 35. 423
Middleton plays on, 15. 310
Nardini plays on, 22. 537
played: at Haymarket entertainment, 39. 382n; at Mrs Keppel's fête, 33. 482; at Old Woman's Oratory, 9. 131; by Nivernais at Esher, 10. 73; by St-Cyr nun, 10. 294; for dancing, from ale-house, 33. 283–4
St-Germain plays, 19. 181, 26. 20
Ussé leaves, to Comtesse de Choiseul-Beaupré, 5. 276
waiter's pedantic remark about, 34. 173
Violinist; violinists:
fingers of, so cold that they miss notes at Massereene's ball, 30. 211
Violin music:
Meinières wishes performance of, were impossible, 4. 257
Violoncello. See Cello
Viomenil, Bn de. See Du Houx, Antoine-Charles
Viper, English sloop:
Conway's letters conveyed by, 37. 512n
Vipers' flesh:
medicine from, 23. 450n
Vipsania Agrippina (d. A.D. 20):
Tiberius's divorce from, 13. 117
Virepoyl. See Vierpyl
Virette. See Virrette
Virgil (Publius Vergilius Maro) (70–19 B.C.), Roman poet:
Addison's compliment to, 16. 269
Æneid, the, by: 2. 289; Anchises and Troy in, 33. 108; beautiful but insipid, 29. 256; Berry, Mary, quotes, 11. 309; Camilla in, 29. 89, 34. 58; defects of, 16. 23, 268–9; Chute paraphrases, 35. 7; Cole quotes, 43.

[Virgil, *continued*]

70; Conway quotes, **37**. 74, 189, 276; Fox, Henry, quotes, **30**. 189; Gray paraphrases, **13**. 150, **14**. 22; HW alludes to, **28**. 25, 454, 43. 377; HW considers, lacking in imagination, **11**. 20; HW corrects quotation from, **15**. 229; HW paraphrases, **13**. 94, **23**. 453; HW quotes, **2**. 245, **9**. 3, **12**. 164, **13**. 85, 86, 87, **18**. 431, **19**. 134, 161, **21**. 213, **23**. 163, **28**. 115, 186, 386, 415, **29**. 23, **33**. 98, 117, **34**. 7, 69, 98, 157, **37**. 583, **39**. 487, **42**. 375; HW studies, **9**. 3; Legge's quotation from, used by Conway, **37**. 81; Montagu mentions, **10**. 200; Montagu quotes, **10**. 174; preserved by Virgil's executors, **20**. 62; requires less talent than creation of 'Falstaff,' **32**. 334; *Sortes Virgilianæ* picks quotations from, **37**. 79; Surrey's version of 4th book of, **42**. 367; Warburton proves legation of Moses by, **16**. 38; West alludes to, **13**. 117, 130, 131, 172; West quotes, **13**. 125; Whaley quotes, **40**. 9, 16

boys at Eton memorize verses of, **2**. 214–15

Caxton cites, as historical authority, **29**. 89

Corneille and Heinsius prefer Lucan to, **16**. 22

Delille translates, **7**. 344, **33**. 378

Dryden's translation of, with Hollar's illustrations, **37**. 299

Eclogues by: Berry, Mary, quotes, **12**. 113; Coke's parody of, **16**. 163; Fox, Henry, quotes, **30**. 190; HW alludes to, **13**. 199; HW paraphrases, **13**. 93, **31**. 333; HW quotes, **10**. 274, **12**. 265, 266–7, **14**. 247, **38**. 454; HW's 'Little Peggy' imitates, **30**. 307, 317; Selwyn quotes, **28**. 271; Williams, Sir C. H., imitates, **30**. 307n, 317; Williams, Sir C. H., quotes, **18**. 48

English schoolboys' study of, their only way of telling the seasons apart, **23**. 305

engraved gem representing, owned by Stosch, **30**. 11

Fox, Lady Caroline, unfamiliar with, **30**. 105

Georgics by: adapted, **33**. 526, **39**. 233; Conway quotes, **37**. 89; George III's activities called, **32**. 132; Gray alludes to, **13**. 143, **14**. 8n; HW alludes to, **13**. 108; HW imitates, **30**. 303–5; HW paraphrases, **28**. 175; HW quotes, **13**. 194–5, **30**. 8, **35**. 109, 195; images ennobled in, **16**. 269; Philippi of, subject of dissertation by Holdsworth, **19**. 139n; West quotes, **13**. 198; Yearsley, Mrs, admires translation of, **31**. 218; Young Pretender's medal quotes, **17**. 19

Glover's *Leonidas* compared to, **37**. 19

grace the chief merit of, **16**. 268–9

Gray reads, at Burnham, **13**. 106

HW alludes to, **28**. 166, **29**. 84

HW fancies, living at Hampstead, **28**. 45

HW mentions, **4**. 215

HW's transcripts from, mentioned by West, **13**. 198

HW will not quote, regarding his journey, **32**. 269

HW wishes more from, than mere harmonious verse, **41**. 28

medal quotes, **17**. 19

Mexico may produce counterpart of, **24**. 62

model of purity and taste, **16**. 257

Montagu misquotes, **10**. 19

More, Hannah, mentions, **31**. 264

Opera, given by Montagu to HW, **43**. 127

Pinkerton depreciates, **29**. 358n

Spence's misinterpretations of, **14**. 20

tomb of, **37**. 59

Voltaire inferior to, **16**. 272

West alludes to, **13**. 118

—— and HW read, together, **13**. 94

Wood's observations on, **41**. 177–8

Virgin; virgins:

HW's verses about, **31**. 120–1

'Virgin and Child,' Domenichino's alleged painting of, *see under* Domenichino

Virginia, pasticcio:

at Haymarket theatre, **25**. 646n

Virginia. See under Crisp, Samuel

Virginia, U. S. A.:

Albemarle, governor of, **20**. 156n

Arnold joins Cornwallis in, **25**. 167

Berkeley, Norborne, governor of, **21**. 313n, **39**. 104

Cornwallis to invade, **24**. 158

De la Warr's account of, **16**. 140

Dunmore expects to resume governorship of, **29**. 184

—— governor of, **28**. 237n

—— tries to involve, in war with the Indians, **41**. 312

events may be expected in, **24**. 206

exports to, **32**. 242

France builds forts on Ohio upon land claimed by gentlemen of, **20**. 440n

French encroachments threaten, **20**. 440, 448, 495

George III wishes to send convicts to, **35**. 535

governorship of: disputed, **23**. 43–4; not settled, **35**. 203; vacant by Albemarle's death, **20**. 461

governor's income at, **20**. 461n

HW's vision of future senate of, **23**. 210

Leslie finds little opposition in, **29**. 90n

—— recalled from, **29**. 90n

Loudoun governor of, **19**. 102n

Montfort asks D. of Newcastle for governorship of, **35**. 201

no one executed in, for treason, **29**. 168n

regiment of, **20**. 455n

regiments sent from Cork to, **20**. 448n

ship from, **24**. 88n

SH more important to HW than boundaries of, **21**. 306

troops in, disbanded, **20**. 455

Virginia cedar. *See under* Cedar

Virginia Gazette:

Washington's report in, reprinted in *London Magazine*, **20**. 449n

Virgin, Mary. *See* Mary

Virgin of the Seven Sorrows. See under Pergolesi

Viri cheese:

recipe for, 4. 60

Virieu-Beauvoir, François-Xavier (ca 1709–82), Comte de; army officer; Lt in the government of Le Havre:

Rodney's alleged notice to, 21. 310

Viriville, Mme de. *See* (?) Fresnel, Françoise-Élisabeth de

Viriville. *See also* Olivier de Sénozan de Viriville

Virot, Charles (1769–95), Vicomte de Sombreuil:

Breton expedition interrupts marriage plans of, 12. 152

Virrette, ——, Swiss:

escaped arrest, and flees assignation to fight Pecquigny, 38. 313

London revisited by, after duel, 38. 322

Pecquigny challenges, after gambling losses, 38. 306–7, 313, 322

St-Germain's toad-eater, denounced and released, 19. 182n

servant of, manages to let him escape officer, 38. 313

Virri. *See* Viry

Virtu:

Conway and Stormont absorbed in, 20. 298

Conway ignorant of, 37. 107

Dalton advises George III about, 21. 478

Frederick, Charles, turns, into fireworks, 37. 297

George III collects, 21. 477–8, 22. 108

HW eschews, 9. 144

HW has a little, to entertain Conway, 37. 110

HW has cartloads of, 37. 107

HW's: Conway would like to have been at unpacking of, 37. 111; HW's sole pleasure, 37. 110

HW's definition of, excludes Gothic antiquities, 43. 118

Mann should cater to George III's taste in, 21. 452, 456–7, 22. 111

—— unwilling to procure, for George III, 21. 456–7, 497, 22. 115

Spence instructs HW in, 40. 34

tongue of Sir John Miller runs over with, 39. 241

Virtue, George. *See* Vertue, George

Virtue; virtues:

disbelieved or without authority now, 25. 373

fashionable at Paris and ancient Rome, 32. 266

French abolish, 31. 401

HW calls, phantoms, 11. 14

HW's fine figure on, 33. 18

HW's reflections on, 21. 541, 28. 156, 32. 347, 38. 130–1

ladies', destroys poetry, 32. 32

More, Hannah, esteems, small, 31. 350

—— promotes, by her writings, 31. 271

Ossory, Cts of, replaces 'Graces' by, 32. 178

Peace takes, to heaven, 38. 130

sales-value of, 32. 40

want of, HW's reflections on, 24. 362

Virtue, Temple of. *See* Honour and Virtue

Virtue Club:

exists in idea only, 32. 6

Virtuoso, The. See under Shadwell, Thomas

Viry, Contessa di ('Mme de Viry'). *See* Montagu, Augusta (d. 1849); Speed, Henrietta Jane (1728–83)

Viry, Francesco Giuseppe (d. 1766), Conte di; Sardinian diplomatist:

Bute outlines peace plans to, 22. 30n

employed in Paris peace treaty, 22. 105

Newcastle informed by, of separate peace treaties, 22. 66n

Sardinian minister to England, 9. 406n, 24. 328n

son of, 9. 406, 41. 342n

Viry, Francesco Maria Giuseppe Giustino di (1736–1813), Baron de la Perrière; Conte di Viry, 1766; diplomatist:

Aigueblanche, enemy of, 6. 476, 477

arrest of, at Susa, 6. 474, 24. 328

banquet, masked ball, and fireworks by, for Ps of Piedmont's wedding, 7. 344, 32. 256, 39. 256

biographical information about, corrected, 43. 95

Boufflers's witticism on seeing, at Mme du Deffand's, 39. 219

career of, 41. 342n

disgrace of, 41. 343n, 43. 102

Du Deffand, Mme, and, 6. 294–5

George III persuades Victor Amadeus III to pardon, 35. 522n

HW's opinion of, 5. 360

Marmora replaced by, 5. 357

marriage of: expected, 9. 406; in England, 24. 328n

pardon of, 24. 328n

recalled, 6. 454, 470, 476, 477, 483

Sardinian ambassador to France, 24. 328n

secret correspondence by, at Turin, to become prime minister, 24. 328n

social relations of, in Paris, 5. 403, 6. 15, 294, 301, 7. 344

wife of, 14. 61n

Viry:

castle of, mentioned by Gray, 14. 123

Vis-à-vis (vehicle):

Englishwoman's child and nurse enter Florence in, drawn by nags and driven by old English coachman, 24. 260

Hertford buys, from Albemarle, and resells it, 38. 160

peer's, 35. 558

Visconti, Caterina, opera singer; 'Viscontina': 'admired more than liked,' 17. 190

Calais visited by, 17. 141

captain of yacht demands song from, 17. 141

Chesterfield jokes about age and weight of, 17. 197

[Visconti, Caterina, *continued*]
Chute prefers, to Bernacchi, **35.** 16
Conway, Bns, to have, sing at assembly, **17.** 334
deteriorates, **19.** 437
HW and Gray expect to hear, in Bologna, **17.** 31n, **30.** 16n
HW meets, at Calais, **30.** 19
HW's opinion of, **9.** 157
HW travels with, **17.** 141
Holdernesse entertains, **18.** 130
London opera directors retain, **17.** 421
London opera directors said to dismiss, **17.** 398, 423
Mann pities, **17.** 240
men should pardon defects of, **35.** 14
Pomfret, Cts of, discusses, **17.** 72
salary of, **17.** 191
Sani, the, as ugly as, **35.** 28
to sing in opera in England, **30.** 5
unpopular in England, **17.** 211
Visconti, Fulvia (d. 1777), m. Marchese Antonio Giorgio Clerici:
(?) child wanted by, **18.** 252
Florence visited by, **18.** 251–2
Lucca baths to be visited by, **18.** 252
Visigoths:
HW compares English to, **20.** 99
Vision, The. See Lesson for the Day, The
Vision; visions:
HW and Montagu like the same kind of, **10.** 291
HW calls, 'the only happiness,' **7.** 357
HW diverts himself with, **35.** 352
HW knows the texture of, too well, **23.** 554
HW says, are never 'pure from annoy,' **25.** 532
HW's, linger in his second childhood, **34.** 184
HW's fondness for, **25.** 133
HW's pleasure in, **10.** 192, 259
HW's preference for, **35.** 366
HW's reflections on, **2.** 337, **24.** 103, 194, **33.** 447
HW tired of, **10.** 184
historic, HW's fondness for, **33.** 42
life itself is, **35.** 352
mortals impelled by, to action, **24.** 521
must be made, to the last, **25.** 604
ought to be cultivated even if in vain, **24.** 327
playthings for boys, **24.** 324
vanity of old people's, **33.** 450
Visit; visits:
'en blanc,' **20.** 584, **24.** 275
hours for, **24.** 426
Visitation, Convent of, at Paris. *See* Filles de la visitation de Ste-Marie
Visitation, Convent of, at San Remo:
evacuated to Villa di San Martino, **19.** 123
Vismes. *See* De Vismes
Visor; visors:
on Lady Caroline Petersham's hat, **9.** 109
Wilkes's squint imitated in, at masquerade, **23.** 193

Vita di Sisto V. See under Leti, Gregorio
Vitæ antiquæ sanctorum. See under Pinkerton, John
Vite di più eccellenti pittori, scultori e architetti. See under Vasari, Giorgio
Vitelli, Mme. *See* Frescobaldi, Maria Anna (d. 1776)
Vitelli, Agnese, m. (1711) Francesco Maria Bagnesi:
(?) Modenese princess gives presents to, **17.** 64
Vitelli, Clemente (d. 1790), Marchese:
Fiesole villa greatly embellished by grandfather of, **20.** 399n
villa and furniture of town house sold by, to pay mother's dowry, **20.** 399
Vitelli family ends with, **20.** 399n
Vitelli, Niccolò (1687–1747):
HW sees Bianca Cappello's portrait in palace of, **20.** 398, 402n
widow of, follows Braitwitz to Naples, **20.** 399
Vitelli, Casa, at Florence:
furniture of, sold, **20.** 399
HW sees Bianca Cappello's portrait at, **20.** 398, 402n, 404
Via de' Renai may be location of, **20.** 398n
Vitellia. See under Jephson, Robert
Vitelli family:
falling into decay, **20.** 402n
Vitellius, Aulus (A.D. 15–69), Roman emperor A.D. 69:
medal of, bought by HW, **26.** 7
Viterbo (Italy):
Austrians at, **18.** 527, 534
Gages assembles troops at, **18.** 556
Gloucester, D. of, entertained at, by Clement XIV's staff, **23.** 388
Montemar, Clarelli, and Ferretti to attend meeting at, **17.** 214–15
Neapolitans on way to Lombardy from, recalled to Naples, **19.** 237
Spaniards from, to join Gages, **19.** 58
Spanish baggage arrives at, **18.** 243
Spanish invalids at, form army, **19.** 55
Vitimillia. *See* Ventimiglia
Vitrification:
of colours, **40.** 238
Vitruvius (Marcus Vitruvius Pollio) (fl. 1st cent.), Roman writer on architecture:
Cumberland gives name of, in Spanish form, **29.** 232
Essex draws from, **1.** 340
Osterley Park's dome would be despised by, **28.** 414
Vitto Pittagorico. See Cocchi, Antonio: *Del vito Pittagorico*
Vittoria, Commendatore, of Naples:
leather shields at SH formerly in collection of, **33.** 518n, **35.** 419n
Vittorio Amadeo II and III. *See* Victor Amadeus
Vittorio Amadeo (1690–1741), Prince de Carignan:
house of, used for gambling, **13.** 165n

Vittorio Amadeo Lodovico Maria Wolfgang (1743–80), Prince de Carignan:
marriage of, reported, **7.** 439
social relations of, with Contessa di Viry, **7.** 352

Vivares, Thomas (b. ca 1735), engraver:
plates by, **2.** 273n

Vive le vin, vive l'amour:
song to air of, **4.** 300–1, **5.** 225

Vivian, John (ca 1729–71), regius professor of history at Oxford:
George II makes, regius professor, **41.** 164n

Viviani, Marchese Luigi (1709–80), Neapolitan agent in Florence; Neapolitan minister to Tuscany, 1758; Spanish envoy to Tuscany 1765–80:
Baiardi's *prodromo* presented by, to Mann, **21.** 142
Botta to be assured by, of Neapolitan-Spanish neutrality, **21.** 270–1
—— told by, that Havana would not be captured, **22.** 89
Charles III promotes, from chargé d'affaires to envoy, **22.** 349–50
courier's non-appearance explained by, **21.** 463
deserts to Spaniards on Montemar's arrival, **20.** 350
Eszterházys entertained by, at festino, **20.** 350–1
Fogliani recommends, to Richecourt, **20.** 350–1
furniture of, sold to pay debts, **20.** 351
HW met, at Craon's, **20.** 350
HW wishes invisible architect of, at SH, **20.** 372
intimate at Casa Craon, **17.** 238–9
language master at Spanish Court, **18.** 129, **20.** 350
low credentials of, exclude him from chambellan's antechamber, **22.** 346
Madrid visited by, **18.** 129
Mann should have bought *Antiquities of Herculaneum* from, **21.** 299
—— told by: about Charles III's behaviour on wife's death, **21.** 441–2; about Spanish-Portuguese clash, **24.** 223; about Young Pretender, **17.** 116
—— to write letter to England citing, as reason for promoting Mann, **22.** 351
ministerial dinner to be given by, **22.** 355, 362
Montemar's pimp, **17.** 239
Neapolitan-Spanish weekly courier service received by, **22.** 349
Porta San Gallo shown by, to San Severino, **20.** 372
Regency to tell, to have Del Monte seized, **20.** 437
Spaniards joined by, **17.** 238–9, **18.** 129
Spanish courier brings news to, of Anglo-Spanish rupture, **21.** 564n

Spanish Court sends South American news to, **24.** 223
Squillace's correspondence with, **22.** 99n, 100
will be *ministre de famille* at Leopold II's wedding, **22.** 319
wishes to be Spanish minister to Francis I, **18.** 129

Viviani, Ottavio (b. 1679), *or* Stefano (b. 1681), painters:
Furnese has pictures by, **26.** 7

Viviani, Palazzo, at Florence:
in Via de' Tornabuoni, **17.** 137n
Zocchi depicts, **17.** 137n

Vivienne, Rue, in Paris:
Marie-Antoinette assigned to, in joke, **8.** 181

Vivret. *See* Virrette

'Vixen, Mrs':
'Coaxer, Mrs,' not to be confused with, **35.** 526

Vizier; viziers, Turkish:
English ministry as changeable as, **35.** 281
Williams, Sir C.H., writes verses about, **23.** 236

Vizir, Grand. *See* Grand Vizir

Vizor. *See* Visor

Vlasiev, ——:
Ivan VI's possible murderer, **22.** 253n

Vocabolario . . . della Crusca. See under Accademia della Crusca

Vocabulary:
HW's reflections on change in, from one generation to another, **25.** 538

Vockerodt, Johann Gotthilf:
Prussian propaganda drawn up by, **30.** 69n

Voelcker, (?) George (d. 1770), (?) valet to George II:
dogs bred by, **23.** 56

Voerst. *See* Van Voerst

Vogelsanck, Isaac (1688–1753), landscape painter:
HW thanks Dalrymple for account of, **15.** 143

Vogt, Johann (1695–1765), bibliographer:
Catalogus historico-criticus librorum rariorum by, **1.** 258

Vogüé, Charles-François-Elzéar (1713–82), Marquis de:
made member of Ordre du St-Esprit, **7.** 14
St-Germain second choice of, **6.** 228

Vogüé, Charlotte-Henriette de, m. (1781) Guillaume-Louis-Camille, Comte de Gand:
marriage of, **6.** 499n

Voice:
HW jokes about pain in his, **30.** 86

Voisenon, Abbé de. *See* Fusée, Claude-Henri de

Voisenon (France):
Voisenon dies at, **6.** 248n

'Voisin, le.' *See* Grave, Charles-François de

Voisins. *See* Gilbert de Voisins

Voiture, Vincent (1598–1648), courtier and letter-writer:
Du Deffand, Mme, prefers HW's style to that of, **3.** 383
HW's acquaintance with letters of, and his opinion of them, **30.** 75

[Voiture, Vincent, *continued*]
HW's letter to be placed with those of, **40.** 173
Voiture; voitures (vehicles):
Beauchamp's, may be drawn by mules, **22.** 336
price of, doubled in France, **11.** 134, 144, 158
Volakia. *See* Wallachia
Volcano; volcanoes:
at Messina, **25.** 374
at Naples, *see* Vesuvius
French philosophers regard, as orderly, **35.** 414
Hamilton, Sir William, investigates, in Italy, **35.** 383
—— should not study, too closely, **35.** 437
——'s paper on, for Royal Society, **35.** 409–10
——'s studies on, **39.** 339
——'s study on, should continue, **35.** 425
—— writes on formation of mountains from, **35.** 412
Pliny killed by, **35.** 414
Voltaire discusses, **35.** 413
Vole (card-game term):
Clive, Mrs, dreads, **35.** 456
—— wins, **35.** 464
term used in quadrille, **17.** 188n
Voltaire (François-Marie Arouet) (1698–1778):
A, B, C, L', by: **4.** 168, 171, 181, **8.** 149, 150, 152; Saurin's verses on, **4.** 179–80
Abrégé de l'histoire universelle by, **43.** 76
Académie française receives letter from, **6.** 354
—— sends delegation to, **7.** 18
activity of, **4.** 411
actors visit, **7.** 18–19
Adam, Père, butt of, **7.** 278
'Address to Kings' ('Avis aux Princes') not by, **32.** 173
Adélaïde du Guesclin by, **7.** 263
Agathocle by, **7.** 39
Aiguillon, Duc d', praised by, **32.** 50
Alembert's correspondence with, **5.** 307, 338, **12.** 9
always says the same things, **4.** 92
Alzire by: **7.** 297, 329, 347; Du Deffand, Mme, criticizes, **4.** 138; Graftons see, performed at Ferney, **32.** 4n; HW likes, **6.** 44, **41.** 294; HW prefers, to Racine's *Iphigénie*, **29.** 111; HW to reread, **5.** 389
'À Madame Lullin' by, **23.** 306
À Monsieur le Chancelier de Maupeou by, **5.** 196
À Monsieur Marmontel by: **5.** 395, 407, 409; HW desires, **5.** 397
anecdote by, about (?) Ds of Marlborough, **37.** 420
Anson's stories believed by, **35.** 284
Appel à toutes les nations by: Dumesnil in *Mérope* described in, **35.** 122n; gravediggers' scene in *Hamlet* disparaged in, **41.** 289n
Aranda's verses from, sent to Ossun, **41.** 203
Argental's correspondence with, **6.** 345, 348

arrives in Paris, **28.** 357, 365
'À une dame' by, quoted by HW, **39.** 518
Barthélemy asks about editions of, **8.** 208
Bastille Day will be forgotten with, **34.** 117
Beaumarchais's edition of, **36.** 242
——'s mémoires please, **6.** 35
Beaune, Rue de, lodging of, **7.** 17
Beauvau finds few letters by, in Mme du Deffand's papers, **36.** 189–90
Bégueule, La, by: Du Deffand, Mme, dislikes, **5.** 232; Voltaire sends, to Mme du Deffand, **5.** 235
Bernis, Cardinal de, friend of, **11.** 4n
Bible 'demolished' by, **31.** 92
body of, transferred from Scellières to Panthéon, **34.** 117n
Boncerf's correspondence with, **6.** 287, **8.** 197–8
Boufflers's style compared by Mme du Deffand to that of, **4.** 289
——'s verses on, **7.** 2
Bourdeaux and Humain martyrs to system of, **6.** 1
Brown's treatment of, **4.** 52
Buirette de Belloy's letter from, enclosed by Hertford, **38.** 521–2
burial of, **7.** 48
buried at Ste-Geneviève, **34.** 117
Burke mentions, **11.** 277
bust of, given to Mme du Deffand by Duchesse d'Aiguillon, **4.** 173–4, **5.** 360, **8.** 20
Byng receives from, Richelieu's letter, **21.** 51, 61
——'s execution deplored by, **28.** 219
Cabales, Les, by, to be sent to HW by Mme du Deffand, **5.** 284, 300
'Caille, Abbé,' pseudonym of, **8.** 149, 151, **41.** 125n
Calas family protected by, **7.** 40
Candide by: Byng's fate mentioned in, **35.** 555; HW alludes to, **10.** 307, **28.** 257, **38.** 473; imitation of, falsely attributed to Voltaire, **21.** 514, 520; in England, 1759, **10.** 349–50; Mason alludes to, **28.** 224, 231; monkey and tiger mentioned in, **43.** 283; Montagu reads, in English translation, **9.** 242; original edition of, published in Geneva, **10.** 349; plot of *Il Re Teodoro* from, **33.** 587; Thunder-ten-tronckh in, **38.** 418
Canonisation de St Cucufin by, **4.** 207
Castle of Otranto has preface written against, by HW, **3.** 256, 261, 270, **4.** 90, 95–9, 102, 107, 129, **6.** 268, **7.** 269, **8.** 141–4
Catherine II buys library of, **8.** 212
—— may be visited by, **4.** 48, 49, 53
—— patroness of, **32.** 31
—— praised by: **3.** 298; to Mme du Deffand's distaste, **3.** 358; to HW's horror, **3.** 299, **7.** 287
——'s apologist, **22.** 253, 570, **23.** 195, 208, 515
——'s ascent to throne called 'a family squabble' by, **25.** 194, 206
——'s conduct edifies, **28.** 475

'chambre de cœur' of, **8**. 215
Charles, Duc d'Orléans's verses might be called 'royal verses' by, **31**. 273
Châtillon, Duchesse de, visits, **6**. 223
Chesterfield praises, **6**. 38
Choiseul, Duc de, praised by, **32**. 50
—— receives letter of, on La Bletterie, **4**. 171, 181
—— receives letter of, on MM. de Pompignan, **3**. 202, 203
—— scandalized by La Bletterie's treatment by, **4**. 105, 113, 171
Choiseul, Duchesse de, corresponds with, indirectly, **4**. 111–12, 181, 207, 223, 244, 405, 411, 443, **5**. 235, **6**. 67, **7**. 64, 67, **8**. 144–9
—— defends La Bletterie to, **8**. 148, 151
—— displeases, **4**. 146
—— receives everything he writes from, **4**. 208
—— receives fable from, **8**. 148
—— receives verses from, **4**. 396
—— 's letter of 15 July 1768 from, **4**. 116–20, 123
—— transmits book and letters from, **4**. 53, 116, 127
—— will not correspond directly with, **4**. 111–12, 181
Choiseuls solicited by, for permission to return to Paris, **28**. 153
Choisy reads pieces and letter by, **7**. 274
Christian VII praises, **4**. 165
—— 's verses from, **3**. 268, **8**. 131
Clairon, Mlle, subject of verses by, **5**. 273, 274
Coke, Lady Mary, visits, **31**. 143
Collection d'anciens Évangiles par l'Abbé B——, by, **4**. 293
Commentaire historique sur les Œuvres de l'auteur de la Henriade by, **6**. 357, 361, 362, 364, 367, 369, **41**. 354n
commentary of, on Beccaria's *Tratto dei diletti e delle pene*, **3**. 173
Condorcet's *Lettre d'un théologien* attributed to, **6**. 88
confession of faith by: **7**. 24–6; HW's opinion of, **7**. 34; verses on, **7**. 31, 39
Congreve ridiculed by, for preferring rank of gentleman to that of author, **21**. 486
Conseils raisonnables à M. Bergier by, **4**. 94, 101, 135
Corneille defended by, **4**. 120, 129
—— edited by, **8**. 141–3, 150
Covelle's verses from, bad, **39**. 230
Craufurd calls on, and finds that he knows no Greek, **22**. 40
—— visits, **4**. 468
Craven, Bns, imitates, in *Modern Anecdote*, **29**. 7
Crébillon condemns irreligion of, **35**. 587
Cromwell's alleged fighting in Holland will be put by, into history, **38**. 442–3
Damer, Mrs, does bas-relief of, **12**. 271
Darget's letters from, **4**. 307
death of: **7**. 46, **16**. 191n, **24**. 387, **28**. 407, 408, 410, 412; rumoured, **7**. 12, **28**. 343, **33**.

6; while railing at Shakespeare, **24**. 536; will be Europe's good night, **24**. 55
death should have been feigned by, after writing *Alzire, Mahomet,* and *Sémiramis*, **42**. 229
Défense de mon oncle, Le, by, **41**. 177n
De l'encyclopédie by, **6**. 153
Denis, Mme, joins, **4**. 293
—— leaves, **4**. 42, 47
—— receives library of, as legacy, **7**. 49–50
—— transmits letter of, on La Bletterie, to Choiseul, **4**. 171, 181
despises his tools, **39**. 386
despots decorated by, **25**. 613–14
Dialogue de Pégase et du vieillard by, sent by Mme du Deffand to HW, **6**. 43, 153
'Diatribe à l'auteur des Ephémerides,' by, **7**. 375
Dictionnaire philosophique by: **8**. 149; Chinese in bookseller's shop in, **33**. 206–7, **34**. 22; Gray has not seen, **14**. 138; religious system advocated in, foolish and absurd, **31**. 69
Dimanche, Le, ou les Filles de Minée by, **6**. 192
Discours aux confédérés de Pologne by, **4**. 135
Discours en vers sur l'homme by, cited by Mme du Deffand, **6**. 367
Dissertation sur la tragédie by: ghost scene in *Hamlet* praised in, **41**. 297n; gravediggers' scene in *Hamlet* disparaged by, **41**. 289n, 295n
'Dizain contre votre grand'maman' by, **4**. 409, 416–17
Docteur Pansophe, Le, attributed to, **3**. 178–9, **43**. 84
doctrines of, **2**. 309
Don Pèdre by: **6**. 149, 156, 167, 170; 'poor performance,' **33**. 140
Doutes historiques by, owned by Mme du Deffand, **8**. 35n
Droits des hommes et les usurpations des Papes, Les, by, **8**. 152
Du Châtelet, Marquise, 'Émilie' of, **8**. 56, 116
—— friend of, **7**. 293
—— mentioned by, **6**. 357
Ducis, successor to, in Académie française, **7**. 48, 100, 118
Du Deffand, Mme, accused by, of attributing verses on Marmontel to him, **7**. 27
—— admires style of, **3**. 113, 144, **4**. 126, 208, **5**. 47, **28**. 420
—— attributes Shuvalov's *Épître* to, **6**. 28
—— cites, **4**. 6, 296, **6**. 140, 460
—— criticizes new volumes of, **4**. 164
—— defends La Bletterie to, **8**. 153
—— defends views of, on dramatic technique, **4**. 135
—— dislikes historical writings of, **6**. 7
—— dislikes newer writings of, **5**. 400
—— displeases, **4**. 146
—— forwards *Castle of Otranto* and *Historic Doubts* to, **4**. 99, 101

[Voltaire, *continued*]

—— hears nothing of, **4.** 138

—— knows 700 or 800 verses of, by heart, **7.** 203

—— makes witticism on, **28.** 468

—— mentions, **3.** 48, **4.** 125, 174, 243

—— misquotes letter by, **43.** 86

—— neglected by, **6.** 43

—— not mentioned by, **6.** 357

—— offers to send writings of, to HW, **4.** 116

—— on good terms with, **4.** 208

—— quotes, **4.** 17, 105, 282, **7.** 120

—— reads, **7.** 178, 180

—— receives Bélesta letter from, **4.** 182

—— receives everything he writes from, **4.** 208

—— receives quarto edition of, from Mme de Luxembourg, **4.** 131, **7.** 2

—— receives two eulogies of, **7.** 426

—— receives verses from, **4.** 396, 408, **7.** 20, 22–3

—— receives works from, **4.** 168

—— requests verses from, for Christmas party, **6.** 115, 118

——'s blindness commented on by, **8.** 67

——'s correspondence with: **3.** 141, 178–80, 188, 190, 298, 301, 319, 388, 406, **4.** 21, 48, 49, 52–3, 59, 62, 97, 99–100, 107, 111–13, 118, 123, 127, 131, 163, 171, 173, 178, 182, 207, 223, 225, 228, 307, 343, 357, 405, 408, 411, 453–4, 468, **5.** 127, 212, 235, 281, 300, 319, 338, 385, 391, 393, 418, 426, **6.** 25, 27, 28, 33, 49, 67, 69, 93, 149, 192, 242–3, 248, 424, 501, **7.** 17, **8.** 147, 151–4, 191, **14.** 150, **36.** 182, **39.** 385–6, **41.** 199; collected, **7.** 59, 62, 64, 67, 109; *see also* Voltaire: letters of

——'s edition of, left to Mouchard, **8.** 8

—— sends Hénault's *Cornélie* to, **4.** 99–100, 105, 111

——'s letter from, of 18 May 1767, praising Catherine II, **3.** 298, 301, 319, 388, 406

——'s opinion of, **3.** 201, **7.** 180

——'s witticism on St-Denis related by, **8.** 60

—— talked of by, to Craufurd, **4.** 468

—— visits, **28.** 366

Dupuits, pretended intermediary between Mme de Choiseul and, **4.** 112, 181, 223, **8.** 148–9

Dupuits, M. and Mme, leave, **4.** 42, 47

Écossoise, L', authorship of, admitted by, **21.** 520

Éléments de la philosophie de Newton by, **41.** 153n

Elizabeth of Russia demands more panegyrics from, **9.** 327

—— gives material to, **9.** 327

Éloge de l'hypocrisie by, **3.** 251, 252

Éloge funèbre de Louis XV received by Mme du Deffand from, **6.** 67

Éloge historique de la raison by, **6.** 153

Enfant prodigue, L', by: **8.** 141; HW likes, **6.** 44

England first popularized by, in France, **24.** 267

English executions in 1746 exaggerated by, in *Précis du siècle de Louis XV*, **35.** 284

English newspapers would supply, with chapter on manners of the time, **33.** 321

English of, defective, though he presumes to criticize Shakespeare, **42.** 121

envious nature of, **28.** 186, 277, 278, 326

epics of, lack fire, **29.** 256

epigram on, quoted, **28.** 253

epigrams of: on George II and Frederick II, **21.** 31; on seeing Bn and Bns Hervey in bed, **31.** 417

epistles of: to Hénault, **4.** 485n; to Querini, **20.** 329

Épître à Boileau by: **4.** 223, 225; criticized, **32.** 35–6

Épître à Horace by: Du Deffand, Mme, to send, to HW, **4.** 276, 281; La Harpe's reply to, **5.** 293, 296; Le Kain to read, at Mme du Deffand's, **5.** 283

Épître à l'auteur du livre des Trois Imposteurs, L', by: **4.** 223, 225, 228, 230, 232, 237, **8.** 155; quoted, **32.** 35–6, 40

Épître à M. Marmontel by, **5.** 395, 397, 407, 409

Épître à M. Pigalle by, sent to HW by Mme du Deffand, **5.** 327–8

Épître à mon vaisseau by, **4.** 101, 105, 111

Épître au Roi de la Chine by, **4.** 489, 493, **28.** 113n

'*Épître au Roi de Prusse*' by: Caracciolo gives, to Mme du Deffand, **5.** 339–40; Du Deffand, Mme, seeks, **5.** 338

Épître by, sent to Lady Ossory, **32.** 307

Épître de Monsieur de V—— en arrivant dans sa terre près du lac de Genève by, mentioned by Gray, **28.** 153n

Épîtres by, **7.** 180

Essai historique et critique sur les dissensions des églises de Pologne by, **3.** 386

Essai sur les mœurs by, quoted, **23.** 387, 523

Essai sur l'histoire générale by, **2.** 333, **35.** 283–4

Essai sur l'histoire universelle by, **43.** 76

Examen de la nouvelle histoire de Henri IV de M. de Bury: mentioned, **4.** 171; suspected of being Voltaire's, **4.** 159

fame of: will last, **33.** 6; will not last, **34.** 117

fatalism favoured by, **31.** 92

Fawkener friend of, **9.** 145n

—— to see, **5.** 435

Faydit de Tersac's letter from, **7.** 34

Ferney may be reoccupied by, **7.** 24

Florian, M. and Mme de, nephew and niece of, **7.** 269

Fontenelle argues with, on naturalness of passions, **7.** 370

forgotten, **7.** 53

Fragments historiques sur l'Inde et sur le général Lally by, to be taken to HW by Palmerston, **5.** 410, 419

France makes peace offer to Frederick II through, **21**. 366n

Franciscans refuse requiem Mass to, **7**. 48

Frederick II asked by, for asylum, **3**. 110

—— does not need, to show him how to write, **21**. 157

—— hymned by, **23**. 515

—— not persuaded by, into a French alliance, **18**. 396n

—— probably pays, in base metal, **23**. 515

——'s addresses should be corrected by, **18**. 500

——'s correspondence with, **5**. 307–8, 338–40, **6**. 307, **34**. 33

—— sends for, **37**. 65

—— sends porcelain bowl to, **5**. 307–8

——'s friendship with, **5**. 340, **24**. 387

—— should make a 'dialogue of the dead' with, **24**. 149

——'s sneers from, may be deleted by editors, **39**. 386

——'s verses called 'royal' by, **31**. 272

——'s verses to, in Cologne Gazette, **21**. 180

—— writes sonnets to, **21**. 171

French abandon, **31**. 43

French parliamentarians idolize, **31**. 69

French poetic excellence said by, to consist in overcoming difficulties, **35**. 466

Fréron enemy of, **3**. 256, **5**. 327, 354, **8**. 157

—— said to have written article on, for Sabatier de Castres's *Trois siècles*, **5**. 314

—— verses on, by, **6**. 274

Galimatias pindarique sur un carrousel donné par l'impératrice de Russie by, **4**. 101

Gaultier, Abbé, seeks conversion of, **7**. 21, 24

—— signs confession of, **7**. 25, 26

Genevese emigrants' watches marketed by, **4**. 411

Geoffrin, Mme, mentioned by, **6**. 357

Gibbon more accurate than, **28**. 243

Graftons call on, on first visit to Geneva, **22**. 40

Gray comments on opinions of, **14**. 187–8

—— detests, **14**. 138

—— loves, in his grander style, **14**. 26

——'s opinion of, **23**. 515

—— will be depreciated by, **28**. 186

Guèbres, Les, by, HW derides plot of, **35**. 122

Gudin's poem would annoy, **4**. 243

Guerre civile de Genève, La, by: condemned by HW, **39**. 230; Du Deffand, Mme, sends, to HW, **3**. 238, 273, **4**. 10, 14, 17, 63–4, 74, 77, 84; Du Deffand, Mme, has poor opinion of, **3**. 277, 285, 295, 298, 301; HW likes, **3**. 295, 301

HW accused by, of officiously sending him books, **13**. 45

HW accuses, of bad taste, **5**. 397

HW attacks, **39**. 44

HW buys bust of, **7**. 410

HW calls: scoffer and impostor, **10**. 184; 'the first genius of Europe,' **41**. 148

HW cites, **2**. 332, 333

(?) HW comments on wit of, **7**. 41

HW compared with, by Mme du Deffand, **3**. 179

HW compares: with Corneille, Racine, Shakespeare, **6**. 44; with Shakepeare, **9**. 356n

HW complimented by: at expense of father, **41**. 152, 354; in letter to Mme du Deffand, **4**. 127

HW consents to printing of Mme du Deffand's correspondence with, **41**. 425

HW defends Shakespeare against, **35**. 558, **41**. 149–58

HW does not like impieties of, **4**. 18

HW does not reveal misconduct of, for fear of hurting Mme de Choiseul, **16**. 199

HW exhorted not to enter into controversy with, **4**. 117, 118, 120, 123

HW jokes about Hume's opinion of letters of, **31**. 119

HW mentions, **6**. 20, **15**. 180

HW more dirtily treated by, than by Hume, **13**. 45

HW neither so great nor so little as, **31**. 270

HW on style and method of, **4**. 129, 214

HW paraphrases, **4**. 174n

HW permits editors of, to have Voltaire's correspondence with Mme du Deffand, **39**. 385

HW prefers Shakespeare to, in preface to *Castle of Otranto*, **3**. 256, 261, 270, **4**. 90, 95–9, 102, 107, 129, **6**. 268, **7**. 269, **8**. 141–4

HW quotes passage from, about Charles V, **23**. 523

HW reads correspondence of, **11**. 28

HW requests verses of, on Lady Ossory, **32**. 4

HW returns epistles of, **32**. 38

HW's comments on Clement XIII welcoming the D. of York will be echoed by, **22**. 180

HW's correspondence with: **4**. 146, 286, **6**. 361, **7**. 387, **8**. 144–6, **41**. 146–59, 354; about *Historic Doubts* and *Castle of Otranto*, **13**. 43, 45; Du Deffand, Mme, eager to know about, **4**. 101–2, 106, 116, 117, 119; *see also* Voltaire: HW's letter from, *and* Voltaire: HW's letter to

HW's epitaph for, **7**. 14, 43. 103

HW's faith in Egyptians weakened by, **41**. 177

HW shares views of, on patriots and statesmen, **32**. 40

HW's letter from, of 6 June 1768, **4**. 102, 104, 113, 117, 120, **41**. 146–7

HW's letter from, of 15 July 1768: **4**. 116–18, 120, **41**. 151–7; HW copies, for Mme du Deffand, **4**. 126, 127; HW discusses, **4**. 119–20, 129; *Mercure de France* prints, **4**. 237, **13**. 45; printed, and may be included in general edition, **41**. 354n, 464–5

HW's letter to, of 21 June 1768: **4**. 90, 104, 113, 117–18, 120, **41**. 148–50; Choiseul, Mme de, approves of frankness of, **4**. 103; Du Deffand, Mme, discusses, **4**. 95–6, 98–9, 117; HW discusses, **4**. 98

[Voltaire, continued]

HW's letter to, of 27 July 1768, **4.** 122–3, 126, **41.** 158–9

HW's letter to Mme du Deffand of 7 May 1770 would please, **4.** 405

HW's opinion of, **4.** 357, **8.** 55, **33.** 6

HW's style resembles that of, **3.** 141, **5.** 142

HW transcribes verses of, for Gray, **14.** 25–6

HW urges Mason to lash, **28.** 277, 279

Hamilton encloses his letter from, **35.** 413

Hardinge likes only the wit of, **35.** 577

——'s correspondence with, **35.** 584

health of, **4.** 307, 468, **6.** 424, **7.** 22, 24, 27, 28, 34–5, 44

Hénault ridiculed by, for omitting him in his will, **41.** 199

—— said to have been praised by, **8.** 151

——'s correspondence with, **7.** 64–5

—— urged by, to enter controversy, **4.** 146, 158–9

Henriade by: Du Deffand, Mme, quotes, **3.** 90; Du Deffand, Mme, reads, **7.** 180; Frederick II mentions, **5.** 308; HW belittles, **28.** 276; Virgil and Lucan better than, **16.** 272

Histoire de Charles XII by, owned by Mme du Deffand, **8.** 34

Histoire de la guerre de 1741 by: Conway seeks, **37.** 420, 421; HW sends, to Bentley, **35.** 264

Histoire de l'Empire de Russie sous Pierre le Grand by: HW prefers *Tancrède* to, **16.** 44; HW's opinion of, **9.** 327

Historic Doubts forwarded by Mme du Deffand to, **4.** 99, 101

—— praised by, **4.** 131, **32.** 341–2, **41.** 152, 353–4

—— requested by, **4.** 120, **5.** 316

history as adjusted by, **34.** 208–9

Homer the subject of, despite ignorance of Greek, **22.** 40

Homme aux quarante écus, L', by, **4.** 53

house bought by, **7.** 39

house to be rented by, **7.** 38

'Huet' pseudonym of, **8.** 152

Hume imitates, **35.** 214

——'s correspondence with, **3.** 178–9, 190

'Impromptu écrit de Genève à Messieurs mes ennemis au sujet de mon portrait en Apollon,' **6.** 130, 137

Ingénu, L', by, **5.** 354

'innkeeper to Europe,' **4.** 52

'Inscription pour une statue de l'Amour, dans les jardins de maisons,' **6.** 157

'Invitation de souper' by: **8.** 196; Du Deffand, Mme, sends, to HW, **6.** 279

Irène (Alexis Comnène) by: crowd expected for opening of, **7.** 29; HW's opinion of, **31.** 270; original name of, *Alexis Comnène,* changed because of harshness, **28.** 366; reading and performance of, hasten Voltaire's death, **28.** 410; reception of, **7.** 30; rehearsed at Voltaire's lodging, **7.** 19, 20,

25, 27; second performance of, **7.** 33; unsuccessful, **7.** 39; Voltaire crowned with laurel at performance of, **28.** 385, **31.** 270; Voltaire writes, in old age, **31.** 270

Italian poet attacks, for pillaging and reviling Shakespeare, **24.** 536

Jesuits abused and praised by, **32.** 213

—— the butt of writings of, **21.** 383, **23.** 515

Jews are better Christians than, **14.** 188

jokes by, about Q. Elizabeth's passion for Essex, **15.** 40n

Keate's poetic epistle to, **14.** 169

Kehl edition of: **7.** 130; prohibited, **33.** 483

La Beaumelle contradicted by, **35.** 283–4

—— subject of verses by, **6.** 274

La Bletterie rudely treated by, **4.** 105, 111–12, 118, 123, 127, 171, **8.** 150, 151, 157

'La Caille, Abbé de,' pseudonym of, **8.** 149, 151, **41.** 125n

La Chalotais's letter from, **11.** 28

Lady Percy's speech in *Henry IV* superior to all of, **42.** 294

La Harpe, M. and Mme de, leave, **4.** 42

La Harpe, M. de, commends 'Diatribe' of, **7.** 375

—— eulogizes, **7.** 172, 426

—— replies to, **5.** 293

——'s verses on, **7.** 2, 8

Lekain asked by, to read poems at Mme du Deffand's, **5.** 282–3, 287–8, 319

letter; letters of: **9.** 262n; Du Deffand, Mme, lends, to Craufurd, **3.** 388, 406, **4.** 231; Du Deffand, Mme, sends, to HW, **4.** 178, 181; to Choiseuls, extant, **28.** 153; to Mme du Deffand, extract from, **4.** 52–3

letter to Rousseau in name of, **1.** 113–14

Lettre . . . à l'académie française by, criticizes *Macbeth,* **41.** 373n

Lettre de M. de Voltaire à l'Académie française by, **6.** 354

Lettres à M. de Voltaire sur La Nouvelle Héloïse by, **15.** 239

Lettres by, bequeathed by Mme du Deffand, **43.** 80

Lettres chinoises, indiennes et tartares à M. Paw par un Bénédictin by, **6.** 285

Lettres de Voltaire à messieurs de la noblesse de Gévaudan by, sent by Voltaire to Mme du Deffand, **5.** 400

Lettres philosophiques by: English writings translated in, **41.** 152n; gravediggers' scene in *Hamlet* disparaged in, **41.** 289n

Lettre sur les panégyriques par Irénée Alethès by, **3.** 298, 301

libel upon, angers him, **7.** 25

library of, left to Mme Denis, **7.** 49–50

Ligne's letter to, **6.** 431

L'Indiscret by, quoted by HW, **28.** 366–7

L'Isle's verses attributed to, **5.** 428

Lois de Minos, Les, by: Du Deffand, Mme, praises, **8.** 191; Du Deffand, Mme, gives opinion of, **5.** 287–8, 322, 325; Du Deffand, Mme, sends extracts from, to HW, **5.** 272–

4; Du Deffand, Mme, to send, to HW, **5.** 322, 325; HW sends, to Lady Ossory, **32.** 100; HW's opinion of, **5.** 334–5; Lekain reads, at Mme du Deffand's, **5.** 283, 287–8, 300, 319; printed, **5.** 320

Lort wishes to see impartial account of, **16.** 200

Louis XIV praised by, for supposed objection to pompous epithets, **7.** 356–7

——'s era approved by, **5.** 397

Louis XVI and Marie-Antoinette may be visited by, **7.** 21

Louis XVI said to have ordered statue of, **7.** 23

——'s reforms praised by, **8.** 197–8

'Louis the Great' discovered by, **40.** 102

Lullin, Mme, verses to, by, thought to be addressed to Mme du Deffand, **6.** 25, 33

Lyttelton calls, an exile, **21.** 486

——'s letter from: **16.** 43; written from his hovel in France, **21.** 486

Macbeth passage ridiculed by, **41.** 373

Maffei's epistle from, **7.** 142

Mahomet by: **7.** 328; coup de théâtre in, **41.** 297; HW likes, **6.** 44, **41.** 294; HW prefers, to Racine's *Iphigénie*, **29.** 111; HW to reread, **5.** 389

Mairan refuses to read works of, **7.** 326

Maître Guignard, ou De l'hypocrisie by, **3.** 251, 252

Malesherbes receives letter of, to Boncerf, **6.** 287

MSS not left by, **7.** 50

Marchand's *Testament* of, **4.** 484, 493, 494, **5.** 8

Marigny orders statue of, **7.** 23

Marmontel mentioned in verses attributed to, **7.** 22–3, 27

——'s ode on unveiling of statue of, **5.** 273

Marseillais et le lion, Le, by: **4.** 161, 163, **8.** 148, 149, 151; Du Deffand, Mme, quotes, **4.** 187, **6.** 313; Du Deffand, Mme, sends, to HW, **4.** 154, 156

Maurepas promises not to molest, **28.** 365

Mémoires of: HW receives, from Lucans from Paris, **39.** 414; HW thinks, genuine but stolen, **31.** 215

Merchant of Venice could mostly have been written by, **34.** 2

Mérope by: **7.** 326, **8.** 142; Dumesnil acts in, **31.** 60; seen by HW in Paris, **35.** 121–2

'meteor of the reading world,' **24.** 387

Micromégas by, Gray asks if HW has read, **14.** 62

Mignot signs confession of, **7.** 25, 26

mistress of, **3.** 237n, **11.** 26n

misuse of talents of, **32.** 36

monastic professions damped by, **34.** 193

Montagu, Mrs, hears invective by, against Shakespeare at Académie française, **24.** 267

Morangiès defended by, **5.** 401

Murville eulogizes, **7.** 172

Nanine by, **4.** 208

Neufchâteau answered by, **6.** 285

——'s epistle to, **6.** 285

new writings of, **4.** 18

not to come to Paris, **4.** 293

Œdipe by: **4.** 100; Joseph II attends, **6.** 443

Œuvres of, owned by Mme du Deffand, **8.** 32, 34

Olimpie by, seen by Hertford, **38.** 351

Olivet, Abbé d', receives letter of, on prosody, **3.** 251, 252

only European author who one wishes would write, **23.** 515

Oreste by, *Hamlet* in French will resemble, **35.** 121

Orphelin de la Chine, L', by, desired by Conway, **37.** 420, 421

Palissot said to have written article on, for *Trois siècles* by Sabatier de Castres, **5.** 314

——'s eulogy of, **7.** 82, 94, 96–7, 180

pamphlet by, sent by Mme du Deffand to Bns Hervey, **3.** 93

Paris forbidden to, **4.** 293, 307

—— may become home of, **7.** 24

—— said to be visited by, **5.** 319

—— visited by, **7.** 17, 24. 356, **28.** 410

parliament of Paris, changes in, will be regretted by, **6.** 118

Patouillet, enemy of, **8.** 156

'patriarch,' **32.** 4

Pauw's controversy with, **34.** 40n

Pélopides, Les, ou Atrée et Thyeste by: **5.** 189, 198; HW ridicules phrase in, **28.** 326

Philosophe, Le, by Chesneau du Marsais, abridged by: Caracciolo brings, **5.** 323; Du Deffand, Mme, and guests read, **5.** 323; Du Deffand, Mme, gives opinion of, **5.** 323

Philosophe ignorant, Le, by: Du Deffand, Mme, asks for, **3.** 200; Du Deffand, Mme, disparages, **3.** 132; HW bored by, **3.** 113

philosophes are not satisfied by, **14.** 144

phrases in Hamlet's 3d soliloquy condemned by, **29.** 370

Pigalle, verses to, by, **5.** 327–8, **7.** 20–1, 23

——'s statue, verses on, **5.** 327–8, 354

Poème sur la loi naturelle by, quoted by Mme du Deffand, **3.** 142, **4.** 105

Poland's ravagers hymned by, **23.** 315

Pompignan may have written article on, for Sabatier de Castres's *Trois siècles,* **5.** 314

'pope of impiety,' **32.** 36

Pope's remark to, on Milton's inability to rhyme, **41.** 151

portraits of friends of, at Ferney, **33.** 377–8

possible reference to, **9.** 305n

posthumous honours of, **7.** 111

'Pot Pourri,' verses by, **4.** 454

Précis du procès du Comte de Morangiès by, **5.** 419

Prédiction tirée d'un ancien manuscrit attributed to: *La Nouvelle Héloïse* ridiculed by, **21.** 514; not by Voltaire, **3.** 110

Princesse de Babylone, La, by, **4.** 53

[Voltaire, *continued*]

Profession de foi des théistes, La, par —— *au R. D.* by, **4.** 135

Prussia negotiates with France through, **21.** 153n

Pucelle, La, by: **3.** 285, **7.** 292, **43.** 224; banned in Béarn, **10.** 192; circulated in MS and then published as *La Jeanne,* **20.** 548; Du Deffand, Mme, cites, **5.** 161; HW criticizes, **20.** 555; HW sends, to Bentley, **35.** 263; indelicacy of, **16.** 272; Mann supposes Wilkes's *Essay on Woman* to resemble, **22.** 192; Mason alludes to, **28.** 399; Voltaire alters, before printing it, **20.** 548

Pyrrhonisme de l'histoire, Le, by, **41.** 146n

Quatrième discours by, quoted by Mme du Deffand, **3.** 319, **4.** 364

Questions sur l'encyclopédie by: Du Deffand, Mme, gives opinion of, **5.** 142; Du Deffand, Mme, reads, **5.** 130, 239; Du Deffand, Mme, receives 6 numbers of, **4.** 411; Du Deffand, Mme, sends, to HW, **5.** 136, 142, 233; HW buys, **7.** 411

Racine defended by, **4.** 129, **5.** 389

——'s *Bérénice* discussed by HW and, **4.** 119–20, 129

Relation de la maladie . . . du jésuite Berthier by, **21.** 383

Relation de la mort du Chevalier de la Barre by, **4.** 101, 135

Relation du bannissement des Jésuites de la Chine by, **4.** 101, 135

religion superior to wit of, **36.** 271

(?) Relongue de la Louptière's verses on confession of, **7.** 31, 39

remark of, on translation, **29.** 156

Remarques sur le Comte d'Essex by, **41.** 56n

Riforma d'Italia, La, criticized by, **8.** 152

Robertson's work sent to, **4.** 343, 357

Rousseau, Jean-Baptiste, too much stressed by, **35.** 284

Rousseau, Jean-Jacques, fame of, compared with that of, **41.** 60

——'s *Julie ou la nouvelle Héloïse* discussed by, **15.** 239

royal personages unpoisoned by, **32.** 313

rumoured financial commission and rank of marquis for, **6.** 242

(?) Sabatier de Castres's article on, in *Trois siècles,* **5.** 313–14

——'s *Tableau philosophique de l'esprit de,* **5.** 79–80

'St-Didier,' pseudonym of, **8.** 149, 151

St-Simon's *Mémoires* have anecdotes that are also found in, **34.** 29

Saurin's verses on, **4.** 179–80

Scythes, Les, by: **3.** 286; Du Deffand, Mme, has poor opinion of, **3.** 281, 285; poorly received, **3.** 276

secretary of, *see* Wagnière, Jean-Louis

Sémiramis by: **4.** 49, **7.** 312; Ayscough imitates, **32.** 342–3; HW likes, **6.** 44, **41.** 294

Sésostris by: based on 'choice of Hercules,'

28. 253; Du Deffand, Mme, sends, to HW, **6.** 275; Du Deffand, Mme, gives opinion of, **6.** 275

Shakespeare and Corneille depreciated by, **41.** 465

Shakespeare and other English writers introduced by, in France, **41.** 152

Shakespeare attacked by, **6.** 345, 348, 354, 373n, **8.** 141, **28.** 275–9

—— criticized by, **40.** 373

—— disparaged by, **32.** 341–2

—— preferred to, by HW, **3.** 256, 261, 270, **4.** 90, 95–9, 102, 107, 129, **6.** 268, **7.** 269, **8.** 141–4

——'s dignifying of vulgar or trivial expressions condemned by, **41.** 295

Shuvalov, André, eulogizes, **7.** 175, 426, 428

Siècle de Louis XIV, Le, [and] *un Précis du siècle de Louis XV* by: **4.** 158, 159, 161, **5.** 7, **8.** 33n, 35n, 149, **22.** 85, **23.** 85; Calvinism subject of epigram in, **17.** 429n; incorporated in *Essai sur l'histoire générale,* **35.** 283

silhouette of, **43.** 94

social relations of, **6.** 281, **7.** 20–1, 22, 24, 27, 35, 36, 39

Socrate by, owned by Mme du Deffand, **8.** 35n

Sorbonne ignores, **7.** 36

sovereigns panegyricized by, for pay, **23.** 195

statement by, that culture has softened human manners, **23.** 387

statue of, unveiled, **5.** 273

story formed by, to suit his opinions, **34.** 208–9

Stratford vindicates English honour from imputations of, **29.** 234n

style of writing of: Du Deffand, Mme, appraises, **6.** 117; HW's style resembles, **3.** 141, **5.** 141

success of, in Paris, **7.** 38–40

successors of, satirized, **7.** 85, 100

summers of, to be spent at Ferney, **7.** 39

Sur la destruction des Jésuites by, sent to HW by Mme du Deffand, **5.** 401

Swiss government and religion endangered by, **35.** 583

Systèmes, Les, by: Du Deffand, Mme, gives opinion of, **5.** 300; Du Deffand, Mme, to send, to HW, **5.** 284, 300

Tactique, La, by: Craufurd to borrow, **5.** 428; Du Deffand, Mme, gives opinion of, **5.** 427, 428, 433; Du Deffand, Mme, receives, from Voltaire, **5.** 426; Du Deffand, Mme, to send, to HW, **5.** 426–8; HW's opinion of, **5.** 430, 432; HW to send, to Lady Ossory, **32.** 169

'Tamponet,' pseudonym of, **8.** 158

Tancrède by: Du Deffand, Mme, mentions rôle in, **4.** 197; HW prefers, to *Histoire . . . de Russie sous Pierre le Grand,* **16.** 44; unsuccessful in Paris, **16.** 44

Taureau blanc, Le, by: Du Deffand, Mme, gives opinion of, **5.** 432–3; Du Deffand,

Mme, sends, to HW, **5.** 414, 416, 419; Du Deffand, Mme, to have, copied for HW, **5.** 408; Garrick produces Mme Celesia's adaptation of, **31.** 152–3; said to be printed, **5.** 432

Théologie portative, La, criticized by, **8.** 152

Thibouville a friend of, **28.** 279n

Traduction du poème de Jean Plokof, conseiller de Holstein, sur les affaires présentes by: **8.** 162–5; Du Deffand, Mme, sends, to HW, **4.** 405, 408

translation discussed by, **29.** 156

Trois empereurs en Sorbonne, Les, by: **4.** 161, 163, 164, **8.** 149, 151, **43.** 89; Du Châtelet sends, to HW, **41.** 125

Tronchin attends, **6.** 22, 24, 26

Turgot's reforms praised by, **8.** 197–8

Universal History by, considered by HW to be Voltaire's chef d'œuvre, **34.** 79; *see also* Voltaire: *Essai sur l'histoire générale*

'unpoisoner' of bygone criminals, **22.** 65, 253

vanity of, **28.** 410

'Vers de M. de Voltaire à Madame la Marquise du Deffand, âgée de quatre-vingt-deux ans.' *See* Voltaire: Lullin, Mme, verses to, by

verse; verses by: **4.** 94, 107, 396, 454; often 'frippery,' **14.** 26; on Choiseul, Duchesse de, **4.** 408, 416–17; on Christian VII, **3.** 268, **8.** 131; on Clairon, Mlle, **5.** 273, 274; on Fréron and La Beaumelle, **6.** 274; on Marmontel's corrections of Quinault, **7.** 22, 27; on Pigalle, **5.** 327–8, **7.** 20–1, 23; on Versoix, **4.** 396–7; on Voisenon, **6.** 248; stupid, **39.** 243; to centenarian lady, **23.** 306; to Frederick II, **21.** 171, 180; to Lady Hervey, in English, published, **31.** 417

verses on: **5.** 354, **7.** 31, 39; ascribed to Dorat, **4.** 172; by Boufflers, **7.** 2; by La Harpe, **7.** 2, 8; by Saurin, **4.** 179–80

verses on Dorat falsely attributed to, **4.** 20

Versoix not connected with, **3.** 393

visitors overwhelm, in Paris, **7.** 18

visits never returned by, **22.** 40

volcanoes discussed by, **35.** 413

volumes still published by, **15.** 133

Walpole, Bns (Cts of Orford), discusses, with Andreasi, **19.** 555

Walpole, Lady, dined with, **41.** 149

Walpole brothers knew, **41.** 146

Warton sends letter of, to HW, who declines to print it, **42.** 121

Wiart takes messages to and from, **7.** 17, 18

will of, **7.** 48

winters of, to be spent in Paris, **7.** 39

writes commentary on treatise, **3.** 173n

'writes volumes faster than they can print,' **41.** 7

writings not produced by, recently, **24.** 62

writings of, repetitious, **28.** 343

Zadig by, hermit in, **41.** 159

Zaïre by: begins with nasal adverbs, **42.** 231; Cibber, Mrs, appears in, **13.** 96; Du Deffand, Mme, reads, **7.** 178; HW dislikes, **5.** 389, **6.** 44

Voltaire (ship):
Piron's verses on, **4.** 122
See also Voltaire: *Épître à mon vaisseau*

Volterra, Bp of. *See* Dumesnil, Joseph (d. 1781)

Volterra (Italy):
Acciaioli's villa near, **20.** 160
alabaster of, not big enough for large vases, **20.** 582
alabaster urns or vases from, *see under* Vase
bishopric of, has high revenue, **19.** 491
chancellor and notary of, avoid Dumesnil, **19.** 493
Dumesnil's attempt to occupy see of, **19.** 490–3
Galluzzi collection at, **25.** 531n
Mann gets vases from, weekly, **17.** 394
nobles of, to be enrolled in two classes, **20.** 192n
Pisan cavaliere sent to, for indiscreet talk about Spaniards, **18.** 46

Volunteer, English privateer:
Kent, Capt., sails, from Leghorn without permission of port authorities, **21.** 274n

Volunteer; volunteers:
in St-Malo attempt, **37.** 536
Irish: address by, **39.** 405–6; Beauchamp's pamphlet addressed to, **39.** 394–7; HW thinks, mostly Roman Catholic, **35.** 379; Irish Parliament resists reforms by, **35.** 382; meeting of, postponed, **35.** 379; *see also under* Ireland
militia booty from *Hazard* shared with, **37.** 236

Vomit, black:
Beauclerk, Lady Diana, ill of, **32.** 77

Vomiting:
HW's, **12.** 194, **34.** 199, 277
James's powder may induce, **36.** 176
occurrences of, **17.** 37, **18.** 153
retchings, **36.** 259

Vonck, François:
Patriotic Committee in Belgium led by, **39.** 456n

Von Ege, ——, Choiseul's musician:
death of, **5.** 403

Von Wallmoden. *See* Wallmoden

Von Wendt. *See* Wendt

Vorese. *See* Varese

Vorontsov, Cts. *See* Skavronska, Anna Carlovna

Vorontsov, ——, 'Rantzau,' natural brother to Ps Dashkov:
seized in Gordon riots, **29.** 60, **33.** 179, **43.** 306

Vorontsov, Alexander Romanovich (1741–1805), diplomatist:
ambassador to England, **22.** 55
(?) Blandford, Lady, rumoured to be marrying, **43.** 331
credentials received by, **22.** 61
HW's correspondence with, over HW's gift to him of (?) *Anecdotes of Painting,* **40.** 308–9
Michell's intrigues with, **38.** 393n

[Vorontsov, Alexander Romanovich, *continued*]
Pelham, Frances, entertains, at Esher, 10. 72–3
uncle tells, to thank George III for Mann's attentions, 22. 203

Vorontsov, Mikhail Illarionovich (1714–67), vice-chancellor of Russia 1744–58; chancellor 1758–63:
at Florence in Princesse de Craon's time, 19. *184*, 21. 248
Bestuzhev could never live near, 22. 11
—— should have replaced, 22. 62
Botta asked by, to get house in Florence for 50 people, 22. 180
Catherine II probably hated by, 22. 195
Craon, Princesse de, quarrels with, 21. 259
Craons to entertain, 19. 184
entourage of, almost equalled by Modenese princess's, 22. 201
Florence to be revisited by, 22. 191, 202, 204
Francis I orders, to be well received at Florence, 19. 184
Frederick II should have been warned against, 22. 61
Halifax tells English diplomatists in Italy to welcome, 22. 173
health of, out of order, 22. 194
hypochondria of, 22. 202
Italy to be revisited by, 22. 173
Ivan VI dethroned by, 22. 62
Keith discusses Russian-Turkish relations with, 21. 247
Mann attends disastrous dinner with, 21. 248
—— entertains, at George III's command, 22. 180, 193–4, 204
Marseille to be visited by, 19. 184n
name of, corrected, 43. 278
Naples to be visited by, for health, 19. 184
nephew and niece of, 22. 55
nephew told by, to thank George III for Mann's attentions, 22. 203
nieces of, 22. 68
Peter III advised by, not to write to Frederick II directly, 22. 11n
—— may banish, to Siberia, 22. 11
—— scolded by, for zeal for Frederick II, 22. 62n
Pisa visited by, 22. 202, 204
Porter's conduct condemned by, 21. 248
postmaster the only companion of, in Florence, 21. 249
Russian revolution feared by, 22. 202, 205
'soul' of the Russian ministry, 21. 247
Uffizi Gallery often visited by, 21. 249
Vienna visited by, 22. 180
wears boots and spurs to dinner table, 21. 248
York, D. of, meets, at Florence, 22. 213–14

Vorontsov, Lt-Gen. Count Roman:
daughter banished to estate of, 22. 55n

Vorontsov, Semen Romanovich (1744–1832), Russian ambassador to England 1785–1806; 'Woronzow':
Hervey, Hon. Frederick William, described by, 42. 359n

house at Richmond lent by, to Comtesse de Boufflers, 11. 76n, 34. 68
minister to England, 11. 323n
SH visited by, 12. 228 *bis*, 234, 43. 160

Vorontsova, ——, m. Count Strogonov:
Mann's ball attended by, because she likes dancing, 22. 204n
travels of, 22. 173n

Vorontsova, Ekaterina Romanovna (1743–1810), m. (ca 1758–60) Prince Mikhail Illarionovich Dashkov:
announcement not made by, until successful, 22. 66
biographical information about, corrected, 43. 91, 128
brother of, seized during Gordon riots, 29. 59–60
Catherine II aided by, 22. *65*
—— at odds with, 4. 483
——'s former favourite, but now disgraced, 23. 242
——'s relations with, 31. 162
—— to hear the horrors of Gordon riots from, 33. 197
Choiseul, Duc and Duchesse de, may entertain, 4. 483
Damer, Mrs, does profiles of daughter of, 12. 272
Du Deffand, Mme, curious to see, 4. 483
England visited by, to put her son in school, 23. 242, 245
HW calls, 'Thalestris,' 33. 172, 179
HW curious to see, 4. 483
HW meets: and describes her, 23. 248–9; at Lady Clermont's, 33. 172; at Northumberland House, 33. 172, 39. 132
HW mentions singing and foreign languages of, 39. 132
London visited by, 29. 59
Mann knew relatives of, in Florence, 23. 245
Northumberlands entertain, at dinner at Northumberland House, 39. 132
Peter III dethroned by conspiracy led by, 10. 38
plots by, 22. 205n
Quaker meeting attended by, 23. 249
Sermon prêché . . . sur la tombe de Pierre a translation by, 23. 249
sister's confidence to, revealed to Catherine II, 22. 68
songs rendered by, 23. 249
SH visited by, 33. 203
verses by, on print of Catherine II, 23. 242

Vorontsova, Countess Elisaveta Romanovna, Peter III's mistress:
brother of, 22. 55
Catherine II said to have declined surrender from, of Order of St Catherine, 22. 58–9
Peter III keeps, as mistress, despite alleged impotence, 22. 57
——'s intention to imprison Catherine II told by, to sister. 22. 68

——'s mistress, **22**. 55, 65
—— would have married, **23**. 215
sister of, **10**. 38
Vorsterman, Lucas (ca 1578– ca 1640), engraver:
Aurelius's portrait said to be engraved by, **16**. 64
copies by, **15**. 95n
print by, **16**. 153n
Vortices:
Descartes's theory of, once fashionable, **20**. 154
Vortigern and Rowena. See under Ireland, William Henry
Vosges mountains:
Val d'Ajol in, **4**. 352n
Voss, Amalie Elizabeth von (d. 1789), cr. (1787) Gräfin Ingenheim:
Frederick William II of Prussia attempts bigamy with, **33**. 555
Vossius, Gerard Jan (1577–1649), Dutch philologist and historian:
(?) Christina's comment on, **31**. 223
De baptismo by, Johnson tries to read in, **33**. 494
Vossius, Isaac (1618–89), Q. Christina's librarian:
(?) Christina's comment on, **31**. 223
Votes of the House of Commons:
French are supposed to know nothing but what appears in, **28**. 357
publishers of, **17**. 425n
See also under Parliament: House of Commons: *Votes* of
Voting:
for pay: HW's reflections on, **25**. 275; in Wallingford borough, **17**. 400n
'noble peer' tries to influence, **19**. 449n
See also under Borough; Election; Elector
Voucher; vouchers:
Bedford, D., always obtains, for transactions in HW's accounts, **41**. 208
Vougny, (?) Monsieur and (?) Madame:
SH visited by, **12**. 240
Vougny, Mme Barthélemy de. *See* Pelée de Varennes, Marie-Louise-Antoinette-Anne
Vougny, Marie-Anne de (d. 1783), m. 1 (1726) Jean-Jacques Amelot, seigneur de Chaillou; m. 2 (1754) Balthazar-Joseph-François-Nicolas-Antoine Urtado, Marquis d'Amezaga:
social relations of, in Paris, **7**. 291, 298, 303, 318
Vous m'entendez bien:
verses to air of, **3**. 348
Vow; vows (votive offerings):
HW's collection of, **15**. 13, 17, 22
Voyage d'Amérique. See Robertson, William: *History of America*
Voyage dans les Alpes. See under Saussure, Horace-Bénédict de
Voyage dans l'hémisphère austral et autour du monde. See under Cook, James
Voyage d'Égypte et de Nubie. See under Norden, Frederik Ludvig

Voyage d'Espagne. See under Caimo, Norberto
Voyage de Sicile. See Brydone, Patrick: *Tour through Sicily and Malta*
Voyage d'Italie:
Du Deffand, Mme, owns, **8**. 35
See also under Richard, Abbé
Voyage du jeune Anacharsis en Grèce. See under Barthélemy, Jean-Jacques
Voyage en Provence. See under Le Coigneux de Bachaumont, François
Voyage en Sibérie. See under Chappe d'Auteroche, Jean
Voyage et les aventures des trois princes de Serendip. See under Mailly, Chevalier de
Voyage pittoresque de la Grèce. See under Choiseul-Beaupré, Marie-Gabriel-Florent-Auguste de
Voyage Round the World. See under Anson, George
Voyages de Gulliver, Les. See Swift, Jonathan: *Gulliver's Travels*
Voyage sentimental. See Sterne, Laurence: *Sentimental Journey*
Voyages et aventures d'une Princesse de Babylone. See Voltaire: *Princesse de Babylone, La*
Voyage to the Pacific Ocean. See under Cook, James
Voyageur françois, Le. See under La Porte, Joseph de
Voyer, Marquise de. *See* Mailly, Jeanne-Marie-Constance de
Voyer, Marc-Antoine-René de (1722–87), Marquis de Paulmy; son of the Marquis d'Argenson; academician:
(?) Ashburnham jealous of, **19**. 454
Bibliothèque des romans edited by, **6**. 400
Boufflers's *Oculist* read by, **7**. 264
HW knows, **39**. 214
HW's correspondence with, **7**. 389
Hénault's *Pièces de théâtre* printed by, **4**. 329
library of, sold to Comte d'Artois, **4**. 264n
Maillebois corresponds with, **23**. 283n
Marie-Antoinette's chancellor, **6**. 52
ministry of war may be given to, **4**. 380, 450
social relations of, in Paris, **3**. 41–2, 49, **7**. 264, 288, 296, 303, 311, 326, 332
Voyer, Marc-Pierre de (1696–1764), Comte d'Argenson; French war minister:
clemency for Young Pretender urged by, **19**. 264n
cost of war department under, **4**. 372
disgrace of: desirable, **21**. 59; rumoured, **21**. 56
divides office of *ministre d'État*, **14**. 153n
Du Deffand, Mme, does 'portrait' of, **8**. 108–9
Frederick II offered monthly subsidy by, **20**. 51n
French declaration of war against England signed by, **20**. 571n
George II angered by letters of, **19**. 271n
—— discusses peace proposals of, with Cabinet, **19**. 264n
government ministry given to, **18**. 32

[Voyer, Marc-Pierre de, *continued*]
haste of, in obeying Dauphin's orders when Damiens attacks Louis XV, draws suspicion, **21**. 48n
letters of, in favour of Jacobites, **19**. 271
Louis XV banishes, **14**. 152
—— dismisses, when no longer under confessor's influence, **21**. 56n
—— receives remonstrances from, about Young Pretender's arrival, **18**. 415
——'s and Mme de Pompadour's love of peace induces, to try to separate them, **20**. 530
Louis XV's devotion to Rome demanded by, as bulwark of monarchy, **21**. 48
Maurepas's disgrace plotted by, **20**. 51n
religious faction led by, **21**. 56
son of, **3**. 42n, **4**. 227n, **19**. (?) 454
Young Pretender meets, **19**. 393n
Voyer, Marc-René (1722–82), Marquis de, Comte d'Argenson's son:
armament for siege taken by, past Lyon, **20**. 536
(?) Ashburnham jealous of, **19**. 454
HW agrees with general opinion of, **4**. 227, 235
(?) HW entertains, at SH, **10**. 278
SH publications given to, **4**. 264
Voyer, Marie-Madeleine-Catherine de (b. 1724), m. (1745) Yves-Marie Desmarets, Comte de Maillebois:
Du Deffand, Mme, pities, for husband's disgrace, **5**. 41
——'s opinion of, **5**. 56
entrées, grandes, given to, **4**. 339
social relations of, in Paris, **3**. 369, **7**. 328, 336, 340
unhappy, **3**. 56
Voyer, René-Louis de (1694–1757), Marquis d'Argenson:
Châteauroux, Duchesse de, causes disgrace of, **5**. 386
(?) Hénault inherits Henri IV's letters from, **7**. 267
Idées . . . venus dans les conférences entre MM. d'Argenson et Wassenaer by, enrages England, **19**. 216n
Loisirs d'un ministre by, desired by HW who praises it, **36**. 249–50
Puisieux replaces, as secretary of state and minister of foreign affairs, **19**. 429n
resignation of, as secretary of state, **19**. 429n
(?) son of, **19**. 454
witticism by, on Vandières's attempt to get *cordon bleu*, **20**. 228
Voyer. *See also* Le Voyer
Voyer d'Argenson de Paulmy, Madeleine-Suzanne-Adélaïde de (1752–1813), m. (1771) Anne-Charles-Sigismond de Montmorency-Luxembourg, Duc de Luxembourg:
Boufflers, Duchesse de, replaced by, **5**. 106
Hénault's social relations with, **7**. 326
Marie-Antoinette's household joined by, **5**. 106

Versailles lodging given to, **5**. 129
Voyer de Chavigny, ——, French army officer: Düsseldorf to be besieged by, **20**. 228n
Vranks. *See* Franks
Vrillière. *See* La Vrillière
Vrillière, Rue de la, in Paris:
'Veau qui tette' in, **13**. 164n
Vriot, Marie-Denise (1742–1817), m. Nicolas Suin:
Beauvau wishes Mme du Deffand to hear, **6**. 237
social relations of, in Paris, **6**. 237, 466
Tartuffe recited by, **6**. 466
Vroom, Hendrik Cornelisz (1566–1640): tapestries designed by, **23**. 242n
Vuide Gousses, Rue de, in Paris:
Louis XV assigned to, in joke, **8**. 181
Vulcan:
Neptune's dispute with, imagined by HW, **33**. 452
Venus's marriage to, **35**. 55
Wolverhampton resembles forge of, **40**. 42
Vulcan, English fireship:
Portsmouth reached by, **30**. 112n
Vulcanian stays:
dangers of wearing, **28**. 294
Vulture, English ship:
Arnold boards, **33**. 239n
Vulture; vultures:
Austrian and Russian eagles become, **24**. 55
battles pleasing only to, **35**. 367
HW and Lady Cecilia Johnston resemble starved, **31**. 26
HW and Mann resemble, in their correspondence, **25**. 327
HW's term: for Catherine II and Frederick II, **35**. 392; for Joseph II, **25**. 410
Prometheus and, **35**. 372
Worsley compared to, **17**. 249
Vuy, ——, Sardinian first commissioner of foreign affairs:
Viry's incriminating letters found with, **24**. 328n
Vyne, the, Hants; John Chute's seat:
alterations at, **9**. 222
Atkynses might bring will to, too late for Anthony Chute to sign it, **35**. 84
Bentley's designs for ante-chapel of, not executed, **9**. 216
(?) ——'s drawing of, **9**. 212
—— should visit, **35**. 185
Carter's monument at, to Speaker Chute, **35**. 231n
chapel at: **9**. 166; Chute should have Masses said in, for England, **35**. 92; HW, Montagu, and Chute have 'Catholic enjoyment' of, **35**. 185; Mann to get 'Last Supper' painting for, **20**. 485, 489, 529, 539; Müntz might execute Bentley's designs at, **35**. 186; Sandys builds, **20**. 485n; stained glass in, **20**. 485n; SH Committee votes for embellishments to, **35**. 185
Chute, Anthony, owns, **17**. 234n, **19**. 458n

Chute, John, at, **9**. 167, 172, 249, 378, **28**. 103, **35**. 252, 256, 265
—— closer to inheritance of, **35**. 58
—— does not execute HW's proposals for, **9**. 216, **35**. 252
—— ill at, **21**. 1
—— inherits, from brother, **9**. 161, **35**. 83–6
—— may be at, **10**. 264
—— of, **14**. 18n, 82n
—— returns from, **35**. 177
——'s bill mentions, **14**. 230
—— sets out for, **35**. 200
——'s house party at, to be deferred, **10**. 98, 100
—— the last of the male line of his family at, **24**. 209n
—— visits, at his brother's death, **20**. 433
Chute, William John, owner of, **35**. 640
Cowslades settled near, **9**. 251n
dampness of, Chute needs braziers more than physicians for, **35**. 109
Gray inquires about, **14**. 80
—— visits, **14**. 83, 84, 92
HW and George and Charles Montagu visit Chute at, **37**. 388
HW considers, too damp for Chute, **35**. 105
HW encourages improvements to, **20**. 449
HW inquires about Montagu's impressions of, **10**. 37
HW lists obstacles to visiting Chute at, **35**. 98
HW's advice about, not taken, **9**. 216, **35**. 252
HW sends to Italy for altar-piece for, **9**. 216
HW's 'Inventionary' about, **35**. 232, 252, 639–40
HW to visit Chute at, **20**. 449, **21**. 1
HW urges Chute to leave, **35**. 67
Montagu's letters forwarded from, **10**. 37, 38, 40
'mouldering estate,' **35**. 58
Müntz's drawings of, **14**. 83, **35**. 89
——'s services to, **35**. 91
—— to visit, **35**. 232
seeds from, sent to Bentley, **35**. 185
view of, **9**. 164
visitors to: Grandison, Vcts, **10**. 97; Gray, **43**. 184; HW, **9**. (?) 88, 162–4, 222, 243, **35**. 185, 249, **38**. 27, **40**. 165, **43**. 184; Montagu, Charles, **10**. 97, **35**. 185, **38**. 27; Montagu, George, **9**. 162, 163, 243, 370, **10**. 37, 38, 75, 97, **35**. 185, **38**. 27; Müntz, **35**. 241, 243, 252, 256
Whithed dies at, **14**. 49n
—— ill at, **20**. 237–8
Vyner, Robert (ca 1685–1777), M.P.:
Mathews's friend, **19**. 33n
Parliamentary motion by, **28**. 401n
Parliamentary debates by: on privately-raised regiments, **26**. 15; on Scotch Bill, **26**. 31, 32
Prussian treaty opposed by, in Parliament, **38**. 7–8
Vyse, Mrs. *See* Howard, Anne

W

W——, Comte Alexandre de. *See* Vorontsov, Alexander
W——, F——:
Friendship, A Poem by, presented by him to HW, **41**. 170
HW's correspondence with, **41**. 170
W——, Cts of:
HW meets, at Chantilly, **35**. 124
W——t——e, Mrs:
(?) Maclaine's mistress, **20**. 169
Waasner Twickle. *See* Wassenaer
Wachmeister, Baron Carl Adam von (1740–1820):
(?) social relations of, with Comtesse de Forcalquier in Paris, **7**. 319
Wachtendonck, Karl Franz (ca 1694–1741), Baron von:
body coach of, **17**. 110
Braitwitz to succeed, temporarily, **17**. 117
Corsini, Cardinal, entertains, **17**. 106
cousin of, maid of honour to Maria Theresa, procures Richecourt's disgrace, **17**. 490
death and burial of, **17**. 109–10, 117
death of, may make Goldsworthys impatient to leave Italy, **17**. 138
disguises himself to meet Ps Triulzi (Trivulzio), **17**. 489–90
Florence visited by, **17**. 40, 95
Goldsworthy, Mrs, cicisbea to, **17**. 146, 186n
—— paid by, **17**. 146–7, 186
—— praises, **17**. 105
Goldsworthys excluded from death-bed of, **17**. 109
ill with malignant fever, **17**. 105, 109
Maria Theresa's troops at Leghorn commanded by, **17**. 467n
Osorio contrasted with, **17**. 186
priests banish pictures and install altars at bedside of, **17**. 109
Richecourt returns to Florence after death of, **17**. 468
—— said to have been frightened by, from Florence by a challenge to duel, **17**. 467
——'s disgrace said to be procured by, **17**. 106, 108, 490
—— tells story about, **17**. 489–90
state coach of, **17**. 260
'Triulzi' (Trivulzio), Ps, mistress of, **17**. 109n
Walpole, Bns, rails at, **17**. 107
Walsegg not to imitate, **17**. 130
Waddes, Alexander:
(?) HW attends auction of prints and drawings owned by, **38**. 371n
Waddilove, Rev. Robert Darley (1736–1828), chaplain of embassy at Madrid 1771–9; Dean of Ripon 1791–1828:
biographical information about, corrected, **43**. 220
Lort encloses letter of, from Madrid, **16**. 179
——'s correspondence with, about *Anecdotes of Painting*, **16**. 168–9, 170

[Waddilove, Rev. Robert Darley, *continued*]
Müntz unknown to, **16**. 168
Waddington, Mrs Benjamin. *See* Port, Georgina Mary Anne
Waddington, Edward (ca 1670–1731), Bp of Chichester, 1724:
Maddox chaplain to, **18**. 246
niece of, **18**. 246n
Wade, George (1673–1748), Gen.; Field Marshal; M.P.:
Arenberg quarrels with, **18**. 441
—— reports Rhine crossing to, **37**. 158
—— to deny desire of, for action, **37**. 183
army of: **19**. 128; slowed by Dutch troops, **37**. 214–15
Black Watch reviewed by, **18**. 236n
cavalry of, pursued rebels, **19**. 186
confined to his room, **37**. 186–7
Conway and Yorke criticize slowness of, **37**. 214
Conway cannot leave, before he leaves Ghent, **37**. 185
—— plays whist with, **37**. 177
——'s commanding officer, **18**. 494n
——'s relations with, **37**. 215
—— to accompany, to Ghent, **37**. 182
Cumberland, D. of, may be joined by, **37**. 214
—— sends Conway to hurry, after the fleeing rebels, **19**. 179
disgrace and defeat of, rumoured at Florence, **19**. 190
Drummond sends proposal to, for exchanging prisoners, **19**. 187, 202
Durand sends express to, **19**. 166
Edinburgh provost sees, at Newcastle, **19**. 175–6
field marshal, **18**. 366
generosity of, to poor gentleman, **20**. 110
George II and Council approve answer of, to Drummond, **19**. 202
George II criticizes, **18**. 494
—— limits the troops allotted to, **19**. 117
—— receives, **18**. 556
HW prefers, to Stair, **18**. 494
HW thinks, superannuated, **30**. 96
Hague, The, to be visited by, **37**. 182
Handasyd sent by, to take Edinburgh, **19**. 159
Hawley to accompany army of, to Scotland, **19**. 193
health drunk to, at Leghorn, **19**. 152
Hessians and British army from Flanders to join, in Yorkshire, **19**. 126–7
house of: auctioned, **9**. 56; Burlington designs, **9**. 56; HW visits, **9**. 56; in Burlington St, **19**. 126n; Montagu compares, to provost's house at Dublin, **9**. 391
independence from government orders demanded by, **19**. 166
Mann expects rebels to be crushed by, **19**. 149
Marlborough might be rivalled by, **18**. 456
named in Secret Committee lists, **17**. 385
Newcastle left by, **19**. 153, 159, 165

noblemen's regiments more effective than army of, in Yorkshire, **26**. 14
Ostend's artillery demanded from England by, **19**. 69
plate stored by, at Antwerp, **37**. 154
quartermaster captured by, **19**. 167
rebel retreat to be intercepted by, **37**. 21
rebels avoid, **19**. 159
rebels not intercepted by, **40**. 55
rebels to be opposed by, **19**. 117, 165, 166
Rubens cartoon bought and sold by, **9**. 56
Scotland to be approached by, from Doncaster, **19**. 137
snuff-box stolen from, at gaming-house, **20**. 110, **43**. 267
Stair may keep, from army command, **19**. 127
Walpole, Sir Robert, buys picture from, **9**. 56
—— writes to, **37**. 167
Wetherby approached by, **19**. 173–4
yacht summoned by, to go to England, **37**. 186
Wade, George (d. ?1758), Lt-Col.:
camp fever and bloody flux of, **40**. 144
Wade, Watson:
SH visited by, **12**. 221
Wadham, Mrs. *See* Petre, Dorothy
Wadham, Nicholas (1532–1609), benefactor of Oxford University:
medal of, **16**. 210
Wadham College, Oxford:
altar-cloth at, by Fuller, **42**. 380n
Thistlethwayte expelled as warden of, **30**. 89n
Waës, Anne-Salomé-Joséphine de (ca 1739–94), m. (1758) Louis-Gabriel des Acres, Comte de l'Aigle:
social relations of, in Paris, with 1st E. Harcourt, **5**. 194
Wafer; wafers (for sealing letters):
Conway mails letter without, **37**. 568
letter sealed with half-ounce of, sure to be read en route, **37**. 573
Wagenfelt, Fredrik:
Swedish war ships to be commanded by, **25**. 60n
Wager, Lady. *See* Earning, Martha
Wager, Sir Charles (ca 1666–1743), Kt, 1709; Adm.; M.P.:
administration not to be influenced by, **18**. 31
Admiralty post refused by, **17**. 346
Bible misquoted by, **17**. 333
Blackburne, Lancelot, subject of stories by, **7**. 368
called an old woman, **17**. 346
death of, **18**. 245–6
election of, declared void, **17**. 220n
English doggedness in sea battles praised by, **18**. 410
flies never killed by, **15**. 70, **35**. 367
Gashry nephew of, **18**. 81n
Goldsworthy may be aided by, **18**. 13, 31, 246
—— recommended by, to D. of Newcastle, **18**. 246n
Gordon given ship by, **17**. 298

Jackson hopes for preferment after death of, 17. *218*

'niece' of, 17. 302n

resignation of, 17. 333

Vernon publishes letters from, 19. 459n

Walpole, Sir Robert, given Greek urn by, 18. 246n

Wager; wagers:

over Paris-Fontainebleau ride, 35. 190

See also under Gambling

Wages and salaries:

arrears in Thomas Walpole's, 15. 326

assistant keeper's, at British Museum, 16. 325

auditor's, 36. 158n

Bengal governor's, 22. 540

Bentley's, in post office, 10. 128

Bishop of Elphin's, 10. 8

Canadian governor's, 21. 540n

cardinal's, from Apostolic Chamber, 23. 118

chancellor's, in Duchy of Lancaster, 33. 412n, 39. 404n

chargé d'affaires's, 18. 17n

Clement, Jane, gets, from Sir Edward Walpole, 36. 319

clerk of the Pells's, 36. 90

clerk of the Pells's, in Ireland, 21. 75n

coachman's, 18. 232n

Cocchi's, in medical post, 21. 194

collector of Customs Inward for Port of London's, 10. 317

collector of customs's, in Philadelphia, 40. 291n

commissioner for Trade and Plantations's, 32. 48n

commissioner of the Treasury's, 17. 332n

Condorcet's, as commissioner of the French Treasury, 39. 487

cook's, at Florence, 19. 357

Customs clerk's, 36. 89

decipherer's, 17. 279n

deputy cofferer's, 30. 207n

deputy park ranger's, 33. 213n

deputy ranger of Rockingham Forest's, 10. 188

diplomatists', 21. 175n

doge of Venice's, 17. 75

Dorset's, for Cinque Ports, 21. 109

dragoon captain's, 37. 93

Dublin Castle constable's, 39. 77

Du Deffand, Mme, pays, to household staff, 4. 386, 8. 46

English private soldier's, 35. 245n

English Resident's, in Tuscany, 18. 17n

first lord of the Treasury's, 17. 333n

Florentine hospital inspector's, 17. 57

gatekeeper's, 3. 49

governor of Canada's, 21. 540n

governor of Grenada's, 32. 280n

governor of Languedoc's, 23. 322

governor of the Royal Military Academy's, 39. 123

governor of Tobago's, 32. 386n

governor of Virginia's, 20. 461n

groom of the Bedchamber's, 17. 493n, 35. 281n

HW jokes about refusal of, 10. 252

HW pays: to domestic employees, 7. 400, 401, 405, 408, 410–13; to printers, 15. 56, 29. 10, 30. 171n, 40. 164

Halifax's, in Board of Trade, 9. 213

Hammond's, as messenger, 17. 275n

Heinel, Mlle, has, 32. 90n

Henrietta Maria's attendants', 41. 160–1

Hill's, from wholesale booksellers, 16. 42

housekeeper's: at Kensington Palace, 43. 132; at Windsor, 43. 132

Irish Exchequer's, 37. 449n

Irish joint treasurer's, 18. 19n

Irish staff officer's, in British army, 9. 257

Irish vice-treasurer's, 18. 20n, 39. 99

Kensington gardener's, 16. 42

labourer's, 10. 240

librarian's, 31. 329n

librettists', 17. 191

lieutenant-general's, 22. 560, 39. 123

lord lieutenant of Ireland's, to be augmented, 10. 18–21

lord of the Bedchamber's, 36. 37n

lord of Trade's, 21. 489n

Lorenzi's secretary's, 17. 157n

Magnan's, 18. 548–9

maid of honour's, 20. 28n, 35. 299

makers of artificial stone receive, 41. 227–9

Mann's secretary's, 17. 156, 190

master-general of the Ordnance's, 39. 123

master of the Harriers's, 35. 201n

master of the Horse's, to P. of Wales, 20. 245n

master of the Rolls's, 38. 468

minister plenipotentiary's, 22. 355n

Montagu, Charles, receives, 9. 257

Müntz's, 9. 259

National Assembly's self-bestowal of, 15. 207–8, 35. 400

naval captains', 32. 99n

of Directeur des places fortifiées, 23. 283

opera singers', 17. 191

Orford's, in Bedchamber and Parks, 32. 133n

paymaster of the Pensions's, 17. 384n

postilions', in France, 37. 41

printer's, 15. 56, 29. 10, 30. 171n, 40. 164

ranger of parks's, 36. 37n

rector of Lowick's, 10. 343

regius professor's, at Cambridge, 39. 106

riding officers' surveyor-general's, 18. 354n

ruspanti's, 17. 273n

secretary of state's, 10. 252

secretary of Académie française's, 5. 209, 222

servants' 'vails,' 20. 89n

Sharpe's, as Cts of Orford's agent, 25. 492

singer's, at the Pantheon, 39. 224

Spanish maid of honour's, 20. 28n

Stanley's, as ambassador to Russia, 30. 233

storekeeper of garrison's, 29. 227, 229

surveyor of the Roads's, 35. 281n

[Wages and salaries, *continued*]
tailor's, **17.** 191
travelling companion's, **21.** 503
treasurer of the Navy's, **29.** 177
unpaid, in France, **39.** 143
valet-secretary's, **17.** 172, 190
Washington's soldiers', **29.** 112
Windsor Castle housekeeper's, **20.** 213n, **30.** 57n
Zouch's, as vicar, **37.** 560
Wagnière, Jean-Louis (1739–ca 1787), Voltaire's secretary:
MS copy of Voltaire's letter to HW in hand of, **41.** 151, 152n, 154n, 156n
Voltaire with, **7.** 20
Wagon; wagons:
American, destroyed, **24.** 309
Bedfordshire, might be sent by Lady Ossory, **32.** 208
child's, Cts Temple takes, from Henrietta Hotham's back, **10.** 116
Downe may bring French heads in, to Cowick, **35.** 293
Dutch, covered with oil-cloth, **38.** 4
early coaches were 'leathern,' **42.** 2
for Southampton: HW to send fish by, to Bentley, **35.** 205; HW to send trees by, to Bentley, **35.** 204
from Brackley, **10.** 81
HW sends mug by, **29.** 38, 41
HW's letter to be sent by coach or, **29.** 66
Hermione's treasure carried in, **22.** 66
Kingston, Ds of, sends treasure in, to Leghorn, **24.** 404
Mason asks HW to send books by, **28.** 63, 300
Montagu to send book by, to London, **10.** 143
—— to send print to HW by, **10.** 303
Northamptonshire, Montagu family portraits to be put aboard, **10.** 85
open, German, Joseph II enters Florence in, **23.** 108
pack horses superseded by, **10.** 348
pictures may be rubbed if carried in, **9.** 250
rebels send cheese and biscuit in, to Carlisle, **37.** 211
road cut up by, **10.** 348
Salisbury, E. of, plans, broad-wheeled, **10.** 348
visible from SH, **20.** 380
Wagoner; wagoners:
Bussy cannot get, on Sunday, **38.** 120
papers from Ragley to be fetched by, **37.** 563
See also under Servant
Wainfleet. *See* Waynefleet
Wainscot; wainscoting:
at Crewe Hall, **10.** 96
at Hurstmonceaux, **35.** 138
at Sissinghurst, **35.** 145
carved, at the Vyne, **35.** 640
Kingston, Ds of, leaves pistol-mark in, **24.** 198
oak, in Mme de Maintenon's apartment at St-Cyr, **10.** 293
of deal, at Osterley, **33.** 237

of House of Commons, **25.** 35
tables of, at Blenheim, **9.** 289
unpainted, at Chatsworth, **9.** 296
wooden partridge attached to, **31.** 80
Waistband; waistbands:
of breeches, **35.** 166
Waistcoat; waistcoats:
Balmerinoch doffs, at execution, **19.** 302
black, worn by *Hamlet* ghost, **20.** 209
blue, in parade, **32.** 331
buff, regimental costume, **9.** 241
cabriolets painted on, **20.** 483
Charles Emmanuel III once the only king in Europe to fight in his, **21.** 277
Cumberland, D. of, makes surgeon change, during operation, **38.** 456
dogskin, **37.** 98
dominoes can be made into, for summer, **38.** 206
Fitzgerald's, lined with gum, **25.** 631
Fitzjames wears, **39.** 9
flannel: French army does not have, **21.** 435; worn by Balmerinoch, **19.** 299
Frederick, P. of Wales, puts on, **20.** 232
green, worn for boar-hunting, **20.** 200n
HW conceals watch in, **29.** 160
HW's: has a little silver in it, **34.** 110; silver, worn for Ds of York's visit to SH, **12.** 12; white and silver, stolen in Paris, **39.** 17; with open sleeves, **11.** 311
HW sends, to Mann, **17.** 152, 193, 433, 473
laced: chairmen wear, **10.** 204; Maclaine steals and sells, **20.** 168; Horatio Walpole (1723–1809) wears, **20.** 342
lace for: **37.** 106; copied from Greek frieze, **22.** 218
Lobkowitz's, gold-fringed, **37.** 289
Maclaine takes, to pawnbroker, **20.** 168
Mann wears: at baptism, **17.** 473; in cold spell, **19.** 391
men may have to dance in, **37.** 55
new, **28.** 131
of purple and silver, with a pink and gold fringe, **30.** 19
Oglethorpe wears, unbuttoned in winter, **31.** 214
Ossory, Lady, gives, to HW, **32.** 219–20
plaid, worn by Frederick, P. of Wales, **20.** 131
satin: **30.** 211; jockeys wear, white, **31.** 108
silk: laced, worn by Palmer, **20.** 396; Montagu asks about stylishness of, **9.** 355
silver, borrowed by Pamfili, **19.** 445
tambour, made by Lady Ossory for Sir Joshua Reynolds, **32.** 220n
trimmed, worn by Hon. Thomas Walpole, **20.** 342
white: men wear, at Reggio fair, **22.** 148; satin, **21.** 399n, **31.** 108; slashed, in Chandos's portrait, **33.** 322; worn at Lord Cholmondeley's wedding, **11.** 255; worn in June, **31.** 305–6
with open sleeves, worn by HW, **11.** 311
Waiter; waiters. *See under* Servant

Waiting-woman. *See under* Servant

Wake, Lady Camilla. *See* Bennet, Lady Camilla

Wake, William (1657–1737), Bp of Lincoln 1705–16; Abp of Canterbury 1716–37:
Atterbury's controversy with, **29**. 156–7
Baker aids work of, on *The State of the Church*, **2**. 348
—— generously treated by, **2**. 348
death of, **15**. 143, **19**. 503n
George I's will surrendered by, **2**. 124
researches encouraged by, **16**. 211n

Wake, Sir William (1742–85), Bt; M.P.:
Shelburne defended by, **29**. 266

Wakefield, Gilbert (1756–1801), scholar:
Gray's elegy translated by, **1**. 388

Wakefield, Yorks:
battle of, **35**. 270
Edward IV built Gothic chapel on bridge at, seen by HW, **35**. 270
HW's letters go to, by mistake, **28**. 147
Spinke, Elizabeth, of, **16**. 1n

Wakefield Lodge, Northants, D. of Grafton's house:
Grafton has meeting at, **7**. 367, **22**. 538n
——'s house, **1**. 129
—— takes Nancy Parsons to, **38**. 435
visitors to Grafton at: Gower, **22**. 538n; Hinchliffe, **10**. 98; Vernon, Caroline Maria, **32**. 313

Wakefield races:
Hertford, Cts of, at, **32**. 83

Wakering, Sir Gilbert, Kt 1604:
Wilkinson. bailiff of, at Essington Manor, serves goose to Lady Townshend, **40**. 77

Walbrook, London:
Heathcote, alderman of, **28**. 372n
St Stephen's in ward of, **28**. 372n

Walby, Robert (d. 1398), Abp of York:
tomb of, **2**. 106

Walcher (d. 1080), Bp of Durham; E. of Northumberland:
titles of, **2**. 182

Walcher (d. 1135), of Lorraine, Prior of Malvern:
tomb of, **2**. 234

Walcot House, (?) Leics:
Montagu inquires about, from Ds of Marlborough's steward, **9**. 245
Roel near, **9**. 245

Walcott (Walcot), Norfolk:
HW's will mentions, **30**. 369

Walcott East Hall *and* Walcott West Hall, manors at Walcott, Norfolk:
HW's will mentions, **30**. 368

Waldaise, ——, Capt.:
captured at Velletri, **18**. 491

Waldeck, Karl August Friedrich (1704–63), Fürst von; field marshal:
army in Flanders led by, **19**. 240
Austrian troops fight limited engagement under, near Breisach, **18**. 304n
Cronström replaces, **19**. 429n
Dutch generals resent being under, **36**. 13n

Fontenoy attempt is the decision of, **36**. 11n
French infiltrate Liège in back of, **30**. 108n
Orange, P. of, disputes with, **19**. 429n
resignation of, after dispute with D. of Cumberland, **19**. 428–9
Rhine crossing attempted by, **37**. 146
Schwartzenberg receives command of, **19**. 428n
Venice said to secure services of, against Austria, **20**. 176

Waldeck, Castle of:
Conway captures, **22**. 25–6, **35**. 315, **38**. 163

Waldegreene. *See* Waldegrave

Waldegrave, Bn. *See* Waldegrave, James (1684–1741)

Waldegrave, Bns. *See* Fitzjames, Henrietta (ca 1667–1730)

Waldegrave, Cts. *See* Leveson Gower, Lady Elizabeth (1724–84); Waldegrave, Lady Elizabeth Laura (1760–1816); Walpole, Maria (1736–1807)

Waldegrave, E. *See* Waldegrave, Geoffrey Noel (b. 1905); Waldegrave, George (1751–89); Waldegrave, George (1784–94); Waldegrave, George Edward (1816–46); Waldegrave, James (1684–1741); Waldegrave, James (1715–63); Waldegrave, John (1718–84); Waldegrave, John James (1785–1835); Waldegrave, William (1788–1859)

Waldegrave, Lady Anna Horatia (1762–1801), m. (1786) Hon. (later Lord) Hugh Seymour-Conway (later Lord Hugh Seymour):
almost drowned, **33**. 47
Ancaster, D. of, dies before marrying, **24**. 494, 498–9, **25**. 75, **33**. 107n, 210, **35**. 498
—— mentions presentiment of death to, **33**. 165
——'s relatives tell, that he would have married her, **24**. 494
Ancaster, Ds of, takes, to Lady Elizabeth Burrell's, **33**. 164
assembly for, at SH, **33**. 61
aunts to supervise, at Windsor and the Pavilions, **24**. 76n
Aylesford, Lady, entertains, at ball, **33**. 283
beautiful, **24**. 498
behaviour of: admired, **36**. 324; said to be condemned, **31**. 200
Berry, Mary, identifies, **11**. 262n
biographical information about, corrected, **43**. 66, 355
Bolton, D. of, visited by, at Hackwood, **33**. 211n
—— visited by sisters and, **31**. 200
brother-in-law and sister to meet, at Weymouth, **35**. 522
Chatham, E. of, asked by, to employ her husband, **11**. 262
Churchill, Sophia, less beautiful than, **25**. 132
Coke, Lady Mary, discusses, **31**. 200
concern of, for stepfather, **32**. 363, 373, 377, 378

[Waldegrave, Lady Anna Horatia, *continued*]
cousin's beauty thought to surpass that of,
25. 508

death of, **43.** 370

Du Deffand, Mme, inquires about, **6.** 328, **7.**
52, 130, 177

Dysart, Cts of, visited by, at Ham House,
39. 311

Dysart, E. of, brutal to, **36.** 327

economy to be made in house but not in
education of, **36.** 328

father provides for, in will, **10.** 62–3

father survived by, **22.** 127

fever in family of, **36.** 288

fiancé's relationship to, **25.** 632n, 647

fortune of, **25.** 132

fracas in Pall Mall seen by, **33.** 335

Gloucester House cannot be shown by, **42.** 464

grandfather might be visited by, **36.** 325

HW at Hampton Court with, **33.** 42

HW attentive to, **36.** 131, 137, 142, 161

HW dances hays with, **33.** 46–7

HW describes, **36.** 150

HW engrossed with, **24.** 315

HW entertains, at dinner, **11.** 323

HW gets news from, about mother and stepfather, **24.** 147

HW goes to Ham with, **39.** 311

HW has no picture of, **36.** 161

HW in charge of, **2.** 55

HW invites, to see Le Texier, **36.** 154

HW praises, **25.** 632

HW regrets erroneous newspaper report of
his bequest to, **15.** 335

HW repeats news sent by, **36.** 209

HW's bequest to, **30.** 356

HW's correspondence with, **36.** 272, 273

HW sees, at Gloucester House, **25.** 68

HW's fête for, at SH, **35.** 494

HW shows illuminations to, **33.** 93

HW spends evenings with, **33.** 2

HW to inform, about D. of Gloucester, **36.**
139

HW visited by, **12.** 158, 160, 169, **32.** 382,
33. 210, 279, 283, **34.** 19

HW wishes, to marry Hon. Horatio Walpole
(1752–1822), **25.** 132–3

HW with, during Gordon riots, **33.** 187

Hackwood visited by, **35.** 522

Harcourt a father to, **35.** 498

Harcourts' kindness to, **35.** 496

Hardinge sees, at Talbot Inn, during shower,
35. 634

health of, better, **33.** 164

Hertford, Cts of, entertains, **33.** 283

Hertford, E. of, charmed with, **39.** 443

—— entertains P. of Wales with, **39.** 439n

—— visited by, at Sudbourne, **39.** 463–4

hostess for HW, **33.** 47

husband's passion for, **39.** 443

Keppel, Mrs, complains about, **36.** 326

Keppels to be visited by, at Windsor, **36.** 152

Keppel-Fitzroy wedding attended by, **33.**
441n

Lennox, Lady George, cares for, **31.** 351–7

Lincoln, Cts of, visited by, **11.** 323

marriage of: **39.** 438n, **43.** 378; has resulted
in HW's meeting George IV at her father-
in-law's and at Leicester House, **25.** 647;
to take place, **25.** 632; Walpole, Thomas,
jr, congratulates HW on, **36.** 235–6

marriage settlement of, **42.** 173–4, **43.** 369

Miller's verses to, **29.** 7n, **33.** 164

mother consoled for absence of, **36.** 323

mother's letters from, **31.** 355, **34.** 247

mourning worn by, for D. of Ancaster, **24.**
494, **33.** 114

North, Lady, entertains, **33.** 284

not to go abroad, **33.** 257

opera attended by, **33.** 335

pistols frighten, **33.** 370

Ranelagh visited by, **25.** 68

Reynolds's painting of sisters and, **29.** 45–6,
138, 285, **35.** 532

rumours of offers refused by, **33.** 91

sister attended by, at birth of daughter, **33.**
504

sister-in-law to be visited by, at Putney Common, **36.** 245

sister less beautiful than, **25.** 68

sister's letter to, **33.** 485

son born to, **31.** 352, **39.** 457

stepfather lodges, at Hampton Court Park,
24. 315

SH entail mentions, **30.** 251

SH visited by, **12.** 225

SH visitors sent by, **12.** 221

Thurlow to lend money for, **36.** 327–8

Waldegrave, William, liked by, **33.** 210, 211

Walpole, Hon. Mrs Robert, less beautiful
than, **25.** 410

Waldegrave, Lady Betty. *See* Leveson Gower,
Lady Elizabeth

Waldegrave, Lady Caroline (1765–1831), dau.
of 3d E. Waldegrave:
Amelia, Ps, leaves legacy to, **33.** 534

Lord Blandford's marriage to, forbidden by
Ds of Marlborough, **11.** 108n, 349

Waldegrave, Hon. Caroline (d. 1878):
HW asks about, **36.** 273

Waldegrave, Lady Charlotte (b. 1789, d. before
15 May 1793):
Aylesford, Lord, accepts guardianship of,
34. 74

biographical information about, corrected,
43. 229, 369

birth of, **34.** 72, 84, 86, **43.** 386

Cornwallis interested in, **36.** 284, 287

—— to be visited by, at Culford Hall, **36.** 287

Thurlow interested in, **36.** 284

well, **34.** 86, **36.** 290

Waldegrave, Lady Charlotte Maria (1761–
1808), m. (1784) George Henry Fitzroy,
styled E. of Euston; 4th D. of Grafton, 1811:

almost drowned, 33. 47

assembly for, at SH, 33. 61

aunts to supervise, at Windsor and the Pavilions, 24. 76n

Aylesford, Lady, entertains, at ball, 33. 283

behaviour of: admired, 36. 324; said to be condemned, 31. 200

birth of, 9. 399, 38. 141

Bolton, D. of, visited by sisters and, at Hackwood, 31. 200, 33. 211n, 35. 522

brother-in-law and sister to meet, at Weymouth, 35. 522

Churchill, Sophia, as handsome as, 25. 132

Coke, Lady Mary, discusses, 31. 200, 239

concern of, for stepfather, 32. 363, 373, 377, 378

cousin's beauty thought to surpass that of, 25. 508

daughter born to, 33. 504

distempered and quite lame, 33. 441n

Du Deffand, Mme, inquires about, 6. 328, 7. 52, 130, 177

Dysart, Cts of, visited by, at Ham House, 39. 311

Dysart, E. of, brutal to, 36. 327

economy to be made in house but not in education of, 36. 328

Egremont's engagement to, 25. 68, 74–5, 77, 544n, 31. 200, 33. 107n, 204–5, 206, 209–10, 451

——'s match with, broken off, 7. 238n, (?) 239, 240, 29. 69, 72, 306

——'s rift with, keeps HW from going to Malvern, 35. 506

endorsement relating to, 33. 484

Euston's engagement to, 33. 441–2, 445

father-in-law approves of, 31. 238, 33. 508

father-in-law treats, well, 36. 241

father provides for, in will, 10. 62–3

father's good sense and temper shared by, 33. 457, 485, 508

father survived by, 22. 127

(?) Fawkener's misconduct wounds, 35. 498

Fitzroy, Mrs, to visit, in Conduit St, 36. 287

fortune of, 25. 132

fracas in Pall Mall seen by, 33. 335

Gloucester House cannot be shown by, 42. 464

—— residence of, 31. 216

Grafton's and Lady Ravensworth's approbation of, 33. 508

grandfather informed by, 36. 200

grandfather might be visited by, 36. 325

HW asked by, for clove-carnations, 33. 567

HW at Hampton Court with, 33. 42

HW attentive to, 36. 131, 137, 142, 161

HW dances hays with, 33. 46–7

HW describes, 36. 149

HW engrossed by, 24. 315

HW gets news from, about her mother and stepfather, 24. 147

HW goes to Ham with, 39. 311

HW has no picture of, 36. 161

HW in charge of, 2. 55

HW invites, to see Le Texier, 36. 154

HW repeats news sent by, 36. 209

HWs bequest to, 30. 356

HW's correspondence with, 31. 216, 35. 529, 36. 116–17, 207, 225, 243

HW sees, at Gloucester House, 25. 68

HWs fête for, at SH, 35. 494

HW's good opinion of, 33. 454, 457

HW shows correspondence of, 31. 200

HW shows illuminations to, 33. 93

HW spends evening with, 33. 2

HW suspected of writing letter for, 31. 209

HW to inform, of D. of Gloucester, 36. 139

HW visited by, 32. 382, 33. 210, 211, 279, 283

HW wishes to marry Hon. Horatio Walpole (1752–1822) to, 25. 132–3

HW with, in Gordon riots, 33. 187

Hackwood visited by, 35. 522

handsome, 25. 132

Harcourt a father to, 35. 498

Harcourts' kindness to, 35. 496

Hardinge sees, at Talbot Inn, during shower, 35. 634

health of: bad cold, 33. 273; recovered, 33. 279, 35. 532

Hertford, Lady, entertains, 33. 283

hostess for HW, 33. 47

Keppel, Mrs, complains about, 36. 326

Keppel-Fitzroy wedding attended by, 33. 441n

less beautiful than her sisters, but more popular with men, 25. 68

marriage of, 25. 544, 554, 33. 451–2, 453, 455, 39. 427

mother consoled for absence of, 36. 323

mother's correspondence with, 36. 117, 143

North, Lady, entertains, 33. 284

not to go abroad, 33. 257

Nuneham Courtenay charms, by its improvements, 35. 529

opera attended by, 33. 335

pistols frighten, 33. 370

pregnant, 36. 241

pretty and sensible, 39. 427

Ranelagh visited by, 25. 68, 33. 189

Ravensworth, Lady, partial to, 33. 485, 496, 34. 104

(?) repartees of, 7. 53

Reynolds's painting of sisters and, 29. 45–6, 138, 285, 35. 532

rumours of offers refused by, 33. 91

Siddons, Mrs, commented on by, 33. 377

stepfather lodges, at Hampton Court Park, 24. 315

SH entail mentions, 30. 351

SH left by, 33. 279

SH to be visited by, for health, 33. 275

Thurlow to lend money for, 36. 328

Waldegrave, William, liked by, 33. 210, 211

Walpole, Hon. Mrs Robert, less beautiful than, 25. 410

witticism by, 32. 411–12

witty, 29. 69

Waldegrave, Hon. Edward William (1787–1809):
  Aylesford guardian to, **34**. 74, **36**. 268
  bereavement of, at father's death, **43**. 386–8
  birth of, impending, **33**. 565
  Cornwallis interested in, **36**. 284, 287
  —— to be visited by, at Culford Hall, **36**. 287
  Eton to be re-entered by, **36**. 289
  health of: well, **36**. 290; whooping-cough, **36**. 272
  mother's attention to, **36**. 266, 270
  SH entail mentions, **30**. 351
  Thurlow interested in, **36**. 287
Waldegrave, Lady Elizabeth. *See* Leveson Gower, Lady Elizabeth (1724–84)
Waldegrave, Lady Elizabeth (1758–1823), m. (1791) James Brudenell, 5th E. of Cardigan, 1790:
  Amelia, Ps, leaves legacy to, **33**. 534
  biographical information about, corrected, **43**. 359
  candidate for vacancy in Queen's Bedchamber, **11**. 367
  house of, in St James's Place, **34**. 110n
  marriage of, **11**. 241, **34**. 110
  Packington visited by, to comfort widowed sister-in-law, **43**. 387
  sister-in-law to be visited by, **36**. 266
  sister of, **11**. 349n
Waldegrave, Lady Elizabeth Laura (1760–1816), m. (1782) George Waldegrave, styled Vct Chewton; 4th E. Waldegrave, 1784:
  affection of, for Bp Keppel, **32**. 410
  afflictions of, **31**. 334
  almost drowned, **33**. 47
  assembly for, at SH, **33**. 61
  aunts to supervise, at Windsor and the Pavilions, **24**. 76n
  Aylesford, Lady, entertains, at ball, **33**. 283
  Aylesfords aid, in her bereavement, **36**. 268, **43**. 387
  —— hospitable to, **36**. 260, 265, 268, 270
  —— visited by, at Packington Hall, **36**. 257–71
  behaviour of: admired, **36**. 324; said to be condemned, **31**. 200
  Berry, Mary, identifies, **11**. 33n
  Boggust met by, at Scarborough, **36**. 284
  Bolton, D. of, visited by sisters and, at Hackwood, **31**. 200, **33**. 210n
  busy with races, quarter sessions, and assizes, **36**. 240
  Carmarthen, M. of, unable to marry, **25**. 75, **33**. 210
  Charlotte, Q., summons, to Windsor, **36**. 247
  children absorb attention of, **36**. 266, 270, 272
  children of, **31**. 334
  Churchill, Sophia, less beautiful than, **25**. 132
  Clement, Jane, corresponds with, **36**. 321
  Coke, Lady Mary, discusses, **31**. 200
  concern of, for stepfather, **32**. 363, 373, 376–7, 378
  Cornwallis writes to, **36**. 284

cousin marries, **25**. 75n, 274, 410n
cousin's beauty thought to surpass that of, **25**. 508
Damer visits, at Navestock, **36**. 239
daughter admired by, **34**. 200
daughter of, born, **33**. 84, 86
Du Deffand, Mme, inquires about, **6**. 328, **7**. 52, 130, 177, 238
Dysart, Cts of, visited by, at Ham House, **39**. 311
Dysart, E. of, brutal to, **36**. 327
economy to be made in house but not in education of, **36**. 328
engagement of, rumoured, **7**. 128
family of, **30**. 350–1, 356–7
father provides for, in will, **10**. 62–3
father survived by, **22**. 127
'female saint,' **31**. 394
Fitzroy, Mrs, visits, **36**. 287
fortune of, **25**. 132
fracas in Pall Mall seen by, **33**. 335
grandfather might be visited by, **36**. 325
HW asked by, to be her son's godfather, **36**. 233–4
HW at Hampton Court with, **33**. 42
HW attentive to, **36**. 131, 137, 142, 161
HW dances hays with, **33**. 46–7
HW describes, **36**. 149
HW engrossed by, **24**. 315
HW expects, at SH, **39**. 437
HW gets news from, about mother and stepfather, **24**. 147
HW goes to Ham with, **39**. 311
HW has no picture of, **36**. 161
HW hears from, of her sister's marriage, **33**. 452
HW hears good accounts of, **33**. 410
HW in charge of, **2**. 55
HW informed by: of fire at Ampthill, **39**. 4–5; of G. F. Fitzroy's marriage, **33**. 441
HW invites, to see Le Texier, **36**. 154
HW lends money to, **36**. 327
HW mentions, **15**. 183, **25**. 272
HW repeats news sent by, **36**. 209
HW's bequests to: lease of his Berkeley Sq. house, **30**. 355–6; money, **30**. 355
HW's correspondence with, **31**. 395, **33**. 374, **34**. 147, **36**. 143, 144, 207, 225, 226, 229–30, 234, 239–40, 242, 257–60, 262, 283–90, 313
HW sees, at Gloucester House, **25**. 68
HW sends letter and news by, **28**. 445
HW sends warrant for venison to, **36**. 289
HW's favourable opinion of, **33**. 348, 374
HW's fête for, at SH, **35**. 494
HW's generosity to, **36**. 270
HW shows illuminations to, **33**. 93
HW's letter from: **33**. 374; tells of Cornwallis's sympathy, **34**. 147
HW's letter from mother of, about husband's illness, **34**. 72
HW's letters censored by, **26**. 38–9, 42
HW's MSS in custody of, **36**. 311

HW spends evening with, **32**. 377, **33**. 2

HW to be visited by, at SH, **36**. 152, 234, 240, 290

HW to inform, of D. of Gloucester, **36**. 139

HW unable to attend baptism of child of, **33**. 416

HW visited by, **10**. 63, **11**. 33, **12**. 50, 51, 209, **16**. 285n, **32**. 382, **33**. 210, 279, 283, 534, 540, **34**. 53, 191, **36**. 330

HW visits, **33**. 408, 441

HW wishes, would go to Navestock, **43**. 388

HW wishes to marry Hon. Horatio Walpole (1752–1822) to, **25**. 132–3

HW with, during Gordon riots, **33**. 187

HW would be pleased to see, **33**. 372

Harcourt a father to, **35**. 498

—— praises, **29**. 356

Harcourt, Cts, invites, to Nuneham with HW as escort, **35**. 492–3, 494

Harcourts' kindness to, **35**. 496

Hardinge sees, at Talbot Inn, during shower, **35**. 634

health of: fever and strangury, **36**. 116–17; 'frets herself pale' over mother's sorrows, **36**. 143, 149; good, at return from Weymouth, **33**. 370; miscarriage rumoured, **35**. 522; perfectly well, **35**. 532; pregnant and not quite well, **33**. 565; recovered, **32**. 304; shock, **36**. 287; weak, **36**. 247; well after birth of daughter, **33**. 405; well at Navestock after birth of son, **33**. 495; well but thin, **33**. 372

Hertford invites, to dinner for P. of Wales, **39**. 43

Hertford, Cts of, entertains, **33**. 283

hostess for HW, **33**. 47

house of, in Mansfield St, **33**. 408n

husband of: dies while she is pregnant, **16**. 310, **43**. 386–8; prizes her, **33**. 402

invited to D. of Gloucester's ball, **5**. 33n

Keppel, Mrs, complains about, **36**. 326

—— treats, well, **36**. 326

London not to be visited by, because of expense, **36**. 330

—— visited by, **31**. 398

looks badly, and should not go to Court, **36**. 325

marriage of, **29**. 216, 245, **31**. 330

Mason expects, to be HW's heir, **29**. 355

—— would like to write epithalamium for, **29**. 248

More, Hannah, concerned for, **31**. 334

—— corresponds with, **31**. 395

—— friend of, **31**. 398

—— gives HW an account of, **31**. 394

—— praises, **31**. 334

—— sends message to, through HW, **31**. 394

—— to meet, at HW's, **31**. 394

—— with, **34**. 203

mother and HW praise ability of, **34**. 75

mother and sister-in-law visit, in her bereavement, **36**. 266, **43**. 387

mother attends, **31**. 334

mother consoled for absence of, **36**. 323

mother gets letter from, about husband's illness, **36**. 260, 262

mother's letter from, reveals pride as well as religion, **36**. 330

mother's letter received by, **32**. 376

mother tells, of praying and weeping, **24**. 323

mother visited by, **12**. 50, 209

mother visits: at Navestock, **36**. 284; at Packington, **36**. 268

name of, corrected, **43**. 350

Navestock to be rented out by, to take house near London, **36**. 273

—— to be visited by, **36**. 225

North, Lady, entertains, **33**. 284

not to go abroad, **33**. 257

opera attended by, **33**. 335

pious composure of, in bereavement, **36**. 265, 268–73, 284, 286, 290, 330

plate of husband's print may belong to, **42**. 413

pregnancy of, **25**. 571, **33**. 565, **34**. 72, 75, 83, **36**. 266, 268, 270

presented at Court, **29**. 249

Ranelagh visited by, **25**. 571, **33**. 189

Reynolds paints sisters and, **29**. 45–6, 138, 285, **35**. 532

rumours of offers refused by, **33**. 91

Scarborough to be visited by, **34**. 53

servants put by, into mourning for Louis XVI, **36**. 285n

sister less beautiful than, **25**. 68

sisters to meet, at Weymouth, **35**. 522

son born to, **33**. 435, **36**. 252

son's death affects, **34**. 199, 200, 203, **36**. 329

son's epitaph proposed by, for Eton chapel, **36**. 285–6

sons put by, in Boggust's house at Eton, **36**. 283–4

staircase to lodgings of, very bad, **31**. 394

stepfather lodges, at Hampton Court Park, **24**. 315

SH bequeathed to heirs of, after Mrs Damer's death, **15**. 336

SH entail mentions, **30**. 350–1

suckles her daughter, **33**. 408

Thurlow lends money for, **36**. 328

Waldegrave, Capt., visits, with HW, **33**. 411

—— liked by, **33**. 210, 211

Walpole, Hon. Mrs Robert, less beautiful than, **25**. 410

Westmorland, Lady, friend of, **12**. 64

Waldegrave, Hon. Emily Susanna Laura (d. 1870):

HW asks about, **36**. 273

Waldegrave, Frances, Lady. See Braham, Frances Elizabeth Anne

Waldegrave, Geoffrey Noel (b. 1905), 12th E. Waldegrave:

HW's MSS owned by, **26**. 44

Waldegrave, George (1751–89), styled Vct Chewton 1763–84; 4th E. Waldegrave, 1784; M.P.:

affairs of, administered in absence of will, 36. 268

Amelia, Ps, tells, of legacies, 33. 534

Aylesfords hospitable to, 36. 260, 265, 270

—— visited by, at Packington Hall, 36. 257–64

Boggust met by, at Scarborough, 36. 284

burial of: 34. 74–5, 36. 268; attended by Finch brothers, 36. 268

Cornwallis may be succeeded by, in India, 36. 256

——'s affectionate remembrance of, 34. 147

cousin marries, 25. 75n, 274, 410n, 584, 29. 245

Damer visits, at Navestock, 36. 239

daughter appeals to, 36. 230

daughter idolized by, 34. 200

death of, 16. 310, 31. 330, 334, 34. 74–5, 36. 264–72, 43. 386–8

discovers officer wounded in Pall Mall, 33. 335

Earlom's mezzotint of, 42. 413n

finances of, may be improved by employment in India, 36. 256

George III and Q. Charlotte show concern over, 34. 84

HW asked by, to be son's godfather, 36. 233–4

HW expects, at SH, 39. 437

HW praises, 25. 584

HW's box destined for, pointed out by HW to Fanny Burney, 43. 369–70

HW's correspondence with, 33. 405, 36. 211, 233–5, 242, 247, 252, 43. 370

HW's note from, about daughter's birth, 33. 405

HW's social relations with, in Paris, 7. 289, 319

HW to be visited by, at SH, 36. 234, 240, 247

HW to see, 33. 374

HW visited by: 11. 33, 16. 285n, 33. 540, 34. 53; with report of Ps Amelia's will, 33. 534

Harcourt informed by, at Windsor, of HW's illness, 35. 537

—— praises, 29. 356

health of: bilious complaint, 36. 258, 259, 262, 263; illness at supper, 36. 230; jaundice, at Lord Aylesford's, 34. 68–9, 72; last illness, 36. 257–64; rheumatism, 36. 234–5

Hertford invites, to dinner for P. of Wales, 39. 438

house of, for 6 months, in Dover St, 33. 554

Master of the Horse to Q. Charlotte, 12. 24n, 33. 448

Murray, Maj., and, 12. 270n

Navestock to be visited by, 36. 225

Nivernais's Jardins modernes given to, 12. 259

Ossory, E. of, friend of, 36. 267, 43. 387

Ossorys' anxiety over, 32. 395

presented at Court, 29. 249n

print of, desired by Bull, 42. 413

prize wife won by, 33. 402

safe in America, 32. 319

Scarborough to be visited by, 34. 53

servants of, in Queen's livery, confuse Sir R. Goodere, 33. 541

sisters-in-law to meet, at Weymouth, 35. 522

son of, born, 33. 435

tutor of, 7. 288

uninjured in Battle of Brandywine, 32. 396

virtuous but poor, 29. 216, 33. 435

widow and HW mourn loss of, 36. 290

wife of, 2. 55n, 10. 62n, 28. 445n, 30. 350

wife praises, 36. 239

Waldegrave, George (1784–94), styled Vct Chewton 1784–9; 5th E. Waldegrave, 1789:

Aylesford guardian of, 34. 74, 36. 268

bereavement of, at father's death, 43. 386

birth of, 33. 435

Cornwallis and Thurlow interested in, 36. 284

death of, 12. 209, 34. 199, 200

epitaph for, proposed by mother for Eton chapel, 36. 285–6

HW's bequest of lease of Berkeley Sq. house mentions, 30. 355–6

(?) HW's letter supposedly to, over contents of box of MSS, 36. 274, 43. 370

HW visited by, 33. 540

health of: cold, 36. 239; well, 33. 540, 36. 229; whooping-cough, 36. 272

monument to, not to be begun yet by grandmother, 36. 329

mother finds, in good health, 36. 229

mother mourns for, 12. 209, 36. 329

mother puts, in Boggust's house at Eton, 36. 283–4

mother's attention to, 36. 266, 270

mother's fondness for, 34. 200

sister quarrels with, 36. 229–30

SH entail mentions, 30. 350–1, 43. 326

Waldegrave, George Edward (1816–46), 7th E. Waldegrave, 1835:

HW's MSS owned by, 26. 40, 43

Waldegrave, Granville (1786–1857), 2d Bn Radstock, 1825:

HW asks about, 36. 273

Waldegrave, Hon. Harriet Anne Frances (d. 1880):

HW asks about, 36. 273

Waldegrave, Lady Henrietta (1717–53), m. 1 (1734) Hon. (later Lord) Edward Herbert; m. 2 (1739) John Beard:

daughter of, 19. 468

generations of family of, 22. 485, 25. 571

HW's footnote about, expurgated, 26. 38, 43. 264

inoculated for smallpox, 22. 127

Waldegrave, Hon. Isabella Elizabeth (d. 1866):

HW asks about, 36. 273

Waldegrave, James (1684–1741), 2d Bn Waldegrave, 1690; cr. (1729) E. Waldegrave; ambassador to Austria 1727–30, to France 1730–40:

death of: 17. 115n; stops son's marriage project with Lady Maria Walpole, 21. 285

generations of family of,. **22**. 485, **25**. 571

Magnan meets, in Paris, **18**. 564

Mann's letter regarding Young Pretender forwarded to, **17**. 13n

Navestock built by, **9**. 243–4

Newcastle, D. of, writes letter to, **2**. 125

Old Pretender's nephew, **17**. 336

peerage of, corrected, **43**. 234

son succeeds, **13**. 31n

subscriptions collected by, for Middleton's *Life of Cicero*, **15**. 4

Thompson formerly chaplain to, **18**. 422

Walpole, Sir Robert, to be impeached for appointing, **17**. 336

Young Pretender's possible journey through France to be stopped after remonstrance by, **17**. 14

Waldegrave, James (1715–63), 2d E. Waldegrave, 1741:

administration post would have been refused by, **10**. 64

(?) at Chesterfield's assembly, **37**. 327

auction of effects of: catalogue of, sent by HW to Montagu, **10**. 97–8, 99, 107, 108, 110; likelihood of high prices at, **10**. 108

brother of, **14**. 121n

Bute not liked by, **22**. 128

—— wished by Leicester House to replace, **20**. 505n

Churchill, Lady Mary, might have married, **21**. 285

colt of, wins sweepstakes at Huntingdon, **38**. 109n

Cumberland, D. of, says that death would be preferred by, to union with Bute and Henry Fox, **10**. 64

daughter (Lady Euston) inherits sagacity and good sense of, **25**. 68, **33**. 457, 485, 508, **36**. 149

daughters of, **11**. 33n, 262n, **24**. 315n, 498n, **25**. 68, 410n, 632n, **30**. 350, 351

death of: **10**. 58–9, **40**. 279, 280; from smallpox, **22**. 126–8, 131; leaves great chasm, **38**. 470; Montagu sends condolences on, **10**. 61–2

Devonshire, D. of, visited by, at Chatsworth, **38**. 19

dirty, **35**. 282n

Drax, Harriet, deserted by, **9**. 166

Egremont's esteem for, **40**. 281, 282

estate of, willed to wife and daughters, **10**. 62–3

father's letter from, **2**. 125

foreign gazettes predict removal of, **20**. 355

Fox, Henry, does not lament death of, **10**. 68

Garter received by, **9**. 215, **35**. 282

George II gives Garter to, alone, **21**. 110, **22**. 572n

—— gives messages to, at Richmond, for P. and Ps of Wales, **20**. 562n

—— notified by, of marriage, **9**. 233

—— notifies Fox through, **20**. 461n

—— orders Hardwicke to present, to George, P. of Wales, **20**. 347n

—— sends message to Leicester House through, **20**. 570n

—— sends messages to P. and Ps of Wales through, **21**. 6n

——'s favourite, **20**. 246, 505

——'s lord of the Bedchamber, **20**. 246n

George III does not lament loss of, **10**. 63

——'s 'governor,' **20**. 345, 347–8, 355, **21**. 285n, **22**. 126n, 128

German gazette announces dismissal of, from George III, despite George II's and D. of Newcastle's favour, **20**. 505

HW entertains, at SH, **9**. 215–16, 233

HW interrupted by, **38**. 119

HW mentions, **9**. 260, **14**. (?) 120

HW misses, **38**. 470

HW played with, in holidays, ca 1729, **25**. 570

HW promotes match of, with Maria Walpole, **13**. 31

HW's chief acquaintance in Albemarle St, **9**. 133n

HW's conversation at death-bed of, **10**. 56

HW's opinion of, **10**. 66

HW's school-fellow, **25**. 570

HW to be entertained by, **9**. 231

HW to entertain, at SH, **9**. 369

HW to visit, **9**. 293, **38**. 74, 180

HW visited by, at SH, **9**. 417

HW visits, at Navestock, **9**. 243–4

Halifax succeeds, in Garter, **22**. 227n

health of: headache, **10**. 55; sickness in stomach, **10**. 55; last illness, **40**. 279; smallpox, **10**. 55–6, 58–9

Holland House dinner to be attended by, **30**. 161

(?) house of, left unwatched in his absence, **9**. 133

income of, mostly dies with him, **22**. 128

James's powders taken by, **10**. 55, 56, 58, 59

jokes with physicians, **10**. 58

kindness of, **10**. 59

knows government secrets but not business procedure, **21**. 98n

lament for, universal, **10**. 63

lived with his grandmother, **25**. 570

marriage of: **7**. 52n, **9**. 234–5; imminent, **9**. 231, 233

Memoirs from 1754 to 1758, HW allowed to read, in MS, **10**. 67–8

ministry under Henry Fox considered hopeless by, **31**. 99

money saved by, **10**. 63

Navestock visited by, on honeymoon, **9**. 235

Newcastle, D. of, said to favour, **20**. 505

opiates given to, **10**. 58

person of, unpleasant, **10**. 56, (?) **21**. 98, **22**. 127, **35**. 282n

Petersham Lodge to be visited by, **31**. 13–14

Piozzi, Mrs, comments on medical treatment of, **10**. 56n

posts refused by, **22**. 131

[Waldegrave, James (1715–63), *continued*]
Rochfords entertain, **9.** 269
seal of, given by wife to his successor, **22.** 164
SH Press visited by, **9.** 215–16
teller of Exchequer, **22.** 126n
tellership of Exchequer profitable to, **10.** 63
to be first lord of Treasury, **21.** 98
Walpole, Sir Edward, writes epitaph on, **38.** 444, 447
Walpole, Maria, rides in coach of, **9.** 233
—— to marry, **21.** 284–5, 287
warden of the Stannaries, **20.** 246, **22.** 126n
wife laments, **10.** 59, 62, 65
wife of, **3.** 57n, **9.** 13n, **11.** 24n, **21.** 98n, 240n
wife recommended to HW's care by, on deathbed, **10.** 56
wife's devotion to, on death-bed, **10.** 56
Wildman's Club in former house of, in Albemarle St, **38.** 294
will of: **10.** 56, 62–3; executed by wife, **10.** 67
witticisms of, **14.** 88, **32.** 411
Waldegrave, Hon. John (1718–84), 3d E. Waldegrave, 1763; army officer; M.P.:
anxiety over military campaign of, **21.** 316
Arthur's Club visited by, **9.** 363
(?) at Chesterfield's assembly, **37.** 327
Bath improves health of, **33.** 374
Bedchamber post denied to, **38.** 433
Bedford faction prefers, to Conway, **39.** 84n
Bedford party wanted mastership of Horse to the Queen for, **30.** 186
cited in order of the day, at Minden, **21.** 316n
colonelcy of, corrected, **43.** 267
daughter-in-law pleases, **33.** 348
daughter of, **11.** 349n
English troops in Germany commanded by, **37.** 555n
Ferdinand, P., commends, to George II, **21.** 316n
—— praises conduct of, at Minden, **35.** 295n
figure of, lean, **9.** 314, 329
Grenville ministry wishes, to suppress riots, **38.** 562
HW called on by, to give news of Fitzroys, **36.** 225
HW mentions, **5.** 75, (?) **10.** 102
HW played with, in holidays ca 1729, **25.** 570
HW sends letter to Cts of Ailesbury through, **38.** 90
HW's school-fellow, **25.** 570
HW summons, to fire, **9.** 363
Halifax suggests commission for, to suppress riot, **30.** 181
house of, endangered by fire, **9.** 363
inoculated for smallpox, **22.** 127
lived with his grandmother, **25.** 570
marriage of: **9.** 115; assisted by E. of Sandwich, **20.** 258
master of the Horse, to Q. Charlotte, **23.** 176, 180
mob pelts, by mistake, **20.** 156
Navestock furniture-pictures bought by, **10.** 108

(?) Portugal to be visited by, **14.** 120n
regiment assigned to, **35.** 295
Rochefort inquiry conducted by, **21.** 155
rumoured to be chamberlain to Q. Charlotte, **38.** 568
Sackville's regiment given to, **21.** 328n
shot at, in battle, **9.** 314
sister-in-law gives her husband's seal to, **22.** 164
sister-in-law told by, of wager about Sandwich losing his head, **38.** 274–5, 281
son of, **11.** 241n, **25.** 75n, 274n
Villinghausen battle involves, **21.** 516n
Waldegrave, Hon. John James (1785–1835), 6th E. Waldegrave, 1794:
Aylesford guardian to, **34.** 74, **36.** 268
bereavement of, at father's death, **43.** 386
birth of: **33.** 495; expected, **25.** 571
Cornwallis interested in, **36.** 284, 287
—— to be visited by, at Culford Hall, **36.** 287
Eton to be re-entered by, **36.** 289
Euston executor to, **36.** 315
—— sells, as executor, HW's MSS, **43.** 139
HW's letters inherited by, **26.** 38–9, 42, 43
HW's MSS owned by, **15.** 33n, **36.** 312–13, 314, 315–16
HW to be godfather to, **36.** 233–4
HW visited by, at SH, **12.** 209
health of: cold and cough, **36.** 239–40; well, **36.** 290; whooping-cough, **36.** 272
Holland, Bn, corresponds with, **36.** 313n
mother puts, in Boggust's house at Eton, **36.** 283–4
mother will be consoled by, **36.** 329
SH entail mentions, **30.** 351
Thurlow interested in, **36.** 284
Waldegrave, Lady Laura. *See* Waldegrave, Lady Elizabeth Laura
Waldegrave, Lady Maria Wilhelmina (1783–1805), m. (1804) Nathaniel Micklethwait:
Aylesford guardian to, **34.** 74, **36.** 268
bereavement of, at father's death, **43.** 386
birth of, **33.** 405, **35.** 532
brothers missed by, **36.** 284
brother's quarrel with, **36.** 229–30
christening of, **33.** 416
Cornwallis interested in, **36.** 284, 287
—— to be visited by, at Culford Hall, **36.** 287
grandmother visited by, **12.** 50
growth of, **36.** 256
HW's bequest of lease of Berkeley Sq. house mentions, **30.** 356
HW visited by, **12.** 50, 51
health of: cold, **36.** 239; well, **36.** 290; whooping-cough, **36.** 272
letter of, proper, **34.** 200
mother finds, in good health and conversation, **36.** 229
mother's attention to, **36.** 266, 270
mother suckles, **33.** 408
temper of, **33.** 565
Thurlow interested in, **36.** 284
unfeeling at brother's death, **36.** 329

Waldegrave, Hon. William (1753–1825), cr. (1800) Bn Radstock; 'Capt. Waldegrave'; naval officer:
affection of cousins for, 33. 272
Ampthill to be visited by, 33. 323
Aylesfords visited by, at Packington Hall, 36. 264–7, 271
Claremont near Waltham Cross the address of, 36. 271, 272
Dutch prizes taken by, 33. 272
HW called on by, 33. 323
HW's correspondence with, 36. 264–7, 271–3, 291, 43. 386–8
HW sees, at Lady Chewton's, 33. 411
HW visited by, 11. 241, 33. 210, 211, 279
health of: harmed by naval service, 33. 279; illness, 33. 323; recovers from accident, 33. 411
'heroic,' 33. 210
legacy to, from Hon. Baptist Leveson Gower, 33. 351
'William the Prudent,' 33. 211
Waldegrave, Hon. William (1788–1859), 8th E. Waldegrave, 1846; naval officer:
Aylesford guardian to, 34. 7, 36. 268
bereavement of, at father's death, 43. 386
birth of, 36. 252
Cornwallis interested in, 36. 284, 287
—— to be visited by, at Culford Hall, 36. 287
health of: well, 36. 290; whooping-cough, 36. 272
mother's attention to, 36. 266, 270
Prudente, La, commanded by, 33. 272n
sister's growth equalled by, 36. 256
SH entail mentions, 30. 351
Thurlow interested in, 36. 284
Waldegrave, Hon. Mrs William. See Van Lennep, Cornelia Jacoba
Waldegrave family:
at the Pavilions, 33. 346
Aylesford's hospitality to, at Packington Hall, 36. 260, 265, 268, 270, 43. 387
Cambridgeshire and Huntingdonshire lands of, 42. 174n
George IV gives dinner for, 25. 647
Gloucester, Ds of, rejects, 36. 323–4
HW has seen 6 generations of, 22. 485
temper of, gentle, 33. 565
transcripts of HW's letters censored by, 26. 38, 39, 42
Waldemar Christian (1622–56), Graf von Schleswig-Holstein; P. of Denmark:
(?) masquerader costumed like, 17. 338
Walden. See Saffron Walden
Waldensians:
Jortin's ardour for, 2. 353
slaughter of, 34. 161
Waldershare, Kent, Furnese's and E. of Guilford's seat:
Dodd and Whaley visit, 40. 5
gardens and belvedere at, 40. 5
Montagu, Charles and George, to visit, 9. 165
Montagu, George, attends ball at, 9. 166

—— predicts government posts for his friends at, 9. 201
—— rides in gardens of, 10. 321
——'s rejuvenation at, 10. 322
—— visits, 10. 319–21
Wale, Margaret (fl. 1760–85), m. 1 Michael Tyson; m. 2 Isaac Crouch:
Cole dines with, 2. 97
—— receives print from, 2. 307
—— returned MS from, 2. 296
Holgate, Mrs, related to, 2. 175
second marriage of, 43. 66
Wale, Samuel (d. 1786), R.A.:
drawings made for HW by, 15. 112, 139, 40. 182n
HW's eagle drawn by, 20. 485, 35. 352
portrait copied by, 15. 162–3
Wales, P. of:
crest of, like Medicis', 7. 279
George III becomes, 20. 239, 246
Young Pretender proclaimed as, 18. 552
See also Arthur (1486–1502); Edward (1330–76); Edward (1453–71); Edward (1473–84); Frederick Louis (1707–51); George II (1683–1760); George III (1738–1820); George IV (1762–1830); Henry Frederick (1594–1612)
Wales, Ps of. See Anne (1456–85); Augusta (1719–72) of Saxe-Gotha; Caroline (1683–1737) of Ansbach; Caroline (1768–1821) of Brunswick Wolfenbüttel; Joan (ca 1328–85)
Wales:
bards of, 35. 252, 40. 101, 105–6
Black Mountain in, visible from Hagley, 35. 148
Cole proposes to visit north of, 1. 34, 87
Conway and family to travel through, 37. 461
Conway's trip through, a uniform 'trot,' 37. 392
counties in, Beaufort tries to wrest lieutenancy of, from Morgan, 23. 174
election in, disputed, 20. 394, 401
estate in, left to George Rice, 33. 162
Ferns, Bp of, crosses on trip from Ireland, 10. 25
Fitzwilliam's servant a native of, 11. 49
Garrick to visit, to superintend a play, 41. 367
genealogies well preserved in, 42. 19
George II orders regiment to be raised in, 21. 311n
Gray's Catalogue should be extended to include antiquities of, 41. 251
——'s Druids might inhabit, 9. 385
——'s odes from, 10. 255
HW regrets not having seen the beauties of, 34. 93
HW's and Montagu's ancestral homes in, 9. 112
HW's Philipps ancestors from, 42. 19
Harcourts and Clio to reunite in, 35. 465
Hardinge's 'Sisyphean labours' in, 35. 575
inhabitants of, all interrelated, 17. 344
Irish couples land in, 11. 37

[Wales, continued]
Jacobite feint towards, 37. 211
Lort plans expedition to, 16. 282
marches of, London as lawless as, 25. 620
Methodist 'seminary' in mountains of, 24. 90–1
Montagu crosses, on return from Ireland, 10. 25
—— crosses mountains of, 9. 385
north of, rebels will perish if they flee to, 19. 179
Ossory, Lady, tours, 34. 92–5
Pennant's *Tour* in, 28. 381
princes of, have uninterrupted male descent, 33. 454
rebellion in, rumoured, 33. 82
rebels in, would have to be supplied from Ireland, 19. 160
Rigby visits Williams in, 30. 88n
Welsh take refuge in precipices of, 42. 2
Wynn a Jacobite in, 19. 310n
—— head of Jacobites in, 30. 292n
—— 'prince' of, 34. 95
See also North Wales
Walff. *See* Walluf
Walgrave. *See* Waldegrave
Walk; walks:
cockleshell, French would introduce, at SH, 9. 168
square cradle, at Drayton, 10. 90
Walkden, Elizabeth:
(?) Worksop arsenal to have been revealed by, 9. 97
Walker, Adam (1726–1821), writer and inventor:
(?) HW promises, not to issue last vol. of *Anecdotes of Painting*, 41. 240n
Walker, Anthony (d. 1692), D.D.:
Εὕρηκα, Εὕρηκα, Warwick, Cts of, commemorated in, 16. 138
Walker, Anthony (1726–65), engraver:
engraves frontispiece to *Life of Edward Lord Herbert of Cherbury*, 1. 71–2, 72, 75, 10. 133n, 15. 112n
engraves heads for Johnson's *Poets*, 29. 413n
(?) HW mentions, 10. 102
HW to write to Bathoe about, 43. 130
not ambitious, 15. 97
(?) Pennant's portrait engraved by, 41. 394n
Walker, Sir Edward (1612–77), Kt; Garter King-at-Arms:
herald, 1. 156
Talbot, Mrs Henry, descended from, 9. 120
tomb of, 9. 120
writings of, 9. 120
Walker, Frances (d. 1788), m. (1757) Rev. Thomas Dampier:
(?) Churchill, Lady Mary, talks with, of Mme du Deffand, 5. 2
(?) Du Deffand, Mme, hears news of Churchills from, 5. 2
(?) social relations of, with Churchills, 6. 207

Walker, John (1674–1747), historian:
Attempt . . . Sufferings of the Clergy . . ., An, by, 2. 354
Walker, John (fl. 1764). *See* Bradley, John
Walker, John, King's Messenger 1758–74:
Vorontsov's letters brought by, 22. 61n
Walker, John (fl. 1778–82), bookseller; publisher:
Lort receives Chatterton's' poems from, with request for more MSS, 16. 177
(?) Paternoster Row, address of, 43. 290
Steevens encourages, 16. 177
(?) *Triumph of Liberty* published by, 43. 290
Walker, Joseph Cooper (1761–1810), antiquary:
college for old maids in Ireland proposed by, 42. 305
Dublin edn of *Mysterious Mother* supervised by, 42. 301
Eccles St, Dublin the address of, 42. 301, 311, 318
essays by, on Irish dress and theatre, 42. 253
HW does not wish *Mysterious Mother* to be revised by, for the press, 42. 305
HW informed by, that Charlemont has stopped Dublin reprint of *Mysterious Mother*, 42. 309
HW receives information from, about art objects, 42. 301–2
HW's correspondence with, 42. 253–6, 301–2, 304–6, 309, 311–12, 318–19, 324–5, 365, 384
HW sends ticket to, 42. 384
HW thanks: for Irish edn of *Mysterious Mother*, 42. 324; for 'Italian pamphlet,' 42. 365; for notes on *Anecdotes of Painting*, and *Royal and Noble Authors*, 42. 304–5; for parcel and letter, 42. 253
health of: indisposition, 42. 325; nervous fever, 42. 318
Holyland Coffee House the address of, 42. 384
Mysterious Mother too greatly favoured by, 42. 365
Paris visited by, 42. 365, 384
SH visited by, 12. 242
Walker, Kitty, courtesan:
Loudoun's mistress, 30. 316
Williams, Sir C. H., had, as mistress, and wrote verses to her, 30. 316
Walker, Richard (1679–1764), Vice-master of Trinity College, Cambridge:
Pope mentions, in *Dunciad*, 1. 227n
print of, 1. 222–3, 227
Walker, Robert (d. ?1658), painter:
Beaufort, Ds of, painted by, 1. 181n
Cromwell's portrait by, 1. 9
Walker, Thomas (ca 1664–1748), Customs commissioner; Surveyor of Crown Lands; M.P.:
biographical information about, corrected, 43. 265
death of, 19. 511
nephew inherits bulk of estate of, 19. 511n
Newmarket frequented by, 19. 511n
painting owned by, 15. 205

surveyor of the roads, and usurer, **19**. 511n

Walpole, Sir Robert, and Lord Godolphin courted by, **19**. 5

Walpole, Robert, 2d E. of Orford inherits Wimbledon house of, **19**. 511n

Walker, Thomas (fl. 1775):
Answer to Mr Fitzgerald's Appeal by, **28**. 189n
duel fought by, **28**. 189n

Walker, W.:
print of, **40**. 236

Walker, William (1621–1700):
reputed executioner of Charles I, **1**. 9n

Walking:
Conway and wife engaged in, at Park Place, **37**. 548
HW's 'Muscovite way of,' **30**. 80

Walking-stick; walking-sticks:
HW discards, **41**. 281
HW falls when rising without, **25**. 555n
HW throws away, **33**. 284
HW uses, **33**. 279
Wren's, slips, **40**. 350

Walkinshaw, Catherine (1715–94):
Bedchamber woman to Augusta, Ps of Wales, **25**. 516
biographical information on, corrected, **43**. 152, 356
HW finds, with Lady Bute, **12**. 43
housekeeper to Ps of Wales, **12**. 43n
sister of, mistress to Young Pretender, **33**. 442

Walkinshaw, Clementina Maria Sophia (ca 1726–1802), cr. (before 22 July 1760) Cts of Alberstroff; mistress to Young Pretender:
daughter not to be accompanied by, **25**. 522
family of, **25**. 516
Gem, Dr, attends, **25**. 516, **26**. 47
HW and Mann call, 'Mrs Walsingham,' **25**. 512, 538n
HW's account of, **33**. 442–3
sister of, **12**. 43n
Young Pretender's daughter by, **25**. 512–14, 516, 521–2, **26**. 46–7

Walkminster. *See* Wachmeister

Wall, Dr:
Hartlebury chapel window designed by, **35**. 149n

Wall, Mr and Mrs:
son of, **20**. 171n

Wall, Eleanor (*or* Ellen) (1662–1732), m. (1680) Sir Theophilus Oglethorpe, Kt, 1685; Charles II's laundress and seamstress, **37**. 353
Portsmouth, Ds of, employs, **37**. 353n

Wall, Patrick (living, 1801), called Comte Patrice de Wall:
command given to, **7**. 147

Wall, Mrs Patrick. *See* Vaudrey, Jeanne-Gabrielle-Catherine de

Wall, Richard (1694–1778), Gen.; Spanish secretary of state; ambassador to England 1748–54:
birth and parentage of, **20**. 171n

Bristol, E. of, assured by, of Charles III's good wishes to England, **21**. 539n
——'s negotiations with, **21**. 548n, 557n, 563n, 564n
Charles III expresses confidence in, **21**. 347
Croix de Frechapelle recommended as lord of the Bedchamber to Ferdinand VI by, **20**. 184n
England not to be supported by, if Charles III supports France, **21**. 333n
English confidence in Charles III urged by, **21**. 347n
English manufacturers said to be lured by, to Spain, **20**. 170–1
English popularity of, **37**. 429
English-Spanish commercial relations discussed by, **19**. 504
fashionable in England, **20**. 51, 426
France asks Frederick Augustus II to urge Q. of Spain to remove, **21**. 347n
Gondomar resembles, **20**. 52
Irish Catholic, **20**. 171, **21**. 347n
Keene brings about elevation of, **21**. 166n
Lobkowitz and Signora Capello accompanied by, **37**. 289
motto of, **35**. 94
recalled to Spain, **20**. 426
Rich, Lady, regrets recall of, **35**. 78–9
Spanish ambassador to England, **19**. 504, **20**. 426n, **21**. 347n
Spanish secretary of state, **20**. 426n
to be secretary of state for foreign affairs in Spain, **20**. 426
witticism of, to Grossatesta, at *Peace in Europe* serenata, **20**. 51–2

Wall; walls:
at Greatworth, **10**. 120
at Ham House, **10**. 306
at Mistley, bad and ill-placed, **30**. 87
English estates no longer concealed by, **20**. 166
hot, in Park Place garden, **39**. 550

Wallace, Lady. *See* Maxwell, Eglantine

Wallace, James, D.D.; writer:
Every Man His Own Letter-Writer by, advertised, **33**. 378

Wallace, James (1729–83), M.P.; solicitor-gen. 1778–80; attorney-gen., 1783:
counsel for Ds of Kingston, **24**. 192, 196, **28**. 261n
Gordon indicted by bill presented to grand jury by, **25**. 98n
solicitor-gen., **39**. 136n

Wallace, Sir James (1731–1803), Kt, 1777; naval officer:
Admiralty sends, to Portsmouth to relieve Jersey, **25**. 111n
Cancale Bay attack by, cripples Nassau's force for Jersey invasion, **39**. 321
ordered to go to Jersey, **29**. 96n

Wallace, Sir William (ca 1270–1305), Scottish patriot:
'Hymn to Liberty' celebrates, **16.** 374
Wallachia ('Volakia'):
Mahmud regains part of, **18.** 53n
Turks lose, to Russia, **23.** 155
Waller, Edmund (1606–87), poet:
Blackburne's favourite poet, **15.** 142
Dorset aided by, in translation, **16.** 6n
Du Deffand, Mme, cites answer of, to Charles II, **3.** 81
elegance of, **2.** 52
English poetic style barbarous until rise of, **16.** 127
engraving of, **16.** 67
engravings to works of, **17.** 358
French elegance added by, to English language, **41.** 297
HW praises small pieces of, **16.** 270
HW quotes, **9.** 228, **15.** 242
Lansdown imitates, **28.** 208n
Morton, Cts of, mentioned by, **30.** 370
'Of His Majesty's Receiving the News of the Duke of Buckingham's Death' by, quoted by HW, **31.** 342
'Of the Last Verses in the Book' by: HW alludes to, **33.** 311; HW quotes, **11.** 364, **33.** 340
'On the Foregoing Divine Poems' by, quoted by HW, **35.** 630
Penshurst celebrated by, **2.** 240, **32.** 30
Pinkerton proscribes, **16.** 270
retort by, to Lady Sunderland, **34.** 226
'Sacharissa' and, **23.** 248, **28.** 464
verses allude to, **28.** 203n
Voltaire introduced, to France, **41.** 152
Waller, Edmund (ca 1699–1771), M.P.:
birth date of, **43.** 243
Bubb Dodington defended by, in Parliament, **17.** 354–5
Case of the Hanover Forces, The, by Chesterfield and, **18.** 123, **35.** 49, **43.** 248
Chesterfield studies public accounts under, **17.** 332n, **30.** 291n
——'s witticism on, **30.** 291n
Court party not joined by, **18.** 118
deafness of, **17.** 332n
diction of, compared to Sternhold's tunes, **30.** 201–2
HW expects his endurance to be tried by, **30.** 81
HW's 'character' of, **30.** 291n
House of Commons abandoned by, because of deafness, **30.** 291n
Lincoln replaces, as Cofferer, **19.** 347
lordship of the Treasury refused by, **17.** 332, **30.** 291n
named in Secret Committee lists, **17.** 385
naval investigation proposed by, in Parliament, **18.** 399–400, 427
Parliamentary motion proposed by, to ask George II to give up Hanover troops, **18.** 355

Ralph's *Of the Use and Abuse of Parliaments* attributed to, **18.** 464
Sandys succeeded by, as Cofferer, **17.** 385n, **18.** 551
Twickenham house of, acquired by Duane, **33.** 200n, **42.** 481
unintelligibility of, **30.** 201
Vindication of a Late Pamphlet, A, by, **18.** 141, **35.** 49
Williams, Sir C. H., writes verse dialogue between Sandys and, **30.** 317
Winnington succeeded by, as Cofferer, **30.** 291n
Waller, Sir Wathen, 1st Bt:
HW's MSS owned by, **36.** 312, 313, 315
Waller, Sir William (ca 1597–1668), Gen.:
Arundel besieged by, **12.** 205n
Parliamentary army under, **9.** 87n
Wallingford, Vct. *See* Knollys, William
Wallingford, Vcts. *See* Law, Mary Katherine
Wallingford, Berks:
election at, **17.** 400
Pentycross, clergyman and schoolmaster at, **2.** 15n, 18–19, **12.** 207, **15.** 287
St Mary's Church at, **2.** 15n, **15.** 287n
'Wallis, Count.' *See* Cornwallis, Edward
Wallis, ——, naval Capt.:
Lee's capture reported by, **24.** 285n
Wallis, ——, (?) Tuscan or Austrian army officer:
infantry of, replaced by Capponi's militia, **17.** 266n
regiment of: **18.** 164, 331n; leaves Leghorn, **17.** 214n
Wallis, Albany (ca 1713–1800), attorney, Norfolk St, London:
believes in Ireland's MSS, **15.** 321
Garrick's correspondence with, **42.** 211n
Shakespeare's mortgage discovered by, **42.** 210n
Shakespeare's mortgage explained by, **31.** 260n
Wallis, John (1616–1703), D.D.; divine and mathematician:
HW confuses, with Dr Willis, **32.** 334
Wallis, Samuel (1728–95), naval captain, 1756:
Tahitian adventure of, **32.** 127–8
Wallmoden, Frau von. *See* Wendt, Amalie Sophie Marianne von
Wallmoden, Adam Gottlieb (1704–52 *or* 56), Oberhauptmann von:
wife of, **9.** 16n
wife's son said to resemble, **18.** 524
Wallmoden, Johann Ludwig von (1736–1811), 'Master Louis'; reputed son of George II; Graf von Wallmoden-Gimborn, 1783; field marshal:
'father's' alleged resemblance to, **18.** 524
Florence visited by, **22.** 327, 354
George II resembled by, **22.** 327
——'s bequest to, **21.** 450n
Mann introduces, at Tuscan Court, **22.** 350, **43.** 280

—— to entertain, at dinner, **22.** 327

messenger sent by, to summon servants from Rome, **22.** 357

returns to Germany by way of Rome, **22.** 362

Walloon Guards ('Gardes Vallones'):

at Campo Santo, **18.** 154, 164

at Leghorn, **19.** 55

at Rome, **18.** 532

casualties in: at Campo Santo, **18.** 154; at Piacenza, **19.** 267, 270

Mariani commands, **18.** 154n

Walloons, The. See under Cumberland, Richard

Wallop, John (1690–1762), cr. (1720) Vct Lymington and (1743) E. of Portsmouth:

Andover election and, **43.** 276

Isle of Wight command to be taken from, **18.** 457

Newcastle, D. of, approaches, to influence Andover borough in favour of Delaval, **21.** 484n

——'s correspondence with, **43.** 276

wife of, **9.** 104n

Wallop, Hon. Mrs John. *See* Griffin, Hon. Elizabeth

Wallpaper:

blue and white striped, at SH, **20.** 382

Bromwich to take samples of, to HW, **37.** 331

crimson predominant colour in, at trial of Lord Cardigan, **19.** 280n

Dutch tiles imitated on, at SH, **20.** 382

Gothic: at SH, **9.** 150; Bentley offers to paint, **35.** 191; fretwork in, in SH hall, **20.** 380, 381; HW will send, to Bentley if he insists, **35.** 196; in Magdalen House chapel, **9.** 273; stone-colour, in SH parlour, **20.** 380

green, in SH closet, **20.** 382

(?) HW asks Dodsley about, **37.** 465

HW orders, **6.** 236, 241, 248, 252, 254

Hertford, Cts of, orders, from London, for Mme de Mirepoix, **39.** 37

in Latimers dining-room, **35.** 234

in SH hall and staircase, **35.** 150, 234

Mann, Galfridus, has, for Horace Mann's room, **20.** 367

merchant of: paid, **6.** 273, 280; wants money, **6.** 266, 269

Montagu does not like, blue, **10.** 309

—— to change, at Greatworth, **9.** 257

pink: HW uses, at Rigby's, **20.** 166; in SH Star Chamber, **40.** 150n

Pitt, Anne, to have, in room, **31.** 99

plain blue, in SH Blue Bedchamber, **35.** 173

red, in SH bedchamber, **20.** 38

treillage paper, with roses and batons, **35.** 483–4

yellow, in SH bedchamber, **20.** 381

See also under Chinese; Indian

Wallsee, Graf von. *See* Colloredo-Melz und Wallsee, Joseph Maria, Graf von

Walluf (Germany):

pandours and hussars cross Rhine at, **37.** 159

Walmer Castle, Kent:

Holdernesse, Cts of, smuggles through, **10.** 288n

Walmoden. *See* Wallmoden

Walnut; walnuts:

Cole's, **2.** 113

'enchanted carpet' packed in, **35.** 49

French garden channels worthy to be navigated by, **35.** 126

more exuberant than their leaves, **34.** 8

Walnut tree; walnut trees:

at SH, damaged by wind, **11.** 159

bent down with fruit, **35.** 397

French strip, for firewood, **39.** 9

HW sees, on Amiens-Clermont road, **7.** 259

proverb alludes to, **31.** 304

Walnut Tree House, Twickenham:

HW bequeaths, to Philip Colomb, **30.** 366

Walpole, Bns (of Walpole). *See* Rolle, Margaret (1709–81)

Walpole, Bns (of Wolterton). *See* Cavendish, Lady Rachel (1727–1805); Lombard, Mary Magdelaine (ca 1695–1783)

Walpole, Lady. *See* Crane, Susan (1632–67); FitzOsbert, Isabel (d. ca 1311); Shorter, Catherine (ca 1682–1737); Skerrett, Maria (ca 1702–38)

Walpole, Mrs:

HW mentions, **10.** 243

Walpole, —— (fl. 1659), 'il Signor Walpoole, Inglese':

president of an academy in Florence, **1.** 127, 128, 130, 131

Walpole, Lady Anne. *See* Osborne, Lady Anne

Walpole, Hon. Anne (1733–97), dau. of 1st Bn Walpole of Wolterton:

(?) dines with HW, **11.** 108

father now willing to disinherit, **36.** 298

mother's bequest to, **36.** 210

not handsome, **36.** 298

parents unwilling to cut off, by entail, **36.** 31, 296

Walpole, Burwell (1675–90), brother of Sir Robert Walpole:

death of, **22.** 26

Walpole, Catherine (ca 1703–22), HW's sister:

Bedford, Mrs Thomas, may have been governess to, **40.** 41n

death of, **22.** 27

portrait of, **30.** 371

Walpole, Hon. Catherine (1750–1831), dau. of 2d Bn Walpole of Wolterton:

(?) Walpole, Hon. Robert, sends muff to, **4.** 335

Walpole, Catherine Margaret (1756–1816), dau. of Hon. Thomas Walpole:

biographical information on, corrected, **43.** 92, 140

brother gets little news from, **36.** 236

brother probably informed by, **36.** 241

brother's visit will make, happy, **36.** 206

Du Deffand, Mme, discusses, with Hon. Thomas Walpole, **5.** 94

[Walpole, Catherine Margaret, *continued*]
father's letter to, 11. 28
HW entertains, at dinner, 11. 108
HW gives *Essay on Modern Gardening* to,
12. 260, 36. 237–8
meritorious, 36. 204
writes well, 36. 241
Walpole, Charlotte (1738–89), dau. of Sir Edward Walpole, m. (1760) Hon. Lionel Tollemache, styled Lord Huntingtower; 5th E. of Dysart, 1770:
'all goodness and good nature,' 32. 398
almost drowned, 33. 47
at Ham House, 33. 346
brother-in-law of, 32. 152
childless, 31. 330
Coke, Lady Mary, characterizes, 31. 315
death of, 11. 56, 57, 59, 60, 67–9, 16. 310, 31.
330, 34. 63
dying, 39. 470
Dysart hears, is 'accomplished,' 9. 312
—— offered part of fortune of, in return for
financial settlement, 9. 312
father entertains, at Waldegrave wedding, 9.
235
father leaves Wimpole St house to, for life,
33. 2n, 36. 126n
father might leave Walpole estates to, 36. 26
father of, 17. 209
father's bounty to, 24. 349
father unlikely to marry because of, 36. 295
Fox, Henry, can send letter to sisters and,
for HW, 30. 136
Gloucester, Ds of, reveals ambitions to, 36.
69n
—— tended by, when mourning first husband, 10. 62, 63
—— too tired to write to, 36. 127
Gloucester, D. of, criticized by, 31. 299
HW attentive to, 36. 15, 17, 34
HW entertained by, at Ham House, 10. 306–7
HW entertains, at SH, 9. 237
HW has, at SH, on brother-in-law's death,
38. 196
HW mentions, 9. 13, 10. 7
(?) HW notifies, of Cts of Orford's death,
25. 123n
HW passes miserable evening with, 32. 377
HW praises, 31. 330
HW's correspondence with, 36. 79–80
HW's epitaph on, 11. 69–70, 31. 314–15, 36.
255
HW's niece, 7. 177n
HW's opinion of, 10. 63
HW's time usurped by, 11. 61
HW to entertain, at SH, 9. 369
HW to give breakfast for sisters and, 30. 132
HW to inform, of D. of Gloucester, 36. 139
(?) HW to visit, at Ham, 31. 275
HW visited by, at SH, 10. 63, 32. 382
HW visits, 33. 480
HW, Waldegrave sisters, and Anna Maria

Keppel go in boat of, at Ham House, 39.
311
Ham House disliked by, 10. 307
—— occupied by, 10. 306–7
health of: declining, 34. 48, 60, 61; illness
and death, 11. 56, 57, 59, 60, 67–8, 69; in
a decay, 34. 46
Helmingham Hall disliked by, 10. 307
Humphry permitted by, to see her pictures
in Wimpole St, 42. 463
Huntingtower , (5th E. of Dysart) asks Dysart
for jointure for, 9. 312
(?) —— interested in medals, 5. 235n
—— marries, 9. 301, 302, 11. 337n, 21. 438–
40, 446
——'s regard for memory of, 36. 268–9, 328
Montagu hopes that HW will take, to SH to
comfort sister, 10. 62
Nivernais's *Jardins modernes* given to, 12. 259
patience of, 11. 56, 68
Ramsay's picture of, 40. 370
sister informs, of Lady Elizabeth Keppel's
engagement, 38. 400
sister-in-law of, 28. 93n
sister less handsome than, 21. 239
sister tended by, in bereavement, 10. 62, 63
sister visited by, 21. 439
sympathy of, for husband's brothers, 32. 398
Tollemache, Hon. William, attached to, 36.
131
Waldegrave girls praised by, 36. 324
Walpole, Dorothy (1686–1726), m. (1713)
Charles Townshend, 2d Vct Townshend:
'Aldermanbury' mistaken by, for 'Alderman
Bury,' 30. 279
HW's godmother, 13. 3
husband of, 2. 124n, 13. 120n, 25. 423n
son of, 9. 32n, 19. 320n
Walpole, Lady Anne, brings up, 9. 32
Walpole, Sir Edward (1621–68), K.B. (?) 1661;
HW's great-grandfather:
daughter of, 12. 267
marriage of, 1. 374
verses by, 1. 52
wife of, 1. 33n
Walpole, Edward (1674–98), Sir Robert Walpole's brother:
death of, 22. 26
Walpole, Hon. Sir Edward (1706–84), K.B.,
1753; HW's brother; M.P.:
Ædes Walpolianæ arouses jealousy of, 20.
41–2, 55
anecdote about Wyndham and Sir Robert
Walpole unknown to, 15. 151–2
annuities and Ryder St house left by, to Margaret and Anne Clement, 36. 156n, 317
appearance of: beautiful without a wrinkle,
25. 462; face unwrinkled, 24. 148; HW
claims, looks younger than his own, 24.
529; sleek, young, and in good colour,
24. 529
Ashton intimate with, 20. 215, 218

'Baron of Englefield Green,' 9. 14, 20
Barron a protégé of, 28. 196n
Bath order esteemed by, 22. 390
birth date of, corrected, 43. 240
Bishop recommended to Pont-de-Veyle by, through HW and Mme du Deffand, 36. 105–7
Boothby recommended by, to Mann, 21. 431, 482
Browne reports Jebb's news of D. of Gloucester to, 36. 138–9, 141
Butler, Bp, patronized by, 28. 458
—— recommended to Hertford at request of, 2. 283n
—— visits, 32. 411–12
—— writes to, 35. 497
Castle Rising might be borough of, 36. 14, 16
Chelsea residence of, 18. 250, 284
children generously treated by, 19. 349
children of, well treated by HW, 36. 15, 17
Clement, Anne, tells, that Ds of Gloucester borrowed from HW, 36. 327
Clement, Jane, corresponds with, quarreling with him, 36. 317–21
—— may convey bad news to, 36. 156–7
—— returns to Pall Mall house of, 36. 321–2
clerk of the Pells, and K.B., 17. 209n, 25. 462n, 26. 52
clerkship of the Pells under, 42. 25–8
Coke family quarrel patched up by, 19. 457
Collier, Susan, housekeeper to, 36. 317n
consoles HW about D. of Gloucester, 32. 378
Conway has not seen, 37. 51
—— recommends to Hertford coolness in dealing with, 37. 373
——'s letter franked by, 37. 36
Coppinger consulted by, about Catherine Daye's purchase, 36. 59
Customs collectorship of HW and, embarrassed by a clerk's embezzling, 35. 493
Customs House place of, 17. 27n, 24. 276, 26. 52–4, 41. 325–9
——'s sale disapproved by, 40. 145
daughter goes to, after husband's death, 10. 59
daughter inherits impetuosity of, 24. 125
daughter of, 2. 31n, 3. 57n, 6. 446n, 9. 61, 11. 24n, 56n, 321n, 12. 136n, 13. 31n, 16. 310n, 17. 209, 21. 239–40, 284–5, 439n, 22. 94n, 127n, 25. 410n, 466n, 508n, 28. 252n, 38. 189n
daughter's dowry from, 36. 35
daughter's letter exhibited by, 23. 415
daughter's letter to, from Verona, 34. 245–7
daughter's marriage settlements entrusted by, to HW, 21. 285
daughter's wedding at house of, 9. 235
daughter visits, 10. 83
death of: 4. 359n, 25. 466, 33. 432, 433; delays HW's payment to Croft, 25. 473; Gloucester, D. and Ds of, hear, from HW, 36. 224; HW to lose place by, 31. 298; makes

HW next heir to E. of Orford, 25. 477n; Mann condoles with HW upon, 25. 473; may soon occur, 25. 462–3; reduces HW's fortune, 16. 275; reduces HW's income, 16. 275n, 29. 325, 327–8, 348, 33. 436n, 36. 223, 39. 289–90; would cause loss of HW's Customs place, 10. 316
death of son-in-law of, 32. 410
diet of, 25. 463
disinterestedness of, in E. of Orford's affairs, 36. 123
Du Deffand, Mme, pleases, by her attentions to Mr Bishop, 6. 160
—— solicited by, in Bishop's behalf, 6. 28n
——'s opinion of, 7. 8
—— thinks, is childless, 6. 31–2
empty title would be inherited by, on nephew's death, 23. 510–11
English visitors to Florence tell, that sister-in-law's health is bad, 23. 505, 512
epitaph by, on E. Waldegrave, 38. 444, 447
family entertained by, at daughter's wedding, 9. 235
father entails estates upon, 36. 295
father gives Pall Mall freehold to, 36. 14n
father loved by, 28. 70, 36. 19
father's bequests to, 13. 15, 19. 32n, 34. 145n, 42. 81
father scolded by, in letter accusing HW of bringing Middleton, 15. 306n, 20. 215
father's estate should go to Cholmondeleys after deaths of HW and, 25. 132
father's ministry supplies anecdotes to, 9. 14
father's retirement wished by, 17. 253, 319
father sups with, after long Parliamentary session, 17. 294
Ferne's alliterative poem mentioned by, 7. 373
fortune of, ample, 25. 466
fortunes of HW and, not paid by 3d E. of Orford after his mother's death, 25. 315–16
Fox, Henry, asks, to employ Windsor tradesmen, 20. 42
—— receives call from, 20. 42
Frederick, P. of Wales, to be attended by, at levee, 17. 338, 369
Frogmore the home of, 9. 56, 20. 42
generosity of, 25. 466
Germain (Sackville) asked by, for Parliamentary bill to pay D. of Gloucester's debts, 36. 130n, 306n, 307n
—— gets letter from, in D. of Gloucester's behalf, 36. 306–8, 309, 327
——'s correspondence with, not to be shown to HW or Bp Keppel, 36. 327
Gloucester, Ds of, cannot persuade, to call on her husband, 23. 461
—— corresponds with, 36. 62, 63, 66–8, 126, 144, 145
—— hesitates to ask, to the Pavilions, 36. 323
—— informs, of her marriage, 23. 415
—— sends black cock pie to, 35. 324

[Walpole, Sir Edward (1706–84), *continued*]
—— speaks tenderly of, 24. 297
—— writes to, revealing her marriage, 5. 247
Gloucester, D. of, asks, to avoid his levee, 36. 68
—— fails to call on, 23. 423
—— orders game and venison to be sent to, 36. 324
—— writes to, 36. 305–9
Gloucester, D. and Ds of, waited on by, 43. 301–2
granddaughter of, 11. 33n
Great Yarmouth borough declined by, 39. 95
HW acts with, in care of nephew, 23. 461
HW advised by, not to attend D. of Gloucester's levee, 36. 70–1
HW agrees with, on place tax on Exchequer place, 40. 154
HW and, conduct business for nephew, 32. 365
HW and Conways annoyed by, over Shorter's will, 37. 372n, 373n
HW arouses jealousy of, 20. 41, 55
HW calls attitude of, unprovoked, 36. 21
HW calls on Cts Waldegrave at house of, 10. 59
HW confused with, by Mrs Hayes, 31. 65
HW deferential to, 36. 17–18
HW differs with, over Castle Rising election, 43. 111
HW eleven years younger than, 24. 529
HW entertained by, 9. 235
HW envies youth and spirits of, 33. 281–2
HW formally asked by, to look after nephew's affairs, 23. 496
HW gets consent of, to manage nephew's affairs, 36. 93
HW impresses age of, on nephew, 24. 372
HW informed by, of daughter's pregnancy and vacant clerkship, 36. 89–90
HW invited by, to meet Mr Bishop, 36. 105
HW less flattered than, 30. 41
HW mentions, 5. 88
HW not aided by, in managing nephew's affairs, 5. 374, 6. 438
HW notifies, of inheritance from uncle, 20. 403
(?) HW notifies, of nephew's recovery, 24. 368
HW not to be surprised if, throws his life away, 39. 88
HW persuaded by, to continue with nephew's affairs, 32. 158
HW persuades, to let Customs House clerks rise by seniority, 24. 358
HW quarrels with, over Castle Rising, 19. 419
HW receives printed writing by, 36. 188
HW's agreement with, on Customs places, broken, 41. 210–12
HW said to foment mother's anger against, 36. 18
HW's breakfast for daughters considered very important by, 30. 132

HW's coolness with: 17. 209n; aggravated by Ashton, 20. 215
HW's correspondence with: 7. 376, (?) 380, 393, 36. (?) 6, 14–21, 22, 23, 34–5, 44, 51–3, 59–60, 62–8, 105–7, 117–27, 133, 138–41, 144–8, 153–5, 157–8, 188, 200–1, 37. (?) 397, 40. 36, 43. 96; MSS of, 36. 313
HW's Customs place depends on life of, 40. 73–4
HW sends red box to, 7. 380, 404
HW sends to, his epitaph on Lady Hervey, 36. 51
HW shares proceeds of Customs place with, 28. 445n
HW should defer to seniority of, 36. 15, 16–17
HW shown by, letter from Ds of Gloucester, 36. 66–8, 69
HW's indebtedness from, must be felt by him, 21. 287
HW's letter to Mann about E. of Orford seen and approved by, 23. 483
HW's place in Customs expires with, 24. 178, 31. 298
HW's references to, censored, 26. 38
HW's relations with, 9. 14, 61, 87, 20. 218
HW surprised that Order of the Bath should be accepted by, 22. 381
(?) HW to be aided by, in house purchase, 36. 201
HW to call on, 25. 123
HW told by, that Harcourt often entertains Bp Butler, 35. 535
HW to meet lawyers at house of, 32. 122
HW visits, 32. 121
half-sister cultivated by, against HW, 36. 19
Handelian quarrels known to, 9. 14
health of: 3. 325, 336, 340, 388, 10. 244, 246; appetite partly restored by the bark, 25. 463; aversion of, to solid food, 25. 462; dangerously ill, 31. 134; dying, 31. 298; fall, 36. 153–4; gout in foot, 36. 205; illness, 7. 318n, 41. 95; Mann condoles with HW on, 25. 469; perfect for many years, 25. 462; relapses, 39. 88; unvaried from 30 to 77, 25. 466
Henderson defended by, in verses against Garrick, 36. 146, 148
High Beech suggested by, for nephew, 36. 121
Highmore's letter to, about Kneller, 43. 349
Houghton visited by, 17. 88
houses of: at Isleworth, 33. 281–2, 36. 205; in Pall Mall, 9. 235, 30. 136; in Wimpole St, 33. 2, 36. 126n
Howe, Hon. Caroline, not to wed, 17. 209, 240
Huntingtower asks, for daughter's hand, 9. 301, 21. 439
Ilay to be asked by, about cobalt and zinc, 18. 250
income of, from Customs post, 10. 317
inquiries of, about cobalt and zinc, 18. 250, 284
Ireland visited by, with Conway, 37. 34n, 35–6

Isleworth house bought by, **36**. 205
Isleworth visited by, **32**. 346
Italian operatic arias owned by, **36**. 53n
Jebb's letter to, about D. of Gloucester, **24**. 319, **36**. 133
—— told by, about Hoffman's medicine in Bates's *Dispensatory*, **36**. 140, 144–5, 147
Keppel, Bp, said to be insolent to, **36**. 321
Keppel, Lady Elizabeth, entertained by, **9**. 235
Keppel, Mrs, given estate, house, and coach by, **24**. 349, 352
—— provided for by, **7**. 5
Keppels entertained by, **9**. 235
K.B., **17**. 209n, **22**. 27, 381n, 390
law to be obeyed literally by, in nephew's affairs, **24**. 295
letter by, about D. of Gloucester's illness, **26**. 50–1
Luxborough may be sold by, **36**. 60
—— visited by, **36**. 66n
Lyttelton addresses eclogue to, **33**. 501n
Mann, Edward Louisa, deputy to HW and, in Customs, **32**. 283, 288
—— to write directly to, about Customs place, **41**. 211
Mann, Sir Horace, asks, about attitude of, to daughter's marriage, **23**. 396, 403
——'s correspondence with, **21**. 431, **23**. 410
——'s power of attorney required by, for Customs House petition, **24**. 209
—— to send paints to, **19**. 368–9
Mann, John, employed by, in Customs House, **24**. 358
Markham's conduct scandalizes, **28**. 313
Marlborough tells, of son's bravery, **21**. 240
Martyn, friend of, **10**. 331
Mason visits, **28**. 196, 200
memory of, failing, **33**. 576–7
Middleton sends compliments to, **15**. 2–3
——'s visit to Houghton resented by, **36**. 19
mistress of, **9**. 302n
mistress tires, **17**. 240
modern miracles in painting and music disparaged by, **25**. 577
Montagu regrets ill health of, **10**. 246
—— to visit, **9**. 13
Montrose asks, about 'every man having his price,' **33**. 277n
Moone sent by, to Eriswell, **36**. 121
musical tastes of, **9**. 14, **10**. 331
Natter patronized by, **16**. 299
North neglects, in treating with Orford over Parks rangership, **36**. 158
——'s arbitration accepted by, for Customs collectorship, **41**. 328–9
Orford, 2d E. of, corresponds with, over Castle Rising borough, **36**. 18
Orford, 3d E. of, encumbers estate to pay father's legacy to, **34**. 145
—— expects, will not press for payment of legacy for fear of being disinherited, **25**. 316, 322–3
—— names, in first will, **16**. 313n
—— not to cause action by, **24**. 316
——'s affairs avoided by, **5**. 374, **6**. 438, **36**. 332, **41**. 266, 379–80
——'s affairs would kill, if he had to assume them, **36**. 123
—— said to have disinherited, **23**. 496
——'s disposal of Rolle lands not to be opposed by, **25**. 148, 156–7
——'s health the only concern of, **36**. 119
——'s heir, **7**. 1
—— should be matter of indifference to, after guarding against consequences of his confederates, **24**. 303
——'s parasites sow distrust against, **24**. 372–3
——'s relations with, **23**. 461
—— thanks, for letting him break Houghton entail, **36**. 163–5
—— told to take advice of, **36**. 297
—— to pay legacy to, **33**. 62
—— to send mourning ring to, **25**. 124
—— unlikely to be survived by, **24**. 372, **25**. 316
Orford, Lady, leaves son to care of HW and, **23**. 464, 487–94, 514
——'s death will not affect, **25**. 123
—— wished by, to look after her son, **23**. 470–1, 476, 481–2, 485–6
Orford estate not coveted by, **25**. 125
Oxford, Bp of, visits, **32**. 411–12
painting, modern, known to, **9**. 14
painting of Gray's tomb given to HW by, **28**. 196
paints, **19**. 268
Pall Mall residence of, **9**. 235, **30**. 136
passions of, warm, **10**. 59
pentachord invented by, **28**. 196, 200, **36**. 53n
Pitt called on by, **19**. 371
play written by, **10**. 11, 15–16
Porter acquainted with, **16**. 217
portrait of Sir Robert Walpole and Legge at house of, **10**. 42
Prescot gives book to, **1**. 299
pun by, on 'Bute,' **10**. 60
Reed and Bp Keppel persuade, to take Jane Clement back, **36**. 320–1
Reeve knew, at Windsor, **40**. 230
reimbursement to, for Waldegrave girls, **36**. 328
Rogers, Charles, dedicates translation of Dante to, **35**. 384n, **42**. 9
Roubiliac patronized by, **2**. 330n
St Albans, D. of, notified by, not to expect support against Henry Fox, **20**. 42
St James's Palace would not be visited by, even if daughter were queen, **36**. 66
Scott, Mrs Samuel, written humorous letter by, **10**. 329–31, **43**. 138
Scotts often visited by, **10**. 330, 331
secludes himself after death of Bp Keppel, **33**. 2
seclusion of, **23**. 460–1
Shorter estate shared by, **9**. 156, **13**. 25, **20**. 403

[Walpole, Sir Edward (1706–84), *continued*]
sketches made by 19. 368n
Sloper's letter from, with thanks for wife's being godmother to Edward Walpole, 43. 365
son-in-law of, 7. 1, 10. 59, 24. 348, 32. 363, 410
son of, 3. 253n, 272n, 21. 240, 23. 300, 307
Spectator imitated by, 36. 188
statute of lunacy not to be taken out by, for E. of Orford, 24. 294, 25. 126
Suckling, cousin of, 24. 178
—— gets agreement from, for accounts of Customs place, 42. 47
—— pays moneys to, from Customs, 24. 231, 237, 36. 328
——'s legacy to, 36. 162
tea seed forgotten by, 18. 284
tea seed to be procured by, 18. 250
temper of, unhappy, 20. 318
Thicknesse's account of, 28. 47
Thirlby, friend of, 13. 19n
—— gets Customs place through, 20. 215n
—— leaves papers to, 20. 215n
—— lives with, 9. 14, 20. 215n
—— preferred by, for biographer of Sir Robert Walpole, 20. 215
town house of, given to Mrs Keppel, 24. 349
unable to attend 3d E. of Orford, 32. 350
unlikely to wed, because of his natural children, 36. 295
Vilett may not get clerkship from, 36. 8on
villa of, HW's partiality for low window in, 34. 195–6
Waldegrave girls may visit, 36. 325
Walpole estates may be left by, to his natural children, 36. 26
will of, leaves most to Mrs Keppel, 25. 466
Wimpole St house of, left to Cts of Dysart and then Mrs Keppel, 33. 2n, 36. 126n
Windsor deanery should be visited by, to see D. of Gloucester, 36. 324
Windsor estate of, 24. 349
witticism by, on Bubb Dodington, 17. 258
Walpole, Edward (1737–71), Lt-Col.; son of Sir Edward Walpole; HW's nephew:
army service of, in Portugal, 38. 179
bravery of, at St-Malo, 21. 240, 246
cornet of the Dragoons, 21. 240n
death of, 5. 57, 63, 23. 300, 307
drinking and gaming the vices of, 23. 300
father entertains, at Waldegrave wedding, 9. 235
father might leave Walpole estates to, 36. 26
father of, 17. 200
father unlikely to marry because of, 36. 295
Forcalquier, Mme de, receives attentions of, 3. 303
HW attentive to, 36. 15, 17
HW mentions, 9. (?) 13, 10. 102
(?) HW returns Conway's sword by, 38. 73
HW's lack of picture of, implies no slight to his memory, 36. 159–62
HW visited by, at SH, 10. 63

(?) Hudson's picture of, given to HW by Ds of Gloucester, 36. 159
Paris visited by, 3. 253, 301
Portugal visited by, 10. 63
Portuguese people condemned by, 10. 63
Rochford fond of, 3. 285
—— occupied with, 3. 253
Sloper, Mrs, godmother to, 43. 122, 365
social relations of, in Paris, 3. 272, 278, 285, 291
Walpole, Elizabeth (1759–1842), dau. of Hon. Thomas Walpole:
biographical information about, corrected, 43. 92
brother gets little news from, 36. 206
brother probably informed by, 36. 241
brother's visit will make, happy, 36. 206
Du Deffand, Mme, discusses, with Hon. T. Walpole, 5. 94
father's letter to, 11. 28
HW entertains, at dinner, 11. 108
HW gives *Essay on Modern Gardening* to, 36. 206
meritorious, 36. 204
writes well, 36. 241
Walpole, Galfridus (1684–1726), postmaster-general 1720–5:
(?) Bell removed from post under, 17. 502n
brother of Sir Robert Walpole, 9. 15n
Walpole, Mrs Galfridus. See Hayes, Cornelia
Walpole, George (1730–91), 3d E. of Orford, 1751; HW's nephew:
actions of, influenced by low rogues, 25. 124–5
affairs of: at Houghton, chaotic, 35. 345; depress HW, 32. 158–9, 160; devolve on HW, 28. 92–4, 116, 143; occupy HW, 31. 172; 'run to ruin,' 32. 118–19
agent of, desires agreement with Sharpe on mother's estate, 25. 150–1
Ailesbury, Cts of, thanks HW and, for (?) plovers' eggs, 37. 484, 485, 489
anecdote told by Penneck probably concerns, 15. 333
appearance of: engaging, 30. 167n; 'look of health and strength,' 42. 344; wild, 9. 241
approaching financial ruin of, 30. 167, 186
Ashburton seat compromised by, 36. 47
balloon ascent encouraged by, 25. 596
Battie attends, 12. 74n, 13. 6n, 23. 540, 546, 25. 126, 43. 58
Bedchamber appointment of: 20. 470, 30. 167n, 36. 187; pressed by great-uncle and promised by Pelham, 20. 470n
Bedchamber duties of, 25. 226
Bedchamber post of, resigned through Hertford, 25. 266, 39. 389
Bedford, D. of, will not be hindered by, in seeking Devonshire lord lieutenancy, 40. 67–8
Beevor attends, at Eriswell, 24. 293, 295, 296
bets made by, at Newmarket, 23. 503
Bewley attends, 16. 121n, 43. 367

Biggin, Blake, Blanchard, Money, and Pilâtre said to be entertained by, **25.** 596n

Boccaccio appreciated by, **25.** 555n

bond of, turned over by Horace Mann II to Hull, **24.** 78

Boone chosen by, to represent Ashburton, **24.** 46–7, **30.** 167n

——'s letter not answered by, **30.** 169

——'s obligations to, **35.** 416

—— the only grateful friend of, **24.** 292

boroughs of: **35.** 416–18; HW comments on elections in, **32.** 212; HW, Hertford, and Portland confer about, **39.** 193; Sharpe recommends sale of, **24.** 52–3; tended by Lucas, **25.** 462

broth forcibly fed to, **36.** 333

broth the only nourishment of, **24.** 505

Burney, Dr Charles, visits, **42.** 333n

busy with races, quarter sessions, and assizes, **36.** 240

Byron's acquittal voted by, **38.** 535

Callington borough in interest of, **39.** 192, **41.** 376

Capper doubts HW's and Chute's good intentions towards, **14.** 221

Carder, Mrs, improves opinion of, of Mozzi, **25.** 168

Castle Rising borough should be sold by, **36.** 47

—— should be borough of, **36.** 14, 16

'Catchem' (dog) may have been stolen during illness of, **39.** 490

Catherine II buys paintings from, **2.** 145–6, 257, **7.** 159, **43.** 68–9

—— may buy Houghton pictures from, **24.** 427–8, 434, 440–1

—— may not pay whole sum to, for Houghton pictures, **24.** 502

——'s portrait received by, **2.** 192

caveat by, against mother's will, **25.** 124, 126, 137, 143, 167, 195, 493, 504, 509

characteristics of, insensibility and insincerity, **30.** 167n

Cheltenham visited by: **20.** 273; in flight from father, **40.** 59

Cholmondeleys not offensive to, **36.** 302

Chute tries to marry, to Miss Nicoll the heiress, **14.** 193–214, **20.** 256–7, 273, **35.** 84

Cipriani does paintings for, **25.** 247

——'s drawings bought by, **36.** 237

——'s pictures vaunted by, though he had sold his others, **25.** 418

claims of, against mother's estate: asserted by Lucas, **25.** 143, 157, 186, 217, 333, 335, 341; chiefly represent repayment of fines on renewal of leases, **25.** 335; exceed her estate's claims against him, **25.** 412; for plate and jewels, **25.** 158; HW does not know, **25.** 176; not to be ready soon, **25.** 191; should be made in justice to father's creditors, **25.** 158

Clermont advises, to pull down Houghton steps, **15.** 327

Clinton barony cannot be transmitted by, to Walpoles, **25.** 165

Clinton barony to be claimed by, **25.** 151, 157, 240, 304

Clinton's alleged portrait desired by, **25.** 151, 227, 240, 304

Cole partial to, **2.** 171

—— sympathetic about, **1.** 313n, 321, **2.** 45

colonel of militia, **9.** 241

commission of lunacy would deprive, of his positions, **23.** 482

'Conjectures on the System of the Universe' by: Courtenay celebrates, in verses, **12.** 94–5; HW has heard of, **34.** 85

contradictions of, called by HW 'emanations of his malady,' **25.** 195

Conway does not wish to injure the prospects of, **37.** 390

—— sorry he did not get recommendations from, for Florence and Rome, **37.** 312

Cony and 'cabal' carry, from Brandon to Houghton in fever, **42.** 356

Cony called 'prime minister' of, **25.** 131

—— employed by, **23.** 560

—— entrusted by, with his affairs, **24.** 310–11

(?) —— preferred by, to HW, **36.** 164

Court attended by, **23.** 460

—— to be visited by, after recovery, **41.** 271n

cousin of, should disillusion him about false friends, **36.** 48

Coutts's friendship with, **42.** 340

creditors of: settlement by, **24.** 246, 272; should get claims before harpies strip him, **24.** 84; suit of, against him, may be terminated by him, **24.** 246; told by Lucas that they may expect large sum from Mozzi, **25.** 286, 439

creditors' composition with, **33.** 62

Crostwick estate the best of HW's inheritance from, **42.** 393

daughter of, by weeding-girl, **25.** 355

death of: **11.** 376, **13.** 11n, **16.** 313n, 314, **34.** 210, **36.** 279, **42.** 338–9; leaves HW much business, **15.** 213, 216, 218, **39.** 494, **42.** 379; overwhelms HW with business, **31.** 363–4; rumoured, **5.** 329–30; without children would involve reversion of barony of Clinton, **25.** 165; would leave empty title to uncle, **23.** 510–11

debts contracted by father to be compounded by, **25.** 148

debts of: **23.** 510, 549, **24.** 78, 82, 440–1, **25.** 155, 158, **36.** 95, 97; at Almack's, **33.** 23; to Manners, **32.** 121

delay in settling mother's affairs welcomed by, **25.** 247

deputy lieutenants for militia of, **39.** 297

Devon and Dorset estates to be bequeathed by, to Rolles, **25.** 148, 156–7

Devon and Dorset estates to have been visited by, **25.** 227

Devonshire property not at present owned by, **40.** 51

[Walpole, George (1730–91), *continued*]

Devonshire's letter from, about Castle Rising seat, 36. 33

disposition and habits of, 20. 482, 23. 560, 24. 295

division of money held by Hoare unlikely to suit, 25. 246

'does not always execute all he intends,' 41. 350

dogs and horses of, sold by HW, 36. 95

dogs of: 43. 151; to be given away, 39. 171; to be sold at Tattersal's, 39. 490

Dorsetshire estate to be sold by, 25. 148

Duane rejected by, 25. 265

Du Deffand, Mme, dislikes conduct of, 7. 40

—— inquires after, 5. 329, 364, 383, 388, 404

—— suggests wife for, 6. 25, 27

elections neglected by, 6. 99n

engaging when present, provoking when absent, 20. 482, 24. 54

England reached by, 20. 251

English people might forget mother's alienation from, 25. 396

entail could be cut off by, 36. 30, 31, 296

Eriswell 'hovel' of, 24. 293, 25. 227

—— revisited by, 25. 227

——'s parsonage inhabited by, 36. 117–25

estate of, involves HW in trouble, 36. 279

estates inherited by, from mother, 2. 257, 30. 169n

executor of father's estate, 25. 446

executors of, pay Dr Ash but not Drs Norford and Monro, 42. 355

falconer of, 32. 355–6

family of, wish for his survival, 41. 261

farm; farms of: let for less than HW could have got, 25. 172; let to a jockey, 24. 52; near Newmarket, 23. 495

father allows, to ride cousin's horses, 18. 70

father's death would injure, 19. 496, 20. 233

father's debts unpaid by, 24. 440, 25. 158

father's will tells, to seek uncles' and great-uncle's advice, 36. 297

Ferrers's trial deserted by, without voting, 9. 279

filly of, in Newmarket sweepstakes, 24. 20n

finances of: 36. 163n; greatly improved by HW, 23. 540, 549, 24. 294, 301, 25. 140, 172; HW not again to manage, 24. 53, 294, 301, 307–8, 25. 143; need attention, 23. 471, 481–2, 488–90, 497–8, 503, 509–11, 515, 521–2, 523, 528–9 (*see also under* affairs of; debts of)

financial dealings of, with great-uncle, 15. 523

financial embarrassment of, 42. 344n, 345

fines on renewal of leases paid to mother instead of, 25. 335

Florence might be visited by, 19. 511

fluctuates between violence and stupidity, 28. 323

footman; footmen of: committed to prison for getting bastard, 25. 355; tells HW of plans for dinner and airing, 36. 122

Fox, Henry, through Boone and HW, seeks political aid from, by offering Parks rangership, 30. 167, 168, 169, 36. 37

friend of: lost at sea, 21. 206; tells HW not to release him, 23. 541

Fronsac aided by, 3. 277

funeral of, 42. 339n, 345

Geneva to be stopping-place of, 20. 7

George II receives, 20. 251n

George III bets with, on having a child before Lowther, 21. 530–1

—— doubts recovery of, 34. 47

—— reviews regiment of, at Kingston, 21. 300n

Glynn and Plumptre attend, 36. 331

goes into country, 23. 551, 24. 372

good qualities and honour of, 14. 50, 204

Gordon, Lord George, as mad as, 25. 355

government posts would be lost by, if committed for insanity, 32. 133

grandfather contrasted with, 25. 418

grandfather doubts legitimacy of, 15. 325

grandfather entailed estates on, 20. 424n, 36. 295–6

grandfather's acts all undermined by, 24. 502–3, 25. 132

grandfather said to have left fortune to, 20. 247

grandfather's creditors make agreement with, 24. 300–1

grandfather's debts compounded by, 24. 440–1

grandmother's bequest to, 20. 418, 424, 436

grandmother slighted by, 20. 482

Greek and Latin not to the taste of, 20. 481

groom advises, to rub his body with sulphur and hellebore, 23. 460

HW absorbed in affairs of, 41. 364, 367

HW acts fairly towards, 25. 125

HW advertises recovery of, 24. 368

HW advised sale of pictures by, to pay father's and grandfather's debts, 24. 434, 440–1

HW advised Sir Horace Mann II to sue, 24. 82, 84

HW and Sir Edward Walpole not to take action over, 24. 316, 41. 380

HW and Sir Edward Walpole not to take out statute of lunacy for, 24. 294, 25. 126

HW and Sir Edward Walpole should be indifferent to, 24. 303, 376

HW and Sir Edward Walpole thanked by, for letting him break Houghton entail, 36. 163–5

HW and Sir Edward Walpole wish mother to take care of, 23. 470–1, 476, 481–2, 485–6

HW arranges affairs of, 5. 411n, 432n

HW as counsel for, must not betray his interests, 25. 565

HW asks if Mann has been paid by, for mother's tomb, 25. 427

HW asks leave of, to show Houghton, **32.** 313

HW as nominee of, cannot altogether side with Mozzi, **25.** 462

HW as referee for, cannot complain of lawyer's delays, **25.** 289

HW attempts to prevent, from sending militia to Norwich, **39.** 297–8

HW attends, **2.** 43n

HW became referee in Mozzi affair solely to save honour of, from public courts, **25.** 445

HW blamed by, for selling horses, **32.** 186n

HW busy with affairs of, **35.** 464

HW buys leasehold estates from executors of, **30.** 347

HW called on by, **23.** 551

HW cannot give Mozzi advice against, **25.** 298

HW condemns Lucas for advising, to contest mother's will, **25.** 315

HW consulted on epitaph by, for mother's monument, **25.** 195

HW consults Sharpe about, **23.** 496, 503, 545–6

HW declares to, that he will be motivated only by fairness, **25.** 217

HW declines financial supervision over, **32.** 355

HW desired by, to visit King's Lynn, **9.** 316

HW detained in London on business of, **41.** 262

HW disappointed in, **20.** 482, **23.** 121

HW dismissed by, **23.** 3–4, **25.** 172

HW distressed by insanity of, **30.** 266

HW does not approve of advice given to, by lawyers, **25.** 147

HW does not approve of contest of mother's will by, **25.** 216

HW does not care for, according to Selwyn, **30.** 266

HW does not covet fortune of, **25.** 125

HW does not reply to letter from, **25.** 247

HW does not wish to inform, of objections to mother's will, **25.** 125

HW, during difficulties over, says that Sir Edward Walpole seems the younger uncle, **24.** 529

HW entertains, at Harris wedding feast, **35.** 217

HW expects bad news of, **33.** 33

HW expects to be dropped as referee by, because of plain dealing, **25.** 184

HW fears, would object to Camden as referee, **25.** 216

HW forgets, as fast as possible, **24.** 440

HW formally asked to look after affairs of, **23.** 496

HW given no cause by, for tenderness, **24.** 372–3

HW glad that Mann did not force mother of, to discuss him, **24.** 320

HW has housed, at High Beech, **24.** 300

HW has probably offended, **25.** 477

HW heir to, **25.** 477n

HW ill-used by, **13.** 26

HW inquires for clergyman to live with, **16.** 171

HW invited by, to Houghton, **23.** 554, **36.** 163–4, 165

HW lacks influence with, **30.** 168

HW leaves, at Newmarket, **9.** 350

HW manages affairs of, **1.** 318, 324, **2.** 45, 55, 73, **5.** 395, 398, 404, 409, 415, **6.** 1, 6, 31–2, 439, 440, 446, **13.** 48–9, **23.** 494, 496–8, 503, 505, 510–11, 516, 521–2, 523, 529, 537, 540–1, 546, 548–9, 554, 560, 565, **24.** 3–4, 19, 294, 301, 307–8, **25.** 140, 143, 172, **28.** 92–4, 116, 143, **31.** 172, **32.** 118–19, 136–43, 158–9, 160, **35.** 416–17, **36.** 91–9, 104, 117–25, **39.** 172–3, **41.** 260–1, 264–6, 376, 378–80

HW may request place for, **38.** 146

HW meets lawyers of, **33.** 404

HW mentions, **9.** 278, **10.** 7, **37.** 418

HW might be summoned by, to King's Lynn, **40.** 113

HW misses, at Houghton, **9.** 350

HW not eager to advise, **25.** 195

HW notifies, of mother's death, **25.** 121, 122

HW offers moose-deer of, to Dr Hunter, **41.** 264–5

HW paid by, his legacy from Sir Robert Walpole, **25.** 637

HW persuades, to visit Court, **9.** 317

HW persuades lawyer, parson, and mistress of, to allow his removal to London, **36.** 118–19

HW pities, for his mother's behaviour, **20.** 439

HW praised by, in letter to mother, **36.** 202

HW praises, **17.** 450, **19.** 510–11, **20.** 6–7, 19, 247, 254

HW preaches to, **24.** 372–3

HW preoccupied with, **32.** 118

HW prevents doctors from separating Martha Turk from, **42.** 336

HW protests his good intentions towards, **14.** 205–6, 213–14

HW quotes from his reply to, **25.** 516

HW regrets claim made by, **25.** 519

HW relinquishes management of affairs of, **6.** 12, 14

HW's and Moone's retrenchments in affairs of, **36.** 97

HW's attempts to prevent ruin of, **30.** 168

HWs care for, repaid with slights, **34.** 130

HW's care twice saved life of, **42.** 335

HW's conduct towards, acknowledged in words but not in practice, **25.** 171–2

HW's correspondence from, notifying annual gift of pewit's eggs, **34.** 130

HW's correspondence with, **6.** 24, **13.** 26, **23.** 467, **25.** 121, 122, 124, 131, 140, 195, 247, 445, 516, **30.** 169n, **36.** 22, 23–7, 33–4, 36–7, 90, 104, 163–5, 190–1, 203, 206, 226, **40.** 60

HW's correspondence with mother about, **23.** 470, 472, 476, 477, 478, 485, 486, 487–8, 493, 495, 509, 512, 514–17, 519, 523, 524, 525, 529, 531–2, 534, 537, 541, 544, 545,

[Walpole, George (1730–91), continued]
548, 552, 557, 558, 560, 563, 24. 52, 58, 66, 70, 83

HW's doing good to, will compensate for his trouble, 35. 590

HW's economies for, at Houghton, 32. 136–43

HW sees, 41. 271

HW sells fen land inherited from, 34. 145

HW's ideas never approved by, or by his lawyers, 25. 315

HW's inheritance as heir-at-law to, 30. 344, 372

HW's letter about, seen and approved by Sir Edward Walpole, 23. 483

HW's letter condemning Sharpe and Lucas will not be shown to, 25. 315

HW's letter to, on St Michael election, 30. 169n

HW's letter to, with account of his political conduct, 13. 26

HW's narrative about proposed marriage of, to Miss Nicoll, 14. 193–214

HW's objections to entail discussed by, with great-uncle, 36. 29

HW's relations with, after mother's death, 25. 121, 122, 123–4, 126, 136–7, 147–8, 155–8, 164–5, 216, 315, 350–1, 511, 515

HW's sale of horses and dogs resented by, 23. 540, 552n

HW surprised that hot weather does not cause, to relapse, 24. 407

HW's visits to, at Houghton, 23. 560, 24. 295, 28. 138, 139, 36. 94–9, 124, 334

HW takes, to Vauxhall, 17. 450

HW takes house for, at Hampstead, 36. 333

HW tells Monro to quit, when it is time to do so, 24. 368

HW the sole administrator of affairs of, 41. 266

HW thinks as little as possible of, 24. 378

HW thinks claim of, wrong, 25. 265

HW to accompany, to Houghton, 32. 190

HW to act justly towards, 25. 289

HW to ask, for ticket for Hardinge to ride in St James's Park, 35. 549, 550

HW to get heirs' consent for managing affairs of, 36. 93–4

HW to meet lawyers of, 33. 372

HW to seek Camden's and Conway's advice about, 25. 125

HW to sign compact with, 28. 445

HW to visit, 6. 27

HW to write to, at Houghton, 36. 34

HW tries to dislodge parasites of, 24. 320

HW tries to dissuade, from entail arrangement, 36. 25–7, 32, 300

HW unable to save, from violent conveyance to Houghton, 42. 344

HW undertakes management of affairs of, 13. 48–9

HW urges, to trust Grafton and T. Townshend more than great-uncle, 36. 27

HW visits, at Houghton, 23. 560, 24. 295, 28. 138, 139, 36. 94–9, 124, 334

HW will not again go to, except in London, 24. 296

HW will not assume title of, till after his burial, 16. 248

HW will not pay for serving, 24. 311

HW will not trouble himself about, 24. 502

HW wishes to keep mother on good terms with, 23. 557

habits of: eating and drinking excessively, 36. 334; injurious to his health, 36. 124; intemperate, 23. 560; intemperate in diet and conduct, 28. 139

Hamilton's interference in boroughs of, displeases HW, 23. 548

Hampstead house occupied by, 23. 495

Hasty Productions by: 34. 85n, 43. 153; epitaph in, 32. 179n

hawking patronized by, 34. 146

health of: apothecary, mistress, and physician predict continuance of insanity, 24. 294; Beevor says, is better, 24. 296; better, 32. 210; engrosses HW's time, 41. 254; eruption, 23. 460; fall from horse, 42. 333n; fever, 24. 293, 34. 130, 137, 36. 124, 335, 336; fever and delirium, 42. 333–4, 335; fever and flux, 36. 120–1; gout, 32. 192; HW hopes for recovery of, 41. 380; ill, 20. 273, 32. 121, 355; insanity, 1. 298–9, 301, 324, 347–8, 2. 43n, 45–6, 49, 55, 73, 170, 5. 321, 326–7, 360, 371n, 6. 437, 438, 12. 94, 95, 15. 135, 136, 324, 23. 460–1, 463, 467, 468, 471, 472, 476, 482, 485, 488–90, 492–3, 495, 505, 521, 529, 24. 293–6, 324, 327, 330, 332, 349, 25. 137, 28. 93, 96, 101, 130, 305–6, 312, (?) 31. 208, 32. 349–50, 34. 30, 129–30, 132, 206, 36. 93–9, 117–25, 331–6, 39. 171–3, 176, 41. 260–1, 364, 367, 43. 367; insanity caused by quack medicines, 13. 48, 49; insanity feared, 33. 59; insanity of, a warning against marriage into insane families, 25. 424n; insanity pronounced incurable by Drs Jebb and Battie, 25. 126; insanity returns, 13. 50; itch, 5. 329n; keeper cures, with apothecary's draught, 24. 372; lame leg, 39. 389; last illness, 36. 279, 336; malady induces contradictory conduct, 25. 195; no better, 32. 365; not well, 32. 97; perfectly well, 41. 271; putrid fever, 42. 343; recovers, 1. 326, 347, 2. 73, 74–5, 5. 403, 6. 4, 8, 14, 17, 24, 7. 38, 23. 539–41, 544, 546, 548, 554, 560, 563, 565, 24. 367, 372, 28. 126, 134, 139, 380, 32. 175, 179, 184, 186, 188, 212, 35. 416, 417, 36. 123–4, 334, 336; recovery of, keeps HW from bothering with elections, 24. 38; recovery of, Mann thinks indicated, 25. 156; relapse expected by, 24. 372; reports of, favourable, 32. 93; seems sinking into idiocy, 32. 368; supposed recovery of, doubted by HW, 25. 195–6; swelled leg may drain head, 25. 266; urinates unconsciously, **36**. 122; worse, **32**. 118

Hertford, E. of, may be shooting with, in Norfolk, **36**. 87

—— 's letter to George III asking that HW's correspondence with, be kept, **39**. 542

—— 's proposed letter to, **39**. 192

High Beech suggested as place for, **36**. 121

Hoare accepts Mozzi's order to pay, **25**. 509, 511

honourable intentions of, foiled by bad advisers, **25**. 181

horse needed for, **15**. 327

horses of: sold, **32**. 131, 133–5, **36**. 95; to be sold, **39**. 171, **41**. 266

Houghton altered by, **36**. 163

—— being refurnished by, with modern pictures, **25**. 247, 316

—— decorated by, with 'scratches,' **25**. 247

—— destroyed by, **25**. 195

—— has relics of madness of, **34**. 206

—— made security by, for £20,000 loan, **15**. 332

—— plundered by, **25**. 132

—— ruined by, **9**. 349

—— seat of, **5**. 391

—— 's exterior 'improved' by, **24**. 427–8

—— 's pictures must be preserved by, **20**. 268

—— 's pictures not prized by, **21**. 208, **25**. 418

—— 's pictures sold by, **2**. 145–6, 171, 192, 257, **13**. 17n, **24**. 427–8, 434, 440–1, 451, 502, 541, **25**. 108, 121, 133, 164, 247, 316, 418, **33**. 86, 486

—— 's sale contemplated by, **20**. 265

house of: in Dover St, **25**. 555n; in Green St, Grosvenor Sq., **32**. 179n; *see also* Eriswell; High Beech; Houghton

Hull, Mayor of, thanks, because his militia begot so many children there, **25**. 355

Hyde and St James's Parks neglected by, **23**. 482n

illness of, reveals human perfidy, **35**. 347

indifference of, **23**. 230

indolence and inattention of, **20**. 418

ingratitude of, towards HW, innocently increased by Mann, **25**. 136–7

inn on Newmarket road visited by, **23**. 460

in the country, **24**. 17

James, Dr, advises, **36**. 332

—— treats, **23**. 460

Jebb, Dr, attends, at Eriswell, **24**. 294

—— treats, **23**. 495, 540, **24**. 294, **25**. 126

jockeys and grooms help ruin estate of, **23**. 511

Knight recommended by, to Mann, **19**. 462

laws of coursing prepared by, for Catherine II, **33**. 312

lawyers of: **41**. 271; delay settlement of affairs with Mozzi, **25**. 161; do not communicate with HW, **25**. 265; may be quickened by Mozzi's presence, **25**. 307; object to Duane as referee, **25**. 235; *see also* Cony, Carlos; Lucas, Charles

letters written by, on recovery, **23**. 539

London never visited by, except to fulfil duties of, in Bedchamber, **25**. 226

—— visited by, **9**. 317

Lucas and Sharpe would probably favour, **25**. 421–2

Lucas delays in transmitting demands of, upon Mozzi, **25**. 172

—— expects, will consent to Duane as referee, **25**. 216

—— instigated, to contest mother's will, **25**. 310, 510

—— may seek approval of, for Duane's nomination, **25**. 216, 217

—— profits by indolence of, **25**. 456

—— reproved by, for delay, **25**. 168, 181

—— 's apparent zeal in cause of, well paid, **25**. 200

—— says, has claims on his mother, **25**. 143

—— , the emissary of, **25**. 227

—— to be tossed in blanket by, **25**. 322, 328

—— to visit, **25**. 286

—— to warn, against acquiescing in mother's will, **25**. 126

—— to write to, **25**. 472

Mackreth brought into Parliament by, **28**. 173

—— named by, in will, **32**. 212n

—— said to have lent money to mother of, thereby becoming M.P. for Castle Rising, **24**. 53n, **42**. 344n

—— unfortunate associate for, **32**. 215

'madman excited by rascals,' **33**. 86

madness of: does not terminate his Bedchamber appointment, **36**. 187; exposes him to malice, **32**. 215

major-general's rank demanded by, **24**. 372

Mann confers with mother about, **23**. 468, 500–1, 503, 515–16, 517, **24**. 17, 318, 353, 368, 376

—— encloses letter for, **25**. 226

—— has no connection with, **25**. 136

—— hopes physique of, will be better than Gardiner's, **18**. 507

—— hopes that HW will not ruin his health taking care of, **24**. 303

—— never mentions, to his mother, **24**. 23

—— not to complain about, to mother, **24**. 47

—— paid by, for mother's tomb, **25**. 436

—— pleased at HW's changed opinion of, **20**. 6–7, 26

—— receives letter from: about Cts of Orford's papers, **25**. 163, 181; about monument, **25**. 219

—— sends drawing to, of mother's monument, **25**. 350

—— to inform Mozzi of inheritance of, **25**. 126

—— to receive mourning ring from, **25**. 124, 206

—— urges HW to forget, **24**. 513

[Walpole, George (1730–91), *continued*]
—— will obey commands of: **25.** 137; concerning mother's monument, **25.** 206
—— wishes HW to explain to, about arms for mother's monument, **25.** 240
—— writes to, **25.** 163
Mann, Horace II, corresponds with, concerning father's debts, **25.** 148, 155, 158
——'s bond from, **24.** 78
—— sues, **24.** 82, 84
Mann family fortunes involved in those of, **20.** 250, **23.** 496
marriage might improve finances of, **20.** 250
marriage not desired by, **14.** 222
marriage of, to Miss Nicoll, prevented by great-uncle, **23.** 367
marriage plans for, **9.** 140n, **12.** 181n, **14.** 193–214
Martinelli's letter to, **25.** 553n, 554–5
men, lions, and weapons desired by, when he was a child, **37.** 73
militia fed by, with onions, **25.** 11
militia led by Windham under, **25.** 11n
militia of, clash with smugglers near Southwold, **39.** 304
militia plagued by, **24.** 451
militia recruits rejected by, for physical defects, **24.** 378n
militia should not be commanded by, because of uncertain health, **39.** 298
militia taken by: to Hull, **25.** 355; to Portsmouth, **21.** 300
militia to be commanded by, **24.** 372
mistress of, *see* Turk, Martha
Molineux aided by, to become M.P., **39.** 96n
Monro diagnoses condition of, **24.** 316
—— praised by, to Martha Turk, **24.** 372
—— reports recovery of, to HW, **24.** 367–8
Montagu reports bad company kept by, **9.** 78
——'s opinion of, **9.** 352
monument to be erected by, to mother, **25.** 195, 213, 219
Moone to approach, about borough for Hon. Henry Seymour-Conway, **39.** 192
Morice is HW's fellow-labourer in affairs of, **25.** 171
mother and grandmother slighted by, **20.** 482
mother and HW unable to rescue, from scoundrels, **24.** 58
mother avoided by, **23.** 224
mother cannot disinherit, **20.** 433
mother condemns: for ingratitude to HW and to her, **24.** 57; for lack of taste in Latin and Greek, **20.** 481
mother corresponds with Sharpe about, **23.** 464, 472, 476, 486, 491–4, 501, 503, 509–10, 514, 516, 525, 548, **24.** 57
mother describes, to Mrs Richmond, **19.** 192
mother fears that recovery of, will not be lasting, **24.** 376
mother gives, power over her boroughs, **24.** 46
mother leaves, to care of HW and Sir Edward

Walpole, **23.** 464, 487–8, 492–3, 496, 514, **24.** 305
mother likes, though continuing to rob him, **20.** 247
mother may meet, in England, **24.** 121
mother may not know condition of, **24.** 330
mother may take, to Italy, **20.** 247
mother neglected by, during lifetime, but now to be honoured by monument, **25.** 195
mother neglects, **5.** 360
mother never inquires after, **24.** 322, 347, 374
mother never inspired by, to tenderness, **24.** 376
mother not to know of HW's break with, **24.** 17
mother resembled by, **17.** 450
mother ruins estate of, **20.** 239
mother's affairs to be honourably settled by, **25.** 144
mother's bequest to Mozzi contested by, **36.** 202
mother's claims on, presented in 'case,' **25.** 162
mother's correspondence with, **23.** 558–9, **24.** 541–2, **25.** 180
mother's correspondence with Mann about, **23.** 472, 476–8, 487, 534, 541, 544, 545, 552, 558, **24.** 305
mother's death brings great estate to, **2.** 257, **25.** 125, 158
mother's death may restore fortunes of, **36.** 99
mother's disposition in favour of Mozzi approved by, **25.** 168, 181
mother sees, **23.** 230
mother's estate and jointure inherited by, **25.** 125
mother's estate to be given to Rolle family by, **25.** 148, 156
mother should have left money in London to, Sharpe thinks, **25.** 154–5
mother should sacrifice jointure to, instead of demanding arrears, **20.** 486
mother shows concern for, **20.** 479, 481, 486
mother slighted by, **20.** 482
mother's memory respected by, **25.** 168
mother's monument erected by, **33.** 300
mother's monument may be forgotten by, because HW did not oppose it, **25.** 213
mother's monument to be superintended by Mann for, **25.** 195, 345, 350
mother's perishable property hardly of interest to, Mann thinks, **25.** 169
mother's portrait should not be given by, to Mozzi, **25.** 502
mother spreads bad reports about, **9.** 78
mother's relationship to Ferrers respected by, **9.** 279
mother's will not to be disputed by, **25.** 124, 172
mother's will omits name of, **25.** 120, 122
mother too far away to aid, **23.** 460

mother wishes Pringle to examine, **23**. 488

mother wounds, by her misconduct, **19**. 39

mourning rings for, **42**. 338n

mourning rings for mother, to be presented by, to his uncles and Mann, **25**. 124

Mozzi advised to divide sum equally with, **25**. 419

—— assured by, of satisfaction, **25**. 181

—— authorizes payment to, by Hoare, **25**. 498, 504

—— favoured by HW over, **25**. 265

—— gives 'Clinton's' portrait to, **25**. 298n

—— imprudently irritates lawyers of, **25**. 216

—— might be unpopular in England for getting inheritance away from, **25**. 396, 404

—— ought to be considerately treated by, **25**. 147

—— receives release from, through Mann, **25**. 527

——'s business with, to be settled when mother's will is proved, **25**. 167

——'s conduct pleases, **25**. 156

——'s correspondence with, **25**. 176, 186, 300, 301–2, 319, 322, 328, 330

—— sends list to, of things taken to Italy by his mother, **25**. 151, 156

——'s negotiations with, over mother's bequests, **25**. 144, 158, 161, 163, 166–7, 335, 439–41, 444–7, 448, 471–2, 495, 498, 504, 509–11, **33**. 274, 281, 288, 300, 302, 452

—— to pay, through Hoare, **25**. 492

—— to send HW a list of mother's demands on, **25**. 158

—— turns mother of, from going from Calais to England to meet him, **23**. 158

mutual entail of, with uncle, contested by HW, **36**. 27–32, 295–304

'my sage nephew,' **33**. 312

Newcastle, D. of, tells, of intended resignation, **30**. 128

Newmarket and the country, principal haunts of, **30**. 167n

Newmarket visited by, **9**. 350

New Park, Richmond, visited by, in holidays, **18**. 70

Nicoll, Margaret, brought to meet, at the Cockpit, **14**. 223

—— does not attract, **14**. 200

—— rejected by, **13**. 23–4, **14**. 57, **20**. 256–7, 262, 265, 273, 278, 425, 431, 435, **21**. 285, **24**. 301, **30**. 168n, **36**. 298, **37**. 321

Norford, Dr, prevents removal of, to Houghton, **42**. 342–3, 356

—— unpaid for attendance on, **42**. 355–6

North administration supported by, **25**. 266

North's letter to: about Parks rangership, **36**. 158; enclosed to HW, **41**. 378–9

Norwich suburbs ordered by, to be burnt in case of invasion, **34**. 48

Orford deeds sought by, **25**. 160

Orford jointure deficiency possibly under scrutiny by, **25**. 176

Ossory, Lord, friend of, **32**. 158

Oxenden reputed father of, **15**. 324

parents' intercourse restricted after birth of, **19**. 203

Parliamentary bill to be introduced by, **33**. 69

Parks rangerships of: **43**. 347, 348, 366, 374; Moone's services to, **43**. 367; to be regulated by his servants, **36**. 158; to be taken away from him, **25**. 266

parsonage rented by, at Eriswell near Barton Mills, **24**. 293

paternity of, dubious, **15**. 324, **23**. 548–9, **25**. 132

Paxton presented by, to livings, **40**. 39n

physicians despised by, **24**. 294

physicians of: listed, **42**. 336n; must be discharged, **28**. 126, 130; (?) reported by Penneck to have advised him to part with housekeeper, **15**. 333; want his friends kept away from him, **23**. 482

Piddletown manor left by, to Martha Turk, **25**. 148n

Piddletown visited by, **25**. 227

planned to leave estates away from HW, **34**. 137

plovers' eggs annually sent to HW by, **25**. 143

pointers of, wanted by Townshend, **41**. 261

politics rarely concern, **30**. 167n

portrait claimed by, allegedly that of a Clinton, **25**. 240

'posthumous piety' of, **25**. 227

races frequented by, **9**. 92n, **38**. 95

'recovery' of, shown by marching to Norwich at head of militia, **34**. 47

regimental costume of, **9**. 241

rents of mother's estates collected by, **25**. 144

resigns as groom of the Bedchamber, **25**. 266

Reynolds offers to buy picture from, **2**. 170n

ring for Mann probably forgotten by, **25**. 206

Rockingham's turkey-geese match with, **21**. 7

rogues beset, **39**. 490

Rolle estate and Walpole estate inherited by, with power to cut off entail, **25**. 164n

Rolle family's Dorsetshire estate might be sold by, **25**. 148

ruined, **20**. 238–9

sailing taken up by, **24**. 38

sale of horses of, **32**. 131, 133–5

sale of Houghton pictures by, declared necessary to pay uncles' fortunes, but they are unpaid, **25**. 316

Sandwich temporarily replaces, in Parks rangerships, **25**. 266n

satisfied with respect to mother's jewels, **25**. 168

Saturday Club and, **43**. 185

secretary of militia compelled by, to read Statius aloud, **24**. 295

servants of: conceal illness, **34**. 130; persist in pilfering, **24**. 521

Sharpe laments conduct of, **24**. 53

[Walpole, George (1730–91), *continued*]
—'s expresses about borough elections unanswered by, 24. 46
—— surprised by Mozzi's employment of him despite connection with, 25. 320, 333
—— thinks Mozzi should divide mother's money in England with, 25. 154–5, 157, 160, 217, 335, 426
—— would probably favour, 25. 421–2
Sherman, Thomas, acquainted with, 29. 228
Shirley, Sewallis, allowed by, to negotiate Parks position, 36. 158
—'s portrait perhaps claimed by, 25. 227
Skrine and Boone chosen by, to represent his boroughs, 24. 46–7
Skrine desired by, to act as agent in affair with Mozzi, 25. 163–4
—— obligated to, 25. 158
—— partial to, 25. 166
sporting interests of, 2. 8
squanders money on whores and parasites, 24. 513
stepgrandfather's death benefits, 36. 47
steward of, from London, 32. 349; *see also* Moone, William; Withers, William
Suckling's legacy to, 36. 162
suicidal attempts of, 23. 495, 505, 24. 293–4, 28. 96
sullen and calm, 28. 315
sum to be claimed by, from Mozzi, may have been settled in advance by lawyers, 25. 335
Swaffham Coursing Society founded by, 42. 333n
sycophants of: divert him from pursuing just thoughts, 25. 148; impertinent to HW, 25. 143; incite him to affront HW, 25. 509; keep outsiders away from him, 25. 137; prejudice him against HW, 25. 125; sow mistrust against uncles, 24. 342–3; 'vultures,' 23. 521; would just have stolen more had his mother died earlier, 25. 108
thoughtless, 20. 26
thoughtlessness and folly of, 14. 70
to go into the country, 23. 551–2
Townshend, George, caricatures, 43. 365
—— condoles with HW on illness of, 42. 332–3
——, Fox's enemy, governs, 30. 169n
Trefusis heir to, in Devonshire, 42. 377
Turin post coveted by, 20. 420n
Turin post declined by, 21. 206
Turin post once requested by, 21. 195, 206
Turk, Martha, and, 43. 151
—— converses with, 36. 122, 124–5
—— has slept with for 20 years, 24. 295
—— joins forehead to, at table in evening, 24. 295
—'s death brings on fever of, 42. 333
—— the Delilah of, 24. 372
—— with, 36. 335
uncles do not covet estate of, 25. 125
uncles' legacies not paid by, after his mother's death, 25. 316, 322–3

uncles' legacies to be paid by, 33. 62
uncles not expected by, to press for payment of their legacies lest they be disinherited, 25. 316, 322–3
uncles' relations with, 23. 461
uncles said to be disinherited by, 23. 496, 25. 477
uncles' tender and disinterested care of, 36. 123
Van Dyck allegedly painted 'Clinton' portrait sent to, 25. 501
'very political,' 39. 221
Walpole, Sir Edward, heir to, 7. 1
—— neglects, 5. 374, 6. 438
Walpole, Horatio (1678–1757), defends his conduct towards, 14. 222–3
—— informs, of quarrel with HW, 13. 217–18
—— lends money to, 36. 296n
—— persuades, to alter settlement of estate, 13. 26
—— reports to HW on attitude of, towards Miss Nicoll, 14. 214–15
Walpole, Horatio (1723–1809), receives angry letter from, about footman, 25. 355
Walpole, Horatio (1752–1822), invites, to be his son's godfather, 25. 418
—— should be heir to, 25. 132
—— with wife invited by, to Houghton in 'frantic' letter, 25. 418
Walpole, Hon. Thomas, nominated by, at Ashburton, 30. 169
whispers to country gentlemen at Houghton, 24. 295
'wild boy,' 19. 496, 20. 26
will of: Cholmondeley-Walpole litigation over, 36. 296n, 297n; HW content with provisions of, 33. 134; HW not to influence, 25. 164; Moone witnesses, 32. 135n; to be read at Houghton, 42. 339
wills of, contradictory, 15. 323–4, 16. 313n, 32. 135n
Windham will not be surprised at conduct of, 25. 11
wishes to make campaign with milita, 2. 75, 77
Withers receives letter from, 24. 367
Wodehouse asks, not to quarter militia at Norwich, 39. 297–8
world believes, to be in his senses, 24. 46
Zincke's portrait of his mother left to, to do as he pleases, 25. 504
Walpole, Hon. George (1758–1835), son of 2d Bn Walpole of Wolterton:
Du Deffand, Mme, discusses, with Hon. Thomas Walpole, 5. 94
Walpole, Hon. Henrietta Louisa (1731–1824), dau. of 1st Bn Walpole of Wolterton:
father now willing to disinherit, 36. 298
(?) HW entertains, at dinner, at SH, 11. 108
mother's bequest to, 36. 210
not handsome, 36. 298
parents unwilling to cut off, by entail, 36. 31, 296

Walpole, Sir Henry de (d. before 1311):
a knight, **15**. 1n
son of, **15**. 1n
widow of, remarries, **1**. 375n, 384, **2**. 3
Walpole, Sir Henry de (fl. 14th cent.):
a knight, **15**. 1n
Walpole, Henry de (fl. 1408):
Calthorpe trustee of, **1**. 33n
Walpole, Henry (d. 1442):
bequest of, **15**. 25
Walpole, Henry (16th cent.):
HW's ancestor, **1**. 376n
Walpole, Col. Horatio (1663–1717), uncle of Sir Robert Walpole:
gift from, as Horace Mann's godfather, **25**. 656n
marries Coke's grandmother, **34**. 38n
Walpole, Horatio (Horace) (1678–1757), cr. (1756) Bn Walpole of Wolterton; diplomatist; M.P.; HW's uncle:
account by, of his case of the stone: (?) Beauvau to have, **7**. 417; Choiseul receives, **4**. 114, 119, 133; Du Deffand, Mme, discusses, with Hon. Thomas Walpole, **4**. 135–6; read before Royal Society, **19**. 510n
Addison, Leonard, a 'creature' of, **14**. 90
ambassador to France, **4**. 119n, **9**. 116n, **31**. 65
ambition and dirt of, **20**. 556
Amigoni and Astley paint family of, **20**. 341–2
Amsterdam gazette attributes naval investigation proposal to, **18**. 427
Answer to the Latter Part of Lord Bolingbroke's Letters on the Study of History by, printed posthumously, **20**. 62n
anecdote of Onslow and, **30**. 301n
anecdote of Spanish ambassador and, **29**. 1
Anson's 'Aquapulca triumph' might please, **30**. 53–4
Appendix by, to Dr Whytt's essay, *see above under* account by, of his case of the stone
avarice and dirt of, **9**. 187, **20**. 42, 81, **21**. 56–7, 62, **30**. 53–4
avarice of, **20**. 42, 81, **21**. 56–7, 62, **30**. 53–4
bathing and fires avoided by, **18**. 47
boasts jokingly about son, **19**. 168
Bolingbroke's *Letters* to be answered by, **20**. 62, 76
breeches shrugged by, **17**. 484
'broken with age and infirmities,' **14**. 197
brother advised by, to decline pension, **17**. 329n, **18**. 465
brother fetched by, from Houghton to Chelsea, **17**. 386
brother imitated by, **19**. 469
brother not allowed by, to visit Ranelagh, **18**. 8
brother of, **30**. 301n
brother put, under obligations, **36**. 28, 30, 295, 297, 298
brother refers to, for facts, **17**. 243n

brother's estate to be diverted by, from brother's grandchildren, **21**. 52
brother's plan for mutual entail rejected by, **36**. 30, 295–6
brother urged by, to resign, **17**. 319
buffoonery of, **9**. 131
Case of the Hessian Forces by, (?) Beauvau to have, **7**. 417
Castle Rising might be borough of, **36**. 14
Cavendish family supports, in breach with HW, **10**. 46
chaplain of, may be critical of HW, **35**. 107
Chesterfield not likely to be more successful than, in Dutch negotiations, **19**. 68
Chetwynd's duel with, **18**. 191–2, 207
childish, **21**. 52
children of, liked by 3d E. of Orford, **36**. 24
Chute blackens character of, **14**. 232
—— tells Miss Nicoll of supposed plot by, **14**. 220
classic commonplaces in praise of *felices agricolæ* quoted by, **30**. 72
cleanliness and warmth avoided by, **18**. 47n
Cleland dismissed by, **35**. 94
Common Sense prints satire on, **17**. 469–70
conduct of, in Nicoll affair, **14**. 57, 193–233
conundrum on Teller's and Auditor's places held by, **19**. 28
Coxe's memoirs of, HW consulted about, **12**. 180–1
cured at 75, **20**. 291
daughters not handsome, now disinherited by, **36**. 298
death of: **21**. 56; vacates son's seat in House of Commons, **36**. 33; would have left 3d E. of Orford hampered by entail, **36**. 25
descendant of, also a descendant of his brother, **25**. 418
Devonshire, D. of, fails to get peerage for son of, **20**. 66–7
drams addressed to, by mistake, **19**. 238
Dresden treaty spoken against but voted for by, **20**. 299n
Dutch gazette read by, **30**. 72
Earle seconded by, **17**. 243
Edinburgh capture reported by, to HW, **19**. 108
embassy of, to Paris, **9**. 116n
entail proposed by, to brother, **15**. 323
entail rejected by, because it omits his daughters, **36**. 31
Etough gets 'lies' about HW from, **40**. 69–70
Fox, Henry, discusses motto with, **35**. 93
Frederick II criticized by, **30**. 72
Frederick, P. of Wales, to be attended by, at levee, **17**. 338, 369
French politics and Fleury influenced by, **33**. 439n
George II said to call, 'a dirty buffoon,' **17**. 243n
Gower's stormy correspondence with, **20**. 563
grandson of: **15**. 325n; Orford, 3d E. of, bound to make, his heir, **25**. 132

[Walpole, Horatio (1678–1757), *continued*]

Gray hopes that highwayman's attack was upon, and not upon HW, 14. 42

HW advises Mann to write to, 19. 484

HW calls: 'old buffoon,' 19. 469; very indifferent character, 15. 323

HW cites, as authority for story about Marlborough, 28. 387

HW confused with, 3. 107n

HW discusses, with Mrs Hayes, 31. 65

HW has cut all acquaintance with, since Nicoll affair, 20. 425

HW hates, 35. 158

HW imagines sister's conversation with ghost of, 9. 351

HW mentions (?) cook of, 35. 65

HW not found very tractable by, 24. 458

HW opposed by, in House of Commons, 13. 20

HW receives marriage settlements from, 20. 250

HW's angry scene with, 14. 204–5

HW's correspondence with, 14. 203–4, 205, 217–18, 36. 10–13, 22–3, 27–32

HW's dislike of, 15. 326

HW's fondness for London and business surprises, 30. 72

HW's godfather, 13. 3

HW's namesake, 28. 433

HW's narrative about Nicoll affair should stay unpublished because of, 20. 278

HW's neglect from nephews should please, 23. 367

HW's obituary of Anthony Chute will be read by, in newspapers, 35. 84

HW's objections to entail discussed by, with 3d E. of Orford, 36. 29

HW's political thermometer, 17. 467

HW's prejudice against, 12. 18

HW's quarrels with, 13. 23, 26–7, 14. 57, 193–233, 17. 243n, 21. 31n, 30. 168n

HW's relations with, 9. 156, 186–7, 351

HW tells, that he looks as if on his way to Aix-la-Chapelle, 18. 305

HW tells nephew to avoid transactions with, 36. 27

HW to speak to, again, about Mann's theory regarding Young Pretender, 19. 210

HW unshocked by Stair's ridicule of, 30. 54

Hartington favours, in Nicoll affair, 35. 160n

health of: bed-ridden, 19. 504; better, 19. 510; going off, 19. 496; mended by soap and lime-water, 19. 510n, 20. 3; stone, the, cured by Dr Whytt, 4. 114n, 19. 510n

Hervey calls, 'a good treaty-dictionary,' 17. 243n

—— does not thank, 9. 116

Hessian and Russian treaties opposed by, 35. 88

Hill courted by, 9. 153

—— leaves nothing to, 9. 153

Houghton visited by, 18. 305, 30. 72

house of, at Wolterton, visited and described by HW, 18. 47

House of Commons cannot spare, 19. 469

—— tells, to 'withdraw,' 17. 431

impeachment of, drawn up, 17. 336, 344

Impostor Detected, The, may have been written by, 20. 62n

indefatigable and healthy, 20. 250

(?) Legge mentions, 37. 424

Leheup brother-in-law to, 19. 111n

longevity of, 9. 186

Magnan not heartily recommended by, 18. 563–4

—— said to be protégé of, 18. 548–9

—— writes to, 18. 549, 563

Malpas, Vct, protests to, over entail of Orford estates, 36. 300–4

Mann aided by, in seeking salary arrears, 19. 474, 21. 483

—— congratulates, on son's wedding, 20. 22

—— defends, 17. 491

—— has seen, 18. 70

—— obtains expense arrears through, 19. 220

——'s correspondence with, 20. 22, 24–5, 419n

——'s godfather, 17. 491n, 20. 419n

——'s memorial to George II drawn up by, 20. 195n

—— thinks, should be prime minister, 20. 419, 425, 431

—— to send orange flower water and dried orange flowers to, 20. 255

Mann, Robert, 'baited' by, to provide for Horace Mann, 18. 308

Middleton's life of Cicero subscribed to by, 15. 7n

motto for: 15. 326; choice of, may arouse HW's ridicule, 35. 93

negotiations of, 33. 302

nephew's estate aided by efforts of, 20. 250, 255

Newcastle, D. of, accused by, of obstructing Mann's appointment, 43. 233

—— approached by, about Mann's salary arrears, 19. 474

—— asked by, to conceal rumour of sham Pretender, 19. 174, 199

—— attacked by, 19. 474n

—— informs, of George II's intention of making him a peer, 21. 56n

Norwich election expenses mortify, 21. 56

notes by, on HW's letter to Capper, 14. 221–4

orange flower water liked by, 19. 330, 20. 255

Orford, 2d E. of, corresponds with, 36. 10

——'s losses could be alleviated by, 14. 50

Orford, 3d E. of, arranges mutual entail with, 36. 24–32, 296–304

—— borrows from, 36. 296n

—— cheated by, of marrying an heiress, 20. 273, 23. 367

—— obligated to, 36. 24

—— said to regret mutual entail with, 36. 31

——'s appointment to Bedchamber pressed by, 20. 470n

——'s financial dealings with, **15**. 323

—— told to take advice of, **36**. 297

Orford entail broken by, defrauding brother's descendants, **23**. 367

Parliamentary Address debated by, **37**. 415

Parliamentary debate by, on privately-raised regiments, **26**. 16

Parliamentary speeches by: called 'Dutch piece,' **37**. 470; his first since brother's fall, **17**. 467; on Aix treaty, **20**. 3; on Dresden treaty, **42**. 494–5; on renewing regiments, **40**. 50

'parts' of, decay, **42**. 495

peerage given to, **17**. 469n, **20**. 556, 563, **35**. 275

peerage rumoured for, **17**. 430–1, 469–70, **19**. 478, **20**. 3

peerage title of, shows he expects Walpole estates, **36**. 300

Pelham, Lady Catherine, to receive orange flower water from, **19**. 330

Pelham, Henry, intimate friend and admirer of, **20**. 420n

Pitt (Chatham) attacked by, over naval appropriations, **19**. 168–9

—— connected with, **35**. 88n

—— rebuked by, for forwardness, **2**. 205

—— thanked by, **19**. 371

play-bill satirizes, **13**. 76n

Pope, Alexander, suppresses poem at wish of, **9**. 116

Ranelagh visited by, with HW, **19**. 371

Receipt to Make a Lord written about, **17**. 469–70

Sandwich's connection with Old Pretender told by, to Pelham, **17**. 231n

saying by, about dogs, **33**. 281

settlements made by, at son's wedding, **19**. 469

Shaw's edition of Bacon dedicated to, **37**. 294n

Shenstone's anecdote of, **1**. 165

sides with HW, **13**. 3n

soap 'mends,' **20**. 3

son; sons of: **2**. 192n, **4**. 133n, **11**. 27n, 97n, **19**. 414n, 469n, **23**. 141n, **25**. 410n

son's horses put to grass in New Park by, **18**. 70

son succeeds, **13**. 27n

Spanish ambassador and, **29**. 1

Stair ridicules, by naming dog after him, **30**. 54–5

'stumping along,' **18**. 305

tailor in Drury Lane farce resembles, **20**. 342

Tower of London rumoured to become prison of, **17**. 299

treaty with Saxony opposed by, in Parliament, **20**. 300, 304–5

unjust uncle, **23**. 497

Voltaire used to know, **41**. 146

Walpole, Hon. Thomas, to be set up by, against Bacon for Norwich, **21**. 56n

whist parties sought by, **20**. 250

Whytt, Dr, cures, of the stone, **19**. 510n

wife of: **9**. 153; called 'Pug,' **18**. 47n

wig snatched off by, to show his gray hair, **19**. 169

William IV of Orange escorted by, **36**. 4n

Williams, Sir C. H., satirizes, in 'Peter and My Lord Quidam,' **30**. 317

Winnington's speech frightens, **17**. 484

witticism by, on Perceval and Edwin, **17**. 272

Walpole, Hon. Horatio (1717–97), ('Horace'; 'Horry'; 'Celadon'; HW), 4th E. of Orford, 1791; M.P.:

acquaintances of, are a few retired elderly folk, **25**. 542

affectations of, joked about by him, **30**. 86

age, old, of: **15**. 133, 138, 142, 144, 151, 154, 165, 185–6, 192, 214, 218, 223, 228, 234, 242, 247, 249, 268, 272, 343, 344, **32**. 4, 37, 43, 53, 66, 103, 238, 316, 320–1, 326, **33**. 117; afraid of being called 'old fool,' **32**. 320; 'almost century of experience,' **12**. 130; 'almost superannuated,' **31**. 356; 'ancient,' **11**. 41, **12**. 33; 'antediluvian,' **12**. 5, 74,; 'an old patriarch,' **32**. 382; 'antique swain,' **32**. 21; 'antiquity and decay,' **33**. 311; a year younger than he thought, **32**. 232; baptized as 'the old HW,' **33**. 227; compared to Berrys, **11**. 60, 181, 330, **12**. 108, 159; compared to Cardigan's, **11**. 242; compared to D. of Clarence's, **11**. 164; compared to Ligonier's, **31**. 8; contemporaries outlived by, **12**. 120; discussed, **11**. 249, 362; divorced from 'young and active world,' **32**. 295; does not diminish love and esteem for those he loves, **31**. 374; 'eight and forty,' **31**. 71; 'elderly Arcadian,' **32**. 114; expects further decay, **33**. 374; fears growing superannuated, **33**. 584; 'forlorn antique,' **11**. 59; French Revolution embitters, **31**. 380; grows quietly old, **32**. 29; has few encumbrances but the gout, **31**. 305; has outlived many of his intimates, **30**. 279; hates to grow old, **32**. 27; infirmities caused by, **12**. 85, 184, 197; 'in the dregs of life,' **11**. 171; just infirm enough to enjoy the prerogatives of old age, **31**. 305; 'lame old Colin,' **11**. 16; 'lame old creature,' **33**. 333; lives to the length of an epic poem, **34**. 14; makes him lazy, **31**. 283; memory failing, **33**. 576–7, **34**. 18, 85, 116; Methusalem, **11**. 51, 67, 364, **31**. 364, **32**. 233, 249, 295, **33**. 130, 389, 452, **34**. 205, 207, 231; middling parts decayed, **31**. 270; mouldering like the joist of an old mansion, **33**. 120; old age marks him for her own, **30**. 272; old and decrepit, **11**. 105; old and lame, **31**. 170; 'old man of the mountain,' **31**. 251; pain to be expected, **12**. 184; 'poor worn-out rag,' **31**. 42; prevents him from visiting Dickensons, **31**. 345; proclaimed by him, **7**. 127, 129; reached by contradicting all advice, **31**. 380; recovery from rheumatism slowed by, **11**. 174; 'rich old alderman,' **33**. 67; short time left, **11**. 112–13, 114, 167,

[Walpole, Hon. Horatio (1717–97), *continued*]
287, 326, 334–5, **12.** 136, 210; 'snail past 74,' **31.** 368; 'Struldbrug,' **32.** 316, 364, **33.** 461, 463, 464, **34.** 13, 64, 205; 'superannuated,' **11.** 1, **12.** 37, 214, **28.** 186, 228, 261, 295, 330, 381, 397, 400, 463, **29.** 49, 55, 82, 91, 136, 140, 250, 282, 290, 298, 330; thankful to be alive at 75, **31.** 359; too ancient to visit anywhere but Ampthill and Park Place, **32.** 408; too old to be improper, **31.** 360; 'too old to care for more than very few friends,' **30.** 173; 'towards eight and twenty,' **30.** 92–3; tranquillity of, interrupted by succession to the title, **31.** 363; 'trumpery old person,' **31.** 274; well-preserved, **31.** 402; wishes to avoid ridicule in, **34.** 210

age of 32 admitted by, as 'elderly,' **20.** 119
aim of, G. J. Williams calls, *monstrari digito prætereuntium*, **30.** 176
ambition never felt by, **25.** 362
ambitions of: not to grow cross, **31.** 69; peace of mind, **31.** 60; retirement, **31.** 69; to please himself without being tied to a political party, **30.** 196
ancestors of, often met violent deaths, **20.** 65
ancestry of: **2.** 47n, 9. 69, **12.** 267; from Charlemagne through Courtenays, **31.** 155
anecdotes told by, authentic, **28.** 116, **29.** 47
antiquarian books to be redeemed by, from reputation for being ill-written, **38.** 152
antiquarian knowledge of, slight, **15.** 154–5
apologies by, for false humility, **23.** 528
appearance of: **4.** 44, **15.** 241; as ghost, will not be changed much from what he is now, **33.** 282; as wrinkled as Methusaleh, **24.** 176; body disappearing, **33.** 507; bones in heap like bits of ivory in game of straws, **31.** 39; bones 'no bigger than a lark's,' **24.** 71; 'bones of a sparrow,' **33.** 304; caducity, **33.** 326; complexion, **32.** 21, **33.** 324; decrepit skeleton, **33.** 434; face described, **11.** 183; face long and yellow, **30.** 92; 'fat and jolly,' **10.** 266; fatter, **24.** 148, **41.** 101; 'featherhood,' **34.** 63; feet small, 9. 293, **32.** 14; flimsy texture, **30.** 192; French reported to admire, **31.** 70, 73–4; Geoffrin, Mme, admires, **31.** 82; 'gherkin' of his family, **33.** 505; gray hair, **32.** 70; HW jokes about, with Conti, **31.** 91; hollow cheeks, **32.** 13; insignificant, **31.** 4; larklike, **31.** 130; lark-like leg, **31.** 37; leanness, **11.** 136; legs thin and gouty, **35.** 588; legs too little except when swelled by gout, **14.** 143; 'like a witch upon my crutch,' **32.** 102; like mummified crane, **32.** 43; 'like Pam's father,' **35.** 304; 'like the picture of a Morocco ambassador,' **35.** 303; limps about, **32.** 109, 114; 'long, lean,' **37.** 110; looked charmingly a month ago, **24.** 176; 'looks very old,' **31.** 140, 130n; meagre, **30.** 8; more emaciated than usual, **38.** 155; Muscovite way of walking, **30.** 80; 'old lean face,' **22.** 136; 'old withered gray pea,' **31.** 58; opposite to Henry Fox's, **30.** 170; pale, **31.** 131; paper frame, **31.** 345; reduced by gout, **30.** 201; shadow, **31.** 359; skeleton, **30.** 204, **31.** 66, 74, **32.** 12, 220, 566; skin and a few bones, **31.** 128; 'starved vulture,' **31.** 26; thighs unsuited to Van Dyck breeches, **35.** 419; thin, **28.** 59, **30.** 39, **31.** 117, 131, **32.** 37, 94, **33.** 225; 251; thin legs, **32.** 21, 25; trips like a pewit or dabchick, **32.** 252, **34.** 118; unchanged, **37.** 110; 'unfinished skeleton of 77,' **42.** 408; unherculean, **31.** 67; unheroic, **31.** 185; 'very fat,' **20.** 57; virtually bald, **31.** 359; walks like a tortoise, **35.** 366; walks badly, **10.** 315; weight, slight, **11.** 19, 70; 'well preserved,' **42.** 170; withered, **10.** 290; 'withered skeleton,' **32.** 12; wrinkled, 9. 269, **10.** 73, **25.** 332, **31.** 72, 74; 'wrinkled Adonis,' **23.** 13; 'wrinkled parchment,' **24.** 148

appetite of, improved by Bath waters, **31.** 130
approbation and resentments of, equally strong, **15.** 333
autopsy permitted by, **15.** 337, **30.** 377
aversions of, to: absurdity, **31.** 97; advice, **10.** 165; affectation, **24.** 213; allegory, **32.** 182; all the professions, **36.** 176; ambition, **24.** 100–1, **35.** 355–6; appearing in public, **12.** 83, 106–7, 148, 184; appearing in public light, **38.** 192; artfulness, **33.** 594; asking favours, **22.** 479–80; asking political favours, **21.** 79; atheism, **31.** 392; attendance at Court, **28.** 34; authors and authorship, **32.** 41, **33.** 41, 492, 543, 574, **34.** 100; authorship, **30.** 152, **35.** 539; authors' vanity, **33.** 537; Bath, **31.** 130–1; beginning journeys, **30.** 260; being a 'party-man,' **16.** 158; being named in subscriptions, **31.** 222, 383; being ridiculous, **34.** 194; black-letter type, **29.** 165; bloodshed, **33.** 167; ceremonious customs, **10.** 145; change of principles, **32.** 349; changing friends, **23.** 425; Christmas, **18.** 367; clergy, **24.** 71, **25.** 441; collected literary works, **16.** 260; compliments, **15.** 126, 272; conquerors, **31.** 44; 'Constantinopolitan jargons,' **31.** 333; Conti, Prince de, **31.** 136; controversy, **28.** 250, 282, 424, **29.** 96, 295, 339–40; conversing with young people, **39.** 296; correcting his writings, **28.** 16–17; correcting proof-sheets, **28.** 88, **29.** 312; correction, **31.** 59; country gentlemen, **37.** 178, **40.** 21; country life, **17.** 443, **35.** 43, **48.** **37.** 107, 109; Court functions, **25.** 307–8; Court life, **25.** 247; Courts, 9. 303–5, **31.** 56, **35.** 511; dining away from home, **39.** 351; disputations, **2.** 67, 229, **33.** 519; disputes, **35.** 112, **42.** 275; dissertations, **32.** 21; diversions, **10.** 231, 24. 86; drugs, 'hot,' **33.** 459; early rising, **40.** 386; elections, **31.** 199, **35.** 357, 398, **36.** 172, 173, 232, **39.** 409–10, **41.** 277; embarking on new scenes, **22.** 111; emotion, **10.** 172; English habits, **31.** 93; entertain-

ing visitors, 35. 43; exercise, 39. 295; 'expeditions,' 30. 60, 62; exultation, 24. 446; family pride, 16. 9; female indelicacy, 31. 76; female novelists, 31. 271; fêtes champêtres, 32. 195; foreign politics, 41. 286; 'fractions of theology and reformation,' 42. 221; France, 37. 103; freethinking, 10. 176; French dissertations on religion and government, 31. 65; French opera, 31. 45; French Revolution, 35. 398 *et passim*; French verse, 42. 230; friendship, 41. 7; gambling, 31. 436; Genoese, the, 18. 179; gifts, 25. 655; gifts from all but closest friends, 24. 475; giving uneasiness to any family, 31. 173; gossip, 11. 60–1, 64–5, 204, 353, 12. 116, 151; gout, 32. 210; hardships of travel, 28. 38–9; heroes, 36. 238; hill-climbing, 11. 106; historians' cold impartiality, 16. 273; hospitality, 39. 434–5; House of Commons, 22. 348, 30. 196, 203, 206, 31. 93, 111; hunting, 35. 387, 40. 21; hurting descendants by publishing blame of their ancestors, 16. 21; inns, 13. 230, 239, 39. 175; Inquisition, the, 31. 324; law, 31. 351; law and lawyers, 13. 5, 14. 212, 28. 93, 278; lawyers, 24. 71, 25. 441, 33. 230; learned men, 41. 52–3; learning, 32. 374, 33. 220, 479, 34. 128; London back parlours in summer, 34. 196; love, 41. 5; lying, 28. 127; lying in state before one dies, 33. 259; madness and extravagance, 31. 69; maintaining a consistent 'character,' 33. 183; making objections, 16. 254; mathematics, 28. 88; meat breakfasts, 40. 386; medicines, 39. 235; metaphysics, 42. 275; Methodists, 32. 185; 'middling writers,' 33. 374; military reviews, 35. 365; mixed company, 10. 231; 'Mr' on title-pages, 14. 65; music, 30. 100; natural history, 35. 427; new acquaintances, 10. 231, 30. 51; news of young people's activities, 35. 361, 369; official biographies, 16. 260; old ideas, 31. 103; ostentation, 22. 480; 'paper-wars,' 15. 59, 62, 38. 35; Parisian dirt, 31. 45–6, 49; Parliament, 24. 101, 32. 210, 36. 109; pen and ink, 38. 251; people who do not write as they talk, 30. 76; pertness of modern French authors, 33. 543; philosophers, 22. 151, 35. 116, 39. 292; physicians, 9. 359, 10. 277, 290, 21. 368, 22. 110, 24. 71, 74, 25. 441, 32. 37, 33. 229, 230, 460, 39. 31; piddling politics, 23. 420; Piozzi, Mrs, 31. 271; political pamphlets, 31. 60, 74; politics, 10. 49, 109, 113, 118, 154, 155, 157, 158, 162, 163, 167, 168, 170, 177, 184, 263, 267, 273, 301, 15. 105, 127, 22. 110, 300, 304, 308–9, 316, 348, 359, 363, 436, 550, 570, 572, 578, 23. 41, 129, 145, 24. 117, 351, 25. 140, 310, 311–12, 365, 476, 483, 604, 30. 196, 211, 31. 39, 105–6, 111, 372, 32. 10, 40, 33. 106, 180, 357, 398, 35. 332, 334, 342, 38. 463, 470, 39. 31, 244–5, 300, 415, 41. 7, 277; post-chaises, 13. 230, 239; praise for his wit, 31. 16–17; prehistoric ages, 16. 302, 305–6; prerogative, 37. 406; priests, 24. 71, 33. 230; princes and princesses, 34. 132; professions of integrity, 37. 416; publicity as an author, 16. 29; public places, 10. 177, 231; public places and active people, 24. 76; questioning of wills, 25. 123; receiving presents, 35. 537; removing landmarks, 25. 541; Richardson's novels, 31. 43; roads, inns, and dirt, 39. 175; royalty, 21. 449, 35. 389; St James's Palace, 35. 227; savants, 35. 116; Saxon architecture, 15. 203; scandal, 11. 213, 12. 159; 'senilia,' 33. 40; sermons, 30. 25; seventeenth-century gravity, 33. 550; sights, 20. 40; sight-seeing, 11. 357; singing in complicated style, 35. 350; slavery, 20. 126, 23. 462, 35. 178; 'smell of paint,' in book reviews, 35. 515; speculation, 33. 571; strangers, 35. 149; systems, 32. 79, 345; talking of young people, 33. 79; talking politics and arguing, 33. 305; torture of animals, 15. 70; trying to please the present age, 39. 277; unsolicited civilities, 10. 106; vanity, 33. 165–6; visiting Houghton, 30. 73; walled parks, 34. 196; war, 18. 422–3, 22. 81, 25. 106, 108, 188, 365, 31. 351, 392, 35. 240, 341, 360–1, 387; whist, 31. 48–9, 65, 79, 89, 35. 112; writing travels, 30. 95

basis of political pronouncements of, explained, 25. 30

Berkenhout requests biography of, 32. 122–3

birthday of, HW gloomy about, 38. 446

birth of, 13. 3

boating accident of, 7. 67

body of: opened by Huitson, after death, and lock of hair removed, 43. 326; to be opened after his death, 15. 337, 30. 377

'Boniface,' 7. 56

book-collecting by, 16. 25

book-seller intends to collect writings and write life of, 16. 259

burial of, to be private, 30. 377

calls himself: 'a dancing senator,' 35. 213; a 'Goth,' 31. 26; 'a Protestant Goth,' 35. 153; 'Anstis of Newmarket,' 32. 142; 'cool, sedate, reasonable,' 38. 97; 'hare with many real friends,' 32. 254; 'most insignificant man alive,' 31. 42; 'old and poor,' 37. 256; 'le fou moquer,' 30. 208; 'philosopher who studies human nature, in its disguises,' 35. 399

'came into the world' at 5 years old, 25. 558

carriage accidents of, 9. 65–6, 195

characteristics of: accounts only for what he understands, 30. 183; admirable company, 31. 146; admires without bounds, 31. 182; affected, 32. 42n; agriculture not understood, 30. 203; all sincerity and says only what he thinks, 38. 160; always agreeable, 31. 147; always employed and never busy, 39. 180; apt to be hurried away by first impressions, 32. 379; apt to say too much

[Walpole, Hon. Horatio (1717–97), *continued*] rather than too little, **31**. 16; a reprobate because he says and does 'whatever came into my head,' **32**. 190–1; aristocrat and placeman for life, **34**. 104; arithmetic poor, **33**. 436, **34**. 78; asserts only what he knows, **30**. 183, 225; avoids 'particularity,' **30**. 40; *bonhommie* lacking, **39**. 295; called 'epicure,' and 'antiquestrian,' **34**. 24; capricious, **39**. 186, 295; careless about non-essentials, **39**. 277; cares more for individuals than for the public, **39**. 393; ceases to be Examiner to become Spectator, **33**. 388; celerity, **10**. 309; character preferred to fortune, **25**. 125; cheated sometimes by tradesmen, **21**. 497; cheerful, **31**. 71; coldness, **11**. 304, **30**. 37; commerce not understood, **30**. 203; common sense, **28**. 88, 130; communicative disposition, **28**. 327, 375; compassion for criminals, **33**. 199; concern for freedom, **33**. 92; consistency, **29**. 329; consistency of principles, **32**. 349; contentedness, **33**. 420, **39**. 244; conversation narrow and barren, with few ideas and many undigested trifles, **33**. 128; could never draw well, **42**. 217–18; curiosity insatiable in Paris, **30**. 204, 215; death not feared, **15**. 335; 'de la vieille cour,' **31**. 73; determinations made on preferences, **30**. 260; discards those who disappoint him, pretending 'they don't exist,' **33**. 546; discriminating in his likes, **19**. 442; disinterestedness, **9**. 203, 317, **13**. 38, **21**. 79, **25**. 210, 260, 276, **35**. 619–20, **36**. 78, 123, 165, 244, **39**. 384, **40**. 154, 183; divested both of vanity and affected modesty, **42**. 310; does not accept political obligations, **30**. 169; does not pretend to be supernatural, **30**. 273; dreads exposing himself to strangers, **33**. 130; eager about trifles, indifferent about anything serious, **39**. 180; earnestness, **11**. 7; easily moved to tears, **28**. 110, 226; East India Co. affairs not understood, **30**. 237–8; ecstatic when really pleased, **30**. 258; effeminacy, **35**. 647; emphasizes ridiculous traits in other characters, **30**. 171; entertaining, **31**. 214; entertaining powers improve rather than decay, **31**. 242; entertains singular 'historic doubts' and 'historic certainties,' **30**. 266; 'epigrammatic brilliancy,' **29**. 358; *étourderie*, **12**. 85, 161; excellent judgment and love of truth, **37**. 197; excessive wit, **35**. 647; false professions not made, **31**. 105; family love and pride, **39**. 296; family pride, **36**. 160; faults and defects numerous, **31**. 257; feelings strong and passionate, **33**. 17; fickle, **31**. 411; **37**. 170; finds conversation difficult with people whose ideas are totally different, **30**. 279; 'fits' of poetry a trouble in the country only, **30**. 100; flattery not his talent, **30**. 333; 'flower of chivalry,' **32**. 100–1; follies, **37**. 170; foolish within limits of absurdity,

39. 79; forgetful, **31**. 113–14; frank, **3**. 320, **4**. 210, **30**. 169; friendships carried to excess, **30**. 77; friendships rarely professed, **30**. 77; full of faults and foibles, **30**. 72; gallantry, **11**. 3; gay, **4**. 33, **5**. 20, **6**. 262; gay and inconsiderate when in Italy, **28**. 69; geometry not understood, **30**. 203; good-humoured, **31**. 71; good-natured, **31**. 349–50; good sense, **37**. 167; good-spirited, **28**. 26; Gothic spirit, **37**. 406; 'Gothic superstition,' **32**. 352; has no talent for business, **34**. 137; hates to dispute and scorns to triumph, **39**. 289; haughtiness of an ancient Briton, **39**. 277; haughtiness of spirit, **39**. 32; head and heart, **33**. 18; heart 'is suspicious, doubtful, cooled,' **41**. 5; heart speaks in compositions, **30**. 131; honour preferred to fortune, **36**. 165; humanity, **31**. 249; humour lacking, **35**. 647; idleness, **15**. 33, 133, 155, 185–6, **28**. 130, 146, 167; idleness of spirits, **31**. 17; ignorance of mechanics and geometry, **21**. 352–3; ignorance of money, racing, and farming, **36**. 96; 'illegible' politics, **35**. 648; impatience, **28**. 268, **31**. 7, 106, 140, **37**. 292, **39**. 386; impatience under praise, **31**. 16; impenetrably dull where common sense is required, **39**. 293; impetuosity, **9**. 286; 'incorrupt,' **36**. 223; indifference, **33**. 1, 420; indifference to peace-time treaties, **20**. 395–6; indifferent to literary fame, **12**. 94; knows own mind, **12**. 4; lacking in candour, **34**. 38; lacks Selwyn's wit, **30**. 210; lacks 'troublesome curiosity,' **38**. 489; lacks vanity or jealousy of authors, **21**. 173; laziness, **28**. 37; *le fou moquer*, **30**. 208; less entertaining than formerly, **31**. 186; less grave than Lyttelton, **32**. 30, 117; likes to hide when dying, **39**. 198; love of truth, **37**. 197, **38**. 39; mathematical knowledge lacking, **11**. 127, **12**. 208, **21**. 352–3, **38**. 359; melancholy, **11**. 174, 180, 189–90, **32**. 214; memory loss due to remembering trifles, **42**. 315; modesty, **30**. 103; monarchical but within limits, **33**. 342n; 'more easily dissatisfied than pleased,' **29**. 261; 'most prejudiced of mankind,' **34**. 38; most troublesome when he has nothing to do, **30**. 34; multiplication table never understood, **39**. 494; music not appreciated but would rear children as musicians, **32**. 182; 'natural and unaffected,' **30**. 100; 'neither young nor old enough for love,' **37**. 110; 'never approves what others approve,' according to Harcourt, **29**. 358; never complains about health, **31**. 308; never had solid understanding or wit, **32**. 327; no affectation, **37**. 79, 296; 'no good friend to reason,' **37**. 198; 'no natural philosopher, no chemist, no metaphysician,' **42**. 363; not a coxcomb, **32**. 21; not a hero or poet, **31**. 22; nothing useful ever studied, **31**. 363; not peevish in gout, **32**. 42; not qualified to treat a subject of importance,

38. 152; old and indolent, 38. 251; 'old scribbling pen, subject to babble,' 42. 287; opinions frequently fantastic, 31. 90; partial to those he loves, 31. 315, 374; passes many lonely hours, 30. 279; patriotic, 10. 111, 263; passionate, 39. 200; passionate principle is attachment to Henry Fox, out of power, 30. 131; passions too prompt and quick, 31. 17; patience, 23. 365, 31. 64, 32. 94, 33. 76, 34. 212; peevishness, 11. 25, 41; 'perishing memory,' 42. 214; perseverance, 10. 307; petty offences easily forgiven, 31. 349–50; philosophical, 32. 274, 326, 39. 180; philosophic only when at ease, 24. 327; philosophy of, to paint thoughts *couleur de rose*, 33. 550; pleasure obtained by not seeing faces he hates, 31. 91; politeness, 15. 322; political disinterestedness, 13. 38, 30. 170; praises indiscriminately when pleased, 31. 299; prefers nonsense to learned discourse, 31. 213; prejudiced in favour of Waldegraves, 31. 200; prejudices acknowledged, 34. 103; prejudices from retired life, 32. 316; prejudices not weakened by age, 15. 333; pride, 28. 156, 29. 237, 33. 574, 584, 37. 416, 39. 277, 495; prides himself on his printing not his writing, 34. 53; prudence, 33. 328, 37. 271; prudent and cautious, 38. 95; punctuality, 11. 97; quaintness in wit, 35. 648; quiet virtues and small faults, 31. 143; respects the characters of the living and the feelings of their children, 42. 122; ridicule feared, 3. 86, 90, 134, 143, 145, 147–8, 148, 150–2, 154, 155, 171, 177, 181, 196, 197, 207, 233, 235, 265, 310, 390–1, 397, 4. 61, 65, 70, 89, 108, 143, 277, 462, 473–6, 5. 2, 20, 22–3, 173, 262, 264, 403–5, 9. 269; said to be shy, 31. 211; scepticism, 16. 23; sedate and deliberate in making decisions, 30. 260; seeks only personal amusement, 33. 549; seeming modesty, really pride, 30. 104; selfishness, 11. 364; sensible to flattery, 30. 104; sensitive plant, 39. 435; sentiments are to him what principles are to others, 39. 86; shrinks and closes up if stranger offers hand, 39. 435; shyness, 1. 343, 9. 77, 77n, 30. 103, 31. 211; sincerity, 30. 169; sincerity and disinterestedness, 29. 217, 330; sincerity doubtful, 31. 184; speaks French indifferently, 32. 21; speculative rather than active, 29. 26; spirits naturally good, 33. 231; spirits never low, 39. 295; spirits not translatable, 31. 43; spirits rather than parts characterized when young, 33. 19; steady political friend, 30. 131; sterling wit, 30. 238; subject to prepossessions, 12. 124; sudden death preferred, 39. 418; superstitious on the favourable side, 39. 336; 'sweet-tempered,' 38. 124; sympathetic, 30. 66; 'taking root at home,' 39. 250; temper kept by keeping it out of everybody's way, 39. 186; temper of, his weakness, 23. 522,

525; too old to care for reputation, 33. 581; too sincere to pretend love, 30. 173; touchy with those he loves, 31. 315, 374; truthful, 3. 92, 107, 311, 313, 368, 403, 4. 6, 104, 5. 180, 295, 10. 159; unalterable in principles, 39. 277; unamiable, 30. 76; unanxious to connect himself with new generation, 30. 279; unaware of his own ridiculous characteristics, 30. 171; understands nothing useful, 31. 331; understands out-of-the-way things, but nothing useful, 33. 545; unheroic, 37. 191; unlike philosopher or *philosophe*, 39. 292; unmusical, 39. 223; unpopular, 30. 76; unsentimental, 37. 191; unsociable, 39. 434; 'unwalking,' 39. 470–1; vanity and hypocrisy wanting, 33. 1; vanity lacking, 42. 108; warmth, gratitude, and sincerity, 31. 17; weaknesses, 37. 170; Whiggism, 10. 164; 'Whig to the backbone,' 37. 406; whims, delicacy, and laziness, 39. 255; 'wicked and unphilosophic bent to laughing,' 40. 385; wit, 31. 249, 313, 349; wit always aimed at, 32. 43n; wit called 'tinsel,' 31. 16, 250; wit unsuccessfully aimed at, 31. 186; would rather be content than in the right, 39. 276; would rather be a philosopher than rich man, 39. 276; 'writative and talkative to those I love,' 33. 59; writes French poorly, 41. 47
character preferred by, to fortune, 25. 125
charity of: for debtors, 40. 123; for Hannah More's protégés, 31. 338; for relief of needy persons, 40. 270, 345; to beggar woman, 9. 93; to relief of French clergy, 31. 383n
clergy reverenced by, in early life, 14. 10
closet of curiosities fitted up by, 17. 213, 241, 322, 324
Cole's encomiums on, 1. 58, 63, 221, 277–8, 299, 359, 369, 370, 373, 2. 5–6, 48, 86–7, 103–4, 198, 200–1, 247, 267, 268, 269, 271
——'s opinion of, 2. 372–3, 374
'Collections for a History of the Manners . . . of England' planned by, 14. 122
collections of, called 'lares and pagods,' 30. 71
comforts of, in old age, 31. 402
compares himself to Orpheus, 11. 21–2
constitution of: bad, 37. 169; tender, 37. 100; 'tender and weak,' 37. 295
costume of: at Birthday Ball, 17. 176, 185, 208, 37. 116; at masquerade, 17. 359, 18. 167, 23. 193; before dressing, 9. 304; clothes stolen, 7. 266; discussed by women at opera, 18. 180; fiddler's hat, 37. 308; flapped hat, 39. 61; for entertaining French visitors, 10. 278; for Waldegrave wedding, 9. 232; in summer, 9. 305; mourning, 10. 310, 311; split shoes, 35. 596; unstudied, 31. 74; winter clothes ordered, 25. 541
county histories disparaged by, 2. 199
Damer, Mrs, loved by, like own child, 25. 184
dances, 13. 201, 17. 185, 19. 18, 33. 284
death of: 12. 215n, 15. 336, 31. 403–4; HW

[Walpole, Hon. Horatio (1717–97), *continued*]
anticipates inventory at time of, **25.** 165;
HW does not fear, **15.** 335; HW reconciled
to thought of, **25.** 201; will be like extinc-
tion of one lamp in an illumination, **24.**
250; will not matter to the world, **25.** 213
decay of faculties observed by, which prevents him from exposing himself, **25.** 332
dedication by, to Bentley's *Reflections*, **9.**
195n
depression of, **10.** 162–4, 320
diet of: 'bumpers to old England' drunk,
35. 5; dinner scanty, **15.** 226n; dinner very
bad, **36.** 285; hartshorn and pears for
supper, **22.** 110, 114; stewed fruit might
be part of, **22.** 114; tea and wine avoided,
23. 76
disclaims power of prophecy, **25.** 252
'disgrace' of, **30.** 82
disposed to publish no more, **1.** 316, **2.** 85,
86–7, 89–90
disposition of: in tolerable humour, **30.** 238;
not in good humour, **30.** 238; peevish, **30.**
172, 265; politics do not affect, **30.** 238;
spirits good, **30.** 238
'dowager' life of, **29.** 153
drawing lessons of, **2.** 222–3
Du Deffand, Mme, compares, to SH, **5.** 34
—— keeps pamphlets mentioning, for him,
3. 207
—— requests 'portrait' of, **4.** 147, 157
——'s farewell to, **7.** 243
——'s hand in marriage asked by, of Mme
de Choiseul, **7.** 321
——'s legacy to: **8.** 7, 26; catalogue of MSS
in, **8.** 7, 44
——'s 'portrait' of, **3.** 185, 189–90, 193–5, 199,
6. 109, **8.** 71–3
——'s 'portraits' by, **8.** 54–6
——'s witticisms given by, **8.** 60
——'s writings criticized by, **8.** 56–9
—— the only one who knows that, is without
mask, **4.** 121
duties of, in Exchequer post, **9.** 117n
economy of, **9.** 204, **10.** 179, **21.** 353–4
effect on, of praise, **2.** 269
election dinner expense of, **43.** 366
'Elzevir Horace' the nickname of, **40.** 104
emolument never asked by, though friends
are in government, **25.** 312
enemies wished by, to feel for others rather
than to suffer, **35.** 489
English gossip about, annoys him, **31.** 70–1,
73–4, 91, 97
epitaph for, by Fitzpatrick, **32.** 89
epitaphs by: on Cutts, **10.** 21; on Gray, **28.**
20, 21, 25; on Lady Beauchamp, **39.** 155–6;
on Lady Dysart, **31.** 314–15, **36.** 255; on
Lady Hervey, **36.** 51; on Lady Ossory's
bullfinch, **29.** 312, 315–16, 318, 320; on
Lancelot Brown, **29.** 286; on Roger Townshend, **40.** 167; on 'Rosette,' **35.** 464

essay by, on Mrs Porter as Clytemnestra, **40.**
27
Eton schooldays of, **9.** 3–4, **40.** 1, 2; *see also
under* Eton
Exchequer House of, in New Palace Yard,
Westminster, **40.** 86
fame not sought by, **28.** 130, **29.** 82–3, 295
family affairs the chief preoccupation of, **24.**
317
family history to be written by, **37.** 234–5
family's fall from prominence will not distress, **17.** 248
family views of, cut off by sale of Houghton
pictures, **25.** 164
Farington's anecdotes of, **15.** 316–38
father's fame goads, to keep himself from
being too insignificant, **9.** 227
favourite child, **25.** 558
favours conferred by, on admirers of the fine
arts, **15.** 259, 262
favours never will be asked by, of cabinet
ministers, **28.** 184, **29.** 230, 242, 246
fears comment on his lodging at convent of
St Joseph, **4.** 391
Felton calls, 'time-honoured Lancaster,' **34.**
10
female relatives' spirits must be kept up by,
when husbands are at war, **24.** 507
finances of: **4.** 359n, **9.** 156, **10.** 278, 317, **36.**
161n; accounting for Customs place, **42.** 47;
annuities sold for 10 times more than he
can pay, **24.** 310; 'a placeman for life,' **34.**
104; as ample as he wishes, **24.** 283; Berkeley Sq. house's cost, **33.** 62–3, 67, **34.** 250–
2; brother's death decreases, **16.** 275, **29.**
325, 327–8, 348, **31.** 298, 436, **36.**
223, **39.** 289–90; coach tax, **41.** 432; controller of the Pipe and clerk of the Estreats,
13. 8; (?) Conway aided by, **39.** 384; Conway offered share of income, **37.** 169–72;
Crostwick estate's income little better than
that from Houghton, **42.** 393; currency in
Arlington St house, **23.** 284; Customs
clerk's theft made good from, **28.** 445, **33.**
63; Customs place, **13.** 7, **17.** 27n, **32.** 283–
4, 288, **33.** 436, **36.** 223, **39.** 289–90; 'dabs'
saved to put in stocks, **21.** 497; Devonshire
burgage-tenures sold to Trefusis, **34.** 184n;
Du Deffand, Mme, concerned over, **3.** 101,
108, 255, 326, 388, **4.** 11–12, 15, **6.** 250; Du
Deffand, Mme, offered share of, **4.** 358–9,
364–6, 375, 379, 403, **5.** 7; Exchequer ushership income, **42.** 327n; expects to receive fortune left him by father, **28.** 445;
expenses never increased till money is at
banker's, **34.** 137–8; father compensates for
loss to brother on Exchequer bills, **37.** 169n;
father's bequests, **13.** 15, **19.** 32n, 447n, **25.**
637, **34.** 145n; father's estates entailed upon
him, **36.** 24–32, 295; father's family leaves
or gives him a total of £7,000, **25.** 637;
father's legacy, **42.** 81; father's legacy paid

to, in full but without full interest, **25**. 637; father's legacy secured to, by 3d E. of Orford, **33**. 62; father's legacy to, not paid, **20**. 250, **25**. 316–17; fortune 'saved by my own prudence,' **36**. 161; gaming losses of, trifling, **33**. 271; HW never seeks addition to, beyond what his father arranged, **35**. 502; HW's frugality safeguards, **38**. 431; Harcourt's interest preferred to establishing of HW's sinecures, **35**. 512; Hertford offers to compensate for Treasury's withholdings from, **38**. 427, 430–1, 434; Hertford's legacy, **34**. 200n; house bills brought to HW every Saturday night by steward or butler, **40**. 258; house in town too expensive to buy, **39**. 289; income, **4**. 359n, **13**. 7–8, 15, **14**. 257, **16**. 275n; income reduced by Exchequer reform, **16**. 275; inherits Houghton estate loaded with mortgages, **16**. 313–14, **42**. 345; lays up money for friends and servants, **39**. 408; losses of, **33**. 272–3; nephew's estate much embarrassed, **42**. 345; 'no money to spare for visions,' **35**. 232; 'not a farthing left' after Parisian purchases, **39**. 62; outlying lands, unconnected with Norfolk, to be sold, **42**. 377; Orford, 2d E. of, paid part of father's legacy to HW, **25**. 637; Paris visit too extravagant for, **38**. 415, 431; patent places a legal property, but income from them may be politically delayed or stopped, **40**. 336; private fortune not to be impaired by expenses as E. of Orford, **34**. 137–8; prudence of, in finances, **33**. 68, **36**. 161, **38**. 431; public sources of, a motive for doing histories for national glory, **40**. 211–12; rise in stocks improves, **33**. 67; saves for his heirs, **39**. 290; servant tax, **41**. 432, 433; Shorter estate shared, **20**. 403 (*see also under* Shorter, Erasmus); short of money, **30**. 149; sinecure places endangered by reform in spending public money, **35**. 501–3, 512; sinecures, **31**. 14; sinecures, HW's application to Pelham concerning, **30**. 119; sinecures to be reduced by brother's death, **31**. 298; £6,000 in the funds, **38**. 381; stocks not to be sold to buy house, **39**. 289; SH construction expenses saved out of his income, **21**. 420; SH improvements cost £105 8s., **20**. 64n; Suckling's legacy, **36**. 162; Suckling to remit money from Customs place, **24**. 231; tax on Exchequer place, **40**. 153–5; 'the poorest Earl in England,' **34**. 136; Treasury may withhold payments, necessitating use of nest-egg, **38**. 415; ushership of Exchequer, **13**. 7; will's distribution of, **15**. 336, **30**. 344–7

first speech by, in Parliament, **17**. 376–7, 404
flattery, subjected to, **12**. 208
follies of, do not include self-love, **31**. 71
fondness of, for: accuracy, **28**. 116, 118; amusements, **28**. 26, 166; 'amusing myself with trifles,' **36**. 249; ancient French ladies, **31**. 61; anecdotes, **20**. 27; animals, **31**. 68; antiquarianism, **21**. 140, **28**. 114, 148, 213, **29**. 360; antiquity, **9**. 250, **10**. 95, 192, 306; architecture, Gothic, **9**. 64, 296; arranging books, **33**. 477; books full of proper names, **42**. 151; bread and butter, **30**. 19; British constitution, **34**. 173; castles, **35**. 396; cats, **31**. 83; children, **32**. 204; collecting curiosities, **33**. 450; company of friends, **28**. 26, 228; conflagrations, **9**. 362; Crammond's tiger, **37**. 383; 'distressed virgins of 5 years old,' **37**. 378; dogs, **28**. 145, **31**. 93, **32**. 204; elderly ladies, **30**. 171, **31**. 61; English historic portraits, **42**. 180–1; English local history, **15**. 253, 267; essences, **18**. 214; faction, **35**. 167n; facts, **25**. 146; fairy tales, **37**. 189; fame, **16**. 260; family portraits, **10**. 67; faro, **38**. 485, 525; Florence, **35**. 48; fountains, **31**. 46; fragrance of flowers, **34**. 123; French life, **32**. 27; genealogy, **28**. 88; House's privileges and liberty of the press, **38**. 225; hurry of business, **30**. 72; idle French books, **30**. 203; impartiality, in writing, **16**. 158; Italy, **37**. 109; last century, **30**. 204; liberty, **39**. 469; lilac-tide, **38**. 554; London, **30**. 72; loo, **28**. 57, 230, **31**. 20, 79, **38**. 525; mansions of ancient families, **30**. 275; masked balls, **38**. 505; masquerades, **23**. 193; maxims, gay and good-hearted, **33**. 395; medals, **16**. 299; memoirs, **31**. 245; nonsense, **32**. 330, 374, **33**. 467, 476, 545, 549, **34**. 170; Norfolk, **40**. 21; novelties, **31**. 103; old errors and prejudices, **32**. 348; old friends and acquaintances, **10**. 140, 231; old stories, **28**. 280; peace, **35**. 235, 240, 341, 366, 367, 398, 400, **36**. 248; pilchards, **31**. 34; piquet, **13**. 154; pleasing Lincoln, **30**. 21; pleasing Selwyn, **30**. 256; pleasures of royalty without cares, **32**. 364; private history, **38**. 213; quartos, **29**. 310; reading, **21**. 156; reading and writing, **28**. 131, 143, 166; redistributing fame, **31**. 200–1; restoration of ancient palaces, **33**. 526; romances, **37**. 126, 150, 189, 203; romping with children, **37**. 484; Scotsmen, **31**. 8; sights, **38**. 171; studies that are *couleur de rose*, **35**. 374; sycamores, **35**. 132; tea, **31**. 75; tranquillity, **23**. 273, 367, **24**. 327, **25**. 331, **28**. 93, 143, **39**. 290; *treillage*, **31**. 46; truth, **15**. 109, 262, **36**. 77–8, **38**. 152; views of moving objects, **34**. 195–6; virtu, **28**. 131, **29**. 328, 349, 360; virtue, **28**. 156; visionary holiday in old age, **33**. 542; visions, **10**. 192, 259, 291, **24**. 103, 194–5, 327, **25**. 133, 604, **33**. 42, 447, **35**. 352, 366; Whigs, **38**. 243; Whig virtues, **38**. 323; writing notes in books, **28**. 292, **29**. 169, 175; writings of Sir C. H. Williams, **30**. 53, 64; writing to Lincoln, **30**. 20; young people, **39**. 244

French learnt by, at Eton, **13**. 6

[Walpole, Hon. Horatio (1717–97), *continued*]
French of, 3. 34, 79, 93, 94, 113, 118, 141, 347, 4. 255, 6. 117, 170, 188, 7. 110
friends of, when dead may be replaced by their children, 40. 181
genealogy of, 2. 47n, 9. 69, 12. 267, 31. 165, 36. 337
genius disclaimed by, 15. 230, 28. 114, 227, 228, 244, 29. 82
ghost of, will be amused to find prudence attributed to him, 37. 271
glad to be unpopular instead of fashionable, 35. 118
Grafton, D. of, godfather to, 20. 120n
habits of: abed till noon, and dresses at 2, 36. 39; abstinence, 9. 291, 10. 68, 162, 163, 182, 22. 257; age makes him lazy, 31. 283; amuses himself foolishly all day long, 31. 93; amuses himself with his own memory, 25. 559; annotating books, 2. 80, 28. 292, 29. 169, 175, 35. 633; appetite indulged indiscreetly, 15. 335; apt to forget gambling debts, 31. 168; at Florence, 37. 78; at Houghton, 18. 36, 30. 81; at Paris, never gets to bed before 2 or 3 A.M., 39. 258; at Paris, stuffs ears with cotton to sleep, 39. 259; attends Parliament constantly but never stays long, 17. 344; avoids everything that would disturb him, 25. 332; awakened early at 9:30, 32. 74; a water-drinker, 2. 291; 'bad hours,' 35. 218; bad man of business, 25. 166; books inadequate to fill after-dinner hours, 36. 285; bottle used, to converse with Norfolk neighbours, 30. 34; bread and butter for breakfast, 35. 342; busy about the most errant trifles, 41. 278; cannot fix his attention to long deductions, 16. 305; card-playing, 37. 86; cautious in making decisions concerning property, 25. 166; ceremonials observed from old-fashioned breeding, 33. 506; charity, 40. 270, 345; church seldom attended, 39. 173; cleanliness, 10. 133; cold baths, 17. 452; coldness, 11. 304; comes home at 10 P.M. because of lack of things to do, 22. 550; 'constantly employed though indeed about trifles,' 40. 288; cool civility to unwelcome visitors, 32. 406; critics ignored, 38. 362; cultivates indifference to the world, 31. 167; dances in same way as at 15, 33. 283; desires company with whom he can talk about his own world, 30. 279; diffidence never felt with friends, 25. 201; dines after Parliament session, 35. 213; dines alone, early, 25. 460; dines alone in dressing-room, 36. 39; dines at 4 when he can, 34. 42; dines earlier than his friends do, 33. 581; dinner not eaten in Parliament, 31. 90, 93; dinner-time his chief hour of business, 38. 232; dipping head in pail of cold water, 21. 168; dirty during attack of gout, 33. 73; discharges his head of anything he has printed, 16. 206–7; disclaims 'all depend-ence, all paying of court,' 40. 336; disregards protection against weather, 28. 182, 241, 29. 1; does not complain about past afflictions and illnesses, 31. 282, 305; does not go out until 8 P.M., 25. 641; 'do not see three persons in three days,' 39. 317; drinking cold water, 39. 162; drinks nothing but cold water, 24. 423; during siesta-time, always drove about deserted Florence, 25. 558; evenings spent alone, 12. 51; 'exercise always hurts me,' 32. 366; face and neck washed in cold water upon waking, 24. 423; faro-playing, 21. 368; favours neither asked nor received, 41. 78; forgives political enemies but never forgets private friends, 26. 28; French spoken only to footman, 37. 110; frugal meals, 10. 239; goes out twice a day, 32. 102; goes to bed after 1 A.M., 38. 183; goes to bed at 10 P.M. 'for once,' 38. 321; grown indolent, 25. 332; grows better 'the more bad I see in my neighbours,' 35. 347; 'hanging in chains' for amusement, 35. 27; hardly stirs out of the house, 25. 209–10; had neither quarrels nor enemies, 25. 310; has room washed though in bed, 39. 186; has to rest until 2 hours before bedtime when recovering from gout, 30. 278; hasty composition, 28. 6; hat never worn, 31. 351, 33. 465, 38. 2; haunts auctions, 21. 368; hears 'everything by seeing everybody,' 32. 89; hides newspaper accounts of executions, 33. 444; hours in bed, 1. 103; hours of rising and retiring, 15. 320; hunting, brewing, reaping and drinking avoided, 18. 8; inaccurate in dates, 11. 26; inclination to please 'all the people you converse with,' 40. 44–5; 'indolence,' 32. 241; indulges himself at home when done with the world, 38. 296; in league with all the sober virtues, 25. 338; in Paris, 31. 93, 109, 41. 1; interested only in necessities not in luxuries, 33. 138; in summer, ignores events since 1600, 40. 288; Italian spoken only to himself, 37. 110; keeps early hours when recovering from gout, 30. 281; late rising, 9. 231, 10. 175, 310, 311, 35. 212; 'laughing at everybody else,' 32. 210; laughs at all serious characters, 19. 4; laughs 'because I do not like to cry,' 35. 347; laughs *with* the world half the time, and *at* it, the rest, 35. 352; lets alum dissolve in his mouth twice a week, 39. 106; lies abed all morning, 21. 368; lies abed longer than the lark, 38. 73; lies late in bed, 9. 231, 10. 175, 310, 311, 31. 36, 90, 93; lies on couch when ill with gout, 31. 62, 128; lives with old women, 41. 277; living single, 37. 110; locks himself up when ill, 39. 184, 186; long autumn evenings the best working hours, 32. 46; loo played till 2 or 3 A.M., 21. 368; loves of old people are life-long, 35. 127; lying in wet room, 39. 162; masks, in Venice, to avoid

dancing, 17. 77; meal hours, 6. 178; morning circle of intimate friends, 29. 353; name not usually put on subscriptions, 31. 383; neither rides nor walks, 39. 437; 'never at home in an evening,' 1. 117; never drinks liqueurs, 21. 222; new acquaintance not sought or encouraged, 25. 338; newsmonger, 11. 29; newspaper at breakfast, 35. 342; newspaper reading, 23. 497; no longer makes overnight journeys, 30. 268; not dressed at 4 P.M., 32. 189; not up at 9:45 A.M., 38. 418; opera box corner occupied by, 36. 39; pampers himself, 11. 287, 311, 325; Parliament attendance followed by assemblies, suppers, and balls, 35. 212–13; 'parti-coloured life,' 32. 298; peevishness, 11. 25, 41; philosophy, 39. 276; plays biribis but does not dance or mask at Reggio, 17. 46; plays loo on Mondays, 38. 265; plays loo till midnight, 36. 39; political disinterestedness, 21. 79, 25. 210, 260, 276; prefers being as young as he pleases, 31. 50; prefers SH to London amusements, 32. 216; presents no longer accepted, 25. 193; prowls about bridge at Florence, after supper, 17. 473; public places avoided except Gloucester House, 25. 242, 247; punctuality, 11. 97; pursuits always light and trifling, 16. 308; quarrels never reciprocated, 38. 358; quiet life at SH, 32. 279; reading, 32. 222–3; reading by candlelight, 21. 139, 147; reading if book provides one passage of interest, 33. 274; reading in a chaise, 21. 139; reads by candlelight only, 16. 20; reads in library at Houghton, 30. 37; reads little, 25. 542; reads only sensible books, 16. 282; reads only for amusement, 16. 304, 32. 374, 34. 195; reads only the most trifling books, 16. 306; reads only what nobody else would read, 41. 278; reads till 3 A.M., 22. 523; reads very little and only for amusement, 34. 195; receives guests at 7 P.M. when recovering from gout, 31. 129; recluse life, 25. 242; regimen, 1. 339, 366, 2. 209–10, 292, 293, 298–9; regimen, temperance, and cold habitually employed to resist gout, 25. 242; renounces dining abroad, 25. 22; reported by L'Isle, 5. 253; retires at 2 A.M., 6. 178; retires early despite fashionable lateness of hours, 25. 247; rises before 11, 17. 335; rising hour, 6. 178n; sauntering in the dew, 33. 278; saunters in slippers till dinner-time, 39. 127; scribbles notes in margins of books, 2. 80, 28. 292, 29. 169, 175, 35. 633; seldom dines abroad, 33. 130, 35. 366; seldom goes out before dinner, 42. 202; seldom goes out before 7 P.M., 32. 279; seldom goes out in the morning, 32. 411, 39. 295, 41. 469; sits in dark corner under window, in House of Commons, 39. 222; sits up late, 31. 90, 93; 'sleep and doze exceedingly,' 33. 144; sleeps at command, 34. 105; sleeps instantly, 34. 195; sleeps

'like a dormouse,' 29. 311; sleeps longer and sounder, 34. 55, (?) sleeps on couch during gout, 31. 120; sleeps 10 hours, 34. 177; sleeps 12 hours, 34. 105; small circle, 33. 271; snuff avoided, 20. 377; 'sober company,' 32. 92; solitary, 34. 18; solitary summers, 32. 295; solitude better than dull company, 32. 94; 'so writative and talkative,' 33. 159; stays home in morning to have spirits to go through the evening, 35. 353; stays out past 1 A.M., 32. 109, 112, 114, 117; stays out till 4 A.M. at Duc de Guines's ball, 32. 117; supper at half an hour after midnight, 38. 371; sups in company, 21. 368; surrounded by family, like a patriarch, 33. 346; takes notes in Parliament, 38. 321; taking dog for walk in Paris gardens, 35. 121; temperance, 28. 93; troublesome to give dinners for foreigners, 33. 353–6; uses infirmities to avoid doing what he dislikes, 30. 280; usually a good sailor, 10. 250; vegetates in one spot, 33. 251; visitors call from 1 to 4 P.M., 34. 107; visitors drop in around 8 P.M., 25. 617; visitors not received during gout, 33. 70–1; visits after dinner, 31. 93; vivid dreams, 10. 295; walks like a tortoise, 33. 366; walks outdoors in slippers with no hat, 9. 225, 10. 163; water-drinking, 2. 291, 9. 300, 337, 10. 266; wine-drinking avoided, 35. 191; writes in bow-window of Round Room, 35. 339; writes when company is in the room, 16. 206; writing on pictures, 9. 225, 10. 12; young people avoided lest he weary them, 32. 246; young people not censured, 33. 567

hair of, given by J. Deere to J. T. Smith of British Museum, 43. 326

handshake of, 3. 348

handwriting of: difficult, 11. 172, 257, 319, 12. 76, 166, 184, 186, 189, 195, 197, 198, 199, 204–5, 209, 211; 'fair,' 10. 165; small, 12. 142, 155, 32. 147, 173; writes without hands, feet, eyes, 32. 94

happiness of, 25. 331–2, 30. 176

hates human race, 3. 216

health of: (1763) 10. 112, (1764) 1. 82, 83, (1765) 10. 157, 177, 183, 185, (1766) 1. 103, 111, 3. 40, 130, 147, 149, 161, 164, 10. 196, 198, 217, 228, (1767) 1. 124, 3. 252, 274, 7. 323–4, (1768) 4. 70, 140, 142, 10. 267, 268, (1769) 4. 277, 283, 293, 417, 10. 284, (1770) 1. 199, 10. 322, (1773) 5. 306, 308, 312, (1774) 6. 7, 34, 85, (1775) 1. 352, 355–6, 373, 6. 224, (1776) 6. 298, 300, (1777) 2. 54, (1779) 2. 163, 167, (1780) 2. 229, 233, (1782) 2. 323, 327, 337, (1784) 31. 217, (1791) 31. 358–9, (1795) 31. 399; able to stamp with both feet on marble hearth, 24. 71, 80; abscesses, 15. 283, 336, 337, 34. 227, 36. 292, 42. 436, 438; abscess in leg, 31. 402; age and gout make engagements uncertain, 35. 536; ague, 1. 301; airings do not benefit, 12. 209; 'a little

[Walpole, Hon. Horatio (1717–97), *continued*]
recovered,' 42. 425; alleviations make him reconciled to pain, 42. 245; almost able to walk up to bed, 39. 478; ankle sprained, 37. 66; ankle swollen, 39. 403; appetite never fails, 34. 105; appetite perfect and slumber marvellous, 25. 558; arm and hand swollen, 15. 260; as broken as if he were 100, 25. 570; bad, 15. 335; bark benefits, 24. 521, 532; bark taken for fever, 2. 7; Bath visit restores, 30. 235; Bath waters improve, 31. 130; Bath waters may aid, 39. 76–7, 78–9, 80, 41. 35, 36, 40; better, 30. 238; better than in the last 5 years, 33. 224; better than 3 years ago, 31. 345; between life and death, 25. 348; bilious attack, 39. 507, 42. 395; bled, 10. 147, 18. 200, 213, 25. 280; bled for influenza, 25. 297; blight in the eye, 33. 561; blind in one eye, 30. 268; bootikins beneficial to, 23. 76, 231, 241, 246, 310, 450, 24. 67, 70–1, 80, 268, 272, 281–2, 421, 463, 479, 494, 25. 149, 242; bootikins used for rheumatism of shoulder, 24. 463; bowel disorder, 12. 37, 38, 47; breast inflammation feared, 24. 426, 433; breast weak, 25. 552; breast, weakest part of, 39. 235; 'broken and weak,' 42. 343; brought to town very ill, 42. 444; bruised from fall, 11. 19, 25, 70, 33. 225, 34. 49, 50, 63–4, 65; bruised in falls, 31. 298, 303, 305, 330; bruises from two falls, 16. 310; can neither ride nor walk, 39. 437; cannot walk farther than snail, 39. 296; carried by servants to bed, 22. 316, 23. 241, 25. 347; chalk in fingers, 12. 76; chalkstone in every finger, 39. 493; chalkstones, 2. 286, 337, 15. 241; chalkstones from finger, 25. 617–18; chalkstones in fingers, 28. 241, 29. 7, 152, 165, 176, 281, 337, 358, 31. 237, 242, 298; 'codicil' of gout, 25. 284; cold and cough, 15. 105; cold and fever, 18. 200, 213; cold cured by SH, 38. 522; cold, fever, and oppression on breast, 25. 280; cold, followed by gout, 25. 343; colds, 1. 85, 89, 301, 2. 317, 318, 7. 266, 10. 147, 148, 180, 11. 143, 17. 197, 218, 18. 94, 115, 147, 174, 365, 546, 21. 139, 22. 42, 285, 348, 506, 23. 450, 28. 348, 353–4, 29. 89, 31. 112, 149, 290, 295, 32. 94, 33. 4, 458, 34. 5, 33, 34, 209, 35. 210, 630, 38. 155, 494, 508, 40. 1, 27, 120, 371, 388, 41. 377; colds rarely afflict, 30. 250; cold weather confines him to room, 42. 443; cold weather improves, 31. 78; confined to bed, 15. 335; constantly flitting gout, 30. 268; consumptive tendency, 15. 337; cough, 1. 85, 89, 2. 317, 10. 26, 18. 135, 23. 450, 25. 555, 30. 277, 31. 290, 34. 5, 34, 35. 630, 38. 155, 508, 39. 166; cramp in left foot in first gout attack, 38. 65; crippled feet, 31. 305; crippled hands, 31. 305, 403; critical state of, 15. 322, 327; declines, 23. 537; delicate, 5. 11; depression of spirits,

12. 210; described, 11. 249; disorder in bowels, 12. 37, 38, 47, 28. 463, 29. 89, 337; disorder in stomach, 36. 319; disorder of, merely nervous, 22. 484; dispiritedness, 38. 65; Du Deffand, Mme, anxious about, 3. 68, 87, 119, 121, 124, 125, 128, 131, 134–41, 145, 147, 150, 153, 154, 159–63, 165, 167–9, 173, 176, 178, 180, 182–5, 192, 194, 220, 221, 223, 225, 232, 248, 265, 267, 281, 307, 316, 322–3, 325, 326, 328, 347, 348, 350, 352–5, 379–81, 384, 386, 397, 398, 401, 4. 34, 81, 109, 116, 147–53, 155, 156, 202, 208, 247, 252, 273, 278, 332, 333, 335, 337, 348, 364, 408, 414, 459–68, 472–4, 476–8, 487, 491, 5. 32, 65, 66, 68, 75, 76, 78, 84, 86, 92, 93, 102, 126, 130, 133, 148, 150, 235–6, 262–3, 271–80, 285–8, 291, 293, 295, 304–5, 308, 312, 318, 321, 324, 326–7, 329, 336, 342, 353, 377, 380, 416, 436, 6. 1, 2, 59, 63, 77, 78, 94, 100, 105–6, 110, 119, 122–6, 140, 165, 178, 196, 198, 238, 264, 265, 267, 269, 271, 274, 283, 295, 298, 305, 309, 370, 371, 373, 382–3, 384, 387–9, 392, 398, 401, 491, 7. 8, 53, 67, 73, 74, 79, 82, 83, 85–8, 90, 105, 106, 137, 147, 188, 193–5, 197, 210, 230, 235, 238; early hours easiest, 31. 368; emaciated, 31. 80; England's damp air injures, more than mode of living, 41. 45–6; eruption in arm, 15. 213; erysipelas, 11. 369, 377; escapes scythe by being low, 39. 62; evenings improve, 31. 129; exceedingly out of order, 31 125; excellent, 12. 51; exercise always hurts, 32. 366; extremely but not dangerously ill, 25. 350; eye improves, 24. 501; eye inflammation, 10. 205, 39. 54, 447, 42. 203; eyes, 18. 135, 148, 365, 386, 21. 139, 41. 8; eyes affected by gout, 33. 106, 118, 120, 352; eyes and memory lost, 42. 101; eyes cured by rum, elderflower water and cold douches, 21. 167–8, 177; eyes differ, 12. 253; eyes formerly strong, 16. 299; eyes grow stronger, 28. 268; eyesight conserved for worthy books, 25. 542; eyesight poor, 16. 299; eyesight strained, 16. 20; eyes incapable of reading faint ink by candlelight, 42. 189; eyes perfect, 31. 305, 374, 402; eyes weak, 9. 227, 230; eyes 'worn out,' 21. 156; eye trouble, 13. 147; eye trouble diagnosed by Dr Cocchi, 21. 147; face swollen, 42. 203; fall, 4. 143, 11. 19, 25, 70, 16. 310, 31. 298, 303, 305, 330, 33. 225, 34. 49, 50, 63–4, 65, 36. 256; fall from rising from chair without stick, 25. 555n; falls down 10 times a day, 31. 72; fatigued after taking the air, 25. 559; fatter, 10. 245, 267; feeble and unable to walk, 15. 333; feels weak, lame, and crippled, 30. 279; feet and legs swelled, 40. 388; feet not quite recovered, 24. 227; fever, 1. 82, 2. 7, 318, 3. 65, 68, 87, 142, 220, 232, 325, 6. 266, 281, 16. 243, 17. 402, 22. 285, 30. 195, 31. 37, 205, 209, 409, 33. 74, 81, 96, 104, 144, 373–4, 413, 419, 427, 35. 529,

38. 236, 508, 39. 3, 401, 43. 169; fever abates, 15. 336; fever and rash, 14. 85, 40. 343; fever nightly, 29. 311; fever remedied by gout, 25. 283; fingers do not write easily, 42. 362; fingers lame, 42. 218; fingers lame in right hand, 25. 370; fingers will serve for chalk pencil, 33. 310; flourishing, 33. 278; forbidden to speak, 24. 426, 433; free from pain, 10. 168; French air said to benefit, 41. 14; frequent illness, 16. 260, 304; giddiness, 39. 76; gnat in the eye, 9, 356; good, 11. 156, 224, 254, 373, 12. 101, 25. 185, 297, 312, 323, 332, 30. 238; gout (general references), 1. 330, 2. 141, 3. 118, 332, 4. 127, 137, 5. 21, 11. 14n, 81n, 13. 48, 51, 14. 115, 140, 142–3, 158, 186–7, 15. 86, 108, 122, 135, 138, 140, 158, 159, 168, 183, 193, 204, 209, 210, 214, 241, 259–60, 274, 283, 337, 344, 16. 132, 180, 199, 200, 202, 246–7, 262, 287, 296, 299, 310, 318, 319, 327, 21. 432, 440, 22. 38, 46, 110, 114, 116, 117, 257, 266, 309, 316, 322–3, 332, 340, 348, 359, 361, 450, 454, 23. 61, 67, 240–1, 243, 246, 251–2, 440, 443, 447, 450, 454, 458, 459–60, 462, 464, 465, 471, 474, 476, 494, 555, 24. 55, 66, 70–1, 80, 83, 174, 178, 184, 189, 268, 270, 272, 274, 278–80, 421, 422, 425, 426, 428, 432, 433, 436, 521, 532, 533, 542, 25. 149, 171, 201, 235, 242, 248, 280, 283, 284, 290, 297, 343, 347–8, 350, 351, 354, 358, 370, 402, 551, 555, 558, 560, 561, 615, 617, 622–3, 28. 51–4, 57, 61, 93, 130, 134 ('biennial'), 145, 164, 167, 179 ('codicil'), 240–1, 247, 250, 258, 268, 443, 462–4, 482, 485, 488 ('codicil') 29. 89, 166, 174–5, 249, 276–7, 279, 298, 337, 353, 358, 361, 366, 30. 281, 283, 298, 337, 353, 358, 361, 366, 31. 411, 35. 303, 317, 330, 331, 338, 340, 366, 372, 395–6, 414, 429, 456–7, 489, 496, 499, 500, 529, 531, 630, 632, 36. 79, 93, 231, 234, 236, 240–1, 244, 250, 275, 38. 65–6, 68, 69, 39. 3, 5, 22–3, 25, 30–1, 37, 54, 59, 112, 131, 156–7, 159, 162, 164, 165, 166, 175, 184, 186, 198–9, 206, 208–9, 216, 225–6, 228–30, 235, 237–8, 244, 274, 317, 401, 402–3, 475, 493–4, 501, 42. 451; gout (arranged by dates), (1755–6) 9. 194, 35. 259–60, 264, (1760) 9. 291–3, (1762) 1. 33, 10. 29–31, (1765) 1. 94, 95, 7. 267–8, 272, 10. 159–65, 167, 179–82, 188, 30. 192, 195, 201–2, 204, 31. 27–41, 58–64, 66–7, 32. 13–14, 21, 23, 42, 40. 385, 386, 388, (1766) 1. 118–20, 3. 124, 134, 135, 138–9, 4. 150, 467, 10. 226–7, 231, 31. 127–9, (1767) 3. 322–3, 325, 10. 245, 246, (1768) 4. 126, 148–52, 155, 158, 160, 165, 169, 10. 266, 267, 269, 31. 140, 41. 165, (1769) 4. 308, 10. 277, 32. 37, (1770) 4. 459–64, 466–70, 474, 479, 10. 319–22, 31. 147–9, 32. 43–4, 41. 184–5, 190, (1771) 5. 133, 148, 150, (1772–3) 1. 285–6, 288, 289, 292, 301, 316, 324, 5. 268, 271–80, 285–6, 293–5, 318, 321, 326, 31. 168–71, 32. 89, 94, 121, 133, 41. 234, 235, 237,

(1774) 6. 12, 17, 77–9, 81, 94, 97, 98, 100, 101, 105, 119, 121–6, 30. 261, 31. 180–1, 41. 280, (1775) 1. 351, 356, 6. 131, 132, 137, 140, 150, 165, 170, 196–8, 203, 41. 284, (1776) 2. 1, 6. 257, 263–4, 266–9, 271, 274, 276, 285, 313, 369, 370, 382–3, 387, 31. 187, 32. 326, 336, 338, 41. 333–4, 336, 339, 343, 351, 42. 138, 157, (1777) 2. 32, 68, 6. 387, 389, 392, 398, 401, 409, 437, 439, 440, 32. 340–1, 344, 402, 41. 355, (1778) 2. 132, 134–5, 7. 1, 83, 85–8, 90, 93, 96, 97, 31. 189–93, 33. 67–70, 72–5, 76, 78, 80, 41. 389, 390, 391, 392, (1779) 2. 139, 178, 7. 100, 105, 106, 176, 192, 196, 197, 199, 235, 31. 198, 33. 83, 90, 106, 117, 118, 120, 122, 124, 141, 143, 144, 148, (1779–80) 2. 254–5, (1780) 2. 261, 41. 406, (1781) 2. 261, 286, 33. 259, 285, 288–9, 307, 309, 310, 41. 456, 457, 462, (1782) 2. 292, 298, 318, 32. 322–3, 352, 373–5, 42. 14, 17, (1783) 31. 204, 33. 378–81, 383, 408, 409, 42. 75, (1784) 33. 456, (1785) 30. 277, 31. 223, 237, 298, 33. 456–9, 42. 127, 128, 157, (1786) 31. 241, 33. 507, 513, 525, 42. 177, (1787) 33. 551, 581, 586, 42. 194, 200, 203, 43. 385, (1788) 31. 276, 282, 288, 34. 4, 5, 12, 14, 42. 214, (1789) 11. 25, 70, 72, 12. 265, 31. 296, 328, 34. 70, 83, 42. 243, 244, 245, 256, 43. 387, (1790) 11. 83, 84, 89, 92, 94, 170, 31. 339, 341–2, 42. 304, 306, (1791) 11. 174, 178, 179, 182, 183, 187, 188, 190, 193, 214, 217, 222, 312, 313, 369, 377, 31. 347, 359, 34. 105, 106, 107, 115, 129, 134, (1792) 34. 142–3, 42. 354, 355, 359, 362, 43. 388, (?) 390, (1793) 12. 4, 31. 392, 34. 188, 193, 42. 396, (1794) 12. 91, 96, 31. 393, 42. 408, (1795) 12. 174, 175, 177, 183–4, 31. 398, 34. 209, 210, 211, 42. 416, (1796–7) 12. 187, 215n, 34. 211, 216–17, 42. 427, 436, 437–9, 442, 444, 447; gout (shortest fit in many years), 25. 242; gout (shortest fit in 10 years) 25. 235; gout as result of being bled for influenza, 25. 297; gout attributed to nerves, 22. 116, 117; gout becomes annual instead of biennial, 24. 272; gout chronic but rarely dangerous, 31. 276; gout compared to Parliamentary ailments, 25. 402; gout connected with politics, 31. 39, 41; gout destructive of his talents, 31. 68; gout expected, 32. 192; gout feared, 32. 366, 33. 4, 51; gout fits frequent but short and tolerable, 31. 345; gout forbids him tea, 31. 75; gout going off in a minuet step, 31. 45; gout gone, 31. 73; gout his only illness, 31. 97; gout if cured might be succeeded by worse ailments, 25. 402; gout in bowels, 25. 555; gout incog. as rheumatism, 33. 120; gout in eye, 39. 332; gout in hands and one arm, 42. 394; gout in head for half an hour, never in stomach, 24. 422; gout in stomach, 33. 259; gout makes writing difficult, 30. 195; gout may force him to leave SH, 31. 75; gout never in his stomach,

[Walpole, Hon. Horatio (1717–97), *continued*]
25. 551; gout no great calamity, 31. 277; gout not envied by Sir Edward Walpole, 36. 154; gout not to be kept from stomach by wine, 35. 264; gout not to be risked by winter return to England, 30. 211; gout ordinarily towards Sept., 4. 337; gout recovering, 40. 380–1, 41. 281–2; gout returns, 30. 200; gout 'rumours,' 36. 41; gout symptoms, 32. 200; gout tendency makes a winter in Paris impossible, 24. 117; gout threats, 36. 165; gout thrown out in several joints, 24. 521; gout would return if in House of Commons, 23. 66; gouty feet, 35. 596; gouty pain in hand, 25. 185; 'great cold and cough,' 42. 191; HW exaggerates badness of, to escape social functions, 25. 22, 332, 595, 611, 647; HW guards, to prevent decrepitude, not to prolong life, 25. 5; HW jokes about, 31. 10; hand muffled up, 25. 552; hand, 'nervous and shaking,' 41. 463; hand shakes, 25. 539; hands lame, 25. 552, 629; hand useless because of gout, 30. 272; hardened against cold, 24. 288; has to be fed, 24. 274; headache, 5. (?) 230–1, (?) 235, (?) 239, (?) 371, 17. 221, 22. 506, 23. 194, 25. 648, 28. 262–3, 32. 132, 38. 380, 39. 76; head thought to be gouty, 39. 3; hearing but little impaired, 31. 305, 402; hearing less sharp, 33. 140; heats gone, 36. 4; 'Herculean weakness,' 34. 211; hobbles, 39. 295; House of Commons's heat improves, 38. 236; ill, 15. 247, 248, 35. 537; ill and weak, 42. 401; ill for two summers, 16. 56; illness, 11. 209, 12. 12, 207; illness at Richmond, 34. 200; ill with vexation and fatigue, 31. 364; impaired by anxiety over nephew, 42. 343–4; improved, 11. 42, 315–16, 319, 371, 12. 189–90, 29. 69; improved by himself, 30. 170; indisposition, 16. 326, 35. 626, 41. 35; infirm, 15. 316, 16. 320, 41. 34; inflammation and swelling of arm, 31. 237; inflammation in bowels, 15. 275; inflammation in face, 28. 179; inflammation of eyes, 18. 117, 21. 131, 139, 147, 24. 501, 513, 31. 112; inflammation of right leg, 34. 227; inflammation of the breast, 33. 75; inflammation of the lungs suspected, 18. 149; influenza, 10. 26, 25. 297, 29. 249, 252, 42. 17; insomnia, 24. 342, 31. 39, 66, 128, 190–1, 409, 35. 374–5, 534, 36. 87; in surgeon's hands, 15. 284; intellect unimpaired for common use, 31. 374; invulnerable stomach, 34. 229; 'iron stomach,' 34. 118, 139; (?) jaundice, 31. 128; joints lame, 11. 89, 12. 170, 25. 354, 29. 218, 280, 283–4, 30. 268, 31. 170, 235, 330, 35. 338–9, 366, 372, 42. 75; lame and weak, 15. 214; lamed by overheating himself, 35. 372; lame hand, 31. 409; lameness, 11. 89, 12. 179, 31. 170, 235, 330; legs swelled, 32. 21; leg swollen from gnat-bites, 38. 102; limbs broken to pieces by gout, 25. 531; lips cut

in coach accident, 39. 454; London air agrees with, 35. 375; London better than SH for, 15. 238, 22. 451, 456–7, 24. 277–8, 288, 33. 427, 428, 39. 165, 166; London's smoke suits, 42. 200; loses use of several joints of fingers, 25. 201; 'low and faint,' 36. 84; 'low and weak,' 34. 211; Mann fears that late hours in Parliament may shatter, 18. 114, 21. 28; Mann's compared to, 24. 532; Mann urges that letter be omitted when it is too painful to write, 25. 1; Mann, Horace II, reports, as perfect, 25. 425; measles, 32. 217; medicines refused, 35. 319; mended, 35. 317; mending fast, 34. 139; mental decay, 29. 136, 153; mind and body want repose, 30. 194; mortification of the bowels, 34. 211; moved from bed by servants, 36. 90; needs aid to climb stairs, 16. 320; nerves, 17. 452, 25. 49; nerves affected by damp, 24. 288; nerves sensitive and spirits low, 33. 157, 159; nerves shattered, 32. 186, 192, 33. 307, 35. 496; nerves very sensitive, 24. 272; nervous, 12. 166, 25. 201; nervous after attack of gout, 33. 157, 311; nervous and lame, 16. 199; nervous fever, 9. 271, 275; nervous in the morning, 25. 539; never ill, 37. 408; night fever, 10. 109, 38. 65; nightly fever and pain in breast, 38. 463–4; 'not able to write,' 41. 38; not allowed to see company, 25. 552; not susceptible to colds, 33. 311; not well, 30. 71; Nuneham gives Mason a good account of, 28. 62; old and broken, 39. 244; oppression on the breast, 16. 243, 288; Orford's illness affects, 24. 373; out of humour, 31. 168; out of order, 16. 247, 35. 582, 41. 36, 437; overtaxed by activity during Gordon riots, 33. 195, 200; pain, 10. 244, 320, 16. 260, 288; pain and swelling in the face, 33. 285; painful and dangerous illness, 42. 439; 'painful disorder,' 42. 416; pain in the breast, 32. 192, 34. 199; pain in the breast and stomach, 22. 110; pain in the eyes, 21. 139; pain in the left wrist, 11. 59; pain in the stomach, 3. 180, 232, 5. 76, 10. 47, 115, 117, 119, 231, 22. 461, 468, 33. 251, 38. 276, 39. 79; pains and weakness, 33. 163; pains in the head and stomach, 38. 65; pains in the stomach and limbs, 22. 450, 454; palpitation of the heart, 15. 327; palpitations, 34. 199; paralytic disorder attributed by gazetteer, 22. 459; Paris stay did not injure, 41. 45; Parliament injures, 38. 511; perspires immoderately and constantly, 24. 423; physic sent by mother, 36. 3, 4; Pitt, Thomas, hopes that fine weather has re-established, 40. 329; poisoned by dirt and vermin, 39. 255; poor, 30. 80; 'poor invalid,' 33. 132; quinsy, 13. 10, 243, 17. 51, 52, 54–5, 66, 21. 369, 30. 17, 42. 204, 43. 169; quite recovered, 30. 238; recovered, 11. 200, 22. 50, 41. 50; recovers more quickly in town than in the country, 33. 415; recovery shown by his resuming a book, 35. 529; regime, 3. 233, 4. 467; 'regiment of disorders,' 39. 341; relapses after change in weather, 31. 149; relapse from talking too much, 31. 192; relapses caused by venturing out too soon, 25. 617; reported ill with paralytic disorder, 1. 118, 31. 127; rheumatic fever, 25. 428, 33. 413, 427, 35. 374, 534; rheumatism, 2. 244, 7. 82, 10. 232, 11. 174, 178, 311, 312, 313, 334, 336, 22. 450, 23. 460, 25. 166, 570, 28. 462, 29. 311, 313, 317, 31. 190, 197, 201, 204–5, 210, 359, 33. 129, 278–82, 322, 409, 412, 419, 428, 34. 105, 106, 112, 125–6, 209, 35. 376, 531, 39. 316, 340, 341, 42. 75; rheumatism in arm, 25. 432; rheumatism in shoulder, 25. 463; 497; rheumatism possibly caused by SH damps, 22. 456–7; riding necessary for, 30. 80, 37. 178; right hand still weak, 25. 5; robust, 22. 396; ruined by years and gout, 35. 372; scandalously well, 33. 438; sciatica, 29. 313, 317, 31. 205; sea air benefits, 23. 227, 311, 318; seasickness, 3. 353, 7. 324, 342, 10. 250, 30. 250, 39. 255, 260; seasickness escaped, 39. 7; sleeps as soon as fever has gone, 25. 620; sleeps in air to improve, 31. 369; sleeps well, 31. 402, 39. 494; sleep the great restorative of, 33. 375; slow fever, 35. 218; sore throat, 28. 179; spectacles used in reading, 35. 455; spirits do not last out the day, 39. 295; stair-climbing difficulties, 31. 394; stomach pain eased by ice-water, 39. 106; stomach pains, 3. 180, 232, 5. 76; stomach sickness, 40. 388; stomach sickness cured by leaving off tea, 39. 30; stomach trouble, 31. 138–9; SH's dampness provokes gout, 22. 451, 24. 277–8, 288; strength does not return, 30. 195; strength returns, 31. 45, 48; strong pulse, 34. 229; suffers from cold, 31. 4; sufficient for HW's needs, 25. 332; sweats, 4. 464, 466–8, 474; swelled finger, 32. 402; swelling, 11. 176; symptoms of palsy, 29. 18; system for preserving, 31. 345; talking forbidden, 31. 367; talking prohibited during attack of gout in chest, 30. 261; teeth can chew nothing solid after coach accident, 39. 454; teeth preserved, 31. 402; teeth sound at near 70, 39. 454; teeth strong, 10. 276; teeth well-preserved, 34. 55–6; teeth will be replaced by colts' teeth when gone, 35. 351; tendency to tumble on nose, 34. 49; 'tender and weak constitution,' 36. 295; tolerably well, 31. 374; 'to live an hundred years longer,' 40. 181; too weak to speak, 30. 281; totters when going down stairs, 24. 81; town agrees better with, than country, 15. 238; trembling hand, 31. 401; 'uneasy posture,' 40. 205; unwell all summer, 30. 272, 273; very nervous but does not catch cold easily, 33. 311; very seriously ill, 30. 277; voice lost, 18. 135, 24. 426, 428; vomiting, 12. 194,

22. 454, 34. 199, 227; weak and broken, 30. 302; 'weak and shattered,' 32. 385; weakened by attention to nephew's affairs, 28. 116, 134, 139; weak frame but strong foundation, 28. 468; weakness, 3. 135, 137, 140, 11. 174, 180, 287, 12. 91, 30. 192, 199, 31. 41, 148, 190, 330; weakness and infirmities, 42. 446; weakness in the breast from gout, 25. 350, 31. 367; weakness on the breast, 42. 254; weakness on the breast 30 years ago, 24. 80; weak on his feet, 24. 327, 337, 342; weight, 1. 124, 2. 184; well as ever, 22. 136; wine avoided to avoid gout, 35. 259, 264

heroic inclinations of, in childhood, 37. 203

hospitality of, limited, 9. 77

hours kept by: 6. 178n; at Florence, 37. 78; at Stowe, 10. 313; calls made at 8 P.M., 12. 159; dinner early, 11. 8, 12. 99; in Paris, 10. 291; late parties, 9. 269; meals, 6. 178; midnight supper, 10. 279; of rising and retiring, 15. 320; rises at noon after balls, 9. 231; rises late and writes letter at 1:30 A.M., 38. 312; supper at 12:30 A.M., 38. 371; unreformed, 38. 418; see also under habits of

house in London may be sought by, 37. 109–10

houses of, see Arlington St: HW's house in; Berkeley Sq.: HW's house in; Strawberry Hill; Windsor

House of Lords not immediately to be entered by, 42. 349

house sought by, 17. 334

inclinations of, 2. 46, 37. 203

indifference of, to peace-time treaties, 20. 395–6

influence of, at Court, seldom employed, 12. 127

in minority, and unlikely to hear news, 22. 256

inoculated for smallpox, 13. 3

intends to die in his bedchamber at SH, 35. 259

Ireland's MSS not believed by, 15. 321

irony the favourite weapon of, 4. 112

Italian learnt by, at Cambridge, 13. 6

judgment of, subject to prepossessions, 12. 124

knowledge of, can reflect no honour on Scottish society of antiquaries, 15. 151, 154–5

languages known to, are English, French, Greek, Italian, and Latin, 41. 294

learning disclaimed by, 21. 368, 28. 88, 114

learning of, superficial, 15. 132, 256

letter of: addressed in another's hand, 24. 72; demanding his letters from Mann, Mann keeps, 20. 397; from Paris not to be specifically answered by Mann, 24. 127; sent to Paris by private hand, 24. 137; takes 7 weeks to reach Florence, 25. 313; to Cts of Orford, Mann keeps copy of, 23. 532; written with left hand, 39. 131

[Walpole, Hon. Horatio (1717–97), *continued*]
letters of: about Nicoll affair, 14. 193–233,
20. 273, 278, 435; always welcome in Warwickshire post-bag, 38. 190; are newspapers,
30. 227, 33. 12; arrive with great speed,
21. 322; as antiquated as the writer, 35.
368; barren in summer, 25. 503; Billings-
gate absent from, unlike political pamphlets, 31. 58; blotted and ill-written, 38.
236, 39. 259; burnt when spread on hearth
to dry, 22. 512, 525; business correspondence, 31. 363–4; business correspondence after nephew's death, 39. 494; complimentary close adhered to in, 30. 269;
contain nothing of consequence, and what
anybody is welcome to see, 25. 185; contain
only what HW believes to be true, 25. 186;
Conway complains about formal salutations
in, 37. 302; Conway knows value of, 37.
121–2; Conway parodies, 37. 345; copies of,
about E. of Orford's affairs, made by HW,
23. 523; customs officials might inspect,
4. 230–1, 234; dates of, for 1760, 21. 450;
deaths and marriages the sources of, 22.
251–2; 'delightful and instructive,' Mann
says, 25. 281; depend upon generals and
admirals, 25. 327; dictated, 24. 423, 426,
428, 25. 350, 615, 616, 39. 229–30; discuss
kingdoms and rulers because common acquaintances are lacking, 21. 329, 24. 206;
Du Deffand, Mme, burns, 7. 69, 249; Du
Deffand, Mme, not to return, 4. 233–4,
237; Du Deffand, Mme, to burn, 7. 59, 64;
Du Deffand, Mme, returns, 4. 279; Du
Deffand, Mme, to return, 4. 229, 230; Du
Deffand, Mme, to return by Conway, 6.
126, 152, 156, 39. 190–1, 198, 234; dwindling, except for a few business and antiquarian ones, 25. 584; Edgcumbe reads
superscription of, 30. 37; erudite, 9. 227;
feigned names in, 13. 55; fit to be seen by
those who have no more rational diversions, 33. 578; from France, indiscreetly
quoted, 41. 7; full of nonsense, 32. 240,
243; Gloucester, Ds of, says, are mere excuses for lack of anything to say, 25. 527,
36. 227–8; Grafton, D. of, praises political
accounts in, 22. 538n; grow shorter, 18.
560; HW and Mann no longer have little
events in common to fill, 21. 295; HW
ashamed of bad French in, 39. 190; HW
asks Lady Ossory not to show, 34. 38; HW
asks Mann to return, 21. 60, 316, 324, 554,
22. 422, 451, 23. 94, 265, 25. 184, 380, 487;
HW asks Montagu to preserve, 9. 2, 275;
HW begs Mann not to entrust, to sots like
Dering, 21. 374–5; HW calls, unoriginal
imitations of Mme de Sévigné and Gray,
28. 217; HW cannot 'compose,' like Pliny
and Pope, 33. 504; HW cannot write 'fine,'
33. 581; HW cautious to write only truths
in, 24. 412, 25. 186; HW does not write,
just to have them shown, 33. 581; HW

fears, will not reach England from Italy,
13. 206; HW forgets by what messenger
Mann is returning, 22. 73; HW gags pen
for those that cross sea, 25. 257; HW glad
to send amusing, to Selwyn, 30. 268; HW
keeps list of dates of, 31. 353; HW knows
Lady Ossory keeps, 32. 385, 33. 53, 34. 46;
HW means what he says in, 24. 493; HW
prides himself in keeping up, despite difficulties, 18. 479–80; HW promises to return, to Mann, 20. 23; HW re-reads, 23.
94; HW's deletions in, 17. 50n, 74n, 91n,
209n; HW sends, by private hand, 22. 294,
308, 24. 137, 25. 309; HW should put covers
on, 37. 578; HW's motives in writing, 21.
263; HW's vanity makes him fear exposure
in, 33. 584; HW the last person to admit,
are 'sensible,' 33. 12; HW will record great
events in, though Mann no longer knows
the background, 21. 551–2; HW would like
to stop writing, from weariness of describ-
ing human folly, 21. 545–6; HW writes, at
Houghton to keep up his English, 30. 34;
HW writes 8 in two days, 32. 281; Hardinge
denies coldness of, 35. 561; Hardinge
praises, 35. 649; Hertford, Cts of, praises,
39. 36; *hors d'œuvre* is HW's term for, 25.
167; inconsequential details will not be
noticed in, 25. 97–8; indifference not a good
ingredient in, 25. 312; information, not general topics, to be the staple of, 24. 456;
in Mann's behalf, not answered, 22. 363;
insipid from his 'decays,' and 'little intercourse' with the world, 35. 296; intervals
between, make Mann anxious about HW's
health, 24. 87; journals, not history, 22.
441; 'kind of history,' 23. 265; lack of
news for, in Paris, 31. 72, 109–10; Leopold
may open, 25. 412n; less frequent from
Paris than from London, 22. 409; like ugly
people, do not grow worse from age, 34.
70; limited to topics of interest to posterity,
24. 451; long continuance of, to Mann,
22. 274; long continuance of, would never
have been predicted, 25. 556; long on the
road, 25. 333; long without content, 31.
57–8; Mann always impatient for, 24. 374;
Mann calls, witty, 17. 270; Mann cherishes
and re-reads, 19. 508, 20. 15, 83, 456; Mann
compares, to Mme de Sévigné's, 20. 83;
Mann could not bear to exchange, for anybody else's, 25. 76; Mann depends on, for
explanation of public events, 24. 408; Mann
finds, necessary to his tranquillity, 24. 388,
390, 396; Mann hopes, will continue even
if there is nothing to say, 20. 397; Mann
may have read a paragraph of, to Dering,
21. 383; Mann needs, for recovery, 25. 607;
Mann praises, 18. 425; Mann reads, first
of those coming in packets, 22. 326, 25.
333; Mann returns, to HW, 20. 15, 23, 54,
441, 456, 471, 485, 21. 113, 118, 124, 413,
565, 22. 88, 141, 145, 152, 326, 477, 483,

490, 23. 296, 309, 491, 24. 100, 165, 246–8, 250, 260, 266, 379, 413, 493, 522, 530, 25. 198, 411, 417, 498, 521, 540, 621, 668; Mann's anxiety to get, and pleasure in reading them, 24. 106; Mann's gratitude for, 25. 657; Mann's greatest consolation and instruction, 24. 396; Mann's reasons for valuing, 20. 283; Mann too weak to answer, 25. 662; Mann unprovoked by delays in, but merely worried about HW's health, 24. 232; Mann wants, back, 19. 508, 20. 15, 218, 397; Mann weeps over, 25. 662; Mann will be punctual in returning, 25. 395; may be intercepted and opened now that HW's niece is married to D. of Gloucester, 23. 537; may seem grave but are really foolish, 22. 373; merit of, is not novelty but confirmation of what is in newspapers, 25. 185–6; middle period of, the most agreeable because of England's victories, 24. 356, 484; Monnerat, David, does not post, if unsealed, 33. 99; Montagu to preserve, 9. 2, 275; more trifling than those of any man living, 38. 94; more unreserved from Paris than when written from England, 24. 123, 134; must be copied, when concerned with E. of Orford's affairs, 23. 523; must be Hebrew to all but Lady Ossory, 34. 97; must contain absurdities, 20. 74; must contain local 'gossipry,' 33. 217; must write themselves or remain unwritten, 30. 80; newspapers may anticipate, but Mann probably opens letters first, 24. 370; newspapers will inform Mann more quickly than, 24. 385; Nivernais pillages expression from, 41. 20; not to include everything that comes into HW's head, 30. 58; often written by proxy, 25. 584; old-fashioned breeding alone prompts, 34. 230; on large paper, 33. 21; on small paper, 34. 99; ordinary small events too trivial to be discussed in, to Mann, 23. 432; Ossory, Lady, reads, to daughters and niece, 34. 35; Ossory, Lady, should not show, 34. 230–1; Ossory, Lady, shows, to Fitzpatrick, 33. 577–8; political predictions in beginnings come true in conclusions of, 38. 564; Pont-de-Veyle's letters as numerous as, 32. 263; poor French insures, against publication, 36. 171–2; Pope's 'studied style' inferior to, 31. 365n; posterity's probable attitude towards, proportioned to frequency of political events, 25. 47; rarer and less informing, 24. 484; rather eras than journals, 25. 108; ready to be sent back to him by any sober traveller, 23. 277; regular recipients of, 38. 94; reports given in, for no more than they are worth, 24. 386; restricted to facts, 25. 79, 146; returned to HW from Paris, 4. 279; ridicule ministers, but Conway sends them unsealed, 37. 568; St Paul is HW's model for, 32. 385; seldom contain anything of consequence, 33. 532;

shorter since more frequent, 24. 450; shorter than Mann's, 18. 560; skim the current of facts, and mark them for Mann's information, 25. 79; sole source of Mann's news from England, 22. 122, 502; sometimes coloured when sent by the post, 24. 493; sometimes too frequent, to those he loves, 28. 327, 400; Strafford overvalues, 35. 360, 371–2, 380–1, 388; style of, changes with politics, 22. 441; take half an hour to write, 33. 38; 'tittle-tattle,' 38. 260; to Chute, disparaged by HW, 32. 306; to Gray, given to Mason for selection and publication, 13. 55; to Jephson on tragedy, 13. 49; to Lincoln, contain the first nonsense that comes into HW's head, 30. 76; to Lincoln, do not contain what he feels, 30. 72; to Mme du Deffand, faithful, 25. 90; to Mme du Deffand, to be returned by Wiart, 36. 171, 179; to Mann, amount to over 800 since he started writing to Mann, 25. 520; to Mann, should not be printed, 33. 546; to Mann, 60 between 1773 and 18 Sept. 1776, 24. 248; to Mann, transcripts of, 26. 36–44; to Mann, wanted for compiling memoirs of George II's reign, 19. 508n; to relations, concerning sister-in-law's death, 25. 122–3; 'to' retained in directions and addresses upon, 30. 269; to the Mayor of King's Lynn on leaving Parliament, 13. 42, 44, 41. 77–9; trifling and superficial, HW thinks, 25. 146; uncensored now that they pass through Conway's office, 22. 309; uniform in sum total, 24. 379; unintelligible to himself after a few years, 34. 46; unnecessary when Lord Ossory is in town, 33. 146, 270, 271, 337; unplanned, 30. 80; Vertot's works resemble, 22. 158; West praises, 13. 172; 'whims' fill gaps in, 33. 367; write themselves and are not composed, 24. 97; writing bons mots enjoyable to HW in, 32. 3; written in bow-window of Round Tower at SH, 23. 315; written only out of decorum, 24. 226; written with left hand during gout, 39. 131

letters received by HW: forwarded by post when HW is out of town, 30. 179; many, to be answered, 30. 95; to be returned to writers living after his death, 29. 355, 30. 367–8

letter-writing in French difficult for, 19. 53

liberty and honour of England the only objects of, 25. 311–12

life of: dedicated to friends, 33. 38; happier than he deserves, and happier than those of millions deserving better, 39. 317; 'insignificant' and his works 'dead and buried,' 41. 255–6; uniform to its first and only principles, 24. 493

literary fame inconsequential to, 12. 94

literary merit denied by, 28. 88, 101

long life of, would never have been predicted in his childhood or youth, 25. 556

[Walpole, Hon. Horatio (1717–97), *continued*]
love affair of, **37**. 122, 126
magazines call, 'ingenious' and 'learned,' **35**. 539
Mann chills, by refusal to come to England, **24**. 176, 182–4, 194
—— does not receive all the writings of, **22**. 273
—— may need all his former gifts to, to furnish Linton, **24**. 175–6
—— promises to accept payment for commissions of, **25**. 465
——'s arrival in England impatiently awaited by, **24**. 173–4
—— says he adores, **24**. 425, 433, 438
——'s commissions forgotten by, **25**. 468
——'s friendship with, like that of Orestes and Pylades, **22**. 274, **23**. 309, **24**. 283, **25**. 5, 9, 312, 615
——'s house inhabited by, for 13 months, **17**. 143n
——'s inviolable affection for, **25**. 192
——'s only friend in England, **24**. 166
——'s relations with: **21**. 72, 79, 89, **22**. 280; friendship of long standing, **25**. 332; HW hopes to be his gazetteer not his philosopher, **25**. 332
—— tells, to put cotton in his ears before putting his head in water, **21**. 177
—— the 'dearest' friend of, **17**. 249
—— thinks, is made for the world, **25**. 34
—— understands hints of, about lack of credit in England, **22**. 370
manners of the age to be recorded by, **9**. 106, 250
manuscripts of: dispersal of, **36**. 310–16; left to E. Waldegrave, **36**. 274
marriage of, reported, **9**. 105
Mason's 'respect' not deserved by, **28**. 155–6, 158–9
medal of, wanted for Q. of Sweden's cabinet, **40**. 214
melancholy thoughts of, **11**. 174, 180, 189–90
memoirs of: possibly alluded to, **28**. 94, 137, 353, **29**. 217; St Michael election in, **30**. 169n
memoranda of, unintelligible except to Kirgate, **34**. 127
memory of: fails, **15**. 182, 218, 242, 334, 335; long, **22**. 484–5; retentive of trifles, **21**. 471; still good though his pen grows old, **23**. 216
military details not understood by, **25**. 153
mind of: little and apt to fluctuate, **24**. 379; naturally more gay than in moral phase induced by nephew, **24**. 301
'miscarriage I was born,' **32**. 192
mock sermon by, for Lady Mary Coke, **31**. 23, **43**. 330
modesty of, about his own works, **9**. 328
Montagu's relations with, **9**. 77, 174–5, **10**. 4, 7–8, 13, 51, 85–6, 140–1, 143, 164–6, 171–2, 184, 195, 268–9, 277–8, 290, 305, 306, 318
Morning Post compliments, **33**. 219–20

'most insignificant man alive,' **31**. 42
motto of, see *Fari quæ sentiat*
narrative by, about Nicoll affair, **14**. 193–233, **20**. 273, 278, 435
nature gave, a statesman's head, but no ambition, **22**. 550
nephews and nieces of: a host, **31**. 354; number 50, **15**. 335; number 56, **25**. 571; numerous, **11**. 245, 255–6, 264, **12**. 260n
nephews of: HW does not interfere with their pleasing themselves, **25**. 331; HW has little joy in, **25**. 331
never good at detailing, **24**. 351
obituary note on himself, **43**. 392
occupations of: adding to SH, **37**. 299, **38**. 59 (*see also under* SH); alone at SH, **38**. 94; amuses himself in sedentary trifling ways, **39**. 276; animal-keeping, **37**. 287; antiquarian, not interesting to others, **32**. 199–200; at Florence, **37**. 78; at SH, **38**. 15–16, 94; attending auctions, **31**. 36, 339; auctions, dinners, loo parties, book sales, and visiting the sick, **38**. 340–1; auctions, politics, visits, dinners, suppers, and books, **38**. 312; birds'–nesting, **32**. 66; book-collecting, **16**. 25; bookseller and printer, **28**. 16, 24, 101, 195; building (*see under* Strawberry Hill); business resulting from nephew's death, **15**. 213, 216, 218; cataloguing his collection, **32**. 216; clipping and pasting prints, **39**. 120; collecting, **15**. 14–15, 23; collecting virtu, **9**. 32, 144, 277–8; 'collects the follies of the age for the information of posterity,' **35**. 236; Conway gives list of, **37**. 299; coursing, **30**. 80–1, **37**. 178, 185; dancing, **9**. 303, **10**. 73; doing good works, **37**. 487; editor and printer, **31**. 7; farming, **37**. 299, **38**. 60 (*see also under* Strawberry Hill); feeding birds and squirrels, **31**. 36; gardening, **37**. 299; **38**. 60; genealogy, **9**. 68–9, 93, 102–3, 218, 291; godfather, **9**. 104, **10**. 22, 23, **11**. 264, **18**. 31, **25**. 92, **33**. 232; going to meadows with Mrs Clive, **38**. 94; Gothic antiquities, **35**. 106; heraldry, **9**. 93, 200, 291; identifying portraits at country houses, **32**. 51; in decline, 'raking' with Mme du Deffand, **30**. 263; informing posterity, **38**. 59; in London, **38**. 312; 'jockey,' **31**. 174; landscaping, **9**. 88, 197; 'making books,' **29**. 290; making songs, **37**. 126; managing E. of Orford's affairs, **15**. 135, 136, **28**. 92–5, 103, 107, 116, 121, 123, 130, 134, 143, 305–6, 308, 323, **31**. 172, 174, 363; Parliament, **15**. 71, 74, 94, 155; pasting prints, **38**. 59; planting, **37**. 292, 296, 301 (*see also under* Strawberry Hill); playing with workmen and animals, **38**. 94; politics, **9**. 227–8, **10**. 49, 111, 118, 157; 'preaching,' **31**. 23; printing (*see* Strawberry Hill Press); Ranelagh attendance, **37**. 164; reading, **9**. 32, 197; reading, writing, forming plans, **35**. 265; riding, **9**. 15; sailing, **9**. 15; scolding ser-

vants, **37**. 209; 'scribbles' about painters, **38**. 94; shopping, **10**. 175; singing, **10**. 94; sitting by the fire, **39**. 497; sitting with Lady Suffolk, **39**. 497; sorting Conway papers, **38**. 59; staying quietly in country house, **39**. 209; 'steward,' **31**. 174; travelling, **37**. 411; trifling, **39**. 417; turns moralist, **38**. 185; Twickenham's history investigated, **32**. 199; 'violent' travel, **10**. 165; Williams, G. J., describes as 'loo and politics,' **30**. 239; will not last above 40 more years, **31**. 36; writes more trifling letters than any man living, **38**. 94; writing, **9**. 197, 227–8, 250, **10**. 152 (*see also under names of HW's publications*); writing memoirs, **35**. 265; writing no more, **15**. 33, 133, 135; writing painters' lives, **38**. 59, 94

old age dreaded by, **10**. 162–3 (*see also under* age of, *and under* Youth and old age)

'old superannuated man, conscious of his decay,' **42**. 229

opera subscription shared by, **17**. 358

Ossory, Lady, gives purse to, **33**. 271

—— has, as intermediary with ex-husband, **33**. 15–16

—— makes, grateful for friendship, **33**. 18–19

—— makes vest for, **32**. 220

—— partial to, **32**. 327

——'s elderly shepherd, **32**. 114

——'s fireside tempts, in long evenings, **33**. 130

——'s letters cheer, **32**. 13, 17

——'s 'Paris,' **32**. 108

papers of, bequeathed to Berrys, **30**. 373

Parliamentary address to George II moved by, in House of Commons, **13**. 23

(?) Parliamentary committee includes, **35**. 208n

Parliamentary conduct of, reviewed, **41**. 77–9

Parliamentary election of, **17**. 73n (*see also under* Callington, Castle Rising, King's Lynn)

Parliamentary motion by, **20**. 222, 227

Parliamentary seconding speech of, undelivered, **13**. 20

Parliamentary speeches by: **17**. 376–7, 404, **18**. 406, **19**. 449n, **20**. 222, 227, 531n, **26**. 25–8, 36. 19; seconding Rigby's petition against Fonnereau, **30**. 331n

Parliamentary voting by: **19**. 154, **20**. 126, **22**. 207n, 208n, **26**. 19, 43. 128; 'neuter,' **37**. 416; on land tax, **22**. 488n, **30**. 243n; on privately-raised regiments, **26**. 19; with minority, **38**. 224

peerage title not immediately assumed by, **29**. 365, **31**. 365, 367

peerage unwelcome to, **15**. 216

(?) pencil drawing by, **10**. 193

philosophy of: **20**. 256, **21**. 539, **22**. 359–60, **24**. 209–10, 213, 301, 327, 373, **32**. 274, 326, **33**. 550, **39**. 180, 223, 308, 317–18; to think of dying but to talk and act as if immortal, **39**. 223

poetic talent disclaimed by, **28**. 17, 241–2, 280, 433, **29**. 312, 316, 319

poetry of, needed more inspiration, **32**. 32

political conduct of: at formation of Rockingham ministry, **30**. 199; explained in letter to E. of Orford, **30**. 169n; indifferent to all but major issues, **38**. 225, 243

political 'frenzy' of, **30**. 177

politically disinterested, **13**. 38

political rôle of, that of prompter rather than actor, **22**. 522

political secrets unknown to, **25**. 185

political views of, have never changed, **29**. 282, 329, 330, 350–2; *see also under* Constitution, English; Court, English; Parliament, Prerogative; Tory; Whig

politics given up by, **29**. 289–90, 292, 297, 314, 317, 350

politics of: accused as plotting republican, **32**. 298; 'an old Whig even in my sleep,' **33**. 339; indifferent to changes in administration, **33**. 338; neither royalist nor republican, **33**. 2, **34**. 173; not 'anti-Gallican,' politically, **33**. 545; not republican, **33**. 342; only unadulterated Whig left in England, **33**. 391; 'rebel and republican,' according to Lady Mary Coke, **33**. 382; speculative not practical politician, **34**. 101; Whiggism founded on constitution not aristocracy, **33**. 342; Whiggism most apparent in *Royal and Noble Authors*, **33**. 276–7; Whiggism of, **10**. 164; *see also under* Whig; Whiggism

politics to be abandoned by, **14**. 143

'portrait' of Duchesse du Maine by, **8**. 114

portrait of, not to be painted in Paris for Conway, **39**. 32

portraits belonging to, anecdote concerning, **12**. 263

portraits of: at the Vyne, **35**. 639; by Ramsay, **31**. 9; by Dance, **15**. 316, 318; by Lawrence, **15**. 321; by Reynolds, **1**. 64n (*see also under* Reynolds, Sir Joshua); by Robinson, **30**. 92–3, 95; by Rosalba, **18**. 243n; requested by Roscoe, **15**. 281

posterity may take, for flatterer, **38**. 176

pride the one vice of, **23**. 528–9

prints of: by MacArdell, **1**. 64, 66, 67, 69, 127, 336–8, **2**. 19, 21, 29, **3**. 360, 376, 386, 396, 399, 402, 404, 405, **4**. 23, 25, 31, 115, **5**. 313, **15**. 196, **25**. 10, **31**. 263, (?) 265; in *Town and Country Magazine*, **2**. 330

private intelligence from foreign courts unavailable to, **24**. 278

privileges of House of Commons defended by, **38**. 225

prophetic powers of, vindicated, **39**. 333

'puny insect,' **35**. 526

purchases of, **31**. 110, 339 (*see also under* Paris)

'Queries Addressed to Every Englishman's Own Feeling' by, printed in *London Chronicle*, **21**. 65n

[Walpole, Hon. Horatio (1717–97), *continued*]
received no favours from any minister but his
father, **25.** 576

reflections by: are *couleur de rose*, **35.** 391;
'Augustan,' **40.** 311; *see also* Acting; Actor;
Affectation; Affluent, the; Age, old; Allitera-
tion; Ambassador; Ambition; America;
Amour; Amusement; Ancestor; Angel; Ani-
mal; Antiquary; Antiquities; Architecture;
Art; Artfulness; Artist; Assassin; Astron-
omy; Atheism; Attorney; Augustan age;
Author; Balloon; Barbarians; Beauty; Be-
nevolent activity; Bigot; Biography; Birth;
Bon mot; Bon ton; Book-collecting; Book-
seller; Bribery, political; British Empire;
Chance; Character; Charade; Chastity;
Cherubim; Childhood; Christian; Church-
man; Church of England, bishops of; City;
Classical art; Clergyman; Collections;
Colour-blindness; Comedy; Commentators;
Common sense; Conqueror; Constitution;
Content and ambition; Controversy; Con-
vent; Correctness; Correspondence; Cos-
metics; Country; Country life; Court;
Court (English); Crime; Criticism, literary;
Cross devout people; Cruelty; Cure; Curi-
osity; Death; Debt; Dedications; Despotism;
Discretion; Dissipation; Divine; Divorce;
Doctrines; Dream; Dress; Dullness; East,
the; Education; Eighteenth century; Elec-
tion; Eloquence; Enemies; England; cli-
mate of; England: comic nature of;
England: decay and ruin of; England: eigh-
teenth-century; England: follies and novel-
ties of; England: madness of; England:
political change in; English, the; Ennui;
Enthusiasm, religious; Envy; Epilogue;
Equality; Equity; Era; Eternity; Exercise;
Exorcism; Experience; Eye; Fact; Faction;
Faith; Fame; Family; Fashion; Feeling;
Felicity; Fidelity; Flattery; Flower; Folly;
Fool; Force; Freedom; French, the; French
Revolution; Friend; Friendship; Funeral;
Futility; Futurity; Gallantry; Gambling;
Genealogy; General; Genius; George I:
HW's reflections on having descendants in
common with; George III: health of; Glory;
God; Gold; Gordon riots; Gossip; Govern-
ment; Grace in writing; Gratitude; Grief;
Handwriting; Happiness; Heart: 'breaking'
of; Hebrew priesthood; Hereditary resem-
blance; Hermetic philosophers; Historian;
History; Honour; Houghton; Human
nature; Humility; Humour; Hypocrisy; Ig-
norance and knowledge; Illness; Illusions;
Imagination; Immortality; Imperialism;
Inconstancy; Indecency; Indifference; In-
gratitude; Insanity; Invention; Invitation;
Irish character; Jesuit: suppression of; Jus-
tice; King; Law; Lawyer; Learning; Letter;
Liberty; Life; Literary fame; Literature;
Louis XVI: death of; Love; Love and

hatred; Love-matches; Magazine; Man;
Manners; March, month of; Marriage;
Martyr; Mathematicians; Matter; Medicine;
Melancholy; Memoir; Merit; Metaphysics;
Mimicry; Minister; Miracle; Mirror; Mis-
chief; Mistresses; Modesty; Monarch; Mon-
archy; Money; Moralizing; Mortification;
Motto; Music; Mystery; Name; Natural
children; Nature; Neighbours; Newspaper;
Newspaper: letters to: Nineteenth century;
Nonsense; Notes; Obligations; Old people;
Opera; Opposition; Orford, earldom of;
Origin of nations; Ostentation; Pain;
Painter; Parent; Paris: people of; Parts
(talents): men of; Passion; Past, present,
and future; Patience; Patriot; Patriotism;
Peace; Peace treaties; Perjury; Perseverance; *Philosophe*; Philosopher; Philosophy;
Physician; Planning for the future; Plea-
sure; Poet; Poetaster; Poetry; Policy;
Political parties; Politician; Politics; Popu-
larity; Posterity; Poverty; Prayer; Preach-
ing; Prediction; Preferment; Prejudice;
Prerogative; Pride; Prince; Prince: health
and prisons of; Prison; Profits; Projector;
Prologue; Propagation; Prophecy; Propor-
tion; Prosperity; Prostitution; Providence,
Divine; Provincial society; Prudence; Public, the; Public taste; Pyramid: Egyptian;
Quack; Quarrel; Queen; Reality; Reason;
Reflections; Reformation, the; Reformer;
Relative; Relativitism; Religion; Remi-
niscence; Research; Resentment; Retirement; Revolution; Rhyme; Riches; 'Rights
of Men'; Riot; Royalty; Rudeness; Rumours, false; Rural life; Sabbatarianism;
Sacrilege; Savage; Saint; Sainthood; Satire;
Science; Scientific discoveries; Scrofula; Se-
clusion; Sects, religious; Self-criticism; Self-
denial; Self-interest; Selfishness; Self-knowl-
edge; Self-love; Sense; Senses, the: varia-
tions in; Sensibility; Sentiment; Serious
matters; Sickness; Singing; Slavery; Sobri-
ety; Social rank; Soldier; Solitary people;
Sonnet; Stage; Stock-jobber; Style, literary;
Suicide; Summer; System; Taste; Tax; Ten
Commandments; Theatre; Time; Title;
Tomb; Trade; Tragedy; Tranquillity;
Translation; Travel; Travellers; Trifles;
Truth; Tyranny; Tyrant; Uncles; 'Uniqui-
ty'; Vanity; Villain; Violence; Virtue;
Vision; Vocabulary; Voting; War; Warfare;
Wisdom; Wit; Woman; Word; World, the;
Wordly grandeur; Writer; Young people;
Youth; Youth and old age; Zeal

relative laughs violently at remarks of, when
HW is ill, **22.** 455

relatives of: HW allowed to see, only briefly,
30. 277; numerous, **32.** 388, **33.** 182, 197,
34. 231

religion of: averse to forcible conversions,
35. 392; devotional fits infrequent but in-

tense, **37**. 206; love of abbeys does not alienate, from Reformation, **35**. 146; St-Cyr abbess doubts sincerity of, **10**. 294
religious opinions of, **17**. 85
residence of, *see under* Arlington St: HW's house in; Berkeley Sq.: HW's house in; Chelsea; Downing St; Strawberry Hill; Windsor
retirement of, from the world, **22**. 111
Rigby comments on reliability of, as a political reporter, **20**. 503n
robbed, **33**. 295–8; *see also under* Maclaine, James
rôle of, as an observer, **20**. 503
royal connections of, **28**. 46–8, 126–7
St James's, Piccadilly, the parish of, **19**. 167n
scientific knowledge of, slight, **15**. 154–5
sea voyages of, **10**. 250, 297
seldom a lucky prophet, **22**. 131
self-analysis of, **5**. 411, 414–15, **31**. 257
self-depreciation by, **31**. 250
sentiments of, well known, **25**. 186
servants of, in 1775, **6**. 214n; *see also under* Servant
signatures of: 'Abbot of Strawberry,' **40**. 125; 'Brantôme,' **32**. 53; 'Constant Correspondent,' **42**. 505; 'Dunce Scotus,' **32**. 297; 'Errat.,' **41**. 221; 'Horace Trismegistus,' **32**. 59; 'Jack the Giant-Killer,' **32**. 175; 'Janus,' **33**. 134; 'Noah,' **35**. 228; 'Phaon the Second,' **32**. 91; 'the Governor of Barataria,' **32**. 211; 'Toby,' **42**. 502; 'Uncle of the late Earl of Orford,' **42**. 339, 340, 341; 'Yo El Rey,' **33**. 378
smells enjoyed by, **18**. 214, 230
society of, very narrow, **25**. 99
spelling difficulties of, **12**. 195
spirits of: destroyed by absurdity, **31**. 97; good, **15**. 325, 327; indecently juvenile, **31**. 45; less nimble than formerly, but never low, **25**. 312; unaffected by gout, **31**. 97; would scarce serve to 'rock the cradle of reposing age,' **24**. 120
spirits still retained, **24**. 176
strength of voice of, altered, **30**. 116
'Strephon's Complaint' by, **39**. 521–2
style of writing of: Alembert attributes, to Mme du Deffand, **3**. 158; Bussy's compared with, **5**. 180–1; clear, **3**. 314–15, **4**. 236; Du Deffand, Mme, admires, **3**. 85, 93, 118, 141, 144, 195, 228, 249, 383, **4**. 104, 145, 221–2, 236, 255, 317, 420, 433, 435, **5**. 217, **6**. 117, 188, 310, **7**. 110; easy, **4**. 431; Williams, G. J., quotes characteristic phrase of, **30**. 238
system of writing: everything found out and practised everywhere, **35**. 226; that 'everything will be found out including the art of living for ever,' **35**. 175
talents and taste of, praised by Roscoe, **15**. 274
temper of, his weakness, **23**. 522, 525
tomb of, HW jokes about, **9**. 312
Townshend, Vcts, compares, to spirit of hart-

shorn, **35**. 227
translation by, of French epigram on Mme de Pompadour, **9**. 249
travels, 'to finish education,' **10**. 167
Treasury bills of, paid the day before Conway's dismissal, **38**. 381–2
Twickenham resident, **42**. 480
uncle hated by, **35**. 158
'unfashionable,' **30**. 62–3
vanity not brought on by genealogical studies of, **10**. 103
verses by: about Temple, **10**. 223; couplet to Hannah More, **31**. 250; 'Epilogue Spoken by Mrs Clive on her Quitting the Stage,' **31**. 141; epigram on war, **33**. 290; 'epitaph' on Lord Lincoln, **30**. 2; for a snuff-box presented to Ps Amelia, **31**. 141; for Mme de Choiseul, **39**. 243; for SH fête, 9 May 1769, **4**. 236–7; in Latin, **9**. 7n; Montagu hears, at SH, **10**. 122; nuptial ode for Lavinia Bingham, **33**. 260–1; on a French book, **31**. 12–13; on Anson's eagerness for Byng's execution, **21**. 66n; on Bess of Hardwick, **9**. 278; on Chevalier Taylor, **31**. 11; on earthquake, **20**. 140; on fountain tree, **10**. 155; on Lady Barrymore, **32**. 144; on Lady Bingley, **20**. 141; on Lady Caroline Petersham, **20**. 140–1; on Lyttelton brothers, drowned at Oxford, **40**. 20; on Lady Mary Coke's erysipelas, **9**. 413; on Mme du Deffand, **8**. 55–6; on Newcastle, Fox, and Leicester House's 'fuction,' **21**. 7n; on Samuel Martin, **34**. 13; on Sandys's peerage, **18**. 357–8, 372; on shells, **32**. 87–8, 95; on the Comtesse de Forcalquier's speaking English, **31**. 96; on visit to Ampthill, **32**. 368, 373–4; on Wolterton, **18**. 47n; paraphrase of Lessing's 'Die Furien' from *Dictionnaire d'anecdotes*, **31**. 120–1, 430; possibly sent to Edgcumbe about Nanny Day, **30**. 109; praised by Ds of Bedford, **32**. 199; satire on clergy, **20**. 134; sent to Lyttelton, **40**. 2; sent to Lady Ossory, **33**. 204; sonnet dedicating *Castle of Otranto* to Lady Mary Coke, **31**. 429; to Berrys, **11**. 1; to Carlisle, **30**. 258; to Conway, **40**. 118; to Conway, on writing better in age than in youth, **39**. 470; to Duchesse de Choiseul, **4**. 133, 138; to French visitors, **10**. 69, 71, 73, 74, 279, 280; to Lady Caroline Petersham and Conway, **10**. 325–7; to Lady Craven, **28**. 247; to Lady Temple, **10**. 115–17, 119; to Pitt, **31**. 15; to Ps Amelia, **4**. 187, 189, **10**. 308, 315–16, 328, **31**. 147; to 'Zelinda,' **39**. 518–20; *see also* 'Advice, The,' 'Noble Jeffrey,' 'Three Vernons, the,' 'When mitred masters,' 'When the moon casts,' 'When Theseus,' 'Where do wit and memory dwell,' *and under other individual titles*
voice of: nearly gone, **17**. 252, **18**. 135; seldom used, **18**. 149; strength of, altered, **30**. 116; 'weak and extinguishing,' **42**. 399
walking avoided by, **22**. 333, **24**. 342

[Walpole, Hon. Horatio (1717–97), *continued*]
walks like a tortoise, 35. 366
Walpoliana supposedly being written by, 31. 281, 283
wants to live alone, 10. 94
'warm friend of republicanism,' 29. 348
Williams, G. J., calls: 'as much a curiosity to all foreigners as the tombs and lions,' 30. 176; 'no minister but near the throne from his connection,' 30. 238
—— thinks pamphlet attack calling him 'prince of cockle shells' will offend, more than grave refutation, 30. 239
will never be connected with any administration, 29. 202, 209–10, 237, 289–90, 314, 317
will of: 5. (?) 244, 36. 310–16; directs that letters of living persons be restored to them, 16. 56; discussed by Farington, 15. 336–8; executed by Lord Frederick Campbell and Mrs Damer, 15. 336; expectant beneficiaries of, 12. 143, 146, 164–5; text of, 30. 344–77; *Times, The,* discusses settlement of SH in, 12. 139, 140, 141, 143
'wine merchant' in Mason's and Harcourt's correspondence, 29. 354–66
wishes of, mostly disinterested, 25. 399
wit disclaimed by, 28. 155
works of: 'commonly written with people in the room,' 14. 167; HW prints, 43. 53; HW's proposed edition of, 1. 150–1, 154; jewels in prose but failing in verse, 35. 648; Mann delighted to contribute towards, 19. 508; printed to forestall posthumous edition, 42. 372–3; *Royal and Noble Authors* being reprinted for, 42. 197; sets of, intended for Eton and King's, 2. 249; *see also under individual titles*
world given up by, 28. 26, 261, 284, 29. 136, 242, 270, 295
writes, prints, and builds to attract attention, 30. 176
writing given up by, 28. 25, 130, 195, 203
writings and buildings of, to be blown away 10 years after his death, 38. 110
writings of: 16. 259; account of C. H. Williams, 30. 159, 311–23; character of Henry Fox, 30. 131–2, 333–5; dictated by youth, spirits, and vanity, 31. 270; epitaph for C. H. Williams, 30. 159; epitaph on Cts of Dysart, 31. 314–15; epitaph on Lady Hervey, 36. 51; HW deprecates value of, 32. 37, 41; HW not to add to, in old age, 31. 270, 32. 385–6, 33. 227; in old age, not to be published, 31. 283; letter to Rousseau under name of K. of Prussia, *see under* Rousseau, Jean-Jacques; 'Life of René of Anjou,' 31. 438–9; 'morsels of criticism,' 3. 281; notes to C. H. Williams's poems, 30. 159; not to be added to for a great while, 30. 152; not valued by him, 28. 71, 88, 195; Ossory, Lady, asks for, 32. 37, 41; 'Patapan,' 30. 287–306; 'Persian Letter' to Lord Lincoln, 30. 35–6; reasons for unexpected

success of, 31. 269–70; Roscoe derives information and amusement from, 15. 274; sermon for Lady Mary Coke, 31. 23, 423–6; 'Spectator No. none,' 32. 78–83; 'Thoughts on Keeping Holy the Sabbath,' 31. 433–7; to be published, 15. 338; trifling, 15. 256–9; unknown correspondents result from, 10. 105; will be forgotten, 15. 230, 272; *see also under individual titles*
writing to be given up by, 15. 33, 133, 135, 39. 276–7
young people entertain, 31. 35
Walpole, Horatio (1723–1809), 2d Bn Walpole of Wolterton, 1757; cr. (1806) E. of Orford, n.c.; M.P.; 'Pigwiggin'; HW's first cousin:
Astley's painting of, in laced coat and waistcoat, 20. 342
avarice of, 20. 42, 81
Castle Rising might be borough of, 36. 14, 16
Chamberlayne tutor to son of, 2. 314
Cholmondeley sued by, over Houghton estate, 16. 313, 36. 297n
daughters of, 4. 335n
'displeased parent,' 36. 143
Du Deffand, Mme, discusses, with Hon. Thomas Walpole, 5. 94
entail could not be cut off by, 36. 31
executor under Maurice Suckling's will, 36. 162
family estate not likely to be dissipated by, 19. 505
father-in-law may get peerage for, 19. 469, 20. 66–7
father jokingly boasts about, in Parliament, 19. 168
father offended at Mann's failure to congratulate him on marriage of, 20. 22
father puts horses of, to graze at New Park, 18. 70
Florence to be visited by, 19. 42
good-natured, 25. 132
Gray hopes that newspaper item refers to, 14. 42
HW acquits, of prosecuting Houghton lawsuit, 15. 323
HW asks, about Thomas Walpoles, 36. 202
HW attends wedding festivities of, 9. 54, 58
HW breaks all relations with family of, 20. 425
HW chosen to succeed, at King's Lynn, 13. 27n
HW complains of bad breath of, 19. 72
HW discusses, with Mrs Hayes, 31. 65
HW formally asked by, to look after 3d E. of Orford's affairs, 23. 496
HW mentions, 39. 171
HW notifies: (?) of Cts of Orford's death, 25. 123n; (?) of 3d E. of Orford's recovery, 24. 368
HW's correspondence with, 36. 158, 162
HW's cousin and namesake, 28. 433
HW told by, about P. of Orange's court, 19. 418

HW to meet, to get his consent to run E. of Orford's affairs, **36.** 93

health of, fever and pain in bowels, **19.** 192

healthy, and likely to inherit, **36.** 296

Heathcote resembles, **20.** 80–1

Houghton lawsuit of, **15.** 323n, **16.** 313

—— visited by, **18.** 70

King's Lynn borough's situation alarms, **39.** 96

—— seat vacated by peerage of, **21.** 57

——'s election left for, **19.** 413–14, 418

letter to HW sent to seat of, **33.** 71

Mann not to lodge, at Florence, **19.** 42, 59, 72

——'s conversazioni attended by, **19.** 83–4

——'s correspondence with, **19.** 42

——'s porter repels, **19.** 59

—— to take notice of nuptials of, **19.** 478

—— would be obliged to air his house if it had been occupied by, **19.** 72

Marchi to restore pictures for, **15.** 325

marriage of: approaching, **19.** 469; fruitful, **36.** 298; Mann to take notice of, **19.** 478; should not affect entail, **36.** 24

Montagu jokes about, **9.** 303

Orford, 2d E. of, promises Parliamentary seat to, **36.** 10

Orford, 3d E. of, should have his trust in false friends shaken by, **36.** 48

—— writes angry letter to, about footman committed to prison, **25.** 355

Parliamentary voting shunned by, **22.** 508n

present at angry scene between HW and Horace Walpole (1678–1757), **14.** 204

'procreated in . . . bed of money and avarice,' **20.** 81

returns to England, **19.** 418

Richmond, D. of, mistakes HW for, **35.** 93

Rome to be visited by, with Turnbull, **19.** 232

—— visited by, **19.** 239

son of, **1.** 312n, **2.** 280, 282, 314, **15.** 317, **25.** 418n, **36.** 121–2, **42.** 389

son of, marries Sophia Churchill, **2.** 280, 282, **25.** 172–3

son's match reluctantly approved by, **25.** 132

Suares, Mme, liked by, **19.** 84

Turnbull tutor to, **19.** 184–5, 192

uncle gives horse to, **18.** 70

Vestris has affair with, **43.** 265

Walpole, Hon. Thomas, sends to, a letter from HW, **36.** 98–9

wife of, **6.** 442n, **15.** 317n, **20.** 42

Walpole, Hon. Horatio (1752–1822), styled Bn Walpole 1806–9; 2d E. of Orford, n.c., 1809; M.P.; 'Col. Walpole':

birth of, **37.** 341

Cavendish gait inherited by, **15.** 317

Chelsea College post accepted by, **33.** 400

contends for second will of 3d E. of Orford, **15.** 323

Du Deffand, Mme, discusses, with Hon. T. Walpole, **5.** 94

election of, at Wigan, **36.** 174

entail could be cut off by, **36.** 31

first marriage of: **2.** 280, 282, **25.** 172–3, **31.** (?) 202, **36.** 202; a love-match, **25.** 132

HW aided by, in caring for 3d E. of Orford, **32.** 349

HW called on by, about Ds of Portland's will, **33.** 484

HW dines with, at Eriswell, **36.** 121–2

HW discusses dog with, **31.** 366

HW displeased with conduct of, in Houghton lawsuits, **15.** 323, 327, 332

HW has, at dinner at SH, **33.** 406

HW revokes order (in his will) to deliver family papers to, **30.** 372

HW's cousin and namesake, **28.** 433

HW's letter from Lady Ossory delivered to, **33.** 71

HW's MSS might have gone to, **36.** 314

HW's opinion of, **25.** 132

HW tries to marry a Waldegrave daughter to, **25.** 132–3

HW visited by, at SH, **11.** 42, **16.** 302, **34.** 57

HW voluntarily confirms 3d E. of Orford's bequest to, **15.** 324

Hastings portrait owned by, **42.** 389

heir-apparent to both branches of the family, **25.** 132

Houghton's reversion not to be further contested by, **15.** 326

Houghton succession lawsuit lost by, **30.** 372

member of Parliament, **33.** 227

music not liked by, **12.** 268

Orford, 3d E. of, invited by, to be son's godfather, **25.** 418

—— invites, to Houghton, in 'frantic' letter, **25.** 418

——'s legacy to, **15.** 324, **34.** 136n

Piddletown estate owned by, **42.** 389

Piddletown manor goes to, **25.** 148n

presented for degree at Cambridge, **1.** 312

sensible and good, **32.** 349

son born to, **25.** 418

tutor of, **2.** 314

(?) Veseys entertain, **12.** 270n

wife of, **2.** 316n, **6.** 189n, **9.** 285n, **15.** 324n

Walpole, Horatio (1783–1858), styled Bn Walpole 1809–22; 3d E. of Orford, n.c., 1822:

birth of, **25.** 418

HW hopes, will be heir of family, **25.** 418

marriage of, **11.** 95n

Orford, 3d E. of, to be godfather of, **25.** 418

Walpole, Mrs Horatio. See Churchill, Sophia (d. 1797); Fawkener, Mary (1788–1860); Lombard, Mary Magdelaine (d. 1783)

Walpole, Sir John de (temp. Henry III): a knight, **15.** 1n

Walpole, John (fl. temp. Edward II): marriage of, **2.** 115

Walpole, John (d. 1507): bequests of, **15.** 2n

Walpole, Sir John (fl. 1646): arms of, **1.** 156

Dugdale, patron of, **1.** 130

Walpole, Hon. John (1787–1859), army officer:
birth of, imminent, **42**. 201n
Walpole, Lambert Theodore (1757–98), son
of Hon. Thomas Walpole; army officer:
brother's letter delivered by, to HW, **36**. 231
brother visited by, **36**. 228
brother will get news from, **36**. 232
Conway cannot aid, **36**. 211
Du Deffand, Mme, discusses, with Hon. T.
Walpole, **5**. 94
meritorious, **36**. 204
Walpole, Laura (ca 1734–1813), m. (1758)
Hon. Frederick Keppel, Bp of Exeter; eldest
daughter of Sir Edward Walpole; HW's niece:
alarmed at daughter's health, **33**. 316
alarmed at discharge of pistols at Toy inn,
33. 370
Albemarle's marriage disappoints, **10**. 304
at Stud House, Hampton Court, **33**. 346
'august and serene,' **12**. 146
Bath visited by, **33**. 2n
belief of, in omens, **33**. 426
Berry, Agnes, discourteously treated by, **12**.
146
Cheltenham to be visited by, **36**. 246
—— visited by, **12**. 146, **31**. 287
children of, **10**. 206n, **30**. 354
Coke, Lady Mary, discusses Cts of Euston
with, **31**. 239
counts passengers on ferry at Richmond, **34**.
195
daughter born to, **36**. 36
daughter of, **11**. 119n, **12**. 136n, **15**. 325, **25**.
410n, 508
daughter pardoned by, after elopement, **25**.
508
drives through London after Gordon riots,
33. 191
Du Deffand, Mme, inquires about, **7**. 177
Dysart, Cts of, mourned by, **34**. 63
father entertains, at Waldegrave wedding,
9. 235
father gives Windsor estate, house, and coach
to, **24**. 348–9, 352
father leaves bulk of fortune to, **25**. 466
father leaves Isleworth house to, **36**. 201n
father leaves reversion of house to, **33**. 2n
father might leave Walpole estates to, **36**. 26
father of, **17**. 209
father provides for, **7**. 5
father unlikely to marry, being deterred by,
36. 295
father wills reversion of Wimpole St house
to, **36**. 126n
fête given by, at her villa at Isleworth, **33**.
481
'fiery furnace,' **39**. 472
Fitzroys to visit, at Isleworth, **39**. 454
—— visit, at Isleworth, **36**. 246
Fox, Henry, can send letter to sisters and, for
HW, **30**. 136
Gloucester, Ds of, confesses marriage to, **5**.
265n

—— hears from, **36**. 325
—— too tired to write to, **36**. 127
HW attentive to, **36**. 15, 17, 34
HW has, at SH on brother-in-law's death,
38. 196
HW mentions, **9**. 13
HW notifies, of Cts of Orford's death, **25**.
123n
HW refuses visit to SH by, **38**. 208
HW's accident at house of, in Pall Mall, **33**.
318–19
HW's attentions to, on death of her husband,
33. 2
HW's bequest to, **30**. 354
(?) HW's medals seen by husband of, **5**. 235
HW speaks of, with good humour, **34**. 230n
HW's relations with, **10**. 63
HW's time usurped by, **11**. 61
HW's uncomplimentary comments on, **12**. 165
HW to entertain, at SH, **9**. 369
HW to give breakfast for sisters and, **30**. 132
HW urged by, to sell burgage-tenures to Lis-
burne, **42**. 376–7
HW visited by: **32**. 382; at SH, **10**. 63, **36**.
150, **38**. 109; in illness, **22**. 455
HW visits, **31**. 210
HW wishes, after sister's death, to visit Cts
of Galloway, **34**. 63n
Hampton Court lodgings of, **33**. 370n
health of: consumption, **9**. 61; 'well and
healthy,' **36**. 150
Hertford, Cts of, gives assembly attended by,
25. 123n
Hertford, E. of, has letter about Drummond's
lodgings (? at Hampton Court) from, **39**.
314
house of, at Isleworth: **33**. 481, 524; let to
Sheridan, **11**. 320–1
husband of: **6**. 446n, **22**. 94n, **28**. 252n, **38**.
189n; dies, **7**. 1, **24**. 348, **32**. 410; ill, **32**. 363
invitation cannot be accepted by, **31**. 410
Keppel to wed, **37**. 551, 553
Lacy House, villa of, **34**. 195n
lives in Pall Mall, **29**. 59
London visited by, after death of husband,
33. 2
marriage of: **10**. 190n, **21**. 239, **23**. 484n;
arranged, **36**. 35; to a Stuart descendant,
21. 285
mother-in-law robbed at door of, **35**. 505
Nivernais's *Jardins modernes* given to, **12**.
259
'noisy,' **12**. 165, 167
Pall Mall house of, altered by Holland, **34**.
189n
park key probably not obtainable from, **35**.
628
pistol-firings at Hampton Court alarm, **35**.
526
prophetic pretensions of, **36**. 230
Ramsay's picture of, **40**. 370
Richmond residence of, **31**. 287
robbery at house of, in Pall Mall, **33**. 318–19

sister informs, of Lady Elizabeth Keppel's engagement, 38. 400

social relations of, 33. 481, 482

SH visited by, 10. 63, 12. 224, 225, 31. 297, 36. 150, 38. 109

Talbot praised by, for rudeness to D. and Ds of Gloucester, 36. 326

Waldegrave, Cts, tended by, in bereavement, 10. 62, 63

Waldegrave, Lady Elizabeth Laura, well treated by, 36. 326

Waldegrave nieces complained about by, 36. 326

Waldegrave nieces to be supervised by, 24. 76n

Waldegrave nieces to visit, at Windsor, 36. 152

Walpole, Lady Maria (Mary) (ca 1725–1801), m. (1748) Col. Charles Churchill; HW's half-sister:

activities of, 9. 71

Amor's name intrigues, 18. 505

Argyll, Ds of, asks Conway about, at Vcts Townshend's, 37. 61–2

astounded at break into HW's house, 5. 53

Berry, Mary, identifies, 11. 97n

Bethell, Mrs, proclaimed as ugly by, in Paris, 9. 139

biographical information about, corrected, 43. 89, 140, 254, 260, 373

Boisgelin, Comtesse de, and Marquise de Boufflers and Mme de Cambis acquaintances of, 5. 23

books left for, by Conway at Smith's, 37. 189

Boutin's garden visited by, 7. 336

Buckingham, Ds of, hints at marriage of Young Pretender to, 17. 139n

Cadogans invite HW to meet, at Caversham, 36. 152–3

Calonne anecdote told by, 11. 44

Champagne visited by, 38. 428

Champion, The, mentions, as Sir Robert Walpole's natural daughter, 18. 33

Charlotte, Q., receives, well, for not championing Ds of Gloucester, 36. 77

children of, 30. 354, 374–5

Choiseul, Duchesse de, would be congenial with, 5. 23

Chute and HW visit, at Chalfont, 35. 233

Chute might be visited by, at the Vyne from Chalfont, 35. 68

comet played by, with HW and Miss Leneve, 18. 33

Conway and wife to entertain, at Park Place with HW, 37. 532–3, 537, 538

Conway and wife visited by, at Park Place, 39. 419n

Conway forwards Mrs Doyne's letter to, 37. 185

—— invites, to Park Place, 37. 379

—— sends compliments to, 37. 122, 132, 138, 148, 151, 154, 158, 177, 199, 205, 212, 215, 219, 222, 233, 247, 253, 265, 476

—— to receive compliments of, 37. 202

Court ladies displeased at rank of, 17. 320n

Court presentation of, 18. 330

(?) Dampier, Mrs, talks of Mme du Deffand with, 5. 2

dances at Robinson's ball, 37. 114

daughter; daughters of: 1. 185n, 312n, 2. 280n, 306n, 21. 279, 24. 320, 25. 132, 418n; marries, 2. 280, 282; to be christened, 9. 104

daughter's elopement distresses, 36. 329

daughter tended by, in pregnancy, 42. 201

desserte imported by, 37. 328

drawing by Miss Hoare of Bath given to HW by, 33. 512

Du Deffand, Mme, disappointed at relinquished Paris visit of, 6. 217

—— has no news of, 5. 71, 79–81, 86, 87, 145, 184, 364, 386, 6. 384

—— hears praises of, 4. 191

—— hopes that daughter's marriage is concern of, 5. 403

—— inquires about, 6. 269, 282, 375, 464, 7. 6, 8, 130, 173, 177

—— not to ask news of HW from, 5. 272

—— receives gifts from, 5. 429, 6. 102, 7. 29

——'s commissions may be executed by, 5. 121, 129

——'s correspondence with, 5. 65, 73, 433, 6. 103, 264, 265, 269, 362, 438, 467

—— seeks news of HW from, 6. 384, 437–8

—— sends messages to, 5. 163, 198, 235, 6. 75, 80, 265, 273, 484, 7. 51, 108

—— sends pastilles to, 6. 325

——'s offer of lodging accepted by, 5. 65, 83, 86

——'s opinion of, 5. 23, 31, 51–2, 56, 73, 6. 375–6

——'s relations with, 5. 31, 37, 120, 7. 110

—— to buy snuff through, 5. 231

Eccardt's painting of, with family, 35. 174

effigy of, carried by mob, 1. 165, 17. 390–1

Englefield, Lady, indignant at HW's small bequest to, 15. 337

entail, as proposed, prejudicial to, 36. 26, 27–8, 296–304

entail of HW's Norfolk estates mentions, 30. 346

father favours, in his will, 36. 24

father gives George II's diamond to, 25. 464

father legitimatizes, 28. 389

father's bequests to, 19. 32n, 104n

father tended by, in illness, 18. 449

favourite child, 26. 28

Fawkener praised by Mme du Deffand to, 5. 435

fifth son born to, just after attendance at opera and ball, 21. 278–9

Fitzwilliam may marry, 17. 177

France may be revisited by, 6. 80, 84

—— may be visited by, 20. 324–5, 339–40, 22. 262

French manners shock, 20. 339–40

[Walpole, Lady Maria, *continued*]

French travels of, **5.** 60, 63, 65, 79, 80, 83, 89

George II's alleged generosity to Sir Robert Walpole not believed by, **25.** 463n

George III grants leave to, from duties at Windsor, **39.** 141

Gloucester, Ds of, told by, of HW's fall, **36.** 256

Gower chooses, as Windsor housekeeper, **38.** 464

'grown old,' and sheds affectation, **30.** 235n

HW accompanies: to shops, **7.** 334, 335; to theatre, **7.** 336

HW accuses, of loving Monticelli, **17.** 487

HW and Conway to visit, at Chalfont, **39.** 173

HW and Conway visit, at Chalfont, **38.** 59

HW defends rights of, **13.** 26–7

HW discussed in presence of, **18.** 180–1, 196

HW encloses letter to, to Hertford, **38.** 464

HW entertains: at dinner, **12.** 38; at Harris wedding feast, **35.** 217; at SH, **33.** 565; at SH breakfast, **35.** 225

HW given Liotard's self-portrait by, **20.** 324n

HW gives news of Montagu to, **4.** 136

HW informed of Fox's health by, **30.** 235

HW jokingly offers, to Chute, **17.** 257

HW mentions, **11.** 101, **12.** 153, **37.** (?) 472

(?) HW notifies, of Cts of Orford's death, **25.** 123n

HW not to mention, **30.** 77–8

HW not to visit, **9.** 71

HW receives Rubens figure from, **5.** 65

HW's bequests to: legacy and annuity, **15.** 336; money, **30.** 354; rent charge, **30.** 372

HW's correspondence with, **7.** 376, 377, 379, 381, 396, **30.** 235, **36.** 22, 23, 32, 38, 43, 44, 114, **37.** 344, 478, 480, **38.** 165, 423

HW sees Fawkener at house of, **39.** 512

HW sends letters by, **7.** 393, **39.** 144, 146, 148

HW sends message to, through Mme du Deffand, **5.** 65

HW sends music to, **7.** 396, 416

HW sends news to Mme du Deffand through, **6.** 264, **7.** 91

HW's flirtation tires, **37.** 126

HW should bring, to Park Place, **37.** 485

HW's letter from, about leaving Paris, **38.** 423

HW's letter to be posted by, at Calais, **38.** 497, 498

HW substitutes for, at Kensington Palace when she is abroad, **16.** 322

HW sups with, **11.** 95, 97, **12.** 46, 149

HW to be repaid through, for purchase, **5.** 21

HW to be visited by: at SH, **38.** 27, 165; with sick daughter, **37.** 378

HW too tired to visit, on first reaching Paris, **35.** 124

HW to receive compliments of, **36.** 113

HW to visit, at Chalfont, **39.** 173, 199

HW visited by, **4.** 173, 191, **11.** 42, 179, 350, **12.** 29, 104, 196, 213, **16.** 302, **32.** 124, **33.** 355, **34.** 107, **37.** 289, **39.** 276

HW visits, **12.** 69, 107, **38.** 59

HW will find, in Paris, **5.** 66, 73, 81–2

HW with, **6.** 76

HW writes to, about opera box, **37.** 478, 480

Harcourt, 1st E., aids, **5.** 86

—— to aid, **5.** 65

harpsichord of, at Houghton, **18.** 317

Hartington may marry, **17.** 176–7

health of, ill, **36.** 329

Hertford asked by, to send discarded English newspapers to her husband, **38.** 495

—— misses, but Cts of Hertford will have dinner for her, **38.** 409–10

Houghton visited by, **17.** 36

housekeeper at Kensington Palace, **10.** 305n, **16.** 322, **43.** 132

housekeeper's salary of, at Windsor, **43.** 132

husband impoverished by lawsuit over fortune of, **40.** 177

husband of, **2.** 292n, **4.** 293n, **13.** 183n

Legge wishes to marry, **9.** 53n, **19.** 458

Le Neve, Isabella, cares for, after mother's death, **21.** 353n, **25.** 609n

Lewisham visited by, **12.** 38, 69, 138

Lillebonne, Comte de, visited by, **5.** 83

——'s attentions to, **36.** 39

lives in Arlington St, **13.** 15n

Lloyd, Rachel, succeeds, at Kensington Palace, **15.** 160n, **38.** 457

London to be visited by, **5.** 184

—— visited by, **35.** 68

Lorraine (probably Nancy) visited by, **38.** 464

Louvet to receive money from, through Mme du Deffand, **6.** 268–9, 271, 273

Mann seeks Pergolesi's *Olimpiade* for, **19.** 95

—— sends flowers to, **17.** 254

Mann, Mary, visits, **17.** 359

marriage of, **18.** 455, **19.** 104, 132, 221, 239, **21.** 353n, **22.** 27, **36.** 296, **37.** 202n, 218, 224

Mazarin, Hôtel de, visited by, **7.** 336

Mingotti to be kept by, in suspense about opera box, **37.** 477–8

(?) miscarriage of, **43.** 122–3

Monaco, P. of, sends respects to, **41.** 213

Montagu sends compliments to, **10.** 142–3

—— sends message to, by HW, **10.** 136

——'s 'old hankerings' for, **10.** 136

mother's marriage agreement affects marriage settlement of, **43.** 176–7

musical ability of, **18.** 316–17

Nancy to become residence of, **22.** 244

Nancy visit delights, **33.** 419

Nicolet attended by, in Paris, **7.** 336

Norfolk ladies visit, in old costumes, **30.** 34

Norsa, Miss, might contaminate, **18.** 249

opera attended by, **18.** 180–1, 196

opera box not taken by, **37.** 477

papal bull might legitimate, if she married Old Pretender's son, **17.** 139

Paris left by, **7.** 336

—— may be visited by, **6.** 213, 462

—— to be left by, **5.** 60, 63

—— to be revisited by, **5.** 76

—— visited by, **5.** 2, 46, **9.** 130, **35.** 123–4, **38.** 423

'Patapan' said to be courting, **18.** 299

Pownall seen by, writing 'character' of Sir Robert Walpole, **42.** 76

pregnant, **9.** 285

rank of earl's daughter given to, **17.** 320, 330, 348

reports the expected marriage of Lady Elizabeth Seymour-Conway, **32.** 358

Richmond visited by, **17.** 330, 359

Rivers, Lady, writes to, **11.** 96

Roissy visited by, **7.** 334

Rueil visited by, **7.** 335

satiric verses on, **17.** 320n

social relations of, in Paris, *see index entries ante* **8.** 551

son born to, **19.** 371, 465, **21.** 278–9

son of: **11.** 264n, **12.** 212n; believed safe, **34.** 219

son's letter from Jamaica received by, **12.** 213

Spa to be visited by, **6.** 206–7

Spa visited by, for waters, **36.** 113

SH left by, **12.** 105, 106

SH to be visited by, **15.** 251

SH visitors sent by, **12.** 230, 232

Suckling's legacy to, **36.** 162

Sunning Hill visited by, **37.** 289

tapestry bought by, **7.** 335

Townshend, Hon. Augustus, said to be in love with, **40.** 47

Townshend, Hon. Mary, to be visited by, at Muffetts, **37.** 202

travels like Tartar princess with all her children, **39.** 146, 148

Versailles visited by, **7.** 334

Viry, Contessa di, needs address of, **41.** 203

Waldegrave might have married, **21.** 285

Wales, Caroline, Ps of, seen by, at Greenwich, **12.** 138–9

Walpole, Sir Edward, converts his jealousy of, into attentions, to spite HW, **36.** 19

Walpole, Hon. Robert, brings, to Mme du Deffand, **5.** 19

—— escorts, **5.** 23

Whiteknights preferred by, to Woburn Farm, **35.** 71

Willes a guardian to, **26.** 28

Windsor Castle promotion of, influences HW's politics, **30.** 176

Windsor Castle servants to be recommended to, by HW, **10.** 137

Windsor Castle's housekeeper, **10.** 136, **36.** 77, **38.** 457

Wolterton visited by, **30.** 80

Walpole, Maria (1736–1807), 2d dau. of Sir Edward Walpole, m. 1 (1759) James Waldegrave, 2d E. Waldegrave; m. 2 (1766) William Henry, cr. (1764) D. of Gloucester; HW's niece:

accounts of, from Rome, are favourable, **24.** 179

Adair and Jebb asked by, to write to Germain, **36.** 130

affronts resented by, **24.** 125

aged by husband's illness, **32.** 389

Albano the summer home of, at Albani's villa, **24.** 214, 247–8

Albemarle, Cts of, calls on, at St Leonard's Lodge, **23.** 433n

—— informs, of daughter's engagement, **38.** 400

Aldobrandini villa to be occupied by, **24.** 186, 190

Almanach royal omits name of, **5.** 320

ambition of, has connected HW with royalty, **28.** 93

Americans supported by, at Rome, **31.** 187

Ansbach visited by, **25.** 413n

appearance of: at wedding, **9.** 235; beauty diminished by grief, **22.** 136; beauty of, **32.** 123; beauty praised by Horace Mann II, **36.** 246; better, **24.** 335; Dalrymple tells Mme du Deffand of beauty of, **36.** 131; fallen away and shrunken, **24.** 332; HW praises, **21.** 239–40, 285; HW thought Mann would be struck by, **24.** 299; Italy's enervating air has altered, **36.** 131, 134; marred by anxiety, **24.** 326; more sublime than her daughter's, **24.** 498; still attracts attention, **25.** 68; thin, **36.** 142; thin and yellow, **36.** 134

Bath visited by, **33.** 2n

Bedford, Ds of, alleges quarrel with, **33.** 588

—— may marry, to Vernon, **38.** 397

bereavement of, may easily be consoled, **22.** 132

Berrys invited by, to the Pavilions, **12.** 21

Bishop Bonner's Ghost praised by, **31.** 318

Bishop not to be employed by, **36.** 106n

Boltons to give ball for, **25.** 22

Bordeaux voyage may be undertaken by, **24.** 360

Boufflers, Cts of, wishes to see, **22.** 136

Bristol, E. of, visits at the Pavilions, **33.** 148

brother-in-law receives husband's seal from, as sign she is not pregnant, **22.** 164

brother-in-law tells, of wager, **38.** 274–5, 281

brother of, **38.** 179

brother's omission from HW's family pictures resented by, as a slight, **36.** 159–62

cares of, concerning her family, **32.** 363

Carlisle ridicules HW's concern for, **30.** 266

Carpenter, Lady Almeria, jealously hated by, **36.** 329

—— lady of the Bedchamber to, **25.** 638n

casino party given by, for son, **36.** 329

chaplain of, **2.** 331

Cheap Repository Tracts to be subscribed to by, **31.** 396

child expected by, in March 1776, **24.** 171

children neglected by, **31.** 200

children of, **10.** 69

Cholmondeley a cousin of, **24.** 319n

Christine meets, at public places only, **24.** 190

Clement, Anne, corresponds with, **36.** 263, 285, 327–30

[Walpole, Maria, *continued*]
Clement, Jane, corresponds with, **36**. 323–7, 330
—— to receive money from, **36**. 320
Coke, Lady Mary, envies marriage of, **23**. 530, 538, **24**. 179n, **33**. 528
—— lays blame on, for Egremont affair, **29**. 74
Colonna recommended by, **7**. 80
Conway and Rockingham do not favour, **36**. 327
Conway and wife anger, by visiting D. and Ds of Cumberland, **36**. 80–1
Conways and Waldegraves rejected as cousins by, **36**. 323–4
Cornwallis's letter to husband lent by, to HW, **36**. 92
Coronation missed by, **9**. 376, 399
courier from, brings news of husband's illness, **32**. 362, 364, 365
courier sent by, to England for Jebb and Adair, **24**. 314, 317
Court admittance demanded by, **33**. 331
Court intrigues avoided by, **25**. 140
Court presentation of, **9**. 235
court of, numerous, **25**. 22
Coventry, Cts of, makes friends with, **9**. 237
—— to be jealous of, **9**. 235, 237
Cumberland, Ds of, to be treated civilly and coolly by, **36**. 88
Cumberland, D. and Ds of, said to pass verse-writing evening with, **36**. 84
Cumberland, D. of, must mortify, by his marriage, **23**. 345
Dalrymple gives report about, **6**. 456
daughter attended by, **31**. 334
daughter born to, **1**. 321n, **5**. 370, **9**. 399, **23**. 483, **28**. 89, **32**. 118, **38**. 141
daughter corresponds with, **31**. 355
daughter gets consent of, to break off match, **25**. 75
daughter of: may be married, **7**. 128; married, **25**. 274
daughter resembles, **26**. 410
daughter's engagement announced to, by courier, **25**. 632
daughter's nuptial contract arranged for, by HW, **32**. 365
daughters of: **2**. 55, **7**. 128, **11**. 262n, **24**. 315n, 498, **25**. 68, 410n, 632, **29**. 45–6, 47n, 69, 249, **30**. 350, 351; dote on her, **32**. 363; inherit her beauty but not her good fortune, **25**. 75; rejected by Bns Walpole for her son, **25**. 132
daughter's wedding attended by, **29**. 245n
daughter told that praying and weeping are the sole occupations of, **24**. 323
daughter visits, **12**. 209n
death of, might result from husband's, **24**. 144
'Death of Cardinal Wolsey' admired by, **11**. 113
despairs of husband's recovery, **28**. 320, 327

dignity has not expelled the good nature of, **24**. 299
Dover embarkation of, **24**. 117n
—— to be left by, for Gloucester House, **43**. 301
—— visited by, **33**. 581n
Du Deffand, Mme, expects Mary Churchill to get a position with, **6**. 34
—— hopes, will visit Paris, **6**. 217
—— hopes Ds of Cumberland will be distinguished from, **5**. 268
—— inquires about, **6**. 153, 177, 181, 187, 189, 328, 463, 464, 467, 474, 475, 477, 488, 491, 494, **7**. 1, 5, 28–9, 42, 52, 60, 130, 177, 199
—— pities, in husband's illness, **5**. 74, 133, **6**. 174, 458, 465, 467, 470
(?) —— sends compliments to, **6**. 186
——'s opinion of, **5**. 33–4, **6**. 215, **7**. 8
Duval's letter from, about D. of Gloucester, **24**. 322n
Dysart, Cts of, hears of ambitions of, **36**. 69n
—— mourned by, **34**. 63
Dysarts visited by, at Ham, **36**. 79–80
Egremont, 2d E., offers house at Petersham to, **40**. 280–2
Egremont, 3d E., pressed by, for larger settlement to wife, **33**. 210n
—— said to be repelled by demands of, **35**. 356
England to be revisited by, but not permanently, **35**. 473
—— to be visited by, **36**. 247
Englefield, Lady, indignant at HW's leaving so much to, **15**. 337
English at Rome attentive to, **24**. 190
English people in France shun, **24**. 125
English visitors received by, at Rome, with great affability, **24**. 247
Exeter, Bp of, hears self-accusations of, **10**. 62
—— tells, of husband's will, **22**. 128
Farington tells of jealousy of, towards Berrys, **15**. 336
father cannot be persuaded by, to call on her husband, **23**. 461
father might leave Walpole estates to, **36**. 26
father not asked to the Pavilions by, for fear of rebuff, **36**. 323
father of, **17**. 209
father praised by, **24**. 297
father's bounty to, **24**. 349
father's correspondence with, **5**. 247, **23**. 415, **26**. 50, **34**. 245–7, **36**. 62, 63, 66–8, 126, 144, 145
father's impetuosity inherited by, **24**. 125
father's letters from: about husband's illness, **26**. 50; announcing her marriage to D. of Gloucester, **5**. 247, **23**. 415; from Verona, **34**. 245–7
father unlikely to marry, being concerned for, **36**. 295
father visited by: after husband's death, **10**. 59; in London, **10**. 83
Ferrers's trial not attended by, **9**. 180

finances of, **36**. 72n

financial provision for, **10**. 62, 67

Florence avoided by, on way to Naples, resulting in four accidents, **25**. 675

—— not visited by, on way to Rome, **24**. 174

—— to be visited by: on way back to Rome, **24**. 298, 312; on way from Rome, **24**. 290

—— visited by, **24**. 296–7

fortitude of, **32**. 123

Fox, Henry, can send letter to sisters and, for HW, **30**. 136

France pays great attentions to, **24**. 125

Frogmore visited by, **10**. 246, 296

Gazette de France calls, D. of Gloucester's wife, **5**. 92–3, **7**. 340

generosity of, too impetuous, **36**. 80

Geneva visited by, on way to Italy, **25**. 314

Genoa visited by, **25**. 628, 637, 638

George III allows no contact with, **25**. 63n

—— indirectly recognizes, **7**. 40

——'s committee inquires into marriage of, **36**. 305n

——'s reconciliation with her husband reported by, **33**. 198

——'s wedding not attended by, **38**. 117

—— to be told of pregnancy of, **36**. 88

—— unwilling to receive, **29**. 67n

—— will never satisfy pride and vanity of, **36**. 108n

girl injured by coach of, **36**. 245

Gloucester, D. of, accompanied by, on outing, **6**. 151n

—— escorts, to Soho ball, dressed as Elizabeth Woodville, **23**. 193

—— gets letter from, composed by HW and sent by Robinson, **38**. 388n

—— invites, to ball for royalty, **5**. 33

——'s relations with, **31**. 26

——'s volunteering must alarm, **7**. 67

good behaviour of, should excuse her marriage, **23**. 437–8

'good sense' of, **10**. 69

Grafton, Ds of, called on by, **38**. 436

Grandison, Cts, entertains, at Frogmore, **10**. 246

—— formerly courted, **36**. 76

Gray encountered by, at SH during Twickenham visit, **43**. 185

Grenville, Mrs, entertains for, **11**. 128

Grenvilles fail to meet, **7**. 347n

Guerchy and Masserano in love with, **38**. 402

HW advises: against her husband's applying to Parliament, **36**. 100–3; to submit entirely to George III, **23**. 434

HW alludes to relations of, with D. of Gloucester, **10**. 310, **31**. 126

HW and Bp Keppel talk politics before, **22**. 164–5

HW and Gray amuse, by reading *Life of Lord Herbert of Cherbury* to her, **10**. 130, **28**. 3n

HW and Lady Hesketh meet at house of, **22**. 467

HW asked by, to communicate her husband's answer to Bn and Bns Holland about their son, **41**. 272–4

HW asks, for permission to call on her husband, **22**. 433

HW at loo party given by, in Pall Mall, **38**. 371

HW attentive to, **36**. 15, 17, 34

HW avoids meeting, at Nuneham, **35**. 456

HW awaits news of, **6**. 472

HW begs Mann not to entertain, at Florence, **25**. 624

HW brings, to Arlington St, **10**. 67

HW calls on, at the Pavilions, **23**. 433–4

HW cares for, after her breast operation, **30**. 171

HW confers with, on business, **42**. 206

HW congratulates, on pregnancy, **36**. 89

HW converses with, at the Pavilions, **36**. 85

HW deplores sorrows of, **5**. 131

HW did not lend money to, **36**. 327

HW disgraced at Court by marriage of, **36**. 323

HW distressed about situation of, if husband dies, **30**. 266

HW entertains, at SH, **9**. 233, **10**. 127

HW expects, **39**. 437

HW expects congratulations on good fortune of, **28**. 48

(?) HW expects discourtesy to Berrys from, **12**. 146

HW franks letter for, **12**. 121

HW gives bedroom to, at SH, **10**. 63

HW has, at SH, on first husband's death, **38**. 196

HW has had but one letter from, since the start of her journey, **24**. 147–8

HW hears from, about husband's illness, **10**. 55

HW informed by, of Gordon riots, **33**. 174

HW informs: of father's death, **36**. 224; of Lady George Lennox's attentions to her daughter, **31**. 353

HW informs Mme du Deffand of pregnancy and travels of, **31**. 182

HW leaves, at first husband's deathbed, **10**. 58

HW may be accompanied by, to Paris, **38**. 343

HW may take, to SH, **10**. 57

HW mentions, **4**. 475, **9**. 13, **10**. 7, (?) 102, **11**. 24, 108, 377, **12**. 13, 116

HW occasionally goes to town to see, **24**. 335

HW praised by, to Mann, **24**. 297

HW probably displeased that pretensions of, are defeated, **31**. 299

HW quotes letter from, **34**. 75

HW recommends, to Mann, **24**. 125, 131

HW refuses to write verses on, **33**. 43

HW, relative of, no asset to her as poet, **32**. 105

HW respects, as Duke's wife, **36**. 84

HW's absence from husband's levee approved by, **36**. 71

[Walpole, Maria, *continued*]

HW's anxiety about, during husband's illness, **32.** 373

HW's bequest to, **15.** 336, **29.** 343n, **30.** 353–4

HW's connection with *Heroic Postscript* might jeopardize, **28.** 126–30

HW's correspondence with: **7.** 395, 396, **24.** 125, **31.** 318, 356, **34.** 72, **36.** 68–78, 80–90, 90, 92, 100–3, 113–15, 116, 117, 125–6, 127, 128–38, 142–3, 148–52, 159–62, 167, 203, 207–10, 226, 235, 243, 244–6, 253–6, 260–3, 268, 275, 287, 289, 292, **43.** 359, 367, 388; MSS of, **36.** 313

HW's 'court,' goes abroad, **33.** 336

HW sees, at Gloucester House, **25.** 68

(?) HW sends letter for, to Mme du Deffand, **6.** 235

HW's fondness for, **28.** 126

HW should conciliate D. of Gloucester for the sake of, **23.** 417

HW's letter from: about declaration of her marriage, **23.** 433; about husband's illness, **24.** 319; about Lady Lucy Mann, **24.** 191; about Pius VI's courtesies, **24.** 174

HW's letters called by, excuses for telling nothing, **36.** 227–8

HW's letter to: acknowledged in letter to Mann, **24.** 250; delivered by D. of Östergötland's officer, **24.** 247; two, to Venice, **24.** 134

HW's offer of hospitality at SH declined by, because of children, **10.** 69

HW's partiality for, **31.** 172

HW spends evening with, **33.** 198

HW's reflections on misfortunes and beauty of, **10.** 59

HW's relationship to, makes inquiries about Octavius's death improper, **25.** 413n

HW's relations with, **5.** 74, 247–8, **6.** 144, 470, 480, **7.** 238

HW's time usurped by, **11.** 61

HW suggests Siena as winter residence for, **24.** 125

HW summoned to the Pavilions by, **31.** 409

HW takes: to London, **10.** 83; to SH after her first husband's death, **10.** 59, 62

HW tells, not to begin grandson's monument yet, **36.** 329

HW to be welcomed by, **36.** 75

HW to entertain, at SH, **9.** 369

HW to frank letter of, to Jane Clement, **36.** 330

HW to give breakfast for sisters and, **30.** 132

HW told by: about Cowper, **25.** 641; about Italian *Castle of Otranto*, **35.** 436; at Pavilions about Ds of Bedford, **33.** 208; in letter that his letters are mere excuses for lack of anything to say, **25.** 527

HW to meet, in London, **2.** 67, 70, **41.** 368

HW to meet court of, in London, **42.** 200

HW to visit, at Navestock, **38.** 74

HW uneasy about pregnancy of, during husband's illness, **24.** 144, 148

HW urges, to take husband to Italy, at once, **24.** 82

HW visited by, **11.** 85, 145, **12.** 21, 84–5, 95, 115, **36.** 328, **38.** 73, 109

HW visits, **33.** 275

HW watches fire from house of, **29.** 55

HW weary of 'royal' connection through, **35.** 463

HW will try to imitate reason of, **34.** 75

HW with, in Gordon riots, **33.** 187

HW wished by, to leave money and SH to her and her family, **36.** 161n

HW would laugh at, if pride did not interfere, according to Selwyn, **30.** 266

HW writes to, to prevent visit to Rome, **24.** 125

Hamilton sends regards to, **35.** 410, 415

handsomest woman in England now that Cts of Coventry is dead, **22.** 128

Harcourt devoted to, **36.** 151

—— entertains, at Nuneham, **35.** 456–7

Harcourts please, by kindness to her daughter, **35.** 494

health of: Adair and Jebb take care of, without bleeding, **36.** 142; bilious disorder, **36.** 328; erysipelas, **36.** 284; fever and sore throat, **21.** 416; good, **36.** 131, 134; ill, **10.** 82–3, **12.** 200; improves, **15.** 327; influenza, **29.** 249; Mann will keep HW informed about, **24.** 172; perfect, **24.** 201; perfect constitution, **24.** 335; perfectly well, **24.** 190; permits her to go out, at Rome, **24.** 184; scabby face, **36.** 328; slight indisposition, **24.** 144, 164; suffers after first husband's death, **10.** 67; very well, **24.** 170; well, **24.** 181

Hertford apologizes for aloofness at meeting, **39.** 344

—— enrages, by telling people not to visit her, **36.** 76–7, 82, 83, 86–7

——'s letter shown to, **36.** 87

—— writes to, about Windsor lodging for Jane Clement, **36.** 323

Heywood fails to tell Mann of situation of, **24.** 317

—— might have been civil to uncle of, **23.** 429

Heywood, Mrs, Bedchamber woman to, **24.** 323n

—— not seen by, for 3 weeks, **24.** 323

history of, compared with romance, **32.** 379

Holland, Bn and Bns, decline offer of husband of, to employ their son, **41.** 272–4

house taken by, at Twickenham, **22.** 136

husband (first) of: **2.** 125n, **21.** 98n; dies, **10.** 56, 59, 62, 65, 130, **22.** 126–8, 131–2; fears that wife may be pregnant, **10.** 56; mourned by wife, **40.** 280; recommends her, to HW, **9.** 56; takes her in coach, **9.** 233

husband (second) of: **5.** 235n, **11.** 63n, 219n; alienation of, from wife, compensated by 'best of daughters,' **36.** 330; and son agonize wife by their illnesses, **35.** 473; asks George

III for state officials to attend wife's accouchement, 36. 92; better, 32. 364, 365; causes wife 7 weeks' confinement by his illness, 32. 373; essential to wife's welfare and happiness, 24. 329; HW secretly flattered by passion of, for wife, 30. 177; hopes his explanation of marriage will convince George III, 36. 305–6; may take wife to southern France, 24. 76; never left by, for 7 weeks, 35. 475; permits wife to visit her daughter, 36. 268; physicians of, give no hope, 24. 74, 76, 39. 248; physicians of, slightly encouraging, 24. 321; plight of, may arouse sympathy for wife, 24. 321; recovery of, reported by wife to her father, 36. 144; said to be dying, 32. 231; seeks provision for wife, 36. 306–7; tells wife to travel home with his body, 24. 326; to arouse pity for wife to get more income, 36. 102–3; to leave wife at Verona, 36. 309; to supplicate George III for aid, 36. 110–11; volunteering of, must alarm wife, 7. 67; will not help wife with her dependants, 36. 106n; wishes for military service in Prussia, distressing his wife, 33. 35–6

Iron's Hill Lodge in New Forest visited by, 24. 360

Italian capitals will probably be avoided by, for fear of embarrassing their monarchs, 24. 130–1

jointure of, from Waldegrave, 22. 127, 36. 137

Keppel, Bp, called on by, at Windsor, 36. 156n

—— hears self-accusations of, 10. 62

—— tells, about husband's will, 22. 128

Keppel, Mrs, comforted by, 32. 410

Kilgore, Mrs, attends, in childbed, 24. 201

Kingsgate may be visited by, 33. 22, 24

Kingston, Ds of, may avoid Rome during sojourn there of, 24. 220

lady in waiting taken by, 4. 9

Lago di Garda to be visited by, for summer, 24. 291

lands at Dover to go to Gloucester House, 36. 154

last Drawing-Room of, before going abroad, 33. 337

Lausanne visited and Geneva to be visited by, 35. 522

Lennox, Lady George, thanked by, for attentions to daughter, 31. 353

Leopold sees, 24. 297

letters by: on husband's recovery, most moving HW has ever read, 32. 373; to Lady Elizabeth Laura Waldegrave on husband's recovery, 32. 376

London reached by, 2. 67, 43. 66

—— visited by, from Tunbridge with tale of pert footman, 38. 421

Louis XV asks D. of York about, 3. 341, 7. 364

Louis XVI invites, to Paris, 24. 125

—— orders royal honours for, 32. 252

——'s invitation to Versailles declined by, 36. 114n

Luttrells suspected by, 36. 84, 85

Lysons, S., surmises that HW will leave SH to, 15. 335

Mann afraid to inquire about, at Rome, 24. 181

—— asks HW to remember him to, 24. 352, 376, 389

—— congratulates, on George III's reconciliation, 25. 65

—— does not owe visit from, to HW, 24. 299

—— hopes to hear of establishment for, 25. 77

—— impressed by beauty of, but still more by her affability and condescension, 24. 306

—— prevented by gout from paying attentions to, at Florence, 24. 290

—— receives gracious answer to his note to, 24. 247, 250

——'s call from, in Florence, 24. 291, 297

——'s correspondence with, 24. 201, 247, 250, 25. 202–3

——'s servants to attend, at theatre, with iced refreshments, 24. 291

—— sympathizes with HW over situation of, 23. 396

—— tells nephew to pay respects to, at Rome, 24. 131

—— told by, that HW would see urns presented to her by Mann at Florence with husband's permission, 24. 453

—— will not give offence elsewhere by attentions to, 24. 290

—— will probably mention passage of, through Florence, 24. 163

Mann, Horace II, awaits, at Florence, 25. 677

—— cordially received by, at Rome, 25. 674

—— probably not known by, to be at Genoa, 25. 638

—— receives regrets by, for rebuff at Genoa, 25. 674

—— to have audience with, 24. 163–4

Maria Louisa receives, though she had determined not to, 24. 298

marriage date of, corrected, 43. 141

marriage (first) of: 9. 167n, 234–5, 23. 284–5, 287; imminent, 9. 231–2; promoted by HW, 13. 31

marriage (second) of: 2. 31, 3. 57, 84, 125, 200, 329n, 4. 5n, 9, 19, 5. 207n, 247–8, 10. 310n, 11. 63n, 349n, 14. 171n, 28. 46n, 93n; alluded to, 32. 65, 33. 441; announced, 5. 247–8, 265, 268, 13. 48; announced to HW, 23. 433; announced to her father, 5. 247, 23. 415, 36. 62–3, 64, 66–8; declared to Bp Keppel, 23. 484; displeasing to HW, 24. 125; George III notified of, by Legrand, 36. 72–3; HW believes, 23. 302; HW hints at, 10. 310; HW opposed to, 36. 64–5, 69–70; HW said to have published, 36. 86; HW's attitude towards, 5. 247–8, (?) 403; HW's letter about, to be shown to George III by Hertford, 39. 161; honour, not

[Walpole, Maria, *continued*]
ambition should be motive for, **36.** 64–71;
known to Leopold, **23.** 308; may result in
HW's letters being opened, **23.** 537; not
foreseen by Sir Robert Walpole, **25.** 133;
offends Lady Mary Coke, **31.** 169; unhappy,
25. 674; valid, **32.** 118
Milan visited by, **25.** 628, 632, 641
mobbed in the Park, **9.** 239–40
Montagu pities, **10.** 61–2
—— praises, **10.** 61, 65
—— wishes print of, **9.** 239
More, Hannah, corresponds with, **31.** 398
name of, as illegitimate child, **23.** 435
Naples visited by, **25.** 675
Navestock visited by, on honeymoon, **9.** 235
newspapers will abuse, **36.** 67
North Briton attacks D. of Gloucester for
marrying, **23.** 165
northern tour of, **35.** 415
Northumberlands exclude, from Alnwick
Castle, **36.** 323
not going abroad, **33.** 233, 257
not pregnant, **10.** 83, 98, 99
'now Lady Waldegrave in all the forms,' **21.**
294
Nunehams solicitous about, **35.** 472, 474, 476
offended but glad at breaking of daughter's
engagement, **33.** 209
Orford, Cts of, graciously received by, **24.**
164, 170, 222
Packington and the Aylesfords praised by,
43. 369
Padua visited by, **24.** 144
Paris and Mme du Deffand not to be seen by,
36. 132
Paris may be visited by: **6.** 461, 471; to see
Mme du Deffand, **36.** 142
Pavilions, the, home of, **7.** 63–4, **12.** 50n, 140n
(*see also under* Hampton Court)
—— to be left by, for Blackheath, **33.** 125
—— visited by, **33.** 22
Pennicott not to read prayers to, at the Pavilions, **36.** 261
—— summoned by, to the Pavilions, **36.** 263
—— with, **36.** 254
Petersham Lodge to be visited by, **31.** 13–14
physicians give no hope to, for husband's recovery, **24.** 74, 76
physicians slightly encourage, about husband's health, **24.** 321
piety and zeal of, **31.** 396
Piozzi, Mrs, comments on HW's partiality to,
10. 69n, 95n
—— comments on marriage of, to D. of
Gloucester, **10.** 310n
Pitt, Anne, writes about, to Cts of Bute, **31.**
187
pity of, for injured girl, more valuable than
crown or ermine, **36.** 245
Pius VI and Roman nobility attentive to, **24.**
190

Pius VI appoints Ps Falconieri to wait on,
24. 164
—— courteous to, **24.** 174
'plaything Court' of, **29.** 193
Poggio Imperiale visited by, to see Tuscan
grand ducal family, **24.** 297
poor aided by, **31.** 396
Portland, D. of, attached to, **38.** 351, 357
pregnant, **5.** 309, 346, **6.** 216n, **9.** 280, 376, **21.**
313, 337, **22.** 128, **23.** 442, 452, **24.** 130, 171,
214, **32.** 249
prohibited from going to Court, **28.** 46n
Provence to be visited by, for winter, **33.** 419
(?) quinze played by, **32.** 187
Ragman's Castle, Twickenham, occupied by,
42. 483
—— taken for, by HW, **10.** 69
Ramsay's portrait of, **30.** 370
Ranelagh visited by, **25.** 68
receives compliments on daughter's wedding,
25. 274
return of, gives HW little trouble, **33.** 581–2
returns to England, **28.** 339
Rochfords entertain, **9.** 269
Rockingham is rude to, **29.** 209
—— snubs, **36.** 199
Roman journey probably already started by,
24. 144
Roman ladies offend, **24.** 247
Roman ladies offended by postponement of
reception of, **24.** 164
Rome may be visited by, **24.** 82, 290, **25.** 618,
623
—— visited by, **24.** 163–4, 170–1, 174, 181,
184, 186, 190, 201, 214, 222, 247, 252, **25.**
674, **31.** 187
St Leonard's Hill occupied by, **5.** 346, **10.** 42n
—— to be visited by, **32.** 132
secludes herself after Bp Keppel's death,
33. 2
Selwyn calls, 'simple Princess,' **30.** 266
servants of, **12.** 24
Sherwin includes, in drawing of beauties,
29. 185
sisters to be told by, of Tavistock's match,
38. 400
sisters try to cheer, **10.** 62, 63
sister visits, **21.** 439
son born to, **24.** 171, 178, **36.** 115–16
son of: **10.** 310n; ill, **32.** 363
Strasbourg visited by: **24.** 134; to see dying
Margravine of Ansbach, **35.** 532
SH to be visited by, **6.** 329
SH visited by, after first husband's death,
22. 127–8
SH visitors sent by, **12.** 235n, 236, 245
Suard calls, Gloucester's wife, **5.** 92–3, **7.** 340
——'s reference to, causes his dismissal, **3.**
158n
suitors for, betted upon at White's, **38.** 403
Talbot rude to, **36.** 326
tells of disturbances in Switzerland, **11.** 85

transcripts of HW's letters about, altered by her daughter, **26**. 38

Trent visited by, **24**. 317, 319, 337

troops reviewed for husband and, **28**. 222n

Tuscany the first Court to receive, due to Mann, **24**. 297–8

Twickenham house of Mrs Pritchard to be taken by, **40**. 282

Vauxhall visited by, **10**. 127

Venetian ambassador's house at Lago di Garda may be taken by, for summer, **24**. 290, 291, 305

Venice visited by, **24**. 125, 134, 291, 305

Vilett aided by, in seeking Ordnance post, **36**. 79–80

Viry, Contessa di, to be visited by, **35**. 522

visits paid by in mornings, goes to assemblies in evenings, **33**. 582

Waldegrave, 2d E., to wed, **21**. 285

Waldegrave, 4th E., illness of, reported by, **34**. 72

Waldegrave, Lady Charlotte Maria, receives letter from, **36**. 117

—— reports sister's illness to, **36**. 143, 149

—— told by, to flee from Helmingham, **36**. 327

Waldegrave, Lady Elizabeth Laura, attended by, **34**. 75

—— left by, before birth of child, **34**. 83

—— reports to, on husband's illness, **36**. 260, 262

——'s letter to, displeasing, **36**. 330

—— visited by, at Packington, in bereavement, **36**. 266, 268, 284, 329, **43**. 387

—— visits, with her daughter, **12**. 50

'Walpole-hastiness' of, **36**. 82

warm, and hurt by indignities, **24**. 125

wedding costume of, **9**. 235

weeps: at husband's martial schemes, **24**. 401; when HW and Bp Keppel discuss politics, **22**. 165

Weymouth visited by, **25**. 203

Wricklemarsh inhabited by, **36**. 246

Walpole, Mary (d. 1686), m. John Wilson: obituary notice of, **12**. 267

Walpole, Mary (1673–1701), m. (1689) Sir Charles Turner, cr. (1727) Bt:

daughter of, **9**. 153n, **14**. 198n

granddaughter of, **15**. 240n

grandson of, **18**. 182

Walpole, Sir Robert, brother of, **9**. 153n

Walpole, Mary (1705–32), HW's sister, m. (1723) George Cholmondeley, styled Vct Malpas 1725–33; 3d E. of Cholmondeley, 1733:

birth date of, corrected, **43**. 115

granddaughter of, **12**. 200n

grandson of, **11**. 88n

husband of, **23**. 217n

posterity of, should succeed HW in her father's estates, **25**. 132, **36**. 27–32

son of, **5**. 177n, **20**. 554n, **22**. 210n, **23**. 316n, **24**. 524n, **25**. 418

Walpole, Hon. Mary (1726–64 *or* 66), m. (1764) Maurice Suckling; HW's first cousin:

(?) bad breath of, **19**. 72

death date of, corrected, **43**. 258

father now willing to disinherit, **36**. 298

Mann sends pastels to, **19**. 368n, 369

not handsome, **36**. 298

parents unwilling to cut off, by entail, **36**. 31, 296

Walpole, Hon. Mary (1754–1840), dau. of 2d Bn Walpole of Wolterton; m. (1777) Thomas Hussey:

(?) HW told by, of Albemarle-Vere relationship, **33**. 386n

(?) Walpole, Hon. Robert, sends muff to, **4**. 335

Walpole, Lady Rachel. *See* Cavendish, Lady Rachel (1727–1805)

Walpole, Ralph de (d. 1302), Bp of Ely 1299–1302:

brother of, **1**. 384n

HW's brass of, **2**. 105, 106, **43**. 67

Walpole, Hon. Richard (1728–98), HW's first cousin; M.P.:

Alexander brothers evade claims of, on their Grenada property, **36**. 172n

American news given to HW by, **32**. 366–7

Cappers did not recommend, to Miss Nicoll, **14**. 218, 220

Castle Rising might be borough of, **36**. 14, 16

Du Deffand, Mme, discusses, with Hon. T. Walpole, **5**. 94

entail could not be cut off by, **36**. 31

Grand Ohio Co. member, **23**. 424n

healthy, and likely to inherit, **36**. 296, 298

involved in Nicoll affair as supposed substitute suitor, **13**. 24, **14**. 57, 203, 207–8, 223, 224

marriage of, **12**. 150n, **28**. 406n

Parliament to be entered by, from Yarmouth borough, **39**. 95n

plain suit worn by, in picture at Wolterton, **20**. 342

rechosen M.P., **36**. 175

Walpole, Richard (1762–1811), son of Hon. Richard Walpole:

Du Deffand, Mme, discusses, with Hon. T. Walpole, **5**. 94

Walpole, Robert (1650–1700), M.P.; HW's grandfather:

account-book of, **17**. 505–6

death of, **22**. 26

estates of, encumbered when son inherited them, **36**. 295

marriage of, **1**. 374

Nestling chaplain to, **1**. 51, 75

Nottingham ale purchased by, **17**. 506

psalm begun by, with reading-glass, **37**. 181

son receives money from, **17**. 506

son succeeds, in estate of over £2,000 yearly, **22**. 25–6

wig bought by, from Wilkins, **17**. 506

Walpole, Sir Robert (1676–1745), K.B., 1725; K.G., 1726; cr. (1742) E. of Orford, n.c.; HW's father; first lord of the Treasury 1715–17, 1721–42:

abilities, integrity, and power of, seldom found combined, in others, **36.** 249

absent from London, **30.** 22

abuse of, stops, **18.** 119

accident of: 'comes of dining with Tories,' **18.** 277n; on Houghton stairs, **18.** 277, 290

accusers of, to be indemnified, **17.** 425

administration of, continues more than 20 years, **13.** 11

Admiralty post held by, under P. George of Denmark, **22.** 26

alleged corruption of, refuted by HW's small inheritance from him, **25.** 637

Amelia, Ps, claims HW would have been murdered by, for impertinence, **10.** 49

—— fishes with, at New Park, **18.** 449

—— questions HW about oratorical ability of, **10.** 50

America's readiness to revolt foreseen by, as chance for foreign interference, **24.** 523

——'s taxation avoided by, **28.** 416

Amhurst and Bolingbroke attack, in the *Craftsman*, **18.** 20n

anecdote about banker and, **15.** 142

anecdote about effigy of, **1.** 165

anecdote about fame of, **11.** 212

anecdote by, of E. of Pembroke at Devonshire House, **16.** 208–9

Anne's speeches written by, **22.** 26

anniversary of birth of, **25.** 604

Anstey chaplain of, **13.** 5n

Anstruther to forward painting to, **18.** 144

Arenberg expected by Mann to see, **18.** 115, 137

Argyll, D. of, managed Scottish elections for, **20.** 5n

—— prevents, from employing Hume Campbell and Marchmont, **20.** 5

——'s regard for, **37.** 31

——'s rudeness expected by, at House of Lords, **17.** 338

Arlington St house of, *see under* house of, in Arlington St

Arlington St house rented by, for HW, **18.** 137

art collections of, *see under* pictures owned by

Ashton, chaplain to, **14.** 234

—— eulogizes, **19.** 29, 40

—— no longer loyal to HW after death of, **20.** 164

——'s essay on death of, **14.** 234

attacks on: by Pelham and Lyttelton, **13.** 19; provoke HW into writing pamphlets, **13.** 21

Augusta, Ps, mistakes Sir Robert Rich for, **18.** 219

aunt of, **21.** 353n

Austrian ambassador at London said to oppose, **17.** 325

'author of all the happiness' of Mann, **17.** 349

autobiography never written by, **20.** 88

ball at Haymarket attended by, **37.** 50

Baltimore tells, that Frederick, P. of Wales, does not refuse to see him, **18.** 8

Barnard leads opposition to, **22.** 252n

Barrington, 1st Vct, and, **2.** 121–2

—— said to have been expelled by, from Parliament, **33.** 470

Bath, E. of (William Pulteney), antagonist of, **13.** 14n, **14.** 87n

—— at odds with, over Hedon election, **17.** 220–1

—— attacked by, **17.** 297

—— attacks, on irrelevant charge, **37.** 91

—— discusses debates with, **17.** 299

—— excluded by, **25.** 605

—— 'friend' of, **9.** 253

—— instrumental in overthrowing, **9.** 394n

—— joked about by, **18.** 25

—— leads opposition to, **17.** 220n

—— mails unsealed letters during administration of, **37.** 568

—— might have executed, **20.** 65

——'s motion for examination of foreign negotiations defeated by, **17.** 250

——'s speech answered by, **17.** 231

——'s triumph over, satirized, **18.** 91

—— tries to undermine, by making Vernon's fleet inactive, **19.** 459

Bath, Order of the, revived by, **22.** 26, 381

Bath knighthood conferred on, **22.** 26, 381n

Bathurst prejudiced against, **25.** 7–8

Bedford, D. of, Berkshire, and Halifax cut, at House of Lords, **17.** 338

Bedford, D. of, opposes, **17.** 247n

Bedford, Grosvenor, appointed by, to Philadelphia customs sinecure, **40.** 291

bed in which death of, occurred, **39.** 285

Benedict XIV's ignorance about, **21.** 125–7, 138

biographical sketch of, by HW, **22.** 25–7

Biron compared to, by HW, **18.** 467, 481

birth-date of, recorded by his mother, **22.** 26n

birthday of, **18.** 298, **30.** 72, **40.** 9

bishops call on, **18.** 537–8

Blackburne discusses Cts of Yarmouth with, **31.** 421

Bladen, supporter of, **17.** 336n

Blakiston pardoned by, for smuggling, **20.** 261n

Bland calls on, **18.** 244

—— friend of, **1.** 52n

——'s translation given by, to Addison, **42.** 18

—— to show Anstey's epigrams to, **40.** 24–5

'Blunderer' a nickname for, **17.** 234

body of, to be opened after death, **26.** 12

Bolingbroke admits, had sole confidence of Q. Caroline, **20.** 6on

——, Pulteney, and Old Pretender excluded by, **25.** 605

Bolingbroke's falsely-boasted abilities annihilated by, **25.** 7

——'s ingratitude to, **20.** 452

——'s *Letters* treat, leniently, **20.** 60–1

——'s opposition may make, a 'martyr,' **20.** 455

—— would have replaced, **20.** 452, 455

Bootle warned by, **17.** 234

Bragge tells, that Correggio painting at Parma is not an original, **18.** 355

brags like any bridegroom, **17.** 272

brother afraid to allow, to go to Ranelagh, **18.** 8

brother and Selwyns advise, to decline pension, **18.** 465

brother fears that HW will accuse him of aping eloquence of, **35.** 93

brother imitates, **19.** 469

brother obtains secretaryship for, to Stanhope in Spain, **36.** 28n

brother of, **17.** 344n, 469n, **19.** 414n, 469n, **30.** 301n

brother's descendant also descended from, **25.** 418

brother should not ascribe motives to, **36.** 31

brother's obligations to, **36.** 28, 30, 295, 297, 298

brother the 'treaty-dictionary' of, for facts, **17.** 243n

brother tries to divert estate from grandchildren of, **21.** 52, **25.** 367

Brunswick-Wolfenbüttel's pension administered through, **2.** 124, **43.** 68

Bubb Dodington attacked by, **17.** 297

—— repeatedly joined and then abandoned, **30.** 292n

——'s desertion of, attacked by Sir C. H. Williams, **30.** 313

——'s panegyric on, **30.** 292n, 316

Buckinger patronized by, **32.** 94n

Buckingham, Ds of, leaves legacy to, **18.** 213

bumpers drunk to, in county election, **35.** 9

Burghley's descendant, **1.** 374

Burke's panegyric on, **34.** 119

burnt in effigy, **25.** 605

Burrell attached to, **24.** 499

business no longer performed by, **17.** 339

busts in collection of, at Houghton, **18.** 326

Bute gets more abuse than, **22.** 42

Cambridge scholarship resigned by, **43.** 55, 247

Cambridge tutor of, **18.** 64

Campbell in Admiralty of, **19.** 256

Canterbury, Abp of, quotes Thuanus to, **17.** 301

Capello talks Latin with, at Lady Brown's, **18.** 459

career of, **22.** 25–7, **42.** 76–82, 248–9

Carlton House thought to be closed to visits of, **18.** 8

Caroline, Q., dines at Chelsea House of, **15.** 333, **43.** 213

—— questions, about hernia, **17.** 276n

—— recommends Butler's book to, **20.** 167

——'s relations with, **31.** 420–1

—— visited by, **37.** 37n

Carteret and Newcastle keep, in ignorance of foreign affairs, **18.** 30

Carteret hates, **37.** 92

—— said to threaten removal of appointees of, **18.** 81

——'s civilities to HW probably intended for, **18.** 527–8

—— sends to, a letter from daughter-in-law, **17.** 441

——'s remark about levees of, **18.** 349

—— thanks: for aid in carrying Hanover troops measure, **18.** 382; for coachman, in Newcastle's presence, **17.** 506

Cecil, William, communicates Jacobite information to, **17.** 479n

Cecil ancestry of, **1.** 374, **33.** 505

censured as much as any one, **40.** 354

Cerretesi entertained by, at Chelsea, **17.** 503, **18.** 14

chairman of Secret Committee: on Q. Anne's last administration, **22.** 26; which condemned Prior, **13.** 186

Champion, The, may be prosecuted by, for mentioning his natural daughter, **18.** 33

chancellor of the Exchequer, **22.** 26

chaplain of, preaches HW's sermon, **13.** 13

chariot cannot be used by, **18.** 538

Chedworth's peerage procured by, **40.** 60n

Chelsea becomes depository for pictures owned by, **18.** 249

—— house of: **9.** 40n, 348n, **13.** 118, **15.** 333, **43.** 213; sold, **43.** 175

—— to be visited by, **17.** 386

Chesterfield enlists Jacobites against, **17.** 134n

—— mentions, **6.** 37

—— quoted and discussed by, **17.** 232

——'s 'portrait' of, **6.** 462, 465

——'s unwitty witticism about not visiting, **30.** 70–1

—— talks with, at George II's levee, **18.** 102

Chetwynd accused by, of wanting to hang him and his brother, **18.** 191

childhood of, **1.** 374

Cholmondeley's correspondence with, **18.** 260

christian names, use of, despised by, **30.** 289n

Churchill, Gen. Charles, always called 'Charles' by, **30.** 289n

—— corresponded with, **2.** 291, **30.** 42, 289n, **43.** 74

—— told by, about Hedon election, **17.** 221

—— would not have dared to approach, about marriage to daughter, **19.** 132

Churchill, Lady Mary, favourite daughter of, **40.** 177

Chute, Anthony and Francis, followers of, **17.** 124n

Chute, Anthony, entertained by, **17.** 301

Chute, Francis, and Robinson voted out of Hedon after fall of, **17.** 234n

Chute, Francis, praised by, **17.** 234

—— suffered from attachment to, **14.** 195

Chute, John, addresses letter to Downing St house of, **35.** 16

[Walpole, Sir Robert (1676–1745), continued]
—— apologizes for not writing to HW on death of, 35. 57–8
—— hopes minority will support, 35. 20
Cleland dismissed by, 35. 94
Clutterbuck disliked by, 30. 293n
—— employed but distrusted by, 17. 391n
——'s succession to Onslow compared by, to Roxburghe's of Montrose, 17. 391n
coachman of, 17. 503, 18. 20–2
Cobham becomes enemy of, 17. 329n
Cobham faction called 'nepotism' by, 17. 451
Cocchi warned by Rucellai not to defend, 18. 133
Coke, Vct, cites foreigners' respect for, 17. 298
—— supports, 17. 247n
—— visits, at Houghton, 18. 254
Coke, Thomas, E. of Leicester, patronized by, 34. 38n
Cole mentions, 15. 313
—— sees Lens at Chelsea house of, 2. 223n
——'s esteem for, 1. 56, 2. 128, 210, 247
collection of, Mann eager to add to, 17. 228
Collins dedicates English Baronage to, 15. 1n
—— receives £200 by order of, 22. 24n
——'s Peerage the best source of facts about, 22. 24
colonies conciliated by, 24. 513–14
'committeeing' of, not possible, 17. 366
complimented, 1. 312
consternation over Patapan's accident amuses, 18. 51
Conway, Bn, and John Selwyn entertained by, at whist, 40. 28
Conway, Henry, corresponds with, 37. 180, 181, 184–5
—— dines with, 37. 51
—— sends respects to, 37. 122, 132, 138, 142, 148, 151, 154, 158, 177
—— talks to, about getting commission, 37. 23–4
Conway nephews and nieces send compliments to, 39. 517
Cork's political connections opposed to, 20. 456–7
—— visits, at Houghton, 20. 456
Cornish boroughs lost by, through Bubb Dodington, 30. 292n
corpulency of, 18. 219
Correggio painting considered by, 17. 167n, 18. 351, 355, 373
Correggio painting should be bought by, 35. 5
courageous, but did not take risks like North ministry's, 39. 330
Court attendance by, 17. 330, 502, 18. 14, 102
'court' of: disparages Vernon's conquests, 30. 29; HW offends, by rebuking Cholmondeley, 30. 31
Coxe receives papers from HW to write life of, 36. 311n

——'s life of, see Coxe, William: Memoirs . . . of Sir Robert Walpole
——'s memoirs of, 12. 180
Craftsman, The, attacks, 17. 83n
—— attacks ancestry of, 9. 26
Craon's offer to expel daughter-in-law rejected by, 17. 326, 359
creditors of: defrauded by Cruwys, 25. 440; to be paid by 3d E. of Orford when Houghton entail is broken, 36. 163
Crostwight bought by, 12. 21n
Cumberland, D. of, requested by, to make Conway his aide-de-camp, 19. 26n
Customs officials respect HW because of, 17. 142
Customs place granted to, by George I, 26. 52–3
Danvers's witticism on, 17. 232
Dashwood cites foreigners' contempt for, 17. 298
daughter-in-law accuses, of having 'bought' her, 20. 439
daughter-in-law disparages, 17. 406, 423, 448
daughter-in-law expects: to be beheaded, 17. 444; to flee to Florence, 17. 450n
daughter-in-law not permitted by, to take earrings out of England, 25. 148
daughter-in-law's conduct of no concern to, 17. 326
daughter-in-law's expectations on death of, 19. 37, 53
daughter-in-law's infidelities known to, 17. 425
daughter-in-law's letter to Carteret shown to, 17. 441
daughter-in-law's marriage portion paid to, 19. 37n
daughter-in-law wears jewels rented by, for George II's coronation, 21. 536
daughters of (illegitimate), 2. 371, 4. 173n, 6. 234n, 20. 346, 28. 389, 36. 53n
daughters of (legitimate or legitimated), 1. 185n, 11. 97n, 19. 104n, 177n, 20. 554n, 21. 285n, 22. 27, 210n, 262n, 23. 217n, 316n, 24. 524n, 25. 418n, 464n, 37. 62, 202n
daughter tends, in illness, 18. 449
Daye, Catherine, inherits advowson from, 36. 53n
death of: 13. 15, 19. 24, 22. 27, 25. 606, 26. 12; Craon condoles with HW on, 40. 53; daughter-in-law gets no mourning for, 19. 42; one of HW's heaviest blows, 22. 226; painless, 19. 32; Riccardi's letter forgotten because of, 19. 73; said to enrich daughter-in-law, 19. 37, 53; should not encourage daughter-in-law to go to England, 19. 38, 46, 48, 49; showed that there was little equity in a point of honour, 24. 155; son's title antedates, 25. 226; to be communicated to Mann by Galfridus Mann, 19. 24, 31, 34; treatment for stone may have caused, 4. 136

debts and legacies of, **19**. 32

debts of, **23**. 310, **30**. 167n, **32**. 141, **36**. 95, 296, **42**. 81

deeds relating to family of, **15**. 1n

Del Nero's statues might be bought by, **18**. 308, 326

descendants of: defrauded by his brother, **21**. 52, **23**. 367; will not all be deprived of his fortune, **25**. 132, 418

Devonshire, D. of, likes, **17**. 176

disgrace of: **17**. 234n, **30**. 291n; cannot injure wife, **17**. 245–6; confers immortality on him, **41**. 201; pleases daughter-in-law, **17**. 360, 367, 393–4

dispersal of collection of, shows folly of perpetuities, **42**. 424–5

distillers called 'sturdy beggars' by, **34**. 229

Domenichino painting desired by, to be sent by man of war, **18**. 79, 89, 123, 144

Domenichino painting expected to please, **18**. 57

Domenichino painting impatiently awaited by, **18**. 63, 79, 89, 144, 181

Domenichino painting inquired about by, **17**. 442

Domenichino painting may come in Dutch ship at wish of, **18**. 89, 123

Domenichino painting pleases, **18**. 303, 308, 351, **35**. 43–4

Domenichino painting surely will go to, **17**. 241

Domenichino painting will be respected for being in collection of, **18**. 285

Dorset, D. of, discusses Hedon election of, **17**. 221

Downing St no longer the address of, **37**. 181, 184

dressing-room of, at Houghton, **9**. 349

Duane said to own papers of, **41**. 119–20

Du Deffand, Mme, asks for print of, **4**. 241, 266

—— mentions, **3**. 108, 278

dukedom suggested for, **18**. 142, 188

Earle patronized by, **15**. 326–7

——'s appointment by, imprudent, **17**. 242n

——'s defeat leads to fall of, **17**. 220n

—— used but distrusted by, **17**. 220n

Eccardt's and Wootton's picture of, **19**. 511, **35**. 173–4

economy pretended by, **9**. 349

Edgcumbe intimate friend of, **17**. 399n, **21**. 259n, **25**. 518

—— visits: at Houghton, **18**. 25; with son, at Houghton, **18**. 245

Edgcumbe family friends of, **42**. 412

Egmont's election triumph during ministry of, **20**. 31

election of committee chairman lost by party of, **17**. 242–3

Electress's affair to be told to, **17**. 241

Ellis shown by, over Houghton, **18**. 25

employment of able people by, opposed because of their low rank, **19**. 448

enemies of: call him 'Father of Corruption,' **33**. 389; convinced by his small estate that he did not plunder England, **19**. 32; exposed after his death, **19**. 459–60; HW 'in love' with, because they seemed patriotic, **21**. 541

England's greatest man, **20**. 254

——'s present follies cannot be blamed upon, **28**. 218

——'s prosperity in time of, **28**. 415–16

English naval actions in Mediterranean not blamed on, **18**. 205

engraving of, in *Ædes Walpolianæ*, **19**. 511

entail by grandson and brother of, would have his approval, **36**. 24

entail devised by, after brother rejected mutual entail, **36**. 30, 295–6

entail proposed by, **15**. 323

entail would set aside daughter and grandchildren of, **36**. 27–8

epigrams upon, **1**. 56, 57

estate inherited by, **22**. 26

estates of, should go to Cholmondeleys after sons' deaths, **25**. 132

Estcourt's 'Jewel of the Tower' satirizes, **33**. 215n

Etough gets preferment from, **14**. 42n

—— marries, to Maria Skerrett, **40**. 69n

Europe would have been saved by, from wars, **18**. 513

'every man has his price' said to be maxim of, **1**. 325, **17**. 343n, **25**. 606, **29**. 359, **33**. 277, **43**. 59

exchequer chest of, **23**. 285

Excise Bill of, **34**. 229

Excise causes clamour in time of, **22**. 129

excise on wine and tobacco dropped by, **13**. 59n

excused from returning calls when prime minister, **24**. 228

exercise abandoned by, **18**. 449

Eyre planted garden of, before 1725, **42**. 131

Fabius compared with, **35**. 62

fall of: coincides with England's, **21**. 138; predicted, **37**. 87

family ruined by, out of excessive vanity, **23**. 497

farmers' accounts received by, **9**. 349

'fat and jolly,' **1**. 126

father gives money to, **17**. 506

father leaves encumbered estates to, **36**. 295

father's account-book found by, **17**. 505

female descendants favoured by, **36**. 24

finances of: **28**. 302, **36**. 163n, 295–6; salary as prime minister, **17**. 333n

first commoner to become K.G. since Charles II's restoration, **22**. 27

fishes at New Park, **18**. 449

Fitzwilliam attached to, **17**. 320n

Fleury friendly with, **22**. 135

[Walpole, Sir Robert (1676–1745), *continued*]

Florentine and Leghorn gossip about, **17.** 146

Florentine disrespect for, condemned by Mann to Richecourt, **18.** 10–11

Florentines fear return of, to power, **18.** 557

—— regard, as Maria Theresa's enemy, **17.** 406

fondness of, for Houghton, **32.** 140

Forbes, Duncan, called on, **37.** 244

Fox, Capt., knows, **18.** 152, 190

Fox, C. J., compared with, **25.** 275–6, 437, **39.** 406

Fox, Henry, calls request of, for pension, 'avaricious,' **18.** 465n

—— first brought into government by, **40.** 88

France may be refuge of, **17.** 360

Francis I considers, as a friend, **18.** 11

—— visits, at Houghton, **17.** 327n

Frederick, P. of Wales, assures, he will not be molested, **17.** 319n

—— graciously receives, on account of speech, **18.** 409, 425

—— injured by, **17.** 320n

—— notified by, of resignation plans, **17.** 319n

—— resenting favour of, declines George II's offers, **35.** 20n

—— said by ballad to have procured fall of, **18.** 80

—— to demand impeachment of, **17.** 329

French politics and Fleury influenced by, **33.** 439n

friends' advice to pursue Excise scheme said to have been rejected by, **39.** 318–19

Furnese an enemy of, **21.** 172n

—— puts high price on Sacchi painting wanted by, **21.** 173

Gage employed by, for intelligence, **30.** 291n

gallery for pictures erected by, at Houghton from HW's directions, **18.** 63

Gardiner not encouraged by, **18.** 509, 563

Garter conferred on, **22.** 27, **23.** 391

Garter ribbon of, **18.** 291

George I converses with, in Latin, **17.** 503n

—— gives Bolingbroke's memorial to, **20.** 455

—— gives Customs place to, **26.** 52–3, **29.** 327n

—— not ungrateful to, **42.** 80

——'s relations with, in last year of reign, **20.** 455

——'s will's suppression blamed on, **2.** 123–6, 127

George II advised by, to give Pulteney a peerage, **34.** 148

—— consults, on Cabinet Council's move against Carteret, **18.** 536

—— cordial to, at levee, **17.** 502, **18.** 14, 102

—— discards, in favour of Newcastle and Hardwicke, **40.** 88

—— embraces, at close of ministry, **17.** 319, 348

—— gives cracked diamond to, **20.** 112

—— gives diamond and crystal bottle to, but not money for Houghton, **25.** 463–4

—— loves and laments, **17.** 339

—— may not permit, to retire, **17.** 287

—— not ungrateful to, **42.** 80

—— persuaded by: to dismiss Granville, **18.** 536n; to insist on Pulteney's going to House of Lords, **17.** 485n; to write financial offers to Frederick, P. of Wales, **17.** 296n

—— said to be allowed by, to go to Hanover if Argyll is ousted, **37.** 61, 69

—— said to have summoned, from Houghton, **18.** 553

——'s alleged letter from, spurious, **34.** 148

——'s gracious reception of daughter-in-law ungracious to memory of, **19.** 72

——'s impotence after fall of, satirized in ballad, **18.** 80–4

——'s last visit from, at St James's Palace, **34.** 148

——'s pension to, at first declined and then accepted, **17.** 329n, **18.** 465

——'s reliance upon, satirized in ballad, **17.** 187–9

——'s rewards to, disprove Florentine attacks, **18.** 11

—— still relies on, **18.** 401

—— supported by, against George I, **22.** 26

—— warned by, against father's carelessness about health, **20.** 232

Gibbon's father in opposition to, **43.** 298–9

Gibson breaks with, over Quaker Bill, **19.** 503n

—— intimate with, **15.** 296n

—— said to be 'pope' of, **17.** 278, **43.** 242

Gin Act opposed by, **20.** 48n

Gloucester's marriage not foreseen by, **25.** 133

Glover's *Hosier's Ghost* a remote cause of resignation of, **31.** 229

Godolphin favours, **22.** 26, 28, **390**

Gordon, Sir William, opposes, over Chippenham election, **17.** 298, **19.** 302

gout not experienced by, **9.** 291

Grafton, D. of, visits, at Houghton, **18.** 245, 254

granddaughter of, to marry a Walpole, **25.** 132

grandson baffles views of, **25.** 133

grandson compounds debts of, **24.** 440–1

grandson contrasted with, **25.** 418

grandson of, **30.** 167n

(?) grandson of, dies, **6.** 494

grandson said to have received fortune of, **20.** 247

grandson sells pictures collected by, **25.** 133

grandson signs agreement with creditors of, **24.** 301

grandson undermines all the acts of, **24.** 502

grandson would benefit more from Nicoll match than from, **20.** 257

gratitude defined by, **43.** 54

Gray angry with, for keeping HW in town, **13.** 119

—— could not have obtained suitable place from, **28.** 70

great chair of, at Houghton, **18.** 68

great-granddaughter of, to marry Wyndham's grandson, **25.** 68

Guards would not have been sent by, to the polls, **25.** 489

Gumley secures post through, **18.** 25

Gustavus Vasa a libel on, **13.** 171n

HW abused for defending, **1.** 57

HW addressed in care of, **37.** 123

HW an infant when ministry of, began, **25.** 558

HW asks, about Mediterranean situation, **17.** 212

HW, as son of, sincere with wife of another prime minister, **41.** 16

HW believed by, to love hunting, **30.** 33

HW, by goodness of, a placeman for life, **34.** 104

HW calls, 'my king,' **30.** 22

HW came into society at 5 years old, thanks to position of, **24.** 228, **25.** 558

HW cannot get used to new name of, **17.** 331

HW compares, with D. of Courland, **30.** 63

HW compensated by, for loss over Exchequer bills, **37.** 169n

HW connected with Court through position of, **12.** 130

HW consults, about Mann's mourning problems, **18.** 191

HW denies accusation against, in *Biographia Britannica,* **15.** 147–8

HW desired by, to return to England, **17.** 55, **40.** 36

HW despite mother's death can be made happy by, **37.** 37

HW discusses, with Hannah More, **31.** 211

HW does not inherit callousness of, **28.** 182

HW does not inherit wisdom of, **24.** 67n

HW does not think unduly well of, **37.** 163

HW entered by, in rolls of Lincoln's Inn, **13.** 5

HW expected by Henry Jones to follow in footsteps of, **9.** 305

HW glad he lacks ambition of, **10.** 168

HW hears from, about Marlborough's 'betrayal' of Brest, **28.** 387

HW hopes, is well, **36.** 1, 2

HW hurried by, to Parliament, **18.** 394

HW inherits furniture from, **9.** 44n

HW jokes to, about uncle's gait in Houghton gallery, **18.** 305

HW laughs with, over raising of Prague siege, **18.** 68

HW may accompany, to Houghton, **17.** 452

HW may not continue to live with, **17.** 478

HW may request, to intercede for Mann with Mann's father, **17.** 27

HW no longer gets flattery after fall of, **35.** 244

HW not to flatter Chesterfield at expense of, **31.** 173–4

HW not to tell, of Mann's shipment till its arrival, **18.** 202

HW not treated partially by, **17.** 270

HW praises, in *Royal and Noble Authors,* **9.** 219, **40.** 171

HW prizes memory of, above 'the greatest rarity,' **42.** 215

HW proud of, for intelligence rather than rank, **16.** 9

HW reaches England at end of 'happy reign' of, **24.** 356

HW received no favours from any minister but, **25.** 276

HW recommends Jackson to, **17.** 186

HW refutes charges against, of corruption, **25.** 605–6, 637

(?) HW reminded of disturbances at fall of, **10.** 35

HW rises early to meet, **17.** 335

HW's affinity to, makes him acceptable as M.P., **36.** 33

HW's association with, **16.** 19

HW saves money by living with, **37.** 170

HW's benefactions from, **36.** 160–1

HW's biographical sketch of, sent to Mann for Lami, **22.** 25–7, 35

HW's cases from Florence directed to, **18.** 177

HW's correspondence with, **17.** 146, **36.** 5–9, **37.** 96

HW's devotion to, amiable but absurd, **35.** 648

HW's devotion to memory of, **28.** 139

HW shows to, Grosvenor Bedford's letter, **40.** 41

HW's illness might alarm, **17.** 51–2

HW's legacy from, **20.** 250, **25.** 315, 637, **28.** 445, **34.** 145n, **43.** 304

HW son of, but not made callous by it, **28.** 182

HW speaks of Mann to, **17.** 373

HW speculates on his housekeeper's being pensioned by, **33.** 394

HW spent last 3 summers of life of, at Houghton, **23.** 121

HW's presence must have helped, **18.** 105

HW's reflections on tomb of, **9.** 348

HW's relations with, **13.** 7–8, 13, 38, **15.** 151–2

HW's reverence for, increases with age, **24.** 507

HW's sinecure places arranged by, **35.** 502

HW's sources of information as good as those of, **18.** 48

HW suspected by brother of getting Middleton to write life of, **20.** 215

HW's veneration for: **1.** 316, **2.** 90, 126, 170; but does not think him perfect, **40.** 354

HW's veneration for memory of, **31.** 174

HW takes, to Ranelagh for first time, **18.** 8

HW to consult, about possible danger to Mann's position, **18.** 31, 382

HW to describe opinion of, about Domenichino painting, **18.** 292, 382

HW to help hang pictures of, **18.** 218

[Walpole, Sir Robert (1676–1745), *continued*]
HW told by Winchilsea to tell story to, 18. 565

HW told he is older than, 17. 294

HW transacts business for, 15. 20

HW urges, to make death-bed request to D. of Cumberland for Conway to be aide-de-camp, 37. 188n

HW weeps over grave of, 32. 145

HW wishes: to buy Correggio painting, 17. 166–7, 373; to buy Domenichino painting, 17. 166–7

HW wishes to have the papers of, 41. 119–20

HW wishes to restore family to glory of, 36. 165

HW writes to, of Hertford's worry over Conway, 37. 23

habits of, at Houghton, 18. 36

Haddock's tactics explained by, 17. 219

Hamond, Mrs Anthony, tells about conduct of, at election, 9. 351

Hampden's correspondence with, 42. 398n

Hanover troop debate not joined by, 18. 356

Hardwicke, 1st E. of, and, 43. 196

Hardwicke, 1st E. of, 'basely betrayed,' 2. 116, 25. 463n, 28. 246n

Hardwicke, 2d E. of, author of *Walpoliana* concerning, 25. 458, 463–4

—— inquires about miniature or wax cast of, 41. 285

Hare, former tutor of, 18. 64

Hare Naylor family invited by, to dinner, 18. 63–4

Hartington entertained by, 17. 176

—— supports party of, 17. 247

head of, on white cornelian, 18. 166n

health of: ague and looseness, 17. 164; apoplexy rumoured, 17. 211; better, 36. 9; bled, 18. 200; bloody water, 18. 538; cold, 18. 159, 449; cold and fever, 18. 200, 213; 'dying' but quite recovered, 30. 29; fall on stairs, 18. 277, 290, 36. 7, 37. 151, 42. 43; fever, 17. 164, 19. 16; fever, slow, 18. 159; flux of water, 19. 16; good as ever, 17. 231, 263; gout not experienced, 9. 291; gout rumoured, 37. 37; gravel, 30. 49; ill at Richmond, 13. 161n; 'indisposition,' 18. 140; insomnia, 17. 171, 36. 7; last illness, 9. 220n, 26. 12; Mann alarmed by, 17. 194, 208; Mann urges HW to preserve, 17. 284; medicines taken by, 18. 555, 566, 19. 13, 26. 12; opiates taken, 19. 16, 26. 12; out of order, 37. 146, 148, 183; recovered, 13. 176, 17. 169, 211, 294, 37. 157; stone in bladder, 18. 538, 555, 566, 19. 16, 21, 22, 29, 22. 27

healths drunk by, to Stair and Carteret, 18. 259–60

Hepburn, physician to, would have bought paintings for him, 40. 226

Hertford to be assured of solicitude of, for Conway, 37. 24

Hertford wedding party fear coarse jokes of, 9. 235

Hervey complimentary to, 40. 18

—— solicits preferment for Middleton from, 15. 292

Hervey, Bns, courts, after shunning him during defeats, 17. 276

Hervey, (?) George, visits, at Houghton, 18. 25

history considered false by, 33. 536n, 34. 128n

Hoadly estranged from, 17. 502n

—— obtains see of Winchester from, 17. 502n

Holland's states-general compliments, 17. 344, 370

Houghton built by, for posterity, 15. 228

—— endangered by sums spent by, on it, 19. 32

—— left by, for Chelsea, 36. 5

——'s cellar on fire in time of, 34. 88

——'s fate and Ds of Gloucester's marriage not foreseen by, 25. 133

—— should have been proportionate to fortune of, 19. 496

——'s illustrious founder, 25. 132

——'s remotest wing may be inhabited by, 18. 449

—— the monument of, 25. 195

—— to be occupied by, 17. 452, 495, 18. 7–8, 442, 458

—— too extravagant for, 42. 81

—— trip must be made by, in a litter, 18. 538

—— visited by, 13. 104n, 17. 142, 330n, 334n, 375, 386, 390, 403, 18. 25, 31–3, 36, 88–9, 341, 458, 467, 481, 37. 167

housekeeper of, 10. 23

house of, at Chelsea, 9. 40n, 348n, 17. 334n

house of, in Arlington St: 9. 348n, 10. 271, 13. 3n, 17. 334n, 33. 340; again thronged with applicants, 18. 381–2; HW describes, 18. 137; Mann asks about, 18. 114; not all paid for, 37. 163n; opposite his former house there, 17. 478; Pelham builds on site of, inherited by Lincoln, 35. 199n; Walpole, Sir Robert, to move to, from Downing St, 17. 440, 478

house of, in Downing St: 9. 348n, 17. 127, 334n, 478, 491, 494–5; accepted by him only as first lord of Treasury, 17. 478; filled with refugees from fire, 17. 496; HW's art objects sent to, 26. 6; things moved from, to Houghton, 17. 495

house of, in St James's Sq., 13. 56, 28. 470n

House of Commons as full as in time of, 25. 368n

—— expels, 2. 121–2

—— lost by, forcing his retirement, 42. 79

—— managed by, against Dr Sacheverell, 22. 26

House of Lords attended by, 17. 335, 338

—— to be entered by, 17. 319, 325, 333

Hulse attends, 18. 538n, 19. 16, 22

Hume hates, for not patronizing scholars, 7. 354

Hume Campbells court and then shun, **20.** 5

hunts at Richmond on Saturdays, **17.** 247n

Hyndford's treachery to Maria Theresa satirized by, **18.** 89

Ilay not acquitted by, of betrayal, **15.** 153

—— said to have betrayed, **17.** 347

——'s betrayal not believed by, **17.** 347n

—— served, 'by managing Scotland,' **17.** 125n

—— shows Old Pretender's letters to Argyll to, **17.** 479

Ilchester and Montfort told by, to bargain for their titles with Cts of Yarmouth, **9.** 51n

impeachment of: drawn up, **17.** 336; not openly hinted by Pulteney and Carteret, **17.** 329; Parliamentary speeches hint at, **17.** 354; started 100 years after rebellion against Charles I, **20.** 315n; talked about, **17.** 114, 366

inscription concerning, on portrait of Catherine II, **2.** 192

intaglio of, Hillier informs HW about, **16.** 169

invasion of England expected by, in 1744, **15.** 133–4

Italian matters never interesting to, **18.** 30

Italian singers enjoyed by, **17.** 274

Italian tour of, rumoured, **17.** 417, 426, **18.** 145, 202, 211–13, 237, 254

Jacobites and Patriots join in opposing, **22.** 93

Jacobites expect House of Commons to thwart, **17.** 203

Jamaica remittance might have been arranged by, **17.** 411

jewels and lands left by, to daughter, **36.** 25n

Johnson wrote speeches for, **11.** 276

Jurin attends, **18.** 538n

——'s medicine used by, **18.** 552, 566, **19.** 13

Keene, Benjamin, attacked in time of, **20.** 198n

—— highly regarded by, **21.** 166

Keene, Edmund, gets preferment from, for promising to wed his illegitimate daughter, **20.** 346

——'s regard for, **2.** 57

Kendal, Ds of, hates, **20.** 455

Kilmarnock pensioned by, **19.** 284

King's Lynn corporation revere memory of, **21.** 57, 62

King's Lynn elects, M.P., **22.** 26

—— re-elects as M.P., despite previous expulsion, **41.** 78

Kippis 'impertinent' to, **2.** 88, 90, 92–3, 98

—— threatens to write severe life of, **15.** 147

knew men, **3.** 250

Labour in Vain mentions, **18.** 19

Lami wishes panegyric of, for publication, **22.** 13, 15

lampoons in streets remind HW of times of, **9.** 192

Lanfranco painting not wanted by, **18.** 275, 296–7, 311

Lansdown composed verses on imprisonment of, in Tower, **31.** 193–4

Lansdowne, M. of, praises, **42.** 327–9

Laocoön of, at Houghton, **18.** 326

last illness of, *see under* health of

last words of, **26.** 12

Latin the only foreign tongue spoken by, **17.** 503

Latin verses by, in *Gratulatio academiæ Cantabrigiensis*, **16.** 224, 226

Leeds, D. of, saved by, **10.** 22n

Legge appointed by, **19.** 457n

—— calls on, **18.** 245

—— loses esteem of, by courting his daughter, **19.** 458

—— private secretary to, introduces Sir C. H. Williams to him, **30.** 311n

Leghorn merchants not thought by, to be safe from Spaniards, **17.** 209

Leghorn rumoured to be visited by, on man of war, **18.** 145

Leicester owes his earldom to, **18.** 441

Lely's portrait of the younger Vane given by, to E. of Darlington, **42.** 125–6

Leneve, Isabella, lived with, to take care of his daughter, **21.** 316, 353n, **25.** 609n

lenient measures preferred by, **23.** 86

Leonidas probably not read by, **37.** 23

letters of: in *Journal encyclopédique*, **3.** 138; in *London Magazine*, **30.** 42; to Churchill, **2.** 291

Letter to the Examiner attributed to, **16.** 139, 370, **40.** 175

levees of, **17.** 318, **18.** 349

Leviathan compared to, by mad parson, **17.** 197

life of: HW unsuited to write, **15.** 146–7, 152, **16.** 18–20; in *Biographia Britannica*, **2.** 117; *see also under* Coxe, William

Lincoln visits, at Houghton, **18.** 245, 248, 254

London clubs drink health of, **18.** 142

London left by, for Houghton, **30.** 49

London sojourn of, soon to end, **18.** 211

London streets and squares confuse, when he returns calls, **24.** 228

lord justice during kings' absences, **22.** 26

Loudoun's correspondence with, over George Townshend, **36.** 7

Lovel tells, of Montemar's alleged arrest, **18.** 29

—— visits, at Houghton, **18.** 254

Lyttelton intimate with close friends of, **20.** 59n

—— moves for secret committee against, **18.** 117

—— tells Bolingbroke not to publish reflections against, **22.** 59

Macaulay, Mrs, abuses, **2.** 127–8

madwoman gives speech to, as Q. Elizabeth, when he comes down from St James's, for opening of Parliament, **24.** 361

Magnan said to have been employed by, **18.** 548

[Walpole, Sir Robert (1676–1745), *continued*]
male succession desired by, **15.** 325

Mann admires, **18.** 478

—— discusses, with Richecourt, **18.** 10–11

—— hopes, will retire, **17.** 287

—— hopes that art shipment will be approved by, **18.** 200

—— identified with party of, at Florence, **17.** 393, **18.** 363

—— pleased by opinion of, concerning daughter-in-law, **18.** 4

—— procures urns and bronzes for, **17.** 24, **18.** 177, 298, 303, 312

—— regrets not having bought Parker's collection for, **18.** 273

—— respects the prophecies of, **19.** 148

——'s account of Corsica pleases, **17.** 163

—— said by Richecourt to be tool of, **18.** 67

—— says, is the only man who could rule England despite opposition, **21.** 106

—— sends excuses to, for diverting courier, **17.** 113

——'s excuse for writing to HW is to convey news to, **18.** 415

——'s fidelity to, **19.** 99

—— should buy paintings for, **35.** 12

——'s respect for, **24.** 513

——'s safety assured by, **18.** 394

—— sure that political crisis will not arouse, from retirement, **18.** 557

—— thanked by: for *bronzo*, **18.** 298; for getting him the Domenichino painting, **17.** 256–7

—— to be provided for by, in case Florence is captured, **17.** 196

—— to bequeath his Sabine to, **18.** 93

—— wishes Newcastle to be approached through, for salary arrears, **18.** 517

—— wishes to know opinion of, on new ministry, **19.** 6

—— wonders how his conduct impresses, **17.** 119

Mann, Edward Louisa, esquire of the Bath to, **24.** 146

—— suffered financial loss through, **24.** 287

Mann, Horace II, disparages, **23.** 340

Mann, Robert, calls on, **18.** 244–5

Mann family owe all to, despite his unpaid debts to them, **24.** 292

Maratti paintings bought by, **10.** 91n, **17.** 56n

Marchmont banished by, **17.** 294n

—— turned out by, for wishing to be head of affairs, **20.** 5n

Maria Theresa owes present English aid to efforts begun by, **18.** 126

——'s interests said to be endangered by, **17.** 335–6, 367, 404, 406, **18.** 5, 126, 363, 382

Marlborough's indiscretion about Brest known to, **28.** 387

marriage of, **13.** 151n

marriage settlements of, sought, **40.** 72–3

Mason offends HW by referring to, **29.** 194, 196–7

Mathews directed by Winchilsea to take care of shipments for, **18.** 330

——'s attachment to, **18.** 153

maxims of, *see* 'Every man has his price'; '*Quieta non movere*'

medals of, **16.** 299–300

medals, satirical, of, **17.** 189, 229, 426, **18.** 45, **21.** 202

melancholy of, **17.** 171

melon seeds sent to, by Mann, **17.** 34, 38

Meredith's pamphlet contains White's anecdotes of, **39.** 318

Middleton seeks preferment from, **15.** 2, 4

—— esteemed by, **15.** 21

—— introduced to, by HW, **15.** 2

——'s interview with, concerning mastership of Charterhouse, **15.** 306

ministerial quarrels composed by, **30.** 49

ministry of: introduced HW at an early age to great figures, **22.** 484; to end, **17.** 318

mobs carry effigies of, **17.** 390

mobs more violent in time of, **20.** 48

mobs would have been anticipated by, **23.** 99

Money ordered by, to look up HW on way back to England, **17.** 108, 115

Monro, old Dr, highly regarded by, **19.** 210

—— recommends change of air and asses' milk to, **33.** 254

——'s appointment as travelling physician due to, **19.** 210

Montagu, D. of, proposed by, as generalissimo, **20.** 79

Montagu, George, prefers times of, to the present, **10.** 239

Montagu, Lady Mary Wortley, writes to, **17.** 98

Monthly Review abuses HW for liking, **13.** 30

Monticelli often dines with, **17.** 487

Morley said to receive money from, for Wallingford election, **17.** 400

Morris's essay dedicated to, **18.** 464

motto of, see *Fari quæ sentiat*

moves to St James's Sq., **28.** 470n

Museum Florentinum to be sent to, **18.** 329

Musgrave's *History* of, **1.** 59, 60, 63

musicians despised by, **17.** 487

Myddelton desires portrait of, from HW, **42.** 215

name of, declines, as Stanhopes grow popular, **17.** 270

Natter's head of, on white cornelian, **40.** 89n

Navy treasurer, **22.** 26

negotiations in peacetime said to be overdone by, **20.** 396

nephew of, **19.** 320n

new attacks on, threatened, **17.** 95–6, 114

Newcastle, D. of, and Carteret do not inform, of foreign affairs, **18.** 30

Newcastle, D. of, discusses HW's attendance at Granville's assembly with, **18.** 562

—— dissatisfied with administration of, **17.** 301n

—— jealous of, **18**. 535
—— said to have betrayed, **18**. 82
—— sends Dettingen news to, **18**. 258
—— served under, **10**. 192n
——'s levee the only one except that of, which HW attended, **28**. 184n
——'s ministerial guests rescued by coachman of, **17**. 503
—— supports friends of, **17**. 336n
Newdigate and Tories met by, in Grosvenor Sq., **18**. 25
new ministers greeted by, at Court, **17**. 502
new ministers speak to, at George II's levee, **18**. 102
New Ode, A, prefers, to new ministers, **18**. 49–52
new Secret Committee proposal does not involve, **18**. 118
newspapers exaggerate illness of, **17**. 165
newspaper slander more mild in time of, **38**. 360
newspapers mention illness of, **18**. 140
Newton's life mentions, **2**. 321
Niccolini wishes to sell Bns Walpole's jewels to, **17**. 217
niece presents Lely portrait to, **41**. 98
Norfolk, D. of, receives portrait from, **35**. 134n
Nugent's alleged bigamy ignored by, **17**. 271n
Old Coachman, The, mentions, **18**. 22
old politicians hate Egmont because of, **20**. 32
Old Pretender excluded by, **25**. 605
——'s handwriting known by, **17**. 479
——'s letters to, shown to George II, **28**. 389
——'s offers to, seen and endorsed by George II, **17**. 479n
——'s party may be encouraged by Frederick, P. of Wales's defeat of, **18**. 361
on prime ministers, **2**. 122–3
Onslow hails Parliamentary triumph over, **18**. 540
—— told by, about Marlborough-Oxford quarrel, **7**. 362
opiates taken by, **19**. 16, **26**. 12
opponents of, propose his retirement, **17**. 299
Opposition accuses, of being Fleury's tool, **33**. 439
—— in time of, not so harmless, **24**. 442
——'s meeting against, at the Fountain, **17**. 329
—— to, **28**. 82n
Orford title chosen for earldom of, **13**. 11, **17**. 333, **43**. 170, 243
Ormond to tell Old Pretender to influence Jacobites against, **17**. 232n
Osterley inspires, to have turrets at Houghton, **34**. 237
Oswald, George, to be authorized by, to pay for picture, **17**. 228
Oswald, James, deserts, **17**. 299
Oxenden once a favourite of, **33**. 222

Oxford, E. of, makes overtures rejected by, **22**. 26
Oxford University opposes, **30**. 87
pamphlet on, sent by Pownall to HW, **42**. 76–82, 84
papers of: lost, **16**. 19, **43**. 216; received by Coxe from HW, **36**. 311n
Parliamentary career of, **22**. 26–7
Parliamentary manipulation taught by, to English kings, **41**. 10
Parliamentary motion for removal of, fails, **17**. 142n, 232n, **30**. 304n, **37**. 87, 89–92, 96
Parliamentary opposition to, **17**. 133n
Parliamentary session over Westminster at close of rule of, **38**. 315
Parliamentary shift said to be feared by, **17**. 203
Parliamentary speeches by: answering Pulteney, **17**. 231–2, **37**. 91–2; in defence of his administration, **17**. 297; on address to George II, **18**. 409
Parliamentary victory of, **37**. 89–92, 96
Parliament said to have been bribed by, **25**. 605–6
——'s ending may prevent future difficulties for, **40**. 40
——'s ending pleases, **17**. 502
——'s opening attended by, from St James's, **24**. 361
party of: Coke, Fitzwilliam, and Hartington support, **17**. 247; Dashwood and Quarendon oppose, **17**. 247; Onslow might have voted for, **17**. 251
'Patapan' interests, **18**. 71
—— said to be 'familiar' of, **18**. 299
Patriots cannot be conciliated by, **17**. 330–1
—— formed in opposition to, **17**. 231n
Paxton called secretary to, **17**. 417
paymaster of the forces, **22**. 26
paymastership profitable to, **42**. 81
peace negotiations of, between England and Prussia described by Mann to Richecourt, **18**. 4–5
peace the delight of, **34**. 19
peerage granted to, **13**. 11, **17**. 318, 325, 333, **22**. 27, **43**. 170, 243
Pelham, 'friend and élève' of, **17**. 329n
—— not to replace, **17**. 319
——'s advice sometimes taken by, against his better judgment, **39**. 318–19
—— secures pension for, **17**. 329n
——'s ingratitude to, attacked by Willes, **19**. 471
—— supports, **17**. 219n
—— told by, to warn George II against George II's Hanoverian policy, **18**. 356n
—— visits, at Houghton, **18**. 245, 248, 254
—— would be warned by, if Bedford's place were in danger, **40**. 41
Pembroke would have been made K.G. by, **20**. 109
Penny's letter read to, by HW, **17**. 257

[Walpole, Sir Robert (1676–1745), *continued*]
pension of: 42. 80; charged to excise on beer, 18. 465n
perpetuation of family the great object of, 25. 156–7
pictures collected by: at Hermitage, 25. 632n; catalogue of, see *Ædes Walpolianæ*; *Gallery of, see under* Boydell, John; placed at Houghton in hopes they would stay there, 24. 441; Pope's epigram alludes to, 30. 4–5; sale of, a blot on his memory, 33. 86; sold, 2. 145–6, 158, 165, 170, 171, 192, 257, 7. 159, 24. 427–8, 434, 440–1; that were not at Houghton, are sold, 20. 261, 268; three sales of, 24. 441, 43. 69; too numerous for Houghton, 17. 340, 18. 249; value of, 2. 159, 168–70, 24. 441, 43. 286; Van Dycks and Lelys among, came from Winchendon House, 30. 371
pictures no longer collected by, 17. 339–40, 462
pictures recommended to, by HW, 17. 166–7
Pitt (Chatham) acquits, in speech, 19. 370
Pitts and Lytteltons deride, for preserving peace, 37. 200
planted trees at Houghton, 1. 374
playbill satirizes, 13. 76n
Pope never reviled, 25. 6
—— seeks aid of, 9. 116n
——'s epigram on, 30. 4–5
——'s letter to, 9. 116n
porter of, told to shoo away mob, 18. 96
portrait owned by, of E. of Surrey, 1. 192, 35. 134
portraits of: 30. 370; at Frogmore, 10. 42; by Richardson, Wootton, and Kneller, 41. 234; by Vanloo, 2. 57; desired by Myddelton from HW, 42. 215; HW lists, 42. 249; sold at auction, 28. 252; to be cleaned and sent to Houghton, 15. 325; Warton buys, 42. 248
Pownall's account of: 1. 293n, 42. 76–82, 84; submitted to HW, 42. 76
Prescot honours memory of, 1. 299, 301, 2. 21
prime ministers after him inferior to, 28. 184
prime ministers discussed by, 2. 122–3
prime ministry would never again be accepted by, 18. 142
print of, in Garter robes, 41. 234
prints of, 42. 249
prisoner in Tower of London, 22. 26, 31. 193–4, 32. 276
prize-taking by ships would have been regulated by, 20. 54, 21. 415
prophecy by: about foreign involvement in American revolt, 24. 523; about rebellions, 19. 118, 148, 24. 356, 25. 606; about ships' prizes, 21. 415
proxy sent by, to House of Lords, 18. 159
Prussian peace negotiations kept secret by, until completion, 18. 5
public benefactions of, discarded like his pictures, 24. 503

'*quieta non movere*' the maxim of, 20. 409, 22. 111, 23. 289, 304, 359, 25. 434, 506, 529, 541, 603, 28. 416, 459, 33. 389
'quiet statesman,' 33. 389
Ralph's *Critical History of the Administration* of, 1. 60
Ranby attends, 18. 538, 26. 12
Ranelagh visited by, 18. 8
Raphael painting not to be bought by, without more information, 18. 250, 254
reading and writing disliked by, 20. 88
religion of, 'fixed,' 20. 167
remarriage of, permitted by son's marriage settlement, 43. 177
reminiscences said to have been written by, 20. 77, 88
resignation of, as prime minister: 9. 199, 13. 11, 15. 306, 17. 332, 28. 48, 70; approved by Mann, 18. 151; daughter-in-law expects congratulations on, 17. 371; desired by his sons, 17. 253, 319; does not end his influence, 17. 335n; followed by offers of dukedoms to others, 21. 26; peerage accompanies, 13. 11
resigns scholarship in King's College, 1. 205
responsibility for Bavarian, Spanish, and Swedish wars disclaimed by, 17. 231–2
rich citizens dine with, on 'rump-days,' 35. 86
Richecourt's insulting remarks about, 18. 4–5
Richmond, D. of, criticizes request of, for pension, 18. 465n
—— defends, in House of Lords, 17. 330
—— not a personal friend of, 17. 319
—— tells, of resigning mastership of the Horse, 17. 319
Richmond (New Park) depository for pictures of, 18. 249
——'s rangership reversion goes to, 20. 125n, 41. 234n
—— to be visited by, 17. 330, 333
—— visited by, 13. 157n, 17. 164, 247n, 335, 358, 18. 136, 430, 449, 455
Rinuccini ascribes Richecourt's disgrace to, 17. 108
Robinson, Luke, suffers for, 19. 371
Robinson, Sir Thomas, gives ball not attended by, 17. 185
Rockingham lacks ministerial power of, 27. 29
Rolfe, Edmund, election agent for, 17. 166n
Ross saved by, from unwelcome post in West Indies, 17. 244
Rowley resembles, 18. 506
—— would respect letter from, asking for Gardiner's promotion, 18. 507
Rubens cartoon bought by, 9. 56
rural life comforts, 36. 9
Rushout opposes, 17. 332n
said to have gout at Houghton, 37. 37–8
St James's Palace not visited by, 17. 403
salary of, as prime minister, 17. 333n
Sandwich's connection with Old Pretender reported to, from Rome, 17. 231n

Sandys angry with, for taking Orford title, **17**. 333
—— orders, to vacate Downing St house, **17**. 495
—— proposes removal of, **17**. 83n
—— ridiculous as successor to, **20**. 518
—— succeeds, in Exchequer post, **18**. 118n
Sandys, Mrs, tells, to quit Downing St house, **17**. 478
Saturday sessions of Parliament instituted on purpose to injure health of, **17**. 247
sayings attributed to: about every man having his price, **1**. 325, **17**. 343n, **25**. 606, **28**. 416, 459, **33**. 277; about majority essential for ministry's continuance, **23**. 190; about ministers seeing too much of human badness, **20**. 77, 88
scholarship at King's College, Cambridge, resigned by, **43**. 55, 247
Scottish and Cornish Parliamentary vote overthrows, **17**. 346n
Scottish partisans of, to defend him, **17**. 338
Scrope will not betray, **17**. 459
scrutoire of, **9**. 349
Scully said to be preparing house for, in Florence, **17**. 426
(?) second marriage of, **13**. 151, 153
second wife compelled by, to burn Lady Mary Wortley Montagu's letters, **34**. 256
secretary at war, **22**. 26
Secret Committee friends expected by, to desert him, **17**. 429
Secret Committee may consist of friends of, **17**. 375
Secret Committee on: **13**. 12, 248, **15**. 148, **30**. 292n, 304n; defeated, **17**. 362–4, 379, 388; fails to harm him, **17**. 390, 420, 421, **22**. 27, **25**. 606; voted on, **17**. 383–6
Secret Committee proposal arouses, **17**. 287
Secret Committee's report does not mention, **17**. 425
self-seeking politicians revile, because he brought prosperity to England, not to them, **25**. 6–7
Selwyn, Mrs, listens to, **17**. 339
Shippen averts impeachment of, **17**. 232n
——'s price unknown to, **17**. 343n
Shuvalov's position compared to that of, **10**. 157
sings ballad and laughs at Prague campaign in his great chair at Houghton, **18**. 68
sister-in-law charges, for his grandson's riding her son's horses, **18**. 70
sister, sisters of, **15**. 240n, **19**. 320n, **25**. 423n
Skerrett, Maria, makes financial agreement with, for their marriage, **43**. 177
——'s marriage to, dated, **14**. 42n, **43**. 182
snores before his curtains are drawn, **17**. 171
snuff-box inscription mentions, **31**. 141
son, sons of, **10**. 11, 332, **20**. 233n, **21**. 121, 126, 127, **22**. 27, **25**. 462n
son's death ruins estate of, **20**. 239

son's match with Margaret Rolle arranged by, **20**. 439, **25**. 156–7
sons of, get Customs benefits, **41**. 326
sons sup with, after long Parliamentary session, **17**. 294
son stores pictures for, **18**. 249
Sortes Virgilianæ drawn for, **37**. 79
Southcote aided by, at Pope's request, **9**. 116n
Spain recommended by, for friendly relations, **21**. 121
speaks without notes, **37**. 91
Spithead expeditions of, **34**. 201
Stanhoe depository for pictures of, **18**. 249
statues needed by, **18**. 326
steward of, **17**. 6n; *see also* Oswald, George
Sturgis opposed to, **17**. 406
subscribes to Middleton's *Life of Cicero*, **15**. 7n
succession to ministry of, **20**. 518
successors should have imitated wise measures of, **24**. 513
successor to, unknown in Norfolk, **40**. 48
Suckling, Rev. Maurice, marries niece of, **9**. 153
Suckling, Capt. Maurice, has obligations to, **36**. 162
—— is greatnephew to, **18**. 152, 182
Suffolk, Cts of, enemy to, **31**. 420
summer residence of, **15**. 4n
Sundon, Bns, discussed by, with HW, **17**. 276
—— discusses Bp Gibson with, at dinner, **17**. 278
—— proposes partnership with, **17**. 277
Surrey's portrait owned by, **1**. 192, **35**. 134
Sutton's remark to Jones when shaving, **38**. 55
Swift's history belittles, **21**. 185
Testament politique (spurious) of: **3**. 200, 201, 207, 209–10, 212, 223, 225; HW's letter commenting on, **3**. 220; reviewed in Fréron's *Année littéraire*, **3**. 209
Thanet, Cts of, makes bon mot about, **37**. 87
Theodore of Corsica falsely claims friendship of, **18**. 187–8, 190, 210, 233
—— never had connections with, **18**. 210, 225
——'s alleged relations with Carteret surprising to, **18**. 210, 225
Thicknesse calls, 'late great minister,' **28**. 47
Thomas, Bp, calls on, **18**. 537–8
three last summers of life of, spent by HW with him at Houghton, **23**. 121
title deeds signed by, as trustee, **40**. 72–3
tomb of, at Houghton, **9**. 348
Tories oppose further prosecution of, **17**. 336
Totnes mayor forwards letter to, **17**. 299
Tower of London rumoured to become again the prison of, **17**. 299
—— the former prison of, **9**. 207, **22**. 26, **32**. 276
Townshend, Vcts, hates followers of, **18**. 497
Townshend, Capt. George, persecuted because related to, **19**. 332
Treasury and Navy posts of, **22**. 26–7

[Walpole, Sir Robert (1676–1745), continued]
Treasury board meets at house of, after his resignation of ministry, 17. 391n
Treasury to be adjourned during absence of, 43. 174
'treat' ordered by, at the Duke's Head, in Norfolk, 18. 260n
Tucker's Case of Going to War lauds, 10. 75
Turk, Martha, a factor in baffling the plans of, 25. 133
Tuscan helplessness to be described to, 17. 267
Tweeddale joins discontented Whigs during administration of, 19. 195n
'Unconnected Whig' praises, 28. 337n
Van Huysum employed by, at Chelsea, 36. 238n
Vernon's published correspondence vindicates, 19. 459–60, 472
——'s success should please, 17. 7
—— toasted by, as joke at Hertford wedding, 9. 235
Villars calls Fleury the tool of, 33. 439
—— mentions, 35. 633
vindication of, before Parliament, 13. 240
virtues of, contrasted with HW's weaknesses, 23. 522, 523, 525
Voltaire compliments HW at expense of, 41. 354
—— considers HW a better writer than, 41. 152
—— used to know, 41. 146
Wade's letter from, does not mention Conway, 37. 167
Waldegrave's appointment by, mentioned in impeachment, 17. 336
Walker, toad-eater to, 19. 511n
Walpole, Sir Edward, ill-treats, because of HW, 36. 19
—— left legacy by, 34. 145n
—— loves, the best, 36. 19
—— receives Pall Mall freehold from, 36. 14n
—— scolds, for letting HW bring Middleton to Houghton, 20. 215
——'s contemplated marriage to Caroline Howe not opposed by, 17. 209
—— was devoted to, 28. 70
Walpole, Horatio (1723–1809) receives horse from, 18. 70
Walpoliana concerning, printed by 2d E. of Hardwicke, 33. 421–2; see also under Yorke, Philip (1720–90)
Walsingham's portrait formerly owned by, 32. 47n
war not to be blamed on, 28. 218
war trophies in Westminster Hall do not make, jealous, 37. 200
Welsh genealogy a compliment to wife of, 33. 454–5
West does not intend to satirize, in Pausanias, 13. 240
Weston a protégé of, 17. 279n

Whaley hopes 'Journey to Houghton' will please, 40. 48–9
——'s 'Journey to Houghton' shown to, by HW, 40. 42
Whigs always supported by, 22. 26
Whitehead, Paul, comments on health of, 17. 252
wife of, 1. 52n, 342n, 4. 59n, 11. 212n, 19. 310n, 22. 27, 24. 71n
Willes, Edward, supported by, for Exeter bishopric, 17. 279
Willes, Sir John, obligated to, 19. 471
—— principal friend of, 26. 28
—— visits, at Houghton, 18. 25
Williams, Sir C. H., contrasts character of, with Pelham's, 30. 318
—— introduced to, receiving his patronage, 30. 311
——'s writings will please, 30. 64
will of, 19. 104n
Wilmington bested by, 33. 422
—— supplanted by, 18. 50n
Windham a Whig of the type of, 24. 424
Winnington's dismissal of Robert Mann violates promise to, 18. 497
——'s only superior, 19. 249
wit of, defined by HW, 15. 146
witticisms by: on Argyll's deserting Oxford's administration, 26. 11; on becoming eunuch, 17. 274; on Newcastle's dinner guests, 17. 506; on Smissaert's remark, 18. 458; to Ranby, on deathbed, 26. 12
Wolterton visited by, 30. 80
worthy of ancestors, 15. 4
would not return to the Treasury, 18. 142
writers employed by, bad, 30. 314
writes from Houghton, 36. 6, 8
Wyndham leads opposition against, 25. 68n
—— not sent by, to the Tower, 23. 289
Wynn an opponent of, 13. 33n
Yonge called fine speaker by, but of trifling character, 17. 233n
Zanetti cheats, 22. 562
Walpole, Robert (1701–51), cr. (1723) Bn Walpole; 2d E. of Orford, 1745; HW's eldest brother:
Amelia, Ps, receives call from, 20. 29
—— succeeds, as ranger of New Park, Richmond, 20. 29n, 125n, 233, 322
arms of, inappropriately placed on proposed monument to wife, 25. 226
'attachment' of, to church and Oxford, 30. 87
auditor of the Exchequer, 17. 299n, 19. 285, 496n, 20. 233n, 26. 52
barony conferred on, 15. 1n
Bath knighthood conferred on, 20. 233n, 22. 27, 381n
Bath order esteemed by, 22. 390
Castle Rising borough controlled by, 30. 330n
Castle Rising borough should be offered by, to Sir Edward Walpole before HW, 36. 14–17

Chesterfield buys Houghton lantern from, **20.** 163

chickens minced by, **9.** 109

Conway not yet seen by, **37.** 51

creditors of, should receive money returned by Mozzi, **23.** 446

Cruwys employed by, **25.** 440n

Customs place for lifetime of, **26.** 52–3, **41.** 326

death of: **9.** 113n, 135n, **13.** 23, **14.** 50, **15.** 323, **20.** 238, 243; approaching, **35.** 67; attributed to carbuncular state of blood, **20.** 413; should not affect entail, **36.** 24; would be fatal to HW, George Walpole, and Galfridus Mann, **20.** 233; would ruin his family, **19.** 496

debts of: **30.** 167n, **32.** 141, **36.** 95, 296, **42.** 81; estate unable to pay off, **19.** 496; son adds to, **23.** 510; son not legally bound to pay, **24.** 440, **25.** 155; son repudiates, **25.** 155, 158; to be compounded by son, **25.** 148

decree obtained by, **25.** 186

diamond earrings (given to wife) later sold by, **25.** 148

(?) discoveries of, may enable him to divorce wife, **37.** 301

Exchequer House of: adjoins House of Commons, **17.** 299n; filled with father's pictures, **18.** 249; improved since his occupancy, **37.** 454

father might have been succeeded by, as prime minister, **40.** 48

father's papers neglected by, **16.** 19

father's retirement wished by, **17.** 253, 319

father sups with, after long Parliamentary session, **17.** 294

finances of, **36.** 163n

Frederick, P. of Wales, talks to, **17.** 386

—— to be attended by, at levee, **17.** 338, 369

gallery of, in Westminster Hall, **19.** 285

Gardiner, Rev. John, chaplain to, at Crostwight, **37.** 183n

Gardiner, Mrs John, unlikely to have been mistress to, **43.** 68

Gardiner, Richard, claims to be son of, **18.** 507, 522, 543

—— to receive letter from, **18.** 522

—— writes to, through Mann, **18.** 507

George I appoints, ranger of Richmond New Park, **17.** 164n

—— makes, Bn and K.G., **22.** 27

George I's and George II's bounty to, **42.** 80

George II notifies, about reversion of Richmond rangership, **20.** 125

government posts of, sinking, **19.** 496

HW explains reference to son of, **20.** 19

HW less flattered than, **30.** 41

HW negotiates with, in Rigby's behalf, **37.** 194n

HW receives condolence calls on death of, **20.** 246

HW receives from, a part of father's legacy, **25.** 637

HW's correspondence with, **30.** 95, **36.** (?) 6, 21, **40.** 36

HW's enemy, **19.** 496

HW's financial relations with, **19.** 447–8

HW should send letter from, in Gardiner's behalf, **18.** 509

HW's income lowered by loss to, over Exchequer bills, **37.** 169n

HW's sermon preached before, **13.** 13

HW told by, not to disturb fish, **9.** 61

health of: boil, **20.** 233; improved, **19.** 504; precarious, **19.** 496, 505; recovered, **19.** 510, **20.** 6, 29; thrush, **20.** 233, 242

Heighington's odes dedicated to, **13.** 84n

horses of, **32.** 131n

Houghton closed by, for economy, **19.** 40

—— visited by, **18.** 88

huntsmen and hounds led by, in fox hunt, **37.** 181

invalids carried by, to Parliament, **17.** 299

jewels taken from wife by, **25.** 162

lantern bought by, at Cholmondeley sale, **20.** 163

lawyers given fees by, in preparation for wife's arrival, **19.** 61

Luxborough chosen by, for M.P., **19.** 419

Mann, Edward Louisa, suffered financial loss through, **24.** 287

Mann, Galfridus, asked by, to ask Horace Mann for proofs of wife's infidelity, **19.** 200

Mann, Horace, hopes that wife does not worry, **19.** 132

—— hopes that wife will not be divorced by, **19.** 80

——'s fidelity to, **19.** 99

—— thanked by, through HW, for news, **19.** 61

Mann, Robert, revokes bequest of debt of, **20.** 302n

Mann family, though inconvenienced by debts of, owes all to his father, **24.** 292

marriage of: **1.** 342n, **25.** 121, **42.** 82, 131; arranged by his father, **25.** 156–7

marriage settlements of: **25.** 440n, **36.** 295–6; permit father's remarriage, **43.** 176–7

master of the Buckhounds, **19.** 496, **20.** 233n

mistress of, see Norsa, Hannah

Montagu may consent to visit Houghton under ownership of, **9.** 77

Norsa, Hannah, entertained by, **9.** 109

not in Norfolk, **40.** 48

Oxford University's request to, about Rigby, to be ignored, **30.** 88

Parliamentary seat promised by, to Horatio Walpole (1723–1809), **36.** 10

Petersham, Lady Caroline, includes, in Vauxhall party, **9.** 109

Philipps, John, presents pedigree to, **13.** 81n

physicians and bark rejected by, **20.** 233

[Walpole, Robert (1701–51), *continued*]
posts held by, **20.** 233n
ranger of New Park, Richmond, **15.** 327, **17.** 503n, **20.** 125, 233n
repairs church at Houghton, **1.** 343
Rowley would respect letter from, asking for Gardiner's promotion, **18.** 507
Shukburghs recommended by, to Mann, **20.** 160
son allowed by, to ride cousin's horses, **18.** 70
son executor of estate of, **25.** 446
son fears to face ire of, by returning from Cheltenham, **40.** 59–60
son of, **36.** 14, 16
son's paternity dubious, **15.** 324
Stanhoe, house of, **18.** 249
Sturgis, friend of, **17.** 70n, 71n
supposed natural son of, **2.** 120n
Surrey's portrait at sale of, **35.** 134
uncle corresponds with, **36.** 10
visitors to, in illness, **19.** 510
Walker's Wimbledon house left to, **19.** 511n
Walpole, Sir Edward, corresponds with, over Castle Rising, **36.** 18
wife cherishes harsh letter from, **19.** 50
wife claims jointure from time of death of, **25.** 162
wife considers, best of his family, **19.** 139
wife dislikes, **9.** 78
wife expects letter from, **19.** 37
wife gets few jewels from, **25.** 148
wife may force, to return her estate to her, **19.** 49–50
wife of, **1.** 342n, **5.** 360n, **9.** 78n, **13.** 227n, **20.** 481n, **21.** 536n, **29.** 106n, **30.** 95
wife restricts intercourse with, after birth of son, **19.** 203
wife said to have received letter from, **19.** 47, 49
wife's allowance from, **19.** 88, 219, 224
wife's divorce would alienate property from, **19.** 88
wife separated from, **36.** 295
wife should be locked up by, **19.** 192
wife's intercepted letters among papers of, **20.** 247–8
wife's jewels mostly retained by, when she went abroad, **25.** 472
wife's jointure said to be in arrears since death of, **23.** 512
wife's motions indifferent to, **19.** 61
wife's negotiations with, **19.** 202–3, 224, 290, 348
wife's portrait by Zincke probably for, **25.** 501
wife's schemes to be told to, by HW, **17.** 389–90
wife to make composition with, **19.** 202
wife to request legal separation from, **19.** 111
wife wounds, by her misconduct, **19.** 38–9
will drawn by, **20.** 238
will of: **13.** 23, **14.** 50; tells son to take uncles' advice, **36.** 297

Walpole, Hon. Robert (1736–1810), youngest son of 1st Bn Walpole of Wolterton; HW's first cousin; secretary of embassy at Paris; English minister to Portugal:
always wins at cards, **4.** 352
Amigoni's and Astley's paintings of, **20.** 341, 342
Angora cat taken by, **4.** 325
arrives: in England from Portugal, **33.** 400; in Paris, **4.** 133
beautiful wife brought home by, **25.** 410–11, 417
Beauvau's praise of Hénault would please, **5.** 54
Boulogne-sur-Seine visited by, **7.** 326
Broglie, Comte de, indignant at, **4.** 374
brother's letter to, to Paris, about Pitt, **39.** 88–9
Castle Rising might be borough of, **36.** 14, 16
Chamier not told by, of Choiseul's invitation, **4.** 301
Choiseul, Duc de, relations of, with, **4.** 306, 311, 344, 378, 461, 480, **5.** 29
Choiseul, Duchesse de, relations of, with, **4.** 161, **5.** 29
Cholmondeley, Mrs Robert, relations of, with, **4.** 257, 328
Cholmondeley daughters to have New Year's gift from, **4.** 328
Churchill, Lady Mary, brought to Mme du Deffand by, **5.** 19
—— escorted by, **5.** 23
courier of, **4.** 190, 191, 193, 198, 205, 310, 383, **5.** 9, (?) 37, **7.** (?) 392
Customs avoidance suggested by, **4.** 439, 453
Diderot describes argument between Ps Dashkov and, **4.** 483n
does not sup, **5.** 13
Du Deffand, Mme, and, mean little to each other, **4.** 241, 242
—— discusses, with Hon. T. Walpole, **5.** 94
—— entertains, at supper, **41.** 195
—— fears, will not return to Paris, **4.** 212, 213, 221
—— hears nothing from, **5.** 129
—— instructed by, in English politics, **4.** 374
—— mentions, **4.** 187, 199
—— receives tea from, **5.** 129–30
——'s correspondence from, **5.** 19, 54, 55, 76, 163, 212, 310, **6.** 39
—— sends letter by, **4.** 209, **5.** 29
—— sends news to, by HW, **5.** 59
—— sends parcels and letters through, **4.** 166, 190, 191, 193, 197, 198, 201, 205–7, 310, 365, 366, 370, 383, 470, 472, **5.** 4, 8, 9
—— shows letters (from HW) to, **4.** 166, 173, 189
——'s opinion of, **4.** 143, 146, 157, 161, 163–4, 182, 190, 210, 212, 213, 245, 256, 257, 274, 301, 306, 309, 327, 366, **5.** 5, 29, 86, 137
—— speculates about views of, on French politics, **4.** 202
—— suggests, as ambassador, **4.** 380

—— suggests that HW share news with, **5.** 51, 62

—— suspects quarrel of, **4.** 280, 281

—— to consult, on sending of pamphlet, **4.** 459

—— to send letter by, **5.** 84, 87

—— wishes HW to know, **4.** 163–4, 190, 202, 203, 209–10

embassy post of, **4.** 161, 311, 343–4, **5.** 29

Englishmen brought to Mme du Deffand by, **4.** 357

entail could not be cut off by, **36.** 31

excuses himself from attending Lady Craven's wedding, **34.** 132–3

financial crisis foreseen by, **5.** 116

financial crisis upsets, **4.** 373, 374

Fontainebleau visited by, **4.** 301, 305

Forcalquier, Mme de, corresponds with, **4.** 224, 231–2

——'s relations with, **4.** 182–4, 221, 240–2, 245

friends of, are not Mme du Deffand's, **4.** 235

Gennevilliers visited by, **4.** 469

Grand Ohio Co. member, **23.** 424n

HW accompanies, to theatre, **7.** 331

HW can send parcels through, **5.** 20, 72

HW has, for dinner at SH, **33.** 406

HW hears news of Mme du Deffand from, **5.** 149

HW inquired after by, **4.** 305

HW is confused with, **14.** 189

HW's correspondence with, **36.** 48–9

HW's correspondence with Mme du Deffand facilitated by, **36.** 48, 49

HW sees, in chaise, in France, **35.** 123

HW sends letter and portfolio by, **4.** 232, 233, 237

HW sends letter by, **7.** 389

HW sends letters through, **4.** 198, 201, **7.** (?) 388, (?) 392

HW's intimacy with Mme du Deffand hidden from, **4.** 133, 138, 143, 206, 392

HW slighted by, **4.** 306, 309, 366

HW's opinion of: **4.** 218, 227; Du Deffand, Mme, understands, **4.** 218; Du Deffand, Mme, wishes to know, **4.** 182, 209–10, 221

HW to be paid by, for Mme de Choiseul's purchases, **5.** 37, 65

HW will learn news from, **5.** 29, 30, 66

Harcourt, Earl, brought to Mme du Deffand by, **4.** 199

has received no letters, **4.** 282

health of, **4.** 138

healthy, and likely to inherit, **36.** 296, 298

housebreaking thought to have happened to, not to HW, **5.** 55

in England, **5.** 33, 37

Lisbon, home of, **5.** 212

marriage of, **7.** 228

minister at Lisbon, **5.** 83

Orford, Cts of, sees, in Paris, **23.** 141

Paris left by, **4.** 209, 212, 480, **5.** 29

—— reached by, **4.** 133

—— to be visited by, **5.** 65, 69, 72, 76, 82

—— visited by, **4.** 233, **5.** 82–3, 86, 89

Portugal to be destination of, **5.** 163

rents house with his brother Thomas, **4.** 211, 212

(?) Richard sent to talk with, **4.** 133

Rochford writes to, to approach Pombal about Jesuit papers, **23.** 533n

Rochford, Cts of, on good terms with, **4.** 173

Rodney's victory reported by, **2.** 192, 193

Rueil visited by, **4.** 245

sad, **4.** 278, 281

sends muff to his niece, **4.** 335

social relations of, in Paris, *see index entries ante* **8.** 552

SH visitor sent by, **12.** 232, 234

tea merchant recommended by, **5.** 231

to return to London, **5.** 87

travels of, **5.** 87

Walpole, Hon. T., loved by, **4.** 211

wife of, **33.** 400

wife's beauty makes, jealous, **25.** 417

Wilkes's news interests, **4.** 184

Walpole, Robert (1768–1834), son of Hon. Richard Walpole:

Du Deffand, Mme, discusses, with Hon. T. Walpole, **5.** 94

Walpole, Mrs Robert. *See* Burwell, Mary (d. 1711); Grosett, Diana (d. 1784); Shorter, Catherine (ca 1682–1737); Stert, Sophia (ca 1769–1829)

Walpole, Susan (1687–1763), m. (1707) Anthony Hamond; HW's aunt:

'beefy,' **35.** 43

birth date of, corrected, **43.** 124

HW mentions, **17.** 140

(?) HW questioned by, at Houghton, **35.** 43

HW rebuked by, at King's Lynn election, **9.** 351

son of, **9.** 26

Walpole, Thomas (d. 1514):

HW's ancestor, **1.** 376n

Walpole, Hon. Thomas (1727–1803), banker; M.P.; HW's first cousin and correspondent:

ambassadorial shifts known by, **5.** 108

Amigoni's and Astley's paintings of, **20.** 341, 342

Ashburton seat to be relinquished by, to replace HW at King's Lynn, **36.** 47n

banker in Paris, **4.** 366n

Beauvau's letter to, **36.** 191–2

Beauvau, Princesse de, orders tea from, **7.** 233, 234

brother devoted to, **4.** 211

brother hears from, of Pitt's power of attorney to wife, **39.** 88–9

business affairs of, **4.** 373, **5.** 100, 107, 116, **7.** 185–6, 201, 202, 204, 228, 242, 431, **36.** 172, 177

Cambis, Mme de, liked by, **7.** 222

Caraman orders locks from, **7.** 233

Carshalton home of, **28.** 456

Castle Rising might be borough of, **36.** 14, 16

Cavendish family allied with, **38.** 546

[Walpole, Hon. Thomas (1727–1803, *continued*)]
Chatham, Cts of, writes to, about Hayes, **36.** 46n
Choiseul's power considered by, infirm, **39.** 34
—— 's relations with, **4.** 378, 461
Colonia's dealings with, **7.** 236
Cordon, Marchesa di, rescued by, in Gordon riots, **25.** 55, **33.** 178
Dalrymple, Sir John, aided by, **28.** 67n
—— perhaps recommended by, **28.** 371
daughters receive letter from, **11.** 28
departure of, from Paris, delayed, **5.** 109–12
Du Deffand, Mme, avoids writing to, **5.** 310
—— consults, about sending contraband, **4.** 453
—— mentions, **7.** 241
—— 's correspondence with, **7.** 222, 224, 449
—— sends letter by, **5.** 108, 113, 120, **7.** 215, 446
—— sends parcels by, **4.** 143, 144, 154, **5.** 103, 104, **7.** 211, 218
—— sends parcels through, **7.** 205, 209–10
—— 's illness reported by, **31.** 229
—— 's opinion of, **5.** 91, 94, 116, **7.** 183, 185, 188–9, 190, 201, 204, 215
—— 's relations with, **7.** 206
—— to have news of HW from, **7.** 230, 234
—— to send parcels by, **7.** 183, 190, 196, 200, 225
—— to send parcels through, **7.** 200, 204
English politics do not interest, **7.** 210
entail could not be cut off by, **36.** 31
father abandons scheme to set up, against Bacon, for Norwich, **21.** 56n
Fox, C. J., regards, highly, **42.** 70
—— to employ son of, when possible, **42.** 70, 73
Gennevilliers visited by, **4.** 469
glad to be away from political turmoil, **36.** 219
Grand Ohio Co. member, **23.** 424n
'Great Broad Street in the City' an address of, **41.** 226
Grenada property of, **7.** 431
Grenville ministry tries to deprive, of contract with French fermiers généraux for tobacco, **38.** 545–6, 556–7
Guines to be interviewed by, **36.** 193–4
HW addresses, at Mme du Deffand's, **36.** 173, 175
HW asked by: to look after 3d E. of Orford's affairs, **23.** 496; to recommend son's friend to Mann, **24.** 488
HW asks, about son, **36.** 276
HW called on by, **39.** 329
HW dines with, at Carshalton, **33.** 110–11, **39.** 331
HW entertains, at dinner, **11.** 108, **33.** 352
HW has news of Mme du Deffand from, **7.** 221
HW has not seen, **5.** 129, 135
HW invites, to SH, **36.** 243
HW receives book from, **36.** 166, 281

HW receives Pitt's letters from, **36.** 45, 46
HW's correspondence with: **2.** 233n, **6.** 341n, **7.** 193, 243–6, 445, **36.** 23, 45–6, 93–9, 164, 166, 168–205, 211–24, 243, 248–50, 275, **39.** 373, **41.** 226, **43.** 100, 366; MSS of, **36.** 314
HW sends letters by, **7.** 378, 458
HW sends parcels by, **7.** 180, 240
HW sends Stoughton's drops to Mme du Deffand by, **7.** 431, 458
HW's intimacy with Mme du Deffand hidden from, **5.** 133, 138, 143
HW's letters to Mme du Deffand to be returned to HW by, **7.** 248–9, 250, 253
HW's set of *Bibliothèque universelle des romans* augmented by, **36.** 195, **43.** 368
HW thanks Hertford for aiding, **38.** 567
HW to meet, to get his consent to managing E. of Orford's affairs, **36.** 93
HW to receive copies of *Bibliothèque universelle des romans* from, **6.** 400n
HW writes guardedly about, **7.** 182
healthy and likely to inherit, **36.** 296
Herries deprives, of tobacco contract, **38.** 546n
house of: at Carshalton, **28.** 456; in Lincoln's Inn Fields, **25.** 55; near Paris, **11.** 27–8
King's Lynn left by, **39.** 96
La Borde linked with, **39.** 34
La Vallière letter not mis-sent to, **5.** 310
law suit of, settled, **36.** 204
Liancourt's sons possibly advised by, **16.** 226n
London to be visited by, **5.** 97, 104
marriage of: to Elizabeth Vanneck, **9.** 105n, **12.** 150n, **28.** 406n, **36.** 298; to Mme de Villegagnon, **4.** 336n, **33.** 587, **36.** 248
Martinelli patronized by, **28.** 99n
Mirepoix, Mme de, orders tea from, **7.** 233, 234
—— receives tea from, **7.** 226
Moone's letters to, about E. of Orford, **23.** 460n, 461n, 463n, **36.** 331
Necker aids affairs of, **36.** 177
—— recommends Turpin to, as lawyer, **36.** 177n
—— 's correspondence with, **7.** 228, 229, 231
—— 's friendship with, **7.** 184, 198, 200, 211, 221, 240
neglect of Parliamentary interest by, alarms brother, **39.** 96
Newcastle's correspondence with, **22.** 101n, 102n
Orford, E. of, nominates, for Ashburton, **30.** 169
Paris left by, **5.** 123
—— reached by, **4.** 133, **7.** 180
—— to be left by, **7.** 187
—— to be visited by, **5.** 137, **7.** 227, 238, 239
—— visited by, **7.** 431, 458
Parliamentary candidate for King's Lynn, **22.** 522n
Pitt (Chatham) asks, to return Hayes to him, **36.** 46
—— converses with, **7.** 273
—— 's correspondence with, **7.** 272, **22.** 93n

——'s quarrel with D. of Bedford described by, **7.** 279

Portsmouth and Plymouth thought by, to be French objectives, **39.** 322

rechosen M.P., **36.** 175

rents house with his brother Robert, **4.** 211, 212

(?) Richard sent to talk with, **4.** 133

Royal Academy dinner attended by, **24.** 92n

(?) Sarsfield's parcel given by, to Mme du Deffand, **7.** 446

servant of, to ask Wiart about Beauclerk's suits, **36.** 192

social relations of, in Paris, *see index entries ante* **8.** 553

son indispensable to, **36.** 202

son's visit will make, happy, **36.** 206

son to explain to, how other son cannot be aided by Conway, **36.** 211

son writes news to, **36.** 192, 213

Spanish war and French expedition not believed by, **39.** 329

Sulivan opposed, at Ashburton, **30.** 169n

Terray said to favour, **5.** 107

tobacco dealt in, by, **5.** 107

Wiart consults, in Mme du Deffand's illness, **7.** 248

—— gives parcels to, for HW, **7.** 250, 253

wife of, **4.** 336n, **10.** 278n, **11.** 96n, 97n

Wilkes's plans discussed by, **7.** 279

Woodfall to call on, in Lincoln's Inn Fields, **41.** 226

Walpole, Thomas (1755–1840), son of Hon. Thomas Walpole; diplomatist:

biographical information about, corrected, **43.** 287

brother visits, **36.** 228

diplomatic post of, pleases father, **36.** 219

Du Deffand, Mme, gives opinion of, **7.** 189

——'s social relations with, **7.** 189, 209, 243, 245, 246, 249, 432, 435

Elector's picture should be drawn by, **36.** 228

father cannot part with, **36.** 202

father hears news from, **36.** 192, 213, 224

father talks about, **5.** 94, **7.** 182, 185

father to hear from, why brother's promotion cannot be arranged, **36.** 211

(?) Fox, C. J., asked by HW to make, under-secretary of state, **42.** 73

—— to employ, when possible, **42.** 70, 73

HW aids, in getting diplomatic post, **36.** 214

HW called on by, **36.** 203–4

HW congratulated by, on Lady Anna Horatia Waldegrave's marriage, **36.** 235–6

HW fond of, **7.** 182, 185, **24.** 488

HW has, at dinner at SH, **33.** 406

HW hears news of father from, **36.** 205

(?) HW hears Paris news from, **33.** 309, **43.** 355

HW hoped to see, **36.** 202, 224

HW invites, to SH, **36.** 276–7

HW may take, to Mme de Boufflers or Bns Mt Edgcumbe, **36.** 276–7

HW praises, **36.** 195–6, 197, 211

HW receives drawing by, of Elector, **36.** 231

HW receives from, her dog and MSS from Mme du Deffand's bequest, **36.** 196

HW regards, as worthy replacement for dead friends, **36.** 185

HW's correspondence with: **36.** 206–7, 227–9, 231–3, 235–8, 240–2, 250–2, 275–7, 279–83; MSS of, **36.** 314

HW sees, at Dacre's, and hopes to see him at SH, **36.** 212

HW's set of *Bibliothèque universelle des romans* augmented by, **36.** 195, **43.** 368

HW to be called on by, to get letter, **36.** 199

HW visited by, **15.** 325–6, **36.** 166, 185, 213

HW wishes that books be sent by, **36.** 241–2

meritorious, **36.** 204

Paris embassy secretaryship might go to, **33.** 420n

Paris visit of, will please his family, **36.** 206

salary of, as envoy, in arrears, **15.** 326

success of, at lotto, **7.** 189

Turnor, friend of, recommended by HW to Mann, **24.** 488

Walpole, Mrs Thomas. *See* Batailhe de Montval, Jeanne-Marguerite (1731–1821); Vanneck, Elizabeth (d. 1760)

Walpole (surname):

pronunciation of, **31.** 232n

spelling of, **31.** 232, **40.** 123

Walpole, Norfolk:

at no great distance from Whaplode, **1.** 378

church at, print of, promised, **2.** 78

Walpole and Ellison:

bankers in New Broad Street, London, **41.** 226n

Walpole, Hon. Thomas, partner in, **41.** 226n

Walpole, Clarke, and Bourne, Lombard St, London:

Walpole, Hon. Richard, partner in, **32.** 366n

Walpole estate:

Orford, 3d E. of, has right to bequeath, to whom he pleases, **25.** 164n (*see also under* Houghton)

Walpole family:

allied with Hamonds and Hostes, **18.** 238n

arms of: **1.** 376, 378, **19.** 421n; on sides of HW's copies of books printed at SH Press, **41.** 467n; to be on Cts of Orford's monument at Leghorn, **25.** 226, 240

branches of, united by Sophia Churchill's marriage to Hon. Horace Walpole (1752–1822), **36.** 202

Chedworth's obligations to, **40.** 60

Chelsea once the home of, **24.** 198

Chute tries to serve, after Whithed's death, **35.** 84

Cocchi respects, **17.** 387

Coke, Lady Mary, envies, for royal marriage, **33.** 528

crest of, a Saracen's head, **32.** 253

early knights in, **15.** 1

entail of estates of, **36.** 24–32, 295–304

[Walpole family, *continued*]
fishing enjoyed by, 18. 256
Fitzroys make another match with, 25. 544
Gardiner to get advancement through, 18. 507, 509
genealogy of, 1. 156, 36. 337
George II's disavowal of civilities to Cts of Orford a just satisfaction to, 19. 144
Gloucester, Ds of, asks if father got messages from, about seeing D. of Gloucester, 36. 324
gossip about, 17. 146
HW asked by, to look after 3d E. of Orford's affairs, 23. 496, 552
HW comments on intermarriages in, 39. 417
HW does not wish to live with, 37. 109
HW fond of his nieces, but can talk little to them, 39. 296
HW hopes 3d E. of Orford, will restore, to former glory, 36. 165
HW hopes to restore, 23. 497
HW inherited little from, 36. 160–1
HW loves the Conways as representing, 37. 110
HW must not ruin himself to restore, 39. 173
HW outlives glory of, 25. 310
HW ridicules expressions of pleasure by, on retirement from power, 30. 72
HW's attempts to retrieve affairs of, well known, 30. 168
HW's hopes for, often disappointed, 24. 373
HW's inheritance or gifts from, 25. 637
HW's pride in, ridiculed, 36. 160
HW's pride in titles of, 2. 374
HW's sacrifices for, 28. 103, 121, 139
HW's satisfaction in serving, his only reward for taking care of 3d E. of Orford, 24. 303
HW twice expunged thoughts of, from his memory, 24. 301
HW will not cheat in behalf of, 23. 528
HW wishes to restore glory of, 36. 165
'hastiness' of, 36. 82
indebted to HW for care of E. of Orford's affairs, 36. 98–9
Jerninghams related to, through FitzOsberts, 42. 110n
jewels of, 25. 144
Magnan boasts of protection from, 18. 548
Mann, Edward Louisa, lost money through, 24. 287
Mann, Sir Horatio, respects, 17. 491n, 20. 486
Mann family always taught to revere, 23. 353, 354
Mann family must always treat, with delicacy, 24. 78
Mann family's indebtedness to, 17. 348
Maynard recommended by, 35. 52
member of, asks HW to print a bulky work, 41. 284
Middleton sends HW charters of, 15. 1–3
——'s praise of, 15. 1–2, 3–4
Montagu's devotion to, 10. 143
Monticelli often entertained by, 17. 487
motto of, 35. 93 (see also *Fari quæ sentiat*)

Orford, Cts of, disparages, 17. 387, 406
—— not notified by, of Sir Robert Walpole's death, 19. 42
—— now mentions, with regard, 20. 479, 481, 486–7
—— said to have received nothing from, 25. 130
—— said to have taken deeds of, to Italy, 25. 160
Orford, 3d E. of, inherits estates of, 25. 164n
——'s affairs may require legal advice for, 36. 120
——'s death would ruin, 23. 461
——'s survival advantageous to, 41. 261
—— to deprive, of Dorsetshire estate, 25. 156–7
papers relating to, to be sent to Houghton after HW's death, 30. 372, 377
perpetuation of, was Sir Robert Walpole's great object, 25. 156–7
Pett owes promotions to, 18. 509
pictures of, not valued enough by Cts of Orford to be taken to Italy, 25. 227
Richecourt disparages, 17. 387, 393–4, 404
Rome unlikely to honour recommendations by, 20. 461
Rowley esteems, 18. 507
Scully said to be preparing house for, in Florence, 17. 426, 450, 18. 14
Stuart descendants marry daughters of, 21. 285
Taylor boasts of patronage from, 20. 458, 461
temper of, violent, 33. 565
Van Dyck portraits owned by, sold for a song, 20. 201
visits to, unfashionable, 30. 63
Voltaire will always remember name of, with esteem, 41. 156
Walpole, Sir Robert, ruined, by his excessive vanity, 23. 497
'warm and imprudent,' 36. 86
Walpole family of Wolterton:
parsimony of, 18. 42
Walpole of Wolterton, Bn. See Walpole, Horatio (1678–1757); Walpole, Horatio (1723–1809)
Walpole of Wolterton, Bns. See Cavendish, Lady Rachel (1727–1805); Lombard, Mary Magdelaine (d. 1783)
Walpole St Peter, Norfolk:
church of, stained glass at, 40. 224–5
Walpole Society (English):
'Vertue Notebooks' printed by, 13. 33, 43. 172
Walpoliana:
HW denies writing, 31. 283
HW's letters might be dignified by title of, 20. 215
Warton, Joseph, tells Hannah More that HW is writing, 31. 281
Yorke, Philip, 2d E. of Hardwicke, is editor of, 21. 129n
See also under Yorke, Philip (1720–90)
Walpoole. *See* Walpole

Walrond family:
arms of, **2**. 36, 40

Walsegg ['Walseck'], Otto (d. 1743), Graf von;
Gen.:
Austrian army in Tuscany commanded by,
17. 117n, 130
Electress called on by, in Florence, **17**. 130
Leghorn to be post of, **17**. 130
Petrillo insults, at burletta, **17**. 130
size of, **17**. 130
Tesi escorted by, **17**. 130

Walsh, Justice:
proclamation read by, to weavers' mob, **38**.
559n

Walsh, Rev. Edward (d. 1628):
succeeds Hilton as vicar, **1**. 223n

Walsh, François-Jacques de (ca 1704–82),
Comte de Serrant:
social relations of, with dowager Comtesse
d'Egmont, **7**. 299

Walsh, John (d. 1766), music printer:
Atalanta score published by, **13**. 103n
Compleat Country Dancing Master published
by, **33**. 284n
Corelli's *Concerti* and Handel's *Six Overtures
for Violins* printed for, **18**. 13n
Handel oratorios to be published by, **24**. 35n

Walsh, John (1726–95), Clive's secretary; M.P.;
scientist:
resigns seat because unable to vote against
Clive or for ministry, **38**. 249

Walsh, Thomas, Chesterfield's valet:
bids at art sale, **32**. 103n

Walsh. *See also* Walsh de Serrant

Walshams, manor in Norfolk:
HW's will mentions, **30**. 368

Walsh de Serrant, Françoise-Élisabeth-Charlotte
de (d. 1793), m. (1775) Charles-Antoine-
Étienne, Marquis de Choiseul:
social relations of, with Comte and Comtesse
de Caraman, **7**. 448

Walsingham. *See* De Grey, Thomas (1748–
1818); De Grey, William (1719–81)

Walsingham, Bns. *See* Irby, Augusta Georgina
Elizabeth (1747–1818)

Walsingham, Cts of. *See* Schulenberg, Petronille
Melusine de

'Walsingham, Mrs.' *See* Walkinshaw, Clementina

Walsingham, Frances (ca 1567–1632), m. 1
(1583) Sir Philip Sidney; m. 2 (1587–90)
Robert Devereux, 2d E. of Essex; m. 3
(ca 1603) Richard Bourke, 4th E. of Clan-
rickarde:
marriages of, **32**. 15, 47

Walsingham, Sir Francis (ca 1532–90), Kt,
1577; statesman:
birth date of, corrected, **43**. 361
Elizabeth, Q., has family picture painted for,
42. 247n
Holdernesse might have surpassed, **35**. 166
Leicester gives portrait to, **35**. 153

prints of, **1**. 180, **32**. 46–7
Scadbury Park house of, in Kent, **32**. 46–7,
35. 153

Walsingham, Hon. Henry Boyle. *See* Boyle,
Henry (d. 1756)

Walsingham, Hon. Mrs Henry Boyle. *See* Martin, Lucia

Walsingham, Hon. Robert Boyle. *See* Boyle
Walsingham, Hon. Robert

Walsingham, Hon. Mrs Robert Boyle. *See* Williams, Charlotte Hanbury

Walsingham, Norfolk:
Bell of, **1**. 183n

Walter, Jane (ca 1752–1840), m. (1779) Isaac
Prescott:
husband's cruelty to, **33**. 424–5

Walter, John (1739–1812), founder of *The
Times*:
Address to the Public, An, by, **29**. 322n
Berrys, subject of panegyric by, **12**. 140
HW's bequest of SH mentioned by, in *The
Times*, **12**. *139*, 140, 141, 143
Hertford, E. of, reported by, to be HW's heir,
12. 146
Jerningham visits, **12**. 140
SH visited by, **12**. 250
Teddington, villa at, taken by, **12**. 139
Times, The, newspaper of, **31**. 265n
Twickenham, damages from storm at, re-
ported by, **12**. 176

Walter, Mrs John. *See* Landon, Frances

Walter, Lucy (? 1630–58), Charles II's mistress:
Hamilton, Lady Archibald, compared with,
9. 16
illegitimate son of, **4**. 114n, **11**. 347n

Walter, Richard (ca 1718–85), naval chaplain:
Anson's *Voyage* edited by, **9**. 55n
daughter of, abused by husband, **33**. 424

Walter. *See also* Rolle Walter

'Walters, Madam Lucy.' *See* Walter, Lucy

Walters, Mrs William. *See* Palliser, Rebecca

Waltham, Bn. *See* Olmius, John

Waltham Cross, Herts:
Claremont near, **36**. 271, 272, **43**. 387
Rooker's drawing of, **2**. 240

Walthamstow, Essex:
Maynard of, **9**. 269n
Tilly's house in, **33**. 67n

Walthers. *See* Wolters

Walton, Mr and Mrs:
SH visited by, **12**. 246

Walton, Sir George (1665–1739), Kt, 1721;
Adm., 1734:
letter by, announcing naval victory, **21**. 297

Walton, Henry (d. 1764), farmer:
Wilkes said to inherit money from, **22**. 281

Walton, Henry (1746–1813):
John Fenn painted by, **43**. 213

Walton, Isaak (1593–1683):
Compleat Angler, The, by: Hawkins's edition
of, **15**. 70; illustrations to, **1**. 174

'Walton, John.' *See* Stosch, Philipp von

Walton, Bucks:
Cole sees Yelverton coat of arms at, **10.** 338
Dicey of, **1.** 332n
Walton Bridge:
model of, in glass, in dessert, **35.** 225
Waltz, Gustavus (fl. 1732–9), bass singer:
sings in *Atalanta*, **13.** 102n
Walworth, Sir William (d. 1385), Kt, 1381; lord mayor of London:
Harley the counterpart of, **23.** 6
Walworth, Durham:
Jenison of, **9.** 33n
Wand; wands:
black and white, of Court party, outvote Camden in House of Lords, **35.** 588
gold, in stained glass, **40.** 224
lord steward's, **23.** 99
white: great officers break, over grave of old king, **21.** 445; holders of, oppress dissenters, **35.** 587; Sandwich carries, at Handel's jubilee, **33.** 468
See also Staff; staves
Wandelein, ——, chemist:
at china factory, **18.** 184n
'Wandering Jew':
HW compares Lady Mary Coke with, **31.** 155
Wandesford, Lady. *See* Montagu, Elizabeth (d. 1731)
Wandesford, Sir Christopher (1656–1707), cr. (1707) Vct Castlecomer; M.P.:
genealogy of, **10.** 352
wife of, **10.** 12n
Wandesford, Christopher (1684–1719), 2d Vct Castlecomer:
wife of, **9.** 196n, **11.** 55n
Wandesford, Christopher (1717–36), 3d Vct Castlecomer:
(?) anecdote about, **10.** 311
Conway alludes to, **37.** 579
HW jokes about 'inconvenience' to, **35.** 91
SH proverb about, **11.** 55–6, **12.** 23, 120
Wandesford, John (1725–84), 5th Vct Castlecomer; cr. (1758) E. Wandesford:
HW's witticism about, **39.** 220, 237
Montagu sees and identifies family miniatures of, **10.** 12
——'s relationship to, **10.** 12
Wandsworth Hill:
Pitt, Mrs George, gives haymaking party at, **38.** 400, 401
Pitt, William, visits Mrs George Pitt at, **22.** 572
Wanfelder, Col.:
Florence visited by, **24.** 113n
Wangenheim, Wilhelmina Sophia von (d. 1750) m. (1715) Gerlach Adolf, Freiherr von Münchhausen:
sugar-figures castrated by, **20.** 125, 144
Wanley, Humfrey (1672–1726), antiquary:
Catalogue of the Harleian Collection by, **30.** 153n
librarian to Lord Oxford, **2.** 145

Wanstead, Essex:
George III and Q. Charlotte visit, **38.** 418
Gray, Sarah, buried at, **13.** 99n
Karl Friedrich mobbed on way to, **20.** 155
Tylney's bequest to the poor of, **25.** 534n
Wanstead House, Essex, E. Tylney's seat:
HW dines at, and describes it, **35.** 238–9
HW pleased by ball at, **21.** 417
Kent's portrait at, **15.** 143
Muzell to visit, **21.** 427
Orford, Cts of, to lodge at, **23.** 120
Tylney always intended to leave, to Long family, **24.** 23
Wantley, dragon of:
ballad of, imitated, **13.** 150, **43.** 176
Gévaudan beast compared with, **22.** 289
Wharncliffe the scene of ballad of, **35.** 268
Wanton Wife of Bath, The, ballad:
HW alludes to, **18.** 8, 23
Waple, John (d. 1763), accountant-general of the Court of Chancery:
Lucchis' money in the name of, **22.** 267
Wapping:
Ames lives in, **1.** 55n
Burr St in, **30.** 61n
coal-heavers' riot in, **23.** 33, 34n
punch to be drunk at, to celebrate Cherbourg capture, **21.** 227
War:
aerial, HW imagines, between balloons, **39.** 425
Algerian-Spanish, **20.** 480, **23.** 118, 120, 121–2, **25.** 26, 416
Algerian-Tuscan: **20.** 472–3, **25.** 270; Regency threatens, **22.** 259; Tuscany cannot support, **20.** 487
Allies-French, *see* War: French-German *below*
alternates with peace, **32.** 7
American-English (American Revolution):
American army in, said to mutiny, **25.** 135; American defeat in, might precipitate French war, **24.** 316; American deputies must be received by Howe to negotiate peace for, **24.** 270; American losses in, might force them to submit, **24.** 274; American retreat probably a wise move, **24.** 282; Americans make no blunders in, **24.** 124; Americans said to be determined upon, **24.** 226; Americans unlikely to make peace overtures for, **24.** 387; battles in, **28.** 206, 215, 411, 433–4, and *passim*; begins, **41.** 302–4; Bennington battle in, **24.** 335; Birmingham wants, to increase munitions manufacture, **6.** 146, **24.** 77; bishops consider, just and necessary, **29.** 159–60; Burgoyne's successes in, **24.** 323; Burgoyne's surrender, **24.** 339–40, 344, 345; campaign in, seems to be over for the winter, **24.** 278; Canadian operations in, **24.** 156–7, 161, 185; Canterbury's loss of tourist trade by, **7.** 342; Carlisle objects to sacrifice of loyal-

ists by peace treaty for, **25**. 365; Catherine II offers troops to England for, **24**. 127; causes of, **29**. 22, 23, 28; Charleston attack, **24**. 236; Clinton-Cornwallis controversy over, **25**. 370; commissaries and threats, to conciliate, **24**. 148; Conway's motions for making peace in, **25**. 244, 251–2, 259, **35**. 615–16, **39**. 353; Cornwallis's operations in, would be facilitated by naval victory over the French, **25**. 150; Cornwallis's successes in, short-lived, **25**. 151–2, 158; Cornwallis's surrender, **25**. 209, 212; Cornwallis's victory will delay peace in, **36**. 197; cost of, **25**. 211, 434, **28**. 358, 361, **29**. 118–19, **33**. 306–7; criminals increase as a result of, **25**. 316, **33**. 353; decided upon, **32**. 228–9; definitive peace treaty to be signed for, **25**. 426–7; Delaware River contests in, **24**. 347, 386; Dundas condemns, **33**. 327; Dutch war provoked by, **25**. 211, 541; Eden and Carlisle stay to negotiate peace for, **24**. 419–20; end of, will save thousands of lives and millions of money, **25**. 209; England almost at last gasp in, **25**. 201; England deserves to suffer the heavy consequences of, **25**. 506; England loses trade by, **25**. 506; England lowered by, **25**. 433; England may hire Russians for, **24**. 127, 324; England may sue for peace in, through France, **24**. 324; England not brought to her senses by, **24**. 310; England rendered by, impotent to keep Austria from taking Holland, **25**. 541; England's losses in, **15**. 157; England's loss of two armies in, almost unprecedented, **25**. 210; England tries to raise a great army for, from Hesse and Brunswick, **24**. 175; England will be ruined by, **24**. 127; England will get nothing from, except its history, forty millions of debt, and three other wars, **25**. 211; English army hardly sets out for, **24**. 193–4, 197; English conquest of Lake Champlain, **24**. 261; English country gentlemen promoted, but balk at its expense, **25**. 5; English credit endangered by, **25**. 310; English defeats in south, in, **24**. 141; English disasters in, **29**. 161–2; English-French war to be joined to, **24**. 348, 349; English inability to continue, will result in war with France, **24**. 335; English losers in, should get titles from provinces they lost, **33**. 421; English may be blockaded, making an end to, **33**. 44; English ministry desires, **6**. 140; English national debt doubled by, **25**. 434; English peace terms for, virtually allow American independence, **24**. 354; English troops should be recalled from, **32**. 399–401; English troops treated with humanity in, **32**. 400; Estaing might shorten, **33**. 306–7; expense of, see cost of; 'fashionable' in England, **28**. 221; France and Spain may join, **32**. 303; France in debt

from participating in, **42**. 252; France may forestall English peace efforts for, **24**. 368–9; France may intervene in, **24**. 268, 523; France spreads news of any English reverses in, **24**. 250, 345; Franklin said to have made peace proposals for, **24**. 281; French invasion of England would embarrass America in peace treaty of, **24**. 392; French war grew out of, **25**. 211; funds for, to be raised, **29**. 109; Gage a general in, **23**. 44n; gazettes and Stormont optimistic over, **24**. 306; Georgia campaigns in, **25**. 306; HW augured ill of, **24**. 355; HW believes, to be near an end, **28**. 350, 448, **29**. 114; HW believes, will last to end of century, **32**. 388; HW cannot discover merit of system which started, **25**. 143; HW cannot wish success to, for it is unjust, **33**. 304; HW condemns, **24**. 452; HW contrasts Seven Years' War with, **28**. 411; HW disapproves of persistence in, **25**. 139; HW expects, to be long, **24**. 158, 484; HW expects a victory or peace in, **33**. 25; HW fears, **39**. 183; HW foresaw miserable conclusion of, **25**. 89; HW hopes, will die of old age, **25**. 308; HW opposes, **28**. 315, **32**. 328, 366; HW says, must stop, **33**. 329; HW's dire predictions about, not unfulfilled, **24**. 282; HW's politics ended with, **33**. 398; HW's predictions at beginning of, **25**. 370; HW unable to grieve over termination of, **25**. 209; HW wishes for peace in, **33**. 129, 160–1, 199; HW wonders about peace for, **35**. 519; Hardinge's honeymoon to outlive, **35**. 595; Hertford wants peace in, at any terms which exclude France, **39**. 304; House of Commons conducts inquiry into, **39**. 321, 325; Howe attacked for receiving American deputies for, **24**. 270; Howe said to be making peace negotiations for, **24**. 261; Howe's withdrawal to Halifax reported in London, **28**. 268–9; 'implicit submission' no longer to be demanded, **25**. 210; incendiary results of, **32**. 346; increases highwaymen in England, **33**. 353; inquiry into conduct of, debated in Parliament, **24**. 351, 474; lesson against extension of power, **33**. 389; *London Gazette* tells lies about, **24**. 232; loses popularity in England, **24**. 205; Mann hopes for accommodation in, **24**. 352; Mann's theories about English failure in, **25**. 76; method of ending, described by Hartley, **29**. 95; ministers responsible for, should be held answerable, if peace terms are humiliating, **25**. 347; naval activity in, **24**. 229; newspapers lie about, **24**. 231–2; newspapers print rubbish during, **25**. 146; news sources lacking for, **24**. 185; New York campaigns, **24**. 229–30, 241, 242–3, 248–9, 255–6, 261; no news of, **32**. 337, 382, 389, 392; North's peace terms for, **24**. 348, 354, 358; opening of, **28**. 135, 174, 178,

[War: American-English, *continued*]
39. 183; Opposition may halt, 36. 222–3; Opposition should have opposed, more strongly, 24. 491; opposition to, mounts, 29. 171, 187, 191, 196; other wars may result from, 24. 287; outbreak of, 24. 109–11; Parliamentary address for peace fails by one vote only, 25. 244; Parliamentary debate over, after Burgoyne's defeat, 24. 341; Parliament eagerly promotes, 24. 81; Parliament may virtually send declaration of, 24. 74–5; Parliament's pacification scheme for, 17. 404; Parliament to vote seamen for, 24. 127; Parliament unable to raise money for, 24. 465; peace articles for, published, 25. 362; peace commissioners fail to stop, 24. 400; peace commissioners for, show that England has knelt, 33. 34; peace expected in, 33. 382; peace for, indicated by rising stocks, 32. 60; peace for, not yet concluded, 25. 354, 355; peace in, 35. 375–6; peace in, abandons American loyalists, 32. 388–9; peace in, complicated by relations with France, 33. 26–7; peace in, delayed, 25. 285, 351; peace in, negotiations for, 24. 359, 362, 387, 25. 279, 311, 341–2, 352; peace in, would make HW happy, 25. 252; peace motion for, by Hartley, 39. 374–5; peace not achieved for, 33. 28–9; peace overtures in, opposed by Americans, 33. 80; peace preliminaries for, signed, 25. 356; peace proposals for, 32. 404, 406, 33. 34, 115, 119, 127; peace proposals for, to be passed by Parliament, 24. 359; peace treaty for, broken off, 25. 259; peace treaty for, said to be offered, 33. 127; peace treaty for, said to be signed, 25. 346; Penn attempts mediation in, 24. 128; Percy may bring accommodation for, 24. 313, 315; perseverance in, announced, 28. 210, 488; politicians to blame for, 24. 490; Portuguese-Spanish clash may complicate, 24. 224; post-war hatred will be nourished by, 24. 287; progress of, (1775) 32. 239, 247, (1776) 32. 318–19, 326, 338–9, 342, (1777) 32. 367, 370, 380, 393, 394, 395–6, 397, 399, 400, 407, 411, 33. 3, 4, (1778) 33. 44, (1779) 33. 150, (1780) 33. 232 (*also* vols 24 – 25 *passim*); progress of, nothing but miscarriages and drawn battles, 25. 164; prolonged frenzy of, endangers England's credit, 25. 309–10; Rhode Island campaign, 24. 281; Rockingham's death may bring revival of, 29. 258; Shelburne uses 'reciprocity' at time of peace after, 25. 519n; Spanish war added to, 24. 484, 25. 211; troops in winter quarters, 24. 349; unpopular, 33. 328; votes for, bought, 29. 127; will be fatal to England, 32. 328; Yorktown ends 'another volume of,' 25. 211; *see also under* America (English colonies in); America (United States of); Boston; Charleston; New York; Philadelphia, etc.

Austrian-Bavarian: peace said to be concluded for, 19. 34, 37; progress of, 17. 151, 194, 203, 289, 315–16; Walpole, Sir Robert, disclaims responsibility for, 17. 231
Austrian-Dutch: compromise may avert, 25. 554, 562; conciliation to avert, 25. 593, 607; Dutch dykes opened in preparation for, 25. 543; European gazetteers disappointed by lack of, 25. 607; France and Prussia may join in, 25. 544; France may aid Holland in, 25. 545, 561; laid aside, 25. 556; Maestricht siege rumoured in, 25. 566; Vergennes involved in, 25. 561
Austrian-Flemish, truce in, 34. 87
Austrian-French: over Spain, 21. 199–200; peace preliminaries of, 19. 487; peace rumoured for, 34. 213; progress of, 9. 33–4, 48, 17. 183, 194, 203, 289, 315–16, 451, 457, 466, 472, 481, 18. 58; progress of, too slow, 34. 217; said to have begun, 17. 119; *see also under* Grand Alliance
Austrian-Genoese: declared, 19. 75; Ferdinand VI said to propose suspension of arms in, 19. 279n; may be declared, 19. 58; peace terms for, 19. 305–6; termination of, 19. 312, 314–16
Austrian-Prussian: accommodation unlikely for, 19. 409; armies too close to avoid, 24. 398; armistice vainly sought to end, 24. 403; battles in, 24. 404; Brabant may be sacrificed by peace in, 39. 474; Charles, P., spoils peace for, 19. 127–8; ended, 17. 456, 472, 482–3, 18. 5; ending of, favours Frederick II, 22. 119; England expects outbreak of, 24. 393; George II may arrange peace for, 17. 76, 87; Joseph II deterred from, 24. 401; Joseph II keeps Frederick II at bay in, 24. 450; large armies accomplish little in, 24. 414; Leopold expects news of, 24. 389; letters from Vienna announce peace for, 24. 454; Maria Theresa halts, 25. 104; outbreak of, possible, 24. 389; peace after, belatedly known to Mann, 17. 496–7; peace for, expected, 22. 118; peace for, not expected, 17. 121, 144; peace rumoured for, 17. 134, 19. 38; peace still expected for, 24. 407; progress of, 9. 198, 205, 206, 234, 10. 36, 22. 51–2, 60
Austrian-Saxon, may end, 17. 466–7
Austrian-Spanish: 9. 33–4, 48; progresses slowly in Italy, 19. 441; *see also under* Spain: army of
Austrian-Turkish: HW hopes Turks will win, 35. 392; represented in ballet, 25. 361n
civil, too high a price for liberty, 39. 469
commerce an excuse for, 22. 39
costliness of: England loses fifteen millions a year by, 25. 317; HW's reflections on, 24. 75; ruinous to England, 25. 201
costs England millions, while they lose, 25. 190–1
Danish-Russian, opening of, 22. 82
Du Deffand, Mme, detests, 7. 56

—— mentions, 4. 495, 5. 9

Dutch-English: American war provoked, 25. 541; armed neutrality may lead to, 33. 259, 264, 268–9; armistice in, rumoured, 25. 188; begins, 29. 89–90, 102; begins in Mediterranean, 25. 120; continuance of, preferred by English to confession of mistake, 25. 143; contradictory reports on, 33. 155–6; definitive peace treaty not yet to be signed for, 25. 426–7; Dutch fleet captured, 33. 154–6; Dutch wealth and settlements hurt by, 25. 150; end of, in sight, 25. 266–7; England brings on, 33. 243; England captures Ceylon settlement in, 25. 277; England makes headway in, only by sufferance of eastern European powers, 25. 201; English manifesto on, sent by Hillsborough to Mann, 25. 112; feared imminent, 33. 158, 243; Feilding's seizure of convoy may precipitate, 25. 3–4; grew out of American war, 25. 211; Holland a feeble enemy in, 25. 149; Holland might abandon, unless profitable, 25. 292; hopes for accommodation in, cease, 25. 108; lie given to English in reply to manifesto, 25. 142; London Gazette announces, 25. 104–5; Mann thinks, can be averted, 25. 8–9; newspapers print rubbish during, 25. 146; no declaration of, 21. 266; peace in, 35. 375–6; peace not likely for, 25. 486; peace not yet declared in, 33. 382; peace preliminaries signed for, 25. 437; peace still hoped for, 25. 116; 'pickpocket war,' 29. 145; preferable to war with Ireland, 25. 5; privateers delighted at prospect of, 25. 108; prizes taken by English in, repaid by wreck on Dutch coast, 25. 134–5; probably averted, 25. 5; reconciliation in, expected, 25. 266–7; (?) rumoured, 36. 247; suspension of arms in, 25. 357; threatened, 21. 260; to begin, 33. 256; victories in, expected, 25. 279; victory at St Eustatius may bring peace in, 25. 139; votes for, bought, 29. 127

Dutch-French: expected, 19. 24; neutrality treaty said to conclude, 19. 67–8; peace preliminaries for, signed at Aix, 19. 479; peace treaty for, signed, 19. 511; said to be declared, 18. 448–9; Wassenaer supposedly brings Dutch peace terms for, 19. 216

England's, lose lives and millions, bringing only debts and taxes, 35. 360–1

England's debt due to two foreign, 42. 497

England's quadruple: managed deplorably for seven years, 25. 347; peace in, mentioned, 25. 272, 276

English-French: adjourned to America, 35. 222; alluded to, 33. 268; America may be saved by, 24. 268; American defeat might precipitate, 24. 316; American developments of, 37. 501–2; American forts fought over in, 20. 506; American-French treaty precipitates, 24. 354–5; America now England's enemy in, 24. 485; American war

to be joined to, 24. 349, 484; American war will alter course of, 24. 287; Argenson's peace proposals for, 19. 264n; armistice for, 19. 480; avoided, 32. 39; backward, 35. 302; Beauvau's regard for HW not to be impaired by, 40. 31; begins, 20. 484; begun at sea, according to HW's predictions, 24. 395; Belle-Isle the author of, 18. 563; Bentley reproaches HW for being amused by, 35. 240; Berlin to arrange accommodation to prevent, 20. 541; blockade rules in, against neutral ships, 21. 273–4; Bute may have become secretary of state in order to put an end to, 21. 488; Canadian battle will probably decide, 21. 327; Carolina's conquest endangered by, 24. 500; Catherine II and Maria Theresa might make peace for, 24. 519–20; Chesapeake naval battle in, 33. 298; Chesterfield ignores, 35. 258; Chichele pushes Henry V into, 35. 287; Choiseul's return to power would reopen, 24. 1; (?) communication with Jersey interrupted by, 9. 179–80; continuation of, preferred by English to confession of mistake, 25. 143; Conway not to take risks at end of, but save himself for the next, 38. 181; correspondence through Holland during, 5. 1; costliness of, to George II, 38. 79; couriers from Paris about peace for, 22. 105; declaration of, 9. 172; declaration of, expected, 18. 394, 422, 20. 504–5, 37. 103; declaration of, imminent, 35. 235; declaration of, sent to Florence by Pucci, 18. 442; declared conditionally, 20. 526; Du Deffand, Mme, believes, to be declared, 7. 31; Du Deffand, Mme, fears, 3. 91n, 4. 314, 315, 342, 347n, 470, 5. 4, 11, 27, 110–11, 345, 6. 366, 380, 392; Du Deffand, Mme, glad, has been averted, 5. 16, 21; Du Deffand, Mme, mentions talk of, 4. 488, 491, 494, 5. 14, 326, 6. 364, 376, 379, 389, 459–60, 7. 3, 4, 7, 9, 11, 15, 17, 18, 26, 28, 36, 39, 40, 44–7, 49, 51, 54, 56; Du Deffand, Mme, not cooled by, in her affection for HW, 7. 169; Du Deffand, Mme, will not speak of, to HW, 4. 484; ending of, in sight, 21. 497–8; England excels France in privateering aspect of, 24. 422, 448; England fears, 24. 226, 33. 14, 27, 30, 34, 129; England on brink of, 24. 350; England should avert, 33. 34–5; England the first to fire cannon in, 20. 488; England to declare, 20. 556; England will continue, in Germany, 21. 456; English culpability for, 32. 366; English feeling about, 33. 28; English fleet prepares for, 20. 468; English inability to continue American war will bring on, 24. 335; English naval preparations possibly for, 24. 253; English probably not victorious in, in Mediterranean, 35. 277; English victory in, unprecedented when on other side of the Rhine, 18. 218; Europe regards, with ungrateful indifference, 20. 585; ex-

[War: English-French, *continued*]

pected in 1742, **17**. 345; extends from Pondicherry to Canada, **21**. 290; Ezekiel's prophecy about, **35**. 218; feared, **33**. 14, 27, 30, 34, 129; Ferdinand's victory in, **38**. 161; Ferdinand's victory will tend to revive, **22**. 47, 81; Flemish revival of, **37**. 178–9; foreign correspondence will be hampered by, **20**. 526; Forth to negotiate in, **33**. 331; France a feeble enemy in, **25**. 149; France anxious to shorten, **33**. 126; France disposed towards, **24**. 273; France does not make preparations for, at Toulon, **23**. 244; France does not want, **10**. 321; France imitates England's piddling style of waging, **24**. 480; France not depleted by, **38**. 212; France prepares for, **20**. 540; France prepares for, though claiming to be peaceful, **24**. 262; France reduced to misery by, **35**. 276; France refuses to end, **21**. 534; France rejects English terms for ending, **21**. 526–7; France ruins her trade and army by, **25**. 7; France says, must begin, **20**. 523; France seems determined on, **24**. 375; France suspends declaration of, **24**. 332; France too cautious to declare, **20**. 490; France wages, differently from Frederick II, **25**. 190; France wants peace for, **22**. 83; France will start, when England is sufficiently undone, **24**. 300; Franco-Spanish naval preparations against Russia almost precipitate, **23**. 474–5; Frederick II tries to avert, **20**. 528; French account of naval clash in, **24**. 402; French aid to America may precipitate, **24**. 316; French avoid decisive battle in, **25**. 156; French bankruptcy may be produced by trade ruin in, **21**. 122–3; French Court not keen for, **24**. 384; French dread Howe's fleet in, **25**. 313; French invasion expected in, **33**. 109; French not enriched nor English impoverished by, **35**. 369; French peace proposals for, considered by Privy Council, **38**. 162; French retreat may mean end of, **38**. 176; French ships captured in, **35**. 251; French should be discouraged from, by defeats in Germany, **21**. 317; French should be forced to make terms in, **37**. 142; French spirit of liberty not quenched by losses in, **38**. 299; French trade suffers from, **21**. 122–3, **24**. 455; Genoa professes impartiality in, **20**. 581; George II said to have declared, **18**. 44; Germany the theatre of, **22**. 35, 43; Gibraltar's relief will delay peace in, **36**. 197; goes to sleep, **35**. 245; grew out of American war, **25**. 211; HW averse to, **35**. 360; HW discredits rumours of, **5**. 355; HW does not expect ending of, **22**. 92; HW dreads, **24**. 342; HW ends letters with wishes for peace in, **25**. 337; HW hopes for peace in, **35**. 302, 308, 310, **35**. 496; HW in 1776 thinks, near, **39**. 288; HW interested in declaration of, **7**. 60; HW ridicules English losses in, **33**. 395; HW's bitter ex-

pectations from, **24**. 364; Hanoverian invasion might deter French from peace overtures in, **21**. 502; Hanover's loss will end, in Germany, **37**. 494; Hastenbeck ends German part of, **37**. 494; hinted at, in Louis XV's alleged letter, **17**. 114; Howe may bring on, by victories in America, **24**. 256; Howe's naval victory off Brest, **34**. 197; imminent, **35**. 352–3; in America, may break out, **20**. 448; inexplicable conduct of French in, **25**. 147; in Germany, always fatal to French in winter campaigns, **20**. 589; in Germany, at a stand, **21**. 291, 440; in Germany, English rôle in, ended, **21**. 306; in Germany, Guadeloupe's capture will not aid, **38**. 14; in Germany, not yet over, **21**. 549; in Germany, Parliament opposes, **21**. 553, **22**. 7; in Germany, seems less interesting than Portuguese war, **22**. 41; in Germany, subject of debate in England, **21**. 549, 553, **22**. 2, 7, 14–15, 30–1; in Germany, tires England, **21**. 466, **22**. 2; in Germany, wanes, **21**. 312, 500; in Germany, will be continued by England, **21**. 456; in India, may spread to Europe, **20**. 448; Ireland attacked in, **34**. 228; Irish civil war not to be added to, **35**. 236; Jersey not captured in, **25**. 127–8; Karl Wilhelm Ferdinand's success in, **38**. 67, 77; lack of declaration of, may facilitate peace, **24**. 399, 414; languor of, **25**. 48; Leghorn merchants anticipate ending of, **22**. 69; London approves of, **20**. 493; London wants English conquests in, retained, **38**. 140; Louis XV's escape from assassination may distract France from, **21**. 48; Mann terrified by prospect of, **24**. 357; Mann will learn peace news of, before HW, **25**. 347; Maria Theresa unlikely to stop, **21**. 389, 502, **22**. 23; Martinique's capture and Peter III's accession do not hasten end of, **22**. 23; military lull in Germany may indicate ending of, **21**. 500; naval clash may begin, **24**. 361; Necker will avert, **34**. 19; negotiations might still prevent, except in America, **20**. 488; Newcastle's dismissal and courteous French answer indicate possible ending of, **22**. 38; newspapers print rubbish during, **25**. 146; Nivernais warns France that adherents of, gain ground in England, **22**. 89; northern monarchs must despise, **25**. 6; not declared, **33**. 28; not yet declared despite French embargo, **24**. 365–6; Opposition attacks, in Parliament, **39**. 508; Opposition may criticize pacification in, **39**. 301–2, 303–4; peace approaches in, **38**. 82; peace articles for, published, **25**. 362; peace celebrations for, **20**. 46–50, **22**. 163; peace congress for, to settle India's ownership, **21**. 527; peace delegates for, **21**. 504, **22**. 55, 69–70, 72, 73, 90, 92–3, **25**. 279, 454–5; peace difficulties in, unintelligible to Mann, **22**. 99; peace for, cannot await Havana's capture, 22. 69; peace for, concluded, 22. 116; peace for, not yet concluded, 25. 354, 355; peace for, opposed, 19. 448–9, 22. 89, 116; peace for, sincerely wanted by D. of Bedford, 22. 92; peace for, to be adhered to, despite change in English administration, 25. 372; peace in, 35. 375–6; peace in, a jack-o-lantern, 38. 185; peace in, awaits France's final answer, 38. 97; peace in, awaits Havana decision, 38. 178; peace in, declared, 33. 381–2, 383; peace in, deferred, 38. 128, 130; peace in, delayed by armies' proximity, 38. 177; peace in, does not advance, 38. 101; peace in, gratifies counties and towns, but not their M.P.s, 36. 209; peace in, hoped for, 25. 183; peace in, hoped for by HW, for Conway's sake, 38. 94, 95; peace in, is England's sole topic, 38. 154; peace in, may be delayed by Havana's capture, 38. 183; peace in, may be joined by Spain, 38. 169; peace in, may be procured by Joseph II and Catherine II, 36. 192; peace in, may result from French starvation, 38. 112; peace in, might be made under walls of Paris, 38. 105; peace in, negotiated by Bedford and Nivernais, 38. 172; peace in, not advanced by Stanley and Bussy, 38. 90; peace in, not too long delayed, 38. 212; peace in, opposed by City of London, 38. 173; peace in, seems certain, 22. 38, 25. 346–7; peace in, talked of, 33. 378, 379; peace negotiations for, 19. 448–9, 21. 546, 22. 54–5, 60, 65–6, 81; peace negotiations for, broken off, 36. 194; peace negotiations for, said to be broken off, 19. 440–1, 464, 22. 81; peace negotiations for, to begin, 25. 279; peace negotiations for, unsettle d'Éon's mind, 38. 243; peace overtures for, from France, 21. 497–8, 38. 162; peace overtures for, through Van Hoey, 19. 264; peace preliminaries for, negotiated at Paris by Fitzherbert, 25. 311; peace preliminaries for, signed, 19. 479–80, 25. 356, 357; peace preliminaries for, to be ratified by France, 25. 362, 365; peace proposals for, supposedly made by Franklin, 24. 281; peace prospects for, 21. 360–1, 25. 342, 359, 366–7; peace prospects for, nearer because of change in English administration, 25. 276; peace rumours for, 19. 218, 225, 21. 365–6, 368–9, 504, 513, 22. 81, 24. 465, 25. 359; peace rumours for, implied by cessation of German war, 21. 500; peace terms (definitive) for, not expected till Parliament meets, 22. 78; peace terms for, not settled enough to be in George II's speech, 37. 296–7; peace terms for, rejected by France, 21. 526–7; peace terms for, unpopular in England, 25. 367–8, 373–4; peace terms from France for, rumoured from France, 25. 359; peace treaty (definitive) for, awaited, 22. 118; peace treaty for, not taken up in Parliament, 20. 30; peace

treaty for, should be influenced by Gibraltar's defence and Rodney's victory, 25. 352; peace treaty for, signed, 19. 511, 22. 95, 25. 426–7; peace treaty for, unpopular with English at Florence, 25. 382; peace would have spared France losses in, 21. 534; Peter III's dethronement may delay peace in, 38. 163–4; Pitt, William (Chatham), content to manage, under D. of Newcastle, 21. 448; politicians to blame for, 24. 490; politics to replace, 38. 142; possibility of, 23. 156; preparations for, 32. 301; progress of, 7. 60, 61, 63, 64, 70, 117, 123, 135, 145, 147–8, 150–2, 157, 158, 166–9, 171–6, 179, 181, 183, 186, 205, 212, 241, 427, 458, 9. 17, 28, 31, 33, 49–51, 54, 168, 178, 181, 183, 192, 193, 198, 214, 217–18, 221, 222, 225–6, 236, 238, 239, 245–6, 249, 250–1, 253, 268, 303–4, 307, 313–14, 353, 364, 369, 377, 392, 405, 10. 20, 22, 29; progress of, nothing but miscarriages and drawn battles, 25. 164; reopened, 9. 168; Rome discusses possibility of, 17. 24; 'rudiments' of, preparing, 35. 208; rumoured, 32. 328; rumoured, from Venice to Florence, 18. 44; Santa Lucia captured in, 33. 94; sea battle begins, 38. 23; Seven Years', 33. 32; slow, 35. 290–1; Spain may join, 20. 491; Spain said to have advised France to continue, 22. 76; Spain subsidizes France to wage, 38. 121; Spain will not be involved in, 20. 487; Spanish mediation might avert, 39. 303; Spanish war added to, 24. 482–4; stock prices fluctuate according to, 21. 497, 504, 22. 81, 24. 179, 282, 361; suspension of arms rumoured for, 18. 245; thought probable, 32. 364; thought unavoidable, 32. 366, 403, 33. 3; threats of, 35. 208, 212, 215, 218–19, 220, 33. 44, 37. 436–7; to be fought in Germany, 22. 35, 43; treaties in, see under Aix-la-Chapelle, Treaty of; Paris, Treaty of; treaty of Fontainebleau in, 35. 614; unavoidable though unwanted, 20. 482–3; undeclared despite hostilities, 18. 276, 283, 24. 390–1, 399, 412, 28. 414–15, 422, 428; undeclared war of succour, 18. 247; unfashionable topic, 35. 222, 254, 263; victory in, would be too dearly bought, 25. 336; Vienna hopes that peace will not be made for, 22. 87

English-Indian, progress of, 11. 251–2, 256

English-Neapolitan: Bourbon family pact may necessitate declaration of, 22. 565; shipping disputes may precipitate, 19. 65

English-Prussian, peace in, expected, 35. 63

English-Russian, threatened but averted, 11. 226–7, 231, 242, 247, 248, 256, 257, 282, 288, 297, 323–4, 336, 25. 118

English-Spanish: 2. 192–5; added to American and French wars, 24. 482–4; Almodóvar's manifesto may precipitate, 33. 102–3; America now England's enemy in, 24. 485; American war will alter course of, 24. 287; anticipated, 11. 74n; averted, 9.

[War: English-Spanish, *continued*]
397, 11. 75, 78, 92, 119–20, 124–5, 127, 130, 134, 173, 21. 172, 23. 297, 304; believed to be averted, 23. 244–5; Bourbon family compact would have riveted, 23. 274; Carolina's conquest endangered by, 24. 500; Charles III does not intend, 24. 492; Charles III may declare, 23. 244–5, 24. 489; Charles III reluctantly declares, 24. 483; conduct of navies in, inexplicable, 25. 147; confusion from, in England and Ireland, 38. 147; continuance of, preferred by English to confession of mistake, 25. 143; declaration of, 21. 560–1, 22. 5, 24. 491, 39. 328, 329; deferred, 38. 120, 145, 147; definitive peace treaty to be signed for, 25. 428; dull, 13. 200; England fears, 24. 226; English administration not blamed for, 24. 491; expense and futility of, 18. 423, 19. 432; fallen into lethargy, 25. 145; feared, 4. 482n, 33. 34, 44, 102–3; first effects of, 24. 496; forgotten in England, 17. 390; France said to have been advised by Spain to continue, 22. 76; French letters predict, 23. 252–3; George III's refusal to appease America causes, 24. 490; Gibraltar's relief will delay peace in, 36. 197; grew out of American war, 25. 211; HW desires, 4. 479, 483; HW inquires about, 13. 217; HW's letters will be made heavy by, 21. 558; HW thinks, inevitable, 38. 121; Hertford's Irish sojourn may be put off by, 38. 145; imminent, 13. 177–8n; languor of, 25. 48; Leopold convinces Joseph II of folly of, 25. 58; Mann hopes, may be averted, 21. 555; Mann persuades Leopold and Maria Louisa to urge Charles III to stop, 25. 42–4, 46; Mann pities George III for having to face, 21. 538; Mann's fear of, 24. 357, 476; may result, without either Court wanting it, 21. 554; newspapers print rubbish during, 25. 146; Orsi faction wants, to be concluded by peace, 17. 263; ought to be employing half of England, 37. 56; outbreak of, 15. 6n; outbreak of, likely, 21. 536–7; Paris and E. of Sandwich expect declaration of, 39. 325; peace in, 35. 375–6; peace in, attacked by newspapers, 23. 274; peace in, declared, 23. 269–70, 33. 381–2, 383; peace in, expected, 38. 169; peace in, hoped for, 25. 183; peace in, may be procured by Joseph II and Catherine II, 36. 192; peace in, rumoured, 36. 184; peace preliminaries for, 25. 356–7, 365; peace said to be made in, 17. 180, 182, 380, 18. 107, 25. 145, 43. 238–9; peace signed for, 22. 95–6; Peterborough's conduct in, 18. 180, 24. 482; Pitt (Chatham) may precipitate, 38. 120–1; Pitt proposes, to Cabinet Council, 38. 131; Pitt reverses his stand on, 20. 222; Pitt should avoid, 21. 544; Pitt's resignation may precipitate, 21. 537–8; poem summarizes, 40. 25–6; politicians to blame for, 24. 490; Portugal the

battle-field of, 22. 34–5, 43; preparations for, 23. 241–2; progress of, 7. 205, 425, 9. 418; progress of, nothing but miscarriages and drawn battles, 25. 164; Repnin said to be going to England to avert, 24. 487; reported naval victory in, 13. 211; rumours of, 7. 128, 129, 145, 148, 152, 20. 491, 25. 98; Spain a feeble enemy in, 25. 149; Spain's reluctance to make peace in, gives English ships a chance to continue, 19. 488–9; Spain wages, differently from Frederick II, 25. 190; Spain will start, when England is enough undone, 24. 300; Spanish avoid decisive battle in, 25. 156; Spanish compliance alone can avert, 23. 246; Spanish fleet may precipitate, 24. 111, 114; Spanish manifesto tries to justify, 21. 563–4; threatened, 9. 389, 392, 416, 24. 459, 495, 33. 34, 44, 571; threatened, over Falkland Islands, 35. 340–1; Torrington's prowess in, 20. 569n; treaties in, *see* Aix-la-Chapelle, Treaty of; Paris, Treaty of; treaty of Fontainebleau in, 35. 614; votes for, bought, 29. 127; Walpole, Sir Robert, disclaims responsibility for, 17. 231

European, may result from East Indian and West Indian disputes, 20. 448

European improvements in techniques of, 25. 105–6, 141–2

excuses offered by nations for waging, 22. 39

Frederick II makes, fashionable for kings, 21. 277

French-Genoese, declared, 12. 62

French-German ('Allies'): campaign in, 34. 182, 185; HW sends Robert Berry news of, 12. 70–1; *see also* Grand Alliance

French-Prussian: ending of, rumoured, 21. 153, 159; Frederick II suggests negotiation to end, 21. 366; progress of, 9. 313, 353; prolongation of, in winter, distresses French troops, 21. 254

French-Sardinian: armistice for, signed, 19. 218n; peace negotiations for, broken off, 19. 441

French-Spanish, rumoured, 7. 127–9

furnish nothing but regrets, 35. 360

Genoese-Sardinian: declared, 19. 75; termination of, 19. 312–14; to be declared, 19. 58

HW calls: a game injuring the cards more than the players, 39. 463; demon of blood, 25. 188

HW compares, with gaming, 30. 274

HW considers, a tragedy, 25. 365

HW detests, 10. 322, 22. 39, 81, 25. 106, 108, 31. 351, 392, 35. 240, 341, 360–1, 387

HW indifferent to, 4. 488

HW's reflections on, 2. 193–4, 12. 23, 30. 274, 35. 235, 240

HW says that the world will never long be free from, 25. 546

HW would rather live in last, than in present, 37. 200

human devastation of, HW's reflections on, 22. 81

hunting is an imitation of, 35. 387

inaction in, the worst fault in war, 21. 519

Indian, in North America, 22. 177, 35. 186

kings' elections cause, in Europe, 42. 496

London usurps right of making, 38. 140

Marlborough's general retorts to alderman's foolish remark about labour of, 21. 198, 24. 29, 414, 25. 340

Modenese-Spanish, may begin over Massa, 17. 35

modern aggressors wage, without pretending it is holy, 25. 400

Montagu dislikes, 10. 321

not to be fought in winter, 37. 132

peace not so catching as, 25. 188

Pisan-Milanese, described by Machiavelli, 11. 250

Pitt (Chatham) insists upon, 38. 131

—— saddles England with, 38. 136

plague may be added to, for destruction of mankind, 25. 304–5

politeness of, 21. 255

Portuguese-Spanish: France to be neutral in, 24. 262n; German war less promising than, 22. 40; outbreak of, expected, 24. 223–4, 253; peace in, 22. 95, 99; progress of, 22. 41, 48, 66, 24. 233–4; Spain pushes, 22. 78; Spain said to have begun, 22. 34; Spain wantonly provokes, 22. 18–19; threatened, 32. 357–8; Tyrawley derides, 22. 70

Prussian-Russian: Elizabeth of Russia's answer to proposed ending of, 21. 368–9; Elizabeth of Russia unlikely to stop, 21. 389; Palzig battle in, 35. 293; progress of, 9. 313; Russian defeat in, alleged, 21. 315; see also under Peter III of Russia

religion used as excuse for, 22. 39

rules of, French accuse English of violating, by use of fireworks, 21. 283

rumour of, in Netherlands, 42. 200

Russian-Swedish: 39. 462–3; HW pleased by, 35. 397, 400; peace treaty for, 18. 275; Vilmanstrand captured in, 17. 155; Walpole, Sir Robert, disclaims responsibility for, 17. 232

Russian-Turkish: 31. 152; accommodation for, may be reached, 23. 161; battle of Tchesmé in, 23. 226–8, 332–3; begins, 23. 70; Catherine II declares, 25. 415; Choiseul dictates gazette article on, 23. 143; contestants in, agree to do nothing, 24. 34; declaration of, 21. 247–8; Dick receives Order of St Anne after termination of, 24. 96; ends without any signal action, 24. 55; fears of, said to be removed, 25. 350; Fox, C. J., said to be responsible for peace in, 25. 486; France blamed by Turkey for causing, 23. 202; France may be involved in, 25. 359–60; France persuades Turkey to begin, 23. 70; George III wants stronger English navy because of, 11. 231n; HW hopes Turks will win, 35. 392; HW knows

nothing about, 25. 427; hostilities in, 4. 188, 203, 6. 397, 8. 162, 11. 161n, 186nn, 28. 382; Joseph II may be prevented by, from coming to Italy, 25. 350; Joseph II to be umpire for, 25. 415; peace comes soon after resumption of hostilities in, 24. 33; peace efforts in, by George III, 11. 282n; peace made in, 23. 420; peace negotiations for, 11. 248n, 297n, 324n; peace negotiations for, broken off, 23. 172–3, 438, 441; peace rumoured in, 39. 180; peace treaty for, 11. 324n; peace treaty for, announced, 24. 40; Pugachev may have contributed to ending of, 24. 35; resembles an armistice, 24. 28; resembles Chancery suit, 23. 432; Rome prays for Turkey's success in, 23. 140; rumours of, 25. 420, 616n; Russian defeat in, 35. 334; Russians at Pisa rejoice over ending of, 24. 84; Russians capture Turkish baggage in, 23. 479; Russian victory in, followed by invasion of Silistria, 23. 478–9; Russia's allies insist on conclusion of, 24. 33; Rutherfurd and Dick act as Russian commissaries during, 24. 453; Sultan averse to, but people and janizaries may precipitate it, 25. 360; Turkish instigators of, might be beheaded, 23. 159; Turkish peace negotiations may end, 23. 469–70; Turks lose provinces in, 23. 160; uneventful, 39. 176

sea, Selwyn's witticism on, 35. 261

Seven Years' War contrasted by HW with war of American Revolution, 28. 411, 29. 33

should be waged within 10 miles, 32. 388

western powers make, clumsily, 39. 371

winter quarters not resorted to, in modern, 21. 316–17, 25. 105

See also under American Revolution; French Revolution; Seven Years War; War of the Austrian Succession; War of the Polish Succession; War of the Spanish Succession; Wars of the Roses, and under names of battles, admirals, and generals

War, Council of, at Florence:
Richecourt, president of, 20. 392

Waræus. See Ware, Sir James

Warasdins:
infantry of, in Lombardy, 17. 266n
Lobkowitz reinforced by, 19. 30

Warbeck, Lady Catherine. See Gordon, Lady Catherine

Warbeck, Perkin (ca 1474–99), pretender to English throne:
Burgundy, Ds of, acknowledges, as nephew, 41. 114
Camden suspects, to be a true Plantagenet, 41. 126
Carte says, was really Richard, D. of York, 35. 607
claim of, perhaps believed by Henry VII, 15. 184
executed, 42. 208n, 255
Gordon family doubt claim of, 15. 121

[Warbeck, Perkin, *continued*]
HW believes, to have been Richard, D. of York, **14**. 163, 176
HW's research upon, praised by Granger, **41**. 133
HW's theory about, **1**. 144, **11**. 347
HW to be persuaded, was not Richard, D. of York, **43**. 200
Hume stresses proclamation of, **14**. 175–6
Leslie treats, as impostor, **14**. 174
marriage of, **15**. 120–1
pretensions of, **15**. 120
proclamation of, **14**. 168, 171, **15**. 119, 120
Simnel thought to be identical with, **42**. 255
Speed's account of, **14**. 173–4, 180
——'s account of, quotes Leslie, **15**. 118–19
Warwick involved with, **2**. 364n, **15**. 222n
wife of, **15**. 121n, **41**. 116, 126–7, 129
Young Pretender may be impersonated by a, **19**. 227, 270
Warblington, Hants:
papal bulls found at, **9**. 98n
Warburg (Germany):
battle of, **38**. 67, 69
Ferdinand's 'victory' at, **35**. 305
Warburghe. *See* Werburgh
Warburton, Hugh (d. 1771), Lt-Gen.:
HW meets, at Ds of Argyll's, and hears of Conway's dismissal, **38**. 375
wife of, dies, **7**. 397
Warburton, Mrs Hugh (d. 1766):
death of, **7**. 397
Warburton, J.:
print of, **40**. 236
Warburton, Jane (ca 1683–1767), m. (1717) John Campbell, 2d D. of Argyll:
Blandford, Marchioness of, called on by, **10**. 94
brother and HW dine with, **38**. 375
brother-in-law of, dies, **9**. 358
Conway asked by, at Vcts Townshend's, about Mary Walpole, **37**. 61–2
cousin of, **10**. 94n
daughter may imitate, **35**. 297, 299
daughter of, to be married, **9**. 36–7
death of, **31**. 133
dines at tavern, at 76, **35**. 297
Dorset entertains, **9**. 368
Guilfords entertain, **9**. 358
HW jokes about Cts of Ailesbury being the equivalent of, **37**. 333
HW meets Bns Milton at house of, **38**. 358
(?) HW mentions, **21**. 503
HW's wearing of flowers in hair questioned by, **10**. 94
health of, **31**. 27
Marriage Bill awaited by, to prevent elopements, **9**. 154
pets constantly discussed by, **9**. 368
Richmond theatre attended by, **9**. 74
Sudbrook the villa of, **23**. 538n
Townshend mocks voice of, **37**. 429–30, 442

—— overwhelms, **37**. 444
Vere's retort to, **9**. 368
Warburton, John (1682–1759), herald; antiquary:
(?) HW jokes about, **38**. 187
MSS of, **2**. 166n
Warburton, William (1698–1779), Dean of Bristol, 1757; Bp of Gloucester 1759–79:
agnosticism of, **22**. 196
Alliance Between Church and State by, cited in 'The Peach in Brandy,' **32**. 63
Anecdotes of Painting felt by, as an attack, **40**. 228–9
archbishopric may be coveted by, since he once headed an atheistic club, **39**. 104
Ashton succeeds, as preacher to Lincoln's Inn, **14**. 236
Bath visited by, **10**. 150
Bentley attacked by, **7**. 354
—— burlesques, **35**. 643
Birmingham edition of Pope proposed by, **13**. 38
Bolingbroke to be answered by, **35**. 167
Brown's relations with, **9**. 221
Butler attacks, in pamphlet, **29**. 134
Castle of Otranto mentioned by, in notes to Pope's *Works*, **41**. 409–10
Churchill dedicates sermons to, **22**. 261–2
—— satirizes, in *The Duellist*, **38**. 290
Critical and Philosophical Enquiry into the Causes of Prodigies and Miracles by: HW has, **40**. 175; Lort has copy of, **16**. 368
Divine Legation of Moses by: **14**. 139; HW jokes about, **10**. 278; HW owns copy of, **13**. 39n; immortality of soul treated in, **32**. 80; Moses's legation proved by Virgil in, **16**. 38
Doctrine of Grace by, HW has copy of, **13**. 39n
Edwards attacks, **9**. 117
Essay on Woman denounced by, **38**. 230
—— purported to have notes by, **38**. 229
HW apologizes to, for altering Pope's couplet, **35**. 101
HW disparages hypotheses of, **35**. 78–9
HW's opinion of, **10**. 150
HW's quarrel with, **13**. 38–9
HW visits, **1**. 341
HW would be despised by, for forsaking Parliament's orators, **38**. 187–8
Hardinge does not love, because of liking Hoadly, **35**. 577
Hawkins disparages, **40**. 228
Hurd imitates, **16**. 34
—— praises notes of, on Shakespeare, **16**. 37
infirmity of, **1**. 341
Johnson's characterization of, more like himself, **29**. 155–6
Julian by: miracle supposedly proved in, **16**. 38; praises Middleton, **15**. 300
Letter to the Editor of the Letters on the Spirit of Patriotism by: answered by Bol-

ingbroke, **20.** 62n; HW binds, in volume of tracts, with *Letter to the Lord Viscount Bolingbroke*, **20.** 65n

Lowth's dispute with, **1.** 108, **10.** 190

Lyttelton, Bp, told by, in House of Lords about refusing Mansfield's invitation to meet Helvétius, **38.** 365

Middleton discusses opinion by, of Roman paganism, **15.** 295

——'s correspondence with, about Moses and Cicero, **15.** 302

Montagu mentions, **10.** 151

Moses said by, to be inspired because he never mentioned a future state, **16.** 352

Newton's planned promotion to London bishopric displeases, **38.** 364–5

Nichols's *Literary Anecdotes* calls, the best letter-writer, **35.** 649

Pitt's name reinstated for Sandwich's in sermons of, **38.** 316

Pope edited by, 9. 116–17, **14.** 3, **29.** 278

——'s *Essay on Man* annotated by, in notes parodied in *Essay on Woman*, **22.** 184

——'s *Works* to contain attack by, on HW, **40.** 228

—— to be defended by, **20.** 62

prefaces by, to Shakespeare, **24.** 267n

Prior Park occupied by, **10.** 228

Quin debates with, **10.** 150

remark by, **2.** 147, **15.** 56n

'Repeal, The,' caricatures, **22.** 400

Shakespeare edition dedicated by, to Mrs Allen, **40.** 228

Sterne patronized by, **15.** 66

Tristram Shandy recommended by, to bench of bishops, **15.** 67

Wilkes attacked by, in speech, **22.** 185

——'s execution at *auto da fé* desired by, **10.** 111

——'s sacrifice wanted by, **22.** 196

—— will appear a martyr in spite of, **38.** 233

Warburton, Mrs William. *See* Tucker, Gertrude

Ward, ——:

(?) Burke brought by, to Mme du Deffand, **5.** 329

(?) Du Deffand, Mme, compares, to Mme Hesse, **5.** 329

—— sends books to HW by, **4.** 42

Ward, Mrs, (?) dau. of James II:

HW inquires about, **5.** 332–4

HW mentions, **5.** 324

La Marck, Comtesse, can find no trace of, **8.** 192

said to be James II's daughter, **5.** 332

Ward, Mrs:

silver chamber pot bought by, **13.** 156

Ward, Mrs (b. ca 1723), femme-de-chambre to Mme de Chambon:

not James II's daughter, **8.** 192

Ward, Ann (d. 1789):

pamphlet printed at press of, **29.** 213n

press of, **28.** 83n

Ward, Artemus (1727–1800), American Maj.-Gen.:

second in command under Washington, **32.** 28

Ward, Cæsar (ca 1711–59), bookseller:

HW hears story of Atterbury's speech from, **13.** 33n

HW knows, **16.** 26

HW's correspondence with, **40.** 130–2

Lyttelton recommends, to HW, **40.** 124

publisher of Parliamentary history, **29.** 294–5

story of Wynne came from, **15.** 111

Ward, John (? 1679–1758), professor:

Lives of the Professors of Gresham College by, cited, **2.** 355

Ward, John (1725–88), 2d Vct Dudley, 1774; M.P.:

landscape effects by, at Teddington, **35.** 389

SH visited by, **12.** 228

Vestris teaches, **33.** 282n

wife of, **11.** 30n

Ward, John (b. ca 1742), Cole's godson:

dines with Cole, **2.** 139, 266

posts letters for Cole, **2.** 266–7

Ward, Mrs John. *See* Plumptre, Dorothea

Ward, Joshua (1685–1761), quack doctor; M.P.:

Churchill treated by, in vain, **37.** 77

Conway, Hon. Jane, treated by, **37.** 19

Edgcumbe treated by, 9. 359

HW describes cures by, **21.** 362–3

HW wants Mann to give a more accurate description to, **21.** 363

Mann inquires about remedy of, **21.** 358

—— tells HW not to consult, **21.** 386

physicians jealous of, 9. 358–9

Ward, Philip, mayor of Oxford:

imprisoned for trying to sell a Parliament seat to Lee and Stapleton, **22.** 584n

Ward, Seth (1617–89), Bp of Exeter 1662–7, of Salisbury 1667–89:

portrait of, offered to HW by Simco, **41.** 388

Ward, Thomas Watson (ca 1718–50), of Great Wilbraham:

marriage of, **13.** 107n

son of, **2.** 139n

Ward, Mrs Thomas Watson. *See* Cutchy, Mary

Ward, W., printer:

London address of, **17.** 83n

Warden of the Stannaries:

Waldegrave replaces Thomas Pitt as, **20.** 246–7

—— was, **22.** 126n

Warder of the Tower of London:

at execution of rebel lords, **19.** 302

stable-boy claimed by, to be son of Lord Kilmarnock, **37.** 268

Wardington, Oxon:

Chamberlayne of, 9. 208n

Wardlaw, Lady. *See* Halkett, Elizabeth

Wardour Castle, Wilts:

Arundell's seat, **21.** 339n

Wardour St Coffee-house, Wardour St, Soho, London:
donations for widow to be received at, **41.** 385n
Wardrobe, Master of the. *See* Great Wardrobe
Wardrobe; wardrobes:
at Cotehele, **39.** 294
Burnet gets Wolsey's hat from, **41.** 332–3
Pesters's, of linen, **37.** 465n
Ware, (?) Catharine (fl. 1761), bookseller:
Dodsley delivers book to, for Zouch, **16.** 43
Ware, Isaac (d. 1766), architect:
death of, **7.** 397
Plans, Elevations, and Sections . . . of Houghton Hall: designs in, **17.** 428n; received by Mann from HW, **17.** 416, **35.** 44–5
Ware, Sir James (1594–1666), antiquary; historian:
Jacobi Waræi aurati de Hibernia et antiquitatibus eius disquisitiones by, lacked by HW, **16.** 9
Whole Works of Sir James Ware, mentions Totnes, **16.** 7, 9
Ware, Herts:
HW visits, **40.** 197
Standon school transferred to, **40.** 198n
Wareham, Dorset:
election at, **19.** 447n, 458, 459n
Hutchins rector of, **40.** 381n
Warehouse, Yorkshire Grey. *See under* Fetter Lane
Warehouse officers:
new arrangement for, **42.** 47
Waren. *See* Warren
Warenne, William de (d. 1089), 1st E. of Surrey:
epitaph on wife of, **2.** 6
Warenne family:
arms of, on monument, **16.** 88
Warfare:
western, contrasted by HW with eastern, **25.** 201
Warfield, Bucks:
Hart of, **4.** 275n, **10.** 291n
Wargrave, Berks:
theatre at, **11.** 101n
Warham, William (? 1450–1532), Abp of Canterbury:
arms of, **35.** 641
portrait of, **1.** 81
tomb of, **1.** 190
Warham All Saints, Norfolk:
HW aids Beloe in soliciting living of, **15.** 216
Warin, Jean (1640–72), painter:
Dupré master of, **7.** 313
Perrault prints portrait and biography of, **7.** 356
Warkton, Northants:
church at: Cole visits and describes, **10.** 339–40; Montagu monuments at, distressingly pagan, **10.** 339–40
Warkworth, Bn. *See* Percy, Hugh (1742–1817)

Warkworth, Bns. *See* Stuart, Lady Anne (1746–ca 1819)
Warkworth, Northants:
gallery of, has armorial glass, **35.** 77
HW and Montagu visit, **35.** 77–8
Holman family owned, **35.** 77
Warkworth Castle, Northumberland:
Northumberlands build at, **20.** 341
Somerset, D. of, owned, but did not occupy it, **20.** 10n
Warley Common:
camp at, **28.** 446n
Warmia, Bp of. *See* Krasicki, Ignatz von
Warner, Capt.:
peace news brought by, **25.** 432n
Warner, Betty:
Warwick induces, to break oath to deceased protector, **18.** 540
Warner, Rev. Ferdinando (1703–68):
Selwyn asked by, to frank letter to HW, **40.** 84n
Warner, Rev. John (1736–1800):
Aix to be visited by, to bring home dowager Cts of Carlisle, **36.** 193, 195
HW sends letter to France by, **36.** 193
Warner, Col. Seth (1743–84), American army officer:
Carleton said to be defeated by, at Longeuil, **24.** 156n
Wooster's letter to, **24.** 185n
War Office:
Conway's orders not delivered at, **38.** 376
Fox, Henry, writes from, **30.** 102–3
War of the Austrian Succession:
HW prefers War of the Spanish Succession to, **37.** 200
literature declines since beginning of, **14.** 14
Spain greatest loser by, but gains by the peace, **37.** 284–5
War of the Polish Succession:
Grotska the last battle of, **20.** 110n
War of the Spanish Succession:
HW prefers, to War of the Austrian Succession, **37.** 200
Noailles's *Mémoires* treat, **28.** 296
Warplesden (Warplesdon). *See* Worplesdon
'Warpool, H.':
HW's name as spelled by Fielding, **40.** 123
Warr. *See* De la Warr
Warrant; warrants:
death, **9.** 46, 197
Fielding refuses to grant, to Richard, **37.** 433
for Byng's execution, **21.** 63
for Sayre's arrest, defective, **24.** 138
for secretary at war's position, **19.** 175
for venison, **10.** 235, 238, 240
general: amendment to Parliamentary question about, **38.** 505; Conway does not regret voting against, **38.** 488; mentioned by Dr Price, **11.** 315; Meredith proposes discussion of, **38.** 488, 490; Meredith's motion against, **38.** 505; outcry against, in counties, **22.** 559;

Parliament discusses, **22.** 274, 283, **38.** 307–9, 315–27, 333–4; Parliament to consider, **38.** 497; Pitt's gout postpones discussion of, **38.** 493; regulation of, expected, **10.** 161; 'sent to devil,' **22.** 312; Temple might support Halifax on, **38.** 563; Townshend, Charles, writes pamphlet on, **38.** 422

HW encloses, to G. Bedford, **40.** 345

Hotham, Henrietta, brings, to Cts Temple, **10.** 116

justice of the peace's, duellists might be confronted with, **38.** 270

of protection, for rescued slave, **31.** 350

Rockingham omits, from complaints, **39.** 122

Warre, Jane (ca 1705–91), m. (1730) Sir Robert Grosvenor, 6th Bt:

house of, at Millbank, Westminster, **24.** 145n

mob breaks glass in coach of, **38.** 560

Molesworth, Henrietta, stays at house of, **22.** 145

Warren, Lady. See Bisshopp, Frances (d. 1804); De Lancey, Susanna (d. 1771)

Warren, ——, m. (1741) John Horncastle:

marriage of, **37.** 104n

Warren, Anne (d. 1807), m. (1758) Charles Fitzroy, cr. (1780) Bn Southampton:

Albemarle St Club suffers from absence of, **32.** 67

Amelia, Ps, entertains, **33.** 416n, **35.** 533n, **38.** 441

aunt of, in wax collection, **32.** 98

beauty of. **32.** 4

Berry, Mary, mistakes, for Mrs George Ferdinand Fitzroy, **12.** 136n

brother-in-law's relations with, **34.** 241–2

Chesterfield's witticism on, **32.** 112

club at Almack's founded by, **10.** 305

Coke, Lady Mary, declines invitation by, to Fitzroy Farm, **32.** 122n

Cornwallis induces, to receive the George Fitzroys, **36.** 225

daughter of: born, **32.** 67; dies, **38.** 561

Dublin visited by, **39.** 37–8

Du Deffand, Mme, does not talk of HW to, **3.** 174, 186

—— entertains, **41.** 41

—— receives mustard from, **6.** 96

——'s commission executed by, **3.** 219, 297, 303

—— sends messages to, **3.** 188, **6.** 90, 96, 98

——'s mistake at departure of, **6.** 154

——'s opinion of, **3.** 157, 162, 208, 251, **6.** 90

——'s social relations with, **3.** 149, 152, 154, 156, 157, **6.** 86, 89

—— to send letter by, **3.** 167

'fiery furnace,' **39.** 472

George III's wedding not attended by, **38.** 117

Guerchy, Comtesse de, brings, to Mme du Deffand, **3.** 149, 152

HW believes, concerning Lady Ossory's verses, **32.** 95

(?) HW entertains, at SH, **10.** 278

HW jokes about fondness of, for shopping, **31.** 125

HW mentions, **10.** 7

HW sees, **3.** 174, 186

HW would like to see, at Park Place, **39.** 101

House of Commons never left by, in long session, **38.** 317

loo played by: at close of confinement, **9.** 238; with HW, **32.** 4

mother of, dies, **32.** 67

Paris left by, **6.** 89

—— visited by, **31.** 125

Pelham, Frances, quarrels with, **32.** 103, 106, 112

Richmond's masquerade attended by, in Turkish dress, **22.** 148

(?) Saturday Club and, **43.** 185

seventh son born to, **32.** 171

son's elopement not forgiven by, **25.** 508

'Thalestris,' **32.** 106

thirteen children of, **25.** 508

Warren, Edward (d. 1760), Irish army officer in Tuscany:

health of, colic, **17.** 223

Modenese princess escorted by, through fortress, **17.** 66

Prujean and Elizabeth Pitt friends of, **20.** 499

Regency council questions, **17.** 223

Warren, Elizabeth Harriet (ca 1760–1826), m. (1777) Thomas James Bulkeley, 7th Vct Bulkeley:

Florence visited by, **25.** 618n

SH visited by, **12.** 235

Warren, Sir George (1735–1801), K.B.; M.P.:

birth date of, corrected, **43.** 350

diamond Bath insignia lost by, at Birthday, **32.** 346

marriage of, **38.** 233

wife of, **9.** 377n

Warren, John (1730–1800), D.D.; Bp of Bangor 1783–1800:

SH visited by, **12.** 227

Warren, Sir John Borlase (1753–1822), cr. (1775) Bt; Adm.:

SH visited by, **12.** 232

Warren, Dr Joseph (1741–75), American Revolutionary Gen.:

HW mistakes, for a clergyman, **32.** 246n

Warren, Sir Peter (ca 1703–52), K.B., 1747; Vice-Adm.; M.P.:

Admiralty candidate, **20.** 17

Anson and Vernon compared with, **20.** 33

birth date of, corrected, **43.** 262

Cape Breton's conqueror, **20.** 33

daughter of, **3.** 149n, **22.** 148n

election of, **19.** 425n

installed as K.B., **20.** 71n

knighted, **19.** 414

Navy Bill opposed by, in House of Commons, **20.** 33

Parliamentary speech by, on Dresden treaty, **42.** 496

ships captured by, off Cape Finisterre, **19.** *410*

Warren, Richard (1731–97), M.D.:
Amelia, Ps, embalmed under direction of, 33. 535n
George III's health reported by, 34. 43n
Gloucester, D. of, attended by, 24. 74, 32. 231
Holland, Lady, attended by, 32. 407
Kingston, Ds of, subject of testimony by, in House of Lords, 24. 151, 28. 234–5
Newcastle, D. of, attended by, 22. 579n
Rockingham attended by, 25. 287–8, 35. 516
Vernon, Miss, attended by, 33. 267
Warren, William (1683–1745), antiquary:
letter of, to Z. Grey cited, 2. 350
Warren, English ship:
French vessels seized by, 19. 230n
Warrender, Lady. *See* Boscawen, Hon. Anne Evelyn
Warrender, Lt-Col.:
Bedford House to be defended by, 38. 559
Warrington, E. of. *See* Booth, George (1675–1758); Grey, George Harry (1737–1819)
Warrington, Lancs:
Lort to go to, 16. 282n
rebels approach, 37. 211
Warrington Bridge:
demolished, 19. 173
Warsaw:
courier from, to Rome, about Cardinal of Bavaria's bishoprics, 22. 119
Craven, Bns, visits, 25. 632, 42. 176n
Durini lately nuncio at, 24. 11
English fleet should sail to, to restore Poland, 23. 475
Frederick Augustus II holds Diet at. 30. 320
Frederick William II of Prussia forced to raise siege at, 12. 105
George II pleased with Sir C. H. Williams's negotiations at, 20. 186n
HW hopes to hear from Sir C. H. Williams from, 30. 116
Monteil, French minister at, 5. 209n
peaceable, if Polish constitution had been allowed, 34. 157
peace expected by, 23. 438
Polish minister at Rome sends express to, 23. 352
Stanislas II entertains Mme Geoffrin at, 4. 214n
—— writes from, 42. 164
Williams, Sir C. H., attends Frederick Augustus II to, 30. 320, 322
—— prefers Turin to, 20. 16n
War ship; war ships. *See* Man of war; Ship of war
Wars of the Roses:
HW enlightens times of, 41. 146
Inquiry into the Doctrine of Libels worthy of, 10. 139
political shifts change interpretation of, 33. 349
thorny for England, 41. 157
uncomfortable period to live in, 24. 117
Warte, M. *See* Ward, ——

Wartensleben, Elisabeth Sophia Frederica von (1764–1817), m. 1 (1785) Joseph Ewart; m. 2 (1799) Rev. John Whitehouse:
York, Ds of, accompanied by, to SH, 12. 11
'Warth, Comtesse de la.' *See* Chudleigh, Elizabeth, Ds of Kingston
Warton, Joseph (1722–1800), D.D.; critic:
Clifton visited by, 31. 281
Colman's *Art of Poetry* dedicated to, 42. 50n
Essay on the Genius and Writings of Pope by, quoted by HW, 29. 178
HW hopes to see, 40. 378
HW returns Voltaire's and Windham's letters to, but declines to print them, 42. 121–3
HW's correspondence with, 40. 376–8, 42. 121–3, 209, 248–9
HW sends *Castle of Otranto* to, 40. 376–7
HW tells, to thank author of essay on mezzotinto, 42. 209
More, Hannah, mistakenly told by, that HW writes *Walpoliana*, 31. 281, 283
—— visited by, at Cowslip Green, 31. 280
(?) 'not the sufferer but the physician,' 42. 123n
(?) poetry of, 42. 103n
portrait of Sir Robert Walpole bought by, 42. 248
Sade's *Pétrarque* and Percy's *Reliques* doubtless to be enjoyed by, 40. 377
World contributions by, 20. 200n
Warton, Sir Ralph:
Moyser, trustee for charity of, 17. 408n
Warton, Thomas (1728–90), poet, critic, and literary historian:
Barrett informs, that he will not use Chatterton MSS, 16. 223
Birthday ode of, 33. 465, 469
brother of, 29. 178n
Bryant and Milles answered by, on 'Rowley' poems, 2. 287–8
Bryant and Milles to be attacked by, 29. 176n
Chattertonian writings of, 33. 319n
Chatterton's death discussed by, 2. 77–8
Colman's *Art of Poetry* dedicated to, 42. 50n
HW accepts offer by, of Beale and Hollar transcripts, 40. 367
HW answers queries of, about Tudor portraits, 40. 365–6
HW's correspondence with, 38. 168, 40. 253–5, 365–6, 367–8, 41. 163–4
HW thanks, for praise, 40. 253–4
history of architecture planned by, 15. 169
History of English Poetry by: 1. 334, 2. 75, 77–8; 43. 60; argument of, 16. 127n; Catcott writes to *Gentleman's Magazine* defending 'Rowley' poems against, 16. 178; Chatterton's 'Rowley' poems discredited in, 28. 381, 429; HW finds 2d volume of, even less entertaining than 1st, 28. 381, 385; HW reads, 32. 193, 33. 8; HWs name mentioned in, 16. 122; Harcourt ancestor mentioned in, 35. 486; Mason wades through, 28. 148, 29. 119; Mason wishes HW would abridge, 29.

120; materials of, more entertaining than book itself, **28.** 140, 142–3; Ossian not sufficiently discredited in, **28.** 148, 154; Ritson's *Observations* on, **2.** 335, 337; statement in, about Oxford books, **28.** 147–8; third volume of, **29.** 101–2, 118

Inquiry into the Authenticity of the Poems Attributed to Thomas Rowley by: **43.** 74; Bryant and Milles answered in, **29.** 183, 186, 195, 206; HW's notes on, **16.** 359; HW's notions about Chatterton confirmed by, **16.** 171

Life of Sir Thomas Pope by: **43.** 57; cited, **1.** 262; resuscitates nothings and nobodies, **28.** 30

Mason possibly alludes to, **29.** 182n

Observations on the Fairy Queen of Spenser by, **1.** 170, **2.** 165, **11.** 62, 63, 68, **43.** 69, 141; HW praises, **40.** 368; notice in, of 'Dance of Death,' **16.** 146; presented to HW, **40.** 253–4

praises everything, **33.** 521

Rowley controversy entered by, **2.** 294n

Spence succeeds, **28.** 124n

work proposed by, **15.** 53n

Warton. *See also* Wharton

Warwick, Cts of. See Beauchamp, Anne (ca 1426–92); Boyle, Lady Mary (1625–78); Ferrers, Philippe de (d. 1384); Hamilton, Elizabeth (ca 1720–1800); Russell, Lady Anne (d. 1604)

Warwick, E. of. *See* Beauchamp, Guy de (ca 1271–1315); Beauchamp, Henry (1425–46); Beauchamp, Richard (1382–1439); Dudley, John (1502–53); Edward (Plantagenet) (1475–99); Greville, Francis (1719–73); Greville, George (1746–1816); Nevill, Richard, (1428–71); Rich, Charles (1616–73); Rich, Edward (1673–1701); Rich, Edward Henry (1698–1721); Rich, Robert (1587–1658); Rich, Robert (1611–59)

Warwick, Guy of. *See* Guy of Warwick

Warwick, Warwickshire:
anti-American address from, **24.** 132n, **39.** 270n, **41.** 311n
assizes and races conflict at, **38.** 16
races at: **21.** 427, **38.** 16, 64; Hertford, E. of, to take HW to, **38.** 18; Hertfords to attend, **9.** 243
rioters tried at, **11.** 320n
St Mary's Church at: Beauchamp chapel in, **9.** 121–2, **32.** 352; tower of, disliked by HW, **32.** 356–7; Wren designed tower only, **40.** 348–9
visitors to: Beauchamp, **10.** 300, **39.** 78; HW, **9.** 121–2; Montagu, George, **10.** 300; Seymour-Conway, Hon. Henry, and Hon. Robert, **10.** 300
Warwick Castle's relation to, **35.** 140
Wise lives at the Priory at, **35.** 77
Wroxhall near, **40.** 345

Warwick, English ship:
at Leghorn, **17.** 455

at Port Mahon, **17.** 285
news brought by, from Quebec, **24.** 339n
West, captain of, **18.** 98n

Warwick, Earls of:
English merchants in India imitate, **22.** 211–12
HW familiar with history of, **39.** 436
Holland House formerly home of, **30.** 114n
Rous's pedigree roll of, at Kimbolton, **1.** 133, 147, **14.** 177, **15.** 123–4, 250n, **35.** 606, **41.** 134–5, 144

Warwick Castle:
arouses HW's Gothic superstition, **32.** 352
Battle Abbey's situation like that of, **35.** 140
Cowslade reports on affairs at, **33.** 170
HW asks if Brooke planted much at, **35.** 77
HW considers, 'first place in the world,' **35.** 408
HW 'had rather possess, than any seat upon earth,' **39.** 435–6
HW reverences, **32.** 357
HW visits, **9.** 121, **10.** 264n
Hamilton, Sir William, writes from, **35.** 411
location of, **42.** 131
MS architectural work at, **41.** 258–9
new eating-room at, **35.** 408
portership of, **15.** 221
portraits at: **32.** 353; examined by Hamilton for HW, **35.** 411–12
visitors to: Conway, **35.** 408; Cowslade, **33.** 170; Fitzpatrick, Lady Anne, **33.** 15–16; HW, **9.** 121, **10.** 264n, **35.** 408; Hamilton, Sir William, **32.** 321, **35.** 411–12; Ossory, Lady, **32.** 352, 360

Warwick family:
arms of, **33.** 350

Warwickshire:
Aylesford jokes about Methodists' ghost attempts in, **10.** 7
colliers from, pay tribute to George III, **32.** 185–6
Conway, Bn, to go to, **40.** 7
Conway, Henry Seymour, to visit, **21.** 228
Conway, Jane, considers going to, **37.** 23
HW and Conway to go to Ragley in, **37.** 556
HW intends visits to Cts of Hertford in, **21.** 128
HW's news is always new in, **38.** 190
HW to visit, **30.** 253
HW visits, **1.** 152, **23.** 57, **35.** 103 (*see also under* Ragley)
Hertford, Cts of, in, **39.** 260
Hertford, E. of, detained in, **39.** 90
Kirgate visits, **29.** 52
Longueville, Vcts, dies in, **10.** 339
Methodists encourage belief in ghosts in, **10.** 7, **22.** 8n
Montagu, D. of, lord lieutenant and custos rotulorum of, **20.** 79n
Packington Hall, Lord Aylesford's seat in, **34.** 68–9
Walpole, Sir Robert, has wife's dowry secured on lands in, **40.** 73n

[Warwickshire, *continued*]
West, James, supposed to be in, **15.** 122
woods of, Hertford averse to burying himself in, **38.** 387
Wroxhall in, **40.** 345
See also Packington Hall; Ragley; Warwick; Warwick Castle
Warwick St, Pall Mall, London:
Chenevix's shop in, **13.** 103n, **18.** 366n
Conway's, not the Warwick St where Ceunot is, **37.** 331
Conway's house in: **11.** 59n, 244n, **20.** 555n, **22.** 587n, **29.** 56, 308, **37.** 470, 493, **39.** 122, 125; HW and Lady Cecilia Johnston regret suppers at. **38.** 142; HW to leave flower picture at, **37.** 475; robbed and set afire, **33.** 583–4; *see also* Little Warwick St
Conway will talk of Rome when back at, **37.** 325
Jerseys not to occupy house in, **12.** 150
Warwick St, Golden Sq., London:
Bavarian ambassador's chapel in, **25.** 54n, **29.** 53n, **33.** 178n
Capezzoli lodges in, **23.** 563n
(?) Ceunot in, **37.** 331n
Edmondson's address, **41.** 93
Kutzleben, Mme, lives in, **11.** 346n
Warwick St, Marylebone, London:
(?) Ceunot in, **37.** 331n
Washed drawing. *See under* Drawing
Washerwoman:
dies in St Martin's roundhouse, **17.** 504
See also under Servant
Washing bed. *See under* Bed
Washington, George (1732–99), American Gen.; President of the United States 1789–97:
army of: casualties of, **24.** 339; demands more pay, **29.** 112; not yet conquered, **29.** 109; reported to be reduced and sickly, **28.** 422; underestimated by English, **39.** 333
Astley's horse-training should be imitated by, in training Congress, **33.** 418
better to send for, than for Lord Chatham, **32.** 399
commission resigned by, **20.** 449n
Congress appoints: 'generalissimo,' **24.** 120, **32.** 248; with stipend he declines, **32.** 248
Cornwallis banqueted by, after surrender, **29.** 184
——'s army surrenders to, **25.** 208–9, **29.** 166n
defeat of: at Brandywine, **32.** 396; not total, **24.** 349; reported, **32.** 392, 393, 394, 395
'dictator,' **6.** 424, **24.** 338, **28.** 293, 323
distinguished in the previous war, **24.** 120
Estaing's troops to cooperate with, **33.** 8n
Fabius and Camillus imitated by, **24.** 287
fort near Pittsburgh surrendered by, to French, **20.** 449n
French capture, and engage him not to serve for a year, **20.** 449–50
Gage's recall attributed to success of, **28.** 219
gains no glory from English retreat, **32.** 380

Gates strengthened by men sent by, **29.** 90
HW considers, great, **39.** 478
HW walks as if watched by, **33.** 81
HW would relinquish William III''s spurs only to, **35.** 478
Howe, Gen., apparently not to dislodge, **24.** 320, 323–4
—— defeats, at Brandywine and Germantown, **24.** 331, 338–9
—— fails to encircle, in Westchester County, **24.** 268–9
—— fails to engage, **28.** 342, 350
—— finds, too well-entrenched to be attacked, **24.** 352
—— intimidated by, **33.** 5
—— retreats after advancing towards, **24.** 323–4
——'s alleged defeat of, doubted by HW, **24.** 334–5
——'s army not increased by battles with, **24.** 336
——'s defeat may be considered best objective of, **24.** 347–8
——'s negotiations with, **24.** 205n, 248n
—— to attack, **33.** 5
—— twice 'gazes at,' **24.** 386
—— twice marches to, without attacking him, **24.** 414
Howes said to have been prevented by, from crossing Delaware to Philadelphia, **24.** 327
ill served by Gen. Lee, **28.** 434
Iroquois with, at Ft Necessity, **20.** 492n
Jumonville killed in skirmish with, **41.** 147n, 159
La Fayette and, **29.** 323
letter of, expresses enjoyment of cannon-balls, **20.** 450
manœuvres of, in New Jersey, **28.** 287
Mirabeau contrasted with, **34.** 111
Monmouth battle must be disappointment to, **24.** 408
New England forces may join, to besiege Clinton, **24.** 342
New Jersey said to be station of, **24.** 338–9
New York's environs said to have been laid waste by, **32.** 354
Paine's *Rights of Man* dedicated to, **11.** 239n
Philadelphia may be invested by, **24.** 361n
report of, in *Virginia Gazette* reprinted in *London Magazine*, **20.** 449n
Rochambeau agrees with, for La Fayette's relief, **25.** 150n
secret correspondence of, with New York informants, **33.** 239
Society of the Cincinnati founded by, **33.** 431
song on Maréchale de Mouchy mentions, **7.** 179
Speaker's mace not respected by, **24.** 356
spies of, **33.** 239n, 240n
supposed revolt of troops under, **25.** 135
talents of, conceded by both sides, **24.** 282
Tryon accuses, of burning New York, **24.** 256n

two generals said to be court-martialled by, **24.** 406

Washington, Durham:
Bland, rector of, **13.** 4n

Washington family:
'a frantic race,' **21.** 397

Wasmes, Baron de. *See* Lannoy, François-Ferdinand de

Wasner, Johann Ignaz (ca 1688–1767), Freiherr von; Austrian minister to England, 1741:
English Opposition said to work with, **17.** 325–6
footman of, brings letter to HW, **19.** 29
George II may be influenced by, **17.** 325
Granville confers with, on Charles VI's death, **26.** 10
HW will not relinquish Riccardi's jewels to, **19.** 74
Richecourt and Toussaint said to have urged, to intercede for Bns Walpole, **19.** 194
Richmond's invitation to, **19.** 308n
Treaty of Worms signed by, **18.** 311n

Wasp; wasps:
Brudenell, Mrs, as a, **30.** 295
English manteau makes women resemble, **30.** 29
HW sees, in April, **25.** 392
Pitt resembles, **35.** 262

Wassenaer, Frederik Hendrik (1701–70), Baron van:
(?) Aix preliminary articles signed by, **19.** 479n

Wassenaer, Jakob Hendrik van (1736–1800):
niece of, his heir, **7.** 92

Wassenaer, Marguerite-Élisabeth-Barbe de (1749–76), m. 1 (1761) Louis-Ernest-Gabriel, Prince de Montmorency; m. 2 (1775) Philippe-Joseph, Comte d'Asson:
daughter of, marries, **7.** 92
second marriage of, **7.** 92

Wassenaer, Unico Willem (1696–1766), Graaf van; Heer van Obdam, Twickel, etc.; Director of the Dutch East India Co.:
(?) Aix preliminaries signed by, **19.** 479n
Holland said to have sent, with peace terms to Paris, **19.** 216
Louis XV to receive Dutch peace plan from **30.** 49n
speech of, hints at restored Franco-Dutch commerce, **19.** 216n

Wassenaer Obdam, Carel Georg (1733–1800), Riksgraaf van; Heer van Twickel:
Joseph II to receive, **25.** 593

Wastell, Elizabeth (d. 1785), m. (1748) Gen. Philip Honywood:
Marie-Josèphe's funeral oration attended by, **7.** 318

Wastell, Rev. Henry (d. 1771):
Scott succeeds, **28.** 465–6n

Watch; watches:
Arthur, Lucile, presents, to national fund, **34.** 67
Arundel takes, to Italy, **21.** 339

captured at Dettingen, **18.** 261
chain for, **21.** 296
Colomb's, valued, **42.** 298
Conway's, **37.** 45
Deard reduces price of, **21.** 314
diamond, given to Farinelli, **38.** 476
enamelled, Bedford, Ds of, sends, to Vcts Bolingbroke for Q. Charlotte, **22.** 104–5
Fairfax's, presented by Parliament after Naseby, **38.** 340n
Ferdinand VI's mania for, **23.** 241
Feronce pulls out, **38.** 287–8
Fleury, Duchesse de, bribes Paris official with, **34.** 165
Florence to send, to Constantinople, **19.** 437
for Choiseul's niece, **4.** 295, 299
George II consults, **31.** 421
—— gives: to Cts of Albemarle, **20.** 111; to Elizabeth Chudleigh, **20.** 57
gold, Mann, Mrs Galfridus, tries vainly to save, from highwayman, **25.** 343–4
gold repeater, presented by Carlisle to Ottoboni, **13.** 214
gold single-cased, Hertford, Cts of, wants, for Vcts Beauchamp and herself, **39.** 117
Gordon rioters snatch, from members of Parliament, **25.** 54
HW and Lady Browne save, from highwayman, **33.** 296
HW mentions, **37.** 472
HW plays with, making it strike, **39.** 3
HW recovers, after robbery, **20.** 99n
HW's, Maclaine offers to return, **40.** 64
HW's coachman''s, stolen by Maclaine, **40.** 64
HW sends, to Mme Grifoni, **17.** 415–16
Harrington's, stolen, **38.** 259
highwaymen take, **33.** 445n
Huntingdon, Cts of, gives, to Whitefield, **35.** 309
makers of, *see* Deards, John *and* William; Ellicot, John; Gray, Benjamin *and* Robert
Northumberland, Ds of, loses, in Gordon riots, **33.** 175
Pius VI's nephew receives, in France, at Princess's' birth, **24.** 470
prices of, **21.** 295–6, 302
repeating, given by Amalia of Modena at Florence, **17.** 64–5, 70
Seymour-Conway, Hon. Henry, buys, from Griegson at Paris, **39.** 117–18
stop: Ferrers gives, to Vaillant, **21.** 401; key to, fits pocket-book, **21.** 402
Turner's, taken by rioters, **33.** 186n
Vere robbed of, **35.** 315
Voltaire has, made at Ferney for Aranda, **41.** 203
woman's repeating, procured by HW for Mann to give to Santini for his sister-in-law, **21.** 293, 295–6, 302–4, 306, 311, 313, 327, 337, 343, 347, 355, **23.** 306

Watch-chain:
HW jokes with Lady Mary Coke about, **31.** 149

Watch-coats:
HW tells G. Bedford to buy, from Mann not Jackson, **40**. 344
Watchmakers:
anecdotes about, **11**. 214–15
Watchman; watchmen:
Arlington St passed by: after 1 A.M., **38**. 183; at 3 A.M., **38**. 394
highwayman nearly kills, **20**. 188
Leveson Gower and Rigby imitate, **20**. 135
of Bristol, **20**. 470
Watch seal; watch seals:
HW copies design for device for, **21**. 314, 322
price of, **21**. 314
Watch-towers:
at Hurstmonceaux, **35**. 137
Watelet Claude-Henri (1718–86), artist, collector, and writer:
boats of, coveted by Mason, **28**. 215
Essai sur les jardins by: **6**. 196, **43**. 99; HW considers, to be absurd and superficial, **28**. 205–6; Mason thanks HW for, **28**. 207; Mason wishes to see, **28**. 200
HW promises to see garden of, **28**. 218
isle and villa of, *see* Moulin-Joli
(?) print by, of Bns Hervey after Cochin, **31**. 417
social relations of, with Mme Geoffrin, **7**. 298
Water:
abundant for Neapolitan gardens, **35**. 439
armies lack, **18**. 471
arquebusade, *see* Harquebusade water
at Bath, makes HW giddy, **39**. 76
at Blackheath, curative, **38**. 406n
bad, at Petraia, **17**. 481
Boscawen's fleet gets, at Gibraltar, **21**. 307, 318
Chute's diet of, **35**. 41
—— takes, with turnips, **18**. 100
cold: gout cured by bathing feet in, **22**. 266, 313, 322, 335–6; gout treated by drinking, **22**. 110, 114, 266, 322, 335, 459, **23**. 246, 252, **24**. 423, 430; HW dips his head in, every morning, **21**. 168
cold spring, for sponging eyes, **18**. 386
Conway fancies drop of, dribbling on forehead, **37**. 124
—— seeks farm with, **37**. 303, 305
drinkers of, unlikely to enlist in army, **37**. 125
England has, outside, and wine within, **39**. 186
Florentine mills lack, **25**. 318
for birds, in Gloucester Cathedral pew, **35**. 154
French do not consider, as article of cleanliness, **31**. 64
Gloucester city supplied with, from hill, **35**. 153
HW amuses himself with parties upon, **37**. 157
HW's opinion of, as a beverage and curative, **31**. 364

hot: Mann puts his feet in, to induce gout, **24**. 457; Mann urged to put his feet into, to cure cold and headache, **24**. 190; Walpole, Bns, soaks legs in, **28**. 153
housekeeper at Castle Howard gives 'Rosette' a basin of, **30**. 258
incrustation by, **42**. 406
Leghorn's supply of, injured by earthquake, **17**. 304
machine for raising, *see under* Machine
Mann's panacea, inside and out, **22**. 459
—— takes, iced, **24**. 430
Mann, Horace II, takes, **25**. 353
More, Hannah, considers, only proper beverage, **31**. 364
nerves 'cured' by, **20**. 389
nymphs provide, for Dublin ballroom fountains, **37**. 412
Orford, Cts of, cannot swallow, **25**. 102
'rainwater from Paris,' **19**. 414
red face from drinking, **35**. 82
Selwyn seeks, from sideboard, **38**. 348
sold on Neapolitan streets during drought, **24**. 479
sugar and, **35**. 473
toast drunk in, in Parliament, **17**. 354
warm, HW takes nothing but, some days when recovering from gout, **39**. 23, 31
See also Bristol water; Geronster water; Harquebusade water; Honey-water; Hungary water; Ice-water; Iron-pear-tree water; Orange flower water; Pepppermint water; Pohen water; Tunbridge Wells, waters of
Water, medicinal. *See under* Watering-places
Water, petrified:
vases of, **10**. 12
Waterage:
expense of, from Florence to Leghorn, **17**. 130
Water-balloons:
literary works compared to, **29**. 295
Waterbeach, Cambs:
Berridge preaches at, **1**. 126n
Cole agrees to take vicarage of, **1**. 121n
—— calls: 'this dirt,' **1**. 130; 'this nasty place,' **1**. 193; 'wretched,' **1**. 122
—— lives at, **14**. 185
——'s house at, **1**. 123n
—— still at, **1**. 156, 159
—— to move to, **1**. 121, 122
faults of vicarage at, **1**. 122, 125, 128, 133, 141, 159, 178n
floods in, **1**. 168
HW proposes to visit, **1**. 124
Methodism in, **1**. 126
rent of house at, **1**. 218
Water-closet; water-closets:
George II dies when leaving, **9**. 311, 312, **35**. 307
Water-colour; water-colours:
at Deane House, **40**. 4
at Welbeck, **35**. 271
Beale's, **32**. 294n

Beauclerk, Lady Diana, paints lilacs in, **42.** 490

Bingham, Cts of, uses, **32.** 155

Carlisle, Cts of, paints in, **23.** 457n

Carmontelle's, of Mmes de Choiseul and du Deffand, **3.** 392n, **43.** 86; *see also under* Carrogis, Louis

HW wants Petitot's portrait of Comtesse de Gramont copied in, **10.** 4

Liotard's, **20.** 362

picture of Comtesse de Gramont in, on snuff-box, **10.** 12

Strange's, **22.** 108n

Walpole, Sir Edward, makes pun about, **10.** 330

Westall's 'Hesiod Instructing the Greeks' in, **12.** 193

See also Berry, Agnes: 'Death of Cardinal Wolsey'

Water container:
for bouquets, **9.** 166

Water Eaton, Bucks:
Wells schoolmaster of **1.** 123n

Waterford, Bp of. *See* Marlay, Richard (d. 1802); Newcome, William (1729–1800)

Waterford, Ireland:
Mason, Aland John, of, **1.** 236n

Waterford, County, Ireland:
Burlington leaves Boyle family estates in, to Lady Charlotte Boyle, **20.** 545n

Whiteboys in, **22.** 24n

Watergall:
imperfection of, **32.** 158, 235, **33.** 72

Water-gruel:
Hardwicke's writings resemble, **33.** 421

Waterhouse, Edward (1619–70), antiquary:
engraving of, **16.** 67

Water-house; water-houses:
at Houghton, **32.** 141, **36.** 95

Wateridge. *See* Waterage

Watering-place; watering-places:
English frequent, **11.** 89

HW's opinion of, **10.** 231

Londoners to flock to, **35.** 323

thronged, **33.** 292

See also Abano; Aix-la-Chapelle; Aix-les-Bains; Bath; Bognor Rocks; Bristol; Buxton; Cheltenham; Harrogate; Pisa; Ramsgate; Scarborough; Spa; Sunning Hill; Tunbridge Wells; Weymouth

Water in the stomach:
Rockingham may have died of, **25.** 287

Waterland, Daniel (1683–1740), D.D.; Master of Magdalene College, Cambridge:
Answer to the Letter to Dr Waterland by, **15.** 295n

Cibber's book might have been written by, **14.** 14

educational method of, **1.** 359

Importance of the Doctrine of the Holy Trinity Asserted, The, by, **14.** 14n, 54–5

Middleton's *Letter* to, **15.** 292, 295, 307

Reflections on the Letter to Dr Waterland attributed to, **15.** 295, **43.** 212

Water Lane, Liverpool:
brewer of, **11.** 278n

Waterman; watermen:
apprenticed, at Richmond regatta, **32.** 318n

Bathoe sends by, to HW, prints and a catalogue, **40.** 290

goldfish to be carried by, to Park Place, **39.** 404

HW and nieces with two, in little boat, **39.** 311

HW's Arlington St maid sends news to SH by, **35.** 229

Hertford offers badge for, to HW for his protégé, **39.** 142

lord chamberlain in charge of, **39.** 142

pun by, on E. of Pembroke's death, **20.** 108

Sandwich bids Hertford tell, to petition Admiralty for release from impressment, **39.** 290–1

weavers may be joined by, **38.** 562n

Waterman's Company:
jury of, to choose regatta winners, **32.** 237n

Watermark; watermarks:
Chatterton's forgeries might have been betrayed by, **16.** 241

Water mill:
Kingston, Ds of, provides, at Calais, to grind for the poor, **31.** 289n

Water music. *See under* Music

Water nymphs. *See under* Nymph

Water pot; water pots:
HW buys, with covers, **37.** 439n

HW jokes about Conway's sending, for him, **37.** 378

Water rocket; water rockets:
at Richmond House, **22.** 148n

Waters, ——:
executor of Cts of Sandwich's will, **40.** 94

Waters, Charles, Cts of Orford's maître d'hôtel:
writes to Florence for a house, **20.** 476

Waters, John, Paris banker:
Boswell's banker, **19.** 507n

(?) Payba claims that Montagu, Taaffe, and Southwell extorted notes from him on, **20.** 288n

Water-souchy:
corn turned to, **35.** 384

goldfish should not be kept like, **35.** 182

Water-tables:
Miller ignores, in building church tower, **35.** 74

Water-works:
at Blathwayt's, **40.** 11

popular despite cold season in London, **17.** 434

See also York Buildings' Waterworks

Watford, Herts:
Woodcock, vicar of, **11.** 141n

Watford, Middlesex:
HW and Rigby dine miserably at miserable inn at, 30. 62
Wathen (Wathan), James (ca 1751–1828), traveller:
(?) SH visited by: 12. 230
Watlington Park, Oxon:
(?) Conway and HW plan to visit, 37. 301
Watson, Adm. *See* Walton, Sir George
Watson, ——:
Florence visited by, 17. 106
Watson, ——, builder:
Dacre's new wing at Belhus constructed by, 41. 360
Watson, Capt. Andrew:
Charlotte commanded by, 24. 335n, 32. 394n
Watson, Brook:
Quebec news brought by, to England, 32. 284n
Watson, Hon. Catherine (d. 1765), m. (1729) Edward Southwell:
death of, 38. 530
(? SH to be visited by, 14. 119
Watson, Charles (1714–57), naval officer:
Princess Louisa commanded by, 19. 410
Watson, Col. (? Daniel):
Hessians conducted to quarters by, 21. 33n
Watson, Henry (d. 1793), surgeon:
Albemarle, Cts of, attended by, 33. 513n
death of, 12. 76n
HW attended by, 11. *180*, 369, 372, 373, 377, 33. 513
HW has, for his hand, 25. 617, 618
HW's gifts from, at SH, 33. 513n
HW's 'oracle,' 11. 369
HW urged by, to take the air, 25. 617, 626
house of, in Rathbone Place, 33. 513n
Watson, James, King's Messenger:
Wilkes arrested by, 38. 197
Watson, James (? 1739–90), engraver:
(?) prints by: 1. 281, 9. 26on; after Romney, 7. 127
Watson, Lewis (ca 1714–45), 2d E. of Rockingham:
HW falls into lap of, at opera, 17. 412, 30. 32
Portland, Ds of, thinks face of, 'prettier for a woman,' 17. 412n
sister of, 14. 119n
wife of, 9. 85n
Watson (formerly Monson), Hon. Lewis (1728–95), cr. (1760) Bn Sondes; M.P.:
Bocchineri, Mme, gives venereal disease to, 20. 36, 447
Hoare does Ganymede for, 20. 86
Mann visited by, 20. 36
marriage of, 37. 339, 341
wife of, 10. 72n
Watson, Hon. Mrs Lewis. *See* Pelham, Grace
Watson, Lewis Thomas (1754–1806), 2d Bn Sondes, 1795; M.P.;
birth of, imminent, 35. 170
Watson, Richard (1737–1816), Bp of Llandaff, 1782:

Cambridge petition supported by, 2. 208
Conway's experiments can be judged by, 39. 552
Cooke attacks, in sermon, 2. 213
Gibbon replies to, 33. 84
(?) Hertford's letter carried by, to England, 38. 331
infidel without knowing it, 42. 449
resigns as chemistry professor at Cambridge, 32. 165n
Talleyrand might pair off with, 34. 138–9
Watson, Rev. Robert (ca 1730–81):
History of the Reign of Philip II by, praised by HW, 15. 136, 32. 339–40, 43. 197
only Scot worthy to write history of William III, 28. 387
Watson, Thomas (1637–1717), Bp of St David's 1687–99:
Baker's correspondence with, 2. 64, 353
Cole's opinion of, 2. 64
convicted of simony, 2. 60, 353
Watson, Thomas (1715–46), 3d E. of Rockingham, 1745:
death of, 19. 224
sister of, 14. 119n
Watson, Thomas (d. 1766) of Berwick:
death of, 7. 397
Watson, Thomas (1743–81), engraver:
(?) print by, 1. 281
Watson, Sir William (1715–87), Kt, 1786; physician:
(?) HW told by, about Herbert's letter, 40. 356
Watson Wentworth, Lady Anne (d. 1769), m. (1744) William Fitzwilliam, 3d E. Fitzwilliam:
dances at Robinson's ball, 37. 114
death of, 7. 398
husband's will slights, 37. 474
jewels of, 30. 50
marriage of, delayed by fiancé's fit, 30. 49–50
relatives feasted by, 30. 50
Watson Wentworth, Charles (1730–82), styled Vct Higham 1734–46 and E. of Malton 1746–50; 2d M. of Rockingham, 1750; prime minister, 1765–6, 1782:
absentee tax opposed by, 23. 524n
administration denounced by, at White's, 38. 180
administration may be foisted upon, 41. 304–5
administration may be led by, 23. 182
administration of, in 1765–6: America and Europe saved by firmness of, 22. 401; American colonies favour, 39. 24; American disputes to be referred by, to Parliament, 22. 407, 408; begins, 35. 331; Coventry said to criticize, 31. 85; dismissal of, 30. 221–2; expected to stand, 14. 141; Fox's and Mackenzie's sacrifices demanded by, 22. 302; HW can desert, now that it is in power, 35. 317; HW leaves, with good wishes, 30. 199; HW much consulted in formation of,

30. 201; HW's influence with, slight, 30. 199; HW tried to prevent some dismissals by, 30. 199; Hertford not conciliatory to, 32. 15n; lasts a year, 31. 121; Mann admires wisdom of, 22. 406–7, 408; Newcastle's discontent with, 30. 196; Pitt (Chatham) attacks, in House of Commons, 31. 117; Pitt charges, with perfidy, 22. 425; Pitt friendly to, 39. 40; Pitt's inability to include Grenvilles strengthens, 22. 436; Pitt turns against, 22. 413–14; resignations by members of, probably to be few, 30. 228; Richmond dissatisfied with his treatment by, 30. 194; Sackville favours, 39. 40; to include members of House of Commons, 22. 311; Townshend, Charles, delays formation of, 31. 39; Townshend, Charles, makes applications to, 30. 193; Townshend, Charles, supports, but with dissatisfaction, 39. 46; Townshend, George, violently opposes, 30. 193; triumphant in Parliament, 22. 381–2; Wilkes's overtures to, 39. 16
administration of, in 1782: accused of republicanism, 29. 215, 217; announced, 25. 261, 262; Burke and C. J. Fox only able members of, 25. 295; called in Paris *malheureux pour la France*, 25. 287; called 'regency,' 29. 238–9; cannot be as bad as predecessor, 25. 264, 276; change from, causes Cholmondeley to resign ambassadorship, 25. 333; change to, was for better, but did not last, 25. 310; did not survive his death, 25. 310; disposed towards independence for America, 25. 285; HW gives, time to breathe before sending Mann news of it, 25. 272–3; HW predicts jolt of, 25. 273, 275; HW's resentment at Conway's neglect of him during formation of, 39. 529–32; hoped by Hamilton to keep him at Naples, 35. 434; list of, 29. 207–8; Mann's acquaintance with members of, 25. 270–1; may be maintained if it can make a tolerable peace, 25. 264; measures of, triumphant, 25. 285–6; must remain united, 29. 222–3, 231, 245; popularity of, probably transient, 25. 275; position of, insecure, 29. 211–12, 214–15, 241, 245; virtue of, their only instrument, 29. 209; Wray named by, as Westminster candidate, 25. 284–5
administration refused by, 22. 543
administration to be accepted by, after negotiations with Bedfords and Grenvilles, 22. 538
American independence favoured by, 28. 349
American independence regarded by, as inevitable, 24. 350n
Antinous bust bought by, at Mead sale, 35. 216–17
Barré's pension signed by, 29. 264
Bedford, D. of, differs with, over Conway, 22. 542n
——'s faction to be reconciled with, by disgusts and by D. of Newcastle, 22. 549

——'s faction wished by, to unite with him, 22. 504n, 505n
bell acquired by HW from, 15. 14n, 16. 254n, 28. 38, 35. 477n
both terms of, as prime minister, very short, 25. 288
breach between Shelburne's Whigs and those of, not healed when they took office, 25. 294
brother of, died of convulsions, 25. 288
Burke, 'governor' of, 23. 209
Bute and Dyson considered by, as his sole enemies, 39. 100
Cabinet requested by, is granted, 25. 261–2
Canadian news distortions resented by, in House of Lords, 32. 284n
cataloguer, 3. 328
Cavendish, Lord John, friend of, 25. 293
—— governs, 30. 232n
Cavendishes think, equal to Chatham, 39. 101
Chatham administration not to include, 10. 222
Cholmondeley recommended by, to succeed E. of Orford in Bedchamber, 25. 266n
constitutional demands of; granted, 25. 261; reluctantly met, 29. 205, 206, 207, 208–9
Conway must despise hartshorn of, 39. 239
——'s and Grafton's treatment from, displeases HW, 35. 512n
Conway's house attended by, for meeting, 22. 432n
——'s intention of resigning known to, 41. 85
—— urged by, to resign, 22. 471–2
Court offends, by appointing another person to treat with him, 25. 261, 380
Court side taken by, in voting, 22. 507–8
Cumberland, Henry Frederick, D. of, cultivated by, for sake of George IV, 36. 200
Cumberland, William Augustus, D. of, summons, 22. 310n
death of: 29. 258, 260, 269, 32. 339, 340, 341, 35. 516–17; not sudden, 25. 287; produces new scene, 25. 293; splits administration, 25. 310; while prime minister, 25. 287–8; will have more consequences than his actions would have had, 25. 288
Devonshire, 4th D. of, by dying, placed, at head of Whigs, 25. 288
—— visited by, at Chatsworth, 38. 19
Devonshire, 5th D. of, might succeed, 25. 289
——'s medals to be seen by, 1. 313n
Dowdeswell chosen by, to move land tax reduction, 22. 487n
'duped and laughed at,' 29. 74
Dyson not a tool of, 29. 143n
Egmont and Northington opposed by, at Cabinet meeting, 22. 425n
faction of: angry at all, 22. 567; at Newcastle House draw up anti-Grenville paper, 22. 566n; Bedford faction meets, at Newcastle House, 22. 541–2; Bedford faction quarrels with, 22. 565; Burke's pamphlet severs, from supporters of bill of rights, 23. 209; Conway connected with, 35. 618; Court

[Watson Wentworth, Charles, *continued*]

majority dashes hopes of, **30**. 243; dine at tavern with G. Grenville, **23**. 115; fluctuate between Conway and G. Grenville, **22**. 495; Fox, C. J., and Cavendishes govern remnant of, **25**. 379; George IV praises, **35**. 520n; Grenville, George, opposes, **22**. 566, 567, 568; Grenville faction does not merge with, **22**. 504; Grenville faction does not tell, of reason for motion in House of Lords, **22**. 507; Grenville faction unites with, for East India Co.'s petition, **22**. 495; HW calls, 'mutes,' **29**. 260; ill humour of members of, **30**. 232; Mason dislikes, **28**. 398; meet at Fitzwilliam's, **25**. 294, 295–6; ministerial changes hoped by, **22**. 489n; ministry to be declined by, unless joined by Grenville and Bedford faction, **41**. 85; moves of, **3**. 261; Newcastle, D. of, to unite, with Bedford faction, **22**. 566; not connected with Grenvilles, **41**. 85; not numerous, **25**. 295; oppose annual Parliaments, **29**. 63; Parliament's dissolution not needed by, **39**. 123; Pitt (Chatham) fails to divide, since most of them resign, **41**. 67n; Pitt may be forced into alliance with Bedford faction by resentment of, **30**. 232; Pitt's faction deserted by, **23**. 199; Richmond, D. of, deserts, **25**. 294, 295; Rigby, Weymouth, and Thurlow betray, **33**. 95n; Rigby, Weymouth, and Thurlow play, against Grafton faction, **24**. 447n; 'time-serving triflers,' **28**. 337; Townshend, Charles, may lead, **22**. 495; warn him of snare laid by Shelburne, **25**. 261

first lord of the Treasury, **3**. 400n, **10**. 161, **25**. 262, **28**. 68n, **29**. 207, 328n, 332

Fitzwilliam the nephew and 'Octavius' of, **25**. 294, **29**. 260n

Florence and Siena visited by, to buy works of art, **20**. 263n

general warrants omitted from compaints of, **39**. 122

George III advised by, not to send for Pitt, **22**. 419n

—— and Shelburne negotiate without consent of, **25**. 372n

George III arrogantly treated by, in negotiations, **22**. 539, 543

—— consents to administration by, **33**. 331n

—— cool towards, **29**. 215, 235

—— did not inquire about health of, **33**. 339–40

—— orders Conway to send dismissal to, **22**. 439n

——'s brothers promised increased pensions by, **22**. 424

——'s memorandum produced by, **22**. 401n

——'s negotiations with, **22**. 538–9, **33**. 332

——'s overtures to, **33**. 251–2

——'s rift with son encourages, **36**. 195

—— tells, that D. of Cumberland's death will make no difference, **22**. 364

Gloucester, Ds of, rudely treated by, **29**. 209

Gloucester, D. and Ds of, not favoured by, **36**. 327

Gloucester, D. of, not permitted by, to lead army, **33**. 331n

Gloucester faction deserted by, for Cumberland one, **36**. 199–200

Gordon rioters threaten, **2**. 224

Gower may succeed, **25**. 289

Grafton, D. of, agrees and disagrees with, **28**. 304

—— almost quarrels with, over amendment to Address, **24**. 534n

——'s letter to, copied by Hertford with HW's corrections, **43**. 376

—— writes to, about George III's intentions, **22**. 539

Grenville, George, and Temple excluded by, **22**. 504n

Grenville, George, breaks with, **22**. 542

—— compared with, **22**. 489

—— may get, in his clutches, **22**. 539

—— must shake hands with, **22**. 572n

—— not likely to acknowledge leadership of, **22**. 504

—— succeeded by, as first commissioner of the Treasury, **22**. 310, **28**. 252n

Grenville alliance wanted by, because unable to cope with opponents in House of Lords, **41**. 88

Grenvilles negotiate with, **22**. 538–9

—— will not allow, to head Treasury, **23**. 181

—— wish to keep, out of Treasury, **41**. 86

Guercino painting at Siena acquired by, through Mann, **20**. 263, 268, 272–3, 313–14

HW buys knife for, **7**. 399

HW deems, unable to get Bath ribbon for Mann, **22**. 359n

HW did not admire, **33**. 342

HW does not admire more, after death, **35**. 517

HW drafts Grafton's letter to, **22**. 539n

HW exchanges Roman coins and medals with, for 'Cellini's' bell, **15**. 14n, **16**. 254n, **28**. 38, **35**. 477n

HW inquires whether, has done anything for G. J. Williams, **30**. 207

HW is not attached to, **29**. 24, 209

HW jokes about C. Townshend and, **30**. 244

HW mentions, **20**. 326

HW not to tell, that his painting has been copied, **20**. 314

HW promises Mason story of, **29**. 61

HW regarded moderately, **39**. 530

HW's correspondence with, **7**. 376, **22**. 395n

HW's opinion of, **10**. 244, **22**. 359n, **25**. 288

HW told by, about purchase of Guercino painting, **20**. 272–3

HW willing to resign empire to, **32**. 176

health of: abscess, **25**. 288; constitution bad, **25**. 288; dangerously ill, **29**. 257, 259; hypochrondria, **25**. 288; improved, **33**. 337; water in stomach, **25**. 287

Hertford, Cts of, sends knives to, **39.** 49
Hertford, E. of, never had the confidence of, **38.** 330
Holdernesse perhaps writing to, **32.** 320
horses loved by, **35.** 267
house defended by, in Gordon riots, **33.** 187
'Le roi Pepin' owned by, **24.** 266n
letters against, **42.** 505
levee of: **10.** 204; attended by only two bishops, **29.** 231
lieutenancy lost by, **22.** 109n
light horse troop to be raised by, **37.** 446n
lives in Grosvenor Sq., **29.** 193
Luttrells cultivated by, **36.** 200
Mann draws on, in favour of Messrs Langlois, **20.** 268n
Markham's public dinner at York races attended by, **28.** 333
Mason hates, **29.** 332
—— mentions, **29.** 67, 79, 281
(?) —— thinks, may be 'put in the wrong,' **28.** 484n
measures insisted upon by, **29.** 214n
medals examined by, **1.** 313n
ministerial triumphs of, keep HW in Paris, **10.** 192
ministers attacked by, in 'lecture' to George III, **29.** 64
ministry of, *see above, under* administration of
Montagu's adherence to, **10.** 194n
'moppet in Grosvenor Square,' **36.** 195
'mute,' **39.** 100
nephew and heir of, **25.** 294, **29.** 260n
Newcastle's political heir, **22.** 579n
Newcastle House meeting arranged by, **22.** 541n
Newmarket visited by, **22.** 97n
no man in public life had fewer enemies, **25.** 288
North's correspondence with, **10.** 215, **32.** 164n
——'s impeachment should have been demanded by, **29.** 280
——'s letter from, on absentee tax, **32.** 164n
—— succeeded by, **2.** 310n
Opposition not to be joined by, though he opposes, **22.** 464, 549
Orford, E. of, has turkey-geese match with, **21.** 7
Parliamentary bill to suspend Habeas Corpus not opposed by, **28.** 283, 333
Parliamentary motion opposed by, **28.** 479n
Parliamentary motions by: **23.** 180; for amendment to Address, **24.** 533n; for Irish relief, **39.** 324n
Parliamentary Opposition too quiet to need, as leader in London, **23.** 546
Parliamentary reforms opposed by, **25.** 29–30
Parliament's dissolution by, would leave Wilkes in control, **23.** 181
'parts' of, not great, **25.** 288

Pitt (Chatham) calls on, though he had formerly been ejected from his house, **23.** 181
—— discourages, **3.** 22n
—— must depend on, **23.** 246
—— refuses prime ministry to, **41.** 304n
——'s coolness with, **24.** 350, **28.** 349, 377
——'s motion supported by, **39.** 246
—— wishes to give prime ministry of, to Temple, **22.** 395n
political activities of, **10.** 236, 244
politics of: begin and end with dinners, **28.** 337; in his ante-chamber, **33.** 337–8
Portland, D. of, rumoured to be successor of, **25.** 289, 295
—— the logical successor to, **25.** 372
power will be engrossed to himself during ministry of, **35.** 512
prime minister, **3.** 400n, **10.** 161, **25.** 262, **28.** 68n, **29.** 207, 328n, 332
prime ministry alone would satisfy, **22.** 504, **24.** 493
prime ministry of, would promote his wife as leader of the Methodists, **35.** 323
Privy Council attended by, during Gordon riots, **33.** 188
protest against Dividend Bill supported by, **22.** 534n
protest meeting against Lord Chatham at house of, **22.** 471n
reconciliation of, with rest of Opposition, **15.** 128n
Regency Bill deserted by, for Newmarket, **38.** 543
Regulating Bill opposed by, **23.** 490n
'Repeal, The,' indicates opposition by, to Stamp Act, **22.** 400
resignation of, as lord of the Bedchamber, **10.** 46, **21.** 99, **22.** 97
resigns, as first lord of the Treasury, **22.** 431–2
(?) retains title, without followers, **35.** 352
Richmond, D. of, influenced by, **30.** 232
—— may succeed, **25.** 289
—— supports, **4.** 374n
Rigby's conversation with, at White's, **22.** 495n
Roman Catholic Relief Bill introduced by, at House of Lords, **33.** 187n
Sandwich attacked by, in House of Lords, **25.** 221
seceding Whigs of, called Junto, **25.** 294
secretaryship of state for America recommended by, **22.** 444n
Serristori, Mme, has as cicisbeo, **20.** 284
Shelburne asks, to give posts to Gower and Weymouth, **25.** 261
—— at odds with, **29.** 63
—— rumoured to be successor to, **25.** 293
——'s rival, **29.** 193n
—— supports, as prime minister, **25.** 261
—— will always contend with, **35.** 513
Shelburne administration may include, **25.** 260n
silly enough to do mischief, **22.** 505

[Watson Wentworth, Charles, *continued*]
sister of: **12.** 20n; elopes, **38.** 456–7
spirit of, comes from pride and hartshorn, **36.** 200
spoke in Parliament only by necessity, **25.** 288
'Stoic' bred by, **32.** 133n
Strafford, cousin and neighbour of, **38.** 180
terms of, deemed to invade rights of the Crown, **25.** 257
Thurlow negotiates with, to form ministry, **25.** 256
—— unlikely to succeed, **25.** 289
to be K. G., **21.** 368
Townshend, Charles, asks, for place for G. J. Williams, **30.** 207n
—— refuses Exchequer and State appointments from, **30.** 193n
Townshend, Thomas, emissary of, hears Pitt's plan for cooperation, **22.** 395n
Treasury headed by, **3.** 400n, **10.** 161, **25.** 262, **28.** 68n, **29.** 207, 328n, 332
Turner, adherent of, **9.** 184n
unable to assume power, **3.** 314n
Unconnected Whig's Address to the Public partial to, **32.** 383
virtues and amiability of, brought him esteem from party and love from friends, **25.** 288
Waldegrave given Garter to mortify, **21.** 110n
Warren, Dr, attends, **35.** 516
wife of, **28.** 342n
Wilkes shunned by, **28.** 337, **36.** 200
Wilton copies statue of Venus for, **20.** 397
witticism by, about Norfolk House's reopening, **37.** 438
Woburn visited by, to confer with Bedford faction, **22.** 538
Yorke, Charles, favoured by, **41.** 86
—— induced by, to reject Seals, **23.** 175, 178
—— makes promises to, **29.** 200n
—— opposed by, in protecting Sir John Dalrymple, **28.** 95
—— the oracle of, **22.** 494
Yorke family attached to, **23.** 178
Yorkshire Association opposed by, **29.** 329n, 352
——'s organization aided by, **43.** 304
Yorkshire meeting attended by, **28.** 488n
Yorkshire meeting did not originate with, **28.** 490n
Zouch, political agent, **16.** 1n
——'s patron, **37.** 560
Watson Wentworth, Lady Charlotte (1732–1810), dau. of 1st M. of Rockingham:
HW acquainted with, in 1753, **12.** 20
Murray, Ladies, bring, to visit HW, **12.** 20
Watson Wentworth, Lady Henrietta Alicia (b. 1737), m. (1764) William Sturgeon:
elopes with footman, tying up her property by deed deposited with Mansfield, **38.** 456–7
Watson Wentworth, Lady Mary. *See* Finch, Lady Mary
Watson Wentworth, Lady Mary, m. (1764) John Milbanke:

aunt displeased at marriage of, **38.** 457
Watson Wentworth, Thomas (1693–1750), cr. (1728) Bn Malton, (1734) E. of Malton, and (1746) M. of Rockingham; M.P.:
biographical information about, corrected, **43.** 112
daughter of, **12.** 20n
death of, from excessive claret, **20.** 208
dukedom may be given to, **9.** 45
express from, in Yorkshire, announces successes against rebels, **19.** 186
HW quarrels with, after he made Conway M.P., **37.** 270
marquessate given to, to appease demand for Garter, **9.** 39
regiment raised by, **19.** 128, **26.** 13, **30.** 98
Rockingham title goes to, **19.** 110, 186n, 244
wife of, **9.** 153n
Yorkshire defence meeting headed by, **19.** 110
Watson Wentworth, Hon. Thomas (1720–34):
death of, from convulsions, **25.** 288
HW remembers, at Eton, **25.** 288
Watson Wentworth family:
Strafford, E. of, not obliged to, **37.** 560
Watteau, Jean-Antoine (1684–1721), painter:
Eccardt's painting of Conway and wife modelled on, **25.** 174n
Esher party resembles painting by, **10.** 73
HW compares West to, **13.** 91
painting by, at Julienne's, **7.** 287
Watts, Amelia (ca 1751–70), m. (1769) Charles Jenkinson:
death of, reported as that of husband, **10.** 316n, 317–19
Watts, Mrs John. *See* De Lancey, Anne
Watts, Mary (d. 1815), m. (1773) John Johnson, Kt, 1765; 2d Bt, 1774:
SH visited by, **12.** 245
Watts, Thomas:
Beaumont Lodge sold to, **1.** 236n
Watts, William (1752–1851), engraver:
Carter's drawing of Croyland to be engraved by, **16.** 194
(?) HW sends information to, **34.** 227
plate by, **2.** 273n
Seats of the Nobility and Gentry, The, by, **2.** 274n
Wauxhall. *See* Vauxhall
Waveney River:
Bungay on, **37.** 406
Palgrave on, **28.** 124n
Wax:
bas relief of, **21.** 105
Beauclerk, Lady Diana, models in, **35.** 425
black: for mourning, **36.** 178; for sealing mourning letters, **17.** 164, **37.** 43
Boyle, Miss, casts babies in, **42.** 204
candles of, *see under* Candle
cast in, of Sir Robert Walpole, **41.** 285
cestrum used on, **9.** 251–2
Florentines offer, to Mann for coronation celebration, **21.** 533
Gosset's head of Hoadly modelled in, **17.** 502n

HW furnishes, 9. 117n
insertion of, beneath broken seal will enable re-sealing of letter, 20. 56
Lucan, Bns, models in, 24. 475
mask of, covers Clement XIV's disfigured face, 24. 43
models in, by Cellini, 25. 215n
seals on, *see under* Seal
sotiltie of, 16. 47
Stanhope, Sir William, thinks that Prince Henry Frederick is a model in, 19. 175
statuary in, *see* Waxwork
torches of, 19. 14, 184, 24. 541
Venice to give present of, to D. of York, 22. 241
Wax painting. *See under* Painting
Waxwork; waxworks:
collection of, by Mrs Wright, 32. 98
monarchs like to sit to a maker of, 23. 539
Rackstrow's, HW does not want to show, to Fleury, 22. 135
statuary in, 38. 198–9
Way, Abigail (d. 1793), m. (1767) John Holroyd (after 1768 Baker Holroyd), cr. (1781) Bn Sheffield and (1816) E. of Sheffield:
Gibbon visited by, at Lausanne, 11. 335
SH visited by, 12. 229
troubles of, in travelling through France, 11. 335
Way, Benjamin (1740–1808), M.P.:
(?) SH visited by, 12. 221
Waymouth. *See* Weymouth
Wayne, Anthony (1745–96), American army officer:
Grey's attack on division of, near Warren Tavern, 24. 336n
Stony Pt surprised by, 24. 519n
troops of, rebel, 25. 135n
Waynflete (*alias* Pattyn), William (ca 1395–1486), Bp of Winchester 1447–86:
Ducarel dates resignation of, as chancellor, 41. 141
laid foundation of learning at Eton, 41. 142
monument of, at Winchester, 35. 250
portrait of, at New College, Oxford, 38. 43–4
Richard III received by, at Magdalen College, 41. 139, 141
Wilson, his descendant, writes biography of, 41. 139
Way of the World, The. See under Congreve, William
Way to Keep Him, The. See under Murphy, Arthur
Weakness on the breast:
occurrences of, 24. 80, 25. 350, 42. 134
Weald:
of Kent, 22. 117
Wealth:
London's evils aggravated by, 23. 151
See also Money; Riches
Weapon; weapons:
pictures of, in Harleian MSS, 40. 217
prohibited in Florence, 17. 136–7

See also Dagger; Gun; Pistol; Sword
Weasel; weasels:
fable of, 37. 7
Weather:
drought, 1. 14, 21, 37, 216; *see also under* Drought
floods, *see under* Flood
fog and damps of Paris equal to London's, 31. 73
HW discusses, to avoid questions, 30. 172
hurricane of 1 Jan. 1779, 2. 135, 136; *see also under* Hurricane
in Paris, 1. 99, 103, 109, 110n, 31. 73
March, 'that Herod of the Almanac,' 2. 149, 151
October, a season to be depended on, 1. 240
sudden change of, causes HW's relapse, 31. 149
See also Climate; Flood; Snow
Weatherall, Mrs Joseph (d. 1794), of Upper Tooting, Surrey:
(?) SH visited by, 12. 234
(?) SH visitors sent by, 12. 234
Weathercock; weathercocks:
HW hopes, will point north-east for Berrys' Channel crossing, 11. 111
HW to watch, for east wind in Yorkshire, 11. 25
shoestrings appropriate to, 9. 294
'wavering weathercockhood' of Ds of Marlborough, 11. 108
See also Weather-glass; Weather house
Weather-glass:
fortune's, 24. 464
HW predicts foul political weather by, 38. 36
HW's letters may be affected by, 24. 379
stock prices are, for predicting war, 11. 247
See also Weathercock; Weather house
Weather house; weather houses:
HW resembles man in, 23. 297
man and woman alternate in, 22. 98n, 33. 297
political change suggestive of that of, 22. 98
See also Weathercock; Weather-glass
Weaver, Mrs William. *See* Douglas, Mary (1718–91)
Weaver. *See also* Weever
Weaver; weavers:
Bedford, D. of, mobbed and wounded by, 22. 301, 38. 558–61
colours displayed by, 22. 301
from Norwich and Essex, 38. 560
George II offered 1,000 men by, 19. 180
George III petitioned by, 22. 301
House of Lords rejects bill for relief of, 22. 301
—— surrounded by, 22. 301
in Spitalfields, can outdo French dancers, 38. 461
insurrection of, in London, 7. 368, 22. 301, 38. 558–61
mob of: besieges Parliament and attacks D.

[Weaver; weavers, *continued*]
    of Bedford and Bedford House, **38.** 558–61; blocks Piccadilly, **23.** 6
    riots against execution of, **23.** 163
    Spanish rioters compared to, **39.** 60
    starving in England, **23.** 476
Weazle, English sloop:
    French snow privateer taken by, **19.** 173n
Webb, Lady. *See* Gibson, Anne (d. 1777); Moore, Helen; Salvin, Mary (d. 1782)
Webb, Capt., of Hampton:
    SH visited by, **12.** 233
Webb, Mrs Bethia (d. 1791 or later), Selwyn's housekeeper; governess to Maria Fagnani: 'dying,' **33.** 348
    Fagnani, Maria, to be under charge of, **7.** 77–8
    Lyon to be visited by, **7.** 133, 137
    Selwyn accompanied by: **7.** 133; at Cleveland Court, **33.** 236
    SH visited by, **33.** 237–8
Webb, Charles, army officer:
    Hertford entrusts letter and mustard-pots for HW to, **38.** 278
Webb *or* Webbe, John (1611–72), architect:
    assistant and executor to Inigo Jones, **21.** 364n
    Gunnersbury built by, **9.** 169n
    Jones, Inigo, master of, **35.** 641
    Vyne portico designed by, **35.** 641
Webb, John (?1730–95), M.P.:
    Gloucester elects, **33.** 227n
Webb, Mary (d. 1731), m. Charles Gerard, 6th Bn Gerard:
    death of, at Joppa, **9.** 244
    Jerusalem visited by, **9.** 244
    portrait of, at Navestock, **9.** 244
Webb, Mary (1697–1768), m. Edward Seymour, 8th D. of Somerset, 1750:
    old and retired, **34.** 240
Webb, Nathaniel (1725–86), M.P.:
    HW does not know, **33.** 183
    Radnor House, Twickenham, bought by, **33.** 183, **42.** 480
Webb, Philip Carteret (?1700–70), M.P.; antiquary:
    'a sorry knave,' **2.** 332, 334
    Essay on Woman obtained by, **22.** 184n, 195n
    Grenville ministry to satisfy, **38.** 321
    House of Commons obtains evidence against, **38.** 316
    ministry to satisfy, **38.** 321
    perjury by, **38.** 297, **39.** 66
    unable to prosecute rioters for burning *North Briton*, **38.** 256–7
    Wilkes asks about perjury indictment of, **38.** 297
Webb, Thomas, of Twickenham; gardener:
    (?) SH visited by, **12.** 242
Webb, W., bookseller near St Paul's, London:
    Blast Upon Blast printed for, **18.** 34n
    Country Girl, The, printed for, **18.** 22n
    Further Report from the Committee of Secrecy printed by, **17.** 476n

Lessons for the Day printed for, **18.** 33n
Old Coachman, The, and *Labour in Vain* printed for, **18.** 18n
Patriots Are Come, The, printed for, **18.** 81n
Webbe. *See* Webb
Webster, Lady. *See* Vassall, Elizabeth
Webster, Dr, surgeon:
    picture sold to, **2.** 216n
Webster, Sir Godfrey (ca 1748–1800), 4th Bt, 1780:
    saves wife from the French, **11.** 331
Webster, Sir Thomas (d. 1751), cr. (1703) Bt:
    Conyers buys Copt Hall from, **9.** 93n
Webster, Sir Whistler (ca 1690–1779), 2d Bt; M.P.:
    HW to frank letter for, **10.** 28
    HW wishes Montagu to write to, about stained-glass window, **9.** 326, 336
    Montagu acquainted with, **9.** 326
    ——'s correspondence with, **9.** 328, 336
Webster family:
    Battle Abbey altered by, **35.** 140
Weddell, Mrs William. *See* Ramsden, Elizabeth
Weddell. *See also* Wedell
Wedderbourn, Maj.:
    Villinghausen news brought by, **21.** 515n
Wedderburn, Alexander (1733–1805), cr. (1780) Bn Loughborough, and (1801) E. of Rosslyn; M.P.; lord chancellor 1793–1801:
    advises placing discretionary powers in hands of the military, **29.** 58n
    attorney-general, **39.** 136n
    bill of conciliation explained by, **41.** 316
    Burke's altercation with, **32.** 401–2
    ——'s breach with, made up, **24.** 341
    ——'s *Reflections* admired by, **34.** 99n
    chief justice of Common Pleas, **33.** 194
    Conway's agreement with, offends Grenville, **41.** 82n
    counsel for prosecution of Ds of Kingston, **28.** 261, 262
    (?) Craven to sue, for affair with wife, **36.** 210
    Dundas's motion withdrawn through aid of, **25.** 35n
    East India Co. inquiry opposed by, **41.** 65n
    East India Co. officer questioned by, about Grand Lama's letter, **25.** 14–15
    Eden abetted by, **29.** 231–2
    elected M.P. for Castle Rising, **1.** 347n, **28.** 173
    flippancies of, severely handled by successors, **25.** 285
    Fox, C. J., arouses sarcasm from, **23.** 291n
    Franklin attacked by, **28.** 141, 142, 417
    —— firmly opposed by, **33.** 173
    Germain, Lord George, said to have, as counsel, **32.** 401
    —— wishes superior rank to that of, **29.** 177n, **32.** 401n
    Gibbon seeks government position through, **35.** 615n
    ——'s patron, **29.** 99

—— toadeater to, 33. 303
Grenville's amendment opposed by, 22. 381n
HW compares, to scavenger, 28. 24
HW indifferent about which coalition is to include, 29. 314, 317
HW sarcastic about patriotism of, 29. 135
HW supposedly quoted by, in House of Commons, 28. 155
Irish conciliation proposed by, 33. 173
Jenkinson's conversation with, 28. 474n
Jersey, Lord and Lady, receive remonstrance from, 12. 150
Kingston, Ds of, opposed by, at her trial, 24. 193, 28. 261, 262
lord chancellor, 15. 216n
Mason satirizes, 28. 432, 435–8, 29. 373–4
——'s counsel, 28. 322n
North's remarks about time-serving affect, 28. 155
Opposition's coalition affected by, 15. 129n
Parliament's dissolution advised by, 33. 222, 36. 174n
'Sawney,' nickname of, 43. 293
sister of, 12. 69n
solicitor-general, 23. 269
threatened in Gordon riots, 33. 184
Thurlow will not sign salary grant of, 33. 332
to be attorney-general, 28. 401
Townshend entertains, at breakfast, 10. 33
Wedderburn, Janet (d. 1797), m. (1761) Sir Henry Erskine, 5th Bt:
death date of, corrected, 43. 374
HW sees, at Lady Bute's, 12. 69
said to be Bedchamber woman to Q. Charlotte, 38. 97
Wedding; weddings:
banquet on day after, 4. 168
before dinner, 9. 235
Bolingbroke's, to take place at camp, 30. 137
clothing given away on, 30. 56
costume for, 9. 235, 10. 198, 11. 255
HW attends, frequently, 11. 264
Lorenzi enjoys, 20. 92
Mann will tell HW about, 18. 56
of poor Florentine girls, 22. 491
opera interfered with by, 18. 59–60
plentiful in London, 38. 379
weeping at, fashionable, 33. 307–8
Wedding clothes:
Ferrers wears, to execution, 9. 283, 21. 399
Wedding coach. See under Coach
Wedding gown:
Elizabeth Chudleigh's, 23. 93
Wedding ring. See under Ring
Wedell, Gen. Karl Heinrich (1712–82):
Dohna succeeded by, 21. 315n
Frederick II joins, 38. 24
—— to be joined by, near Dresden, 21. 257n
Palzig battle of, 30. 156n, 35. 293n
Russians said to be defeated by, 21. 315
Swedes defeated by, at Tarnow and Fehrbellin, 21. 247n
Wedell. See also Weddell

Wedgwood, Josiah (1730–95), potter and modeller; F.R.S.; F.S.A.:
'Druid's mug,' from shop of, sent to Mason by HW, 29. 38, 50
Etruscan chamber at Osterley Park reminds HW of work of, 28. 414
Etruscan vases of, 23. 211
HW's seal made by, 28. 236
Hamilton's portrait in Staffordshire ware of, 26. 46
Harcourt's portrait on plaque by, 35. 477n
Stubbs encouraged by, 29. 137n
Wedgwood, Josiah, jr:
Maer Manor owned by, 42. 146n
Wedgwood and Tassie:
cameos by, 35. 426n
Wedgwood ('Staffordshire') ware:
HW partial to, 6. 429n
(?) HW sends, to Mme du Deffand, 6. 429
Hamilton's portrait in, 26. 46
vases of, 23. 211, 36. 168, 169
Weed; weeds (garden):
Methodists may talk of, 20. 81
Weedemans, ——, hautboy player:
Holdernesse entertains, 18. 131
Weeding-girl. See under Servant
Weeds, widows':
Craon, Princesse de, will try to look well in, 20. 418
Craven, Bns, mourns in, for one day only, 34. 132
Kingston, Ds of, may wear, at trial, 24. 187
Morehead, Mrs, wears, for Hunt, 19. 477
Weeford, Staffs:
Blackbrook Farm at, 41. 232n
Week ends:
Englishmen all go out of town on Saturday, 39. 135
English will not come to town on, 21. 118
—— will not sacrifice, 23. 259
fashionable to leave London for the country on, 20. 63–4
Weekes or Wicks, ——, carpenter:
Bentley's presence at SH wished by, 35. 177
carpenter at Twickenham employed by HW, 35. 221–2
goldfishes' destination guessed by, 35. 221–2
Weekley, Northants:
Hoyland, vicar of, 28. 9n
Weekly Magazine, or Edinburgh Amusement, The:
'Anecdotes of Painting in Scotland' from, 42. 72n
Weemyss. See Wemyss
Weepers:
Court may be wearing, for Stuart's capture, 33. 57
Dutch and English wear, for Princess Royal, 21. 266
HW wears, for Cholmondeley, 10. 310, 311
Lothian wears, for son, 19. 281
Mandeville, Vct, pulls off, at ball, but Marlborough and Lord Charles Spencer do not, 38. 144

[Weepers, *continued*]
Mann wears, for Ps Caroline, **21**. 165, 174
Montagu, D. of, wears, for wife, **32**. 315–16
Pomfret shuns, after father's death, **20**. 390
Weeping willow. *See under* Willow
Weesey. *See under* Vesey
Weever, John (1576–1632), poet; antiquary:
Ancient Funeral Monuments by, **1**. 17, 18–19, 262, **16**. 64, **43**. 43
Cecill's engraving of, **16**. 64
Wegg, Mrs Samuel (d. 1799), of Acton, Middlesex:
SH visited by, **12**. 234
Weidel. *See* Wedell
Weights:
antique bronze: HW's, **15**. 13, 17, 22; Middleton's, **15**. 17, 22
Weil, Ashur (d. 1771), *and* Levi (a physician, d. 1771):
hanged at Tyburn for Slew's murder, **32**. 68n
Weir, Lady Anne. *See* Vane, Lady Anne
Weir, Hon. Charles Hope (1710–91), M.P.:
Vane, Lady Anne, elopes with, **37**. 232
Weissenau (Germany):
Charles, P., crosses Rhine at, **37**. 159
Weissenbruch, ——, of Bouillon, editor of
Journal encyclopédique:
(?) Voltaire's letter to Mme du Deffand shown to, **6**. 27
Weissenburg ('Weissemberg'; 'Weissenbourg'), Germany:
clergy of, protest, **34**. 71n
Coigny defeats P. Charles at, **30**. 60n
Wurmser's victory at, **12**. 40, 51
Weissman, Gen.:
Russians under, cross Danube, **23**. 479n
Welbeck Abbey, Notts, D. of Portland's seat:
'a devastation,' **32**. 375
ball at, **35**. 330
Conway and wife visit, **37**. 477
HW to visit, **9**. 141
Montagu describes visit to, **9**. 141
pictures moved to, **10**. 102n
Portland, D. of, gives masquerade at, **35**. 408
portraits at, **9**. 123n, **15**. 160, 209, **32**. 375, **35**. 270–1
relics at, **9**. 114n
Welbeck St, London:
Dickensons live in, **31**. 367n
Gordon, Lord George, arrested in, **29**. 61n
——'s house in, **25**. 62n, **33**. 194n
Welbourg, Nassau. *See* Nassau-Weilburg
Welby, Leics:
Hartopp of, **11**. 367n
'Welch Harp,' inn (?) near Lichfield:
Conway writes from, **37**. 330
Weld, Edward (1705–61), of Lulworth Castle:
arrest of, **19**. 134
Weld, Edward (d. 1775):
widow of, **25**. 628
Weld, Mrs Edward. *See* Smythe, Maria Anne
Welde, ——:
in Castle St, Dublin, **37**. 332

Welden. *See* Weldon
Welderen, Countess van. *See* Whitwell, Anne
Welderen, Jan Walrad (1725–1807), Count van; Dutch envoy to England 1762–80:
anti-French, **23**. 269–70
Choiseul's designs on Holland not believed by, **23**. 270
Dutch agent in Ireland wished by, **33**. 243n
George III's levee attended by, **33**. 158
HW sends letter by, **7**. 396
leaves England for Holland, **25**. 108
marriage of, **23**. 269n
Petworth visited by, **32**. 154
social relations of, in Paris, with: HW, **7**. 352; Viry, Contessa di, **7**. 350, 352
Suffolk, E. of, answers, regarding Dutch claims, **24**. 424n
Weldon, Anne (d. 1746), m. 1 Sir Robert Bernard; m. 2 Thomas Trevor, 1st Bn Trevor:
genealogy of, **10**. 352
Weldon, Sir Anthony (d. ?1649), writer:
Court and Character of King James I, The, by, **2**. 34, 40, **16**. 162
Weldon, Northants:
Dean between Bulwick and, **12**. 164n
Well; wells:
at Hagley, **35**. 149
Harcourt dies in, **24**. 328
Wellers, Mr (fl. ca 1680):
print of, **1**. 179
Welles, Bns and Vcts. *See* Cecilia *or* Cecily (Plantagenet) (1469–1507)
Welles, John (ca 1448–99), cr. (1485) Bn and (1487) Vct Welles; Henry VII's uncle:
Fenn's unidentified portrait may be of, **16**. 233
marriage of, **16**. 233
relationships of, **1**. 227, **2**. 363, 365
wife of, **1**. 222n
Welles. *See also* Wells
Wellesley, Arthur (1769–1852), cr. (1814) D. of Wellington; army officer; prime minister:
brother of, **2**. 306n
Coronation story about, **9**. 388n
Croker dines at Ham House with, **10**. 307n
Wellesley, Hon. (later Lady) Emily Mary. *See* Cadogan, Hon. (later Lady) Emily Mary
Wellesley, Mrs Gerald Valerian. *See* Cadogan, Hon. (later Lady) Emily Mary
Wellesley, Hon. Henry (1773–1847), K.B., 1812; cr. (1828) Bn Cowley; diplomatist:
arrives in London from Sweden, **12**. 44, 45
Wellesley, Richard (1760–1842), 2d E. of Mornington, 1781; cr. (1799) M. Wellesley:
brother of, arrives in London, **12**. 45
Wellesley. *See also* Wesley
Welleta Georgis, Dowager Empress (Iteghè) of Abyssinia:
Bruce mentions, **39**. 476
Welleta Israel, Ozoro:
Bruce mentions, **39**. 476n
Wellingborough, Northants:
Cole and HW visit, **10**. 88

HW mentions, in itinerary, **10.** 86
inn at, bad, **10.** 88–9
Wells, Bp of. *See* Bath and Wells
Wells, Dean of. *See* Seymour, Lord Francis
Wells, Edward (fl. 1767), schoolmaster:
  draws maps for Cole, **1.** 123
Wells, Phillis (d. 1742):
  death of, **17.** 504
Wells, Winifred, m. (1675) Thomas Wyndham:
  Gramont's *Mémoires* mention, **41.** 242
Wells. *See also* Welles; Württemberg-Oels
Wells, Somerset:
  bishops' palace at, **2.** 135n
  Bristol contrasted with, **40.** 10
  cathedral at, *see* Wells Cathedral
  Dodd and Whaley visit, **40.** 10
Wells Cathedral:
  Gooch prebendary of, **1.** 354n
Wells St, London:
  Dickenson, Mrs, mentions, **31.** 368
Wellwood, Sir Henry Moncreiff:
  'Life of Robert Henry' by, **43.** 198–9
  memoir by, in Henry's *History of Great Britain*, **43.** 208
Wellwood, James (1652–1727), historian:
  letters mentioned by, **15.** 92
Welsbourne, Warwickshire:
  Dewes of, **41.** 188n
Welsh, the:
  Edward I's battles with, **1.** 322–3
  in Gray's *Odes*, **40.** 105–6
Welsh language:
  Carlisle, Bp of, discusses etymologies of, **10.** 210
  HW and Charles Montagu cannot read, **9.** 221
  Müntz transcribes, **9.** 218
Welshmen:
  Williams Wynn tells, that George II was not at Dettingen, **18.** 305–6
Welsted, Leonard (1688–1747):
  Jeffreys's epigram ascribed to, **2.** 202n
Welton, Richard (ca 1692–1726), D.D.:
  Fellowes commissioned by, **13.** 86n
Wemyss, David (1721–87), styled Lord Elcho;
titular 5th E. of Wemyss, 1756:
  Argyll, D. of, appealed to by, for protection, **19.** 272n
  Bologna visited by, **30.** 16
  cruelty of, **19.** 272
  grandfather's will should have prevented, from joining Jacobites, **19.** 148–9
  guards under, at Strath Bogie, **37.** 229n
  health of, salivation, **19.** 248
  Hervey friendly to, at Venice, **19.** 148
  Hesse, Landgrave of, resembles, **9.** 27
  Lincoln implored by, for pardon, **19.** 272
  Mann has seen, at Florence, **19.** 118, 148
  —— hopes, will not escape, **19.** 149
  Paris the refuge of, **19.** 272
  silly, **19.** 118, 148
  Venice to be visited by, **30.** 16
  —— visited by, **19.** 148, 379
  Young Pretender joined by, **19.** *118*

——'s companion on return to France, **19.** 270n
Wemyss, Lady Elizabeth (ca 1718–47), m. (1734) William Sutherland, 17th E. of Sutherland:
  Cromarty in bed with, **19.** 296
Wemyss (later Charteris), Francis (1723–1808), *de jure* 6th E. of Wemyss, 1787:
  grandfather leaves estate to, on condition of his not turning Jacobite, **19.** 148–9
Wemyss, James (1699–1756), 4th E. of Wemyss:
  son of, **19.** 118n, 272n
Wen; wens:
  Francis III's, **20.** 75
Wenbury, Devon:
  Molesworth of, **12.** 152n
Wendover, Bucks:
  borough of, **17.** 425
  election for, **17.** 397
  road through, **1.** 37
Wendt, Amalie Sophie Marianne von (1704–65), m. (1727) Oberhauptmann Gottlieb Adam von Wallmoden; cr. (1740) Cts of Yarmouth, s.j.; George II's mistress:
  Albemarle, Cts of, friend of, **20.** 112
  —— influences, **20.** 269
  (?) at Chesterfield's assembly, **37.** 325
  Bedford's attachment to Sandwich said by, to explain George II's dislike of Bedford, **20.** 235n
  biographical information about, corrected, **43.** 111, 197, 239
  Bouverie buys peerage from, **19.** 419
  Bute's coolness to Pitt noticed by, **21.** 13n
  called 'Madam Vole,' **17.** 188n
  Coke, Lady Mary, friend of, **31.** 70
  —— might meet, **38.** 373
  Conway, Jane, forbids, to see HW, **30.** 83
  Cresset trusted by, **9.** 145n
  Cumberland, D. of, notifies George II through, that he will resign, **30.** 145n
  death of, **7.** 397, **22.** 362, **31.** 70
  Delorain, Cts of, supplanted by, in George II's affections, **18.** 71
  dessert depicts, with George II, **21.** 191
  Devonshire, D. of, approaches, on Conway's behalf, **37.** 542n, **38.** 84n
  fees for creating peers and barons assigned to, **9.** 51
  Finch and Newcastle entertained by, **21.** 460n
  Finch's appointment requested by, **9.** 318
  Fox, Henry, expected by, to decline Treasury, **30.** 128
  George II accompanied by: at review of troops, **9.** 318; to Hanover, **17.** *188*, **37.** 60
  —— advised by, to make D. of Bedford Master of the Horse instead of secretary of state, **20.** 183n
  —— discusses Sackville with, **21.** 320n
  —— does not permit, to show special favour to Cts of Orford, **19.** 111
  —— leaves to, a cabinet and its contents, **9.** 317

[Wendt, Amalie Sophie Marianne, *continued*]
—— said by, to wish D. of Bedford to resign, **20.** 235n
——'s and Q. Caroline's relations with, **31.** 421
George II's bequests to, **9.** 317, **21.** 450, **38.** 79
——'s devotion to, satirized in ballad, **18.** 81
——'s mistress, **15.** 143, **21.** 191n, 443n
——'s rumoured affair with, **13.** 117n
George III asked by, for Finch's appointment, **9.** 318
—— gives George II's bureau contents to, **21.** 450n
Giberne's picture shown to, by his mother, **20.** 90
—— will not be approved by, **20.** 95, 98
HW complimented by, **9.** 305
HW inquires about, at Kensington, **9.** 315
HW mentions, **20.** 326
HW prevents, from playing whist with Cts of Suffolk, **33.** 313
HW's relations with, **9.** 315
HW's witticism to, on robbery of watch, **20.** 112
HW to call on, **9.** 305
Hamilton, Lady Archibald, contrasted with, **9.** 16
Hanover visited by, **17.** 188, **37.** 60
health of: ague, **20.** 88; beyond recovery, **22.** 357; cancer in breast, **22.** 354
Hertford asks, for George II's consent to Bns Hervey's crossing Park, **9.** 305, **38.** 75–6
Holdernesse notified by, of H. Fox's accession, **21.** 100n
Holdernesses to meet, in Holland, **38.** 373
Lodomie's impertinence would be punished by boycott from, **37.** 359
Lorenzi asks about, **20.** 96–7
Mirepoix visits, **20.** 96
Newcastle, D. of, told by: of George II's recovery, **21.** 256n; of Leicester House's confidence in Sackville, **21.** 387n
Northumberlands give supper for, **21.** 191
on the wane, **20.** 212
Orford, Cts of, not taken by, to Court, **19.** 111
palace rooms unobtainable for, **20.** 88
(?) Pitt (Chatham) said to have lived with, **17.** 146
—— urges, to convince George II in favour of Habeas Corpus Bill in return for support of Hessian subsidies, **21.** 205n
Poulett writes to, for intercession with George II, **35.** 224
Powis House former home of, **32.** 106n
Ranelagh proprietor influences, to persuade George II to order jubilee-masquerade, **20.** 47
St James's Palace apartments reoccupied by, **17.** 188n
Schwichelt and Frechapelle fight duel over, **20.** 184
son of, **18.** 524n

Suffolk, Cts of, sees, at review of troops, **9.** 318
summoned on George II's death, **21.** 443
suppers for, **37.** 458
Theodore of Corsica said to be 'uncle' of, **18.** 187, 216
Wendy, Cambs:
Cole's notes on, **1.** 253
Wenham & Co.:
lottery managed by, **5.** 128n
Wenman, Philip (1719–60), 3d Vct Wenman, 1729:
House of Commons seat taken by, **20.** 435n
Wenman, Philip (1742–1800), 4th Vct Wenman, 1760:
Massereene's social relations with, in Paris, **7.** 294
Wentworth, Bn and Vct. *See* Noel, Edward (1715–74)
Wentworth, Bns. *See* Hopton, Anne (1561–1625)
Wentworth, Lady Anne (1713–97), m. (1733) William Conolly:
abstract from title deeds to Twickenham property of, done by lawyer for Astle, **42.** 416
Armstrong, Mrs, house of, described by, **11.** 56
Berry, Mary, identifies, **11.** 283n
birth date of, corrected, **43.** 121
Browne, Lady, to be entertained by, at dinner, **31.** 205
cabinet of medals returned to, by HW, **12.** 164
Copt Hall the home of, at Twickenham, **35.** 346n
Coventry, Cts of, talks with, **9.** 235
daughters of, **31.** 199, **35.** 340n, **38.** 73
deeds owned by, inspected by HW, **42.** 418
HW calls on, at Copt Hall, **35.** 346
HW congratulates, on Gen. Howe's safety, **35.** 352
HW does not expect to meet Lady Browne at house of, **31.** 196
HW entertains, at dinner at SH, **38.** 73
HW has, at Bedford's house for Coronation, **38.** 123
HW hopes, will accompany Lady Browne to Twickenham Park, **31.** 205
HW, Lady Browne, and, return from Twickenham Park with guard, **35.** 355
HW learns news of, **31.** 286–8
HW mentions, **37.** 418
HW's acquaintance with, **41.** 277
HW's correspondence with, **42.** 416, 443
HW sends game from Houghton to, **12.** 164
HW sends message through, **11.** 58n
HW to invite, to SH, **31.** 406
HW unable to wait on, before she goes to London, **42.** 443
health of, better but far from well, **42.** 416
house of, **12.** 58n, **34.** 260
Newcastle, Ds of, often visited by, at Twickenham Park, **35.** 349–50

Staffordshire visited by, to meet daughter, **31**. 199

Strafford's bequest to, **11**. 305n

——'s house to be rebuilt by, **11**. 283

——'s Twickenham house torn down by, and replaced by 'Mt Lebanon,' **35**. 279n

—— told by, of HW's visitors, **35**. 396–7

Twickenham resident, **42**. 482, 485

Wentworth, Darcy:

print of, **40**. 236

Wentworth, Diana (1722–95), m. (1739) Godfrey Bosville:

archbishop complains about, **18**. 286

children of, accepted as Bosville's, **18**. 309n

Chute describes promiscuous behaviour of, **18**. 286

——, Mann, and Whithed disliked by, **35**. 41

Craon complains to Mann about, **18**. 286

English reputation at Florence lowered by, **18**. 309

family of, **18**. 242

Florence visited by, to produce heir, **18**. *238–9*

HW congratulates, on Dettingen victory, **35**. 39, 41

HW considers, a 'beef,' **35**. 44

husband grants separation to, **18**. 309

husband tells, to follow Prole, **18**. 286

Johnson, Dr Samuel, praises, **18**. 242n

Mann called on by, **18**. 238

—— to entertain, **18**. 275

—— to entertain Prole and, **35**. 41

Prole's affair with, **18**. 251, 263, 298

—— to be joined by, **18**. 286, 309

Uguccioni aids, **18**. 242, 251

York the home of, **18**. 242

Wentworth, Lady Harriet. *See* Wentworth, Lady Henrietta

Wentworth, Lady Henrietta ('Harriet') (d. 1786), m. (1743) Henry Vernon:

Amelia, Ps, accompanied by, to SH, **31**. 147

dances at Robinson's ball, **37**. 114

daughter of, **11**. 184n

HW angers, by smiling at daughter's headgear, **38**. 509–10

HW mentions, **37**. 425

Hertford, Cts of, friend of, **38**. 509

Holdernesse, Cts of, entertains, **43**. 304

Kingston, Ds of, seen by, at Colisée in Paris, **24**. 242

lady of Bedchamber to Ps Amelia, **24**. 242n

marriage of, **18**. 342

social relations of, in Paris, with Contessa di Viry, **6**. 364

Wentworth, (?) Hugh (d. ?1787), army officer:

Florence visited by, **18**. 146

from Mathews's ship, **18**. 146

HW does not know, **18**. 166

Lincoln resembles, **18**. 146, 166

Mann must entertain, **18**. 146

Wentworth, Lady Lucy (d. 1771), m. (1747 or 8) Sir George Howard, K.B.:

at Boughton Park, **37**. 212

Boughton Park inherited through, **35**. 279n

Wentworth, Sir Michael, of Woolley:

Hinchliffe, Mrs, daughter of, **31**. 95n

Wentworth, Paul, New Hampshire's London agent:

Congress's petition not presented by, **39**. 231n

Wentworth, Thomas (fl. 1483–4), constable of Queenborough Castle:

portrait of, at Penshurst, **35**. 142

Wentworth, Sir Thomas (1593–1641), cr. (1628) Vct Wentworth, (1640) E. of Strafford; M.P.:

daughter-in-law of, **37**. 559–60

daughter of, **9**. 235n

elegy on death of, **42**. 44

HW satirizes, **18**. 357

HW would like to have seen trial of, **22**. 284

HW writes about, **6**. 430

Ledston belonged to, **35**. 269

letters of, at Ragley, **9**. 224, **35**. 104

only royalist to be esteemed by HW, **35**. 268

perishes before his cause succeeds, **23**. 200

Pitt (Chatham) imitates, **36**. 221

Sandys's hatred of Sir Robert Walpole for taking Orford title resembles Vane's hatred of, for taking Raby title, **17**. 333n

statue of, **35**. 268

tomb of, has paltry figure of him, **35**. 268

tragedy based on life of, **11**. 286n

Van Dyck's portrait of, **35**. 267–8

Wentworth, Thomas (1672–1739), cr. (1711) E. of Strafford, n.c.:

Ashburnham sells Boughton Park to, **35**. 279n

Wentworth Castle built by, **28**. 33n, **35**. 266, 267

widow of, **9**. 15n

Wentworth, Thomas (?1693–1747), army officer; M.P.:

advice by, on privately-raised regiments, **26**. 14

Austrian-Sardinian negotiations to be mediated by, **19**. 401

Austrians hate, for favouring Piedmontese, **19**. 451

—— to be spurred on by, **19**. 406

—— to receive proposal from, about capture of Genoa, **19**. 417

biographical information about, corrected, **43**. 238

Cartagena forts taken by, **17**. 68n

courier of, **19**. 417

failures of, recounted in Smollett's *Roderick Random*, **18**. 143n

Holland visited by, to demand troops, **18**. 400

'Jamaica general,' **18**. 242

niece of, **18**. 242

Piedmontese wish a successor to, **19**. 451

Santiago land attack refused by, **17**. 175

Sinclair to succeed, **19**. 456

troops of, sickened and withdrawn from Cuba, **17**. 175n

Turin visited by, **19**. 401, 406

Vernon will be challenged by, **18**. 143

Wentworth (after 1777, Blackett), Sir Thomas (1726–92), 5th Bt, 1763:

[Wentworth, Sir Thomas, *continued*]
HW to have admitted, at SH, **16.** 55
Wentworth, Sir William (d. 1692):
figure of, in Wentworth Woodhouse library, **35.** 267
Wentworth, William (1626–95), 2d E. of Strafford, 1641:
portrait of second wife of, **37.** 559–60
wife commemorated in inscription by, **35.** 268
Wentworth, Sir William (1686–1763), 4th Bt, 1706; M.P.:
daughter of, **18.** 242
Wentworth, William (1722–91), 2d E. of Strafford, n.c., 1739; HW's correspondent:
Bentley designs Gothic temple for menagerie of, 9. 295, **35.** 279–80, 282, 297, 306, **38.** 72
——'s chimney-piece design disapproved by, **35.** 214
——'s temple design approved by, **35.** 306
Berry, Mary, identifies, **11.** 220n
Boughton Park, seat of, has tower copied from SH, **35.** 279
bow-window built by, at Twickenham house, **35.** 347
bridge built by, **37.** 578
Castle Howard praised by, **30.** 257
(?) Cholmondeley befriended by, **35.** 368
Coke, Lady Mary, informs, of HW's health, **31.** 181
—— mentions HW's conversation with, **31.** 169
—— visits, at Wentworth Castle, **37.** 561
Conway, Anne Seymour, visits, at Wentworth Castle, **35.** 560
Conway, Henry Seymour, and D. of Cumberland entertained by, at Boughton Park, **37.** 212
Conway, Henry Seymour, and HW visit, at Wentworth Castle, **35.** 406
Conway, Henry Seymour, and wife to be visited by, at Park Place, **37.** 483
Conway, Henry Seymour, and wife visit, at Wentworth Castle, **37.** 559–62
Conway, Henry Seymour, has letter from, about bridge, **37.** 578
——'s correspondence with, **37.** 578, **38.** 180, **39.** 185
Craven, Bns, called HW's 'Sappho' by, **29.** 279
Damer, Mrs, should be heard by, speaking epilogue, **35.** 395
death of, **11.** 220
(?) Denbigh, Cts of, builds wall next to Twickenham house of, **35.** 307–8
Devonshire, D. of, leaves legacy to, **38.** 452–3, 455
——'s visit to London puts off visit of, to D. of Norfolk at Worksop, **37.** 578–9
—— to be visited by, at Chatsworth, **38.** 72
Devonshires entertain, at Chatsworth, 9. 295
elections do not interest, **35.** 398
England's destruction not to be blamed on, **35.** 364

family pictures discovered for, by HW, **37.** 559–60
garden of, at Twickenham, HW holds copyhold adjoining, **30.** 366
goods of, to be sold at auction, **11.** 283
Gothic temple in menagerie executed by, 9. 295, **35.** 267, 279–80, 282, 297, 306, **38.** 72
HW abuses patience of, by writing commonplaces, **35.** 371
HW and, visit Lord Thomond, **33.** 387
HW and Conway and wife to visit, at Wentworth Castle, **37.** 472n
HW asks commands of, at Paris, **35.** 316–17, 341, 343
HW calls, 'Adam,' **35.** 335
HW condoles with, on loss of animals, **35.** 377–8
HW congratulates: on Gen. Howe's safety, **35.** 352; on great-nephew's birth, **35.** 345–6
HW describes Wentworth Castle, the seat of, **21.** 429n
HW dines with, **17.** 320
HW disagrees with, on American war, **28.** 232
HW does not mention, to Lady Mary Coke, **31.** 140
HW hopes, will come to London, **35.** 286
HW hopes castle of, is in verdure, **35.** 360
HW hopes Jones's *Muse Recalled* will charm, **35.** 362
HW inquires for, **31.** 109
HW learns of Mason's *Sappho* from, **28.** 342
HW mentions, **10.** 243
HW pities, on illness of wife, **33.** 460
HW proposes to visit, **1.** 66n, 152, 256, 265
HW regrets slow approach of, **35.** 347
HW's correspondence with: **7.** 377, 379, 389, 393, **28.** 109, 230, 232, 236, 274, 411, **31.** 109, 110, 200, **35.** 275–401, **43.** 363; MSS of, **36.** 313
HW sends satiric prints to, **35.** 280
HW's friendship with, **11.** 220, **35.** 332
HW's health subject of inquiries by, **35.** 340
HW's intimate friend, **21.** 452n, **23.** 425
HW's letters overvalued by, **35.** 360, 371–2, 380–1, 388
HW's letter to be franked by, **28.** 385
HW's relations with, **31.** 186
HW takes leave of, **35.** 316
HW thanks: for building Bentley's Gothic structure, **35.** 297; for hospitality at Wentworth Castle, **35.** 278
HW to be given itinerary by, 9. 192
HW to call on, **35.** 353
HW to meet, in London, **35.** 353
HW to receive good wishes from, **28.** 232
HW to visit, **1.** 66n, **2.** 152, 256, 265, 9. 292, **10.** 264, **21.** 429, **22.** 247, **23.** 425, **28.** 37–9, **35.** 318, 329–30, 333, **38.** 64, **39.** 107, 128
HW urges, to come to London, **35.** 349
HW visited by, at SH, for tea, **38.** 362
HW visits, **4.** 137, 141, 142, 9. 295, **11.** 283
HW wishes, to approve of Holbein Chamber, **35.** 298
HW wishes tranquillity for, in woods, **35.** 355

HW would not inflict letters on, except by request, 35. 385
HW writes regularly to, 38. 94
Hertfords visit, at Wentworth Castle, 38. 91
house of, in St James's Sq., 35. 286n
hunting eschewed by, 35. 335
lack of sons should please, since they 'would live to grovel in the dregs of England,' 35. 364
landscaping by, 35. 336
London slowly and reluctantly approached by, 35. 347
——'s troubles will not concern, 35. 335
Luton chapel remembered by, 35. 332–3
Malpas, Vcts, at Twickenham house of, 39. 311
Mann sends scagliola pictures to, 17. 396, 18. 131, 35. 23
Markham visits, 28. 316
Mason's correspondence with, 28. 52, 29. 356
——'s English Garden liked by, 35. 361
—— urges HW to visit, 28. 210
—— visits, or is visited by him, 28. 52, 216, 230, 407, 29. 73
new offices for, rise at Twickenham, 35. 293
Nivernais's Jardins modernes given to, 12. 260
Northumberland House dinner reached by, late, 38. 530
opera-box subscription of, 38. 123
opera will be shunned by, if his box at it is inferior, 38. 127
papers against cruelty to dogs perhaps came from, 39. 428
parson of, to inform HW about Zouch, 37. 559
pheasants of, stolen, 35. 367
retirement unsuitable for, 35. 351
Rockingham, cousin and neighbour of, 38. 180
San Felipe preferred by, to Torcy, 35. 283
scagliola pictures in box sent to, 17. 396, 18. 131
sister of, 6. 364n, 11. 56n, 184n, 12. 164n, 18. 342, 24. 242n
sister tells, of HW's visitors, 35. 396–7
Strawberry Committee's design followed by, for menagerie temple, 35. 297
SH visitor sent by, 12. 232
Suffolk, Cts of, consulted by, about mourning for D. of Devonshire who left him a legacy, 38. 452–3
—— friend of, 35. 320
taste of, shown in improvements to Wentworth Castle, 11. 66
Townshend's retort to wife at dinner of, 37. 430
Twickenham house of, 35. 279, 38. 362, 42. 482
Twickenham visited by, 32. 192
Watson Wentworth family not on good terms with, 37. 560

Welbeck Abbey ball described by, to HW, 35. 330
Wentworth Castle remodelled by, 11. 66, 28. 33n
——'s front to be rebuilt by, 35. 298, 309, 310
——'s new front built by, 35. 407
—— the seat of, 1. 256n
—— unlikely to be taken from, by earthquake, 35. 374
wife and, solitary but happy, 28. 164
wife of, 9. 387n, 30. 327n
wife's health alarms, 38. 180
will of, 11. 305
Worksop celebrations over Minden may be seen by, 35. 293
—— visited by, 35. 270, 280n
—— visit put off by, 37. 578–9
Worsborough near house of, 29. 278
Zouch informed by, of HW's disposal of letters, 16. 56
Wentworth. See also Watson Wentworth
Wentworth, Cambs:
Lagden of, 1. 364n
Wentworth Castle, Yorks, E. of Strafford's seat:
Bentley's Gothic temple for menagerie at, 9. 295, 35. 267, 279–80, 282, 297, 306, 38. 72
—— to design Gothic building for, 35. 267
Berrys to see, 11. 66
bridge at, 37. 560, 578
Clifton Hall compared with, 35. 279
Conway and wife to join HW on trip to, 37. 472n
Conway writes from, 37. 559–62
earthquake unlikely to destroy, 35. 374
front of, to be rebuilt, 35. 298, 309, 310
HW and Conway to visit, 38. 415, 422
HW calls, 'perfectest piece of architecture I know,' 35. 361
HW describes, 35. 266–7
HW hopes, proceeds faster than SH, 35. 315
HW hopes Strafford finds, in verdure, 35. 360
HW longs for floods that pursued him to, 35. 282
HW may visit, 35. 339
HW mentions, 31. 63
HW might leave, sooner than planned, 38. 64
HW not to visit, 28. 83, 167
HW's opinion of, 11. 66–7
HW to accompany Conway and wife to, 35. 333
HW to visit, 1. 66n, 256, 4. 445n, 28. 33, 37, 35. 275, 303, 318, 329–30, 39. 107, 128
HW unable to go to, 38. 68
HW visits, 9. 192n, 295, 10. 264n
HW will see building at, designed by Bentley, 35. 297
HW writes from, 7. 387, 35. 266
Harcourts should visit, 35. 361
Henley bridge worthy to be at, 35. 386
Hertford writes to HW at, 38. 70
landscape and menagerie at, 9. 295
landscape effects at, 37. 560–1

[Wentworth Castle, *continued*]
Mason hopes to see HW at, **28.** 133
menagerie at: **9.** 295; Gothic temple in, *see under* Bentley, Richard (1708–82), *and above under* Bentley's Gothic temple for menagerie at
Strafford, E. of, at, **28.** 210
—— builds new front to, **35.** 407
—— dies at, **11.** 220n
—— probably at, **35.** 390
——'s seat, **1.** 66n, 152
visitors to: Ailesbury, Cts of, **37.** 559–62; Coke, Lady Mary, **37.** 561; Conway, Anne Seymour, **37.** 560; Conway, Henry Seymour, **35.** 406, 407, **37.** 559–62; Devonshire, D. of, **38.** 72; HW, **4.** 137, 141, 142, **7.** 387, **9.** 192n, 295, **10.** 264n, **11.** 283, **35.** 266, 278, 406, 407, **38.** 72; Hertfords, **38.** 91; Markham, **28.** 316; Mason, **28.** 164, 230, 411
Wentworth Fitzwilliam. *See* Fitzwilliam
Wentworth House, Yorks, E. Fitzwilliam's seat:
Berrys decline invitation to, **11.** 60n, 62
George IV and D. of York entertained at, **11.** 59n, 60n
See also Wentworth Woodhouse
Wentworth Woodhouse ('Wentworth House'), Yorks, M. of Rockingham's seat:
Bentley may be condemned to have his design impounded at, **35.** 280
colts and temples at, **35.** 280
Guercino painting in White Dressing-Room at, **20.** 263n
HW visits and describes, **35.** 267–8
Rockingham ill at, **23.** 546n
Strafford tombs in church at, **35.** 268
Wilton's sculptures at, **20.** 397n
Wentzel, Baron, surgeon:
Bedford's cataracts removed by, **22.** 567n, **41.** 110n
Weobley, Herefordshire:
elections at, **19.** 447n, **20.** 31
Werburgh, St:
representation of, **16.** 103
Werff, Adriaen van der (1659–1722), painter. *See* Van der Werff
Werl (Prussia):
Ferdinand's army assembled at, **38.** 15
Werneck, regiment of:
Karl Wilhelm Ferdinand captures, **21.** 355n
Werner (d. 1006):
first Habsburg count, **20.** 409n
Werpup, Georg Anthon (d. 1765), Hanoverian baron:
Hanoverian who attended Q. Charlotte to England, **22.** 306
killed near Rome by overturn of chaise, **22.** 306
Werrington, Devon:
Morice of, **9.** 164n
Werthein, ——:
Mme du Deffand's social relations with, **7.** 341
See also Werthern; Wirter

Werthern, Count:
Mme Geoffrin's social relations with, **7.** 306
Wescote. *See* Westcote
Wesel (Germany):
Karl Wilhelm Ferdinand besieges, **21.** 474n, **38.** 77
siege of, raised, **21.** 444
Voltaire said to have asked asylum at, **3.** 110
Weser (German river):
Cumberland, D. of, forced to cross, **21.** 109
French army crosses, **21.** 117, **37.** 494
Wesket, John (d. 1765), Harrington's porter:
execution of, at Tyburn, wearing white cockade, **38.** 490
goods stolen by, recovered at accomplice's, **38.** 473n
robbery laid to, **38.** 259n
Wesley, Lady Anne (1768–1844), m. 1 (1790) Hon. Henry Fitzroy; m. 2 (1799) Charles Culling Smith:
at Mrs Boyle Walsingham's ball, **42.** 222n
Dorset rumoured to marry, **36.** 240
Wesley, Rev. Charles (1707–88), hymn-writer:
folio of Sir Edward Walpole's Italian operatic arias owned by, **36.** 53n
house in Marylebone given to, **9.** 73n
Indians to be converted by, **17.** 477n
Wesley, Rev. John (1703–91), evangelist; founder of Methodism:
activities of, **1.** 124
actor, like Garrick, **35.** 119
Berridge meets, **1.** 126n
Creek Indians' love of drunkenness noticed by, **17.** 477n
Delamotte travelling companion of, **17.** 477n
HW attends service by, **35.** 118–19
HW dislikes, **2.** 100
HW expects Methodists to decline after death of, **11.** 297
HW hears sermon by, **3.** 159n
(?) Indian's conversation with, **17.** 477
Ingham travels to Georgia with, **17.** 477n
Letter to Dr Middleton on Free Inquiry, A, by, **15.** 297
Madan, follower of, **11.** 12n
opposition to, **11.** 297n
preaches in Moorfields, **25.** 23n
1762 noted by, for conversion of sinners, **22.** 17n
subscription promoted by, for French prisoners, **21.** 367n
Wesley, Charles, travels to Georgia with, **17.** 477n
West St chapel of, **30.** 56n
Wesson. *See* Weston
West, Lt-Col.:
Fitzpatrick succeeds, in army commission, **33.** 7n
West, Miss:
HW mentions, **7.** 142
West, Benjamin (1738–1820), historical painter:
'Delineator' delights, **28.** 329, **29.** 372
—— owned by, **39.** 293

disbelieves in Ireland's MSS, **15**. 321

HW calls painting of George III by, 'sign-post,' **29**. 33

HW's opinion of, **23**. 211, **24**. 93

Houghton pictures to be appraised by, **24**. 441

itemized list owned by, of pictures at Hough-ton, **24**. 441n

pictures by, at Windsor, are 'tawdry,' **11**. 363

Poussin imitated by, in historical paintings, **23**. 210–11

prices of, **23**. 211

Proctor's 'Ixion' admired by, **25**. 577n

St George's Chapel, Windsor, has window designed by, **11**. 363

West, Lady Charlotte (1761–ca 1779), dau. of 2d E. de la Warr:

dancing of, at Duc de Guines's ball, **32**. 116

West, Lady Diana (1731–66), m. (1756) Gen. John Clavering:

(?) Ailesbury, Cts of, to entertain, **37**. 396

death of, **7**. 397

son of, **11**. 48n

West, Lady Frances (1759–77), dau. of 2d E. de la Warr:

dancing of, at Duc de Guines's ball, **32**. 116

West, Hon. George (1733–76), army officer:

(?) Ailesbury, Cts of, to entertain, **37**. 396

Allen carried off by, from opera, **38**. 247

equerry to Edward, D. of York, **37**. 479

HW mentions, **37**. 479

marriage of, **38**. 265

Spencer, Lady Diana, pursued by, **30**. 137

—— will disappoint, by her marriage, **37**. 499–500

West, George John (1791–1869), styled Vct Cantelupe; 5th E. de la Warr, 1795:

uncle of, **11**. 319n

West, Gilbert (1703–56), writer:

Cobham's nephew, **9**. 84

inscriptions by, to Lyttelton and Pitt, **9**. 84

Olympic games described by, **9**. 84

Pindar translated by, **9**. 84, **43**. 115

West, Hon. (later Lady) Henrietta Cecilia (1727–1817), m. (1762) Gen. James Johnston; 'Lady Cecilia Johnston':

Ailesbury, Cts of, asks, to get HW's writings, **38**. 142

(?) —— to entertain, **37**. 396

—— to receive parcels of laces and ribbons from, through HW, **39**. 24

—— visited by, at Park Place, **38**. 165

'anti-divine,' **12**. 148, 152

appearance of, 'starved vulture,' **31**. 26

at Petersham, **33**. 347

Bath visited by, **11**. 289, 350, 352

Berrys told by, about possible house for them, **11**. 26, 42, 55

Campbell, Lady Frederick, visited by, **11**. 265

Catherine II might shock, by preferring crown to husband, **38**. 164

Churchills were to be met by, **38**. 165

Conway to be visited by, at Park Place, **39**. 453

—— told by, of HW's irate letter to oppres-sive parson, **39**. 494

cribbage played at house of, **31**. 298

daughter of, **11**. 237n

'divine,' **12**. 120

fears of, **11**. 284, **12**. 143

French songs of, **38**. 100

George, P. of Wales (George IV), visits, **33**. 299

gossiping tendencies of, **12**. 143, 145

grandson's baptism celebrated by, **12**. 64

HW and, regret Conway's suppers, **38**. 142

HW and Cts of Ailesbury to visit, **38**. 180

HW and Ds of Bedford to dine with, **39**. 456

HW and Majendies call on, **35**. 532

HW calls, 'Lady Ankerstrom,' 'Mother Anker-strom,' **12**. 164, 169

HW dines with, and hears Nuneham news, **35**. 475

HW finds, surrounded by children and animals, **35**. 474

HW has not seen, lately, **35**. 525

HW hears Johnston's praises from, at Con-way's supper, **35**. 305

HW invites: to dinner at SH, **41**. 365–6; to meet Lady Guilford and family, **12**. 164

HW jokes about, **31**. 25–6

HW jokes about effect of Peter III's assassi-nation upon, when newly-wed, **38**. 164

HW jokes about guests of, **31**. 297

HW meets Conway family at house of, to attend play at Ham Common, **33**. 368

HW meets Stonhewer at house of, **29**. 167

HW mentions, **11**. 18, 120, 252, **12**. 152

HW sarcastic about, **12**. 117

HW's correspondence with, **7**. 378, **40**. 241–6, **41**. 365–6

HW sends snuff-box to, **7**. 378

HW's friend, **9**. 28n

HW's letter to be taken by, to Conway, **39**. 420, 422

HW's opinion of, **9**. 270

HW takes, for airings, **12**. 209

HW tells, that she and fiancé are well-suited for a romantic hero and heroine, **40**. 241–6

HW to be visited by, at SH, **38**. 165

HW to entertain, at dinner at SH, **35**. 521

HW to go to, at Ditton, **39**. 390

HW to send partridges to, **12**. 120

HW to visit, with guests, **31**. 217

HW visited by, **11**. 179, 182, 310, **12**. 51, 141–2, 143, 196

HW visits, **11**. 55, 214, 278, **12**. 148, **34**. 62

Hampton the home of, **11**. 23, 284, **12**. 117

health of: cold, **11**. 211; gout, **11**. 214

highwaymen feared by, **33**. 353

Hotham, Miss, visited by, **12**. 154

house of, in South Audley Street, **34**. 142n

inventions of, **33**. 347

lottery at home of, **34**. 142

[West, Hon. Henrietta Cecilia, *continued*]
Lyttelton, Bns, said by, to be in good health, **42.** 200
—— sent parcel by, **7.** 404
Mann has 'flirtation' with, at Florence, **24.** 85
Mendip, Lady, visited by, **12.** 202
Modave gets snuff-box for, **7.** 284
Mordaunt, Lady Mary, visits, at Petersham, **35.** 521
nephew of, **11.** 319
Nuneham, Vct, corresponds with, **35.** 474n
Nuneham Courtenay visited by, **11.** 123
Park Place visited by, **11.** 57, 123, **12.** 169
Piozzi, Mrs, comments upon, **9.** 269n
pregnant, **38.** 179
Seton, Miss, preferred by HW to, **12.** 198
social relations of, with: Anderson, Mrs, **11.** 55; Clive, Mrs, **9.** 269; Coke, Lady Mary, **31.** 297–8; Conway and wife, **11.** 278–9; Damer, Mrs, **11.** 278–9; Farrens, **11.** 278–9; Garrick, Mrs, **11.** 310, 329; HW, **7.** 268, **11.** 48, 153, 350, 351, **12.** 100, **31.** 297–8, **35.** 475; Hervey, Mrs, **11.** 310; Jeffreys, Mrs, **12.** 100; Mt Edgcumbe, Lord, **11.** 278–9; Wheler, Mrs, **12.** 100; Wheler, Sir Charles, **11.** 55, **12.** 100; Wray, Mrs, **12.** 100
son of, **12.** 55n
Tickell, Mrs Richard, invited to lodge with, **12.** 55
Tunbridge visited by, **11.** 89
West, James (1703–72), M.P.; politician; connoisseur; antiquary:
altar-piece owned by, depicting Henry V, **42.** 67n
Antiquarian Society member, **20.** 371n
birth date of, corrected, **43.** 38, 244
Bologna visited by, **20.** 379n
brother-in-law of, **20.** 371
Charles I's execution discussed by, **1.** 8
Cole's poor opinion of, **2.** 334, 354
colic, diarrhœa, and dysentery blamed by, on women, **20.** 379n
collection of: **1.** 8n, 195, 265, **15.** 192n; catalogued by Granger, **1.** 56n; sale of, **1.** 298, 300, 303, 305, 308, 313n, **2.** 354
death of, **1.** 265, 267
Edmund Crouchback's seal bought by, at E. of Oxford's sale, **42.** 266
Granger lists English portrait prints of, **40.** 313
HW buys Henry VIII family group at sale of, **42.** 247–8
HW gives to, a letter to Mann recommending Steavens, **20.** 379
HW informs, of income from Customs place, **26.** 53
HW receives from, Newcastle's proposals about Custom House, **40.** 145
HW's correspondence with, **40.** 311–12
HW sends *Ædes Walpolianæ* to, **20.** 371n
Hereditary Right to the Crown of England Asserted, The, discussed by, **2.** 357
inaccuracy of, **42.** 247–8

Jacqueline's portrait said to be owned by, **42.** 247
Levintz's 'Countess of Desmond' shown by, to Society of Antiquaries, **43.** 59
MS listing officers at Cromwell's funeral owned by, **42.** 127n
MSS of, promised to Ds of Portland and sold to E. of Shelburne, **41.** 253
Martin succeeds, as secretary of the Treasury, **21.** 25
M.P. for St Albans, **20.** 371n
miniature of Q. Margaret owned by, **15.** 122–3
named in Secret Committee lists, **17.** 385
Newcastle's retirement announced by, **22.** 579n
Oxford's library accessible to, **2.** 354, 357
Parliamentary reporting by, **21.** 553n
peerage rumoured for, **38.** 159n
Pelham's secretary, **20.** 371
Pitt (Chatham) accepts a quarter's pension from, **38.** 135
president of Royal Society, **15.** 98n
reversion secured by, for himself and his son, **21.** 26
Rockingham tries to give Navy and Admiralty posts to, to placate Newcastle, **30.** 196n
sale of: **43.** 58; Brander buys Edmund Crouchback's seal at, **42.** 266; HW buys Henry VIII family group at, **42.** 247–8
secretary to the Treasury, **17.** 385n, **20.** 371n
SH visited by, **20.** 371n
treasurer of the Royal Society, **20.** 371n
voted for, as commissioner, **17.** 437
West, James (1742–95), M.P.:
reversion secured for, by his father, **21.** 26
West, Mrs James. *See* Steavens, Sarah
West, Jane (1758–1852), wife of Thomas West; writer:
verses by, **33.** 533
West, John (1693–1766), 7th Bn de la Warr; cr. (1761) E. de la Warr; M.P.:
col. of the Horse Guards, **20.** 137n
daughter of, **9.** 269n, **11.** 18n, **35.** 305n
death of: **7.** 397; leaves vacancy in Bath order, **22.** 417n
earldom granted to, **9.** 341, **21.** 490, **30.** 162
heiress sought by, in City, **35.** 310–11
Mason to visit, **14.** 132
regiment of, **17.** 353
subscription masquerade attended by, dressed as Q. Elizabeth's porter, **20.** 49, **35.** 206
trooper of, prophesies earthquake, **20.** 137, 147, **23.** 261
trooper's wife talks to, of husband's insanity, **20.** 137
York, D. of, entertains, **38.** 476n
West, Hon. John (1729–77), styled Vct Cantelupe 1761–6; 2d E. de la Warr, 1766; army officer:
aide-de-camp to D. of Cumberland, **21.** 78n
(?) Ailesbury, Cts of, to entertain, **37.** 396
Ancaster succeeded by, as Q. Charlotte's Master of the Horse, **22.** 473

chamberlain's post sought by, **10**. 29
Cumberland, D. of, takes, to Hanover, **21**. 78
daughters of, **32**. 116
Effingham's troop of Horse Guards goes to, **38**. 243
Guines's ball attended by, **32**. 116
HW mentions, **9**. 402, 403
Harcourt succeeded by, as chamberlain to Q. Charlotte, **23**. 66
son of, **11**. 319n
vice-chamberlain, at private Court ball, **38**. 143
West, John Richard (1758–95), E. de la Warr, 1783:
marriage of, **5**. 414n
West, Lady Mary. *See* Grey, Lady Mary
West, Mary, m. John Williams:
marriage of, **17**. 5n
Richard West's sister, **13**. 210n
West, Nicolas (1461–1533), Bp of Ely 1515–33:
chapel of, at Ely, **1**. 141
Cole's life of, **1**. 135
West, Richard (ca 1691–1726), lord chancellor of Ireland; M.P.:
birth date of, **43**. 245
daughter of, **17**. 5n
lawyer, **13**. 244
lord chancellor of Ireland, **14**. 234
son of, **13**. 91, **17**. 468n
wife of, **13**. 143n
Williams, secretary and son-in-law of, allegedly has affair with his wife, **13**. 210n, **17**. 5n
West, Richard (1716–42), HW's correspondent; 'Favonius,' 'Zephyrus':
abilities of, appeared early, **28**. 114
'Ad Bacchum' by, sent to HW in letter, **13**. 174
'Ad Pyrrham' by, sent to HW in letter, **13**. 135–6
Ashton's poem on death of, **14**. 234, **17**. 468–70, **28**. 119–20, 124
buried at Hatfield, **14**. 235, **17**. 468n
(?) couplet by, quoted by Conway to HW, **37**. 63, 73
elegy by, sent to Gray, **28**. 97
Gray approves of HW's having set name of, before ode in Dodsley's *Collection*, **14**. 38
——'s conversation with, a failure, **13**. 115
——'s correspondence with, printed by Mason, **28**. 63, 74, 90, 96–7, 99, 105, 107, 114, 124, **43**. 175
——'s *Elegy* written several years after death of, **28**. 117–18
—— sends part of *Agrippina* to, **14**. 12
——'s friendship with, **41**. 268
—— threatens letter in Hebrew to, **13**. 152
'Grotto, The,' by, **13**. 118–19
HW asks, for news of politics and fashions, **13**. 238
HW believes his letters to, destroyed, **28**. 114
HW considers himself inferior to, **28**. 114–15, 122

HW's assistance sought by, for commission in army, **13**. 244–5
HW's correspondence with: **13**. 90–4, 99–101, 107–11, 116–19, 120–36, 144–5, 157–250, **17**. 2n, **43**. 168; MSS of, **36**. 315
HW's love and esteem for, **28**. 99
health of: HW concerned over, **13**. 247–8; improves, **13**. 68; insomnia, **13**. 91; uncertain, **13**. 127
Latin verses of, on Cherokees' visit to Eton, **30**. 94n
law ambitions of, **13**. 244, 247
MS poems by, listed by Gray, **14**. 15–16
Mason revives genius of, **28**. 115, 122
——'s reflections on death of, praised by HW, **28**. 79
member of 'Quadruple Alliance' at Eton, **28**. 120n
memoirs of, in Mason's *Gray*, **28**. 190
military scheme of, **13**. 229, 247
'Monody on the Death of Queen Caroline' by, published in Dodsley's miscellanies, **14**. 234, **17**. 468n, 469n, **28**. 115–16
mother of, said to have affair with Williams, **17**. 5n
Paris visited by, **13**. 247, **43**. 180
Pausanias by: HW comments on, **13**. 241; West acknowledges HW's criticism of, **13**. 244; West sends portion of, to HW, **13**. 239–40, **14**. 249–55
poetic genius of, **17**. 468n
'poetic plumes' borrowed by, **13**. 110
proposal to print edition of poems by Gray and, **14**. 15
reflections by, see Flattery; Poetry, writing of; Translation
reply of, to epigram on Hearne, **14**. 235
returns to Oxford, **13**. 142, 157
'To the Fountain Blandusia' by, sent in letter to HW, **13**. 101
translation from Virgil sent to HW by, **13**. 198, 203
'View from the Thatched House' by, **13**. 157–60
Waldegrave, Cts, quotes, **36**. 290
West, Mrs Richard. *See* Burnet, Elizabeth
West, Sarah (1741–1801), m. (1761) Andrew Archer, 2d Bn Archer, 1768:
Englefield's parody mentions, for painting her face, **33**. 500
HW mentions, **7**. 142
sister of, **7**. 142n
West, Hon. Septimus Henry (1765–93), son of 2d E. de la Warr:
Berrys loved by, **11**. 319
death of, **11**. 319n, **12**. 50
Pisa visited by, **11**. 319
West, Temple (1713–57), naval officer; Cobham's nephew; M.P.:
acquittal of, desired, **20**. 583
Admiralty member, **20**. 25, 583n
Antelope boarded by, for England, **20**. 573n
capt. of the *Dartmouth* and *Warwick*, **18**. 98n

[West, Temple, *continued*]
Francis I's ministers give marks of attention to, 18. 98n
George II coldly receives, as Admiralty lord, 37. 481
—— gives audience to, 20. 583n
government's first witness, at Byng's trial, 20. 583n
Hawke and Saunders sent to Gibraltar to punish, 20. 562
Mann explains Tuscan situation to, 18. 98
—— visited by, in Florence, with naval captains, 18. 98, 99
Pitt (Chatham) selects, for Admiralty, 21. 104n

West, Thomas (1577–1618), 3d (*or* 12th) Bn de la Warr:
Relation of . . . Lord De-La-Warre by: HW mentions, 16. 140; printed by Purchas, 16. 140

West, Thomas (d. 1722), Capt.:
suicide of, 17. 296n
Tom's Coffee-House named after, 17. 296n

West, Thomas (1720–79), Jesuit:
Antiquities of Furness, The, by, 2. 289, 39. 237, 43. 74

West, Mrs Thomas. *See* West, Jane (1758–1852)

Westall, Richard (1765–1836), painter:
Ayton, friend of, 15. 338n
disbelieves in Ireland's MSS, 15. 321
'Hesiod Instructing the Greeks' by, admired by HW, 12. 192–3
Nicol shows HW pictures by, 12. 192
'Sappho Chanting the Hymn of Love' by, 12. 193

Westbrook, Surrey, Oglethorpe's seat:
Lort sees, 16. 196–7

Westcote, Bn. *See* Lyttelton, William Henry

West Drayton, Middlesex:
Spinnage's house at: Montagu asks about, 10. 255–6; stream and fish-ponds near, 10. 256
SH near, 10. 256

Westenra, Jane (d. 1788), m. (1734) John Monckton, 1st Vct Galway:
brag to be played by, out of town, to avoid earthquake, 20. 137

Westerham, Kent:
Wolfe's monument at, 9. 183n

Western, Thomas (1695–1754):
Cole's friendship with, 1. 364n, 43. 62
permits Lagdens to build on waste land, 1. 364

West family:
Stowe visit brings memories of, to HW, 10. 314

West Greenwich:
Kilburne mentions, under Deptford, 16. 80

West Grinstead Park, Sussex:
Burrell of, 1. 162n, 2. 235n, 15. 203n

West Harling, Norfolk:
Croftes of, 2. 219n

West Indiamen (ships), French:
Brest fleet sails to provide convoy for, 12. 73
Howe rumoured to have captured, 12. 75

West India merchants. *See under* Merchant

West Indian, The. See under Cumberland, Richard

West Indian; West Indians:
boroughs contested by, 21. 484
elderly, tells Mann about Tortola lands, 24. 169, 200

West Indies:
Abercromby sails for, 12. 213n
Albemarle's expedition to, 22. 2n, 7n
——'s letters from, not made public, 22. 77–8
American navy half-starves, 24. 229
Blackburne a buccaneer in, 7. 368
Byron may save, if unhurt by Estaing, 24. 447–8
climate of, will not permit British wounded to recover, 25. 278
Clinton said to have embarked and disembarked troops for, 24. 424
Conflans plans to sail from Brest and conduct French convoys from, 20. 579n
Conway averse to dealing with, in state department, 22. 427n
department of, in state department: not relinquished by Pitt, 21. 104; to be restored to Pitt as secretary of state, 21. 488
endangered, 24. 431, 490
England captures wealth in, 19. 92
—— dissatisfied with navigation limits in, established by Aix treaty, 20. 171n
—— may take, when unsuccessful in Europe, 37. 249
—— overruns, 21. 326, 22. 16
—— said to send ships to, 37. 163–4
——'s sugar colonies in, seek to preserve trade with North America, 41. 315n
English capture Dominica in, 21. 516
English expeditions to, 17. 175, 291, 18. 251–2, 278–9, 20. 491, 37. 575n, 580
English fleet from: arrives safely, 24. 391–2, 410, 501; captured, 36. 172; gobbled up by Spaniards, 25. 77–8, 83; safe, 33. 24, 26, 118; taken by Spaniards, 33. 216, 222; *see also under* England: merchant fleets of
English merchants trading with: are to fête Adm. Keppel, 33. 95; Sandwich attacked by, through Germain, for giving captured property to captors, 36. 199n
English ministerial supporters do not want to go to war for, 20. 468
English ships from, not captured, 39. 308
Estaing might be permitted to control, 38. 460–1
fate of, undecided, 33. 215
flowering shrub of, 37. 292
French: American colonies send grain to, 22. 486; negroes needed by, 21. 526n; prizes from, disputed by England with the Dutch, 21. 280
French and Spanish fleets in, 29. 46, 72
French and Spanish fleets unite in, 25. 73

French fleet may attack, **24.** 386

French fleet said to go to, **37.** 556

French fleet sails from Brest to, **25.** 220

French losses in, to be greater than expected, **25.** 286

French may know about undivulged English successes in, **19.** 487–8, 494

French threats to, **37.** 502

governor from Spain in, **17.** 7

governors in, wicked, **21.** 13

Grey, commander-in-chief in, **12.** 91n

Grimaldi rumoured to have Spanish department for, **39.** 36

Guards leave for, **11.** 119

HW fears loss of, **33.** 315–16

HW's interests too narrow to include, **23.** 550–1

HW to entertain guests from, **10.** 107

Halifax demands new secretaryship of state for, **9.** 212

Hamilton and Fitzgerald quarrel in, **37.** 253

heat compared to that of, **33.** 120

Horton carries Nancy Parsons to, **23.** 344n

Kersaint de Coëtnemprem sails to, **21.** 101n

La Clue may try to reach, with Toulon fleet, **21.** 318

Lascelles 'lord' of, **29.** 79

Martin from, **22.** 183n

More, Hannah, wishes Frederik of Denmark had, **31.** 274

naval battles in, **25.** 52, 277–8, 284, **29.** 310n

negro girl to be sent to, by force, from Bristol, **31.** 340

news from, awaited, **21.** 291

Payne from, **23.** 272

Perrier de Salvert sails from Brest to, **20.** 538n

petitions should come from, **41.** 315

Pigot to command English fleet in, **25.** 311n, 318n

Pitt (Chatham) refuses to set up secretaryship of state for, **30.** 135n

probably saved, **24.** 535

Ralegh's expedition to, **14.** 107

regiment for, debated in Parliament, **20.** 531

regiments from, to go to America, **39.** 247

reports from, creditable to England, **33.** 122

Rodney may have gone to, **25.** 17, 24, 99

Ross saved from being sent to, **17.** 244

St Vincent's in, subject of debate, **32.** 99, 100

ship brings news from, to D. of Newcastle, **37.** 246

South Sea Co. sends ship to, annually, **20.** 198n

Spanish fleet sails to, **17.** 17, 20

Spanish ships from, to be intercepted, **37.** 164

Townshend defeats Martinique fleet in, **19.** 186

turnpike bill would be more upsetting than, to Parliament, **23.** 455

war in: HW expected to report upon, **20.** 455; may spread to Europe, **20.** 448

yellow fever in, thought to have killed George Churchill, **34.** 218

Young from, **20.** 327

See also Barbados; Cuba; Dominica; Grenada; Guadeloupe; Havana; Jamaica; Martinique; Porto Rico; St Christopher's (St Kitts); St Vincent; Santa Lucia; Santo Domingo; Tortola

See also under America

West Layton, Yorks:

Robinson of, **11.** 275n, **28.** 35n

Westley. *See* Wesley

West Looe, Cornwall:

HW mentions, **21.** 89

Noel, William, leaves vacancy in, when appointed justice of Common Pleas, **21.** 89n

Trelawny instead of Burrell elected at, **21.** 89n

Westmeath, Ireland:

Roscommon's estate in, now owned by Malone, **42.** 159n

Westminster, Abbot of. *See* Islip, John (d. 1532)

Westminster, Dean of. *See* Pearce, Zachary (1690–1774); Sprat, Thomas (1635–1713); Thomas, John (1712–93)

Westminster, E. of. *See* Murray, Alexander (1712–78)

Westminster, High Bailiff of. *See* Corbett, Thomas; Leigh, Peter; Lever, John

Westminster, M. of. *See* Grosvenor, Robert

Westminster, Edward de. *See* Fitz-Odo, Edward

Westminster, London:

aqueduct for, **40.** 223

Blakiston leads independent electors of, **20.** 261n

bridge built across Thames from Woolstaple in, to Surrey, **20.** 108n

Carter's address in, **16.** 194

chimpanzee to represent, in HW's newspaper parody, **9.** 127

Clive's house in, receives funds from Leadenhall St, **23.** 400n

Court candidates elected by, **19.** 425

Court party cannot find candidate for, **17.** 257

crowd at, awaits Wilkes, **23.** 13

dirt of, **29.** 145

election at: **19.** 425n, **34.** 11–12, 13, **36.** 251, **43.** 368; almost contested, **25.** 284–5; Bedford, D. of, pays for, **20.** 112–13; Burgoyne recommends Petersham as candidate for, **32.** 336; Court institutes scrutiny for, in favour of Wray, to exclude C. J. Fox, **25.** 563n; disputed in Parliament, **38.** 315; Fox, C. J., and Hood oppose Tooke in, **39.** 472–3; Fox, C. J., candidate for, **25.** 11; Fox, C. J., has temporary majority in, **39.** 410; Fox, C. J., likely to be M.P. for, **36.** 174; Fox, C. J., wins, **36.** 177; Fox, C. J., wins though a petition is presented against him, **25.** 488n; Fox, Henry, and Pitt (Chatham) demand investigation of delay in scrutiny at, **20.** 122–3; Gower pays for scrutiny at, **20.** 113; Hood and C. J. Fox returned for, **25.** 563; Hood and Wray oppose C. J.

[Westminster, London, *continued*]
Fox in, **25.** 489, 490–1; Hood's candidacy for, withdrawn, **25.** 585; House of Commons examines, **25.** 502; Mahon and Cotes oppose Court in, **39.** 186; Mann, Horace II, eager about, **25.** 505; Middlesex election bodes ill for, **20.** 131; Mountmorres a candidate for, **28.** 174; Mountmorres defeated as Wilkes's candidate for, **24.** 52; Northumberland, Ds of, wins, for her son and Lord Thomas Clinton, **24.** 51–2; Parliament to settle, **17.** 220, 233, 246, 247, 250, 272, 298, 322; Perceval carries, **17.** 272, **20.** 31; Percy and Lord Thomas Clinton triumphant in, **39.** 196; petitions over, **20.** 223n; returning officers for, **17.** 272n; satiric prints of, **25.** 496; scrutiny at, is England's chief topic, **36.** 231; scrutiny of, **20.** 107–8, 113, 122–3, 156, 223–4; scrutiny of, demolished, **25.** 562; scrutiny of, provoked by royal vengeance, **25.** 565; Sundon's, contested, **17.** 246, 250–2; Trentham opposed by Vandeput in, **20.** 107n; Trentham to be rechosen at, **20.** 100n; Trentham wins, **20.** 107, 156; Wilkes loses, **39.** 196

Exchequer in, **42.** 198
fortune-teller at, **31.** 280
Fox, C. J., has partisans at Amsterdam and Versailles as well as at, **25.** 495–6
Gordon riots begin in, **29.** 51
Guildhall in, **33.** 177
Hare's witticism on, **33.** 7
Hertford too old to enjoy a political contest at, **38.** 336
High Bailiff defines electors at, **20.** 108n
Hood's club in, **34.** 31n
illuminated: **33.** 92–3; for Keppel's arrival, **24.** 443–4, 446
independent electors of, **19.** 387, **20.** 223
Lincoln, E. of, demands election scrutiny for, **36.** 177
London aldermen chosen at, **35.** 334
North ministry may have no candidates for, **24.** 45n
Northumberland, D. of, subscribes for militia to electors of, **33.** 109
Onslow's speech rebuking justices of the peace for election in, **30.** 301n
O'Toole lives in, **1.** 62n
Parliamentary members from, vote for address, **18.** 125
petitions from: **7.** 367; presented by Cooke and Egremont, **20.** 223–4, 235; presented by Pulteney, **17.** 232–3, 298; voted at meeting, **25.** 10–11
Pitt (Chatham) as little heard as the clock at, **37.** 444
Pitt, William II, nominated by, **25.** 278
punch to be drunk at, to celebrate Cherbourg's capture, **21.** 227
remonstrance to Parliament being prepared by, **25.** 218

St John's Church in, Churchill's father was curate at, **7.** 374
Sandys vacates seat for, in Parliament, **23.** 206
theatre in, used by D. of York, Lady Stanhope, and Delavals, **22.** 521
Tracy pursues girls through, **9.** 75
Trinity Hospital's letters patent obtained at, **16.** 83
weavers' mob in, **38.** 559
Wilkes in political control of, **24.** 45

Westminster, Treaty of:
England and Russia sign, **37.** 428, 429
Nivernais's embassy to Prussia made ridiculous by, **20.** 542n
Parallèle de la conduite du Roi contains extract from, **21.** 235n
secret article of, excludes Austrian Netherlands, **20.** 523n

Westminster Abbey (Collegiate Church of St Peter):
abbot of, supposed to be in painting of Henry VII's marriage, **20.** 390
Abergavenny and Selwyn visit, **20.** 181
altar-piece at, **2.** 185, 186n
ambassadors lie unburied at, **22.** 216
ampulla kept in, **14.** 78
Ayloffe's *Account of Some Ancient Monuments in*, **2.** 215
Bath order's installation held in, **20.** 71n, **30.** 82
Blencowe would spurn antiquities of, **10.** 76
Caroline, Q., buried in, **13.** 145n
Caxton may have worked in precincts, **16.** 3
chapter of: and choir, **9.** 322; and dean, **30.** 159; sells spaces for monuments, **38.** 111
Charlotte, Q., has retiring-chamber behind altar of, **21.** 535
Chesterfield's heir to forfeit sums to, if he races or gambles, **32.** 113n
Coke, Lady Mary, visits burial vaults in, when Ps Louisa dies, **24.** 14
Cole objects to pagan mythology in monuments in, **10.** 339–40
Crane, prebendary of, **9.** 399n
Dean of: and chapter, **30.** 159; at opening of Edward I's tomb, **1.** 384n
dedicated to St Peter, **24.** 382n
Edward I's tomb in, opened, **1.** 384n, **24.** 4
Edward III's and consort's effigies in, **12.** 105
Edward the Confessor grants Windsor to, **40.** 223
——'s chapel in, **42.** 87
——'s shrine in, **1.** 244, **2.** 185, 186n, 370
Elizabeth, Ps, to be buried in, **38.** 27n
epitaphs in, do not make epic, **15.** 69
funeral effigies in; **18.** 193n; restored, to attract sight-seers, **38.** 111
Garrick to be buried in, **24.** 435
George II's funeral in, **9.** 322–3
George III refuses burial permit for Ps Carolina of Gloucester in, **36.** 114n

——'s coronation in, **21**. 534–6, **38**. 121–2

glass at, painted by Price, **1**. 21n, 201n

Gray's monument in, **41**. 387

HW does not care to visit, in October, **30**. 82

HW fears to pass schoolboys to see mother's monument in, **35**. 178

HW loves, more than levees, **33**. 172

HW prefers, to Stoke Poges or Pembroke College, for Gray's monument, **28**. 276

HW's design for altar-piece for, **28**. 214, 216

HW's shyness prevents his visiting, **10**. 77n

Handel commemoration in, **11**. 273, **25**. 647–8

——'s music in, **33**. 463

Hargrave's tomb in, provokes epigram, **38**. 31

Henry VII's chapel in: **9**. 322–3; ceiling of, imitated for SH Gallery, **10**. 53; Walpole, Lady, commemorated by monument in, **13**. 25–6, **17**. 212n, **18**. 347, **22**. 98n, **40**. 80

Hough's tomb at Worcester in style of, **35**. 151

Ibbot, prebendary of, **41**. 263n

Islip Chapel in: Bath, E. of, buys Hatton Vault in, and offers to sell unused space in it, **10**. 68; Chatham's monument in, **32**. 98n; stained glass from, **35**. 132

Little Cloisters in, Wilson's address, **41**. 139

Louisbourg colours to be carried to, **37**. 567

Margaret of Anjou crowned in, **14**. 71

Mary, Q. of Scots's effigy in, **15**. 122–3

——'s tomb in, **42**. 321

monks of, **14**. 175

Northesk takes daughters to, **35**. 373

Onslow calls, chapel of ancient English kings, **30**. 291n

Percy family vault in St Nicholas's Chapel in, **41**. 411n

Pitt (Chatham) may be buried in, **24**. 382

'Poets' Corner' in, **28**. 21

Pope's poem on man who shows the tombs in, **32**. 302, **33**. 172

proposal to erect monument in, to Sir C. H. Williams, **13**. 35, **30**. 159

'ragged regiment' at, **9**. 373–4

revenues from Coronation spectators at, **21**. 536

Richard II's effigy in, **12**. 105

Richmond's corpse exhumed from, **20**. 182

'robbed to pay Paul,' **2**. 80

Rochester, Bp of, has gallery in, **25**. 648

St-Denis excels, in ancient monuments, **13**. 163

St Nicholas's chapel in, falling stone from, kills man at Lady Elizabeth Percy's funeral, **38**. 111

Sebert, K., depicted in, **2**. 183, 184–5

sexton shows tombs at, **37**. 107

sightseers at, are referred to HW for information, **9**. 374

spectres in 'lone aisles' of, **30**. 304

Sprat, dean of, **29**. 259n

statues in, **16**. 89, **38**. 126

Suckling, prebendary of, **9**. 153n

tombs and monuments in: 'Coverley, Sir Roger de,' wishes to converse with, **35**. 562; HW does not wish to show, to Fleury, **22**. 135; MS relating to, **28**. 166; object of curiosity to foreigners, **30**. 176; of Anne of Cleves, **2**. 77, 185; of Edward I, **1**. 384n, 24. 4; of Edward III, **2**. 49; of Elizabeth I, **2**. 202; of Gay, **19**. 195n; of Gray, **2**. 101, 103, **28**. 21, **41**. 387; of Mary, Q. of Scots, **42**. 321; of Monck, **38**. 126; of Newton and Shakespeare, by Kent, **35**. 151; of one related to kings, **32**. 312–13; of Roger Townshend, **21**. 421n, **40**. 166–7; of Valence, **38**. 110, **40**. 200–1; of Wolfe, **21**. 421n, **38**. 110, **40**. 200–1; prints of, **2**. 215; shown daily, **38**. 111; shown to visitors, **20**. 181–2

Tudor a monk in, **42**. 20

unpleasant in October for ague victims, **30**. 82

Valence's tomb in, said to be replaced by Wolfe's, **38**. 110, **40**. 200–1

Wales, Augusta, Ps of, erects monument to Stephen Hales in, **20**. 347n

William I gives silver for completing, **40**. 223

Williams, Sir C. H., may have monument in, **13**. 35, **30**. 159

Westminster Association:

Jebb the orator of, **25**. 36n

Westminster Bridge:

Drury Lane Theatre visible from, **12**. 56

HW and Conway cross, on way to Vauxhall, **10**. 279

Keppel family drive over, after Gordon riots, **33**. 191

Pembroke, E. of, asked about 'resting' of, **9**. 52

—— promotes construction of, **9**. 52n

pier of, sinks, **20**. 108

settling of, **9**. 52

Westminster Hall, Westminster, London:

approach to House of Commons through, **17**. 300

Bedford, Grosvenor, has house at gate of, **38**. 123

Byron may not be tried in, **38**. 503

constables, horse guards, and foot guards to protect, during Wilkes's trial, **23**. 12

Coronation banquet in, **9**. 386–9, **21**. 535, **32**. 2

Coronation procession leaves from, and returns to it, **38**. 121–3, 126–7

deeds for breaking Linton entail to be presented at, **24**. 258, 259

Estcourt's ballad mentions, **33**. 215

Ewen-Stanley litigation tried in, **1**. 362

Exchequer building adjoins, **17**. 300n

explosion of gunpowder in, **13**. 104

Ferrers tried in, **9**. 272, **13**. 35n, **21**. 367, 387–9

floor of, raised, **16**. 198

Fox, C. J., harangues meeting at, for voting a petition, **25**. 10–11

[Westminster Hall, *continued*]
galleries in: Lincoln, E. of, has, **9.** 280, 386, **10.** 148, 149; Orford, 2d E. of, has, **19.** 284–5
Gordon, Lord George, tried in, **29.** 103
HW asks Harcourt for ticket to, for Hastings's trial, **35.** 541
HW jokes about, **10.** 253
HW's case against Bisshopp family to be tried in, **35.** 602
HW's reasons for not signing petition at, for reform in expenditure of public money, **35.** 50
Hardinge dares not steal away from, to SH, **35.** 578
—— lacks courage in, **35.** 563
Hastings's trial at: **11.** 273; Sheridan should worry Catherine II and Joseph II at, **35.** 392; Sheridan's speech at, **35.** 391n
illuminated and heated for chairs to pass through, to Exchequer House assembly, **37.** 454
Jebb's rôle at, **25.** 23, 36
Kingston, Ds of, may be tried at, **24.** 87, 151, 187, **32.** 285, **39.** 272–3
—— tried in, **24.** 191–3, 195–6
law suit in, over wager on D. of Cumberland's weight, **20.** 208–9
legal business connected with, **32.** 132
Mme du Deffand's chamber might have resembled, **6.** 386
Middlesex's trial in, **20.** 4–5
Montagu, D. of, forced to produce wife in, **25.** 546n
noble when illuminated, **38.** 126
Onslow calls, parlour of ancient English kings, **30.** 291n
Painted Chamber in, **9.** 388
papers posted at, **9.** 325
Parliamentary petition agreed on at, **25.** 23n
passage from, hung with green baize and lamps, **37.** 454
rebel lords tried in, **9.** 37, 388, **19.** 280–6
satiric prints sufficient to cover, **38.** 180
scaffolds in, for trial of rebel lords, **9.** 37
Sheridan speaks in, against Hastings, **42.** 221n
standards of Blenheim hung in, **25.** 337
statue of Saxon king found under, **16.** 198
Talbot backs horse down, **38.** 128
ticket to, for Coronation, **40.** 202
Townsend, Alderman James, tried in, **23.** 346n
trophies in, **18.** 248, **37.** 200
West's verses mention, **14.** 15
Wilkes's trial in, **23.** 11–13, 29–30
Young Pretender attends Coronation in, **11.** 296
Westminster Hall Gate:
Constitutional Queries burnt at, by hangman, **20.** 222n
near HW's Exchequer house, in Palace Yard, **40.** 87
Westminster Hospital:

Westminster Abbey concerts for benefit of, **25.** 647n
Westminster Palace:
Court of Requests in: Fox, Henry, jokes about releasing HW's 'Muse' in, **30.** 102; HW is silly as soon as he enters, **30.** 104; joins House of Lords and House of Commons, **20.** 123n; Winnington calls praise in, true test of woman's beauty, **30.** 102
House of Commons in: formerly St Stephen's Chapel, **30.** 291n; Onslow calls, private oratory for servants of ancient English kings, **30.** 291n
House of Lords in: HW visits, to hear Onslow's final prorogation speech, **30.** 164; women fill, and stand on benches, at prorogation, **30.** 164
Richard III dates letter from, **41.** 122
Westminster School:
Abercorn at, **42.** 89
Batt at, **11.** 17n
Bedford, Grosvenor Charles and Horace W., of, **42.** 492
Bunbury's drawings done at, **32.** 304n, **34.** 84n
Dashkov to enter, **23.** 242
Freind, headmaster of, **30.** 290
HW receives ticket to Latin play at, **12.** 214
Johnson, former master of, **20.** 345
Markham, headmaster of, **29.** 155n
——'s scholars at, **29.** 155n
Molesworth at, **22.** 140
Murray and Stone at, **20.** 345
nobility at, **32.** 316
schoolboys at: at Vcts Townshend's, **37.** 334; Conway, Anne Seymour, must not keep dormitory at Whitehall for, **37.** 334; epigram on Abbey tomb written by, **38.** 31; HW deterred from visiting Abbey for fear of, **10.** 77n, **35.** 178; to study *Fingal*, **9.** 407
Sprat not educated at, **29.** 259
Westmonasterium. See under Dart, Rev. John
Westmorland, Cts of. *See* Brudenell, Lady Dorothy (ca 1647–1740); Cavendish, Mary (1698–1778); Child, Sarah Anne (ca 1764–93); Cobham, Margaret (d. ca 1470); Gordon, Lady Susan (ca 1746–1814); Mildmay, Mary (ca 1582–1640); Vere, Mary (ca 1611–69)
Westmorland, E. of. *See* Fane, Sir Francis (1580–1629); Fane, John (1685–1762); Fane, John (1759–1841); Fane, Mildmay (1602–66)
Westmorland, county of:
deserted wife left at family mansion in, **11.** 138
lakes of, visited by Mason and Stonhewer, **28.** 106, 108
militia of, in Carlisle, **19.** 159
slate from, on Mason's house, damaged by wind, **28.** 484
West Norfolk Regiment:
encamped on Suffolk coast, **42.** 334n
Westoe Lodge, Cambs:
Keene of, **2.** 57n

Weston, Anne (ca 1747–1838), m. (1774) Horace St Paul:
  health of, 6. 260, 262
  marriage of, 6. *18*, 43. 96
  social relations of, in Paris, 6. 335, 7. 351
  Versailles visited by, 7. 343
Weston, Edward (1703–70), didactic writer:
  HW's mentions of, corrected, 13. 4n, 43. 169
  Junius attacks, 36. 52
  tutor to HW and Townshends, 13. *3–4*
  Walpole, Lady, to receive regards of, 36. 2
  Wolters corresponds with, on political matters, 19. 507n
Weston, Mrs Edward. *See* Fountayne, Anne; Patrick, Penelope
Weston, Richard (ca 1555–1615), jailer:
  executed at Tyburn for Overbury's murder, 16. 163
  Holles fined and imprisoned for conference with, 16. 163
Weston, Richard (1577–1635), cr. (1628) Bn Weston, (1633) E. of Portland; lord high treasurer 1628–35:
  memorandum about Cæsar frightens, 37. 437
  monument to, at Winchester, 35. 250
  portrait of, at Standon, 40. 198
Weston, Stephen (1665–1742), D.D.: Bp of Exeter, 1724:
  death of, 17. 279
  Eton career of, 17. 279n
  son of, 13. *3–4*
  Walpole, Sir Robert, under, at Eton, 17. 279n
Weston, Thomas (1737–76), actor:
  Le Texier has talent of, 39. 273
Weston. *See also* Livingston
Weston, Warwickshire:
  HW visits, 10. 264n, 41. 163n
  Sheldon of, 12. 101n, 16. 195n, 42. 443
  Sheldon sale at, 16. 198
Weston, Le. *See* Livingston
Westphalia:
  army in, will mutiny in cold weather, 21. 435
  Belle-Isle may march to, 26. 23
  Crown Pt politically situated in, 21. 369
  Dauphiness has grace and accent of, 35. 113
  English reverses in, 21. 544
  France to evacuate her conquests in, 21. 527n
  HW jokes about, 9. 378
  Hanover may raise recruits in, 21. 195
  Lippe-Buckeburg leaves, 22. 43
  princes of, could not divert HW from welcoming Berrys, 12. 88
  Theodore of Corsica from, 40. 192
  Twickenham as barren as, 35. 315
'Westphalia':
  HW's nickname for Ham, 31. 191
Westphalia, Treaty of:
  France and Austria renew, in Treaty of Versailles, 21. 96n
  France and Sweden make treaty to guarantee, 21. 96n
  France pretends to be guardian of, 21. 96
West Pt, New York:

  Arnold's plot to betray, to English army, 25. 98n, 29. 124n
West Sheen, Surrey:
  lodge at, 10. 131n
  See also Richmond Palace
West St, London:
  Wesley's chapel in, 30. 56n
Westwick, Norfolk:
  HW's will mentions, 30. 344
Westwood, ——, of Birmingham:
  Conway's experiments to be judged by, 39. 552
Westwood, Pakington's seat:
  Chinese style of, 40. 14
  lake and landscaping at, 40. 14
  Whaley and Dodd visit, 40. 14
Westwood Gate, Knotting, Beds:
  road from, to Market Harborough, 20. 112n
Westwood Park, Worcs:
  Perrot's portrait said to be at, 40. 271, 272
'Wet brown paper.' *See under* Paper
Wetenhall, Edward (1636–1713), Bp of Cork and Ross, 1679, of Kilmore and Ardagh, 1699:
  Wettenhalls recover estate of, 9. 174
  Whetenhall, Mrs Thomas, related to, 9. 174
Wetenhall. *See also* Wettenhall; Whetenhall
Wetherall. *See* Weatherall
Wetherby, Yorks:
  Wade approaches, 19. 173–4
Wettenhall, Nathaniel:
  burial of, 10. 11n
  genealogy of, 10. 352
  HW asks, to seek chairs, 9. 384
  HW entertains, at SH, 9. 233, 10. 121–2
  HW not well known by, 10. 122
  HW sends compliments to, 9. 204, 10. 225
  HW to entertain, at SH, 9. 231
  HW to receive compliments of, 10. 228
  health of, gout, 9. 293
  Montagu, George, brother-in-law of, 9. 118n
  —— to be visited by, at Greatworth, 9. 286, 287, 10. 246
  —— visited by, at Greatworth, 10. 126
  —— visits, at Hankelow, 10. 227
  returns from Greatworth to Hankelow, 9. 293
  SH praised by, 10. 121–2
  Wetenhall estate recovered by, 9. 174
  wife of, 9. 12n, 111n
Wettenhall, Mrs Nathaniel. *See* Montagu, Arabella
Wettenhall. *See also* Wetenhall; Whetenhall
Wexford, Ireland:
  Ponsonbys lose election in, 37. 422–3
Weybridge, Surrey:
  D——, Lady, wishes to go to, 35. 503
  Oatlands near, 9. 169n, 12. 11n
  strolling players in barn at, patronized by Ds of York, 39. 493
  wedding at, 12. 11n
Weyland, Mark (d. 1797), director of Bank of England:
  SH visited by, 12. 235

Weymouth, Vct. *See* Thynne, Thomas (ca 1640–1714); Thynne, Thomas (1734–96)

Weymouth, Vcts. *See* Bentinck, Lady Elizabeth Cavendish (1735–1825); Byng, Hon. Isabella Elizabeth (1773–1830)

Weymouth, Dorset:
Chewtons to meet Waldegrave sisters at, **35.** 522
election at, **17.** 420, 475
English expedition sails from, **21.** 244
HW mistakes Lymington for, **11.** 84, 86
Jordan, mayor of, rewarded with office, **17.** 420n
visitors to: Charlotte, Q., **11.** 32n, 365n, **12.** 198n; Chewton, Lady, **33.** 370; George III, **11.** 32n, 350, 365n; Gloucester, D. and Ds of, **25.** 203; Moira, **12.** 156n; princesses, **11.** 365n
'world' at, **11.** 365

Weymouth, English ship:
Vincent, captain of, dismissed, **21.** 296n

Whaddon, Bucks:
Eyre, vicar of, **1.** 36n

Whaddon Hall, Bucks:
Willis, Browne, lives at, **2.** 326

Whale; whales:
Brown, Lady, as a, **30.** 295
HW jokes about, **39.** 503
ocean infested by, **34.** 155
prints of, **35.** 151

Whaley, Mrs:
Conway hears of, from Hester Thrower, **37.** 62

Whaley, John (1710–45), Fellow of King's College, Cambridge; poet:
Cole's account of, **40.** 3n
Conway sends compliments to, **37.** 19, 36
Davies rambles with, **40.** 42
Dodd's correspondence with, **40.** 43
—'s tutor, **2.** 299n
— tours southern and western England with, **40.** 3–6, 8–17
Dryden's (?) 'Cornaro and the Turk' imitated by, in verse to be sent to HW, **40.** 43–4
epigrams by, **15.** 3n, **40.** 44
HW's correspondence with, **40.** 3–6, 8–17, 22–3, 42–4, 48–50
HW's tutor, **13.** 5, **40.** 50n
'Journey to Houghton' by: HW forgets, **15.** 228n; printed in HW's *Ædes Walpolianæ*, **15.** 228n, **20.** 69; shown to Sir Robert Walpole, **40.** 42; Whaley encloses second part of, to HW, **40.** 49
Kingsland to be visited by, **40.** 42
Poems by, **2.** 299n, **43.** 75
West sends service to, **13.** 100

Whaley. *See also* Whalley

Whalley, Mrs. *See* Jones, Elizabeth

Whalley, John (ca 1699–1748), D.D.; Master of Peterhouse 1733–48:
dies of stone, **15.** 315
Gray's quarrel with, **14.** 41–2

'idle tale' propagated by, about his antagonists, **14.** 4
master of Peterhouse, **15.** 315
Turner belongs to party of, **14.** 1

Whalley, Peter (1722–91):
Bridges's *History and Antiquities of Northamptonshire* edited by, **1.** 7, **2.** 277

Whalley, Thomas Sedgwick (1746–1828), D.D.; traveller and versifier:
More, Hannah, cares for, at Cowslip Green, **31.** 307
(?) — jokes about literary activities of, **31.** 280
wife driven by, in phaeton, **31.** 307
wife's accident distresses, **31.** 307

Whaplode, Lincs:
Walpole not to be confused with, **1.** 378
Walpoles at, **1.** 376n

Whaplode family:
arms of, **1.** 376, 378

Wharncliffe, Yorks:
Wortley Montagu builds lodge at, **35.** 269, **43.** 176

Wharncliffe Lodge:
HW describes, **35.** 268–9

Wharton, Bns. *See* Clifford, Lady Anne (d. 1592); Loftus, Lucy (ca 1670–1717); Wharton, Lady Jane (d. 1761)

Wharton, Cts and Marchioness of. *See* Loftus, Lucy (ca 1670–1717)

Wharton, Gov.:
HW mentions, **38.** 216

Wharton, Sir George (1617–81), 1st Bt; writer:
print of, **1.** 179

Wharton, Rev. Henry (1664–95):
Anglia sacra by, **1.** 15, 16

Wharton, Lady Jane (d. 1761), m. 1 John Holt; m. 2 (1733) Robert Coke; Bns Wharton, s.j., 1738:
brother's letter to, **34.** 6n
death of, **9.** 332
marriages of, **34.** 256
resembles mother's lover, **34.** 256
wealth of, **9.** 332

Wharton, Philip (1613–96), 4th Bn Wharton, 1625:
brother of, **2.** 169n
portrait of, at Wrest, **39.** 139n

Wharton, Philip (1698–1731), 2d M. of Wharton, 1715; cr. (1718) D. of Wharton:
arrested in St James's Park for singing Jacobite song, **42.** 10n
ballad by, **29.** 247, 250, 252, **42.** 10
biographies of, worthless, **16.** 7
convent supposedly entered by, **16.** 6–7
death of, **16.** 6–7
exploits of, well known to HW after Duke left England, **42.** 10
HW confirms story of, **15.** 111
HW's account of, in *Royal and Noble Authors*, **13.** 32, **29.** 294
Lely's portrait of Vane from collection of, **42.** 127–8

Life and Writings of, HW's copy of, **16.** 7n
Poetical Works of, reprint of *Whartoniana*, **16.** 7n
print of, **40.** 237
pun by, **7.** 361
rouses guardian to borrow pin, **34.** 94
sister of, **34.** 256
sister's letter from, **34.** 6n
Stafford, Cts of, friend of, **9.** 119
Twickenham house of, **9.** 119, **42.** 488, 489
Wharton, Samuel:
petition by, for American lands, rejected, **23.** 422n
Wharton, Sir Thomas (1610–84), Kt:
portrait of, **2.** 169
Wharton, Thomas (1648–1716), cr. (1706) E. and (1715) M. of Wharton:
daughter of, **9.** 332n
father of, **39.** 139n
Van Dycks and Lelys collected by, **42.** 126n
Wharton, Thomas (1717–94), M.D.; Gray's friend and correspondent:
Gray's correspondence with, **28.** 64, 69n
—— visited by, **14.** 58
—— visits, **14.** 97
HW is glad to become acquainted with, **29.** 16
Wharton. *See also* Warton
Wharton family:
Walpole, Sir Robert, bought collection of Van Dycks and Lelys belonging to, **30.** 371
Winchendon House, seat of, **30.** 371
Whartoniana:
worthless, **16.** 7n
What D'Ye Call It, The. See under Gay, John
Whateley, Kemble (d. 1780):
HW's accounts with Mrs Coade for artificial stone examined by, **41.** 227, 229
Whately, Thomas (ca 1728–72), politician; M.P.; writer:
Castle Rising allotted to, **36.** 47
Dalrymple, Sir John, friend of, **28.** 92
Grenville entrusts Parliamentary faction to, **39.** 100n
Lort told by, of changed title of book, **16.** 191
Observations on Modern Gardening by: **42.** 131; French and German translations of, **16.** 191, **32.** 55, **35.** 126; Morel's *Théorie des jardins* imitates, **16.** 190
Whately, William (d. 1782), banker:
Temple's duel with, **32.** 167
Whatly. *See* Whateley; Whately
Wheat:
abundance of, in England, **12.** 142, 153
Birmingham millers and engrossers riot on price of, **20.** 585n
Cole raises, **1.** 276
embargo on, Bill of Rights for victims of, **22.** 473n
embargo on export of, **22.** 455n, **35.** 320
England sends quarters of, to Portugal, **20.** 512n
Italian, **1.** 282

price of: lowered, **22.** 460n; makes hair powder expensive, **39.** 184; rises in England, **22.** 455
Turgot's restrictions on, **6.** 321
Wheate, Mrs:
SH visited by, **12.** 240
Wheate, Sir Jacob (ca 1746–83), 5th Bt; naval officer:
brings news, **28.** 457n
Hardy sends news by, **24.** 506n
Sandwich does not believe account by, of combined fleets, **28.** 461
Wheatfield, Mrs, of Ditton:
SH visited by, **12.** 233
Wheatly, Miss, of Walsall:
Shenstone praises, **1.** 309n
Wheatly. *See also* Whately
Wheatsheaf:
brown boar fed with, as if on china, **37.** 348
Wheble, John (1746–1820), publisher of the *Middlesex Journal*:
arrest of, **23.** 279–80
Crosby refuses to arrest, **14.** 189n
Wheel; wheels:
at D. of Richmond's fireworks, **20.** 56
of chaise, **20.** 483
officers broken upon, **21.** 382
Wheelbarrow; wheelbarrows:
Ailesbury, Cts of, envisions daughter in, at SH, **37.** 338
when carrying dead leaves is more lively than HW, **34.** 192
Wheel-chair; wheel-chairs:
gout-sufferers use, at Stowe, **22.** 247
Harrises meet in, **33.** 525
Wheeler, Edward (d. 1761), capt. of the *Isis*:
news brought by, **37.** 555
Wheeler, Mrs John. *See* Winnington, Anne
Wheeler. *See also* Wheler
Wheler, Rev. Sir Charles (1730–1821), 7th Bt, 1799:
HW visited by, **11.** (?) 89, **12.** 21
Johnston, Lady Cecilia, visited by, **11.** (?) 55, **12.** 100
Nivernais's *Jardins modernes* given to, **12.** 260
Richmond visited by, **12.** 21
SH visited by, **12.** 228, 233
SH visitors sent by, **12.** 228
Wheler, Mrs Charles (later Lady). *See* Strange, Lucy
Wheler, Sir George (1650–1723), Kt, 1682:
Journey into Greece, A, by: HW buys, **16.** 158; Winchilsea annotates, **16.** 158
Wheler. *See also* Wheeler
'When Fanny blooming fair.' *See under* Stanhope, Philip Dormer, E. of Chesterfield
'When mitred masters':
HW's verses to Lady Ossory, beginning, **33.** 204
'When the moon casts,' lines by (?) HW:
HW quotes, **12.** 263

'When Theseus from the maid he ruin'd fled,' lines by HW:
  HW quotes, 12. 269
'Where do wit and memory dwell':
  HW's lines on Mme du Deffand, beginning, 8. 55
Wherry; wherries:
  at Richmond regatta, 32. 317n
  Howe does not lose one, 25. 337
  Irish, 24. 302n
  six, loaded with the Court's baggage, 18. 69n
Whetenhall, Thomas:
  Baronetage praises, 9. 118–19
  Gramont's memoirs disparage, 9. 118–19
Whetenhall, Mrs Thomas. See Bedingfield, Elizabeth
Whetenhall. See also Wetenhall; Wettenhall
Whey:
  Berrys drink, 11. 167–8
  Walpole, Sir Edward, takes, 25. 463
  See also Goat's whey
Whichenovre. See Wichnor
Whifield. See Whitefield
'Whig, little.' See Churchill, Anne, Ds of Sunderland
Whig; Whigs:
  abolition of prime ministers would please, 33. 392
  administration of, unlikely, 33. 343
  aldermen of, shun presentation of petition from City of London, 20. 585n
  American, estimated by Chatham, 39. 246
  Anderson's family belongs to, 16. 316
  An Unconnected Whig's Address to the Public pleases HW, 32. 383
  Argyll pleases, by leaving Court, 17. 366
  at Sidney Sussex College, Cambridge, 13. 58
  authors, mentioned by Dr Johnson, 11. 13
  Balchen firm as, 18. 458
  Bedford, D. of, leader of, 17. 247n
  Broad Bottom coalition dupes, 17. 337
  Burke's letter to, 11. 300
  Cambridge, R. O., family of, are, 13. 111
  Cavendish proposes Portland and C. J. Fox as leaders of, 29. 261
  centennial of 1688 to be celebrated by, 34. 31n
  Charles VI's ministers offered bribes by, 7. 354
  Cheshire, suspected by Portland, 43. 305
  Cole's friends, 2. 86
  Conway deserted by, in East India Co. inquiry, 41. 65n
  Conway unattached to either faction of, 25. 294
  Cotton professes to be, 17. 363
  Dalrymple thinks every public man of, deserves hanging, 35. 555
  defection of, mercenary, 29. 27
  discontented, come into place at Sir Robert Walpole's fall, 17. 347n
  divided though triumphant, 35. 518
  English-French commercial treaty opposed by, 36. 249n

English-French commercial treaty should be approved by, 33. 546
Fox, C. J., gives patronage to, by his India Bill, 36. 218n
Fox, Henry, supported by, 20. 412
French, Robert, is, in Irish House of Commons, 37. 410
French parliaments grow into, 38. 245
George II to cherish, 17. 339
Gordon, Thomas, writes for, 15. 293
Grant clan leans towards, 19. 233
HW a, 33. 158
HW a, even in sleep, 33. 339
HW and Ps Amelia discuss, 10. 49–50
HW as, hates all spoils but those of honour, 38. 323
HW describes differences between Tories and, 28. 411–12
HW goes to Parliament only from devotion to, 38. 243
HW impartial towards, 15. 94
HW is, to the backbone, 37. 406
HW likes, for upholding freedom of press, 16. 30
HW settled as, 25. 40
HW's letters to, 9. 305
HW's pains alternate with loyalty as, 33. 163
HW's verses mention, 31. 15
HW the only unadulterated, 33. 391
HW thinks Hertford is betraying, 38. 417
Hampden a 'buffoon,' 20. 224
Hartington calls for, 35. 165–6
Hertford professes principles of, 38. 417
Hessian troops may be detained by, from wish to thwart Pitt and Tories, 21. 34
Highlanders plunder, in Scotland, 16. 375
Hussey speaks in true spirit of, 38. 241
indoctrination by, 42. 403
in Oxfordshire election voting, 35. 192
Jacobites defeated by, in after-rebellion elections, 19. 425
Johnson, Bp, disowned by, 20. 345, 346, 361
ladies indicate preference for, by patching, 16. 258
lawyer discredits his profession if he becomes, 35. 569
Lestock upheld by, 19. 33
Lichfield elected by, to Oxford chancellorship, 22. 72n
London, Middlesex, and Westminster vote for, 19. 425
Mason asks where true ones are to be found, 28. 333
—— says, vie with Tories in wallowing in mire, 29. 39
Minorcan investigation to be used by, in favour of ministry, 21. 77
modern, an old-fashioned Tory is preferable to, 35. 604
Morgan an adherent of, 23. 174
Murray and Stone disowned by, 20. 345, 361
national interests neglected by, for private faction, 35. 215

Newcastle's devotion to, **22**. 579n

old, George III refuses to accept, **25**. 386n

opera directors were, **17**. 191n

Opposition, Lee disobliges, **17**. 451, **43**. 245

Patriots called discontented, **17**. 231n

Pelham attacked, for trying to dismiss Hanover troops, **19**. 17

—— neglects, to court the Tories, **13**. 19

petitioning is characteristic of, **33**. 167

petitions not signed by, **33**. 166–7

Pitt's faction of, do not join Court, **18**. 118

——'s ministry expected by, to be overturned, **34**. 109n

political overturn not engineered by, **10**. 153

Pownall thinks, represent England's Saxon heritage, **42**. 78n

Pulteney pretends to join, **18**. 49–50

pun on, **36**. 209

Pynsent is, **22**. 284

reverses may invigorate, **19**. 118

Rockingham's seceding, called Junto, **25**. 294

—— succeeded Devonshire as leader of, **25**. 288

Scottish, dislike Lord Ilay, **15**. 153

Shelburne's, opposed those of Rockingham, **25**. 294

Stone's tutorship of George III worries, **9**. 144

Thomson celebrates victory of, over Tories, **16**. 375

Tories and, succeeded by new parties, **38**. 140–1

Tories' non-existence affirmed by, **17**. 337, 363

Tory contests with, **38**. 417

Tweeddale among the discontented, **19**. 195n

union of, saves Parliament in 1742, **17**. 118

Walpole, Sir Robert, always loyal to, **22**. 26

—— may be opposed by, **37**. 90

William III not understood by, **28**. 387

Williams, Sir C. H., a steady, **30**. 312

Windham is, of old school, **24**. 524

young, led by Hartington, **20**. 223

See also Parliament: opposition in; 'Whiggism'; Whig-Patriot

Whig Club:

new Association should be different from, **29**. 335

Whig families:

credit lost by, in their own counties, **25**. 488

'Whiggism':

Conway disarms, on the Boyne, **37**. 453

HW's: **10**. 164; cannot include French butchery, **34**. 160; founded on Constitution, **33**. 342; most apparent in *Royal and Noble Authors*, **33**. 277; old-fashioned, **22**. 257; taught to consider France as England's capital enemy, **33**. 167

Oxfordshire election a revival of, **20**. 435

Whig-Patriots:

to come into power, **17**. 319

See also under Patriot; Patriots

Whip; whips:

coachmen crack, in Florence, **17**. 488

Whip-maker:

Hart, Polly, kept by, **10**. 40n

Whipping:

Fuller sentenced to, **16**. 366

Whisk. *See* Whist

Whiskers:

HW jokes about Soubise having, **38**. 101

Wortley Montagu wears, **22**. 113

See also Beard

Whisky; whiskies (vehicles):

at Broadstairs, **12**. 110

Turnham Green man sells only curricles and, **29**. 99

Whisky (beverage):

Conway makes, from potatoes at Park Place, **39**. 551

health of Mlle Morphy drunk in, **37**. 364

Irish do not invite French attackers to drink, **34**. 228

Whisperer, The (periodical):

author of, *see* Moore, William

Conway not to prosecute, for attacking Bute and Ps of Wales, **39**. 124

Mann borrows 6 numbers of, from Leghorn, **23**. 219

Wales, Augusta, Ps of, denounced in, **23**. 196

Whisson. *See* Whiston

Whist:

Amelia, Ps, invites Ds of Bedford to party for, **38**. 344

Bedford, Ds of, plays, with Pecquigny, **38**. 295

Choiseul and Mme du Barry play, with Louis XV, **23**. 157

Compiègne's great pastime, **38**. 408

Conway plays, with Wade, **37**. 177

counters for, **4**. 313

crown, played at Dublin Castle, **10**. 2

Du Deffand, Mme, has guests who excuse themselves to avoid losing money at, **7**. 172

dull, **22**. 555

dull, but the French copy it from England, **40**. 385

English supposed to know, naturally, **22**. 430

faro the alternative to, at Hertford's party, **38**. 298

fashionable in London, **18**. 119, 124, 130, 148

French fondness for, **31**. 48–9, 65, 112, **38**. 408

French imitate, from England, **22**. 555

Gray is learning, **14**. 18

guests play, at SH, **10**. 279

HW dislikes, **31**. 48–9, 65, 89

HW does not play, in Paris, **31**. 48, 79, **32**. 22

HW has not yet learned to play, **18**. 119

HW overwhelmed by, at start of Paris visit, **39**. 12

HW plays: at Fitzroy's farm, **32**. 122; at Lady Lucan's, **33**. 313

HW ridicules, in Paris, **30**. 208

HW's aversion to, **35**. 112

HW tries to supersede, with bilboquet, **18**. 204

Hertford plays, at Fontainebleau, **38**. 448

——'s losses at, trivial compared to gambling in London, **38**. 469

[Whist, *continued*]

Hertfords and Cts of Powis to play, **39**. 285

Italians said to seek English company in order to play, **20**. 175

Jacobite peeresses to play, at Lady Strafford's, **9**. 24

Mann forgets how to play, **22**. 430

—— pretends not to know, **20**. 160

Maria Louisa plays, with Mann and Mrs Hervey, **22**. 430

—— plays, with Vcts Sudley, **23**. 203

mild, compared to other gambling games, **38**. 469

Mirepoix, Mme de, confines herself to, **6**. 393

Montfort plays, before suicide, **35**. 202

Orford, Cts of, plays, **19**. 111

played: **3**. 59, 122, **4**. 250, 295, 297, 301, 302, 352, **5**. 138, **6**. 86, 161, 229, 378, **7**. 102, 119, 125, 135, 172, 262, 267, 302, 304, **9**. 331, 367, **31**. 54, 89, 103, 118, 409; at Petersham, **19**. 166; at Richmond Green, **20**. 63; at Sir Robert Walpole's, **40**. 28; at SH assembly, **33**. 61n; at Vcts Townshend's, **30**. 54; by guests at SH, **10**. 279; by ladies at Stanhope's, **19**. 485; every night in London, **30**. 30

popularity of, at Paris, **32**. 18

Pulteney, Mrs, quarrels with Bn Tullamore over, **40**. 28

Shukburghs addicted to, **20**. 160

six-penny, played at King's Lynn, **9**. 350

Stair plays, at The Hague, **37**. 149–50

Tyrawley comments on, **18**. 148

Walpole, Horace (1678–1757), seeks parties at, **20**. 250

White's Club members play, in country on week-ends, **20**. 63

Williams, Sir C. H., plays, at 7 A.M., **30**. 83

Whistle; whistles:

at Craon's house, solemn, **17**. 79

Whiston, John (1711–80), bookseller; publisher:

HW asks, to send *Royal and Noble Authors* to Zouch, **16**. 22

HW sends Whitworth's *Account of Russia* to, **16**. 16

HW told by, that Zouch does not employ him, **16**. 45

Lort's copies of Northampton's letters at shop of, **16**. 161, 162

Whiston, William (d. before 1742), clerk of records in the Exchequer:

Genealogical History of the House of Yvery finished by, **17**. 272n

Whiston, Rev. William (1667–1752):

Account of the Exact Time When Miracles Ceased, by, **15**. 298

Baker described by, **2**. 344

Bolton, Ds of, converses with, **9**. 22

HW satirizes, in verse, **20**. 134

Historical Memoirs . . . of Dr Samuel Clarke by, **2**. 354

Life and Writings of, mention Chillingworth-Falkland controversy, **16**. 12

Memoirs of, **2**. 354

son of, **16**. 16n

Thirlby writes against, **20**. 215n

unlucky to die before present era, **23**. 81

Whiston, Northants:

Gough to be consulted about, **12**. 270n

Whiston Collection:

Lely's portrait of Vane in, **42**. 125–6

Whitaker, Mrs:

SH visited by, **12**. 228, 236

Whitaker, John (d. ? 1803), M.A.:

Survey of the Doctrine and Argument of St Peter's Epistles, A, by, **15**. 301, 304, **43**. 212

Whitaker, John (1735–1808), historian:

'a Drawcansir,' **1**. 361

Genuine History of the Britons, The, by, **16**. 304n

History of Manchester, The, by, **1**. *361*, 368, 369, **43**. 63

Pinkerton's confutation of, praised by HW, **16**. 304

Whitaker, William (d. 1777), prime sergeant and treasurer of Serjeant's Inn:

HW's correspondence with, **38**. 167

Whitbread, Harriot, sister of Samuel Whitbread:

(?) SH visited by, **12**. 224

Whitbread, Samuel (1720–96), brewer; M.P.:

insolent wealth of, **33**. 268

Whitbread's Brewery:

Wolcot satirizes George III's visit to, **34**. 12n

Whitchester, Lord. *See* Scott, John (1745–9)

Whitchurch, James (d. 1785 *or* 6), of Twickenham:

garden wall of, damaged by storm, **33**. 81

York House, Twickenham, occupied by, **42**. 482

White, —— (d. ca 1742), seaman:

Hervey, William, causes death of, **17**. 275n

White, Mrs:

HW's hostess at Brandon, **18**. 318

wig worn by, over shaved forehead, **18**. 318

White, Mrs, (?) housekeeper to George Montagu:

HW welcomed by, at Adderbury, **10**. 312

White, Benjamin (1725–94), bookseller in Fleet St:

(?) Cole's copy of *Description of Strawberry Hill*, 1774, sold to, **33**. 575–6

(?) Cullum buys Q. Elizabeth's wardrobe account from, **32**. 323

HW wants print of Lady Digby's bust from, **42**. 16

Lort's copies of Northampton's letters at shop of, **16**. 161, 162

(?) Nasmith's *Itineraria* sold by, **2**. 74n

White, Benjamin, jr; bookseller in Fleet St:

SH visited by, **12**. 247

White, Elizabeth (1751–1824), known as Mrs Hartley; actress:

beautiful but without genius, **28**. 61, 110, 183

beauty of, **32**. 106

Caractacus acted by, well, **41**. 362

HW would sacrifice, for Lady Ossory, 32. 108
illness of, causes postponement of *Elfrida*, 28. 362, 364
  Mason's *Elfrida* acted by, 28. 61, 110, 32. *163*
  —— would prefer Mrs Yates to, for *The Mysterious Mother*, 28. 56
White, Rev. George (d. 1751):
  Mercurius Latinus, 15. 297n
  Theological Remarks on Introductory Discourse by, 15. 297
White, George, engraver:
  mezzotint by, of Sir Robert Walpole, 42. 249n
White, George, beggar:
  Reynolds's model, 28. 196
White, Rev. Gilbert (1720–93), naturalist:
  Barrington a correspondent of, 2. 121n
  Pennant, friend of, 1. 328n, 11. 93n
White, John (fl. 1732–8), of Emmanuel College, Cambridge:
  (?) rumoured suicide of, 13. 147
White, John (1699–1769), M.P.:
  anecdote of Sir Robert Walpole told by, 39. 318–19
  birth date of, corrected, 43. 311
  Chatham, object of protest by, 22. 471n
  Parliamentary debate by, on privately-raised regiments, 26. 18
  remark of, on Charles Townshend, 29. 354
White, John (d. 1787), collector:
  coins of, 1. 67–8, 68–9, 43. 47
White, John Campbell:
  Belfast meeting's chairman, 25. 529n
White, Joseph (fl. 1780):
  victim of robbery, 29. 60n
White, Joseph (d. 1791), bookseller:
  (?) Cullum buys Q. Elizabeth's wardrobe account from, 32. 323
  HW commissions, to get books at La Vallière's sale, 36. 216–17, 218, 223
  HW's correspondence with, 42. 93
  HW sends message to, not to bid at sale, 36. 217, 218
  HW's letter conveyed by, 36. 216, 218
  La Vallière sale reported by, to HW, 42. 93
  Nivernais's *Jardins modernes* given to, 12. 259
White, Joseph (1745–1814), orientalist:
  (?) disbelieves in Ireland's MSS, 15. 321
White, Martha (ca 1740–1810), m. (1759) Charles Bruce, 5th E. of Elgin, 1747:
  HW calls 'surfeiting flatterer,' 12. 160
  Udnys visited by, 12. 160
White, R., bookseller in Pall Mall:
  (?) Berry, Mary, sells HW's MSS to, 36. 313n
  subscriptions for *Cheap Repository Tracts* received by, 31. 396
White, Richard, Dublin bookseller:
  Mysterious Mother published by, 42. 301n, 309n, 324n
White, Robert (1645–1703), engraver:
  engravings by, in James I's book, 16. 363
  'greater fame' of, 16. 64
  prints by: 16. 65n; of E. of Cumberland, 1.

355, 357; of Hoskins, 1. 179; of Robert Knox, 2. 134, 140
White, Rowland, steward:
  (?) HW possibly alludes to, 10. 312n
  Montagu to be HW's, at Windsor, 9. 45
White, Mr T. (d. 1769):
  death of, 7. 398
White, William Benoni (d. 1878):
  buys painting from Barrets, 12. 137n
White (colour):
  fashionable in 1795, 12. 179
  Newton said to have called, offensive to eyesight, 18. 228
White Bear, Piccadilly:
  Paine reaches, 11. 319n
Whiteboys (Irish 'levellers'):
  coal-heavers all are, 23. 33, 35. 324
  disturbances by, 22. 24
  France said to have instigated rebellion of, in Ireland, 22. 414
  HW may become, 32. 162
  uprising of, rumoured, 33. 520
Whitebread. *See* Whitbread
Whitechapel, London:
  on HW's route from London to Cambridge, 13. 85n
  poor rates in, 31. 5n
Whitefield, Rev. George (1714–70), Methodist divine:
  activities of, 1. 124
  Berridge meets, 1. 126n
  cant of, 10. 2n
  England tolerates, 25. 23
  Ferrers prayed for by, 9. 284
  ——'s conversion sought by, 21. 398
  Foote satirizes, 9. 326n
  Gibson supported by, 1. 134
  HW expects Methodists to decline when without leadership of, 11. 297
  HW refers to, as Lady Huntingdon's Æneas, 35. 346
  HW satirizes, 20. 134, 31. 34
  Huntingdon, Cts of, angry at finding her watch and trinkets in chamber of wife of, 35. 309
  —— makes, one of her chaplains, 20. 52n
  —— sends, to Ferrers, 21. 398
  Journal of, 13. 192
  London preaching resumed by, after 4 years in America, 20. 52n
  popularity of, 13. 249–50
  preaches at Chelsea (Lady Huntingdon's), 9. 73–4
  'St Whitfield,' preaching of, 32. 227
  Sermons of, only Methodist book owned by HW, 20. 81n
  Shirley, Lady Frances, lured by, from Chesterfield, 10. 2n, 42. 489
  —— opens house to preaching of, during Cts of Huntingdon's absence, 20. 52n
  Townshend, Vcts, makes witticism on, 20. 52, 70

[Whitefield, Rev. George, *continued*]
Venice might be converted by, after its quarrel with Benedict XIV, **20.** 163, 177
vogue of, **9.** 74
Whitefield, Mrs George. *See* Burnell, Elizabeth
Whitefield. *See also* Whitfield
Whitefoord, Caleb (1734–1810), diplomatist and writer:
believes in Ireland's MSS, **15.** 321
New Method of Reading Newspapers, A, by: **10.** 237–9, **43.** 135; Piozzi, Mrs, comments on, **10.** 238n
Whitefriars, London:
Silver St in, **42.** 455n
Whitehall, London:
Amherst's house in, **25.** 110n
banqueting-house at, tapestry in, **16.** 147
blue banners waved in, in Gordon riots, **33.** 177
Chesterfield addresses letter to Pembroke 'in Thames over against,' **31.** 402
Clarendon's premises in, **14.** 216n
congestion at, at Parliament's opening, **9.** 325
Conway, Anne Seymour, shall not keep dormitory at, for Westminster schoolboys, **37.** 334
express arrives at, **40.** 144
fire at, **16.** 322n, **17.** 496, **41.** 191n
France makes peace overtures to, **21.** 499
garden at, slopes to Thames, **20.** 56
George II boards a barge at, for Lambeth, **19.** 39n
Gower's house in, **32.** 295n
HW could not have endured Sackville's ordeal at, **21.** 387
'Holbein Gate' in, **2.** 174, 177
Mason of, **1.** 181n
Pelham does not live in, after children's deaths, **30.** 22
Pelham, Lady Catherine, lives in, **25.** 20n
Pembroke, E. of, swims in Thames near, **42.** 178
Pembrokes live in, **31.** 126
Petitot lodged at, by Charles I, **40.** 238
Richmond, D. of, lives in, **31.** 35, **32.** 237n
——'s fireworks at, **20.** 56, **22.** 148
——'s garden in, to have exhibit of casts from statues, **21.** 173
——'s masquerade at, **22.** 148–9
Robinson has smaller half of Holdernesse House in, **35.** 179n
——'s breakfast at, **35.** 179
Scotland Yard in, **16.** 164
secretary of state's office for southern department moved to, **22.** 176n
soldier who spat at Charles I at trial had probably been most officious when on guard at, **29.** 171
Townshend, Vcts, entertains Westminster schoolboys at, **37.** 334
—— leaves Upper Grosvenor St for, **30.** 58n
Treasury in, **15.** 326

Walpole of Wolterton, Bns, has house in, **25.** 385n
Whithed takes Pembroke's house at, **20.** 142
Whitehall Chapel:
Parker's sermon at, **15.** 298
Whitehall Evening Post:
'Description of the new buildings at Somerset House' in, **16.** 187
(?) HW contributes Anthony Chute's obituary to, **35.** 84
HW's illness reported in, **22.** 459, 461
HW's letter to Langley in, **22.** 531n, **41.** 77n
(?) Mann takes, **22.** 326
ships' prizes mentioned in, **19.** 441
Spain's British policy questioned by, **21.** 544n
Whitehall Gate:
Tracy pursues girls to, **9.** 74
Whitehall Palace:
Burlington, Kent, and others responsible for alterations in plans of, **21.** 363–4
James IV's portrait probably burnt at, **16.** 321
Jones's designs for, **21.** 364n
——'s plan for, imitated at Caserta, **21.** 363
Raphael tapestries at, **16.** 159n
Shakespear, carpenter at, **16.** 197n
Whitehall Stairs:
Cumberland, D. of, and party embark at, **9.** 42
HW embarks at, **9.** 42
Whitehall Yard, London:
Robinson's house in, **35.** 179, **43.** 361
Townshend, Vcts, leases Holdernesse's house in, **40.** 52n
'White Hart,' inn at St Albans:
Cumberland, D. of, said to meet Bns Grosvenor at, **23.** 165n
Hogarth's portrait of Lovat painted at, **19.** 391n
'White Hart,' inn at Windsor:
corpse of Edward Walpole at, **5.** 57n
couples visit, in chaises, **19.** 298
Delany, Mrs, dines at, **33.** 497
White Hart Tavern, Holborn, London:
advertisement gives, as place to give information on Shorter's will, **37.** 372n
Whitehaven:
American privateer attacks, **24.** 377
Whitehead, George (ca 1636–1723), Quaker:
(?) in Stratford's tragedy, **29.** 224
Whitehead, Paul (1710–74), poet:
celebrated Twickenham resident, **35.** 234
Colne Lodge, Twickenham, occupied by, **42.** 486
Discord attributed to, **30.** 49n, **37.** 161n
'infamous but not despicable,' **17.** 252
Manners by, **17.** 211, 252
supper given by, at 'Bedford Head,' **17.** 211
Thompson glorified by, **9.** 66n
Walpole, Sir Robert, angers, by being in good health, **17.** 252
—— opposed by, **17.** 211n
World contributions by, **20.** 395n, 400n

Whitehead, Richard (d. 1733). *See* **Whithed, Richard**

Whitehead, William (1715–85), poet laureate:
Birthday ode's preparation expected to be difficult for, **32**. 247
charade to be guessed by, **35**. 525
Creusa by, praised by HW, **35**. 79
'ethic epistles' by, **34**. 35n
Goat's Beard, The, by, HW finds, inferior to *Variety*, **28**. 281
Gray admires poems of, **14**. 36
—— finds poems of, inferior, **13**. 146
Harcourts accompanied by, at Nuneham, **35**. 531
laureateship of, **28**. 2n
letter of, **9**. 338n
Mason's *Memoirs* of, **29**. 361
Nuneham visited by, **32**. 247
ode by, with music by Boyce for Birthday serenata, **38**. 87
office of, a sinecure, **33**. 314
Shenstone praises, **1**. 309n
talks of anything rather than George III, **33**. 347
Variety, a Tale for Married People by: contains humour but little poetry, **28**. 243; HW considers, his best poem, **28**. 281, **29**. 180
verses on Nuneham by, charm HW and Mason, **29**. 180, 183, 189, 310

Whitehead. *See also* **Whithed**

'White Horse,' Fetter Lane, London:
Cambridge diligence puts up at, **1**. 225n
Essex may be at, **2**. 83

White horse, Saxon:
Fitzpatrick has not altered, **33**. 469

White Horse Cellar, Piccadilly:
Bristol coach leaves from, **31**. 313
stage coaches leave from, **21**. 313

White Horse Inn, Piccadilly:
Williams, John, keeper of, **19**. 388n

Whiteknights, Berks, Englefield's seat:
Englefield of, **2**. 304n
HW visits and describes, **35**. 71
visible from Park Place, **39**. 550

White Lackington, Somerset:
Speke of, **11**. 82n

Whiteladies, Shropshire, Humphrey Penderel's seat:
(?) HW compares, to Meeke's house, **10**. 105

Whitelock, Ann (d. 1771), m. (1721) Gislingham Cooper:
Blandy ghost might be seen by, **37**. 348
Conway and wife to see, at Phillis Court, **37**. 345
Cranstoun might bring more forfeited property to, **37**. 348
Phillis Court sold by, to Freeman, **41**. 219n

Whitelock, A. M. (fl. 1878), of Amboise:
(?) portrait of Mme du Deffand owned by, **8**. 215

Whitelocke, Sir Bulstrode (1605–75), keeper of the Great Seal:
Memorials of the English Affairs by: **40**. 131; books and medals recorded in, **40**. 207; Falkland's wish for clean shirt described in, **40**. 137–8; Hume quotes, about Milton, **35**. 629
Selden persuades, to safeguard Inigo Jones's things, **40**. 208n

Whitemarsh, Pennsylvania:
Washington at, **28**. 342n, **33**. 5

White pine:
HW and Montagu admire, **9**. 177

White Place, Berks:
Leicester of, **1**. 84n

White Plains, N. Y.:
battle of, **24**. 268n, 269n, **28**. 282n

White rod. *See under* **Rod; Staff**

'White rose':
princess of the, **9**. 223

White Rose Court, Coleman St, London:
Lemoine, Ann, bookseller in, **33**. 579n

Whitesand Bay, Cornwall:
invasion lands at, **14**. 176n, **42**. 255n

White's Chocolate House:
tickets for ball delivered at, **13**. 75n

White's Club ('Arthur's'):
Almack's eclipses, as gaming centre, **23**. 187
Arthur of, **20**. 135
bet-book at, says that Burdett will be hanged, **20**. 20
bets laid at, **20**. 185, **28**. 299
Bland's bet with Montfort at, **35**. 258
Brudenell admitted to, in HW's newspaper parody, **9**. 127
Cavendishes whisper politics in, **30**. 238, **41**. 73n
chariots not waiting at, **38**. 459
Chesterfield puts Crébillon's *Sopha* on sale at, **17**. 334
chocolate house the first meeting-place of club of, **25**. 483n
club at Almack's to imitate, **10**. 305
coat of arms for, **9**. 186, 188, **40**. 121
coffee-room at, **9**. 362
Coke spreads his grievances at, **37**. 288
—— to abandon, **9**. 37
Colebrooke, Robert, attends, despite promise to father, **30**. 114
dinner at, extravagant, **20**. 260
Downe at, ridicules English attempt on St-Malo, **37**. 545
drawer employed at, **9**. 133
Drumlanrig's letter left at, for friends to see, **37**. 437n
Edgcumbe finds 'lean hazard' at, **37**. 437
French counterparts of, not separated from newest coffee-houses, **38**. 336
frequenters of: Bath, E. of, **20**. 63; Bedford, D. of, **18**. 124n; Digby, **9**. 362; Fawkener, **9**. 145; Fox, C. J., **35**. 520; Gower, **22**. 472n; HW, **9**. 132, 144–5, 163, 362, **10**. 55, **14**. 9,

[White's Club, *continued*]
19. 261, 35. 357, 38. 494; Hobart, 19. 261; Janssen, 18. 124n; Jeffreys, 9. 145; Lonsdale, 20. 63; Montfort, 20. 169, 35. 202; Selwyn, 9. 133, 145, 202, 10. 259; Waldegrave, 10. 55; Weymouth, 35. 520
gambling at, 17. 36, 38. 469
HW at, preferred hearing of Newmarket instead of elections, 35. 357
HW calls, *Bureau de Bob*, 30. 144
HW compares, with House of Commons, 9. 263
HW does not want to dine at, 40. 151
HW learns Selwyn's address at, 30. 137
HW preferred Newmarket to politics as a topic at, 25. 483
HW's running might be subject of bets at, 38. 65
HW to dine with Lincoln and Edgcumbe at, 30. 51
HW writes from, 9. 144-5, 30. 155-7, 35. 68
in St James's St: 20. 168, 25. 483n, 35. 209; formerly Cts of Northumberland's, 42. 380
Jeffries the contribution of, to politics, 18. 365
John of, angry with HW for his unconcern at Emperor's election, 30. 99
Johnston, James, elected to, 9. 30
Leicester, E. of, returns to, 34. 38
Lincoln, E. of, not to give to Heath at, HW's letter, 30. 41
Macaroni Club absorbs, 10. 139
Maclaine's lodging near, in St James's St, 20. 168
—— visited by Montfort and other members of, 20. 169
Mackreth a former waiter at, 24. 53n, 28. 173, 41. 400
members of, rush in post-chaises to see novelties, 38. 172
Mirepoix sends card inviting chess-players of, 20. 289
Montfort has suppers at, 35. 202
mourning hatchment to be put up at, for deaths of gambling and of Mrs Winnington, 37. 201-2
Old Club at, Dayrolles a member of, 30. 99
Onslow rails at, 18. 289
no separation from, to new coffee-house, 38. 336
notice posted in coffee-room at, 35. 313
parsons scandalized by bets at, about earthquake, 20. 131
Petersham loses at, 20. 140
Pope mentions, 18. 124n
Rigby and Rockingham talk at, 22. 495n
Rockingham at, denounces administration, 38. 180
Rumbold a former waiter at, 25. 400, 29. 122n
Scarbrough watched at, by Lady Kingston, 34. 258
Selwyn falls asleep when at, 38. 482

—— makes witticism at, 9. 202, 29. 206
—— sets Lord George Gordon down at, 33. 169
—— summoned from, 9. 133
——'s wit no longer appreciated at, 10. 259
Stanley dines with HW at, 30. 71
suicides of members of, 9. 173
suppers at, elegant, 19. 261
Taaffe and Wortley Montagu do not belong to, 20. 289
Thomond and Lord Frederick Cavendish confer at, 41. 73
two clubs at, 9. 37, 186, 20. 289
Vernon black-balled at, 20. 301
waiter; waiters at: convicted of robbery, 9. 255-6; Sackville's disgrace discussed by, 38. 20
Waldegrave, Cts, subject of bets at, 38. 403
weather too good to be sauntered away at, 37. 533
whist-players of, play whist in country on week-ends, 20. 63
'young' and 'old' clubs meet separately at, before merger, 20. 301n
White's Hotel, Paris:
Paine arrives at, 11. 319n
Whiteside, Mrs, of Twickenham:
SH visited by, 12. 249
White staff. *See under* Staff; staves
'Whitewash, Gregory':
HW's nom-de-plume, 9. 140
Whitewash:
Bonus uses, on pictures, 10. 285
Cotton, Mrs, contributes, to Gloucester Cathedral, 35. 154
Hurstmonceaux antedates, 35. 138
Irish houses painted with, 9. 390
Montagu, George, dislikes use of, on pictures, 10. 285
Montagu, Lady Mary Wortley, uses, as cosmetic, 37. 81
used on Peterborough Cathedral, 10. 346
used on Prince Arthur's tomb, 35. 150
See also Paint
Whitewashing:
of churches, 18. 480, 24. 527
Whitfield, Anne (d. 1723), m. (1713) Archibald Campbell, cr. (1706) E. of Ilay:
husband of: buries her under the stairs, 17. 506; ill-treats her, 9. 60
Whitfield. *See also* Whitefield
Whitgift, John (? 1530-1604), Abp of Canterbury:
conference of, at Hampton Court, 2. 96, 43. 66
Court idolatry of, 2. 96, 99
Whitham, ——:
Mann, Lady Lucy, aided by, at Majorca, 24. 353n
Whitham, Anne (ca 1761-1824), m. (1780) Gen. James Murray:
escapes to Leghorn from Minorca, 25. 179, 180, 33. 290

husband recommends, to Mann, **25.** 349
pregnant, **25.** 364
Whitham. *See also* Whittam
Whithed (formerly Thistlethwayte), Francis (1719–51), M.P.:
Accademia to be attended by, **18.** 187
Albani introduced to, by Mann, **19.** 59
—— introduces, to Roman society, **19.** 59
——'s protection alone keeps, at Rome, **19.** 196
—— to receive letter of thanks from, **19.** 197
Austrian brutality disgusts, **19.** 279
authorship of literary piece suspected by, **18.** 411
bequests of, **20.** 238, 251
Bologna might be revisited by, for HW's sake, **35.** 22
—— visited by: **19.** 257; to examine Domenichino painting, **17.** 227–8, 233, 240, 241, 312–13, **35.** 5, 13; with HW, **30.** 16
Borghese, Principessa, avoids argument with, **35.** 63
Bosville, Mrs, dislikes, **35.** 41
brother drags out to hunt, **20.** 237
brothers of: 'nasty people,' **14.** 49; obstruct his bequest to Lucchi family, **20.** 312n
Carmelite friar's story to be told by, to HW, **20.** 128
Casa Ambrogi the lodging of, **18.** 109
Castello visited by, **17.** 443, **18.** 1
Chute alarmed by fit of, **18.** 109
—— brings up, **20.** 238
—— despite grief for, tries to help HW's family, **35.** 84
—— helps administer will of, **20.** 246
—— laments, **20.** 256
—— little obliged to, **22.** 268
—— persuades, to provide for Lucchi family, **22.** 265
—— receives small legacy from, **14.** 49
——'s inseparability from, **9.** 54n
——'s 'other half,' **35.** 52
——'s relationship to, **14.** 18, **43.** 181
—— tries to marry fiancée of, to E. of Orford, **20.** 256
—— would have made, his heir, **20.** 238
'Chutehed,' **14.** 18, **19.** 420, 435, and *passim*
Cocchi attends, **18.** 109
—— diagnoses death of, **20.** 244
Correggio painting thought by, to cost more than HW expects, **18.** 370
Craon constantly invites, to play quadrille, **18.** 101
—— entertains, **18.** 132
—— invites, to Petraia, Castello, and Topaja, **17.** 443
(?) Craon, Princesse de, called on by, at Petraia, **17.** 443
Craons to be visited by, at Petraia, **35.** 28
—— to entertain, **18.** 372
—— visited by, at Petraia, **18.** 1
Creti's painting disliked by, **18.** 303
Dagge recommended to, **22.** 268

Dal Borgo entertains, **18.** 406
daughter born to, **18.** 406
daughter of, *see* Lucchi, Sophia
daughter's picture sent to, by Mann, **20.** 244
deaf, **17.** 117
death date of, corrected, **43.** 182
death of: **14.** 197n, **20.** 237–8, 243; HW condoles with Chute on, **35.** 66–7; precipitates Nicoll affair, **14.** 194, 196
Del Sarto painting criticized by, **18.** 214
diet of, **17.** 218
Dunbar tells Romans that Chute is tutor to, **19.** 136
England disappoints, **19.** 329
English captains' gratitude to Mann witnessed by, **18.** 115
English weddings reported to, **18.** 455
'excessively good' to HW, **17.** 365
Firenzuola, the, tires, **17.** 241
Florence left by, **14.** 3n
Florence visited by, **17 – 19** *passim*, **30.** 16, **35.** 3–57, 64, **40.** 57
Florentine house of, *see* Ambrogi, Casa
Ginori, Mme, to entertain, **17.** 161
Giogo, the, crossed by, **17.** 241, 257
Giuseppe's and Riviera's discussion of Young Pretender overheard by, at Petroni's assembly, **19.** 85
Goldsworthy, Mrs, escorted by, to Accademia, **35.** 23
—— with, **17.** 313
good-natured, **19.** 443
Gray's relations with, **14.** 18, 21, 25, 41
—— visits Venice with, **13.** 9
HW and Anthony Chute discuss, **17.** 301
HW and Mann loved by, **35.** 23
HW and Sir Robert Walpole thank, for helping to procure Domenichino painting, **17.** 257
HW asks, to await his return to Florence, **18.** 482
HW asks about, **18.** 123
HW asks about cicisbea of, **18.** 497
HW asks Chute to remember him to, **17.** 365
HW blames, for anti-Jacobite behaviour at Rome, **19.** 139
HW congratulates: on Dettingen victory, **35.** 39; on increase of his family, **19.** 350, 425
HW considered plumper by, **19.** 317
HW finds, in London, **19.** 316
HW gets false notions from, about Mann's health, **19.** 382
HW glad that Mann has regained, **19.** 209
HW impatient to see, in England, **18.** 410, **19.** 224, 272
HW regrets that Mann is soon to lose, **19.** 224
HW relieved by indolence of, in letter-writing, **19.** 442
HW reproached by, for being so English, **19.** 339
HW's absence from *cocchiata* regretted by, **18.** 1

[Whithed, Francis, *continued*]

HW sends regards to, **17.** 143, 177, 346, 392, 421, 440, **18.** 194, 277, 343, 401, 425, 432, 529, **19.** 210, 214

HW's letter to Mann read by Mann to, **17.** 312, **18.** 132

HW's letter to Mann relieves depression of, caused by courier, **19.** 197

HW's remembrance pleases, **35.** 12

HW thanks, **17.** 340

HW to consult, about Young Pretender's movements, **19.** 378

HW told by, about Chute's sister, **20.** 19

HW to receive compliments of, **35.** 63

HW to receive news from, about eagle, **19.** 197

HW to receive regards of, **17.** 218, 294, 382, 418, 428, 474, **18.** 68, 101, 264, **19.** 56, 84, 239

HW to receive respects of, **35.** 6, 10, 12, 15, 22, 23, 30, 33, 36, 42, 53, 56, 63, 66

HW to tell: about affair in Mann's garden, **19.** 499; about Albani's dismissal, **19.** 475

HW visited by, at SH, **19.** 442

HW will laugh with, over Ashburnham's failure, **19.** 420

HW wishes, were safely out of Rome, **19.** 161

Hampshire election won by, **19.** 420

Hampshire to be visited by, **19.** 435

health of: bled, **18.** 109, **20.** 237; clap, **18.** 197; cough, **20.** 237; fever, common, **18.** 138; fit, **18.** 109; gout, **19.** 221, 232

Hervey's conversation with, **19.** 372

Hobart liked by, **19.** 275, 507

—— replaces, **19.** 261

——'s correspondence with, **19.** 365, 382

Houghton gallery should be visited by, **35.** 44, 46

Houghton plans enjoyed by, **17.** 428

house of, burnt, **20.** 185

'infinitely improved,' **19.** 329

in love and wants a whore, **17.** 491

itinerary of: from Florence to England, **19.** 257; from Florence to Rome, **19.** 48–9; from Vienna to Berlin, **19.** 279

Jacobite lies contradicted by, **19.** 135–6

Jacobites might molest, at Rome, **19.** 113

lady discusses Young Pretender with, at Rome, **19.** 97

lean and silent, **17.** 112

leaner and 'pretty,' **19.** 317

lean, pale, deaf, and silent, **17.** 117

Leghorn may be visited by, **18.** 27

London to be visited by, **35.** 66

Lovat's picture sent by, to Mann, **19.** 391

Lucchi, Angiola, arranges Masses for, **20.** 254

—— bears child to, **18.** 333, 368, 406, **22.** 268n

Lucchi family recommended by, to Chute, **22.** 265

Lucchi family's bequests from, revealed to them by Mann, **20.** 251

Mann asks about whereabouts of, **17.** 101

—— borrows money from, for Craon, **18.** 134

—— brags to, of conversation with Richecourt, **18.** 12

—— called on by, **17.** 161, **18.** 140

—— cheered by company of, **19.** 196

—— consults, about model of HW's statue, **18.** 179

—— entertains: at dinner, **18.** 17; at supper, **17.** 218; at tea, **17.** 428

—— excludes, during Theodore's visit, **18.** 187

—— expects, at Florence, **17.** 97, 106, 235, 240

—— grieved at being dropped by, **19.** 443

—— lodges, at his house, **19.** 197

—— praises, **17.** 283–4

—— preferred by, to visiting Rome, **35.** 46–7

—— recommends Moretti to, **20.** 46

—— regrets loss of, **19.** 48, 257, 261, 263

——'s answer to Pucci's remonstrance approved by, **18.** 325

——'s 'apartment over the river' to be occupied by, **17.** 146, 154

——'s correspondence with, **19.** 257, 279, 322, 436, 453, 462

——'s devotion from, **17.** 343

—— sends regards to, **19.** 467, **20.** 93, 162

——'s guests entertained by, at Casa Ambrogi, **18.** 386

——'s hospitality to be attested by, **19.** 349

——'s sale of coffee pot to Mathews advised by, **18.** 472

—— summons, to read HW's letter, **18.** 132

—— to call on, **18.** 109

—— to have tea with, **17.** 161

Mann, Galfridus, accompanies, to select Cholmondeley's pictures, **19.** 405

—— procures seeds for, **20.** 25

—— writes of death of, **20.** 243

Mathews and Villettes laughed at by, **18.** 279

mistress of, *see* Lucchi, Angiola

Modena, Princesses of, discuss HW with, **19.** 257

'more agreeable than Christmas,' **18.** 367

name changed by, from Thistlethwayte, **22.** 268n

Naples visited by, **19.** 171

Nicoll, Margaret, to have married, **20.** 241, 256

Old Pretender said to be offended at, **19.** 136

'one of Orford's crew,' **35.** 25

opera attended by, **18.** 322, **19.** 372

paintings collected by, **20.** 142

Parliament entered by, **19.** 446–7

'Patapan' again to be godfather to expected child of, **18.** 333

Pembroke's house in Whitehall taken by, **20.** 142

Pepi, Signora, may be cicisbea of, **35.** 52

Petersham, Lady Caroline, includes, in Vauxhall party, **9.** 107–10

Petroni's assembly attended by, **19.** 85

Philip, Don, unlikely to harm, **35.** 11

Pisa visited by, **18.** 455

portrait of, in pastel: offered to HW by Mann, 24. 222; painted for Mann, 18. 243
(?) Pucci, Mme, to receive civilities from, 17. 42
Reggio to be visited by, 30. 16
Riccardi's *festino* attended by, 17. 146
Rivera's accusations against English fleet heard by, 19. 120
Roman letter to Goldsworthy amuses, 19. 226
Rome left by: for Florence, 19. 196; too soon, 19. 210
—— may be visited by, 35. 52
—— soon to be revisited by, 19. 171
—— visited by, 19. 48–9, 84, 85, 97, 113, 135–6, 141–2, 171, 196, 209
Rosalba's portrait of, 18. 243n
Sarrazin, Mme, forces, to play quadrille médiateur, 18. 132
seat of, *see* Southwick
Smith informs, of Mann's operation, 35. 4
Stanhope's house admired by, 19. 485
Strozzi family troubles known to, 19. 350
Suares invites, to opera at villa, 35. 5
Suares, Mme, persuades, to back Tesi's opera, 18. 281
subscriber to concert at Florence, 18. 13
Topaja may be visited by, 17. 443
Tunbridge visited by, 19. 436
Ubaldini's apartment occupied by, 17. 146
Uguccioni to introduce, at Baronessa Ricasoli's, 17. 129
valet robs, of money and clothes, 18. 4, 10
Venice left by, 35. 4
—— visited by, 17. 74, 101, 19. 268
Vienna visited by, 19. 207, 257, 279
'Vincenzo's wife' kissed by, 35. 56
Violette's dancing disliked by, 19. 342
Walpole, Sir Robert, congratulated by, on peerage, 35. 25–6
Whithed, Richard, maternal uncle of, leaves estate to him, 14. 18n, 20. 237n
will of: 20. 238, 246, 254; seen by Chute and Galfridus Mann, 20. 251
Winchester assizes to be attended by, 20. 237
Young Pretender hated by, 19. 318
——'s invasion called by, a hoax, 19. 97
——'s progress denied by, at Rome, 19. 142
Whithed *or* Whitehead, Richard (d. 1733):
Whithed, Francis, heir of, 14. 18n, 20. 237n
——'s uncle, 14. 50n, 20. 237n
Whithed. *See also* Whitehead
Whiting; whitings:
HW jokes about, 30. 100
Whitley, Henry:
Bedford, D. of, orders dragoon regiment of, to assemble at Newry, 21. 373n
Whitlow:
Mme du Deffand's lackey ill with, 3. 330
Whitminster, Glos:
Cambridge, Nathaniel, of, 11. 16n, 13. 111n
Whitmore, Lady. *See* Brooke, Frances
Whitmore, John (b. ca 1729), Oxford scholar: to be imprisoned for treason, 20. 6

Whitmore, Sir Thomas (1711–73), K.B., 1744; M.P.:
Bath knighthood given to, 18. 451
wife of, 16. 324n
'Whitnell, la blanche.' *See* Bedingfield, Elizabeth
Whitnell, *philosophe*. *See* Whetenhall, Thomas
Whitsuntide:
exodus from London during, 17. 450
Whittam (*or* Whitham), William, King's Messenger:
arrested, 23. 280–1
Whittington, Richard (d. 1423), Mayor of London:
cat of, discussed by Society of Antiquaries, 13. 47, 32. 84
Foote ridicules Society of Antiquaries' discussion of, 28. 40
Whittington. *See also* Widdrington, Roger
'Whittingtonian':
Pownall is, 1. 293, 43. 57
Whittle, Elizabeth (d. 1696), m. (ca 1754) Sir Stephen Fox, Kt, 1665:
portrait of, 10. 336
Whittlebury Forest, Northants:
Grafton, Ds of, to call at, on way to father's, 38. 435
HW visits, 9. 122
Wakefield Lodge, Grafton's hunting-lodge in, 1. 129, 7. 367, 9. 122, 38. 435
Whittlesey, Cambs:
Moore of, 1. 198n
Whitton, Middlesex:
Gostling, Mrs, addressed at, 41. 437
robbery committed near, 12. 102
Whitton Park, Twickenham:
Gostling builds, 41. 437n
Whitton Place, Middlesex, Sir William Chambers's seat:
Gostling acquires, and sells it to Chambers, 41. 437n
HW inquires about, 15. 287
Ilay lays out the grounds at, 17. 441n
—— owned, 41. 437n
Whitwell, Anne (1721–96), m. (1759) Jan Walrad, Count van Welderen:
Ailesbury, Cts of, will be called wicked by, 38. 99–100
Anne of Orange's maid of honour, 23. 269n
biographical information about, corrected, 43. 132
England left by, for Holland, 25. 108
entertains, 10. 139
(?) Grandison, Cts of, praises, 39. 266
HW meets Kutzlebens at house of, 33. 250
HW mimics mispronunciation by, of French, 38. 100
HW sends parcel to, 7. 379
Hertford, Cts of, engages HW to go to, 39. 159
Whitwell, Elizabeth (1717–76):
burnt to death while saving dog, 6. 337, 43. 100

Whitwell, John. *See* Griffin, Sir John Griffin
Whitworth, Mr:
 HW's correspondence with, **7**. 377
Whitworth, Charles (1675–1725), cr. (1721) Bn Whitworth; diplomatist:
 Account of Russia, An, by, printed at SH: **13**. 29; Conway enjoys, **37**. 578; copies printed of, **43**. 79; HW gives, to Bns Hervey, **31**. 11; HW prints, **9**. 226n, **37**. 552n; HW sends, to Bibliothèque du Roi, **41**. 58n; HW sends, to Montagu, **9**. 226, 227; HW sends, to Zouch, **16**. 16–17; printed for benefit of the Twickenham poor, **28**. 23n
Whitworth, Charles (ca 1721–78), M.P.:
 (?) HW aided by, **40**. 124
Whitworth, Sir Charles (1752–1825), K.B., 1793; cr. (1800) Bn, (1813) Vct, and (1815) E. Whitworth; diplomatist:
 mentioned as envoy, **12**. 248n
 negotiates treaty between Russia and Turkey, **11**. 324n
 wife of, **11**. 206n
Whitworth, Francis (1684–1742), M.P.:
 Legge succeeds, as surveyor of the forests, **17**. 493
Whole Duty of Man, The:
 HW mimics title of, **28**. 154
 Masham, Lady, among supposed authors of, **16**. 137, **40**. 176
 See also under Allestree, Richard
Whole Proceedings. See under Hodgson, Edward
Whole Works of Sir James Ware, The. See under Ware, Sir James
Whood, Isaac (1689–1752), painter:
 painting of Spence by, **14**. 14n
Whooping-cough:
 children's disease, **42**. 412
 occurrences of, **36**. 272
Whore; whores:
 aliases used by, **23**. 520
 Arbuthnot rebukes, **18**. 70
 'capering Madonna' in Italy, **18**. 70
 Cumberland, D. of, has, at lodge at Windsor, **37**. 258n
 Dal Pozzo, Mme, leads life of, **17**. 8on
 Damer, Hon. John, sups with four, at Bedford Arms, **24**. 234
 French, England wastes money on, **37**. 172
 Grafton, D. of, thinks world should be postponed for races and, **39**. 101
 Hamilton jokes on scarcity of, in Ireland, **10**. 11
 Moore's, in coffin chained to his, **20**. 181
 Orford, E. of, squanders money on, **24**. 513
 poxed, Lincoln robbed and infected by, **23**. 378
 'Treaty, The,' implies that Cts of Lincoln was, **21**. 93
 Whithed wants, **17**. 491
Whorwood, Jane:
 Charles I's mistress, **16**. 32n
Whytt, Robert (1714–66), physician:

Essay on the virtues of Lime-Water in the cure of the Stone, An, by, **4**. *114n*, 119n, 133n, **19**. 510n, **43**. 88, 265
Walpole, Horatio (1678–1757), cured by, of the stone, **19**. 510n
Wiart, Auguste-Nicolas-Marie (b. ca 1771); 'Pompom'; son of Mme du Deffand's secretary:
 Bouvart attends, **6**. 409
 Capuchin garb assigned to, **6**. 496–7, **7**. 1–2, 8
 Du Deffand, Mme, amused by, **6**. 206
 —— leaves miniature of, to his mother, **8**. 9, 26
 —— reduced to society of, **6**. 353, 367
 ——'s affection for, **6**. 240, 243, 253, 259, 278, 336, 401, 410, 430
 ——'s financial provision for, **7**. 252, **8**. 6, 10, 39, 44
 ——'s gifts to Mme de Luxembourg presented by, **6**. 249, 496–7, **7**. 1–2
 ——'s opinion of, **6**. 253
 —— visited by, **6**. 189
 education of: **6**. 422, **7**. 447; father to stay in Paris for, **7**. 252
 growing, **6**. 295
 HW given compliments of, **6**. 336
 HW's correspondence with, **6**. 422
 HW to meet, **6**. 212, 215
 hair of, put in medallion by Mme de Luxembourg, **7**. 98
 health of, **6**. 253, 405, 408, 410, 422, **7**. 456
 horse desired by, **6**. 336
 Luxembourg, Mme de, fond of, **7**. 98
 —— gives presents to, **7**. 99, 440
 Marly visited by, **7**. 142
 social relations of, with Duchesses de Choiseul, Gramont, and La Vallière, and Comtesse de Caraman, **7**. 2
Wiart, Jean-François; Mme du Deffand's secretary and valet-de-chambre:
 absent, **5**. 275, 277–8, 439
 Ailesbury, Cts of, argues with, about delivering HW's letter to Mme du Deffand, **6**. 100
 Alembert meets, at Tuileries, **7**. 54
 answers Mme du Deffand's bell, **4**. 83
 armour 'of François I' to be paid for by, **5**. 114, 119–20
 barley sugar given to Conway by, **6**. 120
 Barthélemy to be read to by, **7**. 35
 Beauclerk's suits may be fetched by, from Le Duc, **36**. 192, 196
 blames customs for china breakage, **4**. 338
 Boufflers, Comtesse Amélie de, hints about tea-kettle to, **6**. 9
 burnt in putting out Mme du Deffand's fire, **6**. 176
 Caffieri instructed by, **5**. 301
 Chanteloup visited by, **5**. 237–58
 Choiseul, Mme de, handwriting of, deciphered by, **3**. 81
 Cholmondeley girls seen by, **4**. 369
 Churchill, Lady Mary, gives orders to be executed by, **6**. 266

Cochin's engravings not obtained by, **5.** 283
Colomb asked by, to buy white flannel, **4.** 246
—'s correspondence with, **6.** 124
Conway leaves address with, **6.** 163
copies letters for Mme du Deffand, **3.** 2n
copies in handwriting of, **4.** 99n, 118n, 223n,
   281n, 290n, 307n, 313n, 321n, 428n, 494nn,
   5. 7n, 40n, 69n, 225n, 282n, 284n, 296n,
   382n, 402n, **6.** 1n, 17n, 25n, 65n
country residence avoided by, **7.** 252
custodian of Mme du Deffand's effects, **8.** 31
Du Deffand, Mme, accompanied to Chanteloup by, **5.** 237, 243
—— allots suit to, **6.** 258
—— attended by, to theatre, **4.** 276
—— consults, about poems sent to HW, **5.** 284
—— disputes cost of letter with, **3.** 148
—— hears war news from, **7.** 186
—— loved by, **7.** 251
—— mentions, **3.** 24, 86, 103, 164, 165, 218,
   238, **4.** 39, 125, 201, 373, **5.** 192
—— not reminded by, of news, **7.** 3
—— recalls, to write letter, **7.** 149
—— reminded by: about guests, **7.** 184; of
   account of lit de justice, **6.** 292; of pine-
   apple pâté recipe, **6.** 269
—— rewards, for refusing Craufurd's gratuity, **41.** 4
—'s after-dinner secretary, **6.** 267, **7.** 81
—— sends, on errand, **4.** 182, 206, 225, 368,
   477, **5.** 3, 88–9
—'s financial provision for **7.** 252, **8.** 9, 43,
   44
—'s handwriting deciphered by, **3.** 145, 224
—'s letters to be known only to HW and,
   5. 297
—'s letters written by, **3.** 2n, 6, 107, 116–17,
   292, **4.** 28 *and passim*
—'s mistake about Beauvau's bowl mentioned by, **6.** 175
—'s mistake in distributing HW's *Gramont*
   noticed by, **5.** 305
—'s 'portraits' read to Mme de Genlis by,
   8. 64
—'s repetition noticed by, **5.** 142
—'s writing, when ill, protested by, **3.** 400
—— would like to send, to HW, **3.** 134, 140,
   143, 144, **4.** 66, 149
Dumont, Mme, to be written to by, **3.** 389
Dumont, M., asks news from, **4.** 492
Echlin aided by, **7.** 110, 114, 115, 118, 119,
   121–2, 127, 131, 135, 146
endorsements by, **41.** 16, 42, 100, 136, 342
English bird merchants conducted by, **5.** 229–
   30
fails to make copy of letter, **3.** 80
faithful, **3.** 22
family portraits of, **8.** 16
furniture in chamber of, **8.** 16
goes to central post office, **3.** 352, 353, **4.** 465
gout remedy reported by, **6.** 197
Gramont, Duchesse de, sends letter by, **5.** 363
HW buys lottery ticket for, **3.** 298n

HW buys snuff-box for, **7.** 404
HW given expense account by, **6.** 297
HW mentions, **5.** 88
HW pays, for Churchill, **7.** 411
HW receives report from on: cups and Mme
   du Deffand's finances, **4.** 348–9; Echlin, **7.**
   121–2; engravings, **6.** 345–6; George James
   Cholmondeley's passport, **7.** 87; health of
   Mme du Deffand, **7.** 243–53, **33.** 229; Paris
   hotel lodgings, **6.** 209, 210; wine for Selwyn,
   5. 370–1
HW requests, to return letters to living cor-
   respondents of Mme du Deffand, **33.** 235
HW's acceptance of cup and saucer probably
   remembered by, **36.** 182
HW's accounts with Mme du Deffand kept
   by, **5.** 230
HW's apartment engaged by, **4.** 258, 268, **6.**
   209, 210
HW's apartment to be engaged by, **3.** 16, 221,
   340
HW's bed attended to by, **5.** 120
HW's correspondence with, **2.** 233n, **3.** 140–
   2, 389, 390, **5.** 182, **6.** 236, 238, **7.** 230–1,
   243–53, **36.** 170–1, 172, 173, 177, 178–9, 184,
   186
HW's cups attended to by, **4.** 348–9, 352
HW's dictated letter to Mme du Deffand
   found by, **7.** 101
HW s English deciphered by, **7.** 83
HW's engraving found by, **6.** 368
HW's *Gramont* has errata noticed by, **5.** 313
HW's handwriting may be unrecognizable to,
   6. 132
HWs legacy of MSS from Mme du Deffand
   catalogued by, **8.** 7, 44
HW's letter about Mme de Mirepoix copied
   by, **6.** 13
HW's letter to Mme du Deffand read by,
   6. 101, 410
HW's letters to be read by, only, **4.** 280
HW's letters to be returned by, **6.** 108
HW's letters to Mme du Deffand given to
   Conway by, **6.** 152
HW's meaning incomprehensible to, **6.** 111–
   13
HW's orders executed by, **5.** 130, **6.** 241, 248,
   252, 254
HW's orders will be executed by, **4.** 255, **5.**
   128, 148, 156, 182, 220, 224, 264, **6.** 262,
   7. 110
HW's packages sealed in presence of, **6.** 45
HW to receive *Bibliothèque universelle des
   romans* from, **6.** 400n
HW to receive genealogical note from, **6.** 290
HW to receive reports from, on Mme du Def-
   fand's health, **7.** 243
HW to secure servant through, **6.** 211
HW writes name of, on Selwyn's lottery
   ticket, **30.** 251
health of, **3.** 85, 316, 320, 322, 325, **5.** 19, 288,
   6. 245, 432, 433, 483, **7.** 209, 212

[Wiart, Jean-François, *continued*]

hours of, **4.** 180, 213, 417, **5.** 162, 376, **6.** 267, **7.** 81, 89, *and passim*

Hume-Rousseau memorandum copied by, **3**. 131

incense burner for Mme du Deffand received by, **6.** 341

kept sheaf of copied letters, **8.** 145

La Grange wedding attended by, **4.** 345–6, 346

learns English, **3.** 135, 136, 138, 140, 148, 150, 182–3, **4.** 113, 464

letter by, **4.** 348n

letters copied in hand of, **41.** 28, 33, 100, 136, 146, 148, 158, 342

letters dictated to, **5.** 91n, 92n, *and passim*

Ligne, Princesse de, transmits Duchesse de Choiseul's letter through, **5.** 239–40

(?) lottery ticket of, **4.** 11, 27, **7.** 422, 455

Luxembourg, Mme de, inquired about daily by, **7.** 208

Marly visited by, **7.** 142

Mass to be attended by, **4.** 293

mémoire by, on Lady Fenouilhet's appeal, **5.** 373

(?) Morel, Mme, writes to, **6.** 39

never loses a paper, **3.** 388

note and copy by, **5.** 426n

Panthémont to be visited by, for news of Maria Fagnani, **7.** 148

paper merchant paid by, **6.** 273

paper merchant seeks money from HW through, **6.** 266, 269

'Pompom' as Capuchin, announced by, **7.** 1

——'s education to keep, in Paris, **7.** 252

——'s guardian, **7.** 39

——'s health alarms, **6.** 405, 408, 409

reads letter for Mme du Deffand, **4.** 418, 424

St-Joseph's convent temporary home of, after Mme du Deffand's death, **7.** 250, 253

salary of, **8.** 46

Selwyn gives money for Mme du Deffand to, **7.** 133

——'s correspondence with, **5.** 371n, **6.** 225

——'s lodgings and carriage to be procured by, **7.** 127

—— suggests that Mme du Deffand send, to him, **3.** 393

sends off letter in Mme du Deffand's absence, **4.** 193

snuff-box identified by, **6.** 312

social relations of, with Choiseul, **6.** 162–3

suits of, made from Mme du Deffand's ravelled rags, **4.** 436

tires of Mme du Deffand's chatter, **3.** 49

tires of writing, **5.** 106

Tonton's health to be reported to, **36.** 207

translates: **4.** 63, 122n, 127, 150, 222, 232n, 233, 237–8; Boswell's *Account of Corsica*, **4.** 82, 87, 92, 106, 113, 125, 126; HW's letter to Langley, **3.** 304–5, 312; HW's preface to *Castle of Otranto*, **4.** 99, **8.** 141–3; HW's preface to *Historic Doubts*, **4.** 131; HW's

verses to Ps Amelia, **4.** 187, 189, 201; Voltaire's letter, **4.** 122n

translation of *Historic Doubts* to be made by, **4.** 25, 28

translation of *Mysterious Mother* to be made by, **4.** 93–4, 106, **5.** 270

translation of *Mysterious Mother* to be made under direction of, **5.** 299

transportation time for letter calculated by, **6.** 426

unwilling to write song on Mme du Barry, **5.** 67, 69

Valentinois, Comtesse de, suggested by, as author of 'Sévigné' letter, **3.** 71

Vichy, Marquis and Marquise de, taken walking by, **6.** 283

(?) Voltaire's letter transcribed, not translated by, **4.** 122, **43.** 88

Voltaire's lodging visited by, **7.** 17, 18

waits in vain for Mme du Deffand to dictate, **5.** 385

Walpole, Hon. T., consulted by, in Mme du Deffand's illness, **7.** 248

—— given parcels by, for HW, **7.** 250, 253

Warner may get books for HW from, **36.** 195

weeps at Mme du Deffand's death-bed, **7.** 251

wife of, **5.** 237n

Wilkes compared to Clodius by, **4.** 203

Wiart, Mme Jean-François. *See* La Motte, Françoise

Wibergh, Thomas:

Prior apprehended by, **13.** 187n

Wichnor ('Whichnor'; 'Whichnovre'), Staffs; Offley's seat:

flitch of bacon given at, **9.** 294, **38.** 70–1, **43.** 123

HW visits, **9.** 294, **38.** 70–3

HW writes from, **38.** 70–3

landscape effects at, **9.** 294, **38.** 71

Offley of, **13.** 166n, **38.** 70

spelling of, corrected, **43.** 123

Wickam. *See* William (1324–1404) of Wykeham

'Wicker Chair, The.' *See under* Somerville, William

Wickes, Mr, landlord of house at Teddington:

Armstrong, Mrs, well treated by, **11.** 56

benign and courteous, **11.** 61

HW compares, to Chaucer's host, **11.** 62

HW's negotiations with, **11.** 58–9, 61, 69, 72–3

house of, at Teddington, **11.** 68n

marriage of, **11.** 61

to shoot in Norfolk, **11.** 72

Wickes, Mrs:

former mistress to Gen. Harvey, who called her 'Monimia, **11.** 61

Wickes, Capt. Lambert:

Reprisal, The, commanded by, **32.** 336n

Wickes. *See also* Weeks; Wicks

Wickham, Mr:

SH visited by, **12.** 235

Wickham. *See also* William (1324–1404) of Wykeham

Wicklowes, Suffolk:
Manor of, **1**. 376
Wicks, ——, carpenter:
Montagu asks HW to send, to Hampton Court to pack portraits, **10**. 102
Montagu family portraits packed by, **10**. 104, 107
Wicks. *See also* Weeks; Wickes
Wicquefort, Abraham van (1606–82):
Ambassadeur et ses fonctions, L', by: diplomatic observation not made by, **33**. 489; tale for new edition of, **23**. 125
'Widdrington, Roger':
ballad of *Chevy Chase* refers to, fighting on his 'stumps,' **23**. 264n, **33**. 326, 375, **34**. 106
Pitt resembles, **23**. 264
Widdrington, Sir Thomas (d. 1664), Kt; Speaker of House of Commons:
history of York by, **2**. 114
Widow; widows:
French opera singers omit powder when they act rôles of, **18**. 496
'perishing for want,' perhaps aided by HW, **40**. 345n
'Widow, dainty':
song about, **37**. 565
Widow of Delphi, The. See under Cumberland, Richard
Widville *or* Woodville. *See* Wydevill
Wieland:
Parsons eulogizes, **11**. 177n
Wierix, Jan, engraver:
print attributed to, **15**. 161n
Wife; wives:
More, Hannah, comments on managing and accomplished, **31**. 316
of attempted suicide, young but paralytic, **31**. 337
Wig; wigs:
Adonis: Cumberland, D. of, wears, at George II's funeral, **9**. 322; Mann wears, in portrait, **24**. 27; Maron substitutes, in painting, for Mann's usual wig, **24**. 32; old senators keep, with their robes for days of ceremony, in Rome and Florence, **24**. 32; suited only for younger men, **24**. 27
attorney-general's, opposed to Speaker's coif, **37**. 365
bag: Lyttelton unlikely to wear, **9**. 342; Piozzi, Mrs, comments upon, **9**. 342n
black: generals wear, in Germany, **37**. 143, 291, 292; Pembroke dons, **10**. 17; Sturgis wears, **17**. 461; Wachtendonck disguises himself with, **17**. 489; worn over white hair, **38**. 127
bob, English visitors wear, in Florence, **17**. 132
bob-periwig, Norfolk women wear, of various colours without powder, and call them frontlets, **30**. 34
brown bob, Mrs White wears, **18**. 318
Cenci's, too spruce for Clement XIII to make him cardinal, **21**. 334

Charles III snatches, with hooks, from visitors, **23**. 238
Compton, Lady Margaret, almost loses, **39**. 420
—— has, well-powdered, **32**. 308n
—— wears, **31**. 199n
fashion in, changes, **28**. 208n
flowing, of John Law, **15**. 181
Francis III pulls down, to nose, **20**. 57
——'s, hung on his wen, **20**. 75
from Paris, **37**. 526
full-bottom: French wear, in Louis XIV's reign, **41**. 225; out of style, **18**. 148, **28**. 208
Giovanni Gastone de' Medici's, **25**. 170
Gordon wears flannel under, **17**. 298
great, Mann to wear, at Electress's, **17**. 83
iron, brought by Wortley Montagu from Paris, **20**. 226
judicial, Sewell said to think better under nightcap than under, **35**. 560n
lords', endangered by Gordon rioters, **33**. 175, 176
Lyttelton loses, **15**. 330
Parliament members stripped of, by Gordon rioters, **25**. 54
periwigs, Norfolk ladies think it fashionable to wear, **18**. 318 (*see also under* bob-periwigs *above*)
Portsmouth, Cts of, to wear, at Coronation, **9**. 387
—— wears, and Cts of Exeter discards, **38**. 127
priests forbidden to wear, **24**. 107n
Rutland said to have paid son not to wear, **38**. 481
Sarrazin, Mme, must comb, herself, **18**. 361
—— wore, **18**. 318, **19**. 452
Scott, Mrs, wears, **10**. 329
tie (*or* tye, *or* tied): **38**. 553; Conway wears, frowsy, to masquerade, **37**. 12; Cromwell, Henry, hunted in, **29**. 130; physicians wear, **24**. 71; Piozzi, Mrs, comments on, **9**. 342n; Sandwich wears, **18**. 561
tower: HW wears, **9**. 355; Montagu wishes, **9**. 355
vast, Brown, Sir Robert, sells, in Venice, **25**. 609n
Walpole, Horatio (1678–1757), snatches off, **19**. 169
Walpole, Robert, buys, from Wilkins, **17**. 506
white, old gallants wear, **18**. 501
white with 4 tails, worn by Skinner, **23**. 238
See also Periwig; Perruque; Ramillie
Wigan, John (1696–1739), M.D., 1727; physician and writer:
(?) HW does not recall, **34**. 219
Wigan, Lancs:
Conway stationed at, **37**. 213–15
Haigh Hall near, **16**. 285n
rebels at, **37**. 211n
rebels retreat through, to Lancaster, **19**. 185n
Walpole, Horatio (1752–1822), M.P. for, **36**. 175
Wiggan. *See* Wigan

Wight, Joseph (fl. 1753–65), clerk:
on Armada tapestries, **1.** 13
Wight, Isle of. *See* Isle of Wight
Wignacourt, Marie-Charlotte-Antoinette-Constance-Louise-Françoise de (1750–78), m. (1771) Hyacinthe-Hugues-Timoléon, Comte de Cossé; 'Marquise de Cossé':
social relations of, with Duchesse de la Vallière, **7.** 346
Wilberforce, Miss:
More sisters visited by, at Cowslip Green, **31.** 321n
Wilberforce, William (1759–1833), philanthropist; M.P.:
'Cheap Repository Tracts' aided by circle of, **31.** 395n
HW suggests, should have enfranchisement of negroes started in France, **31.** 331
mechanical sugar cultivation thought practical by, **31.** 328
More, Hannah, visited by, at Cowslip Green, **31.** 321
Pitt's opposition to slave trade inspired by, **31.** 269n
Sierra Leone aided by, **31.** 371n
SH visited by, **12.** 224
Wilbraham, Mr:
SH ticket not used by, **12.** 225n
SH visited by, **12.** 223
Wilbraham, R.:
law chambers of, burnt, **20.** 321n
Wilbraham, Randle (?1695–1770), M.P.; deputy steward of Oxford University:
Balmerinoch seeks, as counsel, **19.** 287
birth date of, corrected, **43.** 261
Wilkes's absence stressed by, in Parliamentary debate on privilege, **38.** 240
Wilbraham, Roger (d. 1829), M.P.; F.R.S.; F.S.A.:
disbelieves in Ireland's MSS, **15.** 321
Wilby, Northants:
Percy, rector of, **15.** 114n
Wilcocks, Joseph (1673–1756), Bp of Gloucester, 1721; of Rochester, 1731:
bishop's palace at Bromley altered by, **35.** 132n
fit for nothing but death, **18.** 201
goldfish of, at Bromley, **35.** 132
HW and Chute visit palace of, at Bromley, **35.** 131–2
York archbishopric predicted for, **18.** 201
York archbishopric refused by, **18.** 203n
Wilcox. *See* Wilcocks
Wilczek, Johann Joseph (1738–1819), Austrian minister to Tuscany:
Gloucester, D. of, might occupy Florentine house of, **23.** 333n
Maria Theresa sends, from Naples to regulate Parma, **23.** 412n
Petraia occupied by, **23.** 296
rank of, **23.** 293
'Wildair, Sir Harry.' *See under* Farquhar, George: *Constant Couple*

Wilder, Thornton:
footnotes by, **43.** 86, 98, 104
Wildman, Thomas (d. 1781):
Lyttelton's conversation with, **15.** 330
Treatise on the Management of Bees, A, by, **15.** 330n, **43.** 213
Wildman's Club, Albemarle St, London:
Élie de Beaumont visits, **38.** 461
Waldegrave's house in Albemarle St occupied by, **38.** 294
Wilhelm (1532–92), Landgrave of Hesse 1567–92:
Elizabeth, Q., sends Palavicini as emissary to, **1.** 4n
Wilhelm (1682–1760), Landgrave of Hesse-Cassel 1730–60 as Wilhelm VIII:
army command given to, **17.** 345
flees to Bremen, **37.** 554
minister of, may go to Cologne, **42.** 494
Strange, Lord, objects to gratuity to, **38.** 8
Wilhelm (1741–2), of Hesse-Cassel:
birth of, **17.** 255
Wilhelm (1743–1821), Hereditary Prince; Landgrave of Hesse-Cassel, 1785, as Wilhelm IX; Elector of Hesse-Cassel, 1803, as Wilhelm I:
Amelia's portrait of her grandmother probably left to, **42.** 180
George III's treaty with, **24.** 175n
Guines, Duc de, gives supper for, **32.** 277
Orford, Cts of, fondles, **19.** 70
'Prince of Hesse', **32.** 277
two brothers of, receive legacies from Ps Amelia, **33.** 534
Wilhelmina Carolina (1743–87), of Orange, Ps, m. (1760) Karl Christian, P. of Nassau-Weilburg:
marriage of, arranged, **38.** 6
Nassau-Weilburg, P. of, woos, **9.** 187–8
Wilhelmine Amalie (1673–1742), of Brunswick-Lüneburg, m. (1699) Joseph I, Holy Roman (German) Emperor, 1705:
death of, **17.** 392
mourning for, **17.** 392, 433
Wilhelmsthal (Germany):
battle of: **38.** 161; French officers captured in English victory at, **31.** 25; Townshend killed at, **9.** 379n
name of, corrected, **43.** 125
Wilkes, John (1725–97), politician:
absent from presentation of London's new remonstrance, **23.** 216
addresses to constituents dated by, from Newgate Prison, **23.** 82
affair of, debated, **15.** 94n
alderman for ward of Farringdon Without, **23.** 81
alderman's dignity may have lulled, into prudence, **23.** 208
alderman's post coveted by, **23.** 206
always revives from his embers, **24.** 45
American affidavits deposited with, **24.** 110n
Amherst and Christian VII eclipse, **23.** 58

amnesty unlikely for, **22**. 305
'and liberty,' **35**. 323
appeal of, to constituents, **23**. 37
appearance of: cross eyed, **10**. 111; squint, **1**. 248
Apsley to tell, that George III does not approve of London's election of him, **39**. 207
arrest of, **15**. 88n
a show for England, **4**. 173
associates of, quarrel with one another, **23**. 297
at end of his reckoning, **23**. 270
attacks by, on religion and government, **33**. 483
at top of the wheel, **24**. 55
attorney-general asked by, for writ of error, **23**. 12
Augusta, Ps of Wales, abused by, **23**. 340n
autobiography being written by, **15**. 246–7
banishment of, silences Temple, **22**. 290
barge of, at regatta, **32**. 238
Beardmore, legal adviser to, **30**. 234n
Beauchamp asked by, to deliver message in Florence, **22**. 281–2
Beauclerk's library discussed by, **6**. 373n
Beckford was political firebrand instead of, **23**. 223
Bedford's and Neville's treatment of, in Paris, **38**. 279, 290
Bentley's *Patriotism* satirizes, **10**. 128n, **14**. 134n
Berlin and Italy to be visited by, **22**. 272
birth date of, corrected, **43**. 86, 128, 146, 278
Boswell sketches, **33**. 462n
Botta criticizes Lorenzi's attentions to, **22**. 282
Brentford election kept quiet by, **23**. 6
—— the capital of, **35**. 324
British Museum's holdings would be increased by motion made by, **24**. 302n
Brown, butler to, to testify, **38**. 292
Bull in election with, **24**. 48
Burke's and Savile's martyrdoms more respectable than that of, **23**. 170
Cambridge committee member, **2**. 208n
Cambridge meeting harangued by, **2**. 207
candidate for lord mayor, **23**. 520n
candidate sent by, to oppose Barret at Dover, **28**. 80
chamberlain of London, **24**. 535
chaplain at Paris embassy must be unable to preach to, without mentioning sins, **38**. 279
Charles I's Day observed as feast by, **6**. 146, **28**. 175n
Chastellux known by, in Paris, **23**. 28
—— talks with, in King's Bench Prison, **23**. 28
Chauvelin, Abbé, compared to, **4**. 342
Chief Justice abused by, in speech, **23**. 12–13
Choiseul has probably tampered with, **23**. 143
Churchill (the poet) dies during visit to, at Calais, **22**. 261
—— friend of, **38**. 233–4

—— said to have written *Essay on Woman* instead of, **38**. 270
——'s death deprives, of materials of history, **22**. 281
——'s works to be edited by, **22**. 261, 292
Clodius compared to, **4**. 203
Cockpit visited by, **38**. 223
Cole dislikes, **2**. 211
—— suggests burial in St Paul's for, **2**. 82
Constantinople post expected by, **39**. 16
conversation and writing of, praised, **22**. 136
Conway known publicly to have defended cause of, **40**. 339
——'s defence of, results in his own dismissal, **22**. 238n
—— supports, **13**. 40n
Cooke given votes by, at Middlesex election, **35**. 324n
Cosway, Mrs, entertains, **33**. 511
courage of, dubious, **38**. 227
Court of Aldermen set aside election of, **23**. 84
Court of Common Pleas delivers, **22**. 137, **38**. 200–1
Court of King's Bench commits, **23**. 19, 22
—— may fine or imprison, **23**. 8
—— may prosecute, **22**. 137
—— tries, in Westminster Hall, **23**. 11–12, 29
Crawford escorts, at Cambridge, **43**. 62
cries in favour of, at opening of Parliament, **23**. 167
Croÿ discusses English freedom of speech with, **22**. 137
Cumberland, D. of, marries daughter of successor of, **5**. 131
daughter of, **7**. 10n, **10**. 311n
dedication by, to *Fall of Mortimer*, **10**. 52
disturbing, **4**. 166
Drury Lane Theatre audience acclaims, **38**. 276
Drury Lane Theatre club attended by, **22**. 185
Du Deffand, Mme, awaits news of, **4**. 193, 227
—— inquires about, **4**. 64, 184
—— makes wager about seat of, in Parliament, **4**. 89, 91, 164, 187, 198
—— mentions, **4**. 197, 239
—— predicts triumph of, **4**. 177
duels avoided by, **38**. 227
dull in Parliament, **22**. 136
Dunn threatens, **22**. 189, **38**. 264–5
Dyson asked impudent question by, **10**. 52
ear-cropping may be punishment of, **22**. 183
Edinburgh celebrates recovery of, **38**. 268
elected sheriff of London, **32**. 52
election successes of, **4**. 204, 205, **6**. 99n, 109
election to be contested by, at Brentford, **10**. 274
English liberties upheld by, **23**. 81
English must see unworthiness of, **23**. 122
English should chastise, **23**. 239
engrosses public attention, **28**. 2n
Éon's 'father,' **22**. 282
Essay on Woman attributed to: author im-

[Wilkes, John, *continued*]

peached because of, **10.** 111; Churchill alleged to have admitted writing, **38.** 270; Court of King's Bench condemns, **38.** 333; HW has never seen, though it lies in House of Lords, **22.** 194–5; House of Lords debates over, **38.** 293–4; House of Lords to try, **22.** 199; Mann surprised at failure to reprint, **22.** 204; Mann wants copy of, **22.** 192; March, E. of, encourages Kidgell to inform against, **23.** 73n; published by Kidgell, **22.** 187; Sandwich denounces in House of Lords, **22.** 184–5, **38.** 229–30; Sandwich hurt by, more than Wilkes, **38.** 243; Wilkes reads, to Sandwich and Le Despenser, **22.** 185

Essex's suicide recommended to, **38.** 202

fails to appear before House of Commons, **22.** 198

fame of, would never have been predicted, **23.** 152

fears poisoned pâté, **4.** 152, 155

Fitzherbert, friend of, **38.** 264n

Forbes challenges, in Paris, **22.** 162–3, 170, 174–5, **38.** 227n, 229

foreign gazettes make much of affair of, **23.** 80

forgotten, **23.** 120

France preferred by, to martyrdom, **22.** 194

French confuse, with Sandwich, **31.** 68

—— endure presence of, though he abused them in print, **22.** 272

friends of, in House of Commons petition against Luttrell, **23.** 114–15

Gazette d'Amsterdam has article on, **4.** 155

general warrant against, **13.** 4n; *see also under* General warrants

George III advised by, not to go to St Paul's, **38.** 199–200

—— and, the 'two kings,' **38.** 324

George III defeated by, **25.** 565

—— lodges complaint against, in Parliament, **22.** 182

—— orders Temple to remove, from militia of Buckinghamshire, **22.** 138

——'s closet might be entered by, **23.** 317

ghost of, in a sea of claret and port, **23.** 5

Glynn, counsel and nominee of, **23.** 30, 78

Gordon riots handled by, with zeal and spirit, **25.** 63

Grande Chartreuse's album has remarks by, **2.** 302, 307, 43. 75

grazier said to have left money to, **22.** 281

Grenville refers to, in speech, **38.** 320

Guildhall meeting does not oppose, **24.** 48n

HW accused by, of flattering the Scots, **13.** 37–8

HW asked by mob if he is for, **23.** 194

HW asks about activities of, in Rome, **22.** 290

HW blames, for upheavals, **32.** 213

HW called on by, at Paris, **10.** 180

HW calls: 'Alderman Catiline,' **23.** 82; 'St Beelzebub,' **23.** 170

HW compares: with Jack Cade, **24.** 536; with Masaniello, **23.** 317, **24.** 535; with Rienzi, **23.** 8, **24.** 536; with Sacheverell, **22.** 263, 360; with Vernon, **23.** 8

HW could convince, that Bute wanted to become pope, **23.** 92

HW forsakes, to go to SH, **38.** 202

HW glad that Methodism was not embraced by, **23.** 87

HW has not yet exchanged visits with, **39.** 17

HW hints to Choiseul's friend that Pitt might be restored by, **23.** 143

HW jokes about revolutionary abilities of, **10.** 58

HW mentions, **3.** 341, **10.** 263, **11.** 208

HW receives θεφραδγου from, **42.** 263

HW remembers unrest caused by, **33.** 190

HW's correspondence with, **42.** 263

HW sees, in hackney chair, **23.** 5

HW shown notes by, on Churchill's works, **10.** 180

HW's opinion of, **10.** 180

HW tired of hearing of, **39.** 98

HW told by, about Col. Clarke, **7.** 357

HW would not have been mentioned by, in *North Briton*, if he had known HW would take it so well, **38.** 193

HW writes letter about, **7.** 378

HW writes symbols of, on gates, to prevent attack by rioters, **10.** 274

habeas corpus by, for two commitments, **38.** 199

Halifax's warrant for treason takes up, **38.** 197

handbills by, **23.** 77

Harley opposes, **23.** 6, 13

health of: recovering from wound, **38.** 243; wounded in duel, **38.** 228, 232; wound prevents Parliamentary appearance, **38.** 297; wound still open, **38.** 280, 297; wound thought to retain piece of cloth, **38.** 259

hearings of, in House of Commons, **10.** 272

Heberden and Hawkins rejected by, in favour of Duncan and Middleton, **38.** 274

Hertford disapproves of writings of, **38.** 244–5

——'s attentions to, at Paris, **38.** 279–80, 289–90, 297–8

——'s chapel at Paris makes, religious, **38.** 243

——'s treatment of, correct, **38.** 289–90

—— suspects, of fostering newspaper attacks on him, **38.** 352–3, 361–2

—— unlikely to entertain, at Paris, as Bedford did, **38.** 274

Hogarth's portrait of, **15.** 142n

Holland House gives public breakfast to support Luttrell against, **25.** 11

Houghton collection recommended by, for purchase, **24.** 304

house of, in Great George St, **38.** 197n

House of Commons and City of London embroiled over, **23.** 279

House of Commons debates over medical attendance for, **38**. 273–4

House of Commons did not dare to allow, to appear before them, **23**. 303

—— expels, **15**. 128n, **22**. 183, 199, **23**. 86, 97

—— quarrels over, **5**. 56n

—— summons, before bar, **23**. 73, 84, 281

—— to choose Luttrell instead of, **23**. 105

House of Lords argues writs of error of, **23**. 83

—— refuses to hear, **23**. 77

Hume exchanges visits with, in Paris, and meets him at Holbach's, **38**. 280n

——'s conversations with, in Paris, **38**. 352

imprisonment of, **4**. 73n

'infamous intoxication' of, **15**. 130

Italy to be visited by: **22**. 263, 272; to write about George III's reign and back to 1688, **38**. 484

Junius papers ascribed to, **23**. 248, 339

Kidgell informs against, **14**. 130n

King's Bench Prison entered by, **23**. 19, 28

ladies eclipse, **23**. 92

legal punishment hard to apply to such mob heroes as, **23**. 143–4

letters of, to Middlesex electors and to his ward, **23**. 213

Letters to Lord Mansfield not written by, **32**. 89

Letter to . . . the Duke of Grafton by, attacks Pitt, **38**. 255n

Letter to the Worthy Electors of . . . Aylesbury by, **38**. 484

London apt to produce figures such as, **11**. 208

London city banquets and sermons attended by, **23**. 208

London Common Council's action on riot concerning, **38**. 262

London election defeats, **23**. 56

London elects, lord mayor, **24**. 45, 48, **39**. 186n, 196

London left by, **38**. 274

London livery's petition protests against rejection of, **35**. 334n, **39**. 114, 115

London, Middlesex, and Westminster politically controlled by, **24**. 45

London's chief topic, **38**. 233

London visited by, when Parliament dissolved, **23**. 5

lord chancellor's retort from, on becoming lord mayor, **39**. 207

lord mayor's election 'as high as he can go,' **39**. 207

lord mayor's election won by, **24**. 45, 48, **39**. 186n, 196

Lorenzi and Botta discuss coming visit of, with Mann, **22**. 282

Louis XVI may be French equivalent of, **24**. 62

—— praised by, **28**. 304

Lovell opposes, **1**. 354n

Luther jovial as, **1**. 241

Luttrell takes place of, in House of Commons, **23**. 344

Mackreth might be proposed by, as Speaker, **39**. 221

manifestos by, against House of Commons, **23**. 205

Mann amazed at defiance of, **22**. 200

—— asks how often House of Commons can reject, after his election, **23**. 96, 110

—— glad of anything that draws attention away from, **23**. 138

—— glad to hear that release of, brought no crisis, **23**. 213

—— hopes, will never sit in House of Commons, **23**. 96

—— hopes that flight of, will end controversies, **22**. 203

—— hopes that Parliament will humble, **23**. 296

—— impatient for sequel to affair of, **23**. 16

—— not surprised by political shifts of, **25**. 23

—— pleased by disappointment of, **23**. 88

—— satisfied with behaviour of, in Florence, **22**. 281

Mansfield threatened by *North Briton* for persecuting, **23**. 28

March, E. of, demanded by, for examination, **10**. 272

——, Sandwich, and Temple demanded by, at bar of House of Commons, **23**. 73–4, 77

Martin denounces, in Parliament, for abusing him in *North Briton*, **38**. 226–7

—— describes affair with, **38**. 270

——practises for duel with, **28**. 71

——'s duel with, **10**. 65n, 111, **22**. 183–4, 192, 198, **28**. 75n, 480n, **38**. 227–9

——'s intercourse with, in Paris, **38**. 280

—— told by, that Paris visit is just to see his daughter, **22**. 198

masquerader dresses as, **23**. 193

Maurepas asks about, **7**. 337

memorials by, in newspapers, **23**. 339

Meredith moves for depositions against, **38**. 307–8

Middlesex elects, **4**. 227n, **10**. 274n, 277, **23**. 6–7, 86, 97, 104–5, **24**. 51, **28**. 46n, **32**. 213n, **39**. 197

——'s sheriffs summon, **23**. 475

mistress supposed to have robbed, **22**. 305

mob of: attacks rivals' coaches, **23**. 461n; does damage, **23**. 6–7

mob reverences, as saint, **10**. 111

mob tries to carry, from prison to Parliament, **23**. 20

Molineux, friend of, **39**. 96n

mottos frequently changed on publications of, **35**. 314

Mountmorres and Mahon defeated as Westminster candidates of, **24**. 51, **28**. 174n

Naples visited by, to write history, **22**. 281, 292, 305

never mentioned, but in debates on Middlesex election, **23**. 186

[Wilkes, John, *continued*]

North, Lord, participates in prosecution of, 10. 216

—— turned into, 32. 99

North Briton edited by: 14. 148n; Augusta, Ps of Wales, attacked in, 22. 53n; Bute's conduct may justify, 22. 396; Bute should be attacked by, for lack of favouritism, 32. 280; Bute will furnish matter for further issues of, 22. 402; condemned to be burnt, but rescued by mob at Cheapside, 1. 52n, 22. 187–8, 38. 256–7, 40. 335, 339; Court of King's Bench condemns, 38. 333; Danish equivalents of, 35. 328; English waste time on, 35. 314 Finch, Lady Charlotte, will not be abused by, 22. 72; Forbes objects to, 22. 162; George III lodges complaint against Wilkes for, 22. 182; George III, with D. of Gloucester and D. of Cumberland, attacked by, 22. 165; Glynn counsel for printers of, 35. 324n; HW attacked in No. 2 of, 13. 37–8; HW encloses, from magazine, 22. 196; HW instigates attack on Fox and himself in, 38. 193; HW may be denounced in, for entertaining E. of March, 38. 175; HW might write, against cold weather, 38. 196; HW recommended to Bute in, 38. 176; HW's praise of Scots ridiculed in, 38. 175n; HW will have copy of, made for Mann, 22. 194; Harris might be arrested for contributing to, 38. 202–3; Junius's attacks exceed, 23. 165; Mann thanks HW for, 22. 204; Mann wishes copy of, 22. 192; Mansfield persecutes printers of, at trials, 38. 433; Mansfield threatened by, for persecution of Wilkes, 23. 28; Martin abused in, 38. 226–7; Norton fails to prove Wilkes to be author of, 22. 189, 38. 259; No. 42 of, HW's opinion of, 10. 52; No. 45 of, 10. 216n, 32. 99, 35. 322–3; Parliamentary proceedings worthy of, 38. 545; printers of, sent to Newgate, 38. 196; publications on, 40. 273; read to House of Commons, 38. 225; Regency Bill resembles, 38. 545; riot on burning of, 38. 256–7; riot over burning of, considered to be a revolution, 22. 200, 209; Russians unlikely to waste time imitating writings of, 22. 60; Sandwich's writings as libellous as, 22. 323; satirizes Coronation, 9. 389n; Scots' second sight derided by, 33. 13n; Solicitor-General cannot prove Wilkes to be author of, 22. 189; unpublished in Wilkes's papers, 38. 199–200; Vergy's French imitation of, 22. 262; *Whisperer* and *Parliamentary Spy* more virulent than, 38. 196; Wilkes corrects, in bed, 38. 232; Wilkes might have used 'boy-bishop' rhymes upon Bp of Osnaburgh in, 38. 369; Wilkes sent to Tower because he accused Bute in, of making George III tell a lie, 22. 136; Wilkes writes, against Bute, 22. 60n; Williams the re-

printer of, 38. 512; Yorke, Charles, pronounces, a libel, 38. 325

North participates in prosecution of, 10. 216

obstacle to delivery of package, 4. 323

Onslow deserts, 28. 395n

Opposition alderman, 35. 334n

——'s support of, shows its unity, 38. 284–5

outlawed, 38. 469

Paoli might join, 23. 142

papers of: said to be illegally seized, 22. 207; seized, 38. 197

Paris visited by, 7. 266, 10. 180, 22. 198, 365, 38. 279, 290, 39. 16–17, 40. 386

Parliamentary debates on depositions and warrants concerning arrest of, 38. 307–9, 324–7

Parliamentary members carried by, 38. 196–7

Parliamentary representation wished by, to be reformed, 24. 187

Parliamentary seat demanded by, 1. 313n

Parliamentary seat to be demanded by, 23. 206

Parliamentary speeches by: about Burgoyne, 32. 400n; advocating British Museum's getting copy of every printed book and acquiring Houghton paintings, 24. 304, 43. 286

Parliament debates over legality of seizing papers of, 22. 207

——'s ending may deprive, of opportunity to vent his rage, 23. 214

—— to hear complaint of, on privilege, 38. 292

—— would be controlled by, if Pitt or Rockingham dissolved it, 23. 181

party of: squabbles over Lord Mayor's appointment, 23. 520; strangely crumbled, 23. 208

pension needed by, 3. 322

pension offered to, 7. 279

Piozzi, Mrs, comments on, 10. 180n

Pitt (Chatham) and Grenville quarrel with, in print, 23. 163

Pitt (Chatham) attacks, 23. 251

—— might not offend, 23. 115n

—— should be satirized by, 38. 255

—— turns against, 39. 255

plotters plan murder of, 38. 268

Potter an associate of, 13. 20n

printer released by, 23. 280

prosecution of, expensive, 41. 313

public speaking not the field of, 23. 86

Pynsent's bequest not believed by, 22. 281

release of, from prison, 4. 402, 405, 23. 205

re-election of, to Parliament, 4. 227n, 10. 274n, 277

remonstrance presented by, to throne, in good form, 24. 89

remonstrance written by, 28. 80

renomination of, urged, 24. 45n

return of, to England, expected, 7. 279, 10. 261n

ridiculous, 23. 246, 251

Rigby attacks Temple over commitment of, 38. 242

rigour against, ill-advised, 23. 86

riots allegedly fomented by, 23. 26

riots in favour of, 4. 73, 75, 10. 272, 22. 187–8

Rockingham shuns, 36. 200

Rockinghamites shun, 28. 337

Rome visited briefly by, 22. 292

Rousseau receives, but later complains about him, 35. 117

Sallust compared with, 38. 188

Sandwich accuses, of writing *Essay on Woman*, 38. 229–30

—— and the Scots forgotten by, to attack Hertford, 38. 362

—— as impious as, and less popular, 38. 233

—— attacks, in House of Lords, over *Essay on Woman*, 38. 293–4

—— demanded by, for examination, 10. 272

—— has, impeached, 10. 111

—— not hated by, 10. 180

Sayre a sheriff under, 24. 138

Scots oppose, 23. 8, 99, 317n

—— put different meaning on '45 than that of, 23. 30

search of secretaries of state's houses, demanded by, 22. 138

Selwin asked by, about Webb's indictment for perjury, 38. 297

Selwyn's witticism to, at Cockpit, on ear-cropping, 38. 223

sentence of: considered mild by Mann, 23. 37; does not arouse mob's sympathy, 23. 33

sent to Tower because of *North Briton* No. 45, 22. 136, 38. 197, 199

sheriff of London, 23. 314, 317, 360, 32. 52

social relations of, in Paris, with: Élie de Beaumont, 7. 286; HW, 7. 267, 269, 291, 306; Helvétius, 7. 289

sometimes lost a day, 35. 338

speeches of, printed by himself, 33. 147

Stanhope, Sir William, intimate with, at Naples, 22. 292

Stanley's health drunk by, in Paris, 38. 484

star of, dimmed, 23. 194

Stowe visit brings memory of, to HW, 10. 314

subscription for benefit of, 23. 92

successor will be named by, for Middlesex, 23. 82

supporters of Bill of Rights not approved by, 23. 114

Talbot fights, for abuse, 9. 389n, 22. 137, 163, 38. 229

Tanucci neglects, at Naples, 22. 292

Temple, Lord, demanded by, for examination, 10. 272

—— friend of, 22. 138, 304

—— not admitted to see, in Tower, 38. 199

—— 's behaviour on commitment of, 38. 242

—— 's reconciliation with Halifax and Sandwich will interest, 22. 303–4

to appear before bar of House of Commons, 23. 82

Tooke, John Horne, disputes with, 23. 263, 274, 314, 31. 151

—— intimate with, 28. 135n

too worthless to keep mob's respect, 23. 15

Tower of London the prison of, 22. 136, 38. 197, 199

Townsend contends with, for Middlesex election, 24. 47

—— supports, 10. 309n

Trelawny compared to, 38. 202

twelve Parliamentary members carried by, 39. 196

unlikely to pick more virtuous representatives than ministers have done, 15. 131

unpopular at Buckingham House, 22. 159

Van to move for expulsion of, from Parliament, 39. 225

verdict of, on Mme du Deffand's wager, 4. 89, 91, 164, 187, 198

'virtue' of, more popular than Pitt's eloquence, 23. 163

volatile in forgetting Sandwich and the Scots, 38. 362

Warburton pictures, in hell, 38. 230

—— 's speech against, 22. 185

—— wishes, burnt at *auto da fé*, 10. 111

weavers' mob incited by friends of, 38. 559n

Westminster seat may be filled by nominee of, 23. 206

Weymouth's letter sent by, to printer, 23. 77

Wilbraham objects to debate on privilege in absence of, 38. 240

will be harmless in House of Commons, 23. 8

Wilmot upholds verdict against, 23. 83

Winckelmann said to have left gold medals to, 23. 113

witticisms by: at Calais, to Croÿ on liberty of the press, 22. 137; on joining the seven bishops, 38. 202; on Lord George Germain, 24. 187, 38. 232

Wood prosecuted by, in Court of Common Pleas, 22. 188, 38. 258–9

wound of: prevents his appearing before House of Commons, 22. 198; recovers, 22. 186

writs of error of, to be tried before House of Lords, 23. 83

Yorke advises commitment of, to Tower, 38. 325

Yorke family opposes, 38. 284

Zoffany's portrait of, with daughter, 33. 138

Wilkes, Mary (1750–1802):

Castille's correspondence with, 7. 10

Cosway, Mrs, entertains, 33. 511

Cumberland, D. of, does not marry, 5. 131

father goes to Paris just to see, 22. 198

HW not to marry, 10. 311

HW visited by, 11. 333

[Wilkes, Mary, *continued*]
post-horses obtained by, at Calais, **23.** 143n
SH visited by, **12.** 248, **33.** 482–3
Zoffany's portrait of, with father, **33.** 138
Wilkes, Robert (ca 1665–1732), actor:
Richelieu, Duc de, reminiscent of age of, **35.** 114
Wilkes. *See also* Wilks
Wilkie, William (1721–72), D.D.; 'Scottish Homer':
Epigoniad by, abused in magazines, **15.** 52, 43. 194
Wilkin, C., engraver:
print by, of Rizzio, **42.** 75n
Wilkins, ——:
Walpole, Robert (1650–1700), buys wig of, **17.** 506
Wilkins, ——, (?) bookseller:
merchant at Bristol, **14.** 31n
previous husband of Mrs Middleton, **14.** 31n, **15.** 310
Wilkins, Mrs. *See* Powell, Anne
Wilkins, Sir Charles (ca 1749–1836):
translation by, **12.** 178n
Wilkins, John (1614–72), Bp of Chester, 1668:
æronautical interests of, may be prophetic, **33.** 418
desire of, to go to moon, **15.** 168
Discovery of a World in the Moon by, **15.** 168n, **39.** 424
Essay towards a Real Character and a Philosophical Language, An, by, **39.** 424–5
flying attributed to, **37.** 550–1
interpreter may be needed by, on reaching moon, **39.** 425
Wilkinson, Capt. (d. 1754):
Cumberland, D. of, employs, **10.** 186
family of, **10.** 186
Wilkinson, Mr:
Nivernais's *Jardins modernes* given to, **12.** 260
Wilkinson, Mrs:
Conway gives money to, **10.** 186
—— to procure pension for, **10.** 186
family of, **10.** 186
Jekyll, Lady Anne, friend of, **10.** 186
Wilkinson, Andrew (1697–1784), M.P.:
Amelia, Ps, says that Winnington is to succeed, **10.** 49
biographical information about, corrected, **43.** 128
Ordnance post lost by, **22.** 109n
Wilkinson, Capt. Andrew (d. 1785), of the *Glasgow*:
L'Oiseau's engagement with, **21.** 292
Tuscans complain about, **21.** 288
Wilkinson, Anne (1738–1803), m. (1771) Thomas Pitt, cr. (1784) Bn Camelford:
'a great fortune,' **32.** 52
courier sent by, to husband at Naples, **24.** 486
Du Deffand, Mme, to meet, **5.** 130
Greville, Mrs, praises, **5.** 130
Hobart, Mrs, entertains, at play at Ham Common, **33.** 370

husband takes, to Italy, **24.** 411
marriage of, expected, **32.** 52
messenger of, delivers Mann's letters to HW, **24.** 498
Mt Edgcumbe, Cts of, informs, of Brest's alleged surrender to Howe, **39.** 506
Wilkinson, James (d. 1736):
Hau Kiou Choaan translated by, **15.** 75n
Wilkinson, James, bailiff to Sir Gilbert Wakering:
goose delivered by, to Vcts Townshend, **40.** 77
Wilkinson, John, M.D.; F.R.S., 1764:
marine belt of, **22.** 332
Wilkinson, Mary (d. 1796), m. (1762) Joseph Priestley:
bigamy may be unfamiliar to, **31.** 328
Wilkinson, Mary (d. 1800), m. (1760) John Smith:
sister of, to marry, **32.** 52
Wilkinson, Montagu:
parents of, **10.** 186
Wilkinson, Pinckney (? 1693–1784), M.P.:
son-in-law takes, to Italy, **24.** 411
Wilkinson, Mrs William. *See* Amphlett, Christina
Wilks, Samuel, examiner of East India Co. correspondence:
Sykes brings, as witness, **23.** 452
Wilks. *See also* Wilkes
Will; wills:
Court of Chancery often sets aside, **22.** 578
French, ill-observed, **36.** 192
gratitude not to be expected from beneficiaries of, **24.** 27
HW involved with, over E. of Orford's affairs, **32.** 121, 122
HW's interest in, **2.** 258, 262, 263
Mann astonished that lawyers so readily undertake to break, **24.** 30
Montfort's, before his suicide, **35.** 202
Paris notary toasts dying man after making, for him, **32.** 260
questioning of, disliked by HW, **25.** 123
Spanish officers make, **17.** 427
Thomond cannot bring himself to make, **24.** 25
See also **34.** 497–8, *and under names of individual testators*
Willebroek. *See* Vilvorde
Willemstad (Netherlands):
Conway encamped near, **37.** 208–9
Dutch troops sail from Shields to, **19.** 221n
English army must escape by, **18.** 457
French to attack, **19.** 455n
Willes, Edward (ca 1693–1773), D.D.; Bp of St David's, 1742, of Bath and Wells, 1743:
'decipherer,' **17.** 279
Exeter bishopric desired by, **17.** 279–80
salary of, as decipherer, **17.** 279n
Walpole, Sir Robert, supports, **17.** 280
Willes, Edward (1723–87), M.P.; judge of Court of King's Bench:
election of, **13.** 20n

Wilkes appears before, **23**. 12

Willes, Sir John (1685–1761), Kt, 1737; Chief Justice of Common Pleas; M.P.:
becomes commissioner of the Great Seal, **20**. 25
Buckingham Assizes Bill aims at, **26**. 27–8
court martial's dispute with, **19**. 328
death of, **9**. 413
friends of, oppose assizes bill, **13**. 20
Grenville never to be forgotten or forgiven by, **19**. 328n
Grenvilles attack, **13**. 19
—— oppose, over Buckingham assizes, **19**. 470–1
insurrections opposed by, **20**. 585
lawyers' army led by, **19**. 180
lord chancellor's post refused by, **19**. 212
Maclaine tried by, at Old Bailey, **20**. 188n
Melcombe entertains, **9**. 373
on circuit, **18**. 25
Parliamentary membership of, corrected, **43**. 246
regiment raised by, among gentlemen of inns of court, **19**. 180n
Walpole, Sir Robert, entrusts daughter to, **26**. 28
—— visited by, at Houghton, **18**. 25

Willes, John (? 1721–84), M.P.:
Parliamentary membership of, corrected, **43**. 264
Pelham's speech against father answered by, **19**. 471

Willes, Margaret (ca 1756–1829), m. (1778) Sir George Howland Beaumont, 7th Bt:
Berry, Mary, identifies, **11**. 220n
eagerness of, **11**. 253
HW visited by, **11**. 220
London, Bp of, visited by, **11**. 253
SH visited by, **12**. 233

Willes. *See also* Wills

Willet, Mr:
at Brentford Butts, **1**. 96n

Willett, Mr:
SH ticket not used by, **12**. 224n

William I (the Conqueror) (1027–87), K. of England 1066–87:
Bayeux tapestries of: **40**. 213; described by Lethieullier, **40**. 221
cherries cheapest since landing of, **34**. 8
Clinton title dates from time of, **18**. 126
currency in time of, **16**. 108
daughter of, **2**. (?) 6, **12**. 263
effigy of, **28**. 100n
English carry branches in battle with, **5**. 199, **35**. 429
Fitzosbern, marshal of, **1**. 387
Ingulph contemporary with, **16**. 195
kitchen of: drawing of, **36**. 38; tiles from, **36**. 38–9
ludicrous print of, **15**. 123
Montfaucon represents, with wife and sons, **40**. 213
Odo, half-brother of, **2**. 182

Peverel, Lady, concubine of, **2**. 175
sea's foretelling the coming of, **16**. 337–8
son of, **35**. 154
statue of, in York Minster, **1**. 276
Westminster Abbey receives silver from, for its completion, **40**. 223
Windsor exchanged by, for other lands, **40**. 223

William II (? 1056–1100) Rufus, K. of England 1087–1100:
Montfaucon represents, **40**. 213
tomb of, at Winchester, **35**. 250

William III (1650–1702), P. of Orange; K. of England 1688–1702:
anecdotes forged against, **28**. 192
Argyll and Cobham promoted by, **26**. 14
artistic taste of, better than his literary taste, as shown by patronizing Kneller and Blackmore, **41**. 191
assassination plot against, **28**. 174
at Battle of the Boyne, **15**. 19n
authentic papers needed for reign of, **42**. 286
avenue planted by, **9**. 380n
birthday of: **33**. 147; celebrated in Dublin, **9**. 401; *Tamerlane* acted on, **19**. 333
Burke's praise of, **34**. 223
Clarendon's anecdotes of, **15**. 148–9
counsel for accused prisoners authorized in reign of, **19**. 396
Dalrymple perhaps offended by HW's treatment of, **14**. 176
England's conquest by, not repeated in Nassau's attack on Jersey, **24**. 472
English constitution should be as pointed out by, **35**. 355
English revolutionaries accompany, from Holland, **16**. 376
Exeter espouses cause of, **15**. 204n
factions bribed by, **25**. 605
Fenwick plots assassination of, **20**. 322n
few men lost by, in 1688 coup, **16**. 376
followers of, to be expelled by Young Pretender, **9**. 23
fortune inherited and half spent by, **7**. 362
France threatened by, with Courtenay's claims, **19**. 310
—— to be humbled by, **25**. 605
gardener to, **2**. 200n
George II imitates, **42**. 496
George III subverts acts of, **28**. 451n
Germain, Sir John, accompanied, to England, **10**. 341
Glencoe massacre in time of, **28**. 451
HW charged with disrespect to, **14**. 162
HW remembered half the remaining Court of, **25**. 558
HW ridicules alleged virtues of reign of, **25**. 605
HW's admiration for, **28**. 307, 387, 388
HW's comment on adherents of, **33**. 305
HW's patron saint, **35**. 477–8
HW tries to discourage Robertson from writing life of, **28**. 386–90

[William III, *continued*]

Halifax's poem on the Boyne mentions, **18.** 266

Hamilton gets retort from, about Scotland, **19.** 103

Hanover, House of, asked by, to give up German lands, **7.** 362

Hardinge a worshipper of, **35.** 582

Hardwicke's remarks on, **35.** 603

health drunk to memory of, at Leghorn, **19.** 152

House of Commons forces new administration on, **33.** 331n

Ireland has spirit of, **33.** 153

Jacobites take oaths to, **2.** 135n

James II's letter to, **35.** 626–7

Kelly confined in Tower since plot against, **19.** 153n

Kneller's portraits of beauties of reign of, at Hampton Court, **30.** 326n

landing of, **16.** 296n

La Rochefoucauld, Charlotte de, proposed to, **7.** 315

letters of, shown to HW by Lady Mary Coke, **31.** 147

Macaulay, Mrs, abuses, **28.** 371

Marlborough's remark from, **28.** 388

medal of, for battle of La Hogue, **21.** 357n

Montagu jokes about cravat of, **10.** 158

Namur taken by, **28.** 296

naval operations in reign of, **21.** 223

Orkney, Lady, favourite of, **34.** 260

papers of, made available to Sir John Dalrymple, **28.** 67n

part of coat of, set in locket, **33.** 338

plot against, **20.** 322n, **28.** 174n

Portland, favourite of, **10.** 4n

——— receives relic from, **9.** 114n

portraits of parents of, at Chantilly, **7.** 260

reign of, **16.** 29n

Remarks on Mr Walpole's Catalogue asperses, **16.** 30

Rochford and Grantham not allowed by: to take Nassau name, **24.** 360; to use Nassau arms, **24.** 370

Scotland given liberty by, **16.** 374

Scots traduce, **29.** 105, 135

Seymour, Sir Edward, retorts to, about D. of Somerset, **18.** 523

Shebbeare writes against, **21.** 39n

shillings coined in reign of, **11.** 3

silver coinage of time of, **16.** 77

Sophia plays loo with, **7.** 362

spurs of, given to HW by Harcourt, **28.** 339, **35.** 477–8, 488; *see also under* Spurs

statue of: **13.** 85–6; at Dublin, **9.** 401

subject of 'chaste and sacred,' **35.** 561

Tamerlane acted on birthday of, **9.** 48n, **19.** 333

times of, serious, **15.** 130

Walpole, Sir Robert, highly admired, **15.** 148

Whitehall Palace burnt in reign of, **16.** 321

William I, ancestor of, **28.** 387n

wounded in battle of the Boyne, **33.** 338

Wren's work at Hampton Court controlled by, **40.** 347, 353

yielded to Parliament, **33.** 331

William IV (1765–1837), cr. (1789) D. of Clarence; K. of England 1830–7:

age of, compared to HW's, **11.** 164

Albany, Cts of, converses with, **11.** 271

(?) ambition of, to be M.P., **34.** 71

anecdote of P. Frederick and, **12.** 255

Barbados and Port Royal visited by, as *Andromeda*'s captain, **25.** 684n

Beauclerk, Lady Diana, entertains, at breakfast, **11.** 341, **43.** 150

birthday of: celebrated by boat-race and ball, **11.** 337, 341, 342, **43.** 150; celebrated with P. of Orange and Mrs Jordan, **12.** 151

birth of, **10.** 167, **32.** 19

Bland, Dorothy, later mistress to, **33.** 507n

Budé governor to, **12.** 9n

conduct of, negative and varied, **34.** 90

father requests provision for, **24.** 371

Finch, Polly, brought to Richmond by, **11.** 63

Garter given to, **22.** 37n, **25.** 273

Gunnersbury visited by, when HW is there, **33.** 406

HW attends party for, **31.** 347

HW describes, **11.** 164

(?) HW's verses for, **12.** 261

HW visited by, **11.** 332

HW visits, **11.** 332

Jordan, Mrs, mistress of, **11.** 352n, **12.** 142

La Luzerne's ball quitted by, early, without dancing, **39.** 465

La Luzerne, Comtesse de, honoured by, at ball at Almack's, **39.** 465n

Leghorn may be visited by, **25.** 590

parents' disagreements with, **39.** 465

(?) Parliamentary ambitions of, **34.** 71

peerage withheld from, **25.** 684

Queensberry's social relations with, **31.** 347

Richmond house of, **11.** 63, 152, 163–4

Richmond house wearies, **34.** 68

Richmond popularity of, **34.** 71–2

Roehampton house taken by, **11.** 70–1, **34.** 68

sails from England to Mediterranean, **25.** 590

Schwellenberg, Mme, called 'old bitch' by, for not curtseying, **39.** 464

SH visited by family of, **12.** 244

Sydney's discussion with, of Clarence dukedom, **25.** 684n

tells brothers he will be king before they are, **34.** 72

Wales, George, P. of (George IV), visits, **12.** 188n

William I (1533–84), P. of Orange:

apotheosis of, by Rubens, **34.** 239

HW considers William III the greatest man since, **28.** 387

(?) witticism by, about fancies of unmarried girls and unmilitary men, **24.** 414

William II (1626–50), P. of Orange:

portrait of, at Chantilly, **21.** 260

William III (1650–1702), P. of Orange. *See* William III, K. of England, *above*

William IV (1711–51), P. of Orange 1732–51; stadtholder, 1747:
army under, at Breda, **37.** 282n
authority of, tottering, **20.** 279
Burdett discovers alleged plot against, **20.** 20
Conway and wife see, in bed with wife and family, **37.** 287, 289
Cumberland, D. of, may be envied by, **19.** 346
death of: **20.** 279, 283, 285; postpones English festivities, **20.** 280
extremely ugly, **37.** 289
Grovestins sent by, to pacify Haarlem, **37.** 286
guns not fired for wedding of, **38.** 288
HW resents being kept from his mother by, **36.** 4
health of: Aix waters taken, **20.** 279; colic and fever, **37.** 286n; imposthume in head, **20.** 283
Holland prevented by, from accepting neutrality, **19.** 408
Karl Friedrich nephew of, **20.** 148
made Stadtholder, **19.** 394, 408
Mann had expected achievements from, **19.** 408
marriage of, **16.** 21n
Newcastle and Sandwich urge, to carry on war against France, **19.** 403n
Quakers address, at Bath, with hats on, **24.** 53n
rejected as member of King's Council, **25.** 680n
Waldeck's dispute with, **19.** 429n
Walpole, Horatio (1723–1809), describes Court of, **19.** 418
wife of, **7.** 354n

William V (1748–1806), P. of Orange 1751–95; Stadtholder:
Anderson, Mrs, dines with, **12.** 143
Austria, Prussia, and France might limit, to a little kingdom near The Hague, **25.** 539
baptism of, **37.** 283
birth of, **19.** 469
Blenheim visited by, **12.** 203
blue ribbon conferred on, **20.** 311
Clarence, D. of (William IV), entertains, **12.** 151
Conway and wife see, **37.** 287
England the refuge of, after French invasion, **34.** 201n
Frederick II intervenes in favour of, **34.** 32n
Frederick William II sends troops to, **39.** 450n, 455n, 457n
Garter installation of, by proxy, **20.** 311n
George III subsidizes, **39.** 448, 450
Hampton Court Palace occupied by, **12.** 140n, 148n, **34.** 213
Johnston, Lady Cecilia, visits, **12.** 148
Nixon appointed apothecary to, **12.** 143
Nuneham and Oxford visited by, **12.** 203
opposition to, tries to depose him, **33.** 562n
SH visited by, **12.** 248
tutors to, **38.** 6
ultimatum issued by, to Brabant, **11.** 130–1
Walter, Mr, to gather news about, **12.** 140
Yorke, Joseph, invests, with Garter at The Hague, **20.** 311n
—— warns, of England's ship-searching, **39.** 347n

'William, Prince.' *See* William (1336–44) of Hatfield; William IV (1765–1837); William Augustus (1721–65), D. of Cumberland; William Frederick (1776–1834), D. of Gloucester; William Henry (1743–1805), D. of Gloucester

'William, Lord.' *See* Gordon, Lord William

William (Plantagenet) (1336–44), P., of Hatfield, 2d son of Edward III:
arms of, **2.** 46, 49
so called from Hatfield, Yorks, **2.** 50
statues of, **2.** 49, 50, 51
tomb of, in York Minster: **1.** 275, **2.** 46; neglected, **28.** 42–3; restoration of, planned by Mason, **28.** 44, and paid for by Mason and HW, **28.** 306–8, 311

William (Plantagenet) (b. 1447), son of Richard, D. of York:
birth of, **1.** 320

William (d. ? 1143) of Malmesbury, historian:
on St Wulfstan and Erwen, **1.** 15–16

William of Worcester. *See* Worcester, William (1415–ca 1482)

William (1324–1404), of Wykeham; Bp of Winchester; lord chancellor:
crozier of, **9.** 289n
HW jokes about Wyatt and, **31.** 342
Lowth's life of, **28.** 30
monument of, at Winchester, **35.** 250
portraits of: at New College, Oxford, **38.** 43–4, 45; at Winchester, **38.** 44, 45
Zouch questions evidence of architecture by, **16.** 35

William, Landgrave of Hesse. *See* Wilhelm

William, Charlotte (b. before 1780), natural dau. of 5th D. of Devonshire; m. —— Heaton:
Devonshire, D. of, said to be father of, **25.** 444, 455
father of, pays Lady Elizabeth Foster to go to France with her, **25.** 459n
Foster, Lady Elizabeth, accompanies, at Florence, **25.** *444*
—— governess to, **25.** 455, 459

William, merchant vessel:
(?) capture of, **21.** 264

William and Mary, yacht:
Calais visited by, to await Lady Cardigan, **17.** 141
Italian singers visit, **17.** 141

William Augustus (1721–65), D. of Cumberland; 'Nolkejumskoi':
Aberdeen occupied by, **19.** 228
—— the station of, while awaiting supplies, **19.** 233
'affronted,' **22.** 303
aides-de-camp of: **11.** 49–50; accompany him to Edinburgh, **19.** 204; accompany him to

[William Augustus, *continued*]

Hulst, 19. 395; and Bedchamber lords accompany, abroad, 21. 78n

Aix treaty's provisions for Maestricht criticized by, 19. 480n

Albemarle (Bury) accompanies, from Hanover, 9. 73

—— a favourite of, 20. 269, 460, 22. 94n, 366n

—— aide-de-camp to, 19. 177, 204, 218

—— and Townshend quarrel over, 9. 319

Albemarle (Bury) escorted by, to Windsor, 20. 460

—— has greater interest with. than Conway does, 37. 220

—— lord of the Bedchamber to, 20. 74n, 459n

—— speaks to, at HW's wish, about Cornwallis's colonelcy, 37. 220

—— tells, of Brudenell's expectations for regiment, 37. 386

Albemarle, Ds of, congratulated by, in Drawing-Room, 22. 94

alderman's witticism on butcheries of, 19. 288

allied armies commanded by, 19. 340n

allowance of, might revert to nephews, 22. 424n

Almack's attended by, after levee and opera, 38. 512

Amelia, Ps, accompanied by, to Stowe, 22. 247n

—— and Francis III discuss corpulency of, 20. 57

Ancram instead of Conway gets dragoon regiment from, 37. 316n

annuities settled on, 19. 284n

Anson's head may replace that of, on street-signs, 37. 272-3

appearance of: fatness increasing, 37. 259; 'fatted calf,' 35. 225; *see also* corpulence of appears in coach at course at Newmarket, 38. 456

arm-chair refused by, 9. 337-8

army adores, 19. 174, 204

army applications come through, 19. 302

army command resigned by, 21. 145

army joined by, at Lichfield, 19. 128n

army left by, 18. 327

army of: Boyd in, 19. 285; in Netherlands, 19. 389; of observation, in Hanover, 21. 73; to be joined by him, 18. 217; to be led against rebels, 19. 166-7; to meet at Stone, 19. 173

army review at Nistelrode pleases, 37. 285-6

army treated tyrannically by, 20. 73n

arrival of, in London from Stade, 37. 512n, 514

Ashe, comptroller of household to, 20. 208n

assistants of, 19. 19-20

Augusta, Ps of Wales, urges, to linger on George III's wedding night, 21. 530

Austrian and Dutch armies' retirement from Flanders not expected by, 37. 296

Austrian appointment of P. Charles in Flanders offends, 19. 288

baggage of, returned from Scotland, 19. 242

ball at Kew attended by, 35. 229

ball given by, 37. 276

Balmerinoch's plea for intercession received by, 9. 46

Banks, Margaret, given ball by, 9. 38, 42, 19. 234n

Barrington acceptable to, as secretary at war, 20. 503n

Bath, E. of, may want to injure, 19. 347

Bath grandmastership coveted by, 20. 120n

Batthyáni to be relieved by, 19. 446n

Beauclerk, Lord Henry, persecuted by, 9. 86

Bedford, D. and Ds of, entertain, 9. 232, 363

Bedford, D. of, and E. of Sandwich might give control of navy to, 20. 222n

Bedford, D. of, supported by, 20. 113, 201

—— visited by, at Woburn, 20. 89

Bedford faction asked by, to respect George III, 7. 369

Bedford faction favoured by, 20. 120, 207

behaviour of, as ranger of Windsor Great Park, disobliges whole country, 20. 73n

Bentley's apology for, 35. 643

——'s design for palace for, unexecuted, 35. 161

biographical information about, corrected, 43. 350

birthday of, 17. 398

Braddock's slowness irritates, 20. 492

Bradford camp unlikely to aid, 37. 492

Brand to attend levee of, 9. 330

brave: at Fontenoy, 19. 44; at Hastenbeck, 21. 119; at Laeffeld, 19. 426

Breda revisited by, 19. 446

brother-in-law may envy, 19. 346

brother not imitated by, 21. 145

Bute opposed by, 38. 186

—— would hardly be attended by, in illness, 38. 344

Byng's sacrifice said to be determined by, 21. 55n

Cabinet changes predicted by, 9. 210

Campbell equerry to, 9. 377n

candle held by, while surgeon opens his knee, 38. 456

captain-generalcy not desired by, 30. 181

captured money lent to, for army use, 37. 236

Carlisle captured by, 19. 193

Carlisle House ball attended by, 38. 291, 296

Cathcart causes accident to, 9. 42-3

(?) —— may influence, 37. 401

cavalry of, in pursuit of rebels, 40. 55

Charles, P., may be replaced by, in Flanders, 19. 324

Charlotte, Q., given away by, at wedding, 21. 529

—— speaks German to, 38. 117

Chesterfield disparages, 6. 37

Churchill's resignation accepted by, 30. 85

Constitutional Queries attacks, 20. 222, 234

Conway aide-de-camp to: 14. 10n, 19. 26, 177,

204, 218; due to Sir Robert Walpole's request through Poyntz, **37.** 188n
Conway and Hawley sent by, **19.** 179
Conway annoyed to find, in Flanders on return, **37.** 295
—— asks leave of, to take wife to Dover, **37.** 291
—— confers with, **37.** 475n
——, Dover, Fitzwilliam, and Lord Frederick Campbell all in service of, **34.** 59n
Conway fights by the side of, **37.** 261
—— goes to Court to see, **37.** 367–8
—— praised by, **37.** 196
—— rushes from Rotterdam to Breda to prepare for, **37.** 281–2
——'s admiration for, pleases HW, **37.** 195–6
——'s anti-Army votes resented by, **37.** 188n
——'s Bedchamber ambitions told to, **37.** 386
——'s horse kicks leg of, at review near Reading, **37.** 382, 383
——'s loyalty to, during regency crisis, **22.** 298n
——'s marriage subject of jokes by, **31.** 278
——'s recommendation from, mentioned by George II to Pelham, **37.** 226
——'s regiment at Laeffeld praised by, **37.** 274
——'s regiment joins army of, **37.** 282
—— summoned by, **37.** 192
—— to be provided with regiment by, **37.** 209
—— told by, that ministers seek to prevent his going to Scotland, **19.** 204
—— visits, at Windsor Lodge, **37.** 382, 386
coolness and intrepidity of, **37.** 191
Coronation proceedings arouse laughter of, **9.** 389n
corpulence of, **18.** 268, **20.** 49, 57, 121, 208–9, **21.** 432
costume of: at George II's funeral, **9.** 322; at masquerade, **20.** 49
counsellors chosen by, said to be unprincipled and wicked, **20.** 73n
Court avoided by, to keep his policy secret, **22.** 102n
Court would not get much quarter from, **22.** 102
Coventry, Cts of, accompanied by, in Hyde Park, **9.** 185
Coventry left by, in search of rebels, **19.** 185n
Cromarty receives rents of, **19.** 284
crowds entertained by, **9.** 337
cruelty of, **19.** 464n
Culloden laurels of, **19.** 246–9, **37.** 238–41
Culloden news sent by, **19.** 247
Cumberland Lodge inhabited by, with whores and aides-de-camp, **37.** 258n
Danish princess supposed to marry, **19.** 20
death of: **7.** 270, 397, **10.** 190n, **14.** 141, **22.** 363–4; announced in Leyden gazette, **22.** 370; leaves vacancy in Bath order, **22.** 417n; reported, **10.** 135; rumoured, **22.** 256, **38.** 444, 445
defeat; defeats of: **9.** 49n, 74, 214, **19.** 42,

21. 119, **35.** 63, **37.** 493–4, 495, 497; irretrievable, **21.** 125; rumoured, **19.** 253
defence of, after Klosterzeven will be difficult, **37.** 514
Dettingen behaviour of, praised, **18.** 258, 259, 279, **35.** 40
Devonshire, D. of, visited by, at Chatsworth, **38.** 19
disappointments of, in Low Countries, **19.** 409
discipline of, strict, **19.** 464
Douglas, 'Mother,' calls, 'Great Sir,' **19.** 52
drums and trumpets enjoyed by, **19.** 20
'Duke of Wales' the nickname of, **19.** 52n
Dunmore subordinate to, **19.** 20
Dunoyer's comment about, to Q. Caroline, **30.** 28
Dutch perform orders of, **19.** 346
Edinburgh insults, **19.** 288
—— to be visited by, on way to Stirling Castle, **19.** 204
—— visited by, **19.** 193n, **37.** 221
Elibank to be sued by, **19.** 284
endangered, **35.** 59
England expects return of, **9.** 52, **19.** 255–6, 271, 442, 495
—— reached by, **21.** 144
English habit worn by, at masquerade, **20.** 49
Euston, Cts of, dances country dances with, at Birthday ball, **37.** 116
Euston visited by, **20.** 373n
expected: in England from Hanover, **30.** 137; in London from Scotland, **30.** 103
exposes himself rashly, at Hastenbeck, **37.** 493–4
Falkirk battle brings, to Scotland, **14.** 2
falls down at ball, **20.** 121
Fawkener secretary to, **19.** 26, 382n, 456n
——'s patron, **29.** 306
Ferrers's trial not attended by, **9.** 280
Finch, Lady Isabella, entertains, at loo party, **38.** 397
fireworks watched by, **20.** 48
Fitzpatrick, Keppel, and H. Fox favoured by, in New Windsor elections, **31.** 19n
Fitzwilliam serves under, **11.** 48n
Flemish campaign may be conducted by, **19.** 240
Florentines condemn, **17.** 360
Fontenoy defeat must mortify, **19.** 42
—— failure of, **35.** 63
—— makes, as popular with men as he is with low women, **19.** 52
—— shows heroism of, **37.** 191
Fort Augustus the objective of, **37.** 249n
Fortrose with, **19.** 233
Fox, Henry, advised by, to remain secretary at war, **20.** 417n
—— attached to, **20.** 224, 412
—— breaks with, **22.** 102, 134
—— favoured by, **21.** 93n
—— hated by George II and Ps of Wales for attachment to, **21.** 6n

[William Augustus, *continued*]

—— persuaded by George II and, to remain secretary at war, 30. 319

—— removed from, 20. 502n

—— seeks reconciliation with, through Albemarle, 30. 201

——'s friend, 30. 107

—— tells, he is surprised at appointment as paymaster, 21. 74n

—— to lay HW's request for George Montagu before, 30. 110–11

—— urged by, to remain secretary at war, 20. 39

France sends seasoned troops against, 21. 94

Frederick II must be envied by, 21. 432

French allegedly defeated by, 40. 95

French army approached by, 21. 117

French army may be engaged by, 37. 489

French defeat, at Hastenbeck, 9. 214, 21. 119

French enmity to, used as excuse to thrash French actor, 18. 305

French enrage, by demanding prisoners' return, 37. 280

French landing to be prevented by, 19. 187

Garter of, to go to Albemarle, 22. 366

generalissimo's post makes, happy, 19. 19–20

George II accompanies, at his entrance into Parliament, 17. 398

—— anxious about, 9. 50

—— believes, to be paying his own expenses, 20. 373

—— commends, in will, 9. 317–18

—— discusses military appointments with, before deciding them, 30. 111

—— might recall, if Young Pretender proved to be a sham, 19. 174, 199

—— orders, to sign Klosterzeven convention but disavows it, 21. 136n

—— receives, badly, 21. 145

—— said to give Hanover to, at instance of Parliament and P. of Wales, 17. 328

——'s bequests to, 9. 317–18, 21. 450, 38. 79

——'s birthday ball opened by, 17. 183n

——'s deed of gift to, 38. 79

——'s funeral attended by, 9. 322–3

——'s gifts of jewels and money to, 21. 450

——'s will opened in presence of, 21. 450n

—— to be accompanied by: to Flanders, 18. 62; to Hanover, 18. 209

—— to be approached by, about regiment for Cornwallis, 37. 220

—— to sacrifice, for obeying him, 30. 142

George III advised by, to retake old ministers, 30. 184

—— appoints, captain-general, 38. 562, 564

—— compliments, on Albemarle's success, 22. 94

—— gives Bath ribbon of, to second son, 22. 578

—— grants offices to friends of, 22. 307

—— hates, 22. 364

—— names, captain-general, 22. 302, 30. 181

—— omits, from Regency, 22. 295

—— reconciled with, 10. 153

—— said to be disliked by, 22. 163

——'s attentions to, 21. 443, 449

—— shows kindness to, 9. 313

——'s regency plans opposed by, 22. 299

—— summons, to form new administration and treat with Pitt, 38. 557–8, 562

—— to see, at Buckingham House, 22. 307n

—— unites with, in hating ministers, 22. 364

George IV's godfather, 38. 174

'girl' lost by, 37. 387

'God Save the King' led by, 9. 81

Gower probably directed by, to propose to George II that nobles recruit for the army, 37. 446

Granville prevents, from having command in Flanders, 19. 287n

——'s and Bolton's appointments probably distasteful to, 20. 207

Great Wardrobe furnishes the Palace for, 20. 373

Grenville criticizes frequent presence of, at Court, 30. 185

HW attacks, in *The Remembrancer*, 20. 73n

HW calls H. Fox the viceroy of, 21. 73n

HW compliments, in epilogue to *Tamerlane*, 13. 16n, 19. 351

HW imagines, tending Bute's sick-bed, 38. 344

HW jokingly suggests that Pitt have regiment under, 35. 281

HW mentions, 20. 292, 37. 479

HW never courted, 39. 530

HW not yet presented to, 30. 27

HW played with, at Leicester House in childhood, 25. 647

HW prefers, to Alexander the Great, 37. 258

HW sends duty to, 36. 2

HW's philosophy might be upset by proximity of, 37. 259

HW's probable source, through Richmond and Conway, for George III's conversation with Bedford and Grenville, 30. 201

HW's relations with, 9. 330–1

HW talks with, at masquerade, 17. 359

HW wishes Fox would send, to avenge defeat at Roucour, 30. 107

Hague, The, visited by, 19. 68, 37. 264

Hamilton's plea for Kilmarnock's pardon rejected by, 9. 46

Hanover to be administered by, 20. 249

—— to be revisited by, 9. 73

—— to be visited by: 18. 276n; to command army of observation, 21. 73, 78

—— visited by, 21. 73n

Hardwicke supports Pitt to keep down Fox and, 20. 412n

Hartington's decision to be notified to, 37. 398n

Hastenbeck defeat of, 37. 493–4, 495, 497

Hawley and Braddock please, by their brutality, 20. 492

Hawley the favourite general and executioner of, **20**. 73

hazard played by: at Bedford House, **35**. 225; in HW's newspaper parody, **9**. 126

Hazard's booty lent to, **37**. 236

head of, replaces Vernon's on signs, **37**. 266, 272

health drunk to, at Leghorn, **19**. 152

health of: bad leg, **9**. 322, **37**. 428, 429, **38**. 444; blindness, **9**. 73, 322; bloated face, **9**. 322; Daffy's Elixir agrees with, **38**. 535; declining, **22**. 288; erysipelas, **22**. 256; fatter, **9**. 73; fever treated by Ranby with bark, **18**. 268n; fits, **38**. 444; gout, **38**. 444, 445; ill, **18**. 279, **42**. 495; mends daily, **38**. 495; not well, **37**. 283; recovered after incision in knee, **38**. 455–6; relapsed, **38**. 523; salivation needed, **19**. 483; shivering fit, **18**. 268; sore throat, **38**. 462; speech altered, **38**. 445; stroke, **9**. 300, 322; stroke of the palsy, **21**. 432; wound in leg, **18**. 258, 268, 340, **21**. 432; wounds received at Fontenoy, **37**. 191

Hertford never had the confidence of, **38**. 330

Hervey's conduct praised by, **26**. 30

Hervey, Felton, groom of the Bedchamber to, **18**. 69n

Hessian troops retained by, **19**. 221n

Hildsley aide-de-camp to, **36**. 13

Holland to be visited by, **19**. 464

—— visited by, **19**. 340, 351

horses brought by, from Flanders for campaign against rebels, **37**. 209

Hulst secretly visited by, before its surrender, **19**. 395

illness of, makes England insecure, **42**. 495

Inverness occupied by, **19**. 247

Inverness magistrates to celebrate birthday of, **9**. 135

Jacobite feint misleads, **37**. 211n

Jacobites claim to have wounded, **19**. 261

—— in official posts in Scotland denounced by, to George II, **20**. 310n

joke by, on Secker, **9**. 318

jovial countenance of, **30**. 73

Karl Wilhelm Ferdinand twice dines with, **38**. 287

Kensington revisited by, **20**. 89n

Keppel, Hon. William, aide-de-camp to, **20**. 459

Kilmarnock accused by, of proposing to murder English prisoners, **9**. 38

—— falsely charged by, **19**. 299–300

Klosterzeven convention concluded by, with Richelieu, **21**. 136n

Königsegg serves, **19**. 19–20

Laeffeld battle fought by, **19**. 409n, 423–4

landau driven by, on course at Newmarket, **38**. 462

La Rochefoucauld, Charlotte de, governess to, **7**. 315n

laundress to, **19**. 427n

Lens, drawing-master to 2. 223n, **13**. 7

Letter from the Cocoa Tree abuses, **22**. 102n

levee of: **37**. 291; HW attends, **38**. 256, 494; Newcastle, D. of, attends, **38**. 256

Lichfield quarters of, **37**. 212

Ligonier to be subordinate to, **19**. 20, 167

limps, **18**. 340

lions and tigers of, at Windsor, **37**. 383

lodge of: HW does not prefer, to Stowe, **10**. 43–4; Montagu prefers, to Stowe, **10**. 42; Montagu visits, **10**. 42

London may give honours to, **19**. 288

—— return of, **19**. 271n

—— saved by, from rebel army, **19**. 178

—— to be visited by, **9**. 27, 30

—— visited by, **9**. 73

loo played by, **9**. 337, 412

losses of, at loo, **9**. 412

Louis XV's peace overtures to, **19**. 430n

Lyttelton collects depositions against, **20**. 240

—— ill-treated by, **20**. 33

Maestricht siege to be relieved by, **37**. 282

Mann admires philosophy of, **22**. 291

—— asked by, for map of Rome, **20**. 459

—— cheered by expulsion of rebels from England by, **19**. 214

—— hopes, will subdue Scotland, **19**. 205, 257

—— hopes for military success by, **21**. 96

—— hopes that rebels will be terrified by, **19**. 218

—— questions tactics of, at Hastenbeck, **21**. 146

—— would have given half his share of Leghorn toasts to, **19**. 151

Mann, Galfridus, to be regimental clothier to, **37**. 231

Mann, James, favoured by, **21**. 50

March, E. of, bets with, **38**. 448

Mary, Ps, to visit, **19**. 295

Mathews's cockade arouses curiosity of, **18**. 522

Methodism subject of bon mot by, **9**. 73

military experience sought by, **19**. 39

militia despised by, **37**. 572–3

Mingotti favoured by, **20**. 557, **37**. 459

minority led by, in House of Lords, **22**. 187

mob hails, **35**. 39

Montagu, Lady Anne, supposedly had affair with, **30**. 62

Montagu, George, regrets reported death of, **10**. 135

Mordaunt receives Pretender's coach from, **9**. 35

Münchhausen conveys George II's orders for, to Steinberg at Hanover, **21**. 136n

—— rebuked by, **21**. 145

Murray's rear-guard attacked by, **19**. 186n

Mutiny Bill receives vote of, **20**. 38

name of, disperses armies, **19**. 209, 213

Navy Bill favoured by, **20**. 33n

Newcastle, D. of, at odds with, **20**. 120

——, Bentinck, and Sandwich to meet with, **19**. 485n

Newcastle, D. of, calls on, **40**. 361

[William Augustus, *continued*]
—— complains to Pelham of ill-usage by, **20.** 120n
—— ignored by, **9.** 232
—— negotiates with Grenville to strengthen himself against, **20.** 72n
—— sees troop review prepared by, **19.** 495
——'s followers will desert to, **21.** 93
—— stands on train of, **9.** 323
—— tells, of elder Horace Walpole's intrigues, **19.** 474n
Newmarket gambling led by, **20.** 373
—— losses of, predictable, **38.** 272
—— may be visited by, instead of army, **37.** 459
—— popularity of, for hospitality and deep gambling, **37.** 352
—— to be visited by, **40.** 361
—— visited by, **22.** 288, 297, 373n, **38.** 444, 445, 527, 535
noblemen's raising light horse troops disapproved by, **37.** 452
'Nolkejumskoi,' HW's cant name for, **35.** 161n
Norfolk, D. and Ds of, entertain, **9.** 331, 337
—— to give ball for, **37.** 454
Norris to be joined by, **13.** 226
Northumberland urges, to make overtures to Pitt and Temple, **22.** 300n
nose-blowing forbidden under window of, **19.** 464
odes to, on Dettingen victory, **35.** 39
Ogilvie, Bns, not allowed by, to see anybody, **37.** 245
Old Pretender survives, **22.** 404
omnipotent, but uses nothing but machines, **20.** 417
opera house taken by, **20.** 557
Opposition leaders summoned by, **22.** 308n
Opposition might be countenanced by, **20.** 300
Opposition persuaded by, to form ministry, **22.** 310
orders of, severe, **19.** 464n
(?) Orford, Cts of, disapproves of German campaign of, **21.** 96
Oxford may make, chancellor, **22.** 72n
Palace, the, at Newmarket houses, at intervals, **20.** 373n
Parliamentary debates expose arbitrary conduct of, **20.** 33
Parliamentary votes influenced by, **9.** 72
Parliamentary voting by, with minority, on *North Briton*, **38.** 247
Parliament entered by, **17.** 398
peace negotiations to be watched by, **19.** 446
Pelham gets ordnance for, **20.** 120
—— writes to, about Conway, **37.** 227
Pitt (Chatham) confers with, **20.** 102
—— explains his Tory ties to, **22.** 101n
—— hints at, **37.** 416
—— jokingly suggested as army subordinate of, **9.** 209

—— rejects proposals of, to form ministry, **22.** 302
——'s conditions made to, in interview, **30.** 188n
——'s letter from, at George III's order, **22.** 307n
—— wants, to be head of army, **22.** 161
Pitt, Mrs George, admired by, **9.** 94
—— loved by, **20.** 58
plotters sure of, **35.** 230
Portuguese princess mentioned as wife for, **21.** 341–2
Poyntz, governor of, **19.** 242n, **20.** 208, **22.** 163n
——, treasurer of, **19.** 242n
—— visited by, **30.** 27
Poyntz family aided by, **20.** 208
presentations to, **31.** 52
Pringle discusses Galfridus Mann's illness with, **20.** 529
—— physician to, **20.** 525, 529
prisoners taken by, **19.** 274
proxy for sister's wedding, **37.** 61
Prussian princess may wed, **18.** 62
rage against, extinguished by that against Mordaunt, **30.** 142
Ranelagh visited by, **17.** 434, **20.** 57n, **30.** 57, **37.** 164
rashness of, in battle, **9.** 50
rebellion to be entirely crushed by, **37.** 228
rebels awaited by, at Stone, **19.** 178
rebels dislodged from Nairn by cavalry of, **37.** 238n
rebels do not forgive, **19.** 296
rebels flee from, **19.** 208–9, 239
rebels pursued by, **19.** 185, 197, 213, 222
recalled, **21.** 136, 150
Regency Bill omits, **38.** 541
Regency Bill opposed by, **20.** 249, 263
Regency Bill subjects Ps of Wales to collaboration with council headed by, **20.** 257n
Regency controlled by, **20.** 491
—— includes, **20.** 239n, 483
—— said to be headed by, **20.** 125, **35.** 225
Remembrancer attacks, **20.** 73
resentment of, complicates debate over Regency Bill, **22.** 299
resignation of, from army commands, **9.** 218, **30.** 145
return of, from Scotland, awaited, **19.** 255–6, 271
rewards for, **19.** 255–6
Reynolds's portrait of, **10.** 79, **40.** 284
Richmond, 2d D. of, says that his children will precede grandchildren of, **19.** 20
——'s fireworks attended by, **9.** 81
Richmond, 3d D. of, and D. of Manchester offer themselves to, **30.** 187
Richmond, 3d D. of, gives masquerade attended by, **22.** 149
—— to consult, on army service, **37.** 541n
Rivett, friend and manager of, **20.** 19
Rochford, Cts of, alienates affections of, **9.** 42

—— loved by, **20.** 58

Rochford, E. of, wears likeness of, on buttons, **9.** 49

Rotterdam said to be visited by, **37.** 281

Royston supported by, for Cambridge high stewardship, **38.** 248n

rumoured to have been ordered to surrender, to protect Hanover, **30.** 143

Russian masquerade attended by, with seraglio, **35.** 206

Sackville sent by, to Saxe about Maestricht siege, **19.** 481

Sandwich and Bedford supported by, against Newcastle, **20.** 113n

Sandwich appointed to Spain, to tie Bute-Fox coalition to, **22.** 103n

—— conceals letter about safety of, **9.** 50–1

—— confers with, **37.** 265

—— gives ball for, **20.** 121

—— intimate with, **20.** 207n

—— no longer friendly with, **10.** 79

——'s house taken by, **9.** 314

—— supported by, **20.** 201

Savoyard girl sent by, to Windsor after she rejected him, **9.** 94

Saxe, Maréchal de, defeats force under, **9.** 49n

—— sends book through, **9.** 52

Schomberg House taken by, **9.** 316

Schutz, G. A., page to, **20.** 15n

Scotland hates, **19.** 288, **37.** 352

—— rather than London may be destination of, **19.** 193

—— the station of, during the rebellion, **19.** 271, 273, 288, 382n, **20.** 240

Scots condemn harshness of, **9.** 34

Scott, Caroline, in service of, **20.** 203n

Scottish bill ignored by, **20.** 311

Scottish disloyalty criticized by, **19.** 228

Scottish sojourn of, likely to be long, **37.** 223

scouting party sent out by, **19.** 233

Secker treads on feet of, **9.** 318

severity of, to rebels, **9.** 34, 86, 93, **19.** 288

sister does not speak tenderly of, **38.** 567

sister tries to prevent, from going to Newmarket, **38.** 445

(?) Spörcken, Gen., sent by, to surprise French troops, **21.** 117n

Stade route followed by, to Hanover, **21.** 78

Stade the ill-judged refuge of, **21.** 146

Strafford entertains, at Boughton Park, **37.** 212

SH visited by, **35.** 161

supper refused by, at Richmond, **9.** 81

Sussex, D. of, as large as, **39.** 504

Temple accuses, of insincerity in negotiating with Pitt, **30.** 184

—— admits to, that he and Pitt were offered *carte blanche*, **30.** 188

Tournai's capture reported by, to D. of Newcastle, **19.** 61n

Townshend, Hon. George, aide-de-camp to, turns against him, **20.** 33

—— caricatures, **37.** 444

—— hostile to, **39.** 46n

—— placed with, **36.** 7n

Trentham visited by, on way to London, **38.** 19

tyrannical behaviour of, **13.** 22n

unpopularity of: **9.** 52, **20.** 240, 243, 322; after Jacobite rebellion, **32.** 347; keeps him from being regent, **20.** 249

Vaneschi disputes with, over opera house, **20.** 557

Vauxhall scene of ball given by, **9.** 42

Vernon's vanished popularity remembered by, when popular himself, **36.** 186

verses compare, with Richard III, **30.** 126

victory by irregular troops will not suit martinet tastes of, **35.** 258n

votes on *North Briton*'s condemnation, **38.** 247

Wade may join army of, **37.** 214

waiter at Carlisle House objects to occupancy by, of Karl Wilhelm Ferdinand's seat, **38.** 296

Waldeck at odds with, **19.** 428–9

Waldegrave's aversion to Bute and Fox described by, **10.** 64

Wales, Frederick, P. of, receives visit from, **19.** 288

weight of, subject of wager and law suit, **20.** 208–9

Whitehall Gate moved by, to Windsor, **2.** 177

Wilkinson, agent of, **10.** 186

will of: **33.** 535n; HW asks about, **31.** 71

Wilmot attends, at Windsor Lodge, **21.** 432n

Wilson, Nanny, mistress to, **19.** 52n

Windsor visited by, **38.** 495, 566

Windsor borough should be resigned to, **31.** 18–19

Windsor Great Lodge perhaps promised by, **31.** 19

Windsor Lodge parties of, to emphasize his and Ps Amelia's support of Bedford and Sandwich against Newcastle, **20.** 120n

witticism on, as prodigal son and fatted calf, **35.** 225

Yarmouth, Cts of, told by, to inform George II of his resignation, **21.** 145n

York, D. of, would precede, in prayers for royal family, **21.** 449

Yorke aide-de-camp to, **37.** 211n

Young Pretender defends, **7.** 274

Zastrow to be replaced by, in charge of army of observation, **21.** 73n

William Frederick (1776–1834), D. of Gloucester, 1805:

annual sum granted to, **7.** 40n

Artois, Comte d' (Charles X), reported in letters of, to be in Flanders, **12.** 118

baptism of, **24.** 181, **36.** 115–16

Bayreuth, Margrave of, godfather to, **24.** 181

birth of: **24.** 171–2, **36.** 115–16; announced to HW, **24.** 178; authenticated, **24.** 172; impending, **32.** 249; may drive Lady Mary Coke to Bedlam, **24.** 179

[William Frederick, *continued*]

Cressen, Barons de, liked by, at Trent, **36.** 129

descendant of both HW and George I, **25.** 248

father asks Margrave of Bayreuth to be godfather to, **24.** 171

father essential to welfare and happiness of, **24.** 329

father pleased with, **36.** 326

father's anxiety for, **33.** 24, **34.** 246

father seeks provision for, **36.** 306, 307

father's plight may arouse sympathy for, **24.** 321

George III demands provision for, **24.** 372, 376

—— permits entering, at Cambridge, **36.** 245n

—— tells sister of, about his being teased, **36.** 329

HW and D. of Gloucester will probably not prefer, to sister, **24.** 302

HW not informed of inoculation of, **32.** 304–5

HW respects princes with name of, **28.** 307n

HW sees, at Gloucester House, **25.** 68

health of: illness, **32.** 363, **35.** 473; inoculated, **25.** 203, **32.** 304–5; not strong, **34.** 246; teeth cut, **24.** 315; well, **24.** 171–2, 181

Humphry's portrait of, at SH, **42.** 71n

Kingsgate not to be visited by, **33.** 24

lands at Dover to go to Gloucester House, **36.** 155

Leopold sees, **24.** 297

Mann kisses, **24.** 306

—— sees, in mother's arms, **24.** 297

—— to be called on by, **24.** 291

mother gives casino party for, **36.** 329

mother's concern for, **33.** 36

mother's 'evil representations' to, **36.** 244n

mother would have trouble in travelling with, if father died, **24.** 326

nurse of, falls, **36.** 142, 149

Piozzi, Mrs, comments on marriage of, **10.** 310n

pretty boy, **24.** 332

Ranelagh visited by, **25.** 68

William Henry (1765–1837), D. of Clarence. *See* William IV, K. of England

William Henry (1743–1805), cr. (1764) D. of Gloucester:

accounts of, from Rome, are favourable, **24.** 179

Adair and Jebb may enable, to finish his journey, **24.** 329

Albani's villa left by, for Rome, **24.** 247–8

Albano to be summer home of, at Albani's villa, **24.** 214

Aldobrandini villa to be occupied by, **24.** 190

Ansbach, Margrave of, supports, with family, **35.** 533n

Ansbach visited by, **25.** 413n

army command denied to, because of wife's exclusion and Rockingham's disapproval, **33.** 331n

army command not expected by, **33.** 198

army leadership denied to, because Sir Edward Walpole revealed Ds of Gloucester's letter, **36.** 71n

attendants of: have no confidence in Mann, **23.** 370; impertinent to Mann, **23.** 377; unworthy, **23.** 357, 364, 384; vainly attempt to regain Mann's favour, **23.** 384

baggage of, goes by sea to England, **23.** 407

ball given by, **5.** 33n

balls frequented by, **21.** 67

Bath visited by: **33.** 2n; with Margrave of Ansbach, **33.** 136

Bayreuth, Margrave of, asked by, to be godfather to son, **24.** 171

Bernis, Cardinal, gives dinner for, **23.** 389

Berry, Mary, identifies, **11.** 62n–63n, 219n

birth of, **18.** 341, 358

Blackheath house of, **33.** 125, 137

Boltons to give ball for, **25.** 22

Bordeaux voyage may be undertaken by, **24.** 360

Bracciano, Duca di, entertains, at concert, **23.** 388

Bristol, E. of, visits, at Pavilions, **33.** 148

Brussels visited by, **33.** 275

Buller, Mrs, intimate with, **11.** 219, 223

Byron's trial attended by, **38.** 535

called 'Gloucester cheese,' **11.** 223

Carlisle ridicules HW's concern for, **30.** 266

Caroline Matilda's disgrace must distress, **23.** 384

Carpenter, Lady Almeria, less courted by, **36.** 329

—— probably caused Horace Mann II's rebuff from, **25.** 638

——'s affair with, **31.** 298

Cato acted by, **21.** 327

Châlons visited by, **6.** 485

chaplain to, **2.** 331, **12.** 75n

character of: compared with Louis XVI's brothers', **32.** 255; to be respected, **23.** 361

Charlotte, Q., led by, to wedding, **21.** 529

——'s Drawing-Room attended by, **31.** 299

Charlton the surgeon of, **23.** 334

children of: please him, **36.** 326; to be inoculated before leaving England, **24.** 82; to have Parliamentary provision, **28.** 380; told by him that Waldegrave may succeed Cornwallis, **36.** 256

Choiseul, Duchesse de, interested in, **6.** 478

Cholmondeley, 4th E. of, accompanies, from Genoa, **23.** 335

—— attends, to Florence, **23.** 353

——'s correspondence with, **36.** 208

——'s rudeness to Mann caused by that of, **23.** 395

—— tells Mann to tell Leopold of plans of, to revisit Florence, **23.** 397

—— to accompany, throughout tour, **23.** 343, 349, 370

—— told by, to visit Florence, **23.** 337

—— totally attached to, **23.** 357

Christine meets, at public places only, **24.** 190

Clement XIV invites, to Rome, and tells nuncio to court him, **23.** 343, 348

——'s hospitality to, **23.** 388–9

—— talks with, in Monte Cavallo garden, **23.** 389

Coke, Lady Mary, criticizes, **31.** 188

—— disapproves of marriage of, **23.** 530, 538, **24.** 179n, **31.** 169, 175

col. of 1st Foot Guards, **42.** 74n

Colonna attached to, **7.** 102

—— recommended by, **7.** 80

——'s recommendation urged by, **7.** 99n

confidence of, in air of Rome not shared by many, **24.** 84

constitution of, always alarming, **24.** 350

consuls visited by, at Genoa and Leghorn, **23.** 347

Conway and Rockingham do not favour, **36.** 327

Conway avoids court of, **33.** 177n

——'s Opposition rôle may displease, **35.** 510n

courier sent by, to Mann, **23.** 331

Court attendance denied to, **23.** 433, 437

Court intrigues avoided by, **25.** 140

court of: numerous, **25.** 22; visited by HW, **32.** 121

Court's relations with, **32.** 389

(?) Covent Garden play attended by, **22.** 199

Coxheath camp visited by, **33.** 24n

Cumberland, Henry Frederick, D. of, and Ds of, may be ill-received at foreign courts because of misbehaviour of, **23.** 502

Cumberland, Henry Frederick, D. of, and Ds of, said to pass verse-writing evening with, **36.** 84

Cumberland, Henry Frederick, D. of, distresses, by marriage, **23.** 395

—— may not be known by, to have married, **23.** 355

—— should not involve, in his politics, **24.** 74

Cumberland, William Augustus, D. of, given house by, **7.** 366

Dalrymple gives report about, **6.** 456

daughter born to, **1.** 321n, **28.** 89n

daughter doted on by, **24.** 86

daughter of: **29.** 47n; to be christened Sophia, **32.** 132

daughter probably will be preferred by, to son, **24.** 302, 306

death of: expected, **5.** 131, 132, **6.** 143, **23.** 374; might have occasioned his wife's, **24.** 144; rumoured from Venice, **24.** 136; rumoured in London, **23.** 343–4; twice falsely announced in newspapers, **25.** 623

desires to be home, **23.** 377

Dick, Sir John, lodges, at Leghorn, **23.** 332, 335, 347

—— notified by, through Rainsford, of marriage, **23.** 437

—— often seen by HW since return of, **24.** 335

—— preferred by, to Mann, as companion, **23.** 395

—— promised Bath knighthood by, but George III can no longer be asked for it, **24.** 85

Dover embarkation of, **24.** 117n

—— to be left by, for Gloucester House, **43.** 301

—— visited by, **33.** 581n

Drawing-Room not attended by, **33.** 198

Drawing-Room of, attended by HW, **35.** 516

Du Deffand, Mme, asks about, **5.** 179, **6.** 236, 463, 467, 474, 475, 477, 488, 491, 494, **7.** 28–9, 42

(?) —— sends compliments to, **6.** 186

dukedom and allowance for, **22.** 264, **38.** 468

Dysart, Cts of, criticizes, **31.** 299

Dysarts visited by, at Ham, **36.** 79–80

Edsir, steward to, assumes parentage of natural child, **36.** 245n

England reached by, **24.** 332, **28.** 339

—— to be destination of, to avoid Italian heat, **24.** 311

—— to be revisited by: **24.** 314, **36.** 247; but not permanently, **35.** 473

English at Rome attentive to, **24.** 190

English packets for, all pass through Mann's hands, **23.** 370

English people in France shun, **24.** 125

English travellers admitted to kiss the hand of, **24.** 163

entrances of, at parties, **38.** 475

equerries, Cholmondeley, Lee, and Jervis accompany, to Florence, **23.** 353

equerries of, see Heywood; Rainsford

essential to family's welfare, **24.** 329

Euston's engagement to stepdaughter of, proposed, **33.** 441

family may be taken by, to southern France, **24.** 76

family to be left by, in Verona, **36.** 309

(?) Fawkener's and Pownall's calls on HW interrupted by, **35.** 498

Ferdinand of Naples and republic of Lucca invite, **23.** 348

Ferrers's trial attended by, **9.** 280

Field Marshal, **12.** 46

fireworks watched by, **20.** 48

firmness and coolness of, **39.** 248

Florence avoided by, **24.** 174, **25.** 675

—— to be visited by, **24.** 290, 290–1, 298, 312

—— visited by, **23.** 353, 405, **24.** 290–1, 296–8

foreign ministers forbidden to visit, **36.** 82

foreign trip of, delayed until he is too ill to travel, **24.** 74

France pays great attentions to, **24.** 125

Frederick II declines offer by, of army service, **24.** 401, 404, 407, 409, 411, **33.** 48

——'s answer to, not arrived, **33.** 44

French fleet's strategy feared by, **33.** 48

Friedrich II of Hesse exchanges visits with, **24.** 275

Garter conferred on, **10.** 32, **22.** 37

[William Henry (1743–1805), *continued*]

Garter installation of, at Windsor, **22.** 79, **38.** 171, 177, 179

Geneva visited by, on way to Italy, **25.** 314

Genoa visited by, **23.** 331–2, 347, **25.** 628, 638

George III and Rockingham promise increased allowance to, **22.** 424–5, 428

George III asked by, for officers to attend wife's accouchement, **36.** 92

—— demands provision for children of, **24.** 372, 376

—— does not intend, to be head of army, **36.** 85

—— does not require, to remarry, **23.** 484

—— generous to, **7.** 40

—— grants audience to, **33.** 198

—— notified by, of marriage, **23.** 433, 437

—— not to be antagonized by, **36.** 306

—— omits, from Regency, **22.** 295

—— prefers, to D. of Cumberland, **36.** 323

—— promises to protect family of, **36.** 145

—— proscribes, **36.** 73, 74

—— rejoices at recovery of, **23.** 347

——'s affection for, **23.** 437

——'s attitude aggravates illness of, **26.** 50

——'s brotherly letter cures, **24.** 326

——'s committee inquires into marriage of, **36.** 305n

—— sends Adair and Jebb to attend, **23.** 356

—— sends leave of absence for, by North, **36.** 308

—— should be given apologetic plea by, for aid, **36.** 110–11

——'s kind letter answered by, with his own hand, **24.** 329, **36.** 136, 137, 144

——'s kind messages to, **24.** 323, **36.** 130

——'s reconciliation with: **7.** 234, **25.** 62–3, 65, **33.** 198, 200–1, **39.** 351; attempted, **29.** 67n; must not be prevented by hasty actions, **36.** 86; rumoured, **28.** 327, **29.** 67–8

—— summons, **34.** 43n

—— to be placated by, to arouse pity, **36.** 102–3

—— unwillingly proscribes, but Q. Charlotte may have insisted, **36.** 77

George IV to be visited by, at Kew, **36.** 167n

German flute played by, **38.** 101n

Giustiniani called on by, to thank him for civilities to D. of York, **23.** 287

Gloucester House under charge of servant of, **42.** 463

Gore family neighbours of, at Castel Gandolfo, **24.** 251

greatcoat worn by, in hackney coach, **35.** 505

great ladies of Rome do not altogether please, **24.** 247

Grenvilles fail to meet, **7.** 347n

Grovestins, Mme de, thought to intrigue with, **5.** 430n, **32.** 93n

HW advises: not to seek financial aid from Parliament, **36.** 100–3, 107–12; to submit entirely to George III, **23.** 434

(?) HW alludes to relations of, with Cts Waldegrave, **31.** 126

HW authorized by, to propose that Miss Keppel go abroad, **33.** 316

HW avoids meeting, at Nuneham, **35.** 456–7

HW awaits news of, **6.** 470, 472

HW begs Mann not to entertain, in Florence, **25.** 624

HW believes that Cts Waldegrave is married to, **23.** 302

HW calls, 'naturally obliging,' **23.** 358

HW calls on: **33.** 159, 275; at Pavilions, **23.** 433–4

HW concerned for wife's situation on death of, **30.** 266

HW congratulates, on wife's pregnancy, **36.** 89

HW declines to convey Mann's invitation to, **23.** 302

HW disliked by, **23.** 404, 549

HW does not wish to sup with, **12.** 46

HW favours Conway over, as commander-in-chief, **29.** 211n

HW feels, should be out of England, **24.** 117

HW has had no letters from, during his journey, **24.** 148

HW informed by: of Gordon riots, **33.** 175; of son's birth, **24.** 178, **36.** 115–16

HW inquires whether Comtesse de Boufflers saw, in Paris, **31.** 126

HW is ill-used by, for not encouraging match with HW's niece, **28.** 126–7

HW makes proper excuse for absence from, **23.** 421

HW mentions, **9.** 278, 402, 403

HW mentions his relationship to, **28.** 307

HW moderates resentments of, **32.** 123

HW owes respect to wife of, **36.** 84

HW pays respects to, **33.** 236

HW pleased by recovery of, **23.** 349

HW praises, **38.** 475

HW receives Meredith's pamphlet from, **39.** 318

HW regrets relationship to, **11.** 80

HW restored to favour of, **24.** 184

HW sarcastically calls, 'sweet,' **11.** 62–3

HW's conversation with, **5.** 265

HW's cool relations with, caused by HW's disapproval of his marriage, **23.** 434

HW's correspondence with, **24.** (?) 134, **36.** 107–12, 114–16, 218, 224

HW's 'Court' goes abroad with, **33.** 336

HW secretly flattered by passion of, for HW's niece, **30.** 177

HW sees, at Gloucester House, **24.** 335, **25.** 68

HW's failure to visit, may be resented, **23.** 416–17

HW shows to, Mrs Jordan's letter, **34.** 143n

HW's respect for, **36.** 160

HW suggests Siena as winter residence for, **4.** 125, 130

HW's will mentions, **30.** 353

HW to beg for print of Ds of Devonshire for, 28. 421
HW to be welcomed by, 36. 75
HW to meet, in London, 2. 67, 70
HW to meet Court of, in London, 42. 200
HW urges Mann to pay court to, 24. 125
HW vexed by rudeness of entourage of, to Mann, 23. 363–4
HW weary of 'royal' connection through, 35. 463
HW would not like to meet, 11. 219
HW writes to Mme du Deffand about, 7. 394
(?) Hampton Court Park keys not given out by, 35. 628
Hampton Court Park's ranger, 11. 62
Harcourt devoted to, 36. 151
—— entertains, at Nuneham, 35. 456–7
(?) —— to reconcile Conway and Lady Ailesbury with, 35. 510
health, not debt, sends, abroad, 36. 327
health of: 5. 74n, 132, 142, 346, 6. 143–4, 150, 151, 238, 456, 470, 479; alarms HW, 23. 361; almost well, 24. 332; asthma, 23. 303, 348, 355, 369, 24. 360, 26. 50–1, 28. 94; better, 23. 375; bloody flux, 23. 336, 24. 135, 31. 188; bones rattle in his skin, 24. 326; bottles of boiling water keep, warm, 36. 139; cold sweats, 36. 138; colic, 23. 332; cough, 24. 82, 86, 350, 360; dangerously ill, 5. 74n, 28. 320, 323, 327, 331; death expected, 32. 230–1, 36. 136, 138, 139, 140, 141; diarrhœa, 23. 332, 334, 336, 342, 369, 36. 133, 138, 141; dying, with shivering fits, 39. 247–8; dysentery, 24. 314, 317, 319, 321, 322–3, 325–6; extremely well, 24. 117; fever, 38. 523; fever and bloody flux, 24. 135; flux, 24. 314; good, 36. 326; good accounts of, 23. 377, 24. 329; grows fat, 24. 214; hæmorrhoids, 26. 50; heats destroy, and damps bad for it, 24. 360; illness, 2. 55, 57, 58–9, 6. 470n, 477n, 32. 123, 274, 362–3; illness at Trent, 36. 128–45; illness at Verona, 34. 245–7; improved, 28. 327, 339, 32. 364, 365, 366, 378, 383, 33. 233, 236, 35. 475, 476; lame, 24. 335; latent cause of illness, 28. 94; Leghorn apothecary provides drugs for, 23. 393; less well than in previous winter, 36. 308; Mann distrusts air of Rome for, 24. 84; Mason inquires about, 28. 90, 322; mother's death and sister's disgrace do not injure, 23. 388; much improved, 23. 384, 388, 32. 379; not able to stand a campaign, 33. 35; not out of danger, 32. 368; out of danger, 23. 336, 346–7, 24. 76, 140, 32. 232; out of order, 24. 350; perfect, 24. 190, 201, 214; permits journey to Rome, 24. 144; physicians fear effects of autumn campaign on, 24. 401; physicians slightly encouraged by, 24. 321, 322–3; precarious state of, should excite pity, 36. 111; probably improved by 'wholesome illness,' 24. 148; purging gone, 36.

126; quite recovered, 24. 144; recovered, 32. 389; reported by Bryant, 35. 472–3; 'risen from the dead,' 32. 372; Rome fixed upon as favourable to, despite HW's dissuasion, 24. 130; sea-bathing may aid, 36. 324; seriously ill, 25. 677; shivering fits, 24. 76, 39. 247–8; sleeps without laudanum, 43. 102; small returns of his disorder, 24. 275; surgeon-page thinks, is past crisis, 24. 315; swelled leg, legs, 23. 355, 369, 36. 138, 139, 141; swelling of leg and arm, 32. 378; swollen from groin to foot, 24. 326; syringe-baths for, 23. 334; ulcer suspected, in large intestine, 23. 337; Venice's heat and nauseous air affect, 24. 314; very bad, 32. 376–7; very ill, 24. 74; very well, 24. 170; well, 24. 163, 181
heart, not sense, lacked by, in mistreating Mann, 23. 500
Hertford knows George III's affection for, 36. 86–7
—— presents Mann's offer to, but it is declined, 23. 302–3, 304
Heywood ought to have been civil to HW without knowledge of, 23. 429
Holland, Bn and Bns, decline offer of, to employ their son, 41. 272–4
horses bespoken by, from Paris for journey, 36. 142
household not provided for, since he inclines towards Opposition, 38. 435
household of, must be exhausted by fatigue and anxiety, 24. 319–20
House of Lords should be urged by, to mediate with George III, 36. 110–11
house reserved for, in Rome, 24. 312
Howard, Sir George, and, 43. 302
Ilchester told by, that Grenville ministry not to resign, 30. 181
inn at Florence to be home of, 25. 677
Italian capitals will probably be shunned by, lest monarchs be embarrassed by his wife, 24. 130–1
Italian winters favourable, and summers unfavourable to, 35. 473
itinerary of: 5. 265, 6. 485; from Gibraltar to Leghorn, 23. 294; from London to Spa, 33. 336n; from Naples, 23. 370; from Rome to England, 24. 252
Jebb deserves full credit for recovery of, 36. 147
Joseph II called on by, 29. 151n
—— might instruct Leopold to make Siena agreeable to, 24. 125
—— might offer Vienna establishment to, 36. 131n, 145n
—— to meet, at Milan, 24. 331
—— to protect, if George III does not, 36. 145
—— visited by, 25. 164
—— voices concern about, 36. 131–2
Keppel, Bp, called on by, at Windsor, 36. 156n

[William Henry (1743–1805), *continued*]

Kingsgate may be visited by, **33**. 22, 24

Kingston, Ds of, may be deterred from Rome by presence of, **24**. 220

La Coast, Louisa Maria, natural daughter of, **36**. 245n

Lago di Garda to be visited by, for summer, **24**. 291

lands at Dover to go to Gloucester House, **36**. 155

last Drawing-Room of, of season, **35**. 516

leaves for Continent, **6**. 181n

Leghorn visited by, **23**. 332–3, 333–7, 341–3, 347–9, 353, 393–4, 404, 405

Leopold asks, to get honours for Cowper, **23**. 502

—— exchanges messages and visits with, **24**. 291, 297–8

—— expected to meet, at Milan, **24**. 331

—— informed by, at Vienna, about marriage, **23**. 308

—— invited, to Florence, at Vienna, **24**. 332

—— probably told by Vienna how to treat, **24**. 129

——'s and Maria Louisa's social relations with, **23**. 294, 304, 331, 332–3, 335, 342, 348, 352–3, 355–6, 357, 405, **24**. 291, 297–8

letter from, to England written in his own hand, **24**. 141

levee of: HW not to attend, **36**. 70–1; HW's absence from, approved by Ds of Gloucester, **36**. 71

Lloyd, Miss, abuses, **31**. 171

lodge in New Forest visited by, **24**. 360

London revisited by, **5**. 247, **43**. 66

Louis XVI's invitation to: to Paris, **24**. 125; to Versailles, declined, **36**. 114n

Lucca invites, **23**. 348

Luttrells' newspaper articles inflame George III against, **24**. 77

Mann advises HW to call on, **23**. 416–17, 421, 426–7, 437–8

—— afraid to inquire about, at Rome, **24**. 181

—— asks HW to convey his gratitude to, **24**. 352

—— called on by, when ill, **24**. 291, 302

—— encouraged by efforts of, to hope for Bath knighthood, **22**. 314

—— gets gracious messages from, from Rome, **24**. 170, 184, 201

—— has not asked if Italy will be revisited by, **24**. 76

—— insists on consultation with Italian physicians over health of, **23**. 393

—— kisses the hand of, **23**. 336, 394

—— might have paid more attention to, in illness, **24**. 141

—— moves furniture to Pisa for use of, **23**. 342

—— offers coaches and theatre boxes to, **24**. 291

—— prevented by gout from paying attention to, at Florence, **24**. 290

—— receives order from, to send him weekly gazette from Florence, **24**. 396

——'s coaches seldom used by, **23**. 395

——'s coolness from: attributed to bad attendants, **24**. 297, 384; attributed to ill health and family troubles, **24**. 395–6; cancelled by warmth at Florence, **24**. 297; caused by Dick, **23**. 367, 404; changed graciously, **23**. 405, **24**. 247; unjustifiable, **23**. 377

—— sends respects to, **24**. 171, 247, 352, 376, 389

——'s house at Pisa arranged for occupancy by, **23**. 342, 347–8, 358, 363–4, 377, 394–5

——'s name probably not mentioned by, to HW, **24**. 453

——'s note from, announcing departure from Rome to Florence, **24**. 291

——'s servants dismissed from, **23**. 348, 394

——'s troublesome guest, **23**. 500

—— tells nephew to pay respects to, at Rome, **24**. 131

—— thanks, at Leghorn, for consenting to visit his Pisa house, **23**. 347

—— told by: of value of a change of air, **24**. 329; to expect a visit from his wife and family, **24**. 291, 297

—— wants HW to invite, to spend Florentine visit in his house, **23**. 294

—— will heed HW's advice about behaviour to, **24**. 131

—— will not give offence elsewhere by attentions to, **24**. 290

—— will probably mention passage of, through Florence, **24**. 163

Mann, Horace II, awaits, at Florence, **25**. 676–7

—— cordially received by, at Rome, **25**. 674

—— does not tell HW about rebuff from, **25**. 637

—— received by, at Rome, **24**. 163

—— receives regrets from, for rebuff at Genoa, **25**. 674

—— repulsed by, at Genoa, **25**. 628, 637, 638

Maria Louisa plays loo with, **23**. 352

marriage of: **2**. 31, **3**. 57n, 84, 200n, **4**. 5n, 9, 19n, **5**. 91n, 207n, 247–8, 268n, **10**. 310, **11**. 349n, **13**. 31n, 48, **14**. 171, **21**. 284n, **23**. 537, **28**. 46n, 93n; alluded to, **32**. 65; announced, **13**. 48, **23**. 415; authenticated, **23**. 483; date of, corrected, **43**. 141; declared to equerries, **23**. 484; George III notified of, by Legrand, **36**. 72–3; HW said to be mysterious on, **33**. 441; HW said to have published, **36**. 86; HW's letter about, to be shown to George III, by Hertford, **39**. 161; must make Parliamentary debate over Royal Marriage Bill very painful, **23**. 396; *North Briton* attacks, **23**. 165; not foreseen by Sir Robert Walpole, **25**. 133; registered in council books, **39.** 170; revealed by wife to her father, **36.** 62–3, 64, 66–8; Royal Marriage Act caused by, **25.** 629; should not make him live like D. of Cumberland, **36.** 67; unhappy, **25.** 674; un-witnessed, **23.** 484; valid, **32.** 118; verified at his request, **5.** 359, 365

Meek attends, **23.** 337, 342

Milan visited by, **25.** 628, 632

mob in Fleet Market robs, **35.** 505

Molini attends, **23.** 394

mother's illness must distress, **23.** 355, 358, 377, 395

musical prodigy at house of, **43.** 351

Naples visited by, **23.** 336, 242, 348, 370, 375, 384, **25.** 675

Neapolitan and Roman experiences of, 'piteous,' **23.** 405

newspapers call, 'D. of Lancaster,' **15.** 329, **22.** 264

nightgown worn by, when receiving Count Thurn, **23.** 352

North and Rochford besought by, for provision for family, **36.** 306

northern tour of, **35.** 415

Northumberlands exclude, from Alnwick Castle, **36.** 323

not promoted, **7.** 39

not to go abroad, **33.** 257

Nugent rebuffed by, **33.** 136–7

Nunehams solicitous about, **35.** 472, 474, 476

nuns pray for recovery of, **32.** 389, **36.** 144

obelisk to, in tableau, **38.** 204

opera attended by, **38.** 289

Opposition attracts, because no provision is made for him, **38.** 435

orange-tree symbolizes brothers and, at ball, **38.** 204

Orford, Cts of, did not like, when he was at Florence, **24.** 175

—— graciously received by, **24.** 170, 222

Padua visited by, **24.** 135–6, 144, 314

page of, sends news, **32.** 379

'page-surgeon' attends, **23.** 393, **24.** 315

Paris may be visited by, **5.** 430, **6.** 461

—— visited by, **31.** 126

Parliamentary Opposition unlikely to aid, **36.** 108–9

Parliament may be asked by, for financial provision, **36.** 100n, 104n

—— not expected by, to pay his debts, **36.** 306–7

Pavilions, The, at Hampton Court occupied by, **12.** 140n, **33.** 22, **38.** 435

—— 'lodge' of, **12.** 13n

—— to be left by, for Blackheath, **33.** 125

pension of, **43.** 281

Piozzi, Mrs, comments on, **10.** 310n

Pisa visited by, **23.** 336, 342, 347–8, 352–3, 355, 356–7, 394–5, 404, 502

Pius VI courteous to, **24.** 174, 190

—— pleased by gift from, of surgical instruments for hospital at Rome, **24.** 129

Pleydell accompanies, **24.** 311

plumper than when at Rome, **24.** 332

Poggio Imperiale visited by, to see Tuscan grand ducal family, **24.** 297

political indiscretions of, make army command unlikely, **38.** 407

Poor Bill supported by, **38.** 529

post-chaise used by, **24.** 314

potatoes craved by, during illness, **32.** 373

preparations and leave-takings of, for death, **23.** 336

Privy Councillors requested by, to witness son's birth, **5.** 265

prohibited from going to Court, **9.** 46n

Protestant mob cheers, **25.** 54n

Provence to be visited by, for winter, **33.** 419

Prussian army service requested by, **7.** 67, 71, **24.** 401, 404, 407, 409, 411, **33.** 32, 38, 48

Quaker would not have been well received by, **24.** 53

quinze the favourite game of, **23.** 356

Ranelagh visited by, **25.** 68, **33.** 189

Regency Bill omits, **38.** 541

rejected as member of Queen's council, **25.** 68on

return of, to England: gives HW little trouble, **33.** 581–2; strongly urged, **24.** 252

Richmond's masquerade not attended by, **22.** 148

riding by, in Kensington Gardens, criticized, **31.** 171–2

Rochford has not told Mann how to behave to, in case of Florentine visit, **24.** 129

Rockingham after rebuff deserts, for D. of Cumberland, **36.** 199–200

Roman assemblies attended by, **24.** 163

Roman nobility attentive to, **24.** 174, 190

Romans insulted by, **23.** 566

Roman visit of, deferred, **23.** 357, 370, **24.** 140, 141, 144

Rome approached by, though he seemed unlikely to want to revisit it, **24.** 129

—— considered by, the best winter residence, **24.** 290

—— the only refuge for Young Pretender and, **36.** 114n

—— to be visited by, **23.** 384, **24.** 82, 123, 130, **25.** 618, 623, **36.** 309

—— visited by, **23.** 396, 405, **24.** 163–4, 170, 174, 181, 184, 186, 190, 201, 214, 222, 247, 252, 290, 291, 332, **25.** 674, **36.** 306–8

sails on frigate commanded by Jervis, **23.** 353

St James's Palace to be home of, **20.** 239

St Leonard's Hill the home of, **10.** 42n

—— to be visited by, **32.** 132

—— visited by, **5.** 346

Saxony, Electress of, discusses Ds of Kingston with, **24.** 25

secludes himself after death of Bp Keppel, **33.** 2

[William Henry (1743–1805), *continued*]
secretary of state's office sends packets to, at Genoa, **23**. 328
servant of, shows letter from Robert Adair, **32**. 378
sister dances with, at private ball, **38**. 143
sister's disgrace will distress, **23**. 384
son born to, **24**. 171–2
son held by, for Mann to kiss, **24**. 306
son of, **10**. 310n
Stainville's social relations with, **6**. 485
stepdaughters lodged by, at Hampton Court Park, **24**. 315
stepdaughters not wanted by, to live with him, **36**. 131n
stepdaughter's wedding attended by, **25**. 274, **29**. 243n
Strasbourg the last place whence news of, reached HW, **24**. 134
—— visited by, to see dying Margravine of Ansbach, **35**. 532
Suard calls Cts Waldegrave the wife of, **7**. 340
surgeon sends gloomy report of, **32**. 376–7
Swiss Guards at Soissons inspected by, **3**. 117
Switzerland to be visited by, **24**. 123
takes proper exercise, **24**. 163
Talbot rude to, **36**. 326
Thurn received by, **23**. 352
travel plans of, **32**. 232
travels slowly in *vettura* from Rome to Florence, **25**. 677
Trent visited by, **24**. 314–15, 317, 319–20, 321, 322–3, 325, 329, 336–7, **26**. 50, **32**. 389, **36**. 128–45
troops reviewed for, **28**. 222n
Udny's letter about, **24**. 311
unable to get command in England, **33**. 35
Ursulines of Trent prayed for, **32**. 389, **36**. 144
Venetian ambassador's house at Lago di Garda may be taken by, for summer, **24**. 290
Venice not to be visited by, **24**. 252
—— to be visited by, at Ascension, **24**. 291
—— visited by, **24**. 125, 130, 134, 305, 314, **36**. 308–9
Verona visited by, **24**. 314, 34. 245–7, **36**. 309
vingt-et-un played by, **24**. 352
visitors not seen by, **23**. 335
visits in morning, goes to assemblies in evening, **33**. 582
Viterbo entertainment of, **23**. 388
votes in House of Lords, **22**. 521
'votre neveu,' **3**. 329
Waldegrave, Cts, escorted by, at Soho ball, dressed as Edward IV, **23**. 193
—— guest of, at ball for royalty, **5**. 33
—— writes letter to, composed by HW, **38**. 388n
Waldegrave, Lady Laura, given in marriage by, **25**. 274
Walpole, Sir Edward, asked by, to avoid his levee, **36**. 68
—— must make first visit to, **36**. 323, 324

—— receives letters from, **36**. 305–9
—— to receive game and venison from, **36**. 324
warm, and hurt by indignities, **24**. 125
Weymouth visited by, **25**. 203
wife accepts Mann's urns with consent of, **24**. 453
wife cannot persuade her father to call on, **23**. 461
wife dares not invite her father, for fear of rebuff to, **36**. 323
wife has no affection for, **36**. 330
wife never leaves, for 7 weeks, **35**. 475
wife not helped by, with her dependents, **36**. 106n
wife of, **3**. 57n, **7**. 340n, **11**. 24n, **21**. 240n, 284n
wife permitted by, to stay with her daughter, **36**. 268
wife told by, to travel home with his body, **24**. 326
wife weeps, but does not oppose martial schemes of, **24**. 401
winter to be spent by, at Rome, **24**. 82, 117
Wricklemarsh occupied by, **36**. 246
Yertzin, Mme, disparaged by, **38**. 407
York, Edward, D. of, dictates letter to, **22**. 553n
—— dying at Monaco may be imitated by death of, at Leghorn, **23**. 345
—— entertains: **38**. 476n; at ball for Ps Amelia, **22**. 270n
—— leaves all to, **7**. 366
——'s last letter to, **7**. 366, **22**. 553n
——'s memory highly regarded by, **22**. 581
—— writes to: about making Mann a K.B., **22**. 235, 241, 318, 581; a letter to be shown to George III, **22**. 561
younger daughter of, dies after inoculation, **24**. 86
Young Pretender met by, in Genoa street, **23**. 343, 345
Williams, Lady. *See* Grenville, Charlotte
Williams, Miss. *See* William, Charlotte
Williams, Lady (fl. 1684):
to make purchases for Nell Gwyn, **1**. 349–50
Williams, Mr:
hypothetical claim of, to Welsh throne, **33**. 454
Williams, Mr:
SH ticket not used by, **12**. 236
Williams, Mrs, fortune-teller from Bath and Bristol:
(?) in Westminster, **31**. 280n
Williams, Anne (d. 1782), m. 1 (1726) Sir William Drake, 6th Bt; m. 2 George Speke:
Keene, Mrs, visited by, **33**. 232
North visits, **10**. 197
'Queen Mother Drake,' **33**. 232
Williams, Arabella (d. 1797), m. (1762) James Hamlyn, cr. (1795) Bt:
Grenville, Mrs, tells HW news of, **11**. 88
returns from Italy, **11**. 88

Williams, Benjamin, HW's printer, 1759:
runs away, **15.** 55, 57, **21.** (?) 300, **43.** 275
SH Press delayed by, **16.** 33
'went away,' **35.** 303n
Williams, Caleb (fl. ? 1693), engraver:
Cole calls attention to, **1.** 46
Nuncius Oris by, **1.** 46n
Williams, Charles (ca 1644–1720), Smyrna merchant:
Williams, Sir Charles Hanbury, heir and godson of, **30.** 311n
Williams, Sir Charles Hanbury (1708–59), K.B., 1744; diplomatist, wit, poet; M.P.; HW's correspondent:
Ansbach, Margrave of, receives Garter ribbon from Anstis and, **30.** 320
Ansbach left by, **20.** 90n
appearance of: Bath robes may make, pink and blooming enough to arouse Vcts Townshend, **30.** 82; vermilion countenance, **30.** 83
Austrian minister and Russian minister negotiate with, **20.** 186–7
ballad possibly by, **9.** 30n
Bath, E. of, injured by pen of, **13.** 14n, **18.** 22n
Bath installation of, **30.** 67, 79, 81, 82, 83
Bath knighthood given to, by Pelham on old promise of Sir Robert Walpole's, **30.** 311
Bath knighthood obtained by, despite Pelham's opposition, **18.** 451
Bath visited by, **18.** 104
Battie cares for, at Kensington, **30.** 322
Bedford, D. of, chooses Rochford instead of, as envoy at Turin, **20.** 58n
Bentley's Chinese plan recommended by, to D. of Bedford, **35.** 177–8
Berlin post may be assigned to, **14.** 10, **19.** 341
Berlin reached by, from Hanover, **20.** 187n
Brown's *Estimate* answered by, **9.** 219
—— threatens, for disclosing his profanity, **9.** 219–21
Brühl quarrels with, **30.** 322
Capuchin, The, by: HW transcribes, for Mann, **18.** 71–3; publication of, **30.** 314
character of, generous and vain, **30.** 312
Cheltenham probably left by, for Coldbrook, **30.** 58
Chesterfield satirized by, **30.** 314
—— sends goldfish to, though Lady Essex does not, **40.** 86n
——'s wit deprecated by, **30.** 70
Churchill, Gen., ridiculed by, in verses about Duck Island, **37.** 75–7
Clytemnestra to Sappho by, **30.** 317
confinement of, at Mrs Clark's, **21.** 183n
Congratulatory Letter, A, perhaps by: **35.** 49–50; generally attributed to Bubb Dodington, **30.** 315–16; HW attributes, to Williams, **30.** 315
Country Girl, The, by, **18.** 22–4, 42, **30.** 314, **43.** 246; see also *Country Maid*
Country Maid, The, author of, **18.** 48

daughter of, **9.** 207n, **11.** 41n, **21.** 53, 312n, 429n
Dear Betty, Come Give Me Sweet Kisses written by, for Cts of Ilchester, **30.** 318
death of, **30.** 322, **33.** 78
design of SH library requested by, for reproduction at Coldbrook, **30.** 147
Dialogue between Samuel Sandys and Edmund Waller, A, by, **30.** 317
died in madhouse, not in Russia, **33.** 78
diplomatic career of: ambassador to Russia, **30.** 322, **35.** 220; envoy extraordinary to Prussia, **20.** 51, **30.** 319–20; envoy at Dresden, **30.** 313; reasons for, **30.** 312–13; second mission to Dresden, **30.** 320–1; special mission to K. of Poland, **30.** 320; Turin embassy vainly sought, **30.** 319–20; unofficial mission to Vienna, **30.** 321
disinclined to return to England, **30.** 116
disliked at St Petersburg, **21.** 53n
distich by: considered unoriginal by Conway, **37.** 360; on Maria Theresa, **16.** 148, **30.** 321, **37.** 353, 360, **43.** 219
Dodsley given messages by, for Dr Brown, **9.** 220
Don Carlos not attempted by, as subject, until mad, **41.** 290
Dresden to be station of, **19.** 347
Eccardt's portrait of, **35.** 174
Edgcumbe does not know address of, **30.** 79
—— presented to James Johnston by, **9.** 30
——'s elegy may be shown to, **30.** 81
—— sends respects to, **30.** 67
——'s letter may be shown to, **30.** 67
Elizabeth, Czarina, offended by, **21.** 53n
enemies of: numerous, **30.** 312; secure Rochford's appointment to Turin, **30.** 319–20
England revisited by, **20.** 90, **21.** 53, 183, **30.** 118, 121, 320, 321–2
epigram by, on Egmont's opposition to Mutiny Bill, **20.** 51, **30.** 319
Epistle to the Right Hon. Henry Fox, An, ('Prudence and Parts') by, **30.** 318
Evening, The, by, **30.** 317
fashionable, **20.** 198
father of, **30.** 311
Fielding, Henry, begs money from, **9.** 84
—— said to have lent play to, **33.** 77–8
Finch family called 'black funereal' in ode by, **21.** 345n
Fourth Eclogue of Virgil Imitated, by, **30.** 307n, 317
Fox, Henry, accepts wager of, that Granville will be president of Council, **20.** 216n
—— and Lady Caroline Lennox married at house of, **18.** 451
Fox, Henry, concerned by illness of, **30.** 71
—— friend of, **9.** 220, **18.** 90n, 451, **21.** 54n, **30.** 313
—— to send HW's letter to, **30.** 114
—— wishes, to go to Turin, **20.** 16
General Churchill's Address to Venus by, **30.** 313

[Williams, Sir Charles Hanbury, *continued*]

George II angered by, allowing Russians to sign treaty first, **30.** 322

—— pleased that Frederick Augustus II was persuaded by, **20.** 186n

—— promised Fox to make, envoy to Berlin, **30.** 319

—— recalls, from Dresden, **20.** 16n

Giles Earle . . . and Geo. Bubb Doddington, Esqrs; a Dialogue, by, **30.** 313–14

granddaughter of, **25.** 577

grandson resembles, **35.** 385

Grub Upon Bubb, A, by, **30.** 316

HW agrees with, about Garrick as 'Hotspur,' **38.** 525

HW annotates verses of, **9.** 255n

HW compares, with Semele, **30.** 159

HW expects to be scolded by, for delay in reminding (?) Selwyn of SH visit, **30.** 118

HW hears anecdotes of, from abroad, after insanity, **39.** 244

HW hopes to entertain, at SH, **30.** 114

HW learns rebus from, **30.** 42

HW loved, **30.** 159

HW mentions, **37.** 175

HW not to write (?) verses at request of, **30.** 81

HW probably informed by, about Brühl, **21.** 320n

HW receives cider from, **30.** 85

HW's account of, **30.** 159, 311–23

HW's correspondence ignored by, after leaving England, **30.** 113

HW's correspondence with: **30.** 47–65, 74, 79–99, 110, 113–16, 118–19, 124, 146–7; MSS of, **36.** 310

HW sends Miss Rigby's verses to, **30.** 118–19

HW's epitaph for, **13.** 35, **30.** 159

HW's goldfish wanted by, **40.** 85

HW 'sold' to, **37.** 157

HW's opinion of: his genius wasted outside England, **30.** 116; 'only man living that can write,' **30.** 64; only true poet in England since Pope's death, **30.** 53

HW's portrait by Robinson to be copied for, **30.** 95

HW's *Royal and Noble Authors* requested by, **30.** 147

HW talks with, at opera, about Fox's wedding, **37.** 157n

HW to write notes to poems of, **30.** 159

HW would be glad to see, **30.** 124

habits of, **30.** 83

Hamburg lady (Mlle John) has affair with, **21.** 183, 194

Hanover visited by, during George II's stay there, **30.** 320

health of: ague, **30.** 82; apoplectic lethargy, **30.** 322; aphrodisiac causes derangement of, **21.** 183; Chesterfield thinks, mad, **21.** 190n; cold, **30.** 48; convulsions, **30.** 322; fever, **21.** 190; illness prevents Houghton visit, **30.** 67–8; insane, temporarily, **9.** 219, 251; insanity, **30.** 322; insanity suspected, **21.** 183, 190; recovered, **30.** 147; said to be ill, **30.** 83; Titley reports on, **21.** 183n; venereal disease, **18.** 104; very ill, **30.** 48

'Hervey and Jekyll,' **30.** 315

Houghton visit planned but abandoned by, **30.** 60, 63–4, 65, 67–8

house of, let, **9.** 39

Hussey's abortive duel with, **30.** 312

Ilchester visited by, **30.** 118

imitation by, of *Donec gratum eram tibi*, Winnington's alteration of, alters Frederick, P. of Wales, **30.** 317

Isabella, or the Morning ('The Toilette or the Morning') by: HW thinks, Williams's best work, **30.** 317; Leicester described in, **25.** 308n

Jamaica remittance agreement witnessed by, **17.** 411

Labour in Vain by: HW transcribes, **18.** 18–20; Mann disparages, **18.** 42

Legge replaced by, in Berlin post, **19.** 457n

letters and verses of, admired, **20.** 186

letters of: inferior to his other works, **30.** 317; ministerial, much admired, **30.** 320; to E. of Lincoln on Mother Hayward's death, **30.** 317

'Letter to Mr Dodsley, A,' by, **30.** 315

'Lord Bath to Ambition' by, **30.** 319

'Maddington Congress' attended by, **30.** 82

Mann dislikes appointment of, to Turin, **19.** 466

——'s praises heard by, in Germany, **20.** 90

—— will prefer letters of, to Villettes's, **19.** 465

Maria Theresa and Elizabeth of Russia reconciled by, **30.** 320

Maria Theresa praised in distich by, **16.** 148, **30.** 321, **37.** 353, 360

Mengs considered by, equal to Carlo Maratti, **20.** 352

—— recommended by, to Mann, **20.** 330–1, 352

Middleton, Mrs, tells, of husband's dislike of dedication, **15.** 304

ministry dislikes, **20.** 16

Montagu embroiled with, **21.** 53

monument may be placed in Westminster Abbey to, **30.** 159

name changed by, for estate, **30.** 311

Newcastle's letter from, on Poland much admired in England, **30.** 320

——'s memorandum indicates Turin as post for, **19.** 456n

New Ode, A ('Nova Progenies'), by: **11.** 246n, **30.** 314; given false ending to hide its authorship, **18.** 52n; HW transcribes, **18.** 48–51; Mann likes, **18.** 78

Ode on the Death of Matzel ('Stanzas on the Death of a Bullfinch Killed by a Cat'), by, **30.** (?) 115, 318

Ode on the Marriage of the Duchess of Manchester by, **9.** 43, 48

odes and other writings of, generally attributed to Bubb Dodington, **30.** 315–16
odes on Pulteney attributed to, **18.** 70
Ode to Henry Earl of Lincoln Wrote in 1742–3 by: **30.** 318; Lincoln called 'joy of womankind' in, **17.** 210n
Ode to Lord Chesterfield by, **30.** 318
Ode to Mr Poyntz by, **30.** 319
Ode . . . to the Earl of Bath, An, by, transcribed by HW, **18.** 73–5
Ode to the Honourable Henry Fox, An, by, **30.** 312
Old Coachman, The, by: HW transcribes, **18.** 20–2; Mann disparages, **18.** 42
Orford, Cts of, may be mentioned in satire by, **30.** 93
Oxford University to send deputation to, **30.** 88
Pandæmonium, The, by, **23.** 236, **30.** 314
Parliamentary vote by, on privately-raised regiments, **26.** 19
Patapan loves odes of, **30.** 55
paymastership of Marines resigned by, after scandal, **19.** 341, **30.** 312
Pelham complimented by, in ode to Lincoln, **30.** 318
—— often slighted, **30.** 312
Peter and My Lord Quidam ('On Legacy Hunters') by, **30.** 316–17
plate of, **18.** 472n
Political Eclogue, A, by, **30.** 317
portrait of, at SH: by Eccardt, **35.** 174; HW hopes Beaulieus did not see, **10.** 106–7; Montagu to hide, on occasion of Cts of Beaulieu's visit, **10.** 107
possible author of additions to HW's 'Lesson for the Day,' **13.** 13n
Prussia sends, away from Berlin post, **38.** 393
Ranby requests, to assure Brown that no personal attack will be made on him, **9.** 220
rebel lords' execution described by, **19.** 298n
reputation of, **30.** 53
return of, from Russia, **21.** 53, 183
returns, on ill-success of Anglo-Russian negotiations, **21.** 53
Rigby accompanies, to Wales, **30.** 330n
—— placed by, with Peg Woffington, **30.** 52n
——'s correspondence with, **30.** 64, 85
—— visits, in Wales, **30.** 88n
Russia's military intentions to be ascertained by, **20.** 187n
—— threatened by, with Prussian attack, **21.** 53n
Sandwich opposed to, as plenipotentiary to Aix, **19.** 456n
Sandys and Jekyll by, **30.** 315
Secret Committee may examine, **17.** 411
self-flattery of, prevents his flattering HW, **35.** 244
Selwyn asks HW to ask his pardon of, **30.** 88
—— replaces, as paymaster of Marines, **19.** 341n
(?) —— to meet, at SH, **30.** 118

—— visited by Rigby and, at Oxford, **30.** 330n
Selwyn family's presence would displease, at Houghton, **30.** 64
1741 by, **17.** 346–7
Simile, A, Published in Geoffrey Broadbottom's Journal perhaps by, **30.** 318
Song on Miss Harriet Hanbury, A, by, **30.** 322
speech by, on Convention of the Pardo, **30.** 311
speeches rarely made by, because he thought he lacked talent, **30.** 311
'speech' of David Morgan in prose by, published, **30.** 319
Statesman, The, attributed to, **18.** 90–1, **30.** 315
Steavens, Thomas, friend of, **20.** 175n
SH visited by, **35.** 177
Tesi, ancient favourite of, **21.** 194
To Mr Garnier and Mr Pearce of Bath by, **30.** 321–2
To the Earl of Bath by: HW quotes, **18.** 320–1; pleases Mann, **18.** 334
To the Rev. Samuel Hill, Canon of Wells by, **30.** 316
Townshend, Vcts, broken with by, after Winnington's death, **30.** 312
—— discusses Anson with, **19.** 13
—— to have cordial reunion with, **30.** 121
Turin post may go to, **19.** 347, 456, 465, 466
Turin preferred to Warsaw by, because of climate, **20.** 16n
Unembarrassed Countenance, The, possibly by, **9.** 30, **33.** 276
Unhappy England, Still in 'Forty-one by, **30.** 319
verse epistle to Lyttelton by, **30.** 313
verses by: early, bad, **30.** 313; political ballads aided by Winnington and Yonge, **30.** 314; to Kitty Walker, **30.** 316; to Mrs Woffington, **30.** 316; to Winnington in Harris's name, **30.** 316
Walker, Kitty, mistress of, **30.** 316
Walpole, Sir Robert, patronized, **30.** 311
Warsaw visited by, **30.** 116, 320
wife ill-treated by, **39.** 244
wife infected by, with venereal disease, **18.** 104n
Winnington corresponds with, **30.** 60, 68
—— friend of, **19.** 250, **30.** 311
——'s death affected, **30.** 312
——'s epitaph written by, **30.** 320
witticisms by: on Onslow's speech to Westminster justices of the peace, **30.** 301n; on Pitt's resignation of Bedchamber, **19.** 27; on Secker and Ds of Kent, **30.** 304n
Woffington, Peg, mistress of, **30.** 52, 316, **39.** 244
—— not deceived by, **39.** 244
Wolters corresponds with, on business, **19.** 507n
World contributions by, **20.** 395n, 400n, **30.** 321

[Williams, Sir Charles Hanbury, *continued*]
writings of: HW anxious to see, **30.** 90, 93;
HW had looked forward to reading, at
Houghton, **30.** 68; HW not to see, until
finished, **30.** 90, 99; HW one of the few
who sees, **30.** 64; HW promised copies of,
30. 53, 85, 93; HW's admiration for, **30.**
53, 64, 93; HW to be content with, instead
of producing his own, **30.** 82; HW will be
pleased to be mentioned in, **30.** 95; Walpole, Sir Robert, will enjoy, **30.** 64; *see also
under individual titles above*
Williams, Charlotte Hanbury (1738–90), m.
(1759) Hon. Robert Boyle Walsingham:
ball given by, at Thames Ditton, **35.** 391,
42. 222
ball guests of, listed, **42.** 222n
biographical information about, corrected,
43. 140
Bishop Bonner's Ghost given to, **31.** 310, 313
chimney-piece designed for house of, at
Thames Ditton, **33.** 573
Christmas spent by, with Mrs Garrick and
Hannah More, **42.** 205
Cowley portrait to be sent by, to SH, **42.** 205
Cowley portrait to be shown by, to HW, **42.**
222
daughter advised by, to have female companion, **31.** 346
daughter decorates Boyle Farm of, **35.** 390
daughter of: **25.** 577n; attentive till her death,
31. 346
Garrick, Mrs, shows to, Monboddo's letter,
33. 363n
HW dines with, at Boyle Farm, **11.** 41
HW regrets missing entertainment by, **42.**
196
HW's correspondence with, **42.** 196–7, 203–5,
222
HW sees, frequently, **31.** 251
HW unable to visit, because of illness, **31.** 217
Hamilton, Mary, invited to visit, **31.** 206
health of: report of 'disorder' probably in-
correct, **31.** 336; suffers terribly, **31.** 336
Hertford's house at Thames Ditton bought
by, **39.** 416
house of, *see* Boyle Farm
library of, **31.** 251
locket shown to HW by, **33.** 338
marriage of, **30.** 323
More, Hannah, provokes, by defending subordination of women, **31.** 370
—— would not have attended fête of, **31.** 266
musicale at Lady Lucan's attended by, **33.** 139
Nivernais's *Jardins modernes* given to, **12.** 259
Penn, Lady Juliana, and daughter dine with,
11. 41
responsibility may be borne by, for Shannon's
contesting Charlotte Boyle's inheritance,
31. 346
robbed, **39.** 416
social relations of, with: Garrick, Mrs, **31.**
206, 213, 217, 228, **35.** 384; Hamilton, Mary,

31. 217; Lucan, Lady, **33.** 139; More,
Hannah, **31.** 213, 228; Penn, Lady Juliana,
and daughter, **11.** 41; Vesey, Mrs, **31.** 214
(?) son disowned by, **31.** 274
SH visited by, **31.** 206
Williams, Christopher. *See* Plumley, Christopher
Williams, Edmund (d. 1752), Capt.:
investigation of, **19.** 25, 32–3
Royal Oak commanded by, **19.** 25n
Williams, Lady Frances [Hanbury]. *See* Con-
ingsby, Lady Frances
Williams, Frances Hanbury (1735–59), m.
(1754) William Anne Holles Capel, 4th E.
of Essex; 'Princess Edward':
ball given by, for D. of York, **21.** 53–4
birth date of, corrected, **43.** 119
Bristol waters prescribed for, **30.** 147
Coldbrook visited by, **30.** 147
Cuzzoni's voice called 'decayed' by, **17.** 359n
death of, **9.** 244, **21.** 312, 429, **30.** 322–3
Edward Augustus, P., (D. of York) object
of song rendered by, **21.** 57
—— pursues, **9.** 207, **21.** 53–4
father arranges marriage of, **30.** 118n
father receives goldfish from, **40.** 86n
Garnier and Peirce attend, **30.** 321
HW asks, to employ Bentley after her mar-
riage to Essex, **35.** 177
HW's correspondence with, **40.** 85
HW sent services by, **30.** 147
HW's goldfish wanted by, **40.** 85
illness of, at Coldbrook, **30.** 321
Lyttelton tells, not to meddle in politics, **21.**
54
marriage of, **30.** 322
(?) Nugent's affair with, **37.** 447
Piozzi, Mrs, comments upon, **9.** 207n
Ranelagh frequented by, **9.** 207
Rochford, Cts of, entertains, at ball, **21.** 57
SH drawn by, from bowling-green, **35.** 177
Yarmouth, Cts of, entertained by, at supper,
37. 458n
Williams, George James ('Gilly') (ca 1719–
1805), wit:
Bath visited by, **30.** 125, 150, 238
designing of coat of arms for White's Club
aided by, **9.** 186
Guilford, Cts of, said by, to fear Coventry's
divorce, **9.** 203
HW and Selwyn may fetch, from Bath, **30.**
150
HW and Selwyn might visit, at Bath, **35.** 89n
HW dines in party with, **30.** 252
HW does not write to, because letters to
Selwyn are shared with him, **30.** 218
HW entertains, at SH, **38.** 276
HW expects, at SH, **32.** 197, **35.** 200
HW hopes, will forgive him for cancelling
Bath visit, **30.** 144
HW hopes to divert, by Paris anecdotes, **30.**
208

HW inquires whether Rockingham has assisted, **30.** 207

HW invites, to call, **30.** 283

(?) HW mentions, **4.** 423

(?) HW plays cribbage with, at Lady Mendip's, **12.** 202, **43.** 157

HW recommends Ossory to, **30.** 207

HW's *Account of the Giants* praised by, and to be sent to Selwyn, **30.** 238

HW's aim called *monstrari digito prætereuntium* by, **30.** 176

HW's correspondence with, **30.** 155

HW sends compliments to, **30.** 143, 172, 207, 211–12

HW's housekeeper's wealth magnified by, **33.** 412

HW's style easily recognized by, **30.** 238

HW supped with by, **30.** 125

HW's visitors prevent, having free conversation with him, **30.** 238

HW tells, of Fox's letter to Albemarle, **30.** 201

HW tells Selwyn's witticism on E. of Pomfret and the Parks to, **30.** 120

HW thought by, more likely to be offended by epithet 'prince of cockleshells' than by grave refutation, **30.** 239

HW told by, that Selwyn likes his *Account of the Giants* and that half Paris is mad about it, **30.** 238

HW visited by, **9.** 186, 417, **11.** 93, **30.** 238, **33.** 197

HW wishes to dine with Selwyn and, **40.** 151

HW would be pleased to see, **30.** 150

Keene, Mrs, visited by, **33.** 232

legacy received by, **30.** 211

letters of, to Selwyn, quoted, **30.** 120, 125, 171, 176–7, 238–9

(?) Mendip, Lady, visited by, **12.** 202

Montagu inquires about, **9.** 267n

news reported by, **33.** 197

Nivernais's *Jardins modernes* given to, **12.** 259

North, Bn, commended by, **9.** 203

—'s confidant, **29.** 206

North, Bns, visited by, **9.** 203

portrait of, by Reynolds, **9.** 417

remark of, on SH, **4.** 251n

Selwyn does not inform, of change in plans, **30.** 151

— urged by, to persuade HW to join Bath visit, **30.** 125

sister of, **10.** 197n

SH may be visited by, **30.** 166

SH visited by, **12.** 223, 250 *bis*, **15.** (?) 327, **30.** 176

Temple-Grenville reconciliation reportedly negotiated by, **30.** 188

Townshend, Hon. Charles, tries to save, from dismissal, **30.** 193n

— writes to Rockingham for place for, **30.** 207n

wife of, **9.** 29n

Williams, Mrs George James. *See* Bertie, Diana

Williams, Helen Maria (1762–1827), writer:

HW calls, 'Jael,' **11.** 320

lacks imagination and novelty, **33.** 533

Letters Written in France in the Summer of 1790 by, **11.** 320n

Poems by, **43.** 150

revolutionary sentiments of, **11.** 320

Williams, Rev. John (fl. 1563):

living of St Mary Abchurch coveted by, **1.** 224

Williams, John (1582–1650), Abp of York:

portrait of, at St John's College, **14.** 114

windows given to Lincoln College by, **16.** 197n

Williams, (?) John (d. before 1775), secretary to Richard West, sr:

HW's 'Dear Witches' mentions, **43.** 178

HW sends letter to Mann through, **17.** 5

HW thanks Mann for civilities to, **17.** 12

(?) Rome visited by, **13.** 210–11

Wales visited by, **13.** 230

Williams, John (fl. 1747), innkeeper in Piccadilly:

assault upon, **19.** 388n

Independents denounced by, **19.** 387n

— should be prosecuted for beating, **19.** 399

Williams, John (ca 1716–79):

HW sees house of, **9.** 66

wife of, **9.** 66n

Williams, John (d. after 1774), printer and bookseller next to the Mitre in Fleet St:

mob hails, when pilloried in New Palace Yard, and gives him a purse, **38.** 512

North Briton Complete printed by, **22.** 195n

trial of, for republishing *North Briton*, **38.** 433n

Williams, Jonathan, (1750–1815):

Franklin's grandnephew and companion, **6.** 383

Williams, Peter, inn-keeper; 'groom':

(?) Ferrers may have injured, **21.** 395

Williams, Rev. Philip (?1695–1749):

letters of, to Z. Grey, cited, **2.** 350

Williams, Rev. R. (fl. 1775):

'The Bard' translated by, **1.** 386, 388

Williams, Renwick (fl. 1790), dancing-master; 'the Monster':

forgotten, **11.** 208

Williams, Robert *or* Roger (fl. 1680), engraver:

print by, of E. of Huntingdon, **1.** 182

Williams, Sophia Wilhelmina (ca 1753–1823), called Sophie Cornelys until 1772:

HW inquires whether, is with Ds of Beaufort at Stoke, **31.** 333

Williams, Watkin:

Digby miniatures bought by HW from descendants of, **23.** 267n, **28.** 180n

Williams, Watkin. *See also* Wynn, Sir Watkin Williams

Williams, Sir William Peere (ca 1730–61), 2d Bt, 1758; M.P.:

death of, **9.** 364, **21.** 505

debts of, **9.** 369

Montagu, Frederick, heir of, **9.** 369

Williamson, Adam (1676 or 7 – 1747), Lt-Gen.; deputy lieutenant of Tower of London:
Balmerinoch ill-treated by, 19. 301
Lovat offers to marry his son to niece of, 19. 380
paper sent to, in behalf of rebel lords, 19. 286
Williamson, Elizabeth Caroline (b. 1731), m. (1760) Daniel Fox:
lived with father in Tower, 19. 376n
Williamson, Sir Joseph (1633–1701), Kt; secretary of state 1674–8; M.P.:
letter ascribed to, 35. 133
Pembroke, Cts of, writes alleged letter to, 9. 125, 10. 336, 35. 133
Williamson, Joseph (fl. 1769):
Sandwich succeeded by, as member of Beefsteak Club, 10. 111n
Williamstadt. See Willemstad
Williams Wynn. See Wynn
Willingham, Cambs:
Cole's tenant forced to move to, 1. 122n
Willingmi, English ship:
Leghorn visited by, from Newfoundland, 24. 246
Willington, Edward Pearce, engineer:
(?) captured by French, 24. 476n
ensigncy for, 39. 52n
Willington family:
Feilding family descended from, 20. 409n
Willis, Browne (1682–1760), antiquary:
Anecdotes of Painting mentions, 40. 228
Baker aids, 2. 351
Byron's verses mention, 2. 162n
Cole presented by, to living at Bletchley, 1. 1n, 71n, 2. 378
Eyre son-in-law of, 1. 36n
HW puts Warburton in company with, 13. 39n
HW suggests life of, 1. 255
'History and Antiquities of Hundreds of Newport and Cotslow,' MS by, 2. 335–6, 338
History of the Mitred Parliamentary Abbies, An, by, 2. 351
Magdalene College receives gift of books from, 2. 351
mansions of, 2. 326
on George Herbert's death, 1. 71
Pennant's error concerning, 2. 325–6, 328
portrait of, 2. 285
print of, 2. 285, 287, 295, 303
Survey of the Cathedrals, A, by, 1. 71, 43. 47
Willis, Francis (1718–1807), M.D.:
George III's health reported by, 34. 43n
——'s illness declared by, to have ceased, 25. 682n
HW confers with, about nephew, 16. 314
Norford, Dr, differs with, about E. of Orford, 42. 333, 342n
Orford, E. of, attended by, at Houghton, 42. 332–4
Willis, Thomas (1621–75), M.D.:
HW confuses, with Dr Wallis, 32. 334

theory of, concerning musical nerve, 32. 334
Willis, Thomas (1743–90):
Browne Willis's grandson, 1. 106n
to have living of Bletchley, 1. 106n
Willock, Mr, of Putney:
SH visited by, 12. 231
Willoughby, Lady. See Bertie, Lady Priscilla Barbara Elizabeth
Willoughby, Cassandra (1670–1735), m. (1713) James Brydges, 9th Bn Chandos, cr. (1714) E. of Carnarvon and (1719) D. of Chandos:
Lund discusses, 30. 61
painter, 30. 61, 62
'patchwork' room composed by, at Cannons, 30. 61–2
Van der Myn's portrait of, drawing husband's portrait, 30. 61
Willoughby, Elizabeth (d. 1560), m. Sir Fulke Greville:
tomb of, at Alcester, 9. 224
Willoughby, Francis (1692–1758), 2d Bn Middleton, 1729; M.P.:
Wollaton Hall, seat of, 35. 279n
Willoughby, George (1742–79), 14th Bn Willoughby of Parham, 1775:
novelty of title of, will soon wear off, 28. 224
Willoughby, Henry (1696–1775), 13th Bn Willoughby of Parham, 1767; Col.:
nephew succeeds, 28. 224n
(?) Wharton's death described by, 16. 6
Willoughby, Hugh (ca 1714–65), (illegally) 15th Bn Willoughby of Parham:
HW dedicates Hentzner edition to, 43. 172
Willoughby, Sir Robert (ca 1385–1452), 6th Bn Willoughby de Eresby; K.G.:
in Margaret of Anjou's escort, 14. 73
Willoughby, Sir Robert (ca 1452–1502), cr. (1491) Bn Willoughby de Broke; K.G.:
Elizabeth of York conducted by, 14. 79
Willoughby, William de (ca 1370–1409), 5th Bn Willoughby, 1396:
marriage of, 42. 139
Willoughby. See also Willoughby de Broke
Willoughby, Lincs:
Bowyer of, 2. 235n
Willoughby de Broke, Bn. See Verney, George (1674–1728); Verney (later, Peyto Verney), John (1738–1816); Verney, Richard (1693–1752); Willoughby, Sir Robert (ca 1452–1502)
Willoughby de Eresby, Bn. See Willoughby, William de (ca 1370–1409)
Willoughby de Eresby, Bns. See Bertie, Lady Priscilla Barbara Elizabeth (1761–1828)
Willow; willows:
in French garden, 28. 220
Lechmere's house shut off by, 35. 152
weeping: at Batheaston, 39. 240; Hannah More compared with, 31. 347; placing of, 9. 177
Will-o-wisp:
peace compared with, 23. 255

Wills, Lt.-Gen. Sir Charles (1666–1741), K.B.; M.P.:
death of, necessitates by-election at Totnes, **17**. 299n
HW mentions, **20**. 441
Windsor property of, **43**. 113
Wills, Haughton (ca 1710–82):
Fame owned by, **19**. 383n
Mann sends medals through, to HW, **21**. 209, 215, 233
Willsbrook, co. Westmeath:
Handcock of, **10**. 16n, **29**. 36n
Wilmington, E. of. *See* Compton, Sir Spencer
Wilmington, Delaware:
English troops land at, and re-embark, **32**. 380
Wilmington, North Carolina:
capture of, reported, **29**. 128n
Wilmot, Mr, lawyer:
papers saved by, from fire, **20**. 321n
Wilmot, Christopher, M.D.:
genealogy of wife of, **10**. 158n, 352
Wilmot, Mrs Christopher. *See* Montagu, Anne
Wilmot, Sir Edward (1693–1786), cr. (1759) Bt; physician:
(?) Cumberland, D. of, attended by, **21**. 432n
Devonshire, D. of, treated by, at Chatsworth, **38**. 419
Frederick, P. of Wales, attended by, **20**. 232
George II said by, to be free from fever, **21**. 188n
——'s health reported by, **21**. 256n
HW attributes patients' deaths to, **9**. 287
HW hears opinion of, on Waldegrave's illness, **10**. 56
Pelham, Lady Catherine, saved by lancing by, **21**. 369
Waldegrave attended by, **10**. 56, **22**. 127n
Wilmot, Elizabeth (1674–1757) m. (1689) Edward Montagu, 3d E. of Sandwich, 1688:
Chesterfield praises, **6**. 38
dies at Paris, **35**. 99–100
Du Deffand, Mme, gives opinion of, **5**. 309
——'s remark about, **7**. 286
Du Maine, Duchesse, said by, to resemble alehouse wall, **7**. 283
effects of, plundered under *droit d'aubaine*, **1**. 89
Ninon de Lenclos's letters to, may be acquired by HW, **31**. 6–7
——'s portrait owned by, **10**. 34n, **35**. 99–100, **37**. 531n
portrait of, by Dahl, **40**. 284
portrait of, in Warwick Castle, **32**. 353
Waters, executor to, to keep Lenclos portrait for HW, **40**. 94
Wilmot, Henry (ca 1710–94), secretary to the lord chancellor:
Harcourt, Cts, requests SH ticket for, **29**. 268
Wilmot, John (1647–80), 2d E. of Rochester; poet:
Bentley calls, 'cousin' in *Epistle to Lord Melcombe*, **9**. 409–11

Charles II grants Twickenham Manor lease to, **42**. 417n
daughter of, **10**. 54n, **35**. 99n, **37**. 531n
Gray's transcripts of letters of, **28**. 165
Greenhill's portrait of, owned by HW, **42**. 206
HW 'transposes' lines by, **18**. 482
Letter from Artemisa, A, by: HW paraphrases, **31**. 111; Mason quotes, **28**. 331
letters of: burnt by Lady St John, **28**. 239–40; transcripts of, **28**. 165; Wolseley correspondence, **16**. 5
poems of, Hinchingbrooke's child to be christened with, **10**. 207
portrait; portraits of: **30**. 370; at Hinchingbrooke, **40**. 283; with monkey, **32**. 353
Portsmouth, Ds of, insulted by, **7**. 353
Sandwich resembles, **28**. 169
Suffolk may have been imitating, **16**. 25
'Upon Nothing. A Poem' by, **12**. 173–4
Voltaire introduced by, to France, **41**. 152
wit of, would be approved only in one half-century, **25**. 308
witty but thoughtless, **33**. 223n
Wolseley friend of, **16**. 5n
——'s letters from, **16**. 5
Wilmot, Sir John Eardley (1709–92), Kt, 1755; chief justice of Common Pleas 1766–71:
becomes commissioner of Great Seal, **21**. 25
health of, will not permit him to accept Seals, **23**. 175
Pratt succeeded by, as chief justice of Common Pleas, **22**. 443
Seals may be thrust upon, **23**. 179
SH visited by, **12**. 222
verdict against Wilkes upheld by, **23**. 83
Vergy swears affidavit before, **22**. 262, **38**. 467
Wilmot, Montagu:
genealogy of, **10**. 352
Wilmot, Sir Robert (ca 1708–72), Kt, 1739; cr. (1772) Bt:
election defeat attributed by, to absences, **17**. 272n
Wilson, Lady. *See* Badger Weller, Jane
Wilson, ——:
Hertford receives HW's *Counter-Address* from, **38**. 424
Wilson, Capt.:
express from St-Malo brought by, in the *Swan*, **21**. 212n
Wilson, Ann, maid:
acquitted as an accomplice in coining, **19**. 242n
Wilson, Arthur (1595–1652), historian:
History of Great Britain by: **16**. 162n, **43**. 45; anecdote in, of Weston's execution, **16**. 163; cited, **1**. 26, **30**. 287n; HW consults, **15**. 83; letters mentioned by, **15**. 92
Wilson, Benjamin (1721–88), painter:
drawing of Thomas Gray by Mason and, **1**. 361n, 367, **28**. 98, 100–1, 141, **29**. 290n
print of, presented by Lort to HW, **16**. 167
Wilson, Christopher (ca 1714–92), D.D.; Bp of Bristol 1785–92:

[Wilson, Christopher, *continued*]
(?) Ducarel communicates letter of, to HW, **40.** 179
(?) HW's correspondence with, **40.** 179–80
SH visited by, **12.** 236
Wilson, Mrs Daniel. *See* Egerton, Beatrix (d. 1779)
Wilson, David, bookseller in the Strand:
Nicol, his nephew, associated with, **42.** 283n
Wilson, Edward (d. 1694):
duel of, with John Law, **15.** 180n
Wilson, Elizabeth, m. (1757) Thomas Bradshaw:
HW tells D. of Richmond to inquire about scandalous pension of, **41.** 311
pension to, **35.** 350n
Wilson, Henry, officer in naval yard:
Cardini accompanies, from Florence to England, **25.** 305n
Wilson, Isabella (1719–73), m. (1739) James Ferguson:
husband's reason for marriage to, **32.** 16
'Wilson, Jasper.' *See* Currie, James
Wilson, John (ca 1627–96):
Chests, The, by, **15.** 198n
Wilson, John (ca 1659–1718) of Knight Thorpe:
wife of, **12.** 267
Wilson, Sir John (1741–93), Kt; judge:
commissioner of the Great Seal, **15.** 216n
Wilson, Mrs John. *See* Walpole, Mary
Wilson, Margaretta Elizabeth (1768–1851), m. (1787) Charles George Perceval, 2d Bn Arden:
SH visited by, **12.** 251
Wilson, Nanny, D. of Cumberland's mistress:
(?) Conway, Hon. Jane, forbids, to see HW, **30.** 83
Cumberland, D. of, takes, as his mistress from Drury Lane stage, **19.** 52
Wilson, Richard (1714–82), painter:
Jenkins, Thomas, at Rome with, **20.** 174n
'Monument of the Horatii' by, **15.** 322n
Wilson, Col. Robert:
Daams, falconer to, **32.** 355n
Wilson, Thomas (?1525–81), lay Dean of Durham:
Discourse Upon Usury by, **1.** 54n
never knighted, **1.** 54, 82
Wilson, Thomas (1663–1755), Bp of Sodor and Man, 1697:
Bible edited by, given by HW to Hannah More, **31.** 399
Wilson, Rev. Thomas (1703–84), D.D.: prebendary of Westminster Abbey 1743–84; rector of St Stephen's Walbrook 1737–84:
appendix by, to Hole's *Ornaments of Churches Considered*: **1.** 21; St Margaret's Church's window defended in, **41.** 142
HW's correspondence with, **41.** 139–43
Macaulay, Mrs, idolized by, **28.** 372
Wilson, Mrs Thomas. *See* Patten, Mary
Wilson, Sir Thomas Spencer (1726–98), 6th Bt, 1760; army officer:

Cornwallis joined by, to attack Red Bank, **33.** 4
daughter of, **11.** 202n
Richmond, D. of, backs, against Peachey, in Sussex election, **39.** 207
Wilson, William, army clothier:
Conway does not know, **37.** 254
Wilton, E. of. *See* Egerton, Sir Thomas
Wilton, ——, father of Joseph Wilton:
plaster-worker at Hedge Lane, Charing Cross, **20.** 392n
son receives article from, **20.** 392
workshop of, in Edward St, Cavendish Sq., **20.** 392n
Wilton, Joseph (1722–1803), sculptor:
Adventurer said to mention, **20.** 395n
artists at D. of Richmond's gallery to be corrected by, **21.** 174n
Capezzoli lives with, **23.** 567
Chambers lives with, at Rome, **20.** 368n
—— returns to England with, **20.** 392n
design submitted by, for Wolfe's tomb, **21.** 428
drawing of design by, for Wood's monument, **41.** 317n
father of, sends him the article mentioning him, **20.** 392
George III's statuary and state coach carver, **20.** 391n
Inspector article praises, **20.** 397
Mann encloses letters to, from two poor fathers, **22.** 418
—— has, in his house, **20.** 391
—— neglected by, despite his hospitality, **22.** 419n
——'s correspondence with, **20.** 520
Paris, Rome, and Florence visited by, **20.** 391n
Pearce tells, to move Aymer de Valence's tomb in Westminster Abbey, **38.** 111
Pitt's bust executed by, **20.** 397n
sculpture by, **20.** 397–8
state coach's carvings by, **22.** 104n
statue by, **28.** 472n
Westminster Abbey examined by, for site of Wolfe's monument, **40.** 200–1
Wood's tombstone executed by, **41.** 318
World article thought by Mann to award praise to, **20.** 392, 395, 397
Wilton House, Wilts, E. of Pembroke's seat:
bridge at: designed by E. of Pembroke, **20.** 109; replica of, in sugar, **9.** 363
Dodd and Whaley visit, **40.** 8
family-piece at, of E. of Pembroke, **41.** 443
HW and Rigby to visit, **30.** 92
HW to visit, **37.** 202
marbles and pictures at, mostly rubbish, **35.** 296
medals not visible at, **16.** 209
Pembroke the owner of, **22.** 9
Pitt's witticism on silly woman's mistake about, **12.** 256

Raphael tapestries at, **16**. 157n, 159n
statuary at, **40**. 8
statues at, adorned with charcoal, **25**. 178
visitors to: HW, **19**. 92n, **35**. 296, **38**. 25,
  40. 165; Montagu, **10**. 284; Rigby, **19**. 92n
Wiltshire, E. of. *See* Boleyn, Sir Thomas (1477–
  1539); Stafford, Edward (1469–99)
Wiltshire:
  Bruce, Lord, inherits Ailesbury's estates in,
    20. 331n
  custom of vails abolished in, **20**. 89n
  HW visits, **1**. 14n
  Parliamentary reform measures not adopted
    in, **29**. 24, 26
  petition from, **7**. 367
  petition to be presented by, **23**. 132
  Pynsent said to be free from, **22**. 276
  Setons move to, **43**. 144
Wilzeck. *See* Wilczek
Wimbledon, Vct. *See* Cecil, Edward (1572–
  1638)
Wimbledon, Surrey:
  Calonne's villa at, **11**. 36n
  HW visits, **9**. 119
  Marlborough, Ds of, has house at, **9**. 119
  Spencer, 1st E., leaves furniture at, to heir,
    33. 428n
  ——'s paintings at, **21**. 173n
  Spencer, John, dies at, **19**. 272n
  Walpole, Robert (1701–51), 2d E. of Orford,
    inherits Walker's house at, **19**. 511n
Wimbledon Common:
  Herbert Lodge near, **39**. 285
Wimborne, Dorset:
  Hanham of, **9**. 167n
Wimpffen, Pierre-Christian (1725–81), Baron
  de:
  Ordre de St-Louis elects, **6**. 412
  social relations of, in Paris, **7**. (?) 284, 286,
    287, 290, 295, 297, 301, 304, 306, 308, 352
Wimpole, Cambs:
  Baker not a visitor at, **2**. 144–5, 361
  —— welcome to, **2**. 348
  Hardwicke may retire to, **20**. 202
  ——'s seat, **2**. 113, 119n, 144n
  Middleton occasionally lived at, **15**. 291n
  Miller designs castle at, **9**. 156n
  Oxford, E. of, has library at, **17**. 357n
  ——'s seat at, **2**. 144, 348
Wimpole St, London.
  residents in: Beauclerk, Aubrey, **10**. 270n;
    Dysart, E. of, **42**. 463; Fry, John, **34**. 143n;
    Pepys, W. W., **11**. 243n, **31**. 228; Walpole,
    Sir Edward, **33**. 2
  Walpole, Sir Edward, leaves house in, to
    daughters, **33**. 2n
  —— wills house in, to Cts of Dysart and then
    to Mrs Keppel, **36**. 126n
  —— writes from, **36**. 126, 155
Wimpsey, Joseph, banker:
  bankruptcy of, **23**. 426
Winbury. *See* Withinbury

Wincanton, Somerset:
  Gapper at Fonthill House at, **42**. 418n
Winchcombe, Glos:
  Montagu's estate near, **9**. 56n, 361n
Winchelsea, Robert de. *See* Robert de Win-
  chelsea
Winchelsea, English ship:
  at Leghorn, **17**. 455, **23**. 233
Winchelsea, Sussex:
  built in squares, **40**. 5
  churches and maritime glory of, departed,
    40. 5–6
  Dodd and Whaley visit, **40**. 5–6
Winchelsea. *See also* Winchilsea
Winchendon ('Winchenton') House, Bucks;
  Wharton's seat:
  painting of, **30**. 371
  Walpole, Sir Robert, bought collection of
    Van Dycks and Lelys from, **30**. 371
  Wharton collection at, **42**. 126n
Winchester, Bp of:
  brothels formerly licensed by, **1**. 137–8
  Newcastle suggested as, **9**. 209, **35**. 281
  See also Andrewes, Lancelot (1555–1626);
    Beaufort, Henry (ca 1375–1447); Foxe *or*
    Fox, Richard (ca 1448–1528); Gardiner,
    Stephen (ca 1483–1555); Hoadly, Benja-
    min (1676–1761); Montagu, James (ca
    1568–1618); North, Hon. Brownlow (1741–
    1820); Swithin, St (d. 862); Thomas, John
    (1696–1781); Trelawny, Sir Jonathan
    (1650–1721); Trimnel, Charles (1663–
    1723); Waynflete, William (ca 1395–1486);
    William (1324–1404) of Wykeham
Winchester, Dean of. *See* Pearce, Zachariah
  (1690–1774); Shipley, Jonathan (1714–88)
Winchester, E. of:
  arms of, **2**. 29
  See also Le Despenser, Hugh (1261–1326)
Winchester, M. of. *See* Paulet, Sir William (ca
  1483–1572)
Winchester, Hants:
  army camp at, **37**. 476n, **28**. 448n
  cathedral at, *see* Winchester Cathedral
  Chelsea connected with diocese of, by bishop's
    house, **9**. 222
  Gregory taken to jail at, **13**. 87n
  HW jokingly suggests D. of Newcastle as
    bishop of, **9**. 209, **35**. 281
  HW visits, and describes it, **35**. 249–50
  Hessian camp at, **21**. 13n
  Lowth archdeacon of, **15**. 302
  Methodists would not like domination of,
    35. 323–4
  Newminster Abbey at, **42**. 223n
  Ossory, Lord, encamped with militia near,
    33. 34–5
  races at, **13**. 89n
  visitors to: Chute, **14**. 83, **35**. 249–50; Dodd
    and Whaley, **40**. 8; George III and Q. Char-
    lotte, **33**. 60n; Gray, **14**. 83; HW, **35**. 249–

[Winchester, Hants, *continued*]

50, 37. 407; Kingston, Ds of, with Merrill and Spearing, 24. 195n

Walpole, Sir Robert, obtains see of, for Hoadly, 17. 502n

Whithed to attend assizes at, 20. 237

William of Wykeham's portrait at, 38. 44

——'s statue or bust at, 38. 45

Wren's palace at, for Charles II, 35. 249, 40. 349, 354

Winchester Bill. *See under* Parliament: acts of

Winchester Cathedral:

Bentley may have used front of, to design 'Mabland,' 35. 249–50

deanery of, resigned by Pearce, 43. 251

Edgar's grants to, 42. 68n

Exeter, Cts of, buried in, 9. 7n

HW admires, 11. 80

Shipley, dean of, 29. 32n

tombs in, 35. 250

Winchester College:

catalogue of, sent by Whaley to HW, 40. 8

Eton superior to, 40. 8

glass at, painted by Price, 1. 201n

Kidgell knew E. of March at, 22. 187n

Waynflete, master of, 41. 140

Whithed at, 13. 146n

'Winchester College, Oxford.' *See* New College

Winchester measure:

quart-pot based on, 1. 279–80

Winchester Palace:

Wren designed for Charles II, 35. 249, 40. 349, 354

Winchilsea, Cts of. *See* Feilding, Lady Frances (d. 1734); Kingsmill, Anne (1661–1720); Palmer, Mary (d. 1757); Seymour, Lady Mary (d. before 1673)

Winchilsea, E. of. *See* Finch, Daniel (1647–1730); Finch, Daniel (1689–1769); Finch, George (1752–1826); Finch, Heneage (ca 1620–89)

Winchilsea. *See also* Winchelsea

Winchilsea family:

Granville, Cts, entertains, 18. 527

Winckelmann, Johann Joachim (1717–68), archæologist:

Description des pierres gravées du feu Baron de Stosch by, dedicated to Albani by Muzell, 21. 186n

Hessenstein met by, at Rome, 22. 291n

in Albani's service, 23. 113

murdered at Trent, 23. 113

Muzell asks Barthélemy to forward letter to, 21. 418n

Wilkes said to have inherited gold medals from, 23. 113

will of, sent to Mann by Albani, 23. 113

Wind; winds:

east: HW dislikes, 9. 130, 262; HW likes, for sake of southeast wind, 10. 78

French fleet dispersed by, 24. 535

high, in Florence, 20. 55

in England, 13. 237, 24. 431

Mann depressed by, 20. 234

northeast, HW jokes about, 10. 262

Rome hurt by, 20. 69

southeast: HW likes, 7. 355, 9. 262, 10. 78

west: cures HW's cold, 31. 295; HW dislikes, 9. 262, 10. 78; Hannah More's 'great physician,' 31. 295

Windam. *See* Windham; Wyndham

Wind-guns:

HW imagines aerial battles with, 39. 425

'Windham, Mr':

Mann's code name for Joseph II, 25. 42–3

Windham, Mr and Mrs, of Norfolk:

anecdote of, 31. 421

Windham, William (1750–1810), statesman; M.P.:

balloon ascent by, 25. 579

Brussels visited by, on return to England, 25. 79

Burney writes to, 42. 330n

Cholmondeley, a friend of, 24. 524

departure of, for Italy, deferred, 24. 527

English victories distress, 25. 50

French Revolution's success predicted by, 34. 65–7

George III indiscreetly discussed by, 25. 524

Gordon rioters will not reconcile Mann with, 25. 55

HW recommends, to Mann, 24. 521, 524

HW regrets that his recommendation of, was so unrewarding to Mann, 25. 79, 518

HW satisfied of virtue of, but not of his knowledge of the world, 25. 40

HW sees, and hears Mann praised, 25. 97

HW sorry that Mann sees so little of, 25. 40

HW takes Mann's remarks about, too seriously, 25. 523–4

health of, recovered, 25. 97

Italian language distasteful to, 25. 50

Italy to be visited by, for health, 24. 521, 524

languages studied by, in Florence, 25. 33

loss of Gibraltar and Port Mahon wished by, as blow to the government, 25. 50

Mann avoided by, for being George III's minister, 25. 40n

—— does not see, as much as was expected, 25. 33, 523–4

—— enjoys meeting, 25. 2–3

—— lately saw, in Italy, 25. 398

——'s dinners and conversazioni attended by, as spectator, 25. 33

—— will see, in theatre boxes, 25. 33

morose notions of Spartan teachers imbibed by, 25. 50

Norfolk gentleman of considerable estate, 24. 521, 524

Norfolk militia gets resignation from, as Lt-Col., because of E. of Orford's troublemaking, 25. 11n

Northington's secretary in Ireland, 24. 521n, 25. 398

Norwich's M.P., 24. 524n, 25. 579

Orford's conduct will not surprise, 25. 11

patriotism of, may be morose, **25**. 40

sentiments suppressed by, in deference to Mann, **25**. 50

Stillingfleet's letter to, **43**. 49

temper of, sour, **25**. 50

Westminster candidacy declined by, **25**. 285n

Whig of the old school, **24**. 524

Windham. *See also* Wyndham

Winding-sheet:

Highland seers will visualize Campbell in, **38**. 7

'Wind in the East,' ballad:

George II's windbound yacht satirized in, **43**. 250

Windmill; windmills:

in France, can be seen by Mary Berry from Prospect House, **12**. 122

Windmill Inn, Salt Hill:

(?) Conway's letter detained by landlady at, **37**. 378

Window; windows:

bow: at Strafford's Twickenham house, **35**. 347; at SH, **35**. 339; Coke, Lady Mary, and Haszlang talk in, **38**. 36; Conway fits up public room with, **37**. 475; Conway's verses on Elizabeth Hervey's, **39**. 470; Hindley's broken by explosion, **39**. 152; Millers' house has, **10**. 233; Pitt, Anne, consults HW about, **31**. 35; to be built at the Vyne, **35**. 640

broken, in E. of Bath's Piccadilly house, unrepaired for 4 years, **30**. 89

carpets hung from, to be dusted, **35**. 458

church, in scene in *King Arthur*, of painted glass, **39**. 133

coach: mob holds flambeaux to, **23**. 194; of glass, **23**. 6, 49, 201–2

curtains for, not permitted by E. and Cts of Bath in servants' rooms, **30**. 89–90

fashion of cutting, down to the ground, **28**. 28

(?) French, higher than English, **31**. 87

French leave open, till supper, **35**. 543

Frenchman encourages English mob to break, **23**. 111

Gothic: at Sandleford Priory, **31**. 321; at the Vyne, **35**. 640

guests open, at Massereene's, because of smoke, **30**. 211

HW prefers prospects through, **39**. 470–1

HW rings for candles, lest mob break, as they did two years before, **25**. 563

HW's broken by mob, **25**. 343

houses in Drury Lane to rent, for Coronation, **38**. 133

illumination of, at Florence, for birth of Cowper's son, **24**. 232

Italian: of paper, in Florence, **24**. 232; unglazed in Montaigne's time, **24**. 16

La Borde's, **31**. 80

laurel stuck in, at Christmas, **38**. 1

Mann's: broken by wind, **20**. 25; on garden side, made into doors, **17**. 499

mob breaks: **35**. 344, **37**. 247, **39**. 60, 152–3;

after Westminster election, **25**. 563, 564, 565

North's and Germain's, broken by mob, **24**. 442

Norton's, broken by mob, **23**. 305

of French émigrés at Richmond, broken by mob, **31**. 386

open, in church, on rainy day, gives HW rheumatism, **31**. 359

painted glass, in every room at SH, **31**. 216

Pitt, Thomas, recommends, removable, for Conway's greenhouse, **38**. 198

plate-glass, **31**. 80

rose: HW's memory of, **9**. 224; Montagu seeks design for, **10**. 11; Montagu's finished, **10**. 18; star-window preferable to, **35**. 154

Selwyn sits in, after dinner, **30**. 69

shop, Almon exhibits Temple's *Inquiry* in, **30**. 237

staircase, **30**. 89

tax on, **21**. 199n, **35**. 468; *see also under* Tax: window

See also Stained glass

Window sashes:

Montagu to replace, at Greatworth, **9**. 257

Winds, Temple of the, at Athens:

'ugly pigeon-house,' **11**. 357

Windsor, Dean of. *See* Booth, Peniston (1681–1765); Keppel, Frederick (1729–77)

Windsor, Vcts. *See* Clavering, Alice (d. 1776); Herbert, Lady Charlotte (1676–1733)

Windsor, Hon. Alice Elizabeth (1749–72), m. (1768) Francis Seymour Conway, styled Vct Beauchamp, 2d M. of Hertford, 1794:

appearance of, **10**. 237

Beauchamp to wed, **22**. 480

death of, **23**. 381, **39**. 153–6

HW's epitaph on, **39**. 155–6

health of: nerves affected, **39**. 142; opium taken, **39**. 149

Hunter, Dr, recalled to, after Dr James fails, **39**. 142

marriage of, expected, **10**. 237

mother-in-law seeks watch for, **39**. 117

wealth of, **10**. 237

Windsor, Hon. Catharine (d. 1742 *or* 3), m. (1741) Mattijs Lestevenon de Berkenroode:

Florence visited by, **17**. 200, 217

Haddock and Vernon discussed by, **17**. 200

Italy bores, **17**. 200–1

Mann's attentions refused by, **17**. 217, 248

Pomfret, Cts of, sister of, **17**. 200

Uguccioni repulsed by, **17**. 217

Windsor, Hon. Charlotte Jane (1746–1800), m. (1766) John Stuart, styled Vct Mount Stuart; 4th E. of Bute, 1792; cr. (1796) M. of Bute:

appearance of, **10**. 237

marriage of, **22**. 465

SH visited by, **12**. 233

wealth of, **10**. 237

Windsor, Edward (1532–75), 3d Bn Windsor:

arms of, **1**. 149

Windsor, Herbert (1707–58), 2d Vct Windsor, 1738; M.P.:
birth date of, corrected, **43**. 241
daughter of, **10**. 237n, **23**. 381n
Nourse challenges, unsuccessfully, **17** 248
—— rebuked by, for slandering Shuttleworth, **17**. 248
Pomfret wins law suit against, **20**. 389n
rebel lords condemned by, **19**. 284
sister will be delighted by ingenuity of, **19**. 303
Windsor, Other Hickman (1751–99), 6th E. of Plymouth, 1771:
fat, sweet-tempered and indolent, **23**. 378
Hertford sends letter through, to Mann, **23**. 373
Windsor, Other Lewis (1731–71), 4th E. of Plymouth:
Ashton tutor to, **13**. 153n, 161, 176n, **14**. 234, **15**. 9n, **20**. 164n
Gray sends compliments to, **13**. 218
voting shunned by, **22**. 508n
Windsor, Berks:
Albemarle at, **31**. 19
—— attends D. of Cumberland at, **20**. 460
Anne, Q., has small house at, **32**. 305
ball at, **29**. 149
Bateman's auction at, *see under* Windsor, Old
'Bell' and 'Mermaid' inns at, **19**. 298n
Belle-Isle imprisoned near, **19**. 18
Booth, Peniston, dean of, **9**. 100n
—— dies, **7**. 396
borough of, Vere should resign, to D. of Cumberland, **31**. 18–19
Burford House at: now Gray Block in Royal Mews, **37**. 242; owned by D. of St Albans, **20**. 42n
Burney, Fanny, cannot receive letter at, **42**. 293
Burnham near, **1**. 328, 334, 337
canon of, **35**. 497
canon's house at, has Plautus quotation on chimney-piece, **20**. 475n
Chalfont Park near, **5**. 2n
Charlotte, Q., charmed with, **23**. 79
Conway, Col., on way to, **32**. 306
Cornwallis, canon of, **13**. 84n
Cumberland, D. of, does not use Bentley's designs for palace at, **35**. 161
—— retires to, **38**. 566
deanery at: Keppel, Bp, writes from, **36**. 321; Walpole, Sir Edward, should visit, **36**. 324
dean of: painting of, at Burghley House, **10**. 346; *see also* Booth, Peniston (1681–1765); Keppel, Frederick (1729–77)
Delany, Mrs, writes from, **42**. 181
Diogenes loves, **37**. 258
Douglas, Bp, lives at, **16**. 317n
Edward the Confessor grants, to Westminster Abbey, **40**. 223
Egerton, Miss, dies at, **12**. 107n
election at, **29**. 80

Fox, Henry, asks Sir Edward Walpole to employ tradesmen at, **20**. 42
Garter installation at, **20**. 311n, **22**. 79, 80
Garter obligations concerning, **20**. 72–3
George III and Q. Charlotte visit Eton from, **22**. 83
George III does not inquire from, on Rockingham's death, **33**. 339
—— gives house at, to Mrs Delany, **33**. 497–8
—— has Keppel defeated at, **36**. 174
—— regulates church fees at, **35**. 497
—— threatened by plot at, **12**. 115, **42**. 411n
—— to receive Clinton's dispatches at, **33**. 306n
(?) Goldwin's verses on, **14**. 27
HW moralizes at, **37**. 257
HW moves philosophy and tea-things at, to SH, **37**. 270
HW seeks to rent house near, **9**. 40
HW sees D. of Cumberland's lions and tigers at, **37**. 383
HW's house at: **14**. 1n, **19**. 298, **43**. 170; HW could send cheese and hare from, **19**. 331; HW seems to prefer, to Birthday, **19**. 348–9; HW takes, **9**. 44, **37**. 255, 256, 258–9, 262–3; HW to spend summer in, **19**. 297; Mann congratulates HW on, **19**. 307; HW will return to, till Parliament meets, **37**. 262; in Priest St, rented from Patrick Jordan, **43**. 112; rent for, **19**. 297n; 'tub,' **13**. 16, **14**. 9; 'tub' as imagined by Conway, **37**. 273; within Castle, **19**. 298
HW writes from, **30**. 106–7
Hamilton, canon of, **11**. 104n
illuminations at, for Keppel's election, **36**. 178
Jeffreys, Mrs, dies at, **12**. 25n
Keppel, Augustus, not elected at, due to George III's opposition, **25**. 86
—— thrown out at election at, **33**. 225, 228
Keppel, Frederick, becomes canon of, **9**. 235n, **21**. 239, **36**. 35, **37**. 551
—— becomes dean of, after Booth's death, **10**. 182, **21**. 239n, **43**. 134
—— dies at, **32**. 410
Keppel, Mrs Frederick, receives estate at, **7**. 5n
Kingdon, Virginia, lamented at, **10**. 203
lodges at, in danger of collapse, **28**. 486
lodgings difficult to procure at, because of earthquake scare, **20**. 137n
mayor of, receives letter from Richard III, **41**. 121–2
Montagu, George, at, **9**. 36, 56, **30**. 106
—— entertains HW at, **9**. 45
—— lives near HW at, **37**. 258
——'s carriage accident at, **10**. 135
—— to prepare HW's house at, **9**. 44
—— visits houses near, **10**. 42
—— writes from, **9**. 20, 100–1
perfumer goes to, for Colomb's effects, **42**. 298

Poor Knights of, **28**. 135, **43**. 296
races at, not to be attended by HW, **19**. 298
St Albans, Ds of, buried at, **17**. 295
St Albans, D. of, owns Burford House at, **20**. 42n
St Leonard's Hill near, **5**. 346n
Savoyard girl sent to, by D. of Cumberland, **9**. 94
Shepherd, canon of, **2**. 226n
Townshend, Vcts, not to visit, **9**. 57
visitors to: Albemarle, **20**. 460, **31**. 19; Beauchamp, **38**. 179; Beauclerk, Lords Henry, Sidney, and Vere, **17**. 295; Burney, Frances, **42**. 171n; Christian VII, **23**. 57n; Chute, **14**. 92; Cumberland, Henry, D. of, and Ds, **32**. 64–5; Gloucester, Ds of, **32**. 410, **36**. 156n; Gloucester, D. of, **36**. 156n; Harcourt, **35**. 537; Hertford, E. and Cts of, **38**. 179; Holland, Bns, **43**. 104; Lort, **16**. 141; Mecklenburg, P. of, **39**. 441; Waldegrave, 4th E., **35** 537; Waldegrave, Cts, called to, for Ps Charlotte's birthday, **36**. 247; Waldegrave, Ladies Anna Horatia and Charlotte Maria, **36**. 152
Waldegrave, 4th E., to visit, **36**. 247
Walpole, Sir Edward, gives estate at, to Mrs Keppel, **24**. 349
—— to support Henry Fox in borough of, **20**. 42
White Hart Inn at, **19**. 298, **33**. 497
William I exchanges, for other lands, **40**. 223
William, P., may prefer Gunnersbury to, **33**. 406
young men leave, to go to France, **1**. 351
See also Windsor, Old; Windsor Castle
Windsor, English ship:
Kinnoull and Thomas Pitt take, to Portugal, **21**. 364n
Windsor, Old, Berks:
Bateman lives at, **1**. 90, 93, 325n, **31**. 36
——'s auction at, **1**. 325n, **32**. 241
——'s offices at, altered by Bentley, **35**. 644
Beaumont Lodge at, **1**. 236
HW may visit Bateman and Bns Hervey at, **31**. 120
Holland, Lady, lives at, **33**. 27, 46
Kent, Ds of, lives at, **30**. 304n
touching scene between Lady Holland and Lady Ossory at, **33**. 50
visitors to: Beauclerk, Topham and Lady Diana, **32**. 241; Craufurd, John, **33**. 46; Fitzpatrick, Richard, **33**. 46; HW, **32**. 241; Hervey, Bns, **31**. 36–7; Ilchester, **31** 36–7; Lloyd, Rachel, **32**. 241; Ossory, Lady, **33**. 49–50
Whitehall Gate moved to Great Park at, **2**. 177
Windsor Castle, Berks:
Anne, Q., lived in house opposite to, **32**. 305
Arblay, Mme d', and husband invited to, **12**. 204
ball at, for George IV's birthday, **11**. 329, **32**. 316n
Beauclerk, Lady Henry, succeeds Mrs Chudleigh as housekeeper of, **20**. 527n
'Beauties' at, painted by Lely: **15**. 96n, 97–8, **30**. 326n, **37**. 242; copies of, at Althorp, **9**. 6; HW seeks copies of, **9**. 34–5
Belle-Isle interviewed by D. of Newcastle at, **19**. 3n
Burney, Fanny, inducted at, **42**. 172
—— may not stoop from, to visit SH, **42**. 170, 173
Cardigan, constable and governor of, **40**. 173n
Cholmondeley, 3d E. of, entertains Lady Walpole and his sisters at his apartment in, **43**. 169
Churchill, Lady Mary, becomes housekeeper at, **30**. 176
—— granted leave from, by George III, **39**. 141
—— housekeeper of, **10**. 136n, 142n, **11**. 42n, **36**. 77, **43**. 132
—— to be housekeeper of, **38**. 457
Clement, Jane, addressed at, **36**. 330
cockades for Adm. Keppel worn on terrace of, **33**. 228
Cumberland, D. of, goes to, **38**. 495
Desmond, Cts of, said to be depicted in painting at, **40**. 108
Drawing-Room at, visited by royal mistresses, **33**. 528–9, **34**. 260
Foldsone, Anne, draws at, **11**. 145
Francavilla statues at, **21**. 480n
George III, plot for assassination of, at, **12**. 115, **42**. 411n
——'s alterations to, **43**. 304
Gloucester, D. of, visits, **25**. 164n
Gower chooses Lady Mary Churchill as housekeeper at, **38**. 464
HW and Conway visit, **11**. 362
HW asks for post at, under Col. Brown, for Bevan, **40**. 173–4
HW did not see James IV's portrait at, **16**. 322
HW romanticizes view of, **9**. 3
HW's house within, *see* Windsor: HW's house at
HW's letter to George III about (?) Houghton pictures sent to, **39**. 337
Harcourt to convey Hervey's pamphlet to, **42**. 360
housekeeper at, might exhibit Bentley's pictures, **35**. 243
housekeeper of, *see* Chudleigh, Elizabeth; Clement, Jane; Lovelace, Hon. Martha; Marriot, Mrs; Walpole, Lady Maria
housekeeper's quarters at, in tower, **43**. 132
housekeeper's revenues at, large, **20**. 213
Hugenien authorized to seek Colomb's effects at, **42**. 298n
kings before Henry III favoured, as residence, **40**. 315

[Windsor Castle, Berks, continued]
Lambeson to get painters for, 1. 156
Lennox, Lady Sarah, should have been at, 33. 299
'Mindas' a mistake for, 16. 10, 16
Montagu goes to, to fetch Margaret Trevor, 10. 135
new furnishings at, 11. 363
paintings at: of Field of Cloth of Gold, 9. 69; of Henry VIII, 9. 99; of Henry VIII's embarkation, to be copied by Grimm, 16. 181; of the Misers, 10. 341; see also portraits at
Penn, Lady Juliana, falls down stairs at, 11. 46
pictures at, 2. 277n, 15. 160, 205, 37. 242
Polignac family presented to George III at, 39. 449
portraits at: of Duns Scotus, 15. 141; of James IV, 16. 322; of Mary, Q. of Scots, 42. 321–2; of Q. Elizabeth, 10. 42n; of Rembrandt's mother, 42. 13
Princesses at, have measles, 36. 246
prints of pictures in, 2. 277
Raphael cartoons at, 16. 168n
royal apartment at, said to be given to pregnant young lady, 20. 278
royal family at, for Bute's and Gloucester's Garter installations, 22. 79
St George's Chapel at: 10. 310n, 11. 6n; depicted at Covent Garden, 32. 66; HW and Conway admire, 11. 362; Hollar's engravings of, 14. 96; melancholy sight for the Keppels, 32. 410; new stalls in, 34. 10–11; paving and decorations at, 40. 220
tapestries displayed by guide at, 9. 18n
Tower of London has early record of chapel at, 40. 220
Trevor, Margaret, dies at, 10. 300n
Winchester Tower at: vacated by Mrs Craster's death, 36. 323; Waldegrave daughters to live in, in winter, 24. 76n
Windsor chair. See under Chair
Windsor forest:
oaks in, might be cut for joint-stools, 35. 161
See also Windsor Great Park; Windsor Park
Windsor Forest. See under Pope, Alexander
Windsor Great Lodge:
Cumberland, D. of, may have promised, 31. 19
See also Windsor Lodge
Windsor Great Park:
Cumberland, D. of, as ranger of, disobliges whole country, 20. 73n
—— ranger of, 10. 43n, 13. 22n
See also Windsor Forest; Windsor Park
Windsor Lodge:
Anne, Q., lived at, 32. 305
Conway visits William Augustus, D. of Cumberland, at, 37. 382, 386
Cumberland, Henry Frederick, D. of, and Ds, arrive at, from Rome, 23. 566n, 24. 3n

Cumberland, Henry Frederick, D. of, moves furniture to, 23. 358n
Cumberland, William Augustus, D. of, attended by Dr Wilmot at, 21. 432n
—— gives parties at, 20. 120n
Fox, Henry, confers with William Augustus, D. of Cumberland, at, 22. 102n
George III may take, 32. 305
See also Windsor Great Lodge
Windsor Ode. See under Cosens, John
Windsor Park:
Cumberland, William Augustus, D. of, at lodge at, 37. 258
disputes about, 9. 135
ploughing-up of, imagined, 34. 215
See also Windsor Forest; Windsor Great Park
Windsor Road:
Gray inquires about, 14. 30
Windstorm:
in England, 13. 237
See also under Wind
Wine:
Addington prescribes, to bring on gout, 22. 505n
Aleatico and Verdea, ordered by Beauchamp from Italy through Mann, 23. 200, 204, 215, 279, 302
Amelia, Ps, serves little of, 32. 308
and hot water, see Negus
at Houghton, 13. 104
booths for, at Ranelagh, 20. 47
Charles III said to drink, with Squillace, 39. 61
Chian, 30. 217
Chute does not drink, 10. 277, 18. 149
——'s temperate use of, brings on gout, 18. 100
clergyman tells Mann to drink, to bring on gout, 22. 335
contraband, 9. 105
Conway takes, 37. 14
Cori has bottle of, 17. 254
Cyprus, preferred by Hobart as restorative, 19. 261
Danvers prefers, to chocolate, 35. 70
Dodd and Whaley have, at Deane House, 40. 5
Du Deffand, Mme, had stock of, 8. 11
Dutch give, to well-behaved soldiers, 37. 276
elections usually bring consumption of, 24. 45, 39. 186
England considers admitting, from France, 7. 375
—— could have grown grapes for, in hot summer, 24. 407
—— has water outside, and, within, 39. 186
Ferrers forbidden to have, on way to execution, 21. 401
——'s allowance of, in prison, shortened, 21. 397
Florence: for Henry Fox, sent in chests by Mann, 21. 156, 164, 187, 189, 304, 309, 313,

353, 375, 383; Grifoni, Mme, displeases HW by offer of, 18. 348, 366, 527; HW's drams mistaken for Fox's, 21. 353; Mazzei to sell, in England, 21. 495; Pembroke buys, from the Rena, 21. 156

French: England wastes money on, 37. 172; improve by crossing the Channel, 21. 233

from Hooker's vineyard, sour, 35. 135

Frontignac, procured by HW for Lady Diana Beauclerk, 42. 450–1

fumes of, confusing, 37. 395

George III and Bute said to drink, together, 39. 61

George III provides, for Mrs Delany, 33. 497

glass of, figuratively thrown by Lord Mark Ker in gentleman's face, 22. 162

Gloucester, D. of, kept warm by, 36. 139

gout driven to stomach by, 24. 423

gout in connection with, 3. 121, 134, 135, 139, 4. 467

gout is produced by, 14. 140–1

gout to be remedied by, 9. 292, 10. 277

HW avoids, 22. 257, 23. 76, 35. 191

HW can take, only very rarely, 28. 420

HW drinks, in Paris, because of filthy water, 14. 142

HW drinks a little: after fatigue in Parliament, 35. 264; and it goes to his gouty foot, 35. 264

HW leaves off, to avoid gout, 35. 259, 264

HW may receive, from Mann, 17. 12

HW offered, at Castle Howard, 30. 258

HW rewards servants with, 11. 33

HW to give pipe of, to Dodd and Whaley at Cambridge, 40. 12

HW tries, for gout cure, 22. 322

Hertford drinks, only, 15. 320

Hertford family are entertained with, at Chester, 39. 18

importation of, from France, suggested by Bentley, 35. 191

Irish overwhelm guests with, 37. 35

local, does not intoxicate, 4. 439

Lucca gives, to D. of York, 22. 221

Mann dilutes, at dinners, 17. 155, 22. 469

—— has avoided, 17. 78, 22. 469

—— serves, to Vorontsov family, 22. 193

—— used to drink too much of, at meals, 17. 78

Mason advises HW to drink, 28. 418

Montagu orders, from Mme Roland, for Grosvenor, 10. 143

Montagu, Charles, drinks, with water at supper, 9. 391

mulled, in Hoffman's medicine, 36. 140

Norfolk squires overindulge in, 35. 42

Orford, 3d E. of, overindulges in, 32. 179, 350, 36. 124

Pomme, Dr, prescribes, 35. 121

sailors often tamper with shipments of, 21. 304

Selwyn chokes on, 38. 348

—— governs Gloucester city by, 35. 153

served: at Versailles ball, 32. 256; in Wroxton library, 35. 72

sweet, Sir Edward Walpole promises, to Mrs Scott, 10. 329

tax on, would be less burdensome than one on tea, 18. 142

Verdea, resembles cider, 23. 204

Walpole, Sir Robert, hands Q. Caroline a glass of, 15. 333

white, callers would expect to be served with, 9. 83

York, D. of, receives, at Rome, 22. 228

Young Pretender lethargic from, 23. 319

—— takes extra dose of, on St Andrew's Day, 25. 100

See also Claret; Côte-rôtie wine; Port; Tokay

Wine cellar; cellars ('wine vaults'):

at Winchelsea, 40. 6

HW's Cloister does not resemble, 35. 110

royal, Arthur removed from clerkship at, 9. 318

Winefride, legendary Welsh saint:

HW deplores obsolescence of, 34. 95

Wine merchant:

Garrick used to be, 17. 435

Giberne becomes, 20. 106n

Harcourt and Mason use, as name for HW, 29. 355–66 passim

Rena, Contessa, wife of, 23. 106n

See also Mazzei, Filippo

Wing; wings:

Salins, Mme, wears, 20. 75n

Wingfield, Sir Anthony (ca 1485–1552), K.G., 1541; controller of the Household, 1550:

portrait of, conceals fingers said to have been cut off by Henry VIII, 35. 248

Wingfield, Edward (1729–64), 2d Vct Powerscourt, 1751:

eye of, only half opened, 38. 155

Hay, Dr, defeated by, at Stockbridge, 21. 73n

wager made by, over Paris-Fontainebleau ride, 35. 190

Wingfield Castle, Suffolk:

tombs at, of D. and Ds of Suffolk, 42. 68n

Tyson visits, 2. 175

Wingfield family:

portrait of, at Boughton House, 10. 341

tombs of, at Letheringham, 35. 248

volumes belong to, 1. 278n

Wingham, Kent:

(?) Bridges writes from, 41. 131

Deane House in parish of, 40. 4

Winkleman. See Winckelmann

Winlaton, Durham:

Crowley removes to, 16. 77n

Winn, Catharine (1708–57), m. Sir Samuel Barnardiston, 5th Bt:

Soame receives MS from, 1. 377

Winn, Sir Rowland (ca 1700–65), 4th Bt, 1722:

marriage and family of, 16. 48n, 49n

More family painting valued by, 16. 49

Winn. *See also* Wynne
Winnington, Anne, m. John Wheeler:
brother avoided by, 19. 250
Methodism of, 19. 250
Winnington, Sir Edward (? 1727–91), cr. (1755)
Bt; M.P.:
Amelia, Ps, questions HW about, 10. 49
biographical information about, corrected, 43. 128
Wilkinson to be succeeded by, 10. 49
Winnington, Henrietta (d. 1761), m. (1736)
Hon. Samuel Masham, 2d Bn Masham, 1758:
HW inquires about, 9. 49
HW sends compliments to, 30. 21
Thompson consulted by, in brother's illness, 19. 249–50
Winnington, Thomas (1696–1746), politician; M.P.:
abstains from voting in Parliament, 17. 484
address against rank for officers of privately-raised regiments to be procured by, 19. 154
alterations by, of Sir C. H. Williams's verses offend Frederick, P. of Wales, 30. 317
anecdote by, about Cts of Abercorn and Ds of Devonshire calling women 'ugly,' 17. 478
Bubb Dodington answered by, 17. 354–5
Carteret's maxim questioned by, 18. 535
chariot of, borrowed by Vcts Townshend for return to London, 30. 70
corruption of, 30. 45–6
death of: 19. 249–50, 257, 30. 302n; Williams, Sir C. H., influenced by, to go abroad, 30. 312
does not speak in debate over privately-raised regiments, 19. 158
Frasi's relations with, 9. 16
Gage discusses his son with, 17. 255
George II asks, to recall Pelham ministry, 19. 212
HW calls: 'man of great parts,' 17. 172n; 'most inconstant, most unfeeling man alive,' 30. 46
HW entertained by, 18. 283
HW jokes about Vcts Townshend's opinion of, 30. 54
HW prefers wit of, to Chesterfield's, 30. 70
HW's unflattering description of, 30. 45–6
Hulse and Thompson consulted by, 19. 250
Lincoln entertained by, 18. 283
Mann, Robert, dismissed by, 18. 479, 496–7
Mathews's friend, 19. 33n
Nugent rebuked by, 17. 431
Parliamentary debates by: on amendment to the Address, 26. 22, 23; on privately-raised regiments, 26. 16, 17, 18
Parliamentary speech by, on renewing regiments, 40. 50
Parliamentary vote by, on privately-raised regiments, 26. 19
paymaster and cofferer of the forces, 9. 32, 17. 172n, 30. 291n
paymastership to go to, 18. 349–50, 356

Pelham succeeded by, as paymaster of Chelsea Hospital, 18. 313n
Pembroke, Cts of, amuses, by her euphemisms, 17. 496
Pitt answered by, 18. 351
political ballads by, with Sir C. H. Williams and Yonge, 30. 314
Quarendon's witticism to, on Bell's release, 17. 503
remark by, about test of women's beauty, 30. 102
remarriage of, may end his affair with Vcts Townshend, 37. 202
resigns as paymaster, 19. 211
Rigby's partner at whist, 30. 54
Stafford entertained by, 18. 283
Thompson, Dr, 'murders,' 9. 66
Townshend, Vcts, at odds with, 37. 232
—— 'cicisbea' of, 9. 32n, 17. 173, 207, 264
—— entertained by, 9. 19, 17. 496
—— induces, to dismiss Robert Mann despite promise to Sir Robert Walpole, 18. 497
—— kept by, 30. 46
—— visited by, 30. 54, 70
Townshend, Hon. Augustus, fights duel with, 17. 172, 207, 264, 37. 112
travel directions by, 30. 65
Waller succeeds, as cofferer, 30. 291n
wife well-treated by, despite strangeness, 37. 202
Williams, Sir C. H., contrasts character of, to Pelham's, 30. 318
—— corresponds with, 30. 60, 68
—— friend of, 19. 250, 30. 311
—— imitates Horace's *Odes* for Vcts Townshend and, 30. 317
——'s verses to, in name of Harris, 30. 316
—— writes epitaph for monument to, 30. 320
wit of: 30. 302; equal to Selwyn's, 15. 331
witticisms by: comparing Betty Warner's lovers to the Ds of Marlborough's legatees, 18. 540; on Churchill daughter, 18. 481; on dining to save dinner, 36. 8; on girl who loved her own sex, 20. 53; on HW's gait, 32. 252, 34. 118; on Pitt's and Chesterfield's turncoat politics, 18. 540; on prudery, 17. 496; on Vcts Townshend's quarrel with Catherine Edwin, 30. 70; on Walpole, Horatio (1678–1757), 19. 28; on young ladies' education at Drury Lane, 34. 89; to Stafford, about Catholicism and fasting, 18. 283
Worcester's instructions to, 18. 103
Winnington, Mrs Thomas. *See* Reade, Love
Winslow, Thomas, of Twickenham:
SH visited by, 12. 230
Winstanley, ——, (fl. 1769), bookseller:
portrait owned by, 1. 175
(?) sells Roscoe's library at auction, 15. 263n
Winstanley, Hamlet (1698–1756), engraver:
self-portrait of, 1. 175
Winstanley, Henry (1644–1703), engineer:

Ground-Platts . . . of Audley End by, at Meade's sale, **35**. 196–7

'wonders or tricks in mechanics' by, at Audley End, **13**. 88

Winstanley, Robert (1710–1804):

(?) observation by, in coffee-house, on recent crime, **20**. 317–18

Winstanley, William (ca 1628–98):

almanac of, **13**. 123n

Winstay. *See* Wynnstay

Winter, Miss:

SH visited by, **12**. 228

'Winter, Mrs':

character in Pinkerton's play, **16**. 253, 256

Winter, John:

silver-plater, **9**. 295n

Winter, Mrs Mary:

(?) stepmother of Robert Mann, **24**. 202n

Winter, Robert, house-painter:

Townshend, Vcts, arrested for failure to pay, **38**. 502n

Winter; winters:

of 1775–6, worst in HW's recollection, **24**. 174

Parliament session equivalent to, in HW's opinion, **25**. 358

sets in, at Florence, in October, **25**. 334

unfavourable to gout-sufferers, **24**. 185

warm but stormy in England, **20**. 16

Winterbottom, Thomas (d. 1752), sheriff of London; lord mayor of London, 1751–2:

Newcastle's controversy with, about Lovat's head, **37**. 267

Winter clothes:

Belle-Isle does not provide, for army, **21**. 435

Florentines wear: in April, **25**. 397; in June, **25**. 281; in October, **20**. 236

HW comes to London to order, **25**. 541

Winter gardens. *See under* Garden

Winter quarters:

cantonments the preliminary stage of, in army, **37**. 207

Frederick II goes into, **21**. 355

modern fighters do not go into, **25**. 105

'Winter's Amusement.' *See under* Anstey, Christopher

Winterslow, Wilts:

Thistlethwayte of, **14**. 49n

Winterslow House, Wilts, seat of Hon. Stephen Fox:

burns, **6**. 8n, **34**. 248

Craufurd to visit, **32**. 174

fire at, **32**. 183, 313n

Fox, C. J., writes from, **41**. 27

Ossorys return from, **32**. 43

plays at, postponed, **32**. 176

theatricals at, **32**. 89n

Winterslow Lodge, Wilts:

confused with Wakefield Lodge, **32**. 313n

Holland, Bn and Bns, temporarily occupy, **32**. 313n

Winter's Tale, The. See under Shakespeare, William

Winterton, Bn and E. *See* Garth Turnour, Edward

Wintertown. *See* Winterton

Winthrop, Mary, m. (1790) John Briscoe of Twickenham:

SH visited by, **12**. 242

Wintzingerode, Hans Sigismund (1717–71), Germany army officer:

to be witness at Lord George Sackville's court martial, **21**. 366

Winwood, Anne (d. 1642), m. (1633) Edward Montagu, 2d Bn Montagu, 1644:

father and son of, **10**. 341

grandmother of D. of Montagu, **14**. 107n

Winwood, Sir Ralph (?1563–1617), Kt; M.P.:

daughter of, **10**. 341

letter to, **14**. 107

Memorials by: Balagny's fight with Pinocin mentioned in, **40**. 357; gives evidence of Northampton's guilt, in Overbury's murder, **16**. 162n

portrait of, at Boughton House, **10**. 341

Wiquefort. *See* Wicquefort

Wire; wires:

Charles III snatches wigs with, **23**. 238

doors of, **39**. 15

for bell, **23**. 392

Wirtemberg; Wirtembergh; Wirtemburg. *See* Württemberg

Wirter, ——, minister from Saxony to France:

Monaco, P. of, has social relations with, in Paris, **7**. 334

Wirter. *See also* Werthein; Werthern

Wirts. *See* Würtz

Wirtumberg. *See* Württemberg

Wirtsbourg. *See* Würzburg

Wisdom:

counteracted by chance, **32**. 344

goddess of, **12**. 23

HW's remarks on, **11**. 14, 62

HW thinks, merely consists in making remarks on folly of others, **25**. 540

human, depreciated by HW who does not claim to have any, **35**. 283

See also 'Wiser'

Wise, Henry (1653–1738), gardener to William III, Q. Anne, and George I:

London's partner, **2**. 200, **29**. 45n, **32**. 354

son of, **32**. 354, **35**. 77

Wise, Matthew (1703–76), of the Priory, near Warwick:

father of, **32**. 354

HW disliked by, for question about gardens, **32**. 354, **35**. 77

lived at the Priory, **32**. 353–4

Warwick Priory's glass given by, to Stowe temple, **35**. 77

Wise. *See also* Wicks

Wiseman, ——, at Lord Sandwich's:

Mann encloses draft from Wiseman at Rome on, **21**. 380n

Wiseman (?Wyseman), Mr (fl. 1740):

[Wiseman (?Wyseman), Mr, *continued*]
HW cannot find, 17. (?) 15, 18, 21, 23
HW discusses (?) Young Pretender's movements with, 17. 18
Mann encloses draft from, at Rome, on Wiseman at Lord Sandwich's, 21. 380n
Mann's correspondence with, 17. 18
Smyth to instruct, in case of Young Pretender's departure, 17. *15*
Wiseman, Mr, of Diss, Norfolk:
SH visited by, 12. 245
'Wiser':
'growing wiser' is 'growing falser,' 7. 360
Wishart, George (1599–1671), Bp of Edinburgh:
History of the King's Majesty's Affairs in Scotland under . . . Montrose by, Montrose not the author of, 16. 7
Wishes, The. See under Bentley, Richard (1708–82)
'Wishfort, Lady,' character in Congreve's *Way of the World*:
Baron d'Albicrac has rôle resembling that of, 7. 272
HW quotes, 12. 103
Wisner, Christian Moritz. *See* Kutzleben, Christian Moritz Wisner
Wissing, William (1656–87), painter:
portrait by, 1. 181n, 183n
print of, by Walker, 15. 97n
Wistowe, William (fl. 1440):
received into fraternity of Bury Abbey, 2. 38
Wit:
Brown's flippancy was once called, 32. 148
fashions in, change, 34. 39
Goldsmith's, in *She Stoops to Conquer*, 32. 108
HW disclaims, 17. 270
HW discusses transitory nature of, 10. 259, 305
HW likes perfect nonsense next to perfect, 32. 467
HW's reflections on, 15. 146, 28. 153–4, 156
Italian language lacks word for, 21. 127
Locke distinguishes between humour and, 35. 647
More, Hannah, discusses, 31. 249
taste in, changes, 25. 308
Witch; witches:
French opera singers omit powder when enacting, 18. 496
HW resembles, upon crutch, 32. 102
HW's 'advertisement' of 'most noble she-witch,' 17. 313n, 26. 9
James I's act against, 30. 295n
——'s curiosity about, 28. 193
pinching of, to loosen their charms, 19. 19
Witchcraft:
becomes fashionable, 31. 319
'Witch of Endor':
HW's name for Ds of Bedford, 38. 380–1
Witenagemot:
HW puns upon, 39. 207, 219
Saxons hold, 10. 274

Witenham Hill. See under Pentycross, Thomas
Witham, Anne (ca 1761–1824), m. (1780) Hon. Gen. James Murray. *See* Whitham, Anne
Witham, Essex:
Charlotte, Q., stays at E. of Abercorn's at, 21. 528, 35. 312, 38. 116
HW visits parsonage at, 9. 93
Karl Wilhelm Ferdinand and Ps Augusta to stay at, in Abercorn's absence, 38. 292
Sayer, vicar of, 9. 93n
Witham, Magna, Essex:
manor of, 9. 93n
Wither ('Withers'), George (1588–1667), poet:
print of, 40. 237
Wither, Henrietta Maria (d. 1790), m. 1 Thynne Worsley; m. 2 Edmund Bramston:
Cowper's annuity to, 23. 416
Elliot, Lady Frances, leaves small legacy to, 23. 416
Montagu desired by, to live in Twickenham, 10. 252
——'s house-search judged by, 43. 135
Withering, William (1741–99), M.D.; botanist and mineralogist at Birmingham:
Waldegrave attended by, 36. 257, 258, 259, 260, 262, 264–5
Withers, William, 3d E. of Orford's steward:
(?) HW urged by, not to move E. of Orford, 24. 293
(?) incompetence of, 32. 141
(?) Orford, E. of, plundered by, 36. 95–6
(?) —— writes to, 24. 367
Withersfield, Suffolk:
Barnard rector of, 1. 155
Withes, manor in Norfolk:
HW's will mentions, 30. 368
Withiam. *See* Withyham
Withinbury, Miss, of Chiras Court:
Pope's elegy said to celebrate hanging of, 42. 123n
Withyham, Sussex:
Dorset, E. of, buried at, 15. 83n
Witley Court, Worcs, Lord Foley's seat:
Foley inherits, 28. 392
Lyttelton offers to take HW to, 35. 149
Wit's Commonwealth; Wits Treasury. See Meres, Francis: *Palladis Tamia*
Wittel, Gaspar Adriaensz van (1653–1736), called Gaspare Vanvitelli *or* Gasparo dagli Occhiali:
Chute envies HW's pictures painted by, 35. 38
HW's pictures by, bought in Italy, 26. 8
Wittenberg, Germany:
Cordus studies at, 14. 126n
Sennert professor of medicine at, 14. 127n
Wittenham Hill. See under Pentycross, Thomas
'Wittol, Sir Joseph.' *See under* Congreve, William: *Old Batchelour, The*
Witton, Norfolk:
HW's will mentions, 30. 344
Witts, Apphia (1743–1840), m. 1 Joseph Peach;

m. 2 (1773) Thomas Lyttelton, 2n Bn Lyttelton:
correspondence by, with father-in-law, thought to be in *The Correspondents*, **28.** 211, **32.** 240, 243
Witz, Konrad:
'Dance of Death' attributed to, **42.** 432n
Witz, De. *See* Dewitz
Wladislaw IV (1595–1648), K. of Poland 1632–48:
proxy marriage of, in Paris, **38.** 83n
Wobersmow, Maj.-Gen.:
Schwerin not captured by, **21.** 247n
Woburn Abbey, Beds, D. of Bedford's seat:
Ancram, Cts of, prefers daughter to be at Charlton instead of, **37.** 543
Bedford, Ds of, at, **10.** 170, **32.** 7
—— holds, till last moment, **33.** 525
—— unlikely to prefer, to political eminence, **30.** 186
Bedford, D. of, acts plays at, **19.** 309n
—— entertains Guerchy and Pecquigny at, **38.** 276, 295
—— expected at, **10.** 170
—— goes to, from Bath without visiting London, **38.** 460
—— returns to, **21.** 199n, **38.** 433
—— spends all his time at, **20.** 201n
——'s seat, **3.** 122n
—— wishes Chinese house at, **35.** 177
—— would never relinquish, **19.** 255
Bedfords retire to, **38.** 565
Chandos's portrait at, **33.** 322
Conway and Hertford to visit Bedford at, **37.** 63
Coventry, Cts of, proposes toast at, **37.** 428, 430
Faustina bust at, **42.** 452
fender at, **22.** 218
HW asks for account from, **34.** 52
HW finds no portrait at, of Cts of Carlisle, **41.** 442–3
HW's catalogue of portraits at, see *Notes to the Portraits at Woburn Abbey*
HW's first visit to, **9.** 123–5, **34.** 126
HW talks of visiting, **30.** 177
Hertford avoids, **39.** 19
Newcastle, D. of, sends express to D. of Bedford at, **30.** 246
painting at, **15.** 192n
parties at, **38.** 109
Pecquigny's misbehaviour at, **38.** 295
pictures at, rearranged since HW saw them, **41.** 252
Pitt (Chatham) sends Gower to, with overtures to D. of Bedford, **22.** 472
portraits at, HW's notes on, **42.** 240; see also *Notes to the Portraits at Woburn Abbey*
Rigby leaves, for Chelmsford, **30.** 222
road to, very bad, **32.** 290
Russells and Keppels at, for Tavistock's wedding, **38.** 401

Shelburnes to visit, immediately after marriage, **30.** 271
Tavistock and fiancée to go to, **38.** 396
visitors to: Boufflers, Mme de, **32.** 14; Cumberland, D. of, **20.** 89; George IV, **34.** 50; Gower, **41.** 70n; Guerchy, **22.** 218; HW, **9.** 123–5, **20.** 281, **34.** 126; Montagu, **10.** 170; Rigby, **41.** 71n; Rockingham, **22.** 538; Vernon, **20.** 301
Woburn Farm, Chertsey, Surrey; Southcote's seat:
a show place, **1.** 44, **2.** 275n
Churchills prefer Whiteknights to, **35.** 71
Conway and wife to visit, **37.** 374
HW praises, **2.** 275n
HW's opinion of, **9.** 71
Southcote, Mrs, leaves, to Bn Petre, **31.** 210n
SH compared with, **9.** 169, **35.** 237
Woburn Park, Beds:
Berkeley sinks in, **35.** 199
Wodehouse, Bns. *See* Norris, Charlotte Laura (d. 1845)
Wodehouse, Sir Airmine (1714–77), Bt:
death of, falsely reported, **7.** 372, 398
Wodehouse, Sir John (1741–1834), 6th Bt, 1777; cr. (1797) Bn Wodehouse; M.P.:
HW and E. of Orford visited by, to prevent quartering militia at Norwich, **39.** 297–8
opposition to, in Norfolk, **12.** 185
Woden:
Christian VII watched over by, **35.** 326
HW's term for SH, **21.** 433
temple of, in stage scenery, **39.** 134
Wodhull, Michael (1740–1816), collector; poet; translator:
Montagu asks HW to give SH tickets to, **10.** 151
—— describes, **10.** 151
Wodrow, Robert:
MSS of, **15.** 109n
Woestyne. *See* La Woestyne
Woffambedue, Cavaliere, Russian officer:
Florence visited by, with Dolgorukov, **23.** 191n
Woffington, Margaret (ca 1718–60), actress:
biographical information about, corrected, **43.** 238, 313, 373
Cæsar takes, **21.** 157
Cholmondeley marries sister of, **19.** 340
Clive, Mrs, and, **17.** 176n
Darnley keeps, **17.** 176, **30.** 52
Foundling well acted by, **19.** 465
HW and Conway dislike, **37.** 113
HW criticizes, **17.** 176
HW has never seen, **30.** 52
Rigby to inform Sir C. H. Williams about, **30.** 52
'Rosetta' acted by, **19.** 405n
Sir Harry Wildair performed by, **17.** 176
sister of, **3.** 299n, **9.** 269n, **19.** 340
Taaffe's bet with, **20.** 289
Teddington residence of, **30.** 52
whole town in love with, **37.** 113

[Woffington, Margaret, *continued*]
Williams, Sir C. H., does not deceive, **39.** 244
—— enamoured of, **30.** 52
—— kept, **30.** 316
—— wrote verses to, **30.** 316
Woffington, Mary (ca 1729–1811), m. (1746) Hon. Robert Cholmondeley (HW's nephew); HW's 'cousine':
Aiguillon, Duchesse d', and, **4.** 238, 240, 242, 245, 477
Angora cat declined by, **4.** 325
apartment occupied by, **8.** 3
Baretti, friend of, **4.** 230–2
Beauvau, Prince de, to give good places to, at Dauphin's wedding, **4.** 402, 407
Beauvau, Princesse de, relations of, with, **4.** 279–80, 461
birth date of, corrected, **43.** 366
Boisgelin, Comtesse de, cordial to, **4.** 477
—— dangerous for, **4.** 326, 327
—— escorts, home, **4.** 327
—— owes money to, **4.** 360, 366, 368–9, 377–8, 423
Boufflers, Marquise de, consulted by, about Comtesse de Boisgelin's debt, **4.** 360
—— cordial to, **4.** 477
—— dangerous for, **4.** 326, 327
—— invites, to play at Mme du Deffand's, **4.** 461
—— pays Comtesse de Boisgelin's debt to, **4.** 423
Buller, Mrs, visited by, **11.** 242, 250
Cambis, Vicomtesse de, cordial to, **4.** 477
—— dangerous for, **4.** 326, 327
Chamier may be asked by, for money, **4.** 369
Choiseul, Duc de, lends lodging to, for Dauphin's wedding, **4.** 402, 407
Choiseul, Duchesse de, plays whist with, **4.** 301
—— sends messages to HW by, **4.** 480
—— sends message to, **4.** 278
—— speaks of, **4.** 328
——'s relations with, **4.** 302, 328, 477, 480
—— would like the purchases made by, **5.** 20
Cholmondeley, 3d E. of, leaves property in trust for sons of, **4.** 423n
—— shocks, by his will, **4.** 423
Cholmondeley, 4th E. of, affects, by his marriage, **11.** 241
——'s wedding excludes, **11.** 256
Cholmondeley, Gen., at odds with, **5.** 200, 203, 210, 212
—— leaves no annuity to, **6.** 225
Clérembault, Mlles de, meet, **4.** 423
clever, **3.** 299
Clive, Mrs, entertains, **9.** 269
Comédie attended by, **4.** 208, 222, 274–5
daughters of, *see* Cholmondeley, Henrietta Maria; Cholmondeley, Hester Frances
daughters with, **4.** 369, 374, 381, 404
daughter taken by, to balls, **4.** 445
does not wish to harbour robe ordered by Craufurd, **4.** 370

Du Deffand, Mme, accompanies, on farewell calls, **4.** 478
—— attributes gift of tea to, **6.** 56
—— begged by, to forsake tea, **36.** 57–8
—— called on by, **36.** 49
—— desired by, to imitate letter of HW's, **4.** 246, 251
—— discusses Bns Grosvenor with, **4.** 310
—— entertains, at supper, **36.** 57
—— finds, a great help, **4.** 238, 239
—— forwards letter to, **4.** 481
—— gives to HW a ring received from, **4.** 487
—— has box and cuffs to return to, **5.** 11
—— has no news of, **4.** 487, 488, **5.** 8, 20, **6.** 75, 379, **7.** 103
—— has not seen, **4.** 336
—— has not seen, alone, **4.** 227
—— hopes to see, again, **4.** 282, 471
—— inquires after, **7.** 6
—— lends money to, **4.** 368, 369, 378
—— mentions, **4.** 234, 342, **5.** 86, 235, **6.** 116
—— proposes to take, to Versailles, **4.** 362
—— provides rooms for, **4.** 217, 223, 225, 226, 271, **5.** 65n
—— receives box of presents and commissions from, **5.** 77
—— relieves depression of, **36.** 50
——'s box at the Comédie to be used by, **4.** 218
——'s commissions executed by, **5.** 82
——'s correspondence with, **4.** 491, 495, **5.** 44, 77, 143, 184, 200, 203, 210, 212, 317, 364, 429, **6.** 41, 56, 165, 248, 250, 253, 440, 441, 451, **7.** 87
—— sends book through, **4.** 212
—— sends gift to, **5.** 309
—— sends letter to HW by, **4.** 478–80
—— sends papers to, **41.** 199
——'s letter to Mrs Greville approved by, **4.** 236
——'s offer to assume Comtesse de Boisgelin's debt refused by, **4.** 367–9
——'s opinion of, **4.** 210, 215, 217, 218, 222, 226, 228, 231, 235, 237, 239, 242, 246, 256, 274, 286, 324, 334, 337, 350, 369, 378, 480, **5.** 69, 73, (?) 191, **6.** 250, 286
——'s relations with, **4.** 231, 239, 285, 286, 288, 300, 306, 324, 337, 350, 360, 367–9, 371, 377, 378, 388, 392, 395, 399, 425, 431, 473, 474, 476, 477, 480, 490, 495, **6.** 280, **7.** 103
——'s servants worried lest customs seize goods of, **4.** 488, 496
—— to give HW's commission to, **4.** 423, 425
—— unable to write to, **41.** 198–9
—— will assist, **4.** 206, 208, 215–16, 226, 238
—— will be consoled by, **36.** 54–5
Élie de Beaumont, Mme, urged by, to send to HW the account of Voisins, **41.** 173–5
English entertained by, **4.** 323, 327
Englishmen brought to Mme du Deffand by, **4.** 357
finances of, **4.** 360, **6.** 225, 234, **7.** 221
Foire Ste-Ovide visited by, **7.** 329

Forcalquier, Mme de, cool to, **4**. 238, 240–1, 284, 306
Fortescues acquaintances of, **4**. 271
French of, weak, **4**. 217, 231, 239, 257
gambles, **4**. 315–17, 324, 327, 328, 331, 337, 352, 360
Gennevilliers may be visited by, **4**. 451
—— visited by, **4**. 447, 450, 458, 469
HW accompanied by, to St-Cyr, **34**. 82
HW accompanies, to theatre, **7**. 325, 326, 328, 331, 332
HW angry with, **7**. 89
HW gives money to, **7**. 408
HW lacks picture of, **36**. 160
HW liked by, **4**. 274, 337
HW meets Dorothy Wrottesley at house of, **33**. 109
HW mentions, **4**. 206
HW receives ring given to Mme du Deffand by, **4**. 487
HW's bequest to, **30**. 356–7
HW's chain for Duchesse de Choiseul admired by, **4**. 365
HW's correspondence with, **4**. 222, 273, 292, 337, 460, 473, 474, 476, **36**. 49–50, 54–8, 61, **43**. 90
HW sends letter by (or about), **7**. 388
HW's English could be translated by, **4**. 464
HW's furniture chosen by, **4**. 435, 457
HW's opinion of, **9**. 270
HW talks with, **4**. 486
HW to hear gossip from, **4**. 451
HW to see play from box of, at Haymarket, **39**. 102
Hamlet attended by, **4**. 281
has no letters from England, **4**. 352
health of, **4**. 224, 272, 282, 283, 285, 293, 334, 337, 378, **36**. 57
Hervey said by, to be in love with Mme du Deffand, **4**. 388
Jonzac, Mme de, cordial to, **4**. 240, 477, 480
—— sends messages to HW by, **4**. 480
La Vallière, Duchesse de, cordial to, **4**. 240, 477
letters for, delivered to Wiart, **4**. 465, 474
lowly birth of, **4**. 206, 208, 231
Malpas liked by, **4**. 235
marriage of, **19**. 340
Mazarin, Hôtel de, visited by, **7**. 332
Mirepoix, Bp of, to have rooms of, **5**. 6, 13
nephew mentioned by, to Mme du Deffand, **39**. 219
not to dine at Lauzun's, **4**. 328
not to sup with Hénault, **4**. 328
Panthémont visited by, **7**. 332
Paris left by, **4**. 480
—— to have been visited by, **5**. 364
—— visited by, **4**. 208
Porquet receives book from, **4**. 454
prize won by, **7**. 329
proverbs acted by, **4**. 277, **7**. 331
reception of, by Mme du Deffand's circle, **4**. 238, 240, 306, 477, 480

Rueil visited by, **4**. 240, 443, **7**. 329
St-Cloud visited by, **4**. 466
St-Cyr visited by, **10**. 292–4, **34**. 82
Sceaux visited by, **4**. 243, 442
sends book to a friend, **4**. 307, 312
sings, **7**. 330
social relations of, in Paris, *see index entries ante* **8**. 559–60
son of, **6**. 440n, **8**. 211n
song of, **4**. 294
SH visited by, **12**. 238
style of writing of, admired by Mme du Deffand, **4**. 495
to have news of Wilkes, **4**. 227
to return to England, **4**. 425, 431, 435, 451, 464, 477, 478
trusts furniture dealers, **4**. 438
Versailles visited by, **7**. 330, **10**. 291–2
Walpole, Hon. Robert, relations of, with, **4**. 257, 328
——'s sadness unexplained to, **4**. 278
Woide, Charles Godfrey (d. 1790), assistant librarian in the British Museum:
death of, **16**. 312n
Wolcot, Dr John (1738–1819), 'Peter Pindar'; satirist:
Barrington ridiculed by, **2**. 164n
Bozzi and Piozzi by: advertised, **25**. 638; Boswell and Mrs Piozzi satirized in, **25**. 638, 640–1; Mann would rather see, than Mrs Piozzi's anecdotes, **25**. 643
material for, in royal visit to Selwyn, **34**. 12
phrase used by, **11**. 103n
Wolczyn, Lithuania, Czartoryski's country house:
(?) Stormont visits, **38**. 33
Wolf; wolves:
Arabian deserts thought to have, **37**. 130
beast of Gévaudan is, **35**. 113, **39**. 14
Catherine II compared to, **31**. 62
Edgar, K., exterminated, **13**. 196
German princes hunt, **25**. 364
on Fiennes arms, **35**. 139
Romulus and Remus nursed by, **13**. 204
'Tory' seized by, **13**. 189–90, **17**. 257, **37**. 43, 47
See also Gévaudan, beast of the
Wolfe, Mrs Edward. *See* Thompson, Henrietta
Wolfe, Maj.-Gen. James (1727–59):
Conway and Mordaunt opposed by, at Rochefort inquiry and court martial, **21**. 267n
Conway not befriended by, **21**. 267
death-bed of, **35**. 556
death of: **21**. 338, **22**. 16n, **24**. 185; makes him popular in England, **38**. 128; retribution for his treatment of Conway, **38**. 38–9
fame of, **31**. 20
force of, against Quebec, **21**. 306n
Gabarus Bay landing forced by, near Louisbourg, **21**. 267n
HW might throw standish at, **38**. 69
HW's opinion of, **21**. 267
hero of Quebec, **9**. 253n

[Wolfe, Maj.-Gen. James, *continued*]
letters of, despairing, **21**. 336
Louisbourg siege shows abilities of, **21**. 267
Maria Theresa should have, instead of Daun, **21**. 428
Mason's suggestions for epitaph for, rejected, **28**. 63
Montgomery less successful than, **24**. 185
monument for: **40**. 201; by Lovell, **9**. 183n; Capezzoli helps Wilton with, **23**. 562n; designed, **21**. 421–2, 428, 436; said to replace Valence's, **38**. 110
Pitt has report from, from Montmorency on the St Lawrence, **21**. 336n
Quebec expedition headed by, **21**. 266–7
Quebec landing of, reported, **21**. 327n
Rochefort inquest attended by, **21**. 155n
Townshend succeeds, **22**. 16n
verses mention, **31**. 16
Wolfembuttle; Wolfenbüttel. *See* Brunswick-Wolfenbüttel
Wolfenbüttel, Duke of:
HW will never scuttle after army of, **35**. 256
See also Brunswick-Wolfenbüttel
Wolfenbüttel (Germany):
MS of Theophilus at, **29**. 6
Wolfeton House, Charminster:
French king said to have stayed at, **37**. 491
Wollaston, Rev. George (1738–1826), D.D.:
(?) SH visited by, **12** 226
Wollaston, William (1660–1724), moral philosopher:
bust of, in the Hermitage, **14**. 39n, **29**. 34n, 296
Wollaston. *See also* Woolaston
Wollaton Hall, Notts:
HW passes, **35**. 279
Smithson builder of, **14**. 111n
Wolley, Edward (ca 1604–84), Bp of Clonfert, 1665:
Charles II's witticism on, **22**. 57, **24**. 52, **33**. 426, **35**. 496
Wollstonecraft, Mary (1759–97), writer and reformer; m. (1797) William Godwin:
HW calls: 'Alecto,' **31**. 397; 'hyena in petticoats,' **31**. 397
HW excommunicates, from his library, **31**. 373
HW's opinion of, **31**. 397
Historical and Moral View of the . . . French Revolution, An, by: attacks Marie-Antoinette, **31**. 397; Beloe gives HW disgusting account of, **15**. 255
Louis XVI seen by, on way to his trial, **43**. 343
Vindication of the Rights of Man by, **11**. 169n, **31** (?) 373
Vindication of the Rights of Women, A, by, **31**. 370, 373
Wolseley, Robert (1649–97), diplomatist:
preface of, to *Valentinian*, **16**. 5
Rochester's correspondence with, **16**. 5

Wolseley, William (1756–1842), Adm.:
at Pitt Place, **28**. 480n
Wolsey, Thomas (?1475–1530), cardinal:
arms of: **35**. 641; on frankincense ship, **32**. 324
arrested at Cawood, **2**. 333n
chicanery of, **2**. 259
Christ Church College members feast, **38**. 62
Cole's MSS concerning, **2**. 192, 247, 250, 251, 252n, 255n, 256, 258–63
copies roof of Beddington at Hampton Court, **33**. 111
died at Leicester Abbey, **2**. 243n
foundations by, at Christ Church, Oxford, **1**. 269
HW hopes, will not disapprove of Beauclerk Tower at SH, **32**. 322
HW owns hat of: **24**. 174, **28**. 313, **29**. 39; given by Cts of Albemarle, **41**. 332–3
HW quotes, **35**. 535
HW quotes speech of, from *Henry VIII*, **32**. 338
Henry VIII and Anne Boleyn at ball given by, **42**. 421
lectures founded by, **1**. 266, 269
Lock's painting of death of, **12**. 268 (*see also* Berry, Agnes: 'Death of Cardinal Wolsey')
masqueraders dressed as, **23**. 193
print of, **1**. 195
print of Beaton in habit similar to that of, **2**. 21
Somerset, D. of, accompanies, on embassy to France, **20**. 39n
stained glass window at Oxford satirizes, **16**. 47
Wolstan, St. *See* Wulfstan, St
Wolston Hall, Essex:
Scott, George, of, **2**. 324n
Wolters, Dirk ('Richard') (1713–71), banker; British agent at Rotterdam:
biographical information about, corrected, **43**. 264
(?) Veers imitates writing of, **19**. 507
Weston, Edward, and Sir C. H. Williams correspond with, **19**. 507n
William V procures HW's *Fugitive Pieces* through, **40**. 286n
Wolterton, Norfolk, seat of 1st Bn Walpole of Wolterton:
at some distance from Broome, **14**. 207n
HW expects owner's duel to appear on fresco at, **18**. 192
HW hopes that Chute's estate will exceed that of, **35**. 85
HW's letter from Lady Ossory sent to, by mistake, **33**. 71
HW's verses on, **18**. 47n
HW visits, **18**. 47, **19**. 72
picture at, of Walpole of Wolterton family, **20**. 341–2
Walpole, Horatio (1678–1757), at, **14**. 224
Walpole, Sir Robert, visits, accompanied by

Lady Mary Walpole and Elizabeth Le Neve, **30**. 80
Wolterton, Walpole of. *See* Walpole
Wolven. *See* Wolvey
Wolverhampton, Staffs:
Whaley visits, **40**. 42
Wolvey, Thomas (d. 1430) *and* Richard (d. 1490):
master masons, **1**. 19
Woman; women:
abandoned, of quality, Mann's English visitors limited to, **20**. 454
addicted to brag and Methodism in England, **20**. 41
at Genoa, pretty, **30**. 1
attendance of, at Court, disapproved of, by HW, **12**. 130
Berry, Mary, thinks occupation important for, **12**. 123
better than men as letter-writers, **20**. 282, **35**. 380–1
Clement XIII orders, to cover their faces in churches, **21**. 292
diplomatic posts held by, **31**. 102
English: are not merely gallant but become street-walkers, **24**. 27; costume of, at Paris opera, unflattering, **30**. 264; get little joy from religion in old age, **20**. 378
Florentine, compared to those of York and Edinburgh, **20**. 427
Florentine archbishop orders, to uncover their breasts in church, **21**. 292
Fox, Henry, fond of, **30**. 335
Francis II taken from care of, before they could give him foolish prejudices, **25**. 282
French: act in Genoese opera, **19**. 505; *see also under* France: ladies of; women of; French, the: women
HW's remarks on, **11**. 267
House of Lords filled with, at prorogation of Parliament, **30**. 164
Italian: act in Genoese opera, **19**. 505; shave their bodies, **19**. 437; soon lose beauty, **23**. 306
Italians punish, lightly, **20**. 356
letters of, superior to men's, **20**. 282, **35**. 380–1
Methodism attracts, **20**. 41, 82
milk of, **24**. 321
nonsense of, common rather than wise, **41**. 277
novelists and poetesses among, in every parish, **36**. 251
old: HW thinks that living with, is worse than living out of the world, **25**. 542; religion used by, as cloak for scandal-mongering, **25**. 584; who cheat at berlan as respectable as patriots who cheat at eloquence, **30**. 221
Piozzi, Mrs, comments on treatment of, **9**. 9n
power of, over husbands, HW's reflections on, **24**. 208
Roman, par and impar played by, **30**. 221

scandal by, HW's reflections on, **18**. 62
spitefulness of, HW's reflections on, **18**. 506
subordination of, approved by Mrs Walsingham and opposed by Hannah More, **31**. 370
treatment of, in England and France, **9**. 9
ugly, provided with mates by fortune, **35**. 462
Woman of the Bedchamber. *See under* Bedchamber (royal)
Wombwell, Lady. *See* Rawlinson, Susanna
Wombwell, George (1734–80), M.P.:
Richmond, D. of, answers speech of, **23**. 547n
Wonder, The. See under Freeman, Susannah
Wondivash, India:
Lally defeats Coote at, **21**. 441n
Wooburn. *See* Woburn
Wood, Anthony [à] (1632–95), biographer:
Archæologia eulogizes, **2**. 347
Athenæ Oxonienses by, **40**. 131; Baker's notes on, **2**. 348, 353–4; cited, **1**. 261, 266, 269; Parker's 'Impartial Account' based on, **20**. 188n; Powell described in, **16**. 159; quoted, **1**. 272–3; Tiptoft not mentioned in, **40**. 298
autobiography of, printed at Oxford in *Lives of those Eminent Antiquaries*, **1**. 255, **28**. 40, **39**. 158
Biographia Britannica on, **2** 92, 342, 350
Bird a friend of, **16**. 36n
Cole's opinions derived from, **2**. 347
HW a combination of Mme Danois and, **2**. 269
History and Antiquities [*Historia et antiquitates*] *of the University of Oxford* by:
Chichele's founding of All Souls quoted from, **35**. 387; Cole asks Gulston for, **1**. 291n; Tiptoft included in, **40**. 298; Waynflete's reception of Richard III described in, **41**. 139–40, 141
'honest,' **2**. 131
inaccuracy of, **1**. 269
Leicester and Amy Robsart described by, **38**. 138
MSS of, transcribed for HW, **35**. 158–9
Oxford's antiquities should be described by, **40**. 12
value of, **1**. 269
Wood, James (fl. 1763–82), Cole's groom; 'Jem'; 'my boy':
child ready to be sworn to, **1**. 297
Cole recommends, **1**. 297
HW to be met by, **1**. 38
on errand to the post, **1**. 114
Wood, Molly:
Cole's cook, **1**. 242n
Wood, Robert (1700–48), of Littleton, Middlesex:
(?) bids on Hogarth's 'Rake's Progress,' **32**. 114
Wood, Robert (?1717–71), archæologist; M.P.:
acquittal demanded by, in House of Commons, **38**. 318
Choiseul entertains, at dinner in Paris, **39**. 89

[Wood, Robert, archæologist, *continued*]
—— prefers, to other English, **39**. 236
classic tastes of, **41**. 175–9
Essay on the Original Genius and Writings of Homer, An: copy of, annotated by Bowyer the printer, **41**. 176n; published by Mrs Wood, **28**. 212; submitted to HW, **41**. 175–9; Wood, Mrs, presents, to HW, **41**. 306–8
French war rumours caused by, **23**. 156n
future travellers' descriptions of England's ruins will resemble books of, **24**. 62
George II's speech sent by, to Mann, **21**. 345n
HW's correspondence with, **41**. 175–9
HW's reflections on Balbec and, **9**. 349
Hertford might have, as secretary in Ireland, **38**. 536
house of, at Meudon, 'perfect ruin,' **31**. 136
House of Commons hears evidence against, **38**. 316
(?) Leeson's secretary, **19**. 13n
Lyttelton, Richard, rejects offer transmitted by, **21**. 507–8, 511
Mann receives news from, of Louisbourg's capture, **21**. 235n
—— 's correspondence with, **21**. 507n
—— 's enclosures from, **21**. 332n
—— 's friendship with, authorizes application for higher rank, **21**. 453
—— writes to, requesting promotion, **21**. 453, 454–5, 463, 483
Mariette likes and admires, **3**. 375
ministry to satisfy, **38**. 321
(?) Orford, Cts of, tells, of her plans and grievances, **20**. 476
Pitt's approaches from, for Mann, **21**. 455, 483, **22**. 469
Ruins of Balbec by, praised by HW, **21**. 173
Ruins of Palmyra by: **10**. 230n, **29**. 268; HW pleased by, **35**. 160; HW praises, **21**. 173; Montagu erroneously attributes, to James Stuart, **10**. 230
secretary of state's office to be under care of, after Egremont's death, **22**. 159n
secretary to Pitt, **16**. 39n
social relations of, in France, **7**. 319, 320, **31**. 136, **39**. 89
tombstone of, at Putney, to be designed by HW, **41**. 245–9, 254–5, 307–8, 317–18
wife of, **6**. 202n
wife wishes tombstone to stress benevolence of, **41**. 249, 254
Wilkes sues, in Court of Common Pleas, **38**. 258–9
—— wins damages from, **22**. 188
Wood, Mrs Robert. *See* Skottowe, Ann (1732–1803)
Wood, Thomas (1708–79):
Hogarth's 'Strolling Actresses' bought by, **32**. 114n
Wood, Thomas (b. 1745), Cole's servant:
Cole calls, 'my servant,' **1**. 314
—— needs, on journey, **1**. 242

—— 's carriage allowed by, to run away, **2**. 179–81
—— 's errands performed by, **1**. 100, 217, 225, 229n, 230, 231, 237, 296, 311, **2**. 15, 63, 65, 68, 118, 142, 158
health of: **1**. 78, 80, 335; ague, **1**. 29–30
sister to be taken by, to Buckinghamshire, **1**. 242
Wood, Thomas (ca 1763–72):
HW designs monument to father and, **28**. 212n
tombstone inscription for, **41**. 248
Wood:
bacon flitch carved in, hangs over chimney at Wichnor, **38**. 71
box of, **30**. 373
figure in, at Gloucester Cathedral, **35**. 154
La Borde's expense for, for fires, **31**. 80
lacking at Florence to build *casotti*, **18**. 270
Lorraine officials sell, **18**. 270
paintings on, **42**. 67, 380n
partridge carved in, attached to wainscot, **31**. 80
sailor mends leg of, **24**. 283–4, 290
sculpture in, **42**. 68
shoes of, *see under* Shoe
snuff-box lined with, between layers of gold, **31**. 113
Soubise, Princesse de, will get, from husband, **21**. 178
staircases should not be built in, **22**. 143
See also Orange-wood; Timber; Tree; *and under* names of trees
Wood; woods (forest):
at Houghton, become forests, **39**. 172
Conway seeks farm with, **37**. 303, 305
hills around Wichnor covered with blue, **38**. 71
of green silk, for ball scenery, **37**. 412
Onslow's insignificant, **30**. 292n
Rhine landscape adorned with, **37**. 150
use of, in landscape design, at Castle Howard, **30**. 257
Woodbine:
at Esher, **10**. 73
in Nuneham garden, **35**. 484n
Woodbridge, Suffolk:
Burwell and Pitman of, **1**. 374n
Hertford's letter sent from, **39**. 433
Woodchester, Glos:
Lysons, Samuel, draws Roman antiquities at, **12**. 198
Roman pavement at, **15**. 251n
Woodcock, Elborough, solicitor in Chancery:
(?) Burney, Frances, advised by, not to have servant's will contested, **42**. 295, 297
testimony of, in House of Lords on Ds of Kingston, **24**. 63n
Woodcock, Elizabeth (d. 1808), m. 1 (1775) Sir John Shelley, 5th Bt; m. 2 (1790) John Stewart, M.D.:
captured and carried to Brest, **12**. 132

Woodcock, John:
wager over ride by, on Newmarket heath, 38. 272n
Woodcock, Mary, m. (1781) Humphrey Ashley Sturt:
Blandford, Lord, visits, 11. 141–2
sister-in-law's letter from, about Lord Blandford, 11. 141–2
Woodcock; woodcocks:
English travellers compared to, 20. 265, 271
HW receives brace of, from Dickensons, 31. 335
Hertford shoots, in Ireland, 39. 45
hunters of, become soldiers, 9. 241
Pembroke, Cts of, calls, 'bird of the wood,' 17. 495–6
Woodcut; woodcuts:
Bowle's 1545 cuts differ from, 40. 306
——'s 'Dances of Death' in, 42. 431–2
Woodcutter; woodcutters:
English, in Bay of Honduras, 38. 432n
Wooddeson, Richard (1745–1822):
elected Vinerian Professor of Common Law at Oxford, 2. 228n
Wood engraving. See under Print; prints
Woodfall, George (fl. 1748–71), printer; bookseller:
Craig's Court, Charing Cross, the address of, 42. 455
HW sends anonymous advertisement to, for Public Advertiser, 42. 455–6
Woodfall, Henry Sampson (d. 1769), editor of Public Advertiser:
brother and son of, 42. 455n
Woodfall, Henry Sampson (1739–1805), printer and publisher:
birth date of, corrected, 43. 296
Conway gives to, notes of speech, 29. 96
HW asks, to print no more of The Mysterious Mother, 42. 85–6
(?) HW's correspondence with, 41. 220–1, 226, 42. 85–6, 498–506
HW urges, to print all letters to him, 42. 498–9
imprisoned for printing libel on Norton, 23. 555, 556
North said to promise indemnity to, for betraying Horne, 23. 557n
Norton's quarrel with, 32. 188–9
Paternoster Row the address of, 41. 226
prints part of HW's Mysterious Mother in Public Advertiser, 33. 429
prosecuted, 28. 135n
(?) trial of, 23. 256n
trial of, for libel, 35. 552n
uncle of, 42. 455n
Walpole, Hon. Thomas, to be called on by, 41. 226
Woodfall, William, printer:
arrested, 23. 280
Woodfall, William (1746–1803), actor and journalist:

Graves's Spiritual Quixote reviewed by, 35. 462
Woodfall's Register:
HW's letter to Burke mentioned in, 34. 100
Woodford, John (d. 1800), army officer:
forced to hide, after Gordon riots, 33. 195
involved in attack on Lord Mansfield's house, 33. 185, 195
threatened by mob in Gordon riots, 33. 185
wife of, 33. 195
Woodford, William (1734–80), American army officer:
English escape from, at Monmouth, 24. 405n
Woodford. See also Woodforde
Woodforde, Rev. James:
Orford, E. of, seen by, at balloon ascent at Norwich, 25. 596n
Woodgate family:
Summer Hill occupied by, 35. 136n
Woodhouse, James (1735–1820), poetical shoemaker:
starvation avoided by, 31. 221n
Woodhouse:
at Drayton, 10. 92, 342
Woodhull, Abraham, American spy:
Washington gets intelligence from, 33. 239n
Woodhull, Nathaniel (1722–76), Brig.-Gen.:
capture of, 24. 249n
Woodlands, near Horton, Dorset:
Hastings of, 42. 389n
Woodman; woodmen:
Lyttelton, Lady, imitates, 42. 200
Woodmason, James (fl. 1773–ca 1798), stationer:
children of, die in fire, 25. 242
Woodmason, James (1773–?82), and Mary (1774–?82):
(?) die in fire, 25. 242
Woodmason, Mary Magdalene, wife of James Woodmason:
children of, die in fire caused by her candle, 25. 242
Wood pigeon; wood pigeons:
bereavement of, 9. 8
ivy liked by, 16. 190
Woodrising, Norfolk:
Crane buried at, 1. 20n
Woodstock, Oxon.:
cheese prices at, 22. 460n
Ditchley near, 9. 289n
Dodd and Whaley visit, 40. 11–12
HW receives steel from, 17. 302
Montagu visits, 10. 309
Ratcliffe and Richard III visit, 41. 141
Rousham near, 28. 45n
trade of, declines, because of competition from Birmingham and Sheffield, 17. 302n
Woodstock St, Oxford Road, London:
house in, pillaged during Gordon riots, 29. 56, 33. 188–9
Wood St, London:
Poultry Compter in, 42. 454
Wood St, Westminster:

[Wood St, Westminster, *continued*]
Carter lives in, **16.** 194
Woodville. *See* Wydevill
Woodward, Mr:
SH visited by, **12.** 250
Woodward, Henry (1714–77), comedian:
Beggar's Pantomime or the Contending Columbines by, first performed in Lincoln's Inn Fields, **18.** 124n
Cumberland's *Brothers* acted by, **32.** 39n
HW reserves rôle for, in *Nature Will Prevail*, **41.** 243
Northington compared with, **38.** 543–4
prologue to *She Stoops to Conquer* spoken by, **32.** 109
She Stoops to Conquer acted by, **41.** 243n
Woodwork:
at SH, **42.** 103
Woodyer, John (1720–1804), Cambridge bookseller:
sales by, of Mason's *Gray*, **1.** 359
subscriptions received by, for Bentham's *Ely*, **1.** 201n
Wookey Hole, Somerset:
Devil's Arse compared to, **40.** 16
Dodd and Whaley visit, **40.** 10
Wool:
export restrictions on, removed, **24.** 542n
factory for, at Abbeville, **37.** 41
price of, falls, **42.** 393
Woolaston, John (b. ca 1672), painter:
Britton's portrait by, **40.** 310
HW ignorant of, **40.** 310
Woolaston. *See also* Wollaston
Woolbeding House, Sussex:
Spencer, Lord Robert, buys, with faro money, and moves Cowdray fountain to it, **43.** 115
Woolcot. *See* Wolcot
Woolett. *See* Woollett
Wooley. *See* Wolley; Woolley
Woollett, William (1735–85), engraver:
Agincourt sends engravings through, **42.** 63, 102
engraver in London, **42.** 102
painting engraved by, **9.** 98n
Rathbone Place, Upper Brook St, the address of, **42.** 63n
Woolley, Mrs Hannah (fl. 1670), afterwards Mrs Challiner; writer on cookery:
print of, **1.** 179, 188, 190
Woolpacks:
covered with scarlet cloth at trials of peers, **19.** 28on
Woolsack; woolsacks:
Ashburnham's wife called, **37.** 438, 450
lord chancellors sometimes carried to, **25.** 347
Mansfield quivers upon, **33.** 175
Woolsey, Robert:
Reflections Upon Reflections by, **11.** 169n
Woolsey. *See also* Wolseley; Wolsey
Woolstaple, Westminster:
bridge across Thames from, to Surrey, **20.** 108n

Woolstencraft. *See* Wollstonecraft
Woolston, Thomas:
trial of, for blasphemy, **35.** 551n
Woolterton. *See* Wolterton
Woolveton, Dorset:
Trenchard of, **11.** 16n
Woolwich, London:
Cromarty, Cts of, visits, to see captured son, **19.** 272
foot regiments embark from, **17.** 410n
Royal Military College at, **28.** 31n; *see also under* Royal Military Academy
Wooster, David (1711–77), American army officer:
Arnold relieved by, at Quebec, **24.** 215n
Montgomery joins, **24.** 157n
Warner's letter from, **24.** 185n
Wootton, Sir Harry. *See* Wotton, Sir Henry
Wootton, Henry:
(?) money embezzled by, from customs office, **35.** 493
Wootton, John (ca 1682–1764), painter:
dates of, corrected, **43.** 250
dogs and landscape supplied by, to Richardson's portrait of Sir Robert Walpole, **41.** 234, **42.** 249n
HW mentions, **37.** 133
'Patapan's' picture by: **43.** 170; Chute asks about, **35.** 38, 41; Chute remembers, **35.** 44–6; to be painted, **18.** 220
Walpole, Sir Robert and Lady, painted by, **19.** 511, **35.** 173–4, **42.** 249
Wootton, Derbyshire:
Rousseau stays at Davenport's house at, **1.** 112n, 113, **3.** 15, 300n, **13.** 41n
Wootton, Norfolk:
HW imagines himself married to heiress of, **18.** 238
Hamond of, **9.** 26n, 351n
Wootton Bassett, Wilts:
rioters lower food prices at, **22.** 460n
Worcester, Bp of. *See* Alcock, John (1430–1500); Babington, Gervase (?1550–1610); Carpenter, John (d. 1476); Earle, John (ca 1601–65); Fletcher, Richard (d. 1596); Hooper, John (d. 1555); Hough, John (1651–1743); Hurd, Richard (1720–1808); Johnson, James (1705–74); Latimer, Hugh (ca 1485–1555); Maddox, Isaac (1697–1759); North, Hon. Brownlow (1741–1820); Pepys, Henry (1783–1860); Wulfstan, St (?1012–95)
Worcester, Cts of. *See* Russell, Anne (d. 1639)
Worcester, E. of. *See* Somerset, Sir Charles (ca 1460–1526); Somerset, Henry (?1495–1549); Tiptoft, John (1427–70)
Worcester, Marchioness of. *See* Child, Rebecca (d. 1712); Leveson Gower, Lady Charlotte Sophia (1771–1854)
Worcester, M. of. *See* Somerset, Edward (ca 1603–67); Somerset, Henry (ca 1577–1646); Somerset, Henry Charles (1766–1835)
Worcester, Marquesses of:
pursuivants instead of heralds serve, **40.** 179

Worcester, William (1415–ca 82), chronicler:
    Annales rerum Anglicarum by, quoted and
        cited, **1**. 319–21, **14**. 70
    *Itineraria Simonis Simeonis et Willelmis de
        Worcestre* by: Nasmith's edition of, **2**. 54,
        57, 73–4, 76–7, 79, 82; quoted, **1**. 175;
        'Rowley' not mentioned in, **2**. 104, 105
    letters by, sent by Fenn to HW, **16**. 241, 243
    'Rowley' not mentioned by, **16**. 124n
Worcester, Worcs:
    battle of: Charles II lectured by Kirk of Scot-
        land on eve of, **23**. 386; Clifford attended
        Charles II at, **35**. 148
    cathedral at, *see* Worcester Cathedral
    Charles II not attended to, by Highlanders,
        19. 107
    Dodd and Whaley visit, **40**. 13–14
    election at, **39**. 197n
    election contests for, **15**. 198n, **35**. 150
    Fanny Burney's uncle at, **42**. 330n
    Gloucester compared with, **35**. 152
    gloves manufactured at, **40**. 13
    HW walks into contested election at, **35**. 150
    Hardinge writes from, **35**. 583
    inn at, invaded by mob, **35**. 150
    instructions of, to Sandys and Winnington,
        18. 103
    'Knight of the Fancy Nose' came from, **29**.
        360
    Lyttelton visits, **42**. 467
    music festival at, **11**. 109, **20**. 338
    paste of, superior to all but that of Saxony,
        for porcelain, **25**. 635
    petition from, **7**. 367, **23**. 132
    Pitt and Legge receive freedom of, **21**. 87
    porcelain from, **6**. 429n, **25**. 635
    Severn River beautiful at, **40**. 13
    shoemaker of, exhibits shoe made for Cts of
        Coventry, **20**. 324
    Walsh offers to resign seat for city of, **38**. 249
Worcester, English ship:
    Keppel joined by, **39**. 306
    (?) Spanish man of war captured by, **17**. 176n
    Spithead reached by, from Gibraltar, **24**. 392n
Worcester Cathedral:
    HW describes, **35**. 150–1
    (?) Hoare does monument in, **20**. 86n
    'mean,' **40**. 13
    three choirs sing in, **20**. 338n
Worcester College, Oxford:
    Clark, Dr George, bequeaths Inigo Jones's
        designs to, **21**. 364n
Worcestershire:
    Bewdley in, **40**. 42
    Collections for the History of, **2**. 154, 266
    HW may visit Lyttelton at, **40**. 2, 7
    HW visits, and prefers it to Kent, **35**. 147
    Nash's history of, **42**. 17
    rioters in, **11**. 317, 319–20
    Winnington buried in, **30**. 320
'Worcestershire Giant':
    HW's term for George Lyttelton, **40**. 88
Word; words:

feelings more powerful than, **12**. 17
HW discusses diversity in meaning of, **11**. 3
Scottish, not included by Mrs Piozzi in *British
    Synonymy*, **12**. 93
See also Hebrew language
Wordsworth, Anne, m. (1771), Harry Verelst:
    marriage of, **28**. 63n
Word to the Wise, A. See under Kelly, Hugh
Work-bags. *See under* Knotting-bags
Work-basket:
    Robinson's ball-room too narrow for, **37**. 55
    Selwyn not to let letter lie in, **30**. 207
Work-box:
    heavy, (?) for SH, **30**. 275
Workman; workmen:
    at SH: HW corrects mistakes of, **31**. 315; un-
        skilled in Gothic construction, **42**. 220
    'finish' a locution of, **37**. 442
    fright of, when Mann's greenhouse collapses,
        20. 94
    George III sees, fall off scaffold at Kew, **20**.
        240
    HW plays with, at SH, **38**. 94
    HW's, at SH, **31**. 315, **37**. 352, 364
    Mann enjoys watching, **20**. 357
    noisy and slow in London, **10**. 271
Works, HW's:
    earnings of, **43**. 138; *see also under* Walpole,
        Horatio (1717–97)
*Works of Celebrated Authors of whose Writings
    There Are But Small Remains, The* (1750):
    reference in, to poem by Tickell, **12**. 260
Works of Mr Alexander Pope. See under Pope,
    Alexander
Works of the English Poets. See under Johnson,
    Dr Samuel
Worksop, Notts, seat of D. of Norfolk:
    arsenal at, to be revealed to Lord R. Sutton,
        9. 97
    'artificial ugly forest of evergreens,' **32**. 375
    Aston near, **29**. 191
    Bess of Hardwick builds, **9**. 298, **40**. 182
    burnt, **9**. 397, **15**. 114, **38**. 141
    'conjuring room' of D. of Norfolk at, **37**. 566
    Conway describes, **37**. 565–6, 572
    HW and Strafford visit, with owner's permis-
        sion, **35**. 270
    Hunloke and Cts of Ailesbury play com-
        merce at, **37**. 565
    landscape effects at, **37**. 565–6, 572
    Mary, Q. of Scots, stays at, **9**. 397
    new menagerie at, **35**. 280
    Norfolk, Ds of, writes from, **41**. 167
    Norfolk, D. of, finishes, **9**. 397
    picture at, **1**. 192
    post from, to Sheffield, passes Mason's door,
        29. 20
    Strafford may revisit, **37**. 579
    —— may see celebrations at, for Minden vic-
        tory, **35**. 293
    turnpike at, **29**. 84n
    visitors at: Conway and wife, **37**. 561, 565;
        HW, **9**. 397, **10**. 264n, **35**. 270; HW, Con-
        way, and E. and Cts of Strafford, **35**. 280n;

[Worksop, Notts, *continued*]
Hillsborough, Cts of, **37**. 566; Strafford, E. of, **35**. 270; York, D. of, **9**. 397

World, The (periodical):
account in, of Devonshire House robbery, **16**. 204
Ailesbury, Cts of, praises HW's number in, **37**. 434, 438, 440
Bentley's, sent to Montagu by HW, **9**. 195
Bishop Bonner's Ghost reprinted in, **31**. 306n
Chesterfield's contributions in, **7**. 319, **9**. 178, 195, **28**. 294, **35**. 199, 257, 258, 339, 586, **37**. 420
—— to contribute to, **20**. 374
Clive, Mrs, praises, **9**. 154
contributors to, **20**. 395n, 400n, **38**. 89
copies of, received at Paris, **7**. 319
Dodsley, Robert, has printed, **20**. 374n
Du Deffand, Mme, asks for copy of, **3**. 113
—— purchases thrice, **4**. 8
George III's statue and Shakespeare Gallery bas-reliefs by Mrs Damer mentioned in, **43**. 167
HW called author of, **9**. 154
HW calls, 'Dodsley's paper,' **30**. 132
HW mentioned in, **34**. 64, 83–4
HW never sees, **34**. 84
HW's character of H. Fox should be printed in, **30**. 132
HW's contributions to: **3**. 93, 136n, 399–400, **6**. 136, **7**. 319, **9**. 154, 167, **13**. 23, **20**. 373–5, 385, 392, 395, 399–400, **35**. 199, 648, **37**. 266n, 434, 438–9, 440, **40**. 75; annotated by Lord Cork, **40**. 76n
HW sends: to Bentley, **35**. 199, 214, 257, 258; to Conway, **37**. 430
HW's low opinion of, **31**. 267
HW's number of, seems to hint at Bute and Ps of Wales, **37**. 438–9
HW's paper in, on street-signs as emblems of glory, **37**. 266n
HW's papers in, may show Chute's influence, **20**. 385
Jenyns's essay in, **29**. 142
Mann welcomes issues of, **20**. 385, 392, 395, 399–400
Merry and Mrs Cowley exchange poems in, **31**. 271n
Moore writes, **35**. 176n
More, Hannah, criticizes style of, **31**. 265
Park Place described in, **39**. 549–52
Pulteney, E. of Bath, contributes to, about Newmarket, **20**. 374
(?) Richmond House theatricals criticized in, **33**. 563
Theodore of Corsica benefited by papers in, **20**. 373–4, **40**. 75
Williams, Sir C. H., writes number for, **30**. 321
Wilton thought by Mann to be praised in, **20**. 392, 395, 397
See also *World Extraordinary, The*
World, the:

Conway would take, like dose of vile medicine, **37**. 176
grows more intrepid, **25**. 105
HW forsakes, except for amusement, **22**. 359
HW holds to, by but few threads, **25**. 116
HW laughs with, half the time, and laughs at it, the rest, **35**. 352
HW's reflection on, as a comedy to those who think, a tragedy to those who feel, **23**. 166, 387, 397, **32**. 315, 344, **33**. 444
HW thinks, can be cured of any folly, but not of being foolish, **25**. 642
inanimate, not appreciated by 'men of wit and pleasure about town,' **41**. 40
insanity of, HW's reflections on, **22**. 570
nine out of ten parts of, intolerable to HW, **35**. 43
'old acquaintance that does not improve upon one's hands,' **35**. 347
senility of, HW's reflections on, **25**. 47
truth not loved by, **38**. 152
See also Life
World As It Goes. See under Combe, William
World Extraordinary, The:
HW's character of H. Fox printed in, **30**. 131n, **38**. 193n
Worldly grandeur:
vanity of, **28**. 103–4
Worlidge, Thomas (1700–66), painter and etcher:
Brown, Lady, wants new peers to sit to, **40**. 90
HW mentions, **20**. 427
Ninon de Lenclos's portrait engraved by, **31**. 5n
style of, fashionable, **14**. 190
Worlingham, Suffolk:
Soley, rector of, **41**. 96n
Worm; worms:
HW does not fish with, **9**. 155
HW wishes, would eat his gardener, **39**. 416
parchment a 'prey' for, **30**. 289
Strafford, Cts of, not to impale, **35**. 335
Temple, Cts, mentions in verses, **10**. 114
'that never dies,' **37**. 67
Wormeston, Fifeshire:
Lindsay of, **40**. 267
Worming:
'Patapan' undergoes, **18**. 317
Worms (Germany):
Condé at, **11**. 295n
Conway encamped at, **37**. 145–7
Worms, Treaty of:
articles of, **18**. 336n
Austrian conquest of Naples said to be promised by, **18**. 444
Bubb Dodington's verses on, **30**. 316
Charles Emmanuel III granted Finale by, **18**. 360
England disregards, **19**. 481
English fleet rejoices at, **18**. 336
English fleet relies on triple alliance of, **18**. 339
Genoese fear consequences of, **18**. 546–7, 554

Lomellini invokes clause of, 19. 67
Maria Theresa promised English naval help by, 18. 470
—— to observe terms of, 19. 481
Mathews expects his cockade by, 18. 522
Parliamentary debate over, expected, 18. 383
signed, 18. 311
Wormsley, Herts:
Fane of, 13. 8n
'Worm tub':
Conway's, 39. 551
Wormwood:
used in tincture for the eyes, 18. 365n
Woronzow. See Vorontsov
Worplesdon, Surrey:
living of, taken: by Apthorpe, 1. 35n, 328, 331n, 334; by Burton, 1. 106, 334; value of, 1. 331n
Cole goes to, 1. 381n
Worsborough, Yorks:
Pope's mother baptized at, 29. 278
Worseley, Mr and Mrs:
SH visited by, 12. 247
Worseley; Worsely. See also Worsley
Worship:
Quaker, conducted in silence, 31. 350
Worship of Priapus. See under Knight, Richard Payne
Worsley, Lady. See Fleming, Seymour Dorothy (fl. 1777–1805); Thynne, Frances (ca 1673–1750)
Worsley, Frances (1694–1743), m. (1710) John Carteret, 2d Bn Carteret, 1695; E. Granville, n.c., 1744:
daughters of, 22. 275n
death of, 18. 255
Hague, The, to be visited by, 18. 209
husband discussed by, 17. 258
mother of, 29. 285
plump, 18. 209
Worsley, Sir Richard (1751–1805), 7th Bt, 1768; M.P.; F.R.S.; F.S.A.:
connivance of, in wife's prostitution, 25. 246
Craven, Bns, shown Otranto picture by, for HW, 34. 36n
Deyverdun travels with, 13. 44
Hampshire election lost by, 28. 488
History of the Isle of Wight, The, by, 2. 272–3, 276, 29. 146–7, 33. 27, 43. 73
jury awards shilling damages to, 25. 246
North's pleasantry on, 25. 246
Parliamentary memberships of, corrected, 43. 305
Reveley accompanies, on travels, 35. 435n, 42. 177n
wife accused by, of adultery, 25. 245
wife leaves, 25. 228
Worsley, Sir Robert (?1669–1747), 4th Bt, 1676; M.P.:
daughter of, 17. 258n, 18. 209n
wife of, 29. 285nn
Worsley, Thomas, of Pidford:
(?) Cardini, servant of, 22. 477, 483, 490–1

(?) HW's letters to be taken by, back to England from Italy, 22. 476–7
Naples visited by, 22. 476–7
Worsley, Thomas (1710–78), equerry to George II; surveyor-general of Board of Works; M.P.:
architectural taste of, 21. 460
Bentley's drawings shown to, 9. 343
biographical information about, corrected, 43. 241, 276
death of, from self-starvation, 24. 428
George III gives orders to, 2. 238n
——'s equerry, 21. 460
(?) —— to be shown Bentley's drawings by, 9. 343
Gough refers to, 2. 240
Mann's acquaintance with, 17. 287, 24. 428
——'s 'death' reported by, to HW, 17. 249, 286–7
master of the Board of Works, 21. 460, 24. 428n
Northumberland House dinner attended by, 38. 529–30
Suares, Mme, has, as cicisbeo, 21. 460
Worsley, Sir Thomas (1728–68), 6th Bt, 1756:
relative of, 22. 476
Worsley, Mrs Thynne. See Wither, Henrietta Maria
Worsley. See also Worseley
Worsley, Lancs:
Bridgwater's canals at, 39. 438
Worsop. See Worksop
Worstead ('Worsted'), Norfolk:
HW's will mentions, 30. 344
Worstead (or Worsted) Vaux. See East Ruston Vaux
Worsted (fabric):
Ailesbury, Cts of, does pictures in, 34. 15, 39. 174, 550
—— does landscape in, for HW at SH, 39. 438
—— to put, on chair frames, 37. 466
HW jokes about Lady Ailesbury's, 39. 174
hangings of, 32. 106
in tapestry, 41. 278
Worth, John, of Diss, Norfolk:
Fenn buys Paston letters from, 16. 231n
Wortham, Hale (d. 1778):
death of, 2. 88
Worthey, George:
victim of highway robbery, 29. 260n
Worthies of England. See under Fuller, Thomas
Worthington, William (1703–78), D.D.:
Historical Sense of the Mosaic Account of the Fall, The, by, 15. 302
Wortley, Edward. See Wortley Montagu, Edward
Wortley, Lady Mary. See Pierrepont, Lady Mary
Wortley, Sir Thomas, Kt:
inscription to, at Wharncliffe, 35. 269
Wortley, Yorks, E. of Bute's seat:
Straffords at, 28. 164
'Wortley':

['Wortley,' *continued*]

Denbigh, Cts of, mistakes 'Wrottesley' for, 9. 395

Wortley Mackenzie, James Archibald. *See* Stuart, James Archibald

Wortley Montagu, Edward (1713–76), traveller; M.P.:

adventures of, better than his writings, 21. 472n

Albemarle bails, but makes no defence for him, 20. 294

Ashe, Elizabeth, goes to France with, 9. 113n

——thought to have married, 20. 289

becomes Mohammedan, 2. 152

Coke's witticism about Parliamentary membership of, 20. 289

daughter said to be placed by, in Roman convent, 22. 113

election of: 19. 450n; corrected, 43. 262

Englishmen worthy only to be directed by, 35. 187

Ethiopia to be visited by, from Italy, 22. 113

extravagance of, 20. 226, 235

faro-banker to Duchesse de Mirepoix, 20. 288

father almost disinherits, 21. 472–3

father gives small allowance to, 20. 226

galleys may be punishment for, 20. 288, 294

imprisoned with Taaffe at Fort l'Évêque, Paris, for robbing Payba, 19. 450n, 20. 287–8, 294, 21. 473n, 43. 263

inherits estate from D. of Kingston, 32. 150

iron wig brought by, from Paris, 20. 226

Kingston, D. of, leaves estate to, 32. 150

Mirepoix, Duchesse de, holds note of, 5. 434

mother accompanied by, from Montélimar to Orange, 18. 567n

mother disinherits, 22. 72n

mother does not supply, 20. 235

mother leaves one guinea to, 22. 81

mother's conversation with, at Geneva, 19. 567

mother's cruel treatment of, 14. 244

mother's relations with, 30. 10

Paris left by, because of promise to avoid father, 20. 226n

Parliament entered by, 19. 450

Payba claims, extorted notes from him, 20. 288n

Rome visited by: to embark at Sicily or Naples for Egypt in search of antiquities, 22. 76–7; when disinherited by mother, 22. 72n

Royal Society elects, 20. 226

Sandwich secures election for, 19. 450n

snuff-boxes collected, and shoe-buckles worn by, with frock, 20. 226

whiskers and Ethiopian costume worn by, 22. 113

White's Club does not include, 20. 289

Wortley Montagu, Mrs Edward. *See* Ashe, Elizabeth; Wortley Montagu, Sally

Wortley Montagu, Lady Mary. *See* Pierrepont, Lady Mary

Wortley Montagu, Mary (1718–94), m. (1736)

John Stuart, 3d E. of Bute; cr. (1761) Bns Mount Stuart, s.j.:

appointment rumoured for, in Q. Charlotte's household, 38. 96

Bedford, Ds of, at odds with, 38. 434

—— opposes, at Anne Pitt's ball, 38. 475

Bentley's *Wishes* attended by, 9. 382

Blandford, Lady, visited by, 32. 278n

Blenheim dances reported by, 38. 462

children of, unfortunate, 24. 378

Coke, Lady Mary, hears from, of Ds of Portland's will, 33. 484n

—— learns anecdotes of the Luttrell family from, 31. 169

comments on Prince Caramanico, 33. 241–2

Court ball attended by, 9. 406, 38. 144

daughter's misconduct mentioned to, 24. 378

death of: feared by HW, 34. 205; HW's loss by, 34. 205, 207; HW's reflections on, 12. 120

Delany, Mrs, has social relations with, 31. 215

fashionable, 9. 344

father's bequest to, 21. 473

father's fortune to be inherited by, 9. 338

footpads rob, near Isleworth, 12. 100

HW and Lady Warwick meet at house of, 34. 199

HW discussed by Lady Mary Coke and, 31. 184

HW jokes about, 10. 23

HW jokes about Anne Pitt and, 31. 57, 67

HW known by, from boyhood, 31. 184

HW meets, 33. 132

HW mentions, 9. 403, 38. 167

HW pities, because of her eccentric mother, 21. 472, 22. 4

HW plays whist with, 33. 313

HW praises, 21. 472

HW praises award of peerage to, 21. 490

HW relates his quarrel with Lady Mary Coke to, 31. 184–5

HW's esteem for, 31. 40–1, 215

HW's sincerity questioned by, 31. 184

HW's verses for George III are sent to, 13. 36

HW thanked by, for Erskine's appointment, 31. 40–1

HW visits, 12. 42–3, 69, 77, 103

health of: gout, 12. 43; illness, 12. 103

Hertford, Cts of, writes to, of wish to serve Q. Charlotte, 38. 104, 113

house rented by, for mother, 22. 3n

Lyttelton's improper conversation before, 15. 330

Macartney expected by, 33. 132

Mann informed by, through HW, that Anne Pitt goes to Pisa, 23. 557

mob throws stones into chamber of, 23. 7

mother bequeaths MSS to, 22. 84

mother of, 32. 91

mother's bequest to, 22. 72

mother's journal burnt by, 14. 242n

mother's letters will be closely guarded by, 22. 84, 141

mother's portrait probably given to, by Ds of Portland, **35.** 271n

mother's unkind treatment of, **14.** 244

Muncaster lets Isleworth house to, **33.** 524n

musicale at Lady Lucan's attended by, **33.** 139

peerage granted to, **9.** 344, **21.** 490

Pitt, Anne, corresponds with, **31.** 41, 187

—— entertains, **32.** 48n

—— friend of, **24.** 378

sits, at Court ball, **9.** 406, **38.** 144

Straffords visit, at Wortley, **28.** 164

SH visited by, **12.** 241

(?) talked of, as 'groom of the stole,' **38.** 96

Warwick, Lady, lives next door to, **34.** 199

Wortley Montagu, Mary (b. ca 1750), natural dau. of Edward Wortley Montagu, jr:

convent at Rome entered by, **22.** 113

Wortley Montagu, Sally (d. 1776), wife of Edward Wortley Montagu, jr:

father-in-law's will refers to, **21.** 472

Wortley Montagu. *See also* Montagu

Wotton, Sir Henry (1568–1639), Kt, 1603; diplomatist:

Boughton Malherbe once owned by, **20.** 166

date of knighthood of, corrected, **43.** 267

definition by, of an ambassador's function, **21.** 276

Flecamore asks, to write sentence in his album, **21.** 276n

HW disparages, **20.** 166

prints of, **1.** 173, 173n, **16.** 66

Venetian senate's relations with, **20.** 198

Wotton, Thomas (d. 1766), bookseller:

English Baronetage by, **9.** 69, 118–19, **15.** 265

Wotton [?Wootton]:

Rigby sees Grenville at, **22.** 538n

Wotton family:

Boughton Malherbe belonged to, **35.** 145

Woty, William:

Graces, The, by, parodies Lord Chesterfield, **32.** 202n

Wouverman. *See* Wouwerman

Wouwerman, Philip (1619–68), painter:

Esher party resembles painting by, **10.** 72

paintings by: at Ham House, **10.** 306; at Julienne's, **7.** 287; at Praslin's, **7.** 353

Wrangel, Vice-Adm.:

Swedish fleet under, **34.** 14n

Wrangel, Carl Henrik (1681–1755), Swedish army officer:

Russians defeat army of, at Vilmanstrand, **17.** 155n

Wrapper; wrappers:

English, rosetti resembles, **42.** 236n

of mazarine, blue, **37.** 78

Wraxall, Sir Nathaniel William (1751–1831), cr. (1813) Bt; M.P.; traveller and memoirist:

explicitness of, in House of Commons, **33.** 276

Parliamentary speech of, as translated in foreign gazettes, must offend sovereigns, **25.** 137–8

name of, corrected, **43.** 298

Short Review of the Political State of Great Britain by, **33.** 557–8, 560–1

talks of himself, **29.** 104

Wray, Sir Cecil (1734–1805), 13th Bt, 1752; army officer; M.P.:

Bellamy, George Anne, mentions, **33.** 465n

Court institutes Westminster election scrutiny in favour of, **25.** 563n

Fox, C. J., and Hood oppose, in Westminster election, **25.** 489, **39.** 410n

Fox, C. J., supports, for Westminster candidacy but later is opposed by him, **36.** 231n

named by new ministers as candidate for Westminster, **25.** 284

very unknown, **25.** 284

Wray, Mrs Daniel. *See* Darell, Mary

Wray, Martha. *See* Ray, Martha

Wray. *See also* Wrey

Wreath of Fashion. See under Tickell, Richard

Wren, Sir Christopher (1632–1723), Kt, 1673; architect:

Benson turns, out of house, **40.** 346–7

buildings by, at corners of Hampton Court's bowling green, **36.** 72n

Charles II rewards, **40.** 349

Chelsea Hospital built by, **15.** 88n

Digby friend of, **40.** 349

drawings and effects of, auctioned, **40.** 348

etching said to be perfected by, **16.** 35

grandson criticizes treatment of, in HW's *Anecdotes of Painting*, **40.** 346–9, 351–4

HW attributes St Mary's, Warwick, to, **32.** 357n

Hampton Court house of, **40.** 347

Hampton Court shows William III's taste, not that of, **40.** 347–8, 353

London fire diverts, to architecture from physic, **40.** 349

Mary II approves of Hampton Court design by, **40.** 348

St Dunstan's tower may not have been designed by, **40.** 348

St Paul's designs by, rejected by Ds of Portsmouth's influence, **40.** 353

St Paul's visited by, rarely, **40.** 350

Scotland Yard house of, **40.** 346

Strong saves, at laying of last stone of St Paul's lantern, **40.** 350–1

Tom Tower at Oxford by, in true Gothic taste, **35.** 154

Warwick tower, but not church, designed by, **40.** 348, 353

Winchester Palace by, for Charles II, **35.** 249, **40.** 349, 354

Wren, Christopher (1675–1747):

father's Hampton Court design shown by, to son, **40.** 348

Parentalia by, **40.** 347, 350, 351

Wren, Christopher (1711–71), grandson of Sir Christopher Wren; of Wroxall Abbey, Worcs:

father shows Hampton Court design to, **40.** 348

[Wren, Christopher (1711–71), *continued*]
grandfather's treatment by HW in *Anecdotes of Painting* criticized by, **40**. 346–9, 351–4
HW's correspondence with, **40**. 345–54
Wren, Stephen (b. 1722):
grandfather's effects sold by, **40**. 348
Wrench, Jacob (ca 1739–1808), draper; deputy of Bridge ward, London:
SH visited by, **12**. (?) 246, 251
Wrestling:
HW prefers not to engage in, **31**. 305
Wrest Park, Beds, E. of Hardwicke's and D. of Kent's seat:
HW considers, ugly, **39**. 139–40
HW visits, **5**. 82n, **9**. 4–5, **33**. 202n
landscape effects at, mended by Brown, **39**. 140
Wrey, Sir Bourchier (?1715–84), 6th Bt, 1726; M.P.:
Banks, Margaret, received opera ticket from, **19**. 234
Mann knew, in Florence, **19**. 238
Orford, Cts of, cousin of, **19**. 238
—— lodges, **19**. 224, 238
—— writes to, at Exeter, **19**. 224
Wrey family:
Bourchiers united with, **19**. 238
Wricklemarsh, near Blackheath:
demolished, **6**. 246
Gloucester, D. and Ds of, occupy, **36**. 246
Wright, Lady. *See* Stapleton, Catherine (ca 1732–1802)
'Wright, Mrs.' *See* Coleman, Sarah
Wright, ——:
Florence to be visited by, **17**. 423
friend of Sir William Turnor and Sir Erasmus Philipps, **17**. 423
imprisoned on suspicion of attacking Lucca, **17**. 449–50, 460
(?) refuses to surrender arms on entering Lucca, **17**. 423n
Wright, ——, architect:
part of Horton designed by, **10**. 334
Wright, ——, banker:
Hill, Father John, employs, as banker, **20**. 533n
Wright, Mrs ——, scandal-monger of Hampton Court:
HW inferior to, as source of news, **31**. 286
HW's last resource for news, **12**. 169
(?) SH visited by, **12**. 222
Wright, Anthony:
HW receipts promissory note of, to Erasmus Shorter, **20**. 403n
Wright (*or* M'Intyre), Denis *or* Dennis (ca 1707–37):
Fotheringham murders, **37**. 33–4
Wright, Capt. Fortunatus (d. 1757), merchant and privateer:
Austria does not permit, to return to Leghorn, **21**. 69n
bondsmen of, summoned to answer damages he may have caused, **19**. 383n

(?) Chute told by, about indecent object in art collection, **35**. 62
Corbet's correspondence with, **19**. 384
English privateer in Mediterranean commanded by, **21**. 20–1
French prizes brought into Malta and Messina by, **21**. 20n
French vow to capture, with special fleet, **21**. 21
Louis XV and Marseille merchants offer rewards for capture of, **21**. 21n
Maltese force, to abandon sailors, **21**. 21n
master of the *Fame*, **19**. 383n
prisoners gently treated by, **21**. 21
prizes taken by, to Porto Ferrajo, **21**. 69
Silva compliments Mann for forcing, to give up captured prize, **19**. 383–4
Turkey Co. makes offer to, **21**. 21
Tuscan government quarrels with England over, **21**. 20
Wright, George (ca 1706–66), *and* George (d. 1804). *See* Wrighte, George
Wright, Henry (ca 1713–94), surgeon; mayor of Bath:
HW declines invitation to attend feast of, **31**. 131
Wright, James (1643–1713), antiquary:
History and Antiquities of . . . Rutland, The, by, **1**. 132, 141, **43**. 49
Wright, Sir James (d. 1803), Kt, 1766; cr. (1772) Bt; English Resident at Venice 1766–74:
intervention of, in Bute-Chatham negotiation, **33**. 64n
ivy admired by, in Boboli gardens, **21**. 457
Mann assured by, of being innocent of trying to supplant him, **22**. 510
—— procures intaglio of Apollo for, **21**. 457n
——'s correspondence with, about possible transfer, **22**. 499–500, 502–3, 510
—— sends ivy seeds to, **21**. 457
uncle asks George III to appoint, to Naples or Florence, **22**. 500
Venice reached by, **22**. 499
—— visited by, on way to Rome and Naples, **21**. 457n
Wright, Rev. John (ca 1699–1768), rector of Euston 1729–68:
HW jokes about, **30**. 38
Wright, John (fl. 1750–ca 1800), coachmaker:
Hatfield Priory seat of, **2**. 174–5, 177
Wright, John (ca 1770–1844), editor:
edition by, of HW's letters, **8**. 216
Wright, John Michael (ca 1623–1700), painter:
Anecdotes of Painting notices, **1**. 171n, **32**. 52
judges painted by, for Guildhall, **40**. 267
Robinson's portrait by, **32** 51n
triple portrait by, of Lacy, **15**. 198
Wright, Mrs Joseph. *See* Lovell, Patience
Wright, Margaret (d. 1803), m. George Farren ('Farran'); actress:
Damer, Mrs, entertains, at supper, **11**. 369, **12**. 76

HW mentions, **12.** 107
HW to entertain, at dinner, **11.** 337
HW visits, **12.** 17, 69
Johnstons entertain, at supper, **11.** 278–9
SH visited by, **12.** 228
Wright, Sir Martin (ca 1693–1767), Kt, 1745; judge of Court of King's Bench:
Murray remanded by, **20.** 249–50
Wright, Mary, (?) maid to Jane Clement:
Walpole, Sir Edward, banishes, **36.** 319, 320
Wright, Sir Nathan (1654–1721), Kt, 1696; lord keeper:
gold purse of, **10.** 332
Gothurst House bought by, **1.** 9, 26
portrait of, at Gothurst, **10.** 332
Wright, Sir Robert (d. 1689), Kt; judge:
Baker preaches before, **2.** 346
Wright, Sir Sampson (d. 1793), Kt, 1782; magistrate:
interrogated in House of Lords, **33.** 176
More, Hannah, involved with, **11.** 253
rioters examined by, at Bow Street, **33.** 179n
Wright, Thomas (d. 1797), printer:
arrested, **23.** 280
Wright. *See also* Wrighte
Wrighte, George (ca 1706–66), M.P.:
birth date of, corrected, **43.** 38
Cole dines with, **1.** 26
Digby portraits owned by, **1.** 9, 26–8
Gothurst seat of, **10.** 332, **41.** 232n
wife of, **10.** 158n
Wrighte, George (d. 1804):
genealogy of, **10.** 352
Wrighte, Mrs George. *See* Jekyll, Anne
Wrighte. *See also* Wright
Wrington, Somerset:
Cowslip Green near, **31.** 231n
Locke born at, **31.** 290
See also Cowslip Green
Wrinkles:
HW's, **25.** 332
HW thinks, are negligible if one is not in pain, **25.** 540
Wriothesley, Elizabeth (d. 1690), m. 1 Joceline Percy, E. of Northumberland; m. 2 (1673) Ralph Montagu, 3d Bn Montagu; cr. (1689) E. of Montagu:
portrait of, **40.** 283
Wriothesley, Henry (1573–1624), 3d E. of Southampton:
Essex friend of, **9.** 123–4, **10.** 104
portraits of: at Bulstrode Abbey, **10.** 104; at Woburn Abbey, **10.** 123–4
Wriothesley, Sir John (d. 1504), Garter King-of-Arms:
HW asks for plate of, **15.** 250
Wriothesley, Lady Rachel (ca 1637–1723), m. 1 (ca 1653) Francis, Lord Vaughan; m. 2 William, styled Lord Russell:
Berry, Mary, writes life of, **20.** 283n
in Stratford's tragedy, **29.** 224, 225
Letters of: **43.** 295; HW wishes D. of Bedford to print, **20.** 282–3; husband's martyr-

dom discussed in, **28.** 85; Mason inquires about, **28.** 84
Tillotson urged by, to accept archbishopric, **20.** 282n
Wriothesley, Thomas (1607–67), 4th E. of Southampton, 1624; lord treasurer:
daughter of, **20.** 282n, **28.** 84n
Fitzwilliam chaplain to, **28.** 85n
lord treasurer, **20.** 282n
portrait of, at Woburn Abbey, **9.** 124
wife of, **1.** 21n, 182n
Wriothesley. *See also* Wrottesley
Wrist; wrists:
Mann has weakness in, **20.** 401
Writ; writs:
of error: Wilkes applies to attorney-general for, **23.** 12; Wilkes's, argued before House of Lords, **23.** 83
of habeas corpus, Hardwicke proposes extending power of granting, to judges in vacation, **37.** 528
of summons to House of Lords: **31.** 363; peers called by, **18.** 126n
Writer; writers:
foolish, find foolish readers, **35.** 462
not the most sensible men, **38.** 208
See also Author
Writing:
easiest when there is nothing to say, **3.** 78
HW's, is just for his own amusement, **25.** 584
Mann fatigued by, **25.** 597
Writing-box:
HW empties, before taking it on journey, **30.** 253
HW keeps banknotes in, at Arlington Street, **23.** 285
HW keeps letters in, **31.** 326
HW's, always has letter to Hertford in preparation, **38.** 414
Morice puts cameo in, **25.** 94
Mozzi shows Cts of Orford's, to Mann, to be opened in lawyer's presence, **25.** 114
Vere's, stolen and broken open, **35.** 315
Writing-desk:
Mason's, **28.** 157
Writing machine:
Mme du Deffand's, **3.** 5, **8.** 64
Writing paper. *See under* Paper
Wroth, Lady. *See* Sidney, Mary (fl. 1604–21)
Wrotham, Norfolk:
manor of, **2.** 159–60
Wrottesley, Lady. *See* Courtenay, Hon. Frances (1747–1828); Leveson Gower, Mary (1717–78)
Wrottesley, Dorothy (1747–1822), m. (1780) Christian, Baron von Kutzleben:
aunt treats, coldly, after marriage, **33.** 252
Bedford, Ds of, not to be accompanied by, **33.** 208
—— visits, **11.** 346
fortune of, **33.** 228
HW meets, at Lady Cholmondeley's, **33.** 109
HW sees, **33.** 250

[Wrottesley, Dorothy, *continued*]
marriage of, 33. 228–9
Wrottesley, Elizabeth (1745–1822), m. (1769)
Augustus Henry Fitzroy, 3d D. of Grafton:
appearance of, compared to that of Marie-
Antoinette, 4. 122, 31. 182, 32. 254, 41.
284, 43. 349
Grafton, D. of, to marry, 23. 121
Shelburne, Cts of, presented at Court by,
33. 139n
stepdaughter's marriage probably a relief to,
32. 351n
Wrottesley, Frances (1743–1811), m. (1769)
Hon. Capt. (later Adm.) Hugh Pigot:
lady in waiting to Ds of Gloucester, 4. 9
Wrottesley, Hon. Harriet (1754–1824), m.
(1779) William Gardiner:
quadrille danced by, 32. 116
Wrottesley, Sir John (1744–87), 8th Bt, 1769;
M.P.; army officer:
news of D. of York's death taken by, to Eng-
land from Monaco, 7. 321, 366, 22. 554
Paris visited by, 22. 554
York, D. of, prayed for by, 7. 366
—— supposedly has, as groom of the Bed-
chamber, 22. 554n
Wrottesley, Lady Mary. *See* Leveson Gower,
Lady Mary
Wrottesley, Hon. Mary (1740–69):
at private Court ball, 38. 143
Charlotte, Q., has, as maid of honour, 32.
147n, 38. 96–7
——'s household to include, 9. 377
HW mentions, 9. 402, 403
'Wrottesley':
Denbigh, Cts of, mistakes, for 'Wortley,' 9.
395
Wroughton, Richard (1748–1822), actor:
Count of Narbonne to be acted by, 41. 455
—— well acted by, 41. 460
Wroughton, Sir Thomas (d. 1787), K.B.; min-
ister to Poland and Sweden:
(?) Mme du Deffand's social relations with,
4. 241
Wrought Silks and Velvets Bill. *See under* Parliament: acts of
Wroxall ['Wroxhall'], Warwickshire:
Wren writes from, 40. 345
Wroxton Abbey, Oxon, E. of Guilford's seat:
Guilford, E. of, lets George Montagu do
honours of, 35. 72
—— to occupy, 10. 263–4
HW and Montagu to visit, 35. 70
Montagu not to visit, 10. 189, 196–7
portrait of Prince Henry at, 34. 189
visitors to: HW, 9. 155, 166; Montagu, George,
9. 36, 248, 261, 352–3, 10. 30, 185, 217, 226,
263–4, 284, 287, 312; Montagu, John, 10.
312
Wulfstan (?1012–95), St; Bp of Worcester
1062–95:
Cole comments on, 1. 15–16
Wulrich, John (fl. 1476):

master mason of King's College, Cambridge,
1. 17
Wurgaon, Convention of:
English make, with Sreemunth Mhade Row
Narrain, 24. 509n
Wurmser, Dagobert Siegmund (1724–97),
Count; Gen.:
army of, 12. 192n
Austrian troops of, 12. 67n
Condé, P. of, defeated by, at Weissenburg,
12. 51
defeat of, in Italy, 12. 209
Fort Louis besieged by, 12. 73n
French force, to retreat, 39. 508n
French send army against, 12. 89
HW wishes, were Cæsar, 12. 56
victories of, reported, 12. 40, 42, 176
Württemberg, Ds of. *See* Bernardin, Franziska
von (1748–1811); Charlotte Augusta Ma-
tilda (1766–1828)
Württemberg, D. of. *See* Friedrich I (1732–97);
Friedrich II (1754–1816); Karl Eugen (1728–
93)
Württemberg, Q. of. *See* Charlotte Augusta
Matilda (1766–1828)
Württemberg (Germany):
Cowper said to be proud of a paltry order
from, 25. 646
ministers from and to, *see under* Minister
Natter born in, 16. 299n
troops of: defeated, 21. 355; France guaran-
teed, by Versailles treaty, 21. 147n
Württemberg-Oels, Friederike Sofie Charlotte
Auguste von (1751–89), m. (1768) Friedrich
August of Brunswick-Wolfenbüttel, D. of
Württemberg-Oels:
(?) Mme du Deffand's social relations with,
7. 449, 460
Würtz von Rudenz, Wolfgang Ignatz (ca 1685–
1774), Marchese di San Pasquale:
captured at San Lazaro, 19. 267
Würzburg, Bp of. *See* Seinsheim, Adam Fried-
rich von (d. 1779)
Wyat, 'old Mr,' of Charterhouse Yard:
Wyatt, Sir Thomas, said to be ancestor of,
41. 231
Wyat, Mr:
SH visited by, 12. 227
Wyat. *See also* Wyatt
Wyatt, Benjamin (d. 1772), farmer and timber
merchant:
death of, 41. 232
Wyatt, Benjamin Dean (1775–ca 1850), archi-
tect:
SH visited by, 12. 247
Wyatt, James (1746–1813), architect:
Belvoir Castle rebuilt by, 2. 281n
dilatoriness of, at Sandleford Priory, 31. 321
dogs modelled by Mrs Damer, praised by, 35.
385
foreman of, 12. 229
Grecian and Gothic styles of, 35. 635
HW admires taste of, 41. 231–2

HW asks: if he is descended from Sir Thomas Wyatt, 41. 231–2; to design offices for SH, 42. 261

HW disagrees with, about position of picture at Lee, 12. 136–7

HW jokes about William of Wykeham and, 31. 342

HW prefers, to Adam, 24. 93

HW recommends, to D. of Norfolk, 12. 205

HW's correspondence with, 41. 231–2, 42. 261

HW to scold, for destruction of Salisbury chapels, 42. 259–60

Kew Palace designed by, 12. 116n

Lee Priory designed by, 11. 59n, 31. 342

——'s library does honour to, 12. 111

Matthews's Gothic taste corrected by, 42. 220

Oxford buildings designed by, 33. 54–5

Pantheon by, shows taste, 28. 31, 102

Ragley altered by, 9. 118n

Salisbury Cathedral altered by, 16. 145n

screen at St George's Chapel, Windsor, worthy of, 11. 362

SH offices built by, 11. 74n

Wyatt, Sir Thomas, ought to be ancestor to, 43. 293

Wyatt, John:
Copt Hall designed by, 9. 93n

Wyatt, Sir Thomas (?1503–42), Kt; poet; diplomatist:
Anne Boleyn's relations with, 1. 261, 270

Bonner abused by, 28. 66

—— accuses, of high treason, 42. 379n

British Museum has MSS by, 42. 370, 379

Cole's notes on, 1. 261–2, 265, 269–70

'Defence' of: Gray asks if HW wants, 14. 117; Gray offers to collate MS of, 14. 116; HW prints Gray's transcript of, 1. 229n, 42. 379

drawing of, 41. 320

HW asks James Wyatt if he is descended from, 41. 231, 232

HW asks Mason to write life of, 28. 27

HW at work on life of, 1. 271, 28. 39–40

HW prints speech of, in Miscellaneous Antiquities, 41. 256

HW's account of, in Miscellaneous Antiquities, 42. 423

HW writes life of, 13. 47, 42. 369–70

Henry VIII's letters from, 42. 370n

Holbein's portrait of, at Kensington Palace, 41. 320

letters of, to Henry VIII, Gray has copies of, 14. 116

lyric by, 28. 191n

of St John's College, Cambridge, 1. 269

papers of, 1. 255

Percy may use HW's drawing of, to have print made, 41. 320

——'s edition of, 41. 320n, 42. 369

print of, 1. 183, 189, 261

proverb used by, 1. 303, 304

said to attend lectures at Oxford, 1. 266, 269

Seven Penitential Psalms by, 42. 368

speech and letters of: copied by Gray, 28. 27; disliked by Mason, 28. 63, 65, 165; disliked by public, 28. 66; HW to print, in Miscellaneous Antiquities, 28. 39–40

speeches by, may be used by Bp Percy, 41. 320

verses in manner of, 1. 357

Wyatt the architect worthy to be descendant of, 28. 31, 43. 293

Wyatt, Sir Thomas (?1521–54):
Cole's notes about, 1. 262, 265, 272

HW asks about, 1. 255

rebellion of: 9. 123n; Proctor publishes tract about, 42. 447, 448

Wyatt family:
portraits of, 41. 231

Wycherley, William (1640–1716), dramatist:
coarseness of dramas by, 33. 564

Country Wife by, adapted by Garrick, 33. 507n

Plain Dealer by: Gray alludes to, 13. 62; 'Widow Blackacre' in, 32. 13

Wycombe, E. See Petty, John Henry (1765–1809)

Wydevill, Anthony (ca 1440–83), 2d E. Rivers, 1469:
beheaded at Pontefract, 35. 269

Dictes and Sayings translated by, 40. 119

Edward IV receives book from, 40. 119n

HW does not acquit Richard III of death of, 15. 183

miniature of Caxton's presentation by, to Edward IV, 41. 112n

Paston letters mention, 33. 559

print of, 1. 140, 16. 1n

widow of, 2. 365

Wydevill, Elizabeth. See Elizabeth (Wydevill or Woodville) (1437–92)

Wydevill, Katharine (b. ca 1458), m. 1 Henry Stafford, D. of Buckingham; m. 2 (ca 1485) Jasper Tudor, cr. (1485) D. of Bedford; m. 3 (1492) Sir Richard Wingfield:
peerage of husband of, corrected, 43. 77

position of, at Henry VII's Court, 2. 363

Wydevill, Richard (d. 1469), cr. (1448) Bn de Ryvers, (1466) E. of Ryvers:
Paston letters mention, 33. 559

Wye, River:
Gilpin's Observations on, 29. 277

More, Hannah, sails down, 31. 320

Wyke, manor of:
Robinson buys, 41. 325n

Wykeham, William of. See William (1324–1404) of Wykeham

Wymondefold, Mrs. See Knight, Hon. Henrietta

Wymondefold, Charles, of Lockinge, Berks:
Child, Josiah, loses action for crim. con. with wife of, 20. 355–6n

Wynch, ——, governor of Bengal:
Rajah of Tanjore deposed by, 23. 561n

Wyndham, ——:
early visitor to Chamouni, 30. 2n

Wyndham, Lady Anne Barbara Frances. *See* Villiers, Lady Anne Barbara Frances

Wyndham, Lady Catherine. *See* Seymour, Lady Catherine

Wyndham, Sir Charles (1710–63), 4th Bt, 1740; 2d E. of Egremont, 1750; M.P.:
appetite of, **22.** 158–9
appointment for, in state department, **9.** 392
Augsburg to have been post of, **21.** 540
Bedford, D. of, may be displeased at appointment of, **38.** 134
Bristol's correspondence with, **21.** 548n, 557n, 558n
brother dies at same age as, **24.** 25
brother of, **22.** 311n
Bute chooses, **21.** 540n
Cabinet Council calls, from Bath, **22.** 96n
Choiseul's peace negotiations with, **22.** 38n
'convert,' **18.** 399
death and property of, **22.** 158–9
Devonshire, D. of, leaves key and staff with, **22.** 96
earldom to revert to, **20.** 81
Edgcumbe's gambling losses amuse, **30.** 56
Egremont title goes to, **20.** 124
extravagance of, **21.** 200
Fox, Henry, has, to supper, **30.** 56n
Fuentes's negotiations with, **22.** 5n
George III said to have been told by, about Bute's resignation plans, **10.** 64–5
Granville tries to get Northumberland title for, **20.** 12, 81
Gray, Sir James, may obtain leave from, to go home in case a transfer to Spain is imminent, **22.** 107n
Grenville recommends, as secretary of state, **31.** 24n
groom of the chambers receives list from, of paintings at Petworth, **40.** 318
HW's correspondence with, **40.** 280–2
Halifax forms triumvirate with Grenville and, **9.** 33n
—— may succeed, **10.** 29
Hardwicke's speech disparaged by, **9.** 38
—— thinks, too sensible to accept secretaryship of state, **21.** 76n
Hartington's hunting trip said by, to indicate Whig security, **9.** 144
health of: apoplectic lethargy, **22.** 17; apoplexy, **35.** 308; recovered, **22.** 33
Henley's advertisements mention, **30.** 56
house built by, in Piccadilly, **9.** 255n, **22.** 96n
kitchen and cellar of, closed to visitors, **40.** 317
lists of portraits at Petworth not found by, **40.** 318
Mann anxious to hear of successor to, **22.** 23
——'s letter to, describes Spain's motives, **22.** 100
Melcombe may succeed, as secretary of state, **22.** 17

Melo assured by, of English aid to Portugal, **22.** 23n
—— seeks English military aid through, **21.** 559n
Monckton's dispatch to, **22.** 16n
Parliamentary address of loyalty to George II seconded by, **18.** 399
Petworth left to, **9.** 97n
—— occupied by, **21.** 76n
pictures added by, at Petworth, **40.** 319
pictures sent by, to be cleaned and framed, **40.** 319
Pitt (Chatham) succeeded by, as secretary of state, **38.** 132, 134
Rigby told by, about Darnley and 'Peg' Woffington, **30.** 52n
—— visits, in Somerset, **30.** 51n
secretary of state, **9.** 392, **21.** 72, 75–6, 98, 540, 541, **22.** 17, 23, 96
Somerset, D. of, leaves borough and estate to, **20.** 11
——'s relations with, **20.** 81n
son of, **9.** 126
supposed Maratti painting bought by, **21.** 172
Townshend, Vcts, quarrels with, **9.** 47
Waldegrave esteemed by, **40.** 281, 282
Waldegrave, Cts, offered Petersham house by, **40.** 280–2
well-bred, **21.** 541
wife of, **9.** 342n, **28.** 286n, **30.** 327n
Wilkes complains to, **22.** 138

Wyndham, Hon. Charles William (1760–1828), M.P.:
(?) alleged daughter of, **11.** 255n
(?) arrest of, for riot, **25.** 565
Keppel, Mrs, entertains, at Isleworth, **33.** 482
Worsley, Lady, has affair with, **25.** 228

Wyndham, Sir Edward (ca 1667–95), 2d Bt: grandson dies at same age as, **24.** 25

Wyndham, Elizabeth (d. 1769), m. (1749) Hon. George Grenville:
Bromfield's letter offends, **40.** 327
brother of, **22.** 311n
death of, **32.** 38
Drawing-Room at George IV's baptism attended by, **38.** 175
grandfather's legacy to, **19.** 11
HW hopes that *Letter from Xo Ho* may divert, **40.** 94
marriage of, **9.** 85

Wyndham, Lady Elizabeth Alicia Maria (1752–1826), m. (1771) Henry Herbert cr. (1780) Bn Porchester and (1793) E. of Carnarvon:
brother's engagement pleases, **33.** 205
lady of the Bedchamber to Q. Charlotte, **12.** 108n

Wyndham, Lady Frances (1755–95), m. (1776) Hon. Charles Marsham, 3d Bn Romney, 1793; cr. (1801) E. of Romney:
accouchement of, **31.** 189
brother's fiancée's family to be visited by, **33.** 20

Wyndham, George (1787–1869), cr. (1859) Lord Leconfield:
Petworth descends to, 9. 97n

Wyndham, George O'Brien (1751–1837), 3d E. of Egremont, 1763:
baptism of, 9. 126
Barrymore, Cts of, might wed, 39. 176
brother of, reared by Lord Thomond, 32. 198
engagement of, rumoured, 6. 190
HW sees, at Gloucester House, 25. 68
Hamilton's bequest to, 12. 202
'libertine,' 6. 190
liveries of, at Petworth, 32. 154
Melbourne, Vcts, said to have had twins and son by, 32. 390n
paintings owned by, at Petworth, unidentified, 40. 317–18
person and fortune of, 25. 68
Petworth the seat of, 12. 206n
Ranelagh visited by, 25. 68
Thomond partial to, 32. 199
——'s will investigated by, 32. 198–9
uncle's real estate goes to, 24. 25
Waldegrave, Lady Charlotte Maria, jilted by, in broken engagement, 7. 238n, 25. 68, 74–5, 77, 544, 29. 69, 72, 306, 31. 200, 33. 107n, 204–5, 206, 209–10, 451
Yorks meeting attended by, 28. 488n

Wyndham, Henry Penruddocke (1736–1819), M.P.:
Bubb Dodington's memoirs published by, 25. 503n
(?) letters of, sent by Warton to HW, 42. 121

Wyndham, Lady Katharine. See Seymour, Lady Catherine

Wyndham, Hon. Percy Charles (1757–1833), M.P.:
Thomond's money expected to go to, 39. 179n
—— takes government of, 32. 198

Wyndham, Thomas (ca 1686–1752), of Clearwell and Cromer; M.P.:
(?) anecdote of, 28. 302–3
birth date of, corrected, 43. 300

Wyndham, Thomas (1696–1777), M.P.:
Bubb Dodington's heir, 22. 80
(?) letters of, sent by Warton to HW, 42. 121

Wyndham, Mrs Thomas. See Wells, Winifred

Wyndham, Sir William (?1688–1740), 3d Bt; M.P.:
anecdote of Sir Robert Walpole and, unknown to HW, 15. 151–2
Anne's chancellor of Exchequer, 39. 179n
birth date of, corrected, 43. 353
Bolingbroke's letter to, 6. 167, 20. 452, 37. 354
chancellor of Exchequer, 25. 68n, 39. 179n
Conway entertained by, 37. 51
daughter of, 9. 85n
Egremont grandson of, 29. 69, 33. 205
grandson of, to marry Sir Robert Walpole's great-granddaughter, 25. 68

HW hears, in House of Commons, 15. 152
Jacobitism of, 20. 60
marriage of, 29. 69n
son dies at same age as, 24. 25
son of, 18. 399, 21. 24n, 39. 179n
Walpole, Sir Robert, opponent of, 25. 68n
—— refuses to send, to the Tower, 23. 289
wife of, 6. 241n, 10. 94n

Wyndham. See also Windham

Wyndham family:
Percy library at Petworth closed by, to visitors, 40. 317

Wyndham family, of Felbrigg, Norfolk:
Mann descended from Edward I through, 20. 13n

Wyndham Knatchbull. See Knatchbull

Wyndham O'Brien (formerly Wyndham), Percy (?1723–74), cr. (1756) E. of Thomond; cofferer; M.P.:
Cavendish, Lord Frederick, talks to, at White's, 41. 73
cofferer, 9. 406, 38. 142
death of, 24. 25
dies intestate, 24. 25, 32. 198
(?) Devonshire, Ds of, confides economies to, 37. 341
Devonshire, Ds of, consults, about proposed peerage, 21. 24n
Devonshires entertain, at Chatsworth, 9. 295
earldom granted to, 9. 203, 21. 24
Egremont's inheritance from, 39. 179
grandfather's legacy to, 20. 11
HW and Strafford visit, 33. 387
HW visits, at Shortgrove, 10. 30
landscape effects of, at Shortgrove, 10. 30
Parliamentary address debated by, 37. 414
Parliamentary speech by, 37. 414
resignation of, as cofferer, 22. 311
Treasury post assigned to, 9. 180
Treasury post left by, 21. 24
uncle leaves estate to, 21. 24n
will not made by, 24. 25

Wynn, Lady. See Grenville, Charlotte

Wynn, Mr:
French not spoken by, 37. 309
Tylney accompanied by, at Paris, 37. 309

Wynn, Dorothy (or Wynn, Frances, m. Henry Soame):
(?) Coventry, Cts of, to be eclipsed by, 9. 256–7
(?) Piozzi, Mrs, comments upon, 9. 256n

Wynn, Lady Henrietta. See Somerset, Lady Henrietta

Wynn, Sir John (1553–1626), Bt; antiquary:
print of, 2. 167n, 170n, 43. 69

Wynn, Sir John (1701–73), 2d Bt; M.P.:
election of: Trevor petitions against, 18. 392n; upheld, 18. 394n
Piozzi, Mrs, comments on, 9. 256n

Wynn, Richard (ca 1588–1649) of Gwydir, 2d Bt, 1662; M.P.:
accounts of, as treasurer to Henrietta Maria, 41. 160–1

Wynn, Thomas (1736–1807), cr. (1776) Bn
  Newborough; M.P.:
  Piozzi, Mrs, comments on, 9. 256n
Wynn, Sir Watkin Williams (?1693–1749), 3d
  Bt, 1740; M.P.:
  Bridgnorth mostly belongs to, 40. 14
  called 'Prince of Wales,' 30. 292n, 34. 95
  defeated in Welsh election, 18. 401
  French insurrection might be led by, 19. 310
  George II said by, to be absent from Det-
    tingen, 18. 305–6
  Jacobite, 17. 243n, 19. 310n, 30. 292n
  Lee seconded by, 17. 243
  Lovat's trial attended by, 19. 381
  named in Secret Committee lists, 17. 385
  Opposition assembly addressed by, at St Al-
    ban's Tavern, 20. 50
  oratorical mannerisms of, 30. 292, 292n
  Parliamentary debate by, on privately-raised
    regiments, 26. 17
  Parliamentary membership of, corrected, 43.
    241
  Parliament entered by, after his petition
    over Denbighshire election, 17. 343–4
  Place Bill to be prepared by, 17. 295n
  Traquair converses with, about Old Pre-
    tender's affairs, 19. 381
  vast estate of, 30. 292n
  Welsh races attended by, 18. 305
Wynn, Sir Watkin Williams (1748–89), 4th Bt,
  1749; M.P.:
  dinner given by, at country house, 23. 64
  father of, called 'Prince of Wales,' 34. 95
  Mann to be accompanied by, at investiture,
    23. 60
  Patch portrays, 26. 45
  play to be acted at Welsh seat of, 41. 367
  Poussin painting bought by, 23. 466
  Powis, Cts of, opposes, in Montgomeryshire
    election, 39. 186–7
  Villiers handsomer than, 39. 152
  Welsh revenue reforms opposed by, 33. 82n
Wynn, Sir Watkin Williams (1772–1840), 5th
  Bt, 1789:
  (?) birth of, 31. 170
Wynn. See also Wynne
Wynne, William:
  Life of Sir Leoline Jenkins, The, by, 1. 114
Wynne, William (1692–1765), sergeant-at-law:
  defence of, printed by Nichols, 29. 294
  denies HW's story about him, 15. 110–11
  said by HW to have borrowed Atterbury's
    speech, 13. 32–3
Wynne, Sir William (d. 1815), Kt, 1788; bar-
  rister; LL.D.; master of Prerogative Court of
  Canterbury:
  counsel for Ds of Kingston, 24. 193, 196,
    28. 261n
  Parson surrogate for, 30. 377
Wynne. See also Winn; Wynn
Wynnstay, Denbighshire, seat of the Wynns:
  Garrick visits, 41. 367n, 368n

HW deplores decline of, 34. 95
  theatre at, 34. 4
Wyrcester or Wyrcestre, Wyllyam (or William)
  of. See Worcester, William
Wyverston (Suffolk):
  Barnardiston of, 1. 189n
Wyvill, Rev. Christopher (1740–1822), political
  writer:
  common sense would be of use to, 29. 197
  delegate from Yorks, 29. 140n
  Irish Committee of Correspondence encour-
    aged by, 29. 314n
  manifesto of, ridiculed by HW, 29. 14–16,
    347
  Mason defends, against HW, 29. 20
  sent to London as deputy, 29. 92n
  speaks at meeting, 28. 490n
  success of, makes him over-confident, 29. 127
  tract of, on removing subscription to Thirty-
    Nine Articles, 29. 25, 26
  Yorkshire Association instituted by Mason
    and, 29. 328n
  ——s historian, 28. 483n
  ——'s organization aided by, 43. 304
Wyvville, packet boat:
  Hartington and staff go to Ireland on, 37.
    392n

                            X

Xavier, ship:
  in Spanish fleet, 17. 286
Xebec; xebecs:
  armed, Jesuits escorted by, 22. 516n
  Dutch, reach Isola Rossa with English war
    ships, 18. 151n
  English have, on Corsican coast, 19. 232
  Spanish: Benedict XIV allows, to enter, 18.
    291; Benedict XIV does not allow, to un-
    load, 18. 296, 300; blockaded at Genoa,
    18. 257; crews flee from, 18. 301; driven
    back by Mathews's ships when about to
    return, 18. 301; escape of, from Civita Vec-
    chia, 18. 296, 300–1; escape of, from Ma-
    jorca to Civita Vecchia, 18. 287, 300;
    repelled from Orbetello, 18. 287
  Sultan should send, to Leghorn with HW's
    letters, 11. 161
  Turkish, defeated by Russians, 23. 234
  See also Postillion
Xenophon (b. ca 430 B.C.), Greek general and
  historian:
  New York may produce counterpart of, 24. 62
  on Spartan permission of robbery, 15. 227
  shines after defeat, 32. 171
Xerxes (d. 472 B.C.), K. of Persia:
  Greeks' battle with, 37. 19
  HW's name for George III, 38. 315
  'removal' of Mt Athos by, 15. 225
Xeuxis (d. ca 40 B.C.), Greek painter:
  composition piece of, 30. 324
Ximenes, Leonardo:
  Fantoni's criticism of, 22. 527n

Ximenes d'Aragona, Marchesa di. *See* Scarlatti-Rondinelli, Elena Vittoria

Ximenes d'Aragona, Ferdinando (d. 1816), Marchese d'Esch, Priore di Romagna:
England to be visited by, **23**. 25
mother of, **23**. 25

Ximenes de Cisneros, Francisco (1436–1517), Abp of Toledo; cardinal:
Polyglot Bible of, **42**. 240

Xo Ho. *See Letter from Xo Ho, A*, by HW

Y

Y.:
verses on SH by, **2**. 78, 79n

Y, Charlotte-Louise-Thérèse d', m. (1770) Louis-Armand de Rogres, Marquis de Champignelles:
(?) SH visited by, **12**. 250

Y, G. *See* Yeates, George

Yacht (*or* Yatch); yachts:
Caroline Matilda to travel in, **23**. 409
Charlotte, Q., reaches Suffolk coast on, **38**. 115–16
George II orders his, for Hanover visit, **19**. 483n
HW describes, at Twickenham boat-race, **11**. 86
HW sails to Dover in, **17**. 142
Karl Wilhelm Ferdinand's, seen by sea-captain near Holland, **38**. 312
Kingston, Ds of, has, **24**. 333, **32**. 390
Newcastle, D. of, finds, too small for his travelling gear, **19**. 484–5
royal, being expedited, **29**. 202, 204
Wade summons, **37**. 186
See also Charlotte; Fubbs; Katherine; William and Mary

Yamacraw Indians:
Oglethorpe brings party of, to England, **30**. 94, **43**. 314
outlawed Creeks, settled near Savannah, **42**. 236n

Yarborough, Bn. *See* Anderson Pelham, Charles

Yardley, (?) Edward, printseller in New Inn Passage, Clare Market:
'A Modern Venus' published by, **35**. 512n
(?) Kirgate aided by, in printing *Jardins modernes*, **42**. 135n

Yarmouth, Cts of. *See* Fagnani, Maria Emily (1771–1856); Ingram Shepheard, Isabella Anne (1760–1834); Wendt, Amalie Sophie Marianne von (1704–65)

Yarmouth, E. of. *See* Seymour-Conway, Francis (1743–1822); Seymour-Conway, Francis Charles (1777–1842)

Yarmouth, Norfolk:
address from, to George III, ill-attended, **41**. 311n
Bedford, D. of, windbound at, **9**. 32, 34
Carteret puts in at roadstead of, **18**. 80
Galbret ordered to, **21**. 336n

HW visits, **40**. 21
Heighington organist at, **13**. 84n
man of war to convey Houghton pictures from, **43**. 68–9
Norfolk militia should be quartered at, **39**. 298
Orford, E. of, high steward of, **23**. 482n
Pitt and Legge receive freedom of, **21**. 87
squadron sent to cruise between Flushing and, **21**. 336n
Townshend, Charles, cannot be re-elected from, **21**. 26
Walpole, Sir Edward, declines to be M.P. for, **39**. 95
Walpole, Hon. Richard, to be M.P. for, **39**. 95

Yarmouth, English ship:
French ships pursued by, **19**. 411
Portsmouth reached by, **30**. 112n
West Indies fleet convoyed by, **24**. 392n

Yasous I (the Great), K. of Abyssinia 1680–1704:
Bruce mentions, **39**. 476

Yasous II, K. of Abyssinia 1729–53:
Abuna cannot be installed by, because money all spent on Venetian mirrors, **39**. 476
Bruce mentions, **39**. 476

Yatch. *See* Yacht

Yate, Ann, m. Robert Foote:
(?) HW gives breakfast to, at SH, **39**. 475
SH visited by, **11**. 81n

Yate, Richard:
Letter in Defence of Dr Middleton, A, by, **15**. 298, 300

Yates, Mrs, of Twickenham:
SH visited by, **12**. 221, 223, 229, 230, 239, 240, 241

Yates, Mrs James. *See* Swan, Anne

Yates, Sir Joseph (1722–70), Kt, 1763; judge of Court of King's Bench:
Wilkes appears before, **23**. 12

Yates, Lowther (d. 1798), Master of St Catharine's College:
vice-chancellor, **2**. 241n

Yates, Richard (ca 1706–96), actor:
Cumberland's *Brothers* acted by, **32**. 39n
(?) *High Life Below Stairs* acted by, **31**. 14n
School for Scandal acted by, **41**. 363

Yates, Mrs Richard. *See* Graham, Mary Ann

Yates. *See also* Yeates

Yatman (Yateman), Mr, apothecary:
(?) witnesses Miss Gunning's oath, **11**. 205

Yawning at dull play:
Mme du Deffand's witticism on, **8**. 60

Yearly Chronicle for 1761. See under Baldwin, Henry

Yearsley, John (d. 1803), labourer:
deed by, relinquishing wife's profits, **31**. 244n
wife's money protected from, **33**. 537

Yearsley, Mrs John. *See* Cromartie, Ann

Yeast:
medicinal use of, **3**. 125

Yeates, George (fl. 1660), engraver:
print by, of Bp Montaigne, **1**. 149

'Ye British Dames':
  verses to, **33.** 125
Yecla, Prior of San Juan:
  Madrid rioters convey demands to Charles III by, **39.** 63
Yeldham, Essex:
  Platel rector of, **10.** 331n
Yellow fever:
  Alexander the Great and Cæsar would look badly after, **21.** 290
  Churchill, George, thought dead of, **34.** 218
  Dupin de Chenonceaux dies of, **3.** 369n
Yellow ribbon. *See under* Ribbon
Yelverton, Anne (d. 1698), m. 1 (1655) Robert Montagu, 3d E. of Manchester; m. 2 (1688) Charles Montagu, cr. (1714) E. of Halifax:
  genealogy of, **10.** 351
  portrait of, **10.** 338
Yelverton, Lady Barbara (1760–81), m. Edward Thoroton Gould:
  appearance of, **10.** 339
  title of Grey might go to, **10.** 339
Yelverton, Barry, Irish attorney-general:
  Irish Parliamentary activity of, **39.** 350n
  Irish Parliamentary legislation regulated by bill by, **25.** 682n
  Irish Parliamentary resolution by, **25.** 453n
  Rutland threatens prosecution by, on national congress elections, **25.** 529n
Yelverton, George Augustus (1727–58), styled Vct de Longueville; 2d E. of Sussex, 1731:
  (?) at Chesterfield's assembly, **37.** 327
  Court position of, as Bedchamber lord to George III as P. of Wales, **10.** 339, **20.** 247
  death and burial of, in London, **10.** 339
  HW compares, to captive in Glover's *Boadicea*, **9.** 158
  HW's acquaintance with, **15.** 115
  hostage at Paris, **10.** 339
  pension of, **10.** 339
Yelverton, Sir Henry (1566–1629), Kt; M.P.:
  portraits of, **10.** 338
Yelverton, Henry (1728–99), 3d E. of Sussex, 1758:
  appearance and halting speech of, **10.** 339
  army training of, **10.** 339
  Easton Maudit, seat of, **10.** 338
  family, finances, and marriage of, **10.** 339
  hostage at Paris, **4.** 347n
  Percy does not agree with, **15.** 114–15
Yelverton, Mrs Henry. *See* Hall, Hester
Yelverton family:
  Bp Morton's relations with, **10.** 339
  coat of arms of, **10.** 338
  Easton Maudit, seat of, **10.** 88n
  monuments of, at Easton Maudit, **10.** 338–9
Yelverton library:
  locked up, **15.** 114
Yenikale, in the Crimea:
  Turks refuse, to Russia because of its mosques, **23.** 469
Yeo, Richard (d. 1779), painter:
  Scotts often visited by, **10.** 330, 331

Yeomen of the Guard ('Gentlemen Pensioners'):
  Berkeley said to get position in, **18.** 143
  changes in command of, **17.** 457, 492, **18.** 551, **21.** 25
  Dorset succeeds Falmouth as captain of, **25.** 241
  Edgcumbe, captain of, **25.** 518n
  George II's coffin carried by, at funeral, **9.** 322
  HW calls, 'band of pensioners,' **25.** 241
  Montagu, D. of, captain of, **20.** 79n
  Newcastle, D. of, dragged upstairs by, **35.** 169
  picture of, at Hatfield, **40.** 199
  Torrington appointed captain of, **19.** 221n
  See also Bathurst, Allen (1684–1775), Bn Bathurst; Hobart, John (1723–93), Bn Hobart
Yertzin, 'Countess,' of Mecklenburg-Strelitz:
  Charlotte, Q., ashamed of, **38.** 401
  Frederick II receives box on the ear from, **38.** 402
  Guerchy entertains, **38.** 407
  HW mentions, **22.** 239
  Northumberland House assembly attended by, **38.** 401, 402
  William Henry, P., disparages, **38.** 407
Yew; yews (taxus):
  clipped, preferable to modern landscape oddities, **35.** 389
  pyramidal, at Drayton, **10.** 90
  trimmed, at Hampton Court, **33.** 42
Yoddrall, —:
  Mann escorted by, **23.** 60n
Yolande (1428–83) d'Anjou, m. (1444) Ferry, Comte de Vaudemont; Duchesse de Lorraine, 1473:
  age of, in 1444, **14.** 76
  painting of, **14.** 69
Yonge, Lady. *See* Cleeve, Anne (d. 1833); Howard, Hon. Anne (d. 1775)
Yonge, —, apothecary:
  Waldegrave got medicine from, **36.** 259
Yonge, Sir George (1733–1812), 5th Bt, 1755; M.P.; secretary at war 1782–94:
  Hotham, Miss, entertains, **12.** 154
  Jacobins' detection reported by, **12.** 25
  Jeffreys, Mrs, visited by, **12.** 25
  Newcastle, D. of, consulted by, about cider counties' opposition, **38.** 459n
  resignation of, from Admiralty, **23.** 180, **39.** 122
Yonge, Jane (d. 1783):
  Blandford, Marchioness of, called on by, **10.** 94
  HW's joke about Bedford's wearing flowers taken seriously by, **10.** 94
  SH visited by, **31.** 127
Yonge, Philip (ca 1709–83), Bp of Norwich, 1761:
  death of, **33.** 400
Yonge, Sir William (ca 1693–1755), 4th Bt; 1731; M.P.; versifier:
  Bedford, D. of, attacks, **17.** 336

Cornish petition presented by, **17**. 233

death of, **20**. 518, **33**. 400, **35**. 245

Earle proposed by, **17**. 243

Frederick, P. of Wales, wants Harrington to receive letter in presence of, **19**. 175

HW identifies, **34**. 257

impeachment of, intended, **17**. 344

Marriage Bill opposed by, **20**. 383n

Murder Preventing Act presented to House of Commons by, **20**. 317n

Newcastle, D. of, supports, **17**. 336n

Parliamentary bill proposed by, **19**. 396

Parliamentary committee headed by, **19**. 387n

Parliamentary debate by, on privately-raised regiments, **26**. 13, 15, 16, 17, 18

Parliamentary membership of, corrected, **43**. 240

Parliamentary speeches by, **17**. 297, **40**. 50, **42**. 496

political ballads by, with Winnington and Sir C. H. Williams, **30**. 314

vice-treasurership of Ireland rumoured for, **37**. 219

vice-treasurer of Ireland, **19**. 155, 256, **20**. 518

Walpole, Sir Robert, calls, a fine speaker but of trifling character, **17**. 233n

wife of, **10**. 122n

Yonge. *See also* Jong; Young

'Yorick':

Hamlet's soliloquy on, **25**. 7

York, Abp of. *See* Blackburne, Lancelot (1658–1743); Bowet, Henry (d. 1423); Dawes, Sir William (1671–1724); Drummond, Robert Hay (1711–76); Gilbert, John (1693–1761); Harsnett, Samuel (1561–1631); Herring, Thomas (1693–1757); Hutton, Matthew (1693–1758); Kemp, John (ca 1380–1454); Markham, William (1719–1807); Rotherham, Thomas (1423–1500); Walby, Robert (d. 1398); Wolsey, Thomas (ca 1475–1533)

York, Archbishops of:

Cawood Palace belongs to, **2**. 334

York, Cardinal (*or* Cardinal of). *See* Henry Benedict Maria Clement (Stuart) (1725–1807)

York, Dean of. *See* Fountayne, John

York, Ds of. *See* Frederica Charlotte Ulrica Catherina (1767–1820); Holand, Joan de (ca 1380–1434); Hyde, Anne (1637–71); Isabel (ca 1355–92) of Castile; Mowbray, Lady Anne de (1472–81); Nevill, Lady Cecily (1415–95)

York, D. of. *See* Edmund (Plantagenet) (1341–1402); Edward (Plantagenet) (ca 1373–1415); Edward Augustus (1739–67); Frederick (1763–1827); Henry Benedict Maria Clement (Stuart) (1725–1807); James II (1633–1701); Richard (Plantagenet) (1411–60); Richard (Plantagenet) (1473–ca 83)

York, Dukes of:

bagnios and taverns will be frequented by, **20**. 155

York, Mr (fl. 1776), upholsterer:

Cole buys Delft vase from, **2**. 16, 20

York. *See also* Yorke

York, Yorks:

archbishopric of: Herring receives, **18**. 201n, 203; refused by several bishops, **18**. 203

assembly at, Irish girls fit to appear at, **37**. 336

Berrys receive letters at, **12**. 83–4, 85

'Black Swan' at, **28**. 56

'Blue Boar' at, animals exhibited at, **28**. 91

Bosville, Mrs, lives in, **18**. 242

Burgh moves to, **28**. 199n

Carlisle, E. of, dying at, **37**. 561

Cathedral at, *see* York Cathedral

Christian VII to visit, **23**. 41

—— unable to see races at, **23**. 48, **39**. 108

circulating library at, **28**. 148

Clough of, **7**. 116n

Coney St in: **16**. 26n; Ward bookseller in, **15**. 111n

Cope's defeat becomes known at, **19**. 126

'dullest of all provincial towns,' **28**. 23

election; elections at, **17**. 301, **28**. 173, **39**. 197

HW may get book from Cæsar Ward at, **16**. 26

HW to visit, **28**. 37

HW writes from, **30**. 256

Herbert attends Charles I at, **16**. 5

Hoyland at, **28**. 11

Kaye, prebendary of, **29**. 40n

London as quiet as, **31**. 5

——'s example followed by, with regard to Pitt, **21**. 546

Lord Mayor and aldermen of, to hear Mason's sermon, **28**. 362

lunatic asylum at, **16**. 210

Mason in residence at, **28**. 83, 133, 198, 231, 244, 352, 452, 471, 473, **29**. 17n, 93, 143, 153–4, 275–6

——'s pamphlet published at, **16**. 210

—— to return to, **35**. 368

Middleton educated at, **15**. 305

minster at, *see* York Cathedral

mob at, destroys house, **33**. 96

Peckitt of, **1**. 145n

petitions from, **7**. 368

physician from, joins rebels, **19**. 180

post-house at, **11**. 18, 47

Press at: *English Garden* printed at, **28**. 231, 234, **29**. 93, 120, 213; *Poems and Memoirs of Gray* printed at, **28**. 83, 87, 163; slow but sure, **29**. 195, 248

races at, **1**. 233, **11**. 50, 58, 59, 62, **23**. 48, **28**. 333, 429, 459, **30**. 234, **34**. 64n, **35**. 329, **37**. 562

remoteness of, **28**. 260

Rockingham Club at, **28**. 362

Salisbury, E. of, drives coach to, **10**. 348

Smelt's speech at, **29**. 1n

theatre at, **11**. 64n

Thompson, M.P. for, **34**. 257

[York, Yorks, *continued*]
'Tory town,' 28. 362
Warbeck, Perkin, issues proclamation at, 14. 176, 15. 120
Ward writes from, 40. 130
women of, compared to those of Florence, 20. 427
York, County of. *See* Yorkshire
York, House of (dynasty of Dukes of York):
and Lancaster, HW jokes about, 38. 468
Croyland chronicler no enemy to, 14. 163
Henry VII and Henry VIII behead heirs of, 42. 208
history of, like that of highway robbers, 41. 157
lawful line, 15. 174
wars of, 11. 296
York Buildings, London:
Adelphi bounded by, 28. 102n
Henderson's house in, 42. 4n
Poulett's house in, 35. 224n
York Buildings Co.:
miners settled by, at Strontean, 26. 31
York Buildings Waterworks, London:
obelisks make Wentworth Woodhouse resemble, 35. 267
Trinity symbolized by, 35. 156
York Cathedral ('York Minster'):
bell of, tinkles Mason to prayers, 28. 181
choir screen of, 28. 100, 106, 108, 254, 259–60
estate given to, by Q. Philippa, 28. 42
Eyre residentiary of, 2. 23n
HW's opinion of, 1. 275–8
history of construction of, 16. 49
Kaye preaches in, 29. 40
live princes were not slighted by chapter of, 1. 276
Mason finds cold of, intolerable, 28. 369, 29. 275–6
—— holds prebend in, 29. 349
——'s anthem-book for, 29. 190
—— writes Fast Day sermon for, 28. 351–2
monument to Dealtry in, 28. 97
opinions of, 1. 10
organ in, 16. 47, 48
roof of, being repaired, 28. 84
statues of kings on screen of, 1. 276
Tatton, prebendary of, 2. 304n
William of Hatfield's tomb in, 1. 275, 2. 46; *see also under* William (1336–44), of Hatfield
York Courant:
advertisement in, 28. 90
Yorke, ——:
farm of, at Twickenham, 42. 417
Yorke, Miss —— (d. 1759):
death of, 21. 312
Yorke, Amabel (1751–1833), Bns Lucas, 1797; cr. (1816) Cts de Grey; m. (1772) Alexander Hume Campbell, styled Vct Polwarth; cr. (1776) Bn Hume:
HW dislikes behaviour of, 33. 242
sister of, 33. 242

Yorke, Caroline (1765–1818), m. (1790) John Eliot, 2d Bn Eliot, 1784; cr. (1815) E. of St Germans:
HW receives etchings by, through Bull, 42. 237n, 238
HW's correspondence with, 42. 238
Yorke, Catherine (1732–1815) m. (1772) James John Clavering, K.B., 1776:
HW sees, at Lady Bute's, 12. 69
Yorke, Hon. Charles (1722–70), lord chancellor, 1770; M.P.; solicitor-gen. 1756–61; attorney-gen. 1762–3, 1765–6:
amendments to Wilkes case approved by, 38. 325
attorney-general, 9. 413, 22. 263, 268, 443
attorney-general's place resigned by, 10. 109, 110, 22. 443, 38.. 285
bereavements of, 21. 312
biographical information about, corrected, 43. 197, 270
Clarke does not leave fortune to, 38. 468
Conway opposed by, 41. 66
Court and Opposition both ridicule, 38. 472
Court will not be rejoined by, while Norton is attorney-general, 38. 285
Dalrymple, Sir John, protected by, 28. 95
daughter of, 42. 237n, 238
death of, 4. 311, 349, 23. 178, 187, 25. 463n, 39. 121
Dowdeswell's motion advised by, 22. 495n
Du Deffand, Mme, inquires about, 4. 347
East India Co. inquiry opposed by, 41. 65n
father's death confines, 22. 211
father secures reversion of clerkship for, 9. 42
'fugitive from the Muses,' 35. 575
George III and Grafton offer post of lord chancellor to, 23. 178
George III told by, that he will not serve under Camden, 22. 443n
Grafton influenced by acceptance or refusal of, 23. 182
Grenville anxious about 'trimming' of, 22. 494
HW cares not about politics of, 38. 511
(?) HW mentions, 20. 326
HW's couplet on Opposition's being deserted by Charles Townshend and, 38. 496–7
HW threatens to write about death of, 25. 463n
Hardwicke drives, to despair, 29. 200
law chambers of, burnt, 20. 321n
life precedency over solicitor-general taken by, 38. 472
lord chancellor is needed after death of, 39. 121
lord chancellor's post coveted by, 23. 175, 178
lord chancellor's post first declined and then accepted by, 23. 174, 175–6, 178, 188
Mauduit's pamphlet defended by, in Parliament, 21. 458n
Newcastle, D. of, angers, by preferring Pitt in privilege dispute, 38. 285

Norton answered by, in Parliamentary debate, 38. 325
—— opposes, in debate, 22. 283n
—— opposes promotion of, 23. 176
—— succeeded by, as attorney-general, 22. 443, 38. 468
obstructions to be expected from, 41. 87
opinion of, on Cts of Orford's claim, 25. 162, 169, 186
Opposition favours Pratt over, in privilege dispute, 38. 285
—— joined by, 14. 137n, 38. 318
Parliamentary adjournment proposed by, 38. 318
Parliamentary speeches by, 22. 208, 38. 248, 325
Parliament not attended by, on first day of session, 23. 178
patent of precedence accepted by, over De Grey, 22. 268–9
Pitt (Chatham) opposed by, in Parliamentary debate over Wilkes, 22. 187n
—— prefers Pratt (Camden) to, as lord chancellor, 38. 285
——'s administration not to include, 10. 222
——'s summons to Pratt reportedly displeases, 30. 227
political conduct of, 'mean,' 30. 234
position of, may be removed because of Court opposition, 10. 64
Pratt (Camden)'s opinion on privilege opposed by, in Parliament, 38. 241
——'s peerage offends, 30. 196n
'prim,' 10. 109
profession may be abandoned by, because of Camden's appointment, 30. 234
'rapid history' of, 15. 130
resignation of: as attorney-general, 10. 109, 110, 22. 443, 38. 285; probable, 30. 229; since he cannot be lord chancellor, 22. 443–4
Richmond, D. of, names, for lord chancellor, but HW prefers him as lord president, 41. 86
Rockingham favours, 41. 86
—— has attachment of, 23. 178
——'s oracle, 22. 494
—— the obstacle to lord chancellorship for, 23. 175
Rockingham ministry has no assurance that attorney-generalship will be accepted by, 30. 196
Rockingham ministry's resignation delayed by, 22. 432n
Rolls would be taken by, were salary raised, 38. 471–2
Sackville believed by, to be entitled to court martial, 21. 366n
seals declined by, 22. 420n
solicitorship suggested for, 20. 202
Somers's papers in collection of, lost in fire, 20. 321–2, 331–2
son of, 2. 219

Townshend, Hon. Charles, concerts trimming plan with, 38. 502
'very cautious,' 41. 66
wife of, 9. 244n
Wilkes's committal to Tower recommended by, 38. 325
Yorke, Hon. Mrs Charles. See Freeman, Catherine; Johnson, Agneta
Yorke, Hon. Elizabeth (1725–60), m. (1748) George Anson, cr. (1747) Bn Anson:
absurd utterances of, 9. 89–90
brag played by, 9. 90
death of, 21. 416, 429, 35. 302
generosity of, 35. 302
husband's relations with, 20. 13, 35. 206
marriage annulment of, rumoured, 9. 90
marriage of, 9. 54
minuets danced by, at Sandwich's ball, 20. 121
witticisms about virginity of, 20. 13, 21. 66
Yorke, Hon. James (1730–1808), Bp of St David's 1774–9, of Gloucester 1779–81, of Ely 1781–1808:
preaches Hospital Sermon at Cambridge, 2. 331
Queensberry, Ds of, dines with, 32. 297
Yorke, Hon. John (1728–1801), M.P.:
becomes lord of Trade, 21. 490
Cambridgeshire seat offered to, 1. 199
Chatham administration not to include, 10. 222
Parliament not attended by, on first day of session, 23. 178
position of, may be removed because of Court opposition, 10. 64
resigns from Board of Trade, 10. 110
Yorke, Hon. Sir Joseph (1724–92), K.B., 1761; cr. (1788) Bn Dover; diplomatist; M.P.:
Affry's false report of French defeat sent by, 37. 469
athletic activity of, 30. 280
Bedford orders dragoon regiment of, assembled at Newry, 21. 373n
Cambridgeshire seat offered to, 1. 199
capture of Dutch fleet advised by, 33. 155
chaplain of, 2. 69
Cleve's capture and Wesel's siege announced by, 38. 77
Conway's letters unanswered by, 38. 420
Cumberland, D. of, has, as aide-de-camp, 37. 211n
dragoon regiment of, in Ireland, 39. 111
Dutch to receive memorial from, 33. 243n
Dutch troops reportedly demanded by, 21. 299n
Ferdinand's victory announced by, 21. 314
Fitzwilliam's bequest to, 11. 49–50, 34. 59
French invasion threat not believed by, 21. 297n
George II hears false victories announced by, 21. 319
George III attended by, 11. 258n

[Yorke, Hon. Sir Joseph, *continued*]

Hanover might be ceded by, if England lost the war, 21. 499

Howard, Lt-Gen., reports victory to, 22. 46n

Jones, John Paul, writes letter to, 33. 257–8

Maddison, private secretary to, 42. 73n

Mann might correspond with, at The Hague, 21. 129

—— told by, about Dutch-English trade pact, 21. 269

marriage to Crasteyn's heiress jokingly suggested for, 9. 230

marriage to rich Dutchman jokingly suggested for, 9. 232

memorial against Holland, and Hardwicke's counter-declaration to Dutch, delivered by, 21. 280n

Minden victory announced by, to George II, 35. 292

Newcastle, D. of, offended by failure of, to write, after Newcastle's retirement, 38. 420

news of Zorndorf battle sent by, 21. 237n

newspapers call, a great man, 29. 114, 118, 128

not yet returned from Holland, 25. 116

Parliamentary memberships of, corrected, 43. 274, 317

Parliament not attended by, on first day of session, 23. 178

peerage of, pleases Gen. Fitzwilliam, 31. 287

Pitt and Newcastle agree on, as negotiator with France, 21. 355n

position of, may be removed because of Court opposition, 10. 64

Princess of Orange reported by, to have dropsy in head, 21. 260n

Prussian defeats reported by, as victories, 30. 156, 158

recall of, from The Hague, rumoured, 38. 263–4

regiment of, from Ireland to be augmented, 20. 474n

Rockingham has attachment of, 23. 178

secretary of English embassy at Paris, 4. 347n

Stormont may be replaced by, at Paris, 24. 179

William V invested with Garter by, at The Hague, 20. 311n

—— warned by, of England's ship-searching, 39. 347n

Yorke, Lady Margaret (1731–69), m. (1749) Gilbert Heathcote, 3d Bt, 1759:

death of, 7. 398

marriage of, 20. 80

opera attended by, 32. 28

Yorke, Mary Jemima (1757–1830), m. (1780) Thomas Robinson, 2d Bn Grantham, 1770:

HW calls, 'silly ugly prude,' 33. 426

HW's opinion of, 33. 242

Holdernesse, Lady, entertains, 33. 242

marriage of, 33. 202

omens and, 33. 426

portrait of grandmother of, falls, 33. 426

Yorke, Philip (1690–1764), cr. (1733) Bn Hard-

wicke, and (1754) E. of Hardwicke; lord chancellor 1737–56; M.P.:

address against use of Hanoverian troops opposed by, 18. 159

Amelia, Ps, denies Richmond Park ticket to, 9. 135, 20. 322

Anson follows, 20. 135

—— son-in-law of, 35. 170

—— would have Navy treasurership according to demands of, 21. 93

avarice of, 21. 39n, 30. 141

ballad satirizes, 18. 82–3

Bath's Court presentation arouses jealousy of, 20. 80

(?) Bedford, D. and Ds of, entertain, 9. 363

bill against clandestine marriages gets support of, 20. 383

Birch receives living from, 1. 107n

Bootle's appointment approved by, on condition that Glenorchy receive post, 17. 487

Bunbury's motion attacks, 22. 8n

Bute advised by, to be secretary of state, 21. 488

Bute and D. of Newcastle join, against Pitt, 21. 539n

Byng re-investigation opposed by, in House of Lords, 21. 64–5

——'s courage contrasted to behaviour of, 21. 67

——'s recall of hostile witnesses disapproved by, 21. 45n

Cabinet Council's temporizing on Spain due to, 21. 537n

Cambridge high steward, 38. 248

Capper hopes, will appoint guardian soon, for Miss Nicoll, 14. 221

—— threatened with disapprobation of, 14. 208

'Chancellor Shylock,' 30. 141

Chesterfield's praise of, excessive, 28. 303

Chute is directed by, to return Miss Nicoll to her guardians, 14. 195

Chutes not permitted by, to see Miss Nicoll alone, 14. 229

Clarendon title rumoured for, 35. 170

Cocks's volunteering might be encouraged by, 37. 571

Conway urges, to drop Stone from Irish Regency, 20. 503n

country visit of, 21. 74

Court attended by, and Opposition dinners may be shunned, 38. 195

—— opposed by, but Opposition alienates him by opposing his son, 38. 284–5

daughter of, 20. 121n, 21. 416n

daughter of, married, 9. 54–5

death of: 22. 211, 38. 340–1; expected, 10. 109, 22. 219n, 38. 243

Denbigh's appointment not opposed by, 9. 334

earldom for, expected, 9. 33

Egremont thought by, too sensible to accept secretaryship of state, 21. 76n

English success attributed by HW to loss by, of absolute power, 21. 499
Essay on Woman debated by, 38. 230n
evidence against Byng communicated to Anson by, 21. 23n
explosion resented by, as a libel, 13. 104
faction of, 21. 27
financial advancement of, 9. 42
Fox, Henry, disliked by, 21. 23n
—— expected by, to decline Treasury, 30. 128
—— hated by, 20. 412, 21. 87
—— offered secretaryship of state by, 35. 88
—— opposed by, 20. 383
—— opposes, on Marriage Bill, 37. 365
—— permitted by, to join ministry, 35. 168
—— supposedly inspired Shebbeare's attack on, 21. 39n
——'s warfare with, 9. 149
—— writes apologetic letters to, after Pelham's death, 20. 412n
Fox-Newcastle reconciliation attempted by, 35. 169
George II discards Sir Robert Walpole in favour of D. of Newcastle and, 40. 88
—— entrusts, with formation of new ministry, 20. 411n
—— orders, to present Waldegrave to P. of Wales, 20. 347n
——'s speech drafted by, 21. 344n
——'s wealth compared to that of, 9. 317
—— tells, of not going overseas, 30. 48n
—— wants Newcastle and, to manage his affairs, 20. 502n
George III talks with, at levee, 21. 530
groom of chambers to Lady Fitzroy would be ridiculous post for, 9. 181
HW calls, 'merciful and disinterested legislator,' 30. 140
HW did not admire, 23. 265
HW does not 'connect' with, 10. 111
HW mentions, 9. 211, 37. 479
HW should include in future *Royal and Noble Authors*, 40. 159
HW suggests bigamy for, 9. 231
habeas corpus revision opposed by, 21. 182n
habeas corpus writ privilege extended by, to judges on vacation, 37. 528
Harcourt's complaints to be heard by, 20. 343
Harrington visits, to ask how he has offended George II, 20. 207n
Hartington's policy deemed by, a concession to Boyle, 37. 398n
health of: dangerously ill, 22. 169n; quack medicine relieves, 38. 258; recovering, 38. 276; relapsed, 38. 327; rupture suspected, 38. 260
Hertford asks about illness of, 38. 245
—— loved by, next to his own children, 38. 420, 427
House of Lords formerly subservient to, 22. 109–10
'immensely rich,' 22. 211
incompetence of, 30. 141

in political minority, 10. 111
Inquiry into the Doctrine attacks, 22. 274n
jealousy of, 20. 80, 412
'Jew who loves human blood better than anything but money,' 30. 141
Jones, nephew of, 21. 26
libel a favourite subject with, 35. 551
Lyttelton's verses inspire verses from, 9. 342
mace of, 17. 174
Mann must now read manifesto of, 21. 286
Mansfield (William Murray)'s draft warrant for Schroeder's release upheld by, 21. 12n
—— upheld by, against Pratt, 21. 205
Marriage Bill 'cooked up' by, 9. 147
—— defended by, 9. 149, 20. 383
—— not extended by, to Ireland, 37. 407
—— revised by, 37. 407
Maurepas resembles, 7. 278, 30. 205, 214, 39. 215
may be lord president, 20. 3, 302
may be lord privy seal, 21. 92–3, 541
may be lord treasurer, 20. 412
may retire to Wimpole, 20. 202
Militia Bill clogged with absurdities and hardships by, 21. 137n
(?) Montagu refers to, 10. 142
Mordaunt's execution probably intended by, 30. 140, 141
Mountrath, Cts of, visited by, 17. 135
Murray, Sir John, examined by, 19. 288n
Newcastle, D. of, advised by: about retiring, 22. 37n; to urge Regency provision on George II, 20. 239n
—— asked by, to put Anson in Privy Council, 20. 135n
—— may be joined by, in opposition, 22. 98, 107, 109
—— prevented by, from joining Henry Fox, 21. 87
—— proposes, as lord chancellor, 21. 86n
——'s coalition with Pitt announced by, at Kensington, 21. 103
—— suggests, as lord privy seal, but Bute disagrees, 21. 541n
—— tells, of Maria Theresa's difficulties, 17. 144n
—— to be succeeded by, as high steward of Cambridge, 20. 19
newspapers laud, 19. 293
Nicoll affair heard before, 14. 197, 198–9, 212–13, 230–1
Nicoll affair referred by, to Master in Chancery, 14. 201
Northington abuses, 22. 109
Onslow's dispute with, 9. 149
opinion of, on Ferrers's will, 21. 398
Oxford, E. of, sells Wimpole to, 2. 144n
Parliamentary speech by, on Habeas Corpus, 37. 529
Parliament's dissolution advised by, 19. 412n
Pelham forced by, to support Marriage Bill, 37. 364
Piozzi, Mrs, comments on, 9. 342n

[Yorke, Philip (1690–1764), *continued*]

Pitt's popularity alarms, **21**. 87

——'s Spanish war proposal opposed by, **38**. 131n

——'s terms taken to George II by, **21**. 109n

—— supported by, to keep down Fox and D. of Cumberland, **20**. 412n

Pitt-Newcastle-Fox coalition arranged by, **30**. 135n

poet laureate's post predicted for, **9**. 345

Pratt thought by, inexperienced, **21**. 205n

preferment awaited by, **21**. 104

prime minister's post may go to, **35**. 165

privy seal rumoured for, **38**. 132

rebel lords tried by, **19**. 280–1, 283, 287, 293

regent, **18**. 209n

resigns as lord chancellor, **9**. 202, **19**. 211, **20**. 3, **21**. 17, 25

restoration of *Maria Theresa* due to, **21**. 285n

Robinson to entertain, **17**. 174

Rochefort expedition planned by, **21**. 117n

Salter, chaplain and tutor in household of, **31**. 427n

Sandwich wants to succeed, as high steward of Cambridge, **38**. 248

Sandys succeeds, as Speaker of the House of Lords, **21**. 25

Seals refused, but Presidency or Privy Seal might be accepted by, **21**. 92–3

Secker recommended by, as archbishop, **21**. 185n

——'s gift from, for arranging his son's marriage, **30**. 304n

Selwyn imitates voice of, before Lovat's corpse, **37**. 268

Seymour, Sir Edward, denied Somerset title by, **20**. 139

Shebbeare attacks, **21**. 39

son of, **2**. 331n, **18**. 351

sons claim, forced them into Opposition, **38**. 472

sons forced by, to resign, **10**. 110

speech by, at Jacobite trials, **9**. 38, 38–9

Talbot's death makes, lord chancellor, **37**. 70

temptations resisted by, **22**. 104

Townshend, George and Charles, recommended by, to George II, **21**. 104n

Vaneschi intimate with, **35**. 229

verses attack, **30**. 125

Walpole, Sir Robert, and, **15**. 99, **43**. 196

Walpole, Sir Robert, betrayed by, **2**. 116, **25**. 463n

wand of, **9**. 38–9

war's continuation urged by, **30**. 109n

war would be waged by, as slowly as Chancery suit, **21**. 261

Westminster election returns said by, to be illegally made out, **17**. 272

wife of, **9**. 39n

Yorke, Sir Joseph, delivers counter-declaration of, to the Dutch, **21**. 280n

Yorke, Philip (1720–90), styled Vct Royston 1754–64; 2d E. of Hardwicke, 1764; M.P.:

Addenbrooke's Hospital's president, **2**. 331

Address seconded by, **18**. 351

Anecdotes of Painting apparently wanted by, **41**. 284, 285

'an old goody,' **33**. 422

apologizes for printing letter about Jane Shore, **2**. 108, 115

Biographia Britannica, 2d edn, inscribed to, **2**. 342

Birch's letter to, **43**. 170

Blenheim visited by, **10**. 309

brother advised by, about becoming lord chancellor, **23**. 178

brother driven by, to despair, **29**. 199–200

Cambridge high stewardship sought by, **10**. 309, **14**. 133

Cambridgeshire election and, **1**. 198n, 199, 200

Cole dislikes, **2**. 113, 263–4, 265, 266

——'s life of, **2**. 226n

Cumberland, D. of, supports, for Cambridge high stewardship, **38**. 248n

death of, falsely reported, **33**. 400

Ewin favoured by, for chancellorship, **2**. 51

Exchequer post of, **12**. 100n

father-in-law of, **17**. 487

Garnett's letters to, **41**. 224n

generally disliked, **2**. 119, 120

Grantham, Lord, son-in-law of, **33**. 422

Grub St kennels searched by, for anecdotes about Sir Robert Walpole, **25**. 464

HW apologizes for being 'squab' about Mann's commission for, **21**. 539

HW asked by, to print *Letters from and to Sir Dudley Carleton*, **16**. 276

HW calls, oaf, **25**. 463

HW courted by, to see Conway papers, **2**. 109

HW disparages, **2**. 268

HW informs, about Sévigné family, **41**. 257–9

HW receives Bourchier extract from, **41**. 224

HW refuses request of, about Carleton letters, **2**. 109–10, 113, 116, **16**. 276, **29**. 183

HW refuses to bother about picture for, **21**. 538

HW returns letters to, and thanks him for print and verses, **41**. 364

HW returns MS volume to, **41**. 270

HW's coolness with, **15**. 98–9

HW's correspondence with, **40**. 125, **41**. 234, 237, 239–42, 257–9, 265–6, 270, 271–2, 283–6, 364–5, **43**. 277

HW sends play and poems to, **41**. 352

HW's enemy, **2**. 109–10, 111, 115–16

HW should include, in future *Royal and Noble Authors*, **40**. 159

HW shown drawings sent by, and sends him *Mysterious Mother*, **41**. 240–1

HW's relations with, **28**. 246

HW thanked by, for (?) *Royal and Noble Authors*, **40**. 125

HW threatens, if he writes about Sir Robert Walpole, **25**. 463n

HW to hunt for papers wanted by, **41**. 266

HW to permit Sir Robert Walpole's portrait to be copied for, **41**. 234
HW to tell story of, **32**. 229
HW unable to give unpublished volume of *Anecdotes of Painting* to, **41**. 239–40
Hardinge wishes his father's book to be printed by, **35**. 606
health of, gout, **41**. 271
'historically curious and political,' **21**. 129
house of, in St James's Sq., **25**. 116n, **33**. 202n, 400n
(?) Janssen's painting like one owned by, **7**. 337
Jenyns attached to, **29**. 198, 200
—'s verses dedicated to, **28**. 86n
later E. of Hardwicke, **21**. 538n
Letters from and to Sir Dudley Carleton published by: **1**. 379–80, 386, **2**. 263, **21**. 129n, 43. 63; HW refuses request to print, **2**. 109–10, 113, 116, **16**. 276, **29**. 183
Mann did not want HW to speak to, about picture, **21**. 545
—— might send unusual documents to, **21**. 129
—'s letters from: about Jesuits' correspondence relating to Gunpowder Plot, **25**. 458; with anecdotes of Sir Robert Walpole, **25**. 458
—— tries to get painting for, **21**. 532
MSS transmitted to, **15**. 133n
marriage of: arranged by Secker, **30**. 304n; to D. of Kent's heiress, **37**. 70–1
Milles encouraged by, to reply to *Historic Doubts*, **28**. 246
Miscellaneous State Papers published by, **2**. 66n, 75, 77, 263, **16**. 171, **28**. 381, **35**. 603, **41**. 237
nephew of, **2**. 219n
Newcastle, D. of, confers with Pitt at house of, **21**. 92n
—— reportedly recommends, as secretary of state, **30**. 185
—— suggests, for Board of Trade, **30**. 185n
Oxford rôle of, **10**. 309
Parliament not attended by, on first day of session, **23**. 178
position of, may be removed because of Court opposition, **10**. 64
retinue and equipage of, **10**. 309
Rockingham has attachment of, **23**. 178
Royal and Noble Authors annotated by, **16**. 364n
St James's Sq. the address of, **41**. 240, 241, 285
Sandwich contests Cambridge high stewardship with, **10**. 142n, **22**. 219, **38**. 341n, 355, 360, 362–3
Seals declined by, **22**. 420n, **23**. 263n
Walpoliana published by, **2**. 261–5, 276–7, **21**. 129n, **25**. 458, 463–4, **33**. 421–2, **43**. 72
wife of, **9**. 230n
Wrest dining-room made by, **39**. 139n
Yorke, Charles, resigns against wish of, **38**. 285

Yorke, Philip (1757–1834), 3d E. of Hardwicke, 1790; M.P.:
M.P. for Cambridgeshire, **2**. 219, **35**. 612n
Yorke, Mrs Philip. *See* Campbell, Jemima (1722–97)
Yorke. *See also* York
Yorke family ('House of Yorke'):
avarice of, **22**. 269
Cambridge contest for high steward will fix, in Opposition, **38**. 341
Coronation shunned by, because of Cts of Hardwicke's death, **38**. 122
father said by, to have forced them into Opposition, **38**. 472
Gray inquires about doings of, **14**. 137
Grenville ministry will not be rejoined by, **38**. 327
HW accuses, of marrying for money, **9**. 230–1
HW attacked by a supporter of, **14**. 166
HW has no connection with, **21**. 538
HW owes no particular attentions to, **33**. 502
HW's dislike of, **21**. 538n
House of Commons defers to, **38**. 325
Mauduit's book inspired by faction of, **21**. 458
minority may be joined by, in East Indian dispute, **22**. 473
Mountrath, Lady, makes no bequests to, **30**. 223
Opposition joined by, **38**. 318, 459
—— left by, **38**. 468
—— may be joined by, after Wilkes affair, **38**. 285
—— never joined by, unless with hope of success, **22**. 98
—— opposed by, over Wilkes, **38**. 284
Rockingham's adherents, **23**. 78
sons of, **43**. 187
very powerful, **21**. 129
Wilkes opposed by, **38**. 284
Yorke, Charles, wished by, to become lord chancellor, **23**. 178
Yorke (*or* York) Farm (*or* House). *See under* Twickenham
York House, Pall Mall:
York, D. of, lives in, **22**. 270n
York House, the Strand:
style of, to return, **18**. 316
Yorkshire:
Beauchamp visits Irvine in, **39**. 265
Berrys to visit, **34**. 49
—— visit, **11**. 13, 16, 19, 25, 41, **12**. 6n, 10, 21, 24, 32, 50, 57, 58, 64, 69, 74, 90, **31**. 341, **34**. 194
Blanshard has estate in, **38**. 442
Brooke writes account of families of, **29**. 278
Bruce, Lord, inherits Ailesbury's estates in, **20**. 331n
(?) Castle Howard in, **37**. 359
coin-clipping prevalent in, **23**. 498
committee of, Saville tries to humour, **25**. 18
Conway and wife may visit, **37**. 547, 551
Cowick is Downe's seat in, **35**. 293

[Yorkshire, *continued*]
Danby from, **24.** 94
dialect of, retained by Middleton, **15.** 305
Downe from, **20.** 200n
East Riding of: found defenceless by Carmarthen, **28.** 471; Mason returns from, **28.** 310
HW envies verdure of, **35.** 315
HW hopes rains extend to, **35.** 360
HW jokes about, as 'desert,' **35.** 336
HW mentions, **11.** 38, 258, **12.** 15, 16
HW prevented from visiting, **9.** 292
HW to visit, **1.** 66, **9.** 192, 193, **16.** 43, **30.** 253
HW travels in, contrasting it to Nottingham, **35.** 266–72
HW unable to visit, **28.** 211, 214
HW visits, **1.** 152n, 275n, **20.** 585, **23.** 57, 425, **31.** 140, 168, **35.** 278
Harrogate in, visited by Lady Ailesbury, **37.** 553
Hartington acquires estates in, by marriage, **20.** 66n
Herring and Malton head defence meeting in, **19.** 110
Herring's speech to, on threatened invasion, **19.** 126
inn at, crowd waits at, to see Ds of Hamilton enter post-chaise, **20.** 317
instructions from, **21.** 13n
Kew pagoda may be visible in, **35.** 308
Lascelles defeated in election in, **36.** 177
Malton sends express from, **19.** 186
Mason comes from, **31.** 201
may present petition, **23.** 132
men from, alone dare to attack boars, **20.** 200n
Milbanke from, **20.** 200n
Militia Bill riots in, **21.** 137n
militia of, attacked in Northumberland, **9.** 341
Muzell to visit clergyman in, **21.** 427
Napier's regiment raised in, **37.** 446n
North Riding, Mason to make visits in, **29.** 50
Opposition in, proved practicable, **29.** 79
Piers a rich gentleman of, **24.** 148
plain taste in, **28.** 165
quarries of, good for Gothic, **35.** 266
reform should not be countenanced by, **35.** 382
remonstrances from, **28.** 487, **29.** 149
riots in, **21.** 137n, **35.** 285
Rokeby in, **24.** 282n
Russian fleet on coast of, **23.** 146
Schroeder affair elicits instructions from, **35.** 291n
Strafford, E. of, calls Castle Howard one of finest places in, **30.** 257
—— in, **23.** 425
—— might be robbed by rioters in, **35.** 285
—— returns to, **35.** 290
—— tries to landscape hill and vale in, **35.** 336
troops from Flanders land in, **19.** 134

Tullie has estate in, **23.** 498
Twickenham scarcely closer than, to news, **35.** 349
Wade to be joined in, by Hessians and army from Flanders, **19.** 126–7
West Riding, beauties of, seen from Mason's study, **28.** 33
Wetherby in, **19.** 173–4
would have petitioned earlier, **33.** 167
Yorkshire, waters of. *See* Harrogate
Yorkshire Association:
active because of resignation of Sir George Savile, **29.** 321n
American war opposed by, **29.** 160
becomes a county quarrel, **29.** 95
Burke's bill dissatisfies, **29.** 109
committee for: activities of, **28.** 490; Mason a member of, **29.** 1, 12; Mason tires of, **29.** 313, 317; resolutions of, temperate, **29.** 213, 217, 221, 222, 225–6, 228; resolutions passed by, **29.** 74–5, 92
deputies of, cannot petition Parliament, **29.** 121
HW accuses, of censuring his father, **29.** 196–7
HW calls, 'pert and ignorant cabal,' **29.** 351
HW hopes Mason will be able to control, **29.** 16, 25
imitators of, **25.** 6n
Lascelles defeated by, **29.** 79, 229, 248
Mason alludes to, **29.** 280
—— busy with, **29.** 280n, **35.** 523
—— describes plans of, **28.** 483–4
—— wastes time on, **29.** 316, 319, 321, 323
meetings of, **28.** 490, **29.** 140–1, 169–70, 276
organization of, **43.** 304
Parliamentary reform advocated by, **29.** 15, 16, 20, 24, 214n, 221, 328n
petition presented by, **28.** 491
resolutions of, **29.** 74n
Richmond's conduct towards, puzzling, **29.** 67
Rockingham opposes, **29.** 329n, 352
Savile active in, **25.** 18n
support of 'great barons' not welcomed by, **28.** 488, 490, **29.** 1
Wyvill and Mason institute, **29.** 328n, 347
Wyvill's manifesto for, ridiculed by HW, **29.** 14–16, 347
Yorkshire Grey warehouse. *See under* Fetter Lane
York St, Covent Garden, London:
Baker in, **1.** 12n
Best lives in, **10.** 286
Blackstone's warehouse in, **23.** 476n
Yorktown, Virginia:
Cornwallis's surrender at: **25.** 208–9, 210–11, 212, **29.** 166n, 192n; Germain blames, on navy, **25.** 241n
Youlgreave, Derbyshire:
Barker, vicar of, **1.** 362n
Younas Bey. *See* Yūnūs Bey
Young, Lady. *See* Taylor, Elizabeth
Young, Mr:

Bland hires, **30.** 84

(?) Fitzroy, Lady Caroline, interested in, **30.** 84

Young, Mr:

HW mentions, **10.** 224

Young, Mr:

puns, **41.** 7

social relations of, in Paris, **7.** 284, 285, 289, 293, 296, 299, 300, 301, 306, 309–10, 316

Young, Admiral:

Rodney's proxy at Westminster, **33.** 227n

Young, Anne ('Sukey') (d. 1759), m. (1748) Hon. Richard Fitzpatrick:

husband to introduce, to Ds of Bedford, **37.** 289

Young, Arthur (1741–1820), agriculturist:

Annals of Agriculture collected and published by, **34.** 85n

Marlay visited by, **9.** 379n

Orford's treatise published by, **12.** 94n

Young, Edward (1683–1765), D.C.L.; poet:

Bubb Dodington and, **12.** 255

——'s verses corrected by, **28.** 242n

Centaur Not Fabulous by, 'nonsense,' **15.** 56n

Conjectures on Original Composition by: HW describes Addison's death from, **9.** 236; Piozzi, Mrs, comments upon, **9.** 236n

Conway does not read, **37.** 576

death of, **38.** 530

HW denies saying of, that fame is mankind's universal passion, **25.** 545

Night Thoughts by: **12.** 255; French translation of, **4.** 232; Williams, Sir C. H., writes 'A Letter to Mr Dodsley' on allusion to Wilmington in, **30.** 315; Yearsley, Mrs, familiar with, **31.** 218

(?) print of, **40.** 236

Revenge, The, by: **41.** 296; acted, **19.** 468

Richardson told story of 'Marcella' to, **34.** 37n

Universal Passion, The, by, mentions Bns Hervey, **31.** 417

Works of, reprinted, **35.** 284–5

Young, Edward (1689–1773), Bath King-of-Arms:

daughter of, **17.** 431n, **20.** 58n

Young, Isabella (d. 1791), m. (1757) Hon. John Scott:

Ezio acted by, **38.** 466–7

Young, James (d. 1789), naval Capt.:

Admiralty orders, to sail from Port Mahon in the *Colchester* for Byng's trial, **20.** 590n

Byng accused by, **20.** 586, 590–1

George III's remonstrance from, for Keppel trial, **24.** 432n

Trepid, ship of, almost sunk, **20.** 591

Young, Lucy (ca 1723–73), m. (1740) William Henry Nassau de Zuylestein, 4th E. of Rochford:

adopts husband's natural daughter, **3.** 325

Aiguillon, Duchesse d', exchanges gifts with, **4.** 312–13

Augusta, Ps of Wales, had, as maid of honour, **17.** 431n, **20.** 58n

ball given by, **21.** 57

beauty of, faded, **20.** 378

biographical information about, corrected, **43.** 83, 112

Bologna and Venice to be visited by, **20.** 376n

Boufflers, Comtesse de, mentions, **3.** 172

Bunbury, Lady Sarah, thanks, **3.** 224

childless, **3.** 325

Coke, Lady Mary, corresponds with, **31.** 134

Compiègne visited by, **3.** 319, 333

Cumberland, D. of, gives ball to pique, **9.** 42

—— in love with, **20.** 58

——, with D. of York, interrupts duet of, with Cts of Essex, **21.** 57

dances without stays, **35.** 213

death of, not to be regretted, **5.** 264

Du Deffand, Mme, discusses gift for, **4.** 312–13, 316–17

—— does not suit, **3.** 229–30, 311

—— does not understand, **4.** 173, 190, 207

—— receives gift from, **4.** 312–13

—— sees little of, **3.** 292, **4.** 16

——'s opinion of, **3.** 208, 263, 278, 392, **4.** 16, 199, 211

——'s parcel expedited by, **3.** 201

Edward Augustus, D. of York, entertained by, **9.** 269

Florence to be visited by, **20.** 370, 376

Forcalquier, Mme de, considers, witty, **41.** 162

—— correspondent of, **3.** 333

—— friend of, **3.** 303, 309, 311, 315, 333, 337, 392, **4.** 207, 211, 231–2

Friedrich Wilhelm of Hesse in love with, **9.** 42, **20.** 58

gaiety of, **20.** 76

Garrick's dinner includes, **35.** 244

George III's coronation attended by, **9.** 269

HW admires appearance of, at Coronation, **9.** 387, **38.** 126

(?) HW asked by, for motto for ruby ring received from Lord (?) Thanet, **35.** 215

HW avoids, **9.** 88

HW describes, **20.** 58

HW entertained by, **9.** 269

HW entertains, at SH, **9.** 168, 215–16

HW mentions, **3.** 342

HW's verses to, **3.** 208, **9.** 216

HW wishes Mann were more struck by beauty of, **20.** 389

health of, **3.** 283, 285, 286, 291

Hesse, Landgrave of, enamoured of, **9.** 42, **20.** 58

hours of, late, **9.** 269

Huntingdon entertained by, **9.** 269

husband, dupe of, **9.** 49

husband no longer faithful to, **30.** 378

Mann entertains, at Florence, **20.** 378

marriage of, **17.** 431

Maynard, Lady, and Morrison entertained by, **9.** 269

Narbonne, Vicomtesse de, friend of, **3.** 333

Paris left by, **4.** 233

[Young, Lucy, *continued*]
—— to be left by, **4.** 211, 224, 228, 232
—— to be visited by, as ambassador's wife, **41.** 41
Rome reached by, from Turin, **20.** 370n
Rueil visited by, **7.** 320
St Osyth, seat of, **9.** 88
sees no one during husband's illness, **4.** 68
small talk of, **32.** 148–9
social relations of, in Paris, **31.** 134, 136; *see also index entries ante* **8.** 561
subscription masquerade attended by, in vast beauty, **20.** 49
suspected of complicity with La Vauguyon and Jesuits, **4.** 199, 203
to remain in Paris, **4.** 190
Turin to be residence of, **20.** 58, 76
Waldegraves entertained by, **9.** 269
Walpole, Charlotte, entertained by, **9.** 269
Walpole, Hon. Robert, on good terms with, **4.** 173
witticism by, to (?) Charlotte Dyve, at Bns Hervey's, **37.** 454–5
Young, Margaret (fl. 1760–86), HW's housekeeper at SH:
Amelia, Ps, gives gratuity to, **10.** 82
bed at SH to be described by, **28.** 42
Description of SH printed to aid, in showing SH to visitors, **42.** 39
dinner at SH hard to organize by, **39.** 404
Du Deffand, Mme, admires good-heartedness of, **5.** 396
fawn presented by, to HW, **33.** 208
grows rich from 'vails,' **28.** 406
HW feigns hand of, **30.** 282
HW jokes about suitors for, to get her riches, **33.** 411–12
HW mentions, **5.** 75, **6.** (?) 418
HW proposes, as 'necessary woman,' **33.** 394
HW's disappearance to be reported by, **33.** 507
HW's instructions to, about visitors to be admitted, **43.** 163n
HW told by, to see balloon, **25.** 579
HW to tell, to admit Wentworth, **16.** 55
HW to write to, to admit Beauchamp to SH, **39.** 154
'hoary-headed,' **33.** 507
loves all creatures, **32.** 208
no scholar but by rote, **2.** 317
Pentycross begs, for interview with HW, **12.** 207
Perkins, Mr, does not tip, **2.** 222n
powder-mills explosion reported by, **32.** 75
prays to St Rainbow, **33.** 402
requests to HW conveyed by, **32.** 122
robbery heard by, **33.** 476
room of, over Holbein Chamber at SH, **33.** 476
'Rosette' attended by, **32.** 160
SH chimney fire detected by, **38.** 175
SH damage lamented by, **32.** 76

SH shown by, to visitors, **1.** 166, 265, **2.** 41, 316, **32.** 76, **39.** 106
Sulkowsky's gratuity to, **33.** 280
superstitious, **32.** 76
'tattling,' **33.** 281
ticket required by, to show SH to visitors, **35.** 635
'Tonton's' foot dressed by, **39.** 370
very ill, **1.** 264
Young (*or* Youngson), Margaret Caroline (ca 1745–97), m. (ca 1762) Valentine Rudd; mistress of Daniel Perreau and James Boswell:
acquittal of, after refusing her lawyer a clear story, **24.** 152–4
biographical information about, corrected, **43.** 285, 349
London apt to produce, **11.** 208
memoirs of, are town news, **28.** 289
play attended by, in Lord Lyttelton's chariot, **32.** 286
reluctant mercer paid by, for brocaded silk, **24.** 153–4, 167
Richard III might have been aided by, **41.** 323
talked of, **32.** 261
testifies against Perreau brothers, **28.** 192
Young, Mary *or* Polly (ca 1749–99), m. (1766) François-Hippolyte Barthélemon:
in burletta company, **22.** 474n
Young, Matthew (1750–1800), D.D., Bp of Clonfert 1798–1800:
Gothic architecture's origins traced by, **42.** 305
Young, Sarah (1731–91), m. (1748 *or* 1749) Thomas Chatterton; mother of the poet:
Chatterton claims to be a burden to, **16.** 125
death of, **34.** 149
documents said to have been made by, into thread papers, **16.** 356
HW urges Chatterton to cultivate profession for sake of, **16.** 128
letter from HW in possession of, **34.** 149
Young, Susanna. *See* Young, Anne
Young, Sir William (1725–88), cr. (1769) Bt; Lt-Gov. of Dominica:
boasts of his wealth, **20.** 331
Florence visited by, **20.** 327, 331
organ, electrical instruments, and pictures bought by, **20.** 331
sugar cane of, damaged by hurricane, **20.** 331
weekly concert given by, at Florence, **20.** 327
'West Indian,' **20.** 327
Young, Mrs William. *See* (?) Taylor, Elizabeth
Young. *See also* Yonge; Younge
Younge, Elizabeth (ca 1744–97), actress; m. (1785) Alexander Pope:
agrees, after delay, to act in Jephson's *Count of Narbonne*, **33.** 302
Count of Narbonne acted by, **33.** 308n, **41.** 453, 456, 459–60
HW begs, to improve Miss Satchell's performance, **41.** 460

HW charmed with, in *Count of Narbonne*, **39**. 387

HW persuades, to act in Jephson's play, **29**. 166, 167, **41**. 446–7

HW's correspondence with, **33**. 302, **41**. 446–7, 453

HW's solicitations to, **41**. 462

Siege of Berwick, The, interrupted by illness of, **12**. 69–70

——, performance in, admirable, **12**. 83

SH visited by, **12**. 237

Younge. *See also* Yonge; Young

Younger, Elizabeth (d. 1762), m. Hon. John Finch:

marriage and daughter of, **19**. 389

Young people:

conversational difficulties with: HW's reflections on, **23**. 350–1, 364–5; Mann's reflections on, **23**. 357

displaced by those yet younger, **35**. 352

Du Deffand, Mme, does not know what to say to, **5**. 2

HW cannot write for, or talk to, **28**. 25, 228, 280

HW likes, but cannot live with them, **39**. 244

HW not amused by, **35**. 361, 369

HW's reflections on, **25**. 307–8

HW uninterested in, except those related to him, **39**. 317

'Young Pretender, The.' *See* Charles Edward (Stuart)

Youth:

age less tolerant than, to differing customs, **35**. 370

death begins with end of, **22**. 462

disadvantages of, **31**. 305–6

Du Deffand, Mme, on, **3**. 320–1

French persist in, when old, **35**. 115–16

HW on, **3**. 317–18, **11**. 62

older people cannot converse with, **39**. 149

parade and ridicule may be outlived and forgiven in, **39**. 79

See also Youth and old age

Youth and old age:

HW's reflections on, **9**. 2–3, 228–9, 410–11, 416, **10**. 109, 163, 171–2, 184, 191–2, 267, 269, 270, 289, 291, 298, 305, **18**. 498–9, **22**. 462, **23**. 237, 364–5, **24**. 219, 359, **25**. 109, 332, 502, **33**. 20

Montagu's reflections on, **9**. 352, **10**. 143–4, 177–8, 321

See also Age, old

Ypres, France:

communication with, reopened, **18**. 416

French almost capture, **18**. 456

—— attack, **37**. 155–6

—— mine, **19**. 482n

Maria Theresa said to have given, to the French, **21**. 117

siege of, delayed, **18**. 463

Ysabeau, ——:

attends session of parliament of Paris, **8**. 174

Ysenburg. *See* Isenburg

Ysenburg-Birstein, Christian Ludwig (1710–91), Graf zu; Hessian army officer:

Montagu wishes London's censure of England's war conduct sent to, **9**. 201

Yucatan (Mexico):

governor of, tries to stop English wood-cutting in Honduras, **38**. 432n

Yūnūs Bey (d. 1756), son of Bey of Tunis:

father's wives massacred by, and his eyes put out, **20**. 319n

Husain ben 'Alī killed by, **20**. 319n

rebellion of, **20**. 319

Yusupov, Prince Nikolai (1750–1831), diplomatist; collector:

SH visited by, **28**. 269

Yvery, history of house of. *See under* Perceval, John (1683–1748)

Yvetot. *See* 'Roi d'Yvetot'

Yvetot, Prince d'. *See* Albon, Claude-Camille-François d'

Yvetot, Princesse d'. *See* Castellane, Angélique-Charlotte de

Z

Zaballi, Abate:

Mann entertains, **17**. 104

Zabern, Rohan's château:

Hussars seize, **18**. 293

Zaccaria, St Antonio Maria (1502–39):

Barnabiti founded by, **14**. 20n

Zacchia, Emilio (d. 1605), cr. (1598) Cardinal San Marcello:

Shirley engages, to support James, **15**. 80

Zacchiroli, Abbé Francesco:

Description de la galeria royale de Florence by, (?) requested by HW from Mann, **25**. 531

Zadig. See under Voltaire

'Zadok the Priest.' *See under* Handel, George Frideric

Zaffre:

Saxony produces, **18**. 184n

Zafir Bey, Turkish naval officer:

Repulin Bacha commanded by, **23**. 228n

Zagarola:

Lobkowitz marches to, **18**. 447

Zaïde. See under Pioche de la Verne, Comtesse de la Fayette

Zaïre. See under Voltaire

Załuski, Józef Jedrzej (1702–74), Bp of Kiev:

Russians remove, **22**. 574

Zambault *or* Zambo, ——:

Conquête des Pays-Bas by, owned by Mme du Deffand, **8**. 34

Zambeccari, ——, aeronaut:

balloon ascent by, **25**. 579n

Zambeccari, ——, m. Count Pironi:

brother's intercession liberates, from Spanish captors, **18**. 257

Zambeccari, Conte, Spanish minister at Bologna:
Montemar said by, to be going to Naples, 18. 2
Regency council's reply sent to, by Vernaccini, 17. 281
sister liberated by, 18. 257
Traun may seize, 18. 257
Zambeccari, Francesco, Monsignore:
alleged Domenichino painting owned by, acquired by HW through Mann, 17. 167, 199, 226–7, 240, 241, 256–7, 267–8, 442, 462, 18. 57–8, 67, 285, 35. 12
Bolognese pronunciation of name of, 17. 167n
collection of, at Bologna, to be sold, 17. 167
HW visits house of, to see 'Domenichino' painting, 18. 308
originality of Domenichino painting believed by, 35. 17, 18
price asked by, 35. 17
receipt given by, for painting, 18. 57–8, 67
rich, 17. 227
'Zamore':
Lekain acts part of, 7. 297
Zamperini, Anna Maria (b. ca 1752, living 1780), Venetian singer:
biographical information about, corrected, 43. 283
followers of, applaud, 32. 39
has no voice, 32. 39
Hobart prefers, to Lavinia Guadagni, 23. 271
——'s mistress, 23. 271
Zamperini, Giandomenico, Antonia, and Maria:
probably Anna Maria Zamperini's parents and sister, 43. 283
Zanaida. See under Bach, J. C.; Bottarelli, G. G.
Zanetti, Conte Antonio Maria (1680–1757), collector:
cameo owned by, of tiger: HW wants, 21. 562; Mann often reminds Murray of, 22. 116; Mann will write to Venice about, 22. 6; Murray has not found, 22. 14
Marlborough said to have bought gems from, 21. 561–2, 22. 6
Regent of France employs, to buy pictures, 21. 562n
Walpole, Sir Robert, cheated by, 21. 562
Zanetti, Conte Antonio Maria (1706 or 1716–78):
birth date of, corrected, 43. 277
Marlborough's purchases from, 21. 561–2, 22. 6
negotiations for purchase of Francis III's art collection conducted by, 19. 314n
Zanetti, Girolamo Francesco:
Dichiarazione di un antica papiro by, 42. 240n
Zanovitch, Premislos (b. ca 1747), 'Prince Scanderbeck'; sharper:
Lincoln, E. of, cheated by, 23. 368, 378
Zante:
possible revolt by, against Turks, 23. 146n
vice-consul at, see Forrest, ——

Zara. See Hill, Aaron: Tragedy of Zara; Voltaire: Zaïre
Zarlino, Gioseffe (1517–90), musicologist:
Opere, Mann to send to Hawkins, 21. 467
Zastrow, Karl Anton Leopold von (? 1710–79), or Ludwig von (1680–1761), Prussian army officer:
Cumberland, D. of, to replace, in command of army of observation, 21. 73n
Frederick II resents appointment of, 21. 73n
Granby's battle with, 22. 86n
Zatta, Antonio, (?) Venetian publisher:
Dimostrazione printed by, 21. 476n
Museum Mazzuchelianum published by, 22. 14n
Zatta ('Zattee'):
melon variety, 20. 170
Zavallios, ——, Spanish minister at Rome:
Charles III presses Clement XIV through, to suppress Jesuits, 23. 413n
Zeal:
convert-making, is lacked by HW, 24. 281
true name of, is Plunder, 33. 192
Zealand. See Zeeland
Zebecque. See Xebec
Zebra; zebras:
Q. Charlotte's: Heroic Epistle mentions, 28. 45, 81; stuffed skin of, exhibited, 28. 90–1
Zebra, English ship:
Tollemache, captain of, 32. 165n
Zecchin; zecchins ('zecchini'):
exchange in, unfavourable to English in Florence, 19. 433
value of, 17. 82n, 273n, 19. 433n
Zeeland, Cts of. See Jacoba or Jacqueline (1401–36)
Zeeland (Holland):
George II orders the Royal Scots to the relief of, 19. 395n
Huske writes to George II from, 9. 50
Pitt orders Mann to send letters through Flushing in, 21. 141n
Zeerleder, Ludwig von (1772–1840), Swiss banker:
(?) SH visited by, 12. 246
Zelada, Francesco Saverio de (1717–1801), cardinal:
congregation on Jesuits includes, 23. 507n
Jesuits' suppression by brief drafted by, 23. 473n
Sertor given money by, to retire to Florence, 24. 73n
Zelanti:
at Conclave of 1774, 24. 59n, 73n
cardinals' faction, governed by conscience, 17. 5n
couriers sent by, to Germany, Spain, and France, 24. 79n
Pius VI belonged to, 24. 86n
Zélé, Le, French ship:
Minorca said to be objective of, 25. 48n
Zelinda:
HW's verses to, 37. 81, 84–5, 39. 518–20

Zell, Ds of. *See* Desmier d'Olbreuse, Éléonore (1639–1722)

Zell, D. of. *See* George William (1624–1705)

Zell (Celle), Germany. *See* Celle

Zelmire. See under Buyrette de Belloy, Pierre-Laurent

Zen, Alois (b. ca 1734), sharper:
Lincoln, E. of, cheated by, **23**. 368, *378*

Zennoni, Don. *See* Somodevilla y Bengoechea, Zenón de

Zeno, Apostolo (1668–1750), poet:
Gianguir by, **18**. 96, 104
Lucio Vero by, **23**. 547n, **35**. 468
Mitradate by, **14**. 10, **43**. 181

Zeno, Pietro Caterino:
Crescimbeni's *Dell' Istoria* annotated by, **40**. 299n

Zephyr:
Flora wooed by, **30**. 328

'Zephyrus.' *See* West, Richard

Zerbst. *See* Anhalt-Zerbst

Zetter, Paul (ca 1600–ca 1667):
engraving by, **14**. 114n

Zicavo, Corsica:
Colonna, Bianca, collects deserters at, **17**. 147n

Zieten, Hans Joachim von (1699–1786), Prussian army officer:
supply train under, taken by Austrians, **21**. 224n, **37**. 549n

Zinc:
Bristol has factory for, **18**. 184n
deposits of, in Cornwall, Derbyshire, and Cumberland, **18**. 184n
Ginori wishes, from England, for painting china, **18**. 184, 202, 216, 250, 283–4, 323
Mann, Galfridus, thinks, is mineral water, **18**. 216
pewter by-product, **18**. 323
Walpole, Sir Edward, hears that, is in Lancashire, **18**. 284
—— to ask Ilay for, **18**. 250

Zincke, ——:
name of, is on document concerning Berkeley Sq. house, **34**. 250

Zincke, Christian Frederick (1685–1767), miniature painter:
Chandos's miniature by, given by Harcourt to HW, **35**. 447n
Cowley's miniature by, in HW's collection, **18**. 347n, **22**. 523, **33**. 110
HW mentions, **37**. 133
Lucan, Bns, copies, **41**. 418n
miniature by, **9**. 20n, **18**. (?) 347
Orford, Cts of, painted by, on snuff-box, **25**. 501–2, 504
Orléans, Duchesse d', miniature of, by, **18**. 347n
Queensberry, Ds of, miniature of, by, **33**. 110
Walpole, Sir Robert, painted by, **42**. 249

Zingari (gipsies):
Monte Santa Maria inhabited by, **20**. 424, 428

Zingho. See Zinc

Zingist. *See under* Dow, Alexander

Zink. *See* Zincke

Zinzendorff. *See* Sinzendorff

Zipoli, Caterina, singer:
Caffarelli's witticism to, **19**. 438

Znaim:
Francis I commands Austrian forces at, **17**. 143n

Zobeide. See under Cradock, Joseph

Zocchi, Giuseppe (1711–67), painter:
Gerini patron of, **17**. 57n
Mann sends view of Florence by, to HW, **17**. 57, 58
Scelta and *Vedute* by, **43**. 235

Zodiac:
HW thanks, for approach of April, **31**. 386
Heinel, Mlle, seems to be dancing in, **35**. 344

Zoffanii. *See* Zoffany

Zoffany, John (1733–1810), painter:
Charlotte, Q., said to have sent, to Florence to paint Tribune scene, **24**. 540
Farren, Elizabeth, painted by, **43**. 357
Foote and Garrick painted by, **23**. 435n
gates of Florentine baptistery to be copied by, in gesses, **23**. *430*
George III sends, to Florence to do view of Tribune in Uffizi, **23**. 430, 436n, 519, **24**. 33–4, 539
HW criticizes, **23**. 435–6, **24**. 92–3, 526–7, 529, 539
HW goes to studio of, to see 'Tribune' painting, **24**. 526–7
HW praises 'Tribune' painting by, **33**. 137–8
'Hogarth of Dutch painting,' **24**. 92–3
Italians think, was hanged for bigamy, **24**. 539
Mann criticizes, **24**. 33–4
——'s portrait to be inserted by, into painting of Tribune, **23**. 519
—— tortured by, to appear before Leopold and Maria Louisa to be painted, **24**. 540
Mann, Horace II, testifies to good likeness of uncle's portrait by, **24**. 529
many portraits painted by, at Florence, **24**. 33–4
may return to England or go to Russia, **23**. 92
painting by, of Florentine 'Tribune': **43**. 284; Florentine criticisms of, **24**. 539; has faulty perspective, **24**. 539; increased in historic value by recent alterations in Tribune, **25**. 177
painting by, of Holy Family, at Royal Academy exhibit, **24**. 92
Patch's engravings charm, **23**. 430
portrait of Tuscan grand ducal family taken by, to Vienna, **24**. 92n
position of Queen's painter enables, to take down any picture in Florentine galleries, **24**. 540
robbed near Twickenham, **33**. 298
Wilkes and daughter painted by, **33**. 138

Zoffany, Mrs John. *See* Eiselein, Maria Juliana Antonia; Thomas, Mary

Zondadari. *See* Chigi Zondadari

Zoppio, Melchiorre (fl. 1588):
Accademia dei gelati founded by, **13**. 193n

Zopyrus, courtier of Darius:
mutilates himself to betray Babylon to Darius, **34**. 41

Zorndorf (Germany):
Austrians, Russians, and Prussians all sing Te Deums for alleged victory at, **21**. 246, 317
battle of: **21**. 236, 237, 241; Conway hears of, **37**. 566; Russians give and accept no quarter at, **21**. 255
Frederick II defeats Russians at, **37**. 562–3
—— sends 'Relation' of, to Finckenstein, **21**. 241n

Zoroaster:
'legislator of society in its infancy,' **33**. 418
'mystic doctrines' of, **32**. 58

Zouch, Anne (1724–59), m. (1753) Rev. William Lowther:
death of, **16**. 33

Zouch, Rev. Henry (ca 1725–95), antiquarian; HW's correspondent:
(?) *Anecdotes of Painting* presented to, **14**. 120
Bath may be visited by, **16**. 54
Bristol may be visited by, **16**. 40
Conway inquires about, for HW, **37**. 559–60
eyes of, weak, **16**. 51
HW asked by, to aid navigation proceedings in Parliament, **16**. 28–9
HW asks, for aid on Vertue's MSS, **16**. 26
HW gives SH Lucan to, **15**. 72, **16**. 41, 42, 43
HW praises modesty of, **16**. 8–9
HW's correspondence with, **9**. 227n, **16**. 3–56, **36**. 310
HW sends *Anecdotes of Painting* to, **14**. 120, **16**. 45–6
health of, HW hopes, is better, **16**. 54
Rockingham, Lady, has, as chaplain, **35**. 323n
salary and fortune of, under Rockingham's patronage, **37**. 560
spectacles worn by, **16**. 51
SH Lucan received by, late, **15**. 72

Zoutman, J. A., Dutch Vice-Adm.:
Dutch fleet under, **25**. 300n

Parker's battle with, on Dogger Bank, **25**. 176n

Zuccarelli, Francesco (1702–88), painter:
paintings by, in Colebrooke's sale, **23**. 569n

Zuccari, Federico (ca 1543–1609), painter:
copies by, **15**. 95n
Mary, Q. of Scots, said to be painted by, **42**. 321
paintings by, in Caprarola palace, illustrated in *Illustri fatti Farnesiani*, **25**. 403n
portraits by: of Burghley, Bn, **10**. 346; of Elizabeth, Q., **37**. (?) 531; of 'Queen Elizabeth's Giant Porter,' **20**. 49n, **35**. 206; of Tollemache, **16**. 285n; of Walsingham, Sir Francis, **32**. 47

Zuccari, Ottaviano:
Illustri fatti Farnesiani has no paintings by, **25**. 403n

Zuccari, Taddeo (1529–66), painter:
paintings by, in Caprarola palace, illustrated in *Illustri fatti Farnesiani*, **25**. 403n

Zucchero. *See* Zuccari

Zucchi, Signora. *See* Kauffmann, Maria Anna Angelica Catherine

Zuchmantel, François-Antoine-Pacifique (ca 1715–70), Baron de:
death of, **7**. 423

Zudcote:
mail put ashore at, **24**. 302n

Zufager, sword of Hali:
Lincoln's 'manhood' to be more piercing than, **30**. 36

Zulestein:
William III compels E. of Rochford to take name of, instead of Nassau, **24**. 360

Zulestein. *See also* Nassau de Zuylestein

Zung, Francisco, Col.:
captured at Velletri, **18**. 493

Zurich, Switzerland:
canton of, prepares against invasion, **18**. 290

Zutphen, Holland:
deputies of, complain about P. Ferdinand's crossing the Rhine, **21**. 222n

Zuylestein. *See* Nassau de Zuylestein

Zweibrücken, D. of. *See* Karl August (1746–95)

Zweibrücken-Birkenfeld, Pfalzgräfin von. *See* Maria Franziska Dorothea (1724–94)